Taxation and Business Planning for Real Estate Transactions

Taxation and Business Planning for Real Estate Transactions

Second Edition

Bradley T. Borden

PROFESSOR OF LAW
BROOKLYN LAW SCHOOL

CAROLINA ACADEMIC PRESS
Durham, North Carolina

ISBN 978-1-5221-0530-5
e-ISBN 978-1-53100-078-3
LCCN 2016956308

Carolina Academic Press, LLC
700 Kent Street
Durham, North Carolina 27701
Telephone (919) 489-7486
Fax (919) 493-5668
www.cap-press.com

Printed in the United States of America

To Sam and Claire

Contents

Table of Cases

Table of Statutes and Treasury Regulations

Table of Other Authorities

[References are to pages and note numbers.]

Books

Websites

Acknowledgments

In attempting to acknowledge all the people who have contributed to this book and its companion client files, I will invariably leave someone out, and I offer my apologies in advance for such oversight. I have been blessed with tremendous mentors, friends, family, associates, research assistants, students, and others who made direct and indirect contributions to this project. In particular, my wife Sam and daughter Claire support my efforts to write. I would be lost without them. Several people have been important mentors—their tutelage regarding the law, writing about the law, and the practice of law are an important part of all I do. They include Stanley Blend, Erik Jensen, and Marty McMahon. Margaret Robertson helped compile and edit the cases, rulings, and other primary-source legal material that appeared in the first edition of this book and provided valuable feedback on the content. Her work ethic and skill were very important to the production of this book. Sarah Cranganu provided invaluable secretarial support throughout this project. Her creativity, skill, and diligence helped solve many problems relating to the compilation and presentation of the material. She created a plat map in a way that was useful for one of the companion client files and the foundation of the client-file method. Bobbi Bullock helped prepare the original manuscript for submission. Richey Wyatt and Lucky DeFries helped me develop the entity and loan documents that appear in the client file. Quintin Nelson prepared the diagrams. Deborah Launer and the people at Civic Research Institute granted permission to reproduce documents published in one of their books. Paul Caron and the editorial board of the Graduate Tax Series and Leslie Levin at LexisNexis helped refine the idea and scope of the project. Cristina Gegenschatz edited the final manuscript of the first edition and prepared it for publication. Students who have taken the course over the last several years have used the materials both in pre- and post-publication form and have pointed out errors and provided excellent ideas for improving them. I thank all of these people and more for their assistance and encouragement. I nonetheless retain full responsibility for the contents of this book.

Introduction

This casebook and its companion client files focus on transactional tax planning in the real estate context. To adequately provide tax-planning advice, attorneys must be familiar with the transactional tax attorney's analytical process. Transactional tax attorneys must recognize opportunities for tax planning and address issues that such planning may raise. Recognizing opportunities and addressing issues generally require a thorough understanding of the transaction and the relevant law. Knowledge of the law often derives from legal research and an in-depth study of primary-source legal resources, such as statutes, cases, regulations, and rulings. Legal research generally begins with treatises or articles that address the questions relevant to the tax-planning opportunity. That initial research leads the attorney to primary-source legal resources. The attorney then must interpret the law and apply it to a set of facts and provide advice. The advice helps clients structure transactions. Generally, such work results in a finished product in the form of a memorandum or letter to the client or a legal document such as a contract.

This book and the accompanying client files provide tax professors various alternatives for teaching their respective courses. Professors can choose to use the casebook alone to teach the legal concepts in a more traditional lecture-oriented course setting, but the casebook and companion client files provide the opportunity to adopt the client-file method of teaching and learning.[1] The client-file method uses a general real-life fact pattern to create a tax-planning context. For instance, one client file presents facts related to a suburban subdivision and another one presents the facts for a conversion of an apartment building to condominiums. The client-file has a series of memoranda that ask questions related to the fact pattern that require students to study and apply the relevant legal materials. The memoranda also direct students to applicable chapters in the casebook. The casebook commentary provides an overview of relevant concepts and directs students to the relevant legal resources. Thus, the materials embrace the transactional attorney's analytical process. They also provide for various forms of adaptability, as the substantive material in the casebook can facilitate the analysis of various fact situations that can appear in different client files. Professors can choose to use any single published client file for the entire semester, pick and choose materials from one or more client files, or use the casebook as the background for a lecture-style course.

---

1. See Bradley T. Borden, Using the Client-File Method to Teach Transactional Law, 16 Chap. L. Rev. 101 (2013).

The fact patterns in the client files may appear relatively simple at first glance, but they are filled with nuances and provide students the opportunity to do sophisticated tax planning. The questions in the client-file memoranda help students begin asking the appropriate questions and identifying and considering the relevant issues. The questions are often more general than questions found in typical tax law casebooks. Nonetheless, a proper analysis of most questions requires detailed knowledge of the factual context in which a question arises and the relevant law. The analyses should result in very specific answers and recommendations. The boundary of the questions may not always appear to be clear and some questions may appear to overlap. Nonetheless, the questions should help students begin an analysis and start to develop skills that will help them identify issues in a nebulous practice environment that most tax planners face. As students continue to work with the fact pattern in a client file, they also gain an appreciation for the complex nature of real estate transactions, the myriad issues that such transactions raise, the extent of legal knowledge that they must obtain to properly competently advise clients with respect to transactions, and the manner in which business aspects of a transaction work together with legal advice to affect the decisions that property and business owners make.

To replicate the research process, each chapter of the casebook provides commentary that could be similar to (but perhaps less detailed than) material typically found in treatises, articles, and other secondary sources of the law. The commentary introduces ideas and legal concepts that apply to the questions and directs the reader to relevant primary legal authority. Ultimately, the students must carefully study, interpret, and apply relevant law to the issues raised by the questions in the client files. The commentary cites primary legal sources in the footnotes. The chapters reproduce relevant case law and rulings, but students will have to access the cited tax statutes and regulations in sources outside of the casebook. The knowledge students will need to properly approach the material is largely contained in the primary authority. In fact, students generally will not be able to fully understand and answer the questions until they have carefully studied the relevant law.

The casebook is organized to introduce the practice setting and provide background in the first several chapters. Chapter 1 provides a general overview of transactional tax practice. It emphasizes that thoroughly understanding a client matter and the relevant law is critical to giving competent tax advice. Chapter 1 encourages students to spend time thinking about fact patterns presented by as client matters (such as the ones replicated in companion client files) and considering the work a successful tax plan will require. It discusses issues that a tax planner must consider when deciding whether to accept tax planning work. To adequately address such questions, students will have to understand the fact scenario and contemplate advice they will give. To do that, they will generally have to consider the table of contents, which lists the topics that will be important in providing advice with respect to fact patterns in the companion client files. Chapter 1 also includes provisions of Rules of Professional Conduct. Invariably, ethical issues arise in tax-planning engagements, and having the rules handy when such issues arise helps resolve ethical questions.

Chapter 2 reviews general income tax concepts that govern the tax treatment of gains and losses from the sale of real property. Students may have studied aspects of these rules in their introductory tax courses, but this chapter provides an opportunity to consider the rules in greater detail and to study the nuances of the rules. Concepts such as amount realized and adjusted basis can become complex when applied to facts that often arise in the practice setting, which the client files help illustrate. The different tax rates that apply to capital gains also add some complexity to the computation of tax from the sale of property and can affect tax-planning strategies. Chapter 2 provides an opportunity to study how the law can apply different rates to different types of long-term capital gain and how capital losses might offset those various types of gains for purposes of applying the various rates. The complexity of the application of the material in this chapter may surprise some students. In introductory courses, students often study the taxation of gain and loss at a fairly high level, but this chapter provides the opportunity for a more in-depth study.

Chapters 3 and 4 provide background regarding the types of legal and tax entities the property owners might consider using to hold their property. Choice of entity considerations should not consume the course, but issues relating to state-law entities and tax entities often arise when planning for real estate transactions. These chapters contain a significant amount of commentary to introduce topics and concepts. Students also must consider general provisions of state law, tax law, and the entity's governing document to adequately consider the questions arise with respect to choosing an entity. The focus in these chapters is to introduce concepts and provide background information. Chapter 3 cites to several provisions of the uniform and state entity laws. Access to those laws will help students analyze issues presented in Chapter 4 and may help in subsequent chapters as state-law issues arise. If most students in the course have already completed business law and business tax courses, the chapters may be less relevant to the class and require little or no attention. A more thorough review may be appropriate if many students have not studied those topics, but the materials provide sufficient descriptions and resources for students to analyze the questions presented in the client files. Chapter 3 also provides an opportunity to consider some of the ethical issues that attorneys face when advising entities and their members.

Chapter 5 explains basic finance principles and provides an opportunity to consider how tax affects financial analyses and business decisions. Although tax attorneys may not have traditionally provided financial advice, clients expect tax attorneys to understand the language property owners use to discuss their investments, and many entity agreements now adopt financial concepts that require attorneys to know financial principles. Consequently, many transactional attorneys now must be familiar with finance concepts. Furthermore, when discussing matters with clients, attorneys often must make rough estimates of tax effects to facilitate the decision-making process and illustrate the effect of taxes. To be able to competently respond in discussions with clients, attorneys must be familiar with basic finance concepts and have some proficiency with basic tax computations. Chapter 5 introduces concepts with which transactional attorneys should be familiar, provides opportunities to consider the effect tax will have on a real estate investment and transaction decisions, and allows students to practice using those concepts. Finally, by working with numbers, students develop familiarity with numeric aspects that arise with respect to almost all transactions.

Chapter 6 introduces students to the standards of tax practice. Tax attorneys often find themselves between a proverbial rock and hard spot. They feel pressure from clients to reduce their clients' tax liabilities. Tax attorneys also must adhere to statutory and regulatory standards. Chapter 6 introduces the standards of tax practice, which students will have to consider as they enter subsequent chapters that require them to provide tax-planning advice. Transactional tax attorneys must learn to balance duties they owe to clients with duties they owe to the system, as expressed in standards of tax practice. Although the ethics of tax practice warrant a course unto itself, the concepts are vital to tax-planning practices, and a brief review will reinforce the importance of the standards and prepare students to apply them in the practice setting that arises in subsequent chapters.

Chapters following Chapter 6 provide the legal authority that students will use to plan ownership and transactional structures for situations described in the client files. The amount of commentary in some of the chapters is minimal because the relevant primary-source material contains the law, describes its application, explains important tax concepts, and introduces important tax-planning ideas. The focus in these subsequent chapters is on ownership and transactional structures that best serve the objectives of real-estate investors. Thus, capital-gain and gain-deferral planning take center stage. Much of the law relating to property ownership and character of gain recognition is found in cases. Consequently, much of the early chapters on tax planning are predominantly case oriented. Students will find many of their planning ideas as they read the cases.

Obtaining favorable gain characterization and gain deferral are two very important aspects of real estate tax planning. Chapters 7 and 8 focus on gain characterization. The determination of the character of gain often depends upon whether property is a capital asset or dealer property, which is governed by numerous fact-intensive cases. Chapter 7 presents several of those cases. Chapter 8 discusses a structure that property owners often adopt to help lock in as much capital gain as possible. That structure typically requires an entity to issue an installment note, so the chapter discusses the installment-method of accounting for gains and the issues that arise when the transferee is related to the transferor. The primary planning strategy for locking in some capital gain in the development context appears in the case law that the chapter reproduces. Although many planning structures come from prior transactions that may appear in cases, students should begin to think about how they can apply the law to come up with their own planning ideas. The materials in the client files provide opportunities for students to start down that path.

Section 1031 is a very important part of tax planning for real estate transactions as it drives much of the structuring in real estate acquisitions, ownership, and dispositions. Several of the chapters following Chapter 8 focus on various aspects of section 1031 planning, but often that planning requires understanding other tax con-

cepts. For instance, leases and construction have become important to the more sophisticated section 1031 transactions. Two chapters (Chapter 9 on accounting for
real estate improvements and Chapter 14 on leases) are devoted to two of those topics
to lay the groundwork needed to seriously consider leasehold improvements exchanges
and other topics. Professors wishing to focus on traditional real-estate tax topics can
focus on those chapters that cover such topics and focus less on the chapters that
cover some of the more sophisticated section 1031 planning structures.

Chapter 14 on leases appears in the midst of chapters that cover various section
1031 planning structures. Leases can be complicated arrangements, and the material
in Chapter 14 provides the opportunity to cover them from various perspectives. The
use of leases in section 1031 exchanges makes understanding the transactional aspects
of leases critical for some section 1031 structures, such as improvements exchanges
and leasehold improvements exchanges, covered in Chapter 15. Chapter 16 is the
final chapter on section 1031. It provides the primary authority for some of the most
common situations that arise in relation to section 1031 — proximate business transactions. Chapter 17 provides an overview of real estate investment trusts (REITs), a
real estate investment vehicle that continues to grow in popularity. Chapter 18 presents
materials on loss limitation rules, such as the passive-activity-loss rules and at-risk
rules. It also discusses the loss nonrecognition requirement in section 1031. Finally,
Chapter 19 provides a brief overview of foreign investment in U.S. real property.

The client files include practice materials, such as entity and loan documents that
may be important in the tax-planning process. A significant portion of real estate law
is found in the contracts. Often tax planners must consider existing documents to determine whether a particular tax-planning transaction is feasible. The best-laid tax
plans may be frustrated by provisions in governing documents, if the tax planner fails
to consider the relevant documents and plan accordingly. The inclusion of documents
in the client files provides an opportunity to study them in the planning process. The
documents are not necessarily intended to be models of perfection. In studying the
documents, students may find that particular language does not adequately serve
clients. They may recommend changes that would improve the documents.

For the most part, each chapter of the casebook is self-contained. Nonetheless, to
a certain extent, some chapters will work better after studying earlier chapters. For
instance, before studying Chapter 8 to begin planning to preserve capital gains, students will most likely need the background on capital assets in Chapter 7. Furthermore, the client files often build on work that relates to prior chapters. For instance,
the memo in the client file that relates to a particular chapter could lead to a structure
that appears in subsequent memos that relate to other chapters. Thus, even though
chapters of the casebook may be self-contained, classes that use a client file may find
that proceeding in sequence often leads to the best result. Other chapters, such as
Chapter 12 relating to the qualified intermediary industry and risks associated with
hiring qualified intermediaries, do not necessarily affect general transactional planning,
so some professors may choose to skip it to devote more time to subsequent chapters
that focus on transactional planning.

The rationale for the casebook's planning perspective is fourfold. First, many students will enter private practice after completing their formal study of law. The market will require that they possess the tax-planning skills this casebook and the accompanying client files are designed to teach. Second, the classroom provides an opportunity to teach the techniques of responsible tax planning. Undoubtedly, every lawyer will be exposed to ideas and techniques that violate the standards of tax practice and professional ethics. By covering such topics in a law school course, students can learn the rules and be prepared to face charlatans in practice and adhere to the highest standards of tax practice and rules of ethical conduct. Third, students who enter government service will gain an understanding of tax-planning techniques that exist in private practice. With that understanding, they will be better prepared to draft rules that accomplish the government's objectives. Finally, studying the rules in a practice setting will help reinforce the rules and provide an opportunity to study them in the broader context in which they are most relevant and help them be closer to practice ready at the time of graduation. Such exposure should aid in learning and retaining the material.

Now, a note regarding the reproduced materials. The casebook reproduces several different types of materials. First, it reproduces cases and Internal Revenue Service publications. The casebook generally notes redacted material with ellipses and asterisks. In some situations, however, it deletes footnote citations that provide information that is not important to the relevant issue or that reproduce statutory and regulatory material that the casebook cites in the commentary. Generally, the casebook does not note such omissions. The casebook slightly modifies some citations in the reproduced cases and rulings to eliminate string citations, add dates, and make other minor changes to case names to conform with the citation style used throughout the casebook. The casebook also modifies section headings in the cases as appropriate to improve the readability of the case and promote uniformity. The casebook reproduces all cases and rulings cited in the commentary, but some reproductions may appear in a chapter different from the one citing it. In such situations, the citation refers to the chapter that reproduces the resource.

Second, the casebook does not reproduce provisions from the Internal Revenue Code or Treasury Regulations or sections of state-law entity statutes. All section references are to the Internal Revenue Code, unless provided otherwise. Students must have access to those resources to properly analyze the questions. Third, the client files that accompany the casebook present several sample documents, some of which are reproduced with permission from the original publisher, as indicated in those materials.

Taxation and Business Planning for Real Estate Transactions

Chapter 1

Real Estate Transaction Setting

I. Commentary

This chapter introduces general concepts that apply to transactional real estate tax attorneys. Transactional tax attorneys must know applicable laws, understand the client's fact situation, and be able to apply the law to help clients solve problems. Before beginning tax and business planning of any transaction, an attorney must anticipate some of the issues that the transaction will raise. The topics in other chapters of the book foreshadow the potential complexity of problems attorneys face with single transactions and the amount of work a single engagement will require from an attorney.

Attorneys hear from current and potential clients at various stages of their dealings. In some situations, clients may have entered into agreements and have taken steps to start fairly significant real estate projects at the time they call an attorney for advice related to their project. Several factors may delay their search for competent advice. They may have had a unique opportunity to acquire property and acted as quickly as possible to close on the acquisition at terms they found desirable. Perhaps the speed with which they closed on the property prevented them from searching for adequate counsel. They may have relied upon the expertise of a non-lawyer, such as a broker (in some jurisdictions), who might be part of the investment group, to negotiate the acquisition of, contract for, and ultimately acquire the property. The project they are contemplating may be new to them and they may not have fully anticipated its scope, and they may have failed to realize the myriad tax and legal issues it presents. Whatever the cause, clients often seek advice after they have taken steps to acquire property and begun some work to develop or market it.

Other clients call attorneys as they begin to contemplate entering into transactions. Regardless of the stage at which attorneys hear from clients, they must be prepared to assist the client. If the client has proceeded with insufficient legal advice, the attorney may have to help rectify prior actions, which may include helping the client ensure that the property is held in the proper legal entity and the purpose for holding the property is properly stated. Furthermore, attorneys must understand their roles and responsibilities in transactions with which they provide advice.

A. Role of Transactional Attorneys

Attorneys fill an important role as transactional advisors. They bring legal knowledge and skills to a transaction. They do not, however, merely use that knowledge and those skills to answer questions and solve problems clients present. Often, attorneys must use legal knowledge and skills to raise questions that a lay person would not know to ask. Thus, the attorney must critically appraise clients' situations, solicit information, raise issues, and make suggestions that the client may not anticipate.

The attorney must be aware of the setting in which a transaction occurs and be knowledgeable about the business and economic aspects of the transaction. Nonetheless, the client makes all business decisions. The attorney provides information and advice that assists the client with those decisions.[1] In doing so, attorneys must consider and appropriately address rules of professional ethics. If more than one party to a transaction seeks counsel together, the attorney must determine if representing all of them in the transaction raises a prohibited conflict of interest or other concerns.[2] If so, the attorney must identify who the client is and provide advice accordingly.[3] If not, the attorney must follow rules of professional ethics in advising all of the parties.[4] Making such decisions requires the attorney to properly identify conflicts of interests and anticipate the potential growth of a multiple-party arrangement.

After practicing in a particular area of law for some time, an attorney may develop an expertise in the area of law and have a fairly comprehensive understanding of particular types of transactions. An attorney in such a situation will have an appreciation for the amount of work and the level of expertise a particular engagement will require. Nonetheless, a seasoned attorney may be approached to handle a transaction that is new to the attorney, or an attorney that is just starting a practice may be approached to assist with a transaction that is new to the attorney. In each situation, the attorney must be able to anticipate the complexity of a project for the practical purpose of entering into an engagement letter with the potential client and for estimating the amount of time and costs the engagement will require. The attorney must also assess whether the work is something for which the attorney has the required level of professional competence and to which the attorney can devote the requisite amount of time.[5] As a general matter, the attorney may not contract away liability for giving bad advice,[6] so the stakes can be high. An attorney who fails to adhere to the ethics rules

---

1. *See* N.Y. COMP. CODES R. & REGS. tit. 22, § 1200.0 (2015) (see r. 2.1, addressing the scope of services an attorney provides).

2. *See* N.Y. COMP. CODES R. & REGS. tit. 22, § 1200.0 (2015) (see r. 1.7(a)); Montgomery v. eTreppid Technologies, LLC, 548 F. Supp. 1175 (D. Nev. 2008) (discussing the types of organizations that can be clients); United States v. International Brotherhood of Teamsters, 961 F. Supp. 665 (S.D.N.Y. 1997) (discussing the relationship of conflicts of interests and attorney-client privilege).

3. *See* N.Y. COMP. CODES R. & REGS. tit. 22, § 1200.0 (2015) (see r. 1.13, allowing an attorney to represent an organization; r. 4.3, providing rules for dealing with unrepresented clients).

4. *See* N.Y. COMP. CODES R. & REGS. tit. 22, § 1200.0 (2015) (see r. 1.7(b)).

5. *See* N.Y. COMP. CODES R. & REGS. tit. 22, § 1200.0 (2015) (see rs. 1.1 & 1.3).

6. *See* N.Y. COMP. CODES R. & REGS. tit. 22, § 1200.0 (2015) (see r. 1.8(h)).

may be subject to discipline that could range from admonition by disciplinary counsel to disbarment by the court.[7]

Transactional attorneys who do not exercise the appropriate standard of care could also be liable under malpractice or other claims brought by their clients.[8] Attorneys can be liable for malpractice if the client establishes the attorney owed the client a duty, the attorney breached that duty, and the breach caused damages.[9] An attorney's duty to a client is to exercise "the ordinary and reasonable skill and knowledge commonly possessed by a member of the legal profession...."[10] This standard of care considers what typical attorneys know and do, so it may be different from the standards set by the rules of professional ethics.

B. Business of Real Estate Development

Real estate developers make money by acquiring large pieces of real estate, developing it to some extent, and selling or leasing the developed property. One type of development is residential subdivision. Real estate developers plan to make a profit by acquiring and subdividing property. They then sell many of the subdivided lots to builders. The builders will build homes on the lots and sell the homes to customers, most of whom will use them as personal residences. To make a profit on those sales, the revenue they receive must exceed the cost to acquire and subdivide the lots. Real estate developers may also plan to construct improvements and either sell the improvements or rent them as commercial or residential real estate. Often developers contract for the construction of buildings that they can lease or sell to retailers or businesses. Thus, they may look to profit from owning and managing commercial real estate. The return in the form of rent or sales must justify the costs to construct and manage such properties.

Real estate development can be horizontal or vertical. If the development is horizontal, the developers will build on lots that are side by side. Horizontal development is typical in suburbia, as developers create entire subdivided neighborhoods, which may include retail and commercial areas on the periphery of the development. Vertical development would be more common in urban areas. Vertical development occurs when a developer constructs a high rise or acquires an existing building, converts it into an apartment coop or condominiums, and then sells or leases the individual units to customers. Many legal, tax, and economic principles apply to both types of real estate developments. Attorneys who represent real estate developers must be fa-

---

7. *See* MONT. RULES FOR LAWYER DISC. ENFORCEMENT rs. 8 & 9.

8. *See* Thomas D. Morgan, *Sanctions and Remedies for Attorney Misconduct*, 19 S. ILL. U. L.J. 343 (1995).

9. *See Developments in the Law — Lawyers' Responsibilities and Lawyers' Responses: II. Lawyers Responsibilities to the Client: Legal Malpractice and Tort Reform*, 107 HARV. L. REV. 1557, 1558–74 (1994); Jacob L. Todres, *Malpractice and the Tax Practitioner: An Analysis of the Areas in Which Malpractice Occurs*, 48 EMORY L.J. 547 (1999).

10. *See* Endless Ocean, LLC v. Twomey, Latham, Shea, Kelly, Dubin & Quartararo, 979 N.Y.S.2d 84, 87 (App. Div. 2d Dept. 2014).

miliar with the business, legal, and tax aspects of the transactions regardless of the setting in which the client operates.

In particular, attorneys must be familiar with the potential profitability of the proposed plan. If the plan will be profitable, the attorney should be prepared to provide tax advice that will benefit the developer in times of profitability. If the plan does not mature as anticipated, the developers may incur losses. Such a change in circumstances could affect the advice the attorney provides. Thus, the attorney must be aware of the business arrangement when providing advice to real estate developers.

II. Primary Legal Authority

New York Rules of Professional Conduct

(selected provisions)[11]

PREAMBLE: A LAWYER'S RESPONSIBILITIES

[4] The legal profession is largely self-governing. An independent legal profession is an important force in preserving government under law, because abuse of legal authority is more readily challenged by a profession whose members are not dependent on government for the right to practice law. To the extent that lawyers meet these professional obligations, the occasion for government regulation is obviated.

[5] The relative autonomy of the legal profession carries with it special responsibilities of self-governance. Every lawyer is responsible for observance of the Rules of Professional Conduct and also should aid in securing their observance by other lawyers. Neglect of these responsibilities compromises the independence of the profession and the public interest that it serves. Compliance with the Rules depends primarily upon the lawyer's understanding of the Rules and desire to comply with the professional norms they embody for the benefit of clients and the legal system, and, secondarily, upon reinforcement by peer and public opinion. So long as its practitioners are guided by these principles, the law will continue to be a noble profession.

Scope

[8] The Rules provide a framework for the ethical practice of law. Compliance with the Rules, as with all law in an open society, depends primarily upon understanding and voluntary compliance, secondarily upon reinforcement by peer and public opinion and finally, when necessary, upon enforcement through disciplinary proceedings. The Rules do not, however, exhaust the moral and ethical considerations that should inform a lawyer, for no worthwhile human activity can be completely defined by legal rules.

---

11. The New York statutes are codified at N.Y. Comp. Codes R. & Regs. tit. 22, § 1200.0 (2015). The preamble and comments are part of N.Y. State Bar Ass'n, Res. on Prof'l Standards for Attorneys in N.Y. State, *available at* http://www.nysba.org/professionalstandards/.

RULE 1.1: COMPETENCE

(a) A lawyer should provide competent representation to a client. Competent representation requires the legal knowledge, skill, thoroughness and preparation reasonably necessary for the representation.

(b) A lawyer shall not handle a legal matter that the lawyer knows or should know that the lawyer is not competent to handle, without associating with a lawyer who is competent to handle it.

(c) A lawyer shall not intentionally:

(1) fail to seek the objectives of the client through reasonably available means permitted by law and these Rules; or

(2) prejudice or damage the client during the course of the representation except as permitted or required by these Rules.

Comment

Legal Knowledge and Skill

[1] In determining whether a lawyer employs the requisite knowledge and skill in a particular matter, relevant factors include the relative complexity and specialized nature of the matter, the lawyer's general experience, the lawyer's training and experience in the field in question, the preparation and study the lawyer is able to give the matter, and whether it is feasible to associate with a lawyer of established competence in the field in question. In many instances, the required proficiency is that of a general practitioner. Expertise in a particular field of law may be required in some circumstances. One such circumstance would be where the lawyer, by representations made to the client, has led the client reasonably to expect a special level of expertise in the matter undertaken by the lawyer.

[2] A lawyer need not necessarily have special training or prior experience to handle legal problems of a type with which the lawyer is unfamiliar. A newly admitted lawyer can be as competent as a practitioner with long experience. Some important legal skills, such as the analysis of precedent, the evaluation of evidence and legal drafting, are required in all legal problems. Perhaps the most fundamental legal skill consists of determining what kinds of legal problems a situation may involve, a skill that necessarily transcends any particular specialized knowledge. A lawyer can provide adequate representation in a wholly novel field through necessary study. Competent representation can also be provided through the association of a lawyer of established competence in the field in question.

[4] A lawyer may accept representation where the requisite level of competence can be achieved by adequate preparation before handling the legal matter. This applies as well to a lawyer who is appointed as counsel for an unrepresented person.

Thoroughness and Preparation

[5] Competent handling of a particular matter includes inquiry into and analysis of the factual and legal elements of the problem, and use of methods and procedures

meeting the standards of competent practitioners. It also includes adequate preparation. The required attention and preparation are determined in part by what is at stake; major litigation and complex transactions ordinarily require more extensive treatment than matters of lesser complexity and consequence. An agreement between the lawyer and the client may limit the scope of the representation if the agreement complies with Rule 1.2(c).

Retaining or Contracting with Lawyers Outside the Firm

[8] To maintain the requisite knowledge and skill, a lawyer should (i) keep abreast of changes in substantive and procedural law relevant to the lawyer's practice, (ii) keep abreast of the benefits and risks associated with technology the lawyer uses to provide services to clients or to store or transmit confidential information, and (iii) engage in continuing study and education and comply with all applicable continuing legal education requirements under 22 N.Y.C.R.R. Part 1500.

ABA Model Rules of Professional Conduct Comment[12]

Maintaining Competence

[8] To maintain the requisite knowledge and skill, a lawyer should keep abreast of changes in the law and its practice, including the benefits and risks associated with relevant technology, engage in continuing study and education and comply with all continuing legal education requirements to which the lawyer is subject.

RULE 1.2: SCOPE OF REPRESENTATION AND ALLOCATION OF AUTHORITY BETWEEN CLIENT AND LAWYER

(a) Subject to the provisions herein, a lawyer shall abide by a client's decisions concerning the objectives of representation and, as required by Rule 1.4, shall consult with the client as to the means by which they are to be pursued. A lawyer shall abide by a client's decision whether to settle a matter. In a criminal case, the lawyer shall abide by the client's decision, after consultation with the lawyer, as to a plea to be entered, whether to waive jury trial and whether the client will testify.

(b) A lawyer's representation of a client, including representation by appointment, does not constitute an endorsement of the client's political, economic, social or moral views or activities.

(c) A lawyer may limit the scope of the representation if the limitation is reasonable under the circumstances, the client gives informed consent and where necessary notice is provided to the tribunal and/or opposing counsel.

(d) A lawyer shall not counsel a client to engage, or assist a client, in conduct that the lawyer knows is illegal or fraudulent, except that the lawyer may discuss the legal consequences of any proposed course of conduct with a client.

(e) A lawyer may exercise professional judgment to waive or fail to assert a right or position of the client, or accede to reasonable requests of opposing counsel, when doing so does not prejudice the rights of the client.

---

12. ABA Model Rules of Professional Conduct, comment to r 1.1.

(f) A lawyer may refuse to aid or participate in conduct that the lawyer believes to be unlawful, even though there is some support for an argument that the conduct is legal.

(g) A lawyer does not violate these Rules by being punctual in fulfilling all professional commitments, by avoiding offensive tactics, and by treating with courtesy and consideration all persons involved in the legal process.

Comment

Allocation of Authority Between Client and Lawyer

[2] Clients normally defer to the special knowledge and skill of their lawyer with respect to the means to be used to accomplish their objectives, particularly with respect to technical, legal and tactical matters. On the other hand, lawyers usually defer to their clients regarding such questions as the expense to be incurred and concern for third persons who might be adversely affected. On occasion, however, a lawyer and a client may disagree about the means to be used to accomplish the client's objectives. Because of the varied nature of the matters about which a lawyer and client might disagree, and because the actions in question may implicate the interests of a tribunal or other persons, this Rule does not prescribe how such disagreements are to be resolved. Other law, however, may be applicable and should be consulted by the lawyer. The lawyer should also consult with the client and seek a mutually acceptable resolution of the disagreement. If such efforts are unavailing and the lawyer has a fundamental disagreement with the client, the lawyer may withdraw from the representation. See Rule 1.16(c)(4). Likewise, the client may resolve the disagreement by discharging the lawyer, in which case the lawyer must withdraw from the representation. *See* Rule 1.16(b)(3).

Agreements Limiting Scope of Representation

[6] The scope of services to be provided by a lawyer may be limited by agreement with the client or by the terms under which the lawyer's services are made available to the client. When a lawyer has been retained by an insurer to represent an insured, for example, the representation may be limited to issues related to the insurance coverage. A limited representation may be appropriate because the client has limited objectives for the representation. In addition, the terms upon which representation is undertaken may exclude specific means that might otherwise be used to accomplish the client's objectives. Such limitations may exclude actions that the client thinks are too costly or that the lawyer regards as repugnant or imprudent.

[6A] In obtaining consent from the client, the lawyer must adequately disclose the limitations on the scope of the engagement and the matters that will be excluded. In addition, the lawyer must disclose the reasonably foreseeable consequences of the limitation. In making such disclosure, the lawyer should explain that if the lawyer or the client determines during the representation that additional services outside the limited scope specified in the engagement are necessary or advisable to represent the client adequately, then the client may need to retain separate counsel, which could result in delay, additional expense, and complications.

Illegal and Fraudulent Transactions

[9] Paragraph (d) prohibits a lawyer from counseling or assisting a client in conduct that the lawyer knows is illegal or fraudulent. This prohibition, however, does not preclude the lawyer from giving an honest opinion about the consequences that appear likely to result from a client's conduct. Nor does the fact that a client uses advice in a course of action that is illegal or fraudulent of itself make a lawyer a party to the course of action. There is a critical distinction between presenting an analysis of legal aspects of questionable conduct and recommending the means by which a crime or fraud might be committed with impunity.

[10] When the client's course of action has already begun and is continuing, the lawyer's responsibility is especially delicate. The lawyer is required to avoid assisting the client, for example, by drafting or delivering documents that the lawyer knows are fraudulent or by suggesting how the wrongdoing might be concealed. When the representation will result in violation of the Rules of Professional Conduct or other law, the lawyer must advise the client of any relevant limitation on the lawyer's conduct and remonstrate with the client. *See* Rules 1.4(a)(5) and 1.16(b)(1). Persuading a client to take necessary preventive or corrective action that will bring the client's conduct within the bounds of the law is a challenging but appropriate endeavor. If the client fails to take necessary corrective action and the lawyer's continued representation would assist client conduct that is illegal or fraudulent, the lawyer is required to withdraw. *See* Rule 1.16(b)(1). In some circumstances, withdrawal alone might be insufficient. In those cases, the lawyer may be required to give notice of the fact of withdrawal and to disaffirm any opinion, document, affirmation or the like. *See* Rule 1.6(b)(3); Rule 4.1, Comment [3].

[13] If a lawyer comes to know or reasonably should know that a client expects assistance not permitted by the Rules of Professional Conduct or other law, or of the lawyer intends to act contrary to the client's instructions, the lawyer must consult with the client regarding the limitations on the lawyer's conduct. See Rule 1.4(a)(5).

Refusal to Participate in Conduct a Lawyer Believes to be Unlawful

[15] In some situations such as those described in paragraph (d), a lawyer is prohibited from aiding or participating in a client's improper or potentially improper conduct; but in other situations, a lawyer has discretion. Paragraph (f) permits a lawyer to refuse to aid or participate in conduct the lawyer *believes* to be unlawful, even if the conduct is arguably legal. In addition, under Rule 1.16(c)(2), the lawyer *may* withdraw from representing a client when the client persists in a course of action involving the lawyer's services that the lawyer reasonably *believes* is criminal or fraudulent, even if the course of action is arguably legal. In contrast, when the lawyer *knows* (or reasonably should know) that the representation will result in a violation of law or the Rules of Professional Conduct, the lawyer *must* withdraw from the representation under Rule 1.16(b)(1). If the client "insists" that the lawyer pursue a course of conduct that is illegal or prohibited under the Rules, the lawyer must not carry out those instructions and, in addition, may withdraw from the representation under Rule 1.16(c)(13). If the lawyer is representing the client before a tribunal, additional rules may come into

play. For example, the lawyer may be required to obtain the tribunal's permission to withdraw under Rule 1.16(d), and the lawyer may be required to take reasonable remedial measures under Rule 3.3 with respect to false evidence or other criminal or fraudulent conduct relating to a proceeding.

Fulfilling Professional Commitments and Treating Other with Courtesy

[16] Both Rule 1.1(c)(1) and Rule 1.2(a) require generally that a lawyer seek the client's objectives and abide by the client's decisions concerning the objectives of the representation; but those rules do not require a lawyer to be offensive, discourteous, inconsiderate or dilatory. Paragraph (g) specifically affirms that a lawyer does not violate the Rules by being punctual in fulfilling professional commitments, avoiding offensive tactics and treating with courtesy and consideration all persons involved in the legal process. Lawyers should be aware of the New York State Standards of Civility adopted by the courts to guide the legal profession (22 NYCRR Part 1200 Appendix A). Although the Standards of Civility are not intended to be enforced by sanctions or disciplinary action, conduct before a tribunal that fails to comply with known local customs of courtesy or practice, or that is undignified or discourteous, may violate Rule 3.3(f). Conduct in a proceeding that serves merely to harass or maliciously injury another would be frivolous in violation of Rule 3.1. Dilatory conduct may violate Rule 1.3(a), which requires a lawyer to act with reasonable diligence and promptness in representing a client.

RULE 1.3: DILIGENCE

(a) A lawyer shall act with reasonable diligence and promptness in representing a client.

(b) A lawyer shall not neglect a legal matter entrusted to the lawyer.

(c) A lawyer shall not intentionally fail to carry out a contract of employment entered into with a client for professional services, but the lawyer may withdraw as permitted under these Rules.

Comment

[1] A lawyer should pursue a matter on behalf of a client despite opposition, obstruction or personal inconvenience to the lawyer, and take whatever lawful and ethical measures are required to vindicate a client's cause or endeavor. A lawyer must also act with commitment and dedication to the interests of the client and in advocacy upon the client's behalf. A lawyer is not bound, however, to press for every advantage that might be realized for a client. For example, a lawyer may have authority to exercise professional discretion in determining the means by which a matter should be pursued. *See* Rule 1.2. Notwithstanding the foregoing, the lawyer should not use offensive tactics or fail to treat all persons involved in the legal process with courtesy and respect.

[2] A lawyer's work load must be controlled so that each matter can be handled diligently and promptly. Lawyers are encouraged to adopt and follow effective office procedures and systems; neglect may occur when such arrangements are not in place or are ineffective.

[3] Perhaps no professional shortcoming is more widely resented than procrastination. A client's interests often can be adversely affected by the passage of time or the change

of conditions; in extreme instances, as when a lawyer overlooks a statute of limitations, the client's legal position may be destroyed. Even when the client's interests are not affected in substance, unreasonable delay can cause a client needless anxiety and undermine confidence in the lawyer's trustworthiness. A lawyer's duty to act with reasonable promptness, however, does not preclude the lawyer from agreeing to a reasonable request for a postponement that will not prejudice the lawyer's client.

[4] Unless the relationship is terminated, as provided in Rule 1.16, a lawyer should carry through to conclusion all matters undertaken for a client. If a lawyer's employment is limited to a specific matter, the relationship terminates when the matter has been resolved. If a lawyer has served a client over a substantial period in a variety of matters, the client sometimes may assume that the lawyer will continue to serve on a continuing basis unless the lawyer gives notice of withdrawal. Doubt about whether a client-lawyer relationship still exists should be clarified by the lawyer, preferably in writing, so that the client will not mistakenly suppose the lawyer is looking after the client's affairs when the lawyer has ceased to do so. If a lawyer has handled a judicial or administrative proceeding that produced a result adverse to the client and the lawyer and the client have not agreed that the lawyer will handle the matter on appeal, Rule 1.16(e) may require the lawyer to consult with the client about the possibility of appeal before relinquishing responsibility for the matter. Whether the lawyer is obligated to prosecute the appeal for the client depends on the scope of the representation the lawyer has agreed to provide to the client. *See* Rule 1.2.

RULE 1.5: FEES AND DIVISION OF FEES

(a) A lawyer shall not make an agreement for, charge, or collect an excessive or illegal fee or expense. A fee is excessive when, after a review of the facts, a reasonable lawyer would be left with a definite and firm conviction that the fee is excessive. The factors to be considered in determining whether a fee is excessive may include the following:

   (1) the time and labor required, the novelty and difficulty of the questions involved, and the skill requisite to perform the legal service properly;

   (2) the likelihood, if apparent or made known to the client, that the acceptance of the particular employment will preclude other employment by the lawyer;

   (3) the fee customarily charged in the locality for similar legal services;

   (4) the amount involved and the results obtained;

   (5) the time limitations imposed by the client or by circumstances;

   (6) the nature and length of the professional relationship with the client;

   (7) the experience, reputation and ability of the lawyer or lawyers performing the services; and

   (8) whether the fee is fixed or contingent.

(b) A lawyer shall communicate to a client the scope of the representation and the basis or rate of the fee and expenses for which the client will be responsible. This information shall be communicated to the client before or within a reasonable time after commencement of the representation and shall be in writing where required by statute or court rule. This provision shall not apply when the lawyer will charge a regularly represented client on the same basis or rate and perform services that are of the same general kind as previously rendered to and paid for by the client. Any changes in the scope of the representation or the basis or rate of the fee or expenses shall also be communicated to the client.

(c) A fee may be contingent on the outcome of the matter for which the service is rendered, except in a matter in which a contingent fee is prohibited by paragraph (d) or other law. Promptly after a lawyer has been employed in a contingent fee matter, the lawyer shall provide the client with a writing stating the method by which the fee is to be determined, including the percentage or percentages that shall accrue to the lawyer in the event of settlement, trial or appeal; litigation and other expenses to be deducted from the recovery; and whether such expenses are to be deducted before or, if not prohibited by statute or court rule, after the contingent fee is calculated. The writing must clearly notify the client of any expenses for which the client will be liable regardless of whether the client is the prevailing party. Upon conclusion of a contingent fee matter, the lawyer shall provide the client with a writing stating the outcome of the matter and, if there is a recovery, showing the remittance to the client and the method of its determination.

(d) A lawyer shall not enter into an arrangement for, charge or collect:

   (1) a contingent fee for representing a defendant in a criminal matter;

   (2) a fee prohibited by law or rule of court;

   (3) a fee based on fraudulent billing;

   (4) a nonrefundable retainer fee; provided that a lawyer may enter into a retainer agreement with a client containing a reasonable minimum fee clause if it defines in plain language and sets forth the circumstances under which such fee may be incurred and how it will be calculated; or

   (5) any fee in a domestic relations matter if:

      (i) the payment or amount of the fee is contingent upon the securing of a divorce or of obtaining child custody or visitation or is in any way determined by reference to the amount of maintenance, support, equitable distribution, or property settlement;

      (ii) a written retainer agreement has not been signed by the lawyer and client setting forth in plain language the nature of the relationship and the details of the fee arrangement; or

      (iii) the written retainer agreement includes a security interest, confession of judgment or other lien without prior notice being provided to the client in a signed retainer agreement and approval from a tribunal after notice to the adversary. A lawyer shall not foreclose on a mortgage placed on the marital residence while the spouse who consents to the mortgage remains the titleholder and the residence remains the spouse's primary residence.

(e) In domestic relations matters, a lawyer shall provide a prospective client with a Statement of Client's Rights and Responsibilities at the initial conference and prior to the signing of a written retainer agreement.

(f) Where applicable, a lawyer shall resolve fee disputes by arbitration at the election of the client pursuant to a fee arbitration program established by the Chief Administrator of the Courts and approved by the Administrative Board of the Courts.

(g) A lawyer shall not divide a fee for legal services with another lawyer who is not associated in the same law firm unless:

(1) the division is in proportion to the services performed by each lawyer or, by a writing given to the client, each lawyer assumes joint responsibility for the representation;

(2) the client agrees to employment of the other lawyer after a full disclosure that a division of fees will be made, including the share each lawyer will receive, and the client's agreement is confirmed in writing; and

(3) the total fee is not excessive.

(h) Rule 1.5(g) does not prohibit payment to a lawyer formerly associated in a law firm pursuant to a separation or retirement agreement.

Comment

[1A] A billing is fraudulent if it is knowingly and intentionally based on false or inaccurate information. Thus, under an hourly billing arrangement, it would be fraudulent to knowingly and intentionally charge a client for more than the actual number of hours spent by the lawyer on the client's matter; similarly, where the client has agreed to pay the lawyer's cost of in-house services, such as for photocopying or telephone calls, it would be fraudulent knowingly and intentionally to charge a client more than the actual costs incurred. Fraudulent billing requires an element of scienter and does not include inaccurate billing due to an innocent mistake.

[1B] A supervising lawyer who submits a fraudulent bill for fees or expenses to a client based on submissions by a subordinate lawyer has not automatically violated this Rule. In this situation, whether the lawyer is responsible for a violation must be determined by reference to Rules 5.1, 5.2 and 5.3. As noted in Comment [8] to Rule 5.1, nothing in that Rule alters the personal duty of each lawyer in a firm to abide by these Rules and in some situations, other Rules may impose upon a supervising lawyer a duty to ensure that the books and records of a firm are accurate. *See* Rule 1.15(j).

Basis or Rate of Fee

[2] When the lawyer has regularly represented a client, they ordinarily will have evolved an understanding concerning the basis or rate of the fee and the expenses for which the client will be responsible. In a new client-lawyer relationship, however, an understanding as to fees and expenses must be promptly established. Court rules

regarding engagement letters require that such an understanding be memorialized in writing in certain cases. *See* 22 N.Y.C.R.R. Part 1215. Even where not required, it is desirable to furnish the client with at least a simple memorandum or copy of the lawyer's customary fee arrangements that states the general nature of the legal services to be provided, the basis, rate or total amount of the fee, and whether and to what extent the client will be responsible for any costs, expenses or disbursements in the course of the representation. A written statement concerning the terms of the engagement reduces the possibility of misunderstanding.

Terms of Payment

[4] A lawyer may require advance payment of a fee, but is obliged to return any unearned portion. *See* Rule 1.16(e). A lawyer may charge a minimum fee, if that fee is not excessive, and if the wording of the minimum fee clause of the retainer agreement meets the requirements of paragraph (d)(4). A lawyer may accept property in payment for services, such as an ownership interest in an enterprise, providing this does not involve acquisition of a proprietary interest in the cause of action or subject matter of the litigation contrary to Rule 1.8(i). A fee paid in property instead of money may, however, be subject to the requirements of Rule 1.8(a), because such fees often have the essential qualities of a business transaction with the client.

[5] An agreement may not be made if its terms might induce the lawyer improperly to curtail services for the client or perform them in a way contrary to the client's interest. For example, a lawyer should not enter into an agreement whereby services are to be provided only up to a stated amount when it is foreseeable that more extensive services probably will be required, unless the situation is adequately explained to the client. Otherwise, the client might have to bargain for further assistance in the midst of a proceeding or transaction. In matters in litigation, the court's approval for the lawyer's withdrawal may be required. *See* Rule 1.16(d). It is proper, however, to define the extent of services in light of the client's ability to pay. A lawyer should not exploit a fee arrangement based primarily on hourly charges by using wasteful procedures.

Division of Fee

[7] A division of fee is a single billing to a client covering the fee of two or more lawyers who are not affiliated in the same firm. A division of fee facilitates association of more than one lawyer in a matter in which neither alone could serve the client as well. Paragraph (g) permits the lawyers to divide a fee either on the basis of the proportion of services they render or if each lawyer assumes responsibility for the representation as a whole in a writing given to the client. In addition, the client must agree to the arrangement, including the share that each lawyer is to receive, and the client's agreement must be confirmed in writing. Contingent fee arrangements must comply with paragraph (c). Joint responsibility for the representation entails financial and ethical responsibility for the representation as if the lawyers were associated in a partnership. *See* Rule 5.1. A lawyer should refer a matter only to a lawyer who the referring lawyer reasonably believes is competent to handle the matter. *See* Rule 1.1.

Disputes over Fees

[9] A lawyer should seek to avoid controversies over fees with clients and should attempt to resolve amicably any differences on the subject. The New York courts have established a procedure for resolution of fee disputes through arbitration and the lawyer must comply with the procedure when it is mandatory. Even when it is voluntary, the lawyer should conscientiously consider submitting to it.

RULE 1.6: CONFIDENTIALITY OF INFORMATION

(a) A lawyer shall not knowingly reveal confidential information, as defined in this Rule, or use such information to the disadvantage of a client or for the advantage of the lawyer or a third person, unless:

    (1) the client gives informed consent, as defined in Rule 1.0(j);

    (2) the disclosure is impliedly authorized to advance the best interests of the client and is either reasonable under the circumstances or customary in the professional community; or

    (3) the disclosure is permitted by paragraph (b).

"Confidential information" consists of information gained during or relating to the representation of a client, whatever its source, that is (a) protected by the attorney-client privilege, (b) likely to be embarrassing or detrimental to the client if disclosed, or (c) information that the client has requested be kept confidential. "Confidential information" does not ordinarily include (i) a lawyer's legal knowledge or legal research or (ii) information that is generally known in the local community or in the trade, field or profession to which the information relates.

(b) A lawyer may reveal or use confidential information to the extent that the lawyer reasonably believes necessary:

    (1) to prevent reasonably certain death or substantial bodily harm;

    (2) to prevent the client from committing a crime;

    (3) to withdraw a written or oral opinion or representation previously given by the lawyer and reasonably believed by the lawyer still to be relied upon by a third person, where the lawyer has discovered that the opinion or representation was based on materially inaccurate information or is being used to further a crime or fraud;

    (4) to secure legal advice about compliance with these Rules or other law by the lawyer, another lawyer associated with the lawyer's firm or the law firm;

    (5)(i) to defend the lawyer or the lawyer's employees and associates against an accusation of wrongful conduct; or

      (ii) to establish or collect a fee; or

    (6) when permitted or required under these Rules or to comply with other law or court order.

(c) A lawyer shall exercise reasonable care to prevent the lawyer's employees, associates, and others whose services are utilized by the lawyer from disclosing or using confidential information of a client, except that a lawyer may reveal the information permitted to be disclosed by paragraph (b) through an employee.

Comment

Scope of the Professional Duty of Confidentiality

[2] A fundamental principle in the client-lawyer relationship is that, in the absence of the client's informed consent, or except as permitted or required by these Rules, the lawyer must not knowingly reveal information gained during and related to the representation, whatever its source. See Rule 1.0(j) for the definition of informed consent. The lawyer's duty of confidentiality contributes to the trust that is the hallmark of the client-lawyer relationship. The client is thereby encouraged to seek legal assistance and to communicate fully and frankly with the lawyer, even as to embarrassing or legally damaging subject matter. The lawyer needs this information to represent the client effectively and, if necessary, to advise the client to refrain from wrongful conduct. Typically, clients come to lawyers to determine their rights and what is, in the complex of laws and regulations, deemed to be legal and correct. Based upon experience, lawyers know that almost all clients follow the advice given, and the law is thereby upheld.

[3] The principle of client-lawyer confidentiality is given effect in three related bodies of law: the attorney-client privilege of evidence law, the work-product doctrine of civil procedure and the professional duty of confidentiality established in legal ethics codes. The attorney-client privilege and the work-product doctrine apply when compulsory process by a judicial or other governmental body seeks to compel a lawyer to testify or produce information or evidence concerning a client. The professional duty of client-lawyer confidentiality, in contrast, applies to a lawyer in all settings and at all times, prohibiting the lawyer from disclosing confidential information unless permitted or required by these Rules or to comply with other law or court order. The confidentiality duty applies not only to matters communicated in confidence by the client, which are protected by the attorney-client privilege, but also to all information gained during and relating to the representation, whatever its source. The confidentiality duty, for example, prohibits a lawyer from volunteering confidential information to a friend or to any other person except in compliance with the provisions of this Rule, including the Rule's reference to other law that may compel disclosure. *See* Comments [12]-[13]; *see also* Scope.

Use of Information Related to Representation

[4B] The duty of confidentiality also prohibits a lawyer from using confidential information to the advantage of the lawyer or a third person or to the disadvantage of a client or former client unless the client or former client has given informed consent. See Rule 1.0(j) for the definition of "informed consent." This part of paragraph (a) applies when information is used to benefit either the lawyer or a third person, such as another client, a former client or a business associate of the lawyer. For example, if a lawyer learns that a client intends to purchase and develop several parcels of land, the lawyer may not (absent the client's informed consent) use that information to buy a nearby parcel that is expected to appreciate in value due to the client's purchase, or to recommend that another client buy the nearby land, even if the lawyer does not reveal any confidential information. The duty also prohibits disadvantageous use of confidential information unless the client gives informed consent, except as permitted or required by these Rules. For example, a lawyer assisting a client in purchasing a parcel of land may not make a competing bid on the same land. However, the fact that a lawyer has once served a client does not preclude the lawyer from using generally known information about that client, even to the disadvantage of the former client, after the client-lawyer relationship has terminated. *See* Rule 1.9(c)(1).

Disclosure Adverse to Client

[9] A lawyer's confidentiality obligations do not preclude a lawyer from securing confidential legal advice about compliance with these Rules and other law by the lawyer, another lawyer in the lawyer's firm, or the law firm. In many situations, disclosing information to secure such advice will be impliedly authorized for the lawyer to carry out the representation. Even when the disclosure is not impliedly authorized, paragraph (b)(4) permits such disclosure because of the importance of a lawyer's compliance with these Rules, court orders and other law.

[10] Where a claim or charge alleges misconduct of the lawyer related to the representation of a current or former client, the lawyer may respond to the extent the lawyer reasonably believes necessary to establish a defense. Such a claim can arise in a civil, criminal, disciplinary or other proceeding and can be based on a wrong allegedly committed by the lawyer against the client or on a wrong alleged by a third person, such as a person claiming to have been defrauded by the lawyer and client acting together or by the lawyer acting alone. The lawyer may respond directly to the person who has made an accusation that permits disclosure, provided that the lawyer's response complies with Rule 4.2 and Rule 4.3, and other Rules or applicable law. A lawyer may make the disclosures authorized by paragraph (b)(5) through counsel. The right to respond also applies to accusations of wrongful conduct concerning the lawyer's law firm, employees or associates.

RULE 1.7: CONFLICT OF INTEREST: CURRENT CLIENTS

(a) Except as provided in paragraph (b), a lawyer shall not represent a client if a reasonable lawyer would conclude that either:

    (1) the representation will involve the lawyer in representing differing interests; or

    (2) there is a significant risk that the lawyer's professional judgment on behalf of a client will be adversely affected by the lawyer's own financial, business, property or other personal interests.

(b) Notwithstanding the existence of a concurrent conflict of interest under paragraph (a), a lawyer may represent a client if:

    (1) the lawyer reasonably believes that the lawyer will be able to provide competent and diligent representation to each affected client;

    (2) the representation is not prohibited by law;

(3) the representation does not involve the assertion of a claim by one client against another client represented by the lawyer in the same litigation or other proceeding before a tribunal; and

(4) each affected client gives informed consent, confirmed in writing.

Comment

General Principles

[1] Loyalty and independent judgment are essential aspects of a lawyer's relationship with a client. The professional judgment of a lawyer should be exercised, within the bounds of the law, solely for the benefit of the client and free of compromising influences and loyalties. Concurrent conflicts of interest, which can impair a lawyer's professional judgment, can arise from the lawyer's responsibilities to another client, a former client or a third person, or from the lawyer's own interests. A lawyer should not permit these competing responsibilities or interests to impair the lawyer's ability to exercise professional judgment on behalf of each client. For specific Rules regarding certain concurrent conflicts of interest, see Rule 1.8. For former client conflicts of interest, see Rule 1.9. For conflicts of interest involving prospective clients, see Rule 1.18. For definitions of "differing interests," "informed consent" and "confirmed in writing," see Rules 1.0(f), (j) and (e), respectively.

[2] Resolution of a conflict of interest problem under this Rule requires the lawyer, acting reasonably, to: (i) identify clearly the client or clients, (ii) determine whether a conflict of interest exists, *i.e.*, whether the lawyer's judgment may be impaired or the lawyer's loyalty may be divided if the lawyer accepts or continues the representation, (iii) decide whether the representation may be undertaken despite the existence of a conflict, *i.e.*, whether the conflict is consentable under paragraph (b); and if so (iv) consult with the clients affected under paragraph (a) and obtain their informed consent, confirmed in writing. The clients affected under paragraph (a) include all of the clients who may have differing interests under paragraph (a)(1) and any clients whose representation might be adversely affected under paragraph (a)(2).

Identifying Conflicts of Interest

[7] Differing interests can also arise in transactional matters. For example, if a lawyer is asked to represent the seller of a business in negotiations with a buyer represented by the lawyer, not in the same transaction but in another, unrelated matter, the lawyer could not undertake the representation without the informed consent of each client.

[8] Differing interests exist if there is a significant risk that a lawyer's exercise of professional judgment in considering, recommending or carrying out an appropriate course of action for the client will be adversely affected or the representation would otherwise be materially limited by the lawyer's other responsibilities or interests. For example, the professional judgment of a lawyer asked to represent several individuals operating a joint venture is likely to be adversely affected to the extent that the lawyer is unable to recommend or advocate all possible positions that each client might take because of the lawyer's duty of loyalty to the others. The conflict in effect forecloses alternatives that would otherwise be available to the client. The mere possibility of

subsequent harm does not itself require disclosure and consent. The critical questions are the likelihood that a difference in interests will eventuate and, if it does, whether it will adversely affect the lawyer's professional judgment in considering alternatives or foreclose courses of action that reasonably should be pursued on behalf of the client.

Personal-Interest Conflicts

[10] The lawyer's own financial, property, business or other personal interests should not be permitted to have an adverse effect on representation of a client. For example, if the probity of a lawyer's own conduct in a transaction is in serious question, it may be difficult or impossible for the lawyer to give a client detached advice. Similarly, when a lawyer has discussions concerning possible employment with an opponent of the lawyer's client or with a law firm representing the opponent, such discussions could materially limit the lawyer's representation of the client. In addition, a lawyer may not allow related business interests to affect representation, for example, by referring clients to an enterprise in which the lawyer has an undisclosed financial interest. *See* Rule 5.7 on responsibilities regarding nonlegal services and Rule 1.8 pertaining to a number of personal-interest conflicts, including business transactions with clients.

[11] When lawyers representing different clients in the same matter or in substantially related matters are closely related, there may be a significant risk that client confidences will be revealed and that the lawyer's family relationship will interfere with both loyalty and professional judgment. As a result, each client is entitled to know of the existence and implications of the relationship between the lawyers, before the lawyer agrees to undertake the representation. Thus, a lawyer who has a significant intimate or close family relationship with another lawyer ordinarily may not represent a client in a matter where that other lawyer is representing another party, unless each client gives informed consent, as defined in Rule 1.0(j).

Interest of Person Paying for Lawyer's Services

[13] A lawyer may be paid from a source other than the client, including a co-client, if the client is informed of that fact and consents and the arrangement does not compromise the lawyer's duty of loyalty or independent judgment to the client. See Rule 1.8(f). If acceptance of the payment from any other source presents a significant risk that the lawyer's exercise of professional judgment on behalf of a client will be adversely affected by the lawyer's own interest in accommodating the person paying the lawyer's fee or by the lawyer's responsibilities to a payer who is also a co-client, then the lawyer must comply with the requirements of paragraph (b) before accepting the representation, including determining whether the conflict is consentable and, if so, that the client has adequate information about the material risks of the representation.

Informed Consent

[18] Informed consent requires that each affected client be aware of the relevant circumstances, including the material and reasonably foreseeable ways that the conflict could adversely affect the interests of that client. Informed consent also requires that the client be given the opportunity to obtain other counsel if the client so desires.

See Rule 1.0(j). The information that a lawyer is required to communicate to a client depends on the nature of the conflict and the nature of the risks involved, and a lawyer should take into account the sophistication of the client in explaining the potential adverse consequences of the conflict. There are circumstances in which it is appropriate for a lawyer to advise a client to seek the advice of a disinterested lawyer in reaching a decision as to whether to consent to the conflict. When representation of multiple clients in a single matter is undertaken, the information must include the implications of the common representation, including possible effects on loyalty, confidentiality and the attorney-client privilege, and the advantages and risks involved. *See* Comments [30] and [31] concerning the effect of common representation on confidentiality.

[19] Under some circumstances it may be impossible to make the disclosure necessary to obtain consent. For example, when the lawyer represents different clients in related matters and one client refuses to consent to the disclosure necessary to permit the other client to make an informed decision, the lawyer cannot properly ask the latter to consent. In some cases the alternative to common representation is that each party obtains separate representation with the possibility of incurring additional costs. These costs, along with the benefits of securing separate representation, are factors that may be considered by the affected client in determining whether common representation is in the client's interests. Where the fact, validity or propriety of client consent is called into question, the lawyer has the burden of establishing that the client's consent was properly obtained in accordance with the Rule.

Revoking Consent

[21] A client who has given consent to a conflict may revoke the consent and, like any other client, may terminate the lawyer's representation at any time. Whether revoking consent to the client's own representation precludes the lawyer from continuing to represent other clients depends on the circumstances, including the nature of the conflict, whether the client revoked consent because of a material change in circumstances, the reasonable expectations of the other clients, and whether material detriment to the other clients or the lawyer would result.

RULE 1.13: ORGANIZATION AS CLIENT

(a) When a lawyer employed or retained by an organization is dealing with the organization's directors, officers, employees, members, shareholders or other constituents, and it appears that the organization's interests may differ from those of the constituents with whom the lawyer is dealing, the lawyer shall explain that the lawyer is the lawyer for the organization and not for any of the constituents.

(b) If a lawyer for an organization knows that an officer, employee or other person associated with the organization is engaged in action or intends to act or refuses to act in a matter related to the representation that (i) is a violation of a legal obligation to the organization or a violation of law that reasonably might be imputed to the organization, and (ii) is likely to result in substantial injury to the organization, then the lawyer shall proceed as is reasonably necessary in the best interest of the organization. In determining how to proceed, the lawyer shall give due consideration to the seriousness of the violation and its consequences, the scope and nature of the lawyer's representation, the responsibility in the organization and the apparent motivation of the person involved, the policies of the organization concerning such matters and any other relevant considerations. Any measures taken shall be designed to minimize disruption of the organization and the risk of revealing information relating to the representation to persons outside the organization. Such measures may include, among others:

(1) asking reconsideration of the matter;

(2) advising that a separate legal opinion on the matter be sought for presentation to an appropriate authority in the organization; and

(3) referring the matter to higher authority in the organization, including, if warranted by the seriousness of the matter, referral to the highest authority that can act in behalf of the organization as determined by applicable law.

(c) If, despite the lawyer's efforts in accordance with paragraph (b), the highest authority that can act on behalf of the organization insists upon action, or a refusal to act, that is clearly in violation of law and is likely to result in a substantial injury to the organization, the lawyer may reveal confidential information only if permitted by Rule 1.6, and may resign in accordance with Rule 1.16.

(d) A lawyer representing an organization may also represent any of its directors, officers, employees, members, shareholders or other constituents, subject to the provisions of Rule 1.7. If the organization's consent to the concurrent representation is required by Rule 1.7, the consent shall be given by an appropriate official of the organization other than the individual who is to be represented, or by the shareholders.

Comment

The Entity as the Client

[1] An organizational client is a legal entity, but it cannot act except through its officers, directors, employees, members, shareholders and other constituents. Officers, directors, employees and shareholders are the constituents of the corporate organizational client. The duties defined in this Rule apply equally to unincorporated associations. "Other constituents" as used in this Rule means the positions equivalent to officers, directors, employees, and shareholders held by persons acting for organizational clients that are not corporations.

[2A] There are times when the organization's interests may differ from those of one or more of its constituents. In such circumstances, the lawyer should advise any constituent whose interest differs from that of the organization: (i) that a conflict or potential conflict of interest exists, (ii) that the lawyer does not represent the constituent in connection with the matter, unless the representation has been approved in accordance with Rule 1.13(d), (iii) that the constituent may wish to obtain independent representation, and (iv) that any attorney-client privilege that applies to discussions between the lawyer and the constituent belongs to the organization and may be waived by the organization. Care must be taken to ensure that the constituent understands that, when there is such adversity of interest, the lawyer for the organization cannot provide legal representation for that constituent, and that discussions between the lawyer for the organization and the constituent may not be privileged.

Acting in the Best Interest of the Organization

[3] When constituents of the organization make decisions for it, the decisions ordinarily must be accepted by the lawyer, even if their utility or prudence is doubtful. Decisions concerning policy and operations, including ones entailing serious risk, are not as such in the lawyer's province. Paragraph (b) makes clear, however, that when the lawyer knows that the organization is likely to be substantially injured by action of an officer or other constituent that violates a legal obligation to the organization or is in violation of law that might be imputed to the organization, the lawyer must proceed as is reasonably necessary in the best interest of the organization. Under Rule 1.0(k), a lawyer's knowledge can be inferred from circumstances, and a lawyer cannot ignore the obvious. The terms "reasonable" and "reasonably" connote a range of conduct that will satisfy the requirements of Rule 1.13. In determining what is reasonable in the best interest of the organization, the circumstances at the time of determination are relevant. Such circumstances may include, among others, the lawyer's area of expertise, the time constraints under which the lawyer is acting, and the lawyer's previous experience and familiarity with the client.

Concurrent Representation

[12] Paragraph (d) recognizes that a lawyer for an organization may also represent a principal officer or major shareholder, subject to the provisions of Rule 1.7. If the corporation's informed consent to such a concurrent representation is needed, the lawyer should advise the principal officer or major shareholder that any consent given on behalf of the corporation by the conflicted officer or shareholder may not be valid, and the lawyer should explain the potential consequences of an invalid consent.

RULE 2.1: ADVISOR

In representing a client, a lawyer shall exercise independent professional judgment and render candid advice. In rendering advice, a lawyer may refer not only to law but to other considerations such as moral, economic, social, psychological, and political factors that may be relevant to the client's situation.

Comment

Scope of Advice

[1] A client is entitled to straightforward advice expressing the lawyer's honest assessment. Legal advice often involves unpleasant facts and alternatives that a client may be disinclined to confront. In presenting advice, a lawyer endeavors to sustain the client's morale and may put advice in as acceptable a form as honesty permits. Nevertheless, a lawyer should not be deterred from giving candid advice by the prospect that the advice will be unpalatable to the client.

[2] Advice couched in narrow legal terms may be of little value to a client, especially where practical considerations, such as cost or effects on other people, are predominant. Purely technical legal advice, therefore, can sometimes be inadequate. It is proper for a lawyer to refer to relevant moral and ethical considerations in giving advice. Although a lawyer is not a moral advisor as such, moral and ethical considerations impinge upon most legal questions and may decisively influence how the law will be applied.

[3] A client may expressly or impliedly ask the lawyer for purely technical advice. When such a request is made by a client experienced in legal matters, the lawyer may accept it at face value. When such a request is made by a client inexperienced in legal matters, however, the lawyer's responsibilities as advisor may include the responsibility to indicate that more may be involved than strictly legal considerations. For the allocation of responsibility in decision making between lawyer and client, see Rule 1.2.

[4] Matters that go beyond strictly legal questions may also be in the domain of another profession. Family matters can involve problems within the professional competence of psychiatry, clinical psychology or social work; business matters can involve problems within the competence of the accounting profession or of financial or public relations specialists. Where consultation with a professional in another field is itself something a competent lawyer would recommend, the lawyer should make such a recommendation. At the same time, a lawyer's advice at its best often consists of recommending a course of action in the face of conflicting recommendations of experts.

Offering Advice

[5] In general, a lawyer is not expected to give advice until asked by the client. However, when a lawyer knows that a client proposes a course of action that is likely to result in substantial adverse legal consequences to the client, the lawyer's duty to the client under Rule 1.4 may require that the lawyer offer advice if the client's course of action is related to the representation. Similarly, when a matter is likely to involve litigation, it may be advisable under Rule 1.4 to inform the client of forms of dispute resolution that might constitute reasonable alternatives to litigation. A lawyer ordinarily has no duty to initiate investigation of a client's affairs or to give advice that the client has indicated is unwanted, but a lawyer may initiate advice to a client when doing so appears to be in the client's interest.

RULE 4.2: COMMUNICATION WITH PERSON REPRESENTED BY COUNSEL

(a) In representing a client, a lawyer shall not communicate or cause another to communicate about the subject of the representation with a party the lawyer knows to be represented by another lawyer in the matter, unless the lawyer has the prior consent of the other lawyer or is authorized to do so by law.

(b) Notwithstanding the prohibitions of paragraph (a), and unless otherwise prohibited by law, a lawyer may cause a client to communicate with a represented person unless the represented person is not legally competent, and may counsel the client with respect to those communications, provided the lawyer gives reasonable advance notice to the represented person's counsel that such communications will be taking place.

(c) A lawyer who is acting *pro se* or is represented by counsel in a matter is subject to paragraph (a), but may communicate with a represented person, unless otherwise prohibited by law and unless the represented person is not legally competent, provided the lawyer or the lawyer's counsel gives reasonable advance notice to the represented person's counsel that such communications will be taking place.

Comment

[4] This Rule does not prohibit communication with a represented party or person or an employee or agent of such a party or person concerning matters outside the representation. For example, the existence of a controversy between a government agency and a private party or person or between two organizations does not prohibit a lawyer for either from communicating with nonlawyer representatives of the other regarding a separate matter. Nor does this Rule preclude communication with a represented party or person who is seeking advice from a lawyer who is not otherwise representing a client in the matter. A lawyer having independent justification or legal authorization for communicating with a represented party or person is permitted to do so.

[7] In the case of a represented organization, paragraph (a) ordinarily prohibits communications with a constituent of the organization who: (i) supervises, directs or regularly consults with the organization's lawyer concerning the matter, (ii) has authority to obligate the organization with respect to the matter, or (iii) whose act or omission in connection with the matter may be imputed to the organization for purposes of civil or criminal liability. Consent of the organization's lawyer is not required for communication with a former unrepresented constituent. If an individual constituent of the organization is represented in the matter by the person's own counsel, the consent by that counsel to a communication will be sufficient for purposes of this Rule. In communicating with a current or former constituent of an organization, a lawyer must not use methods of obtaining evidence that violate the legal rights of the organization. *See* Rules 1.13, 4.4.

Client-to-Client Communications

[11] Persons represented in a matter may communicate directly with each other. A lawyer may properly advise a client to communicate directly with a represented person, and may counsel the client with respect to those communications, provided the lawyer complies with paragraph (b). Agents for lawyers, such as investigators, are not considered clients within the meaning of this Rule even where the represented entity is an agency, department or other organization of the government, and therefore a lawyer may not cause such an agent to communicate with a represented person, unless the lawyer would be authorized by law or a court order to do so. A lawyer may also counsel a client with respect to communications with a represented person, including by drafting papers for the client to present to the represented person. In advising a client in connection with such communications, a lawyer may not advise the client to seek privileged information or other information that the represented person is

not personally authorized to disclose or is prohibited from disclosing, such as a trade secret or other information protected by law, or to encourage or invite the represented person to take actions without the advice of counsel.

RULE 4.3: COMMUNICATING WITH UNREPRESENTED PERSONS

In communicating on behalf of a client with a person who is not represented by counsel, a lawyer shall not state or imply that the lawyer is disinterested. When the lawyer knows or reasonably should know that the unrepresented person misunderstands the lawyer's role in the matter, the lawyer shall make reasonable efforts to correct the misunderstanding. The lawyer shall not give legal advice to an unrepresented person other than the advice to secure counsel if the lawyer knows or reasonably should know that the interests of such person are or have a reasonable possibility of being in conflict with the interests of the client.

Comment

[1] An unrepresented person, particularly one not experienced in dealing with legal matters, might assume that a lawyer is disinterested in loyalties or is a disinterested authority on the law even when the lawyer represents a client. In order to avoid a misunderstanding, a lawyer will typically need to identify the lawyer's client and, where necessary, explain that the client has interests opposed to those of the unrepresented person. As to misunderstandings that sometimes arise when a lawyer for an organization deals with an unrepresented constituent, see Rule 1.13(a), Comment [2A].

[2] The Rule distinguishes between situations involving unrepresented parties whose interests may be adverse to those of the lawyer's client and those in which the person's interests are not in conflict with the client's. In the former situation, the possibility that the lawyer will compromise the unrepresented person's interests is so great that the Rule prohibits the giving of any advice apart from the advice to obtain counsel. Whether a lawyer is giving impermissible advice may depend on the experience and sophistication of the unrepresented party, as well as the setting in which the behavior and comments occur. This Rule does not prohibit a lawyer from negotiating the terms of a transaction or settling a dispute with an unrepresented person. So long as the lawyer has explained that the lawyer represents an adverse party and is not representing the person, the lawyer may inform the person of the terms on which the lawyer's client will enter into an agreement or settle a matter, prepare documents that require the person's signature, and explain the lawyer's own view of the meaning of the document or the lawyer's view of the underlying legal obligations.

Montana Rules for Lawyer Disciplinary Enforcement
(selected provisions)[13]

Rule 8. Grounds for Discipline.

A. Reasons for Discipline. Discipline may be imposed for any of the following reasons:

---

13. MONT. LAWYER DISC. ENFORCEMENT RULES.

(1) Acts or omissions by a lawyer, individually or in concert with any other person or persons, which violate the Rules of Professional Conduct or the disciplinary rules adopted from time to time by the Supreme Court.

(2) Any act committed by an attorney contrary to the highest standards of honesty, justice, or morality, including but not limited to those outlined in Title 37, chapter 61, parts 3 and 4, MCA, whether committed in such attorney's capacity as an attorney or otherwise.

(3) Conduct which results in conviction of a criminal offense.

(4) Conduct which results in lawyer discipline in another jurisdiction.

(5) Violation of the terms of any discipline or disciplinary order.

(6) Failure to promptly and fully respond to an inquiry from Disciplinary Counsel, an investigator, or the Commission, or failure to justify such refusal or nonresponse.

(7) Willful contempt of court and failure to purge the contempt.

B. **Relationship to Criminal Proceedings.** Acquittal of a charge of crime, plea bargain, conviction of a lesser crime, or dismissal of a charge of crime after deferred imposition of sentence shall not constitute a bar to lawyer discipline for that act, nor shall conviction in a criminal proceeding be a condition precedent to the institution of disciplinary proceedings for that act.

Rule 9. Discipline and Sanctions.

A. **Forms of Discipline.** Discipline may take one or more of the following forms:

(1) Disbarment. "Disbarment" means the unconditional termination of any privilege to practice law in this State and, when applied to any attorney not admitted to practice law in this State, means the unconditional exclusion from the admission to or the exercise of any privilege to practice law in this State.

(2) Suspension from the practice of law for a definite period of time or for an indefinite period of time with a fixed minimum term. "Suspension" means the temporary or indefinite termination of the privilege to practice law in this State and, when applied to any attorney not admitted to practice law in this State, means the temporary or indefinite exclusion from the admission to or the exercise of any privilege to practice law in this State.

(3) Public censure.

(4) Admonition administered by an Adjudicatory Panel of the Commission.

(5) Probation.

(6) Requirement of restitution to persons financially injured.

(7) Reimbursement to the Lawyers' Fund for Client Protection.

(8) Assessment of the cost of proceedings, investigations, and audits. Whenever costs of proceedings are assessed by the Supreme Court as part of the discipline imposed upon a lawyer, the Disciplinary Counsel shall assemble

and serve upon the lawyer an itemized list of those costs. The lawyer shall then have ten days thereafter in which to file written objections with the Commission on Practice and, if so desired, request a hearing before an Adjudicatory Panel on whether the amount of such costs is reasonable and necessary. An Adjudicatory Panel shall thereafter recommend an amount of costs to be imposed, and shall file its recommendation with the Supreme Court, which shall then issue an appropriate order assessing costs.

    (9) Interim suspension pending final determination of discipline.

B. **Discipline Criteria.** The following factors shall be considered in determining discipline to be recommended or imposed:

    (1) The gravity and nature of the duty violated, including whether the duty is owed to a client, to the public, to the legal system, or to the profession;

    (2) The lawyer's mental state;

    (3) The actual or potential injury caused by the lawyer's misconduct;

    (4) The existence of aggravating or mitigating factors; and

    (5) The existence of prior offenses.

C. **Probation.** A lawyer against whom disciplinary proceedings are pending may be placed on probation by the Supreme Court or, with the lawyer's concurrence, by an Adjudicatory Panel. The probation shall be for such time and upon such terms and conditions as are determined appropriate in the case. Discipline may be imposed for violation of any of the terms and conditions of such probation, including satisfactory completion of a diversion or treatment program.

Montgomery v. eTreppid Technologies, LLC

United States District Court, D. Nevada
548 F. Supp. 2d 1175 (2008)

ORDER

VALERIE P. COOKE, UNITED STATES MAGISTRATE JUDGE.

Before the court is eTreppid Technologies, LLC's ("eTreppid") points and authorities in support of its assertion of the attorney-client privilege against Dennis Montgomery (#427). Also before the court is Dennis Montgomery ("Montgomery") and the Montgomery Family Trust's ("the Trust") (collectively the "Montgomery Parties") memorandum of points and authorities showing that eTreppid's attorney-client privilege objections should be overruled in their entirety (#428 and #429). Both eTreppid and Montgomery filed replies (#438 and #439). eTreppid additionally filed a supplement and errata to their supplement (#s443–445). The court has thoroughly reviewed the record and the parties' submissions and concludes that eTreppid may withhold attorney-client privileged communications from Montgomery.

I. HISTORY & PROCEDURAL BACKGROUND

Plaintiffs in this action are Dennis Montgomery and the Montgomery Family Trust, members of eTreppid (#7). Defendants and counter-claimants are eTreppid Technologies, LLC, a limited liability company registered in the State of Nevada, and Warren Trepp, a member of eTreppid. *Id.* eTreppid is "in the business of developing and marketing software for various applications" (#393).[14]

The Montgomery Parties' main claim is that eTreppid unlawfully used and sub-licensed certain software that Montgomery invented and developed, and for which the Trust owns copyrights (#7). eTreppid's primary counter-claim is that between December 2005 and January 2006, Montgomery knowingly destroyed and/or deleted software from eTreppid's computers and servers, and also stole a complete copy of the software for his personal use and benefit (#393). eTreppid claims that by stealing the software, Montgomery misappropriated eTreppid's trade secrets. *Id.*

This dispute involves the Montgomery Parties' discovery requests, which eTreppid asserts implicate the attorney-client privilege. Montgomery claims that as a member and former manager of eTreppid, he is a "joint client" with eTreppid for the purposes of the attorney-client privilege; as such, eTreppid may not assert the attorney-client privilege against him with respect to privileged communications created during the time he was a manager and member of eTreppid (#428). eTreppid's position is that it is the sole client for the purposes of the attorney-client privilege, that the ability to assert or waive the privilege belongs to current management, and that Montgomery is no longer current management as he is adverse to eTreppid and has been since 2006 (#427). As the parties were unable to resolve this issue, the court ordered that the parties file simultaneous briefs setting out their respective views (#419).

II. DISCUSSION

A. Attorney–Client Privilege

"The attorney-client privilege is one of the oldest recognized privileges for confidential communications." *Swidler & Berlin v. U.S.,* 524 U.S. 399, 403, 118 S.Ct. 2081, 141 L.Ed.2d 379 (1998). Its main purpose is "to encourage full and frank communication between attorneys and their clients and thereby promote broader public interests in the observance of law and the administration of justice." *Upjohn Co. v. United States,* 449 U.S. 383, 389, 101 S.Ct. 677, 66 L.Ed.2d 584 (1981). The privilege extends to "confidential disclosures made by a client to an attorney in order to obtain legal advice ... as well as an attorney's advice in response to such disclosures." *U.S. v. Chen,* 99 F.3d 1495, 1501 (9th Cir.1996).

Only the holder of the attorney-client privilege may waive it. *Tennenbaum v. Deloitte & Touche,* 77 F.3d 337, 340–41 (9th Cir.1996). The privilege is not absolute and may be waived or lost under certain circumstances. *Weil v. Investment/Indicators, Research*

---

14. [1] This case has a very involved history, much of which is irrelevant to the current issues before the court. Therefore, the court does not here list all the claims and/or parties involved in this action and sets out only the facts necessary to the immediate issues.

& Management, 647 F.2d 18, 24 (9th Cir.1981) (privilege waived upon voluntary disclosure to third-party); *see also In re Napster, Inc. Copyright Litigation,* 479 F.3d 1078, 1090 (9th Cir.2007) (privilege lost due to crime-fraud exception). Because it impedes "the full and free discovery of the truth, the attorney-client privilege is strictly construed" and "'applies only where necessary to achieve its purpose.'" *United States v. Talao,* 222 F.3d 1133, 1140 (9th Cir.2000) (quoting *Weil,* 647 F.2d at 24 and *Fisher v. United States,* 425 U.S. 391, 403, 96 S.Ct. 1569, 48 L.Ed.2d 39 (1976)).

B. Analysis

The essential issue here is whether, over the objections of eTreppid, Montgomery has the right to access attorney-client privileged communications for the time period during which Montgomery served as a manager and active member of eTreppid. The issue turns this question: who is the client for purposes of the attorney-client privilege?

The parties generally agree that the attorney-client privilege belongs to the "client," and that only the "client" may assert or waive the privilege. However, the parties disagree as to who the client is. eTreppid takes the "entity is the client" position, arguing that eTreppid, as a limited liability company ("LLC"), is the sole client. Montgomery contends that the "joint client exception" applies here — he agrees that eTreppid is a "client," but argues that as an individual member and former manager of eTreppid, he is also a "client" such that eTreppid may not assert the privilege against him.

1. Preliminary Issues

Before delving into the principle issue, the court must address two preliminary matters. First, the parties disagree as to whether there exists federal common law sufficient to resolve the relevant issues. Second, the parties differ as to whether an LLC should be treated as a corporation or a partnership for the purposes of the attorney-client privilege.[15]

---

15. [2] A third preliminary issue involves how to treat each specific communication, particularly those related to Douglas Frye, who, in addition to being an eTreppid member, is eTreppid's manager and in-house counsel. Montgomery claims that before the court may rule on the issue of privilege, eTreppid must meet its burden of proving that each particular document/communication is protected by the attorney-client privilege. Montgomery argues that because eTreppid failed to produce a privilege log setting out which communications it claims are privileged, eTreppid has failed to meet its burden; therefore, eTreppid has waived its privilege.

The court is aware that eTreppid has not produced a privilege log. However, the current briefs are not before the court upon a motion to compel discovery. Instead, the court ordered simultaneous briefing on this narrow issue: whether eTreppid may assert the attorney-client privilege against Montgomery — who, while still technically a member of eTreppid, has not been active in its management since he adversely parted ways with eTreppid over two years ago — to prevent him from obtaining certain communications during discovery. To the extent that the parties address issues pertaining to particular documents and attorneys, the court finds these arguments premature.

The court concludes below that eTreppid may assert the attorney-client privilege against Montgomery. After eTreppid produces a privilege log and the parties confer, should the parties still disagree as to which communication are privileged, they may bring the particular communications to the court's attention for *in camera* review. *See Gottlieb v. Wiles,* 143 F.R.D. 241, 248 (D.Colo.1992) (after ruling on whether the former director was entitled to the corporation's privileged communications, the court ordered counsel to prepare a privilege log of all materials it planned to withhold on the

a. Jurisdiction and Applicable Law

Both parties agree that the federal law of privilege applies (#428, p. 3; #438, p. 6). However, Montgomery asserts that there is no applicable federal common law addressing the joint client exception to the attorney client privilege; therefore, the court should look to Nevada or California law (#428, p. 3). eTreppid contends that there exists federal law sufficient to resolve the issues presented (#427).

This case is before the court on the basis of federal question jurisdiction. In cases involving a federal question and pendant state law claims, the federal law of privilege applies. *Agster v. Maricopa County,* 422 F.3d 836, 839 (9th Cir.2005); *see also* Fed.R.Evid. 501. Although the court looks first to federal common law, the court may also look to state privilege law "if it is enlightening." *Tennenbaum,* 77 F.3d at 340. If neither state nor federal law is on point, the court should issue an opinion "in light of reason and experience." *Roberts v. Heim,* 123 F.R.D. 614, 622 (N.D.Cal.1988) (citing *Trammel v. United States,* 445 U.S. 40, 100 S.Ct. 906, 63 L.Ed.2d 186 (1980)); *see also* Fed.R.Evid. 501. Thus, the court will look primarily at federal common law, but may also rely on state law, particularly Nevada and California, in making a determination on the issues presented.[16]

b. Is a Limited Liability Company more analogous to a Corporation or a Partnership?

The second issue is whether eTreppid, as an LLC, should be treated as a corporation or a partnership for the purposes of the attorney client privilege. There is no case law, state or federal, that is directly on point; thus, this is an issue of first impression. eTreppid argues that federal courts have routinely treated LLCs as corporations; as such, the court should apply corporations law (#427). Montgomery contends that, particularly on the facts of this case, an LLC is more like a partnership because co-members of an LLC owe each other fiduciary duties just as partners in a partnership owe each other fiduciary duties; therefore, the court should apply partnership law (#428).

---

basis of privilege and noted that if the parties disagreed after reviewing the privilege log, the parties could submit the documents to the court for *in camera* review). The court anticipates that eTreppid, as stated in its brief, will be reasonable in making such privilege determinations. *See* # 427 ("To be sure, eTreppid understands that not all communications between eTreppid and Frye are privileged. It goes without saying that in order for a communication to be protected under the attorney-client privilege, the communication must be confidentially made pursuant to the obtaining or rendering of legal services from a duly licensed attorney acting as such. Clearly, due to Frye's position as manager of eTreppid, many communications between Frye and eTreppid will concern issues unrelated to legal services.").

16. [3] As set out in further detail below, the court undertook an in-depth review of the case law cited by each of the parties, and further conducted its own independent research. While the court acknowledges that neither the Supreme Court nor any of the Circuit Courts of Appeals have specifically addressed the joint client exception to the attorney-client privilege, especially with respect to the particular circumstances presented in this case, a number of federal district courts have addressed very similar issues. The court finds that for the most part, it has adequate federal law at its disposal to make determinations in this case. However, as noted, the court's determinations may be guided by referencing state law as well.

An LLC is a relatively new hybrid business entity that has the characteristics of both a corporation and a partnership, but is not characterized as either. *Lattanzio v. COMTA*, 481 F.3d 137, 140 (2d Cir.2007); *see also In re Tri–River Trading, LLC*, 329 B.R. 252, 267, n. 16 (8th Cir. BAP 2005). While LLCs offer members the same protection from personal liability as corporations offer their shareholders, *see Ditty v. CheckRite, Ltd.*, 973 F.Supp. 1320, 1335 (D.Utah 1997), unless otherwise indicated, LLCs are generally treated as partnerships for tax purposes. *McNamee v. Department of the Treasury, Internal Revenue Service*, 488 F.3d 100, 107 (2d Cir.2007) (citing IRS rules and publications). One commentator has stated that an LLC borrows from a partnership the characteristics of informal operation, internal governance by contract, direct participation by members, and no taxation at the entity level. *See* William Meade Fletcher, 1A Fletcher Cyclopedia of the Law of Corporations, *Classification and Kinds of Corporations, Limited Liability Companies* § 70.50 (2007). From a corporation, an LLC borrows the characteristics of member protection from personal liability, the requirement that organizers file articles of organization with the secretary of state, a corporate form of governance if the LLC elects to be governed by managers, and an operating agreement analogous to corporate bylaws. *Id.* An LLC has an existence separate from its members and managers. *Abrahim & Sons Enterprises v. Equilon Enterprises, LLC*, 292 F.3d 958, 962 (9th Cir.2002) (applying California law and stating "Members own and control most LLCs, yet the LLCs remain separate and distinct from their members.").

In support of his position, Montgomery cites *Wortham & Van Liew v. Superior Court*, 188 Cal.App.3d 927, 233 Cal.Rptr. 725 (1987), in which the court analyzes California's joint client exception (#428). The *Wortham* court held that in the context of a partnership, partners owe each other fiduciary duties. *Wortham*, 188 Cal.App.3d at 932, 233 Cal.Rptr. 725. Further, the court held that since all partners are entitled to a wide range of documents related to the partnership, an attorney who represents the partnership also represents each partner jointly as to any partnership business. *Id.* However, while this may be true regarding partnerships, *Wortham* fails to enlighten the court as to whether an LLC should be treated as a partnership or a corporation for purposes of the attorney-client privilege.

The court is aware of only two cases, neither of which is factually on point, that have addressed how an LLC is treated with respect to the attorney-client privilege. *See Moore v. Commissioner of Internal Revenue*, T.C. Memo.2004–259 (2004) (federal tax court applying the law of corporations to an LLC for the purposes of the attorney-client privilege); *see also In re Tri–River Trading, LLC*, 329 B.R. 252 (8th Cir. BAP 2005) (Eighth Circuit bankruptcy appellate panel treating an LLC as a corporation for the purposes of the attorney-client privilege).[17]

In *In re Giampietro*, 317 B.R. 841, 845–47 (D.Nev.2004), a bankruptcy court applying Nevada law held that an LLC should be treated as a corporation for purposes of the "alter ego" doctrine, which results in "piercing the corporate veil" and finding

---

17. [4] The court will discuss both of these cases in further detail below.

the individuals behind the corporation personally liable. *Id.* at 845–47. The court stated: "Even though the Bankruptcy Code does not explicitly mention limited liability companies, as the Code was adopted before such entities were widely-used, most courts and commentators agree that they are analogous to corporations...." *Id.* at n. 3; *see also Ditty*, 973 F.Supp. at 1335 (applying Utah corporate law to an LLC for purposes of the alter ego doctrine). In *In re Senior Cottages of America*, 482 F.3d 997 (8th Cir.2007), the Eighth Circuit held that an LLC should be treated as a corporation for purposes of determining whether a bankruptcy trustee had standing to assert claims against an LLC's former attorneys. *Id.* at 1001. The Eighth Circuit compared Minnesota's LLC statutory provisions to its corporate provisions, and held that the two entities share many of the same properties. *Id.*

A number of states have also applied corporate law to LLCs. In *PacLink Communications v. Superior Court*, 90 Cal.App.4th 958, 109 Cal.Rptr.2d 436 (2001), a California court held that LLC members must bring a derivative action against the LLC, similar to corporate shareholder derivative actions, where the claim is that LLC assets were injured. *Id.* at 963–64, 109 Cal.Rptr.2d 436; *see also Blanton v. Prins*, 938 So.2d 847, 852–53 (Miss.App.2005) (applying corporate shareholder derivative rules to an LLC). Further, a Virginia court applied the corporate "business judgment rule" to the managers of a Virginia LLC, stating "there is no basis to apply a different rule to managers seeking protection from liability...." *Flippo v. CSC Assoc. III, L.L.C.*, 262 Va. 48, 56–7, 547 S.E.2d 216 (2001); *see also In re Tri–River Trading, LLC*, 329 B.R. 252, 267–68 (8th Cir. BAP 2005) (treating an LLC like a corporation pursuant to Missouri law for the purposes of the business judgment rule). Additionally, an appellate court in Ohio applied corporations law to an LLC in determining whether to disqualify an attorney on the basis of a conflict of interest. *Legal Aid Society of Cleveland v. W & D Partners I, LLC*, 162 Ohio App.3d 682, 834 N.E.2d 850, 854–55 (2005). California has codified the corporate "alter ego" doctrine for LLCs, *see* Cal. Corp.Code § 17101(b) (2004), while other states have applied the doctrine to LLCs through the common law. *Milk v. Total Pay and H.R. Solutions, Inc.*, 280 Ga.App. 449, 634 S.E.2d 208 (2006).

Montgomery argues that an LLC is more closely analogous to a partnership because, like partners in a partnership, members of an LLC owe each other fiduciary duties (#428, p. 4). Montgomery cites a New York District Court case for the proposition that "co-members of an LLC owe fiduciary duties to each other." *Id.* (citing *At the Airport v. ISATA, LLC*, 438 F.Supp.2d 55, 65 (E.D.N.Y.2006)). Regardless of the truth of that statement, Montgomery has not cited one case that holds that an LLC is similar to a partnership based on the fiduciary duty members owe each other. Indeed, Montgomery fails to cite any case law applying the law of partnerships to an LLC. Instead, Montgomery supports his argument only by generally comparing eTreppid's LLC organizational structure to a partnership.

eTreppid contends that even if the court found that eTreppid operates like a partnership, under federal common law, partnerships and limited partnerships are treated as corporations for purposes of the attorney-client privilege. The court agrees. *See*

Hopper v. Frank, 16 F.3d 92, 94–7 (5th Cir.1994) (holding that the attorneys' representation was of the limited partnership "entity," and stating that "there is no logical
reason to distinguish partnerships from corporations or other legal entities in determining the client a lawyer represents."); *see also United States v. Campbell,* 73 F.3d 44,
47 (5th Cir.1996) (holding that only the bankruptcy trustee for the limited partnership—not the general partner—had the power to assert or waive the attorney-client
privilege on behalf of the limited partnership, and stating that a "limited partnership,
like a corporation, is an inanimate entity that can act only through its agents. Accordingly, the same rule that applies to corporations in bankruptcy should apply to
a bankrupt limited partnership."); *see also In re Bieter Company,* 16 F.3d 929, 935 and
n. 7 (8th Cir.1994) (holding that the partnership entity is the client for the purposes
of the attorney-client privilege and stating that "Once it is recognized ... that the
privilege applies to the corporate form of organization there seems no basis for limiting
it to corporations, as distinct from unincorporated associations, partnerships, or sole
proprietorships") (citations and quotations omitted).

In addition to case law, the court also conducted an extensive review of eTreppid's
1998, 1999 and 2001 Operating Agreements ("OA") (#429, Exhibits A–C).[18] The OA
reveals that eTreppid elected to be classified as a partnership for federal tax purposes.
Id., Exhibits A–B, sec. 10.6.1; Exhibit C, sec. 9.6.1. However, as to the management
of eTreppid, the OA states that eTreppid is managed by, and all company powers are
vested in, a management committee. *Id.,* Exhibits A–C, sec. 6.1 and 6.2. The management committee has "the general powers and duties of the management typically vested
in the board of directors and the office of the chief executive officer of a corporation."
Id. The LLC's manager conducts the day-to-day operations at the direction and under
the oversight of the management committee. *Id.,* sec. 6.1. The manager has "the general
powers and duties of management typically vested in the office of a chief operating officer of a corporation." *Id.,* sec. 6.3. In January 1999, the manager was also given the
title of "President" of eTreppid. *Id.,* Exhibits B–C, sec. 6.3. The OA contains specific
limitations on the powers of the management committee and the manager, requiring
member action for certain important duties. *Id.,* Exhibits A–C, sec. 6.4.

In the original 1998 OA, Montgomery was designated as eTreppid's manager. *Id.,*
Exhibit A sec. 6.1.1. However, from January 1999 on, Douglas Frye was designated
as eTreppid's manager, and Montgomery was designated as eTreppid's chief technology
officer. *Id.,* Exhibit B, sec. 6.1.1 and 6.1.3. As of January 1999, the management committee consisted of Douglas Frye, Warren Trepp and Dennis Montgomery. *Id.,* Exhibits
B–C, sec. 6.1.4. From inception, Warren Trepp acted as the chair of the management
committee. *Id.,* Exhibits A–C, sec. 6.1.5.

The Operating Agreement indicates that eTreppid conducts business more like a
corporation than a partnership. eTreppid's organization is based on a corporate struc-

---

18. [5] eTreppid's original Operating Agreement is dated September 28, 1998 (#429, Exhibit A).
The Operating Agreement was amended and restated on January 1, 1999 (#429, Exhibit B), and again
on November 1, 2001 (#429, Exhibit C). The court here sets out only provisions relevant to the issues
at hand.

ture, with the Management Committee being compared to a corporate board of directors and a chief executive officer, and the manager being compared to a president and chief operating officer. The management committee acts by vote and makes policies and procedures, similar to a corporate board of directors. The committee then oversees eTreppid's manager in carrying out those policies and procedures, just as a board of directors oversees corporate officers. Members, like corporate shareholders, have no personal liability. eTreppid also has a resident agent similar to a corporation, had to file articles of organization with the Nevada Secretary of State like a corporation files articles of incorporation, and has an Operating Agreement akin to corporate bylaws. The only comparison to a partnership is eTreppid's tax treatment.

Further, while none of the cases the court reviewed is exactly on point, taken together with eTreppid's Operating Agreement, they are instructive. Federal and state courts have consistently applied the law of corporations to LLCs, including for the purposes of piercing the corporate veil, the "alter ego" doctrine, determining standing, the "business judgment rule," and derivative actions. Federal courts have also treated partnerships and limited partnerships as corporations for the purposes of determining the attorney-client privilege. Montgomery has not called to the court's attention any cases applying partnership law to an LLC. Therefore, the court concludes that eTreppid should be treated as a corporation pursuant to federal common law.

2. Main Issue

a. Corporations and the Attorney-Client Privilege

It is well established that the attorney-client privilege attaches to both individuals and corporations. *Upjohn Co. v. United States,* 449 U.S. 383, 390, 101 S.Ct. 677, 66 L.Ed.2d 584 (1981). However, "special problems" arise in the administration of the attorney-client privilege to corporations. *Commodity Futures Trading Commission v. Weintraub,* 471 U.S. 343, 348, 105 S.Ct. 1986, 85 L.Ed.2d 372 (1985). With regard to this issue, the Supreme Court has stated:

> As an inanimate entity, a corporation must act through its agents. A corporation cannot speak directly to its lawyers. Similarly, it cannot directly waive the privilege when disclosure is in its best interest. Each of these actions must necessarily be undertaken by individuals empowered to act on behalf of the corporation....

> For solvent corporations, the power to waive the corporate attorney-client privilege rests with the corporation's management and is normally exercised by its officers and directors. The managers, of course, must exercise the privilege in a manner consistent with their fiduciary duty to act in the best interests of the corporation and not of themselves as individuals.

> The parties also agree that when control of a corporation passes to new management, the authority to assert and waive the corporation's attorney-client privilege passes as well. New managers ... may waive the attorney-client privilege with respect to communications made by former officers and directors. Displaced managers may not assert the privilege over the wishes of current

managers, even as to statements that the former might have made to counsel concerning matters within the scope of their corporate duties.

Id. at 348–49, 105 S.Ct. 1986 (internal citations omitted).

b. The Joint Client Exception

Joint clients are clients who are represented by the same attorney on a matter of common legal interest. Paul R. Rice, *Attorney-Client Privilege in the United States* § 4:23 (2008). With respect to corporations, the joint client exception theory is that there is one collective corporate client which includes the corporation and each individual member of the board of directors rather than just the corporation alone. *Id.* The theory is that because directors are collectively responsible for the management of a corporation and a corporation is an inanimate entity that cannot act without humans, it is consistent with a director's role and duties that the director be treated as a joint client when legal advice is rendered to the corporation through one of its directors. *Milroy v. Hanson,* 875 F.Supp. 646, 649 (D.Neb.1995). Courts have come down on both sides of this issue.[19]

c. Divergent Positions

(1) The "Entity is the Client"

Some courts have held that the sole client is the corporate entity or organization. In *Milroy v. Hanson,* 875 F.Supp. 646 (D.Neb.1995), a former director and minority shareholder of a closely held corporation sued the directors and majority shareholders seeking liquidation of the corporation. The plaintiff sought company documents, but the defendants refused to produce them, arguing that they were protected by the attorney-client privilege. *Id.* at 647. The court rejected a line of cases, which had held that the joint client exception applied to such a situation. *Id.* at 648–49. The court found that those cases:

> make a fundamental error by assuming that for a corporation there exists a "collective corporate 'client'" which may take a position adverse to "management" for purposes of the attorney-client privilege. There is but one client, and that client is the corporation. *Weintraub,* 471 U.S. at 348, 105 S.Ct. at 1990. This is true despite the fact that a corporation can only act through human beings. As the Supreme Court has stated, "for solvent corporations" the "authority to assert and waive the corporation's attorney-client privilege" rests with "*management.*" *Weintraub,* 471 U.S. at 348–49, 105 S.Ct. at 1991 (emphasis added). A dissident director is by definition not "management" and, accordingly, has no authority to pierce or otherwise frustrate the attorney-client privilege when such action conflicts with the will of "management."

---

19. [6] The court notes that both parties cited numerous cases to support their respective positions. In this order, the court does not list all of these cases but assures the parties that it has reviewed each of these holdings.

Id. at 649. The *Milroy* court found that the fact that the plaintiff former director had not filed suit in his fiduciary role as a corporate director to benefit the company, but rather in his individual role to benefit himself, made it even less likely that the plaintiff was entitled to the company's privileged documents. *Id.* at 650.

In *Dexia Credit Local v. Rogan*, 231 F.R.D. 268 (N.D.Ill.2004), the largest creditor of a bankrupt corporation sued the corporation's former CEO and managers for fraud. *Id.* at 277. The former CEO moved to compel production of documents withheld under the attorney-client privilege. *Id.* The court held that "the [attorney-client] privilege does not belong to the individual agents of the corporation seeking the advice; the privilege belongs to the corporation because the corporation is the client. That is the rule in federal courts...." *Id.* (citing *Weintraub*). The court noted that once the former CEO left the corporation, his right to access attorney-client privileged documents terminated. *Id.* It was of no matter that he had been employed at the time the documents were originally created because the privilege belonged to the corporation and did not depart with former officers who left the company. *Id.*

Other courts have taken the same position. *Bushnell v. Vis Corp.*, 1996 U.S. Dist. LEXIS 22572, 1996 WL 506914, *8 (N.D.Cal.1996) (unreported) (stating that the suggestion that the corporation is a joint client with its directors is "erroneous" and holding that a former director has no right to the corporation's attorney-client privileged documents); *In re Marketing Investors Corp.*, 80 S.W.3d 44, 50 (Tex.App.1998) (finding the *Milroy* line of cases most persuasive and holding that when the corporation terminated its former president, his right to view attorney-client privileged documents ceased); *Genova v. Longs Peak Emergency Physicians, P.C.*, 72 P.3d 454, 462–63 (Colo.App.2003) (agreeing with *Milroy* and stating "although plaintiff's status as a former director would have entitled him to learn privileged information when he was a director, he would then have been duty bound to keep such information confidential. He would not have been entitled alone to assert or waive the privilege on behalf of [the corporation]"); *Lane v. Sharp Packaging Systems, Inc.*, 251 Wis.2d 68, 640 N.W.2d 788, 800–04 (2002) (holding that a former director is not by definition "management" and does not have the right to access attorney-client privileged documents against the will of current management).

(2) The Collective Corporate Client

A second line of cases has embraced the joint client exception for corporations. In *Gottlieb v. Wiles*, 143 F.R.D. 241 (D.Colo.1992), a former director and CEO sued the corporation. The corporation withheld documents from the plaintiff during discovery based on the attorney-client privilege. The court stated "It is certainly true that the attorney-client privilege belongs to the corporation, or its Trustee, and that [the plaintiff] has no power to either assert or waive it" on behalf of the corporation. *Id.* at 247. However, the court stated that whether the plaintiff could assert or waive the privilege on behalf of the corporation was not the dispositive issue—the issue was whether he could access those privileged documents that had been originally created during the time he had been a director and officer. *Id.* The court noted that while the plaintiff had been a director, he was "squarely within the class of persons who could receive communications" from the corporation's counsel "without adversely impacting the privileged or confidential nature of such material." *Id.* The court compared this situation to one in which two parties jointly retain a single attorney, and noted that when those joint clients later become adverse, neither is permitted to assert the attorney-client privilege against the other as to communications occurring while they had a common interest. *Id.* Thus, the court held that former director and CEO had the right to access the documents that had been created while he was a director and officer at the corporation. *Id.*

Other courts have come to the same conclusions as the *Gottlieb* court. *Kirby v. Kirby,* 1987 Del. Ch. LEXIS 463, 1987 WL 14862, *7 (Del.Ch.1987) (unreported) (holding that the directors of a closely held corporation, collectively, were the client and that joint clients may not assert the attorney-client privilege against one another); *Harris v. Wells,* 1990 U.S. Dist. LEXIS 13215, 1990 WL 150445, *3-4 (D.Conn.1990) (unreported) (holding that because the corporation's directors are entrusted with the responsibility of managing the corporation, the corporation's directors hold the attorney-client privilege and therefore cannot assert the privilege against each other); *Glidden Company v. Jandernoa,* 173 F.R.D. 459, 473–74 (W.D.Mich.1997) (directors have a right to access attorney communications relating to the time that they served as directors); *Inter-Fluve v. Montana Eighteenth Judicial District Court,* 327 Mont. 14, 112 P.3d 258, 264 (2005) (closely held corporation and directors were joint clients because a corporation can act only through its agents; therefore, the corporation could not assert the attorney-client privilege against its joint client directors).

d. Which Position is Most Persuasive?

The Ninth Circuit has not spoken on this subject. Indeed, none of the Circuit Courts of Appeals appear to have directly addressed the joint client exception under the facts of this case. However, in the context of a criminal case, the Ninth Circuit held that the defendant, a former director of a corporation, had hired the law firm to represent the corporate entity and not the director in his individual capacity as a director. *United States v. Plache,* 913 F.2d 1375, 1381 (9th Cir.1990). Thus, the corporate entity was the client. *Id.* The Ninth Circuit concluded that because the corporation itself was the client, the former director, as a "displaced" manager, had no power to assert the attorney-client privilege to prevent the corporation's attorney from testifying against him. *Id.*

The court acknowledges that *Plache* is a criminal, not a civil, case. Moreover, the *Plache* facts are the inverse of the present case: in *Plache,* the former director claimed he was a joint client in order to assert the attorney-client privilege on behalf of the corporation. In the present case, Montgomery does not seek to assert the attorney-client privilege on behalf of the corporation — instead, he seeks to prevent eTreppid from asserting the privilege against him. Despite the fact that *Plache* is the opposite of the present situation, the court finds the conclusion that the corporation is the client instructive. This court concludes that, given the opportunity, the Ninth Circuit would likely reject the premise that directors are joint clients with the corporation.

The court also finds *Moore v. Commissioner of Internal Revenue,* T.C. Memo, 2004–259 (2004) instructive. In *Moore,* the petitioners argued that because an LLC is an entity and can act only through humans, the individual members of an LLC were the "clients" for the purposes of the attorney-client privilege. *Id.* at *4. The tax court rejected that position and held that the LLC was the sole client of the attorney. *Id.* at *3–4. Noting that the power to waive a corporation's attorney-client privilege normally belongs to the officers and directors, the court held that this power belonged only to the *current* management of the LLC. *Id.* at *3 (quoting *Weintraub,* 471 U.S. at 348–49, 105 S.Ct. 1986).

Additionally, while *Milroy* may not be the "majority" position, as eTreppid asserts, the court notes that many more courts have rejected the reasoning in *Gottlieb* than in *Milroy.* The court further notes that in *Kirby,* the seminal case supporting the joint client exception line of cases, the court relied on absolutely no authority at all. *Kirby v. Kirby,* 1987 Del. Ch. LEXIS 463, 1987 WL 14862 (Del.Ch. 1987) (unreported).

In *In re Tri-River Trading, LLC,* 329 B.R. 252 (8th Cir. BAP 2005), an individual and a corporation formed an LLC and were the sole members. *Id.* at 257. The individual member and the LLC eventually sued the corporate member and the corporation's president and manager. *Id.* at 258. One attorney represented both the individual member and the LLC in that suit. *Id.* In a later bankruptcy action, the bankruptcy court prohibited the LLC's state court attorney from testifying as to communications he had with the LLC. *Id.* at 259. Instead, the attorney was permitted to testify only as to the advice he gave to the individual member during the state court action. *Id.* The Eighth Circuit bankruptcy appellate panel overturned. *Id.* Without explanation, the court assumed that the individual member and the LLC were joint clients. *Id.* at 268–69. The court concluded that there is no expectation of privacy between adverse joint clients for communications the clients receive during the time they had a common interest and held that the attorney should have been allowed to testify as to his communications with the LLC. *Id.*

The court in *Tri-River* cited neither *Milroy* nor *Gottlieb.* Further, the *Tri–River* court relied on a First Circuit case in holding that individual member and the LLC were joint clients—yet, this court's review of the First Circuit case reveals that it did not touch upon the issues pertinent to this case, namely, whether a former director could access attorney-client privileged documents from the corporation. *Id.* at 269 (citing *FDIC v. Ogden Corp.,* 202 F.3d 454, 461 (1st Cir.2000)).[20]

---

20. [7] Montgomery also makes the argument that Nevada law recognizes the joint client exception to the attorney-client privilege. *See* NRS 49.115(5) ("There is no privilege … as to a communication relevant to a matter of common interest between two or more clients if the communication was made by any of them to a lawyer retained or consulted in common, when offered in an action between any of the clients."). Before this clause applies, however, one must qualify as a "client" in the first instance, which, obviously, is the primary issue involved. Nevada's definition of "client" is "a person, including a public officer, corporation, association or other organization or entity, either public or private, who is rendered professional legal services by a lawyer, or who consults a lawyer with a view to obtaining professional legal services from him." NRS 49.045. Although it appears that either an individual or an entity such as an LLC may be a client, this definition does not assist the court in determining

Based on all of these considerations, the court concludes that the *Milroy* line of cases are more persuasive. It makes sense that the corporation is the sole client. While the corporation can only communicate with its attorneys through human representatives, those representatives are communicating on behalf of the corporation, not on behalf of themselves as corporate managers or directors. Moreover, the court finds very convincing the language in *Weintraub*, which states that the privilege belongs to the corporation, can be asserted or waived only by management, and that this power transfers when control of the corporation is transferred to new management.

Also important to the court's decision is the fact that Montgomery, like the former director in *Milroy*, is not suing on behalf of eTreppid or in his capacity as a former manager or officer. Rather, Montgomery is suing to benefit himself individually— a perfectly acceptable position, but not one which should entitle him to eTreppid's attorney-client privileged communications. Like the "dissident" director in *Milroy*, Montgomery is now adverse to eTreppid and may not obtain privileged documents over the objection of current management. Moreover, even though Montgomery would have had access to such documents during his time at eTreppid, he still would have been duty-bound to keep such information confidential.

The court concludes that eTreppid is the sole client; therefore, eTreppid holds the attorney-client privilege. Only current management may assert or waive such privilege. Although he is still a member of eTreppid, Montgomery is not part of eTreppid's current management (#s443–445). As such, Montgomery may not access eTreppid's attorney-client privileged communications.

III. CONCLUSION

The court concludes as follows:

1. The federal law of privilege applies, although the court may look to state law if instructive;

2. Limited liability companies, and particularly eTreppid under the facts of this case, are most analogous to corporations; therefore, the law of corporations applies for purposes of the attorney-client privilege;

3. Montgomery is not a joint client with eTreppid. eTreppid is the sole client for purposes of the attorney-client privilege; and

4. eTreppid holds the attorney-client privilege and may assert or waive the privilege against Montgomery.

Based on the foregoing and for good cause appearing:

IT IS ORDERED that eTreppid may assert the attorney-client privilege in response to Montgomery's discovery requests;

---

whether Montgomery is a "client" *in conjunction with* eTreppid. The court's research reveals no Nevada case law on this topic. Montgomery requests that the court turn to *Wortham* because it discusses California's joint client exception which is similar to Nevada's. However, as noted, *Wortham* involves a partnership rather than a corporation, and the court does not view *Wortham* as applicable.

IT IS FURTHER ORDERED that eTreppid produce a privilege log that includes all documents and communications for which it intends to assert the attorney-client privilege. In doing so, eTreppid must carefully consider Douglas Frye's role as eTreppid's full-time manager and part-time in-house counsel;

IT IS FURTHER ORDERED that after conferring, should the parties disagree that certain documents and/or communications are attorney-client privileged, the parties may submit these documents and/or communications to the court, *in camera,* with arguments supporting their respective positions.

IT IS SO ORDERED.

United States v. International Brotherhood of Teamsters

United States District Court, S.D. New York
961 F. Supp. 665 (1997)

OPINION

Edelstein, District Judge:

This opinion emanates from the voluntary settlement of an action commenced by plaintiff United States of America (the "Government") against, *inter alia,* defendants International Brotherhood of Teamsters ("IBT") and the IBT's General Executive Board embodied in the voluntary consent order entered March 14, 1989 (the "Consent Decree"). The goal of the Consent Decree is to rid the IBT of the hideous influence of organized crime through a two-phased implementation of the Consent Decree's various remedial provisions.

In the first phase of the Consent Decree, these provisions provided for three court-appointed officers: the Independent Administrator to oversee the Consent Decree's provisions, the Investigations Officer to bring charges against corrupt IBT members, and the Election officer to supervise the electoral process that led up to and included the 1991 election for IBT office. In the second phase of the Consent Decree, the Independent Administrator was replaced by a three-member Independent Review Board, but the position of Election Officer remained, and was authorized to supervise the 1996 IBT elections.

Currently before this Court is *Application No. IX of the Election Officer For A Declaratory Judgment Regarding Claim of Privilege* ("Application IX"). For the following reasons, this Court finds that Application IX should be granted.

BACKGROUND

Under the terms of the Consent Decree, the Election Officer has the responsibility to investigate, to evaluate, and, in the event of a violation, to remedy all protests concerning IBT elections. *See* (Rules for the 1995–96 IBT International Union Delegate and Officer Election, Art. XIV, ("Election Rules").) On February 4, 1997, after Ron Carey ("Carey") was re-elected as IBT President over James Hoffa, Jr. ("Hoffa"), Hoffa filed an election protest with the Election Officer asserting that certain contributors to the Campaign to Re-elect Ron Carey (the "Carey Campaign") were made by "employers" under the Election Rules, and that therefore their contributions were prohibited under the Election Rules. (Declaration of Barbara Zack Quindel In Support of Election Officer Application IX, *United States v. International Bhd. of Teamsters,* 88 Civ. 4486 ("Quindel Decl.") ¶ 4 (Apr. 10, 1997).) Upon receipt of this protest, the Election Officer commenced an investigation into its allegations. *Id.*

Since June 8, 1995, the New York law firm of Cohen, Weiss & Simon ("CW&S" or the "firm") has acted as counsel to the Carey Campaign. (Declaration of Susan Davis, *United States v. International Bhd. of Teamsters,* 88 Civ. 4486 ("Davis Decl. II") ¶ 1 (Apr. 15, 1997).) Jere B. Nash III ("Nash") of Jackson, Mississippi was the Carey Campaign's Campaign Manager during the 1996 IBT election. (Quindel Decl. ¶ 5.) In the course of the Election Officer's investigation into the protest concerning the contributions to the Carey Campaign, Susan Davis ("Davis"), a partner at CW&S, informed the Election Officer that Davis and other attorneys at her firm had communications with Nash relevant to the Election Officer's investigation. *Id.* Davis further informed the Election Officer that IBT President Carey, the Carey Campaign's authorized representative, had instructed Davis to disclose her firm's communications with Nash to the Election Officer, waiving the Carey Campaign's attorney-client privilege as to those communications. *Id.*

Davis represents that Carey authorized CW&S on behalf of the Carey Campaign, to cooperate fully with the Election Officer and to provide the Election Officer with access to all information relevant to the campaign contribution investigation. (Davis Decl. II ¶ 13.) Nash, however, contends that his communications with CW&S are subject to his personal attorney-client privilege, and that CW&S may not disclose those communications to the Election Officer without Nash's explicit waiver, which he refuses to provide. (Opposition of Jere Nash to Election Officer Application IX, *United States v. International Bhd. of Teamsters,* 88 Civ. 4486 ("Nash Opp.") at 1–2 (Apr. 15, 1997).) CW&S is willing to disclose the substance of all its communications with Nash. (Davis Decl. II ¶ 13.) Because of Nash's assertion of privilege, however, CW&S, after conferring with its own outside counsel, has elected not to reveal the substance of any of its communications with Nash absent an order from this Court. *Id.*; (Declaration of Susan Davis, *United States v. International Bhd. of Teamsters,* 88 Civ. 4486 ("Davis Decl. I") ¶ 4 (Apr. 9, 1997).)

The communications at issue took place on several occasions during March 1997. (Davis Decl. I ¶ 5.) On March 6, 1997, a CW&S associate was present during a telephone conversation in which Mr. Nash was questioned by an Election Office investigator regarding the alleged campaign contribution violations. *Id.* ¶ 5(a). On March 7, 1997, CW&S asked Nash to meet at the firm's offices on Saturday March 8, or Sunday March 9, 1997, in order to discuss the campaign contributions. *Id.* ¶ 5(b). Nash was unable to meet on either of those dates, but agreed to meet that Monday, March 10, 1997. *Id.* On March 10, 1997, four CW&S attorneys, Stanley Berman ("Berman"), Stephen Presser ("Presser"), Nathaniel Charney ("Charney") and Davis, met with Nash at CW&S's offices. *Id.* ¶ 5(c). Davis asserts that at this meeting she "informed Mr. Nash that [CW&S] had asked to speak with him as counsel to the Carey Campaign and that [CW&S] w [as] investigating allegations concerning the [election protest] that had recently been brought to the attention of the Carey Campaign on behalf of the [Carey] [C]ampaign and Ron Carey." *Id.* Davis also declares that the CW&S attorneys present at this meeting informed Nash that their conversations were "privileged," by which the attorneys assumed that the privilege belonged to the firm's client, the Carey Campaign, not to Nash. *Id.* This assumption, however, was never communicated to Nash. (Hearing Transcript, *United States v. International Bhd. of Teamsters,* 88 Civ. 4486 ("Tr.") 22 (Apr. 17, 1997).) Nash was also cautioned at the meeting that his disclosure of the substance of the meeting to individuals "outside the Carey Campaign could alter the 'privileged' nature" of the communications made during the meeting. (Davis Ded. I ¶ 5(c).) Once again, however, the CW&S attorneys "understood this privilege to belong to the Carey Campaign rather than to any individual employed by the Carey Campaign," and, once again, they neglected to inform Nash of their understanding. *Id.*

On March 12, 1997, CW&S attorneys Berman, Presser and Charney had a brief telephone conversation with Nash. *Id.* ¶ 5(d). At the end of this phone call, Nash asked the attorneys whether this conversation had been privileged. *Id.* Nash was advised by Berman and Presser that it was privileged, but, yet again, the attorneys did not explain that, in their view, the privilege belonged to the Carey Campaign, not to Nash. *Id.* On March 13, 1997, CW&S "engaged and consulted outside counsel concerning the status of [its] conversations with Mr. Nash and other legal issues that the firm had encountered in connection with the [election] protest" regarding the allegedly illegal campaign contributions. *Id.* ¶ 5(e). On March 14, 1997, Davis informed Nash that CW&S "was making a full report to Ron Carey concerning [CW&S's] conversations with Mr. Nash on March 10, 1997, and March 12, 1997." *Id.* ¶ 5(f). Nash did not object to the firm's disclosure, and acknowledged that he was aware that the firm would report the communications to Carey. *Id.* On March 18, 1997, CW&S informed Nash that he should "consider engaging personal counsel with respect to further inquiries of him from [the Election Officer]." *Id.* ¶ 5(g). Nash asserts that, upon hearing this information, he stated his belief that CW&S was his personal counsel. (Declaration of Jere Nash In Opposition to Election Officer Application No. IX, *United States v. International Bhd. of Teamsters,* 88 Civ. 4486 ("Nash Decl.") ¶ 4 (Apr. 15, 1997).) In response to Nash's statement, Davis "told Mr. Nash that CW&S represented the Carey Campaign as an entity, rather than individuals within the campaign," and that the firm had never represented Nash individually. (Davis Decl. II ¶ 11.)

Through both telephone and personal communications over the course of the next week, CW&S attorneys apprised the Election Officer and the United States Attorney's Office of the firm's situation with Nash. *Id.* ¶¶ 5(h)-(1). On March 19, 1997, Davis informed the Election Officer that Nash would likely engage personal counsel and that "certain of [the firm's] conversations with Mr. Nash were arguably subject to privilege claims by Mr. Nash, that [the] firm had sought advice of counsel with respect to those privilege issues, and that the firm believed that such privilege issues should be resolved through a prompt judicial proceeding." *Id.* ¶ 5(h). On March 21, 1997,

Davis confirmed to the Election Officer that Nash had, in fact, engaged personal counsel and asserted the attorney-client privilege over his March 10 and 12, 1997, conversations with the CW&S attorneys. *Id.* ¶ 5(i). Davis also notified the Election Officer that "the firm had explained to the U.S. Attorney's [O]ffice that the appropriate course of action was to seek judicial resolution of such claims before a court of competent jurisdiction." *Id.* On March 22 and 26, 1997, Davis and Presser met with the Election Officer to describe "the facts and circumstances surrounding Mr. Nash's privilege claim," CW&S's own consultation with counsel, the need for "prompt judicial resolution of Mr. Nash's claim," and the "proper procedural approach" to such a resolution. *Id.* ¶¶ 5(j), (l). On March 24 and 27, 1997, CW&S attorneys met with at least one unidentified Assistant United States Attorney to discuss Nash's privilege claim, as well as a possible judicial resolution of it. *Id.* ¶¶ 5(k), (m).

On April 10, 1997, the Election Officer filed the instant application with this Court. The Election Officer's application seeks, pursuant to her authority under the Consent Decree, a declaratory judgment that Nash possesses no attorney-client privilege with respect to his communications with CW&S. (Quindel Decl. ¶ 1.) Because of the importance of a prompt adjudication of this issue to the Election Officer's ongoing investigation into the alleged improprieties of the Carey Campaign, this Court set an expedited submission schedule and held a hearing ("the hearing") concerning this matter on April 17, 1997.

At the hearing, this Court made two preliminary rulings before proceeding to the core issue of the validity of Nash's asserted privilege. First, this Court granted Nash's unopposed motion to intervene as of right under Federal Rule of Civil Procedure 24(a)(2), based on this Court's finding that the hearing jeopardized Nash's interest in his asserted attorney-client privilege. (Tr. 3.) Second, relying upon the substantial body of case law affirming this Court's jurisdiction over all facets of the Consent Decree, this Court rejected Nash's challenge to this Court's jurisdiction to issue a declaratory judgment adjudicating this matter to assist the Election Officer's investigative responsibilities under the Consent Decree. *Id.* at 7–8. Finally, after hearing lengthy testimony and argument, this Court found that Nash cannot assert the attorney-client privilege over his communications with CW&S, and granted the Election Officer's application in summary fashion. *Id.* at 85–86. The authority and reasoning supporting this Court's two preliminary rulings are fully set forth on the record, *id.* at 3–8, and therefore, they require no further explanation here. The instant Opinion and Order is thus dedicated to fully explaining the legal and factual foundations for this Court's determination that Nash cannot invoke the attorney-client privilege to protect his communications with CW&S regarding the allegations of improper campaign contributions.

DISCUSSION

This Court must resolve three distinct issues in the instant Opinion and Order: (1) whether Nash may assert the attorney-client privilege over his communication with CW&S; (2) whether a declaratory judgment should issue adjudicating Nash's ability to assert that privilege; and (3) whether CW&S breached its ethical obligations under New York's Code of Professional Responsibility. This Court will address each of these questions individually.

I. THE ATTORNEY–CLIENT PRIVILEGE

The attorney-client privilege applies so that

> (1) [w]here legal advice of any kind is sought (2) from a professional legal advisor in his capacity as such, (3) the communications relating to that purpose, (4) made in confidence (5) by the client, (6) are at his instance permanently protected (7) from disclosure by himself or the legal advisor (8) except the protection [can] be waived....

In re Richard Roe, Inc., 68 F.3d 38, 39–40 (2d Cir.1995) (Winter, J.) (citing *United States v. Kovel*, 296 F.2d 918, 921 (2d Cir.1961)) (Friendly, J.) (citing 8 Wigmore, Evidence §2292 (McNaughton Rev.1961)). Permitting clients to speak to their attorneys in confidence is designed "to encourage full and frank communication between attorneys and their clients in order to promote the public interest in the observance of the law and the administration of justice." *Upjohn Co. v. United States*, 449 U.S. 383, 389, 101 S.Ct. 677, 682, 66 L.Ed.2d 584 (1981). The privilege, however, conflicts with the principle that the public has a right to "every man's evidence," and therefore must be "strictly confined within the narrowest possible limits consistent with the logic of its principle." *In re Horowitz*, 482 F.2d 72, 81 (2d Cir.1973) (Friendly, J.); *see also University of Pa. v. Equal Employment Opportunity Comm'n*, 493 U.S. 182, 189, 110 S.Ct. 577, 582, 107 L.Ed.2d 571 (1990); *United States v. Schwimmer*, 892 F.2d 237, 244 (2d Cir.1989), *aff'd*, 924 F.2d 443 (2d Cir.), *cert. denied*, 502 U.S. 810, 112 S.Ct. 55, 116 L.Ed.2d 31 (1991); *Diversified Indus., Inc. v. Meredith*, 572 F.2d 596, 602 (8th Cir.1977) ("[w]hile the privilege, where it exists, is absolute, the adverse effect of its application on the disclosure of truth may be such that the privilege is strictly construed"). With these principles in mind, this Court must determine whether Nash may invoke the attorney-client privilege over his communications with CW&S. In so doing, this Court is confronted with two issues, each of which will be addressed separately: (1) the legal standard controlling whether an employee's communications with corporate counsel are subject to the employee's personal attorney-client privilege, and whether Nash meets that standard; and (2) if Nash's communications with CW&S are privileged, whether he waived that privilege.

A. The Appropriate Legal Standard

It is undisputed that CW&S was the Carey Campaign's counsel, and, therefore, that the Carey Campaign as an organization may assert the attorney-client privilege over its communications with CW&S. *See Upjohn*, 449 U.S. at 389, 101 S.Ct. at 682, 66 L.Ed.2d 584 (attorney-client privilege applies to corporations and other inanimate entities). However, where an attorney represents an inanimate entity, such as an election campaign, the application of the attorney-client privilege can be problematic because the entity cannot directly assert or waive the privilege, but can do so only through its agents. *See Commodity Futures Trading Comm'n v. Weintraub*, 471 U.S. 343, 347, 105 S.Ct. 1986, 1991, 85 L.Ed.2d 372 (1985); *see also Diversified Indus.*, 572 F.2d at 602. In this context, courts often are asked to determine "whether the privilege extends to communications by or to all classes of [the entity's] agents or employees[,] or whether the privilege is limited to communications by or to only limited classes of such agents or employees." *Diversified Indus.*, 572 F.2d at 596. The Supreme Court has grappled with this issue on several occasions, but has not yet established a clear standard by which such privileges are judged. *See, e.g.,* Michael A. Waldman, *Beyond Upjohn: The Attorney-Client Privilege in the Corporate Context,* 28 Wm. & Mary L.Rev. 473, 476–89 (1987) (discussing Supreme Court decisions concerning organization attorney-client privilege). The case at bar, however, presents a rather different question. Here, this Court is not asked to determine whether the Carey Campaign may assert the attorney-client privilege over the communications of Nash, its campaign manager. Rather, the issue squarely before this Court is whether Nash may assert the privilege on his own behalf to protect his communications with the Carey Campaign's counsel, CW&S, when the Carey Campaign has stated that it will not invoke the privilege on its own behalf.

As the Election Officer and the Government point out, it is a general rule that "any privilege that attaches to a communication between a corporate officer and a corporate attorney concerning matters within the scope of the officer's duties or relating to the corporation's affairs belongs to the corporation, not to the individual officer." (Govt. Letter at 5); (E.O. Memo at 4–5); *see, e.g., United States v. Demauro,* 581 F.2d 50, 55 (2d Cir.1978); *In re O.P.M. Leasing Svcs., Inc.,* 13 B.R. 64, 67 (S.D.N.Y.1981) (Weinfeld, J.). Nevertheless, the Government and the Election Officer each acknowledge that courts have recognized exceptions to this general rule, but have articulated no clear standard setting forth the circumstances in which that exception applies. Unsurprisingly, the Election Officer and Nash each ask this Court to apply a different standard.

The Election Officer contends that this Court should adopt a rigorous standard for determining when an employee may invoke the attorney-client privilege over communications with corporate counsel which requires the employee to "prove [that] the attorney represented the person as an individual, rather than as a representative of the entity." (E.O. Memo at 5.) As an example of such a standard, the Election Officer offers In re *Grand Jury Investigation No. 83–30557,* 575 F.Supp. 777 (N.D.Ga.1983). Reasoning that "the attorney-client privilege is a narrowly tailored exception to the rule of full disclosure" of "every man's evidence," the *In re Grand Jury* court set forth a standard which requires the employee seeking to assert a personal privilege over communications with corporate counsel to establish: (1) that he approached corporate counsel to obtain legal advice; (2) that he clearly indicated that he was seeking legal advice in an individual, rather than a corporate, capacity; (3) that corporate counsel, aware of the potential conflict, agreed to represent him in an individual capacity; (4) that he understood his communications were confidential; and (5) that the substance of the conversation did not concern matters related to the employee's official duties or the affairs of his employer. *Id.* at 780.

Nash, on the other hand, urges this Court to apply a more lenient legal standard to determine whether an employee of an entity may assert the attorney-client privilege over communications made by the employee to the entity's counsel. (Nash Memo at

4–7.) Nash contends that the Election Officer's proposed standard unfairly places the burden upon the "layman untrained in the law ... to identify potential conflicts in a context where an attorney seems to be acting in the individual's interest." *Id.* at 6. Accordingly, Nash argues for a standard which permits an individual to assert the attorney-client privilege where the individual "had a reasonable belief he was making confidential disclosures to attorneys who were acting on his behalf." *Id.* at 4. Nash then asserts that, as Campaign Manager, it was reasonable for him to believe that the Carey Campaign's attorneys were his personal attorneys and that CW&S's assurances that his communications were privileged made it reasonable for him to believe that CW&S did, in fact, represent him individually. *Id.* at 11–12.

To this Court's surprise, research has revealed that the Second Circuit has not yet confronted the issue of an employee's attempted assertion of a personal attorney-client privilege over communications with his employer's counsel, and, as a result, this Court is left without binding authority establishing the appropriate standard by which to adjudicate the case at bar. The facts of this case, however, relieve this Court from the responsibility of holding that either the standards proffered by the parties or some other rule controls this Court's resolution of the instant dispute. Instead, assuming *arguendo* the applicability of Nash's reasonable belief standard, this Court finds that Nash could not reasonably have believed that CW&S was his personal counsel, or that his communications with the firm were confidential.

The communications at issue occurred in the context of CW&S's investigation, on behalf of the Carey Campaign, into allegations of improper campaign contributions. *See* (Davis Decl. I ¶ 5(c)); (Davis Decl. II ¶¶ 6–9.) At the March 10, 1997, meeting between CW&S and Nash, Davis asserts that she "informed Mr. Nash that [CW&S] had asked to speak with him *as counsel to the Carey Campaign* ... [and] that [CW&S] needed to interview him *on behalf of the campaign* concerning the subject of [the alleged improper campaign contributions]." (Davis Decl. II ¶ 7 (emphasis added)). In addition, when CW&S informed Nash that Nash's communications with CW&S were "privileged," they did so in a manner which made it clear that the privilege existed for the benefit of its client, the Carey Campaign, not for Nash. At the March 10, 1997, Presser "cautioned Mr. Nash that the disclosure of our conversation with *persons outside the Carey Campaign* could alter the 'privileged' nature [of the meeting]." (Davis Decl. I ¶ 5(d) (emphasis added).) Likewise, Nash's conduct manifests his awareness that any privilege which existed over his communications with CW&S belonged to the Carey Campaign and Carey. On March 14, 1997, Davis informed Nash that CW&S "was making a full report to Ron Carey concerning our conversations with Mr. Nash on March 10, 1997[,] and March 12, 1997," and Nash "did not object to the firm's disclosure of those conversations to Mr. Carey and acknowledged that he was aware that [CW&S] w[as] reporting to Mr. Carey on such conversations." *Id.* ¶ 5(f).

This Court finds that a reasonable person in Nash's situation could not have believed that CW&S represented him individually, or that he personally possessed an attorney-client privilege over his communications with CW&S. Nash was informed, prior to his making the communications he now seeks to protect, that CW&S was speaking with him in the course of their investigation on behalf of the Carey Campaign. In addition, Nash was told that his communications could be disclosed to others within the Carey Campaign, and that they would be disclosed to Carey. A reasonable person could not have believed that he possessed a personal privilege while acknowledging that the information he claims to be privileged could be, and was, shared with third parties. These facts effectively undercut Nash's claim that he reasonably believed that CW&S was his personal counsel and that he possessed a personal privilege over his communications with them. *See Polycast Technology Corp. v. Uniroyal, Inc.,* 125 F.R.D. 47, 49 (S.D.N.Y.1989) (second corporate officer's presence during conversation between another officer and corporate counsel "underscored the fact that [counsel] was providing advice to a corporate, rather than an individual, client"). Accordingly, this Court finds that, even if this Court were to adopt the lenient standard Nash proposes—which it does not—Nash cannot establish that he possessed an attorney-client privilege over his communications with CW&S.

Even though this Court need not settle upon a standard governing situations in which an employee seeks to assert a personal attorney-client privilege over communications with his employer's counsel, in an effort to be thorough, this Court observes without deciding that Nash's reasonable belief standard appears inappropriate. That standard would create an unworkable, overly broad privilege which would thwart both the precept that the privilege is to be narrowly construed, *see Horowitz,* 482 F.2d at 81; *In re Grand Jury Investigation,* 575 F.Supp. at 779, and the principle that the attorney-client privilege is intended to encourage clients' disclosure to attorneys to assist their compliance with the law. *See Upjohn,* 449 U.S. at 389, 101 S.Ct. at 682. First, as noted above, the general rule is that the attorney-client privilege belongs exclusively to an employer with respect to employees' communications with the employer's counsel, *see In re O.P.M. Leasing Svcs.,* 13 B.R. at 67, with an unclear exception which the parties urge this Court to define. Adopting the reasonable belief standard to define that exception would vastly expand the attorney-client privilege's applicability by making it available to every employee who purports to have a reasonable belief that his employer's counsel gave him personal advice. Such an exception is contrary to the narrow construction that courts are required to give the attorney-client privilege.

Moreover, this extraordinarily broad privilege would permit an employee to frustrate an internal investigation by his employer's counsel simply by claiming that his communications with counsel were based on a reasonable belief that counsel represented him. If that were so, the investigating attorneys would be precluded from disclosing the employee's communications to the employer, thus thwarting the investigation. Erecting such a wall between an employer and his counsel contravenes the attorney-client privilege's grounding principle—to facilitate compliance with the law by encouraging open and candid communication between attorneys and their clients. For these reasons, the reasonable belief standard appears to this Court to be overly broad, unworkable and contrary to well-established principles underlying the attorney-client privilege.

B. Waiver

The Government contends that "[e]ven assuming *arguendo* that Mr. Nash somehow possessed a personal attorney-client privilege based on his conversations with [CW&S], the disclosure of the content of such conversations to Mr. Carey eliminated any such privilege." (Govt. Letter at 4.) No other party, either by submission or by oral argument, has addressed the impact of Nash's knowing disclosure of his communications to Carey on Nash's claim of privilege.

Waiver of an attorney-client privilege is a question of fact. *See* 3 Joseph M. McLaughlin, *et al.,* Weinstein's Federal Evidence § 503.09[1] (2d ed.1997). The attorney-client privilege is waived if the "holder of the privilege voluntarily discloses or consents to disclosure of any significant part of the matter or communication" over which the privilege is claimed. *In re Kidder Peabody Sec. Litig.,* 168 F.R.D. 459, 468 (S.D.N.Y.1996); *see also Westinghouse Elec. Corp. v. Republic of Philippines,* 951 F.2d 1414, 1424 (3d Cir.1991); *United States v. Rockwell Int'l,* 897 F.2d 1255, 1265 (3d Cir.1990) ("the attorney-client privilege does not apply to communications that are intended to be disclosed to third parties or that are in fact so disclosed"); 3 Weinstein's Federal Evidence § 503.09[1] ("Any disclosure of a lawyer-client communication to a third party for purposes inconsistent with maintaining confidentiality waives the attorney-client privilege as to that disclosure"). Moreover, disclosure of a privileged communication waives the privilege as to all other communications on the same subject. *See Rockwell Int'l,* 897 F.2d at 1265, 3 Weinstein's Federal Evidence § 503.09[1].

In the instant case, even if Nash once possessed a personal privilege with respect to his communications with CW&S regarding the campaign contribution investigation, this Court finds that he knowingly waived that privilege. The uncontroverted evidence clearly establishes that Davis informed Nash of CW&S's intention to "mak[e] a full report to Ron Carey" concerning Nash's communications with CW&S, and that Nash neither objected nor sought to prevent that disclosure. (Davis Decl. I ¶ 5(f).) This Court finds that Nash's failure to object serves to waive any privilege he may have had over all of his communications with CW&S concerning the campaign contribution investigation.

II. DECLARATORY JUDGMENT

Having found that Nash cannot assert an attorney-client privilege over his communications with CW&S, this Court must briefly consider whether to grant the Election Officer's application for a declaratory judgment, see 28 U.S.C. § 2201 ("Section 2201"), regarding Nash's claim of privilege. Section 2201 authorizes courts in "case[s] of actual controversy within its jurisdiction [with certain exceptions not relevant here] to declare the rights and other legal relations of any interested party seeking such declaration." *Id.* The issuance of a declaratory judgment rests within this Court's discretion. *See Agency Rent a Car Sys. v. Grand Rent a Car Corp.,* 98 F.3d 25, 32 (2d Cir.1996); *Wilton v. Seven Falls Co.,* 515 U.S. 277, ——, 115 S.Ct. 2137, 2143, 132 L.Ed.2d 214 (1995).

In the case at bar, this Court found above that this Court possesses jurisdiction over this matter pursuant to its oversight of the Consent Decree. In addition, this Court finds that Nash's assertion of privilege impacts the Election Officer's investigative ability, and that the issuance of a declaratory judgment precluding Nash from doing so will greatly assist the Election Officer in the fulfillment of her duties under the Consent Decree. This, in turn, will promote the objectives of the Consent Decree itself, as it will help determine the existence of illegal conduct within the recent Teamsters election. This Court therefore finds that the Election officer's application for a declaratory judgment should be granted.

III. CODE OF PROFESSIONAL RESPONSIBILITY

At the hearing, Nash questioned CW&S's compliance with the New York Code of Professional Responsibility (the "Code"). (Tr. 77–80.) Specifically, Nash asserted that Disciplinary Rule 5–109 ("DR 5–109") sets forth the ethical rule applicable to the case at bar, and required the CW&S attorneys to inform Nash that they represented the Carey Campaign, not Nash. *Id.* at 78. CW&S did not address its compliance with DR 5–109 in its submissions or at the hearing. However, the firm does assert, and no one disputes, that it complied with Ethical Consideration 5–18 and Disciplinary Rule 4–101(B) of the Code. *See* (Memorandum of Law Submitted on Behalf of Cohen, Weiss & Simon In Response to the Election Officer's Application No. IX, *United States v. International Bhd. of Teamsters,* 88 Civ. 4486 at 5–7 (Apr. 16, 1997).) The only disputed ethical violation, therefore, is CW&S's compliance with DR 5–109. This Court takes seriously its duty to ensure the unwavering ethical conduct of the attorneys who appear before it, and therefore will consider whether, as Nash asserts, the CW&S attorneys breached DR 5–109, and, if so, the disciplinary action which should be taken against them.

Effective September 1, 1990, the Appellate Division of the New York Supreme Court adopted the Disciplinary Rules of the Code of Professional Responsibility under Title 22 of the New York Code, Rules and Regulations (the "Disciplinary Rules"). 22 N.Y.C.R.R. pt. 1200 (West 1997). These Disciplinary Rules are "applicable to all attorneys admitted to practice in New York State," 29 N.Y. Jud. Law app. (McKinney 1997 Supp.), are "mandatory in character," and set forth "the minimum level of conduct below which no lawyer can fall without being subject to disciplinary action." 29 N.Y. Jud. Law app. Preliminary Statement (McKinney 1992). DR 5–109, "Conflict of Interest—Organization as Client," provides:

> (a) When a lawyer employed or retained by an organization is dealing with the organization's directors, officers, employees, members, shareholders or other constituents, and it appears that the organization's interests may differ from those of the constituents with whom the lawyer is dealing, *the lawyer shall explain that the lawyer is the lawyer for the organization and not for any of the constituents.*

22 N.Y.C.R.R. § 1200.28 (1997) (adopting DR 5–109) (footnote omitted) (emphasis added). Davis is admitted to practice law in New York, (Tr. 14), and for purposes of

the instant Opinion and Order this Court assumes that the other CW&S attorneys implicated in this matter are members of the New York bar. As a result, each of them is subject to the mandatory ethical conduct requirements of DR 5–109.

On its face, DR 5–109 simply requires an attorney who has an organization as a client to be cognizant of potential conflicts between the interests of the organization, and the organization's individual employees. *See* 22 N.Y.C.R.R. § 1200.28. When the attorney recognizes such a conflict, he must explain to the employee with whom he is dealing that the attorney represents the organization, not the employee. *See id.* The text of the rule, however, leaves unaddressed at least one consideration which is important to the case at bar. DR 5–109 does not inform attorneys specifically when they must explain to an employee that the attorney represents the employer, not the employee. The rule simply states "when" a lawyer becomes aware of such a conflict, he must make the required explanation to the employee. This Court observes, however, that "when" could mean "immediately and without hesitation," it could mean "after thinking it over for a few days," or it could mean "anytime at all, just as long so it is done."

The timing issue aside, this Court finds that, in the instant case, CW&S did, in fact, comply with the minimal facial requirements of DR 5–109. On March 18, 1997, Davis informed Nash that he should obtain his own counsel and that CW&S represented the Carey Campaign rather than Nash personally. (Davis Decl. II 11.) This Court makes this finding reluctantly, however, and does so only because DR 5–109 does not clearly state when CW&S had to inform Nash that it did not represent him personally.

The following sequence of events demonstrates the reason for this Court's reluctance. Nash's communications with CW&S which he seeks to protect took place on March 10 and 12, 1997. (Davis Decl. I ¶¶ 5(c)-(d). On March 13, 1997, CW&S consulted its own outside counsel "concerning the status of [the firm's] conversations with Mr. Nash and other legal issues that the firm had encountered in connection with [the campaign contribution investigation])." *Id.* ¶ 5(e). On March 14, 1997, Davis informed Nash that CW&S would disclose the firm's communications with Nash to Carey, and Carey did not object. *Id.* ¶ 5(f). Not until March 18, 1997, did CW& inform Nash that he should engage personal counsel. *Id.* ¶ 5(g). It was only after Nash expressed his surprise that CW&S was not his counsel, that CW&S explained to Nash that the firm represented only the Carey Campaign, not Nash. (Davis Decl. II ¶ 11.) CW&S thus recognized its own interest in hiring outside counsel on March 13, 1997, but inexplicably delayed five days before it informed Nash that it did not represent him—and even then, did so only in response to Nash's question. Even more troubling, however, is that CW&S informed Nash that he should hire his own lawyer one day *after* Davis elicited Nash's waiver of privilege. Were it not for this Court's findings above that there are two independent reasons that Nash cannot assert an attorney-client privilege, this Court would refer the CW&S attorneys to the Committee on Grievances for this district. *See* (Local Rules of the United States District Courts for the Southern and Eastern

Districts of New York, Local Civil Rule 1.5(a), (b) (1997).) Because this Court's finding that Nash cannot assert the privilege does not hinge solely upon his waiver, CW&S's conduct is not the sole proximate cause of Nash's inability to assert the privilege. Nevertheless, CW&S's conduct amply justifies this Court's reluctance in finding that CW&S complied with DR 5–109.

While CW&S's conduct may have complied with the letter of the Code of Professional Responsibility, it clearly trampled its spirit. The Code's Preamble reads in relevant part:

> Lawyers, as guardians of the law, play a vital role in the preservation of society.... A consequent obligation of lawyers is to maintain the highest standards of ethical conduct.

> Each lawyer must find within his own conscience the touchstone against which to test the extent to which his actions should rise above minimum standards. But in the last analysis it is the desire for the respect and confidence of the members of this profession and of the society which he serves that should provide to a lawyer the incentive for the highest possible degree of ethical conduct. The possible loss of that respect and confidence is the ultimate sanction.

29 N.Y. Jud. Law app. Preamble (McKinney 1992). This Court finds that CW&S's conduct in the instant matter did not rise at all above the minimum standards of conduct established by DR 5–109. While that may be sufficient to avoid sanction, it is far from the sound, ethical practice of law which courts, clients, and all others who come into contact with our legal system have a right to expect from attorneys who hold themselves out as "guardians of the law."

CONCLUSION

IT IS HEREBY ORDERED THAT Application IX of the Election Officer for a declaratory judgment that Nash may not assert an attorney-client privilege over his communications with Cohen, Weiss & Simon is GRANTED.

SO ORDERED.

Endless Ocean, LLC v. Twomey, Latham, Shea, Kelley, Dubin & Quartararo

Supreme Court of the State of New York
Appellate Division, Second Department
979 N.Y.S.2d 84 (2014)

OPINION

In an action to recover damages for legal malpractice, the plaintiff appeals from (1) an order of the Supreme Court, Westchester County (O. Bellantoni, J.), dated June 4, 2012, which granted the defendants' motion to dismiss the complaint pursuant to CPLR 3211(a), and (2) a judgment of the same court dated July 5, 2012, which, upon the order, is in favor of the defendants and against the plaintiff dismissing the complaint. * * *

The plaintiff commenced this action to recover damages allegedly sustained as a result of the defendants' legal malpractice. As alleged in the complaint, the plaintiff retained the defendants to represent it in connection with the sale of certain real property and a related exchange of "like-kind property" pursuant to the Internal Revenue Code (see 26 USC § 1031). According to the allegations in the complaint, the plaintiff, based upon the defendants' advice, selected LandAmerica 1031 Exchange Services, Inc. (hereinafter LandAmerica), as the qualified intermediary to hold a portion of the sale proceeds, totaling $5.5 million, for the exchange of like-kind property pursuant to 26 USC § 1031. The complaint alleged, inter alia, that the defendants negligently represented the plaintiff inasmuch as they reviewed, and advised the plaintiff to execute, an agreement with LandAmerica, under which the exchange funds were to be held in a commingled account and not a qualified escrow account or trust. Soon after the sale proceeds were transferred to LandAmerica, its parent corporation, LandAmerica Financial Group, Inc., declared bankruptcy. According to the complaint, the plaintiff's funds were frozen for several years during the bankruptcy proceedings, and the plaintiff lost a portion of the funds because they were not held in a qualified escrow account or trust. The complaint further alleged that the plaintiff could not defer the taxes on the capital gains from the initial sale, as it did not have access to its funds to purchase a replacement property within the required 180-day period.

Prior to answering, the defendants moved to dismiss the complaint pursuant to CPLR 3211(a)(1) based on documentary evidence, and pursuant to CPLR 3211(a)(7) for failure to state a cause of action. The Supreme Court granted the defendants' motion to dismiss the complaint on both grounds.

The Supreme Court improperly granted the defendants' motion to dismiss the complaint based on documentary evidence. A motion to dismiss a complaint pursuant to CPLR 3211(a)(1) may be granted only if the documentary evidence submitted by the moving party utterly refutes the factual allegations of the complaint, "conclusively establishing a defense as a matter of law" (*Goshen v. Mutual Life Ins. Co. of N.Y.*, * * * 774 N.E.2d 1190). Here, the retainer agreement submitted by the defendants did not conclusively establish a defense as a matter of law (*see Harris v. Barbera*, * * * 947 N.Y.S.2d 548; *Rietschel v. Maimonides Med. Ctr.*, 921 N.Y.S.2d 290 * * *).

"On a motion to dismiss the complaint pursuant to CPLR 3211(a)(7) for failure to state a cause of action, the court must afford the pleading a liberal construction, accept all facts as alleged in the pleading to be true, accord the plaintiff the benefit of every possible inference, and determine only whether the facts as alleged fit within any cognizable legal theory" (*Breytman v. Olinville Realty, LLC*, * * * 864 N.Y.S.2d 70; *see Leon v. Martinez*, 84 N.Y.2d 83, 87 * * *). "Whether the complaint will later survive a motion for summary judgment, or whether the plaintiff will ultimately be able to prove its claims, of course, plays no part in the determination of a prediscovery CPLR 3211 motion to dismiss" * * *.

To succeed in a legal malpractice action, "a plaintiff must show that the defendant attorney failed to exercise the ordinary reasonable skill and knowledge commonly possessed by a member of the legal profession and that the attorney's breach of this professional duty caused the plaintiff's actual damages" (*Stuart v. Robert L. Folks & Assoc., LLP,* * * * 965 N.Y.S.2d 149 [internal quotation marks omitted]; *see Conklin v. Owen,* * * * 900 N.Y.S.2d 118; *Lamanna v. Pearson & Shapiro,* * * * 843 N.Y.S.2d 143).

Here, construing the complaint liberally, accepting the facts alleged in the complaint as true, and according the plaintiff the benefit of every possible inference, as we are required to do, the plaintiff stated a cause of action to recover damages for legal malpractice (*see Palmieri v. Biggiani,* * * * 970 N.Y.S.2d 41; *Kempf v. Magida,* * * * 832 N.Y.S.2d 47). The plaintiff alleged in the complaint that the defendants were negligent in failing, inter alia, to advise it to keep its exchange funds in a qualified escrow account or trust, and that this negligence was a proximate cause of its damages. The defendants' contentions that it was the conduct of the plaintiff's manager and unforeseeable events that were the proximate causes of the plaintiff's damages, and that the defendants did not depart from the standard of care, concern disputed factual issues that are not properly raised and resolved on a motion to dismiss a complaint pursuant to CPLR 3211(a)(7). * * * Accordingly, the defendants' motion to dismiss the complaint should have been denied.

Chapter 2

Taxable Gain and Loss

I. Commentary

Basic income tax concepts apply in the real estate context, so a brief review of some of the most basic concepts will help set the stage for discussing more complex aspects of taxation and business planning for real estate transactions. Income tax is a percentage of taxable income.[1] The computation of income tax (i.e., a person's tax liability) thus requires determining taxable income. Taxable income is gross income minus deductions.[2] Gross income is defined broadly to include any "accession[] to wealth" that is "clearly realized, and over which [a person has] complete dominion."[3] More specifically, gross income includes items such as compensation for services, interest, dividends, and gains from the disposition of property.[4] The law also excludes some items from gross income even though they may come within the broad definition of gross income or be listed as an item of gross income.[5] Taxpayers can only claim deductions that are specifically granted by a provisions of the Internal Revenue Code.[6] Common deductions include deductions for ordinary and necessary business expenses,[7] the deduction for interest,[8] and the depreciation deduction.[9] The Internal Revenue Code also specifically denies deductions for some expenditures. For example, a taxpayer must capitalize amounts paid to acquire or improve property.[10]

Taxable gains and losses are a significant component of the tax situation of many real estate owners. Property owners must include gains from dealings in property in gross income,[11] unless the gain is otherwise excluded or qualifies for nonrecognition

---

1. *See* I.R.C. §§ 1(a)–(d), 11(a).

2. *See* I.R.C. § 63.

3. *See* Comm'r v. Glenshaw Glass Co., 348 U.S. 426, 431 (1955) (not reproduced in this book).

4. *See* I.R.C. § 61(a).

5. *See, e.g.,* I.R.C. §§ 102(a) (excluding the value of gifts from gross income); 103(a) (excluding interest on state and local bonds from gross income); 108(a) (excluding income from the discharge of indebtedness from gross income); 121(a) (excluding gain from the sale of a principal residence);

6. *See* I.R.C. §§ 62(a), 63(a), 161, et seq.

7. *See* I.R.C. § 162.

8. *See* I.R.C. § 163.

9. *See* I.R.C. §§ 167, 168.

10. *See* I.R.C. § 267(a).

11. *See* I.R.C. § 61(a)(3). Dealings in property include sales and exchanges. *See* Treas. Reg. § 1.61-6(a).

treatment.[12] To deduct losses from the disposition of property, the loss must satisfy the conditions of one of the deduction-granting provisions.[13] After computing gains and losses and applying them correctly to compute taxable income, a taxpayer then must determine the rates that apply to the gain. Gains and losses are either ordinary or capital in nature.[14] Stated simply, long-term capital gains generally qualify for tax rates that are lower than the rates that apply to ordinary income,[15] so property owners generally prefer that their gains be characterized as long-term capital gains. Because the deductibility of capital losses is subject to limitations, property owners generally prefer that losses be ordinary. This chapter discusses the computation of gains and losses and the tax treatment of the different types of gains and losses. Other chapters introduce the law that determines the character of gains and losses.

A. Computing Taxable Gains and Losses

Property owners and attorneys often view the financial aspects of transactions differently. Many property owners consider the amount they invest in property and the return they receive on their investment.[16] Consequently, property owners often focus on cash they contribute to a real estate venture and cash they receive from the venture. In other words, property owners typically do not consider the amounts they borrow as part of their investment.[17] That view is different from the tax perspective of a transaction. Tax law provides that gain realized is the excess of the amount realized on the disposition of property over the property's adjusted basis.[18] As the discussion below reaffirms, amount realized includes liability relief that results from the transfer of property.[19] Often attorneys must explain to clients that tax law computes taxable gain and loss differently from the manner in which property owners determine their profitability.

Generally, an attorney can provide rough estimates to clients to illustrate the tax consequences that result from disposing of real property. For example, if a client believes that 100,000 square feet of non-depreciable property will sell for $4.50 a square foot and the client purchased the property for $2.75 a square foot, the attorney can roughly estimate the amount of gain the client will realize on this transaction. The amount realized would be $450,000 (100,000 square feet times $4.50 a square foot). The adjusted basis appears to be $275,000 (100,000 square feet times $2.75 a square

---

12. *See* I.R.C. §§ 61(a); 1001(c). Subsequent chapters cover gain and loss recognition and non-recognition in significant depth.

13. *See* I.R.C. § 161. Section 165 is the typical granting provision for losses on the disposition of property.

14. *See* I.R.C. § 64.

15. *See* I.R.C. § 1(h)(1).

16. *See infra* Chapter 5 (discussing the financial aspects of real estate investments and transactions).

17. *See infra* Chapter 5 (discussing the financial aspects of real estate investment).

18. *See* I.R.C. § 1001(a).

19. *See infra* Part I.B.

foot). By subtracting the estimated adjusted basis from the estimated amount realized, the attorney can estimate that gain on such a transaction would be $175,000 ($450,000 − $275,000 = $175,000).

Rough Estimate of Potential Gain

Amount realized (100,000 ft.2 x $4.50/ft.)	$450,000
Adjusted basis (100,000 ft.2 x $2.75/ft.)	($275,000)
Estimated potential gain	$175,000

With such basic information, the parties can estimate the amount of tax liability that may result from the disposition of the property. For example, if the tax rate that applies to the gain is 35%, the disposition of the property might generate $61,250 of tax liability for the owner ($175,000 of gain times the 35% tax rate). If the gain qualified for favorable long-term capital gains rates, the amount of tax liability might be $26,250 ($175,000 of gain times the 15% tax rate).

Potential Tax Liability

	Ord. Inc.	Cap. Gain
Estimated potential gain	$175,000	$175,000
Estimated tax rate	x 35%	x 15%
Estimated tax liability	$61,250	$26,250

These values allow the taxpayer to compute the potential tax savings that result from obtaining favorable long-term capital gain treatment.

Potential Tax Savings from Planning

Tax liability with no planning	$61,250
Potential tax liability with planning	($26,250)
Potential tax savings	$35,000

The $35,000 difference between the two potential tax liabilities represents the tax savings that could result from competent tax planning in some situations.

Subsequent chapters provide opportunities to learn some tax-planning techniques for real estate transactions and ownership. Before receiving tax advice with respect to a particular transaction, property owners will be interested to know the potential tax savings such advice may provide. They will likely compare that amount to the amount of legal fees they will incur to structure a transaction to obtain tax savings. A property owner would likely pay some amount considerably less than $35,000 for tax planning that would save $35,000 of taxes. Thus, tax attorneys must be able to determine and communicate the potential tax savings their planning will have for their clients. That planning begins with being able to compute gain and loss, which often requires an in-depth understanding of what amount realized and adjusted basis include.

1. *Amount Realized*

Stated generally, amount realized includes the sum of money and fair market value of property received on the disposition of property.[20] Amount realized also includes liability from which the property owner is relieved on the disposition of the property.[21] For purposes of computing amount realized, tax law treats recourse and nonrecourse liabilities differently,[22] so tax advisors must be able to determine whether liabilities exist, whether the property owner is relieved of the liability as part of the disposition, and what type of liability is relieved.[23] If the liability relief results in cancellation of indebtedness income, the property owner may be able to exclude that portion of the liability relief from gross income.[24] Amounts paid to sell property reduce the amount realized.[25]

2. *Adjusted Basis*

The adjusted basis of property is the cost of the property adjusted as provided in the statute.[26] The cost of property includes amounts borrowed to acquire the property.[27] If a property owner sells a portion of a large piece of property, the property owner must apportion part of the property's total basis to the sold portion.[28] Adjustments to the basis of property can either increase or decrease the adjusted basis.[29] The rules governing the adjustments to basis can become complex.

Capital expenditures that relate to the property increase the adjusted basis of the property.[30] As a general rule, a capital expenditure (i.e., an expenditure for which the

---

20. *See* I.R.C. § 1001(a).

21. *See* Commissioner v. Tufts, 461 U.S. 300 (1983); Crane v. Commissioner, 331 U.S. 1, 67 S. Ct. 1047, 91 L. Ed. 1301 (1947); Treas. Reg. § 1.1001-2(a)(1).

22. *See* Ghel v. Commissioner, 102 T.C. 784 (1994); Treas. Reg. § 1.1001-2(c), Ex. (7), (8).

23. *See infra* Chapter 5 (discussing the distinction between loans and other arrangements).

24. *See* I.R.C. § 108. If the property owner is a tax partnership, the analysis must consider whether the analysis to exclude is done at the tax-partnership level or the member level. *See* Chapter 4 (discussing tax aspects of tax partnerships).

25. *See* Treas. Reg. § 1.263(a)-1(e).

26. *See* I.R.C. § 1011(a) (providing that the definition of adjusted basis of property begins with the basis as determined under one of four different rules, including section 1012); I.R.C. § 1012 (providing that the basis of property is its cost).

27. *See* Commissioner v. Tufts, 461 U.S. 300 (1983); Crane v. Commissioner, 331 U.S. 1, 67 S. Ct. 1047, 91 L. Ed. 1301 (1947).

28. *See* Fairfield Plaza, Inc. v. Commissioner, 39 T.C. 706 (1963); Treas. Reg. § 1.61-6(a).

29. *See* I.R.C. § 1016.

30. *See* I.R.C. § 1016(a)(1).

property owner cannot take a deduction currently, as opposed to costs to repair and maintain property, which a property owner may deduct[31]) is any amount paid to acquire or improve property.[32] The issue of whether an expenditure is a cost to improve or repair has been the subject of numerous court cases, but Treasury has promulgated regulations that attempt to codify that body of case law (often referred to as the "repair regs" or "TPR (tangible property repair) regs"). Now, tax advisors generally turn the regulations to determine whether an amount paid is a non-deductible capital expenditure that becomes part of the property's basis or a deductible repair or maintenance expense.

The application of the repair regs requires careful study. Treasury framed the regulations with respect to units of property.[33] The regulations have an extensive definition of unit of property.[34] Identifying the unit of property is an essential part of the analysis of an expenditure. For instance, if a building is a unit of property, and an elevator is part of the building, then replacing the elevator could be an improvement to the building. If so, the cost would be added to the building's adjusted basis. If the elevator is a unit of property, however, then the cost of the new elevator would be an acquisition cost and would be the basis of the elevator. The rules determine what constitutes a unit of property.

After identifying the unit of property, the analysis should focus on whether an expenditure is an improvement. The repair regs identify costs of (i) betterments, (ii) restorations, and (iii) adaptations as costs that property owners must capitalize.[35] The rules are subject to two safe harbors: (i) the safe harbor for small taxpayers,[36] and (ii) the safe harbor for routine maintenance.[37] The analysis of expenditures related to the property requires working through the rules. The examples often help clarify the text of the regulations. If an expenditure comes within one of the definitions of the types of improvements, the property owner must capitalize the amount paid for the improvement, unless one of the safe harbors apply. If the expenditure is not for an improvement or if one of the safe harbors applies, the property owner might otherwise be able to deduct the expenditure.

Depreciation deductions also affect the adjusted basis of property.[38] A property owner can take depreciation deductions only if the property is subject to exhaustion or wear and tear (including obsolescence) and the property owner holds it for in-

---

31. *See* Treas. Reg. § 1.162-4(a).

32. *See* I.R.C. § 263(a)(1); Treas. Reg. § 1.263(a)-1(a), (d). Property owners also must capitalize both direct and indirect costs incurred to construct property. *See infra* Chapter 9 (discussing I.R.C. § 263A).

33. *See* Treas. Reg. § 1.263(a)-3(d) (requiring property owners to capitalize amounts paid to improve a unit of property).

34. *See* Treas. Reg. § 1.263(a)-3(e).

35. *See* Treas. Reg. § 1.263(a)-3(j), (k), (l).

36. *See* Treas. Reg. § 1.263(a)-3(h).

37. *See* Treas. Reg. § 1.263(a)-3(i).

38. *See* I.R.C. § 1016(a)(2). Even if a property owner does not take the correct amount of depreciation deductions, the rules require an adjustment to basis equal to the amount of allowable depreciation deductions. *See* I.R.C. § 1016(a)(2) (flush language).

vestment or uses it in a trade or business.[39] To calculate allowable depreciation deductions, a person must determine the applicable depreciation method, the applicable recovery period, and the applicable convention.[40] The calculation of depreciation deductions becomes more complicated if the property has been improved.[41]

B. Taxation of Gain and Loss

Gain and loss from the sale of property can be ordinary income or capital gain.[42] The character of gain and loss derives from the character of the property. Gain and loss from the sale of a capital asset is capital.[43] Gain from the sale of property used in a trade or business can also be capital.[44] Long-term capital gain qualifies for favorable tax rates; ordinary income and short-term capital gain are taxed at ordinary rates.[45] Determining the tax that applies to long-term capital gain requires working through section 1(h). For high-income taxpayers (the type that typically seeks tax advice from attorneys), that section uses a multiple-tier structure that removes net capital gain from taxable income, and taxes the balance of taxable income at ordinary rates.[46]

Section 1(h) breaks net capital gain down into various components and taxes those components at various rates. It does this by using adjusted net capital gain. Adjusted net capital gain is net capital gain minus 28%-rate gain and unrecaptured section 1250 gain.[47] Net capital gain is the excess of net long-term capital gain over net short-term capital loss.[48] Net capital gain for high-income taxpayers is taxed at 20%,[49] 28%-rate gain is taxed at 28%,[50] and unrecaptured section 1250 gain is taxed at 25%.[51] Each of these gains are long-term capital gains, but different rates apply to them. Tax advisors must do the analysis necessary to determine what constitutes 28%-rate gain and unrecaptured section 1250 gain to determine what rates will apply to long-term capital gain.[52] Applying section 1(h) to long-term capital gain can be challenging if the gain

---

39. *See* I.R.C. § 167(a). Because land is not subject to wear and tear, it does not qualify for the depreciation deduction. *See* Treas. Reg. § 1.167(a)-2.

40. *See* I.R.C. § 168(a)-(d).

41. *See* I.R.C. § 168(i)(6).

42. *See* I.R.C. § 64.

43. *See* I.R.C. § 1222. *See also* I.R.C. § 1221 (defining capital asset); *infra* Chapter 7 (discussing the definition of capital asset).

44. *See* I.R.C. § 1231(a).

45. *See* I.R.C. § 1(h). The rates that apply to ordinary income range from 15% to 39.6%. *See* I.R.C. § 1(a)-(d), (i)(2), (3).

46. *See* I.R.C. § 1(h)(1)(A).

47. *See* I.R.C. § 1(h)(3).

48. *See* I.R.C. § 1222(11).

49. *See* I.R.C. § 1(h)(1)(D).

50. *See* I.R.C. § 1(h)(1)(F).

51. *See* I.R.C. § 1(h)(1)(E).

52. *See* I.R.C. §§ 1(h)(4) (defining 28%-rate gain); 1(h)(6) (defining unrecaptured section 1250 gain).

includes unrecaptured section 1250 gain, but the application may be a bit more intuitive, if one remembers that unrecaptured section 1250 gain is attributed to depreciation deductions that the property owner took with respect to the property being sold.

Individuals can deduct capital losses only to the extent of their capital gains plus $3,000.[53] Deductible capital losses in effect reduce the amount of capital gains that are subject to tax, regardless of the temporal nature (i.e., long-term versus short-term) of either the losses or gains. The temporal nature of the losses may, however, affect the order in which they offset the various types of long-term capital gain. For instance, for purposes of applying tax rates to long-term capital gain, net short-term capital loss offsets long-term capital gain in the following order: (1) 28%-rate gain, (2) unrecaptured section 1250 gain, and (3) regular long-term capital gain.[54] On the other hand, to the extent that long-term capital gain exceeds net short-term capital loss, for purposes of applying tax rates to long-term capital gain, long-term capital losses effectively offset long-term capital gains in the following order: (1) regular long-term capital gain, (2) 28%-rate gain, and (3) unrecaptured section 1250 gain.[55]

C. Tax on Net Investment Income

In addition to paying the tax on taxable income, taxpayers who have more than the threshold amount of adjusted gross income must pay a 3.8% Medicare surtax on their net investment income.[56] Three types of income come within the definition of net investment income: (1) interest, dividends, annuities, royalties, and rents (Type-1 Income), subject to an active-business exception; (2) other income from a passive activity and from trading in financial instruments or commodities (Type-2 Income); and (3) net gain from the disposition of property (Type-3 Income), subject to an active-business exception.[57] Under the active-business exception that applies to Type-1 Income, items of income are excluded from net investment income if they derive from any type of trade or business that is neither a passive activity nor trading in financial instruments or commodities.[58] Under the active-business exception that applies to Type-3 Income, gain is excluded from net investment income if the property was held

---

53. *See* I.R.C. § 1211(b).

54. *See* I.R.C. §§ 1(h)(4)(B)(ii), 1(h)(6)(A)(ii). Carried-over long-term capital loss applies in the same order. *See* I.R.C. §§ 1(h)(4)(B)(iii), 1(h)(6)(A)(ii).

55. *See* I.R.C. §§ 1(h)(1) (applying the 28% rate to residual income); 1(h)(3) (excluding unrecaptured section 1250 gain and 28%-rate gain from the definition of adjusted net capital gain); 1(h)(6) (defining unrecaptured section 1250 gain as the excess of gain attributable to straight-line depreciation allowable with respect to property over the sum of collectibles loss and net short-term capital loss and long-term capital loss carry forward net of 28%-rate gain); 1(h)(4) (defining 28%-rate gain without reference to current long-term capital losses).

56. *See* I.R.C. § 1411(a), (b).

57. *See* I.R.C. § 1411(c); Treas. Reg. § 1.1411-4(a), (b).

58. *See* I.R.C. § 1411(c)(2).

in a trade or business that is neither a passive activity nor trading in financial instruments or commodities.[59] Thus, if Type-1 Income derives from passive activities or does not derive from any trade or business, it would come within the definition of net investment income. For instance, dividends an individual receives from an investment portfolio would come within the definition of net investment income. If, however, Type-1 Income (such as interest or rent) derives from the ordinary course of an active trade or business, the income will not be part of net investment income. Similarly, gain from the sale of property held in a non-passive, non-trading business would not come within the definition of net investment income. The definition of net investment income adopts the section 469 definition of passive activity for purposes of defining the scope of the active-business exception.[60]

The regulations provide rules for determining how to test whether the active-business exception applies in various situations. If an individual receives Type-1 Income, the determination of whether the active-business exception applies is made at the individual level.[61] If a partnership or S corporation (i.e., passthrough entity[62] is engaged in a trade or business and has Type-1 Income, the determination of whether the income derives from a passive activity is made at the member level.[63] By contrast, the determination of whether the income derives from a trade or business of trading in financial instruments or commodities is made at the entity level.[64] The entity must, however, be engaged in a trade or business for Type-1 Income to derive from a trade or business. Thus, if a partnership that is not engaged in a trade or business receives dividends, those dividends will come within the definition of net investment income, regardless of the members' business activity.[65] If a partnership is engaged in a trade or business, the question becomes whether the partnership's trade or business is a passive activity with respect to the members of the partnership, and that determination is made at the member level.[66] Similar rules apply to the active-business exception that applies to Type 3 Income.[67] Partnership and S corporation interests generally are not property held in a trade or business, so gain from the sale of such property generally would be net investment income.[68] Nonetheless, a look-through rule applies that requires the selling member to consider net gain that would be allocated to the member if the entity sold all of its assets for fair market value immediately before the transfer of the interest.[69]

---

59. *See id.*
60. *See* I.R.C. § 1411(c)(2)(A).
61. *See* Treas. Reg. § 1.1411-4(b)(1).
62. *See infra* Chapter 4 (discussing taxation of income of passthrough entities).
63. *See* Treas. Reg. § 1.1411-4(b)(2)(i).
64. *See* Treas. Reg. § 1.1411-4(b)(2)(ii).
65. *See* Treas. Reg. § 1.1411-4(b)(3), *Example 1.*
66. *See* Treas. Reg. § 1.1411-4(b)(3), *Examples 2, 4*; (d)(4).
67. *See* Treas. Reg. § 1.1411-4(d)(4)(i)(B)(2), (3).
68. *See* Treas. Reg. § 1.1411-4(d)(4)(i)(B)(1).
69. *See* I.R.C. § 1411(c)(4).

II. Primary Legal Authority

Commissioner v. Tufts

United States Supreme Court
461 U.S. 300 (1983)

FACTS

On August 1, 1970, respondent Clark Pelt, a builder, and his wholly owned corporation, respondent Clark, Inc., formed a general partnership. The purpose of the partnership was to construct a 120-unit apartment complex in Duncanville, Tex., a Dallas suburb. Neither Pelt nor Clark, Inc., made any capital contribution to the partnership. Six days later, the partnership entered into a mortgage loan agreement with the Farm & Home Savings Association (F & H). Under the agreement, F & H was committed for a $1,851,500 loan for the complex. In return, the partnership executed a note and a deed of trust in favor of F & H. The partnership obtained the loan on a nonrecourse basis: neither the partnership nor its partners assumed any personal liability for repayment of the loan. Pelt later admitted four friends and relatives, respondents Tufts, Steger, Stephens, and Austin, as general partners. None of them contributed capital upon entering the partnership.

The construction of the complex was completed in August 1971. During 1971, each partner made small capital contributions to the partnership; in 1972, however, only Pelt made a contribution. The total of the partners' capital contributions was $44,212. In each tax year, all partners claimed as income tax deductions their allocable shares of ordinary losses and depreciation. The deductions taken by the partners in 1971 and 1972 totaled $439,972. Due to these contributions and deductions, the partnership's adjusted basis in the property in August 1972 was $1,455,740.

In 1971 and 1972, major employers in the Duncanville area laid off significant numbers of workers. As a result, the partnership's rental income was less than expected, and it was unable to make the payments due on the mortgage. Each partner, on August 28, 1972, sold his partnership interest to an unrelated third party, Fred Bayles. As consideration, Bayles agreed to reimburse each partner's sale expenses up to $250; he also assumed the nonrecourse mortgage.

On the date of transfer, the fair market value of the property did not exceed $1,400,000. Each partner reported the sale on his federal income tax return and indicated that a partnership loss of $55,740 had been sustained.[70] The Commissioner of Internal Revenue, on audit, determined that the sale resulted in a partnership

---

70. [1] The loss was the difference between the adjusted basis, $1,455,740, and the fair market value of the property, $1,400,000. On their individual tax returns, the partners did not claim deductions for their respective shares of this loss. In their petitions to the Tax Court, however, the partners did claim the loss.

capital gain of approximately $400,000. His theory was that the partnership had realized the full amount of the nonrecourse obligation.[71]

Relying on *Millar v. Comm'r*, 577 F.2d 212, 215 (3d Cir. 1978), *cert. denied*, 439 U.S. 1046, the United States Tax Court, in an unreviewed decision, upheld the asserted deficiencies. 70 T.C. 756 (1978). The United States Court of Appeals for the Fifth Circuit reversed. 651 F.2d 1058 (1981). That court expressly disagreed with the *Millar* analysis, and, in limiting *Crane v. Comm'r, supra*, to its facts, questioned the theoretical underpinnings of the *Crane* decision. We granted certiorari to resolve the conflict. 456 U.S. 960.

Section 752(d) of the Internal Revenue Code of 1954, 26 U.S.C. §752(d), specifically provides that liabilities incurred in the sale or exchange of a partnership interest are to "be treated in the same manner as liabilities in connection with the sale or exchange of property not associated with partnerships." Section 1001 governs the determination of gains and losses on the disposition of property. Under §1001(a), the gain or loss from a sale or other disposition of property is defined as the difference between "the amount realized" on the disposition and the property's adjusted basis. Subsection (b) of §1001 defines "amount realized": "The amount realized from the sale or other disposition of property shall be the sum of any money received plus the fair market value of the property (other than money) received." At issue is the application of the latter provision to the disposition of property encumbered by a nonrecourse mortgage of an amount in excess of the property's fair market value.

ANALYSIS

In *Crane v. Comm'r, supra*, this Court took the first and controlling step toward the resolution of this issue. Beulah B. Crane was the sole beneficiary under the will of her deceased husband. At his death in January 1932, he owned an apartment building that was then mortgaged for an amount which proved to be equal to its fair market value, as determined for federal estate tax purposes. The widow, of course, was not personally liable on the mortgage. She operated the building for nearly seven years, hoping to turn it into a profitable venture; during that period, she claimed income tax deductions for depreciation, property taxes, interest, and operating expenses, but did not make payments upon the mortgage principal. In computing her basis for the depreciation deductions, she included the full amount of the mortgage debt. In November 1938, with her hopes unfulfilled and the mortgagee threatening foreclosure, Mrs. Crane sold the building. The purchaser took the property subject to the mortgage and paid Crane $3,000; of that amount, $500 went for the expenses of the sale.

Crane reported a gain of $2,500 on the transaction. She reasoned that her basis in the property was zero (despite her earlier depreciation deductions based on in-

---

71. [2] The Commissioner determined the partnership's gain on the sale by subtracting the adjusted basis, $1,455,740, from the liability assumed by Bayles, $1,851,500. Of the resulting figure, $395,760, the Commissioner treated $348,661 as capital gain, pursuant to §741 of the Internal Revenue Code of 1954, 26 U.S.C. §741, and $47,099 as ordinary gain under the recapture provisions of §1250 of the Code. The application of §1250 in determining the character of the gain is not at issue here.

cluding the amount of the mortgage) and that the amount she realized from the sale was simply the cash she received. The Commissioner disputed this claim. He asserted that Crane's basis in the property, under § 113(a)(5) of the Revenue Act of 1938, 52 Stat. 490 (the current version is § 1014 of the 1954 Code, as amended, 26 U.S.C. § 1014 (1976 ed. and Supp. V)), was the property's fair market value at the time of her husband's death, adjusted for depreciation in the interim, and that the amount realized was the net cash received plus the amount of the outstanding mortgage assumed by the purchaser.

In upholding the Commissioner's interpretation of § 113(a)(5) of the 1938 Act,[72] the Court observed that to regard merely the taxpayer's equity in the property as her basis would lead to depreciation deductions less than the actual physical deterioration of the property, and would require the basis to be recomputed with each payment on the mortgage. 331 U.S., at 9–10. The Court rejected Crane's claim that any loss due to depreciation belonged to the mortgagee. The effect of the Court's ruling was that the taxpayer's basis was the value of the property undiminished by the mortgage. *Id.*, at 11.

The Court next proceeded to determine the amount realized under § 111(b) of the 1938 Act, 52 Stat. 484 (the current version is § 1001(b) of the 1954 Code, 26 U.S.C. § 1001(b)). In order to avoid the "absurdity," see 331 U.S., at 13, of Crane's realizing only $2,500 on the sale of property worth over a quarter of a million dollars, the Court treated the amount realized as it had treated basis, that is, by including the outstanding value of the mortgage. To do otherwise would have permitted Crane to recognize a tax loss unconnected with any actual economic loss. The Court refused to construe one section of the Revenue Act so as "to frustrate the Act as a whole." *Ibid.*

Crane, however, insisted that the nonrecourse nature of the mortgage required different treatment. The Court, for two reasons, disagreed. First, excluding the nonrecourse debt from the amount realized would result in the same absurdity and frustration of the Code. *Id.*, at 13–14. Second, the Court concluded that Crane obtained an economic benefit from the purchaser's assumption of the mortgage identical to the benefit conferred by the cancellation of personal debt. Because the value of the property in that case exceeded the amount of the mortgage, it was in Crane's economic interest to treat the mortgage as a personal obligation; only by so doing could she realize upon sale the appreciation in her equity represented by the $2,500 boot. The purchaser's assumption of the liability thus resulted in a taxable economic benefit to her, just as if she had been given, in addition to the boot, a sum of cash sufficient to satisfy the mortgage.[73]

---

72. [3] Section 113(a)(5) defined the basis of "property ... acquired by ... devise ... or by the decedent's estate from the decedent" as "the fair market value of such property at the time of such acquisition." The Court interpreted the term "property" to refer to the physical land and buildings owned by Crane or the aggregate of her rights to control and dispose of them. 331 U.S., at 6.

73. [4] Crane also argued that even if the statute required the inclusion of the amount of the nonrecourse debt, that amount was not Sixteenth Amendment income because the overall transaction had been "by all dictates of common sense ... a ruinous disaster." Brief for Petitioner in *Crane v. Comm'r*, O.T.1946, No. 68, p. 51. The Court noted, however, that Crane had been entitled to and

In a footnote, pertinent to the present case, the Court observed: "Obviously, if the value of the property is less than the amount of the mortgage, a mortgagor who is not personally liable cannot realize a benefit equal to the mortgage. Consequently, a different problem might be encountered where a mortgagor abandoned the property or transferred it subject to the mortgage without receiving boot. That is not this case." *Id.*, at 14, n. 37.

This case presents that unresolved issue. We are disinclined to overrule *Crane*, and we conclude that the same rule applies when the unpaid amount of the nonrecourse mortgage exceeds the value of the property transferred. *Crane* ultimately does not rest on its limited theory of economic benefit; instead, we read *Crane* to have approved the Commissioner's decision to treat a nonrecourse mortgage in this context as a true loan. This approval underlies *Crane's* holdings that the amount of the nonrecourse liability is to be included in calculating both the basis and the amount realized on disposition. That the amount of the loan exceeds the fair market value of the property thus becomes irrelevant.

When a taxpayer receives a loan, he incurs an obligation to repay that loan at some future date. Because of this obligation, the loan proceeds do not qualify as income to the taxpayer. When he fulfills the obligation, the repayment of the loan likewise has no effect on his tax liability.

Another consequence to the taxpayer from this obligation occurs when the taxpayer applies the loan proceeds to the purchase price of property used to secure the loan. Because of the obligation to repay, the taxpayer is entitled to include the amount of the loan in computing his basis in the property; the loan, under § 1012, is part of the taxpayer's cost of the property. Although a different approach might have been taken with respect to a nonrecourse mortgage loan,[74] the Commissioner has chosen to accord it the same treatment he gives to a recourse mortgage loan. The Court approved that choice in *Crane*, and the respondents do not challenge it here. The choice and its resultant benefits to the taxpayer are predicated on the assumption that the mortgage will be repaid in full.

---

actually took depreciation deductions for nearly seven years. To allow her to exclude sums on which those deductions were based from the calculation of her taxable gain would permit her "a double deduction ... on the same loss of assets." The Sixteenth Amendment, it was said, did not require that result. 331 U.S., at 15–16.

74. [5] The Commissioner might have adopted the theory, implicit in Crane's contentions, that a nonrecourse mortgage is not true debt, but, instead, is a form of joint investment by the mortgagor and the mortgagee. On this approach, nonrecourse debt would be considered a contingent liability, under which the mortgagor's payments on the debt gradually increase his interest in the property while decreasing that of the mortgagee. *Note, Federal Income Tax Treatment of Nonrecourse Debt*, 82 Colum. L. Rev. 1498, 1514 (1982); Lurie, *Mortgagor's Gain on Mortgaging Property for More than Cost Without Personal Liability*, 6 Tax. L. Rev. 319, 323 (1951); *cf.* Brief for Respondents 16 (nonrecourse debt resembles preferred stock). Because the taxpayer's investment in the property would not include the nonrecourse debt, the taxpayer would not be permitted to include that debt in basis. *Note*, 82 Colum. L. Rev., at 1515; *cf. Gibson Products Co. v. U.S.*, 637 F.2d 1041, 1047–1048 (5th Cir. 1981) (contingent nature of obligation prevents inclusion in basis of oil and gas leases of nonrecourse debt secured by leases, drilling equipment, and percentage of future production).

We express no view as to whether such an approach would be consistent with the statutory structure and, if so, and *Crane* were not on the books, whether that approach would be preferred over *Crane's* analysis. We note only that the *Crane* Court's resolution of the basis issue presumed that when property is purchased with proceeds from a nonrecourse mortgage, the purchaser becomes the sole owner of the property. 331 U.S., at 6. Under the *Crane* approach, the mortgagee is entitled to no portion of the basis. *Id.*, at 10, n. 28. The nonrecourse mortgage is part of the mortgagor's investment in the property, and does not constitute a coinvestment by the mortgagee. *But see* Note, 82 Colum. L. Rev., at 1513 (treating nonrecourse mortgage as coinvestment by mortgagee and critically concluding that *Crane* departed from traditional analysis that basis is taxpayer's investment in property).

When encumbered property is sold or otherwise disposed of and the purchaser assumes the mortgage, the associated extinguishment of the mortgagor's obligation to repay is accounted for in the computation of the amount realized.[75] *See U.S. v. Hendler,* 303 U.S. 564, 566–567. Because no difference between recourse and nonrecourse obligations is recognized in calculating basis,[76] *Crane* teaches that the Commissioner may ignore the nonrecourse nature of the obligation in determining the amount realized upon disposition of the encumbered property. He thus may include in the amount realized the amount of the nonrecourse mortgage assumed by the purchaser. The rationale for this treatment is that the original inclusion of the amount of the mortgage in basis rested on the assumption that the mortgagor incurred an obligation to repay. Moreover, this treatment balances the fact that the mortgagor originally received the proceeds of the nonrecourse loan tax-free on the same assumption. Unless the outstanding amount of the mortgage is deemed to be realized, the mortgagor effectively will have received untaxed income at the time the loan was extended and will have received an unwarranted increase in the basis of his property.[77] The Commissioner's interpretation of § 1001(b) in this fashion cannot be said to be unreasonable.

---

75. [6] In this case, respondents received the face value of their note as loan proceeds. If respondents initially had given their note at a discount, the amount realized on the sale of the securing property might be limited to the funds actually received. *See Comm'r v. Rail Joint Co.,* 61 F.2d 751, 752 (2d Cir. 1932) (cancellation of indebtedness); *Fashion Park, Inc. v. Comm'r,* 21 T.C. 600, 606 (1954) (same). *See generally* J. Sneed, The Configurations of Gross Income 319 (1967) ("[I]t appears settled that the reacquisition of bonds at a discount by the obligor results in gain only to the extent the issue price, where this is less than par, exceeds the cost of reacquisition").

76. [7] The Commissioner's choice in Crane "laid the foundation stone of most tax shelters," Bittker, *Tax Shelters, Nonrecourse Debt, and the Crane Case,* 33 Tax. L. Rev. 277, 283 (1978), by permitting taxpayers who bear no risk to take deductions on depreciable property. Congress recently has acted to curb this avoidance device by forbidding a taxpayer to take depreciation deductions in excess of amounts he has at risk in the investment. Pub. L. 94-455, § 204(a), 90 Stat. 1531 (1976), 26 U.S.C. § 465; Pub. L. 95-600, §§ 201–204, 92 Stat. 2814–2817 (1978), 26 U.S.C. § 465(a) (1976 ed., Supp. V). Real estate investments, however, are exempt from this prohibition. § 465(c)(3)(D) (1976 ed., Supp. V). Although this congressional action may foreshadow a day when nonrecourse and recourse debts will be treated differently, neither Congress nor the Commissioner has sought to alter Crane's rule of including nonrecourse liability in both basis and the amount realized.

77. [8] Although the Crane rule has some affinity with the tax benefit rule, see Bittker, *supra,* at 282; Del Cotto, *Sales and Other Dispositions of Property Under Section 1001: The Taxable Event, Amount*

The Commissioner in fact has applied this rule even when the fair market value of the property falls below the amount of the nonrecourse obligation. Treas. Reg. § 1.1001-2(b), 26 CFR § 1.1001-2(b) (1982);[78] Rev. Rul. 76-111, 1976-1 Cum.Bull. 214. Because the theory on which the rule is based applies equally in this situation, *see Millar v. Comm'r*, 67 T.C. 656, 660 (1977), aff'd on this issue, 577 F.2d 212, 215–216 (3d Cir. 1978), *cert. denied*, 439 U.S. 1046;[79] *Mendham Corp. v. Comm'r*, 9 T.C. 320, 323–324 (1947); *Lutz & Schramm Co. v. Comm'r*, 1 T.C. 682, 688–689 (1943), we have no reason, after *Crane*, to question this treatment.[80]

Although this indeed could be a justifiable mode of analysis, it has not been adopted by the Commissioner. Nor is there anything to indicate that the Code requires the Commissioner to adopt it. We note that Professor Barnett's approach does assume that recourse and nonrecourse debt may be treated identically.

The Commissioner also has chosen not to characterize the transaction as cancellation of indebtedness. We are not presented with and do not decide the contours of the cancellation-of-indebtedness doctrine. We note only that our approach does not fall within certain prior interpretations of that doctrine. In one view, the doctrine rests on the same initial premise as our analysis here—an obligation to repay—but the doctrine relies on a freeing-of-assets theory to attribute ordinary income to the debtor upon cancellation. *See Comm'r v. Jacobson*, 336 U.S. 28, 38–40; *U.S. v. Kirby Lumber Co.*, 284 U.S. 1, 3. According to that view, when nonrecourse debt is forgiven, the debtor's basis in the securing property is reduced by the amount of debt canceled, and realization of income is deferred until the sale of the property. See *Fulton Gold Corp. v. Comm'r*, 31 B.T.A. 519, 520 (1934). Because that interpretation attributes income only when assets are freed, however, an insolvent debtor realizes income just to the extent his assets exceed his liabilities after the cancellation. *Lakeland Grocery Co. v. Comm'r*, 36 B.T.A. 289, 292 (1937). Similarly, if the nonrecourse indebtedness exceeds the value of the securing property, the taxpayer never realizes the full amount of the obligation canceled because the tax law has not recognized negative basis.

Realized and Related Problems of Basis, 26 Buff. L. Rev. 219, 323–324 (1977), the analysis we adopt is different. Our analysis applies even in the situation in which no deductions are taken. It focuses on the obligation to repay and its subsequent extinguishment, not on the taking and recovery of deductions. *See generally Note*, 82 Colum. L. Rev., at 1526–1529.

78. [9] The regulation was promulgated while this case was pending before the Court of Appeals for the Fifth Circuit. T.D. 7741, 45 Fed. Reg. 81743, 1981-1 Cum.Bull. 430 (1980). It merely formalized the Commissioner's prior interpretation, however.

79. [10] The Court of Appeals for the Third Circuit in Millar affirmed the Tax Court on the theory that inclusion of nonrecourse liability in the amount realized was necessary to prevent the taxpayer from enjoying a double deduction. 577 F.2d, at 215; *cf.* n. 4, *supra*. Because we resolve the question on another ground, we do not address the validity of the double deduction rationale.

80. [11] Professor Wayne G. Barnett, as *amicus* in the present case, argues that the liability and property portions of the transaction should be accounted for separately. Under his view, there was a transfer of the property for $1.4 million, and there was a cancellation of the $1.85 million obligation for a payment of $1.4 million. The former resulted in a capital loss of $50,000, and the latter in the realization of $450,000 of ordinary income. Taxation of the ordinary income might be deferred under § 108 by a reduction of respondents' bases in their partnership interests.

Although the economic benefit prong of *Crane* also relies on a freeing-of-assets theory, that theory is irrelevant to our broader approach. In the context of a sale or disposition of property under § 1001, the extinguishment of the obligation to repay is not ordinary income; instead, the amount of the canceled debt is included in the amount realized, and enters into the computation of gain or loss on the disposition of property. According to *Crane*, this treatment is no different when the obligation is nonrecourse: the basis is not reduced as in the cancellation-of-indebtedness context, and the full value of the outstanding liability is included in the amount realized. Thus, the problem of negative basis is avoided.

Respondents received a mortgage loan with the concomitant obligation to repay by the year 2012. The only difference between that mortgage and one on which the borrower is personally liable is that the mortgagee's remedy is limited to foreclosing on the securing property. This difference does not alter the nature of the obligation; its only effect is to shift from the borrower to the lender any potential loss caused by devaluation of the property.[81] If the fair market value of the property falls below the amount of the outstanding obligation, the mortgagee's ability to protect its interests is impaired, for the mortgagor is free to abandon the property to the mortgagee and be relieved of his obligation.

This, however, does not erase the fact that the mortgagor received the loan proceeds tax-free and included them in his basis on the understanding that he had an obligation to repay the full amount. *See Woodsam Associates, Inc. v. Comm'r*, 198 F.2d 357, 359 (2d Cir. 1952); Bittker, 33 Tax. L. Rev., at 284. When the obligation is canceled, the mortgagor is relieved of his responsibility to repay the sum he originally received and thus realizes value to that extent within the meaning of § 1001(b). From the mortgagor's point of view, when his obligation is assumed by a third party who purchases the encumbered property, it is as if the mortgagor first had been paid with cash borrowed by the third party from the mortgagee on a nonrecourse basis, and then had used the cash to satisfy his obligation to the mortgagee.

Moreover, this approach avoids the absurdity the Court recognized in *Crane*. Because of the remedy accompanying the mortgage in the nonrecourse situation, the depreciation in the fair market value of the property is relevant economically only to the mortgagee, who by lending on a nonrecourse basis remains at risk. To permit the taxpayer to limit his realization to the fair market value of the property would be to recognize a tax loss for which he has suffered no corresponding economic loss.[82]

---

81. [12] In his opinion for the Court of Appeals in *Crane*, Judge Learned Hand observed: "[The mortgagor] has all the income from the property; he manages it; he may sell it; any increase in its value goes to him; any decrease falls on him, until the value goes below the amount of the lien.... When therefore upon a sale the mortgagor makes an allowance to the vendee of the amount of the lien, he secures a release from a charge upon his property quite as though the vendee had paid him the full price on condition that before he took title the lien should be cleared...." 153 F.2d 504, 506 (2d Cir. 1945).

82. [13] In the present case, the Government bore the ultimate loss. The nonrecourse mortgage was extended to respondents only after the planned complex was endorsed for mortgage insurance

Such a result would be to construe "one section of the Act ... so as ... to defeat the intention of another or to frustrate the Act as a whole." 331 U.S., at 13.

In the specific circumstances of *Crane*, the economic benefit theory did support the Commissioner's treatment of the nonrecourse mortgage as a personal obligation. The footnote in *Crane* acknowledged the limitations of that theory when applied to a different set of facts. *Crane* also stands for the broader proposition, however, that a nonrecourse loan should be treated as a true loan. We therefore hold that a taxpayer must account for the proceeds of obligations he has received tax-free and included in basis. Nothing in either § 1001(b) or in the Court's prior decisions requires the Commissioner to permit a taxpayer to treat a sale of encumbered property asymmetrically, by including the proceeds of the nonrecourse obligation in basis but not accounting for the proceeds upon transfer of the encumbered property. *See Estate of Levine v. Comm'r*, 634 F.2d 12, 15 (2d Cir. 1980).

Relying on the Code's § 752(c), 26 U.S.C. § 752(c), however, respondents argue that Congress has provided for precisely this type of asymmetrical treatment in the sale or disposition of partnership property. Section 752 prescribes the tax treatment of certain partnership transactions, and § 752(c) provides that "[f]or purposes of this section, a liability to which property is subject shall, to the extent of the fair market value of such property, be considered as a liability of the owner of the property." Section 752(c) could be read to apply to a sale or disposition of partnership property, and thus to limit the amount realized to the fair market value of the property transferred. Inconsistent with this interpretation, however, is the language of § 752(d), which specifically mandates that partnership liabilities be treated "in the same manner as liabilities in connection with the sale or exchange of property not associated with partnerships." The apparent conflict of these subsections renders the facial meaning of the statute ambiguous, and therefore we must look to the statute's structure and legislative history.

Subsections (a) and (b) of § 752 prescribe rules for the treatment of liabilities in transactions between a partner and his partnership, and thus for determining the partner's adjusted basis in his partnership interest. Under § 704(d), a partner's distributive share of partnership losses is limited to the adjusted basis of his partnership interest. 26 U.S.C. § 704(d) (1976 ed., Supp. V); see Perry, Limited Partnerships and Tax Shelters: The Crane *Rule Goes Public*, 27 Tax L. Rev. 525, 543 (1972). When partnership liabilities are increased or when a partner takes on the liabilities of the partnership, § 752(a) treats the amount of the increase or the amount assumed as a contribution by the partner to the partnership. This treatment results in an increase

---

under §§ 221(b) and (d)(4) of the National Housing Act, 12 U.S.C. § 1715 *l* (b) and (d)(4) (1976 ed. and Supp. V). After acquiring the complex from respondents, Bayles operated it for a few years, but was unable to make it profitable. In 1974, F & H foreclosed, and the Department of Housing and Urban Development paid off the lender to obtain title. In 1976, the Department sold the complex to another developer for $1,502,000. The sale was financed by the Department's taking back a note for $1,314,800 and a nonrecourse mortgage. To fail to recognize the value of the nonrecourse loan in the amount realized, therefore, would permit respondents to compound the Government's loss by claiming the tax benefits of that loss for themselves.

in the adjusted basis of the partner's interest and a concomitant increase in the §704(d) limit on his distributive share of any partnership loss. Conversely, under §752(b), a decrease in partnership liabilities or the assumption of a partner's liabilities by the partnership has the effect of a distribution, thereby reducing the limit on the partner's distributive share of the partnership's losses. When property encumbered by liabilities is contributed to or distributed from the partnership, §752(c) prescribes that the liability shall be considered to be assumed by the transferee only to the extent of the property's fair market value. Treas. Reg. §1.752-1(c).

The legislative history indicates that Congress contemplated this application of §752(c). Mention of the fair market value limitation occurs only in the context of transactions under subsections (a) and (b).[83] The sole reference to subsection (d) does not discuss the limitation.[84] While the legislative history is certainly not conclusive, it indicates that the fair market value limitation of §752(c) was directed to transactions between a partner and his partnership.[85] A. Willis, J. Pennell, & P. Postlewaite, Partnership Taxation §44.03, p. 44–3 (3d ed. 1981); Simmons, Tufts v. Commissioner: *Amount Realized Limited to Fair Market Value*, 15 U.C. Davis L. Rev. 577, 611–613 (1982).

By placing a fair market value limitation on liabilities connected with property contributions to and distributions from partnerships under subsections (a) and (b), Congress apparently intended §752(c) to prevent a partner from inflating the basis of his partnership interest. Otherwise, a partner with no additional capital at risk in the partnership could raise the §704(d) limit on his distributive share of partnership losses or could reduce his taxable gain upon disposition of his partnership interest. See Newman, *The Resurgence of Footnote 37:* Tufts v. Commissioner, 18 Wake Forest L. Rev. 1, 16, n. 116 (1982). There is no potential for similar abuse in the context of §752(d) sales of partnership interests to unrelated third parties. In light of the above, we interpret subsection (c) to apply only to §752(a) and (b) transactions, and not

---

83. [15] "The transfer of property subject to a liability by a partner to a partnership, or by the partnership to a partner, shall, to the extent of the fair market value of such property, be considered a transfer of the amount of the liability along with the property." H.R. Rep. No. 1337, 83d Cong., 2d Sess., A236 (1954); S. Rep. No. 1622, 83d Cong., 2d Sess., 405 (1954).

84. [16] "When a partnership interest is sold or exchanged, the general rule for the treatment of the sale or exchange of property subject to liabilities will be applied." H.R. Rep. No. 1337, at A236–A237; S. Rep. No. 1622, at 405. These Reports then set out an example of subsection (d)'s application, which does not indicate whether the debt is recourse or nonrecourse.

85. [17] The Treasury Regulations support this view. The regulations interpreting §752(c) state: "Where property subject to a liability is contributed by a partner to a partnership, or distributed by a partnership to a partner, the amount of the liability, to an extent not exceeding the fair market value of the property at the time of the contribution or distribution, shall be considered as a liability assumed by the transferee." §1.752-1(c). The regulations also contain an example applying the fair market limitation to a contribution of encumbered property by a partner to a partnership. *Ibid.* The regulations interpreting §752(d) make no mention of the fair market limitation. §752-1(d). Both regulations were issued contemporaneously with the passage of the statute, T.D. 6175, 1956-1 Cum. Bull. 211, and are entitled to deference as an administrative interpretation of the statute. *See* Comm'r v. South Texas Lumber Co., 333 U.S. 496, 501.

to limit the amount realized in a sale or exchange of a partnership interest under §752(d).

When a taxpayer sells or disposes of property encumbered by a nonrecourse obligation, the Commissioner properly requires him to include among the assets realized the outstanding amount of the obligation. The fair market value of the property is irrelevant to this calculation. We find this interpretation to be consistent with *Crane v. Comm'r*, 331 U.S. 1, and to implement the statutory mandate in a reasonable manner. *National Muffler Dealers Assn. v. U.S.*, 440 U.S. 472, 476.

Crane v. Commissioner

United States Supreme Court
331 U.S. 1 (1947)

FACTS

Petitioner was the sole beneficiary and the executrix of the will of her husband, who died January 11, 1932. He then owned an apartment building and lot subject to a mortgage,[86] which secured a principal debt of $255,000.00 and interest in default of $7,042.50. As of that date, the property was appraised for federal estate tax purposes at a value exactly equal to the total amount of this encumbrance. Shortly after her husband's death, petitioner entered into an agreement with the mortgagee whereby she was to continue to operate the property—collecting the rents, paying for necessary repairs, labor, and other operating expenses, and reserving $200.00 monthly for taxes—and was to remit the net rentals to the mortgagee. This plan was followed for nearly seven years, during which period petitioner reported the gross rentals as income, and claimed and was allowed deductions for taxes and operating expenses paid on the property, for interest paid on the mortgage, and for the physical exhaustion of the building. Meanwhile, the arrearage of interest increased to $15,857.71. On November 29, 1938, with the mortgagee threatening foreclosure, petitioner sold to a third party for $3,000.00 cash, subject to the mortgage, and paid $500.00 expenses of sale.

Petitioner reported a taxable gain of $1,250.00. Her theory was that the "property" which she had acquired in 1932 and sold in 1938 was only the equity, or the excess in the value of the apartment building and lot over the amount of the mortgage. This equity was of zero value when she acquired it. No depreciation could be taken on a zero value.[87] Neither she nor her vendee ever assumed the mortgage, so, when she sold the equity, the amount she realized on the sale was the net cash received, or $2,500.00. This sum less the zero basis constituted her gain, of which she reported half as taxable on the assumption that the entire property was a "capital asset".[88]

---

86. [1] The record does not show whether he was personally liable for the debt.

87. [2] This position is, of course, inconsistent with her practice in claiming such deductions in each of the years the property was held. The deductions so claimed and allowed by the Commissioner were in the total amount of $25,500.00.

88. [3] *See* §117(a)(b), Revenue Act of 1938, c. 289, 52 Stat. 447, 26 U.S.C.A. Int. Rev. Code, §117. Under this provision only 50% of the gain realized on the sale of a 'capital asset' need be taken into account, if the property had been held more than two years.

The Commissioner, however, determined that petitioner realized a net taxable gain of $23,767.03. His theory was that the "property" acquired and sold was not the equity, as petitioner claimed, but rather the physical property itself, or the owner's rights to possess, use, and dispose of it, undiminished by the mortgage. The original basis thereof was $262,042.50, its appraised value in 1932. Of this value $55,000.00 was allocable to land and $207,042.50 to building.[89] During the period that petitioner held the property, there was an allowable depreciation of $28,045.10 on the building,[90] so that the adjusted basis of the building at the time of sale was $178,997.40. The amount realized on the sale was said to include not only the $2,500.00 net cash receipts, but also the principal amount[91] of the mortgage subject to which the property was sold, both totaling $257,500.00. The selling price was allocable in the proportion, $54,471.15 to the land and $203,028.85 to the building.[92] The Commissioner agreed that the land was a "capital asset", but thought that the building was not.[93] Thus, he determined that petitioner sustained a capital loss of $528.85 on the land, of which 50% or $264.42 was taken into account, and an ordinary gain of $24.031.45 on the building, or a net taxable gain as indicated.

The Tax Court agreed with the Commissioner that the building was not a "capital asset." In all other respects it adopted petitioner's contentions, and expunged the deficiency.[94] Petitioner did not appeal from the part of the ruling adverse to her, and these questions are no longer at issue. On the Commissioner's appeal, the Circuit Court of Appeals reversed, one judge dissenting.[95] We granted certiorari because of the importance of the questions raised as to the proper construction of the gain and loss provisions of the Internal Revenue Code.[96]

ANALYSIS

The 1938 Act,[97] § 111(a), 26 U.S.C.A. Int. Rev. Code, § 111(a), defines the gain from "the sale or other disposition of property" as "the excess of the amount realized

---

89. [4] The parties stipulated as to the relative parts of the 1932 appraised value and of the 1938 sales price which were allocable to land and building.

90. [5] The parties stipulated that the rate of depreciation applicable to the building was 2% per annum.

91. [6] The Commissioner explains that only the principal amount, rather than the total present debt secured by the mortgage, was deemed to be a measure of the amount realized, because the difference was attributable to interest due, a deductible item.

92. [7] *See* supra, note 4.

93. [8] *See* § 117(a)(1), Revenue Act of 1938, *supra*.

94. [9] 3 T.C. 585. The Court held that the building was not a "capital asset" within the meaning of § 117(a) and that the entire gain on the building had to be taken into account under § 117(b), because it found that the building was of a character subject to physical exhaustion and that petitioner had used it in her trade or business. But because the Court accepted petitioner's theory that the entire property had a zero basis, it held that she was not entitled to the 1938 depreciation deduction on the building which she had inconsistently claimed. For these reasons, it did not expunge the deficiency in its entirety.

95. [10] 153 F.2d 504 (2d Cir. 1946).

96. [11] 328 U.S. 826.

97. [12] All subsequent references to a revenue act are to this Act unless otherwise indicated. The relevant parts of the gain and loss provisions of the Act and Code are identical.

therefrom over the adjusted basis provided in § 113(b)...." It proceeds, § 111(b), to define "the amount realized from the sale or other disposition of property" as "the sum of any money received plus the fair market value of the property (other than money) received." Further, in s 113(b), 26 U.S.C.A. Int. Rev. Code, § 113(b), the "adjusted basis for determining the gain or loss from the sale or other disposition of property" is declared to be 'the basis determined under subsection (a), adjusted ... ((1)(B)) ... for exhaustion, wear and tear, obsolescence, amortization ... to the extent allowed (but not less than the amount allowable)...." The basis under subsection (a) "if the property was acquired by ... devise ... or by the decedent's estate from the decedent", § 113(a)(5), is "the fair market value of such property at the time of such acquisition."

Logically, the first step under this scheme is to determine the unadjusted basis of the property, under § 113(a)(5), and the dispute in this case is as to the construction to be given the term "property". If "property", as used in that provision, means the same thing as "equity", it would necessarily follow that the basis of petitioner's property was zero, as she contends. If, on the contrary, it means the land and building themselves, or the owner's legal rights in them, undiminished by the mortgage, the basis was $262,042.50.

We think that the reasons for favoring one of the latter constructions are of overwhelming weight. In the first place, the words of statutes—including revenue acts—should be interpreted where possible in their ordinary, everyday senses.[98] The only relevant definitions of "property" to be found in the principal standard dictionaries[99] are the two favored by the Commissioner, i.e., either that "property" is the physical thing which is a subject of ownership, or that it is the aggregate of the owner's rights to control and dispose of that thing. "Equity" is not given as a synonym, nor do either of the foregoing definitions suggest that it could be correctly so used. Indeed, "equity" is defined as "the value of a property ... above the total of the liens...."[100] The contradistinction could hardly be more pointed. Strong countervailing considerations would be required to support a contention that Congress, in using the word "property", meant "equity", or that we should impute to it the intent to convey that meaning.[101]

In the second place, the Commission's position has the approval of the administrative construction of § 113(a)(5). With respect to the valuation of property under that section, Reg. 101, Art. 113(a)(5)-1, promulgated under the 1938 Act, provided that "the value of property as of the date of the death of the decedent as appraised for the purpose of the federal estate tax ... shall be deemed to be its fair market value...." The land and building here involved were so appraised in 1932, and their appraised value—$262,042.50—was reported by petitioner as part of the gross estate.

---

98. [13] Old Colony R. Co. v. Comm'r, 284 U.S. 552, 560 (1932).

99. [14] See Webster's New International Dictionary, Unabridged (2d Ed.); Funk & Wagnalls' New Standard Dictionary; Oxford English Dictionary.

100. [15] See Webster's New International Dictionary, supra.

101. [16] Crooks v. Harrelson, 282 U.S. 55, 59 (1930).

This was in accordance with the estate tax law[102] and regulations,[103] which had always required that the value of decedent's property, undiminished by liens, be so appraised and returned, and that mortgages be separately deducted in computing the net estate.[104] As the quoted provision of the Regulations has been in effect since 1918,[105] and as the relevant statutory provision has been repeatedly reenacted since then in substantially the same form,[106] the former may itself now be considered to have the force of law.[107]

Moreover, in the many instances in other parts of the Act in which Congress has used the word "property", or expressed the idea of "property" or "equity", we find no instances of a misuse of either word or of a confusion of the ideas.[108] In some parts of the Act other than the gain and loss sections, we find "property" where it is unmistakably used in its ordinary sense.[109] On the other hand, where either Congress or the Treasury intended to convey the meaning of "equity," it did so by the use of appropriate language.[110]

A further reason why the word "property" in § 113(a) should not be construed to mean "equity" is the bearing such construction would have on the allowance of deductions for depreciation and on the collateral adjustments of basis.

§ 23(l) permits deduction from gross income of "a reasonable allowance for the exhaustion, wear and tear of property ..." §§ 23(n) and 114(a), 26 U.S.C.A.

---

102. [17] *See* §§ 202 and 203(a)(1), Revenue Act of 1916; §§ 402 and 403(a)(1), Revenue Acts of 1918 and 1921; §§ 302, 303(a)(1), Revenue Acts of 1924 and 1926; § 805, Revenue Act of 1932, 26 U.S.C.A. Int. Rev. Code, §§ 811, 812.

103. [18] *See* Reg. 37, Arts, 13, 14, and 47; Reg. 63, Arts. 12, 13, and 41; Reg. 68, Arts. 11, 13, and 38; Reg. 70, Arts 11, 13, and 38; Reg. 80, Arts. 11, 13, and 38.

104. [19] *See* City Bank Farmers' Trust Co. v. Bowers, 68 F.2d 909 (2d Cir. 1934), *certiorari denied*, 292 U.S. 644; Rodiek v. Helvering, 87 F.2d 328 (2d Cir. 1937); Adriance v. Higgins, 113 F.2d 1013 (2d Cir. 1940).

105. [20] *See also* Reg. 45, Art. 1562; Reg. 62, Art. 1563; Reg. 65, Art. 1594; Reg. 69, Art. 1594; Reg. 74, Art. 596; Reg. 77, Art. 596; Reg. 86, Art. 113(a)(5)-1(c); Reg. 94, Art. 113(a)(5)-1(c); Reg. 103, § 19.113(a)(5)-1(c); Reg. 111, § 29.113(a)(5)-1(c).

106. [21] § 202(a)(3), Revenue Act of 1921; § 204(a)(5), Revenue Act of 1924; § 204(a)(5), Revenue Act of 1926; § 113(a)(5), Revenue Act of 1928; § 113(a)(5), Revenue Act of 1932; § 113(a)(5), Revenue Act of 1934; § 113(a)(5), Revenue Act of 1936; § 113(a)(5), Revenue Act of 1938; § 113(a)(5), Internal Revenue Code, 26 U.S.C.A. Int. Rev. Code, § 113(a)(5).

107. [22] Helvering v. R. J. Reynolds Co., 306 U.S. 110, 114 (1939).

108. [23] *Cf.* Helvering v. Stockholms Enskilda Bank, 293 U.S. 84, 87 (1934).

109. [24] Sec. 23(a)(1), 26 U.S.C.A. Int. Rev. Code, § 23(a)(1), permits the deduction from gross income of "rentals ... required to be made as a condition to the continued use ... for purposes of the trade or business, of property ... in which he (the taxpayer) has no equity." Sec. 23(l) permits the deduction from gross income of "a reasonable allowance for the exhaustion, wear and tear of property used in the trade or business...." *See also* § 303(a)(1), Revenue Act of 1926, c. 27, 44 Stat. 9; § 805, Revenue Act of 1932, c. 209, 47 Stat. 280.

110. [25] *See* § 23(a)(1), supra, note 24; § 805, Revenue Act of 1932, supra, note 24; § 3482, I.R.C., 26 U.S.C.A. Int. Rev. Code, § 3482; Reg. 105, § 81.38. This provision of the Regulations, first appearing in 1937, T.D. 4729, 1937-1 Cum. Bull. 284, 289, permitted estates which were not liable on mortgages applicable to certain of decedent's property to return "only the value of the equity of redemption (or value of the property, less the indebtedness)...."

Int.Rev.Code, §§ 23(n), 114(a), declare that the "basis upon which depletion exhaustion, wear and tear ... are to be allowed" is the basis "provided in section 113(b) for the purpose of determining the gain upon the sale" of the property, which is the § 113(a) basis "adjusted ... for exhaustion, wear and tear ... to the extent allowed (but not less than the amount allowable)...."

Under these provisions, if the mortgagor's equity were the § 113(a) basis, it would also be the original basis from which depreciation allowances are deducted. If it is, and if the amount of the annual allowances were to be computed on that value, as would then seem to be required,[111] they will represent only a fraction of the cost of the corresponding physical exhaustion, and any recoupment by the mortgagor of the remainder of that cost can be effected only by the reduction of his taxable gain in the year of sale.[112] If, however, the amount of the annual allowances were to be computed on the value of the property, and then deducted from an equity basis, we would in some instances have to accept deductions from a minus basis or deny deductions altogether.[113] The Commissioner also argues that taking the mortgagor's equity as the § 113(a) basis would require the basis to be changed with each payment on the mortgage,[114] and that the attendant problem of repeatedly recomputing basis and annual allowances would be a tremendous accounting burden on both the Commissioner and the taxpayer. Moreover, the mortgagor would acquire control over the timing of his depreciation allowances.

Thus it appears that the applicable provisions of the Act expressly preclude an equity basis, and the use of it is contrary to certain implicit principles of income tax depreciation, and entails very great administrative difficulties.[115] It may be added that the Treasury has never furnished a guide through the maze of problems that arise in connection with depreciating an equity basis, but, on the contrary, has consistently

---

111. [26] Secs. 23(n) and 114(a), in defining the "basis upon which" depreciation is "to be allowed", do not distinguish between basis as the minuend from which the allowances are to be deducted, and as the dividend from which the amount of the allowance is to be computed. The Regulations indicate that the basis of property is the same for both purposes. Reg. 101, Art. 23(1)-4, 5.

112. [27] This is contrary to Treasury practice, and to Reg. 101, Art. 23(1)-5, which provides in part: "The capital sum to be recovered shall be charged off over the useful life of the property, either in equal annual installments or in accordance with any other recognized trade practice, such as an apportionment of the capital sum over units of production." *See* Detroit Edison Co. v. Comm'r, 319 U.S. 98, 101 (1943).

113. [28] So long as the mortgagor remains in possession, the mortgagee cannot take depreciation deductions, even if he is the one who actually sustains the capital loss, as § 23(l) allows them only on property "used in the trade or business."

114. [29] Sec. 113(b)(1)(A) requires adjustment of basis 'for expenditures ... properly chargeable to capital account.... '

115. [30] Obviously we are not considering a situation in which a taxpayer has acquired and sold an equity of redemption only, i.e., a right to redeem the property without a right to present possession. In that situation, the right to redeem would itself be the aggregate of the taxpayer's rights and would undoubtedly constitute "property" within the meaning of § 113(a). No depreciation problems would arise. *See* note 28.

permitted the amount of depreciation allowances to be computed on the full value of the property, and subtracted from it as a basis. Surely, Congress' long-continued acceptance of this situation gives it full legislative endorsement.[116]

We conclude that the proper basis under § 113(a)(5) is the value of the property, undiminished by mortgages thereon, and that the correct basis here was $262,042.50. The next step is to ascertain what adjustments are required under § 113(b). As the depreciation rate was stipulated, the only question at this point is whether the Commissioner was warranted in making any depreciation adjustments whatsoever.

Section 113(b)(1)(B) provides that "proper adjustment in respect of the property shall in all cases be made ... for exhaustion, wear and tear ... to the extent allowed (but not less than the amount allowable....)." The Tax Court found on adequate evidence that the apartment house was property of a kind subject to physical exhaustion, that it was used in taxpayer's trade or business, and consequently that the taxpayer would have been entitled to a depreciation allowance under § 23(l), except that, in the opinion of that Court, the basis of the property was zero, and it was thought that depreciation could not be taken on a zero basis. As we have just decided that the correct basis of the property was not zero, but $262,042.50, we avoid this difficulty, and conclude that an adjustment should be made as the Commissioner determined.

Petitioner urges to the contrary that she was not entitled to depreciation deductions, whatever the basis of the property, because the law allows them only to one who actually bears the capital loss,[117] and here the loss was not hers but the mortgagee's. We do not see, however, that she has established her factual premise. There was no finding of the Tax Court to that effect, nor to the effect that the value of the property was ever less than the amount of the lien. Nor was there evidence in the record, or any indication that petitioner could produce evidence, that this was so. The facts that the value of the property was only equal to the lien in 1932 and that during the next six and one-half years the physical condition of the building deteriorated and the amount of the lien increased, are entirely inconclusive, particularly in the light of the buyer's willingness in 1938 to take subject to the increased lien and pay a substantial amount of cash to boot. Whatever may be the rule as to allowing depreciation to a mortgagor on property in his possession which is subject to an unassumed mortgage and clearly worth less than the lien, we are not faced with that problem and see no reason to decide it now.

At last we come to the problem of determining the "amount realized" on the 1938 sale. Section 111(b), it will be recalled, defines the "amount realized" from "the sale ... of property" as "the sum of any money received plus the fair market value of the property (other than money) received," and § 111(a) defines the gain on "the sale ... of property" as the excess of the amount realized over the basis. Quite obviously, the

---

116. [31] *See* note [22].

117. [32] *See* Helvering v. F. & R. Lazarus & Co., 308 U.S. 252 (1939); Duffy v. Central R. Co., 268 U.S. 55, 64 (1925).

word "property", used here with reference to a sale, must mean "property" in the same ordinary sense intended by the use of the word with reference to acquisition and depreciation in § 113, both for certain of the reasons stated heretofore in discussing its meaning in § 113, and also because the functional relation of the two sections requires that the word mean the same in one section that it does in the other. If the "property" to be valued on the date of acquisition is the property free of liens, the "property" to be priced on a subsequent sale must be the same thing.[118]

Starting from this point, we could not accept petitioner's contention that the $2,500.00 net cash was all she realized on the sale except on the absurdity that she sold a quarter-of-a-million dollar property for roughly one per cent of its value, and took a 99 per cent loss. Actually, petitioner does not urge this. She argues, conversely, that because only $2,500.00 was realized on the sale, the "property" sold must have been the equity only, and that consequently we are forced to accept her contention as to the meaning of "property" in § 113. We adhere, however, to what we have already said on the meaning of "property", and we find that the absurdity is avoided by our conclusion that the amount of the mortgage is properly included in the "amount realized" on the sale.

Petitioner concedes that if she had been personally liable on the mortgage and the purchaser had either paid or assumed it, the amount so paid or assumed would be considered a part of the "amount realized" within the meaning of § 111(b).[119] The cases so deciding have already repudiated the notion that there must be an actual receipt by the seller himself of "money" or "other property", in their narrowest senses. It was thought to be decisive that one section of the Act must be construed so as not to defeat the intention of another or to frustrate the Act as a whole,[120] and that the taxpayer was the "beneficiary" of the payment in "as real and substantial (a sense) as if the money had been paid it and then paid over by it to its creditors."[121]

Both these points apply to this case. The first has been mentioned already. As for the second, we think that a mortgagor, not personally liable on the debt, who sells the property subject to the mortgage and for additional consideration, realizes a benefit in the amount of the mortgage as well as the boot.[122] If a purchaser pays boot, it is immaterial as to our problem whether the mortgagor is also to receive money from the purchaser to discharge the mortgage prior to sale, or whether he is merely

---

118. [33] *See* Maguire v. Comm'r, 313 U.S. 1, 8 (1941). We are not troubled by petitioner's argument that her contract of sale expressly provided for the conveyance of the equity only. She actually conveyed title to the property, and the buyer took the same property that petitioner had acquired in 1932 and used in her trade or business until its sale.

119. [34] U.S. v. Hendler, 303 U.S. 564 (1938); Brons Hotels, Inc., 34 B.T.A. 376 (1936); Walter F. Haass, 37 B.T.A. 948 (1938). *See* Douglas v. Willcuts, 296 U.S. 1, 8 (1935); 101 A.L.R. 391.

120. [35] *See* Brons Hotels, Inc., supra, 34 B.T.A. at page 381.

121. [36] *See* U.S. v. Hendler, supra, 303 U.S. at 566.

122. [37] Obviously, if the value of the property is less than the amount of the mortgage, a mortgagor who is not personally liable cannot realize a benefit equal to the mortgage. Consequently, a different problem might be encountered where a mortgagor abandoned the property or transferred it subject to the mortgage without receiving boot. That is not this case.

to transfer subject to the mortgage—it may make a difference to the purchaser and to the mortgagee, but not to the mortgagor. Or put in another way, we are no more concerned with whether the mortgagor is, strictly speaking, a debtor on the mortgage, than we are with whether the benefit to him is, strictly speaking, a receipt of money or property. We are rather concerned with the reality that an owner of property, mortgaged at a figure less than that at which the property will sell, must and will treat the conditions of the mortgage exactly as if they were his personal obligations.[123] If he transfers subject to the mortgage, the benefit to him is as real and substantial as if the mortgage were discharged, or as if a personal debt in an equal amount had been assumed by another.

Therefore we conclude that the Commissioner was right in determining that petitioner realized $257,500.00 on the sale of this property.

The Tax Court's contrary determinations, that "property", as used in § 113(a) and related sections, means "equity", and that the amount of a mortgage subject to which property is sold is not the measure of a benefit realized, within the meaning of § 111(b), announced rules of general applicability on clear-cut questions of law.[124] The Circuit Court of Appeals therefore had jurisdiction to review them.[125]

Petitioner contends that the result we have reached taxes her on what is not income within the meaning of the Sixteenth Amendment. If this is because only the direct receipt of cash is thought to be income in the constitutional sense, her contention is wholly without merit.[126] If it is because the entire transaction is thought to have been "by all dictates of common-sense … a ruinous disaster", as it was termed in her brief, we disagree with her premise. She was entitled to depreciation deductions for a period of nearly seven years, and she actually took them in almost the allowable amount. The crux of this case, really, is whether the law permits her to exclude allowable deductions from consideration in computing gain.[127] We have already showed that, if it does, the taxpayer can enjoy a double deduction, in effect, on the same loss of assets. The Sixteenth Amendment does not require that result any more than does the Act itself.

---

123. [38] For instance, this petitioner returned the gross rentals as her own income, and out of them paid interest on the mortgage, on which she claimed and was allowed deductions. *See* Reg. 77, Art. 141; Reg. 86, Art. 23(b)-1; Reg. 94, Art. 23(b)-1; Reg. 101, Art. 23(b)-1.

124. [39] *See* Comm'r v. Wilcox, 327 U.S. 404, 410 (1946); Bingham's Trust v. Comm'r, 325 U.S. 365, 369–372 (1945). *Cf.* John Kelley Co. v. Comm'r, 326 U.S. 521, 527, 698 (1946); Dobson v. Comm'r, 320 U.S. 489 (1943).

125. *Ibid*; *see also* § 1141(a) and (c), I.R.C., 26 U.S.C.A. Int. Rev. Code, § 1141(a, c).

126. [40] Douglas v. Willcuts, supra, 296 U.S. at page 9; 101 A.L.R. 391; Burnet v. Wells, 289 U.S. 670, 677.

127. [41] In the course of the argument some reference was made, as by analogy, to a situation in which a taxpayer acquired by devise property subject to a mortgage in an amount greater than the then value of the property, and later transferred it to a third person, still subject to the mortgage, and for a cash boot. Whether or not the difference between the value of the property on acquisition and the amount of the mortgage would in that situation constitute either statutory or constitutional income is a question which is different from the one before us, and which we need not presently answer.

Gehl v. Commissioner

United States Tax Court
102 T.C. 784 (1994)

OPINION

TANNENWALD, JUDGE:

Respondent determined deficiencies in petitioners' Federal income tax for the years 1988 and 1989 in the amounts of $6,887.00 and $13,643.00, respectively. The sole issue is the proper treatment of the excess of the fair market value over basis of property, transferred by petitioners to a creditor in partial satisfaction of a debt.

All the facts have been stipulated and are found accordingly. Petitioners resided in Cascade, Iowa, at the time they filed their petition.

As of December 30, 1988, Production Credit Association (Production) held a recourse note from petitioners with a balance due of $152,260. At that time, petitioners were unable to make the required payments. Pursuant to a restructuring agreement, petitioners transferred to Production on December 30, 1988, 60 acres of farm land having a fair market value of $39,000 and a basis of $14,384 and, on January 4, 1989, an additional 141 acres having a fair market value of $77,725 and a basis of $32,080. Pursuant to the agreement, petitioners also paid $6,123 in cash to be applied towards the outstanding balance, and their remaining debt to Production was forgiven. Petitioners were not debtors under Title 11 of the U.S.Code (the bankruptcy code) at any time during 1988 and 1989 but were insolvent both before and after the transfers and the discharge of indebtedness. Respondent concedes that the amount of the indebtedness in excess of the fair market value of the transferred land constitutes income from the discharge of indebtedness excludable under section 108.[128]

Respondent contends that the transfers in partial satisfaction of petitioners' indebtedness constitute gains taxable under sections 61(a)(3) and 1001, that such gains do not constitute income from discharge of indebtedness, and that therefore they are not excludable under section 108. Petitioners contend that, because of their insolvency, they realized nothing of value from the gains in question, that such gains should be characterized as income from discharge of indebtedness under section 61(a)(12) and that therefore they are excludable under section 108. We hold for respondent.

It is well settled that a transfer of property by a debtor to a creditor in satisfaction, in whole or in part, of an indebtedness constitutes a "sale or exchange" under section 1001 and that the excess of the fair market value over basis of the property applied against the indebtedness constitutes taxable gain. *Allan v. Commissioner,* 86 T.C. 655, 659–660 (1986), affd. 856 F.2d 1169, 1172 (8th Cir.1988); *Freeland v. Commissioner,* 74 T.C. 970 (1980). The question before us is whether such excess herein should be

---

128. [1] Unless otherwise indicated, all statutory references are to the Internal Revenue Code in effect during the years in issue, and all Rule references are to the Tax Court Rules of Practice and Procedure.

treated as "gains derived from dealings in property" includable in gross income under section 61(a)(3) or as "discharge of indebtedness" within the meaning of section 61(a)(12) excludable under section 108, because of petitioners' insolvency. Section 108 provides in pertinent part:

SEC. 108(a). Exclusion from Gross Income.—

(1) In general.—Gross income does not include any amount which (but for this subsection) would be includible in gross income by reason of the discharge (in whole or in part) of indebtedness of the taxpayer if—

(B) the discharge occurs when the taxpayer is insolvent,

At the outset, we note that petitioners' obligation was recourse and not nonrecourse, and that respondent has conceded that the amount of the gain represented by the excess of the amount of the debt over the fair market value of the property transferred constitutes cancellation of indebtedness not includable in gross income because of petitioners' insolvency. Under these circumstances, only the amount of the gain represented by the excess of such fair market value over basis is at issue, and we need not and do not resolve any issue of bifurcation[129] in the context of either recourse or nonrecourse indebtedness. Compare *Estate of Delman v. Commissioner,* 73 T.C. 15 (1979), with *Danenberg v. Commissioner,* 73 T.C. 370 (1979), and Rev.Rul. 76-111, 1976-1 C.B. 214, with Rev.Rul. 90-16, 1990-1 C.B. 12; see Cunningham, "Payment of Debt with Property—The Two-Step Analysis after *Commissioner v. Tufts,*" 38 Tax Law. 575 (1985).[130]

Our path to decision involves an analysis of the interplay between section 1.1001-2(a)(2) and (c) *Example (8),* Income Tax Regs.,[131] and section 1.61-12, Income Tax

---

129. [2] We note that this bifurcation has "not always been clearly defined" and that earlier cases have been described as reflecting "some confusion". See *Estate of Delman v. Commissioner,* 73 T.C. 15, 31 & n. 6 particularly (1979); see also Cunningham, "Payment of Debt with Property—The Two-Step Analysis after *Commissioner v. Tufts,*" 38 Tax Law. 575 (1985); Del Cotto, "Basis and Amount Realized Under *Crane:* a Current View of Some Tax Effects of Mortgage Financing," 118 U.Pa.L.Rev. 69, 87–88 (1969); Eustice, "Cancellation of Indebtedness and the Federal Income Tax: A Problem of Creeping Confusion," 14 Tax L.Rev. 225, 247 (1959). We further note that the Supreme Court has declined to deal with the issue of bifurcation. See *Commissioner v. Tufts,* 461 U.S. 300, 310, n. 11 (1983).

130. [3] See also brief of Wayne G. Barnett, Amicus Curiae, in *Commissioner v. Tufts,* 461 U.S. 300 (1983), for a detailed explanation of the two-step analysis.

131. [4] Sec. 1.1001-2, Income Tax Regs., provides in pertinent part:

(a) Inclusion in amount realized.—(1) * * *

(2) Discharge of indebtedness. The amount realized on a sale or other disposition of property that secures a recourse liability does not include amounts that are (or would be if realized and recognized) income from the discharge of indebtedness under section 61(a)(12). For situations where amounts arising from the discharge of indebtedness are not realized and recognized, see section 108 and § 1.61-12(b)(1).

* * *

(c) *Examples.* * * *

Example (8). In 1980, F transfers to a creditor an asset with a fair market value of $6,000 and the creditor discharges $7,500 of indebtedness for which F is personally liable. The

Regs.[132] In *Danenberg v. Commissioner, supra* at 385–386, we held that, despite the existence of insolvency both before and after the transfer, the taxpayer realized gain to the extent of the excess over basis of the fair market value of the transferred property which was used to satisfy the indebtedness and that such gain did not constitute income from discharge of an indebtedness. See also *Gershkowitz v. Commissioner,* 88 T.C. 984, 1016 (1987); *Estate of Delman v. Commissioner, supra* at 32.

Petitioners seek to distinguish *Danenberg* on the ground that the transfers therein were to third parties and not to the creditor. In point of fact, part of the property transferred (the Meloland stock) in that case was to a nominee of the creditor who simply stood in the shoes of the creditor and did not constitute a third party as did transferees of other property. See *Danenberg v. Commissioner,* 73 T.C. at 374, 386; Cunningham, *supra* at 613. Moreover, our analysis in *Danenberg* was constructed in the context of our observation, that:

> Case law is clear that when a debt is discharged or reduced upon the debtor's transfer of property to his creditor or a third party, such transaction is treated as a sale or exchange of the debtor's assets, and not as a mere transfer of assets in cancellation of indebtedness. * * * [*Danenberg v. Commissioner,* 73 T.C. at 380–381; fn. and citations omitted.]

Thus, *Danenberg* is a compelling precedent, as is *Estate of Delman v. Commissioner, supra,* insofar as the issue of taxable gain versus income from discharge of indebtedness is concerned. In resolving that issue, both cases rejected the test of lack of economic gain because of insolvency, *Danenberg v. Commissioner, supra* at 380–382, or, in other words, the absence of any freeing of petitioners' assets, *Estate of Delman v. Commissioner, supra* at 31–33.

Petitioners' reliance on *Dallas Transfer & Terminal Warehouse Co. v. Commissioner,* 70 F.2d 95 (5th Cir.1934), revg. 27 B.T.A. 651 (1933), and *Lakeland Grocery Co. v. Commissioner,* 36 B.T.A. 289 (1937), is misplaced. Those cases were decided upon the basis of the impact of insolvency on the transaction as a whole without any consideration of the possibility of bifurcation of the transaction between the gain and the discharge of indebtedness elements.[133] Moreover, we note that both of these cases and other cases which speak in the same vein[134] involved taxable years com-

---

amount realized on the disposition of the asset is its fair market value ($6,000). In addition, F has income from the discharge of indebtedness of $1,500 ($7,500 – $6,000).

132. [5] Sec. 1.61-12, Income Tax Regs., provides in pertinent part:
(b) Proceedings under Bankruptcy Act. (1) Income is not realized by a taxpayer * * * by virtue of an agreement among his creditors not consummated under any provision of the Bankruptcy Act, if immediately thereafter the taxpayer's liabilities exceed the value of his assets. * * *

133. [6] See comments on *Dallas Transfer & Terminal Warehouse Co. v. Commissioner,* 70 F.2d 95 (5th Cir.1934), revg. 27 B.T.A. 651 (1933), in Trower, Federal Taxation of Bankruptcy and Workouts, par. 2.04[3][b], at 2-75–2-76, and par. 5.05[6], at 5–38 n. 127 (1993).

134. [7] *Turney's Estate v. Commissioner,* 126 F.2d 712 (5th Cir.1942), revg. a Memorandum Opinion of this Court dated Sept. 25, 1940; *Commissioner v. Simmons Gin Co.,* 43 F.2d 327 (10th

mencing prior to January 1, 1939, and were decided before the first statutory provision dealing with income from the discharge of indebtedness was enacted in 1939 as section 22(b)(9) by section 215 of the Revenue Act of 1939, ch. 247, 53 Stat. 875. Substantially the same comment applies to *Main Properties, Inc. v. Commissioner,* 4 T.C. 364, 384–385 (1944), in respect of the taxable year ending November 30, 1939, and *Texas Gas Distributing Co. v. Commissioner,* 3 T.C. 57 (1944), in respect of a 1941 taxable year but in which no reference is made to the 1939 statutory enactment. Moreover, both these cases appear to have dealt with arrangements with all, as distinguished from one or some, creditors, a position in which different considerations may be involved. An arrangement with all creditors also appears to have been present in *Brutsche v. Commissioner,* 65 T.C. 1034, 1063 (1976), which quotes from *Texas Gas.* Thus, even if not overtaken by subsequent events, see *infra,* these cases are distinguishable and clearly do not support a departure from *Danenberg v. Commissioner, supra.*

It cannot be gainsaid that the early judicial history in respect of the gain from a sale or exchange with income from discharge of indebtedness has not been exemplary in its message. See *Estate of Delman v. Commissioner,* 73 T.C. at 31 & n. 6 particularly; Cunningham, "Payment of Debt with Property—The Two-Step Analysis after *Commissioner v. Tufts,*" 38 Tax Law. 575, 622 (1985). But we are of the view that the cases reflecting that history have been overtaken by subsequent judicial pronouncements which have sapped them of much, if not all, of their vitality.[135] See *Hicks v. Commissioner,* 47 T.C. 71, 74 (1966).

As we see it, paragraphs (3) and (12) of section 61(a) are separate, independent, and not overlapping provisions in respect of the includability of a particular item in income. *Danenberg v. Commissioner, supra.* Consequently, the first steps in analyzing the consequences of a transfer of property in satisfaction of an indebtedness, in whole or in part, are to determine whether (1) gain or loss occurred under section 61(a)(3), and/or (2) there was cancellation of indebtedness under section 61(a)(12). *Danenberg v. Commissioner, supra* at 380; see also *Home Builders Lumber Co. v. Commissioner,* 165 F.2d 1009 (5th Cir.1948), affg. a Memorandum Opinion of this Court dated Dec. 9, 1946; Cunningham, *supra* at 623. Only after it is determined that the latter provision applies does one reach the question of the impact of insolvency and therefore the applicability of section 108. This approach conforms precisely to the language of section 108(a)(1) which applies only to income "which (but for this subsection) would be includible in gross income by reason of the discharge

---

Cir.1930), affg. 16 B.T.A. 793 (1929); *Springfield Industrial Building Co. v. Commissioner,* 38 B.T.A. 1445 (1938); *Quinn v. Commissioner,* 31 B.T.A. 142 (1934).

135. [8] Contributing to this consequence are the substantial revisions of the statutory provisions dealing with income from discharge of indebtedness which were made by section 108, enacted as part of the Internal Revenue Code of 1954, and by the amendments thereto in the Bankruptcy Tax Act of 1980, Pub.L. 96-589, 94 Stat. 3389. See Eustice, "Cancellation of Indebtedness and the Federal Income Tax: A Problem of Creeping Confusion," 14 Tax L.Rev. 225, 272–276 (1959); Trower, Federal Taxation of Bankruptcy and Workouts, par. 3.01 at 3-3–3-8 (1993).

* * * of indebtedness of the taxpayer", see *supra* p. 4. In this connection, we think it significant that section 108, by its terms, is the exclusive exception from "the general rule that gross income includes income from the discharge of indebtedness". Sec. 108(e)(1); see Trower, Federal Taxation of Bankruptcy and Workouts, par. 3.02, at 3-8–3-9 (1993).

In sum, we reaffirm *Danenberg v. Commissioner, supra,* and hold that section 1.1001-2, Income Tax Regs., see *supra* note 4, accurately reflects the proper treatment of the elements involved where property is transferred by the debtor to a creditor having a fair market value in excess of basis but less than the amount of a recourse debt and which is reflected in respondent's position herein. See also *Michaels v. Commissioner,* 87 T.C. 1412, 1415 (1986); *Bressi v. Commissioner,* T.C.Memo. 1991-651, affd. without published opinion 989 F.2d 486 (3d Cir.1993); Trower, *supra,* par. 5.05[3], at 5–30. Accordingly, the gains in question do not constitute "income from discharge of indebtedness" under section 61(a)(12) and are therefore not excludable under section 108.

In order to take into account an adjustment resulting from a concession by respondent in respect of the excess of the indebtedness above the fair market value of the property transferred, see *supra* p. 785, *Decision will be entered under Rule 155.*

Fairfield Plaza, Inc. v. Commissioner

United States Tax Court
39 T.C. 706 (1963)

FACTS

Petitioner is a West Virginia corporation, organized on March 31, 1955, with its principal office in the city of Huntington, Cabell County, W. VA. Petitioner's income tax returns for the taxable years 1957 and 1958 were filed with the district director of internal revenue, Parkersburg, W. Va.

S. Grady Risen, secretary-treasurer and one of the principal stockholders of petitioner, has been in the real estate business in Huntington since 1927. Prior to petitioner's incorporation, Risen had become familiar with a tract of land of approximately 10 acres, lying between 16th and 17th Streets in Huntington, occupied by the West Virginia Paving & Pressed Brick Co. On or about October 15, 1954, Risen had an aerial photograph made of the property. On April 13, 1955, 13 days after its incorporation, petitioner purchased the entire tract occupied by the brickyard, consisting of 453,921 square feet. After purchasing the tract, petitioner intended to develop it into a drive-in shopping center.

Total cost of the entire shopping center, including development expenditures, was as follows:

Real estate	$100,000.00
Commissions	5,000.00
Interest	4,500.00
Taxes	420.08
Legal	820.00
Insurance	201.04
Grading	23,016.80
Engineering	705.73
Additional costs, 1957	8,856.72
Miscellaneous	23.50
Total	143,543.87
Less: Credits, rebates, and scrap sales	3,018.11
Total	140,525.76

In 1955, when petitioner purchased the shopping center, an excavation was located on the eastern two-thirds of the tract near the southern edge, where the brick company had been extracting clay. On the western portion of the tract were located the six kilns, plant, brick shed, and office building of the brick company, covering approximately one-third of the tract. No buildings were located on the other two-thirds of the property.

In line with its plan of developing a drive-in shopping center, petitioner graded the entire tract. In the process, the excavation made by the brick company was filled in with dirt removed from high portions of the tract. All of the brick company's buildings were removed, and the trace was made level except for a narrow hill area along a portion of the southern edge.

The grading and leveling was completed in 1956, at a total cost of $23,016.80.

Petitioner believed that the use for which the property was best suited was a shopping center, although one other use was considered. As a part of its plan of development, petitioner hired an engineer to prepare maps outlining the uses of various parts of the property as a shopping center. Certain areas were set aside for buildings, for parking, and for entrances and exits. Petitioner intended to erect the store buildings, complete the necessary paving and lighting, and then rent the buildings to tenants.

Prior to the summer of 1956, petitioner entered into negotiations with the Big Bear Stores Co., hereinafter sometimes called Big Bear, for the leasing of a portion of the tract fronting on 17th Street. Petitioner encountered difficulty in obtaining financing for the building to be constructed for Big Bear, and in May 1957 Big Bear offered to buy outright that portion of the tract.

By a deed dated June 17, 1957, petitioner conveyed 126,611.47 square feet of the easterly portion of the tract to Big Bear for $100,000. Of this purchase price, $50,000 was held in an escrow account pending completion of paving and lighting to be performed by petitioner on the remainder of the tract not sold to Big Bear.

On petitioner's income tax return for the year 1957, a cost basis of $91,237.25 was allocated to the Big Bear tract. Petitioner calculated such basis by computing pro rata land cost at 33 cents per square foot for a total of $41,237.25 and by adding the escrow fund of $50,000 to cost.

The respondent, in his notice of deficiency, determined that the escrow fund was not an allowable addition to petitioner's cost basis of the Big Bear tract, and further determined that the correct cost basis of said tract was $38,738.74, or 27.567 percent of the cost of the total tract.

In the summer of 1957, following the sale of the Big Bear tract, petitioner deeded, without charge, a strip of its western frontage on 16th Street amounting to 16,526 square feet, to the State Road Commission of West Virginia. Such gift of land was made so that the State could widen 16th Street along the western end of the tract, thus providing easier access to the shopping center. Such widening was completed prior to June 14, 1958.

After the sale to Big Bear, petitioner still intended to retain ownership of the remainder of the shopping center, and to construct and lease stores thereon.

Despite such intention, petitioner, by deed dated June 16, 1958, sold the western portion of the shopping center, hereinafter sometimes called the Paisley tract, consisting of 128,937 square feet, to Orion M. Paisley, Walter F. Williams, and Herman E. Martin for $150,000.

The sales price of the Paisley tract was 150 percent of the sales price of the Big Bear tract. The tracts were substantially equivalent in size. In preparing petitioner's income tax return for the year 1958, Grady Risen calculated cost basis of the Paisley tract at 50 cents per square foot, or $64,468.80.

The respondent, in his notice of deficiency, determined that the correct cost of the Paisley tract was $43,481.48, or 30.942 percent of the original cost, plus $1,320.85 of additional costs incurred in 1958, for a total of $44,802.33.

In its deeds to Big Bear and Paisley, petitioner granted travel and parking easements across its retained tract, to each grantee. In each deed petitioner reserved equivalent easements for travel and parking across the property conveyed to Big Bear and Paisley. Each deed recited the intention of the petitioner to operate the drive-in shopping center as a unit, and required each grantee to maintain uniform paving and lighting, keep such areas in repair, and confine all buildings to the areas designated on maps attached to each deed. Without easements, petitioner had no access to the retained center parcel.

Between June 1957, when the Big Bear tract was sold, and June 1958, when the Paisley tract was sold, petitioner added $4,710.03 to its land development account. The record does not reveal how much of such figure represented costs incurred separately as to each of the two remaining tracts, nor how much was incurred in connection with both portions as a unit, nor the amount expended in 1957 and the amount expended in 1958, nor the amounts involved in the items claimed by petitioner to constitute the $4,710.03.

In his notice of deficiency respondent determined that petitioner's allowable basis of the Paisley tract included $1,320.85 of additional costs incurred in 1958.

In connection with the sale of the Paisley tract, petitioner incurred expenses of $8,503.94, which were reported as expenses of sale on its 1958 income tax return. Respondent has allowed such expenses of sale in full.

By the time the paving and lighting on petitioner's retained tract commenced, as specified in the escrow agreement with Big Bear, petitioner had already sold the Paisley tract, under a deed obligating Paisley to pave and light its own portion of the shopping center.

Both Big Bear and Paisley paved and illuminated their own respective tracts, as required in the deeds by which petitioner conveyed each parcel to them. Petitioner paved and illuminated only the retained tract.

Petitioner did not know what the cost of its own paving and lighting would be until the year 1958. No contracts for the performance of such work had been entered into prior to such year. In December 1958 and January 1959, petitioner paid $40,146.32 to various contractors in payment of the paving and lighting on its retained tract.

On its 1957 income tax return, petitioner included, as part of the proceeds of the Big Bear sale, the $50,000 fund held in escrow. Such fund was not released to petitioner until December 23, 1958.

As of January 1 of each of the following years the following assessed valuations were carried on the land books and records of the office of the Cabell County assessor:

1957	
Fairfield Plaza land	$25,200.00 (entire tract)
1958	
Fairfield Plaza land	$25,200.00 (less Big Bear tract)
Big Bear land	$27,500.00
1959	
Fairfield Plaza land	$49,320.00(less Big Bear and Paisley tracts)
Big Bear land	$32,770.00
Paisley land	$36,780.1

The foregoing valuations include only the land, exclusive of improvements such as buildings, paving, or lighting.

The basis to be allocated to the Big Bear property is $41,437.94. The basis to be allocated to the Paisley property is $54,831.38.

Petitioner is not entitled to allocate any portion of the $50,000 escrow fund to the basis of the Big Bear or Paisley tracts.

The $50,000 held in escrow must be added to petitioner's capital gain in 1958, the year in which it was actually released to petitioner, and not included in 1957.

In 1955 petitioner purchased a 10-acre tract of real estate, located between 16th and 17th Streets in Huntington, W. Va., with the intention of developing the property into a shopping center. After grading had been completed, negotiations were begun with Big Bear Stores Co. pursuant to which petitioner was to build and lease to Big Bear a store on approximately 30 percent of the property, which portion has frontage on 17th Street.

Petitioner had difficulty in obtaining financing for the building, and in 1957 sold this easterly portion of the tract to Big Bear for $100,000, $50,000 of which was placed in escrow pending petitioner's completion of paving and lighting on the remainder of the tract.

In 1958 the western 30 percent of the tract, which has frontage on 16th Street, was sold to Paisley and associates for $150,000.

The parties agree that the $50,000 placed in escrow in the Big Bear sale should be taken into income in 1958.

The purchase price to petitioner in 1955 of the whole trace, including the basic cost of the land, commissions, interest, taxes, and legal fees and insurance, was $110,941.12. In addition, petitioner spent a net of $29,584.64 for engineering, grading, and other miscellaneous items which are to be capitalized. The first issue involves the allocation of the above amounts in the computation of the bases of the two parcels sold to Big Bear and Paisley, respectively.

It is the position of respondent that the allocation must be made as of the 1955 purchase date and that since the petitioner then intended to use the land for a shopping center the only proper method of allocation is on the basis of square footage. Respondent reasons that reciprocal easements for access and the very nature of a shopping center support his assertion that no portion of the property has a value greater than that of any other.

ANALYSIS

We agree with respondent that the allocation of basis is to be made as of 1955. *Ayling v. Comm'r*, 32 T.C. 704 (1959). It is the proper method of allocation which remains in issue.

Section 1.61-6, Income Tax Regs., provides that "When a part of a larger property is sold, the cost or other basis of the entire property shall be equitably apportioned among the several parts,...." Such "equitable" apportionment demands that relative values be reflected. Accordingly, if one parcel is of greater value than another, apportionment solely on the basis of square footage appears inappropriate. *Biscayne Bay Islands Co. v. Comm'r*, 23 B.T.A. 731 (1931); *Cleveland-Sandusky Brewing Corp.*

v. Comm'r, 30 T.C. 539 (1958); *and see* 3-A Mertens, Law of Federal Income Taxation, §. 21.12, p. 43. It is, of course, true that petitioner bears the burden of demonstrating the applicability of an allocation of basis other than that reflected in respondent's determinations.

We are satisfied from the evidence presented that despite the fact the property was to be used as a shopping center, thus having an integrated value, each lot or portion thereof reflecting upon each other portion, the land fronting on 16th Street, which was sold to the Paisley group, had a greater value than that reflected by a simple allocation of cost on the basis of square footage. Sixteenth Street is one of Huntington's main thoroughfares. Any business fronting thereon is inevitably in the public eye. Two expert witnesses testified that the Paisley property had a value equal to the remainder of the tract. Despite petitioner's intentions in 1955, we are satisfied that this property had a fair market value in excess of the approximately 30.9 percent of original cost assigned thereto by respondent. On the basis of all of the evidence, we have concluded that 40 percent of cost is allocable to the Paisley parcel. While we have not rested our conclusion thereon, it is significant that the sales price realized on the sale of the Big Bear parcel which fronts on the less-traveled 17th Street. Nothing in the evidence warrants a conclusion that the value of the 16th Street property increased so markedly from 1955 to 1958 that such a percentage difference is explained thereby. Yet, respondent valued the Big Bear and Paisley parcels almost equally.

The opinion of the experts did not differ greatly with respect to the relative value of the Big Bear parcel. Taking into account its frontage on 17th Street as well as its accessibility by reason of easements across the remainder of the tract, we have determined that the Big Bear parcel had a basis of 30 percent of the cost of the entire tract.

Respondent has argued that since the witnesses called by petitioner did not specifically testify with respect to allocation as of 1955, their testimony should be wholly disregarded. Petitioner contends, however, that there was little or no change in the relative values of the parcels between 1955 and 1959. Such a posture of the facts is consistent with respondent's own position, for his valuation as of 1955 reflects relative values which very closely parallel the relative values disclosed by the county assessor's records as of 1959, upon which respondent places some emphasis. Thus, we are satisfied that the relative values of the properties remained fairly constant over the period in question and that the testimony of the expert witnesses called by petitioner is not to be disregarded.

What we have said thus far resolves the allocation issue only in connection with those costs incurred as part of the purchase price or clearly measurable thereby. Such costs total $110,941.12. There remains $29,584.64, consisting of grading and leveling expenses, engineering costs, and other related amounts incurred after purchase of the property. Petitioner has introduced no evidence to demonstrate that these costs may be apportioned or allocated to the Big Bear and Paisley tracts in any proportions other than those originally determined by respondent. Moreover, since these costs appear to have been incurred principally to fill and grade the excavation in the center parcel, allocation of some 41 percent thereof to that portion of the tract does not seem excessive. Accordingly, respondent's determinations with respect to allocation of these costs, to wit, 27.567 percent to the Big Bear parcel and 30.942 percent to the Paisley parcel, are sustained.

Respondent has allowed petitioner an addition to the Paisley basis of $1,320.85 for additional costs incurred with respect to that parcel in 1958. Petitioner has introduced no evidence from which any change in this amount can be determined. Respondent's determination with respect thereto is sustained.

The remaining question involves the $50,000 placed in escrow in 1957 upon sale of the Big Bear parcel. The parties now agree that the amount in question is $40,146.32, the actual cost to petitioner for paving and lighting the center tract. While it has been held that improvements made to specific parcels or contracted for with respect to specific parcels may be added to the basis thereof, *Mackay v. Comm'r*, 11 B.T.A. 569 (1928); *Cambria Development Co. v. Comm'r*, 34 B.T.A. 1155 (1936), and that costs of improvements to a subdivision as a whole may be allocated among the parcels thereof, *Biscayne Bay Islands Co., supra*, improvements to property retained by the petitioner which may be sold at a later date may not be added to basis of another parcel in the tract. *Colony, Inc. v. Comm'r*, 26 T.C. 30 (1956), *aff'd.*, 244 F.2d 75 (6th Cir. 1957), reversed on other grounds 357 U.S. 28 (1958). *Cf. Biscayne Bay Islands Co., supra. Cf. also Estate of M. A. Collins v. Comm'r*, 31 T.C. 238 (1958). Accordingly, since it is uncontested that the $40,146.32 was spent entirely on improvements placed on the center or retained parcel of the tract, no portion of that amount may be allocated to the basis of the Big Bear tract alozne or to the Big Bear and Paisley parcels.

The matter of a net operating loss carryover from 1957 to 1958 depends upon the disposition of the above issues.

Chapter 3

Overview of State-Law Entities

I. Commentary

Generally, real estate owners prefer not to hold title to real property directly. The direct ownership of real property exposes the owners to liabilities that may arise with respect to the property. To avoid such liability exposure, owners generally form a legal entity and cause the legal entity to take title to the property.[1] States provide several types of legal entities that investors may choose from in structuring the acquisition of property. Attorneys must be aware of the legal and tax attributes of the various legal entities to advise investors regarding their choice of legal entity. Those attributes will affect the entity that attorneys recommend their clients use and can also affect transactions that occur between the entity and its members.

A. Legal Attributes of State-Law Entities

Investors generally must choose from a list of four general types of legal entities: (1) general partnerships, (2) limited partnerships, (3) limited liability companies, and (4) corporations. States may require a filing to form some legal entities.[2] States generally defer to the agreements among members of some entities,[3] but they provide default rules that govern issues not covered in the agreements.[4] Thus, attorneys must be prepared to carefully draft the documents that govern any legal entity with multiple members, or they must help their clients understand the default rules that will govern

---

1. The various forms of legal entities may have different formation requirements. *See, e.g.,* U.P.A. § 202, U.L.P.A. § 201; U.L.L.C.A. § 201; Del. Corp. Act § 101. Each state enacts its own partnership act, limited partnership act, and limited liability company act, and many of them have adopted versions of the uniform acts. This chapter does not reproduce the acts, but they are available online generally at www.uniformlaws.org. The cited versions of the specific acts are available at the following cites: U.P.A. (1997) at http://www.uniformlaws.org/shared/docs/partnership/upa_final_97.pdf; U.L.P.A. (2001) at http://www.uniformlaws.org/shared/docs/limited%20partnership/ulpa_final_2001rev.pdf; U.L.L.C.A. (2006) at http://www.uniformlaws.org/shared/docs/limited%20liability%20company/ullca_final_06rev.pdf. The chapter refers to the cites to the Delaware Corporate Act, which is available at http://delcode.delaware.gov/title8/c001/.

2. *See, e.g.,* U.L.P.A. § 201; U.L.L.C.A. § 201; Del. Corp. Act § 101.

3. *See, e.g.,* Elf Atochem N. Am., Inc., v. Jaffri, 727 A.2d 286 (Del. 1999); Allen v. Amber Manor Apartments Partnership; 95 Ill. App. 3d 541 (1981).

4. *See* U.P.A. § 103; U.L.P.A. § 110; U.L.L.C.A. § 110.

their entity. In choosing a legal entity, investors should consider, among other things, the extent to which the entity provides liability protection, the transferability of interests in the entity, and the management flexibility the entity provides. The tax classification of the entity is also important, but the next chapter considers that issue.

1. Liability Protection

One attribute property owners seek in choosing an entity to hold property is liability protection. Corporations and limited liability companies provide liability protection for all of their members.[5] If the members properly manage the entities, they will not be liable for the entities' liabilities.[6] The only loss such members may incur is their investment in the entity. Thus, if real estate investors form a limited liability company and contribute cash to the entity, the creditors of the entity may be able to claim the owners' contributions in the event a claim arises against the entity. The entity's creditors generally may not, however, proceed against the members' individual assets.

Limited partnerships provide liability protection only for the limited partners.[7] Thus, general partners may be liable for any of the limited partnership's liabilities.[8] The ultimate owners of the property may limit the liability of the general partner by forming a corporation or limited liability company that will act as the general partner. The unlimited liability of general partners, or the cumbersome structure required to limit that liability, often makes the limited partnership an unattractive choice of entity. Nonetheless, other factors may overwhelm those apparent shortcomings and make the limited partnership the entity of choice in some circumstances.

General partnerships provide no liability protection for their members, so each member is jointly and severally liable for the partnership's liabilities.[9] For this reason, property owners often choose an entity other than a general partnership to hold title to their property. Property owners may, however, choose to use a general partnership if they otherwise hold property in entities that provide liability protection. For example, if Ali, Bobbi, and Cris each had a separate legal entity (such as a limited liability company) in which they held property, they may combine the ownership of those properties using a general partnership with the limited liability companies as partners. The limited liability companies would protect Ali, Bobbi, and Cris from the liabilities of the general partnership, but other assets of the limited liability companies would be subject to claims of the general partnership's creditors. Consequently,

---

5. *See* U.L.L.C.A. §304; Del. Corp. Act §282 (limiting the liability of a stockholder of a dissolved corporation); §325 (implying that a specific provision of the corporate act must impose liability on a stock holder).

6. *But see* ASB Allegiance Real Estate Fund v. Scion Breckenridge Managing Member, LLC, 2012 Del. Ch. LEXIS 109, 2012 WL 1869416 (Del. Ch. 2012) (discussing potential liability for breach of fiduciary duties).

7. *See* U.L.P.A. §303.

8. *See* U.L.P.A. §404.

9. *See* U.P.A. §306.

the parties may hesitate to form such a general partnership, if it will expose other assets to claims of the general partnership's creditors.

2. Transferability of Interests

Another factor the parties may consider in choosing an entity is the transferability of the interests in the legal entity. Most likely, they will prefer to restrict the transfer of the interests. A group of owners may intend a project to be just among themselves. Therefore, they may prefer that no one else (including spouses and children of members of the group) enter the arrangement, so they may consider whether one type of entity grants them greater control of the transferability of the interests. They may, however, later decide to admit additional members to help finance the subdivision and construction of commercial buildings. Finally, they may prefer to restrict the powers of a creditor of a member who may obtain a judgment against the member.[10] The inability to foresee all contingencies requires the attorney to exercise great care when drafting buy-sell agreements for the entity.

3. Management Flexibility

Management flexibility is the extent to which the members of an entity may choose their management structure. Corporate law generally is more rigid than the laws governing the other types of entities.[11] Corporations generally must have shareholders who elect a board of directors.[12] The board hires officers to manage the corporation.[13] Such rules prohibit shareholders from acting in their capacity as shareholders on behalf of the corporation. State law governing limited partnerships will generally prohibit a limited partner from acting in the capacity of a limited partner on behalf of the limited partnership.[14] The laws governing limited liability companies provide significant flexibility. For example, members of a limited liability company can directly manage the limited liability company, or they can elect managers to manage the company.[15] All members of general partnerships have a right to manage the general partnership, unless otherwise provided in the governing documents.[16] Attorneys must be aware of the various management options when advising clients regarding the appropriate choice of legal entity.

B. Drafting Considerations

Once the parties choose the type of entity they will form to hold the property, the attorney must draft the governing documents to reflect the parties' intent. Often the

---

10. *See* U.P.A. §§ 503, 504; U.L.P.A. §§ 701–703; U.L.L.C.A. §§ 501–503 (limiting the powers of members' transferees).

11. *But see* DEL. CORP. ACT § 341 *et seq.* (providing significant leeway for close corporations).

12. *See* DEL. CORP. ACT § 151.

13. *See* DEL. CORP. ACT §§ 141, 142.

14. *See* U.L.P.A. § 302.

15. *See* U.L.L.C.A. § 407.

16. *See* U.P.A. §§ 301, 303.

parties will be hesitant to discuss issues that should be a part of the entity's governing documents. The hesitancy may have several sources. Perhaps the parties fear that discussing issues with each other will imply a sense of distrust. They may feel that if they suggest certain things (such as buy-sell provisions) be put in writing that they will offend other members of the group. They may not anticipate all of the potential issues that may arise, so they may not know to plan for them by including provisions in the governing documents that address the issues. Attorneys must be aware that clients do not always appreciate the need for sophisticated governing documentation for their entities. Attorneys must anticipate potential problems when drafting the governing documents. After practicing for several years, attorneys will gain experience that will help them anticipate potential issues. New attorneys must draw from the experience of others and use careful reflection to anticipate and address potential issues.

Attorneys should consider several items when drafting governing documents. Good documents should include buy-sell provisions that govern the transfer of interests in the entity. The provision should anticipate transfers upon death, divorce, or other actions by one or more of the members. It should also consider the appropriate settlement mechanism or disposition of interests in the event of gridlock among the members. The governing document should also address the allocation of tax and economic items and include a provision addressing distributions from the entity and the manner in which the entity will be liquidated. The document should also address capital contribution requirements, if any, of the members. Attorneys should also anticipate other potential issues and include provisions in the governing documents as needed to address those issues, and they should be leery of using form documents without carefully reviewing them.[17]

C. Transactions Between Entities and Members

Often complex ownership and transactional structures require property to move between entities and their members and between entities controlled by the same members. The movement of property raises numerous issues. For example, the movement of money or property may appear to be a contribution or distribution, but could be another type of arrangement.[18] Movement of property can also raise other types of legal issues. For instance, entering the chain of title of property can expose a person to liability that may arise with respect to the property. Transferring direct ownership of property also requires a deed and perhaps expensive title work. Nonetheless, tax and business planning often require the transfer of property to or from an entity. Attorneys must be familiar with how such transfers occur and with the issues that such transfers raise. Often, attorneys use simple diagrams to illustrate the flow

---

17. *See, e.g.,* ASB Allegiance Real Estate Fund v. Scion Breckenridge Managing Member, LLC, 2012 Del. Ch. LEXIS 109, 2012 WL 1869416 (Del. Ch. 2012).

18. *See* Mizrah v. Cohen, 104 A.D.3d 917 (N.Y. App. 2d Dept. 2013).

Figure 3.1 Formation of Hidong LLC

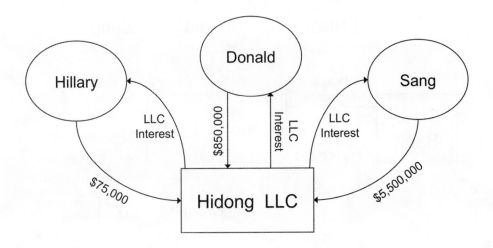

of property and other items that occur as part of any transaction between entities and their members. Such diagrams help the attorney visualize transactions, anticipate unforeseen problems, and explain transactions to clients. The following discussion illustrates how a hypothetical limited liability company might use contributed and borrowed money to acquire property.

Assume that Hillary, Donald, and Sang form Hidong LLC to acquire property. The members contribute the money to Hidong LLC in exchange for interests in the limited liability company. The transfer of money from the members to Hidong LLC thus appears to be a contribution to Hidong LLC,[19] and that money represents the members' initial contributions. Figure 3.1 illustrates the formation of Hidong LLC.

Following the formation of Hidong LLC, State Bank transfers $10,000,000 to Hidong LLC in exchange for a note from Hidong LLC and a security interest in Hidong LLC's property. That transaction would be a loan. Hidong LLC uses the member contributions and loan proceeds to acquire property for $14,000,000. Figure 3.2 illustrates the acquisition of the property. Notice that following the acquisition, Hidong LLC owns the property, subject to the bank's security interest. Hillary, Donald, and Sang each have an interest in Hidong LLC as determined in the operating agreement.

---

19. *See* U.L.L.C.A. §§ 102(2), 404, 405.

Figure 3.2 Hidong LLC's Acquisition of Property

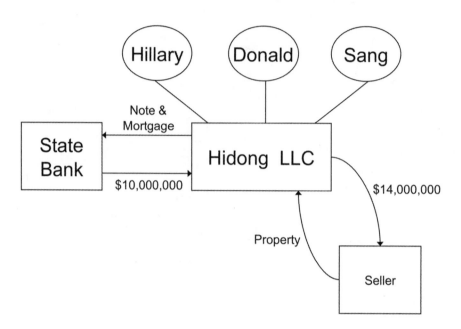

These very simple transactions illustrate the general manner in which property and other items flowed as part of the transactions. The diagrams are fairly general, and may not accurately reflect specific aspects of the transactions. In reality, Hidong LLC may never take possession of the loan proceeds. Instead, those proceeds may go directly to the seller at closing. Such detail was not needed in these diagrams, however, because they show the general flow of property and other items. Determining the appropriate level of detail requires professional judgment and often depends upon what an attorney is communicating and to whom such communication is directed.

Diagrams will often help illustrate transactions and the structure parties will use to own, develop, and transfer property. When drawing such diagrams, understand that a person generally must pay consideration of some sort to acquire property. Hidong LLC transferred membership interests to Hillary, Donald, and Sang in exchange for their contributions. It transferred a note in exchange for the loan proceeds, and it transferred money in exchange for property. Be sure to always pay attention to the flow of property and other items that occur as part of every transaction.[20] Such attention is critical to planning.

---

20. Distributions can also move property between entities and their members. *See, e.g.,* U.L.L.C.A. §§ 102(4), 404, 405. Members and entities may also enter into other transactions. *See, e.g.,* U.L.P.A. § 112.

II. Primary Legal Authority

Elf Atochem N. Am., Inc. v. Jaffari

Supreme Court of Delaware.

727 A.2d 286 (Del. 1999)

VEASEY, CHIEF JUSTICE:

This is a case of first impression before this Court involving the Delaware Limited Liability Company Act (the "Act"). The limited liability company ("LLC") is a relatively new entity that has emerged in recent years as an attractive vehicle to facilitate business relationships and transactions. The wording and architecture of the Act is somewhat complicated, but it is designed to achieve what is seemingly a simple concept—to permit persons or entities ("members") to join together in an environment of private ordering to form and operate the enterprise under an LLC agreement with tax benefits akin to a partnership and limited liability akin to the corporate form.

This is a purported derivative suit brought on behalf of a Delaware LLC calling into question whether: (1) the LLC, which did not itself execute the LLC agreement in this case ("the Agreement") defining its governance and operation, is nevertheless bound by the Agreement; and (2) contractual provisions directing that all disputes be resolved exclusively by arbitration or court proceedings in California are valid under the Act. Resolution of these issues requires us to examine the applicability and scope of certain provisions of the Act in light of the Agreement.

We hold that: (1) the Agreement is binding on the LLC as well as the members; and (2) since the Act does not prohibit the members of an LLC from vesting exclusive subject matter jurisdiction in arbitration proceedings (or court enforcement of arbitration) in California to resolve disputes, the contractual forum selection provisions must govern.

Accordingly, we affirm the judgment of the Court of Chancery dismissing the action brought in that court on the ground that the Agreement validly predetermined the fora in which disputes would be resolved, thus stripping the Court of Chancery of subject matter jurisdiction.

FACTS[21]

Plaintiff below-appellant Elf Atochem North America, Inc., a Pennsylvania Corporation ("Elf"), manufactures and distributes solvent-based maskants to the aerospace and aviation industries throughout the world. Defendant below-appellee Cyrus A.

---

21. [1] Since this is an appeal from a dismissal under Court of Chancery Rule 12(b)(1) for lack of jurisdiction, we must confine ourselves to the allegations of the complaint and exhibits thereto, which must be accepted as true for purposes of the motion to dismiss. See Harman v. Masoneilan Int'l, Inc., Del.Supr., 442 A.2d 487, 488 (1982). None of these allegations has been established by proof. As the Court of Chancery's decision notes, no factual statements in that court's decision constitute a finding of fact that would have any preclusive effect in California or elsewhere. See Elf Atochem North America, Inc. v. Jaffari, et al., C.A. No. 16320, 1998 WL 326596 (June 9, 1998), Letter Op. at 8, n. 9. The same applies to this Opinion.

Jaffari is the president of Malek, Inc., a California Corporation. Jaffari had developed an innovative, environmentally-friendly alternative to the solvent-based maskants that presently dominate the market.

For decades, the aerospace and aviation industries have used solvent-based maskants in the chemical milling process. Recently, however, the Environmental Protection Agency ("EPA") classified solvent-based maskants as hazardous chemicals and air contaminants. To avoid conflict with EPA regulations, Elf considered developing or distributing a maskant less harmful to the environment.

In the mid-nineties, Elf approached Jaffari and proposed investing in his product and assisting in its marketing. Jaffari found the proposal attractive since his company, Malek, Inc., possessed limited resources and little international sales expertise. Elf and Jaffari agreed to undertake a joint venture that was to be carried out using a limited liability company as the vehicle.

On October 29, 1996, Malek, Inc. caused to be filed a Certificate of Formation with the Delaware Secretary of State, thus forming Malek LLC, a Delaware limited liability company under the Act. The certificate of formation is a relatively brief and formal document that is the first statutory step in creating the LLC as a separate legal entity.[22] The certificate does not contain a comprehensive agreement among the parties, and the statute contemplates that the certificate of formation is to be complemented by the terms of the Agreement.[23]

Next, Elf, Jaffari and Malek, Inc. entered into a series of agreements providing for the governance and operation of the joint venture. Of particular importance to this litigation, Elf, Malek, Inc., and Jaffari entered into the Agreement, a comprehensive and integrated document[24] of 38 single-spaced pages setting forth detailed provisions for the governance of Malek LLC, which is not itself a signatory to the Agreement. Elf and Malek LLC entered into an Exclusive Distributorship Agreement in which Elf would be the exclusive, worldwide distributor for Malek LLC. The Agreement provides that Jaffari will be the manager of Malek LLC. Jaffari and Malek LLC entered into an employment agreement providing for Jaffari's employment as chief executive officer of Malek LLC.

The Agreement is the operative document for purposes of this Opinion, however. Under the Agreement, Elf contributed $1 million in exchange for a 30 percent interest

---

22. [4] See 6 Del.C. § 18-201.

23. [5] See 6 Del.C. § 18-201(d), which provides:

   A limited liability company agreement may be entered into either before, after or at the time of the filing of a certificate of formation and, whether entered into before, after or at the time of such filing, may be made effective as of the formation of the limited liability company or at such other time or date as provided in the limited liability company agreement.

24. [6] See the definition section of the statute, 6 Del.C. § 18-101(7), defining the term "limited liability company agreement" as "any agreement … of the … members as to the affairs of a limited liability company and the conduct of its business," and setting forth a nonexclusive list of what it may provide.

in Malek LLC. Malek, Inc. contributed its rights to the water-based maskant in exchange for a 70 percent interest in Malek LLC.

The Agreement contains an arbitration clause covering all disputes. The clause, Section 13.8, provides that "any controversy or dispute arising out of this Agreement, the interpretation of any of the provisions hereof, or the action or inaction of any Member or Manager hereunder shall be submitted to arbitration in San Francisco, California...." Section 13.8 further provides: "No action ... based upon any claim arising out of or related to this Agreement shall be instituted in any court by any Member except (a) an action to compel arbitration ... or (b) an action to enforce an award obtained in an arbitration proceeding...." The Agreement also contains a forum selection clause, Section 13.7, providing that all members consent to: "exclusive jurisdiction of the state and federal courts sitting in California in any action on a claim arising out of, under or in connection with this Agreement or the transactions contemplated by this Agreement, provided such claim is not required to be arbitrated pursuant to Section 13.8"; and personal jurisdiction in California. The Distribution Agreement contains no forum selection or arbitration clause.

General Summary of Background of the Act

The phenomenon of business arrangements using "alternative entities" has been developing rapidly over the past several years. Long gone are the days when business planners were confined to corporate or partnership structures.

Limited partnerships date back to the 19th Century. They became an important and popular vehicle with the adoption of the Uniform Limited Partnership Act in 1916. Sixty years later, in 1976, the National Conference of Commissioners on Uniform State Laws approved and recommended to the states a Revised Uniform Limited Partnership Act ("RULPA"), many provisions of which were modeled after the innovative 1973 Delaware Limited Partnership (LP) Act. Difficulties with the workability of the 1976 RULPA prompted the Commissioners to amend RULPA in 1985.[25]

To date, 48 states and the District of Columbia have adopted the RULPA in either its 1976 or 1985 form.[26] Delaware adopted the RULPA with innovations designed to improve upon the Commissioners' product.[27] Since 1983, the General Assembly has amended the LP Act eleven times, with a view to continuing Delaware's status as an innovative leader in the field of limited partnerships.

The Delaware Act was adopted in October 1992. The Act is codified in Chapter 18 of Title 6 of the Delaware Code. To date, the Act has been amended six times with a view to modernization. The LLC is an attractive form of business entity because it combines corporate-type limited liability with partnership-type flexibility and tax

---

25. [11] Robert J. Haft and Peter M. Fass, The Limited Partnership as an Investment Vehicle for Tax-Advantaged Investments, in Tax-Advantaged Securities § 15.01 (1996).

26. [12] *See* Revised Uniform Limited Partnership Act (1976) with the 1985 Amendments, Table of Jurisdictions Wherein Act Has Been Adopted.

27. [13] *See* Haft & Fass, *supra* note 11, at § 15.01.

advantages.[28] The Act can be characterized as a "flexible statute" because it generally permits members to engage in private ordering with substantial freedom of contract to govern their relationship, provided they do not contravene any mandatory provisions of the Act.[29] Indeed, the LLC has been characterized as the "best of both worlds."[30]

The Delaware Act has been modeled on the popular Delaware LP Act.[31] In fact, its architecture and much of its wording is almost identical to that of the Delaware LP Act.[32] Under the Act, a member of an LLC is treated much like a limited partner under the LP Act.[33] The policy of freedom of contract underlies both the Act and the LP Act.[34]

In August 1994, nearly two years after the enactment of the Delaware LLC Act, the Uniform Law Commissioners promulgated the Uniform Limited Liability Company Act (ULLCA).[35] To coordinate with later developments in federal tax guidelines regarding manager-managed LLCs, the Commissioners adopted minor changes in 1995.[36] The Commissioners further amended the ULLCA in 1996. Despite its purpose to promote uniformity and consistency, the ULLCA has not been widely popular. In fact, only seven jurisdictions have adopted the ULLCA since its creation in 1994.[37] A notable commentator on LLCs has argued that legislatures should look to either the Delaware Act or the Prototype Act created by the ABA when drafting state statutes.[38]

---

28. [14] See 1 Larry E. Ribstein & Robert R. Keatinge, Ribstein and Keatinge on Limited Liability Companies, § 2.02, at 2 (1998); Martin I. Lubaroff & Paul M. Altman, Delaware Limited Liability Companies, in Delaware Law of Corporations & Business Organizations, § 20.1 (R. Franklin Balotti & Jesse A. Finkelstein eds., 1998).

29. [15] See 1 James D. Cox et al., Corporations, § 1.12, at 1.37–.38 (1999).

30. [16] Lubaroff & Altman, supra note 14, at § 20.1.

31. [17] The Delaware LP Act is codified in Chapter 17 of Title 6 of the Delaware Code, and the Delaware LLC Act is codified in Chapter 18 of Title 6 of the Delaware Code.

32. [18] See Lubaroff & Altman, supra note 14, at § 20.3

33. [19] See id. (citing 6 Del.C. §§ 18-209, 18-301, 18-302, 18-305, 18-306, 18-501, 18-502, 18-603, 18-607, 18-705, 18-803, 18-804, 18-1001, and 18-1101(c)).

34. [20] See id. at § 20.4; compare 6 Del.C. § 18-1101(b) ("It is the policy of ... [the LLC Act] to give the maximum effect to the principle of freedom of contract and to the enforceability of limited liability company agreements.") with 6 Del.C.§ 17-1101(c) ("It is the policy of ... [the LP Act] to give maximum effect to the principle of freedom of contract and to the enforceability of partnership agreements.").

35. [21] Jennifer J. Johnson, Limited Liability for Lawyers: General Partners Need Not Apply, 51 Bus.Law. 85, n. 69 (1995). In addition to the ULLCA, a Prototype Limited Liability Company Act ("Prototype Act") was drafted by the Subcommittee on Limited Liability Companies of the ABA Section of Business Law. The Prototype Act was released in the Fall of 1993 and has formed the basis for several LLC statutes enacted since that time. See id.

36. [22] Carter G. Bishop, The Uniform Limited Liability Company Act: Summary & Analysis, 51 Bus.Law. 51 (1995).

37. [23] To date, the seven jurisdictions that have adopted the ULLCA are Alabama, South Dakota, the U.S. Virgin Islands, Hawaii, South Carolina, Vermont, and West Virginia. See Uniform Limited Liability Company Act (1995), Table of Jurisdictions Wherein Act Has Been Adopted and additional information provided by the Uniform Law Commissioners (Mar. 17, 1999).

38. [24] See Larry E. Ribstein, A Critique of the Uniform Limited Liability Company Act, 25 Stetson L.Rev. 311, 329 (1995).

Policy of the Delaware Act

The basic approach of the Delaware Act is to provide members with broad discretion in drafting the Agreement and to furnish default provisions when the members' agreement is silent.[39] The Act is replete with fundamental provisions made subject to modification in the Agreement (*e.g.* "unless otherwise provided in a limited liability company agreement....").[40]

Although business planners may find comfort in working with the Act in structuring transactions and relationships, it is a somewhat awkward document for this Court to construe and apply in this case. To understand the overall structure and thrust of the Act, one must wade through provisions that are prolix, sometimes oddly organized, and do not always flow evenly. Be that as it may as a problem in mastering the Act as a whole, one returns to the narrow and discrete issues presented in this case.

Freedom of Contract

Section 18-1101(b) of the Act, like the essentially identical Section 17-1101(c) of the LP Act, provides that "[i]t is the policy of [the Act] to give the maximum effect to the principle of freedom of contract and to the enforceability of limited liability company agreements." Accordingly, the following observation relating to limited partnerships applies as well to limited liability companies:

> The Act's basic approach is to permit partners to have the broadest possible discretion in drafting their partnership agreements and to furnish answers only in situations where the partners have not expressly made provisions in their partnership agreement. Truly, the partnership agreement is the cornerstone of a Delaware limited partnership, and effectively constitutes the entire agreement among the partners with respect to the admission of partners to, and the creation, operation and termination of, the limited partnership. Once partners exercise their contractual freedom in their partnership agreement, the partners have a great deal of certainty that their partnership agreement will be enforced in accordance with its terms.[41]

---

39. [25] *See* Lubaroff & Altman, *supra* note 14, at §20.4. According to Lubaroff & Altman, "the Act gives members virtually unfettered discretion to define contractually their business understanding, and then provides assurance that their understanding will be enforced in accordance with the terms of their limited liability company agreement." *Id*

40. [26] See, e.g., 6 Del.C. §§18-107, 18-204(b), 18-209(b), 18-301(d), 18-302(d), 18-304(a) & (b), 18-402, 18-403, 18-404(d), 18-502(a) & (b), 18-503, 18-504, 18-605, 18-606, 18-702(a), (b) & (d), 18-704(b), 18-801(a)(4) & (b), 18-803(a), and 18-804(a)(2) & (3). For example, members are free to contract among themselves concerning management of the LLC, including who is to manage the LLC, the establishment of classes of members, voting, procedures for holding meetings of members, or considering matters without a meeting. See Lubaroff & Altman,supra note 14, at §20.4.

41. [27] Martin I. Lubaroff & Paul Altman, *Delaware Limited Partnerships* §1.2 (1999) (footnote omitted). In their article on Delaware limited liability companies, Lubaroff and Altman use virtually identical language in describing the basic approach of the LLC Act. Clearly, both the LP Act and the LLC Act are uniform in their commitment to "maximum flexibility." *See* Lubaroff & Altman, *supra* note 14, at §20.4.

In general, the commentators observe that only where the agreement is inconsistent with mandatory statutory provisions will the members' agreement be invalidated.[42] Such statutory provisions are likely to be those intended to protect third parties,[43] not necessarily the contracting members. As a framework for decision, we apply that principle to the issues before us, without expressing any views more broadly.[44]

Mizrahi v. Cohen

Supreme Court of New York, Appellate Division, Second Department
104 A.D.3d 917 (2013)

Judges: RANDALL T. ENG, P.J., REINALDO E. RIVERA, PLUMMER E. LOTT, ROBERT J. MILLER, JJ. ENG, P.J., RIVERA, LOTT AND MILLER, JJ., concur.

OPINION

In an action, inter alia, to recover damages for breach of fiduciary duty and breach of contract, and for the judicial dissolution of the subject limited liability company, the plaintiff appeals from so much of an order of the Supreme Court, Kings County (Demarest, J.), dated January 12, 2012, as, after a nonjury trial, directed dismissal of the causes of action to recover damages for breach of fiduciary duty and breach of contract, and denied, in effect, his application for an order authorizing him to purchase the defendant's interest in the limited liability company upon its dissolution, and the defendant cross-appeals, as limited by his brief, from so much of the same order as granted, in effect, the plaintiff's application for judicial dissolution of the limited liability company and directed that, upon dissolution, certain contributions of the plaintiff to the limited liability company are to be treated as loans to the limited liability company.

Ordered that on the Court's own motion, the notices of appeal and cross appeal are treated as applications for leave to appeal and cross-appeal, and leave to appeal and cross-appeal is granted ... and it is further,

Ordered that the order is modified, on the law and the facts, by deleting the provision thereof denying, in effect, the plaintiff's application for an order authorizing him to purchase the defendant's interest in the limited liability company upon its dissolution, and substituting therefor a provision directing that the plaintiff may purchase such interest within 60 days after a determination by the Supreme Court as to the value of such interest; as so modified, the order is affirmed insofar as appealed and cross-appealed from, without costs or disbursements, and the matter is remitted to the Supreme Court, Kings County, for further proceedings and for a determination thereafter as to the value of the defendant's interest in the limited liability company.

The plaintiff and the defendant are the sole members of a limited liability company (hereinafter LLC). The plaintiff is a dentist and the defendant is an optometrist. The LLC was formed for the purpose of the construction and operation of a mixed-use commercial/residential building. The parties did not initially execute an LLC operating

---

42. [28] *See* Ribstein & Keatinge, *supra* note 14, at §4.16, at 27.

43. [29] *See id.*

44. [30] See Paramount Communications Inc. v. QVC Network Inc., Del.Supr., 637 A.2d 34, 51 (1994) ("It is the nature of the judicial process that we decide only the case before us....").

agreement (hereinafter LLC agreement). In 2000, several months after the LLC was formed, the parties purchased a parcel of real property, upon which they intended to construct the building. At the closing of title, the property seller or lender required an LLC agreement. The attorney who represented both the plaintiff and defendant at the closing then drafted an LLC agreement.

The LLC agreement provided that the parties each own a 50% membership interest in the company. However, the LLC agreement did not set forth the amount of the parties' initial capital contributions. The LLC agreement also provided that, after the "initial capital contributions" by the parties, no member would be required to contribute additional capital unless required by a vote of all of the members of the company. The LLC agreement provided that no member "shall have the right to receive any return of any Capital Contribution," subject to certain exceptions that are not relevant here. The LLC agreement provided that the LLC may be dissolved only upon the happening of certain specified events. Upon dissolution, the assets were to be distributed first to creditors of the LLC, and then to the members, in proportion to their respective ownership shares.

The parties contributed approximately equal funds toward the down payment on the parcel of real property. The construction of the building was largely financed by a construction loan. At some point, the parties refinanced that loan and obtained a mortgage loan. In 2006, the construction was completed, and both parties moved their professional offices into the building.

Through approximately 2003, the parties made approximately equal capital contributions to the LLC. After that, however, the contributions by the plaintiff greatly exceeded those of the defendant. It is undisputed that, over time, the plaintiff contributed approximately $1.4 million in capital to the company, while the defendant contributed approximately $317,000 in capital to the company. At a hearing, an accountant for the LLC testified that the LLC experienced net operating losses in each year from 2006 through 2010, and through the first half of 2011, when the hearing was held. The accountant testified, inter alia, that the LLC would have failed, if not for the use of proceeds of the mortgage loan and capital infusions by the plaintiff, which were used to cover its operating expenses.

The plaintiff commenced this action, inter alia, to recover damages for breach of fiduciary duty and breach of contract, and for the judicial dissolution of the LLC. The plaintiff also sought an order authorizing him to purchase the defendant's interest in the LLC upon its dissolution.

The Supreme Court did not err in directing dismissal of the cause of action to recover damages for breach of fiduciary duty. Contrary to the plaintiff's contention, that cause of action was not properly brought in the plaintiff's individual capacity....

Contrary to the defendant's contention, the LLC agreement is ambiguous and, therefore, parol evidence of the parties' course of dealing is admissible to supplement and interpret the terms of that agreement.... Further, the evidence of the parties' conduct with respect to capital contributions did not constitute a prior oral agreement or an impermissible oral modification of the contract.

Nevertheless, the Supreme Court did not err in directing dismissal of the cause of action to recover damages for breach of contract. Even considering the evidence of the parties' conduct regarding capital contributions, the plaintiff failed to establish the existence of a binding agreement as to the parties' responsibility for such contributions. Therefore, the plaintiff failed to show a breach of any such agreement....

The Supreme Court did not err in granting, in effect, the plaintiff's application for judicial dissolution of the LLC. Under the circumstances presented, it is not reasonably practicable for the LLC to continue to operate, as continuing the LLC is financially unfeasible (*see* Limited Liability Company Law § 702; *see also Matter of 1545 Ocean Ave., LLC*, 72 AD3d 121, 131, 893 NYS2d 590 [2010]).

Contrary to the defendant's contention, the Supreme Court did not err in determining that if the assets of the company are to be liquidated, then the capital contributions of the plaintiff are to be treated as loans to the LLC to the extent that those contributions exceeded those made by the defendant. Although the LLC agreement provided that a member does not have the right to receive any return of capital contributions, the LLC agreement also provided for the repayment of debts of the LLC upon dissolution. The record, including an affidavit submitted by the defendant, establishes that the parties intended that the capital contributions by the plaintiff were to be treated as loans to the LLC to the extent that those contributions exceeded those made by the defendant. In addition, the LLC agreement is silent as to the issue of equalization of capital contributions. Under these circumstances, the Supreme Court did not err in directing that such contributions are to be treated as loans to the LLC....

The Supreme Court should have granted, in effect, the plaintiff's application for an order authorizing him to purchase the defendant's interest in the LLC upon its dissolution. The Limited Liability Company Law does not expressly authorize a buyout in a dissolution proceeding.... Nonetheless, in certain circumstances, a buyout may be an appropriate equitable remedy upon the dissolution of an LLC.... Under the facts of this case, the remedy of a buyout by the plaintiff is appropriate.... Contrary to the defendant's contention, the provisions of the LLC agreement regarding dissolution of the LLC do not preclude an order authorizing a buyout upon the judicial dissolution of the LLC pursuant to Limited Liability Company Law § 702.... Accordingly, the matter must be remitted to the Supreme Court, Kings County, for further proceedings and for a determination thereafter as to the value of the defendant's interest in the LLC.

Eng, P.J., Rivera, Lott and Miller, JJ., concur.

Allen v. Amber Manor Apartments Partnership

Appellate Court of Illinois
95 Ill. App. 3d 541 (1981)

Perlin, J.

Defendants-appellants Amber Manor Apartments Partnership, William J. Brant, Jr., L. Cosby Bernard, Jr., and Lewis J. Scheer appeal from an order of the circuit court of Cook County which granted a motion by plaintiff-appellee, Franklin G. Allen, for partial summary judgment declaring Allen a limited partner of the Amber Manor Apartments Partnership. We consider whether the trial court erred in granting Allen's motion for partial summary judgment.

The following factual allegations emerge from the pleadings, affidavits and discovery depositions. On or about November 1, 1971, defendants Sauk Properties, Inc., Hyman Clapman, Willard Gassel and Duane F. Linden entered into a limited partnership agreement for the purpose of constructing and operating a qualifying housing development under the National Housing Act. The partnership was designated the Amber Manor Apartments Partnership. On or about February 27, 1972, defendants-appellants, William J. Brant, Jr., L. Cosby Bernard, Jr., and Lewis J. Scheer, entered into an agreement which provided for the admission of Brant, Bernard and Scheer as limited partners.[45] During the period of November 1971 through December 1974, Amber Manor Apartments Partnership acquired an interest in certain real estate in Hobart, Indiana, and obtained certain financing for the construction of an apartment complex.

In December 1974 additional financing was required to pay outstanding construction debts, to complete construction and provide working capital. During the latter part of 1974 representatives of Brant, Bernard, Scheer, Clapman, Linden and Amber Manor Apartments Partnership met with representatives of plaintiff-appellee, Franklin Allen, and other interested investors. Thereafter Allen, the other investors, Brant, Bernard, Scheer, Clapman, Cassel, Linden, Sauk Properties, Inc., and Eugene Storry executed an agreement which is the subject of this action.[46]

The agreement provides, *inter alia*: (1) that each of the new limited partners (Allen and the other investors) "agree to pay into the capital of Amber [Manor Apartments Partnership] the amount of money set opposite his name, the aggregate total of which constitutes FIVE HUNDRED THOUSAND ($500,000) DOLLARS, provided the terms and provisions of this Agreement are met, as evidenced by promissory notes"; (2) that Brant, Bernard and Scheer "shall be the sole General Partners of Amber prior to December 31, 1974, and shall continue as sole General Partners until 'completion of the Project'";[47] (3) that "Storry shall become a General Partner of Amber * * * upon Completion of the Project"; (4) that each of the new limited partners "agree to loan to the General Partners, jointly and severally, the amount of money set opposite his name, the aggregate total of which constitutes FIFTY THOUSAND ($50,000.00)

45. [1] Although not crucial to the issue before us on appeal, but for the purpose of factual accuracy, the pleadings, affidavits and depositions contain a reference that due to some failure to comply with formal requisites of Indiana partnership law Brant, Bernard and Scheer became general partners.

46. [2] The agreement states "THIS AGREEMENT entered into this 27th day of December, 1974 * * *." Allen alleges in his complaint that the agreement was entered into on December 27, 1974. Defendants-appellants, Amber Manor Partnership, Brant, Bernard and Scheer, in their answer to Allen's complaint admit that the agreement was executed but deny that it was executed on December 27, 1974.

47. [3] There is a lengthy definition of the term "Completion of the Project" contained in the agreement which need not be recited.

DOLLARS, which loan shall be evidenced by a Promissory Note from the General Partners to the New Limited Partners, bearing interest at 6% per annum, due and payable on or before December 31, 1975,[48] subject to acceleration upon the escrow dispursement [*sic*] pursuant to the Completion of the project, secured by an assignment of collateral reasonably acceptable to Storry, with a net fair market value of at least $50,000.00"; (5) that the "General Partners shall loan such $50,000.00 to Amber to be used for: (a) the redemption of the interest of Salk [*sic*] Properties, Inc., Talandis Construction Company, and Vytantes Talandis in the Partnership; and/or (b) the Project"; (6) that the "capital contributions from the New Limited Partners shall be due and payable within thirty days following notice from the General Partners of the Completion of the Project; provided, however, such notice may not be given sooner than June 15, 1975 nor later than January 31, 1976"; (7) that "[i]f the completion of the Project does not occur on or before January 31, 1976, then the obligation of the New Limited Partners to: (a) make any capital contribution, or (b) pay any monies whatsoever with respect to either Amber or the Project, shall terminate."

The agreement further provides that "[t]he New Limited Partners are hereby admitted to Amber as of January 1, 1974 on the following basis:

(a) The participation in the profits and losses of Amber shall be allocated among the parties hereto in the following manner:

(i) For the calendar year 1974:

Party	Percent of Profits and Losses
Old Limited Partners	0%
New Limited Partners	100%

(ii) For: (a) calendar year 1975; and (b) calendar year 1976 and subsequent years, *if* the Completion of the Project does *not* occur:

Party	Percent of Profits and Losses
Old Limited Partners	51%
New Limited Partners	49%

(iii) For the calendar year 1976 and subsequent years, *if* the Completion of the Project occurs:

Party	Percent of Profits and Losses
Old Limited Partners	47-1/2%
Storry	5%
New Limited Partners	47-1/2%

(b) The net cash flow generated from the operations of the Project shall be distributed among the parties hereto in the following manner and in accordance with the following priorities:

(i) For the calendar year 1974:

---

48. [4] The promissory notes provide that the loan shall become due and payable on or before January 31, 1976.

Party	Percent of Cash Flow
New Limited Partners	47-1/2%
Old Limited Partners	52-1/2%

(ii) For the calendar year 1975 and subsequent years, if the Completion of the Project occurs:

(a) First, an amount equal to 11% of the cash capital contribution of the New Limited Partners as of the escrow disbursement pursuant to the Completion of the Project, less any cash capital contribution returned to the New Limited Partners prior to June 30, 1976, pursuant either to Paragraph 7 or by a return of capital from Amber, shall be distributed among the New Limited Partners on a non-cumulative basis.

(b) Second, an amount equal to the amount distributed to the New Limited Partners pursuant to Subparagraph (a) above shall be distributed among Old Limited Partners on a non-cumulative basis.

(c) Third, an amount equal to 5% of the amount distributed to the New Limited Partners and the Old Limited Partners pursuant to Subparagraph (a) and (b) above shall be distributed to Storry on a non-cumulative basis.

(d) Fourth, any amounts due to the New Limited Partners pursuant to Paragraph 7 hereof.[49]

(e) Fifth, all amounts in excess thereof shall be distributed as follows:

Storry	5%
Old Limited Partners	47-1/2%
New Limited Partners	47-1/2%

(iii) For the calendar year 1975 and subsequent years, *if* the Completion of the project does *not* occur; all of the Cash Flow shall be distributed to the Old Limited Partners on a non-cumulative basis."

The agreement also provides that:

"The General Partners hereby represent to Storry and the New Limited Partners that the net tax losses of Amber to be reported for Federal Income Tax purposes for the calendar year 1974 are not less than FOUR HUNDRED SEVENTY-FIVE THOUSAND ($475,000.00) DOLLARS and that such losses have been determined in accordance with good accounting practices and will be subscribed to by the accounting firm of Altschuler, Melvoin and Glasser or any of the eight largest public accounting firms. To the extent that the net federal income tax losses of Amber for the calendar year 1974 are less than $475,000.00, the required aggregate cash capital contributions of the New Limited Partners shall be proportionately reduced by an amount equal to 50% of the amount by which such net federal income tax loss are less than $475,000.00."

---

49. [5] Paragraph 7 concerns the distribution of net proceeds in the event the Project is refinanced by increasing the amount of the loan from Bell Federal Savings and Loan.

On December 30, 1974, an amended certificate of limited partnership was recorded in the office of the recorder of Lake County, Indiana. The amended certificate listed Allen and the other new limited partners and set forth the terms and provisions of the agreement. The amended certificate was signed by David Rosenthal as "Attorney-In-Fact" for Brant, Bernard and Scheer, and by Eugene Storry for Allen and the other new limited partners.

Pursuant to the agreement Brant, Bernard and Scheer executed a promissory note dated December 30, 1974, in the amount of $50,000 due and payable on or before January 31, 1976. On January 27, 1975, Alfred C. McClure, one of the attorneys for Brant, Bernard, Scheer and Amber Manor Apartments Partnership, sent a letter to Jeffery Rubenstein (an attorney for Allen and the other new limited partners). In that letter Mr. McClure requested that the "remainder of $50,000" be forwarded to him. In a letter dated March 18, 1975, Mr. McClure informed Mr. Rubenstein that the remainder of the $50,000 loan was "release[d]."[50]

Allen's complaint alleges that $450,000, "funds for [the] capital contributions," was placed in escrow. In their answer, Brant, Bernard, Scheer and Amber Manor Apartments Partnership neither admitted nor denied the allegation but demanded strict proof thereof.

On January 24, 1975, Brant filed a report of sale pursuant to section 4(G) of the Illinois Securities Act reporting the sale of limited partnership interests to Allen and the other new limited partners. The report listed each new limited partner's name, address, the extent of his interest. The date of sale listed for each of the new limited partners is either December 27, 1974, December 28, 1974, December 29, 1974, December 30, 1974, or December 31, 1974. In the report Brant noted that:

> "The limited partnership units are sold in exchange for commitments by the purchasers to make contributions to the capital of Amber Manor Associates in the following amounts if and only if certain conditions are satisfied in 1975. Each purchaser has made a loan to the general partners of Amber Manor Associates in the amount of 10% of such capital contribution."

The partnership income returns (IRS Form 1065) for the calendar years 1974, 1975, 1976, 1977 and 1978 listed, on Schedule K-1, Allen and the other new limited partners as limited partners.

On April 1, 1976, Allen filed a complaint for accounting, specific performance, injunction and declaratory judgment. Allen requested that the court declare that the agreement is valid, binding and enforceable upon all parties; that Amber Manor Apartments Partnership is a duly organized and validly existing limited partnership under the laws of the State of Indiana; and that Allen and the other persons designated in the agreement as new limited partners are, in fact, limited partners of Amber Manor Apartments Partnership. Pursuant to Allen's motion for partial summary judgment, the court found that "the Agreement dated December 27, 1974 * * * is a

---

50. [6] The letter provides no explanation of the meaning of "release[d]."

valid and enforceable Agreement * * * [and] there was adequate consideration for such Agreement on the part of the 'New Limited Partners.'" The court adjudged and decreed Allen "to be and to have been a limited partner in the Amber Manor Apartments Partnership, an Indiana Limited Partnership, as of January 1, 1974 pursuant to the terms of the said Agreement dated December 27, 1974." Defendants Brant, Bernard, Scheer and Amber Manor Apartments Partnership appeal from this order. Defendants Clapman, Gassel, Linden, Sauk Properties, Inc., and Eugene Storry have not appealed.

Limited partnerships were unknown at common law; they are exclusively a creature of statute. Their main purpose is to permit a form of business enterprise, other than a corporation, in which persons could invest money without becoming liable as general partners for all debts of the partnership ... The fundamental difference between the liability of general partners and limited partners under these statutes is that the former are responsible *in solido* for the debts and obligations of the firm, without regard to the amounts contributed by them to the capital, while the latter is not personally liable if the statute has been complied with, because his cash contribution is substituted for a personal liability ... A limited partnership is in the nature of an investment ... Through his contribution, the limited partner becomes entitled to share in the profits and losses of the partnership, though his share of the losses will not exceed the amount of capital initially contributed by him to the enterprise.... The word "contributions" as used in the Uniform Limited Partnership Act (hereinafter referred to as the ULPA) as adopted in Indiana (Ind. Code Ann. §23-4-2-1 *et seq.* (Burns 1972)), is limited to the contribution made by a limited partner at the time of formation of the partnership for the benefit of the partnership's creditors. Section 17 of the ULPA delineates the extent of the limited partner's investment in the business: it makes him liable to the partnership:

"(1) For the difference between his contribution as actually made and that stated in the certificate as having been made; and

(2) For any unpaid contribution which he agreed in the certificate to make in the future at the time and on the conditions stated in the certificate."

However, when the limited partner makes the contribution, he is placing that amount at risk ... He is not permitted to insure that risk or to guarantee a return to himself by taking some form of security.... He may not vie with creditors for the assets available to pay the partnership's obligations. Thus a limited partner is prohibited from taking collateral to secure repayment of his capital contribution. To do so would give him an unfair priority over the creditors of the partnership contrary to the express provisions of section 16(1) of the ULPA:

"(1) A limited partner shall not receive from a general partner or out of partnership property any part of his contribution until

(a) All liabilities of the partnership, except liabilities to general partners and to limited partners on account of their contributions, have been paid or there remains property of the partnership sufficient to pay them,

(b) The consent of all members is had, unless the return of the contribution may be rightfully demanded under the provisions of paragraph (2), and

(c) The certificate is cancelled or so amended as to set forth the withdrawal or reduction."

See Kramer v. McDonald's System, Inc. (1979), 77 Ill. 2d 323, 332.

The creation of a limited partnership is not a mere private, informal, voluntary agreement as in the case of a general partnership, but is a public and formal proceeding which must follow the statutory requirements of the ULPA.... Section 2 of the ULPA as adopted in Indiana mandates that a certificate of partnership be signed by the parties, acknowledged, and recorded with the county recorder of the county in which the principal place of business of the partnership is located. Section 2 requires that the certificate set forth 14 designated partnership details, including the name of the partnership, the character and location of the business, the identity of the general and limited partners, the terms of the partnership, the cash contributions made by the limited partners, and such additional contributions, if any, which the limited partners have agreed to make in the future. The principal function of the certificate is to give third persons notice of the essential features of the limited partnership.... The certificate is a statutory prerequisite to the creation of a limited partnership and until it is filed, the partnership is not formed as a limited partnership ... However, the recording requirement is meant to protect the public, and parties to the partnership are not bound by the terms of the certificate simply because it is recorded....

A partnership is, of course, a contractual relationship to which the principles of contract law are fully applicable.... An agreement to form a partnership may be made by the parties, but such an agreement does not of itself create a partnership.... One of the essential elements for formation of a contract is a manifestation of agreement or mutual assent by the parties to the terms thereof. The failure to agree upon or even discuss an essential term of a contract may indicate that the mutual assent required to make or modify a contract is lacking.... Whether a partnership exists is always a matter of fact which must depend on the intention of the parties....

It appears from the argument of defendants-appellants (Brant, Bernard, Scheer and Amber Manor Apartments Partnership) that it is their understanding that "the [agreement] provides that [Allen's] interest, if any, in Amber Manor [Apartments Partnership] would vary depending on whether or not the project was completed by January 31, 1976." It appears that Allen's understanding of the agreement is that his status as a limited partner is unaffected by whether the project was completed by January 31, 1976. The threshold dispute is not whether the project was actually completed but whether the parties intended the formation of the limited partnership to occur prior to, or only upon, the completion of the project.

As we noted above, it appears that Allen's interpretation of the agreement, and perhaps his intention at the time of the execution of the agreement, is that his status as a limited partner is unaffected by whether the project was completed by January

31, 1976. In support of his interpretation, Allen points out that paragraph 4 of the agreement provides that "the New Limited Partners shall not be obligated to make *any* capital contributions unless the Completion of the Project occurs prior to January 31, 1976." (Emphasis supplied.) Paragraph 4 also provides that:

> "If the Completion of the Project does not occur on or before January 31, 1976, then the obligation of the New Limited Partners to:
>
> (a) make any capital contribution, or
>
> (b) pay any monies whatsoever with respect to either Amber or the Project, shall terminate."

Allen also points out that the agreement sets forth the extent of the interest of the new limited partners for the calendar years 1974, 1975, 1976 and subsequent years, and with respect to each of those time periods, the agreement makes different provisions, depending upon whether the project was completed.

We note that Allen's interpretation of the agreement would bestow upon him the status of limited partner and the attendant right to share in the profits and losses of the partnership without making a contribution and placing that amount at risk. Allen cites no authority for this type of agreement, and our research has revealed no authority which would sanction such an agreement, if such an agreement was actually intended by the parties.

As previously noted, it appears to be defendants-appellants' interpretation, and perhaps their intention at the time of the execution of the agreement, that Allen's interest, if any, would vary depending upon whether the project was completed by January 31, 1976. In support of this interpretation they also rely upon paragraph 4 of the agreement and argue that no limited partnership could be formed in the absence of any capital contribution. Although defendants-appellants have not so argued, those portions of the agreement which delineate the extent of the limited partners' interest in the event the project is not completed by January 31, 1976, may have been intended to take effect in the event that Allen and the other designated new limited partners chose, even though not obligated, to make their capital contributions even if the project was not completed by January 31, 1976.

We are also unable to ascertain from the pleadings, depositions, affidavits and documents whether the parties intended the $50,000 to be a contribution to the capital of the limited partnership or a loan to the general partners. As we noted earlier, the word "contributions" as used in the ULPA is limited to the contribution made by a limited partner at the time of the formation of the partnership for the benefit of the partnership's creditors....

Allen's and the other investors' transfer of the $50,000 was made at the time of the alleged formation of the limited partnership. This is revealed in the agreement which provides:

> "Each of the New Limited Partners [Allen and the other investors] agree to loan the General Partners [Brant, Bernard and Scheer], jointly and severally,

the amount of money set opposite his name, the aggregate total of which constitutes FIFTY THOUSAND ($50,000.00) DOLLARS, which loan shall be evidenced by a Promissory Note from the General Partners to the New Limited Partners, bearing interest at the rate of 6% per annum due and payable on or before December 31, 1975, subject to acceleration upon the escrow dispursement [sic] pursuant to Completion of the Project, secured by an assignment of collateral reasonably acceptable to Storry, with a net fair market value of at least $50,000.00. The General Partners shall loan such $50,000.00 to Amber to be used for: (a) the redemption of the interest of Salk [sic] Properties, Inc., Talandis Construction Company, and Vytantes Talandis in the Partnership; and/or (b) the Project."

The promissory note, executed by Brant, Bernard and Scheer on December 30, 1974, makes reference to the agreement and provides that the note shall be due and payable on or before January 31, 1976, subject to acceleration upon the escrow disbursement. Moreover, it is alleged by Allen, and neither admitted nor denied by defendants-appellants, that $450,000 was placed in escrow. Pursuant to the agreement, the purported loan was due and payable at the completion of the project, on or before January 31, 1976. The disbursement of the $450,000 in the escrow account was also to occur at the completion of the project, on or before January 31, 1976. Since the difference between the $450,000 in escrow and the required capital contribution of $500,000 due from the new limited partners is equal to the $50,000 amount to be returned to the new limited partners, it can be as reasonably inferred that the $50,000 was intended as a loan as it can be inferred that it was intended as an initial capital contribution, which the new limited partners sought to secure in contravention of the ULPA. In addition, we note that after the agreement was executed, and even after this action was commenced, Allen apparently claimed his deductible share of the partnership's loss on his individual tax returns for 1974, 1975, 1976, 1977 and 1978 as reflected by Schedule K-1 of IRS Form 1065.

At oral argument Allen advanced, apparently for the first time, the theory that the "old limited partners" merely "assigned" their limited partnership interests Allen and the other "new limited partners," and that the requirements of the ULPA do not apply to the "assignment" of a limited partner's interest subsequent to the formation of the limited partnership. Allen has cited no authority for this proposition, and we are unaware of any authority which would support this proposition.

It is our opinion, based upon the foregoing, that the agreement is ambiguous and that the intent of the parties cannot be ascertained from the language of the agreement. The intent of the parties as to whether a partnership was in fact formed and as to the time of the formation of the partnership is in dispute; and fair-minded persons could draw different inferences from the facts not in dispute. Thus a triable issue exists, and summary judgment is inappropriate....

Accordingly, we reverse the judgment of the circuit court of Cook County and remand the cause for further proceedings not inconsistent with the views expressed herein.

Reversed and remanded.

ASB Allegiance Real Estate Fund v. Scion Breckenridge Managing Member, LLC

Court of Chancery of Delaware, New Castle
2012 Del. Ch. LEXIS 109, 2012 WL 1869416

MEMORANDUM OPINION

Laster, Vice Chancellor.

Entities affiliated with ASB Capital Management, LLC sued to reform the capital-event waterfall provisions in a series of agreements governing real estate joint ventures managed by affiliates of The Scion Group, LLC. The erroneously drafted provisions called for Scion to receive incentive compensation known as a "promote" even if the joint ventures lost money. Scion seeks to enforce the agreements as written, and its affiliates advance counterclaims for breach of fiduciary duty, breach of the implied covenant of good faith and fair dealing, and breach of contract. In this post-trial opinion, I find that the plaintiffs have proved their entitlement to reformation by clear and convincing evidence and enter judgment in their favor on the defendants' counterclaims.

I. FACTUAL BACKGROUND

The case was tried on March 12–15, 2012. My factual findings rest on a record that included more than 300 documentary exhibits and twenty-five deposition transcripts. Nine fact witnesses and two experts testified live at trial.

Each of the ASB witnesses testified candidly and credibly. Despite obvious personal and professional embarrassment, each witness detailed his or her role in contributing to the scrivener's error in the capital-event waterfall provision. Each described how the standard transactional technique of duplicating the prior deal precedent then focusing only on terms that needed changing caused the perpetuation of the error in subsequent joint venture agreements. The ASB witnesses and their expert explained cogently how the resulting provision departed from settled real estate practice and produced an economically irrational result.

The Scion witnesses' testimony was at best self-serving. Robert and Eric Bronstein, who co-founded and remain the principals of Scion, were not credible witnesses. Rob,[51] the majority owner of Scion, was the Bronstein brother who took responsibility for negotiating Scion's business deals. In contemporaneous, pre-litigation emails, Rob demonstrated a willingness to say whatever he thought would close the deal on the terms he wanted, irrespective of any correlation with historical fact. Although more restrained at trial, his testimony had a similar feel.

Eric, an attorney who owns a minority stake in Scion, serves as the firm's Executive Vice President and General Counsel. He and ASB's lawyers at DLA Piper LLP worked

---

51. [1] For clarity, I refer to the brothers Bronstein by their first names. I use "Rob" for Robert Bronstein to distinguish him from Robert Bellinger of ASB and because the parties used that shortened form in their contemporaneous communications.

to memorialize the deal terms that Rob and ASB negotiated. Eric advanced two contradictory accounts at trial. In one version, he negotiated changes to the capital-event waterfall provision as the authorized representative of Scion and obtained the disproportionately pro-Scion change, fully aware of its implications. In the other version, he lacked sophistication in real estate matters, innocently asked about the capital-event waterfall provision, and naively believed that DLA Piper accurately scrivened the deal. It is one thing to plead claims in the alternative; it is quite another to testify in the alternative about your own role, knowledge, and intentions.

Scion's expert witness fared worse. He could not offer any plausible justification for the mistakenly drafted capital-event waterfall provision. He later admitted that he was "simply looking back in hindsight and speculating and trying to come up with some argument that supports some consideration that would justify" the provision as written. Tr. 767–68.

A. Scion and ASB Form a Business Relationship.

Rob and Eric co-founded Scion in 1999. Rob previously worked as a vice-president for a Chicago-based real estate services and consulting firm, where he consulted for a number of major corporate and institutional real estate investors. Eric was a partner at Jaffe Raitt Heuer & Weiss, a Detroit law firm with over 100 lawyers. Eric focused on commercial real estate transactions, including the formation of a $100 million real estate joint venture and multiple real estate financings. Eric later served as senior group counsel for Johnson Controls, the world's largest automotive interior supplier, where he supervised $5 billion a year in business transactions.

Scion specializes in the student housing industry. Converting a building that leases unfurnished apartments without utilities to furnished, utilities-included student housing is potentially lucrative. This is because unlike traditional rental properties, student housing is leased by the bed. "[I]f three people live together, they're on their own separate contract, even though they share a living room and kitchen." Tr. 328 (Rob). Student housing also provides relatively reliable cash flows. Between 2002 and 2006, Scion served as the sponsor or developer on fifteen student housing real estate joint ventures in which Scion made equity investments totaling $12.2 million.

In 2006, former ASB managing director Keyvan Arjomand cold-called Rob Bronstein. ASB is a registered investment adviser that serves as an investment manager for approximately 150 pension funds. As part of its diversification strategy, ASB maintains a real estate investment portfolio. At the time of trial, ASB managed seventy-five real estate investments, sixty-seven of which were joint ventures. It was Arjomand's role to find attractive real estate investment opportunities. Arjomand was particularly interested in student housing, which he believed offered attractive risk-adjusted returns, and he contacted Rob after learning that Scion was soliciting investors for a student housing project.

Between January 2007 and January 2008, ASB-advised pension funds entered into five joint ventures for the ownership, operation, and development of student housing with special purpose entities wholly owned by Scion. Each ASB/Scion venture is a

Delaware limited liability company: University Crossing Apartments, LLC; Millennium Bloomington Apartments, LLC; Breckenridge Apartments, LLC; 2040 Lofts, LLC; and Dwight Lofts, LLC.

For each deal, Rob negotiated the economic terms for Scion. Arjomand served as Scion's primary contact at ASB and negotiated with Rob. ASB President Robert Bellinger actively oversaw the negotiations and personally approved each venture. The joint ventures were subject to further approval by ASB's Real Estate Investment Advisory Committee (the "Investment Committee"). When evaluating a given investment, the Investment Committee did not review actual transaction documents, but instead considered the investments based on an internally drafted Investment Committee memorandum summarizing the deal terms.

Rob left the "wordsmithing" of the agreements to Eric. Tr. 257 (Rob). ASB relied on DLA Piper, a large, international law firm. Barbara Trachtenberg, a partner experienced in real estate joint ventures, headed the DLA Piper team. Trachtenberg was heavily involved in the initial joint venture agreement for the University Crossing deal. After that, she ceded much of the drafting responsibility on later deals to Cara Nelson, an associate who "had been working on [real estate joint venture] deals for a couple of months and was just starting to get introduced" to their terms. Tr. 186 (Nelson).

B. The Core Joint Venture Terms

Real estate joint ventures follow a recurring pattern with the same basic players: a promoter, who provides the bulk of the capital, and a sponsor, who typically finds the deal and manages the property. In each of the five ASB/Scion joint ventures, ASB served as the promoter, provided at least 99% of the capital, and retained at least 99% of the equity. Scion served as the sponsor and invested no more than 1% of the capital. As sponsor, Scion earned a management fee for overseeing the day-to-day operations of the properties, as well as a leasing fee and an acquisition fee. Scion primarily earned fees through incentive compensation that took the form of a promoted interest, or "promote."

A promote pays a sponsor an agreed-upon portion of the cash flows generated by operations or by a capital event such as a sale or refinancing of the joint venture property. The promote is triggered once the project clears a specified hurdle known as the "preferred return." Once the preferred return has been reached, the promote grants the sponsor a share of profits disproportionately greater than that sponsor's ownership stake. The promote thus incentivizes the sponsor to achieve higher levels of profitability.

Real estate professionals commonly discuss promotes using industry shorthand, in which the economics are described as "an X over a Y." In this formulation, the X refers to the disproportionate share of profits that the sponsor will receive. The Y refers to the preferred return on capital that the investment must achieve to trigger the promote. For example, the phrase "20% over an 8%" means the sponsor would receive 20% of incremental profits after the project generated an 8% preferred return.

C. The Initial ASB/Scion Joint Ventures

During the discussions leading up to the first joint venture, Arjomand and Rob Bronstein negotiated Scion's compensation using the industry shorthand for promotes. By email dated October 2, 2006, Arjomand proposed a "20% above an 8% preferred return." JX 7. Rob replied the following day that he was "probably okay with the promote structure." *Id.* Neither side questioned the meaning of the industry shorthand or sought to clarify whether Scion would get its greater share of profits if ASB did not receive back its capital. Bellinger explained at trial that the 8% preferred return was designed to motivate Scion to achieve above-average profitability: "In most of these investments, the target return on cost at stabilization was around 6-1/2 to 7 percent.... So the notion was that if [Scion] hit that 8 percent, everyone is doing well. We're exceeding the expectations." Tr. 21. The notion was not for Scion to do well following a capital event even if ASB suffered a significant loss.

The University Crossing LLC Agreement incorporated the promote and preferred return as proposed by Arjomand and agreed to by Rob. The relevant portion of the capital-event waterfall provision, which the parties labeled the Sale Proceeds Waterfall, called for distributions to be made in the following order:

> (ii) Second, among the Members in proportion to the Unrecovered 8% Preferred Return Amounts of the Members at such time, until such time as each Member's Unrecovered 8% Preferred Return Amount has been reduced to zero;
>
> (iii) Third, among the Members in proportion to the Invested Capital of the Members at such time, until such time as each Member's Invested Capital has been reduced to zero;
>
> (iv) Fourth, (x) the Remaining Percentage to the Members in proportion to each Member's respective Percentage Interests at such time, and (y) the Promote Percentage to Venture Partner.

JX 20, § 4.2. I have omitted the first tier because the parties agree it is not relevant to their dispute. The University Crossing LLC Agreement defined the Promote Percentage and the Remaining Percentage as 20% and 80%, respectively. *Id.* § 1.1.

In simplified terms, the Sale Proceeds Waterfall calls for distributions in proportion to the members' respective percentage equity investments, approximately 99% for ASB and 1% for Scion, until each member receives an 8% preferred return on that investment. Distributions then continue at a ratio of 99:1 until each member receives back the capital it invested in the venture. Only after invested capital is returned does Scion receive a promote payment equal to 20% of excess profits, with the members continuing to receive the remaining 80% pursuant to their 99:1 equity-ownership ratio.

The parties' second venture, Millennium Bloomington Apartments, LLC, followed closely on the heels of the University Crossing deal. In the University Crossing deal, ASB paid Scion an acquisition fee of $150,000 and a property management fee equal to 5% of gross revenue. Rob asked for higher acquisition and management fees on the Millennium deal, but ASB refused. The compensation for the Millennium deal mirrored the University Crossing terms.

D. The Parties Agree on a Two-Tier Promote for Scion.

Although ASB rejected his request for greater fees on the Millennium deal, Rob continued to seek greater compensation for Scion. Increasing the promote percentage provided an alternative means to that end. One way for a sponsor like Scion to make increasing the promote percentage attractive to an equity investor is to create a second tier of promote that will be triggered after the project achieves a higher preferred return. In this structure, the project only pays out the larger promote if the equity investor also makes more money.

In March 2007, Rob suggested a two-tier promote on a joint venture opportunity called Case Western Triangle Apartments. In his Case Western proposal, Rob suggested that Scion receive "20% of returns above an 8% preferred return—and 30% of returns above 12%." JX 28. Neither Rob nor Arjomand asked about the industry shorthand or whether Scion could earn its promote if ASB did not receive back its capital. Quite obviously, the second level of promote contemplated an additional level of incentive compensation *on a profitable deal*. It meant that "if the project generated returns so great as to give ASB a return of 12 percent on its capital, [Scion would] receive an even greater disproportionate share of the returns above a 12 percent second hurdle...." Tr. 239 (Rob).

During the same period, Arjomand encouraged Rob to focus on the promote as a way to achieve potentially greater compensation. By email dated March 20, 2007, Arjomand told Rob that Arjomand's boss, Bellinger, "wants to try to structure deals with lower fees but appropriate incentive comp so that partners are less incented by fees to do deals, and more by the upside they can earn in their promote and through ongoing good management at the properties...." JX 29. Rob responded that "[w]e respect [Bellinger's] point that he doesn't want deals too front-loaded, and of course, if we didn't believe in the deals and our ability to make money on the promotes, we wouldn't be even considering them in the first place. Therefore, we don't mind trading one for the other." JX 30. In a March 30, 2007 memorandum, Rob proposed a two-tier promote for future deals similar to the aborted Case Western proposal: "Once [an] 8% return has been achieved, Scion will receive 25% of the proceeds (75% to [ASB]) until [ASB] realizes a 12.0% cumulative annual return, above which Scion will receive 50% of proceeds (50% to [ASB])." JX 32.

Arjomand and Rob continued to negotiate the two-tier promote before finally agreeing on terms. By email dated May 9, 2007, under the subject heading "ASB/Scion General Deal Parameters Going Forward," Arjomand set forth "a summary of what I believe both sides have agreed to." JX 35. The email stated: "**Promote**—On an unlevered deal, 20% over an 8%, and 35% over a 12%. On a levered deal, 20% over a 9%, and 35% over a 15%." *Id.* Rob replied by email the following day: "Yes, I agree with all this. Thanks." *Id.* Arjomand forwarded the email agreement to the entire deal team on May 22, adding "[b]elow are the basic economics of our deal format with Scion on a go forward basis...." JX 41 (the "May 2007 Terms").

E. The Breckenridge Joint Venture

After agreeing on the May 2007 Terms, Scion and ASB worked on the Breckenridge joint venture. DLA Piper prepared the initial draft of the Breckenridge LLC Agreement by starting with the Millennium LLC Agreement as a template, then making deal-specific adjustments.

Nelson circulated the first draft on June 14, 2007. The draft did not reflect the May 2007 Terms. Although DLA Piper revised both the operational cash flow waterfall and Sale Proceeds Waterfall to add the second tier of preferred return, each waterfall continued to provide for only one level of promote. Eric emailed back the same day:

> I may not have read it correctly, but I think the distribution paragraphs (both operational proceeds and liquidation proceeds) seem to be missing language applying the "Promote Percentage" split after the first-tier preferred return has been achieved but before the second-tier has been reached. As I read it now, it looks like it measures the first-tier preferred return ... and then goes straight to the second-tier preferred return before invoking the "promote" split....

Contrary to one version of Eric's testimony, in which he claimed to have negotiated the change in the promote, Eric did not offer this comment to alter the economic terms for the Sale Proceeds Waterfall. He rather sought to memorialize accurately the two-tier promote agreed upon by Rob and Arjomand.

In response to Eric's comment, Nelson revised the waterfall provisions. When she circulated the next draft of the Breckenridge LLC Agreement on June 15, 2007, the missing first-tier promote appeared after the first preferred return but *before* the return of capital in the Sale Proceeds Waterfall. Placing the promote in this position meant that Scion would begin to earn its promote immediately after the preferred return, before ASB and Scion received back their capital. Therefore on a money-losing deal, after the initial 8% preferred return, Scion effectively would receive 20% of every dollar that ASB originally invested.

Despite the dramatic economic consequences of placing the promote in this position, no one commented on the change. Eric reviewed the Sale Proceeds Waterfall in detail following Nelson's June 15 email. He noted that the first-tier promote now appeared before the return of capital, and he understood the favorable implications of the error for Scion. Tr. 462, 472 (Eric). Eric admitted that Scion did not provide any consideration for the placement of the first-tier promote before the return of capital, Tr. 462–63, but he claimed implausibly as part of his negotiation story that it was normal for opposing counsel to give away a significant deal point for nothing. Tr. 467. Given the allocation of responsibility at Scion between Rob and Eric, it is not credible that Eric was negotiating a change in the Sale Proceeds Waterfall. Eric did not play that role, and Rob testified that he did not instruct Eric to seek to elevate the promote before the return of capital. Tr. 259. Rob claimed not to recall being aware of the placement of the first-tier promote before 2010. Tr. 264.

Trachtenberg, the lead DLA Piper attorney, cannot recall whether or not she read the June 14 and June 15 drafts of the Breckenridge LLC Agreement before they were circulated. She admitted that if she read the June 14 draft, she "didn't focus on what the language was there, because it's just wrong. It's a terrible translation of the [May 2007 Terms]." Tr. 140. Nelson conceded that at the time of the Breckenridge deal, she lacked the experience necessary to understand the terms of the promote. She only learned of the mistake in the Sale Proceeds Waterfall when Trachtenberg explained it to her in fall 2010.

As outside legal counsel, DLA Piper did not have authority to make substantive changes to the economic agreement between the business principals. As Nelson explained, "lawyers don't negotiate the basic economics of a deal. That's just not something that lawyers do.... [The basic economic deal terms] are discussed between business people at the business level in every deal." Tr. 196. And placing the first-tier promote before the return of capital was not just a change in the basic economics; it was a radical departure that promised Scion promote compensation even if ASB lost 80–85% of its invested capital. Tr. 459 (Eric).

Eric responded by email on June 19. He attached a draft that changed wording in the Sale Proceeds Waterfall from "each Member," which referred to Scion and ASB, to "the Fund," which refers to ASB alone. JX 45. Eric explained in the June 19 email that he made the change because "Scion would achieve its own 'Second Preferred Return' (12–15%) before the time that the Fund does. But Scion achieving the Second threshold doesn't matter; rather the test for the next split level (65/35) is whether the Fund achieves the higher preferred return." *Id.* Eric's change addressed his concern that Scion, by virtue of the 20% promote payment being disproportionate to its invested capital, would achieve its second preferred return before ASB and that payment of the first-tier promote to Scion might stop until ASB caught up and received its second preferred return. Eric's June 19 email did not address or reference that the draft placed the promote before the return of capital. Nelson signed off on Eric's change later that evening. Except for the June 19 alteration, ASB and Scion executed the Breckenridge LLC Agreement with the Sale Proceeds Waterfall as circulated by Nelson on June 15.

The executed version of the Breckenridge Sale Proceeds Waterfall reads as follows:

(ii) Second, among the Members in proportion to the Unrecovered First Preferred Return Amounts of the Members at such time, until such time as each Member's Unrecovered First Preferred Return Amount has been reduced to zero;

(iii) Third, (x) the Remaining Percentage [80%] to the Members in proportion to each Member's respective Percentage Interest at such time, and (y) the Promote Percentage [20%] to Venture Partner [Scion] until such time as the Fund's Unrecovered Second Preferred Return Amount has been reduced to zero; and

(iv) Fourth, among the Members in proportion to the Invested Capital of the Members at such time, until such time as each Member's Invested Capital has been reduced to zero;

(v) Fifth, (x) the Remaining Percentage [65%] to the Members in proportion to their respective Percentage Interest at such time, and (y) the Promote Percentage [35%] to Venture Partner.

JX 76, § 4.2. Because the parties erroneously placed Paragraph Third before Paragraph Fourth, the first-tier promote falls before the return of the members' invested capital. This mistake also puts the "and" in a linguistically odd place. If Paragraph Third and Paragraph Fourth were reversed and renumbered, the waterfall would reflect the May 2007 Terms and, conveniently, the "and" would fall into place.

The ASB Investment Committee approved the Breckenridge deal based on an internal memorandum summarizing the deal terms. The memorandum summarized the Sale Proceeds Waterfall as it should have been drafted, with the return of invested capital coming before the first-tier promote.

Bellinger testified that he reviewed parts of the Breckenridge LLC Agreement before approving it, but admitted that he did not read the agreement carefully. Bellinger also admitted that he overlooked the placement of the first-tier promote in the Sale Proceeds Waterfall. He noted that "once someone points out the mistake, it's very obvious that it's wrong." Tr. 42–43.

In the fall of 2007, the parties amended and restated the Breckenridge LLC Agreement to incorporate provisions related to the assumption of certain mortgage financings. The amendment did not relate to the waterfalls or the promote, and the parties did not discuss them.

F. The 2040 Lofts Joint Venture

The next joint venture was 2040 Lofts, LLC. Trachtenberg was on vacation, and Nelson took the lead on drafting the agreement. She electronically copied the Breckenridge LLC Agreement, then made deal-specific changes. The only changes to the Sale Proceeds Waterfall were to replace the word "First" with "8%" in two places and the word "Second" with "12%" in one place. JX 49, § 4.2. Nelson made these changes because 2040 Lofts was an unlevered deal, and the May 2007 Terms called for lower hurdles on an unlevered deal. Neither ASB nor Scion reviewed the Sale Proceeds Waterfall in any meaningful respect. Everyone assumed that the Breckenridge LLC Agreement reflected the deal terms and that everything should stay the same unless the principals negotiated a change.

As with the Breckenridge deal, the ASB Investment Committee approved the 2040 Lofts LLC Agreement based on a memorandum that described return of capital as preceding the first-tier promote in the Sale Proceeds Waterfall. In the actual 2040 Lofts LLC Agreement, the return of capital came after the first-tier promote, as in the Breckenridge LLC Agreement.

Neither Bellinger nor Trachtenberg read the 2040 Lofts LLC Agreement carefully before approving the deal. Bellinger relied on Trachtenberg. Trachtenberg relied on Nelson. Nelson thought the Breckinridge LLC Agreement accurately reflected the agreed-upon ASB/Scion deal structure and believed she had duplicated it for 2040 Lofts, subject to minor, deal-specific alterations like the unlevered hurdle rates.

In May 2009, the Allegiance Fund, the entity that was the ASB member in the 2040 Lofts deal, transferred its membership interest down to EBREF Holding Company, LLC, a wholly owned subsidiary. The transfer allowed ASB to use its interest in 2040 Lofts as collateral for a line of credit. In documenting the transfer and the admission of EBREF as the new member of 2040 Lofts, ASB and Scion did not focus on or discuss the placement of the first-tier promote ahead of the return of invested capital. At the time, ASB did not know there was anything there to discuss.

G. The Dwight Lofts Joint Venture

The fifth and final joint venture was Dwight Lofts, LLC. Nelson again electronically copied the Breckenridge LLC Agreement, then made deal-specific changes. The only edits to the Sale Proceeds Waterfall consisted of replacing "Fund" with "Fund Member." JX 79, §4.2. The first-tier promote remained incorrectly placed before the return of invested capital.

Neither ASB nor Scion reviewed the Sale Proceeds Waterfall in any meaningful respect. Neither Bellinger nor Trachtenberg read the Dwight Lofts LLC Agreement carefully before approving the deal. Once again, everyone assumed that the Breckenridge LLC Agreement reflected the agreed-upon deal structure, that the Dwight Lofts LLC Agreement duplicated the Breckenridge LLC Agreement, and that everything stayed the same except for minor deal-specific modifications.

Effective March 3, 2008, ASB and Scion amended the Dwight Lofts LLC Agreement (the "Dwight Amendment") to modify a put provision. Paragraph 4 of the Dwight Amendment states: "Except as set forth herein, the terms and provisions of the [Dwight Lofts LLC Agreement] are hereby ratified and confirmed and shall remain in full force and effect." JX 97. Nothing in the Dwight Amendment changed the Sale Proceeds Waterfall. Before executing the amendment, Scion and ASB did not have any discussions about the Sale Proceeds Waterfall, the placement of the first-tier promote, or the economic implications of its location. At the time, ASB and DLA Piper did not know about the error. Only Scion did.

H. The Automatic Lofts Deal

After the 2040 Lofts joint venture but before the Dwight Lofts joint venture, Scion and ASB entered into a sixth deal for a project known as Automatic Lofts. For tax reasons, Scion could not participate as either an equity holder or a lender, so Automatic Lofts was not structured as a traditional joint venture. Instead, Scion participated as property manager and loan servicer, and the parties agreed to structure Scion's compensation in these roles to "mimic" Scion's joint venture compensation under the May 2007 Terms, including the two-tier promote. *See* JX 69 (email from Eric to deal team asking whether "Scion's 'upside' compensation (mimicking our usual economics) [is] being written in a side agreement … ?").

Because of the need for a new set of documentation, Trachtenberg was heavily involved for DLA Piper. She recommended re-casting Scion's two-tier promote as an "Incentive Fee" paid pursuant to an Incentive Management Agreement. By email dated August 28, 2007, Arjomand explained to Rob that the "[i]ncentive management fee ... is meant to mimic the Scion/ASB promote structure. In this case, ... 20% over a 9% preferred return and 35% over a 15% preferred return...." JX 62. Rob responded that the approach was "probably fine," but argued that the deal should use the lower, unlevered preferred return hurdles of 8% and 12%. *Id.*

To mimic the preferred return concept, the Incentive Management Agreement employed an internal rate of return ("IRR") formulation. The Incentive Management Agreement provides that cash flows "from the operation and/or disposition" of Automatic Lofts would be first distributed "in an amount sufficient to yield ST-Park [an ASB affiliate] a eight percent (8%) Internal Rate of Return." JX 74, §4(a). After ST-Park achieved an 8% IRR, proceeds would be distributed "(i) twenty percent (20%) to [Scion] and eighty percent (80%) to ST-Park, until ST-Park has achieved an aggregate twelve percent (12%) Internal Rate of Return; (ii) then, thirty-five percent (35%) to [Scion] and sixty-five percent (65%) to ST-Park." JX 74. Under an IRR formulation, Scion necessarily earns a promote only *after* the return of invested capital.

When reviewing the Automatic Lofts agreement, Eric silently accepted the placement of the return of capital *before* the first-tier promote. If Eric truly believed that Scion and ASB had a deal in which Scion received the promote *pari passu* with ASB's return of capital, he would have objected to the change. When asked about the subject at trial, the Bronstein brothers feigned naivety. Eric claimed that he "had not encountered the [term 'internal rate of return'] prior to that evening." Tr. 495. Rob testified that he thought IRR was a "Microsoft Excel formula." Tr. 278. Neither assertion is credible. I find that the Bronstein brothers accepted the IRR formulation in the Automatic Lofts deal because they knew it was right and that the different Sale Proceeds Waterfalls in the Breckenridge and 2040 Lofts LLC Agreements were wrong.

I. ASB Learns About the Mistake.

On June 12, 2010, Scion exercised a put right in the 2040 Lofts LLC Agreement. At that point, ASB had contributed $47.3 million in capital to the venture and Scion had contributed $479,000. The parties agreed that the venture was underwater and had a fair market value of $35.5 million. On August 30, 2010, Eric informed ASB that the purchase price for the put was $1.83 million. This figure included a promote of $1,556,356.92. If correct, then Scion would receive a gain of 282%; ASB would be left with an investment valued at $32.96 million, representing a loss of $14.41 million or roughly 30%. Without the promote, Scion's buyout price would have been only $347,792.46, in which case Scion would suffer a proportionate loss.

By the time Scion exercised the put, Arjomand had left ASB. James Darcey, who was in charge of the Scion relationship, responded to Eric's purchase-price calculation less than half-an-hour after receiving it: "I'm confused. Does your calculation suggest that Venture Partner (Scion) is due $1.8 million? It seems odd to me that an investment into which we together invested over $47 million and which is now valued at $35.5 million would generate a promote." JX 167. Eric invoked the Sale Proceeds Waterfall: "[W]e prepared our calculation to follow the LLC Agreement precisely, so I believe it is correct." *Id.*

After receiving Eric's response, Darcey emailed Rob to ask if the business deal for 2040 Lofts was different than for University Crossing. Rob responded:

> [T]his was the business deal we negotiated through Keyvan Arjomand in 2007. It was different than the [University Crossing] and Millennium structure, for several reasons—we brought to ASB an off-market deal, our acquisition fee was reduced, we left our proceeds in but still had to pay capital gains tax, our management fee was lowered, etc. Therefore our deal was structured with more back-end compensation

Id. As Rob was forced to admit at trial, virtually every statement in this email was false. Scion's acquisition fee was not reduced relative to the University Crossing or Millennium deals. Scion did not leave any proceeds in the Breckenridge deal and did not pay any capital gains taxes. And Scion's management fee was not lower than the University Crossing and Millennium deals.

After the email exchanges with Rob and Eric, Darcey and Bellinger examined the Sale Proceeds Waterfall and identified the scrivener's error. Bellinger called DLA Piper and "had a very, very tough conversation." Bellinger was "incredibly upset that this had happened because it was clear what the document said, and that it was just wrong." Tr. 44–45. ASB subsequently put DLA Piper on notice of a malpractice claim.

On July 22, 2010, Scion exercised its put right under the Dwight Lofts LLC Agreement. ASB contributed approximately $78.5 million in capital to Dwight Lofts; Scion contributed approximately $790,000. Scion calculated the price for the put rate as $3.38 million. This figure included a promote of approximately $2.6 million. If correct, then Scion would receive a gain of 328%. ASB believes that Scion is due only $1.26 million.

J. The Dwight Lofts Summer Leasing Dispute

By late 2009, ASB had grown dissatisfied with Scion's property management capabilities. Effective March 15, 2010, ASB removed Scion as Dwight Lofts' property manager.

During the period leading up to Scion's removal, ASB and Columbia College of Chicago were negotiating a master lease for Dwight Lofts. ASB and Scion agreed that a master lease was highly desirable. Rob noted that revenue from the proposed ten-month master lease would equal twelve months of revenue generated from non-master lease tenants. After months of difficult negotiations, ASB and Columbia College consummated a master lease in April 2010.

As noted, Scion exercised its put right under the Dwight Lofts LLC Agreement in July 2010. Between December 2009, when ASB gave Scion notice that it would be terminated, and July 22, 2010, when Scion exercised the put right, Rob sent a series of emails to ASB about ways that Dwight Lofts could increase its summer revenue. It is clear that Rob sent these emails in anticipation of a dispute over the value of the put right.

Two types of summer leasing exist at Dwight Lofts: generic summer leasing and extended summer leasing. Under a generic summer lease, a tenant leases a bed in

Dwight Lofts from June 1 until July 31, the period of time not covered by the Columbia College master lease. Under an extended summer lease, a tenant leases a bed in Dwight Lofts for a period that overlaps the Columbia College master lease, either beginning in May or extending into August.

In his emails, Rob advocated strenuously that ASB should re-open discussions with Columbia College and seek permission for extended summer leases, and in May 2010 he provided a detailed memorandum identifying measures that ASB and its new property manager, Campus Advantage, could take to maximize summer revenue. Rob wrote follow-up emails on May 21 and 25 offering to speak personally with Columbia College about the possibility of extended summer leasing. ASB declined, believing it would be unwise to approach Columbia about extended summer leasing after recently executing the master lease. Darcey told Rob that "[w]e are focus[ing] on building a strong, professional and long-term relationship with Columbia and believe a proactive effort at this time to renegotiate their lease start date for some or all of their beds will complicate their transition into the property and cause un-necessary and counterproductive stress." JX 153.

Without telling ASB, Rob contacted Mark Kelly, the Columbia College Vice President of Student Affairs. Rob claims that Kelly said Columbia College would be pleased to make extended summer leasing arrangements with Dwight Lofts. During his deposition, Kelly could not recall making any such statement and said he "would dispute" Rob's recollection. Kelly Dep. at 35.

On July 22, 2010, Scion exercised its put right under the Dwight Lofts LLC Agreement. Scion valued the joint venture at $96.63 million, a figure that assumed a 75% summer occupancy rate generating an additional $525,000 of revenue in both June and July. JX 140. ASB disputed Scion's valuation, arguing that there was no historical basis for Scion's summer revenue estimates.

Because the parties could not agree on a valuation for the joint venture, Section 6.4.5 of the Dwight Amendment called for the parties to appoint jointly one independent appraiser. Scion and ASB engaged Craig Schumacher of CB Richard Ellis. Scion submitted projections to Schumacher that assumed a 90% occupancy rate in June and July. ASB's projections were based on historical summer leasing rates and assumed a 25% occupancy rate. Using projections that fell in between, Schumacher valued Dwight Lofts at $97.5 million, more than Scion's figure.

Both ASB and Scion rejected Schumacher's appraisal. Under the Dwight Lofts LLC Agreement, the next step was a three-appraiser process in which each side selected its own appraiser and those two appraisers selected a third appraiser. All three appraisers prepared appraisals, and the average of the two closest appraisals would be used as the property's fair market value. ASB selected Nancy Myers of Integra Realty Resources. Scion selected Chris Myers (no relation) of Argianas & Associates, Inc. Chris Myers and Nancy Myers selected Appraisal Resource Counselors ("ARC") to conduct the third appraisal. The Integra appraisal assumed a stabilized summer occupancy rate of 20%, projected $278,678 in stabilized summer revenue, and valued

Dwight Lofts at $90.0 million. The Argianas appraisal assumed a stabilized summer occupancy rate of 35%, projected $431,760 in stabilized summer revenue, and valued Dwight Lofts at $90.7 million. The ARC appraisal is not in the record. The Integra and Argianas appraisals were the closest, and averaging those two produced a fair market value of $90.35 million for Dwight Lofts, less than Schumacher's figure.

At some point after summer 2010, Campus Advantage approached Columbia College about extended summer leasing and reached an oral agreement to permit it. Scion contends that an informal oral agreement was reached in September 2010 and that ASB withheld this information from the appraisers. ASB contends that the informal agreement was not reached until March 2011.

Jacqueline Pingel, general manager of Dwight Lofts for Campus Advantage, backed up ASB's position. Pingel explained that although she discussed generic summer leading with a Columbia College representative in August and September 2010, she first discussed extended summer leasing with Columbia College in January 2011 and only reached an informal oral agreement in March 2011.

II. LEGAL ANALYSIS

ASB seeks an order reforming the Sale Proceeds Waterfalls. Scion seeks to enforce the agreements as written and has counterclaimed for damages. Both sides invoke contractual fee-shifting provisions to recover their legal fees and costs.

A. Equitable Reformation

The Court of Chancery has the power "to reform a contract in order to express the 'real agreement' of the parties involved." *Cerberus Int'l, Ltd. v. Apollo Mgmt, L.P.*, 794 A.2d 1141, 1151 (Del. 2002) (quoting *Colvocoresses v. W.S. Wasserman Co.*, 26 Del. Ch. 333, 28 A.2d 588, 589 (Del. Ch. 1942)).

> There are two doctrines that allow reformation. The first is the doctrine of mutual mistake. In such a case, the plaintiff must show that both parties were mistaken as to a material portion of the written agreement. The second is the doctrine of unilateral mistake. The party asserting this doctrine must show that it was mistaken and that the other party knew of the mistake but remained silent.

Id. at 1151 (footnote omitted). "Regardless of which doctrine is used, the plaintiff must show by clear and convincing evidence that the parties came to a specific prior understanding that differed materially from the written agreement." *Id.* at 1151–52. "The clear and convincing evidentiary standard is 'an intermediate evidentiary standard, higher than mere preponderance, but lower than proof beyond a reasonable doubt.'" *Id.* at 1151 (quoting *In re Tavel*, 661 A.2d 1061, 1070 n.5 (Del. 1995)). ASB has met its burden of proof.

1. The Specific Prior Contractual Understanding

Reformation requires the existence of a specific prior contractual understanding that conflicts with the terms of the written agreement. The prior understanding "provides a comparative standard that tells the Court of Chancery 'exactly what terms to insert in the contract rather than being put in the position of creating a contract for the parties.'" *Id.* at 1152 (quoting *Collins v. Burke*, 418 A.2d 999, 1002 (Del. 1980)). The prior understanding "need not constitute a complete contract in and of itself." *Id.* (finding prior specific understanding based on handwritten note "This looks fine" on proposed term sheet); *see also* Restatement (Second) of Contracts § 155 cmt. a (1981) ("The prior agreement need not, however, be complete and certain enough to be a contract."). Reformation is available even when "'the antecedent expressions ... [were] no more than a part of the contract that is in the preliminary process of [being made].'" *Cerberus*, 794 A.2d at 1152 n.40 (alterations in original) (quoting Arthur Linton Corbin et al., *Corbin on Contracts* § 614 (2001)).

The May 2007 Terms constitute a specific prior contractual understanding that provides the necessary foundation for reformation. Using industry terms of art, Arjomand proposed terms to Rob: "On an unlevered deal, 20% over an 8%, and 35% over a 12%. On a levered deal, 20% over a 9%, and 35% over a 15%." JX 35. Rob responded: "Yes, I agree with all this." *Id.* Arjomand forwarded the terms to the deal team in an email entitled "ASB / Scion General Deal Parameters Going Forward," noting that it contained "the basic economics of our deal format with Scion on a go forward basis...." JX 41.

The evidence at trial established that a "promoted interest" or "promote" is a term of art that inherently contemplates the return of invested capital when used in the context of a capital event. ASB's expert explained that a promote refers to a share of the profits or upside from a project. In the capital event context, profit or upside is necessarily calculated by subtracting the cost of the investment from the proceeds of the capital event. Invested capital is one such cost. Accordingly, the return of invested capital precedes the promote in a capital-event waterfall provision. Scion's expert admitted that in twenty-five years of real estate experience, he had never heard of a deal in the real estate industry in which a promote was paid before the return of capital in a capital-event waterfall provision.

In agreeing to terms, the parties operated based on the established industry meaning of a "promote." They reflected this understanding in the two most heavily negotiated agreements: the University Crossing LLC Agreement and the Automatic Lofts Agreement. University Crossing was the first ASB/Scion joint venture. Trachtenberg personally drafted the agreement and placed the return of capital before the promote in the Sale Proceeds Waterfall. The Automatic Lofts deal was the only investment not structured as a joint venture. ASB and Scion employed teams of people to ensure that the economic structure "mimick[ed]" Scion's usual "upside compensation." JX 69 (internal quotation marks omitted). Trachtenberg played a major role in the drafting process. Here too, the promote appears after the return of capital in the capital-event waterfall provision.

I credit the ASB witnesses' testimony about the meaning of a promote and the terms of their agreement with Scion. Their testimony and the economic structure they contemplated make sense as a coherent whole. By contrast, I reject the Scion witnesses' testimony as self-serving and internally contradictory. The economic structure the Scion witnesses described does not make sense in the context of the parties' negotiations or the transactions as a whole.

Based on the trial record, I am convinced that the May 2007 Terms constitute a specific prior understanding that the return of capital was to come before the payment of promote compensation in the Sale Proceeds Waterfall. ASB proved the existence of this specific prior understanding by clear and convincing evidence.

2. Mistaken Belief

ASB proved at trial that it entered into the Breckenridge, 2040 Lofts, and Dwight Lofts LLC Agreements (together, the "Disputed Agreements") in the mistaken belief that the Sale Proceeds Waterfalls reflected the May 2007 Terms. The contemporaneous documentary evidence includes the internal ASB Investment Committee memoranda, which explain the Sale Proceeds Waterfalls in terms consistent with the May 2007 Terms. Consistent with its mistaken understanding, ASB reacted with confusion and disbelief to Scion's put calculation. Darcey described it as "inconceivable that [Arjomand] would agree to pay a promote on a deal that lost principal." JX 167. Bellinger promptly had "a very, very tough conversation" with DLA Piper and put the firm on notice of a malpractice claim. Tr. 44. Bellinger and Trachtenberg testified credibly to their belief about how the Sale Proceeds Waterfalls should have read, and Bellinger testified credibly that he was "incredibly upset that this had happened because it was clear what the document said, and that it was just wrong." Tr. 44–45.

3. Knowing Silence

ASB proved at trial that Scion knew that terms of the Sale Proceeds Waterfalls as written did not reflect the May 2007 Terms but intentionally remained silent. At trial, Eric tried to walk a fine line. He admitted that he identified the placement of the first-tier promote before the return of capital in the June 15 draft of the Breckenridge LLC Agreement and recognized the favorable implications of the placement for Scion. He further admitted that he remained silent. He therefore tried to construct accounts in which he did not intentionally remain silent. In one account, he negotiated the change and thought DLA Piper gave it away. In a conflicting account, he naively believed that DLA Piper properly drafted the provision.

Eric is a sophisticated real estate attorney with significant real estate joint venture experience. I am convinced that he intentionally remained silent in an effort to capture an undeserved benefit for Scion. I reject Eric's contrary accounts as not credible. Having evaluated Eric's demeanor, I am convinced that Eric recognized the scrivener's error and tried to take advantage of the mistake.

"Delaware law states the knowledge of an agent acquired while acting within the scope of his or her authority is imputed to the principal." *Albert v. Alex. Brown Mgmt. Servs., Inc.*, 2005 Del. Ch. LEXIS 133, 2005 WL 2130607, at *11 (Del. Ch. Aug. 26, 2005). "[I]t is the general rule that knowledge of an officer or director of a corporation will be imputed to the corporation." *Teachers' Ret. Sys. of La. v. Aidinoff*, 900 A.2d 654, 671 n.23 (Del. Ch. 2006). This basic principle of agency law applies with equal force to LLCs. Eric acted on behalf of the Scion LLC members in his capacity as

Scion's Executive Vice President and General Counsel. Eric's knowing silence and intent are imputed to them.

B. Scion's Affirmative Defenses

Scion raises three affirmative defenses in an effort to avoid reformation: (i) Bellinger failed to read the agreements; (ii) ASB ratified the agreements; and (iii) ASB has unclean hands. I reject each defense.

1. Failure to Read

Bellinger testified that he read portions of each Disputed Agreement, but that he does not recall how much he read. Scion attacked Bellinger's testimony by pointing to (i) the absence of any email or other communication conveying the document and (ii) differences between the signature pages and the agreements, such as different document stamps, that suggested the use of a form signature page. To rehabilitate Bellinger, ASB introduced a copy of a June 19, 2007, email from Nelson to ASB employees Ashley Earnest and Larry Braithwaite attaching a draft of the Breckenridge LLC Agreement and instructing them to provide it to Bellinger. ASB had withheld the June 19 email as privileged and did not log it. I therefore will exclude the email from the record and decline to consider it. I will not go further and grant Scion an adverse inference contrary to Bellinger's testimony.

Having considered Bellinger's testimony and the overall context of the negotiations, I believe that Bellinger read the University Crossing agreement in its entirety and was familiar with its terms. After that, I believe Bellinger relied on Trachtenberg and Arjomand to advise him about any changes, brief him on new terms, and provide him with any portions that he needed to read. Delaware law does not require that a senior decision-maker like Bellinger read every agreement *in haec verba*.[52] I find that Bellinger adequately and properly oversaw the negotiation process and was informed about the terms of the joint venture agreements as negotiated by the parties.

Even assuming Bellinger did not read the agreements before approving them, that would not bar equitable reformation. "Reformation is not precluded by the mere fact that the party who seeks it failed to exercise reasonable care in reading the writing...." Restatement (Second) of Contracts § 155 cmt. a.[53] Although declining to rule on the

---

52. [2] *See In re Walt Disney Co. Deriv. Litig.*, 907 A.2d 693, 749 n.424 (Del. Ch. 2005), ("[A] board of directors need not read '*in haec verba* every contract or legal document that it approves, but if it is to successfully absolve itself from charges of [violations of the duty of care], there must be some credible evidence that the directors knew what they were doing, and ensured that their purported action was given effect.'" (second alteration in original) (quoting *Smith v. Van Gorkom*, 488 A.2d 858, 883 n.25 (Del. 1985), *overruled on other grounds by Gantler v. Stephens*, 965 A.2d 695 (Del. 2009))), *aff'd*, 906 A.2d 27 (Del. 2006).

53. [3] This is the majority rule. *See, e.g., Albany City Sav. Inst. v. Burdick*, 87 N.Y. 40, 46–47 (1881) ("It has certainly never been announced as the law in this State that the mere omission to read or know the contents of a written instrument should bar any relief by way of a reformation of the instrument on account of mistake or fraud."); *Pioneer Res., LLC v. D.R. Johnson Lumber Co.*, 187 Ore. App. 341, 68 P.3d 233, 251 (Or. Ct. App. 2003) ("[A] party's failure to read a document, by itself, will generally not constitute gross negligence sufficient to bar reformation."); *Wash. Mut. Sav. Bank v. Hedreen*, 125 Wn.2d 521, 886 P.2d 1121, 1127 (Wash. 1994) (en banc) (affirming grant of refor-

issue specifically, the Delaware Supreme Court in *Cerberus* indicated support for the Restatement (Second) approach and noted that "[a]ny mistake claim by definition involves a party who has not read, or thought about, the provisions in a contract carefully enough." *Cerberus*, 794 A.2d at 1154 (citing Restatement (Second) of Contracts Sections 155 and 157, but "tak[ing] no position on whether, under certain circumstances, a party's misconduct could bar a reformation claim").

Finding little support in reformation jurisprudence, Scion cites avoidance cases for the proposition that "'failure to read a contract in the absence of fraud is an unavailing excuse or defense and cannot justify an avoidance, modification or nullification of the contract or any provision thereof'" *Graham v. State Farm Mut. Auto. Ins. Co.*, 1989 Del. Super. LEXIS 46, 1989 WL 12233, at *2 (Del. Super. Jan. 26, 1989) (quoting *Standard Venetian Blind Co. v. Am. Empire Ins.*, 503 Pa. 300, 469 A.2d 563 (Pa. 1984)), *aff'd*, 565 A.2d 908 (Del. 1989); *see also Hicks v. Soroka*, 55 Del. 424, 188 A.2d 133, 140–41, 5 Storey 424 (Del. Super. 1963) ("'If one voluntarily shuts his eyes when to open them is to see, such a one is guilty of an act of folly (in dealing at arm's length with another) to his own injury; and the affairs of men could not go on if courts were being called upon to rip up transactions of that sort.'" (quoting *Judd v. Walker*, 215 Mo. 312, 114 S.W. 979, 980 (Mo. 1908))). In citing these authorities, Scion overlooks a fundamental difference between the remedies of avoidance and reformation. Unlike avoidance, "[a]n agreement subject to reformation is not voidable, and cannot be disaffirmed." *In re Schick*, 232 B.R. 589, 599 n.11 (Bankr. S.D.N.Y. 1999). The remedy of equitable reformation does not void an agreement but rather corrects an error by conforming the as-written document to the agreed-upon understanding.

Section 157 of the Restatement (Second) further explains the rationale for the different rules:

> Generally, one who assents to a writing is presumed to know its contents and cannot escape being bound by its terms merely by contending that he did not read them; his assent is deemed to cover unknown as well as known terms. The exceptional rule stated in the present Section with regard to reformation has no application to the common case in which the term in question was not the subject of prior negotiations. It only affects cases that come within the scope of § 155 [When Mistake Of Both Parties As To Written Expression Justifies Reformation], under which there must have been an agreement that preceded the writing. In such a case, a party's negligence in failing to read the writing does not preclude reformation if the writing does not correctly express the prior agreement.

---

mation despite bank's failure to carefully read lease). The minority rule bars reformation where a party fails to read the agreement. *See, e.g., Monroe Guar. Ins. Co. v. Langreck*, 816 N.E.2d 485, 490 (Ind. Ct. App. 2004) ("Equity should not intervene and courts should not grant reformation if the party seeking reformation failed to read the instrument or, if it was read, failed to give heed to its plain terms."); *Pierides v. GEICO Ins. Co.*, 2010 N.J. Super. Unpub. LEXIS 851, 2010 WL 1526377, at *4 (N.J. Super. Ct. App. Div. Apr. 19, 2010) ("Reformation will not be granted based upon a mistake resulting from the complaining party's own negligence." (internal quotation marks omitted)).

Restatement (Second) of Contracts § 157 cmt. b. Although the Restatement (Second) discusses these principles under the heading of mutual mistake, they apply equally to a unilateral mistake coupled with knowing silence.

Consequently, assuming Bellinger failed to read the Disputed Agreements, it would not foreclose ASB's claim for equitable reformation. ASB still could prove by clear and convincing evidence, as it has, that the contracts failed to match the parties' specific prior understanding.

2. Ratification

Ratification requires "[k]nowledge, actual or imputed, of all material facts" and "may be implied from conduct, as well as expressed by words." *Frank v. Wilson & Co., Inc.*, 27 Del. Ch. 292, 32 A.2d 277, 283 (Del. 1943). In discussing ratification's sister doctrine of acquiescence, this Court explained that

> [w]hen a man with full knowledge, or at least with sufficient notice or means of knowledge of his rights, and of all the material circumstances of the case, freely and advisedly does anything which amounts to the recognition of a transaction, or acts in a manner inconsistent with its repudiation, ... there is acquiescence, and the transaction, although originally impeachable, becomes unimpeachable in equity.

Papaioanu v. Comm'rs of Rehoboth, 40 Del. Ch. 557, 186 A.2d 745, 749–50 (Del. Ch. 1962) (internal quotation marks omitted).

For purposes of reformation, however, stricter rules apply. Rather than imputed or constructive knowledge, ratification of a contract subject to reformation requires actual knowledge of the error.[54] The higher standard recognizes that a party otherwise entitled to equitable reformation based on mistake nearly always could have discovered the erroneous provision. The mistaken party unwittingly believes, however, that the provision is accurate. That is the point of the mistake. Accordingly, ratification does not preclude reformation unless the ratifying party actually knew of the error.

Scion identifies nine separate occasions in its post-trial brief when the plaintiffs ostensibly affirmed their intent to be bound by the Disputed Agreements despite having constructive or imputed knowledge of the scrivener's error in the Sale Proceeds

---

54. [4] *Fitzgerald v. Cantor*, 1998 Del. Ch. LEXIS 199, 1998 WL 781188, at *2 (Del. Ch. Oct. 28, 1998) (granting motion to amend pleadings to add reformation claim on grounds that "[t]he context of the particularized reformation claims suggests no information from which one could infer the circumstances that allegedly constituted mutual mistake, fraud or unilateral mistake with [the plaintiff's] knowing silence were different by the time of ratification or reaffirmation"); *see also Elliott v. Sackett*, 108 U.S. 132, 142, 2 S. Ct. 375, 27 L. Ed. 678 (1883) (granting equitable reformation of warranty deed in favor of buyer despite buyer having made two payments under unreformed contract); *Knight v. Elec. Household Utils. Corp.*, 133 N.J. Eq. 87, 30 A.2d 585, 587 (N.J. Ch. 1943) ("After a party *becomes aware* of a mistake in a written contract, if he acquiesces in the contract as written, he loses his right to reformation." (emphasis added)), *aff'd*, 134 N.J. Eq. 542, 36 A.2d 201 (N.J. 1944); *Merriam v. Nat'l Life & Accident Ins. Co.*, 169 Tenn. 291, 86 S.W.2d 566, 569 (Tenn. 1935) ("It is the general rule that reformation will be denied on the ground of ratification only when there is full knowledge of the facts by the party against whom ratification is invoked; and, to make ratification effective, the party must have ratified the instrument as it was, and not as he thought it was.").

Waterfalls. These occasions include the execution of the 2040 Lofts and Dwight Lofts LLC Agreements and the drafting and execution of the Dwight Amendment, which "ratified and confirmed" the Dwight Lofts LLC Agreement. In each case, ASB's ostensibly ratifying act occurred before August 30, 2010, when ASB first acquired actual knowledge of the scrivener's error. Accordingly, Scion has not carried its burden to demonstrate that ASB ratified the error in the Sale Proceeds Waterfalls of the Disputed Agreements.[55]

3. Unclean Hands

"The question raised by a plea of unclean hands is whether the plaintiff's conduct is so offensive to the integrity of the court that his claims should be denied, regardless of their merit." *Gallagher v. Holcomb & Salter*, 1991 Del. Ch. LEXIS 148, 1991 WL 158969, at *4 (Del. Ch. Aug. 16, 1991) (Allen, C.), *aff'd sub nom. New Castle Ins., Ltd. v. Gallagher*, 692 A.2d 414 (Del. 1997). "The Court invokes the doctrine when faced with a litigant whose acts threaten to tarnish the Court's good name." *Nakahara v. NS 1991 Am. Trust*, 718 A.2d 518, 522 (Del. Ch. 1998) (applying the doctrine in indemnification and advancement dispute after determining plaintiffs "acted in bad faith, underhandedly, in a manner deserving condemnation, wrongfully, without permission, and surreptitiously with an aim at subverting the judicial process" (alteration, footnotes, and internal quotation marks omitted)). "The Court of Chancery has broad discretion in determining whether to apply the doctrine of unclean hands." *SmithKline Beecham Pharms. Co. v. Merck & Co., Inc.*, 766 A.2d 442, 448 (Del. 2000). "The equitable doctrine of unclean hands is not strictly a defense to which a litigant is legally entitled." *Gallagher*, 1991 Del. Ch. LEXIS 148, 1991 WL 158969, at *4.

Scion argues that in a September 20, 2010 letter, Bellinger told Scion that ASB would pay $347,909.52, representing the undisputed portion of Scion's interest in 2040 Lofts, if Scion agreed to correct the Disputed Agreements. When Scion refused, ASB did not pay the undisputed amount until May 18, 2011. Scion claims the eight-month delay constitutes unclean hands sufficient to bar ASB's reformation claim.

Perhaps ASB should have paid the undisputed amount to Scion earlier than it did. The delay, however, "was not so material as to deprive plaintiff[s]" of the requested relief. 1991 Del. Ch. LEXIS 148, [WL] at *1. Moreover, ASB cured its misconduct when it paid Scion the undisputed amount plus statutory prejudgment interest. *See Gen. Elec. Co. v. Klein*, 36 Del. Ch. 275, 129 A.2d 250, 252 (Del. Ch. 1956) (Seitz, C.) ("The repentant sinner, especially where he has been duly punished, is not un-

---

55. [5] In post-trial briefing, Scion asserted for the first time that ASB's transfer in May 2009 of its membership interest in 2040 Lofts from the Allegiance Fund to EBREF constituted a novation. Scion now argues that EBREF must establish *its own* prior understanding with Scion in order to obtain reformation. EBREF is a wholly owned subsidiary of the Allegiance Fund. Neither the Allegiance Fund nor EBREF has any employees; ASB acts for both entities. To the extent EBREF needed its own prior understanding, that understanding was the same as ASB's. ASB executed the agreement on behalf of EBREF unaware of the scrivener's error in the Sale Proceeds Waterfall. The reformation analysis therefore applies with equal force to EBREF and the 2040 Lofts LLC Agreement post-transfer.

welcome in equity."). On the facts of this case, an eight-month delay of payment followed by full payment plus statutory prejudgment interest does not threaten to tarnish this Court's good name such that reformation of the Disputed Agreements should be denied.

C. The Dwight Lofts Counterclaims

ASB removed Scion as Managing Member of Dwight Lofts effective March 15, 2010. Scion contends that after its removal, ASB breached its fiduciary duties by suppressing Dwight Lofts' summer revenue and failing to inform the appraisers of an oral agreement with Columbia College that allowed extended summer leasing. Scion asserts that, for the same reasons, ASB breached the implied covenant of good faith and fair dealing. Neither argument has merit.

1. Breach of Fiduciary Duty

Under the Dwight Lofts LLC Agreement, the Managing Member owes fiduciary duties to the company and its members. Section 5.1.1(i) of the Agreement states:

> The Managing Member shall exercise the power and authority granted to it under this Agreement and shall perform its duties as Managing Member under this Agreement in good faith, in a manner Managing Member reasonably believes to be in the best interests of the Company and with such care as a prudent real estate professional in a like position would use under similar circumstances. The Managing Member acknowledges and agrees with the Company and the other Members that it is undertaking fiduciary duties and responsibilities to the Company and each of its Members identical to those a general partner undertakes in a limited partnership to its limited partners under the statutes and case law of the State of Delaware applicable to a limited partnership form of business organization. The Managing Member shall not, by intentional act or intentional failure to act, commit gross negligence, willful misconduct, a material breach of fiduciary duty, fraud, misapplication of funds, theft, misappropriations of a Company asset or intentional misrepresentation

JX 82, § 5.1.1(i). Under Section 5.2, a member will not be held liable for damages arising out of acts or omissions (i) "in good faith on behalf of the Company or the Members," (ii) "reasonably believed ... to be within the scope of the authority granted to such Member by this Agreement," and (iii) "reasonably believed ... to be in the best interests of the Company or the Members." *Id.* § 5.2. Section 5.2 does not eliminate liability if acts or omissions are "the consequence of fraud, gross negligence, or willful misconduct

I assume for purposes of analysis that ASB became the *de facto* Managing Member after removing Scion from that position effective March 15, 2010, and that ASB took on fiduciary duties in that capacity. Regardless, ASB did not act willfully, recklessly, or with gross negligence to suppress Dwight Lofts' summer revenue.

Dwight Lofts and Columbia College entered into the master lease in April 2010. At the time, summer leasing for 2010 did not rank high on anyone's priority list. Rob agreed that it was more important to focus on getting the master lease. Only later did

Rob argue that ASB should revisit the lease and seek a concession on extended summer leasing. ASB declined to re-trade the master lease, believing that such a request would "complicate [Columbia's] transition into the property and cause un-necessary and counter-productive stress." JX 153. I credit ASB's explanation and good faith.

Scion also contends that ASB and Columbia College agreed orally in September 2010 to allow extended summer leasing, but hid that information from the appraisers to depress Dwight Lofts' value. Pingel testified that Campus Advantage only reached an informal oral agreement on extended summer leasing in March 2011. Tr. 1163–65. I credit her testimony, which is supported by contemporaneous documents. *See* JX 219 (email dated March 11, 2011 in which Columbia representative notes that "Columbia would be okay" with informal extended summer leasing plan).

The evidence at trial demonstrated that ASB (i) acted reasonably and in good faith to maximize Dwight Lofts' summer revenue within the constraints of the master lease with Columbia College and (ii) participated in the appraisal process in good faith and with candor. Accordingly, ASB did not breach any fiduciary duties that I assume for purposes of this claim it owed to Scion as *de facto* Managing Member.

2. The Implied Covenant of Good Faith and Fair Dealing

Scion reframes its breach of fiduciary duty count as a breach of the implied covenant of good faith and fair dealing. For reasons similar to those set forth above, ASB did not breach the implied covenant. "The implied covenant of good faith and fair dealing inheres in every contract and requires a party in a contractual relationship to refrain from arbitrary or unreasonable conduct which has the effect of preventing the other party to the contract from receiving the fruits of the bargain." *Kuroda v. SPJS Hldgs., L.L.C.*, 971 A.2d 872, 888 (Del. Ch. 2009) (internal quotation marks omitted). "Wielding the implied covenant is a 'cautious enterprise.'" *Lonergan v. EPE Hldgs., LLC*, 5 A.3d 1008, 1018 (Del. Ch. 2010) (quoting *Nemec v. Shrader*, 991 A.2d 1120, 1125 (Del. 2010)). The doctrine should not be used to "rewrite the contract" that a party now regards as "a bad deal." *Nemec*, 991 A.2d at 1126.

As set forth above, ASB did not suppress the value of Dwight Lofts. ASB and Scion agreed to forego potential summer revenue in favor of securing the master lease. ASB participated in good faith in the contractual appraisal process and submitted reasonable estimates of summer revenue based on historical occupancy rates. Scion's projections were higher and more speculative. With input from both Scion and ASB, the appraisers used their own summer occupancy projections that fell between the ASB and Scion estimates. ASB did not hide an oral agreement about summer leasing from the appraisers. At the time of the appraisals, there was no such agreement. ASB did not engage in any other arbitrary or unreasonable conduct that prevented Scion from receiving the fruits of its equity interest in Dwight Lofts. Accordingly, ASB did not breach the implied covenant of good faith and fair dealing.

D. Scion's Breach of Contract Counterclaims

Scion's three remaining counterclaims seek to enforce the Sale Proceeds Waterfalls as they appear in the Disputed Agreements. Because I grant reformation, Scion's request for relief runs counter to the terms of the agreements. Judgment is entered against Scion on these counterclaims.

E. ASB Is Entitled to Costs And Expenses

Having prevailed in this litigation, ASB is entitled to recover its costs and expenses under the contractual fee-shifting provisions in the Disputed Agreements. The provisions state:

> In the event that any of the parties to this Agreement undertakes any action to enforce the provisions of this Agreement against any other party, the non-prevailing party shall reimburse the prevailing party for all reasonable costs and expenses incurred in connection with such enforcement, including reasonable attorneys' fees....

See, e.g., JX 82, §9.9. Scion argues that even if ASB prevails, it is not entitled to fees because an action for reformation is not an "action to enforce the provisions of the Agreement." Scion further argues that ASB did not "incur" costs or expenses because DLA Piper has not been billing ASB for its fees.

Scion's technical arguments do not prevent enforcement of the contractual fee-shifting provisions. The term "Agreement" in Section 9.9 refers to the parties' actual agreement. It does not mean the erroneous agreement that contained a scrivener's error. ASB proved in this action that the Disputed Agreements incorrectly memorialized the parties' actual agreement. Scion breached the parties' actual agreement by attempting to enforce versions that it knew were incorrect. Through this lawsuit, ASB enforced the parties' actual agreement and became entitled to fees under Section 9.9.

The purpose of the contractual fee-shifting provision is to allocate the burden of contract enforcement between the breaching party and the non-breaching party. Arrangements that the non-breaching party may have made internally or with third parties to minimize or lay off its own burdens do not affect the breaching party's liability. If, for example, ASB had obtained litigation insurance such that its fees and expenses were covered by an insurer, that fact would not eliminate Scion's obligation under the fee-shifting provision. Either ASB or the insurer by subrogation could enforce the fee-shifting provision. Here, the non-breaching side of the case caption litigated the dispute at significant cost, albeit a cost that DLA Piper and ASB have allocated between themselves. The contractual fee-shifting provision obligates the breaching side of the caption to bear that cost, regardless of the allocation between DLA Piper and ASB.

III. CONCLUSION

ASB has demonstrated by clear and convincing evidence that (i) the May 2007 Terms constituted a specific prior understanding that promote compensation would be paid only after the return of capital in a capital event, (ii) the ASB Members executed the Disputed Agreements under the mistaken belief that the Sale Proceeds Waterfalls reflected the May 2007 Terms, and (iii) the Scion Members knew that the waterfalls did not reflect the May 2007 Terms but intentionally remained silent. ASB is therefore entitled to reformation of the Sale Proceeds Waterfalls in the Disputed Agreements.

The relevant portion of the Sale Proceeds Waterfall in the Breckenridge LLC Agreement is hereby reformed to read:

> (ii) *Second*, among the Members in proportion to the Unrecovered First Preferred Return Amounts of the Members at such time, until such time as each Member's Unrecovered First Preferred Return Amount has been reduced to zero;

> (iii) *Third*, among the Members in proportion to the Invested Capital of the Members at such time, until such time as each Member's Invested Capital has been reduced to zero;

> (iv) *Fourth*, (x) the Remaining Percentage to the Members in proportion to each Member's respective Percentage Interest at such time, and (y) the Promote Percentage to Venture Partner until such time as the Fund's Unrecovered Second Preferred Return Amount has been reduced to zero; and

> (v) *Fifth*, (x) the Remaining Percentage to the Members in proportion to their respective Percentage Interest at such time, and (y) the Promote Percentage to Venture Partner.

The Sale Proceeds Waterfalls in the 2040 Lofts and Dwight Lofts LLC Agreements are reformed in parallel fashion to reflect the return of capital before payment of the promote.

Judgment is entered in favor of ASB on Scion's counterclaims. ASB is entitled to recover the fees and expenses its side incurred in the action. ASB would be entitled to costs in any event as the prevailing party.

Within ten days, the parties shall submit an order implementing these rulings. The order shall provide conforming language for the 2040 Lofts and Dwight Lofts LLC Agreements. If possible, the parties shall specify a dollar amount of fees and costs to which ASB is entitled. Any dispute over the amount should be presented promptly for the Court to resolve.

Chapter 4

Overview of Tax Entities

I. Commentary

Entity taxation is the topic of several difficult upper-level law school and graduate tax courses. This chapter provides an overview of aspects of entity taxation to introduce the uninitiated to general concepts of the respective regimes that are important to real estate transactional tax attorneys. To introduce the material in an efficient manner, the chapter does not cover many of the details that support the general concepts in this chapter. A person with a serious interest in a real estate transactional practice should seek opportunities to study entity taxation, especially partnership taxation, in depth. The overview in this chapter will provide sufficient background to enable students to address basic issues that arise in the transactional context related to the problem in this book, but it cannot substitute for full courses on partnership or corporate taxation.

Tax law has its own entity classification system. An entity's tax classification can affect the overall tax liability of an arrangement. As a general rule, all state-law corporations are tax corporations.[1] Other types of state-law entities are tax partnerships by default if they have multiple members, or they are disregarded if they have a single member.[2] Arrangements that are tax partnerships or disregarded by default may elect to be tax corporations.[3] Transactional attorneys must know whether a tax entity is subject to an entity-level tax or whether the entity's tax items flow through to the members, who report and pay tax on those items. Transactional attorneys must also be aware of the tax consequences that arise from various transactions, including the formation of an entity, contributions to an entity, operations of an entity, distributions from an entity, liquidation of an entity, and other transactions involving the ownership of an entity. The tax treatment of each of those types of transactions often depends upon the tax classification of the arrangement.

Transactional attorneys must consider the following items when advising clients with respect to the proper choice of entity.

1. Will the transfer of property to or from an entity result in taxable gain or loss?

---

1. *See* Treas. Reg. § 301.7701-2.
2. *See* Treas. Reg. § 301.7701-3.
3. *See id.*

2. If a person transfers money or property to an entity in exchange for an interest in the entity, what basis will the person take in the interest in the entity?[4]

3. If an entity receives property in exchange for an interest in the entity, what basis will the entity take in the property received?[5]

4. If an entity distributes property to one of its members, will either the entity or the distributee recognize gain on the distribution?

5. If a person receives property from an entity as a distribution, what basis will the person take in that property?

6. How do distributions affect the distributee's basis in the entity?

7. If an entity is a flow-through entity, how does it allocate tax items to its members?

8. What effect do allocations have on the members' bases in their interests in the entity?

9. What effect do the liabilities of an entity have on the members' bases in their interests in the entity?

10. Do tax-item allocations affect the members' legal rights and obligations in the entity?

11. How does the choice of entity affect employment taxes?

The following discussion provides a brief overview of the rules that help answer such questions for the various types of tax entities. The discussion illustrates the importance of the choice of tax entity in real estate transactions, reinforces basic entity tax concepts, and posits that tax partnerships are generally the preferred choice of entity for real estate investors.

A. Tax Corporations

Tax corporations come in one of two forms: (1) C corporations or (2) S corporations. C corporations are subject to an entity-level income tax, and distributions from the corporation generally are subject to income tax.[6] The two levels of tax make C corporations unattractive to many property owners. Consequently, C corporations find little use in real estate transactions. S corporations are not subject to tax at the entity level.[7] All of the tax items of an S corporation flow through to the members of the S corporation, who report the items on their individual tax returns in proportion to their ownership interests in the entity.[8] An entity must be a tax corporation (either by default or election) and meet several requirements to be an S corporation.[9] The

---

4. The basis of an interest in an entity is often referred to as the "outside basis."

5. The basis an entity takes in property is often referred to as the "inside basis."

6. *See* I.R.C. §§ 11, 301.

7. *See* I.R.C. § 1363(a).

8. *See* I.R.C. § 1366. The items flow through in proportion to ownership interests in the corporation. I.R.C. § 1366(a)(1).

9. *See* I.R.C. § 1361.

rules governing the formation, contributions, distributions, liquidation, transfer of interests, and reorganization that apply to C corporations apply to S corporations, unless the law specifically provides otherwise.[10] Corporate formations can be tax free, but if not properly structured, they can be taxable.[11] The basis rules defer the gain not recognized on formation.[12] Many distributions from corporations are subject to tax, and the corporation recognizes gain on the distributions of appreciated property.[13] Because those rules apply to S corporations, contributions to and distributions from S corporations may be taxable. The following discussion illustrates the general rules governing contributions to and distributions from corporations.

Assume Deb owns DEB Apartment. DEB Apartment is worth $8,000,000 and Deb has a tax basis of $1,000,000 in it. She would recognize $7,000,000 of gain if she were to sell DEB apartment for cash.[14] Instead, she would like to contribute it to an entity that provides limited liability. She decides to contribute it to a corporation, which she named DEB Corp. She will recognize no gain on the contribution because she will be the sole shareholder following formation.[15] In exchange for contributing DEB Apartment to the corporation, Deb will receive all of the stock of the corporation. Her basis in the stock will be the $1,000,000 basis she had in DEB Apartment.[16] DEB Corp's basis in DEB Apartment will likewise equal the $1,000,000 basis that Deb had in it. The following table summarizes the tax consequences that would result when Deb contributed DEB Apartment to DEB Corp.

Formation of Single-Member C Corporation

Deb's gain recognized	$0
Deb's basis in the stock received	$1,000,000
DEB Corp's basis in DEB Apartment	$1,000,000

Because DEB Apartment is worth $8,000,000, DEB Corp would recognize $7,000,000 if it were to sell DEB Apartments immediately following the contribution. The stock in Deb's hands should also be worth $8,000,000, so she too would recognize $7,000,000 of gain if she sold all of the stock in the corporation. Thus, the contribution to the corporation converted a single built-in gain into two built-in gains.

---

10. *See* I.R.C. §1371.
11. *See* I.R.C. §351.
12. *See* I.R.C. §§358, 362.
13. *See* I.R.C. §§301, 302, 311(b).
14. *See* I.R.C. §1001.
15. *See* I.R.C. §351. Section 351 is an exception to the general rule in section 1001(c) requiring gain recognition.
16. *See* I.R.C. §358(a).

Consider what would happen if Deb later decided to liquidate the corporation and receive DEB Apartment in a liquidating distribution. Assume DEB Apartment would be worth $10,000,000 on the date of distribution, Deb's basis in the DEB Corp stock would still be $1,000,000, and the corporation's basis in DEB Apartment would be $1,000,000. DEB Corp would recognize $9,000,000 of gain on the distribution and pay tax on that gain.[17] Deb would also recognize $9,000,000 of gain on the distribution.[18] Deb would take a $10,000,000 basis in DEB Apartments.[19]

Liquidation of Single-Member C Corporation

DEB Corp's gain recognized	$9,000,000
Deb's gain recognized	$9,000,000
Deb's basis in property received	$10,000,000

If Deb had formed DEB Corp as an S corporation, DEB Corp would still recognize gain on the distribution, but the gain would flow through to Deb.[20] Deb's basis would increase as a result of the gain flowing through to her,[21] so she would recognize no gain on the distribution and take a $10,000,000 basis in the property.[22] The distribution would also decrease her basis in her DEB Corp stock by $10,000,000.[23]

Now assume that Eddie and Fran wish to form Edran Corp. Eddie will contribute $1,000,000 of cash, and Fran will contribute Big Lot worth $1,000,000 with a $100,000 basis to Edran Corp. The formation will qualify for nonrecognition, so Fran will not recognize gain on the formation.[24] Eddie will take a $1,000,000 basis in the stock she receives,[25] and Fran will take a $100,000 basis in the stock she receives.[26] Edran Corp will take a $100,000 basis in Big Lot.[27]

---

17. *See* I.R.C. § 11 (imposing a tax on corporate income); I.R.C. § 311 (treating a distribution of appreciated property as a sale by the corporation for the property's fair market value). If DEB Corp had sold the property for its fair market value, its amount realized would have been $10,000,000. With an adjusted basis of $1,000,000, its gain realized would have been $9,000,000. *See* I.R.C. § 1001 (governing gain and loss recognition on the disposition of property).

18. *See* I.R.C. § 302. This example assumes DEB Corp had other assets to satisfy the tax liability. Often the distribution will be net of taxes paid by the corporation. It also assumes that the distribution would be a dividend to Deb.

19. *See* I.R.C. § 334(a).

20. *See* I.R.C. § 1366(a).

21. *See* I.R.C. § 1367(a).

22. *See* I.R.C. §§ 302, 334(a), 1368. If her basis in her Edran Corp stock was less than $10,000,000, she would recognize a gain on the distribution. *See* I.R.C. § 1368(b)(2).

23. *See* The distribution cannot, however, reduce her basis in her DEB Corp stock below zero. *See id.*

24. *See* I.R.C. § 351.

25. *See* I.R.C. § 1012.

26. *See* I.R.C. § 358(a).

27. *See* I.R.C. § 362(a).

Formation of Multi-Member C Corporation

Eddie's gain recognized	$0
Fran's gain recognized	$0
Eddie's basis in Edran Corp stock	$1,000,000
Fran's basis in Edran Corp stock	$100,000
Edran Corp's basis in Big Lot	$100,000

After several years, Edran Corp purchases Raw Land for $200,000. When it is worth $400,000, Edran Corp distributes it to Eddie. Edran Corp will recognize $200,000 of gain on that distribution and owe tax on that gain (assuming Edran Corp is a C corporation).[28] If Edran Corp is a C corporation, the distribution could be a dividend to Eddie,[29] and Eddie's basis in the Raw Land would be $400,000.[30] If the distribution is a dividend to Eddie, it would not affect her basis in the Edran Corp stock.

Distribution from Multi-Member C Corporation

Edran Corp's recognized gain	$200,000
Dividend income to Eddie	$400,000
Eddie's basis in Raw Land	$400,000

If Edran Corp were an S corporation, the $200,000 it recognizes on the distribution would flow through to Eddie and Fran, i.e., Edran Corp would not pay tax on the gain, but Eddie and Fran would.[31] Assuming Eddie and Fran each own half the stock of Edran Corp, they would each report $100,000 of the gain on their respective tax returns.[32] They would also increase the bases of their stock in Edran Corp by the amount of the allocations.[33] Eddie would take a $400,000 basis in Raw Land upon receipt,[34] and she would not recognize gain on the distribution, assuming Eddie's basis in her Edran Corp stock exceeded $400,000.[35] The distribution would decrease Eddie's basis in the Edran Corp stock by $400,000.[36] Because S corporations can have

---

28. *See* I.R.C. § 311(b).
29. *See* I.R.C. § 301.
30. *See* I.R.C. § 301(d).
31. *See* I.R.C. § 1363, 1366.
32. *See* I.R.C. § 1366.
33. *See* I.R.C. § 1367(a).
34. *See* I.R.C. § 301(d).
35. *See* I.R.C. § 1368(a), (b). Nonrecognition on the distribution assumes that Edran Corp has no accumulated earnings and profits. Accumulated earnings and profits could trigger dividend income to Eddie. *See* I.R.C. § 1368(c). If Eddie's basis in her Edran Corp stock was less than $400,000, Eddie would recognize gain on the distribution in an amount equal to the excess of the fair market value of the property over the basis. *See* I.R.C. § 1368(b)(2).
36. *See* I.R.C. § 1367(a)(2). If Eddie's basis in the stock were less than $400,000, however, her basis in the stock would not go below zero. *See id.*

only one class of stock,[37] when Edran Corp makes the distribution to Eddie, it must make an equal distribution to Fran.[38] Assuming Fran's basis in her Edran Corp stock exceeds the amount of the distribution she receives, she will recognize no gain, but the distribution will reduce her basis in the Edran stock.

Distribution from Multi-Member S Corporation

Edran Corp's gain recognized	$200,000
Eddie's share of Edran Corp's gain	$100,000
Fran's share of Edran Corp's gain	$100,000
Eddie's basis in Raw Land	$400,000

Consider the consequence that results if Edran Corp admits Giorgio as a new member several years after Eddie and Fran form it. Giorgio contributes New Property to Edran Corp in exchange for Edran Corp stock representing a one-third interest in Edran Corp. New Property is worth $500,000 and Giorgio has a $200,000 basis in it. Edran Corp recognizes no gain on the admission of Giorgio.[39] Because Giorgio does not control the corporation,[40] however, the nonrecognition rules would not apply, and Giorgio would recognize $300,000 of gain on the contribution.[41]

Finally, assume that Gwen, Henri, and Ian wish to form Ghean Corp, which will elect to be an S corporation. Gwen will contribute $1,000,000 of cash, Henri will contribute Real Property worth $1,000,000 with a $200,000 basis, and Ian will manage the corporation. Each person will take 100 of the 300 shares that Ghean Corp will issue on formation. The formation of Ghean Corp does not qualify for nonrecognition because the persons contributing property do not control the corporation immediately following formation (Ian is not a part of the control group because he contributes services).[42] Thus, Henri will recognize $800,000 of gain and Ian will have $1,000,000 of compensation income on the formation of Ghean Corp.[43]

---

37. *See* I.R.C. § 1361(b)(1)(D).

38. *See* Treas. Reg. § 1.1361-1(l)(1), -1(l)(2)(i).

39. *See* I.R.C. § 1032.

40. *See* I.R.C. § 368(c) (defining control for purposes of section 351 as owning at least eight percent of the vote and stock of the corporation).

41. Giorgio's gain recognized equals the difference between the $500,000 gain recognized (the fair market value of the Edran Corp stalk she received) the $200,000 basis she had in New Property. *See* I.R.C. § 1001.

42. *See* I.R.C. §§ 351, 368.

43. Henri's gain will equal the difference between the $1,000,000 of Ghean Corp stock he receives and the $200,000 basis he had in Real Property. *See* I.R.C. § 1001. Ian will have compensation income on the date of formation equal to the fair market value of the stock received, assuming it is not subject to a substantial risk of forfeiture. *See* I.R.C. §§ 61, 83; Treas. Reg. § 1.61-2(d)(1). Because each party received one-third of the Ghean Corp stock, the amount of stock each person receives will be of equal value. Gwen and Henri each transferred something worth $1,000,000 to Ghean Corp in exchange for their shares of stock. The amount of stock they each received therefore must be worth $1,000,000.

Ghean Corp will not recognize gain on the formation.[44] It will take a basis in Real Property equal to the property's $1,000,000 fair market value.[45] It may qualify for a deduction with respect to the distribution of stock it issues to Ian.[46] Gwen, Henri, and Ian will each take a $1,000,000 basis in the Ghean Corp stock they receive.[47]

Formation of a Multi-Member S Corporation (control requirement fails)

Ghean Corp's gain recognized	$0
Gwen's gain recognized	$0
Henri's gain recognized	$800,000
Ian's compensation income	$1,000,000
Ghean Corp's basis in Real Property	$1,000,000
Ghean Corp's deduction	$1,000,000
Gwen's basis in Ghean Corp's stock	$1,000,000
Henri's basis in Ghean Corp's stock	$1,000,000
Ian's basis in Ghean Corp's stock	$1,000,000

The uninitiated often think that tax corporations are unattractive from a tax perspective solely because of the double tax they impose. They may react to such thinking by recommending an S corporation as a viable choice of tax entity because it would not be subject to an entity-level tax. This discussion reveals, however, that contributions to and distributions from any type of tax corporation could trigger gain recognition. Tax and business planning in real estate transactions often require the movement of property from one entity to another. In the transactional planning context, gain recognition on contribution and distribution make corporations especially unattractive. The following discussion illustrates that moving property between tax partnerships is often tax free. That aspect of tax partnerships coupled with other aspects generally make tax partnerships the preferred choice of entity in real estate transactions.

B. Tax Partnerships

Tax partnerships are not subject to income tax.[48] All of the tax items of a tax partnership flow through to the partners, who report the tax items on their individual

---

Because Ian received the same amount of stock, it must be worth $1,000,000 also. Often one or side of a transaction will help indicate the value of the other side of the transaction.

44. *See* I.R.C. § 1032.

45. *See* I.R.C. § 362(a).

46. *See* I.R.C. § 83(h) (requiring that the expense be deductible under section 162); Treas. Reg. § 1.83-6(a)(4) (disallowing a deduction if the distribution constitutes a capital expenditure).

47. *See* I.R.C. § 358 (providing that basis in stock equals the basis of property contributed plus the gain recognized by the contributor); I.R.C. § 1012 (providing that basis equal the cost of property); Treas. Reg. § 1.61-2(d)(2)(i) (providing that the basis of property received in exchange for services equals the amount paid for the property plus the gain recognized by the service provider on receipt of the property).

48. *See* I.R.C. § 701.

tax returns.[49] The character of a tax partnership's tax items are determined at the tax-partnership level and that character flows through to the members.[50] Tax partnerships compute taxable income in the same manner that individuals do, but tax partnerships must separately state and allocate tax items that may affect the members differently depending upon the members' individual tax situations outside the tax partnership.[51] For example, the amount of a charitable contribution that an individual can deduct depends upon the individual's adjusted gross income,[52] so some members of a tax partnership may be able to deduct their distributive shares of a tax partnership's charitable contributions while other members may not. Consequently, tax partnerships must separately state any charitable contributions they make.[53] Tax rules grant members of tax partnerships significant leeway in allocating tax items to members.[54]

If the ownership interests of a tax partnership change during the tax partnership's taxable year, the tax partnership will have to properly allocate tax items to the periods preceding and following the change of ownership interests.[55] Treasury has promulgated regulations to assist with allocations when ownership interests change. Those regulations provide a ten-step process for allocating items.[56] Tax partnerships generally can choose between using the interim closing method or the proration method to allocate items in the year of a change of ownership interests.[57] Because the tax partnership can choose between the two methods, the members of tax partnerships will most likely be interested to know how the two methods will affect their respective tax liabilities.

Contributions to and distributions from tax partnerships generally are not taxable.[58] Instead, the members and the tax partnership take the basis of contributed property,[59] preserving built-in gain or loss of contributed property. The exception to this rule is a contribution of services for a capital interest in the tax partnership.[60] To avoid the tax on contributions of services, service members may consider taking a profits-only interest in the tax partnership, which often is not taxable upon receipt.[61] The flow-through treatment and flexibility to allocate tax items make tax partnerships a popular choice of entity for real estate investors. Other aspects of tax partnerships, such as the effect tax-partnership liabilities have on partners' outside bases and ad-

---

49. *See* I.R.C. §§ 701–704.

50. *See* I.R.C. § 702(b).

51. *See* I.R.C. § 703(a); Treas. Reg. §§ 1.702-1, 1.703-1.

52. *See* I.R.C. § 170.

53. *See* I.R.C. § 702(a)(4).

54. *See* I.R.C. § 704; Bradley T. Borden, *The Allure and Illusion of Partners' Interests in a Partnership*, 79 U. Cin. L. Rev. 1077 (2011).

55. *See* I.R.C § 706(d).

56. *See* Treas. Reg. § 1.706-4.

57. *See* Treas. Reg. § 1.706-4(a)(3)(iii).

58. *See* I.R.C. §§ 721, 731. *But see* I.R.C. § 752 (providing that changes in partners' shares of tax-partnership liability may cause gain or loss on contributions or distributions).

59. *See* I.R.C. §§ 722, 723.

60. *See* Treas. Reg. § 1.721-1(b).

61. *See* Rev. Proc. 93-27, 1993-2 C.B. 343.

justments of inside bases on transfers of tax-partnership interests, add to the attractiveness of tax partnerships. Because tax practitioners focus on the tax classification of arrangements, they often refer to an entity that is taxed as a partnership as a "partnership," even though it might be a state limited liability company.[62] A more accurate term is "tax partnership." Owners of partnerships are partners, and owners of limited liability companies are members. This chapter refers to owners of tax partnerships as members.

Consider the different results that obtain if the parties above form a limited liability company (which does not elect to be a tax corporation) instead of a corporation. Gwen agrees to contribute $1,000,000 of cash, and Henri agrees to contribution Real Property (worth $1,000,000 with a $200,000 basis) to Ghean LLC, and Ian agrees to manage it. Gwen and Henri each receive 100 ownership units in Ghean LLC, granting them each a one-half interest in the capital of Ghean LLC and a one-third interest in its profits. Henri receives a one-third interest in the profits of Ghean LLC. The partnership formation rules do not have a control requirement similar to that in corporate tax law, so Gwen, Henri, and Ghean LLC do not recognize gain on the transaction.[63] The nonrecognition rules do not, however, apply to a person who contributes services to the tax partnership,[64] but a person who receives a profits-only interest in a tax partnership generally does not recognize gain on the receipt of that interest.[65] Because neither Henri nor Ian has income on the formation of Ghean LLC, they prefer the tax partnership over the tax corporation alternative.

Because Henri did not recognize gain on the contribution of Real Property, Ghean LLC should take a basis in Real Property equal to the $200,000 basis Henri had in the property.[66] Gwen's basis in her Ghean LLC interests would be $1,000,000,[67] Henri's

---

62. *See* Treas. Reg. § 301.7701-1 through -3.

63. *See* I.R.C. § 721.

64. *See* Treas. Reg. § 1.721-1(b)(1).

65. *See* Rev. Proc. 93-27, 1993-2 C.B. 343. The transfer of profits-only interests to Ian makes the tax-partnership scenario different from the corporate scenario. The one-third interest that Ian took in the corporation is analogous to a capital interest in a tax partnership. The profits-only interest may, however, more closely resemble the intent of the parties because Gwen or Henri probably would not want a portion of their contributions to be distributed to Ian if Ghean LLC liquidated immediately after formation. The transfer of an equity interest in a corporation that bestows the equivalent of a profits-only interest on a service provider would, however, be taxable. The transfer of a capital interest in a tax partnership in exchange for services can trigger gain recognition to the service provider and a deduction for the partnership. *See* William S. McKee, William F. Nelson & Robert L. Whitmire, Federal Taxation of Partnerships and Partners, Ch. 5 (2015) (discussing transfers of tax-partnership interests in exchange for services). The accounting rules for such transactions are complicated and beyond the scope of these materials. As a general matter, however, they may cause Henri to recognize some gain (resulting from a deemed transfer of an interest in his property) on the admission of Ian. That gain should be offset by the deduction allocated to Henri.

66. *See* I.R.C. § 723. If Ghean LLC immediately sold Real Property for its $1,000,000 fair market value, it would recognize the $800,000 built-in gain and would allocate all of that to Henri, the member who contributed it. *See* I.R.C. § 704(c).

67. *See* I.R.C. § 1012.

basis in his Ghean LLC interests would be $200,000,[68] and Ian's basis in his Ghean LLC interest would be $0.[69] Ian would recognize income only as the partnership allocates income to him.

Formation of a Tax Partnership

Ghean LLC's gain recognized	$0
Gwen's gain recognized	$0
Henri's gain recognized	$0
Ian's income	$0
Gwen's basis in Ghean LLC interests	$1,000,000
Henri's basis in Ghean LLC interests	$200,000
Ian's basis in Ghean LLC interests	$0
Ghean LLC's basis in Real Property	$200,000

If the bases the members take in their interests differs from the fair market value of those interests, the members will have unrealized gain or loss in those interests, and the tax partnership will generally have unrealized gain or loss in the property it receives in contribution. Generally, the character of gain or loss that the tax partnership will recognize when it disposes of property will depend upon the purpose for which the tax partnership holds the property, unless such treatment could be abusive.[70] Furthermore, tax partnerships generally must allocate pre-contribution gain and loss to the contributing member at the time the tax partnership recognizes such gain or loss.[71]

Ghean LLC could admit a new member who would recognize no gain or loss on the contribution of property,[72] even though the person acquired a minority interest in Ghean LLC. The law would treat the contribution of property by a new member in the same manner that it treated Henri's contribution. Thus, Ghean LLC's basis in the contributed property would equal the contributing partner's basis in that property, and the contributing partner's basis in the Ghean LLC interest would also equal the basis of the contributed property.

Assume that six years after formation Ghean LLC acquires New Building for $500,000. Two years later when New Building is worth $750,000, Ghean LLC distributes it to Gwen. At the time of the distribution, Gwen's basis in her Ghean LLC interests is $1,000,000.[73] Neither the tax partnership nor Gwen will recognize gain

---

68. *See* I.R.C. § 722.

69. *See* Treas. Reg. § 1.61-2(d)(2)(i).

70. *See, e.g.,* I.R.C. § 724(a)–(c) (imposing specific character requirements on gains and losses recognized by a tax partnership on the disposition of certain types of contributed property).

71. *See* I.R.C. § 704(c); Treas. Reg. § 1.704-3.

72. *See* I.R.C. § 721.

73. A member's basis in a tax-partnership interest equals that member's basis determined under section 722, adjusted for allocations of income and loss and distributions. *See* I.R.C. § 705(a).

on the distribution.[74] Gwen would take the tax partnership's $500,000 basis in New Building,[75] and she would reduce her basis in her tax-partnership interests by that amount.[76] (Contrast that result with the result of a distribution in complete liquidation of a member's interest in a tax partnership.[77]) After the distribution, Gwen's basis in her Ghean LLC interests would be $500,000. As result of taking Ghean LLC's basis in the distributed property, Gwen will take the property with unrealized gain (i.e., the difference between the basis she has in the property and its fair market value).[78]

Distribution from a Tax Partnership

Ghean LLC's gain recognized	$0
Gwen's gain recognized	$0
Gwen's basis in New Building	$500,000
Gwen's basis in Ghean LLC interests	$500,000

In this example, neither the tax partnership nor the distributee member recognized gain or loss. A member of a tax partnership may, however, recognize gain or loss on a distribution of cash from a tax partnership. If a distribution of cash exceeds the member's basis in the tax-partnership interest, the member recognizes gain to the extent of that excess.[79] A member may recognize loss on a liquidating distribution of cash, if the amount of distributed cash is less than the basis of the member's interest in the tax partnership.[80]

The rules governing contributions to and distributions from a tax partnership allow for the tax-free movement of property to and from the tax partnership. The partnership tax allocation rules are, however, the heart of partnership taxation. A real estate transactional attorney should know those rules well. At a minimum, such attorney should understand how allocations may affect the legal rights and obligations

---

74. *See* I.R.C. §731(a), (b). A member can recognize gain if the tax partnership distributes money that exceeds the partner's basis in the tax partnership and in other limited circumstances. *See* I.R.C. §731(a)(1), (2).

75. *See* I.R.C. §732(a)(1). The basis the member takes in distributed property could equal the partner's basis in the tax-partnership interest, if the distribution is made in liquidation of the tax partnership or if the partner's basis in the partnership is less than the tax-partnership's basis in the property. *See* I.R.C. §732(a)(2).

76. *See* I.R.C. §733.

77. *See* I.R.C. §732(b).

78. That unrealized gain a member of a tax partnership takes in distributed property should reflect the character of the unrealized gain that the tax partnership had in the property. *See, e.g.*, I.R.C. §1250(d)(5); Treas. Reg. §1.1250-3(c)(3). Although the character of gain or loss recognized by a distributee member of a tax partnership upon disposition of distributed property will normally depend upon the distributee's holding purpose, rules prevent the abusive use of the distribution rules to change the character of income or loss that the distributee would recognize on the disposition of certain types of property. *See, e.g.*, I.R.C. §735(a).

79. *See* I.R.C. §731(a)(1).

80. *See* I.R.C. §731(a)(2).

of partners. To understand the legal consequences of allocations, one must know the difference between tax items and economic items. Tax items are amounts the law requires taxpayers to report on tax returns. Economic items are metrics that express economic activity. Members and their advisors should understand that allocations of economic items could affect their economic rights and obligations in the tax partnership. They also must understand the effect of tax-item allocations.

Often tax items have corresponding economic items. For example, compensation paid by a tax partnership to an employee has a corresponding section 162 deduction. Gain recognized on the disposition of raw land should correspond to the economic appreciation in the value of the land. Generally, the allocation of a tax item should match the allocation of the corresponding economic item. To illustrate, assume that Andres, Sarah, and Kim are equal members of Anraim LLC, which allocates tax and economic items equally among its members. If Anraim LLC were to pay $3,000 of compensation to an employee to perform accounting services, Andres, Sarah, and Kim would each understand that they would be entitled to $1,000 less of tax-partnership assets upon liquidation. They would each also report $1,000 of a compensation deduction on their individual returns. Similarly, if Anraim LLC recognized $300,000 of gain on the disposition of a portion of its property, Andres, Sarah, and Kim would each be entitled to an additional $100,000 upon liquidation because Anraim LLC allocates all items of gain equally to the partners. Each of Andres, Sarah, and Kim should also include $100,000 of taxable gain on their individual tax returns.

Even though the allocation of economic items and their corresponding tax items seems intuitive, the partnership tax allocation rules are quite complex. The complexity derives in part from tax items that do not correspond to economic items. One such tax item is the depreciation deduction. Tax law grants the owner of improved property a depreciation deduction.[81] The owner of the property may take that deduction even if the property appreciates in value. Thus, the depreciation deduction does not correspond with an economic item; a tax partnership must nonetheless allocate the depreciation deduction to its members. The law allows the tax partnership to allocate such items in accordance with the partners' interests in the tax partnership or in any manner that has substantial economic effect.[82]

"Substantial" and "economic effect" are technical tax terms. The test for substantiality attempts to prevent abusive allocations.[83] The regulations provide a safe harbor that will ensure the allocations have economic effect.[84] In studying that safe harbor, notice how the allocation of tax items can affect partners' legal rights and obligations

---

81. *See* I.R.C. §§ 167, 168.
82. *See* I.R.C. § 704(b).
83. *See* Treas. Reg. § 1.704-1(b)(2)(iii). That test is beyond the scope of these materials.
84. *See* Treas. Reg. § 1.704-1(b)(2)(ii)(*b*). Allocations may have economic effect, even if they do not come within the economic effect safe harbor. *See* Treas. Reg. § 1.704-1(b)(2)(ii)(*d*) (describing the alternate test for economic effect); Treas. Reg. § 1.704-1(b)(2)(ii)(*i*) (describing test for economic effect equivalence).

in the tax partnership. To satisfy the economic effect safe harbor, a tax-partnership agreement must include the following three mandates.[85]

1. The tax partnership must maintain capital accounts in accordance with rules in the regulations.

2. The tax partnership must make liquidating distributions in accordance with positive capital account balances.

3. Members must be unconditionally obligated to restore deficit capital account balances.

The capital account maintenance rules require adjustments for tax-item allocations.[86] Because the distribution rules and deficit restoration rules depend upon the capital account balances, adjustments to the capital accounts affect the partners' rights and obligations in a tax partnership. Consequently, the allocation of tax items can affect partners' rights and obligations in a tax partnership.

A simple example illustrates how tax-item allocations can affect partners' rights and obligations in a tax partnership. Assume two partners, each with a $500,000 capital account balance, agree to allocate all of the depreciation deduction to one member and to allocate everything else equally. The tax partnership has $100,000 of depreciation deduction, which it allocates to the one partner.[87] The allocation reduces the partner's capital account balance to $400,000. If the tax partnership then sells the depreciable property for $200,000 of gain, it will allocate $100,000 to each partner. After the allocation the member who took the depreciation deduction will have a $500,000 capital account balance (original $500,000 balance minus $100,000 depreciation deduction plus $100,000 of gain), and the other member will have a $600,000 capital account balance (original $500,000 balance plus $100,000 of gain). If the tax partnership then liquidated, the member would receive different amounts on the liquidation. The difference would be attributable to the depreciation deduction (the tax-item allocation), which reduced one partner's capital account balance, but not the other's.

The effect of tax-item allocations can be even more pronounced. Assume, for example, that the depreciation deduction is $800,000 and causes the member to have a $300,000 deficit capital account balance (original $500,000 minus $800,000 depreciation deduction). The tax partnership sells the property for $200,000 of gain and allocates $100,000 to each partner. The member who took the depreciation deduction would have a $200,000 deficit capital account balance following that allocation ($300,000 deficit plus $100,000 of gain). The other member would have a $600,000 capital account balance (original $500,000 balance plus $100,000 of gain). If the tax partnership liquidated, the member with the deficit capital account balance would have to contribute $200,000 to the tax partnership. That would be a problem if the

---

85. *See* Treas. Reg. § 1.704-1(b)(2)(ii)(*b*).

86. *See* Treas. Reg. § 1.704-1(b)(2)(iv)(*b*).

87. This example assumes that the allocations will pass the test for substantiality. *See* Treas. Reg. § 1.704-1(b)(2)(iii).

tax partnership were a limited liability company, and the members thought they would not be liable for additional capital contributions.

These examples illustrate that bad results may obtain if the partners' attorneys simply put boilerplate tax provisions in the tax-partnership agreement to satisfy the economic effect safe harbor. There are other methods to ensure that the allocations have substantial economic effect or are in accordance with the partners' interests in the tax partnership.[88] Those methods are beyond the scope of these materials, but every transactional real estate attorney should be familiar with them, or work with someone who is. They should also know that failure to adequately consider these rules could also limit the amount of deductions that a member is allowed.

Another distinguishing aspect of partnership taxation deserves attention in this context. A partner's share of tax-partnership liabilities can affect the partner's basis in the tax partnership. Determining the partners' shares of tax-partnership liabilities is a complicated undertaking, most of which is beyond the scope of this book.[89] Readers should know generally, however, that if a tax-partnership liability is recourse to the members of a tax partnership, the members' shares of the liability generally equals the amount of the liability for which they bear the economic risk of loss.[90] If, on the other hand, the liability is nonrecourse to the partners, the members' shares of the tax partnership's liabilities will often equal their shares of tax-partnership profits.[91] An increase in a partner's share of tax-partnership liabilities is treated as a contribution by the member to the tax partnership, which increases the partner's basis in the tax partnership.[92] A decrease in a partner's share of tax-partnership liability is treated as a distribution by the tax partnership to the partner, which decreases the partner's basis in the tax partnership and could trigger gain recognition.[93] These rules can be both detrimental and beneficial to partners.

These rules could trigger gain recognition on the contribution of encumbered property. For example, if the amount by which a partner's personal liability decreases as part of a contribution exceeds the basis of contributed property, such excess could be gain to the contributing partner.[94] Careful planning could help members avoid

---

88. *See* Treas. Reg. §1.704-1(b)(2)(ii)(*d*), -1(b)(2)(ii)(*i*); Treas. Reg. §1.704-1(b)(3).

89. *See* Treas. Reg. §1.752-1through -3.

90. *See* Treas. Reg. §1.752-1, -2.

91. *See* Treas. Reg. §1.752-3(a)(3). The regulations governing the allocation of nonrecourse liabilities adopt a three-tier approach. The first tier (Treas. Reg. §1.752-3(a)(1)) applies if the tax partnership has had nonrecourse deductions, which would happen if the basis of tax partnership assets dipped below the amount of outstanding tax-partnership liability. The second tier (Treas. Reg. §1.752-3(a)(2)) applies if a member of the tax partnership had contributed property or a new member joined at a time when the tax partnership had property. If those first two tiers do not apply, the tax partnership allocates nonrecourse liabilities under the third tier, i.e., in accordance with the members' interests in the profits of the tax partnership.

92. *See* I.R.C. §§722, 752(a).

93. *See* I.R.C. §§731(a)(1), 752(b).

94. *See* Treas. Reg. §§1.707-5, 1.752-1.

this outcome. The partnership liability rules can also allow tax partnerships to borrow money and distribute the proceeds tax free to its members. For example, if a tax partnership owns property that has appreciated significantly, it may be able to convince a bank to lend it money with the property as collateral for the loan. Assuming each member has a share of that new tax-partnership liability, each partner's basis in the tax partnership will increase by an amount equal to the partner's share of tax-partnership liability. The tax partnership could then distribute the proceeds to the members tax free. Contrast that result with that of an S corporation. If the arrangement were an S corporation, the corporation's loan would not affect the shareholders' bases in their corporate stock. A distribution of the loan proceeds could exceed their bases in the corporate stock and trigger gain recognition.

One final distinguishing aspect of partnership taxation deserves mention in this context. To appreciate this partnership tax rule, consider the basis rules that apply to a purchaser of an interest in a tax corporation. The purchaser of the interest takes a cost basis in the interest.[95] The purchase does not, however, affect the basis of property in the corporation. This result could be particularly troubling for a purchaser of an interest in an S corporation. For example, assume that OP LLC, an S corporation, owns a piece of property worth $500,000 with a $100,000 basis. Ollie and Polly are equal members of OP LLC, and they each have a $50,000 basis in their respective interests in OP LLC. Ollie sells his interest in OP LLC to Quintin for $250,000 and recognizes $200,000 of gain on the transfer. Quintin takes a $250,000 basis in the OP LLC interests. OP LLC then sells its property, recognizes $400,000 of gain, and allocates $200,000 each to Polly and Quintin. Quintin would likely be disappointed to recognize a portion of the gain.

The result could be different if, instead of electing OP LLC to be a tax corporation, Ollie and Polly allow it to be a tax partnership. They could have caused OP LLC to make a section 754 election. If a section 754 election is in effect when a tax-partnership interest changes hands by virtue of a sale or transfer upon death of a partner, the tax partnership can increase the basis of its property to account for the transfer.[96] As a result, if OP LLC held property worth $500,000 with a $100,000 basis when Ollie sold all of his interests to Quintin, the tax partnership could increase the basis of its property by $200,000, with respect to Quintin. If the tax partnership later sold the property for $500,000, that basis increase would result in Quintin recognizing no gain on the transfer. Similarly, a person who receives a tax-partnership interest upon the death of a member will take a fair market value basis in that property.[97] If the tax partnership has a section 754 election in effect, it can step up the basis of its property with respect to the transferee to eliminate the gain the member would otherwise recognize on the disposition of tax-partnership property.

---

95. *See* I.R.C. § 1012.
96. *See* I.R.C. § 743(b).
97. *See* I.R.C. § 1014(a).

C. Employment Tax Considerations

Choice of entity decisions must include employment tax considerations. Employment tax considerations may justify using a corporation for some real estate situations. Often the ownership of real estate coincides with providing services. For example, a group of property owners may own several apartment complexes. They may form different legal entities to own each complex and create one separate legal entity. Such an arrangement would require the management company to enter into management agreements with the several entities that own property. The management company would then receive management fees from those other entities. The entities that hold the property would undoubtedly be tax partnerships for all the reasons discussed above. The management entity would hold little, if any, property. Most of the factors that suggest that an entity should be a tax partnership apply to arrangements that hold property. Consequently, those factors would not weigh heavily in the choice of entity decision regarding the management company. The management entity might therefore consider being a tax corporation. Because of the double-tax problem of C corporations, the owners would elect to make it an S corporation, if they chose the corporate form. The primary factor that may affect choice of entity for the management company could be employment taxes.[98]

Anyone who has been employed should recognize that employers withhold amounts for Social Security and Medicare taxes. Self-employed individuals must also pay those taxes. For self-employed individuals, the rate for the Social Security tax generally is 12.4% and for the Medicare tax is 2.9%.[99] The Social Security tax is subject to a wage limit, so it only applies to self-employment income up to a certain amount, which is adjusted for inflation.[100] Compensation is subject to the same rates and limits, but employers pay half of each tax and employees pay the other half.[101] If an entity is closely held, the owners of the entity bear the full cost of employment taxes paid on their compensation. Consequently, the full rates are relevant when planning to limit employment tax liability for the owners of closely held businesses.

The question in employment tax planning for closely held businesses is whether allocations to members and shareholders are subject to self-employment tax. Amounts allocated to general partners are subject to self-employment tax.[102] Amounts allocated to a limited partner are not subject to self-employment tax, unless they are guaranteed

---

98. The entities that hold property would not provide services, so the income from those pro properties would not be subject to employment taxes.

99. *See* I.R.C. § 1401(a), (b).

100. *See* I.R.C. § 1402(a), (b). The wage limit was $118,500 for 2015 and 2016. *See* U.S. Social Security Administration, *Contribution and Benefits Base, available at* http://www.ssa.gov/oact/cola/cbb.html.

101. *See* I.R.C. §§ 3101, 3111. An individual may, however, deduct one-half of the self-employment taxes. *See* I.R.C. § 164(f). Members of tax partnerships are not employees for purposes of withholding employment taxes. *See* Rev. Rul. 69-184, 1969-1 C.B. 256.

102. This assumes that the tax partnership carries on an active trade or business. *See* I.R.C. § 1402(a).

payments for services performed by the limited partner.[103] The treatment of allocations to members of limited liability companies is uncertain. Income allocated to shareholders of S corporations and dividends paid to shareholders of S corporations are not subject to self-employment tax.[104] The choice therefore comes down to limited partnerships and S corporations.[105] Limited partnerships are a bit cumbersome. To obtain limited liability, the owners of a limited partnership must form a limited liability company or corporation to be the general partner. That structure makes limited partnerships a bit less attractive then an S corporation.

Employment-tax planning implicates the adage that "pigs get fat, but hogs get slaughtered." Owners of an active business may not be able to completely eliminate the employment tax, but they can minimize it. For instance, an S corporation should pay a reasonable compensation to shareholders who perform services for the corporation and distribute the remainder as a dividend. A reasonable amount paid as compensation will be subject to the employment tax, but the portion paid as a dividend will not be subject to employment tax.[106] The following example illustrates a possible planning technique to reduce employment taxes for owners of a closely held business.

Margo and Nan own several office buildings in separate legal entities. They wish to centralize the management of those buildings, so they form Management LLC, which elects to be an S corporation. Margo and Nan each own fifty of the 100 ownership units in Management LLC. Management LLC enters into management agreements with all of the entities that own Margo and Nan's office buildings. Margo and Nan are the president and vice president, respectively, of Management LLC. Management LLC hires several employees and contractors to help with the upkeep and maintenance of the properties and to work in the management office. Before paying Margo and Nan, Management LLC has $450,000 of net income. Management LLC must pay Margo and Nan for the services they perform as officers. Management LLC will distribute to Margo and Nan any cash flow that remains after it pays their compensation (assume that cash flow, before compensation paid to Margo and Nan, equals the $450,000 of net income). Reasonable compensation for people who perform functions similar to those Margo and Nan perform is between $90,000 and $130,000.

Consider the consequences of different compensation arrangements that Management LLC may enter into with Margo and Nan. Management LLC could pay $225,000 to each of Margo and Nan as compensation. That full amount would be subject to the 2.9% Medicare tax,[107] so the Medicare tax would be $13,050 ($450,000 x 2.9%). Assuming the Social Security wage limit is $118,500, at 12.4%, the Social Security

---

103. *See* I.R.C. § 1402(a)(13).

104. *See* I.R.C. § 1402(a)(2); Rev. Rul. 59-221, 1959-1 C.B. 225.

105. A limited liability company or other legal entity that elects to be an S corporation would provide the same opportunities that a state-law corporation provides.

106. *See* Watson v. United States, 107 A.F.T.R.2d 311 (S.D. Iowa 2010).

107. This example combines the employer and employee portion of the tax because Margo and Nan, as the sole shareholders of Management Corp, will bear the cost of both portions.

portion of the employment tax would be $29,388 ($118,500 x 12.4% x 2). Thus, total employment tax would be $42,438. Alternatively, Management Corp could pay a reasonable compensation to each of Margo and Nan and distribute the balance to them as dividends. Assume it pays Margo $97,000 and pays Nan $93,000, and both of those amounts are reasonable compensation for the services they perform. The total compensation paid to Margo and Nan will be $190,000. Because the amount paid to each of Margo and Nan is below the Social Security wage base, the entire amount will be subject to the Social Security and Medicare taxes. The Social Security portion of the tax will be $23,560 ($190,000 x 12.4%) and the Medicare portion will be $5,510 ($190,000 x 2.9%). The total employment tax will therefore be $29,070 ($23,560 + $5,510). Planning therefore appears to reduce Margo and Nan's aggregate employment tax liability by $13,368 ($42,438 − $29,070).

If Management LLC pays no compensation to Margo and Nan, perhaps the IRS and courts would recast all of the distributions to them as compensation, and the entire $450,000 would be subject to employment taxes.[108] Therefore, Margo and Nan cannot merely cause Management LLC to distribute all positive cash flow to themselves as dividends and avoid paying employment tax on the entire amount. To avoid some employment tax, they should cause Management LLC to pay them a reasonable compensation. The ability to affect the amount of distributions to owners that are subject to employment tax makes tax corporations more attractive than tax partnerships in this narrow area.

D. Disregarded Arrangements and Changing Tax Classification

Tax classification of entities is, for the most part, governed by the check-the-box regulations. Those regulations require first determining whether an arrangement is an entity separate from its owners.[109] paraN121E3 If an arrangement is such a separate entity, then it is either a tax corporation, a tax partnership, or a disregarded entity. A separate entity is a tax corporation by default if it is a state-law corporation.[110] A separate entity that is not a state-law corporation is a tax partnership by default if it has more than one member and is a disregarded entity if it has just one member, but such entities can elect to be tax corporations.[111] An arrangement that is not a separate entity, is disregarded for tax purposes.

Tax law does not recognize disregarded arrangements as entities separate from their members. A common type of disregarded arrangement is a single-member limited liability company or other non-corporate entity.[112] For example, a single-member

---

108. The IRS may, however, recharacterize only a portion of the distribution as compensation. *See* Watson v. United States, 107 A.F.T.R.2d 311 (S.D. Iowa 2010) (recharacterizing only a portion of a distribution as compensation).

109. *See* Treas. Reg. § 301.7701-1.

110. *See* Treas. Reg. § 301.7701-2(b).

111. *See* Treas. Reg. § 301.7701-3.

112. *See* Treas. Reg. § 301.7701-3.

limited liability company is a disregarded arrangement, unless it elects to be a corporation. Another common disregarded arrangement in real estate ownership is a tenancy-in-common. If an arrangement is a tenancy-in-common for tax purposes, tax law will treat each member as owning an undivided interest in the property and tax the owner of the interest on tax items attributable to that interest. The arrangement will not qualify for the partnership tax allocation or other rules. Even though an arrangement is a tenancy-in-common under state law, however, tax law may treat it as a tax partnership. Distinguishing between disregarded arrangements and tax partnerships can be a difficult task.[113] Attorneys must be aware of the case law that governs the distinction between tax partnerships and disregarded arrangements to help clients avoid unintended classification.

Factors that affect the choice between a disregarded arrangement and a tax partnership are often subtle,[114] and the preference for one form is often difficult to determine in advance. Section 1031 (a topic covered in several subsequent chapters) may tip the scale for some real estate investors. For example, a person may transfer real property and wish to use the proceeds from such a sale to acquire like-kind replacement property with another investor. An interest in a tax partnership is not like-kind to real property, so it is not viable replacement property. Instead of forming a tax partnership to acquire the replacement property, each person could acquire a tenancy-in-common interest in the property. A tenancy-in-common interest in real property can be like kind to other real property, so the investors may prefer to own property as tenants in common instead of in a tax partnership. Ensuring that the co-ownership arrangement is not a tax partnership requires care.

Because tax classification does not depend solely on the state-law classification of an entity,[115] business owners may change a tax classification without altering the legal classification of an entity.[116] For example, the admission of another member to a disregarded single-member limited liability company will make that entity a tax partnership. A two-member limited liability company can elect to be a tax corporation without changing its state law identity. The change in tax classification can have serious tax consequences,[117] so attorneys must be aware of the consequences of actions when advising a course of action.

E. Choice of Entity for Real Estate Owners

This discussion should illustrate that tax partnerships will almost always be the choice of entity for real estate investors. Tax partnerships are not subject to double

---

113. *See* Bradley T. Borden, *Open Tenancies-in-Common*, 39 Seton Hall L. Rev. 387 (2009); Bradley T. Borden, *The Federal Definition of Tax Partnerships*, 43 Hous. L. Rev. 925 (2006).

114. *See* Bradley T. Borden, *The Federal Definition of Tax Partnerships*, 43 Hous. L. Rev. 925, 957–969 (2006). The single member of a limited liability company may prefer the entity to be a tax corporation for employment-tax-planning purposes, for the reasons discussed above.

115. *See* Treas. Reg. § 301.7701-1 through -4.

116. *See* Treas. Reg. § 301.7701-3(c), (f).

117. *See* Treas. Reg. § 301.7701-3(g).

taxation. They allow parties to join together tax free. They allow new members to join existing tax partnerships tax free. They provide leeway in allocating items of income and loss. Partners' bases in tax partnerships increase to reflect increases in tax-partnership liabilities. The basis of tax-partnership property can increase the transfer of a partnership interest. Finally, tax partnerships can distribute property tax free. All of these features make tax partnerships the ideal choice of entity for almost all real estate ventures. This chapter introduced basic concepts of partnership taxation. Anyone interested in advising real estate investors should invest more time to master the intricacies of partnership taxation. The material in the following chapters requires an understanding of the general concepts covered in this chapter. Subsequent chapters, however, focus more closely on tax issues that arise on transfers of property to unrelated parties.

II. Primary Authority
David E. Watson, P.C. v. United States
United States District Court, Southern District of Iowa
107 A.F.T.R.2d 311 (2010)

On or about February 5, 2007, the United States of America ("Defendant" or "Government") recharacterized dividend and loan payments from David E. Watson, P.C. ("DEWPC" or "Plaintiff") to its sole shareholder and employee, David E. Watson ("Watson"), as wages. In light of this recharacterization, Defendant assessed additional employment taxes, interest and penalties against Plaintiff for each of the eight calendar quarters in 2002 and 2003. DEWPC paid the fourth quarter 2002 assessment of $4,063.93 on or about April 14, 2007 and filed a claim for refund of that amount on or about June 27, 2007. Defendant denied Plaintiff's request for a refund on or about November 16, 2007.

Plaintiff filed the above-captioned action on October 31, 2008, contending that the assessments against it were illegal, and requesting a refund of the amount paid. Defendant filed an Answer and Counterclaim on February 12, 2009, resisting Plaintiff's request for refund, and requesting Judgment against Plaintiff in the amount of $44,457.39 for additional assessments, penalties, and interest for the seven additional quarters in 2002 and 2003 for which Plaintiff did not make payment. The Court held a bench trial in the case on August 27, 2010. On September 27, 2010, the parties submitted proposed findings of fact and conclusions of law. The matter is fully submitted.

I. CONSIDERATIONS ON REVIEW

Federal Rule of Civil Procedure 52(a) requires that in all cases tried without a jury or with an advisory jury, "the court shall find the facts specially and state separately its conclusions of law thereon." In determining the credibility of the witnesses and the weight to be accorded their testimony, the Court has taken into consideration: the character of the witnesses, their demeanor on the stand, their interest, if any, in the result of the trial, their relation to or feeling toward the parties to the trial, the probability or improbability of their statements as well as all the other facts and circumstances given in evidence. *Clark v. U.S.*, 391 F.2d 57, 60 (8th Cir.1968). With these considerations in mind, the Court finds facts and makes conclusions of law as articulated herein.

II. FINDINGS OF FACT

A. Stipulated Facts

The parties have stipulated to many of facts in this case. Pursuant to the parties' stipulation, the Court finds the following facts in this case:

- David Watson ("Watson") graduated from the University of Iowa in 1982, with a bachelor's degree in business administration and a specialization in accounting.
- Watson became a Certified Public Accountant ("CPA") in 1983, and received a master's degree in taxation from Drake University in 1993.
- Between 1982 and 1992, Watson practiced accounting at two different accounting firms, one of which was Ernst & Young, where he began specializing in partnership taxation.
- After leaving Ernst & Young, Watson became a 25% shareholder in an accounting firm called Larson, Watson, Bartling & Eastman ("LWBE").
- The remaining 75% of LWBE was owned by Tom Larson, Jeff Bartling, and Dale Eastman.
- On October 11, 1996, Watson incorporated DEWPC, an Iowa Professional Corporation.
- DEWPC is a validly organized and existing corporation, properly recognized as a separate entity for federal tax purposes.
- Watson, at the times relevant to this action, and at all times generally, is the only individual who is or has ever been an officer, shareholder, director, or employee of DEWPC.
- Watson's employment with DEWPC was, at all relevant times, governed by the terms and conditions of an Employment Agreement.
- DEWPC has elected to be taxed as an S Corporation since the time of its inception.
- After incorporating DEWPC in 1996, Watson caused DEWPC to become a 25% shareholder in LWBE, replacing Watson's own, individual shareholder status in DEWPC.
- The other partners in LWBE undertook similar action, such that LWBE became owned by DEWPC, Thomas E. Larson, P.C., Jeffrey T. Bartling, P.C., and Dale A. Eastman, P.C., rather than by Watson, Larson, Bartling, and Eastman individually.
- By 1998, Paul Juffer, P.C. had become a partner and Dale A. Eastman, P.C. had ceased being a partner, such that LWBE changed its name to Larson, Watson,

Bartling, & Juffer, LLP ("LWBJ"). DEWPC remained a partner in LWBJ after the name change.

- Watson is not personally a partner or employee of LWBJ; rather, he provides accounting services to LWBJ and its clients as an employee of DEWPC.

- In the relevant years, 2002 and 2003, Watson could not practice accounting other than through LWBJ.[118]

- In 2002 and 2003, Watson received $24,000 designated as salary from DEWPC and paid employment taxes on that amount.

- DEWPC's 2002 and 2003 cash income came exclusively in the form of distributions from LWBJ.

- Watson is the only person to whom DEWPC distributed money in 2002 or 2003.

- There is no tax statute, regulation, or other rule that requires DEWPC to pay any minimum salary to Watson.

- There is no minimum amount of compensation that DEWPC was required to pay to Watson before it could declare and pay a dividend to Watson.

- On or about April 14, 2007, the United States received a payment of $4,063.93 from DEWPC, representing additional tax and related penalty and interest assessments made against DEWPC by the United States for the calendar quarter ending December 31, 2002.

- Though DEWPC designated that the payment of $4,063.93 be applied to the tax liability for the fourth quarter of 2002, the IRS erroneously applied the payment to the first quarter of 2002.

- The parties agree that the erroneous application of Plaintiff's tax payment to the first quarter of 2002, rather than the fourth quarter of 2002, does not operate to deprive this Court of subject-matter jurisdiction.

B. Additional Findings of Fact

Though the facts to follow were not stipulated to by the parties, the Court finds that they have been amply proven or established by evidence and testimony at trial.

1. David Watson.

- DEWPC regularly held shareholder meetings, at which Watson (DEWPC's only shareholder, employee, and officer) was the only participant.

- Watson testified that, when LWBE first started, he received zero salary due to the startup nature of the company.

- At the October 6, 1997 shareholder meeting, DEWPC authorized an annual salary for Watson of $12,000 for 1998. DEWPC also approved payment to Watson

---

118. [1] The accounting work that Watson performed did not change significantly after LWBE became LWBJ.

of "dividends in the amount of available cash on hand after payment of compensation and other expenses of the corporation."

• Watson testified that the partners agreed to a $12,000 annual salary for each in 1998 because "we had determined as a group that, as a minimum, we should have enough cash flow on hand in any given period to pay $1,000 a month to each partner, whether it was good times or bad."

• At the October 2, 2000 shareholder meeting, DEWPC authorized an annual salary for Watson of $24,000 for 2001. DEWPC also approved payment to Watson of "dividends in the amount of available cash on hand after payment of compensation and other expenses of the corporation."

• DEWPC approved the same salary and dividend arrangement with respect to Watson ($24,000 salary plus dividends) at its October 1, 2001, October 7, 2002, and October 6, 2003 shareholder meetings.

• Watson testified at trial that the reason his compensation was set at $24,000 for the years 2002 and 2003 was because the partners of LWBJ "got together and discussed what we felt that we could pay on a regular and continuous basis regardless of the seasonability of our business." Watson further testified that the partners agreed that "regardless of whether it's a good economy or bad economy ... we felt that we'd grown to the point that, for each of the partners, that we could pay $2,000 a month for sure and then we'd have that cash available."

• Watson testified that his salary for the last several years (post-dating the tax years at issue in this case) has been $48,000, again because the partners of LWBJ agreed that the business' cash flow was sufficient to pay a "minimum of $4,000 per month whether it was good times or bad."

• LWBJ maintained a "co-employer" relationship with Merit Resources, whereby twice a month, LWBJ submits funds to Merit Resources, and Merit Resources sends out payroll checks after accounting for relevant deductions. Hence, Watson's paychecks and W-2s are issued by Merit Resources.

• The gross revenues of LWBJ for 2002 were $2,349,556, and the gross revenues for LWBJ for 2003 were $2,949.739.

• Watson's gross billings to clients were approximately $197,682.21 in 2002, and $200,380.36 in 2003.

• Watson testified that LWBJ has approximately 30 employees, and that approximately 26–27 of those employees bill time to clients.

• Watson further testified that the partners of LWBJ incur substantially more of the expenses of the firm than any other employees, due to larger offices, more travel, and greater educational costs.

• Watson testified that there are adverse effects of setting his salary at $24,000 annually for the relevant years, including lesser 401(k) contributions and matching, and lower Social Security contributions.

- Watson testified that when he set his salary at $24,000, he was not concerned that he was doing anything improper with regard to the payment of employment taxes because: 1) the salary was set for a business purpose; and 2) because the partners were "vaguely familiar" with case law where S corporation and C corporation distributions were recharacterized, but did not believe such case law was applicable to LWBJ because of differing fact patterns.

- Watson, through DEWPC, received profit distributions from LWBJ totaling $203,651 for 2002. Specifically, Watson received profit distributions of $36,151 during the first quarter of 2002; $55,000 during the second quarter of 2002; $26,500 during the third quarter of 2002; and $86,000 during the fourth quarter of 2002.

- Watson, through DEWPC, received profit distributions from LWBJ totaling approximately $175,470, with payments totaling $43,867.50 in each of the four quarters of 2003.

- Watson is an experienced and successful Certified Public Accountant, and has advertised on the internet as having "significant experience in the taxation of S corporations."

- Watson has taught in Drake University's MBA program and keeps up on developments in the tax law.

- Watson is aware of IRS Circular 230, which provides that return preparers cannot take a position on a tax return unless there is a realistic possibility of the position being sustained on its merits.

- LWBJ routinely advises S corporations on taxation issues.

- Payment of a lower wage results in the payee owing less employment ("FICA") taxes.

- Watson has no documents reflecting conversations with other members of LWBJ regarding setting salaries, and no other members of LWBJ testified on the matter at trial.

- Watson and the other partners of LWBJ did not "research the tax issues" when they put the structure of LWBJ together.

- Watson testified that he and the other LWBJ partners did not raise their salaries to $48,000 in 2007 as a result of being audited on August 25, 2006, and did not consider factors identified in case law as relevant to setting salaries due to the different factual settings in the case law.

- Watson testified that when setting his salary, he did not look at what comparable business paid for similar services.

- Watson maintained at trial that the IRS has no authority whatsoever to reclassify dividends as wages in a situation where $12,000 or $5,000 in wages were paid, but agreed that a salary of a penny could be reclassified.

- Watson was not surprised to discover that he was paying himself less salary than that typically made by a recent college graduate in accounting.

- Watson testified that he would not hire himself out to someone else for $24,000 per year without having ownership in the business.
- Watson testified that he is aware that the IRS has taken a public position that S Corporation employees must be paid reasonable compensation, but does not believe that there is statutory authority to support the IRS's position that wages must be reasonable.

2. Igor Ostrovsky.

- Igor Ostrovsky is a general engineer[119] for the IRS, who offered testimony at trial regarding the fair market value of Watson's accounting services in 2002 and 2003.
- Ostrovsky holds bachelor of science degrees in electrical engineering and mathematics and a Masters of Business Administration with concentration in finance, all from the University of Minnesota.
- Ostrovsky has acted as an expert for the IRS in evaluating the reasonableness of taxpayer compensation on an estimated 20–30 cases.
- Ostrovsky has made presentations regarding issues of reasonable compensation in his role as an engineer with the IRS.
- Ostrovsky has testified three times in court on issues of reasonable compensation.
- Ostrovsky is a member of the National Association of Certified Valuation Analysts.
- Ostrovsky testified that he did not share his expert report with anyone at the IRS and that no one at the IRS attempted to influence his testimony in any way.
- Ostrovsky is competent to render an expert opinion regarding the fair market value of Watson's accounting services, and is qualified as an independent expert in the field of compensation, specializing in the fair market value of S corporations and other corporate entities, based on his experience training, and education.
- Ostrovsky's expert opinion is that for the years 2002 and 2003, the fair market value of Watson's accounting services to DEWPC and LWBJ were $91,044 per year.
- In reaching his opinion, Ostrovsky evaluated the financial performance of both Watson and LWBJ.
- Relying on the Risk Management Association ("RMA") annual statement studies Ostrovsky opined that DEWPC was "significantly more profitable than comparably sized firms, accounting firms, and they were as much as ten times more profitable than comparable firms," and that LWBJ was "at least three times more profitable than comparably sized firms in the[ ] accounting field."

---

119. [3] Ostrovsky testified that a general engineer for the IRS serves as a consultant on audits, and assists revenue agents in the valuation of businesses, depreciation, tangible and intangible assets, and reasonable compensation, amongst other things.

- Ostrovsky also found that the Leo Troy Almanac of Business and Industrial Financial Ratios, which contains tax return data on all C and S corporations, supports a conclusion that DEWPC was "considerably more profitable than its peers" and that LWBJ "was at least twice as profitable as [its] peers."

- Ostrovsky additionally looked at information relating to compensation for accountants in rendering his expert opinion.

- Relying on a survey published by the University of Iowa regarding starting salaries for new accounting graduates, Ostrovsky opined that Watson's salary of $24,000 was lower than: 1) the median reported starting salary for new graduates in 2002 ($40,000); 2) the median reported starting salary for new graduates in 2003 (just under $40,000); and 3) the minimum reported offer for an accounting graduate in 2002 ($26,000).

- Using compensation data from Robert Half International, a placement agency for individuals in accounting and finance, Ostrovsky determined that compensation for individuals in positions subordinate to that of Watson was significantly higher than the compensation Watson claimed in 2002 and 2003. In reaching this conclusion, Ostrovsky deemed Watson, an individual with approximately 20 years of accounting experience as akin to a director/manager, defined by the Half survey as a person with 11-plus years of experience. Persons in positions of lesser experience to that of the director/manager position had a range of compensation in 2002 from between the "middle sixties to almost $90,000." Ostrovsky made adjustments to account for region and education.

- Ostrovsky also relied on the portion of the Management of an Accounting Practice ("MAP") survey, conducted by the American Institute of Certified Public Accountants, relevant specifically to the Iowa Society of CPAs. The MAP survey indicated that an average "owner" (defined as both an investor in and an employee of a firm) in a firm the size of LWBJ would receive approximate $176,000 annually, reflecting both compensation and return on investment. A director (defined as solely an employee with no investment interest) would realize approximately $70,000 compensation annually.

- To properly determine a comparable salary for Watson, free of "return on investment," Ostrovsky evaluated billing rates for owners and directors and found that owners billed at a rate approximately 33% higher than did a director. Accordingly, Ostrovsky increased the director's estimated compensation by 33% to obtain an estimated comparable salary for someone in Watson's position of approximately $93,000. Ostrovsky then reduced this amount to $91,044 to account for certain untaxable fringe benefits.

- Ostrovsky believes his estimate, providing that reasonable compensation for Watson would have been approximately $91,044 for each of 2002 and 2003, to be an "extremely conservative determination."

- Ostrovsky concedes that part of the reason LWBJ appears more profitable than its comparators is because it pays lower salaries. Ostrovsky did not evaluate how

LWBJ or DEWPC's profitability would look after the recharacterization of dividends as wages.

- Ostrovsky's opinion changed over time as he became aware of more facts regarding Watson's engagement with DEWPC and LWBJ following Watson's deposition, and as he identified some errors in his initial calculations.

- Ostrovsky's opinion is based on analyzing Watson as a de facto partner in LWBJ, not based on his status in relation to the smaller DEWPC.

- Ostrovsky's opinion of the fair market value of Watson's services was based on an average billing rate, rather than on Watson's actual billing rate.

3. Daniel Olson.

- Daniel Olson testified via deposition designations.

- Olson testified that the amount of compensation properly paid to Watson would be determined the same regardless of whether DEWPC had S or C corporation status.

- Olson testified that the United States does not take the position that any special rules are applicable to DEWPC or to Watson, or that there is any tax, statute, regulation, or other rule that would require DEWPC to pay Watson any minimum amount of compensation.

- Olson testified that the sole basis for Defendant's position that portions of the 2002 and 2003 dividend payments to Watson should be recharacterized as wages is Defendant's belief that DEWPC paid Watson an unreasonably low salary.

- Olson testified that the Defendant does not contend that DEWPC failed to properly authorize loans or dividend payments to Watson.

- Olson testified that the Defendant does not contend that there is any minimum amount of compensation that DEWPC must pay Watson before it can pay him dividends; rather, Defendant contends only that FICA taxes be paid on the fair value of services provided by Watson to DEWPC.

- Olson testified that the Defendant believes the primary reason for setting Watson's salary at $24,000 was to minimize Social Security tax.

- Olson testified that, in reaching its determination, the Defendant "didn't look to intent. We looked to the fair value of the services provided by the shareholder employee to determine the amounts that were subject to Social Security tax."

- Olson testified that setting Watson's salary low could have had a negative impact on his later entitlement to Social Security benefits.

III. LEGAL CONCLUSIONS

The Federal Insurance Contributions Act ("FICA") imposes "on every employer an excise tax, with respect to having individuals in his employ, equal to [a certain] percentage[] of the wages paid by him with respect to employment." 26 U.S.C.

§ 3111(a). The term "wages" is defined broadly by FICA as "all remuneration for employment."[120] 26 U.S.C. § 3121(a). Thus, an employer, such as DEWPC, is required to pay FICA tax on all wages paid to its employees. *See HB & R, Inc. v. U.S.*, 229 F.3d 688, 690 (8th Cir.2000). An employer is not, however, obligated to pay FICA tax on "other types of employee income, such as dividends." *Id.* There is no dispute in this case that Watson was an employee of DEWPC. There is, likewise, no dispute that if the funds paid to Watson are properly characterized as dividends, DEWPC need not pay FICA taxes on them, but that if the funds are properly recharacterized as wages, DEWPC would be required to pay FICA tax.

The IRS assessments against DEWPC are "entitled to a legal presumption of correctness." *U.S. v. Fior D'Italia, Inc.*, 536 U.S. 238, 242 (2002). Thus, DEWPC bears the burden to prove by a preponderance of the evidence that the IRS tax assessments are incorrect, as well as to prove what the correct assessments should be. *See Armstrong v. U.S.*, 366 F.3d 622, 625–26 (8th Cir.2004) (citing *IA 80 Group, Inc. v. U.S.*, 347 F.3d 1067, 1071 (8th Cir.2003)); *Mattingly v. U.S.*, 924 F.2d 785, 787 (8th Cir.1991). DEWPC additionally bears the burden of proving that the wages paid to Watson were reasonable. *RTS Inv. Corp. v. Comm'r*, 877 F.2d 647, 650 (8th Cir.1989) ("The determination of what is reasonable compensation is a question of fact.... The burden of proving reasonableness of compensation is on the taxpayer."). The fact that the United States is defending this suit using a different methodology than the one it used in making its initial assessment against DEWPC is of little import, and does not change the Court's analysis. *See Blansett v. U.S.*, 283 F.2d 474, 478 (8th Cir.1960) ("[A] deficiency assessment may be sustained upon any legal ground supporting it, even though the Commissioner did not rely thereon when the assessment was made. If the assessment is right on any theory it must be sustained." (citing *Helvering v. Gowran*, 302 U.S. 238 (1937)).

DEWPC contends that it unquestionably intended to pay Watson compensation of $24,000 per year, and that amounts distributed to Watson in excess of that amount are properly classified as dividends and/or loans. DEWPC points out that the United States has stipulated that it does not have the authority to require DEWPC to pay Watson any particular minimum salary before it can pay dividends to Watson. According to DEWPC, the United States' ability to assess additional employment taxes is limited to taxing payments which were intended to be compensatory in nature. Thus, DEWPC maintains, as it did at summary judgment, that it is the intent of DEWPC that controls whether funds paid to Watson are categorized as wages or as dividends. DEWPC claims its intent is evidenced by Watson's testimony and trial evidence showing that DEWPC opted to pay Watson $24,000 annually for "legitimate business reasons, and not for the purposes of reducing [DEWPC's] employment tax liability, and therefore, [DEWPC] and Watson's classification of the distributions to

---

120. [4] The definition of "wages" contains numerous exceptions, none of which are applicable in the present case. See 26 U.S.C. § 3121(a)(1)-(23).

Watson in excess of $24,000.00 per year as dividends should not be ignored." Pl.'s Proposed Findings of Fact & Conclusions of Law (hereinafter Pl.'s Br.) at 6.

As it did at summary judgment, DEWPC cites *Electric & Neon, Inc. v. Comm'r*, 56 T.C. 1324 (1971), *Paula Construction Co. v. Comm'r*, 58 T.C. 1055 (1972), and *Pediatric Surgical Associates, P.C. v. Comm'r*, T.C. Memo 2001-81 (Apr. 2, 2001), in support of its position. After evaluating each of those cases in its summary judgment order, the Court determined that the cases were inapposite, because in each of those cases, "the taxpayer was attempting to recharacterize funds, whereas in the present case, it is the Government that is attempting to recharacterize the funds." The Court noted that the distinction was discussed in the 1993 edition of the *Akron Tax Journal*:

> The courts and the Service seem to have adopted a double standard. In the context of taxpayer attempts at recharacterization, "intent" has dominated the decisions. But the courts have found intent irrelevant where the Service is arguing for recharacterization. This outcome may be justified to the extent the taxpayer is distorting the actual character of payments received from the corporation for tax advantage.

(quoting Harrington, Kirsten, *Employment Taxes: What Can the Small Businessman Do?* 10 Akron Tax J. 61, 69 (1993)). The Court further stated that the incentive for S corporations to distort the actual character of payments to its shareholders/employees to obtain a tax advantage had been recently articulated by Judge Richard A. Posner:

> The distinction between accounting profits, losses, assets, and liabilities, on the one hand and cash flow on the other is especially important when one is dealing with either a firm undergoing reorganization in bankruptcy or a small privately held firm; in the latter case, in order to avoid double taxation (corporate income tax plus personal income tax on dividends), the company might try to make its profits disappear into officers' salaries. *See Menard, Inc. v. Comm'r*, 560 F.3d 620, 621 (7th Cir.2009). The owners of a Subchapter S corporation, however, have the oppositive incentive—to alchemize salary into earnings. A corporation has to pay employment taxes, such as state unemployment insurance tax and social security tax, on the salaries it pays. A Subchapter S corporation can avoid paying them by recharacterizing salary as a distribution of corporation income.

(quoting *Constr. & Design Co. v. United States Citizenship & Immigration Servs.*, 563 F.3d 593, 595–96 (7th Cir.2009)).

The Court reaffirms the analysis it undertook in evaluating DEWPC's motion for summary judgment. DEWPC's assertion that its own intent controls the characterization of funds paid to Watson is only minimally supported by the case law it cites, and is undermined by relevant IRS rulings and case law that are more in line with the facts of this case than *Electric & Neon, Paula,* or *Pediatric Surgical Associates, P.C.* First, in a 1974 Revenue Ruling, two sole shareholders of a corporation sought advice on whether they would incur liability for employment taxes on facts similar to the present case. Rev. Rul. 74-44, 1974-1 C.B. 287. The shareholders "performed services for the corporation. However, to avoid the payment of Federal employment taxes, they drew no salary from the corporation but arranged for the corporation to pay them "dividends" [in an amount equal to] the amount they would have otherwise received as reasonable compensation for services performed." *Id.* The IRS stated that the dividends "were reasonable compensation for services" performed by the shareholders "rather than a distribution of the corporation's earnings and profits." *Id.* Accordingly, the dividends would properly be characterized as "wages" for which "liability was incurred for the taxes imposed by [FICA and other federal employment taxes]." *Id.* This conclusion comports with an earlier Revenue Ruling stating:

> Neither the election by the corporation as to the manner in which it will be taxed for Federal income tax purposes nor the consent thereto by the stockholder-officers has any effect in determining whether they are employees or whether payments made to them are "wages" for Federal employment tax purposes.

Rev. Rul. 73-361, 1973-2 C.B. 331.

Of the relevant case law, the Court finds *Joseph Radtke, S.C. v. U.S.* and *Spicer Accounting, Inc. v. U.S.* particularly persuasive. In *Joseph Radtke, S.C.,* the district court determined that certain funds designated as dividends were actually compensation for which an S corporation owed employment taxes. 712 F. Supp. 143 (E.D. Wis.1989). Radtke, a Wisconsin attorney, had created an S corporation to provide legal services in Milwaukee. *Id.* at 144. Radtke was the firm's sole director, shareholder, and full-time employee, but he took no salary, receiving instead $18,225 in dividend payments from the corporation in 1982. *Id.* Since Radtke received the funds as dividends, rather than as wages, the corporation did not pay employment taxes on them. *Id.* The IRS recharacterized the funds as wages and assessed FICA and other employment taxes on them, along with penalties and interest. *Id.* at 145. In concluding that the funds were properly recharacterized as wages rather than dividends, the district court stated:

> I am not moved by the Radtke corporation's connected argument that "dividends" cannot be "wages." Courts reviewing tax questions are obligated to look at the substance, not the form, of the transactions at issue. *Frank Lyon Co. v. U.S.,* 435 U.S. 561, 573 (1978). Transactions between a closely held corporation and its principals, who may have multiple relationships with the corporation, are subject to particularly careful scrutiny. *Tulia Feedlot, Inc. v. U.S.,* 513 F.2d 800, 805 (5th Cir.1975). Whether dividends represent a distribution of profits or instead are compensation for employment is a matter to be determined in view of all the evidence. *Cf. Logan Lumber Co. v. Comm'r,* 365 F.2d 846, 851 (5th Cir.1966) (examining whether dividends were paid in guise of salaries).
>
> In the circumstances of this case—where the corporation's only director had the corporation pay himself, the only significant employee, no salary for substantial services—I believe that Mr. Radtke's "dividends" were in fact

"wages" subject to FICA and FUTA taxation. His "dividends" functioned as remuneration for employment....

An employer should not be permitted to evade FICA and FUTA by characterizing all of an employee's remuneration as something other than "wages." *Cf. Greenlee v. U.S.*, 661 F.Supp 642 (D. Colo. 1985) (corporation's interest-free loans to sole shareholder constituted "wages" for FICA and FUTA where loans were made at shareholder's discretion and he performed substantial services for corporation). This is simply the flip side of those instances in which corporations attempt to disguise profit distributions as salaries for whatever tax benefits that may produce.

Id. at 146. Radtke appealed the district court's decision to the Seventh Circuit, which framed the issue as, "whether, based on the statutes and unusual facts involved, the payments at issue were made to Mr. Radtke as remuneration for services performed." *Joseph Radtke, S.C. v. U.S.*, 895 F.2d 1196, 1197 (7th Cir.1990). "As the district judge determined, these payments were clearly remuneration for services performed by Radtke and therefore fall within the statutory and regulatory definitions of wages." *Id.*

Relying on Radtke and the Revenue Rulings cited supra, the Ninth Circuit also determined, in a case remarkably similar to the one at bar, that payments designated as dividends can properly be recharacterized by the IRS as wages subject to federal employment taxes. *See Spicer Accounting, Inc. v. U.S.*, 918 F.2d 90 (9th Cir.1990). Spicer, a licensed public accountant, was the president, treasurer, and director of an S Corporation, Spicer Accounting, Inc. *Id.* at 91. Spicer and his wife were the only stockholders in the corporation, and Spicer performed substantial services for the corporation. *Id.* at 91–92. Spicer had an arrangement with the corporation whereby he would "donate his services to the corporation" and "withdraw earnings in the form of dividends." *Id.* at 91. For tax years 1981 and 1982, the IRS recharacterized dividend payments to Spicer by the corporation as wages, and assessed taxes, penalties, and interest against the corporation for unpaid employment taxes. *Id.* The Ninth Circuit affirmed the characterization of payments to Spicer as wages, emphasizing that it is the substance rather than the form of the transaction that matters, and noting that "salary arrangements between closely held corporations and its shareholders warrant close scrutiny." *Id.* at 92. Citing to *Radtke*, the *Spicer* court found that, "regardless of how an employer chooses to characterize payments made to its employees, the true analysis is whether the payments are for remunerations for services rendered." *Id.* at 93. According, "Mr. Spicer's intention of receiving the payments as dividends has no bearing on the tax treatment of these wages." *Id.*

Other courts have reached conclusions similar to those in *Radtke* and *Spicer*. For instance, in *Veterinary Surgical Consultants v. Comm'r*, the United States Tax Court rejected a petitioner's argument that amounts paid to its sole shareholder were distributions of corporate net income rather than wages. 117 T.C. 141, 145 (2001).

Dr. Sadanaga performed substantial services on behalf of petitioner [the S corporation]. The characterization of the payment to Dr. Sadanaga as a distribution of petitioner's net income is but a subterfuge for reality; the payment constituted remuneration for services performed by Dr. Sadanaga on behalf of petitioner. An employer cannot avoid Federal employment taxes by characterizing compensation paid to its sole director and shareholder as distributions of the corporation's net income, rather than wages. Regardless of how an employer chooses to characterize payments made to its employees, the true analysis is whether the payments represent remunerations for services rendered.

Id. at 145–46. Likewise, in *JD & Associates, Ltd. v. U.S.*, Jeffrey Dahl, the sole shareholder, officer, and director of the plaintiff S corporation, received an annual salary of $19,000.00 in 1997 and $30,000.00 for each of 1998 and 1999. No. 3:04-cv-59, at 4 (D.N.D. May 19, 2006) (available in Def.'s App. to Summ. J. at 146–56). Dahl also received dividends of $47,000 for 1997, $50,000 for 1998, and $50,000 for 1999. *Id.* at 5. As in the present case, the IRS determined that Dahl's salary was unreasonably low, and assessed employment taxes, interest, and penalties against the corporation after recharacterizing portions of the dividend payments as wages to Dahl. *Id.* at 1. Applying an Eighth Circuit test to determine whether Dahl's compensation was reasonable, the district court concluded it was not and upheld the tax assessments against the corporation. *Id.* at 9–11.

Upon review of the law, the Court holds that the characterization of funds disbursed by an S corporation to its employees or shareholders turns on an analysis of whether the "payments at issue were made ... as remuneration for services performed." *Radtke*, 895 F.2d at 1197. This approach conforms with well settled jurisprudence holding that tax consequences are governed by the economic realities of a transaction, not by the form of the transaction or labels given it by the parties. *See, e.g., Boulware v. U.S.*, 552 U.S. 421, 430 (2008) ("The colorful behavior described in the allegations requires a reminder that tax classifications like "dividend" and "return of capital" turn on "the objective economic realities of a transaction rather than ... the particular form the parties employed."") (quoting *Frank Lyon*, 435 U.S. at 573); *Pinson v. Comm'r*, T.C. Memo 2000-208 (July 6, 2000) ("As a general rule, the substance of a transaction controls tax treatment." (citing *Gregory v. Helvering*, 293 U.S. 465, 469–70 (1935)); *True v. U.S.*, 190 F.3d 1165, 1173–74 (10th Cir.1999) (stating that "substance over form" is a "fundamental tax principle [that] operates to prevent the "true nature of a transaction from being disguised by mere formalisms, which exist solely to alter tax liabilities"" (quoting *Comm'r v. Court Holding Co.*, 324 U.S. 331 (1945)); *Leisure Dynamics, Inc. v. Comm'r*, 494 F.2d 1340, 1345 (8th Cir.1974) ("For tax purposes, we must concern ourselves with actualities rather than the refinements of title; our concern is with the substance, not form."). Thus, a determination of whether funds are "remuneration for services performed," must be made "in view of all the evidence." *Radtke*, 712 F.Supp. at 145. While intent is unquestionably a consideration in the analysis, it is by no means the only one. Other relevant considerations include, but are not limited to: 1) the employee's qualifications; 2) the nature, extent and scope of the employee's work; 3) the size and complexities of the business; 4) a comparison of salaries paid with the gross income and the net income; 5) the prevailing general economic conditions; 6) comparison of salaries with distributions to stockholders; 7) the prevailing rates of compensation for comparable positions in comparable concerns; 8) the salary policy of the taxpayer as to all employees; and 9) in the case of small corporations with a limited number of officers the amount of compensation paid to the particular employee in previous years. *See Charles Schneider & Co., Inc. v. Comm'r* 500 F.2d 148, 152 (8th Cir.1974) (identifying factors to be considered in determining the "reasonableness of compensation").

After considering the trial testimony, and all exhibits and evidence in this case, the Court finds Watson's assertion that DEWPC "intended" to pay Watson a mere $24,000 in compensation for the tax years 2002 and 2003 to be less than credible. Indeed, the Court is convinced upon the entire record that substantial portions of the distributions from LWBJ to DEWPC, and in turn to Watson were, in fact, "remuneration for services performed." Watson is an exceedingly qualified accountant, with both bachelor's and advanced degrees and with approximately 20 years experience in accounting and taxation. He worked approximately 35 to 45 hours per week as one of the primary earners in a reputable and well-established firm, which had earnings well in excess of comparable firms, with over $2 million in gross revenues for 2002 and nearly $3 million in gross revenues for 2003. Tr. at 30, 68, 78; Exs. 12– 13. A reasonable person in Watson's role within LWBJ would unquestionably be expected to earn far more than a $24,000 salary for his services. As such, the $24,000 salary Watson opted to pay himself as DEWPC's sole shareholder, officer, and employee, is incongruent with the financial position of LWBJ and in light of Watson's experience and contributions to LWBJ, and when compared to the approximately $200,000 in distributions DEWPC received in each of 2002 and 2003. Moreover, the $24,000 salary is low when compared to salaries that could reasonably be expected to be earned by persons with experience similar to that of Watson, and holding a position such as Watson held in a firm comparable to LWBJ. Indeed, upon evaluation of all of the facts and circumstances in this case, the Court is convinced that DEWPC structured Watson's salary and dividend payments in an effort to avoid federal employment taxes, with full knowledge that dividends paid to Watson were actually "remuneration for services performed." *See, e.g., Tool Producers, Inc. v. Comm'r*, 97 F.3d 1452 (6th Cir. 1996) (unpublished opinion) ("In determining the intent behind a corporate distribution, we have held that a court should 'look not to mere labels or to the self-serving declarations of the parties, but to more reliable criteria of the circumstances surrounding the transaction.'" (quoting *Jaques v. Comm'r*, 935 F.2d 104, 107 (6th Cir.1991)); *Electric & Neon*, 56 T.C. at 1340 (finding that a corporation may deduct the amount of compensation that it pays so long as it "actually intended" to pay the relevant funds as compensation, but noting that "whether such intent has been shown is, of course, a factual question to be decided on the basis of the particular facts and circumstances of the case"); *Paula*, 58 T.C. at 1058–59 ("It is now settled law that only if payment is made with the intent to compensate is it deductible as compensation. Whether such intent has been demonstrated is a factual question to be decided on the basis of the particular facts and circumstances of the case." (internal citations omitted)).

The Court further finds the testimony of Igor Ostrovsky to be abundantly reasonable and credible. Ostrovsky's calculations, though they changed somewhat over time due to his receipt of additional information, are amply supported in their methodology and reach a well-reasoned conclusion as to what constitutes a "reasonable" salary for Watson under the facts and circumstances of this case. Accordingly, the Court adopts Ostrovsky's calculations and finds that, for each of the years 2002 and 2003, the reasonable amount of Watson's "remuneration for services performed" was $91,044. This amount is $67,044 more than the $24,000 annual salary paid by DEWPC to Watson, and DEWPC, accordingly, is obligated to pay the appropriate FICA taxes, interest, and penalties on the recharacterized amounts.

Having established that DEWPC owes FICA taxes, penalties and interest on an additional $67,044 for each of the tax years 2002 and 2003, there remains one additional issue. Specifically, since taxes are imposed on a quarterly, rather than on an annual, basis, there still exists the question of whether the $67,044 should be imposed as wages ratably throughout each of the two years. DEWPC argues that, based on the Government's initial assessments, the amount of compensation would all be taxable only in the first two quarters of each tax year, with the remainder of funds paid to Watson comprising distributions only in the third and fourth quarters. According to Plaintiff's calculations, this would result in DEWPC only owing employment taxes, interest and penalties for recharacterized wages in the first two quarter of each tax year, meaning that DEWPC should succeed on its claim for a refund for the fourth quarter of 2002. The Court disagrees. An evaluation of the record demonstrates that Watson was paid his allotted $24,000 salary in equal installments throughout the course of each tax year, with payments occurring in each of the four quarters of 2002 and 2003. The designated "distribution" payments were also made in installments throughout the year, with payments occurring in each of the four quarters of 2002 and 2003. Plaintiff offers no legal support for the proposition it would now have the Court adopt, i.e., that Watson received all his remuneration for services rendered in the first two quarters of each tax year. Indeed, had Watson's "salary" been set at $91,044 to begin with, he undoubtedly would have received such salary in ratable installments throughout each year, as virtually all salaried employees do. Accordingly, the Court finds that, unless the parties agree otherwise, the additional $67,044 in compensation should be applied ratably throughout each of the two years, with $16,761 in additional compensation attributed to each of the eight quarters of 2002 and 2003.

IV. CONCLUSION

For the reasons stated herein, the Court concludes that Plaintiff's $24,000 salary in 2002 and 2003 was unreasonable. The Government's recharacterization of $67,044 in dividend payments to Watson for each of the tax years 2002 and 2003 is amply supported by the evidence, as an annual salary of $91,044 for Watson is reasonable on the specific facts and circumstances of this case. Accordingly, DEWPC fails on its claim for refund of all taxes paid for the fourth quarter of 2002,[121] and the United States has prevailed on its counterclaim that DEWPC owes additional employment taxes, penalties and interest on a $91,044 salary for Watson for 2002 and 2003. The parties shall submit a joint proposed judgment, with final calculations of employment taxes, interest and penalties owed, based on the Court's findings of facts and conclusions of law within thirty days of the date of this Order.

Revenue Procedure 93-27

1993-2 C.B. 343

SECTION 1. PURPOSE

This revenue procedure provides guidance on the treatment of the receipt of a partnership profits interest for services provided to or for the benefit of the partnership.

SEC. 2. DEFINITIONS

The following definitions apply for purposes of this revenue procedure.

.01 A capital interest is an interest that would give the holder a share of the proceeds if the partnership's assets were sold at fair market value and then the proceeds were distributed in a complete liquidation of the partnership. This determination generally is made at the time of receipt of the partnership interest.

.02 A profits interest is a partnership interest other than a capital interest.

SEC. 3. BACKGROUND

Under section 1.721-1(b)(1) of the Income Tax Regulations, the receipt of a partnership capital interest for services provided to or for the benefit of the partnership is taxable as compensation. On the other hand, the issue of whether the receipt of a partnership profits interest for services is taxable has been the subject of litigation. Most recently, in *Campbell v. Commissioner*, 943 F.2d 815 (8th Cir. 1991), the Eighth Circuit in dictum suggested that the taxpayer's receipt of a partnership profits interest received for services was not taxable, but decided the case on valuation. Other courts have determined that in certain circumstances the receipt of a partnership profits interest for services is a taxable event under section 83 of the Internal Revenue Code. *See, e.g., Campbell v. Comm'r*, T.C.M. 1990-236, *rev'd*, 943 F.2d 815 (8th Cir. 1991); *St. John v. U.S.*, No. 82-1134 (C.D. Ill. Nov. 16, 1983). The courts have also found that typically the profits interest received has speculative or no determinable value at the time of receipt. *See Campbell*, 943 F.2d at 823; *St. John*. In *Diamond v. Comm'r*, 56 T.C. 530 (1971), *aff'd*, 492 F.2d 286 (7th Cir. 1974), however, the court assumed that the interest received by the taxpayer was a partnership profits interest and found the value of the interest was readily determinable. In that case, the interest was sold soon after receipt.

---

121. [6] The Court notes that, depending on the final tax calculations, DEWPC may be entitled to a partial refund of tax payments made for the fourth quarter of 2002. This is because the Government initially recharacterized more of the dividends as wages, and the assessments were issued on these higher amounts. Ultimately, however, since DEWPC will owe additional sums for the other seven quarters of 2002 and 2003, any potential refund would be offset by additional amounts owed.

SEC. 4. APPLICATION

.01 Other than as provided below, if a person receives a profits interest for the provision of services to or for the benefit of a partnership in a partner capacity or in anticipation of being a partner, the Internal Revenue Service will not treat the receipt of such an interest as a taxable event for the partner or the partnership.

.02 This revenue procedure does not apply:

(1) If the profits interest relates to a substantially certain and predictable stream of income from partnership assets, such as income from high-quality debt securities or a high-quality net lease;

(2) If within two years of receipt, the partner disposes of the profits interest; or

(3) If the profits interest is a limited partnership interest in a "publicly traded partnership" within the meaning of section 7704(b) of the Internal Revenue Code.

Revenue Ruling 69-184

1969-1 C.B. 256

Bona fide members of a partnership are not employees of the partnership within the meaning of the Federal Insurance Contributions Act, the Federal Unemployment Tax Act, and the Collection of Income Tax at Source on Wages (chapters 21, 23, and 24, respectively, subtitle C, Internal Revenue Code of 1954). Such a partner who devotes his time and energies in the conduct of the trade or business of the partnership, or in providing services to the partnership as an independent contractor, is, in either event, a self-employed individual rather than an individual who, under the usual common law rules applicable in determining the employer-employee relationship, has the status of an employee. Sections 1402(a) and 3121(d)(2) of the Code.

Remuneration received by a partner from the partnership is not "wages" with respect to "employment" and therefore is not subject to the taxes imposed by the Federal Insurance Contributions Act and the Federal Unemployment Tax Act. Such remuneration also is not subject to Federal income tax withholding.

Revenue Ruling 59-221

1959-1 C.B. 225

Advice has been requested whether the undistributed taxable income required to be included in the gross income of shareholders of a small business corporation which has made an election pursuant to subchapter S of the Internal Revenue Code of 1954 not to be subject to Federal income tax, constitutes net earnings from self-employment to the shareholders for purposes of the tax imposed under the Self-Employment Contributions Act of 1954 (chapter 2, subtitle A, Internal Revenue Code of 1954.)

Section 64 of the Technical Amendments Act of 1958, Public Law 85-866, 72 Stat. 1606, at 1650, added subchapter S to chapter 1 of the Internal Revenue Code of 1954, effective for taxable years beginning after December 31, 1957. This subchapter contains sections 1371–1377 of the Code which pertain to the election of certain small business corporations as to taxable status.

Section 1372 of this subchapter provides, in effect, that any small business corporation, as defined in section 1371, may elect not to be subject to the income tax imposed by chapter 1 of the Code.

Section 1373 of the Code provides that each person who is a shareholder of an electing small business corporation on the last day of a taxable year of such corporation shall include in his gross income, for his taxable year in which or with which the taxable year of the corporation ends, the amount he would have received as a dividend, if on such last day there had been distributed pro rata to its shareholders by such corporation an amount equal to the corporation's undistributed taxable income for its taxable year. This section provides further that an amount so included in a shareholder's income shall be treated as an amount distributed as a dividend on the last day of the taxable year of the corporation.

Section 1402 of the Self-Employment Contributions Act of 1954 (chapter 2, subtitle A, Internal Revenue Code of 1954) provides in part as follows:

> (a).... The term "net earnings from self-employment" means the gross income derived by an individual from any trade or business carried on by such individual, less the deductions allowed by this subtitle [subtitle A] which are attributable to such trade or business, plus his distributive share (whether or not distributed) of income or loss described in section 702(a)(9) from any trade or business carried on by a partnership of which he is a member;....

> (c) The term "trade or business," when used with reference to self-employment income or net earnings from self-employment, shall have the same meaning as when used in section 162....

From the above-defined terms it is apparent that income not resulting from the conduct of a trade or business by an individual or by a partnership of which he is a member is not includible in computing the individual's net earnings from self-employment. Amounts which must be taken into account in computing a shareholder's income tax by reason of the provisions of section 1373 of the Code, are not derived from a trade or business carried on by such shareholder. Neither the election by a corporation as to the manner in which it will be taxed for Federal income tax purpose nor the consent thereto by the persons who are shareholders results in the consenting shareholder's being engaged in carrying on the corporation's trade or business. Accordingly, amounts which a shareholder is required to include in his gross income by reason of the provisions of section 1373 of the Code should not be included in computing his net earnings from self-employment for Self-Employment Contributions Act purposes.

Chapter 5

Financial Aspects of Real Estate Development

I. Commentary

Real-estate developers and investors must decide how to finance the acquisition and possible development of property. The decision regarding the appropriate form of financing will require legal advice. Attorneys must be prepared to help property owners understand the legal and tax differences between debt and equity. They must be prepared to prepare the necessary documents for either type of financing.

Attorneys generally do not give advice regarding financial aspects of an investment, but they should have general familiarity with finance principles to understand the property owners' objectives and the feasibility of a project. They also must know how taxes affect financial calculations. Such knowledge will help the attorney know what legal advice will be relevant to the property owners. Understanding the feasibility of a project will also help the attorney know whether the project is large enough to support the legal fees the attorney will charge to provide advice with respect to a project.

A. Legal Attributes of Debt and Equity

The line between debt and equity is not always clear, but the two general types of financing have traditional characteristics. The contracts entered into between the parties to a financing arrangement will establish the parties' rights and obligations. The parties' rights and obligations determine whether an arrangement is debt or equity. Owners of debt generally have a right to receive a fixed rate of interest on the amount they lend. The terms of the loan also generally provide that the borrower will repay the principal according to a fixed schedule or at a specified future date. The lender may take a security interest in a specific piece of property or all of the assets of the borrower. If the lender takes a security interest in a piece of property, the lender may impose restrictions on the transferability of the property, but the lender generally does not participate in the management of the property. Holders of debt also have priority in liquidation of an entity.

The two general types of debt are recourse debt and nonrecourse debt. A debt is recourse if the lender can proceed against all of the assets of the borrower if the borrower defaults. A debt is nonrecourse if the lender can only proceed against a specific piece of collateral if the borrower defaults. The distinction can be very important when considering the tax consequences of debt-financed transactions.[1] The way to test whether a loan is recourse or nonrecourse is to consider the rights a lender would have if the borrower were to default on the loan.

Owners of equity generally participate in the profit of a company and have a vote. Thus, instead of receiving a fixed rate of interest on an investment, the owners of equity receive dividends (if the arrangement is a corporation) or shares of profit (if the arrangement is a partnership or limited liability company) based upon the entity's performance. Some forms of equity may provide the holder with preferred distributions, if funds are available to make distributions. Generally, equity holders do not have a right to repayment of their contribution at a fixed time. Equity holders generally receive stock or some other form of ownership interest in the entity that provides them a vote or other rights in the management of the borrower. Owners of equity have residual claims to an entity's assets, i.e., they are paid upon liquidation only after creditors get paid. Distinguishing between debt and equity can be very difficult in some instances. These general guidelines would be insufficient in such situations, and an attorney would have to become familiar with the law governing the definitions of debt and equity to confidently opine about some financing arrangements.

B. Tax Attributes of Debt and Equity

The fundamental tax difference between debt and equity is the entity that makes interest payments on debt may deduct the amount paid, whereas it may not deduct payments made with respect to equity. That distinction is very important if the entity is a C corporation. If the entity is a tax partnership or S corporation, the distinction may be less important, but the distinction can still be relevant. In such flow-through tax entities, the distinction may affect the amount of income and deductions that are allocated to the members.[2] Whether a finance arrangement is debt or equity for tax purposes is not always obvious based upon the multiple-factor tests used by courts,[3] and attorneys must carefully craft finance documents to ensure the financing arrangement reflects the parties' intent.

C. Basic Finance Principles

Potential tax savings are only one factor that property owners must consider when planning a particular transaction. Some property owners are so intent upon mini-

---

1. *See, e.g.,* I.R.C. §§ 705, 722, 731, 752, and Treas. Reg. §§ 1.752-1 through -3 (describing the effect changes in partnership liabilities have on the partners).

2. *See* I.R.C. §§ 707(a) (providing that certain transactions with partners are to be treated as transactions with non-partners for tax purposes), 1366 (describing the pass through of S corporation tax items to shareholders).

3. *See, e.g.,* Slappey Drive Industrial Park v. United States, 561 F.2d 572 (5th Cir. 1977). Several commentators have discussed the federal tax distinction between debt and equity. *See, e.g.,* Thomas D. Greenaway & Michelle L. Marion, *A Simpler Debt-Equity Test,* 66 Tax Law. 73 (2013). William T. Plumb, *The Federal Income Tax Significance of Corporate Debt: A Critical Analysis and a Proposal,* 26 Tax L. Rev. 369 (1971).

mizing their tax liability that they may forget that the tax tail should not wag the business dog. The most favorable tax treatment may not correspond with the most favorable business deal. Property owners and their attorneys must remember the distinction between the business arrangement and tax planning. Nonetheless, tax issues permeate most aspects of real estate transactions, and competent tax planning and advice can help improve the profitability of a real-estate transaction and inform decisions property owners must make. The tax aspects of a transaction are also relevant to the financial analysis of the transaction. Property owners or their accountants will generally do the financial analysis of a property, but attorneys should have a basic understanding of concepts that are important to the property owners and be prepared to discuss how tax issues may affect financial analyses.

Individual investors often will not focus on the full value of the property if they are partners in a real estate venture or if the venture is debt-financed. Instead, individual investors will focus on amounts they invest individually in property and consider the return on their individual investments. For example, if an investor borrows $800,000 and pays $200,000 to acquire a $1,000,000 property, the investor will focus on the return on the $200,000, not the entire $1,000,000. The lender will focus on the return on the $800,000. The investor's focus is very important when analyzing the economic performance of an investment.

Parties' Foci

Amount of loan (bank's focus)	$800,000
Owners' investment (investor's focus)	$200,000
Purchase price	$1,000,000

Simple facts help illustrate the investor's focus. Assume the investor who invested $200,000 and borrowed $800,000 later sells the property for $1,200,000. The investor will have to use $800,000 of that $1,200,000 to repay the outstanding balance of the loan.[4] That will leave the investor with $400,000. The investor invested $200,000 in the property and now has $400,000, so the investor's return is $200,000. That is 100% of the investor's original investment.[5] That far exceeds the return on the total invested by the investor and the lender. The total investment was $1,000,000, and the $200,000 return is only 20% of that total. The loan thus helps the investor leverage the original $200,000 investment and realize a potentially significant return.

---

4. The investor will also pay interest on the loan. This example disregards interest payments to simplify the illustration of the investor's general financial analysis. The example below incorporates interest payments into the analysis.

5. The return is merely a percent of the amount invested. It is the dollar amount of the return on investment divided by the amount invested multiplied by 100. The dollar amount of the return on investment was $200,000 and the amount invested was $200,000. Dividing $200,000 by $200,000 returns one, which, multiplied by 100, is 100%.

Use of Sales Proceeds

Total sales proceeds	$1,200,000
Loan repayment	($800,000)
Balance to investor	$400,000

Dollar Return on Investment

Balance received on sale	$400,000
Amount invested	($200,000)
Dollar return on investment	$200,000

Basic Return on Investment

$200,000 (dollar return on investment) ÷ $200,000 (amount invested) = 100%

That simple example illustrates the concept of leveraging an investment and the general manner in which investors measure their return on investment. The actual computation of the return on investment can, however, be quite complicated. To accurately compute the return on an investment, investors must (1) account for costs, such as the after-tax cost of interest paid on the loan and tax liability; (2) consider the extent to which taxable gain affects the return; (3) realize that the passage of time affects the rate of return on investment; and (4), if the property is depreciable, consider the effect depreciation deductions have on the return. After considering each of these points in turn, consider how they all work together to help determine the investor's return.

Undoubtedly, the lender will require the investors to pay interest on the $800,000 loan. Assume the interest is a simple annual rate of 6% and that the interest is due at the end of each year and the principal is due in 10 years or, if earlier, on the date the investors dispose of the property.[6] Investors often can deduct the amount of

---

6. Loan terms can, of course, vary significantly from loan to loan and transaction to transaction. In this example, the loan has simple interest. The loan agreement could, however, provide for compound interest, which means that the borrower would pay interest on interest that accrues between interest payments. For instance, a loan could provide for annual interest payments with 6% interest compounding semiannually. If that were the case, the interest computation would divide into two parts. The first part would be interest for the first half of the year, which would be 3% of the $800,000 loan balance, or $24,000. That amount would then be subject to interest for the second half of the year. Thus, the interest for the second half of the year would 3% of the $800,000 loan balance and the $24,000 of interest for the first half of the year, or $24,720. The parties can set the interest to compound more frequently or set the payments to occur at different intervals of time. Attorneys must be aware of the concepts associated with interest to help ensure that the loan documents accurately reflect the parties' understanding of the transaction. The discussion of net present value in this chapter illustrates the effect of compound interest.

In this simplified example, the principal is due in one installment. Loans can also provide for regular payments that include principal and interest. Most people use such loans to purchase automobiles or homes. The interest portion of installment payments is based upon the outstanding principal balance at the time of the installment payment. The portion of the installment payment that is not interest reduces the principal balance of the loan. Because the principal balance is greater

interest paid, which will reduce the investor's taxable income.[7] When computing the return on investment, an investor should therefore consider the after-tax cost of the interest. To illustrate, assume an investor pays $48,000 of interest after one year and that the individual's tax rate is 40%. Because the investor deducts the $48,000 of interest, the payment of interest reduces the investor's tax liability by the amount of the deduction multiplied by the tax rate, or $19,200. Because the interest deduction reduces the investor's tax liability, the investor's after-tax cost of paying the interest equals the $48,000 of interest paid minus the $19,200 tax liability reduction, or $28,800. The interest paid will reduce the investor's return on investment by the amount of the after-tax cost of the interest.

Tax Effect of Interest Deduction

Interest paid and deducted	$48,000
Tax rate	x 40%
Tax reduction attributed to interest deduction	$19,200

After-Tax Cost of Interest

Interest paid	$48,000
Tax reduction attributed to interest deduction	($19,200)
After-tax cost of interest	$28,800

The tax an investor pays on gain recognized on the disposition of the property will also reduce the investor's return. Assuming the gain is $200,000 and does not qualify for favorable capital-gains rates, the investor will owe $80,000 ($200,000 of taxable gain times the investor's 40% tax rate) of tax on the disposition of the property.[8] The investor must account for the after-tax cost of interest and the tax from the gain on disposition when determining the return on the investment. Therefore, the investor must reduce the $200,000 return on the investment by the $28,800 of the after-tax cost of interest and the $80,000 of tax on the gain. As a result of those reductions the return becomes $91,200, or 45.6% of the original investment.

---

at the beginning of the loan, a greater portion of the installment payment goes to interest at the beginning of the loan. As loan payments progress the amount of each installment that goes to principal also increases. Borrowers and lenders often use amortization tables to identify the portion of each installment payment that goes to interest and the portion that goes to principal. The Note and Security Agreement in the Practice Materials at the end of this chapter includes an authorization, which illustrates these points.

7. *See* I.R.C. §§ 63, 163(a). The deduction allowed in section 163(a) is subject to the limits in sections 163(d), if the interest is investment interest. *See also* Rev. Rul. 84-131, 1984-2 C.B. 37 (providing rules governing the application of the limit in the partnership context). The owners of real property will generally pay property tax, which may also be deductible. *See* I.R.C. § 164.

8. This example assumes the investor sells the property one year after acquiring it.

After-Tax Dollar Return on Investment

Dollar return on sale of property	$200,000
Tax paid on sale	$80,000
After-tax cost of interest	$28,800
Tax effect on return on investment	($108,800)
After-tax dollar return on investment	$91,200

After-Tax Basic Return on Investment

$91,200 (after-tax dollar return on investment) ÷ $200,000 (amount invested) = 45.6%

That return still appears to be very good, but not as good as the 100% return determined without considering the interest paid and the tax consequences of the transaction. Tax significantly affected the investor's return on investment. To understand the nuances of a transaction and property owners' objectives, tax attorneys must be aware of how taxes affect the financial aspects of a transaction. They also must understand how time affects the profitability. The passage of time makes the financial aspects of a transaction more complicated.

1. Internal Rate of Return

Up to this point, the discussion has used the term "return on investment" generally. Often investors are concerned more specifically about the internal rate of return of an investment.[9] The internal rate of return of an investment considers the time value of money. The underlying theory of the time value of money is that a dollar today is worth more than a dollar in the future. Rates of return must take into account the passage of time between the time a real estate investor invests in property and the time the investor recognizes income or gain from the property. Internal rate of return is the rate that makes the present value of cash flows equal zero. To illustrate, the investor in the running example obtained a 46% internal rate of return by selling the property for $1,200,000 one year after acquiring it. If the investor sold the property two years after acquiring it, paid interest both years, and had the same $91,200 after-

---

9. The finance principles discussed in this chapter may have subtly different meanings for different people. To properly draft documents, attorneys must be familiar with the concepts generally and know what the parties intend the meaning of terms to be with respect to specific transactions. Using a term such as "internal rate of return" in documents without defining it accurately may create ambiguity and lead to future contention among the parties. *See, e.g.*, Bradley T. Borden, *XIRR Guessing Games and Distribution Waterfalls*, Bus. L. Today (online) (Jan. 2016) (discussing the shortcomings of the XIRR function when used to compute IRR hurdles in distribution waterfalls). A downside of internal rate of return is that it can return multiple values. For instance, the number of possible values returned in computing internal rate of return equals the number of times the signs of the cash flow changes. Thus, if the sign changes twice (e.g., negative for a cash outflow changing to positive for a cash inflow and then changing again to negative for a cash outflow), the internal rate of return will generate two possible answers. *See id.* For this reason, investors may prefer to use net present value instead of internal rate of return.

tax dollar return on investment at the time of sale, the investor's internal rate of return would be 22%.[10] Realizing the same gain one year later significantly affects the individual's internal rate of return because of the time value of money. Calculators and computers facilitate the computation of the internal rate of return.[11]

Investors use the internal rate of return to assess the attractiveness of an investment. If an investor can estimate the amount and timing of a property's outlays and receipts, the investor can estimate the property's internal rate of return. To make investment decisions, the investor can compare internal rates of return of multiple possible investments. For example, if the investor estimated that the property would sell after four years for $1,200,000, the investor could estimate that the property's internal rate of return would be 4%.[12] If that amount is less than the investor would earn purchasing bonds or other investments, the investor may decide to not purchase the property but instead to invest in bonds.

2. Net Present Value

Another useful financial tool is the net present value of an investment. The net present value of an investment allows an investor to compare present outlays to the present value of an investment's future cash flows. To compare present outlays with future cash flows, the investor must estimate or project future cash flows and then must discount the projected future cash flows to present value to account for the time value of money.[13] Recall that when computing the internal rate of return, the investor used outlays and subsequent returns to determine the rate of return. The internal rate of return reflects the annual return that an investor would have to realize to obtain the future dollar returns. To compute net present value, the investor must assume some rate of return (referred to as a discount rate) and be able to estimate the amount and timing of outlays and receipts. An investor's opportunity cost of capital is an appropriate discount rate. Using the discount rate, the investor can compare the amount of present outlays to the value of projected future cash flows in present-value terms. If the present value of the projected future cash flows does not exceed the amount of current outlays, the investor may decide not to proceed with an investment. These concepts generally only make sense when applied to examples.

---

10. This is based upon the calculation described in the Practice Materials at the end of this chapter. As discussed in the Practice Materials at the end of this chapter, the tax rate may change if the individual holds the property for more than one year before selling it, and the individual must also account for another year of interest payments. Thus, the return would likely be different if some of the assumptions change.

11. The Practice Materials at the end of this chapter explain how to use Microsoft Excel to compute internal rate of return and net present value for the property.

12. *See infra* Practice Materials at the end of this chapter.

13. Projecting future cash flows obviously is not an exact science. Investors may base projections on historic information, such as year-over-year growth of revenue and expense items and use some form of historic growth to predict future growth of such items. Projections should also account for anticipated changes to market conditions. For instance, revitalization of an area may positively affect rent revenues, so investors may base projected rent revenue partly on historic data but also account for potential bump in revenues based upon an anticipated change in market conditions.

To begin the examination of net present value, consider an investment of $100,000 that has a 5% return, compounded annually. For example, an individual could purchase a five-year certificate of deposit (CD) that provides for 5% annual compound interest. At the end of the first year, the CD would have a $105,000 balance (the original $100,000 deposit plus $5,000 of interest). The CD would earn 5% interest on the $105,000 balance during the second year ($5,250), so the balance at the end of the second year would be $110,250. Thus, a $100,000 investment with a 5% compounded annual return would be worth $110,250 after two years.

Effect of Compound Interest

Original investment	$100,000
Year 1 interest (5% of $100,000)	$5,000
Balance at the end of Year 1	$105,000
Year 2 interest (5% of $105,000)	$5,250
Balance at the end of Year 2	$110,250

Net present value reverses that process. In computing net present value, one asks what a future dollar amount would be worth in present value terms. For example, one could ask what $110,250 received two years from now would be worth in today's dollars assuming a 5% discount rate. The example above illustrates that if a person invests $100,000 today compounded annually at 5%, the $100,000 would be worth $110,250 in two years. Thus, the net present value of $110,250 to be received two years from now must be worth $100,000 today. The net present value of $110,250 received in two years is therefore $100,000, assuming a 5% discount rate.

Now consider how a real estate investor may use net present value to assess a proposed development. Assume a real estate investor has $490,000 to invest. One potential investment requires the investor to pay $100,000 for a piece of property at the beginning of Year 1 and pay $390,000 at the end of Year 2 for a newly constructed building on the property.[14] In Year 3, investor will receive $40,000 of rent on the property; pay $5,000 in maintenance expenses, $1,200 in property taxes, $7,000 in management fees, and $1,800 in utilities; and have $10,000 depreciation deduction.[15] In computing the property's net present value, the investor will naturally focus on the property's projected cash flow (rent receipts and operating expenses).

The tax liability will also affect the property's cash flow, so it must factor into the computation of net present value. In Year 3, the investor will compute taxable income by subtracting the deductible operating expenses and $10,000 depreciation deduction

---

14. For the sake of simplicity, the example assumes the builder accepted payment in full at the end of the second year, after the construction was completed. The example also assumes that the property owner does not pay property tax.

15. The computation of depreciation assumes the straight-line method for nonresidential rental property, but does not account for the appropriate convention. *See* I.R.C. § 168 (governing the computation of depreciation). The actual computation of depreciation for most analyses will be more complicated.

from the $40,000 rent received, so the investor's taxable income will be $15,000. Assuming the investor's tax rate is 40%, the investor will owe $6,000 of income taxes on the taxable income of the property.

Tax Liability from Operations

Gross income		
Rental income		$40,000
Deductions		
Maintenance Expense	$5,000	
Property Taxes	$1,200	
Management Fees	$7,000	
Utilities	$1,800	
Depreciation deduction	<u>$10,000</u>	
Total deductions		<u>($25,000)</u>
Taxable income		$15,000
Tax rate		<u>x 40%</u>
Tax liability		$6,000

Investors and entities also track cash flow from their investment and financing activities. Statements of cash flows can follow the indirect method or the direct method. Under the indirect method, the statement of cash flows begins with net income (or it could begin with taxable income, if the investor does not separately compute net income). Investors then adjust net income to reflect amounts that affect net income but do not represent cash flows. For instance, net income includes an adjustment for depreciation, but depreciation is not a cash flow item. Consequently, the indirect method requires adding depreciation deductions to net income to compute the cash flows for the period. They also adjust net income for cash flow items that do not affect net income. For instance, capital outlays are cash flow items that do not affect net income. Similarly, cash contributions to and from an entity do not affect the entity's net income, but they do affect cash flow. Those items must be added to or subtracted from net income, as appropriate, to determine the total cash flows for the year under the indirect method.

The direct method of presenting cash flows does not start with net income. Instead, it merely presents cash outflows and cash inflows from the different categories. Cash flows from operating activities include items such as receipts from customers, clients, or tenants (inflows); dividend and interest income; compensation paid to employees (outflows); overhead expenses, such as utilities, insurance, marketing, and administrative expenses (outflows); taxes (outflows); and interest (outflows). Cashflows from investing activities include items such as purchase of property, plant, and equipment (outflows); capital improvements (outflows); purchase of investment assets (outflows); and proceeds from the sale of property or investment assets (inflows). Financing activities include items such as contributions to an entity (inflows to the entity); distributions from the entity (outflows to the entity);[16] loan proceeds (inflows); repayment of loan principal (outflows). Both types of cash flow statements can present information about cash on hand at both the beginning and end of the relevant period. Both types of cash flow statements also generally divide cash flows among operating activities, investing activities, and financing activities.

The figures from the simple investor example of the computation of tax liability provide the basis for creating a simple statement of cash flows. The cash inflows from operations include the $40,000 of rent received and outflows include the $15,000 of operating expenses and the $6,000 of tax liability. Assume the investor also paid $5,000 for a capital improvement to its property and took out a $12,000 loan at the end of the year. The statement of cash flows would also include those amounts. The investor's statement of cash flows, using the direct method, would appear something as follows for Year 3.

Cash Flow Statement for Years of Operation

Cash Flows from Operations

Rent Received	$40,000
Maintenance Expense	($5,000)
Property Taxes	($1,200)
Management Fees	($7,000)
Utilities	($1,800)
Income Tax	($6,000)
Net Cash Flows from Operations	$19,000

Cash Flows from Investments

Sale or Disposition of Property	$0
Sale or Maturity of Investment	$0
Tax on Sale of Property or Investment	$0
Purchase of Property	$0
Capital Improvements	($5,000)
Net Cash Flows from Investments	($5,000)

Cash Flows from Financing

Loan Proceeds	$12,000
Loan Repayment	$0
Net Cash Flows from Financing	$12,000
Net Cash Flows	$26,000

---

16. For a person who contributes money to an entity, the contributions would generally be outflows for investment activity, and the distributions from the entity would be inflows from investment activity.

Assume that the investor's projected net cash flow in Years 5 through 12 are as follows: Year 4: $14,500; Year 5: $15,050; Year 6: $15,000; Year 7: $15,750; Year 8: $16,125; Year 9: $16,500; Year 10: $16,250; Year 11: $16,000; Year 12: $16,650; Year 13: $16,825; Year 14: $17,000. To compute the net present value of this investment, the investor must also consider the future selling price of the asset. Assume, for example, that the investor could sell the building at the end of Year 15 for $1,200,000. The investor will receive that amount, net of taxes attributed to the taxable gain. Because the property was depreciable, the investor expects a portion of the gain will be unrecaptured section 1250 gain, taxed at 25%, and the remaining gain will be taxed at 20%.[17] Over the 13 years since the construction of the building, the owner was entitled to $130,000 of depreciation deductions.[18] Thus, the adjusted basis of the building and land would be $360,000, and the investor would recognize $840,000 on the disposition of the property.

Gain Recognized on Disposition

Amount realized	$1,200,000
Adjusted basis	($360,000)
Gain recognized	$840,000

Of the gain recognized, $130,000 would be unrecaptured section 1250 gain subject to a 25% tax rate, so the tax liability for that portion of the gain would be $32,500. The remaining $710,000 of gain recognized would be subject to a 20% tax rate, so the tax liability for that portion of the gain would be $142,000. The investor's total tax liability on the gain would therefore be $174,500.

Tax Liability on Disposition

$130,000 of section 1250 gain at 25%	$32,500
$710,000 of capital gain at 20%	$142,000
Tax liability on disposition	$174,500

The investor's after-tax net cash flows from investments would be $998,520 in Year 15.[19] In Year 15, the investor also would have $19,000 of net cash flow from operations, including an interest payment and repayment of the $1,000 balance remaining on

---

17. *See* I.R.C. §§ 1(h), 1231, 1250. The example assumes that the investor's regular long-term capital gain is taxed at the 20% capital-gain rates that apply to high-income taxpayers and that the 3.8% Medicare surtax does not apply because the investor is engaged in a business not described in I.R.C. § 1411(c)(2) with respect to the property. *See* I.R.C. § 1411.

18. This example assumes that the investor placed property in service on the first day of Year 3 and sold it on the last day of Year 15, without taking into account the convention that might apply to the property.

19. The investor should either include a separate line item for tax on the sale of investment property or present cash from the sale of the property net of tax. This analysis lists the tax as a separate line item.

the loan. Thus, the investor's total net cash flows for Year 15 would be $1,025,500. Net cash flows for the year would be $1,043,500.

Cash Flow in Year of Disposition

Cash Flows from Operations

Rent Received	$40,000
Maintenance Expense	($4,550)
Property Taxes	($1,200)
Management Fees	($7,000)
Utilities	($1,800)
Interest	($50)
Income Tax	($6,000)
Net Cash Flows from Operations	$19,000

Cash Flows from Investments

Sale or Disposition of Property	$1,200,000
Sale or Maturity of Investment	$0
Tax on Sale of Property or Investment	($174,500)
Purchase of Property	$0
Capital Improvements	$0
Net Cash Flows from Investments	$1,025,500

Cash Flows from Financing

Loan Proceeds	$0
Loan Repayment	($1,000)
Net Cash Flows from Financing	($1,000)
Net Cash Flows	$1,043,500

Once the investor knows the projected cash flows for each year of the investment, the investor can compute the net present value of the investment. Computers and calculators facilitate the computation of net present value.[20] In this case, the net present value, assuming a 5.5% discount rate, appears to be $$133,050.[21] The investor can compare that amount to other investment alternatives and choose the one that has the highest net present value.

3. Capitalization Rate

The simplest finance tool this chapter covers is the capitalization rate (real estate investors often refer to this concept as the "cap rate"). The cap rate is a simple financial tool because it does not incorporate time value of money principles. Instead, it merely

---

20. The Practice Materials at the end of this chapter provide a brief tutorial on computing net present value using Microsoft Excel.

21. *See infra* Practice Material at the end of this chapter.

relies upon the property's first year net operating income and the property's value. Consequently, cap rate is only useful for income-producing property.

A property's cap rate is its first year's net operating income divided by the property's value. The value generally would be the purchase price. Stated generally, net operating income of real estate is the property's gross rent receipts minus operating expenses and income taxes. Individual investors will, of course, focus on the cap rate with respect to their individual interests in property. Thus, if an individual borrows to purchase property, the individual should focus on the cap rate of the individual's investment, not on the cap rate of the total purchase price. The individual's cap rate would equal payments the individual receives from the property divided by the amount invested. Partners may compute cap rate by dividing distributions they receive from the partnership by the amount they contribute to the partnership.

To illustrate the computation of cap rate, consider an individual who borrows $800,000 at a simple 6% interest rate and uses $200,000 to acquire a $1,000,000 piece of property. That individual should focus on the cap rate for the $200,000. Assume the property is expected to have annual gross rent receipts of $100,000, deductible expenses of $35,000 (which includes interest payments), and a $20,000 depreciation deduction. The individual's income tax rate is 40%. The taxable income from the property will equal the gross receipts minus the expenses and the depreciation deduction, or $45,000. The individual's tax liability for that amount will be $18,000.

Tax Liability

Gross income		
Rental income		$100,000
Deductions		
Operating expenses	$35,000	
Depreciation deduction	$20,000	
Total deductions		($55,000)
Taxable income		$45,000
Tax rate		x 40%
Tax liability		$18,000

The projected net operating income for the first year is $100,000 minus the $35,000 operating expenses and $18,000 tax liability, or $47,000.

Projected Net Operating Income

Gross receipts		$100,000
Expenditures		
Operating expenses	$35,000	
Tax liability	$18,000	
Total expenditures		($53,000)
Projected net operating income		$47,000

The cap rate will be that amount divided by the $200,000 the individual invested, or 23.5%.

Cap Rate

$47,000 (projected net operating income) ÷ $200,000 (amount invested) = 23.5%

The individual can use the cap rate of this property and different properties to compare their relative values, even if the properties have different selling prices or different net operating income. An investor can also compute cap rate without taking depreciation and tax rates into account, if they are similar across properties.

4. Application of Finance Concepts to Real Estate Joint Ventures

Many real estate ventures include multiple members who have the common objective of buying real estate, holding it for some period of time, and selling it. Some such ventures may also have the objective of developing or redeveloping the property. Some members of the venture may be actively involved in managing the venture and others may be passive. Each member could have a unique method of measuring the financial performance of the venture. Some may take an entity view of the venture and perceive the venture itself as the investment and measure of the financial performance of the contributions to and distributions from the venture.[22] Other members may take an aggregate view of the venture and measure financial performance of the venture with respect to allocations of profits and losses. If the venture is a flow-through entity, as a general rule, members should consider tax allocations when performing financial analyses of the venture. Real estate ventures may therefore present interesting analytical puzzles for investors.

II. Primary Legal Authority

Slappey Drive Industrial Park v. United States

United States Court of Appeals, Fifth Circuit
561 F.2d 572 (1977)

FACTS

Spencer C. Walden, Jr. is a successful real estate developer in Albany, Georgia, a city of some 100,000 located less than 50 miles southeast of Plains. Acting primarily through the partnership of Walden & Kirkland, Walden has developed numerous residential subdivisions and various commercial properties. This case concerns a subset of his activities.

---

22. *See, e.g.,* Bradley T. Borden, *The Overlap of Tax and Financial Aspects of Real Estate Ventures,* 39 Real Est. Tax'n 67 (1st Quarter 2012).

Among the properties Walden has developed are several tracts originally owned by his father-in-law, J. T. Haley, and Haley's descendants. [Footnote omitted.] With Walden directing organizational efforts, members of the Haley family formed six corporations over a fifteen year period. Those corporations were Pecan Haven, Inc. (Pecan Haven), Lake Park, Inc. (Lake Park), Sherwood Acres, Inc. (Sherwood), Lake Park Additions, Inc. (Additions), Forest Estates, Inc. (Forest Estates) and Slappey Drive Industrial Park, Inc. (Slappey). Each of these is a party to this case. The other corporate party is Cairo Developers, Inc. (Cairo Developers), which Walden formed in conjunction with two individuals not members of the J. T. Haley family.

Walden was the moving force behind each of these corporations. He was president of each enterprise, and his partnership, Walden & Kirkland, handled their development work. All but Slappey were to develop residential subdivisions; Slappey's project was an industrial park.

On this appeal the government asserts that Additions was formed primarily for tax-avoidance purposes and that Sherwood and Additions held certain property for sale rather than for investment. The government further contends that purported debts that each corporation owed its shareholders should receive equity treatment. The debts arose from eight transfers of land (ostensibly credit sales) and three transfers of money (ostensibly loans) that the shareholders made to the corporations. We develop the facts relevant to these contentions by discussing the corporations in the order of their incorporation, referring to the contested transfers by alphabetical labels.

The tax years in question are those ending in 1961 through 1965, though some of the actions involve fewer years. The taxes contested in these suits total about $350,000 plus interest, and the amount of tax liability affected in these and other years will presumably run much higher. Because the facts are crucial in cases of this type, we set them forth in plentiful detail. Our discussion may rank with any drug on the market as a cure for insomnia, though we trust that our version of "the Waldens" will prove more lively than a current Thursday night television series.

Pecan Haven. Pecan Haven was formed in June 1947. The shareholders were Walden (1 share), his wife Cornelia Haley Walden (59 shares) and her twin sister Loretta Haley (60 shares). They paid $12,000 for their shares. Pecan Haven developed several tracts obtained from Loretta and Cornelia and later developed a tract purchased from their father J. T. Haley.

Transfer A occurred July 26, 1960. Spencer Walden transferred 69.435 acres to the corporation in exchange for its $65,000 five-year 3% installment notes. Appellants assert that the corporation's book net worth at that time was $83,000 and that its "true" net worth, taking into account the appreciated value of its real estate holdings, was $476,000. The corporation failed to make timely payments of principal or interest, and $20,000 remains outstanding.

Lake Park. J. T. Haley's three children Joel T. Haley, Jr., Cornelia and Loretta organized Lake Park in November 1950 intending to develop lands they held jointly.

They took equal shares of the corporation's stock, for which they paid a total of $28,000. The corporate books reflected the contributions as $9,000 paid-in capital and.$19,000 paid-in surplus. The corporation immediately acquired land from its shareholders that it developed.

Transfer B occurred September 7, 1954. The shareholders transferred 100 acres to the corporation in exchange for $10,000 cash and a $40,000 demand note bearing 4% interest. Appellants contend that at the time of the transfer the corporation's net worth was $50,000 and that its "true" net worth was $78,000. Lake Park made irregular principal payments and retired the note in 1959. The corporation did not pay interest as provided in the note, making only a single $2,500 interest payment in 1956.

Sherwood. The Lake Park shareholders Joel, Cornelia and Loretta formed Sherwood in September 1954. Each took one-third of the new corporation's stock, for which they paid a total of $21,000. The next day they made transfer C, conveying to the corporation 48 acres in which each owned a one-third undivided interest. In exchange the corporation paid $6,000 cash and an $18,000 demand note bearing 4% interest. The corporation made irregular principal payments and a single interest payment, retiring the debt in 1960.

By the time of the second contested Sherwood transaction, Joel had died, leaving to his wife Katherine and his two children equal portions of his stock and the remaining property owned in conjunction with the other shareholders. This new lineup of shareholders made transfer D in January 1960. In exchange for 126.48 acres, the corporation issued five-year 3% notes to each shareholder totaling $189,720.02. Appellants assert that at that time the corporation had a book net worth of $62,000 and a "true" net worth of $206,000. Sherwood made irregular principal and interest payments, and a $32,000 balance remains outstanding. [Footnote omitted.]

Transfer E occurred in December 1964 when Sherwood's shareholders conveyed an additional 84.252 acres to the corporation. In exchange they received five-year 5% notes totaling $126,000. Appellants contend that the corporation had a $117,000 book net worth and a $240,000 "true" net worth. In September 1965 the corporation retired the notes held by Katherine and her two children. The corporation has made no payments on the notes held by Loretta and Cornelia. The corporation made an interest payment to Katherine and her children in 1965 and made annual interest payments to Loretta and Cornelia from 1967 through 1971.

On July 7, 1965, Sherwood sold.99 acres of the tract it had received in 1954 from its shareholders. The land was part of 3.71 acres that the corporation had not divided into residential lots and which were identified on the recorded plat as "reserved for business" and described in the corporate books as a "land reserve." Texaco, the purchaser, had initiated negotiations for the sale; Sherwood had not solicited buyers. Texaco used the land for a gas station. Sherwood originally reported the profit on the Texaco sale as ordinary income but now seeks capital gains treatment.[23]

---

23. [7] Sherwood contended in the court below that a portion of the 1960 transfer from its shareholders had also been held for investment. Sherwood carried the property on its books as "Land In-

Additions. In June 1959 Loretta, Cornelia and Katherine formed Additions, each taking one-third of its shares and contributing a total of $36,900 paid-in capital. Katherine's two children did not participate. The shareholders and Katherine's children immediately made transfer F, conveying 268.8 acres to the corporation in exchange for five-year 3% notes totaling $368,200. [Footnote omitted.] The corporation made no principal or interest payments until 1964. From 1964 until 1969 it made annual interest payments. It has made a single principal payment, for $5,000 in 1965.

Transaction G occurred August 2, 1961. Loretta advanced the corporation $61,250, taking in return its one-year 5% note. The corporation made its first payment on the note in 1964 and retired the note in 1965.

After conducting a topographical survey of the land it had received from its shareholders in 1959, Additions discovered that nearly three acres could not be incorporated into the planned residential subdivision because of drainage problems. The corporation abandoned its initial plan regarding this tract and did not subdivide it into lots. The corporation did not break the parcel out separately on its books but carried it in the same account that included all undeveloped land. In 1963 Georgia Power Company approached Additions and bought two acres for a substation, and the City of Albany contacted Additions and purchased the remainder of the tract for a pumping station. Georgia Power paid $7,500 for its parcel and the city $2,500. Additions claims that this land had been held for investment, making capital gains treatment appropriate.

Forest Estates. In September 1959 Loretta Haley and Marjorie Scherberger formed Forest Estates, each taking half its stock, for which they paid a total of $25,000. They immediately effected transfer H, conveying to the corporation 43.93 acres that they owned jointly in exchange for five-year 4% notes totaling $100,000. Forest Estates made no principal payments on the notes until 1971, and $70,000 remains outstanding. The corporation made small and irregular interest payments from 1961 through 1967. Forest Estates suffered losses in 1965 and 1966 and apparently abandoned development plans.

Cairo Developers. Spencer C. Walden, Jr., George M. Kirkland, Jr., and J. Norwood Clark formed Cairo Developers in April 1961. Kirkland was Walden's partner in Walden & Kirkland. Clark was a real estate broker from Cairo, Georgia, who owned the bulk of the land that Cairo Developers was to develop. Each organizer took one-third of the corporation's stock, paying in a total of $5,100. From May 1961 through January 1964, the corporation received ostensible loans from the three shareholders, the Walden & Kirkland partnership, a corporation that Walden and Kirkland owned, and two of Walden's children. These advances together constitute transfer J. [Footnote omitted.] Most of these notes were due in one year; a few were payable on demand. The corporation made no payments of principal or interest until 1971.

---

vestment" and on the recorded plat did not subdivide the tract into lots. The corporation made five sales from the area for residential usage in the fiscal years ending in 1964 and 1965. Sherwood has apparently abandoned its claim for capital gains treatment of these sales.

Slappey. On July 7, 1962, Cornelia Haley Walden organized Slappey, paying $9,000 for all its issued stock. On July 9 she transferred the stock in equal segments to her three children. The next day Cornelia made transfer K, conveying 80.78 acres to the corporation in exchange for $6,366.50 cash and an eight-year 4% note for $75,000. Slappey planned to develop the land for industrial and commercial establishments. The corporation made irregular principal and interest payments, failing to pay the debt on its due date.

Transfer L occurred May 27, 1963. Each of the three shareholders advanced the corporation $5,000 in exchange for one-year 6% notes. Slappey has made no payments of principal or interest on these notes.[24]

Overview. We may assume, as appellants contend, that in each ostensible sale of property to a corporation the price reflected the fair market value. Nonetheless, the recurring pattern in regard to all the loans has been the corporations' failure to adhere to the announced repayment schedules. Although the corporations did make some principal and interest payments, in not a single case did the payments conform to the terms included in the notes. In addition, Spencer Walden's deposition testimony makes clear that the creditor-shareholders viewed their situation not at all as normal creditors would. The shareholders entered no objections to the passing of payment dates and requested payments only when the corporations had "plenty of cash." In explaining the willingness to tolerate delinquencies even when interest was not being paid, Walden candidly stated that the individuals were more concerned with their status as shareholders than in their status as creditors.

ANALYSIS

The tax code provides widely disparate treatment of debt and equity. In regard to a typical transfer at issue here, involving an individual's transfer of property to his corporation in exchange for the instrument in question, the classification as debt or equity may affect the taxation of the original transaction,[25] the resulting bases and hence the taxation of subsequent transfers,[26] and the taxation of payments the cor-

---

24. [10] The characterization of this transaction as debt or equity apparently does not affect any of the tax years in question here. Although the corporation originally claimed a deduction for an $82.50 accrual of interest in 1963, it now concedes that the amount is not deductible because it was not paid within 21/2 months of the fiscal year's close. *See* 26 U.S.C. § 267. The characterization of the transaction retains significance, however, with respect to payments the corporation may make in the future.

25. [12] *See* I.R.C. § 351. That section provides that no gain or loss is recognized when persons transfer property to their controlled corporation solely in exchange for "stock or securities." The term "stock" would include the instruments here if they were characterized as equity. The term "securities" might or might not extend to them if characterized as debt; the term encompasses some debt instruments but not others. As an alternative to its argument that the transactions here are equity, the government contends that even if characterized as debt the property transfers come within § 351 as "securities." In light of our acceptance of the government's primary argument, we need not pass on its alternative contention.

26. [13] *See, e.g.,* I.R.C. § 362. In the instant case the transferring shareholders' bases in their land were significantly lower than the sales prices. Thus the difference between new basis and carryover basis is important.

poration makes to the shareholder with respect to the instrument.[27] In the case at bar debt classification would greatly benefit the taxpayers.

Unfortunately, the great disparity in the tax treatment of debt and equity does not derive from a clear distinction between those concepts. The problem is particularly acute in the case of close corporations, because the participants often have broad latitude to cast their contributions in whatever form they choose. Taxpayers have often sought debt's advantageous tax treatment for transactions that in substance more closely resembled the kind of arrangement Congress envisioned when it enacted the equity provisions. *See Nassau Lens Co. v. Comm'r*, 308 F.2d 39, 44–46 (2d Cir. 1962). Thus the labels that parties attach to their transactions provide no guarantee of the appropriate tax treatment. *See, e.g., Tyler v. Tomlinson*, 414 F.2d 844, 850 (5th Cir. 1969); *Berkowitz v. U.S.*, 411 F.2d 818, 820 (5th Cir. 1969).

Articulating the essential difference between the two types of arrangement that Congress treated so differently is no easy task. Generally, shareholders place their money "at the risk of the business" while lenders seek a more reliable return. *See Midland Distributors, Inc. v. U.S.*, 481 F.2d 730, 733 (5th Cir. 1973); *Dillin v. U.S.*, 433 F.2d 1097, 1103 (5th Cir. 1970). That statement of course glosses over a good many considerations with which even the most inexperienced investor is abundantly familiar. A purchaser of General Motors stock may bear much less risk than a bona fide lender to a small corporation. *See Fin Hay Realty Co. v. U.S.*, 398 F.2d 694, 697 (3d Cir. 1968).

Nevertheless, the "risk of the business" formulation has provided a shorthand description that courts have repeatedly invoked. Contributors of capital undertake the risk because of the potential return, in the form of profits and enhanced value, on their underlying investment. Lenders, on the other hand, undertake a degree of risk because of the expectancy of timely repayment with interest. Because a lender unrelated to the corporation stands to earn only a fixed amount of interest, he usually is unwilling to bear a substantial risk of corporate failure or to commit his funds for a prolonged period. A person ordinarily would not advance funds likely to be repaid only if the venture is successful without demanding the potential enhanced return associated with an equity investment. *See Curry v. U.S.*, 396 F.2d 630, 634 (5th Cir.), cert. denied, 393 U.S. 967; *DuGro Frozen Foods, Inc. v. U.S.*, 481 F.2d 1271, 1272 (5th Cir. 1973).

These considerations provide only imperfect guidance when the issue relates to a shareholder's purported loan to his own corporation, the usual situation encountered in debt-equity cases. It is well established that shareholders may loan money to their corporations and achieve corresponding tax treatment. *See U.S. v. Snyder Bros. Co.*, 367 F.2d 980, 983 (5th Cir. 1966), cert. denied, 386 U.S. 956; *Rowan v. U.S.*, 219 F.2d 51 (5th Cir. 1955). When making such loans they could hardly be expected to ignore their shareholder status; their motivations will not match those of potential lenders who

---

27. [14] The corporation may deduct interest on indebtedness, *see* I.R.C. §163, but if the transaction is characterized as equity, ostensible interest payments become non-deductible dividends. In general, the recipient is not taxable on loan principal payments but is taxable if the transaction constitutes equity; in that instance the purported principal payments come in for dividend treatment. *See* I.R.C. §316.

have no underlying equity interest. The "risk of the business" standard, though, continues to provide a backdrop for our analysis. While we should not expect a creditor-shareholder to evidence motivations and behavior conforming perfectly to those of a mere creditor, neither should we abandon the effort to determine whether the challenged transaction is in substance a contribution to capital masquerading as debt.[28]

Rather than attempt to measure concrete cases against an abstract formulation of the overriding test, we have identified numerous observable criteria that help place a given transaction on one side of the line or the other. We have always recognized, however, that the various factors are not equally significant. "The object of the inquiry is not to count factors, but to evaluate them." *Tyler v. Tomlinson*, 414 F.2d 844, 848 (5th Cir. 1969). Each case turns on its own facts; differing circumstances may bring different factors to the fore. *See In re Indian Lake Estates, Inc.*, 448 F.2d 574, 579 (5th Cir. 1971); *Tomlinson v. The 1661 Corp.*, 377 F.2d 291, 295 (5th Cir. 1967).

With that preliminary caveat, we note the factors that prior cases have identified:

(1)   the names given to the certificates evidencing the indebtedness;

(2)   The presence or absence of a fixed maturity date;

(3)   The source of payments;

(4)   The right to enforce payment of principal and interest;

(5)   participation in management flowing as a result;

(6)   the status of the contribution in relation to regular corporate creditors;

(7)   the intent of the parties;

(8)   "thin" or adequate capitalization;

(9)   identity of interest between creditor and stockholder;

(10) source of interest payments;

(11) the ability of the corporation to obtain loans from outside lending institutions;

(12) the extent to which the advance was used to acquire capital assets; and

(13) the failure of the debtor to repay on the due date or to seek a postponement.

Estate of Mixon v. U.S., 464 F.2d 394, 402 (5th Cir. 1972).[29] As indicated above, these factors are but tools for discerning whether a transaction more closely resembles the type arrangement for which Congress provided debt or equity treatment.[30]

---

28. [15] In emphasizing the usefulness of comparing the challenged transaction to the type arrangement that a disinterested lender would have entered, the Third Circuit has noted that disregarding the shareholder-lender's personal interest in his own corporation is fairer than presumptively construing all such transactions adversely to the shareholder. *See* Fin Hay Realty Co. v. U.S., 398 F.2d 694, 697 (3d Cir. 1968).

29. [16] The list is not exhaustive; our cases undoubtedly mention considerations that have yet to take a number. Congress has recently authorized the Secretary to promulgate regulations setting forth appropriate factors. *See* I.R.C. § 385. For the time being, however, we must rely on our own pronouncements.

30. [17] The issue is primarily one of law. We must uphold the district court's findings of basic facts unless clearly erroneous, but the ultimate characterization of the transactions as debt or equity receives no such protection. *See* Estate of Mixon v. U.S., 464 F.2d 394, 402–03 (5th Cir. 1972).

In the case at bar the most telling of the *Mixon* factors is the corporate debtors' consistent failure to repay the debts on the due dates or to seek postponements. More generally, that failure and the corresponding absence of timely interest payments combine with Walden's testimony regarding the parties' view of their relationships to make clear that these transactions were in substance not at all the type arrangements for which debt treatment is appropriate.

The individuals' failure to insist upon timely repayment or satisfactory renegotiation indicates that the compensation they sought went beyond the announced interest rate, for an investor would not ordinarily undertake such a risk for so limited a return. *See Tyler v. Tomlinson*, 414 F.2d 844, 850 (5th Cir. 1969). The failure to insist that the corporations pay the interest that the agreements provided underscores the inference; "a true lender is concerned with interest." *Curry v. U.S.*, 396 F.2d 630, 634 (5th Cir.), cert. denied, 393 U.S. 967. *See also National Carbide Corp. v. Comm'r*, 336 U.S. 422, 435 n. 16. When a corporate contributor seeks no interest, it becomes abundantly clear that the compensation he seeks is that of an equity interest: a share of the profits or an increase in the value of his shareholdings. *See Estate of Mixon v. U.S.*, 464 F.2d 394, 409 (5th Cir. 1972).

Walden's testimony confirms these conclusions. He acknowledged that the individuals sought payments of principal or interest only when the corporations had "plenty of cash" and that the investors did so because they were more concerned with their status as shareholders than as creditors. That statement of how the individuals viewed their situation corresponds almost perfectly to the classic equity situation. A corporation normally declares dividends only when it has "plenty of cash." Shareholders ordinarily acquiesce in such dividend policies because their primary concern is the health and long-term success of the enterprise. Walden's statement indicates that the individuals here possessed precisely those motivations and that they believed it appropriate for the corporations to decide when to make payments on the same basis that corporations customarily make dividend decisions. *See Berkowitz v. U.S.*, 411 F.2d 818, 821 (5th Cir. 1969). The taxpayers' pattern of conduct belies any intention to structure their affairs as parties to a debt transaction ordinarily would. In the circumstances here, these factors indicate that all the transactions should be characterized for tax purposes as equity arrangements.

In reaching this conclusion we have not ignored the other factors our cases have identified. Appellants place particular reliance on the intent of the parties. Here, appellants contend, the form in which the parties cast the transactions conclusively demonstrates their intent to create a debt relationship. In relying so heavily on this factor, however, appellants misconceive its import. The question is not whether the parties intended to call their transaction "debt" and thus to achieve advantageous tax treatment; that a person wants to pay less tax rather than more provides little basis for discerning how much tax Congress decided he should pay. Instead, the relevant inquiry is the actual manner, not the form, in which the parties intended to structure their relationship. If the intended structuring accords with the type arrangement that qualifies for taxation as debt, that intent supports a finding of debt. Here, however, the parties intended to structure their relationship in a manner placing funds at the prolonged risk of the businesses; they intended decisions whether to make payments on the advances to be based on the criteria usually associated with dividend decisions. To the extent that intent is relevant, it favors equity classification.[31]

Another *Mixon* factor to which appellants look for support is the extent to which the advance was used to acquire capital assets. They argue that here the corporations used none of the advances for that purpose. Instead, appellants note, the corporations used the contributions primarily for land, which constitutes the inventory of these real estate development firms. Whatever force this factor might have in other settings, appellants here can garner little support from it. Most of these advances, while perhaps not used for capital assets, nonetheless served "to finance initial operations." *Plantation Patterns, Inc. v. Comm'r*, 462 F.2d 712, 722 (5th Cir. 1972). *See Aqualane Shores, Inc. v. Comm'r*, 269 F.2d 116 (5th Cir. 1959) (shareholder's credit "sale" of land to real estate development corporation held to constitute equity contribution). Providing the bulk of the necessary first assets without which a corporation could not begin functioning is as traditional a usage of capital contributions as is purchasing "capital assets."

Another factor from *Mixon* that sometimes proves most instructive is the identity of interest between creditor and stockholder. Courts and commentators have often discussed this criterion under the rubric "proportionality." When each shareholder owns the same proportion of the company's stock as he does of the ostensible shareholder debt, the parties' framing of the transaction contributes little to the analysis. *See Fin Hay Realty Co. v. U.S.*, 398 F.2d 694 (3d Cir. 1968). In that situation the owners' decision regarding how much of their contribution to cast as equity and how much as debt does not affect the distribution of control over the company. Non-tax considerations may play little role in the choice, and reviewing courts accordingly must scrutinize carefully the resulting transaction. When, on the other hand, an individual holds different percentages of the corporation's stock and shareholder debt, the casting of debt in that form ordinarily will affect substantial non-tax interests. There is thus reason to believe that the parties' debt characterization has substance as well as form.[32]

---

31. [18] Walden testified that the corporations intended to repay the indebtedness. Even accepting that testimony as true, the parties' conduct makes clear that they intended to repay only after a prolonged period, at which time repayment would be likely only if the enterprises had proved successful. Thus they intended to repay in the same sense that corporations might intend their dividends eventually to total up to the original price of the stock. Walden's testimony in this regard provides only the barest support for debt classification.

32. [19] Even when a corporation incurs bona fide debt, of course, the opportunity to advance the funds and earn the corresponding return provides both tax and other advantages to the shareholder. Individual shareholders may therefore insist upon receiving their share of such advantages. Thus "proportionality" justifies courts in applying careful examination of the transactions but is not necessarily inconsistent with a finding of bona fide debt.

Appellants argue in the case at bar that many of the challenged transfers exhibited imperfect proportionality and that some displayed none at all.[33] While that argument would carry weight in the usual case, it has little force here. The disproportional holdings all occurred among close relatives. Although we do not treat the various shareholding members of the J.T. Haley family as an indivisible unit, neither do we treat them as unrelated individuals. For all that appears in this record, relations among the various family members were completely harmonious. Because shareholding family members were thus less likely to attribute major significance to departures from strict equality in their positions, the instances of disproportionate debt and equity holdings provide a much weaker inference than they ordinarily would that the ostensible debt was in fact what it purported to be.[34]

Finally, appellants strenuously urge that the level of the corporations' capitalization does not undermine their position. We have not, however, based our decision on the inadequacy of the corporate capitalization. While some of the purported loans were made to corporations with woefully inadequate capital, others were not. In some cases, as the taxpayers note, capitalization was adequate.[35] These facts strengthen our

----

33. [20] Transfers B, C, H and L exhibited perfect proportionality; each shareholder took the same percentage of shareholder debt as he or she held of the corporation's stock. Transfers D and E originally showed complete proportionality but became somewhat disproportional when the corporations made principal payments in different amounts to the different shareholders. Transfer F was not completely proportional; Katherine's children made loans but held no shares. Treating Katherine and her children as a unit, however, transfer F exhibited perfect proportionality. Similarly, transfer K evidenced no proportionality but was totally proportional treating Cornelia and her children as a unit. Transfer J was only roughly proportional. While different shareholders (or their businesses) made advances at different times, each of the three equal shareholders put up roughly one-third of the funds when considered in conjunction with their other loans to the corporation. Transfer G was not proportional; a one-third shareholder made the entire advance. Transfer A was completely disproportional; Spencer made the loan but held no stock.

34. [21] In *Estate of Mixon v. U.S.*, 464 F.2d 394 (5th Cir. 1972), we examined proportionality by looking to the family attribution provisions of I.R.C. §318. *See* 464 F.2d at 398 n. 3, 409. Even using those provisions to increase the individual's shareholdings, he held only 15.3% of the corporation's stock while making 80% of the challenged advance. Thus taking the view of attribution most favorable to the government in that case, the low proportionality favored the taxpayer. In the case at bar, unlike in *Mixon*, the approach taken to attribution affects the direction in which the proportionality factor cuts. We think the proper approach is the practical one outlined in the text. Rather than rigidly apply the §318 attribution rules an approach that *Mixon* does not require and that would contravene the limitation of that section to "those provisions ... to which (it is) expressly made applicable," I.R.C. §318(a) we treat the familial relationships as factors affecting the impact to be accorded the results of the proportionality inquiry. We of course accord careful scrutiny to intra-family transactions. *See Dillin v. U.S.*, 433 F.2d 1097, 1103 (5th Cir. 1970).

35. [22] Taxpayers urge that these businesses involved little risk and therefore needed little capital. The apparent failure of Forest Estates, however, belies their assertion. The ventures incurred development expenses running into six figures and required as much as two or three years to begin receiving any revenues by selling lots. These considerations demonstrate the inadequacy of, for example, the initial capitalizations of $5,100 for Cairo Developers, $9,000 for Slappey, and $21,000 for Sherwood. Thus the capitalization factor favors the government with respect to transfers made to those corpo-

conclusion as to some transactions, weaken it for others. They do not, however, suffice to change the conclusion we have derived from the parties' pattern of conduct and from Walden's testimony.[36]

Because the parties to the transactions in question intended to conduct and did conduct their affairs in a manner that the tax code labels equity rather than debt, taxation of the transactions as equity is appropriate. Contrary to appellants' assertions, in reaching that result we do not disapprove their decisions concerning how to organize the corporations, and we do not substitute our business judgment for theirs. We merely announce the tax consequences that attach to their decisions. While appellants are correct that they were free to decide without our supervision how much of the corporate financing to derive from loans and how much from capital contributions, they were not free to decide for themselves what tax consequences would attach to their conduct.

Revenue Ruling 84-131

1984-2 C.B. 37

ISSUE

How is the limitation of interest on investment indebtedness in section 163(d) of the Internal Revenue Code applied to partners and shareholders in S corporations after the amendment of sections 163(d) by the Subchapter S Revision Act of 1982 I.R.B. L. 97-354, 1982-2 C.B. 702?

FACTS

Situation 1 — In 1983, Partnership PRS has two partners, A and B, who share equally in profits, losses, and capital. PRS incurred indebtedness in order to purchase

---

rations upon their formation. In regard to transfers made at later times, however, we agree with appellants that net worth, not initial capitalization, provides the relevant data. *See* Tomlinson v. The 1661 Corp., 377 F.2d 291, 299 n. 18 (5th Cir. 1967). At the time of transfer E. Sherwood's net worth was $117,000. That figure would become much greater if we were to take into account the appreciated value of Sherwood's real estate holdings or if we added the amounts of the earlier purported debts (originating from transfers C and D) that we reclassify as equity. We need not decide the propriety of these steps, for we agree with appellants that in any event Sherwood's capitalization at the time of transfer E was adequate.

36. [23] The *Mixon* factors not discussed in text carry little weight in this case. The source of principal and interest payments and the questionable availability of similar loans from outside lenders provide slight support to the government. That most of the obligations possessed fixed maturity dates would favor appellants had they not consistently ignored those dates. Similarly, the individuals' legal right to enforce payment does not aid appellants in light of the apparent understanding, as manifested in observable behavior, that they would not enforce those rights. The lenders already controlled corporate management; that they derived no more control as a result of the ostensible loans does not cut against the equity classification. *See* Dillin v. U.S., 433 F.2d 1097, 1101 (5th Cir. 1970). Finally, that appellants did not subordinate their loans to other corporate obligations, *see* note 11 *supra*, provides slight support for appellants but does not undermine the conclusion we have drawn from the more significant indicia discussed in text.

taxable investment securities and paid interest on this indebtedness. A also incurred indebtedness in order to purchase taxable investment securities for A's own account. The interest on A's investment indebtedness, when added to A's distributive share of the interest on PRS's investment indebtedness, exceeds the limitation on investment interest provided in section 163(d)(1) of the Code. B incurred no indebtedness to purchase or carry personal investments, and B's distributive share of PRS's investment interest does not exceed the limitation in section 163(d)(1).

Situation 2—In 1983, Corporation X elected S corporation status under section 1362 of the Code. X had two shareholders, C and G, who each owned 50 percent of the X stock. X incurred indebtedness in order to purchase taxable investment securities and paid interest on this indebtedness. C also incurred indebtedness in order to purchase taxable investment securities for C's own account. The interest on C's investment indebtedness, when added to C's pro rata share of the interest on X's investment indebtedness, exceeds the limitation on investment indebtedness under section 163(d)(1) of the Code. G incurred no indebtedness to purchase or carry personal investments, and G's pro rata share of X's investment interest does not exceed the limitation under section 163(d)(1).

LAW AND ANALYSIS

Section 163(a) of the Code generally allows a deduction for all interest paid or accrued within the taxable year on indebtedness.

Section 163(d)(1) of the Code provides that, in the case of a taxpayer other than a corporation, the amount of investment interest otherwise deductible is limited, in the following order, to (1) $10,000 ($5,000 in the case of a separate return by a married individual) plus (2) the amount of the net investment income (as defined in § 163(d)(3)(A)). An additional amount may be deductible in the case of property of the taxpayer subject to a net lease.

Section 163(d)(3)(A) of the Code defines "net investment income" as the excess of investment income over investment expenses.

Section 163(d)(3)(D) of the Code defines "investment interest" as interest paid or accrued on indebtedness incurred or continued to purchase or carry property held for investment.

Section 163(d)(4) of the Code was amended by the Subchapter S Revision Act of 1982, P.L. 97-354, 1982-2 C.B. 702, effective for taxable years beginning after December 31, 1983. The amendment struck former subparagraphs (B) and (C) of § 163(d)(4) and redesignated former subparagraph (D) of that section as subparagraph (B). Prior to being stricken, § 163(d)(4)(B) provided, in part, that each partner of a partnership shall take into account separately that partner's distributive share of the partnership's investment interest and the other items of income and expense taken into account under § 163(d). Prior to being stricken, former § 163(d)(4)(C) provided, in part, that the investment interest paid or accrued by an electing small business corporation and the other items of income and expense that would be taken into account if § 164(d) applied to the corporation are treated as investment interest paid or accrued by the shareholders of the corporation and as items of such shareholders and shall be apportioned pro rata among the shareholders in a manner consistent with former § 1374(c)(1).

Under § 702(a)(7) of the Code, each partner, in computing the partner's income tax, must take into account separately the partner's distributive share of certain items of income, gain, loss, deduction, or credit to the extent provided in the Income Tax Regulations under § 702. Under § 702(b), the character of any item included in a partner's distributive share under § 702(a)(7) is determined as if the item were realized directly from the source from which realized by the partnership, or incurred in the same manner as incurred by the partnership.

Under § 1.702-1(a)(8)(ii) of the Income Tax Regulations, each partner must take into account separately the partner's distributive share (as determined under § 704 and the regulations thereunder) of any partnership item that, if separately taken into account by any partner, would result in an income tax liability for that partner different from that which would result if that partner did not take the item into account separately. Under § 1.702-1(a)(8)(iii), each partner must aggregate the amount of the partner's separate deductions and the distributive share of partnership deductions separately stated in determining the amount allowable to the partner of any income tax deduction as to which a limitation is imposed.

Thus, § 702 of the Code and corresponding regulations require that a partnership's investment interest be treated in the same manner as was required under former § 163(d)(4)(B); that is, the partner's distributive share of the partnership's investment interest expense must be separated from other partnership items and combined with the partner's individual investment interest expense to determine whether § 163(d)(1) of the Code limits the partner's interest deduction.

Under § 1366(a)(1)(A) of the Code, a shareholder of an S corporation, in determining the income tax for the shareholder's taxable year in which the taxable year of the S corporation ends, must take into account the shareholder's pro rata share of the corporation's items of income (including tax-exempt income), loss, education, or credit, the separate treatment of which could affect the liability for tax of any shareholder. Under § 1366(b), the character of any item concluded in a shareholder's pro rata share under § 1366(a)(1) is determined as if the item were realized directly from the source from which realized by the corporation, or incurred in the same manner as incurred by the corporation.

The Report of the House Committee on Ways and Means and the Report of the Senate Committee on Finance, H.R. Rep. No. 97-826, 97th Cong., 2d Sess. 14 (1982), 1982-2 C.B. 730, 736, and S. Rep. No. 97-640, 97th Cong., 2d Sess. 15 (1982), 1982-2 C.B. 718, 724, respectively, both give investment interest as an example of an item whose separate treatment could affect the liability of individual shareholders and must therefore be stated separately.

Thus, the committee reports explaining § 1366 of the Code indicate that investment interest is treated in the same manner as it was treated under former § 163(d)(4)(C), that is, an investment interest paid or accrued by the shareholders of the corporation to be apportioned pro rata among such shareholders.

HOLDINGS

Situation 1: A and B must take into account their respective distributive shares of PRS's investment interest separately from their distributive shares of other deductible expenses. A's investment interest is greater than the limitation prescribed in § 163(d)(1) of the Code, so A may not deduct investment interest in excess of such limitation. B's investment interest is less than the limitation prescribed in § 163(d)(1), so B's investment interest is fully deductible, provided B itemizes deductions.

Situation 2: C and G must take into account their respective pro rata shares of X's investment interest separately from their pro rata shares of other deductible expenses of X. C's investment interest is greater than the limitation prescribed in § 163(d)(1) of the Code, so C may not deduct investment interest in excess of such limitation. G's investment interest is less than the limitation prescribed in § 163(d)(1), so G's investment interest is fully deductible, provided G itemizes deductions.

III. Practice Material

A significant amount of finance theory supports the calculations that spreadsheets do fairly quickly. Spreadsheets also make assumptions, which if altered, would alter the computation of the various finance concepts. Every transactional attorney would benefit from additional knowledge of finance and more sophisticated spreadsheet skills. This brief discussion provides an introduction for those with no finance background and those who may not have used finance recently.

A. Tips for Computing Internal Rate of Return

One way to compute internal rate of return (IRR) is to use Microsoft Excel. The setup is crucial when using a computer spreadsheet such as Excel. The setup requires you to enter information needed to determine the IRR of an investment. The information includes amounts spent on the investment and amounts received from the investment. Amounts spent on an investment include the initial outlay for the investment and any additional expenditures, such as interest or management costs paid during the life of an investment. Amounts received from the investment include amounts such as rent, if the property has rental income, and amounts realized on the disposition of property.

Excel spreadsheets consists of cells. The cells are labeled horizontally with letters and vertically with numbers. For example, the cell on the top left of a spreadsheet is labeled A1. To use the spreadsheet, you must input information in the cells. The information you input in the cells will consist of labels, numerical values, and formulas.

The example in the commentary provides information that helps illustrate the computation of IRR using Excel. In that example, the investor's initial outlay was

$200,000, the investor also paid interest, and received sale proceeds on the eventual sale of the property. To set up the computation of IRR for the sale of property at the end of one year, input the following the labels; A1: IRR, C1: Investment, D1: Year 1, B2: Outlays, B3: Receipts, and B4: Total.

	A	B	C	D
1	IRR		Investment	Year 1
2	Outlays			
3	Receipts			
4	Total			

Next, enter the numerical information from the transaction. That information includes the amount the investor invested ($200,000), the after-tax cost of interest ($28,800), and the after tax receipts on the sale of the property ($320,000). Enter outlays into Excel as negative values and enter inflows as positive values. When you input information, remember that you must identify outflows as negative amounts. Also do not use dollar signs or commas when you input information (if you desire numbers to have such characteristics, you can use the cell properties feature to include them). Input the following information in the appropriate cells: C2: -200000, C3: 0, D2: -28800, D3: 320000.

	A	B	C	D
1				
2		-200000	-28800	
3		0	320000	
4				

Next, input the formulas. Total the columns for the investment and Year 1. Excel has a formula that totals the numbers in a column (=SUM(cell:cell)), and it has a formula for determining IRR (=IRR(cell:cell). Input the following formulas in the appropriate cells: C4: =SUM(C2:C3), D4: =SUM(D2:D3), and A2: =IRR(C4:D4).

	A	B	C	D
1				
2	=IRR(C4:D4)			
3				
4			=SUM(C2:C3)	=SUM(D2:D3)

If you entered the information correctly, cell A2 should show an IRR of 46%. The formula you entered in cell A2 used the information in cells C4 through D4 (represented in the formula by the notation C4:D4) to determine the IRR. Your spreadsheet should look something like this:

	A	B	C	D
1	IRR		Investment	Year 1
2	46%	Outlays	-200000	-28800
3		Receipts	0	320000
4		Total	-200000	29120

With these basic tools, you can explore the consequences that will result if the individual held the property for more than one year. Assume for example that the individual sold the property at the end of the second year for the same $1,200,000. The gain the individual recognizes on the sale would remain $200,000, but, if the gain qualifies for long-term capital gain treatment, the tax rate on the gain would be 20% instead of 40%. The individual would owe $40,000 of tax, and the individual's after-tax receipts would be $360,000. In Year 1, the individual would still have the same outlay for interest, but would have no receipts. In Year 2, the individual would have $28,800 of after-tax outlays for interest and would have $360,000 of after-tax receipts on the sale of the property.

To compute the IRR based on the new facts, you must add an additional column for Year 2. For Outlays in Year 2 enter -28800 and for after-tax Receipts enter 360000. Total that column as you did for the other columns and modify the IRR formula in cell A2 to ensure that it accounts for the additional year of activity (i.e., change it to be: =IRR(C4:E4)). The IRR based on these new facts should be 22%, and the spreadsheet should look something like this:

	A	B	C	D	E
1	IRR		Investment	year 1	year 2
2	22%	Outlays	-200,000	-28,800	-28,800
3		Receipts	0	0	360,000
4		Total	-200,000	-31,200	331,200

With these simple skills, you can now estimate what the IRR would be if the individual were to hold the property for more than two years. For example, if the amount of gain remained constant and was subject to a 20% tax, you could determine that the IRR would be 10% and 4% if the individual held the property for three years or four years, respectively.

Microsoft Excel also includes an XIRR function, which computes IRR based upon dates cash flows occur and the amount of cash flows. The XIRR function therefore allows a person to compute IRR if cash flows occur at other than regular intervals. When used to compute the internal rate of return of projected future cash flows, the XIRR function appears to be very capable, for the most part. Drafters of distribution waterfalls of partnerships and LLCs appear to be using XIRR frequently to define internal rate of return for the purpose of determining waterfall hurdles. The XIRR function is less suited for that type of use and can lead to confusion.[37]

B. Tips for Computing Net Present Value

Microsoft Excel facilitates the computation of net present value. The example in the commentary provided that an investor was considering spending $100,000 to purchase property at the beginning of Year 1. At the end of Year 2, the investor would spend $390,000 for a building constructed on that property. For Years 3 through 15, the developer planned to receive the net cash flows presented above and to receive $1,061,000 at the end of Year 15 from the disposition of the building and land.[38] This is the information the investor needs to compute the net present value of the property.

To compute the net present value using Excel, first input the labels into the spreadsheet. The labels will simply be the net present value, the initial investment, and Years 1 through 15. Input those labels in Row 1 using the following cells: A1: NPV, B1: Investment, C1: Year 1, D1: Year 2, and E1 through Q1: Year 3 through Year 15.

Next, input the information from the example. The initial investment was $100,000. In Year 2, the developer paid $390,000 for the building. At the end of Year 3 the investor received net cash flow of $26,0000. At the end of Year 15, the developer re-

---

37. *See, e.g.,* Bradley T. Borden, *Math Behind Financial Aspects of Partnership Distribution Waterfalls,* 145 TAX NOTES 305 (Oct. 20, 2014).

38. The cash flows for Years 4 through 13 come from the presentation above. *See supra* Part 1.C.2.

ceived $1,043,500 in after-tax proceeds from the sale of the property and net cash flow. Recall that Excel recognizes payments as negative numbers and receipts as positive numbers. Input this information in Row 2 using the following cells: B2: -100000, C2: 0, D2: -390000, E2 through P2: relevant net cash flows from above, and Q2: 1043500.

With this information in the spreadsheet, you can now compute the net present value of the investment. The computation will include all the net cash flows from the time of the initial investment through Year 15 (cells B2 through Q2). The net present value computation also requires a discount rate. The discount rate should usually reflect the market rate of return that the developer can expect to obtain from other investments. Assume that rate of return is 5.5%. The net present value function in Excel is =NPV(rate, cash flow). In this example, the rate is 5.5%, but you must input that amount as a decimal, or 0.055. The cash flow is in cells B2 through Q2. You can input that as B2:Q2. Thus, input the following formula in A2: =NPV(0.055,B2:Q2). The information you enter should look something like this:

	A	B	C	D	E	...	P	Q
1	NPV	Invest-ment	Year 1	Year 2	Year 3	...	Year 14	Year 15
2	=NPV(0.055,B2:Q2)	-100000	0	-390000	26000	...	17000	1043500

This will return a net present value of $133,050.

Chapter 6

The Role of the Real Estate
Tax Attorney

I. Commentary

Because most transactions raise tax issues, attorneys must be aware of the standards that govern taxpayer reporting and the tax-practice standards that govern tax advisors. Tax advisors owe a duty to both the tax system and to their clients. They must balance those duties when providing tax advice. Ultimately, clients make decisions about courses of action and reporting positions they will take, but attorneys must provide accurate information about the law that helps their clients make decisions, and they must avoid aiding wrongdoing.

A. Property Owners' Tax-Planning Objectives

Property owners generally have three or four tax-planning objectives. If they acquire or own depreciable real property, they will generally want to recover the cost of the property as quickly as possible through depreciation deductions.[1] The tax-planning objective of all property owners, including those with depreciable property, will be to obtain favorable tax treatment on the disposition of property. As discussed in Chapter 2, favorable tax treatment often depends upon the amount and character of gain or loss recognized on the disposition. In some situations, the property owners can defer or exclude gain. Gain deferral and exclusion are generally preferable to gain recognition. If the disposition of property will result in taxable loss, however, the owners will often prefer to accelerate the recognition of the loss instead of deferring it.

Attorneys giving tax advice therefore must be aware of the consequences of a particular transaction and the property owner's situation to know how to help the property owner accomplish objectives. For example, if a property owner has significant losses to offset gains, recognizing gains currently may be better than deferral. Thus, attorneys generally should obtain some general information beyond the current transaction when providing tax advice.

Although property owners often focus on tax planning when they prepare to dispose of property, the manner in which they acquire and hold property will often affect

---

1. *See* I.R.C. §§ 167, 168 (governing depreciation deductions).

the tax treatment on disposition of the property. Thus, attorneys must consider the property owners' tax objectives when assisting them with the acquisition and ownership of property, and they must help property owners understand the importance of structuring the ownership of property to help obtain desired tax results.

1. Amount and Character of Gain or Loss

Recall from Chapter 2 that section 1001 determines the amount of gain or loss that a taxpayer realizes on the disposition of property.[2] Gain realized is the excess of amount realized over the property's adjusted basis.[3] If the amount realized is apparent,[4] the only way to affect the gain or loss a property owner will realize is to consider the property's adjusted basis. The basis of property is not always obvious. For example, in the case of a real-estate developer, the basis of specific tracts of land may vary depending upon costs incurred to improve or subdivide the property and the fair market value of the property at the time of acquisition. Various factors may affect the manner in which the owners allocate the purchase price to the basis of different portions of the property.[5]

The character of gain or loss will also be important to property owners. Long-term capital gain generally qualifies for favorable tax treatment.[6] Short-term capital gain and gain from the sale of inventory are subject to ordinary income rates.[7] Thus, to obtain favorable tax treatment on the disposition of property, property owners must hold the property long enough to satisfy the long-term-holding-period requirement, and the property must be a capital asset. The manner in which property owners hold property and the activities that they engage in with respect to the property will determine whether the property is a capital asset and will affect the character of gain they recognize on the disposition of the property. Attorneys must be familiar with the rules governing the classification of property to provide advice regarding the acquisition and holding of the property to help ensure it is classified as a capital asset. Chapter 7 covers the classification of property.

2. Gain Deferral

Property owners who will realize gain on the disposition of property will generally prefer to defer the gain, if possible. Several types of dispositions qualify for gain deferral. Of particular interest to property owners are installment sales and like-kind exchanges.[8] The deferral rules that apply to transfers to and from tax entities become

---

2. *See* I.R.C. § 1001(a).

3. *See id.*

4. Generally, however, the amount realized will be the sum of the fair market value of property received, money received, and debt relief in exchange for the property. *See* I.R.C. § 1001(b); Treas. Reg. § 1.1001-2(a). Closing and other costs may, however, affect the amount realized. *See* Ward v. Commissioner, 224 F.2d 547 (9th Cir. 1955); Treas. Reg. § 1/263(a)-2(e).

5. *See* Fairfield Plaza, Inc. v. Commissioner, 39 T.C. 706 (1963), *reproduced supra* Chapter 2; Rev. Rul. 79-276, 179-2 C.B. 200.

6. *See* I.R.C. §§ 1(h)(1)(C), 1221(a), 1222, 1231.

7. *See* I.R.C. §§ 1(h)(1)(A), 64, 1221(a), 1222, 1231.

8. *See* I.R.C. §§ 453, 1031; *infra* Chapters 8 & 10.

important if property moves to or from entities under common control.[9] Gain deferral provisions often defer gain through basis-carryover rules, which preserve gain or loss by requiring property owners to take a basis in acquired property that is equal to the basis of the transferred property.[10] The purpose for which a property owner holds property will affect the application of deferral provisions,[11] so attorneys must help property owners ensure that the manner in which they hold property accurately reflects their intent. Chapter 8 covers installment sales, and several chapters cover like-kind exchanges.

3. Income Exclusion

Nonrecognition rules provide that property owners do not have to recognize gain at the time they dispose of property. Nonetheless, the basis-carryover rules preserve the gain in other property (e.g., replacement property, installment note, or entity interest). The subsequent disposition of the other property could trigger the deferred gain. Gain deferral distinguishes nonrecognition rules from income exclusion rules. Income exclusion rules provide that a taxpayer will not recognize income on a certain transaction, and they have no mechanisms to defer the excluded income. Therefore, taxpayers prefer income exclusion over gain deferral. Exclusion rules that may apply to owners of real estate include the exclusion of cancellation-of-indebtedness income and perhaps the exclusion of gain on the sale of a principal residence.[12] Of those two rules, the exclusion for cancellation-of-indebtedness income is more likely to be relevant to attorneys giving tax advice to real-property owners. The exclusion for cancellation-of-indebtedness income becomes relevant in the transactional setting if a property owner disposes of property subject to a recourse liability and the amount of the recourse liability exceeds the property's value.[13]

B. Standards Governing Tax Reporting

Property owners and their advisors must consider the owners' objectives in light of rules governing tax reporting and tax practice. Property owners will generally be interested in the standards governing their tax reporting because failure to adhere to the standards may result in penalties. Taxpayers must, of course, avoid making false or fraudulent statements with respect to tax-reporting positions.[14] Most taxpayers should

---

9. *See, e.g.,* I.R.C. §§ 351, 721 (providing nonrecognition rules for contributions to corporations and partnerships); I.R.C. §§ 301, 302, 311, 731 (providing rules for distribution from corporations and partnerships).

10. *See, e.g.,* I.R.C. §§ 301(d), 358, 362, 722, 723, 732, 1031(d).

11. *See, e.g.,* I.R.C. §§ 453(l) (providing that installment-sale treatment is not available for dealer dispositions), 1031(a)(1) (requiring property to be held for productive use in a trade or business or for investment).

12. *See* I.R.C. §§ 108, 121.

13. *See* Treas. Reg. § 1.1001-2(c), *Example (8).*

14. *See* I.R.C. § 6663 (imposing civil penalties for underpayment of taxes due to fraud); I.R.C. §§ 7206, 7207 (imposing criminal penalties for false or fraudulent actions with respect to tax reporting).

know that making false or fraudulent statements is illegal. Their main interest will often be to know the weight of authority that they need to support reporting positions. Failure to rely upon the appropriate weight of authority may result in penalties.[15]

Taxpayers will want to avoid the accuracy-related penalty for underpayments, which penalty is 20% of the underpayment.[16] That penalty applies to many situations,[17] but in tax planning, the substantial-understatement penalty (a subset of the accuracy-related penalty) is particularly important. The substantial-understatement penalty applies if the amount of an understatement exceeds a certain threshold.[18] The rules reduce the amount of the understatement if substantial authority supports the reporting position or if the taxpayer adequately discloses a reporting position that has a reasonable basis.[19] Thus, even though a taxpayer may have to pay tax and interest with respect to a reporting position, the taxpayer may not have to pay the substantial-understatement penalty. To advise taxpayers with respect to reporting positions, attorneys must be familiar with the weight of authority required for a position to have substantial authority or reasonable basis. The regulations define those concepts.[20] Items the regulations identify as providing substantial authority may not have precedential value for a substantive position.[21]

The ultimate decision regarding the position a taxpayer will take on a tax return is the taxpayer's. Attorneys can advise taxpayers with respect to consequences that may result from particular positions, but taxpayers must make the final decision.[22] Several factors may affect a taxpayer's decision. For example, a taxpayer's risk tolerance will be important. Some taxpayers will want to avoid any negative interaction with the IRS and only take positions on tax returns if they are very confident that the IRS will respect the position. Other taxpayers will be interested in taking positions, even if there is some doubt about whether the IRS will challenge the position, as long as they will not be assessed penalties. Only individual taxpayers will know the level of

---

15. *See* Long Term Capital Holdings v. United States, 330 F. Supp. 2d 122 (D. Conn. 2004) (discussing various penalties and measures taxpayers must take to avoid the penalties).

16. *See* I.R.C. § 6662(a).

17. *See* I.R.C. § 6662(b) (listing the situations that give rise to the penalty).

18. *See* I.R.C. § 6662(d)(1), (2) (defining substantial understatement).

19. *See* I.R.C. § 6662(d)(2)(B). Taxpayers may also avoid the accuracy-related penalty if there is a reasonable cause for a position they took and they acted in good faith with respect to the position. *See* I.R.C. § 6664(c)(1). *See also* Ringgold Tel. Co. v. Comm'r, T.C. Memo. 2010-103 (holding that the taxpayer acted with reasonable cause and in good faith by relying upon the advice of an accountant regarding the valuation of property); Treas. Reg. § 1.6664-4 (discussing reasonable cause and good faith). *But see* I.R.C. § 6662(b)(6) (imposing strict liability for transactions that lack economic substance under section 7701(o)); I.R.C. § 7701(o) (codifying economic substance doctrine).

20. *See* Treas. Reg. § 1.6662-3(b)(3), (c) (defining reasonable basis and the method for disclosing positions that are contrary to the regulations); Treas. Reg. § 1.6662-4(d) (defining substantial authority); Treas. Reg. § 1.6662-4(e) (providing rules for adequate disclosure). *See also* Long Term Capital Holdings v. United States, 330 F. Supp. 2d 122 (D. Conn. 2004) (discussing penalties and the weights of authority).

21. *See, e.g.*, AmerGen Energy Co., LLC v. United States, 94 Fed. Cl. 413 (2010) (discussing whether private letter rulings have precedential value).

22. *But see* Circular 230, § 10.34(c) (presenting the tax advisor's obligation to provide certain information to clients).

risk that they will tolerate. To make the decision, however, taxpayers must receive informed counsel from their tax advisor.

C. Standards Governing Tax Advisors

Attorneys providing tax advice must follow the general rules of professional responsibility, and they must adhere to tax-practice standards that are specific to tax advisors as set forth in statutes and Circular 230. Attorneys may feel pressure from clients to provide advice that will reduce the amount of tax the client must pay. An attorney who provides advice that does not have adequate legal support or that is false or fraudulent may be subject to penalties or sanctions.[23] If an attorney fails to recognize provisions in the law that allow a client to pay less tax, perhaps the client will have a malpractice claim against the attorney. Thus, providing tax advice requires attorneys to get the answer right. Attorneys giving tax advice may not merely advise clients to take conservative positions that require the payment of the most taxes. On the other hand, attorneys also must have adequate legal support to advise a client to take a position that reduces tax liability. That dilemma makes tax practice challenging.

II. Primary Legal Authority

Ward v. Commissioner

United States Court of Appeals, Ninth Circuit

224 F.2d 547 (1955)

FACTS

Before us are the petitions of Dwight A. Ward and Hanna P. Ward to review decisions of the Tax Court entered on August 13, 1953, 20 T.C. 332 decreeing that there were deficiencies in the petitioners' income taxes for the year 1946 in the respective amounts of $8051.46 and $2444.45. The determination of the Tax Court was made on petitions from a determination of the Commissioner of Internal Revenue finding deficiencies in the respective amounts of $11,221.46 and $1,965.95.

Petitioners are husband and wife, the wife's case being here merely because of her community interest under California law. Throughout the proceeding the record in the husband's case was used as that in the wife's case, because this controversy arose out of the business carried on by the husband as one of the partners in a commercial enterprise.

The reference to "taxpayer" will mean petitioner Dwight A. Ward.

For many years prior to November 1, 1945, taxpayer was an equal partner with his two brothers Harry Ward and D. T. Ward in a partnership which conducted the business of manufacturing refrigerators under the name of 'Ward Refrigerator & Mfg.

---

23. *See* I.R.C. § 6694; Circular 230. The statutory penalties apply to tax return preparers, which could include advising attorneys. *See* I.R.C. § 7701(a)(36); Treas. Reg. §§ 1.6694-1, 301.7701-15.

Co.', at Los Angeles, California. Because of disputes as to the management of the business between the taxpayer and his two brothers, the two brothers filed, on November 1, 1945, in the Superior Court of the State of California, for the County of Los Angeles, a petition for the dissolution of the partnership and the appointment of a receiver. On the same day, the Court appointed R. E. Allen receiver, and ordered him to operate the business, and, upon proper application to the Court, to sell it.

The business was sold at a public sale to taxpayer's two brothers for the price of $820,000.00, the Order confirming the sale being entered by the Court on February 14, 1946. Taxpayer had a one-third interest in the partnership. The cost basis of his one-third interest in the partnership on the date of sale was $140,756.64. His one-third share was $211,111.26. Taxpayer received the proceeds from the sale on the dates and in the amounts following: February 5, 1946, to April 3, 1946, $2,800.00; March 12, 1946, $14,500.00; April 22, 1946, $173,000.00; April 25, 1946, $2,785.17; May 14, 1946, $956.46; January 2, 1947, $2,073.34; January 2, 1947, $14,926.66, and, some time in 1947, $69.63, making a total of $211,111.26.

The purchase price for the taxpayer's partnership interest was paid to the receiver in cash about May 14, 1946. The payment of $17,000.00, consisting of the two amounts paid on January 2, 1947, was delayed because of a notice of attachment served on Allen, the receiver, by Walter Webb in an action instituted by him against the taxpayer for personal services alleged to have been rendered to him personally, and not to the partnership, during the two years prior to April, 1946. The attachment was issued on April 19, 1946, after the filing of the complaint. Upon being served with the statutory notice, the receiver drew a check for $17,000.00 upon the receivership funds to himself as trustee, which he deposited in a separate bank account as a special trust account to abide the outcome of the action. Appropriate entries on the receiver's books to reflect the segregation of the amount were made. The receivership fees were paid to Allen on April 5, 1946. However, as is customary when funds are in the hands of the receiver to take care of contingencies that might arise later, he was not actually discharged until March 21, 1947.

Taxpayer excluded $17,069.63 from the reported selling price of the partnership interest, but used the total cost basis as an offset in computing the amount of taxable gain reported in his return.

After a trial of the issues in Webb v. Ward, the Court awarded to the plaintiff $11,000.00, subject to the offset of an amount claimed to have been paid to Webb by Ward. After discussions with the Court and negotiations between counsel, it was agreed that payments of $8926.66 should be offset against the award, and a final judgment was entered in favor of Webb, on January 2, 1946, for the sum of $2073.34. On the same day the attachment was released, and the receiver paid to Webb the amount of his judgment and gave to taxpayer a check for the balance in the trust account, $14,926.66. The Tax Court found that taxpayer's gain in the sale, including the amount of $17,000.00, was realized in 1946, although payment of the amount was deferred, by reason of the attachment, until 1947. Section 111, Internal Revenue Code of 1939, 26 U.S.C., 1952 ed., § 111.

The taxpayer has challenged the correctness of this finding as well as of the findings disallowing the sum of $4000.00 paid to Benjamin S. Parks, attorney, and $5000.00 paid to Roy C. Seeley, appraiser, claimed as deductions. Instead, the Tax Court allowed these sums as offsets against the selling price. For convenience of treatment and to avoid repetition, a more detailed analysis of the facts relating to these two matters will be given further on in the opinion. For the moment, we advert to certain general legal principles which apply to the situation.

Since 1948, the findings of the Tax Court have the same force as those of the "decisions of the district courts in civil actions tried without a jury". 26 U.S.C. § 1141(a). This section applies to reviews of the decisions of the Tax Court the rule that "findings of fact shall not be set aside unless clearly erroneous, and due regard shall be given to the opportunity of the trial court to judge of the credibility of the witnesses." Rule 52(a), Federal Rules of Civil Procedure, 28 U.S.C.

This Court, in giving effect to the mandate of the Congress, expressed in the Amendment of 1948, has stated that it is not our function to retry cases on review, and that we will not disturb a finding or conclusion of the Tax Court "unless clear error appears". *National Brass Work, Inc., v. Comm'r*, 205 F.2d 104, 107 (9th Cir. 1953). [footnote omitted]

Another principle to be borne in mind is that upon a sale incidental to the dissolution of a partnership, whether by agreement of the parties or through judicial proceeding,—in fact, through any of the methods provided by State law,—the distributive shares received by the partners after sale are not income, but gain upon the sale of a capital asset within the meaning of § 117(a) and (b) of the Internal Revenue Code, 26 U.S.C., 1952 ed., 117(a) and (b). *See, Stilgenbaur v. U.S.*, 115 F.2d 283, 286–287 (9th Cir. 1940); *U.S. v. Adamson*, 161 F.2d 942 (9th Cir. 1947); *Hatch's Estate v. Comm'r*, 198 F.2d 26, 29 (9th Cir. 1952).

As the transaction upon which taxes were assessed was a sale upon dissolution of a partnership through court action in a proceeding in the State courts, California Corporations Code, § 15032, in which, for the purpose of dissolution and sale of the property, a receiver was appointed, it is well to state that, under California law, a receivership is an ancillary proceeding. California Code of Civil Procedure, § 564 et seq. The receiver in California is an officer of the court whose possession of property is that of the court for the benefit of all persons who may show themselves to be entitled to it. *Adams v. Haskell*, 6 Cal. 113 (1856); *Pacific Ry. Co. v. Wade*, 91 Cal. 449, 454–456 (1891); *Tapscott v. Lyon*, 103 Cal. 297 (1894); *Highland Securities Co. v. Superior Court*, 119 Cal. App. 107, 112–114, (1931); *Chiesur v. Superior Court*, 76 Cal.App.2d 198, 199, 200–201 (1946). When a receiver is appointed to sell the property of a partnership, he holds the proceeds of the sale for distribution to the parties entitled to them.

These general considerations must be borne in mind in determining the matters before us. For, while, generally, state rules are not necessarily binding in federal tax matters, where taxable situations arise from relationships entered into under state law, their nature and the rights of the parties under such law must be kept in view in determining the incidence of federal taxation. This is especially true in considering the first problem before the Court, — the refusal of the Tax Court to overturn the determination of the Commissioner that the taxpayer was taxable in 1946 upon his full share of the purchase price received for the sale of the partnership business, and in not allowing deduction from the amount received in 1946 of the sum of $17,000.00 attached in the hands of the receiver in the action instituted by Webb on April 19, 1946. California Code of Civil Procedure, §§ 537, 542(6).

Here again, it will be helpful to consider the nature of attachments. Under California law, an attachment is an auxiliary proceeding. It may be issued at the time of issuing the summons and its object is to attach the property of the defendant "as security for the satisfaction of any judgment that may be recovered, *unless the defendant gives security* to pay such judgment...." California Code of Civil Procedure, § 537. (Emphasis added.)

The attachment is merely a sequestration of the debtor's funds to abide the judgment. They still remain the property of the debtor and title to them passes to the attaching creditor only after a judgment in his favor has been entered, in which case the lien of the attachment is merged into that of the judgment. *Kinnison v. Guaranty Liquidating Corp.*, 18 Cal.2d 256 (1941); *Puissegur v. Yarbrough*, 29 Cal.2d 409 (1946); *Pintel v. K. N. H. Mohamed & Bros.*, 107 Cal.App.2d 328 (1951). The lien extends only to the interest of the debtor at the time of the levy, and the attaching creditor "obtains only a potential right or a contingent lien." *Puissegur v. Yarbrough*, supra, 29 Cal.2d at page 412.

The Supreme Court has approved this description of the lien created in California by attachment as "apt", adding:

> The attachment lien gives the attachment creditor no right to proceed against the property unless he gets a judgment within three years or within such extension as the statute provides. Numerous contingencies might arise that would prevent the attachment lien from ever becoming perfected by a judgment awarded and recorded. Thus the attachment lien is contingent or inchoate — merely a *lis pendens* notice that a right to perfect a lien exists.

U.S. v. Sec. Tr. & Savings Bank, 340 U.S. 47, 50, (1950). (Emphasis in text)

The same case states that while a state court's classification of a lien, although entitled to weight, is subject to reexamination by the federal courts, nevertheless "if the state court itself describes the lien as inchoate, this classification is 'practically conclusive.'" 340 U.S. at page 50.

We now return to the specific problems before us as reflected in the Tax Court's decision.

The Tax Court found that the transaction which formed the subject of the action in which the attachment was issued was "a wholly unrelated claim". Whether this language properly describes the transaction or not, these undisputed facts appear from the record: The receivership was auxiliary to the dissolution of a partnership through court action. California Corporations Code, § 15302. A receiver was appointed to effect the dissolution. The sale of the business of the partnership and its purchase by two of the partners, the brothers of the taxpayer, was the judicial means for terminating the partnership and awarding to taxpayer his share of the purchase price after deducting the costs of the receiver's operation of the business prior to the sale, his expenses of administration and such claims as were presented and allowed in the course of administration. The cost basis of taxpayer's one-third interest in the partnership on the date of sale was $140,756.64. The sale was for $820,000.00. The taxpayer's one-third share of the net proceeds of the sale was $211,111.26, without taking into account the effect on it, if any, of the action instituted by Webb and the levy under the attachment proceedings in it. The taxpayer's entire share of the proceeds, excepting the sum of $17,000.00, was paid to him between February 5, 1946, and May 11, 1946. The money garnisheed was deposited by the receiver in a separate trust account. The garnishment conformed to California law. Money in the law's custody is not, ordinarily, subject to garnishment. However, if a person is entitled *to a definite distributive share* of a fund in the law's custody, one of his creditors may, under California law, garnish it in the hands of the officer, such as a receiver or court clerk having the custody. *Dunsmoor v. Furstenfeldt*, 26 P. 518 (1891); *Widenmann v. Weniger*, 130 P. 421 (1913); *Youtz v. Farmers' etc., Nat. Bank*, 160 P. 855 (1916); *City of Los Angeles v. Knapp*, 70 P.2d 643 (1937). So when the plaintiff in the action against Ward served the receiver with a notice of garnishment, that officer properly set aside, in a special trust fund, the amount claimed. California Code of Civil Procedure, § 544. The action in which the attachment was issued was not against the partnership, but against the taxpayer for services claimed to have been rendered to him personally. Neither the other partners, as individuals, nor the partnership, as an entity, were made parties to the action or served with any process in it. Nor were any of their funds garnisheed. In the circumstances, the Tax Court was correct in ruling that the taxpayer realized his share of the purchase price in 1946, and that the postponement of the actual possession by him of $17,000.00 of his share of the proceeds of the sale did not arise from a condition inherent in the sale.

It is an accepted principle in the law of income taxation that if, in order to reduce funds to the taxpayer's actual possession, action beyond his control is required, there is no realization. This situation arises when, for instance, approval of a court in order to withdraw money deposited in the court's registry by the Government in a condemnation proceeding is required, *Nitterhouse v. U.S.*, 207 F.2d 618, 620 (3rd Cir. 1953) — or the taxpayer, being the executor of an estate, has to determine whether the interests of the estate warrant immediate payment to himself of money allowed him by order of court. *Weil v. Comm'r*, 173 F.2d 805, 808–809 (2d Cir. 1949). In such instances, the failure of the taxpayer to make the legal showing in order to secure court approval for withdrawal of funds deposited or to exercise his own discretion in favor of immediate payment to himself, does not justify charging him with the income *he might have* received but for his *failure to act*. See, *North American Oil Co. v. Burnet*, 1932, 286 U.S. 417, 424 (1932); *Comm'r v. Wilcox*, 327 U.S. 404, 409 (1946). Had the court in which the receivership was pending delayed distribution of the proceeds of the sale until the disposition of the litigation between Webb and the taxpayer, the act would have been one beyond the control of the taxpayer. But the withholding by the receiver, out of the taxpayer's share, of the amount garnisheed until the following year arose not from any of the conditions of the sale or the orders of the court in which the receivership was pending, but from the fact of attachment in a personal action against the taxpayer in which a levy sequestered the funds. The sale had been completed before the attachment was issued and the levy made and the entire amount of the taxpayer's share, including the money garnisheed, was actually available for payment to him. U.S. Treasury Regulation 111, § 29.42-2; *McEuen v. Comm'r*, 196 F.2d 127 (5th Cir. 1952).

Which means that the conditions for the application principle adverted to do not exist. *U.S. v. Pfister*, 205 F.2d 538, 541 (8th Cir. 1953).[24]

So the Tax Court was justified in holding that the amount garnisheed under the Writ of Attachment was realized in 1946, although not actually paid over to the taxpayer until January, 1947. Which brings us to the other two items in the Tax Court's decisions which are under attack.

The Tax Court found that after the other brothers filed suit to dissolve the partnership, the taxpayer engaged the services of Benjamin S. Parks as his attorney, who rendered services between the early part of December, 1945, and February 8, 1946, during which period he devoted most of his time to the taxpayer's affairs, continuing to represent him, when necessary, until January, 1947. During the taxable year, the taxpayer paid to Parks sums aggregating $10,000.00. Parks' services were not limited to strictly legal problems. He assisted the taxpayer in his efforts to secure financial backing in order to buy out his two brothers. Parks secured the assistance of a Mr. W. C. Graham of San Francisco, who bid up the property and only ceased bidding when his final bid of $815,000.00 was overbid by the taxpayer's brothers, who bid $820,000.00. In conjunction with the sale, Graham insisted that the services of Roy C. Seeley be secured for the appraisal of the property. The taxpayer paid to the Company of which Seeley was a member $5000.00 for the services, under an agreement which provided, in effect, that the taxpayer would guarantee and pay a minimum

---

24. [2] In *Parkford v. Comm'r*, 133 F.2d 249, 251 (9th Cir. 1943), this Court stated:
"The situation of the taxpayer would not be different taxwise had the sum owing been seized by a creditor through process of garnishment after it had been earned. The taxpayer obtained the economic benefit of the income through its disbursement to his creditors, although he denies receiving any benefit because, he says, he was entitled to his discharge regardless of whether the creditors received anything. But we think the latter circumstance is immaterial. The net result of petitioner's argument is that the portion of the fee received by the trustee, although undeniably income to somebody, was legally income to nobody. We conclude that since the income accrued to the taxpayer he must account for it in his return. The taking over of the amount by the trustee for the payment of debts was the final step by which the taxpayer obtained the fruits of the accrual."
(Emphasis added.) The Court was considering the effect of the claim of a trustee in bankruptcy to a commission earned by the bankrupt. Hence the statement as to the effect of the garnishment was, in a sense, obiter. But it aptly illustrates a situation in which, although the taxpayer has no actual possession of the income, it nevertheless accrues to him. So the language correctly described a situation such as that confronting us here, and is justly anticipatory of, and spells out, the ruling to be made.

fee of $5000.00 to Seeley if the assets were sold to someone other than Graham and at a figure of more than $800,000.00 gross. Pursuant to this agreement, the Roy C. Seeley Company made several value analyses of land, buildings, machinery and inventory of the partnership business. As a consequence of Parks' and Seeley's efforts and services, Graham became interested in purchasing the business and agreed to bid up to $800,000.00 for the business, and taxpayer, in turn, agreed to exchange his one-third interest in the partnership for one-third of the common stock of a corporation to be organized and which was to operate the business if Graham's bid acquired it. Taxpayer also agreed to be active in the new business and to become a director of the corporation. Petitioners each deducted one-half of the $5000.00 as a miscellaneous deduction.

Although the Tax Court treated these two items separately, we shall treat them together, because their solution depends upon the application of the same principles. The Tax Court allowed as a deductible business expense under § 23(a)(1)(A) of the Internal Revenue Code, 26 U.S.C. § 23(a)(1)(A) $6000.00 of Parks' fee. But $4000.00 of it was allowed only as an offset against the selling price,—an expenditure made in connection with the sale of a capital asset. *See, Coke*, 17 T.C. 403 (1951), affirmed in *Comm'r v. Coke*, 201 F.2d 742 (5th Cir. 1953). It also allowed as an offset the $5000.00 fee paid to Seeley. It is not disputed that services of this type that are not compensable as commissions in sales are proper offsets. *Spreckels v. Helvering*, 315 U.S. 626 (1942), affirming *Spreckels v. Comm'r*, 119 F.2d 667 (9th Cir. 1951); *Comm'r v. Covington*, 120 F.2d 768, 770 (5th Cir. 1941). But it is insisted that these amounts should have been treated as deductible non-business expenses paid "for the production or collection of income", under § 23(a)(2) of the Internal Revenue Code, 26 U.S.C., 1952 ed. § 23(a)(2). To be deductible as such, expenses must "bear a reasonable and proximate relation to the production of income or to the management, conservation or maintenance of property held for the production of income." *U.S. v. Lykes*, 188 F.2d 964, 967 (5th Cir. 1951).[25]

And where the expenditures were fees paid to an attorney to represent a taxpayer in a dispute as to the amount due on an option agreement, *Naylor v. Comm'r*, 203 F.2d 346 (5th Cir. 1953), or to litigate on behalf of a dissenting stockholder who was seeking to recover the cash value of the stock of a corporation merged with another corporation, *Heller v. Comm'r*, 147 F.2d 376 (9th Cir. 1945), the facts complied with these tests. But here, the two "agreeing" partners and the taxpayer, who was the "dissident" partnership as a going concern. Parks was employed to assist in securing a person who would finance the taxpayer in his attempt to purchase. He helped interest Graham who insisted that Seeley's services be secured. Seeley was promised a fee of $5000.00, if Graham was not the purchaser and the bid exceeded $800,000.00. Gra-

---

25. [3] In affirming the case, *Lykes v. U.S.*, 343 U.S. 118, 124 (1952), the Supreme Court approved the test that to be deductible, expenditures must be "proximately related to the production of income". *And see, McDonald v. Comm'r*, 323 U.S. 57 (1944); *Cobb v. Comm'r*, 173 F.2d 711, 714 (6th Cir. 1949), the ruling in which was approved in *Lykes v. U.S., supra*, 343 U.S. 124. Certiorari was denied earlier, *Cobb v. Comm'r.*, 338 U.S. 832.

ham's highest bid was $815,000.00. He allowed a final $5000.00 raise in this bid to thwart the acquisition of the property by himself and the taxpayer. So the services of Parks and Seeley merely enabled the taxpayer to sell his interest in the property at a greater profit. They were not ordinary and necessary business expenses or non-business expenses incurred in the production or collection of income. In this respect, *Cobb v. Comm'r*, supra, Note 3, which has the approval of the Supreme Court, is very revealing. There, an attorney had been employed to represent the taxpayer in a claimed gift tax deficiency on account of interests in income-producing realty given to married daughters. The services of the attorney resulted in a reduction of the gift tax deficiency. It was argued that the amount so paid was deductible as ordinary and necessary expense incurred "for the production or collection of income." The contention was rejected, the Court saying:

> The true criterion would seem to be that, to become deductible under the statute, the expense must be in proximate relation to the production or collection of income or to the care and conservation of property held to produce it. The paring of the deficiency in the taxpayer's gift tax through the efforts of his attorneys was beneficial to him, in that he was not forced to sell other income-producing property, but the expense to that end is not appropriately classifiable as an expense directly incurred in conserving such property. The opinion in the Bingham case declares that section 23(a)(2) is in pari materia with section 23(a)(1), permitting the deduction of ordinary and necessary expenses *directly connected with or approximately resultant from the conduct of the business,* and that section 23(a)(2) provides for a class of coextensive non-business deductions, except that the expenses need not be incurred in a business but only in the production of income or in the conservation or management of property held for the production of income.

(Emphasis in text.) *Cobb v. Comm'r*, supra, Note 3, 173 F.2d at page 714.

In the case before us, the payments for Parks' and Seeley's services were, in effect, a capital expenditure to help the sale. *Cf. Brown v. Comm'r*, 215 F.2d 697, 700–701 (5th Cir. 1954); *Shipp v. Comm'r*, 217 F.2d 401 (9th Cir. 1954). Their efforts were "beneficial" to the taxpayer in that by the raising of the bid, he secured a higher price for his share. Hence, the expenditures were a legitimate offset against the cost of the property sold. But they cannot be classified as deductible expenses under § 23(a)(1)(A) or § 23(a) (2).

In the reply brief filed on behalf of the taxpayer, the object sought to be attained by the payment of the $9000.00 is stated in this manner:

> The $9000.00 in question was paid so that petitioners would have a bidder at the sale which would accomplish the purpose either of acquiring the business by an organization in which petitioners would be part owners or of increasing the price for which their interest would be sold. The first purpose was not realized but the second purpose became a fact in that the partnership business was sold for $820,000.00 instead of $450,000.00 which was the first bid of petitioner's brothers.

This being the taxpayer's own appraisal of the purposes for which Parks and Seeley were employed and what their employment achieved, it may be accepted as correct.

It follows that the ultimate result of the employment was the sale of the partnership assets at a higher price. The result thus achieved is, therefore, no different than that derived by the employment of a selling agent, and paying him a commission to secure a buyer at a desired price. Here the taxpayer did not buy, he sold. And the efforts of his agents helped increase the sale price of the property, and, consequently, the value of his distributive share. So the tax Court was right in treating these expenditures as commissions.[26]

Amergen Energy Co., LLC v. United States

United States Court of Federal Claims

94 Fed. Cl. 413 (2010)

OPINION

Plaintiff filed its complaint on February 20, 2009. Discovery is underway, but disputes have arisen. The primary dispute before the court at this time concerns plaintiff's requests for admission regarding the PLRs issued to the sellers of the nuclear power plants. In essence, plaintiff asserts that these PLRs are relevant to the issue it must prove to win its case:

These Requests for Admission would demonstrate that the factual and related legal questions regarding whether the decommissioning liabilities at issue in this case were fixed and reasonably determinable at the time they were assumed by [plaintiff and] have already been determined [in the sellers' PLRs], and would allow the Court to resolve on summary judgment the core legal issue in this case, which is whether [plaintiff] may include in its tax basis of each facility the nuclear decommissioning liability it assumed as part of the purchases, thus avoiding a trial and conserving judicial resources.

Pl.'s Mot. at 7. In plaintiff's view, the PLRs issued to the sellers of the nuclear power plants constitute evidence that the decommissioning liabilities assumed by plaintiff were fixed and reasonably determinable in amount at the time of the purchases. *Id.* at 18 ("The United States has already decided [in the PLRs issued to the

---

26. [4] The facts in the case before us are different from those in *Parker*, 1943 1 T.C. 709, relied on by the taxpayer. There the taxpayer employed an attorney to investigate certain mining property. The attorney made no charge for the investigation. However, after a favorable report, he advised the petitioner and others to advance money, advancing some himself, for the operation of the mine as a joint venture. The venture proving unsuccessful, the Court allowed the money advanced as a deductible loss "in a transaction for profit." The venture having been abandoned and a loss incurred, it was clearly deductible under § 23(a)(2). We fail to see how the reasoning of this case can be applied to a situation like the one before us in which, on a forced judicial sale, upon dissolution of a partnership in what was a profitable going business, the efforts of a lawyer and an appraiser succeeded in raising the price at which the business was sold, thereby "benefiting" the taxpayer by "increasing" the value of his share.

sellers] that the nuclear decommissioning liabilities that are at issue in this case are fixed and reasonably determinable.").

Defendant opposes plaintiff's motion, and argues that the PLRs in question are irrelevant to plaintiff's claims in this suit:

> [A]n investigation into the reasons why the IRS did or did not make certain statements in various private letter rulings, as well as any attempt now to interpret and understand the qualifications to those statements, and to compare the much more limited set of (untested) factual representations made to the IRS ten years ago to the actual, and much more complete, record that will be presented here, can have no bearing on the issues in this case.

Def.'s Opp. at 3. As to other requests for admission not related to the PLRs issued to the sellers, defendant argues that responding to those requests cannot proceed until more progress on discovery has been made. Id. at 3–4. Plaintiff's motion appears to address only the requests for admission related to the sellers' PLRs, Pl.'s Mot. at 7–8, and does not clearly state a position as to other requests for admission.

DISCUSSION

* * *

III. Relevance of Private Letter Rulings to This Case

The parties clearly disagree as to the relevance of a private letter ruling, issued by the IRS to one taxpayer, to the litigation of a different tax claim brought by another taxpayer. Plaintiff's argument is founded on assumptions that the court cannot endorse. First, plaintiff states that "[t]he Court of Federal Claims ... has ruled repeatedly that PLRs can be relevant to ongoing litigation, and many cases have explicitly considered PLRs as evidence." Pl.'s Mot. at 8. This statement does not give a full picture of this court's, or other courts', consideration of PLRs in tax cases.[27]

A. Statutory Guidance and Caselaw Regarding the Relevance of PLRs

Private letter rulings, like certain other written determinations issued by the IRS, "may not be used or cited as precedent." I.R.C. §6110(k)(3) (2006). Most courts, therefore, do not find private letter rulings, issued to other taxpayers, to be of prece-

---

27. [6] The court notes that plaintiff relies extensively on *Int'l Bus. Machs. Corp. v. U.S.*, 343 F.2d 914 (Ct. Cl. 1965) (IBM), a case with thirty negative citing references on Westlaw, and omits any reference to the precedential limitation of the holding of that case to its facts. *See, e.g., Fla. Power & Light Co. v. U.S.*, 375 F.3d 1119, 1124 (Fed. Cir. 2004) ("We need not decide whether the appellant would be entitled to relief under IBM, however, because the decision in IBM was effectively limited to its facts by subsequent decisions of the Court of Claims....") (citations and footnote omitted). Plaintiff perhaps believes that this case falls within the fact pattern of IBM. Nonetheless, plaintiff should have alerted the court to the binding precedent limiting the scope of the holding of IBM, so that the weight to be accorded IBM was clear. *See, e.g., Jewelpak Corp. v. U.S.*, 297 F.3d 1326, 1333 n.6 (Fed. Cir. 2002) (stating that "officers of our court have an unfailing duty to bring to our attention the most relevant precedent that bears on the case at hand—both good and bad—of which they are aware") (citations omitted). Plaintiff could not have been unaware of this binding precedent, because another case upon which plaintiff greatly relies discussed, at length, the limits placed on the holding of IBM. *See Vons Cos. v. U.S.*, 51 Fed. Cl. 1, 10 & nn. 9–10 (2001), modified in part by *Vons Cos. v. U.S.*, 89 AFTR 2d 301 (Fed. Cl. 2001).

dential value in deciding the tax claims before them. *See, e.g., Lucky Stores, Inc. & Subsidiaries v. Comm'r*, 153 F.3d 964, 966 n.5 (9th Cir. 1998) ("Taxpayers other than those to whom such rulings or memoranda were issued are not entitled to rely on them.") (citations omitted); *Liberty Nat. Bank & Trust Co. v. United States*, 867 F.2d 302, 304–05 (6th Cir. 1989) (noting that "private letter rulings are directed only to the taxpayer who requested the ruling [and] … may not be used or cited to as precedent"); *David R. Webb Co. v. Comm'r*, 708 F.2d 1254, 1257 n.1 (7th Cir. 1983) (stating that "private letter rulings … may not be used or cited as precedent") (citation omitted); *Fla. Power & Light Co. v. United States*, 56 Fed. Cl. 328, 332 (2003) (*Florida Power I*) (stating that "private letter rulings have no precedential value in that they do not represent the IRS's position as to taxpayers generally and thus are irrelevant in the context of litigation brought by other taxpayers") (citations omitted), *aff'd*, 375 F.3d 1119 (Fed. Cir. 2004) (*Florida Power II*); *Abdel-Fattah v. Comm'r*, 134 T.C. No. 10, (2010) (declining to consider private letter rulings offered by the plaintiff in support of his tax claim). But see *Glass v. Comm'r*, 471 F.3d 698, 709 (6th Cir. 2006) (acknowledging that under section "6110(k)(3), a Private Letter Ruling cannot be used as precedent," but nonetheless commenting that "a recent [private letter] ruling provides persuasive authority for refuting the Commissioner's argument" in that case); *Thom v. U.S.*, 283 F.3d 939, 943 n.6 (8th Cir. 2002) ("Although private letter rulings have no precedential value and do not in any way bind this court, 26 U.S.C. §6110(k)(3), we believe they are an instructive tool that we have at our disposal."); *ABC Rentals of San Antonio, Inc. v. Comm'r*, 142 F.3d 1200, 1207 n.5 (10th Cir. 1998) ("While private letter rulings are not binding authority, they may be cited as evidence of administrative interpretation.") (citations omitted); *Taproot Admin. Servs., Inc. v. Comm'r*, 133 T.C. 202, 237 n.10 (2009) (permitting the submission of a "private letter ruling as evidence of the practice of the Commissioner"). This court in *Vons Cos. v. United States*, 51 Fed. Cl. 1 (2001) (*Vons I*), modified in part by *Vons Cos. v. U.S.*, 89 AFTR 2d 301 (Fed. Cl., 2001), examined section 6110(k)(3) and relevant caselaw and noted that the use of PLRs in tax litigation is limited.[28] *Vons I*, 51 Fed. Cl. at 9–11 & nn.9–10. *Vons I* concluded that "most courts have refused to consider private letter rulings as any form of precedent." *Id.* at 9.

The *Vons I* court provided an excellent summary of relevant caselaw regarding the uses of private letter rulings issued to taxpayers other than the plaintiff in a tax case:

> Private letter rulings and technical advice memoranda, in accordance with section 6110(k)(3) of the Code, may not be used or cited in any precedential way and thus, a fortiori, may not be used to support, in any fashion, an argument that one interpretation of the Code is more authoritative than another. Rather, such rulings and memoranda may be relied upon not for their

---

28. [7] The modification of Vons I altered language regarding revenue rulings, not private letter rulings, and may have incorrectly indicated the paragraph where the substituted language should be inserted. See *Vons Cos. v. U.S.*, 89 AFTR 2d 2002-301, at 1 (indicating, perhaps in error, that "[t]he first two sentences in the second full paragraph under Part II.B (page 12) of the order...." should be replaced).

substance, but only as indication: (i) of the IRS' administrative practice (i.e., that it has issued rulings regarding a particular subject); or (ii) that, under the *IBM* decision, the Commissioner has abused his discretion under [26 U.S.C. §7805(b) (2006)] in issuing different rulings to two directly competing taxpayers. More extensive use or citation of such rulings not only flatly ignores the plain language of section 6110(k)(3), but also threatens the careful compromise struck by the Congress in enacting that section—one that recognizes the functional relationship between allowing the IRS to use a streamlined review process to issue such rulings and memoranda on a relatively expedited basis in exchange for assurances that those documents will have no precedential impact except as to the taxpayers to which they are issued.

Vons I, 51 Fed. Cl. at 12 (citing *Int'l Bus. Machs. Corp. v. U.S.*, 343 F.2d 914 (Ct. Cl. 1965) (*IBM*)). To summarize the impermissible uses of PLRs identified in *Vons I*, which are really variations on a single theme, PLRs cannot be used or cited as precedent; they cannot be used to advance a particular interpretation of the Internal Revenue Code (I.R.C. or Code); and they cannot be used "for their substance." *Id.* For the sake of simplicity, the court refers to such impermissible uses of PLRs as the use of PLRs as precedent. To summarize the permissible uses of PLRs identified in *Vons I*, PLRs may be used as evidence of the administrative practice of the IRS, and may, in certain instances, be used in abuse of discretion cases governed by *IBM*.

Assuming that the court understands plaintiff's arguments, plaintiff does not seek to use the private letter rulings in question to establish the administrative practice of the IRS, one of two permissible uses of PLRs.[29] Instead, in the court's view, plaintiff seeks either to impermissibly rely on the PLRs as precedent, or wishes to use the PLRs as evidence of an abuse of discretion, as PLRs were found to be evidence of an abuse of discretion in *IBM*. If *IBM* were indeed applicable to the facts of this case, use of private letter rulings would be permissible as evidence that the IRS had "issu[ed] different rulings to two directly competing taxpayers." *Vons I*, 51 Fed. Cl. at 12. Neither of plaintiff's proposed uses of PLRs is permissible in this case.

B. Private Letter Rulings Cannot Be Used as Precedent in This Case

Plaintiff's motion could be read as an attempt to present a case for using certain private letter rulings as precedent, although plaintiff disavows such an intent. See Pl.'s Reply at 9 (asserting that plaintiff "has not cited the PLRs as legal precedent").

---

29. [8] Plaintiff references a number of private letter rulings and concludes that "[a]s far as [plaintiff] has been able to determine, the IRS has never ruled that a decommissioning liability is not fixed and reasonably determinable, and, as far as [plaintiff] can determine, none of these rulings have been revoked." Pl.'s Mot. at 6. Although this assertion tangentially implicates the administrative practice of the IRS, plaintiff's arguments focus on the holdings of these private letter rulings, not on the evidence of IRS administrative practice that might be contained therein. For example, plaintiff argues that some of its requests for admission are proper when they ask defendant to confirm that IRS private letter rulings have stated that "the nuclear decommissioning liabilities at issue in this litigation are fixed and reasonably determinable." Id. at 13. The scope of this type of request for admission goes far beyond a desire to ascertain the administrative practices of the IRS; the topic of the request is the substance of those private letter rulings, not the practice of issuing them.

Plaintiff justifies its requests for admission by citing "at least 47 PLRs," and asserts that every PLR cited found nuclear power plant decommissioning liabilities to be fixed and reasonably determinable at the time of sale. Pl.'s Mot. at 4–6. Plaintiff suggests that the PLRs "would allow the court to resolve the remaining legal questions [in this case] on summary judgment." Pl.'s Mot. at 8. Plaintiff also surveys caselaw concerning the use of PLRs in litigation, and implies that courts routinely rely on PLRs for their decisions. Pl.'s Reply at 7 (citing cases). To the extent that plaintiff intends to rely on PLRs as precedent, i.e., for their substance or for their value in interpreting the I.R.C., the requests for admission submitted to defendant are improper because they seek to rely on PLRs for an impermissible purpose. See, e.g., *Hanover Bank v. Comm'r*, 369 U.S. 672, 686 (1962) (noting that taxpayers "are not entitled to rely upon unpublished private rulings which were not issued specifically to them") (citations omitted); *Vons Cos. v. U.S.*, 55 Fed. Cl. 709, 718 (2003) (*Vons II*) (rejecting arguments based on PLRs because "[t]he truth of the matter is that the IRS "positions" to which [plaintiff] refers were never intended to be relied upon by any taxpayers except those to which the rulings were directed").

C. The PLRs Are Not Evidence Relevant to This Case

1. IBM

Plaintiff strives mightily to squeeze this case into the factual pattern provided by *IBM*. Pl.'s Mot. at 19 ("[Plaintiff] is in the same position as IBM."). To the extent that *IBM* survives as precedent binding on this court, *see Florida Power II*, 375 F.3d at 1124–25 & n.10 (limiting the holding in *IBM* to its facts, and noting, but not deciding, the question of whether *IBM* had been "effectively overruled" by *Dickman v. Comm'r*, 465 U.S. 330, 343 (1984)), the facts of this case do not resemble *IBM* and *IBM* is thus of no avail to plaintiff. *IBM* concerned fundamental inequities in the conduct of the IRS toward two competing sellers of large computers. One corporation was relieved of excise taxes on the large computers it sold for six and a half years, whereas *IBM* was required to pay such taxes for the same period, despite having sought a favorable private letter ruling relieving it of the excise tax within a few months of the issuance of such a letter to its competitor. 343 F.2d at 915–17. There was no dispute that the I.R.C. required the payment of the excise taxes in question. Id. at 917.

The issue before the Court of Claims was whether the competitor should reap the comparative advantages of an erroneous private letter ruling along with the IRS delays that prevented IBM from obtaining a similar ruling, so that the competitor's excise tax liability was applied only prospectively, while IBM had to suffer the comparative disadvantages of a retroactive application of its excise tax liability. In those circumstances, the court stated that "[e]quality of treatment is so dominant in our understanding of justice that discretion [to apply tax liabilities retroactively], where it is allowed a role, must pay the strictest heed." Id. at 920. The *IBM* court held that it was an abuse of discretion to thus favor the competitor over IBM, and that the provision of the I.R.C. that allowed retroactive application of the tax laws, 26 U.S.C. § 7805(b), did not permit such unfettered discretion. 343 F.2d at 920 (stating that the IRS "does not have carte blanche"). In the *IBM* case, the Court of Claims found "a manifest and unjustifiable discrimination against the taxpayer" and ordered the IRS to refund IBM's excise taxes for the relevant period. Id. at 923, 925.

To summarize IBM, then, a taxpayer plaintiff who (1) learns of a favorable private letter ruling issued to its direct competitor, (2) promptly attempts to secure a similar letter, (3) encounters significant delay in obtaining a ruling from the IRS, (4) pays taxes for a lengthy period during which time its competitor is relieved from paying the same taxes due to an erroneous private letter ruling, (5) sues once that competitor's favorable ruling has been revoked only prospectively whereas its own tax liability has been applied retroactively, would likely be able to show that the IRS abused its discretion under I.R.C. §7805(b). Cf. *Florida Power II*, 375 F.3d at 1124–25 & n.12 (recounting most of these facts, and noting in particular the delays encountered by IBM in obtaining its private letter ruling). Here, there is no allegation that the private letter rulings issued to the sellers of the nuclear power plants were erroneous (indeed, they are reputed to be just the opposite), or that unfair retroactive application of the tax laws is at issue in this case. *Vons I*, 51 Fed. Cl. at 10 (noting that *IBM* "applies only where ... the taxpayer denied the favorable ruling is arguing that the Commissioner abused his discretion under section 7805(b) by failing to apply a new legal position only prospectively") (citations omitted). Because *IBM* has been limited to its specific facts and since plaintiff's tax situation fails to reflect *IBM*'s factual scenario, *IBM* provides no support for the relevance of private letter rulings to this case.

2. Oshkosh

Plaintiff also relies extensively on *Oshkosh Truck Corp. v. U.S.*, 123 F.3d 1477 (Fed. Cir. 1997). Plaintiff quotes this statement from *Oshkosh*: "[U]nless there is a rational reason for different treatment, similarly-situated taxpayers should be treated similarly." Id. at 1481. Oshkosh concerned the unfavorable tax treatment of Oshkosh's sales of trucks to the government, when the sales of certain trucks and trailers by other manufacturers received more favorable tax treatment. The United States Court of Appeals for the Federal Circuit held that the IRS abused its discretion by applying its own regulations differently to similarly-situated taxpayers. *Id.*

Although the cited comment in *Oshkosh* implies that inconsistent rulings issued to similarly-situated taxpayers might be additional grounds for overturning an IRS ruling on tax liability in some circumstances, *Oshkosh* should not be read too broadly. The result in *Oshkosh* restrained the Department of the Treasury from frustrating the intent of Congress, as that intent was expressed in one section of the Code. 123 F.3d at 1481. A Treasury regulation had exempted certain sales from the increased taxes imposed in that code section. Because the sales by Oshkosh "did not involve the problem that Congress intended to reach" with the increased taxes required by that code section, the exemption of other manufacturers' sales, but not Oshkosh's sales, was arbitrary and unsupportable. *Id.* The lesson of *Oshkosh* is that "drawing an arbitrary distinction between similarly-situated taxpayers" may not survive judicial review, *Florida Power II*, 375 F.3d at 1125 n.13, if the distinction is not supported by the

Code. *Oshkosh* nowhere discusses private letter rulings, and cannot be interpreted to support plaintiff's motion.[30]

Plaintiff interprets Oshkosh as placing a general ban on inconsistent rulings in similar cases, and states that it "is entitled to explore the possibility that it is being subjected to unequal treatment." Pl.'s Reply at 12; *see also* Pl.'s Mot. at 18 (citing *Computer Scis. Corp. v. U.S.*, 50 Fed. Cl. 388 (2001) (*Computer Sciences*), for the proposition that "it [i]s improper for the IRS to treat similarly-situated taxpayers differently without a rational basis for the difference"). As this court said in *Vons I*, however, "the manifest weight of precedent rejects a "least common denominator" notion of federal taxation, in which the law that the Congress actually enacts can be short-circuited and disregarded any time the IRS has afforded a single taxpayer or even a group of taxpayers treatment more favorable than the law provides." 51 Fed. Cl. at 10 n.10. If plaintiff is entitled to the tax treatment it requests in this suit, that entitlement will come from the Code, not from a comparison with private letter rulings issued by the IRS. See *Oshkosh*, 123 F.3d at 1481 (rejecting the government's position because its interpretation of the relevant tax provision was inconsistent with the intent of Congress). If plaintiff is not entitled to the tax treatment it requests, a comparison with PLRs, correct or erroneous, is irrelevant. See *Vons II*, 55 Fed. Cl. at 718 (noting that "nothing prevent[s] the IRS from "changing" its position, provided that its "new" view is supported by the [relevant tax] statute"); *see also* Def.'s Opp. at 9–10 (citing cases disregarding PLRs as precedent). Plaintiff's reliance on *Oshkosh* does not further its contention that PLRs are relevant to this case.

3. The Sellers' PLRs Do Not Bind the IRS

Plaintiff also suggests that "the PLRs [cited by plaintiff] are likely binding on Defendant in this action." Pl.'s Mot. at 8. This statement is not supported by the weight of authority consulted by the court.[31] Indeed, there is no plausible reading of precedent that supports this view. *See, e.g., Am. Stores Co. v. Comm'r*, 170 F.3d 1267, 1270 (10th Cir. 1999) ("It is well settled that [private letter rulings] do not bind the Commissioner or this court.") (citations omitted); *Florida Power I*, 56 Fed. Cl. at 334

---

30. [9] The court, in the context of this discovery dispute over PLRs, need not reach the issue of whether plaintiff, as a purchaser of nuclear power plants, is "similarly-situated" to sellers of nuclear power plants, in regards to the tax treatment of assumed decommissioning liability.

31. [10] Plaintiff relies on *IBM* and *Oshkosh*, among other authorities, for its theory that defendant is bound in this case by its private letter rulings issued to other taxpayers. See Pl.'s Mot. at 13, 17–19. For the reasons stated in this opinion, *see supra*, the facts in *IBM* are distinguishable from this case and *IBM* does not support plaintiff's contentions. See *Florida Power II*, 375 F.3d at 1124 (limiting the holding in *IBM* to its facts). Similarly, for the reasons stated in this opinion, see supra, *Oshkosh* cannot be used to exempt plaintiff from tax treatment imposed by the Code, or to estop defendant from correctly applying the Code. See *Auto. Club of Mich. v. Comm'r*, 353 U.S. 180, 183–84 (1957) ("The doctrine of equitable estoppel is not a bar to the correction by the Commissioner of a mistake of law.") (citations omitted); *Vons II*, 55 Fed. Cl. at 718 ("[I]t is axiomatic that the IRS simply is not estopped from changing its views of the law, even retroactively and even if a taxpayer has relied to its detriment on the earlier position." (citing *Dixon v. U.S.*, 381 U.S. 68, 72–73 (1965); *Vons I*, 51 Fed. Cl. at 6)). Precedent does not hold that the United States, in this case, is bound by its previous rulings in the PLRs, correct or incorrect, that were issued to the sellers of the nuclear power plants.

(stating that a "plaintiff cannot claim entitlement to a particular tax treatment on the basis of a [private letter] ruling issued to another taxpayer" (citing Hanover Bank, 369 U.S. at 686)).

Plaintiff relies, in support of its contention that defendant is bound by PLRs issued to other taxpayers, on decisions by this court which rely on IBM and Oshkosh. *See* Pl.'s Mot. at 18 (citing Computer Sciences, 50 Fed. Cl. at 388; *Bunce v. U.S.*, 28 Fed. Cl. 500, 509 (1993), *aff'd*, 26 F.3d 138 (Fed. Cir. 1994) (table)). The court notes that decisions in other cases before this court are not binding in this proceeding. *See W. Coast Gen. Corp. v. Dalton*, 39 F.3d 312, 315 (Fed. Cir. 1994) ("Court of Federal Claims decisions, while persuasive, do not set binding precedent for separate and distinct cases in that court.") (citations omitted). To the extent that plaintiff's reading of *Computer Sciences* asserts that defendant is bound by PLRs issued to other taxpayers, this court agrees with the *Vons I* court that such a reading goes against binding precedent. *See Vons I*, 51 Fed. Cl. at 10 n.10. *Bunce*, on the other hand, discussed *IBM* only in the particular context of the IRS's discretion in reaching settlements with taxpayers, and has no applicability to the facts of this case. Thus, plaintiff, despite its citations to Computer Sciences and Bunce, has not overcome strong contrary authority in *Florida Power I, Vons I* and *Vons II* which indicates that the government is not bound in this case by PLRs issued to other taxpayers.

The only other case extensively cited by plaintiff is *Corelli v. Comm'r*, 66 T.C. 220 (1976). Pl.'s Mot. at 11, 18; Pl.'s Reply at 4–8. *Corelli* is cited by plaintiff as support for the proposition that the sellers' PLRs are relevant to this case, and for the proposition that the government is bound by the sellers' PLRs. *Corelli* also held that requests for admission concerning a PLR issued to another taxpayer must be answered by the IRS. Because *Corelli* is often cited by plaintiff, the court has examined this case for its persuasive value. *See, e.g., Southland Royalty Co. v. U.S.*, 22 Cl. Ct. 525, 530 (1991) ("Although Tax Court decisions are not binding on [this] Court, the court will follow these decisions if the underlying rationale is persuasive.") (citation omitted).

The court notes first that no other court has relied upon *Corelli* to hold that PLRs are relevant or binding, or that requests for admission regarding PLRs must be answered by the IRS. In fact, *Corelli* has been cited only once by a court, as support for this phrase: "even if the private letter rulings [sought by the petitioner in that case] can be viewed as potentially relevant." *Davis v. Comm'r*, 69 T.C. 716, 722 (1978). In *Davis*, the Tax Court noted in an explanatory footnote the somewhat unusual holding of Corelli: "a private letter ruling issued by respondent to an applicant other than the taxpayer, but covering contractual arrangements among taxpayer and others was held relevant in the determination of whether the taxpayer's actions were due to negligence or intentional disregard of rules and regulations." 69 T.C. at 723 n.10.

Mr. Corelli sought discovery and admissions related to a private letter ruling issued to another taxpayer as part of his defense against a negligence penalty for underpayment of income taxes. *Corelli*, 66 T.C. at 221. The private letter ruling was issued to an accounting firm, and discussed the contractual relationships between Mr. Corelli, the Metropolitan Opera, and foreign corporations which appear to have been agents or impresarios arranging for Mr. Corelli to perform "personal services" for the Metropolitan Opera.[32] *Id.* at 221–22. One of the issues before the Tax Court was whether Mr. Corelli's reliance on the private letter ruling issued to the accounting firm would preclude a finding of negligence or intentional disregard of tax rules and regulations. *Id.* at 223.

The unique facts of *Corelli* might present some corollaries if this were a case of negligence penalties that might or might not be justified, depending on the contents and circumstances of a private letter ruling issued to one of the parties to an employment arrangement. As it is, however, Mr. Corelli's circumstances are distinguishable from this case, and, in any event, *Corelli* does not provide persuasive authority as to the relevance or binding nature of the sellers' PLRs in this action. For these reasons, the court rejects plaintiff's reliance on Corelli, for any purpose, including its ruling compelling the IRS to answer requests for admission regarding a PLR issued to another taxpayer.

4. Plaintiff's Status, as an Interested Party or as a Buyer, Does Not Render the PLRs Relevant

Plaintiff argues that its status as an interested party in the transactions that were the subject of the PLRs somehow makes those PLRs relevant to its tax claims in this suit. Pl.'s Mot. at 16; Pl.'s Reply at 10. Plaintiff relies solely on private letter rulings, issued in entirely different contexts, as support for this contention. As stated supra, private letter rulings are not precedential and this court accords them no precedential weight. Furthermore, plaintiff has not convinced the court that its status as an interested party in other taxpayers' requests for PLRs renders the PLRs issued to those taxpayers relevant to this case.

Plaintiff next contends that "[s]ection 6110(k)(3) does not bar reliance on a PLR by a taxpayer whose tax liability is directly involved in a ruling." Pl.'s Reply at 8. In essence, plaintiff argues that AmerGen's status as the buyer of nuclear power plants renders the PLRs issued to the sellers of those nuclear power plants relevant, because the sellers' PLRs implicate the transaction involving AmerGen. Pl.'s Mot. at 12–13, 18–19; Pl.'s Reply at 8. Plaintiff relies on a variety of authorities for this proposition, none of which are binding on this court and all of which appear to be distinguishable on their facts. None of these cases persuades the court that the PLRs in question have any relevance to the issues to be decided in this case. Those PLRs cannot, in these circumstances and under binding precedent, determine the result in this case and are thus irrelevant. *See, e.g., Florida Power I*, 56 Fed. Cl. at 334 (stating that "plaintiff cannot claim entitlement to a particular tax treatment on the basis of a ruling issued to another taxpayer" (citing *Hanover Bank*, 369 U.S. at 686)).

---

32. [11] Franco Corelli was a celebrated Italian tenor.

IV. Proper Use of Requests for Admission

The court has found that the facts of this case are not within the factual bounds of the ruling in *IBM*. In addition, the court has found that the PLRs issued to the sellers of the nuclear power plants are irrelevant to the subject matter. In these circumstances, it is clear that requests for admission related to the sellers' PLRs are objectionable. *See, e.g., Shakespeare Co. v. United States*, 389 F.2d 772, 777 (Ct. Cl. 1968) (denying the production of private letter rulings to a plaintiff in part because "no court has held a private ruling binding on the government against other taxpayers") (citations omitted); *Vons I*, 51 Fed. Cl. at 10 (noting that "IBM only ever so slightly expands the realm in which private letter rulings may be used or cited"); *Cederloff*, 105 AFTR 2d 2010-601, at 2 (denying requests for admission as to the treatment of other taxpayers, because "[e]ven if these requests were admitted, … Plaintiff's law suit would be no more likely to prevail"). The PLRs at issue here are irrelevant and defendant shall not be required to respond to requests for admission regarding these PLRs.[33]

Plaintiff points to *Vons I* as an example of this court requiring the IRS to respond to requests for admission regarding private letter rulings issued to other taxpayers. Pl.'s Mot. at 11–12; Pl.'s Reply at 16–17. The court reproduces one of plaintiff's contentions in this regard:

> In *Vons [I]*, which Defendant asserts supports its position, the Court required the defendant to answer requests for admission to establish the authenticity of certain PLRs, and *specifically noted that the PLRs were relevant* to determine whether "under the *IBM* decision, the Commissioner has abused his discretion under section 7805(b) of the Code in issuing different rulings to two directly competing taxpayers." 51 Fed. Cl. at 12.

Pl.'s Reply at 16 (emphasis added and unrelated footnote omitted). The court has searched *Vons I*, a rather lengthy and thorough opinion, for a sign that the *Vons I* court "specifically noted that the PLRs [sought by the plaintiff in that case] were relevant." Pl.'s Reply at 16. Instead, the court found this statement regarding two PLRs sought by the plaintiff in that case:

> Because these documents [including two PLRs] are not the originals issued by the IRS and *because they have potential relevance to the case, albeit limited,* plaintiff's admission requests seeking to confirm the genuineness of these documents are appropriate….

Vons I, 51 Fed. Cl. at 14 (emphasis added).

It is clear from the court's ruling in *Vons I* that certain private letter rulings were potentially relevant, either to establish an administrative practice of the IRS, or to determine the applicability of the holding of IBM to the facts and arguments in that case. See *Vons I*, 51 Fed. Cl. at 12 (noting that these two uses of private letter rulings

---

33. [12] Nor shall defendant be compelled to authenticate these PLRs in the manner proposed by plaintiff. See Pl.'s Reply at 15–17; Def.'s Opp. at 7–8.

were permitted, but that PLRs could not be relied upon "for their substance"). Plaintiff in this case cannot rely on *IBM* and does not seek to establish evidence of an administrative practice of the IRS, as discussed supra. Instead, plaintiff asks this court to rely upon the substance of the PLRs issued to the sellers of the nuclear power plants, a use of PLRs not condoned by *Vons I*. Plaintiff's reliance on *Vons I* is misplaced.

V. Statute Restricting Disclosure of Taxpayer Information

The court briefly notes defendant's argument that even if the sellers' PLRs were relevant, plaintiff's requests for admission run afoul of 26 U.S.C. §6103 (2006). According to defendant, §6103 "prohibits the disclosure of the identity and other identifying information about recipients of private letter rulings." Def.'s Opp. at 13. As plaintiff points out, there are exceptions to the confidentiality requirements of §6103(a) allowing disclosure in judicial proceedings, which are found in §6103(h)(4)(B)–(C). Pl.'s Mot. at 20–21; Pl.'s Reply at 3–5. Plaintiff assures the court that this case falls within §6103(h)(4)(C), and cites two Tax Court cases, neither of which cites, never mind discusses, §6103(h)(4)(C). Pl.'s Reply 4–6. The court finds that neither party has adequately briefed the applicability of §6103 to the facts of this case.

In *Vons I*, the court applied §6103 to that plaintiff's requests for admission concerning certain private letter rulings and other documents. 51 Fed. Cl. at 15–19. After discussing certain ambiguities found in §6103, and engaging in a thorough consideration of the legislative history of the statute, the court found that §6103 prevented disclosure of what might have been relevant information contained in those PLRs and other documents. Id. at 19 (stating that just "because a document meets the evidentiary relevancy standard does not mean that it also meets the disclosure requirements" of §6103(h)(4)(B)). Here, the parties have barely scratched the surface of the text of the statute, have cited no relevant cases, and have offered only one sentence fragment of relevant legislative history. *See* Pl.'s Reply at 4. Because the court has determined that the requested PLRs are not relevant in the first instance, the court will not decide, on this record, if §6103 imposes another barrier to plaintiff's requests for admission.[34]

CONCLUSION

For all of the above reasons, the court denies plaintiff's motion. To the extent that plaintiff's motion might have included a challenge to defendant's responses that cited a need to conduct further discovery before otherwise responding to plaintiff's requests for admission, such a challenge is also denied.[35] To the extent that plaintiff's reply

---

34. [13] A court's decision to approve disclosure of taxpayer information under 26 U.S.C. §6103(h)(4)(C) appears to be case specific. *See, e.g., Lebaron v. U.S.,* 794 F. Supp. 947, 951–53 (C.D. Cal. 1992) (analyzing whether the disclosed tax return information would directly affect the resolution of issues in that case); *Heimark v. U.S.,* 14 Cl. Ct. 643, 647–51 (1988) (same).

35. [14] Defendant's responses numbered 23, 29, 46, 52, 69, and 75 state that "[t]he United States is currently conducting discovery concerning this issue." The sufficiency of the responses citing this rationale does not appear to have been directly challenged by plaintiff.

brief might request that the court compel defendant to answer plaintiff's first set of interrogatories and second request for document production, that request is denied as well. The court urges the parties to cooperatively resolve further discovery issues as expeditiously as possible.

Long Term Capital Holdings v. United States
United States District Court, District of Connecticut
330 F. Supp. 2d 122 (2004)

I. SUMMARY

Petitioners Long-Term Capital Holdings ("Holdings"), Long-Term Capital Management L.P. ("LTCM"), Long-Term Capital Portfolio L.P. ("Portfolio"), Long-Term Capital Fund,[36] Eric Rosenfeld, and Richard Leahy filed petitions under 26 U.S.C. §6226(a)(2) seeking (a) readjustment of the IRS denial of $106,058,228 in capital losses for petitioners' 1997 tax year in connection with the sale by Portfolio on December 30, 1997 of preferred stock for $1,078,400 with a claimed basis of $107,136,628, and (b) a determination that the IRS imposition of penalties pursuant to 26 U.S.C. §6662(a), (b)(1-3), (h) was erroneous. Jurisdiction is conferred by 28 U.S.C. §1346(e). The Court's findings of fact and conclusions of law set out in this opinion are based on the bench trial held June 23, 2003–July 30, 2003.

Petitioners' claim that Portfolio sold stock on December 30, 1997 with a tax basis one hundred times in excess of its fair market value arises from two separate sets of transactions. The first set is comprised of nine cross border lease-stripping transactions, five of which utilized a master lease or wrap lease structure and were termed "Computer Hardware Investment Portfolio" ("CHIPS") and four of which utilized a sale/lease back structure and were termed "Trucking Investment Portfolios" ("TRIPS").

In the CHIPS transactions, Onslow Trading and Commercial LLC ("OTC"), an entity incorporated under the laws of the Turks and Caicos Islands, purportedly leased from General Electric Capital Computer Leasing ("GECCL") computer equipment already subject to existing leases to end-users and then immediately subleased its

---

36. [1] Holdings, organized in 1995 under the Delaware Revised Uniform Limited Partnership Act ("DRULPA"), was LTCM's general partner in 1997 and is currently and was during 1996 and 1997 LTCM's tax matters partner. LTCM, organized in 1994 under DRULPA, is currently and was during 1996 and 1997 the tax matters partner of Long-Term Capital Partners L.P. ("LTCP" or "Partners"). LTCM was owned by the twelve managing partners of Long Term and their families. LTCP was organized in 1994 under the DRULPA. Portfolio was organized in 1994 under the laws of the Cayman Islands, and, in 1996 and 1997, was a privately organized pooled investment vehicle, also referred to as a hedge fund. LTCM, LTCP, and Portfolio were all treated as partnerships for federal tax purposes during 1996 and 1997 with their principal place of business located in Greenwich, Connecticut. Unless specification is necessary, Holdings, LTCM, Portfolio, and LTCP will be referred to collectively as "Long Term".

rights in the equipment to U.S. based partnerships. The new sublessees then prepaid 92.5% of the rent due under the subleases. The prepayments, totaling tens of millions of dollars, were made with loans to the U.S.-based partnerships from Barclays Finance & Leasing B.V. ("Barclays") and were guaranteed by GECCL. OTC, formed under foreign laws and resident in the United Kingdom, paid no U.S. taxes upon receipt of the rent prepayments and deposited them into a Barclays branch bank account. OTC then exchanged the master leases, the subleases and the bank accounts with the prepayment deposits for preferred stock in certain U.S. corporations; OTC received approximately $1,000,000 in preferred stock for every $100,000,000 of prepayments and lease positions it gave up. OTC's transfer was timed to be prior to accrual of rent under the subleases such that under UK law OTC paid no taxes on the prepayments. Pursuant to 26 U.S.C. §§ 351, 358, these exchanges were claimed to be tax free exchanges and OTC claimed an adjusted basis in the preferred stock tranches it received of approximately $100,000,000.

In the TRIPS transactions, Wal-Mart sold fleets of trucks to NationsBanc and First American National Bank, the banks leased the trucks to OTC, and OTC subleased the trucks back to Wal-Mart. Wal-Mart guaranteed OTC's obligations to the banks and prepaid a percentage of the rent due under the sublease. In TRIPS I, the prepayment was 92.5% of the rent due, approximately $27 million, which OTC deposited in a bank account. Again, before the sublease rent accrued, OTC exchanged its lease positions and bank deposits for preferred stock of American corporations. The ratio of exchange again approximated $1 of preferred stock received for every $100 of lease positions and prepayment deposits given up.

OTC, in a purported transaction under 26 U.S.C. § 721, contributed to Long Term the tranches of preferred stock it received from the TRIPS and CHIPS transactions, which had a fair market value of approximately $4 million and a claimed basis of $400 million, in exchange for a Long Term partnership interest. OTC subsequently sold its partnership interest to Long Term and withdrew from the partnership. Long Term then had Portfolio sell a portion of the contributed TRIPS and CHIPS stock to purportedly generate the claimed losses in dispute in this case and those losses were allocated to Long Term under the loss allocation rules of U.S. partnership tax law.

For the reasons set forth below, the Court finds that the transaction in which OTC and Long Term engaged lacked economic substance and therefore must be disregarded for tax purposes, and, in the alternative, must be recast under the step transaction doctrine as a sale of preferred stock by OTC to Long Term resulting in an adjustment in Long Term's basis in the preferred stock to Long Term's purchase price. With respect to penalties, the Court rejects Long Term's contention that it satisfied the requirements of the reasonable cause defense to such penalties by obtaining legal opinions, and upholds the IRS application of 40% gross valuation misstatement and 20% substantial understatement penalties related to Long Term's claim of basis in OTC's contributed stock. Accordingly, the petitions are DENIED in all respects.

III. DISCUSSION

* * *

D. Penalties

The Government maintains that any underpayment of tax resulting from adjusting Long Term's inflated basis in the stock contributed by OTC is subject to a 40% penalty for gross valuation misstatement, *see* 26 U.S.C. §6662(a), (b)(3) and (h), and, in the alternative, a 20% penalty for substantial valuation misstatement, *see id.* §6662(a) and (b)(3), a 20% penalty for negligence or disregard of rules or regulations, *see id.* §6662(a) and (b)(1), or a 20% penalty for substantial understatement of income tax, *see id.* §6662(a) and (b)(2). Long Term contests the applicability of these accuracy-related penalties principally on the grounds that obtaining the Shearman & Sterling and King & Spalding opinions satisfies the reasonable cause exception of 26 U.S.C. §6664(c)(1). It also maintains that it satisfies the statutory limitations on the scope of each penalty, namely, that there is no valuation misstatement on its tax return, it did not act negligently but acted as a reasonable and prudent person, and it had substantial authority for its tax return position. For the reasons that follow, the Court concludes that the IRS determination with respect to the 40% penalty for gross valuation misstatement should be sustained and, in the alternative, the 20% penalty for substantial understatement should be sustained. There is no need to reach the negligence penalty issue.

1. Burden of Proof

26 U.S.C. §7491(c) provides,

> (c) Penalties. Notwithstanding any other provision of this title, the Secretary shall have the burden of production in any court proceeding with respect to the liability of any individual for any penalty, addition to tax, or additional amount imposed by this title.

Petitioners argue that this provision places the burden of production on the Government regarding their liability for accuracy-related penalties. *See* Pets.' Mem. [Doc. # 145] at 6–7. If applicable, such burden would require the Government "initially [to] come forward with evidence that it is appropriate to apply a particular penalty to the taxpayer ... [but not] to introduce evidence of elements such as reasonable cause or substantial authority." H.R. Conf. Rep. 105–599, at 241; *see generally e. g., Higbee v. Commissioner,* 116 T.C. 438, 446, 2001 WL 617230 (2001). The Government, however, points to the contrast in terminology between §7491(c) — "with respect to the liability of any *individual* for any penalty ... imposed by this title" (emphasis added) — and §7491(a)(1) — "with respect to any factual issue relevant to ascertaining the liability of the *taxpayer* for any tax imposed by subtitle A or B" (emphasis added), arguing that Congressional selection of two different terms in the same statutory enactment must be presumed to have been deliberate. *See* Opp'n [Doc. # 158] at 7–8. The Government urges that since "[i]n a TEFRA action, the partnership, and not the individual partners, is the taxpayer, ... §7491[(c)] is inapplicable to this case because Petitioners are not individuals." *See id.* at 8.

The Government's interpretation has substantial appeal. There is undeniably a difference between § 7491(a)(1) and § 7491(c) as originally enacted in 1998, and such contrast appears to rise to the level of substantive terminological difference in light of Congress' demonstrated ability to distinguish elsewhere in the same enactment between "taxpayers'" as an all encompassing category and subsets of that category, including partnerships, corporations, trusts, and individuals, *compare e.g.*, 26 U.S.C. § 7491(a)(2)(C)("in the case of a partnership, corporation, or trust, the taxpayer ...") *with* § 7491(b)("In the case of an individual taxpayer....").[37] *See e.g., United States v. Gayle*, 342 F.3d 89, 92–93 (2d Cir. 2003) (*quoting Saks v. Franklin Covey Co.*, 316 F.3d 337, 345 (2d Cir. 2003))(statute's "plain meaning can best be understood by looking to the statutory scheme as a whole and placing the particular provision within the context of that statute.").

On the other hand, at least two arguments support petitioners' view. First, the Government's interpretation is at odds with the legislative history of § 7491(c):

> ... in any court proceeding, the Secretary must initially come forward with evidence that it is appropriate to apply a particular penalty to the *taxpayer* before the court can impose the penalty.... Rather, the Secretary must come forward initially with evidence regarding the appropriateness of applying a particular penalty to the *taxpayer*; if the *taxpayer* believes that, because of reasonable cause, substantial authority, or a similar provision, it is inappropriate to impose the penalty, it is the *taxpayer's* responsibility (and not the Secretary's obligation) to raise those issues.

H.R. Conf. Rep. 105–599 at 241 (emphasis added). The Court has not located and the parties have not cited any explanation of why this language of the conference agreement was not replicated in the statutory language.

Second, although weaker, § 7491(c)'s "*with respect to* the liability of any individual" (emphasis added)[38] could arguably be viewed as applying to petitions filed pursuant to 26 U.S.C. § 6226(a) where denial will indirectly result in penalty liability for one or more partners who are also individuals. Recognizing that such petitions seek "readjustment of ... partnership items," 26 U.S.C. § 6662(a), if the partnership is considered the taxpayer, this argument points to statutory provisions illustrating the close relationship between the readjustment action and the partners of the partnership, in which each partner of the partnership, with certain exceptions, is treated as a party to the readjustment action, *see* 26 U.S.C. § 6226(c), (d), the tax treatment of such partnership items and the applicability of any penalty is determined in the readjustment action, *see* 26 U.S.C. § 6221, and assessments are made against partners after the readjustment action becomes final, *see* 26 U.S.C. § 6225. However, this argument is weakened by

---

37. [95] *See* 26 U.S.C. § 7701(a)(14) ("The term 'taxpayer' means any person subject to any internal revenue tax.") *and* § 7701(a)(1) ("The term 'person' shall be construed to mean and include an individual, a trust, estate, partnership, association, company or corporation").

38. [96] "With respect to" is defined as "with reference to" or "as regards," WEBSTER'S NEW INTERNATIONAL DICTIONARY 2128 (2d unabridged ed.1959).

explicit statutory and regulatory provisions that preserve partner level defenses for proceedings subsequent to disposition of a readjustment petition, *see e.g.* 26 U.S.C. § 6230(c)(1)(c), (4); Treas. Reg. § 1.6662-5(h)(1), and the fact that a partnership may be comprised completely or in part of partners who are not individuals.[39]

In addition, focus on the legislative purpose for the enactment of § 7491 yields ambiguous results. The Senate Report states that the reason for the enactment was to correct the "disadvantage" faced by individuals and small business taxpayers "when forced to litigate with the Internal Revenue Service." S. Rep. 105-174 at 44. To that end, § 7491(a) was supported by the "belie[f]" that, if the statutory conditions are met, "facts asserted by individual and small business taxpayers ... should be accepted," and § 7491(c) because "[t]he Committee also believes that, in a court proceeding, the IRS should not be able to rest on its presumption of correctness if it does not provide any evidence whatsoever relating to penalties." *See id.* Given these premises, it would be arguably inconsistent to conclude that, just like individuals, small business taxpayers organized under various structures qualifying, for example, as partnerships or S Corporations for federal tax purposes, were to be afforded the benefit of the burden shifting provision of § 7491(a) but, unlike individuals, not afforded the benefit of § 7491(c) imposing the burden of production in the penalty context on the Secretary. On the other hand, interpreting "individual" in § 7491(c) as encompassing taxpayers such as partnerships and corporations would give the subsection far broader scope than the plain meaning of the statutory language used. Members of those classifications which are not "small," and which are explicitly excluded from the benefit of burden shifting when litigating the merits of their tax liabilities, *see* § 7491(a)(2)(C)(excluding from burden shifting benefit of § 7491(a)(1) partnerships, corporations, or trusts with net worth in excess of $7,000,000 at the time an action is filed), would receive the advantage of the burden imposing benefit in the penalty context.

If it were necessary to decide the applicability of § 7491(c) in this case, the Court would conclude that the Government has the stronger position. The language of § 7491(c) is unambiguous, particularly within the context of § 7491 as a whole, even though it is in contrast with the language of its legislative history. *See e.g. Russello v. U.S.,* 464 U.S. 16, 20 (1983) ("If the statutory language is unambiguous, in the absence of a clearly expressed legislative intent to the contrary, that language must ordinarily be regarded as conclusive.") (quotations omitted). However, because the Government has met any burden of production it may have in this case, even under petitioners' view of § 7491(c), by coming forward with evidence demonstrating the

---

39. [97] In one tax controversy involving a corporate taxpayer, the Tax Court appears to have assumed that § 7491(c) places the burden of production with respect to penalties or additions to tax on the Government, *see* Maintenance, Painting & Construction, Inc. v. Comm'r, 86 T.C.M. (CCH) (Sept. 17, 2003), and, in another, the Government conceded as much, *see* Charlotte's Office Boutique, Inc. v. Comm'r, 121 T.C. 89, 109–110 and n.11, (2003). In neither case is there discussion of the differences between § 7491(a) and § 7491(c).

appropriateness of penalties, resolution of whether such burden is appropriately imposed is unnecessary.

2. Gross Valuation Misstatement

A 40% penalty is imposed on any underpayment of tax exceeding $5,000 that is attributable to a "gross valuation misstatement." 26 U.S.C. §6662(a), (b)(3), (e)(2), (h)(1).[40] As relevant here, a gross valuation misstatement exists if "the value of any property (or the adjusted basis of property) claimed on any return of tax imposed by chapter 1 is 400 percent or more of the amount determined to be the correct amount of such valuation or adjusted basis (as the case may be)...." 26 U.S.C. §6662(e)(1)(A), (h)(2)(A)(i).

Long Term reported on its 1997 return losses of $106,058,228 resulting from the sale of a portion of the preferred stock contributed by OTC. Embedded in that number are claims that the stock sold for fair market value of $1,078,400 and had an adjusted basis of $107,136,628. The Court's application of the step transaction doctrine to the OTC transaction has the effect of imputing to Long Term a cost basis in the Rorer and Quest stock of approximately $1 million and thereby making Long Term's claimed adjusted basis well in excess of 400 percent of the amount determined to be the correct adjusted basis.[41]

---

40. [98] The dollar limitation element is not applicable to a petition for readjustment under 26 U.S.C. §6226(a) but applies at the taxpayer level. *See* Treas. Reg. §1.6662-5(h)(1).

41. [99] The Court's economic substance ruling, which has the effect of disregarding for tax purposes the contributions of stock to LTCP by OTC and the subsequent sale of OTC's partnership interest to Long Term, thereby producing a basis of zero for the contributed stock in the hands of Long Term and a claimed adjusted basis in the preferred stock of not just 400 percent but infinitely more than the amount determined to be the correct basis, *see* Treas. Reg. §1.6662-5(g), may also provide grounds for sustaining the gross valuation misstatement penalty. What is difficult is the issue of whether any tax deficiency resulting from the basis claimed by Long Term is "attributable" to the misstatement of basis, as required by 26 U.S.C. §6662(b)(3), (h)(1), or, as argued by Long Term, to the disallowance of the partnership transactions. The Second Circuit in *Gilman*, 933 F.2d at 151–52, considered and approved application of a valuation misstatement penalty in the context of an inflated purchase price from which claimed depreciation and interest deductions are derived at least in part. The assumption appears to be that, had the purchase price been lower, the chance at a pre-tax profit would have been correspondingly increased. "In that way, the overvaluation of the computer equipment contributed to the Court's conclusion that the transaction lacked economic substance." *Id.* at 151. Where, as here, the taxpayer seeks to obtain capital losses by acquisition of property with a basis purported to be in excess of the property's fair market value, the taxpayer will have no incentive to inflate the property's fair market which would thereby reduce the sought after tax benefit; in fact, understatement would be the more likely motivation to increase the claimed tax loss. To the extent some nexus is required under the reasoning of *Gilman* to this different context to demonstrate how Long Term's claimed basis contributed to the absence of economic substance, such a nexus is possibly satisfied here because the differential between the stock's value and its claimed basis drove the entire OTC/Long Term transaction, including Long Term's outlay of expense in order to obtain the perceived built-in tax Losses. In that way, the high basis motivated Long Term's expenditures, which in turn provide the cornerstone evidence supporting a conclusion of lack of economic substance, and thus may be said to have contributed to the Court's holding. The Court does not reach whether its economic substance holding would sustain the gross valuation misstatement penalty because the penalty is appropriately sustained on the application of the step transaction doctrine.

3. Substantial Understatement of Income Tax

A 20% penalty is imposed on any underpayment of tax attributable to "any substantial understatement of income tax." 26 U.S.C. §6662(b)(2). The term "understatement" generally means the excess of the amount of tax required to be shown on the return over the amount of tax shown on the return. *See* 26 U.S.C. §6662(d)(2)(A). An understatement is substantial if the amount of the understatement exceeds the greater of 10 percent of the tax required to be shown on the return or $5,000. *See* 26 U.S.C. §6662(d)(1)(A).

In calculating the understatement, the taxpayer is permitted a reduction for that portion attributable to "the tax treatment of any item by the taxpayer if there is or was substantial authority for such treatment," 26 U.S.C. §6662(d)(2)(B)(i), or "any item if the relevant facts affecting the item's tax treatment are adequately disclosed in the return or in a statement attached to the return and there is a reasonable basis for the tax treatment of such item by the taxpayer." 26 U.S.C. §6662(d)(2)(B)(ii)(I & II). However, the reduction rules are modified "in the case of any item of a taxpayer other than a corporation which is attributable to a tax shelter," 26 U.S.C. §6662(d)(2)(C)(i): no reduction is available for adequate disclosure and, to be entitled to a reduction on grounds of substantial authority for any item, the taxpayer must also have "reasonably believed that the tax treatment of such item by the taxpayer was more likely than not the proper treatment." 26 U.S.C. §6662(d)(2)(C)(i)(I & II). The term "tax shelter" for these purposes includes "any ... plan or arrangement if a significant purpose of such ... plan[] or arrangement is the avoidance or evasion of Federal income tax." 26 U.S.C. §6662(d)(C)(iii)(III). Treasury regulations define "tax shelter" as "any ... plan or arrangement, if the principal purposes of the ... plan or arrangement, based on objective evidence, is to avoid or evade Federal income tax," Treas. Reg. §1.6662-4(g)(2)(i), and set out that a principal purpose is tax avoidance if it exceeds any other purpose and that tax shelters are "transactions structured with little or no motive for the realization of economic gain." *Id.* It is the taxpayer's burden to prove substantial authority or reasonable belief; the Government has no burden in this regard. *See* H.R. Conf. Rep. 105-599 at 241.

Long Term argues that it had substantial authority for claiming a basis of $107,136,628 on its tax return for the Rorer and Quest stock, but does not address whether it had a reasonable belief that its treatment of the basis on its return was more likely than not the proper treatment, apparently assuming that the OTC transaction was not a "tax shelter."[42]

---

42. [100] As appears to have been assumed by both parties, the calculation of the understatement and whether it is substantial are not issues for determination at the entity level in a petition filed pursuant to 26 U.S.C. §6226. *See* Govt.'s Trial Brief [Doc. # 132] at 164–65 ¶203; Pets.' Trial Brief [Doc. #133] at 137–40. Rather, as both require reference to each partner's tax return, such calculations are partner level determinations and thus, to the extent attributable to a partnership item, subject to contest in a subsequent refund action. *See* 26 U.S.C. §6230(c)(1)(C), (4); Treas. Reg. §§301.6221-1(d), 301.6231(a)(5)-1(e), 301.6231(a)(6)-1(a)(3).

As an initial matter, the Court's determination that Long Term entered the OTC transaction without any business purpose other than tax avoidance and that the transaction itself did not have economic substance beyond the creation of tax benefits makes the transaction a "tax shelter" for purposes of the understatement penalty. Acquisition of the claimed basis in the Rorer and Quest stock was the purpose for the transaction and thus is attributable to it. *See* Treas. Reg. § 1.6662-4(g)(3).[43] Accordingly, the partners of Long Term are not entitled to a reduction of any understatement attributable to the claimed basis and corresponding losses unless Long Term both had substantial authority for the claimed basis when it filed its return and a reasonable belief that more likely than not the basis was as claimed. Long Term had neither.

a. Substantial Authority

"The substantial authority standard is an objective standard involving an analysis of the law and application of the law to relevant facts." Treas. Reg. § 1.6662-4(d)(2). It exists where "the weight of the authorities supporting the treatment is substantial in relation to the weight of authorities supporting contrary treatment." Treas. Reg. § 1.6662-4(d)(3)(i). Weight is determined in light of the particular facts and circumstances of the case at hand and the weight accorded any particular authority depends on its relevance and persuasiveness. *See* Treas. Reg. § 1.6662-4(d)(3)(i & ii). The definition of what constitutes "authority" is explicitly limited to written determinations provided to the taxpayer and legal sources (including statutes, regulations, case law, legislative history, etc.). *See* Treas. Reg. § 1.6662-4(d)(3)(iii & iv).

Notwithstanding the regulations' explicit cabining of "authority" to legal sources, disagreement has arisen both within and among the federal courts of appeal regarding whether evidence offered by the taxpayer unsuccessfully on the merits nevertheless may qualify in certain circumstances as authority for purposes of the substantial understatement penalty analysis, and, if so, when such evidence can be considered substantial. *See Kluener v. Comm'r*, 154 F.3d 630, 637–41 (6th Cir. 1998) (2–1 decision); *Streber v. Comm'r*, 138 F.3d 216, 222–23, 227–29 (5th Cir. 1998) (2–1 decision); *Osteen v. Comm'r*, 62 F.3d 356, 358–60 (11th Cir. 1995).[44] The majority opinions in those cases agree that evidence may constitute authority (only *Kluener* analyzes the relevant regulatory provisions) but disagree on the meaning of "substantial" in this context.

Osteen concluded that evidence can be authority based on its view that "application of a substantial authority test [was] confusing in a case of this kind" where once the taxpayer loses on the factual finding—finding a profit motive would permit deductions and finding no profit motive would deny deductions—the taxpayer must then lose on "what would seem to be a legal issue [the threshold penalty determination]."

---

43. [101] In addition, Long Term did not disclose on its return the relevant facts affecting the basis of the Rorer and Quest stock or the corresponding claimed losses.

44. [102] Both *Osteen* and *Streber* deal with 26 U.S.C. § 6661 and its implementing regulations. Those provisions do not appear materially different from those under consideration in the present case.

Osteen, 62 F.3d at 359. Thus, *Osteen* concluded that "the regulations ... are unsatisfactory in application to an all or nothing case of this kind." *Id.*[45]

Kluener concluded that evidence may constitute authority based on *Osteen*, interpretation of applicable regulations, and policy considerations. It interpreted the regulations directing application of the law to relevant facts, *see* Treas. Reg. § 1.6662-4(d)(2), and weighing authorities "in light of the pertinent facts and circumstances," Treas. Reg. § 1.6662-4(d)(3)(i), as "command[ing] ... examin[ation of] relevant facts...." *Kluener*, 154 F.3d at 638, reasoning that the regulations (*see* Treas. Reg. § 1.6662-4(d)(3)(iii & iv)) only distinguish between the types of legal sources that constitute legal authority and the types that do not and therefore do not comment on factual evidence. *Kluener* was motivated by "policy concerns" where, as in *Osteen*, discrediting the taxpayer's evidence was tantamount to assessing a substantial understatement penalty. *See id.* at 638–39.[46]

These decisions do not distinguish between the terms "relevant facts" and "facts and circumstances" in the regulatory language and the "evidence" offered by the taxpayer. The former exist only as found by the trial court, not a taxpayer, who can only present evidence from which "facts" are found. The regulation at issue, Treas. Reg. § 1.6662-4(d) defines "authority" only as legal sources. *See* Treas. Reg. § 1.6662-4(d)(3)(iii). As emphasized by the dissent in *Streber*, "Noticeably absent from this list of potential sources of authority is any mention of factual evidence favorable to the taxpayer's position." *See Streber*, 138 F.3d at 228 (King, J., dissenting). *Kluener*'s gloss on the regulation's otherwise unambiguous language is unconvincing. The regulatory language is clear and thus the presumption should be in favor of the unambiguous meaning unless other parts of the regulatory scheme direct review of the taxpayer's evidence. None do.

In fact, the section of the regulation relied on in *Kluener* as support for its interpretation includes the following statement: "Conclusions reached in ... opinions rendered by tax professionals are not authority. The authorities underlying such expressions of opinion *where applicable* to the facts of a particular case, however, may give rise to substantial authority for the tax treatment of an item." Treas. Reg. § 1.6662-4(d)(3)(iii) (emphasis added). Similarly, written determinations from the IRS provided to a taxpayer are authority unless "[t]here was a misstatement or omission of a material fact or the facts that subsequently develop are materially different from the facts on which the written determination was based." Treas. Reg. § 1.6662-

---

45. [103] In *Osteen* the Commissioner did not argue to the contrary and the opinion notes that there was no case law to provide guidance. *See Osteen*, 62 F.3d at 359. *Streber* simply adopted *Osteen*, explicitly noting that the Government did not make a legal challenge to *Osteen*'s holding but rather attempted to distinguish the case on its facts. *See Streber*, 138 F.3d at 223 and n. 14.

46. [104] The *Osteen/Streber* and *Kluener* majorities disagreed, however, on the meaning of "substantial." *Osteen/Streber* adopted a standard under which substantial authority from a factual standpoint is lacking only if a merits decision for the taxpayer would have to be reversed at the appellate level as clearly erroneous. *See Streber*, 138 F.3d at 223; *Osteen*, 62 F.3d at 359. *Kluener* disagreed, holding that "'substantial authority' requires a taxpayer to present considerable or ample authority, whereas *Osteen* requires him to present only some evidence." *Kluener*, 154 F.3d at 639.

4(d)(3)(iv)(A)(1). Opinions rendered by tax professionals and private letter rulings from the IRS are based on the taxpayer's representations and submitted evidence. Yet the regulations explicitly take into account that the "facts of a particular case" or the "facts that subsequently develop" may require a result different than the submissions relied upon by the taxpayer (e.g. personal expressions of intent such as "Kluener's personal notes indicat[ing] that he decided to withdraw the proceeds only after meeting with bank officials," *Kluener*, 154 F.3d at 636; *see also id.* at 639.). In such cases, the regulations direct disregard of such opinion sources as authority.

The regulations also state that "the taxpayer's belief that there is substantial authority for the tax treatment of an item is not relevant in determining whether there is substantial authority for that treatment." Treas. Reg. § 1.6662-4(d)(3)(I). This provision which would be rendered a nullity if a taxpayer's testimony of his or her profit motive can be considered as authority in a case where, if credited, a decision on the merits would be rendered in favor of the taxpayer since "substantial authority" in such context would necessarily merge with belief in the existence of a profit motive. Finally, the regulations direct that little weight be given to an authority if it "is materially distinguishable on its facts." Treas. Reg. § 1.6662-4(d)(3)(ii). Such provision would have little force if it means authority is given only little weight when materially distinguishable from the evidence offered by the taxpayer since the taxpayer could simply manufacture weight by, for example, testifying as to his or her profit motive and citing the authorities holding the existence of a profit motive sufficient in a particular context.

In sum, the regulation permits a taxpayer to escape penalties where the taxpayer can cite legal sources that would hold for the taxpayer on the merits of identical or closely analogous facts if the same were found by the court, even if such legal authority was rejected during determination of the taxpayer's liability.[47] It does not permit consideration as authority rejected evidence offered by the taxpayer, even in cases in which the merits of the taxpayer's tax liability and the threshold application of a substantial understatement penalty are decided jointly merely by making fact findings.[48]

---

47. [105] A textbook example would be the taxpayer's reliance in a refund suit filed in one circuit on application of precedent from another to undisputed facts where the Government urges application of conflicting precedent from yet a third circuit and all agree that no precedent controls.

48. [106] In similar vein, Judge Wellford wrote in dissent in *Kluener*:

I would affirm the Tax Court's assessment of the penalty in this case under the standard endorsed by the majority. The appellants argue that "substantial authority" existed to support their tax treatment of the horse sales. The legal authority upon which the appellants rely is the same as that relied upon to challenge the deficiency itself. The appellants cite cases which hold "that funding of corporate operations [is] a valid business purpose." I do not disagree with this legal premise. The appellants' argument, however, presupposes that Kluener in fact transferred the proceeds of the horses to APECO to fund corporate operations. We have unanimously found that Kluener had no valid business purpose in the transfer of the horses. In essence, the appellants' entire argument regarding the penalty is a factual one, and it must rise or fall depending on the disposition of the deficiency issue. Because the absence of a valid business purpose undermines the appellants' legal arguments, the argument that "substantial authority" existed for their tax treatment of the horses must fail.

Kluener, 154 F.3d at 640–41 (Wellford, J., dissenting).

The mischief resulting from use of evidence as authority is shown when analyzed under the summary judgment standard propounded by *Osteen* and *Streber*, as persuasively set forth in the *Streber* dissent:

> [T]he majority's construction of the substantial authority standard implies that, in many circumstances, if a taxpayer is able to survive summary judgment, he is shielded from liability for substantial understatement penalties because substantial authority—in the form of some evidence—supports his tax position. Moreover, when a taxpayer's entitlement to a particular tax benefit hinges upon facts that will be elucidated by witness testimony, the taxpayer need only lie about the facts that would entitle him to the benefit in order to shield himself from liability for a substantial understatement penalty resulting from his improperly claiming the benefit. In such a circumstance, the taxpayer's testimony would constitute some evidence indicating his entitlement to the benefit, and, the majority opinion in this case notwithstanding, it is doubtful that we would be in a position on appeal to conclude that the trial court would have clearly erred had it credited the taxpayer's testimony. Surely Congress did not intend to impose such a toothless penalty for substantial understatement of tax liability.[49]

Streber, 138 F.3d at 228 and n. 3. Moreover, the Court notes that the concerns in *Osteen, Streber*, and *Kluener* about the potential for mechanical application of the substantial understatement penalty based on the underlying merits determination are misplaced. Other penalties, such as valuation misstatement, are intended to apply in mechanical fashion, inquiring only as to the magnitude of error in the taxpayer's claimed value or adjusted basis, and the taxpayer may defend against a substantial understatement penalty by assertion of the reasonable cause and good faith defense of 26 U.S.C. § 6664(c), which provides for consideration of a taxpayer's motives and reliance on facts that ultimately turn out to be incorrect, *see infra* Part III.D.4.

Since the Court has found that the OTC transaction is devoid of objective economic substance and subjective business purpose, Long Term has not and cannot cite authority, much less substantial authority, for the proposition that a taxpayer may claim losses from a transaction in which the taxpayer intentionally expends far more than could reasonably be expected to be recouped through non-tax economic returns in a transaction the sole motivation for which is tax avoidance. The cases relied on by Long Term, principally *Frank Lyon, Newman*, and *UPS* are not authority

---

49. It is worth noting that the majority's construction of the substantial authority standard also provides a disincentive for taxpayers to settle with the IRS in situations in which they are potentially liable for substantial understatement penalties. If the taxpayer is able to create a fact issue about which reasonable minds could differ regarding his entitlement to a particular tax benefit, he can avoid liability for substantial understatement penalties. In some circumstances, this heightened incentive may be sufficiently strong that it convinces the taxpayer to proceed to trial rather than settle the dispute.

supporting the OTC transaction as having genuine economic substance but are "materially distinguishable," Treas. Reg. § 1.6662-4(d)(3)(ii), from it. By contrast, the clear and pre-existing on-point authority of *Goldstein* and *Gilman*[50] preclude Long Term's tax treatment of the sale of the Rorer and Quest stock. Similarly, with respect to the Court's application of the step transaction doctrine, there is no authority for claiming losses on the sale of the Rorer and Quest stock approximately 100 times in excess of the cost basis to Long Term. The "authority" offered on this point by Long Term was based on the rejected factual claim that no agreement or understanding existed between OTC and Long Term prior to OTC's contributions that OTC would sell its partnership interest to LTCM, the rejected legal contentions that the independent economic substance of LTCP and Portfolio and their valid and substantial business purposes precluded operation of the step transaction doctrine under *Vest*, *Weikel*, and *DeWitt*, and that *Grove* and *Greene* precluded the Court's recast of the OTC transaction.[51]

b. Reasonable Belief

In addition, the partners of Long Term are not entitled to a reduction of any understatement attributable to the claimed basis and corresponding losses because Long Term lacked a reasonable belief that more likely than not the basis was as claimed. There was no evidence or argument at trial that Long Term itself "analyze[d] the pertinent facts and [legal] authorities ... and in reliance upon that analysis, reasonably conclude[d] in good faith that there [was] a greater than 50-percent likelihood that the tax treatment of the item [would] be upheld if challenged by the [IRS]." Treas. Reg. § 1.6662-4(g)(4)(i)(A). To the contrary, Long Term repeatedly urged that it relied just upon the analysis of the "should" level opinions issued by Shearman & Sterling and King & Spalding, and thus, to establish reasonable belief, Long Term must demonstrate its reasonable good faith reliance on those opinions. *See* Treas. Reg. § 1.6662-4(g)(4)(i)(B). Such showing is impossible in light of the Court's conclusion *infra* that Long Term failed to satisfy its burden of proof to satisfy the requirements of Treas. Reg. § 1.6664-4(c)(1). *See* Treas. Reg. § 1.6662-4(g)(4)(ii) (" ... in no event will a taxpayer be considered to have reasonably relied in good faith on the opinion of a professional tax advisor for purposes of paragraph (g)(4)(i)(B) of this section unless the requirements of § 1.6664-4(c)(1) are met.").

---

50. [107] The Court recognizes that the fact that *Goldstein* and *Gilman* are Second Circuit decisions does not count against Long Term in the substantial authority calculus. *See* Treas. Reg. § 1.6662-4(d)(3)(iv)(B).

51. [108] While not pressed at trial, Long Term in its trial brief cites several informal memoranda and electronic mail purported to be advice provided to the IRS exam team from the IRS National Office during the course of the examination of Long Term to show that the National Office believed that Long Term had substantial authority for its return position. *See* Pets.' Trial Brief [Doc. # 133] at 138–40. However, Long Term does not claim that the cited documents may be considered as "authority" for purposes of the substantial authority analysis, and indeed they may not. *See* Treas. Reg. § 1.6662-4(d)(3)(iii).

. . .

Long Term principally seeks to avoid imposition of accuracy related penalties by reliance on 26 U.S.C. §6664(c)(1), which provides, "No penalty shall be imposed under this part with respect to any portion of an underpayment if it is shown that there was a reasonable cause for such portion and that the taxpayer acted in good faith with respect to such portion." The entity level inquiry relevant to this TEFRA proceeding is whether Long Term had reasonable cause for and acted in good faith with respect to claiming approximately $100 million in losses from the sale of the Quest and Rorer stock. *See* Treas. Reg. §1.6664-4(d); *supra* note 100. Long Term bears the burden of production and proof on its reasonable cause defense. *See* H.R. Conf. Rep. 105-599 at 241.

"The determination of whether a taxpayer acted with reasonable cause and in good faith is made on a case-by-case basis, taking into account all pertinent facts and circumstances. Generally, the most important factor is the extent of the taxpayer's effort to assess the taxpayer's proper tax liability." Treas. Reg. §1.6664-4(b)(1). Neither reliance on the advice of a professional tax advisor nor on facts that, unknown to the taxpayer, are incorrect necessarily demonstrates or indicates reasonable cause and good faith. *See id.*

However, "[r]eliance on professional advice[] or other facts ... constitutes reasonable cause and good faith if, under all the circumstances, such reliance was reasonable and the taxpayer acted in good faith." *Id.*

> Advice is any communication, including the opinion of a professional tax advisor, setting forth the analysis or conclusion of a person, other than the taxpayer, provided to (or for the benefit of) the taxpayer and on which the taxpayer relies, directly or indirectly, with respect to the imposition of the section 6662 accuracy-related penalty. Advice does not have to be in any particular form.

Treas. Reg. §1.6664-4(c)(2). Before a taxpayer may be considered to have reasonably relied in good faith on advice, two threshold requirements must be satisfied: (1) the advice must be based upon all pertinent facts and circumstances and the law as it relates to those facts and circumstances, including taking into account the taxpayer's purpose for entering into a transaction and for structuring a transaction in a particular manner, and is not adequate if the taxpayer fails to disclose a fact that it knows, or should know, to be relevant to the proper tax treatment of an item; and (2) the advice must not be based on unreasonable factual and legal assumptions (including assumptions as to future events) and must not unreasonably rely on the representations, statements, findings, or agreements of the taxpayer or any other person, including a representation or assumption the taxpayer knows, or has reason to know, is unlikely to be true, such as, an inaccurate representation or assumption as to the taxpayer's purposes for entering into a transaction or for structuring a transaction in a particular manner. *See* Treas. Reg. §1.6664-4(c)(1).

Long Term claims it reasonably relied in good faith on the advice of Shearman & Sterling and King & Spalding in claiming losses from Portfolio's sale of the Quest and

Rorer stock. There are at least four separate grounds for concluding that Long Term has failed to carry its burden to show that all pertinent facts and circumstances demonstrate reasonable and good faith reliance on the advice of King & Spalding and therefore Long Term may not avoid penalties by taking refuge in 26 U.S.C. § 6664(c).[52]

a. Receipt and Content of King & Spalding Advice

Long Term cannot satisfy its burden to establish applicability of the reasonable cause defense if it cannot prove it received the King & Spalding' opinions prior to April 15, 1998. Similarly, proof of the content of those opinions and corresponding analysis is necessary to an evaluation of threshold requirements for reasonable good faith reliance on advice, whether the advice was based on all pertinent facts and circumstances and the law related to them and was not based on unreasonable factual or legal assumptions. There is no reliable basis in the record from which to conclude that, prior to claiming losses from the sale of the Rorer and Quest stock on its 1997 tax return, Long Term actually received the opinions from King & Spalding on which it claims to have relied and, even assuming it timely received some form of "opinion," there is inadequate evidentiary basis for accurately determining what it consisted of and what substantive analysis undergirded it.

Long Term's proof problems stem from the fact that, prior to April 15, 1998, King & Spalding's advice was apparently conveyed to Noe and Long Term exclusively by oral communication from Kuller and is purportedly memorialized in writing prior to that date only by an electronic mail Noe wrote to his own file the day before Long Term's 1997 tax return was due, April 14, 1998. *See* Pets.' Ex. 346. The e-mail, reprinted in full *supra* at Part II.D.8., is essentially comprised of conclusory statements that the losses generated from the sale of the Rorer and Quest stock should be allocated to LTCM and mere parroting of the language of Treas. Reg. § 1.6664-4(c) (such as, King & Spalding "considered all pertinent facts and circumstances and the current U.S. Federal Income tax law and administrative practice as it relates to such facts and circumstances." *See id.*). The King & Spalding written opinion was not issued until January 27, 1999, over nine months after Long Term claimed the losses, and, while Noe testified he received drafts of it prior to its issuance, he did not testify he ever received any drafts before Long Term's tax return was filed. There was no corroborative evidence offered regarding the existence or timing of his receipt of such drafts.

The King & Spalding written opinion provided three opinions to Long Term, *see* Pets.' Ex. 357 at 28–29, and followed up each opinion with a corresponding "discussion and analysis" section: the first opinion related to Portfolio's tax basis in OTC's preferred stock (*see* Pets.' Ex. 357 at 29–42); the second opinion related to Portfolio's recognition of loss upon sale of the Rorer and Quest stock (*see id.* at 42–49); and the third opinion

---

52. [109] Because the claimed basis in the Rorer and Quest stock purportedly derived from the CHIPS and TRIPS transactions, reasonable good faith reliance on advice from both Shearman & Sterling and King & Spalding would be required for Long Term to establish its reasonable cause defense. The Court does not reach whether Long Term reasonably relied in good faith on advice from Shearman & Sterling.

related to allocation to LTCM of the built-in loss recognized upon Portfolio's sale of the Rorer and Quest stock (*see id.* at 50–79). The written opinion states, "[t]he opinions set forth herein confirm oral opinions provided to you prior to March 15, 1998." *Id.* at 79. Noe testified that all three opinions had been given to him orally before he wrote his April 14, 1998 e-mail. At trial, however, Kuller admitted that the oral opinion he rendered to Long Term in March 1998 was essentially the third of the three opinions set forth in the King & Spalding opinion, *see* Tr. [Doc. # 186] at 2151:16–17, which is corroborated by Noe's e-mail, stating in pertinent part,

> In deciding how to properly allocate the loss, I had discussions with Mark Kuller of King & Spalding. Mark, on this date, has orally confirmed that King & Spalding will issue an opinion *that the allocation of such Loss, as described above, should be sustained; that is, it is properly allocable to LTCM.*

Pets.' Ex. 346. This language tracks the third of the opinions set forth in the King & Spalding written opinion. Notably absent from the e-mail is any mention of the purported 26 U.S.C. §721(a) non-recognition contribution transactions of OTC to LTCP and LTCP to Portfolio, the subject of the first opinion, or recognition of loss by Portfolio upon sale of the Rorer and Quest stock, the subject of the second opinion. This is significant because the Court's holdings on liability, applying the step transaction doctrine and finding lack of economic substance in the OTC Transaction, are the subject of the King & Spalding first and second opinions, and Long Term makes no showing it ever saw these analyses before filing its tax return. *See* Pets.' Ex. 357 at 30–37, 44–49.

In addition, Noe's testimony about advice received from Kuller prior to Long Term's filing was either too vague or inconsistent to provide a basis for evaluating whether and what advice was actually received, much less whether it was based on unreasonable legal or factual assumptions or covered the law applicable to the OTC transaction. For example, Noe repeatedly emphasized that, prior to the tax return deadline, Kuller was intimately involved with every aspect of the OTC transaction, had all documents related to it, and discussed all aspects of the transaction with Noe, including the topics of substantive law covered by the final written King & Spalding' opinion. Noe at times even appeared to suggest that the exact substance of what was set forth in the final written opinion was provided to Long Term before it claimed the losses. However, on cross examination, a fuller picture emerged and Noe admitted that he could not remember discussing with Kuller the specific representations and assumptions set forth in the final written opinion and on which its conclusions depend, *see* Pet.'s Ex. 357 at 16–27 (for example that LTCM expected to derive a material pre-tax profit from OTC's investment in LTCP, *see id.* at 20), suggested that he could not recall whether such assumptions were in drafts he reviewed, *see* Tr. [Doc. # 171] at 799:3–6, conceded that he had not read all authorities cited in the final written opinion, and acknowledged that he could not recall whether he was concerned about the absence of Second Circuit authority in the opinion or whether he had even discussed with Kuller whether Second Circuit authority should be relied upon. Thus, the record does not permit using the content of the King & Spalding written opinion as a proxy for the analysis underlying any advice King & Spalding rendered to Long Term prior April 15, 1998.

With one notable exception, Kuller's and Scholes' testimony are both too vague to provide sufficient content for evaluating the basis of advice received before claiming losses. The one exception was Kuller's exhaustive and detailed testimony of his purported discussions with Noe regarding a material pre-tax profit analysis of the OTC transaction. If such conversations actually took place, they would constitute concrete analysis from which the Court could assess whether the advice provided prior to claiming losses, at least with respect to the Court's economic substance holding, was based on unreasonable legal assumptions or otherwise failed to take into account pertinent facts and circumstances and the law relevant thereto. However, as already discussed, the Court has concluded that such conversations either never took place in the time period claimed or were so embellished at trial by Kuller's testimony that it is impossible to ferret out reality. *See supra* Part II.D.8.b.

Accordingly, the Court holds that Long Term has failed to prove that the King & Spalding' advice on which it claims to have relied when it claimed losses on its 1997 tax return, at least as related to the Court's holdings on economic substance and the step transaction doctrine, had been rendered to it prior to the claiming of those losses such that it could have in fact relied upon such advice. The King & Spalding' advice thus cannot form the basis of a reasonable cause defense. In the alternative, the Court holds that Long Term has not satisfied its burden to prove entitlement to the reasonable cause defense as it is unable to prove the content of any advice actually received from King & Spalding before claiming losses from the sale of the Rorer and Quest stock for the purpose of showing it was based on all pertinent facts and circumstances and not on unreasonable assumptions.

b. King & Spalding's Written Opinion

Assuming, arguendo, that the King & Spalding' written opinion dated January 27, 1999, had been provided to Long Term prior to April 15, 1998, Long Term cannot prove that such advice meets the threshold requirements for reasonable good faith reliance, and the preponderance of evidence otherwise does not demonstrate that Long Term reasonably relied in good faith on King & Spalding' advice.

The first page of the King & Spalding opinion states that it was prepared as part of Long Term's litigation strategy in anticipation of possible future litigation over the claimed losses, language sounding like a predicate for assertion of an attorney work product privilege against disclosure, which Kuller testified was its purpose. The opinion's timing and stated purpose casts doubt on its contents as serving the purpose of providing a reasoned opinion on the application of tax law to the facts of the OTC transaction for client guidance in future actions.

The substance of the King & Spalding opinion does not provide a basis for concluding that the advice rendered to Long Term was based on all pertinent facts and circumstances or does not unreasonably rely on unreasonable factual assumptions. While the opinion states that it relies on assumptions and representations expressly made by Long Term, including that Long Term entered the OTC transaction for business purposes other than tax avoidance and reasonably expected to derive a material pre-tax profit from it and that there was no preexisting agreement on the part of OTC to sell its partnership interest to LTCM, it makes no effort to demonstrate, factually or analytically, why it was reasonable to rely on those assumptions and representations. Moreover, there is no evidence, such as internal King & Spalding memoranda, revealing King & Spalding' analysis of the claimed non-existence of an agreement on the part of OTC to exercise its put option or any breakout of Long Term's claimed expectation of profit or business purpose. As seen in the Court's discussion above, particularly the existence of evidence clearly contrary to certain representations regarding the settlement payment to Turlington, *see supra* Part III.B.4.c., a reasonably diligent analysis of all facts and circumstances would have revealed at least some of those assumptions to be unreasonable and unsupportable.

The King & Spalding written opinion also fails to demonstrate that its advice was based on the law related to the OTC transaction and not based on unreasonable legal assumptions. There is no citation to Second Circuit authority in the opinion, notwithstanding Long Term's continual residence in the Second Circuit and the obvious, central applicability of *Goldstein, Gilman, Grove, Blake,* and *Greene.* Furthermore, there is little, if any, of what could be characterized as legal analysis of the economic substance of the OTC transaction. What little there is essentially quotes a sentence from *Frank Lyon,* observes that the subjective business purpose/objective economic substance test emerged from that decision, and concludes that the OTC transaction passes muster because Long Term "instructed [King & Spalding] to assume" that both OTC and Long Term had business purpose for and a reasonable expectation of material pre-tax profit from the transaction. *See* Pet.'s Ex. 357 at 45–46. As set forth above, however, the Supreme Court's decision in *Frank Lyon* is highly fact sensitive and cannot simply be applied to just any set of facts. For example, before *Frank Lyon* could be relied on as support for the OTC transaction, in which the star attraction was a foreign entity not subject to U.S. taxes and thus one that could not use the $170 million in U.S. tax savings it was carrying, some explanation would have to be devoted to the Supreme Court's explicit consideration that the parties to the *Lyon* transaction had no differential in their respective tax rates or other special tax circumstances. *See supra* note 89.

The King & Spalding written opinion further contains minimal legal analysis of the application of the end result test for purposes of step transaction analysis. The opinion's treatment of *Esmark* is shallow; after brief discussion of the basic facts and step transaction holding of the tax court, King & Spalding opines:

> *Esmark* strongly supports respecting the form of the transactions described herein as a contribution of Preferred Shares followed by the sale of the Partners' Interest to LTCM. As in *Esmark,* the Service's potential re-characterization (a sale of the Preferred Shares to LTCM followed by a contribution of the Preferred Shares by LTCM to Partners) involves the same number of steps as the route chosen by LTCM, Partners, and OTC. In both cases, the route

chosen by the taxpayers produces a more tax beneficial result than the one potentially suggested by the Service.

Pets.' Ex. 357 at 32. It contains no comparison of the facts in *Esmark* to those of the OTC transaction, merely an extraction of a talismanic test that compares the numerosity of the steps of what was purportedly done versus the steps proposed in a re-characterization. As discussed above, *Esmark*'s derivation of such mechanical step transaction analysis from *Grove* is questionable, *see supra* note 94, but more importantly *Esmark*'s reliance on *Grove* as the basis for its holding, *see Esmark*, 90 T.C. at 196–97, makes it all the more surprising that the King & Spalding opinion omits any discussion of that Second Circuit decision.

After some discussion of authorities, the opinion concludes that "where the new corporation was found to have independent economic significance or a valid business purpose, the form of the transactions has been respected," Pets.' Ex. 357 at 36, with supporting citation to *Vest, DeWitt,* and *Weikel*:

> You have instructed us to assume that at all times from August 1, 1996 through the date hereof, each of Partners and Portfolio operated for valid and substantial business purposes with the objective of realizing a material pre-tax profit and possessed independent economic substance, and that each is expected to do so for the foreseeable future. The end result test therefore should not apply to the present case.

As discussed above, even if this assumption were factually correct, application of the end result test would not be legally precluded, as is apparent from *Vest* and *DeWitt* and exhaustively analyzed in *Associated*.[53] This assumption that the end result test would not be properly applied is a paradigmatic example of an unreasonable legal assumption within the meaning of Treas. Reg. § 1.6664-4(c)(1)(ii).

Finally, no other evidence such as companion memoranda discussing the application of the Second Circuit's decisions in *Goldstein, Gilman, Grove, Blake,* and *Grove,* or the Tenth Circuit's decision in *Associated* to the actual facts of the OTC transaction was offered to show research for King & Spalding's legal analysis and opinions. Such background research does not involve obscure or inaccessible caselaw references, is basic to a sound legal product, especially for "should" level opinion and a premium of $400,000. With hourly billing totals exceeding $100,000 there could not have been research time constraints.

---

53. [110] This is an example of the selective discussion of authority that appears in the King & Spalding' written opinion, which bolsters its appearance as an advocacy piece not a balanced reasoned opinion with the objective of guiding a client's decisions. One would expect that this comprehensive Tenth Circuit opinion from 1991 critiquing *Weikel* and accurately describing *Vest* should be considered before citation to the latter authorities as supporting the inapplicability of the step transaction doctrine. In this regard, the Court notes that *Associated* is the first case listed in the citing references of *Vest* in Westlaw and there it is labeled with three stars to demonstrate discussion as opposed to mere citation or mention; similarly, *Associated* is the sole case listed in the negative indirect history of *Weikel* in Westlaw where it is also marked with three stars.

In essence, the testimony and evidence offered by Long Term regarding the advice received from King & Spalding amounted to general superficial pronouncements asking the Court to "trust us; we looked into all pertinent facts; we were involved; we researched all applicable authorities; we made no unreasonable assumptions; Long Term gave us all information." The Court's role as factfinder is more searching and with specifics, analysis, and explanations in such short supply, the King & Spalding effort is insufficient to carry Long Term's burden to demonstrate that the legal advice satisfies the threshold requirements of reasonable good faith reliance on advice of counsel.

There was other evidence in the record suggesting the absence of reasonable good faith reliance on legal advice. Noe discussed the King & Spalding advice with other partners only to the extent of informing them that King & Spalding would render a "should" level opinion. There was no evidence that any partners other than Scholes has ever read the King & Spalding opinion, only that the principals specifically discussed that "should" level opinions would provide penalty protection. Merton was unaware of what assumptions, if any, were made by King & Spalding. Rosenfeld erroneously believed Long Term had a written opinion from King & Spalding at the time of the OTC transaction, apparently based on Scholes informing him that King & Spalding had issued a "should" level opinion.

c. Long Term's Lack of Good Faith

There is a fourth reason Long Term has not qualified itself for the reasonable cause defense, namely, its apparent steps to conceal the tax losses from the sale of the Rorer and Quest stock on the tax returns to thereby potentially win the audit lottery and evade IRS detection. Long Term reported the losses as "Net Unrealized Gains" on line 6 of Schedule M-1 of its 1997 tax return. *See e.g.*, Pets.' Ex. 319; 332. As Noe conceded, the M-1 schedule is designed to notify the IRS of differences in book income/loss and tax income/loss. Line 6, on which Long Term reported the losses, calls for income recorded on the books not included in tax income. Line 7, by contrast, calls for deductions not charged against book income. On its return, Long Term combined Line 6 and Line 7 to produce one number, netting out the losses against other capital gains, and put the composite number on Line 6.

In an internally prepared draft copy of Portfolio's return, Long Term initially described the composite as "Net Capital Gains/Losses," *see* Govt.'s Ex. 321, which at least truthfully reveals that the composite number included capital losses. Long Term then sent the draft to Price Waterhouse. While the draft was at Price Waterhouse, Will Taggart of Coopers & Lybrand, who had worked under Noe's supervision when Noe was with that firm, advised Long Term to re-characterize the composite number as "Net Unrealized Gains." Price Waterhouse concurred. Noe provided no testimony regarding the reasoning of Price Waterhouse or Coopers & Lybrand but explained that he believed line 7 of the M-1 was not applicable because the tax losses were not "deductions" as called for by that line but were losses used to offset capital gains and thereby reduce the partners' taxes.

Noe's explanation of Long Term's use of the term "Net Unrealized Gains" on line 6 is a transparent attempt to conceal Long Term's efforts to keep the huge tax losses claimed from raising a red audit flag. Long Term sold the Quest and Rorer stock and claimed losses from the sale so there was nothing "unrealized" about them. Furthermore, Long Term certainly did not pass the losses through to partners as "gain", rather it used them to reduce the partners' tax liability. The sale of the Rorer and Quest stock resulted in virtually no action on Long Term's books, and, the little activity there constituted a *loss*, not, as reported by Long Term, "*book income* not included [in taxable income]." If Noe and the collaborating consultants were properly concerned about accurately reporting the technical difference between a loss that offsets gain and thereby reduces taxes and a deduction that reduces taxes, Long Term should have put the amount in line 7 and labeled it to that effect, e.g., "tax losses offsetting gains." There is no justification for reporting approximately $106,000,000 in tax losses under the misleading titles and labels used. Given that Long Term's characterization contravenes a central purpose for the M-1 schedule — to notify the IRS of tax losses not charged to book income, it is of little moment that its disingenuous choices were counseled or encouraged by consultants.

* * *

Ringgold Telephone Company v. Commissioner

United States Tax Court
99 T.C.M. (CCH) 1416 (2010)

FACTS

Some of the facts and certain exhibits have been stipulated. The stipulations of fact are incorporated in this opinion by reference and are found as facts. Petitioner was a Georgia corporation at the time the petition was filed.

Petitioner provides telecommunications services to customers in Georgia and Tennessee.

Before tax year 2000, petitioner was taxed as a C corporation for Federal income tax purposes. Petitioner made a valid election to be classified as an S corporation for Federal income tax purposes effective January 1, 2000.

Petitioner's Interest in CRC and CHAT

On January 1, 2000, petitioner owned a 25-percent partnership interest in Cellular Radio of Chattanooga (CRC) (hereinafter we will refer to petitioner's partnership interest in CRC as the CRC interest). As of January 1, 2000, the other partners in CRC, each with a 25-percent interest, were BellSouth Mobility, Inc. (BellSouth), Trenton Telephone Co., and Bledsoe Telephone Co.

As of January 1, 2000, CRC's primary asset was a 29.54-percent limited partnership interest in the Chattanooga MSA Limited Partnership (CHAT), which provided wireless telecommunications service in Chattanooga, Tennessee.

Before September 30, 2000, CHAT's general partner was Chattanooga CGSA, Inc. Effective October 1, 2000, CHAT's general partner was Chattanooga CGSA, L. L.C.

Both of the successive general partners were, at all times relevant to this proceeding, wholly owned by BellSouth, and hereinafter they collectively are referred to as Chattanooga CGSA. As the only general partner of CHAT, Chattanooga CGSA was the only partner with the authority to request additional capital contributions and make distributions of partnership profits.

From January 1 through November 27, 2000, CHAT was owned as follows:

Ownership Interest (percentage)

Partnership	General partnership	Limited partnership	Total
Chattanooga CGSA	40	15.31	55.31
Alltel Cellular Associates of South Carolina Limited Partnership		15.15	15.15
CRC		29.54	29.54

At all times between January 1 and November 27, 2000, petitioner indirectly owned a 7.385-percent interest in CHAT as a result of petitioner's 25-percent partnership interest in CRC and CRC's 29.54-percent limited partnership interest in CHAT.

BellSouth acquired petitioner's 25-percent interest in CRC on November 27, 2000. Before that date, BellSouth owned 62.7 percent of CHAT—7.385 percent through its interest in CRC and 55.31 percent through its ownership of Chattanooga CGSA. Through its ownership of Chattanooga CGSA, BellSouth controlled CHAT.

The interests of petitioner and BellSouth in CHAT by virtue of their ownership of interests in CRC and Chattanooga CGSA before November 27, 2000, were are as follows:

Ownership interest (percentage)

	CHAT via Chattanooga CGSA	CHAT via CRC	CHAT total
BellSouth	55.31	7.385	62.695
Petitioner		-7.385	7.385

On January 1, 2000, CRC interests were not publicly traded, and petitioner's right to sell its 25-percent interest in CRC was subject to a right of first refusal in favor of the other CRC partners.

On January 1, 2000, partnership interests in CHAT were not publicly traded.

Reporting of Built-In Gain on the Sale of the CRC Interest

On September 30, 1999, at petitioner's request, the certified public accounting firm Warinner, Gesinger & Associates, L.L.C. (Warinner), issued a report using 1998 financial data that valued the CRC interest of petitioner at approximately $4,600,000 (September 1999 report).

In early 2000, Phil Erli (Mr. Erli), then the general manager of petitioner, requested that Warinner prepare a revised valuation report to correct arithmetical errors in the September 1999 report and to include more recent data in the valuation analysis. On February 15, 2000, Warinner issued a revised report on the basis of financial data through September 30, 1999, which estimated the value of the CRC interest to be approximately $2,600,000 (February 2000 report).

At the time that Mr. Erli requested the February 2000 report, he was not aware of the existence of the built-in gains tax and the impact that the determination of fair market value would have on that tax.

Petitioner's management did not become aware of the built-in gains tax until sometime in late 2000 or early 2001.

In March of 2000, petitioner engaged the investment banking firm Robinson-Humphrey Co., L.L.C. (Robinson-Humphrey), to identify potential buyers and to market the CRC interest. Robinson-Humphrey prepared an offering memorandum, which was provided to prospective purchasers and listed the value of the CRC interest as approximately $7 million. Robinson-Humphrey's compensation was contingent on the sale price of the CRC interest; accordingly, it had an incentive to try to generate a high sale price. The Robinson-Humphrey memorandum was prepared for marketing purposes rather than as an objective assessment of value.

Petitioner did not expect to get an offer of $7 million for its interest. Indeed, petitioner's management had decided that it would accept as little as $2 million for the CRC interest.

On July 6, 2000, BellSouth offered to purchase the CRC interest for $5,022,929, subject to working capital adjustments as of the date of closing.

Petitioner received no other offers to purchase the CRC interest. The other partners in CRC did not exercise their rights of first refusal with respect to the offer made by BellSouth.

Petitioner accepted BellSouth's offer on July 11, 2000, and the sale of the CRC interest to BellSouth was completed on November 27, 2000, for $5,220,043.

Petitioner timely filed a Federal income tax return on Form 1120S, U.S. Income Tax Return for an S Corporation, for the 2000 tax year.

On its 2000 Form 1120S, petitioner reported the amount of recognized built-in gain attributable to the CRC interest using a fair market value as of January 1, 2000 (the valuation date), of $2,600,000, the amount determined by the February 2000 report. Petitioner used the valuation of the CRC interest contained in the February

2000 report on the advice of Stephen Henley, a certified public accountant petitioner consulted to review its 2000 Federal income tax return.

Respondent sent petitioner a notice of deficiency dated August 3, 2007, that determined a deficiency of $925,260 and a penalty pursuant to section 6662(a) of $185,052. The deficiency resulted from respondent's determination that the fair market value of the CRC interest was $5,243,602[54] rather than the $2,600,000 shown on petitioner's 2000 Federal income tax return.

ANALYSIS

I. Valuation of the CRC Interest

The issue we must decide is the fair market value of the CRC interest on the valuation date; i.e. on January 1, 2000, the effective date of petitioner's subchapter S election.

A. Built-In Gains Tax

Section 1374 imposes a tax on built-in gains—gains accrued while an asset is held by a C corporation which later makes a subchapter S election. An S corporation's gain upon disposition of an asset generally is treated as built-in gain to the extent that the fair market value of that asset on the first day of the first taxable year for which the corporation's subchapter S election is in effect exceeds that asset's adjusted basis on such date. § 1374(d)(1). If an asset with built-in gain is sold during the 10-year period beginning on such date, the S corporation will be taxed on the built-in gain. § 1374(a), (d)(7).

The parties agree that petitioner is subject to built-in gains tax under § 1374 on the sale of the CRC interest. Respondent asserts that the fair market value of the CRC interest on the valuation date was $5,220,423, the price for which the interest was sold to BellSouth on November 27, 2000. Petitioner contends that the value of the CRC interest on the valuation date was $2,980,000.

B. Fair Market Value Standard

The standard for valuation is fair market value, which is defined as the price that a willing buyer would pay a willing seller, both persons having reasonable knowledge of all relevant facts and neither person being under a compulsion to buy or to sell. *See U.S. v. Cartwright*, 411 U.S. 546, 551 (1973) (applying the standard set forth in § 20.2031-1(b), Estate Tax Regs.). The standard is objective, using a hypothetical willing buyer and seller who are presumed to be dedicated to achieving maximum economic advantage in any transaction involving the property. *See Estate of Newhouse v. Comm'r*, 94 T.C. 193, 218 (1990). The objective willing buyer, willing seller standard must be achieved in the context of market and economic conditions on the valuation date. *Id.*

The valuation of stock is a question of fact resolved on the basis of the entire record. *See Ahmanson Found. v. U.S.*, 674 F.2d 761, 769 (9th Cir.1981); *Estate of New-*

---

54. [2] We note that Schedule 2 to the notice of deficiency, Explanation of Adjustments, states that the value of the CRC interest is determined to be $5,220,423. However, Schedule 3 to the notice of deficiency uses the value of $5,243,602 in calculating the built-in gains tax.

house v. Comm'r, supra at 217. The trier of fact must weigh all relevant evidence to draw the appropriate inferences. *See Comm'r v. Scottish Am. Inv. Co.*, 323 U.S. 119, 123–125 (1944); *Helvering v. Nat. Grocery Co.*, 304 U.S. 282, 294–295 (1938); *Estate of Newhouse v. Comm'r, supra* at 217.

In valuing unlisted securities, "actual arm's length sales of such stock in the normal course of business within a reasonable time before or after the valuation date are the best criteria of market value". *Estate of Andrews v. Comm'r*, 79 T.C. 938, 940 (1982); *See also Estate of Davis v. Comm'r*, 110 T.C. 530, 535 (1998). Where the value of unlisted stock cannot be determined from actual sale prices, its value generally is to be determined by taking into consideration a host of factors, including, among others, the company's net worth, prospective earning power, and dividend-paying capacity. *See, e.g., Estate of Davis v. Comm'r, supra* at 536.

As is customary in valuation cases, the parties offered expert opinion evidence to support their opposing valuation positions. In such cases, we evaluate the opinions of experts in the light of the demonstrated qualifications of each expert and all other evidence in the record. *See Estate of Christ v. Comm'r*, 480 F.2d 171, 174 (9th Cir.1973), *affg.* 54 T.C. 493 (1970); *Parker v. Comm'r*, 86 T.C. 547, 561 (1986). We have broad discretion to evaluate "'the overall cogency of each expert's analysis.'" *Sammons v. Comm'r*, 838 F.2d 330, 334 (9th Cir.1988) (quoting *Ebben v. Comm'r*, 783 F.2d 906, 909 (9th Cir.1986), *affg. in part and revg. in part* T.C. Memo.1983-200), *affg. in part and revg. in part on another ground* T.C. Memo.1986-318.

We are not bound by the formulas and opinions proffered by an expert witness and may accept or reject expert testimony in the exercise of sound judgment. *See Helvering v. Nat. Grocery Co., supra* at 295; *Estate of Newhouse v. Comm'r, supra* at 217. Where necessary, we may reach a determination of value on the basis of our own examination of the evidence in the record. *See Silverman v. Comm'r*, 538 F.2d 927, 933 (2d Cir.1976), *affg.* T.C. Memo.1974-285; *Estate of Davis v. Comm'r, supra* at 538. Where experts offer divergent estimates of fair market value, we decide what weight to give these estimates by examining the factors they used in arriving at their conclusions. *See Casey v. Comm'r*, 38 T.C. 357, 381 (1962).

We have broad discretion in selecting valuation methods, *see Estate of O'Connell v. Comm'r*, 640 F.2d 249, 251 (9th Cir.1981), *affg.* on this issue and *revg. in part* T.C. Memo.1978-191, and in evaluating the weight to be given the facts in reaching our conclusion because "finding market value is, after all, something for judgment, experience, and reason", *Colonial Fabrics, Inc. v. Comm'r*, 202 F.2d 105, 107 (2d Cir.1953), *affg.* a Memorandum Opinion of this Court. Moreover, while we may accept the opinion of an expert in its entirety, *see Buffalo Tool & Die Manufacturing Co. v. Comm'r*, 74 T.C. 441, 452 (1980), we may be selective in the use of any part of such opinion, or reject the opinion in its entirety, *see Parker v. Comm'r, supra* at 561. Because valuation necessarily results in an approximation, the figure at which this Court arrives need not be one as to which there is specific testimony if it is within the range of values that may properly be arrived at from consideration of all the evidence. *See Estate of O'Connell v. Comm'r, supra* at 252; *Silverman v. Comm'r, supra* at 933.

C. The Parties' Expert Testimony

Petitioner's expert witness, William E. King (Mr. King), prepared a report (King report) that concludes that the value of the CRC interest was $2,980,000 on the valuation date. Respondent's expert witness, Steven C. Hastings (Mr. Hastings), prepared a report (Hastings report) that concludes that the value of the CRC interest was $5,155,000 on the valuation date.

Mr. King is a certified public accountant and is accredited in business valuation by the American Institute of Certified Public Accountants. Mr. King has substantial experience in valuing telecommunications entities. Since 1998 Mr. King's work has been focused on the telecommunications industry, and Mr. King's company provides, on average, between 35 and 45 valuations per year related to telecommunications businesses. Mr. King testified that in any given year he spends between 25 percent and 75 percent of his time working on telecommunications valuations. On the basis of his experience in telecommunications valuation, Mr. King was able to factor in the specific conditions and outlook of the telecommunications industry, as well as the economic outlook in general, existing on the valuation date.

Mr. Hastings is a certified public accountant but is not accredited specifically in business valuation. Mr. Hastings worked in the area of business valuation during the late 1980s and early 1990s before leaving to work in other areas of finance. Mr. Hastings returned to business valuation work in 2006, and he testified that about 95 percent of his billable hours are currently spent on valuation issues. However, Mr. Hastings had never valued a telecommunications company before preparing his expert report in the instant case. Consequently, Mr. Hastings took a more mechanical approach to the valuation of the CRC interest, relying heavily on historical data without significant adjustment to reflect prevailing market conditions in the telecommunications industry on the valuation date.

Mr. King valued the CRC interest using both a business enterprise value analysis and a distribution yield analysis. The business enterprise value analysis incorporated four valuation methods (capitalization of income method, discounted future income method, guideline company method, and guideline transaction method). The capitalization of income method applied a capitalization rate of 13.6 percent to CHAT's determined net cashflows for four distinct periods preceding the valuation date. The discounted future income method applied discount rates ranging from 14.33 percent to 17.03 percent to CHAT's projected annual net cashflows for each of the years during a 10-year period ending on December 31, 2009, and a 17.03-percent discount rate to CHAT's residual value. The guideline company method reflected prices paid for companies similar to CHAT and whose stock was traded in a public market. The guideline transaction analysis reflected transactions involving the acquisition of privately held entities similar to CHAT. The resulting values derived under these four enterprise valuation methods, and the weights assigned to each, were as follows:

Method	Value of CHAT	Weight (percentage)
Capitalization of income	$44,902,000	50
Discounted future income	34,516,000	30
Guideline company	32,471,000	10
Guideline transaction	26,528,000	10
Concluded enterprise value	38,735,000	

On the basis of the above, Mr. King determined in his report that, on the valuation date, the total business enterprise value of CHAT was $38,735,000, the fair market value of CRC's interest in CHAT was $11,442,000, and the fair market value of the CRC interest was $2,861,000. In his report, Mr. King then applied a 5-percent lack of marketability discount and concluded that the appropriate business enterprise valuation of the CRC interest was $2,718,000.

Using the distribution yield analysis, Mr. King estimated the value of CHAT by applying a capitalization factor of 12.41 percent that reflected a 5-percent marketability discount to CHAT's net after-tax distributions for the 3 years before the valuation date (1997 through 1999). On the basis of the distribution yield analysis, Mr. King determined that the fair market value of the CRC interest on the valuation date was $3,243,000. In his report, Mr. King weighted the business enterprise analysis and the distribution yield analysis equally to arrive at a fair market value of $2,980,000 for the CRC interest.

In his report, Mr. Hastings valued the CRC interest by considering three business enterprise valuation methods (discounted cashflow method, merger and acquisition method, and guideline company method) to determine the fair market value of CHAT. Using the discounted cashflow method, Mr. Hastings applied a 14-percent discount rate to CHAT's projected annual income for each of the years during a 10-year period ending on December 31, 2009. Mr. Hastings used the merger and acquisition method to reflect transactions involving acquisitions of privately held entities comparable to CHAT. Mr. Hastings used the guideline company method to reflect prices paid for companies which were engaged in a business similar to CHAT and whose stock was publicly traded. In his report, Mr. Hastings determined that the guideline company method potentially overstated the value of CHAT and gave it no weight. Mr. Hastings concluded that the discounted cashflow method and the merger and acquisition method should be weighted equally. The resulting values derived under these three methods were as follows:

Valuation Method	Value of CHAT	Weight (percentage)
Discounted cashflow	$98,900,000	50
Merger & acquisition	115,900,000	50
Guideline company	127,800,000	0
Concluded value	107,400,000	

On the basis of the above, Mr. Hastings, in his report, determined that the total value of CHAT was $107,400,000, applied a 35-percent marketability discount, and concluded that the value of a 7.385-percent equity interest in CHAT on January 1, 2000, was $5,155,000. He also concluded that a multilevel discount was not appropriate and concluded that the value of the CRC interest on the valuation date was $5,155,000.

In his report, Mr. Hastings did not consider CHAT's distribution history when preparing his valuation analysis, and respondent asserts that Mr. King's use of a distribution yield analysis in his report was inappropriate. Specifically, respondent contends that a distribution yield analysis is appropriate only where the company being valued has been distributing almost all of its net income. Relying on § 25.2512-2(f)(2), Gift Tax Regs., and Rev. Rul. 59-60, 1959-1 C.B. 237, respondent further asserts that dividend-paying capacity, not dividends paid or distributed, should be used to value closely held stock. Respondent contends that a distribution yield analysis will understate the value of a company's stock when the company is not paying out all of the cash that it has available for dividends. It is important to note that while dividend-paying capacity may well be more important than actual dividends paid or distributed when determining the value of a controlling interest in a closely held business, this Court has recognized that "Dividends paid can be more important than dividend-paying capacity in appraising minority interests because a minority shareholder cannot force the company to pay dividends even if it has the capacity to do so". *Barnes v. Comm'r*, T.C. Memo.1998-413 (citing PRATT, ET AL., VALUING A BUSINESS: THE ANALYSIS AND APPRAISAL OF CLOSELY HELD COMPANIES 227 (3d ed.1996)).

D. Sale Price of the CRC Interest as Evidence of Fair Market Value

Since a reasonably contemporaneous arm's-length sale is the best evidence of value, we must decide whether the sale of the CRC interest to BellSouth meets that criterion. During July 2000, approximately 6 months after the valuation date, petitioner and BellSouth entered into an agreement for the purchase of the CRC interest. Petitioner sold the CRC interest to BellSouth on November 27, 2000, for $5,220,043. Respondent contends that the best evidence of the value of the CRC interest on January 1, 2000, is the subsequent sale of that interest to BellSouth on November 27, 2000. Petitioner contends that the sale of the CRC interest to BellSouth did not reflect arm's-length pricing between a willing and informed hypothetical buyer and seller and that the sale price must be disregarded or adjusted. Petitioner further contends that BellSouth would have paid more than an average hypothetical buyer for the CRC interest because BellSouth already owned a controlling interest in CHAT, the primary asset of CRC.

In deciding whether the sale of the CRC interest to BellSouth is probative evidence of its value on the valuation date, we first consider whether the sale was within a reasonable time after the valuation date. The price at which the CRC interest sold was fixed by a formula agreed to 6 months after the valuation date. Petitioner has not established, and does not argue, that there were intervening circumstances that would have affected value between the valuation date and the sale date, and neither party asserts that the sale date was not within a reasonable time after the valuation date. We conclude, on the basis of the record, that the sale of the CRC interest to BellSouth occurred within a reasonable time after the valuation date and that there were no intervening events that would have affected value between the valuation date and the sale date.

We next consider whether the sale to BellSouth was an arm's-length sale in the normal course of business. The evidence indicates that BellSouth was an unrelated buyer acting in its own self-interest when it purchased the CRC interest. Neither party argues that the sale to BellSouth was not an arm's-length transaction. We conclude, on the basis of the record, that the sale of the CRC interest was an arm's-length sale in the normal course of business.

Finally, even though we have concluded that the sale of the CRC interest to BellSouth was an arm's-length transaction, we consider whether unique characteristics of the transaction persuade us to adjust the sale price in our valuation analysis. Petitioner argues that if we use the BellSouth purchase price as evidence of the value of the CRC interest on the valuation date, that purchase price must be adjusted to reflect "special circumstances surrounding the buyer, the seller, or the transaction generally that could have skewed the sale price from a measure of true fair market value that would have been reached between a hypothetical buyer and seller absent those circumstances". We agree with petitioner that in the instant case we should consider the unique characteristics of the actual buyer, seller, and transaction. See *Epic Associates 84-III v. Comm'r*, T.C. Memo.2001-64; *Hansen v. Comm'r*, a Memorandum Opinion of this Court dated July 28, 1952; §20.2031-2(e), Estate Tax Regs.

Petitioner contends that the sale price must be adjusted because "BellSouth was a truly unique buyer that would have likely valued the CRC interest at a higher price than literally anyone else in the world based on its unilateral control of CHAT". Additionally, petitioner contends that we must consider BellSouth's history of submitting "high bids" in order to discourage exercise of rights of first refusal.

E. Whether the BellSouth Sale Price Included a Control Premium

Petitioner argues that, as a matter of law, the fair market value of a minority interest in a business cannot be ascertained by reference to what a controlling interest holder would pay for the interest because a controlling interest holder would place a greater value on a minority interest than would a hypothetical purchaser who lacks control. Petitioner therefore contends that the BellSouth purchase price reflects a "control" value to BellSouth and must be disregarded or discounted in determining the fair market value of the CRC interest to a hypothetical buyer who did not control CHAT as BellSouth did.

Respondent counters with the argument that BellSouth already controlled CHAT before its acquisition of the CRC interest and did not gain any additional measure of control over CHAT by virtue of its purchase of the CRC interest. Consequently, respondent contends, BellSouth would not have paid a control premium for the CRC interest but instead would have paid only what any other buyer would have paid for a minority interest in CRC. Respondent, therefore, argues that the BellSouth sale price reflects a discount for lack of control.

According to petitioner, valuing the CRC interest by reference to the BellSouth sale price, without applying a discount for lack of control, would violate the precedent of this Court and the Court of Appeals for the Eleventh Circuit.[55] Petitioner contends that *Estate of Bright v. Comm'r*, 658 F.2d 999 (5th Cir.1981) (en banc),[56] and *Estate of Andrews v. Comm'r*, 79 T.C. 938 (1982), prohibit the Commissioner from valuing an interest on the basis of its value to a person who already holds a controlling interest without applying a discount for lack of control.

In *Estate of Bright*, the decedent and her husband owned, as community property, a 55-percent interest in each of several closely held corporations. The issue in *Estate of Bright* was the valuation of the decedent's one-half of that community property interest. The Commissioner argued that the proper valuation method was to value the entire 55-percent interest, including a control premium, and then take one-half thereof. The Court of Appeals for the Fifth Circuit held that family attribution did not apply to lump the decedent's minority interest with the interest of her husband to create a controlling interest for valuation purposes. *Id.*

In *Estate of Andrews v. Comm'r, supra*, the issue was the valuation of a decedent's 20-percent interest in each of four closely held corporations. As there had been no sales of interests in the corporations being valued within a reasonable time before or after the valuation date, this Court valued the stocks indirectly by weighing net worth, prospective earning power, dividend-paying capacity, and other relevant factors. *Id.* at 940. The portion of the *Estate of Andrews* Opinion on which petitioner relies addresses whether a control discount should be applied to that indirectly determined value. *Id.* at 951. The Commissioner's position in *Estate of Andrews* was that a control discount should not be applied if family members control a corporation. *Id.* at 952. Because all the shareholders, including the decedent, were family members and shared in control, the Commissioner argued that no discount should be allowed in valuing the decedent's 20-percent interest. *Id.* Citing *Estate of Bright v. Comm'r, supra*, this Court rejected the family attribution argument and applied a minority discount in determining the value of the decedent's minority interests. *Id.* at 956.

We do not agree that either *Estate of Bright* or *Estate of Andrews* controls the valuation issue in the instant case as a matter of law. In both *Estate of Bright* and *Estate of Andrews*, the question was not whether a majority shareholder would pay a premium for a minority interest in an entity that it controlled but whether family attribution should apply to prevent the application of a lack of control discount even though the

---

55. [3] The Tax Court follows the law of the Court of Appeals to which an appeal would lie if the law of that circuit is on "all fours". *Golsen v. Comm'r*, 54 T.C. 742, 757 (1970), *affd.* 445 F.2d 985 (10th Cir.1971). Absent stipulation to the contrary, any appeal of the instant case would be to the Court of Appeals for the Eleventh Circuit. *See* § 7482(b)(1)(B).

56. [4] The Court of Appeals for the Eleventh Circuit has adopted as binding precedent certain decisions of the former Court of Appeals for the Fifth Circuit. *See Bonner v. City of Prichard*, 661 F.2d 1206, 1209 (11th Cir.1981) (en banc); *Stein v. Reynolds Sec., Inc.*, 667 F.2d 33 (11th Cir.1982). However, as discussed below, because *Estate of Bright v. Comm'r*, 658 F.2d 999 (5th Cir.1981), is not on "all fours" with the instant case, we need not consider whether it would be binding precedent in the Eleventh Circuit.

interest being valued was a minority interest. Neither *Estate of Andrews* nor *Estate of Bright* involved an actual, contemporaneous sale of an interest in any of the entities being valued as is present in the instant case. In both *Estate of Bright* and *Estate of Andrews*, the Commissioner's position was that a minority interest in a closely held corporation should be valued with a control premium. Those are not the circumstances of the instant case. Respondent concedes that the CRC interest was a minority interest and that a minority discount is appropriate in valuing that interest.[57] As discussed above, respondent contends that the minority discount is reflected in the Bell-South sale price.

For the foregoing reasons, we conclude that neither *Estate of Bright v. Comm'r, supra,* nor *Estate of Andrews v. Comm'r, supra,* establishes that a controlling shareholder would necessarily be willing to pay a premium for a minority interest in a corporation that it already controlled. Accordingly, we do not agree with petitioner that we must, as a matter of law, apply a lack of control discount to the actual sale price of the CRC interest because the buyer, BellSouth, controlled CHAT.

We next consider whether petitioner has proved that, under the particular circumstances present, the CRC interest would have been more valuable to BellSouth than to another investor who was merely acquiring a minority interest. We find nothing in the record to support petitioner's assertion. To the contrary, petitioner's own expert, Mr. King, indicated that BellSouth had no incentive, from a control perspective, to buy the CRC interest. Mr. King testified at trial that "it's already been indicated that BellSouth had no reason to buy this. There was no control element that … was associated with this." He further stated that "there's no reason for it, they already had control. They already had operating control of the partnership." Accordingly, we conclude that petitioner has not established that BellSouth paid a control premium for the CRC interest.

F. Whether Rights of First Refusal Affected the Sale Price

We next consider whether, as petitioner contends, there is evidence that BellSouth paid a premium for the CRC interest in order to discourage the exercise by the other CRC partners of their rights of first refusal. The sale of the CRC interest was subject to a right of first refusal in favor of the three nonselling partners of CRC. Mr. King testified that, in his extensive prior experience dealing with BellSouth and its successor entities, once BellSouth determines that a transaction is strategic it will "do whatever it takes to win" including submitting high bids to discourage exercise of rights of first refusal. Regarding the CRC purchase, Mr. King stated that "In other words, they wanted to make sure that they put an offer out that was sufficient enough to essentially discourage Bledsoe Telephone Company and Trenton Telephone Company from exercising their right of first refusal."

We found Mr. King's testimony to be credible, and there is no evidence contradicting his testimony in that regard. Consequently, we conclude that the BellSouth sale price should be adjusted to reflect the likelihood that BellSouth viewed the CRC

---

57. [5] The parties disagree as to what the appropriate minority discount is and as to when and how that discount should be reflected in the different valuation methodologies.

interest as a strategic acquisition and was willing to pay a premium to avoid exercise of the rights of first refusal of the other CRC partners. For the foregoing reasons, we conclude that the BellSouth sale price is probative, but not conclusive, evidence of the value of the CRC interest on the valuation date.

G. Fair Market Value of the CRC Interest

Because we find that the BellSouth sale price is probative, but not conclusive, evidence of the value of the CRC interest on the valuation date, we have also carefully considered all of the other evidence in the record in arriving at a determination of the fair market value of the CRC interest. In making a determination of value, we have considered the sale of the CRC interest to BellSouth and the valuation reports of Mr. King and Mr. Hastings, as well as all the other relevant factors, including the unique characteristics of BellSouth as a purchaser, the business climate on the valuation date, the double-tiered partnership structure, and the dividend and capital call history of CRC.

We found petitioner's expert, Mr. King, to be the more persuasive of the two expert witnesses. As discussed above, his experience in the field of telecommunications valuation allowed him to tailor his analyses to reflect industry conditions existing on the valuation date. Additionally, Mr. King's analysis considered the distribution history of CHAT, a factor ignored by Mr. Hastings but likely to be an important consideration for a purchaser of a minority interest. Finally, the Court found Mr. King's testimony at trial to be credible and persuasive. Accordingly, we place great weight on Mr. King's expert report. However, we do believe that Mr. King failed to adequately consider the sale to BellSouth in his analysis, and we take that sale into account in reaching a determination of value.

We accept the values determined by Mr. King in his business enterprise valuation analysis and his distribution yield analysis and his decision to weight those factors equally in valuing the CRC interest. However, we have also determined that it is appropriate to include a third factor in the analysis; i.e., the BellSouth sale price. After considering all of the evidence in the record, we conclude that the values yielded by the business enterprise analysis ($2,718,000), the distribution yield analysis ($3,243,000), and the BellSouth sale price ($5,220,423) should be weighted equally in arriving at the value of the CRC interest. Weighting each of those numbers equally results in a value of $3,727,141. On the basis of the foregoing considerations and the entire record, we conclude that the fair market of the CRC interest as of the valuation date was $3,727,142.

II. Substantial Understatement Penalty

A taxpayer may be subject to an accuracy-related penalty of 20 percent of any underpayment which is attributable to a substantial understatement of income tax. § 6662(a) and (b)(2). For an S corporation, there is a substantial understatement of income tax if the amount of the understatement for the tax year exceeds the greater of 10 percent of the amount required to be shown on the return or $5,000. § 6662(d)(1)(A). Pursuant to § 7491(c), the Commissioner generally bears the burden of production for any penalty, but the taxpayer bears the ultimate burden of proof. *Higbee v. Comm'r*, 116 T.C. 438, 446 (2001).

The accuracy-related penalty does not apply where it is shown that there was substantial authority for the position taken by the taxpayer. §6662(d)(2)(B)(i). The accuracy-related penalty also does not apply to any part of an underpayment of tax if it is shown that the taxpayer acted with reasonable cause and in good faith. §6664(c)(1). That determination is made on a case-by-case basis, taking into account all the pertinent facts and circumstances. §1.6664-4(b)(1), Income Tax Regs. Taxpayers bear the burden of proving that they had reasonable cause and acted in good faith. See *Higbee v. Comm'r, supra* at 446; *Dollander v. Comm'r*, T.C. Memo2009-187. Relevant factors include a taxpayer's efforts to assess his proper tax liability, including the taxpayer's reasonable and good-faith reliance on the advice of a professional such as an accountant. §1.6664-4(b)(1), Income Tax Regs.

Respondent determined that petitioner is liable for a substantial understatement penalty pursuant to §6662 of $185,052. Because we conclude below that petitioner acted with reasonable cause and in good faith, it is unnecessary to determine the precise amount of the understatement resulting from our determination of the value of the CRC interest.

Petitioner contends that it is not liable for an accuracy-related penalty because it acted in good faith and reasonably relied on the advice of Mr. Henley in reporting the value of the CRC interest. Respondent asserts that petitioner did not act reasonably and in good faith because it disregarded two appraisals and the actual sale price, all of which would have resulted in a value for the CRC interest higher than that which was reported on petitioner's 2000 income tax return.

Mr. Erli, who was petitioner's general manager in 2000, testified that he was not an expert in tax matters, and that, in fact, tax was one of his areas of weakness. For that reason, Mr. Erli suggested that petitioner should bring in someone to consult on its tax returns. Consequently, Mr. Henley, a certified public accountant specializing in tax, was hired to review petitioner's tax returns. It was Mr. Henley who first raised the issue of built-in gains tax. Mr. Erli's uncontradicted testimony establishes that the decision to use the $2.6 million valuation of the CRC interest from the February 2000 report was based on the advice of Mr. Henley. We conclude that it was reasonable for petitioner to rely on the advice of Mr. Henley in determining the valuation of the CRC interest to report on its income tax return

Mr. Henley testified that he was made aware of the sale to BellSouth, but that he did not recommend that petitioner use the sale price in determining the value of the CRC interest on the valuation date. On the basis of the testimony of Mr. Erli and Mr. Henley, it appears that petitioner did not provide Mr. Henley with the September 1999 report or the Robinson-Humphrey memorandum. All of the evidence indicates that the February 2000 report was an update of the September 1999 report to correct errors and incorporate more current data. Respondent does not dispute that the September report contained errors, nor does respondent contend that the February 2000 report did anything more than correct errors and incorporate more recent financial information. We conclude that there was no reason for petitioner to have provided Mr. Henley with an appraisal that contained errors and outdated financial information when a more current version of that same report was available. Furthermore, we conclude that the Robinson-Humphrey memorandum was prepared primarily as a marketing tool, not as an objective valuation of the CRC interest. Consequently, we conclude that petitioner did not act in bad faith when it failed to provide Mr. Henley with the September 1999 report and the Robinson-Humphrey memorandum.

For the foregoing reasons we conclude that petitioner acted with reasonable cause and in good faith in relying on the advice of Mr. Henley regarding the valuation of the CRC interest. Because we so conclude, we need not reach the question of whether petitioner's position was supported by substantial authority. We hold that petitioner is not liable for a substantial understatement penalty under § 6662.

OPINION

On the basis of the foregoing, we conclude that the value of the CRC interest on January 1, 2000, was $3,727,142 and that petitioner is not liable for a substantial understatement penalty.

* * *

Treasury Department Circular No. 230

31 C.F.R., Subtitle A, Part 10

§ 10.0 Scope of part.

(a) This part contains rules governing the recognition of attorneys, certified public accountants, enrolled agents, enrolled retirement plan agents, registered tax return preparers, and other persons representing taxpayers before the Internal Revenue Service. Subpart A of this part sets forth rules relating to the authority to practice before the Internal Revenue Service; subpart B of this part prescribes the duties and restrictions relating to such practice; subpart C of this part prescribes the sanctions for violating the regulations; subpart D of this part contains the rules applicable to disciplinary proceedings; and subpart E of this part contains general provisions relating to the availability of official records.

* * *

§ 10.2 Definitions.

(a) As used in this part, except where the text provides otherwise—

(1) *Attorney* means any person who is a member in good standing of the bar of the highest court of any state, territory, or possession of the United States, including a Commonwealth, or the District of Columbia.

(2) *Certified public accountant* means any person who is duly qualified to practice as a certified public accountant in any state, territory, or possession of the United States, including a Commonwealth, or the District of Columbia.

(3) *Commissioner* refers to the Commissioner of Internal Revenue.

(4) *Practice before the Internal Revenue Service* comprehends all matters connected with a presentation to the Internal Revenue Service or any of its officers or

employees relating to a taxpayer's rights, privileges, or liabilities under laws or regulations administered by the Internal Revenue Service. Such presentations include, but are not limited to, preparing documents; filing documents; corresponding and communicating with the Internal Revenue Service; rendering written advice with respect to any entity, transaction, plan or arrangement, or other plan or arrangement having a potential for tax avoidance or evasion; and representing a client at conferences, hearings, and meetings.

(5) *Practitioner* means any individual described in paragraphs (a), (b), (c), (d), (e), or (f) of § 10.3.

(6) A *tax return* includes an amended tax return and a claim for refund.

(7) *Service* means the Internal Revenue Service.

(8) *Tax return preparer* means any individual within the meaning of section 7701(a)(36) and 26 CFR 301.7701-15.

§ 10.3 Who may practice.

(a) *Attorneys.* Any attorney who is not currently under suspension or disbarment from practice before the Internal Revenue Service may practice before the Internal Revenue Service by filing with the Internal Revenue Service a written declaration that the attorney is currently qualified as an attorney and is authorized to represent the party or parties. Notwithstanding the preceding sentence, attorneys who are not currently under suspension or disbarment from practice before the Internal Revenue Service are not required to file a written declaration with the IRS before rendering written advice covered under § 10.37, but their rendering of this advice is practice before the Internal Revenue Service.

* * *

§ 10.21 Knowledge of client's omission.

A practitioner who, having been retained by a client with respect to a matter administered by the Internal Revenue Service, knows that the client has not complied with the revenue laws of the United States or has made an error in or omission from any return, document, affidavit, or other paper which the client submitted or executed under the revenue laws of the United States, must advise the client promptly of the fact of such noncompliance, error, or omission. The practitioner must advise the client of the consequences as provided under the Code and regulations of such noncompliance, error, or omission.

§ 10.22 Diligence as to accuracy.

(a) *In general.* A practitioner must exercise due diligence—

(1) In preparing or assisting in the preparation of, approving, and filing tax returns, documents, affidavits, and other papers relating to Internal Revenue Service matters;

(2) In determining the correctness of oral or written representations made by the practitioner to the Department of the Treasury; and

(3) In determining the correctness of oral or written representations made by the practitioner to clients with reference to any matter administered by the Internal Revenue Service.

(b) *Reliance on others.* Except as modified by §§ 10.34 and 10.37, a practitioner will be presumed to have exercised due diligence for purposes of this section if the practitioner relies on the work product of another person and the practitioner used reasonable care in engaging, supervising, training, and evaluating the person, taking proper account of the nature of the relationship between the practitioner and the person.

* * *

§ 10.27 Fees.

(a) *In general.* A practitioner may not charge an unconscionable fee in connection with any matter before the Internal Revenue Service.

(b) *Contingent fees—*

(1) Except as provided in paragraphs (b)(2), (3), and (4) of this section, a practitioner may not charge a contingent fee for services rendered in connection with any matter before the Internal Revenue Service.

(2) A practitioner may charge a contingent fee for services rendered in connection with the Service's examination of, or challenge to—

(i) An original tax return; or

(ii) An amended return or claim for refund or credit where the amended return or claim for refund or credit was filed within 120 days of the taxpayer receiving a written notice of the examination of, or a written challenge to the original tax return.

(3) A practitioner may charge a contingent fee for services rendered in connection with a claim for credit or refund filed solely in connection with the determination of statutory interest or penalties assessed by the Internal Revenue Service.

(4) A practitioner may charge a contingent fee for services rendered in connection with any judicial proceeding arising under the Internal Revenue Code.

(c) *Definitions.* For purposes of this section—

(1) *Contingent fee* is any fee that is based, in whole or in part, on whether or not a position taken on a tax return or other filing avoids challenge by the Internal Revenue Service or is sustained either by the Internal Revenue Service or in litigation. A contingent fee includes a fee that is based on a percentage of the refund reported on a return, that is based on a percentage of the taxes saved, or that otherwise depends on the specific result attained. A contingent fee also includes any fee arrangement in which the practitioner will reimburse the client for all or a portion of the client's fee in the event that a position taken on a tax return or other filing is challenged by the In-

ternal Revenue Service or is not sustained, whether pursuant to an indemnity agreement, a guarantee, rescission rights, or any other arrangement with a similar effect.

(2) *Matter before the Internal Revenue Service* includes tax planning and advice, preparing or filing or assisting in preparing or filing returns or claims for refund or credit, and all matters connected with a presentation to the Internal Revenue Service or any of its officers or employees relating to a taxpayer's rights, privileges, or liabilities under laws or regulations administered by the Internal Revenue Service. Such presentations include, but are not limited to, preparing and filing documents, corresponding and communicating with the Internal Revenue Service, rendering written advice with respect to any entity, transaction, plan or arrangement, and representing a client at conferences, hearings, and meetings.

* * *

§ 10.29 Conflicting interests.

(a) Except as provided by paragraph (b) of this section, a practitioner shall not represent a client before the Internal Revenue Service if the representation involves a conflict of interest. A conflict of interest exists if—

(1) The representation of one client will be directly adverse to another client; or

(2) There is a significant risk that the representation of one or more clients will be materially limited by the practitioner's responsibilities to another client, a former client or a third person, or by a personal interest of the practitioner.

(b) Notwithstanding the existence of a conflict of interest under paragraph (a) of this section, the practitioner may represent a client if—

(1) The practitioner reasonably believes that the practitioner will be able to provide competent and diligent representation to each affected client;

(2) The representation is not prohibited by law; and

(3) Each affected client waives the conflict of interest and gives informed consent, confirmed in writing by each affected client, at the time the existence of the conflict of interest is known by the practitioner. The confirmation may be made within a reasonable period of time after the informed consent, but in no event later than 30 days.

(c) Copies of the written consents must be retained by the practitioner for at least 36 months from the date of the conclusion of the representation of the affected clients, and the written consents must be provided to any officer or employee of the Internal Revenue Service on request.

* * *

§ 10.32 Practice of law.

Nothing in the regulations in this part may be construed as authorizing persons not members of the bar to practice law.

§ 10.33 Best practices for tax advisors.

(a) *Best practices.* Tax advisors should provide clients with the highest quality representation concerning Federal tax issues by adhering to best practices in providing advice and in preparing or assisting in the preparation of a submission to the Internal Revenue Service. In addition to compliance with the standards of practice provided elsewhere in this part, best practices include the following:

(1) Communicating clearly with the client regarding the terms of the engagement. For example, the advisor should determine the client's expected purpose for and use of the advice and should have a clear understanding with the client regarding the form and scope of the advice or assistance to be rendered.

(2) Establishing the facts, determining which facts are relevant, evaluating the reasonableness of any assumptions or representations, relating the applicable law (including potentially applicable judicial doctrines) to the relevant facts, and arriving at a conclusion supported by the law and the facts.

(3) Advising the client regarding the import of the conclusions reached, including, for example, whether a taxpayer may avoid accuracy-related penalties under the Internal Revenue Code if a taxpayer acts in reliance on the advice.

(4) Acting fairly and with integrity in practice before the Internal Revenue Service.

(b) *Procedures to ensure best practices for tax advisors.* Tax advisors with responsibility for overseeing a firm's practice of providing advice concerning Federal tax issues or of preparing or assisting in the preparation of submissions to the Internal Revenue Service should take reasonable steps to ensure that the firm's procedures for all members, associates, and employees are consistent with the best practices set forth in paragraph (a) of this section.

§ 10.34 Standards with respect to tax returns and documents, affidavits and other papers.

(a) *Tax returns.*

(1) A practitioner may not willfully, recklessly, or through gross incompetence

(i) Sign a tax return or claim for refund that the practitioner knows or reasonably should know contains a position that

(A) Lacks a reasonable basis;

(B) Is an unreasonable position as described in section 6694(a)(2) of the Internal Revenue Code (Code) (including the related regulations and other published guidance); or

(C) Is a willful attempt by the practitioner to understate the liability for tax or a reckless or intentional disregard of rules or regulations by the practitioner as described in section 6694(b)(2) of the Code (including the related regulations and other published guidance).

(ii) Advise a client to take a position on a tax return or claim for refund, or prepare a portion of a tax return or claim for refund containing a position, that

    (A) Lacks a reasonable basis;

    (B) Is an unreasonable position as described in section 6694(a)(2) of the Code (including the related regulations and other published guidance); or

    (C) Is a willful attempt by the practitioner to understate the liability for tax or a reckless or intentional disregard of rules or regulations by the practitioner as described in section 6694(b)(2) of the Code (including the related regulations and other published guidance).

(2) A pattern of conduct is a factor that will be taken into account in determining whether a practitioner acted willfully, recklessly, or through gross incompetence.

(b) *Documents, affidavits and other papers*

(1) A practitioner may not advise a client to take a position on a document, affidavit or other paper submitted to the Internal Revenue Service unless the position is not frivolous.

(2) A practitioner may not advise a client to submit a document, affidavit or other paper to the Internal Revenue Service

(i) The purpose of which is to delay or impede the administration of the Federal tax laws;

(ii) That is frivolous; or

(iii) That contains or omits information in a manner that demonstrates an intentional disregard of a rule or regulation unless the practitioner also advises the client to submit a document that evidences a good faith challenge to the rule or regulation.

(c) *Advising clients on potential penalties*

(1) A practitioner must inform a client of any penalties that are reasonably likely to apply to the client with respect to

(i) A position taken on a tax return if

    (A) The practitioner advised the client with respect to the position; or

    (B) The practitioner prepared or signed the tax return; and

(ii) Any document, affidavit or other paper submitted to the Internal Revenue Service.

(2) The practitioner also must inform the client of any opportunity to avoid any such penalties by disclosure, if relevant, and of the requirements for adequate disclosure.

(3) This paragraph (c) applies even if the practitioner is not subject to a penalty under the Internal Revenue Code with respect to the position or with respect to the document, affidavit or other paper submitted.

(d) *Relying on information furnished by clients.* A practitioner advising a client to take a position on a tax return, document, affidavit or other paper submitted to the Internal Revenue Service, or preparing or signing a tax return as a preparer, generally may rely in good faith without verification upon information furnished by the client. The practitioner may not, however, ignore the implications of information furnished to, or actually known by, the practitioner, and must make reasonable inquiries if the information as furnished appears to be incorrect, inconsistent with an important fact or another factual assumption, or incomplete.

* * *

§ 10.35 Competence.

(a) A practitioner must possess the necessary competence to engage in practice before the Internal Revenue Service. Competent practice requires the appropriate level of knowledge, skill, thoroughness, and preparation necessary for the matter for which the practitioner is engaged. A practitioner may become competent for the matter for which the practitioner has been engaged through various methods, such as consulting with experts in the relevant area or studying the relevant law.

* * *

§ 10.36 Procedures to ensure compliance.

(a) Any individual subject to the provisions of this part who has (or individuals who have or share) principal authority and responsibility for overseeing a firm's practice governed by this part, including the provision of advice concerning Federal tax matters and preparation of tax returns, claims for refund, or other documents for submission to the Internal Revenue Service, must take reasonable steps to ensure that the firm has adequate procedures in effect for all members, associates, and employees for purposes of complying with subparts A, B, and C of this part, as applicable. In the absence of a person or persons identified by the firm as having the principal authority and responsibility described in this paragraph, the Internal Revenue Service may identify one or more individuals subject to the provisions of this part responsible for compliance with the requirements of this section.

(b) Any such individual who has (or such individuals who have or share) principal authority as described in paragraph (a) of this section will be subject to discipline for failing to comply with the requirements of this section if

(1) The individual through willfulness, recklessness, or gross incompetence does not take reasonable steps to ensure that the firm has adequate procedures to comply with this part, as applicable, and one or more individuals who are

members of, associated with, or employed by, the firm are, or have, engaged in a pattern or practice, in connection with their practice with the firm, of failing to comply with this part, as applicable;

(2) The individual through willfulness, recklessness, or gross incompetence does not take reasonable steps to ensure that firm procedures in effect are properly followed, and one or more individuals who are members of, associated with, or employed by, the firm are, or have, engaged in a pattern or practice, in connection with their practice with the firm, of failing to comply with this part, as applicable; or

(3) The individual knows or should know that one or more individuals who are members of, associated with, or employed by, the firm are, or have, engaged in a pattern or practice, in connection with their practice with the firm, that does not comply with this part, as applicable, and the individual, through willfulness, recklessness, or gross incompetence fails to take prompt action to correct the noncompliance.

* * *

§ 10.37 Requirements for other written advice.

(a) *Requirements.*

(1) A practitioner may give written advice (including by means of electronic communication) concerning one or more Federal tax matters subject to the requirements in paragraph (a)(2) of this section. Government submissions on matters of general policy are not considered written advice on a Federal tax matter for purposes of this section. Continuing education presentations provided to an audience solely for the purpose of enhancing practitioners' professional knowledge on Federal tax matters are not considered written advice on a Federal tax matter for purposes of this section. The preceding sentence does not apply to presentations marketing or promoting transactions.

(2) The practitioner must

(i) Base the written advice on reasonable factual and legal assumptions (including assumptions as to future events);

(ii) Reasonably consider all relevant facts and circumstances that the practitioner knows or reasonably should know;

(iii) Use reasonable efforts to identify and ascertain the facts relevant to written advice on each Federal tax matter;

(iv) Not rely upon representations, statements, findings, or agreements (including projections, financial forecasts, or appraisals) of the taxpayer or any other person if reliance on them would be unreasonable;

(v) Relate applicable law and authorities to facts; and

(vi) Not, in evaluating a Federal tax matter, take into account the possibility that a tax return will not be audited or that a matter will not be raised on audit.

(3) Reliance on representations, statements, findings, or agreements is unreasonable if the practitioner knows or reasonably should know that one or more representations or assumptions on which any representation is based are incorrect, incomplete, or inconsistent.

(b) *Reliance on advice of others.* A practitioner may only rely on the advice of another person if the advice was reasonable and the reliance is in good faith considering all the facts and circumstances. Reliance is not reasonable when—

(1) The practitioner knows or reasonably should know that the opinion of the other person should not be relied on;

(2) The practitioner knows or reasonably should know that the other person is not competent or lacks the necessary qualifications to provide the advice; or

(3) The practitioner knows or reasonably should know that the other person has a conflict of interest in violation of the rules described in this part.

(c) *Standard of review.*

(1) In evaluating whether a practitioner giving written advice concerning one or more Federal tax matters complied with the requirements of this section, the Commissioner, or delegate, will apply a reasonable practitioner standard, considering all facts and circumstances, including, but not limited to, the scope of the engagement and the type and specificity of the advice sought by the client.

(2) In the case of an opinion the practitioner knows or has reason to know will be used or referred to by a person other than the practitioner (or a person who is a member of, associated with, or employed by the practitioner's firm) in promoting, marketing, or recommending to one or more taxpayers a partnership or other entity, investment plan or arrangement a significant purpose of which is the avoidance or evasion of any tax imposed by the Internal Revenue Code, the Commissioner, or delegate, will apply a reasonable practitioner standard, considering all facts and circumstances, with emphasis given to the additional risk caused by the practitioner's lack of knowledge of the taxpayer's particular circumstances, when determining whether a practitioner has failed to comply with this section.

(d) *Federal tax matter.* A Federal tax matter, as used in this section, is any matter concerning the application or interpretation of—

(1) A revenue provision as defined in section 6110(i)(1)(B) of the Internal Revenue Code;

(2) Any provision of law impacting a person's obligations under the internal revenue laws and regulations, including but not limited to the person's liability to pay tax or obligation to file returns; or

(3) Any other law or regulation administered by the Internal Revenue Service.

* * *

§ 10.50 Sanctions.

(a) *Authority to censure, suspend, or disbar.* The Secretary of the Treasury, or delegate, after notice and an opportunity for a proceeding, may censure, suspend, or disbar any practitioner from practice before the Internal Revenue Service if the practitioner is shown to be incompetent or disreputable (within the meaning of § 10.51), fails to comply with any regulation in this part (under the prohibited conduct standards of § 10.52), or with intent to defraud, willfully and knowingly misleads or threatens a client or prospective client. Censure is a public reprimand.

(b) *Authority to disqualify.* The Secretary of the Treasury, or delegate, after due notice and opportunity for hearing, may disqualify any appraiser for a violation of these rules as applicable to appraisers.

   (1) If any appraiser is disqualified pursuant to this subpart C, the appraiser is barred from presenting evidence or testimony in any administrative proceeding before the Department of the Treasury or the Internal Revenue Service, unless and until authorized to do so by the Director of the Office of Professional Responsibility pursuant to § 10.81, regardless of whether the evidence or testimony would pertain to an appraisal made prior to or after the effective date of disqualification.

   (2) Any appraisal made by a disqualified appraiser after the effective date of disqualification will not have any probative effect in any administrative proceeding before the Department of the Treasury or the Internal Revenue Service. An appraisal otherwise barred from admission into evidence pursuant to this section may be admitted into evidence solely for the purpose of determining the taxpayer's reliance in good faith on such appraisal.

(c) *Authority to impose monetary penalty* —

   (1) *In general.*

      (i) The Secretary of the Treasury, or delegate, after notice and an opportunity for a proceeding, may impose a monetary penalty on any practitioner who engages in conduct subject to sanction under paragraph (a) of this section.

      (ii) If the practitioner described in paragraph (c)(1)(i) of this section was acting on behalf of an employer or any firm or other entity in connection with the conduct giving rise to the penalty, the Secretary of the Treasury, or delegate, may impose a monetary penalty on the employer, firm, or entity if it knew, or reasonably should have known of such conduct.

   (2) *Amount of penalty.* The amount of the penalty shall not exceed the gross income derived (or to be derived) from the conduct giving rise to the penalty.

   (3) *Coordination with other sanctions.* Subject to paragraph (c)(2) of this section —

      (i) Any monetary penalty imposed on a practitioner under this paragraph (c) may be in addition to or in lieu of any suspension, disbarment or censure and may be in addition to a penalty imposed on an employer, firm or other entity under paragraph (c)(1)(ii) of this section.

(ii) Any monetary penalty imposed on an employer, firm or other entity may be in addition to or in lieu of penalties imposed under paragraph (c)(1)(i) of this section.

§ 10.51 Incompetence and disreputable conduct.

(a) *Incompetence and disreputable conduct.* Incompetence and disreputable conduct for which a practitioner may be sanctioned under § 10.50 includes, but is not limited to —

* * *

(4) Giving false or misleading information, or participating in any way in the giving of false or misleading information to the Department of the Treasury or any officer or employee thereof, or to any tribunal authorized to pass upon Federal tax matters, in connection with any matter pending or likely to be pending before them, knowing the information to be false or misleading. Facts or other matters contained in testimony, Federal tax returns, financial statements, applications for enrollment, affidavits, declarations, and any other document or statement, written or oral, are included in the term "information."

* * *

(11) Knowingly aiding and abetting another person to practice before the Internal Revenue Service during a period of suspension, disbarment or ineligibility of such other person.

(12) Contemptuous conduct in connection with practice before the Internal Revenue Service, including the use of abusive language, making false accusations or statements, knowing them to be false, or circulating or publishing malicious or libelous matter.

(13) Giving a false opinion, knowingly, recklessly, or through gross incompetence, including an opinion which is intentionally or recklessly misleading, or engaging in a pattern of providing incompetent opinions on questions arising under the Federal tax laws. False opinions described in this paragraph (a)(13) include those which reflect or result from a knowing misstatement of fact or law, from an assertion of a position known to be unwarranted under existing law, from counseling or assisting in conduct known to be illegal or fraudulent, from concealing matters required by law to be revealed, or from consciously disregarding information indicating that material facts expressed in the opinion or offering material are false or misleading. For purposes of this paragraph (a)(13), reckless conduct is a highly unreasonable omission or misrepresentation involving an extreme departure from the standards of ordinary care that a practitioner should observe under the circumstances. A pattern of conduct is a factor that will be taken into account in determining whether a practitioner acted knowingly, recklessly, or through gross incompetence. Gross incompetence includes conduct that reflects gross indifference, preparation which is grossly inadequate under

the circumstances, and a consistent failure to perform obligations to the client.

(14) Willfully failing to sign a tax return prepared by the practitioner when the practitioner's signature is required by Federal tax laws unless the failure is due to reasonable cause and not due to willful neglect.

(15) Willfully disclosing or otherwise using a tax return or tax return information in a manner not authorized by the Internal Revenue Code, contrary to the order of a court of competent jurisdiction, or contrary to the order of an administrative law judge in a proceeding instituted under § 10.60.

* * *

§ 10.52 Violations subject to sanction.

(a) A practitioner may be sanctioned under § 10.50 if the practitioner—

(1) Willfully violates any of the regulations (other than § 10.33) contained in this part; or

(2) Recklessly or through gross incompetence (within the meaning of § 10.51(a)(13)) violates §§ 10.34, 10.35, 10.36 or 10.37.

* * *

§ 10.79 Effect of disbarment, suspension, or censure.

(a) *Disbarment.* When the final decision in a case is against the respondent (or the respondent has offered his or her consent and such consent has been accepted by the Internal Revenue Service) and such decision is for disbarment, the respondent will not be permitted to practice before the Internal Revenue Service unless and until authorized to do so by the Internal Revenue Service pursuant to § 10.81.

(b) *Suspension.* When the final decision in a case is against the respondent (or the respondent has offered his or her consent and such consent has been accepted by the Internal Revenue Service) and such decision is for suspension, the respondent will not be permitted to practice before the Internal Revenue Service during the period of suspension. For periods after the suspension, the practitioner's future representations may be subject to conditions as authorized by paragraph (d) of this section.

(c) *Censure.* When the final decision in the case is against the respondent (or the Internal Revenue Service has accepted the respondent's offer to consent, if such offer was made) and such decision is for censure, the respondent will be permitted to practice before the Internal Revenue Service, but the respondent's future representations may be subject to conditions as authorized by paragraph (d) of this section.

(d) *Conditions.* After being subject to the sanction of either suspension or censure, the future representations of a practitioner so sanctioned shall be subject to specified conditions designed to promote high standards of conduct. These conditions can be imposed for a reasonable period in light of the gravity of the practitioner's violations. For example, where a practitioner is censured because the practitioner failed to advise the practitioner's clients about a potential conflict of interest or failed to obtain the clients' written consents, the practitioner may be required to provide the Internal Revenue Service with a copy of all consents obtained by the practitioner for an appropriate period following censure, whether or not such consents are specifically requested.

Revenue Ruling 79-276
1979-2 C.B. 200

ISSUE

May the taxpayer use a cost recovery method of accounting for reporting income from sales of apartments that have been converted into condominiums?

FACTS

X corporation is in the business of converting rental apartment buildings into condominiums. This business consists of purchasing suitable apartment buildings, modernizing and improving the apartment units and facilities, and selling the individual units.

In January 1978, X purchased an apartment building for 50,000x dollars. X made numerous improvements to the building at a cost of 15,000x dollars and began selling apartment units in July 1978. As of December 31, 1978, X, a calendar year taxpayer, had sold nearly half the units for 40,000x dollars.

In determining the income to be reported from the sale of condominium units, X wished to adopt a cost recovery method of accounting. Under this method, no income is reported until all of the cost is recovered. Thus, X would treat the 40,000x dollars received in 1978 as a recovery of basis in the property so that no income would be reported and X would have a basis in the remaining property of 25,000x dollars $(65,000x - 40,000x = 25,000x)$.

LAW AND ANALYSIS

Under section 1.446-1(a)(2) of the Income Tax Regulations, no method of accounting is acceptable unless, in the opinion of the Commissioner, it clearly reflects income.

Under section 1.61-6(a) of the regulations, which concerns gain derived from dealings in property, when part of a larger property is sold, the cost or other basis of the entire property shall be equitably apportioned among the several parts, and the gain realized or loss sustained on the part of the property sold is the difference between the selling price and the cost or other basis allocated to such part. The sale of each part is treated as a separate transaction and gain or loss shall be computed separately on each part. Thus, gain or loss shall be determined at the time of sale of each part and not deferred until the entire property has been disposed of.

In Rev. Rul. 74-479, 1974-2 C.B. 148, the taxpayer's business consists of purchasing entire manufacturing plants that have been permanently shut down and selling the personal property and leasing the real property. The taxpayer bought a plant and equipment for 35,000x dollars, of which 6,500x dollars was allocated to personal property consisting of thousands of items. After selling 5,000x dollars of the personal property the taxpayer wished to treat the 5,000x dollars as a recovery of basis so that no income would be reported and the taxpayer would have a 1,500x dollar basis in the remaining property.

Rev. Rul. 74-479 provides that the use of such a cost recovery method of accounting is not appropriate because it was possible for the taxpayer to inventory each item on a cost basis and indicate a selling price for each item. Use of a cost recovery method of accounting is appropriate only in situations in which it is practically impossible to apportion the cost or other basis to property. See *Fasken v. Commissioner,* 71 T.C. 650 (1979); *William T. Piper v. Commissioner,* 5 T.C. 1104 (1945), *acq.,* 1946-1 C.B. 4, *Inaja Land Co. v. Commissioner,* 9 T.C. 727 (1947), *acq.,* 1948-1 C.B. 2.

Example (1) of section 1.61-6(a) of the regulations provides that a dealer in real estate who acquires a 10-acre tract for $10,000 and divides it into 20 lots must equitably apportion the $10,000 cost among the lots so that on the sale of each, the dealer can determine the taxable gain or deductible loss.

In the present situation, the purchase of an apartment building for sale as condominium units is analogous to the purchase of a large tract of real estate for subdivision. In both situations, a large parcel of real property is purchased and resold as a number of smaller parcels. Both situations are subject to similar risks and both require that the developer accept the burdens of carrying the unsold portion during a sales period of uncertain duration. Furthermore, it is possible for X to apportion the basis of the building to each apartment unit.

HOLDING

The taxpayer may not use a cost recovery method of accounting for reporting income from sales of apartments that have been converted into condominiums.

Chapter 7

Tax Characterization of Property

I. Commentary

As discussed in earlier chapters, property owners generally prefer to recognize long-term capital gain on the disposition of property because long-term capital gain is subject to favorable tax rates.[1] A property owner generally must satisfy two requirements to recognize long-term capital gain on the disposition of property. First, the property owner must hold the property long enough to satisfy the holding-period requirement. Second, the property must be a capital asset.

A. Holding-Period Requirement

The Internal Revenue Code provides that a property owner must hold property for more than one year to qualify for long-term capital gain treatment on the disposition of property.[2] Determining the holding period should not be too difficult, but the rules governing property acquired in an exchange or other nonrecognition transaction require some thought.[3] Attorneys must also be aware of the tax rules that determine whether a person holds a piece of property. Legal title is one of many factors that determine ownership for tax purposes.[4] Attorneys providing advice with respect to the holding period must be familiar with the concept of tax ownership to ensure that any arrangement that delays the transfer of title does not transfer the benefits and burdens of ownership, frustrating the property owners' objectives.

B. Capital-Asset Requirement

The Internal Revenue Code defines capital asset generally,[5] but most of the law governing the definition of capital asset is found in cases. The cases are fact intensive, so an attorney advising a property owner with respect to the capital-asset requirement must become familiar with numerous cases that consider the definition. Generally,

---

1. *See* I.R.C. §1(h). Gain from the sale of property used in a trade or business may also qualify for capital gain treatment. *See* I.R.C. §1231.
2. *See* I.R.C. §1222.
3. *See* I.R.C. §1223.
4. *See* Grodt & McKay Realty, Inc. v. Comm'r, 77 T.C. 1221 (1981).
5. *See* I.R.C. §1221.

in the case of real estate, the question is whether the property is inventory (dealer property) or a capital asset. Several judicial decisions hold that the property in question is inventory,[6] and several hold that property is a capital asset.[7] Often, the facts in the cases appear to be similar, so attorneys must read several cases and pay particular attention to facts and factors judges rely upon to reach their conclusions. Attorneys also must pay attention to whether certain facts and factors are more important than others. Consequently, distinguishing between dealer property and capital assets often is a labor-intensive process.

II. Primary Legal Authority
Gartrell v. United States
United States Court of Appeals, Sixth Circuit
619 F.2d 1150 (1980)

FACTS

Appellee Dr. Francis E. Gartrell was Director of Environmental Planning for the Tennessee Valley Authority from 1956 until his retirement in 1973. Mrs. Gartrell is a housewife. On November 28, 1956, the taxpayers purchased for $2,362.50 a one-fourth undivided interest in a tract of land on the shores of Watts Bar Lake in Roane County, Tennessee. Contemporaneously, a Mrs. Hollis purchased another one-fourth interest in the tract. The remaining one-half interest was owned by E. Wayne Gilley.[8] Dr. Gartrell stated that his interest was purchased as a long-term investment to help "provide adequate income after retirement." He owned no other business real estate and never had a license as a real estate broker.

The tract of land was named the Lake Harbor Subdivision by the taxpayers and their co-owners. The property was surveyed during 1958 and 1962. No improvements were made by the owners except the construction of a few gravel roads. In 1958 a public auction resulted in the sale of 19 lots. Sales were scattered during succeeding years, averaging approximately 2.6 sales per year.

The present suit involves the proceeds from three lots and a tract sold in 1973.

* * *

---

6. *See, e.g.,* Suburban Realty Co. v. United States, 615 F.2d 171 (5th Cir. 1980); Biedenharn Realty Co. v. United States, 526 F.2d 409 (5th Cir. 1976); U. S. v. Winthrop, 417 F.2d 905 (5th Cir. 1969). *See also* Priv. Ltr. Rul. 83-38-114 (June 23, 1983).

7. *See, e.g.,* Gartrell v. United States, 619 F.2d 1150 (6th Cir. 1980); Gudgel v. Comm'r, 273 F.2d 206 (6th Cir. 1959); Buono v. Comm'r, 74 T.C. 187 (1980); Gangi v. Comm'r, 55 CCH T.C.M. 1048 (1987).

8. [1] The record indicates that this one-half interest may have been purchased or given to the children of E. Wayne Gilley. The trust instrument of August 1958, discussed in Part IV of this opinion, was signed by Gilley and his wife, Lois D. Gilley. For the purpose of this opinion, we assume that the one-half interest was owned by Gilley.

In *Broughton v. Comm'r*,[9] 333 F.2d 492, 495 (6th Cir. 1964), District Judge Frank W. Wilson, sitting as a visiting judge on this court, wrote a Sixth Circuit opinion applying the clearly erroneous rule in a case involving the ultimate question of whether real estate was "property held by the taxpayer primarily for sale to customers in the ordinary course of his trade or business." Judge Wilson speaking for this court said:

> Section 1221(1) of the Internal Revenue Code of 1954, in defining "capital assets" for the purpose of determining capital gains and losses, excludes from the category of capital assets "property held by the taxpayer primarily for sale to customers in the ordinary course of his trade or business." The gain from the sale of property which is excluded from the definition of capital assets is taxable as ordinary income. Thus, the initial issue for determination is whether the Tax Court was correct in holding that the lots held respectively for Mr. Broughton and Mrs. Broughton were held primarily for sale to customers in the ordinary course of their trade or business. This issue is essentially a factual one, the determination of which necessarily depends upon the facts and circumstances in each particular case and no one fact or circumstance is controlling.

Bauschard v. Comm'r, 279 F.2d 115 (6th Cir. 1960).

A factual determination by the Tax Court upon the issue now before this Court may not be set aside upon appeal unless it is clearly erroneous. *U.S. v. United States Gypsum Company*, 333 U.S. 364 (1947), rehearing denied, 333 U.S. 869 (1948).

In *Philhall v. U.S.*, 546 F.2d 210, 214 (6th Cir. 1976), this court said:

> The appellee contends that the ultimate determination as to whether the property was held "primarily for sale to customers" under the facts of a particular case is to be treated as a legal rather than a factual determination. As authority it cites a Fifth Circuit case, *Biedenharn Realty Co. v. U.S.*, 526 F.2d 409 (5th Cir. 1976). Biedenharn is the latest in a long line of Fifth Circuit cases so holding. No other Circuits are cited as adhering to that view. This Circuit has taken the position that the ultimate issue is a factual one. *Mathews v. Comm'r*, 315 F.2d 101 (6th Cir. 1963); *Bauschard v. Comm'r*, 279 F.2d 115 (6th Cir. 1960); *Dougherty v. Comm'r*, 216 F.2d 110 (6th Cir. 1954). The determination of whether the tract of land was held primarily for sale hinges on the intent of the parties. Ascertaining this intent, including weighing the statements of the parties, is within the province of the finder of the facts. There is no reason in the present case for this court to reconsider our prior holdings.

* * *

---

9. [2] This opinion is cited three times in the brief of the Government in the present case.

In *United States Steel Corporation v. Fuhrman*, 407 F.2d 1143, 1145 (6th Cir. 1969), cert. denied, 398 U.S. 958 (1970), this court held in an admiralty case that the findings of fact of the district judge, sitting without a jury, are to be reviewed under the clearly erroneous standard notwithstanding the fact that the entire appellate record consisted of depositions, written reports and other written evidence, and no oral testimony was offered.

We refuse to depart from the clearly erroneous standard of review in the present case.

In the alternative the Government contends that there is no substantial evidence in the record to support the findings of the district court.

In determining this issue, the statute according preferential treatment to capital gains is to be construed narrowly "so as to protect the revenue against artful devices." *Comm'r v. P. G. Lake, Inc.*, 356 U.S. 260, 265 (1958).

* * *

The taxpayers have the burden of proving that the IRS classification of the proceeds of the sale as ordinary income is erroneous. *Welch v. Helvering*, 290 U.S. 111, 115 (1933); *Mathews v. Comm'r*, 315 F.2d 101, 106 (6th Cir. 1963).

In *Mathews v. Comm'r*, 315 F.2d 101, 107 (6th Cir. 1963), this court set forth the following factors to be considered in determining whether properties are held for the primary purpose of sale to customers in the ordinary course of business:

> It is well settled that the question whether property sold by a taxpayer at a profit was property held by the taxpayer primarily for sale to customers in the ordinary course of his trade or business, within the meaning of the statute, is essentially a question of fact. *Bauschard v. Comm'r*, 279 F.2d 115 (6th Cir. 1960). No single factor or test is dispositive. Among the factors considered are: (1) the purpose for which the property was acquired; (2) the purpose for which it was held; (3) improvements and their extent, made to the property by taxpayer; (4) frequency, number and continuity of sales; (5) the extent and substantiality of the transactions; (6) the nature and extent of taxpayer's business; (7) the extent of advertising to promote sales, or the lack of such advertising; and (8) listing of the property for sale directly or through brokers. *Kaltreider v. Comm'r*, 255 F.2d 833 (3d Cir. 1958). While petitioner may well have purchased and held certain of these properties for investment rather than for sale in the ordinary course of business, it was for the Tax Court, under all of the circumstances of the case, to draw its conclusions as to whether any of such purchases by the taxpayer were for investment, or was property held for sale in the ordinary course of business. The facts, and inferences to be drawn from the facts, are for the fact finder, which, in this case, is the Tax Court. On review of the Tax Court's findings and conclusions, we cannot say that they are clearly erroneous, and that is the criterion by which an appellate court must adjudicate the case.

* * *

District Judge Wilson considered each of these factors in arriving at his conclusion in the present case. His findings of fact with respect to the factors are as follows:

> The determination of whether or not a taxpayer holds property primarily for sale in the ordinary course of business is essentially a question of fact. *Bauschard v. Comm'r*, 279 F.2d 115, 117 (6th Cir. 1960). The Court must consider the eight factors which are to be weighed in making that factual determination. *Mathews v. Comm'r*, 315 F.2d 101, 107 (6th Cir. 1963).

1. and 2. The purpose for which the property was acquired and held. The plaintiff Francis E. Gartrell testified that he acquired and held the property as a long-term investment and as a means of supplementing his retirement income. He acknowledges, however, that he did realize gain on the property before his retirement.

3. Improvements, and their extent, made to the property by the taxpayer. In 1958, 1959 and 1962 the land was surveyed and subdivided and gravel roads were constructed on the tract. No other improvements to the property were made during the period in question by any of the original holders of interests in the tract.

4. Frequency, number and continuity of sales. The plaintiff sold lots in the property in accordance with the following table:

Year	Number of Sales	Number of Lots
1956	0	0
1957	0	0
1958	1	19
1959	1	1
1960	3	7
1961	0	0
1962	10	12
1963	1	2
1964	1	1
1965	3	8
1966	2	2
1967	2	4
1968	1	2
1969	5	7
1970	0	0
1971	4*	7*
1972	4	6
1973	2**	4**
1974	1	3
1975	4	4

* 6 Lots and Tract II
** 3 Lots and Tract I

5. The nature and substantiality of the transactions. The transactions were carried out by real estate or auction companies and as a result of personal contacts of other holders of interests in the property.

The substantiality of the transactions is illustrated by an examination of the income generated by the sale of the property as compared with the salary income of the plaintiff Francis E. Gartrell. From 1956 until his retirement in 1973, Francis E. Gartrell was a full-time employee of the Tennessee Valley Authority (TVA). His average annual income from TVA during that period was $21,361 and ranged from a low of $12,790 in 1956 to a high of $35,500 in 1973. His average annual income from the sale of the Lake Harbor Subdivision property was $1,815 and ranged from a low of zero in 1956, 1957 and 1961 to a high of $6,414 in 1972. The average ratio of his income from the Lake Harbor property to that from his TVA employment was 8.5% and ranged from a low of 0% in 1956, 1957 and 1961 to a high of 23.5% in 1962.

Moreover, the plaintiff has realized a large proportion of the gain on the property during the years since his retirement and those immediately preceding his retirement. Approximately 40% of the total income derived from the property during 1956–1976 was realized after Francis E. Gartrell's retirement in 1973. An additional 28% was realized during the years 1971–1973.

6. The nature and extent of the taxpayer's business. As noted previously, the plaintiff Francis E. Gartrell was a full-time employee of TVA from 1956 until his retirement in 1973. In retirement, he is a part-time consultant with TVA. The record is silent as to Mabel L. Gartrell's occupation. The plaintiffs purchased no real estate (other than a principal residence) for sale during the period 1956 to 1973. The plaintiff Francis E. Gartrell did maintain records of the sales of the Lake Harbor Subdivision Property.

7. The extent of advertising to promote sales or the lack of such advertising. The plaintiff Francis E. Gartrell placed advertisements in connection with the 1958 auction sale in eight East Tennessee newspapers and on one Chattanooga, Tennessee radio station. Other newspaper advertisements were placed in 1960, 1962 and 1964 and in 1961 a sign was placed on the property identifying it as property for sale. No other advertising activities were engaged in by the plaintiffs.

8. Listing of the property for sale directly or through brokers. The plaintiffs engaged as agents for the sale of the property some four individuals or real estate agencies.

CONCLUSION

It is the opinion of the Court that the facts in the present case do not support the conclusion that the Lake Harbor Subdivision property was held by the plaintiffs "primarily for sale to customers in the ordinary course of (their) trade or business" within the meaning of that phrase in 26 U.S.C. §§ 1221 and 1237. It is the opinion of the Court, therefore, that the gain realized by the plaintiffs from the sale of the property that is the subject of this lawsuit should have been treated as capital gain for the purpose of computing federal income taxes. Accordingly the District Director of Internal Revenue in Memphis, Tennessee acted in error and illegally by assessing an adjustment to the plaintiffs' taxes for the year 1973 in so far as that adjustment was made after a computation of the plaintiffs' tax liability on the sale of part of the property in question at ordinary income rates. (Footnote omitted).

The Government contends that the District Judge "merely paid ... lip service" to the factors enumerated in Mathews, supra, "or perhaps misinterpreted them." To the contrary, we conclude that the district court correctly interpreted and applied the Mathews factors in the present case.[10]

On the record before us, this court cannot hold that the foregoing findings of fact by the district judge are clearly erroneous. To the contrary, we conclude that they are supported by substantial evidence and must be affirmed.

In August 1958, the taxpayers and their co-owners of the land here in question established a revocable trust, naming themselves as beneficiaries. E. Wayne Gilley, one of the co-owners, was named as trustee. The trust instrument recited that Gilley and his wife owned a one-half interest, the taxpayers a one-fourth interest and Georgia P. Hollis a one-fourth interest.

The purpose was stated as follows:

> Whereas. Beneficiaries have this day conveyed in trust to the Trustee the above-described land with full power and right of disposition as enumerated therein to simplify real estate transactions involving the property described and to eliminate the necessity and relieve all the parties hereto, except E. Wayne Gilley, individually and as trustee from executing various documents required in such real estate transactions.

The Government contends that the trust instrument supports its position that the intention and purpose of taxpayers was to hold the property for sale in the ordinary course of business. Emphasis is placed upon the fact that the district judge did not mention the trust in his findings of fact. The taxpayers assert that the trust was established after their experience with the auction sale of 1958, when it was necessary for each of the co-owners to sign the deeds to all the nineteen tracts sold; that the purpose of the trust was to authorize the trustee to sign deeds and any other necessary instruments without the necessity of multiple signatures; and that the trust had no effect whatsoever on the tax status of the owners or the issue of whether the taxpayers held the property primarily for sale to customers in the ordinary course of their trade or business. Presumably this was the conclusion of the district judge, who did not mention the trust in his opinion, even though the trust instrument is a part of the record, was attached as an exhibit to the answers filed by taxpayers to the Government's interrogatories, was submitted by the Government in support of a motion for summary judgment, and was a topic of oral argument by the attorneys.

---

10. [3] As author of the Sixth Circuit opinion in *Broughton v. Comm'r, supra,* 333 F.2d 492 (6th Cir. 1964), sitting as a visiting judge, Judge Wilson demonstrated comprehensive familiarity with this area of the law of federal income taxation.

We conclude that the language of the trust instrument does not support the Government's contention that the grantors were engaged in business through a trust.

The provisions of a "grantor" trust may be such that it does not affect the tax status of the grantor. *Cf. Helvering v. Clifford*, 309 U.S. 331 (1940); *Acuff v. Comm'r*, 296 F.2d 725 (6th Cir. 1961). The trust instrument in the present case, by its language, did not express an intention to create a separate entity for tax purposes. It simply authorized one of the co-owners of the real estate, in his capacity as trustee, to execute deeds and other documents on behalf of all the grantors, who in turn received their respective shares of net proceeds of sales as if no trust had been created.

The Government, in the alternative, urges that the decision of the district court be vacated and the case be remanded for further exploration of the issue concerning the trust. We conclude that the language of the trust instrument speaks for itself and that the tax status of the beneficiaries remained the same as if no trust had ever been created.

Suburban Realty Co. v. United States

United States Court of Appeals, Fifth Circuit
615 F.2d 171 (1980)

FACTS

Suburban Realty Company was formed in November, 1937 to acquire an undivided one-fourth interest in 1,742.6 acres of land located in Harris County, Texas ("the property"). Suburban received its interest[11] in the property in exchange for all of its stock from four individuals who had themselves acquired the property in a foreclosure proceeding brought against the property as a result of a default in the payment of certain bonds, the payment of which was secured by the property. Suburban's corporate charter states that it was formed to erect or repair any building or improvement, and to accumulate and lend money for such purposes, and to purchase, sell, and subdivide real property, and to accumulate and lend money for that purpose.

The five transactions whose characterization is in dispute here concern six tracts of unimproved real estate sold from the property by Suburban between 1968 and 1971.[12] On its tax returns, Suburban originally reported profits from these sales, as

---

11. [2] The remaining three-fourths undivided interest was held by two individuals who acquired their interest at the same time that Suburban's shareholders acquired their interest. Mr. George Hamman owned an undivided one-half interest, which ultimately passed to the Hamman Foundation. Mrs. Mary Alice Talbot owned the remaining undivided one-fourth interest.

12. [4] The parties stipulated that the sales were as follows:

Date	Acreage	Sales Price
December 31, 1968	4.5	$56,250
July 31, 1969	6.25	93,285
July 31, 1969	6.0225	90,225
July 31, 1969	17.50	262,282
1970 [sic]	5.6944	39,799
April 14, 1971	4.375	65,675

well as all of its other real estate sales, as ordinary income. Later, Suburban filed a claim for refund asserting that these six tracts, as well as three similar tracts sold later, were capital assets, and that profits from these sales were entitled to capital gain treatment. The Internal Revenue Service denied Suburban's claim as to the sales here in issue. Suburban then instituted this action for a refund of $102,754.50. The district court, in a non-jury trial, rendered a decision against Suburban and entered a judgment dismissing Suburban's complaint. Suburban appealed.

* * *

A. Overall activities.

1. Total Sales Activity From the Property.

Between 1939 and 1971, Suburban made at least 244 individual sales of real estate out of the property. Of these, approximately 95 sales were unplatted and unimproved property legally suitable for commercial development for any other purpose, and at least 149 sales were from platted property restricted to residential development. In each of these 33 years, Suburban concluded at least one sale; in most years, there were four or more sales. Suburban's total proceeds from real estate sales over this period were $2,353,935. Proceeds from all other sources of income amounted to $474,845.[13] Thus, eighty-three percent of Suburban's proceeds emanated from real estate sales; only seventeen percent flowed from all other sources.

2. North Loop Freeway.

In 1957, the Texas Highway Department proposed that the limited access superhighway now known as the North Loop would be located from east to west across the property. In 1959 and 1960, Suburban sold at least two parcels out of the property to the Texas Highway Department for the purpose of constructing this highway. The location of the highway had a dramatic effect on the price of land in the area. Land which had been selling for between three and five thousand dollars per acre prior to announcement of the highway rose in value to between seven and twelve thousand dollars per acre.

* * *

B. Specific portions

1. Houston Gardens.

In 1938, Suburban and the other owners of the property formed a separate corporation, Houston Gardens Annex, Inc. ("Houston Gardens"), to plat and sell a parcel in the northeast quadrant of the property. The stock ownership in Houston Gardens was in the same proportion as ownership interests in the property i.e., Suburban and Mrs. Talbot each owned one-quarter of the stock of Houston Gardens; Mr. Hamman owned one-half of the stock. Houston Gardens owned approximately

---

13. [8] This includes dividend income ($54,165), rent and lease income ($15,732), and sales of lumber from its lumber yard ($11,939). The source of the remaining proceeds, approximately $400,000, is not apparent.

200 or 250 lots, which were generally sold in bulk to builders. These sales covered as many as 20, 30, or even 50 lots at a time. By 1961, Houston Gardens had sold all but two of its lots, and it was then liquidated. Houston Gardens never engaged in advertising, used brokers or real estate agents, or employed a sales organization at any time during its existence.

2. Homestead Addition.

Certain portions of the property, located near its center, were designated as Homestead Addition Sections One, Two, Three, and Four. Little was done with Homestead Addition Section One except for platting it and running a few utility lines up to it.

Homestead Addition Section Two, however, was the primary subject of Suburban's activities. In July, 1948, Suburban acquired 100 percent ownership of Homestead Addition Section Two by exchanging cash and other land for the other owners' interests. Immediately thereafter, Suburban commenced development of Homestead Addition Section Two. The area was platted, streets and sewers were put in, and a sewage disposal plant was built nearby.[14] Suburban also built a lumberyard in Section Two.[15] At the instance of one of the individuals whom Suburban hired to collect water bills and notes on houses and to manage the lumberyard, Suburban also built eleven houses in Section Two in the early 1950's. The last was built by 1955, and none was sold later than 1958. Between 1948 and 1966, Suburban sold 252 subdivided lots out of Section Two. About half of these lots were sold in bulk to builders 10, 15, or 20 lots at a time.[16]

Homestead Addition Sections Three and Four were platted for residential use by Suburban in 1951. This area was never developed by Suburban, however. In 1961 the plats were withdrawn and cancelled. This had the effect of eliminating restrictions which prevented commercial use of the land. Subsequently, the real estate within Sections Three and Four was sold to commercial and industrial users.

3. Other Parcels.

The remainder of the property appears to have been treated as one undifferentiated bulk by Suburban. It is from this undifferentiated, undeveloped remainder that the sales at issue here were made. There are no specific findings by the trial court, and there appears to be no evidence of record from which we could ourselves make findings, concerning the number and frequency of sales of real estate from other parts of the property. Rather, the evidence concerning annual sales groups all sales made by Suburban, including

---

14. [11] A utility company was formed by Suburban, Mr. Hamman, and Mrs. Talbot to maintain the water and sewage system. By 1961, the system had been sold to the City of Houston, and the utility company was liquidated.

15. [12] In 1961 or 1962, the lumberyard was sold, having already been dormant for some years.

16. [14] There is no finding by the court below, or any record evidence that we can locate, concerning the number of individual transactions employed to sell the 252 lots. This lack of evidence may be attributable to Suburban's failure to record separately transactions from the various Homestead Addition Sections or even to separate Homestead Addition sales from non-Homestead sales. Alternatively, the paucity of evidence may merely reflect incompleteness of the records submitted to the district court.

sales from the Homestead Addition Sections, together. However, it is clear that throughout the period 1939–1971, sales were being made from the remainder of the property.

ANALYSIS

Our analysis of this case must begin with *Biedenharn Realty Co., Inc. v. U.S.*, 526 F.2d 409 (5th Cir. 1976).... *Biedenharn* is this Court's latest (and only) en banc pronouncement concerning the characterization of profits of a real estate business as ordinary income or capital gain. The decision answers the characterization question by evaluating certain "factors" often present in cases of this ilk.[17] *Biedenharn* attempts to guide the analysis in this area by assigning different levels of importance to various of the "factors." Substantiality and frequency of sales is called the most important factor. *Biedenharn*, 526 F.2d at 416. Improvements to the land, solicitation and advertising efforts, and brokerage activities also play an important part in the *Biedenharn* analysis.

The question before us today, put into the *Biedenharn* framework, can be stated as follows: when a taxpayer engages in frequent and substantial sales over a period of years, but undertakes no development activity with respect to parts of a parcel of land, and engages in no solicitation or advertising efforts or brokerage activities, under what circumstances is income derived from sales of undeveloped parts of the parcel ordinary income?

The *Biedenharn* framework allows us to ask the question, but gives us little guidance in answering it. In the principal recent cases, there has always been a conjunction of frequent and substantial sales with development activity relating to the properties in dispute.... The conjunction of these two factors "will usually conclude the capital gains issue against (the) taxpayer." *Biedenharn*, 526 F.2d at 418. Judge Wisdom has recently written that "ordinary income tax rates usually apply when dispositions of subdivided property over a period of time are continuous and substantial rather than few and isolated." *Houston Endowment*, 606 F.2d at 81. Also, it has been explicitly stated that the factor which will receive greatest emphasis is frequency and substantiality of sales over an extended time period. *See Biedenharn*, 526 F.2d at 417. However, substantial and frequent sales activity, standing alone, has never been held to be automatically sufficient to trigger ordinary income treatment. In fact, we have continual reminders of the fact that "specific factors, or combinations of them are not necessarily controlling," *Biedenharn*, 526 F.2d at 415, quoting *Thompson v. Comm'r*, 322 F.2d 122, 127 (5th Cir. 1963), quoting *Wood v. Comm'r*, 276 F.2d 586, 590 (5th Cir. 1960).

* * *

---

17. [16] In the *U.S. v. Winthrop*, 417 F.2d 905, 910 (5th Cir. 1969), the following factors were enumerated: (1) the nature and purpose of the acquisition of the property and the duration of the ownership; (2) the extent and nature of the taxpayer's efforts to sell the property; (3) the number, extent, continuity and substantiality of the sales; (4) the extent of subdividing, developing, and advertising to increase sales; (5) the use of a business office for the sale of the property; (6) the character and degree of supervision or control exercised by the taxpayer over any representative selling the property; and (7) the time and effort the taxpayer habitually devoted to the sales.

Today, we must go into territory as yet unmapped in this Circuit. Suburban's case is at once more favorable to the taxpayer than Biedenharn's and less so. It is more favorable because, with respect to the particular parcels of land here at issue, it is undisputed that Suburban undertook no development or subdivision activity. It is less favorable because Biedenharn was continually engaged in business activities other than real estate sales, whereas Suburban was for many years doing little else. Following the *Biedenharn* framework alone, we would be left with yet another essentially ad hoc decision to be made. We could justify a decision for either party, yet remain confident that we were being fully consistent with the analysis in *Biedenharn*. However, although there will always remain a certain irreducible ad hoc-ishness in this area, we are now firmly convinced that the uncertainty can be substantially reduced by turning to the divining rod of capital gains versus ordinary income the statute itself.

* * *

The ultimate inquiry in cases of this nature is whether the property at issue was "property held by the taxpayer primarily for sale to customers in the ordinary course of his trade or business." 26 U.S.C.A. § 1221(1). In our focus on the "tests" developed to resolve this question, we have on occasion almost lost sight entirely of the statutory framework. The "tests" or "factors," whether they be counted to number seven, see *Winthrop*, 417 F.2d at 910, or to number four, see *Houston Endowment*, 606 F.2d at 81, have seemingly acquired an independent meaning of their own, only loosely tied to their statutory pier. Some years ago, Judge Brown cautioned us against this tendency:

> Essential as they are in the adjudication of cases, we must take guard lest we be so carried away by the proliferation of tests that we forget that the statute excludes from capital assets "property held by the taxpayer primarily for sale to customers in the ordinary course of his trade or business." *Thompson*, 322 F.2d at 127. See *Biedenharn*, 526 F.2d at 424 (Roney, J., specially concurring).

The tendency to overemphasize the independent meaning of the "factors" has been accompanied by, perhaps even caused by, a tendency to view the statutory language as posing only one question: whether the property was held by the taxpayer "primarily for sale to customers in the ordinary course of his trade or business." This determination was correctly seen as equivalent to the question whether the gain was to be treated as ordinary or capital. However, probably because the question "is the gain ordinary" is a single question which demands an answer of yes or no, the courts have on occasion lost sight of the fact that the statutory language requires the court to make not one determination, but several separate determinations. In statutory construction cases, our most important task is to ask the proper questions. In the context of cases like the one before us, the principal inquiries demanded by the statute are:

1) was taxpayer engaged in a trade or business, and, if so, what business?

2) was taxpayer holding the property primarily for sale in that business?

3) were the sales contemplated by taxpayer "ordinary" in the course of that business?[18]

We by no means intend to suggest that we disagree with anything decided by the recent Fifth Circuit decisions. *Biedenharn* guides our decision-making process. But after the relevant three independent statutory inquiries are pried apart, it becomes apparent that the central dispute in *Biedenharn* was a narrow one: was Biedenharn Realty Company holding the land in dispute "primarily for sale?" The majority, applying the Winthrop factors, decided this question in the affirmative. The dissent, emphasizing the continuing farming activities being conducted by Biedenharn, see *Biedenharn*, 526 F.2d at 425 & n.5, 426 (dissenting opinion), disagreed as to this conclusion.

In fact, once the inquiry is redirected towards the statutory inquiries, the ultimate relevance of the *Biedenharn* factors becomes apparent. It will remain true that the frequency and substantiality of sales will be the most important factor. But the reason for the importance of this factor is now clear: the presence of frequent and substantial sales is highly relevant to each of the principal statutory inquiries listed above.[19] A taxpayer who engages in frequent and substantial sales is almost inevitably engaged in the real estate business. The frequency and substantiality of sales are highly probative on the issue of holding purpose because the presence of frequent sales ordinarily belies the contention that property is being held "for investment" rather than "for sale." And the frequency of sales may often be a key factor in determining the "ordinariness" question.

The extent of development activity and improvements is highly relevant to the question of whether taxpayer is a real estate developer. Development activity and improvements may also be relevant to the taxpayer's holding purpose, but, standing alone, some degree of development activity is not inconsistent with holding property for purposes other than sale. The extent of development activity also seems to be only peripherally relevant to the "ordinariness" question.

Thus, under the statutory framework, as under *Biedenharn*, the extent of development activity and improvements, although an important factor, is less conclusive than the substantiality and frequency of sales.

Solicitation and advertising efforts are quite relevant both to the existence of a trade or business and to taxpayer's holding purpose. Thus, their presence can strengthen the case for ordinary income treatment. *See Biedenharn*, 526 F.2d at 418. However, in cases like *Biedenharn*, their absence is not conclusive on either of these statutory

---

18. [19] In other types of cases, or even in real estate cases with different factual patterns, other questions may be crucial. For example, whether the contemplated purchasers were "customers" of the taxpayers, or whether business activity is to be imputed to taxpayer so as to be considered "taxpayer's business," could be an important inquiry. Yet other inquiries may be demanded by the statutory language in other contexts. Here, the key questions are those set out above.

19. [21] This truth is suggested in *Biedenharn*: "The frequency and substantiality of Biedenharn's sales go not only to its holding purpose and the existence of a trade or business but also support our finding of the ordinariness with which the Realty Company disposed of its lots." 526 F.2d at 416.

questions for, as we noted there, "even one inarguably in the real estate business need not engage in promotional exertions in the face of a favorable market."

We need not comment individually on each of the other *Biedenharn-Winthrop* factors. It should be apparent that each factor is relevant, to a greater or lesser extent, to one or more of the questions posed by the statute along the path to the ultimate conclusion.

Having laid the framework for the requisite analysis, we must now apply that framework to the facts here. We must decide whether Suburban was engaged in a trade or business, and, if so, what business; whether Suburban was holding the properties at issue here primarily for sale; and whether Suburban's contemplated sales were "ordinary" in the course of Suburban's business.

* * *

Once it is perceived that the ultimate legal conclusion of capital gain or ordinary income involves several independent determinations, it can be easily seen that some of the determinations are predominantly legal conclusions or are "mixed questions of fact and law," whereas others are essentially questions of fact. Thus, the question of taxpayer's purpose or purposes for holding the property is primarily factual, as is the question of which purpose predominates. Similarly, the "ordinariness" of the contemplated sales is mainly a fact question. The question of whether taxpayer was engaged in a trade or business involves the application of legal standards concerning what constitutes a trade or business to the facts concerning taxpayer's activities, and therefore is best characterized as a "mixed question of fact and law", The ultimate legal conclusion, based on these factual and legal conclusions, of whether the property was "held primarily for sale to customers in the ordinary course of his trade or business" cannot be appropriately characterized in this scheme at all because, as noted above, there are several subsidiary questions which, separately answered, lead to the ultimate conclusion.

A. Was Suburban in the real estate business?

This is a relatively simple issue. The question is whether taxpayer has engaged in a sufficient quantum of focused activity to be considered to be engaged in a trade or business. The precise quantum necessary will be difficult to establish, and cases close to the line on this issue will arise.

Happily, we need not here define that line. It is clear to us that Suburban engaged in a sufficient quantity of activity to be in the business of selling real estate. Suburban's sales were continuous and substantial. It completed at least 244 sales transactions over the 33-year period 1939–1971. This averages to over 7 transactions per year. Proceeds from these sales exceeded 2.3 million dollars.

Suburban does not claim to have been engaged in any business other than real estate; rather, it claims that during the periods at issue it simply "did not carry on a trade or business." Br. for Appellee at 20. Were additional support necessary for our conclusion, we would point to Suburban's own statements on its tax returns over the years that its principal business activity was "development and sales of real estate." These statements are by no means conclusive of the issue. *See Thomas v. Comm'r*,

254 F.2d 233, 236–37 (5th Cir. 1958). However, we believe they show at least that if Suburban is engaged in a trade or business, that business is real estate.[20] And Suburban's activities over the years were sufficient to convince us that it cannot sustain its contention that it was never engaged in any "trade or business" at all.

Here, Suburban's argument is of an entirely different character. Suburban suggests no business other than real estate dealing, but claims that it was engaged in no business at all.

Suburban relies heavily on the insignificance of its subdivision and development activity and the total absence of any advertising or sales solicitation activity on its part. However, the first two absences do not concern us at all. We need not decide whether its subdivision and development activities were sufficient to compel the conclusion that Suburban was in the real estate development business.[21] We rely solely on Suburban's real estate sales business.

The presence of any sales solicitation or advertising activity would certainly be relevant to the issue of whether Suburban was in the business of selling real estate. Strenuous, but largely unsuccessful, attempts to sell might compel the conclusion that a taxpayer with very few sales transactions was nonetheless in the business of selling. But the absence of such activity does not compel the opposite conclusion. *Thompson*, 322 F.2d at 126.

Suburban also seeks solace from the fact that it never purchased any additional real estate to replenish acreage it sold. As is the case with the presence of sales activity, the presence of such purchases tends to demonstrate that a taxpayer is engaged in a real estate business, but their absence is not conclusive:

> The fact that (taxpayer) bought no additional lands during this period does not prevent his activity being a business. (Taxpayer) merely had enough land to do a large business without buying any more. *Biedenharn*, 526 F.2d at 417, quoting *Snell v. Comm'r*, 97 F.2d 891 (5th Cir. 1938).

Additionally, Suburban points to its commencement of an investment program in securities in 1966. By itself, this cannot affect our conclusion that Suburban was in the real estate business. It merely demonstrates that, commencing in 1966, Sub-

---

20. [29] In *Thomas*, we went to some length to demonstrate that the fact that Thomas designated his occupation as a Real Estate Broker and as a Registered Real Estate Broker was not conclusive in determining the character of the holding of property of the taxpayer sold by him. *See Thomas*, 254 F.2d at 236–37. Thomas did earn brokerage commissions on sales of certain properties where his role was that of a middleman or go-between; i.e., a broker. This fact, we said, was not of great significance in determining whether dealings in property owned by the taxpayer were to be characterized as investments or as "sale(s) to customers in the ordinary course of (his) trade or business." Put otherwise, it might be said that an admission that one is a real estate "broker" does not automatically concede that one is also a "dealer" in real estate. Thomas was a real estate broker, but as to deals in which he was a principal, he successfully argued that he was an investor rather than a dealer.

21. [30] If Suburban was ever in this business, it certainly had withdrawn by 1961, when the plats for Homestead Addition Two were withdrawn and cancelled, as no development activity had occurred since 1955.

urban was also engaged in investing in securities. As stated earlier, the presence of other types of activities does not prevent taxpayer's real estate activities from being considered a business.

Suburban also contends that, if it was ever in the real estate business, it had exited that business long before 1968, the time of the first transaction here at issue. Even if this is true, it cannot affect our ultimate conclusion. The statutory language does not demand that property actually be sold while a taxpayer is still actively engaged in its trade or business for ordinary income treatment to be required. Rather, it demands that the property have been held primarily for sale in that business.[22] To that inquiry we now turn.

B. What was Suburban's primary purpose for holding the properties whose characterization is here in dispute?

Put into the framework being used here, Suburban's contention concerning holding purpose is two-fold. Principally, it argues that, at the time of the sales in dispute, the properties were not being held for sale. Alternatively, it contends that it "originally acquired its property as an investment…, and it continued to hold it for investment purposes." Br. for Appellant at 7.

We reject Suburban's statement of the legal principle upon which its first argument is premised. It simply cannot be true that "the decisive question is the purpose for which (the property) 'primarily' was held when sold." Br. for Appellant at 15 (emphasis omitted). At the very moment of sale, the property is certainly being held "for sale." The appropriate question certainly must be the taxpayer's primary holding purpose at some point before he decided to make the sale in dispute.

There is language in the cases that supports the proposition we are here rejecting. For example, the Tax Court has stated explicitly that "the determining factor is the purpose for which the property is held at the time of sale." *Eline Realty Co.*, 35 T.C. 1, 5 (1960). See *Maddux Construction Co.*, 54 T.C. 1278, 1286 (1970).

* * *

We caution that our agreement with the Tenth Circuit on the question of the timing of the holding purpose inquiry should not be understood to indicate our agreement with its ultimate conclusion. If external events change the holding purpose for certain property from "for sale" to "for investment," we might well still find that the gains were ordinary because the property had been acquired and held "primarily for sale to customers in the ordinary course of (taxpayer's) trade or business." Conversely, as indicated in *Biedenharn*, an initial purpose to hold for investment might "endure () in controlling fashion notwithstanding continuing sales activity." *Biedenharn*, 526 F.2d at 421. As noted there, such an opening would most generally exist

---

22. [33] The question of exit from a business is intimately tied to, although independent of, the "holding purpose" inquiry. Exit from active business can be strong evidence of a change in holding purpose. The holding purpose question, as well as the timing of its inquiry, are discussed immediately below.

"where the change from investment holding to sales activity results from unantici-pated, externally induced factors which make impossible the continued pre-existing use of the realty." *Id.* On the facts of Tri-S, we might well have concluded that taxpayer was "wholesaling" property held "primarily for sale to customers in the ordinary course of his trade or business," so that ordinary income treatment would be ap-propriate. This "wholesaling niche" would be the converse of the "liquidation niche" left open by *Biedenharn.*

* * *

The "holding purpose" inquiry may appropriately be conducted by attempting to trace the taxpayer's primary holding purpose over the entire course of his ownership of the property. *See Malat v. Riddell,* 383 U.S. 569 (1966); *Devine v. Comm'r,* 558 F.2d 807 (5th Cir. 1977).[23] Thus, the inquiry should start at the time the property is acquired. We seek to divine the taxpayer's primary purpose for acquiring the property. In this case, we are willing to assume, as Suburban argues, that the property was ac-quired principally as an investment.[24] We then seek evidence of a change in taxpayer's primary holding purpose. Here, such evidence is plentiful and convincing.

We express no opinion on the resolution of this issue, for it is unnecessary to our decision. We find Suburban's primary holding purpose to be "for sale" both at the relevant moment of time, if the first proposed test is appropriate, and over most of the period of Suburban's ownership of the property, if the second proposed test is appropriate. See ensuing discussion in text.

The property was acquired in December, 1937. Houston Gardens Annex, Inc. was formed in 1938 to plat and sell a portion of the property. Sales commenced by 1939,

---

23. [36] It is not clear to us from the *Malat* decision whether "primarily" means "predominates at a certain point of time" or "predominates over the life of taxpayer's ownership of the asset." This could be critical if, for example, a taxpayer held a piece of property primarily for sale over many years, but then, shortly but not immediately before sale, switched his primary holding purpose to one of investment. If the appropriate measure of "primarily" is at a fixed instant of time, this taxpayer would be entitled to capital gain treatment if the other requirements of § 1221 are met. However, tax-payer's "primary holding purpose" over the length of his ownership of the asset would still be "for sale," and, if this is the proper test, ordinary income treatment would be mandated.

24. [37] There is considerable evidence to the contrary. Suburban's corporate charter clearly con-templates an active real estate business rather than passive investment status. This is not conclusive, because "the exercise of a (corporate) power and not the possession of it is the material factor to be weighed in testing whether a corporation is in a particular business." *Alabama Mineral, supra,* 250 F.2d at 872. More importantly, Suburban's activities, commencing soon after acquisition of the property, are convincing evidence that it did not originally acquire the property primarily for invest-ment. Thus, the same facts which convince us that any initial investment holding purpose was soon overborne by Suburban's desire to sell, see discussion in text, also make us highly skeptical of Suburban's claim to have initially intended to hold the property primarily for capital appreciation. The trial court adopted this theory, stating "the pattern of (Suburban's) acquisition and subsequent activities indicates that the plaintiff never had any other idea than to periodically sell the property to its customers." In future cases, we would expect such fact findings to be followed unless clearly erroneous. We are reluctant to follow that course here because of the extreme confusion the cases have previously exhibited concerning what is fact and what is law in this area. *See* pp. 180–181, *supra.*

and sales were transacted in each year thereafter. From 1946 through 1956, approximately 17 sales per year occurred. Proceeds from sales exceeded $8,500 each year, and were as high as $69,000 (in 1952). Also during this period, the development activity pertaining to Homestead Addition Two was occurring. This development activity clearly contemplated, and was accompanied by, sales.

All of these factors convince us that, by the mid-1940's at the latest, and probably much earlier, Suburban's primary holding purpose was "for sale." We need not decide the precise moment. Were it necessary to our decision, we quite likely would be unwilling to accept Suburban's contention that the property was initially acquired for investment.

With its primary holding purpose through the 1940's and 1950's fixed at "for sale," Suburban is then entitled to show that its primary purpose changed to, or back to, "for investment." Suburban claims that this shift occurred either in 1959, when its officers and directors discussed liquidation; in 1961, when Rice University became a stockholder of Suburban, further liquidation discussions were held, and the plats were withdrawn; or, at the latest, in 1966, when further liquidation discussions were held and Suburban began investing in securities.

We view this determination to be a closer call than any of the others in this case. The frequency of sales did drop off after the late 1950's. Suburban had discontinued its development activities.[25] Also, 1961 was the year the plats for Homestead Additions Three and Four were withdrawn.

This withdrawal of plats could be quite significant. Unlike liquidation discussions,[26] which were apparently a dime a dozen for Suburban, withdrawal of the plats was an action taken by Suburban which may evince a different relationship to its land. The critical question is whether this withdrawal indicated that henceforth the land was being held principally as an investment or simply showed that Suburban was attempting to maximize sales profits by selling to commercial users.

The continuing sales activity is strong evidence that the latter interpretation is the correct one. Moreover, the trial court found that the withdrawal evinced "an attempt to maximize profits from the sale of real estate and to capitalize on the new North

---

25. [38] These two factors are probative of a changed holding purpose, as they tend to demonstrate a different corporate attitude towards the real estate. They are not conclusive of this issue, however.

26. [39] We attach no independent significance to "liquidation discussions." As we said in *Biedenharn*, "a taxpayer's claim that he is liquidating a prior investment does not really present a separate theory but rather restates the main question ... under scrutiny." *Biedenharn*, 526 F.2d at 417. Suburban uses the term "liquidation" to refer to discussions about winding up Suburban as a corporate entity and distributing its assets, as well as discussions about converting its investments into cash. Discussions about each of these matters may evidence a change in holding purpose, but a corporation's actions may speak louder than "its" words. The latter is the case here. When investigating a corporation's intent, courts must be skeptical of words spoken at board meetings. paraN122EA

Although Suburban uses the word "liquidation" in an effort to place itself in *Biedenharn*'s "liquidation niche," *Biedenharn*, 526 F.2d at 417, that concept is not applicable here. Rather, it refers to the possibility that a holding purpose other than "for sale" might be found to continue through a period of relatively substantial sales activity when "unanticipated, externally induced factors ... make impossible the continued pre-existing use of the realty." Id. at 421.

Loop Freeway which would cross (Suburban's) property." Thus, we conclude that Suburban's primary purpose for holding the property remained "for sale" at the time of the transactions here disputed.[27]

Suburban does not explicitly contend that its primary purpose for holding the specific parcels at issue here was different from its purpose for holding the property as a whole. However, it does attempt to rely to some degree on the lack of development activity relating to the parcels here at issue. Although in some circumstances a taxpayer in the real estate business may be able to establish that certain parcels were held primarily for investment, the burden is on the taxpayer to establish that the parcels held primarily for investment were segregated from other properties held primarily for sale. The mere lack of development activity with respect to parts of a large property does not sufficiently separate those parts from the whole to meet the taxpayer's burden. *Cf. Houston Endowment*, 606 F.2d at 81 (pattern of sales activity with respect to entire tract determines characterization of individual sales). The lack of development activity with respect to the parts of the property here at issue is at least equally consistent with a primary motivation to maximize immediate sales profits as it is with a primary motivation to hold for investment.

C. Were the sales contemplated by Suburban "ordinary" in the course of Suburban's business?

We need say no more on this question than quote from the discussion of this issue in *Winthrop, supra*:

> The concept of normalcy requires for its application a chronology and a history to determine if the sales of lots to customers were the usual or a departure from the norm. History and chronology here combine to demonstrate that (taxpayer) did not sell his lots as an abnormal or unexpected event. (Taxpayer) began selling shortly after he acquired the land; he never used the land for any other purpose; and he continued this course of conduct over a number of years. Thus, the sales were ... ordinary.

417 F.2d at 912. The same is true here.

Having relied on the language of § 1221 itself to determine that the assets here at issue were not capital assets, we must return for a moment to the query posed at the outset. In this case, as we have demonstrated, sales of the type here in dispute were precisely what Suburban's business was directed towards. In other words, the profits garnered from these sales arose from the ordinary operation of Suburban's business.

---

27. [42] Some of our skepticism over Suburban's claim to have changed its holding purpose stems from the fact that it points to so many separate times when its purpose may have changed. This leads us to believe that Suburban was merely gradually shifting its strategies as market conditions changed in an effort to maximize sales profits. We do not reject outright the possibility that a sequence of events separate in time may indicate a gradual change in holding purpose from "for sale" to "for investment." However, we would be more likely to find a "change of purpose" argument convincing if a discrete event were followed by a string of zero's in the annual sales column figures, especially if this were followed by a sale of the remainder of taxpayer's property in a small number of transactions.

At the same time, however, these profits did not arise principally from the efforts of Suburban. Rather, they arose from the same historical, demographic, and market forces that have caused the City of Houston to grow enormously during the years Suburban held the land. Shrewdly, Suburban held on to much of its land. It only sold relatively small portions year by year. Thus, by 1968, market forces and the location of the North Loop Freeway had driven up the value of Suburban's land.[28] We must decide whether the policies motivating lower tax rates on capital gains and the controlling precedents expressing those policies require that we ignore the plain language of § 1221 and hold for Suburban.

The key cases we must explore here number three. First is *Malat v. Riddell*, 383 U.S. 569 (1966) (per curiam). It lends us no aid. As we have previously stated, it suggests that profits cannot arise from both "the (ordinary) operation of a business" and "appreciation in value accrued over a substantial period of time." Yet here we have profits which fall squarely into both categories.

We thus turn to the two cases from which the *Malat* court quotations are taken, *Comm'r v. Gillette Motor Transport, Inc.*, 364 U.S. 130 (1960), and *Corn Products Refining Company v. Comm'r*, 350 U.S. 46 (1955). In *Gillette*, the Supreme Court said:

> This Court has long held that the term "capital asset" is to be construed narrowly in accordance with the purpose of Congress to afford capital-gains treatment only in situations typically involving the realization of appreciation in value accrued over a substantial period of time, and thus to ameliorate the hardship of taxation and the entire gain in one year.

364 U.S. at 134. We note that the quoted language does not state that all gains emanating from appreciation in value over a substantial period of time are to be treated as capital gains. Rather, it states the logical converse of that proposition; i.e., that capital gain treatment will be proper only if the gain emanates from appreciation in value. Instances of gain emanating from appreciation being treated as ordinary income are not inconsistent with this proposition.

We also note the Supreme Court's recognition of the attempt by Congress to avoid taxing income earned over a period of years in one year. In Suburban's case, although it is true that with respect to each individual parcel of land there is a "bunching" effect, taxation of the overall gains from the property as a whole has been spread over a long period of years. Thus, the "bunching" effect has been minimized. Last, we note the Supreme Court's admonition to construe the term "capital asset" narrowly. *Id.*

---

28. [43] Suburban's evidence demonstrated that the normal net profit on sales by a developer is approximately thirty-three percent, whereas Suburban's profit on the sales here in issue approximated ninety-five percent. Since Suburban did nothing to enhance the value of the parcels here at issue, and since we can take notice of the often rapid rise in real estate prices as cities expand, we accept Suburban's contention that its profits on these sales emanated from market forces and Suburban's patience rather than any other value-enhancing activities performed by Suburban.

Further support for a narrow construction of the term "capital asset" and a broad interpretation of its exclusions comes from Corn Products, the third key case in this area. *See Corn Products*, 76 S.Ct. at 24. More importantly, the Supreme Court in *Corn Products* squarely stated:

> Congress intended that profits and losses arising from the everyday operation of a business be considered as ordinary income or loss rather than capital gain or loss.

It is this type of profit that is before us today.

We thus conclude that § 1221(1) should be construed in accord with its plain meaning, and that, if the other requirements of § 1221(1) are met, when the ordinary business of a business is to make profits from appreciation in value caused by market forces, those profits are to be treated as ordinary income. Such is the case here.

* * *

Biedenharn Realty Company, Inc. v. United States

United States Court of Appeals, Fifth Circuit
526 F.2d 409 (1976)

FACTS

Because of the confusing state of the record in this controversy and the resulting inconsistencies among the facts as stipulated by the parties, as found by the District Court, and as stated in the panel opinion, we believe it useful to set out in plentiful detail the case's background and circumstances as best they can be ascertained.

A. The Realty Company

Joseph Biedenharn organized the Biedenharn Realty Company in 1923 as a vehicle for holding and managing the Biedenharn family's numerous investments. The original stockholders were all family members. The investment company controls, among other interests, valuable commercial properties, a substantial stock portfolio, a motel, warehouses, a shopping center, residential real property, and farm property.

B. Taxpayer's Real Property Sales—The Hardtimes Plantation

Taxpayer's suit most directly involves its ownership and sale of lots from the 973 acre tract located near Monroe, Louisiana, known as the Hardtimes Plantation. The plaintiff purchased the estate in 1935 for $50,000.00. B. W. Biedenharn, the Realty Company's president, testified that taxpayer acquired Hardtimes as a 'good buy' for the purpose of farming and as a future investment. The plaintiff farmed the land for several years. Thereafter, Biedenharn rented part of the acreage to a farmer who Mr. Biedenharn suggested may presently be engaged in farming operations.

1. The Three Basic Subdivisions

Between 1939 and 1966, taxpayer carved three basic subdivisions from Hardtimes-Biedenharn Estates, Bayou DeSiard Country Club Addition, and Oak Park Addition-covering approximately 185 acres.[29] During these years, Biedenharn sold 208 subdivided Hardtimes lots in 158 sales, making a profit in excess of $800,000.00. These three basic subdivisions are the source of the contested 37 sales of 38 lots. Their development and disposition are more fully discussed below.

a) Biedenharn Estates Unit 1, including 41.9 acres, was platted in 1938. Between 1939 and 1956, taxpayer apparently sold 21 lots in 9 sales. Unit 2, containing 8.91 acres, was sold in 9 transactions between 1960 and 1965 and involved 10 lots.

b) Bayou DeSiard Country Club Addition, covering 61 acres, was subdivided in 1951, with remaining lots resubdivided in 1964. Approximately 73 lots were purchased in 64 sales from 1951 to 1966.

c) Oak Park Units 1 and 2 encompassed 75 acres. After subdivision in 1955 and resubdivision in 1960, plaintiff sold approximately 104 lots in 76 sales.

2. Additional Hardtimes Sales

Plaintiff lists at least 12 additional Hardtimes sales other than lots vended from the three basic subdivisions. The earliest of these dispositions occurred in November, 1935, thirteen days after the Plantation's purchase. Ultimately totaling approximately 275 acres, most, but not all, of these sales involved large parcels of non-subdivided land.

C. Taxpayer's Real Property Activity: Non-Hardtimes Sales

Plaintiff's own submissions make clear that the Biedenharn Realty Company effectuated numerous non-Hardtimes retail real estate transactions. From the Company's formation in 1923 through 1966, the last year for which taxes are contested, taxpayer sold 934 lots. Of this total, plaintiff disposed of 249 lots before 1935 when it acquired Hardtimes. Thus, in the years 1935 to 1966, taxpayer sold 477 lots apart from its efforts with respect to the basic Hardtimes subdivisions....

Unfortunately, the record does not unambiguously reveal the number of sales as opposed to the number of lots involved in these dispositions. Although some doubt exists as to the actual sales totals, even the most conservative reading of the figures convinces us of the frequency and abundance of the non-Hardtimes sales.... Moreover, Biedenharn has sold over 20 other properties, a few of them piecemeal, since 1923.

Each of these parcels has its own history. Joseph Biedenharn transferred much of the land to the Realty Company in 1923. The company acquired other property through purchases and various forms of foreclosure. Before sale, Biedenharn held some tracts for commercial or residential rental. Taxpayer originally had slated the Owens acreage for transfer in bulk to the Owens-Illinois Company. Also, the length of time between acquisition and disposition differed significantly among pieces of realty. However, these variations in the background of each plot and the length of

---

29. [6] In 1938, A. G. Siegfried, Inc., prepared a plat for all of the Hardtimes Plantation. B. W. Biedenharn testified that he thought that this particular plat was used only for a single 1939 sale. However, a copy of the blueprint read in conjunction with plaintiff's answers to interrogatories indicates that the Siegfried plat formed the basis for the entire first Biedenharn subdivision, Biedenharn Estates Unit 1, from which the Realty Company eventually sold 21 lots....

time and original purpose for which each was obtained do not alter the fact that the Biedenharn Realty Company regularly sold substantial amounts of subdivided and improved real property, and further, that these sales were not confined to the basic Hardtimes subdivisions.

D. Real Property Improvements

Before selling the Hardtimes lots, Biedenharn improved the land, adding in most instances streets, drainage, water, sewerage, and electricity. The total cost of bettering the Plantation acreage exceeded $200,000 and included $9,519.17 for Biedenharn Estates Unit 2, $56,879.12 for Bayou DeSiard County Club Addition, and $141,579.25 for the Oak Park Addition.

E. Sale of the Hardtimes Subdivisions

Bernard Biedenharn testified that at the time of the Hardtimes purchase, no one foresaw that the land would be sold as residential property in the future. Accordingly, the District Court found, and we do not disagree, that Biedenharn bought Hardtimes for investment. Later, as the City of Monroe expanded northward, the Plantation became valuable residential property. The Realty Company staked off the Bayou De-Siard subdivision so that prospective purchasers could see what the lots 'looked like.' As demand increased, taxpayer opened the Oak Park and Biedenharn Estates Unit 2 subdivisions and resubdivided the Bayou DeSiard section. Taxpayer handled all Biedenharn Estates and Bayou DeSiard sales. Independent realtors disposed of many of the Oak Park lots.... Taxpayer delegated significant responsibilities to these brokers. In its dealings with Faulk, Biedenharn set the prices, general credit terms, and signed the deeds. Details, including specific credit decisions and advertising, devolved to Faulk, who utilized on-site signs and newspapers to publicize the lots.

In contrast to these broker induced dispositions, plaintiff's non-brokered sales resulted after unsolicited individuals approached Realty Company employees with inquiries about prospective purchases. At no time did the plaintiff hire its own real state salesmen or engage in formal advertising. Apparently, the lands' prime location and plaintiff's subdivision activities constituted sufficient notice to interested persons of the availability of Hardtimes lots....

The Realty Company does not maintain a separate place of business but instead offices at the Biedenharn family's Ouachita Coca-Cola bottling plant. A telephone, listed in plaintiff's name, rings at the Coca-Cola building. Biedenharn has four employees: a camp caretaker, a tenant farmer, a bookkeeper and a manager. The manager, Henry Biedenharn, Jr., devotes approximately 10% of his time to the Realty Company, mostly collecting rents and overseeing the maintenance of various properties. The bookkeeper also works only part-time for plaintiff. Having set out these facts, we now discuss the relevant legal standard for resolving this controversy.

ANALYSIS

* * *

The Code defines capital asset, the profitable sale or exchange of which generally results in capital gains, as "property held by the taxpayer." 26 U.S.C. § 1221. Many exceptions limit the enormous breadth of this congressional description and consequently remove large numbers of transactions from the privileged realm of capital gains. In this case, we confront the question whether or not Biedenharn's real estate sales should be taxed at ordinary rates because they fall within the exception covering "property held by the taxpayer primarily for sale to customers in the ordinary course of his trade or business." 26 U.S.C. § 1221(1).

* * *

Assuredly, we would much prefer one or two clearly defined, easily employed tests which lead to predictable, perhaps automatic, conclusions. However, the nature of the congressional "capital asset" definition and the myriad situations to which we must apply that standard make impossible any easy escape from the task before us. No one set of criteria is applicable to all economic structures. Moreover, within a collection of tests, individual factors have varying weights and magnitudes, depending on the facts of the case. The relationship among the factors and their mutual interaction is altered as each criteria increases or diminishes in strength, sometimes changing the controversy's outcome. As such, there can be no mathematical formula capable of finding the X of capital gains or ordinary income in this complicated field.

* * *

We begin our task by evaluating in the light of Biedenharn's facts the main Winthrop factors—substantiality and frequency of sales, improvements, solicitation and advertising efforts, and brokers' activities—as well as a few miscellaneous contentions. A separate section follows discussing the keenly contested role of prior investment intent. Finally, we consider the significance of the Supreme Court's decision in *Malat v. Riddell.*

A. Frequency and Substantiality of Sales

Scrutinizing closely the record and briefs, we find that plaintiff's real property sales activities compel an ordinary income conclusion. In arriving at this result, we examine first the most important of Winthrop's factors—the frequency and substantiality of taxpayer's sales. Although frequency and substantiality of sales are not usually conclusive, they occupy the preeminent ground in our analysis. The recent trend of Fifth Circuit decisions indicates that when dispositions of subdivided property extend over a long period of time and are especially numerous, the likelihood of capital gains is very slight indeed. *See U.S. v. Winthrop,* 417 F.2d 905 (5th Cir. 1969); *Thompson v. Comm'r,* 322 F.2d 122 (5th Cir. 1963). Conversely, when sales are few and isolated, the taxpayer's claim to capital gain is accorded greater deference. *Cf. Gamble v. Comm'r,* 242 F.2d 586, 591 (5th Cir. 1957); *Brown v. Comm'r,* 143 F.2d 468, 470 (5th Cir. 1944).

On the present facts, taxpayer could not claim "isolated" sales or a passive and gradual liquidation. *See Gamble,* supra; *Dunlap v. Oldham Lumber Company,* 178 F.2d 781, 784 (5th Cir. 1950); *Brown,* supra. Although only three years and 37 sales (38 lots) are in controversy here, taxpayer's pre-1964 sales from the Hardtimes acreage as well as similar dispositions from other properties are probative of the existence of sales "in the ordinary course of his trade or business." *See* Levin, *Capital Gains or Income Tax on Real Estate Sales*, 37 B.U. L. Rev. 165, 170 & n.29 (1957). *Cf. Snell v. Comm'r*, 97 F.2d 891 (5th Cir. 1938). As Appendix I indicates, Biedenharn sold property, usually a substantial number of lots, in every year, save one, from 1923 to 1966. Biedenharn's long and steady history of improved lot sales at least equals that encountered in *Thompson v. Comm'r*, 322 F.2d 122 (5th Cir. 1963), where also we noted the full history of real estate activity. Supra at 124–25. There taxpayer lost on a finding that he had sold 376 1/2 lots over a 15 year span — this notwithstanding that overall the other sales indicia were more in taxpayer's favor than in the present case. Moreover, the contested tax years in that suit involved only ten sales (28 lots); yet we labeled that activity "substantial." The frequency and substantiality of Biedenharn's sales go not only to its holding purpose and the existence of a trade or business but also support our finding of the ordinariness with which the Realty Company disposed of its lots. These sales easily meet the criteria of normalcy set forth in *Winthrop*.

Furthermore, in contrast with *Goldberg v. Comm'r*, 223 F.2d 709, 713 (5th Cir. 1955), where taxpayer did not reinvest his sales proceeds, one could fairly infer that the income accruing to the Biedenharn Realty Company from its pre-1935 sales helped support the purchase of the Hardtimes Plantation. Even if taxpayer made no significant acquisitions after Hardtimes, the "purpose, system, and continuity" of Biedenharn's efforts easily constitute a business.

The fact that he bought no additional lands during this period does not prevent his activities being a business. He merely had enough land to do a large business without buying any more.

Citing previous Fifth Circuit decisions including *Goldberg v. Comm'r*, 223 F.2d 709, 713 (5th Cir. 1955), and *Ross v. Comm'r*, 227 F.2d 265, 268 (5th Cir. 1955), the District Court sought to overcome this evidence of dealer-like real estate activities and property "primarily held for sale" by clinging to the notion that the taxpayer was merely liquidating a prior investment. We discuss later the role of former investment status and the possibility of taxpayer relief under that concept. Otherwise, the question of liquidation of an investment is simply the opposite side of the inquiry as to whether or not one is holding property primarily for sale in the ordinary course of his business. In other words, a taxpayer's claim that he is liquidating a prior investment does not really present a separate theory but rather restates the main question currently under scrutiny. To the extent the opinions cited by the District Court might create a specially protected "liquidation" niche, we believe that the present case, with taxpayer's energetic subdivision activities and consummation of numerous retail property dispositions, is governed by our more recent decision in *Thompson v. Comm'r*.

* * *

B. Improvements

Although we place greatest emphasis on the frequency and substantiality of sales over an extended time period, our decision in this instance is aided by the presence of taxpayer activity—particularly improvements—in the other Winthrop areas. Biedenharn vigorously improved its subdivisions, generally adding streets, drainage, sewerage, and utilities. These alterations are comparable to those in *Winthrop*, supra at 906, except that in the latter case taxpayer built five houses. We do not think that the construction of five houses in the context of Winthrop's 456 lot sales significantly distinguishes that taxpayer from Biedenharn. In *Barrios Estate v. Comm'r*, 265 F.2d 517, 520 (5th Cir. 1959), heavily relied on by plaintiff, the Court reasoned that improvements constituted an integral part of the sale of subdivided realty and were therefore permissible in the context of a liquidating sale. As discussed above, Biedenharn's activities have removed it from any harbor of investment liquidation. Moreover, the additional sales flexibility permitted the Barrios Estate taxpayer might be predicated on the forced change of purpose examined in section IV. Finally, in *Thompson*, *supra*, the plaintiff's only activities were subdivision and improvement. Yet, not availing ourselves of the opportunity to rely on a Barrios Estate type "liquidation plus integrally related improvements theory," we found no escape from ordinary income.

C. Solicitation and Advertising Efforts

Substantial, frequent sales and improvements such as we have encountered in this case will usually conclude the capital gains issue against taxpayer. *See, e.g., Thompson*, *supra*. Thus, on the basis of our analysis to this point, we would have little hesitation in finding that taxpayer held "primarily for sale" in the "ordinary course of [his] trade or business." "[T]he flexing of commercial muscles with frequency and continuity, design and effect" of which *Winthrop* spoke, is here a reality. This reality is further buttressed by Biedenharn's sales efforts, including those carried on through brokers. Minimizing the importance of its own sales activities, taxpayer points repeatedly to its steady avoidance of advertising or other solicitation of customers. Plaintiff directs our attention to stipulations detailing the population growth of Monroe and testimony outlining the economic forces which made Hardtimes Plantation attractive residential property and presumably eliminated the need for sales exertions. We have no quarrel with plaintiff's description of this familiar process of suburban expansion, but we cannot accept the legal inferences which taxpayer would have us draw.

The Circuit's recent decisions in *Thompson*, supra at 124–26, and *Winthrop*, implicitly recognize that even one inarguably in the real estate business need not engage in promotional exertions in the fact of a favorable market. As such, we do not always require a showing of active solicitation where "business … [is] good, indeed brisk," *Thompson*, and where other *Winthrop* factors make obvious taxpayer's ordinary trade or business status. Plainly, this represents a sensible approach. In cases such as Biedenharn, the sale of a few lots and the construction of the first homes, albeit not, as in *Winthrop*, by the taxpayer, as well as the building of roads, addition of utilities, and staking off of the other subdivided parcels constitute a highly visible form of advertising. Prospective home buyers drive by the advantageously located property, see the development activities, and are as surely put on notice of the availability of lots as if the owner had erected large signs announcing "residential property for sale." We do not by this evaluation automatically neutralize advertising or solicitation as a factor in our analysis. This form of inherent notice is not present in all land sales, especially where the property is not so valuably located, is not subdivided into small lots, and is not improved. Moreover, inherent notice represents only one band of the solicitation spectrum. Media utilization and personal initiatives remain material components of this criterion. When present, they call for greater Government oriented emphasis on *Winthrop*'s solicitation factor.

D. Brokerage Activities

In evaluating Biedenharn's solicitation activities, we need not confine ourselves to the *Thompson-Winthrop* theory of brisk sales without organizational efforts. Unlike in *Thompson* and *Winthrop* where no one undertook overt solicitation efforts, the Realty Company hired brokers who, using media and on site advertising, worked vigorously on taxpayer's behalf. We do not believe that the employment of brokers should shield plaintiff from ordinary income treatment. Their activities should at least in discounted form be attributed to Biedenharn. To the contrary, taxpayer argues that "one who is not already in the trade or business of selling real estate does not enter such business when he employs a broker who acts as an independent contractor. *Fahs v. Crawford*, 161 F.2d 315 (5 Cir. 1947); *Smith v. Dunn*, 224 F.2d 353 (5 Cir. 1955)." Without presently entangling ourselves in a dispute as to the differences between an agent and an independent contractor, *see generally* Levin, *supra*, we find the cases cited distinguishable from the instant circumstances. In both Fahs and Smith, the taxpayer turned the entire property over to brokers, who, having been granted total responsibility, made all decisions including the setting of sales prices. In comparison, Biedenharn determined original prices and general credit policy. Moreover, the Realty Company did not make all the sales in question through brokers as did taxpayers in Fahs and Smith. Biedenharn sold the Bayou DeSiard and Biedenharn Estates lots and may well have sold some of the Oak Park land. In other words, unlike Fahs and Smith, Biedenharn's brokers did not so completely take charge of the whole of the Hardtimes sales as to permit the Realty Company to wall itself off legally from their activities.

E. Additional Taxpayer Contentions

Plaintiff presents a number of other contentions and supporting facts for our consideration. Although we set out these arguments and briefly discuss them, their impact, in the face of those factors examined above, must be minimal. Taxpayer emphasizes that its profits from real estate sales averaged only 11.1% In each of the years in controversy, compared to 52.4% in Winthrop. Whatever the percentage, plaintiff would be hard pressed to deny the substantiality of its Hardtimes sales in absolute terms (the subdivided lots alone brought in over one million dollars) or, most importantly, to assert that its real estate business was too insignificant to constitute a separate trade or business.[30] The relatively modest income share represented by Biedenharn's real property dispositions stems not from a failure to engage in real estate sales

---

30. [35] This Court has repeatedly recognized that a taxpayer may have more than one trade or business for purposes of Internal Revenue Code § 1221(1). *See, e.g., Ackerman v. U.S.*, 335 F.2d 521, 524 (5th. Cir. 1964); *Gamble v. Comm'r*, 242 F.2d 586, 591 (5th. Cir. 1957); Fahs v. Crawford, 161 F.2d 315, 317 (5th. Cir. 1947).

activities but rather from the comparatively large profit attributable to the Company's 1965 ($649,231.34) and 1966 ($688,840.82) stock sales. The fact of Biedenharn's holding, managing, and selling stock is not inconsistent with the existence of a separate realty business. If in the face of taxpayer's numerous real estate dealings this Court held otherwise, we would be sanctioning special treatment for those individuals and companies arranging their business activities so that the income accruing to real estate sales represents only a small fraction of the taxpaying entity's total gains.

Similarly, taxpayer observes that Biedenharn's manager devoted only 10% of his time to real estate dealings and then mostly to the company's rental properties. This fact does not negate the existence of sales activities. Taxpayer had a telephone listing, a shared business office, and a few part-time employees. Because, as discussed before, a strong seller's market existed, Biedenharn's sales required less than the usual solicitation efforts and therefore less than the usual time. Moreover, plaintiff, unlike taxpayers in *Winthrop, supra* and *Thompson, supra*, hired brokers to handle many aspects of the Hardtimes transactions — thus further reducing the activity and time required of Biedenharn's employees.

Finally, taxpayer argues that it is entitled to capital gains since its enormous profits (74% To 97%) demonstrate a return based principally on capital appreciation and not on taxpayer's "merchandising" efforts. We decline the opportunity to allocate plaintiff's gain between longterm market appreciation and improvement related activities. *See generally* S. Surrey, W. Warren, P. McDaniel, H. Ault, 1 Federal Income Taxation 1012 (1972). Even if we undertook such an analysis and found the former element predominant, we would on the authority of *Winthrop, supra* at 907–908, reject plaintiff's contention which, in effect, is merely taxpayer's version of the Government's unsuccessful argument in that case.[31]

IV.

The District Court found that "[t]axpayer is merely liquidating over a long period of time a substantial investment in the most advantageous method possible." 356 F. Supp. at 1336. In this view, the original investment intent is crucial, for it preserves the capital gains character of the transaction even in the face of normal real estate sales activities.

* * *

While the facts of this case dictate our agreement with the Internal Revenue Service's ultimate conclusion of taxpayer liability, they do not require our acquiescence in the Government's entreated total elimination of *Winthrop*'s first criterion, "the nature and purpose of the acquisition." Undoubtedly, in most subdivided-improvement situations, an investment purpose of antecedent origin will not survive into a present

---

31. [37] In *Galena Oaks Corp. v. Scofield*, 218 F.2d 217, 220 (5th. Cir. 1954), the Court said: "Congress intended to alleviate the burden on a taxpayer whose property has increased in value over a long period of time. When, however, such a taxpayer endeavors still further to increase his profits by engaging in a business separable from his investment, it is not unfair that his gain should be taxed as ordinary income."

era of intense retail selling. The antiquated purpose, when overborne by later, but substantial and frequent selling activity, will not prevent ordinary income from being visited upon the taxpayer. *See, e.g., Ackerman v. U.S.*, 335 F.2d 521 (5th Cir. 1964); *Thompson v. Comm'r*, 322 F.2d 122 (5th Cir. 1963); *Galena Oaks Corp. v. Scofield*, 218 F.2d 217 (5th Cir. 1954); *Brown v. Comm'r*, 143 F.2d 468 (5th Cir. 1944). Generally, investment purpose has no built-in perpetuity nor a guarantee of capital gains forever more. Precedents, however, in certain circumstances have permitted landowners with earlier investment intent to sell subdivided property and remain subject to capital gains treatment. *See, e.g., Cole v. Usry*, 294 F.2d 426 (5th Cir. 1961); *Barrios Estate v. Comm'r*, 265 F.2d 517 (5th Cir. 1959); *Smith v. Dunn*, 224 F.2d 353 (5th Cir. 1955).

* * *

In a sense, we adhere to our own admonitions against efforts at reconciling and making consistent all that has gone before in the subdivided realty area. But in so avoiding a troublesome and probably unrewarding task, we are not foreclosed from the more important responsibility of giving future direction with respect to the much controverted role of prior investment intent, nor are we precluded from analyzing that factor's impact in the context of the present controversy.

We reject the Government's sweeping contention that prior investment intent is always irrelevant. There will be instances where an initial investment purpose endures in controlling fashion notwithstanding continuing sales activity. We doubt that this aperture, where an active subdivider and improver receives capital gains, is very wide; yet we believe it exists. We would most generally find such an opening where the change from investment holding to sales activity results from unanticipated, externally induced factors which make impossible the continued pre-existing use of the realty. *Barrios Estate*, supra, is such a case. There the taxpayer farmed the land until drainage problems created by the newly completed intercoastal canal rendered the property agriculturally unfit. The Court found that taxpayer was "dispossessed of the farming operation through no act of her own." Similarly, Acts of God, condemnation of part of one's property, new and unfavorable zoning regulations, or other events forcing alteration of taxpayer's plans create situations making possible subdivision and improvement as a part of a capital gains disposition.[32]

However, cases of the ilk of *Ackerman*, supra, *Thompson*, supra, and *Winthrop*, supra, remain unaffected in their ordinary income conclusion. There, the transformations in purpose were not coerced. Rather, the changes ensued from taxpayers' purely voluntary responses to increased economic opportunity—albeit at times externally created in order to enhance their gain through the subdivision, improve-

---

32. [40] A Boston University Law Review article canvassing factors inducing involuntary changes of purpose in subdivided realty cases enumerates among others the following: a pressing need for funds in general, illness or old age or both, the necessity for liquidating a partnership on the death of a partner, the threat of condemnation, and municipal zoning restrictions. Levin, *Capital Gains or Income Tax on Real Estate Sales*, 37 B.U. L.Rev. 1965, 194–95 (1957). Although we might not accept all of these events as sufficient to cause an outcome favorable to taxpayer, they are suggestive of the sort of change of purpose provoking events delineated above as worthy of special consideration.

ment, and sale of lots. Thus reinforced by the trend of these recent decisions, we gravitate toward the Government's view in instances of willful taxpayer change of purpose and grant the taxpayer little, if any, benefit from *Winthrop*'s first criterion in such cases.

* * *

Clearly, under the facts in this case, the distinction just elaborated undermines Biedenharn's reliance on original investment purpose. Taxpayer's change of purpose was entirely voluntary and therefore does not fall within the protected area. Moreover, taxpayer's original investment intent, even if considered a factor sharply supporting capital gains treatment, is so overwhelmed by the other *Winthrop* factors discussed *supra*, that that element can have no decisive effect. However wide the capital gains passageway through which a subdivider with former investment intent could squeeze, the Biedenharn Realty Company will never fit.

V.

The District Court, citing *Malat v. Riddell*, 383 U.S. 569 (1966), stated that "the lots were not held ... primarily for sale as that phrase was interpreted ... in *Malat*...." 356 F. Supp. at 1335. Finding that Biedenharn's primary purpose became holding for sale and consequently that *Malat* in no way alters our analysis here, we disagree with the District Court's conclusion. *Malat* was a brief per curiam in which the Supreme Court decided only that as used in Internal Revenue Code § 1221(1) the word "primarily" means "principally," "of first importance." The Supreme Court, re-manding the case, did not analyze the facts or resolve the controversy which involved a real estate dealer who had purchased land and held it at the time of sale with the dual intention of developing it as rental property or selling it, depending on whichever proved to be the more profitable. *Malat v. Riddell*, 347 F.2d 23, 26 (9th. Cir. 1965). In contrast, having substantially abandoned its investment and farming intent, Bieden-harn was cloaked primarily in the garb of sales purpose when it disposed of the 38 lots here in controversy. With this change, the Realty Company lost the opportunity of coming within any dual purpose analysis.

We do not hereby condemn to ordinary income a taxpayer merely because, as is usually true, his principal intent at the exact moment of disposition is sales. Rather, we refuse capital gains treatment in those instances where over time there has been such a thoroughgoing change of purpose ... as to make untenable a claim either of twin intent or continued primacy of investment purpose.

OPINION

Having surveyed the Hardtimes terrain, we find no escape from ordinary income. The frequency and substantiality of sales over an extended time, the significant im-provement of the basic subdivisions, the acquisition of additional properties, the use of brokers, and other less important factors persuasively combine to doom taxpayer's cause. Applying *Winthrop*'s criteria, this case clearly falls within the ordinary income category delineated in that decision. In so concluding, we note that *Winthrop* does not represent the most extreme application of the overriding principle that "the definition of a capital asset must be narrowly applied and its exclusions interpreted broadly." *Corn Products Refining Co. v. Comm'r*, 350 U.S. 46, 52 (1955). *See also Comm'r v. P. G. Lake, Inc.*, 356 U.S. 260, 265 (1958). *Accord, Winthrop, supra* at 911.

We cannot write black letter law for all realty subdividers and for all times, but we do caution in words of red that once an investment does not mean always an investment. A simon-pure investor forty years ago could by his subsequent activities become a seller in the ordinary course four decades later. The period of Biedenharn's passivity is in the distant past; and the taxpayer has since undertaken the role of real estate protagonist. The Hardtimes Plantation in its day may have been one thing, but as the plantation was developed and sold, Hardtimes became by the very fact of change and activity a different holding than it had been at its inception. No longer could resort to initial purpose preserve taxpayer's once upon a time opportunity for favored treatment.

United States v. Winthrop

United States Court of Appeals, Fifth Circuit
417 F.2d 905 (1969)

FACTS

The taxpayer, Guy L. Winthrop was the owner of certain property in the environs of Tallahassee, Florida, known as Betton Hills. The property had been in his family since 1836. Winthrop first received a share of the property in 1932 upon the death of his mother. Additional portions of the property were received by him in 1946, 1948, and 1960 through inheritance and partition. As the city of Tallahassee expanded, its city limits were extended to incorporate most of the Winthrop property and the taxpayer began to sell lots for homesites. The first subdivision was undertaken in 1936, and the first sales were made in that year. Thereafter, eight other subdivisions were platted and developed by the taxpayer. Each subdivision was platted separately and the taxpayer endeavored to sell most of the lots in one subdivision before another was developed. The process was one of gradual orderly development of the property through the various subdivisions. Each was surveyed and platted. The streets were graded and paved at Winthrop's expense. Electricity and water facilities were installed; and in some subdivisions sewer lines were built, again at Winthrop's expense, although this was eventually repaid out of the utility bills incurred by homeowners who moved into the subdivisions. Moreover, the taxpayer participated in building five houses for sale in the addition in order to assist other purchasers in obtaining F.H.A. loans to finance their homes.

In selling the lots Winthrop neither advertised nor engaged brokers. The customers primarily came to his home to conduct the sale negotiations since he did not even have an office. He did however, purchase an annual occupational license as a real estate broker from the City of Tallahassee from 1948 through 1963. Despite this low pressure and informal selling technique, the parties stipulated that Winthrop was primarily engaged in selling the Betton Hills property and that though he was a civil engineer by profession, he did little work of this type during the period in question save that done on the Betton Hills property. Furthermore, Winthrop's technique, although unorthodox, was apparently effective. Commencing with the year 1945 and ending in December, 1963, approximately 456 lots were sold in Betton Hills. The profit and other income realized by Winthrop from the sale of these lots from 1951 through 1963 was $483,018.94 or 52.4% of his total income during that period.

The taxpayer reported the profits from these sales as capital gains up until 1953. In that year the Commissioner determined that Winthrop was liable for self employment taxes with respect to his real estate sales. His accountant thereafter listed the sales of Betton Hills property, and expenses connected with those sales, as profits from a business or profession and for the years 1953 through 1963 the taxpayer and his wife paid taxes on these profits at ordinary income rates. In addition, the taxpayer paid self employment taxes for these years on the income derived from the sale of Betton Hills real estate, and such a tax was paid for him in 1963 by his executrix. On his income tax returns for the years 1953 through 1962 the taxpayer listed his occupation as "real estate and engineer." He also listed his occupation in a similar manner on motel registration cards during his extensive travels within the period in question.

After Mr. Winthrop's death in 1963, Mrs. Winthrop, individually and as executrix of Mr. Winthrop's estate, filed claims for a refund for the years 1959 through 1963 in the amount of $57,630.96, asserting that the gains from the sale of the subdivided properties should have been treated as capital gains rather than ordinary income, as originally reported on the tax returns for those years. The Commissioner disallowed these claims and this suit followed. The court below agreed with Mrs. Winthrop's contention and ordered the refund. From this adverse judgment the government appeals. Agreeing with the government, we reverse the decision of the district court and hold that the profits received by the taxpayer from the sales of the property in question were ordinary income.

ANALYSIS

The government's first argument in support of its contention that the district court erred in granting capital gains treatment to the taxpayer is founded upon the proposition that capital gains treatment is available only where the appreciation in value is the result of external market changes occurring over a period of time. In other words, the government argues that where the appreciation is due to the taxpayer's efforts, all profit should be reported as ordinary income. In statutory terms the government argues that the subdivided land ceased to be a "capital asset" when the taxpayer improved the land through his own efforts by platting the lots, paving streets, and installing utilities. Although recognizing that subdivided land is not expressly removed from the "capital asset" category by the exclusionary provisions of I.R.C. 1221 unless such land is held primarily for sale to customers in the ordinary course of business, the government, nevertheless, maintains that its taxpayer efforts rule has, in effect, been read into the statute by the courts. In support of this argument the government relies principally on the following language from *Corn Products Refining Co. v. Comm'r*, 350 U.S. 46 (1955):

Congress intended that profits and losses arising from the everyday operation of a business be considered as ordinary income or loss rather than capital gain or loss. The preferential treatment provided by 117 applies to transactions in property which are not the normal source of business income. It was intended "to relieve the taxpayer from ... excessive tax burdens on gains resulting from a conversion of capital investments, and to remove the deterrent effect of those burdens on such conversions." *Burnet v. Harmel*, 287 U.S. at page 106.

Id. at 52.

We think the preceding language from Corn Products fails to support the taxpayer efforts rule advanced by the government. The case does support the proposition that an asset may not be a capital asset for tax purposes even though not expressly excluded from that status by I.R.C. § 1221, but the opinion neither mentions nor deals with assets improved by the taxpayer's effort. Rather, it dealt with daily operational profits in the ordinary course of the taxpayer's business. Further, the other cases discussed in the government's brief in support of this novel interpretation of Corn Products do not adopt the taxpayer efforts rule.

* * *

If the universality and sweep which the government reads into the Corn Products message is in fact the gospel word in capital gains cases, it has not yet come through nor been heard by the Fifth Circuit. Indeed, the cases are many where taxpayer efforts have contributed to value and have been accorded capital gains treatment. *U.S. v. Temple*, 355 F.2d 67 (5th Cir. 1966); *Comm'r v. Ponchartrain Park Homes, Inc.*, 349 F.2d 416 (5th Cir. 1965); *Cole v. Usry*, 294 F.2d 426 (5th Cir. 1961); *Barrios' Estate v. Comm'r*, 265 F.2d 517 (5th Cir. 1959); *Smith v. Dunn*, 224 F.2d 353 (5th Cir. 1955); *Goldberg v. Comm'r*, 223 F.2d 709 (5th Cir. 1955). As this court said in *Barrios' Estate, supra*:

> The idea of selling a large tract of land in lots embraces necessarily the construction of streets for access to them, the provision of drainage and the furnishing of access to such a necessity as water. It is hardly conceivable that taxpayer could have sold a lot without doing these things. To contend that reasonable expenditures and efforts, in such necessary undertakings are not entitled to capital gains treatment is to reject entirely the established principle that a person holding lands under such circumstances may subdivide it for advantageous sale. 265 F.2d at 520.

We therefore conclude that this blanket interdiction of capital gains treatment where there has been any laying on of hands is belied by the past decisions of this court.

While we are in disagreement with the government's first argument concerning taxpayer efforts, we find its second argument, that the land in question was primarily held for sale in the ordinary course of business and, therefore, was not a capital asset under 1221, persuasive. In holding against the government on this point the court below appears to have placed particular emphasis upon the following facts: (1) The proceeds from the sales of the property were not reinvested in real estate; (2) the taxpayer had other investments, none of which involved the sale of real estate; (3) the subdivided property was acquired by inheritance, not by purchase for the purpose of resale; (4) the taxpayer's holding period was twenty-five years; (5) the taxpayer maintained no office, made most of the sales from his home, spent no time whatever promoting sales and did not advertise; and (6) the purchasers came to him and he was selective in making the sales.

In relying on these factors the court below was obviously following earlier suggestions by this court that such facts are relevant in determining the ultimate question of whether or not the land in question was held primarily for sale to customers in the ordinary course of business.... In condensed form the tests mentioned most often are: (1) the nature and purpose of the acquisition of the property and the duration of the ownership; (2) the extent and nature of the taxpayer's efforts to sell the property; (3) the number, extent, continuity and substantiality of the sales; (4) the extent of subdividing, developing, and advertising to increase sales; (5) the use of a business office for the sale of the property; (6) the character and degree of supervision or control exercised by the taxpayer over any representative selling the property; and (7) the time and effort the taxpayer habitually devoted to the sales. *Smith v. Dunn, supra*, 224 F.2d at 356.

Despite their frequent use, this court has often declared that these seven pillars of capital gains treatment "in and of themselves ... have no independent significance, but only form part of a situation which in the individual case must be considered in its entirety to determine whether or not the property involved was held primarily for sale in the ordinary course of business (source cited)." *Cole v. Usry, supra*, 294 F.2d at 427.... Moreover, in *Thompson v. Comm'r, supra*, this court remarked concerning these "tests":

> Essential as they are in the adjudication of cases, we must take guard lest we be so carried away by the proliferation of tests that we forget that the statute excludes from capital assets "property held by the taxpayer primarily for sale to customers in the ordinary course of his trade or business". 26 U.S.C.A. 1221. 322 F.2d 122.

In the instant case the trial court found that these test facts, about which there is no disagreement, compelled a finding of the ultimate fact that the holding was not primarily for sale in the ordinary course of the taxpayer's business. In weighing the arguments on this point this court recognizes that the characterization of the taxpayer's manner of holding lands is a question of fact. The district court's finding on this ultimate issue, however, is not to be garrisoned by the clearly erroneous rule. Though it has factual underpinnings this ultimate issue is inherently a question of law. Obeissance to the clearly erroneous rule must yield when the facts are undisputed and we are called upon to reason and interpret. This is the law obligation of the court as distinguished from its fact finding duties.

* * *

We think, therefore, that even though we accept as true the fact findings of the court below, it is nevertheless incumbent upon this court to inquire into the ultimate conclusion of law reached by that court. In so doing, our analysis of the undisputed facts leads us to the contrary conclusion, that the taxpayer did hold the land in question primarily for sale to customers in the ordinary course of business, and thus, under I.R.C. § 1221 is not eligible for capital gains treatment on the profits made from the sale of this land.

OPINION

In analyzing a case of this sort no rubrics of decision or rubbings from the philosopher's stone separate the sellers garlanded with capital gains from those beflowered in the garden of ordinary income. Each case and its facts must be compared with the mandate of the statute. In so doing we note that the enunciations of the Supreme Court are clarion as they enjoin us to construe narrowly the definition of a capital asset and as a corollary interpret its definitional exclusions broadly.... We therefore approach first the issue of whether or not Winthrop held the property "primarily for sale" as that phrase is used in § 1221.

It is undisputed that Winthrop inherited the first portion of the Betton Hills land in 1932. By 1936 the first sales had been made and further subdivisions were under way. Mrs. Winthrop's testimony indicates that, except for the subdividing and selling, the land was not used by the taxpayer. According to her, a city employee was allowed to live there, but this was rent free. Later, another city employee rented a small house for $40.00 a month but "not the land." Rather they "granted him the right to plant some corn." On the other hand, her testimony was equally clear in showing that the taxpayer's activities regarding the land, such as paving the streets and having utilities installed, were done with the express purpose of making it more saleable. She testified that he built houses on some of the lots in order to make FHA financing available to prospective purchasers of other lots. Moreover, she built some houses on the lots because "if a person built a house and there was a house nearby, somebody wanted the lot, because people like neighbors."

There were, therefore, no multiple, dual, or changes of purpose during the relevant years of Winthrop's Betton Hills sales. The taxpayer, long before the tax payers in question, had as his sole motivation the sale of Betton Hills, lot by lot, year by year, transaction by transaction. The evidence is clear and uncontradicted that the lots were at all times held by Winthrop "primarily for sale" as that phrase was interpreted by the Supreme Court in *Malat v. Riddell*, 383 U.S. 569 (1966).

Holding primarily for sale, however, is by itself insufficient to disqualify the taxpayer from capital gains privileges. The sales must also be made in the ordinary course of the taxpayer's trade or business. The next issue, therefore, is whether the taxpayer's activities constituted a trade or business. We think that they did. The magnitude and continuity of his operations and design all point to these sales being part of a business. This was a planned program of subdividing and selling, lasting over a quarter of a century. It constituted Winthrop's principal activity and produced over one-half of his income during the years in question. This was no minuscule operation in terms of transactions or profits. Unlike the sellers in *Smith v. Dunn*, *supra*, the taxpayer here devoted a substantial amount of his time, skill and financial resources to developing and selling the property. He thereby became engaged in the business of subdividing real estate for sale. One need not be a static holder to qualify for capital gains treatment, but the flexing of commercial muscles with frequency and continuity, design and effect does result in disqualification because it indicates one has entered the business of real estate sales. *Thompson v. Comm'r*, 322 F.2d 122 (5th Cir. 1963); *Galena Oaks Corp. v. Scofield*, 218 F.2d 217 (5th Cir. 1954).

The taxpayer has made much over the fact that no office was used, no brokers were employed, no time was spent promoting sales, and no advertising was used. While advertising, solicitation and staff are the usual components of a business, they are not a necessary element in either the concept or the pragmatics of selling. Here it is evident that the taxpayer was quite successful in selling the lots without the assistance of these usual props. It is not necessary that customers be actively and fervently and frenetically sought. Winthrop had lots to sell and not mousetraps, so they beat a way to his door to buy his lots. As the court remarked in *Thompson v. Comm'r*, *supra*, which involved a similar lack of promotional activity, "merely because business was good, indeed brisk, does not make it any less in the ordinary course of such a good business." 322 F.2d at 124. Winthrop was in the business of selling lots in Betton Hills, even though his salesmanship was unorthodox and low pressure. The sales were out of his lots, and were made to customers, though these customers sought him out rather than having been pursued.

In addition, we think the sales were ordinary in the course of this business. The concept of normalcy requires for its application a chronology and a history to determine if the sales of lots to customers were the usual or a departure from the norm. History and chronology here combine to demonstrate that Winthrop did not sell his lots as an abnormal or unexpected event. He began selling shortly after he acquired the land; he never used the land for any other purpose; and he continued this course of conduct over a number of years. Thus, the sales were not only ordinary, they were the sole object of Winthrop's business. It is this singleness of purpose which distinguishes Winthrop's sales from those in *Barrios' Estate*, *supra*, *Consolidated Naval Stores*, *supra*, *Ross*, *supra*, and *Goldberg*, *supra*, all relied on by the taxpayer. It is true, as the taxpayer asserts, that in each of these cases there was considerable sales activity. However, in each the property had been used for some other purpose and the sales ensued only when this primary purpose was abandoned. Here there was no change of purpose.

Winthrop's subdividing was not adventitious, but on the contrary was consistently advertent. While Winthrop probably would not have qualified as the salesman of the year in any of the years in controversy in Tallahassee and its environs, the sales were routine and ordinary, not a result of an abandoned activity on the land. Sale was the prime purpose of the holding and the sales were made in the ordinary course of the taxpayer's business. We conclude, therefore, that the taxpayer is not entitled to capital gains treatment on the profit made from the sales of land during the years 1959 through 1963. The judgment of the district court is … [r]eversed.

Gudgel v. Commissioner

United States Court of Appeals, Sixth Circuit
273 F.2d 206 (1959)

FACTS

In 1940, long prior to the tax years, the petitioners acquired 17 1/2 acres of land in Jefferson County, Kentucky, on which they built a house, barn and silo, and proceeded to operate thereon a dairy farm. The acreage not so used was devoted to pasture. In 1943, they acquired 19 1/2 additional adjoining acres, which they fenced in 1944 for pasture and hay. Later in that year, the State of Kentucky extended Ralph Avenue through their property, dividing it approximately into halves. In 1945, the petitioners purchased an additional 14.7 acres, adjoining the land previously acquired, and leased other adjoining land for grazing and hay production. In 1948, or 1949, the petitioners received an offer from someone by the name of Fey who wished to construct a house upon part of their land and, at his solicitation, sold him five lots abutting on the south side of Ralph Avenue, as extended. Later in 1949, petitioners placed an advertisement in a Louisville newspaper, offering lots for sale and about a dozen crude signs were put upon the fence line bearing the inscription "Lots". Still later, they sold three additional lots abutting on the south side of Ralph Avenue. In 1950, the petitioners sold five lots abutting on the north side of Ralph Avenue and one additional lot abutting on the south side of Ralph Avenue. In that same year, they opened up Likens Avenue into the remaining portion of their land south of Ralph Avenue, dedicating the roadway to public use, after having the abutting land surveyed and subdivided into residential building lots. Two of these lots were sold in 1950. In that year, they acquired a tract of land located 1200 feet from the subdivided property, on which they constructed a small shopping center.

In 1951, the first tax year, the petitioners sold thirteen lots on Likens Avenue and one on the north side of Ralph Avenue. In 1952, they opened Gudgel Road into that part of the property north of Ralph Avenue, dedicated it to public use and had the abutting land surveyed and subdivided into residential building lots. That year, they sold one tract abutting on the south side of Ralph Avenue and ten lots abutting on Gudgel Road. In 1952, the second tax year, the Illinois Central Railway Company approached the petitioners with an offer to purchase 5.72 acres of land for use as a right-of-way across the farm. Gudgel testified, without contradiction, that the Railroad wanted to buy just enough to lay the track which would require about a third of an acre. He insisted that they buy the whole tract but after some talk about putting a viaduct underneath the railroad, so he could get to the west side of his farm, the Railroad said it would be impossible, but 'if I would stake off the land west of there—west of the railroad—they would take the remaining property that I had left over to correspond with my property plan." The petitioners then sold the Railroad the 5.72 acres of land. Since the railroad ran at right angles to Ralph Avenue, it divided the farm into four irregular sections.

When in 1944, Ralph Avenue was continued to accommodate the traffic from Rubber Town, it wasn't, at first, too big a problem crossing the road. When they started running three and four shifts, working twenty-four hours a day, the traffic was terrific. It would take three or four men to move the cattle and "the people just had no respect whatever for my livestock." It was then that the petitioners started to dispose of their farm. Asked what effect the sale to the railroad had, the response was, "Well, it just put me out of business." In the three tax years, a total of forty eight lots were sold. While they opened the roads for access by the purchasers, they made the very minimum of improvements. They installed no water lines and the purchasers dug their own individual wells. After the vendees started to build, they themselves arranged for connection with the electric light company. The area was zoned for heavy industry and factories moved into the neighborhood. The lot owners began fighting the smoke from Rubber Town. In selling to prospective homeowners, the petitioners took what they could get as a down payment, with installments sometimes of $20.00 per month. Neither Gudgel nor his wife had ever been in the real estate business, they had no real estate license, they bought no land prior to 1941, and bought none subsequent to the tax years. Their reason for letting a real estate man sell some of the lots was that he owed them money and the lots were to be sold on the understanding that the commissions would be applied upon his indebtedness. They had sold the real estate agent four lots upon which the agent built houses, just to get rid of them because the land was getting stale and was going "sour". Gudgel placed one advertisement of "Lots For Sale" in a newspaper and the crude signs placed on the fence line had the single designation, "Lots".

ANALYSIS

Section 117(a) of the Internal Revenue Code of 1939, 26 U.S.C. § 117(a), defines "capital assets" as property held by the taxpayer (whether or not connected with his trade or business), but does not include the taxpayer's stock in trade or other property of a kind which would properly be included in the inventory of the taxpayer, if on hand at the close of the taxable year, or "property held by the taxpayer primarily for sale to customers in the ordinary course of his trade or business."

The principal issue is whether, during the tax years 1951, 1952 and 1953, the Gudgel farm land had been held by the petitioners primarily for sale to customers, in the ordinary course of trade or business. Gudgel's attack upon the Tax Court's decision rests primarily on his assertion that he was forced to liquidate his farm and his activities were directed only to that end. The Government urges that this contention is a factual rather than a legal attack upon the Court's finding, resting upon three asserted premises: 1) That the area around the farm was zoned for heavy industry, 2) that the State in 1944 extended Ralph Avenue across the farm, and 3) that the Illinois Central Railroad in 1952 continued its right-of-way across the farm so as to divide it into quarters and that these three events made it impossible for Gudgel to continue the operation of his dairy farm.

The Tax Court reasoned that no one of these factors had any material bearing upon Gudgel's asserted desire to liquidate the farm. It is, however, common experience that where the character of a neighborhood undergoes substantial change, it is usually the result not of an isolated circumstance but derives from cumulative changes that affect the desirability of land for the purpose for which it was originally purchased. Gudgel's complaint is not primarily the extension of Ralph Avenue but from the greatly increased use of it due to the zoning of the area for factory purposes, which made it difficult for him to move his stock and, so, made uneconomical the carrying on of his farm activities. The building of a railroad track across his farm was the climax of his troubles in operating the farm. The totality of interference with his dairy activities provides an eminently reasonable ground for finally concluding that he could not economically operate his farm as a dairy, and called for its liquidation.

The Tax Court's ultimate finding that Gudgel was engaged in the real estate business during the tax years is based primarily upon the undisputed fact that Gudgel sold during the tax years forty eight lots, opened streets to furnish access to purchasers, and reaped a profit of more than $51,000 on farm land he purchased between 1940 and 1945, and began subdividing it by an isolated sale in 1948 or 1949.

This brings us to a consideration of the scope of our power of review in tax litigation. By Title 26 U.S.C. §7482, the United States Courts of Appeals were given exclusive jurisdiction to review decisions of the Tax Court " ... in the same manner and to the same extent as decisions of the district courts in civil actions tried without a jury". This is substantially an application of the old equity rule and is the subject matter of Rule 52(a) of the Federal Rules of Civil Procedure, 28 U.S.C., which recites that "findings of fact shall not be set aside unless clearly erroneous, and due regard shall be given to the opportunity of the trial court to judge of the credibility of the witnesses." There has been a difference of opinion as to whether the reason for the rule conditions its application. The courts have almost invariably, in applying the rule, cited the reason for its existence, and absent the reason; that is, where there is conflicting evidence, it requires a judgment as to the good faith, truthfulness and candor of witnesses. It is felt, however, in many cases, that the Court of Appeals is as well qualified as the District Judge, or the Tax Court, to draw inferences and conclusions from undisputed facts without subjecting them to the test of the "clearly erroneous" rule.

* * *

If we are right in our appraisal of the scope of review, where there are no disputed evidentiary facts, it becomes necessary to determine whether the lots sold during the tax years by the petitioners constituted property held by the taxpayers primarily for sale to customers in the ordinary course of the petitioners' trade or business; in other words, whether they had put themselves in the category of real estate dealers by the nature and extent of their transactions. The response of the taxpayers is that it became uneconomical to use the farm as a dairy and that they had embarked upon an orderly course of liquidation of their farm property. It was pointed out in *Consolidated Naval Stores Co. v. Fahs*, 227 F.2d 923, 926 (5th Cir. 1955), that there are usually factors casting weight upon each side of the question and in many instances the issue becomes a close one and no single fact will be decisive in the usual case. The Tenth Circuit, and perhaps others, have undertaken a catalogue of the circumstances to be considered, which included the purpose for which property was acquired, the activity of the taxpayer and his agents with respect thereto, the making of improvements to the property, conducting a sales campaign, the frequency and continuity of sales, as well as other factors reasonably tending to show that the transactions were in furtherance of liquidation or in the course of the taxpayers' occupation or business.

We see no occasion to enlarge upon this catalogue. The purpose of the petitioners in acquiring the land for a dairy farm is not in dispute. It was conceded in argument that if they had sold the farm as a single unit their profits must have been classed as capital gains. Their first sale was at the solicitation of the purchaser. It clearly did not put the taxpayers into the real estate business. Five years were to elapse without further transactions, clearly indicating the desire to use the property as a farm. When they did subdivide and began the sale of lots, their purpose was similar to that of the taxpayer in *Barrios' Estate v. Comm'r*, 265 F.2d 517 (5th Cir. 1959), who found his 165 acres unsuitable for farming and thereupon proceeded to subdivide and sell residential lots. The decision was that the taxpayers' purpose was to liquidate a capital asset. The minimum improvements that the taxpayers put upon the property, in providing access to the purchasers of lots, was merely an attempt to dispose of their holdings advantageously in an orderly, business-like manner. *Riedel v. Comm'r*, 261 F.2d 371 (5th Cir. 1958); *Home Co. v. Comm'r*, 212 F. 2d 637, 639 (10th. Cir. 1954); *Yunker v. Comm'r, supra.*

The respondent draws the distinction between the instant case and *Yunker* because Yunker attempted to sell the entire tract and was reluctant to subdivide. It is not a valid distinction, in the light of *Barrios' Estate v. Comm'r, supra; Smith v. Dunn*, 224 F.2d 353 (5th Cir. 1955); *Camp v. Murray*, 226 F.2d 931 (4th. Cir. 1955). The point made by the respondent that the non-farm income greatly exceeded their farm income during the tax years would seem to emphasize the fact that their activities in dairying subjected them to disturbing interruptions by the changing character of the area. It is not, therefore, a controlling factor. It must be noted that they acquired no additional land for the purpose of subdividing. Their purchase of the site for a shopping center near the farm is as consonant with the purpose of liquidation as it would be to entering upon a real estate business and there is no evidence that the market site was sold or offered for sale. The sale of forty eight lots over a period of three years did not put the petitioners in the real estate business, in view of the cases that have permitted capital gains treatment. *Berberovich v. Menninger*, 147 F.Supp. 890 (D.C. E.D. Mich. 1957); *Barrios' Estate v. Comm'r, supra; Smith v. Dunn, supra; Camp v. Murray, supra.* *Dillon v. Comm'r*, 213 F.2d 218 (8th. Cir. 1954), involved twenty sales in one year and *Smith v. Dunn* dealt with the sale of fifty one lots in two years. Indeed, the Court's finding of facts concedes that the total number of sales involved may be comparatively small but that alone is not conclusive. Taking it all in all, we conclude that the Court was in error in assuming that these dairy farmers, by their activities, had placed themselves in the real estate business during the tax years.

* * *

HOLDING

Reversed and remanded to the Tax Court with instructions to permit the profits on the sale of the land herein involved to be given the status of capital gains.

Grodt & McKay Realty, Inc. v. Commissioner

United States Tax Court

77 T.C. 1221 (1981)

FACTS

Respondent determined the following deficiencies in petitioners' income taxes:

Petitioner	Docket No.	Year	Deficiency
Grodt & McKay Realty, Inc	16210-79	1976	$6,885.24
		1977	13,567.83
Davis Equipment Corp	4852-80	1976	3,171.43
		1977	4,464.49

The issues for decision are:

(1) Whether transactions in which petitioners purportedly purchased cattle were bona fide sales or sham transactions;

(2) In the alternative, whether petitioners' cattle-breeding activities were activities engaged in for profit;

(3) In the alternative (a) whether nonrecourse purchase-money notes used to purchase the cattle were so contingent as to (1) prohibit their inclusion in petitioners' bases for depreciation and investment tax credit purposes, and (2) prohibit deductions for interest payments thereon; and (b) whether petitioners are entitled to deduct management fees in excess of the amounts allowed by respondent.

Some of the facts have been stipulated and are found accordingly.

Grodt & McKay Realty, Inc. (Grodt & McKay), and Davis Equipment Corp. (Davis Equipment) each had its principal place of business in Des Moines, Iowa, when it filed its petition. Both Grodt & McKay and Davis Equipment keep their books and file their income tax returns using the accrual method of accounting and the calendar year. During all relevant times, both corporations were taxed as regular corporations.

Grodt & McKay is an Iowa corporation primarily engaged in the sale of real estate. During 1976, Paul O. Grodt was the president and sole shareholder of Grodt & McKay. During 1977, Grodt owned 80 percent of Grodt & McKay's outstanding stock, and the remaining 20 percent was owned by a trust established by Grodt for the benefit of his heirs.

Davis Equipment is an Iowa corporation primarily engaged in the retail sales and servicing of fertilizer application equipment. During all relevant times, Roger L. Davis was the president and sole shareholder of Davis Equipment.

On December 8, 1976, T.R. Land & Cattle Co., Inc. (Cattle Co.), issued a private placement memorandum describing a private offering of an investment opportunity in a cattle-breeding program. The memorandum detailed Cattle Co.'s intention to establish a large-scale cattle-breeding program by selling 35 "units" of cattle at $30,000 per unit, with each unit consisting of five breeding cows. Cattle Co. proposed to retain all management responsibility for the cattle,[33] and it offered to finance up to $28,500 of the purchase price with a promissory note payable out of the profits from the cattle-breeding operations. A "Sales Agreement," a "Management Agreement," a "Promissory Note," and a "Security Agreement" made up the basic instruments embodying the arrangement between purchasers and Cattle Co.[34]

On December 9, 1976, Grodt & McKay executed documents pursuant to which it purchased[35] two units of cattle in Cattle Co.'s program for $30,000 per unit. On December 11, 1976, Davis Equipment purchased one unit of cattle for $30,000.

Under the provisions of the sales agreements, petitioners' units of breeding cattle[36] consisted of five purebred Angus cows (the basic herd). Cattle Co. agreed to promptly replace any nonbreeder[37] in the basic herd with a cow of comparable quality.

Grodt & McKay's purchase price of $60,000 was payable as follows: $2,000 cash on execution of the sales agreements and the balance ($58,000) in the form of a nonrecourse promissory note. Davis Equipment agreed to pay $1,500 cash on execution of the sales agreement and the balance of the $30,000 purchase price ($28,500) in the form of a nonrecourse promissory note. Petitioners remained liable on the promissory notes whether or not Cattle Co. performed under the management agreement.

Pursuant to the sales agreements, Cattle Co. agreed that it would, whenever possible, artificially inseminate each cow in the basic herd with semen from a quality bull that would hopefully improve the calf crop of the basic herds. The sales agreements contained the following warranties and guaranties, and the following provisions regarding early termination of the management agreements:

2. The animals in the Basic Herd are represented and warranted to be breeders capable of being registered with the Black Angus Association. The Herd will remain reg-

---

33. [2] The memorandum specifically states that Cattle Co.'s management services are optional. However, the management services were considered an integral element of the arrangement between Cattle Co. and purchasers of the units, and the memorandum and the proposed agreements fully contemplate that the management services will be part of the overall undertaking.

34. [3] The specifics of the cattle-breeding program as explained in the memorandum (including the sample documents attached thereto) are materially different from some of the provisions of the program found in the actual documents executed by petitioners. For this reason, the text of our findings of fact will rely on the actual documents executed.

35. [4] Use of such terms as "purchase," "sale," "own," "petitioners' herds," "interest," "principal," "price," "downpayment" and "management fee," should not be construed as carrying any conclusion as to the legal effect of the documents or transactions involved.

36. [5] The sales agreements contain no definition of "breeding cattle." The memorandum, on the other hand, states that "Each animal in the basic herd will be between 1 and 12 years of age at the time of sale and will be mature for breeding." Black Angus heifers generally reach breeding age between 18 and 20 months.

37. [6] The sales agreements define a nonbreeder as a cow or heifer which does not become pregnant after six consecutive breeding attempts or within 6 months of the date of the sales agreement, whichever occurs first. An agreement to replace a nonbreeder is standard practice in the industry.

istered with the Black Angus Association under the name of the Seller or its nominee for the benefit of the Buyer.[38]

* * *

9. Seller [Cattle Co.] agrees that, commencing with the fiscal year (January 1 to December 31) starting on the first January 1 to follow the execution of this Agreement, if for any reason whatsoever, the Basic Herd shall have less than an 80% annual live calf birth rate and if such deficiency shall not have been offset by calves born from the date of entry into a Program in excess of the 80% minimum for that year, then Seller shall promptly transfer to Buyer and add to Buyer's Herd a sufficient number of animals of a quality comparable to the progeny of other Basic Herds managed by Seller to the extent necessary to make up such net deficiency. The animals so transferred to make up any deficiency shall be approximately 50% heifer calves and 50% bull calves.

10. Seller agrees to forthwith replace any animal in the Basic Herd which shall, prior to its tenth (10th) birthday, die or be lost by theft or disappearance. The aforesaid obligation to substitute animals shall apply not only to the animals in the Basic Herd but also to any animal substituted therefor in accordance herewith. All substitutions shall be of comparable quality to the animal for which they are substituted.

11. In the event Buyer desires to remove his or its Herd from Seller's care and management, Buyer agrees to release Seller of all obligations under the Sales Agreement and Management Agreement. Seller agrees to release the Herd on the terms set forth below. Seller agrees that upon written notice from the Buyer to remove his or its Herd from Seller's management together with full payment of the Purchase Price (Note and accrued interest, where applicable), payment of 50% of the Progeny or Herd value determined as set forth below and payment of Management Agreement fees prorated to the date of Herd removal, Seller shall arrange, within 30 days, for the Herd to be prepared for shipment and delivery. If the Program is terminated within 30 days of the date of entry therein, no management fees will be paid by the Herd Owner. Buyer will pay all costs of preparation and shipment. If Buyer exercises his or its right under this Section, Seller agrees to reduce the Purchase Price and/or the outstanding principal balance of the Note, if applicable, in the following manner:

   (a) If Buyer takes delivery of the Herd in 1977, such reduction shall equal Twenty Thousand Dollars ($20,000.00).

---

38. [7] The American Angus Association issues registration certificates for purebred Angus cattle and records such certificates in the American Aberdeen-Angus Herd Book. These certificates contain information on the registered cow, including its name and registration number, the name of its record owner, and provisions for subsequent transfer of its registration on the records of the American Angus Association. The registration certificates for the purebred cattle designated as part of petitioners' basic herds all indicate Cattle Co. as the record owner. All of the registration certificates for the purebred progeny of the basic herds list Cattle Co. as the first owner and do not reflect any subsequent owners. None of the certificates indicate that Cattle Co. held title in a fiduciary or other capacity for the benefit of petitioners.

(b) If Buyer takes delivery of the Herd in 1978, such reduction shall equal Fifteen Thousand Dollars ($15,000.00).

(c) If Buyer takes delivery of the Herd in 1979, such reduction shall equal Seven Thousand Five Hundred Dollars ($7,500.00).

In the event Buyer terminates this Agreement during the first three calendar years of a Program, he will be required to pay the Company [Cattle Co.] 50% of the Progeny value as additional management fees. Thereafter, the Buyer will be required to pay the Company 50% of the Herd value as additional management fees. Both values will be determined by an independent third party selected by the Company. In the event that both this and the Management Agreement are terminated within 30 days of their execution, all sums paid by the Herd Owner will be refunded.

The Company will defend one test case at its own expense if its cattle breeding programs are challenged by the IRS. If such case is lost and if a Herd Owner thus loses his tax benefits the Company will, if the Herd Owner so elects, buy the Herd from the Herd Owner. That is, the Company will refund any principal or interest payments, or management fees (all of which shall be net of tax savings from which the Herd Owner has benefited, based on the assumption he is in a 50% tax bracket). In exchange therefor the Herd Owner will transfer his entire Herd to the Company, and the Sales Agreement, Management Agreement and Note will be mutually terminated. If the Herd Owner elects to thus resell his Herd he may recapture certain depreciation and investment credit deductions. (See "Recapture" above). The ability of the Company to buy back the Herd will be dependent on its financial viability. (See "Risk Factors-1. Financial Condition of the Company.")[39]

Finally, each sales agreement provides that it, the management agreement, the security agreement, and the promissory note constitute the entire understanding between petitioners and Cattle Co. and cannot be amended or terminated, orally, and shall be interpreted under the law of Iowa.

The promissory notes executed by petitioners call for the payment to Cattle Co. of $58,000 by Grodt & McKay and $28,500 by Davis Equipment, together with interest at the rate of 7 percent per annum. The promissory note executed by Davis Equipment provided for the payment of principal and interest as follows:

WITH RESPECT TO PRINCIPAL

* * *

An amount equal to seventy-five percent (75%) of the total net proceeds (gross sales less commissions, sales costs and brokerage fees), resulting from the sale or other income derived from the animals in the Maker's Herd (as

---

39. [8] These last two paragraphs were taken directly from the memorandum. Whether the references to portions of the memorandum incorporate them in the sales agreements is not an issue in this case.

such term is defined in the certain Sales Agreement and Management Agreement between the Maker and the Company) in accordance with the Sales Agreement and Management Agreement will be applied first towards the payment of interest and then toward the reduction of principal until the principal balance of this Note has been paid in full.

The Maker has no personal liability of any kind whatsoever for the principal amount referred to above and in the event of default in payment of the amount, the Company will look only to the collateral (as that term is defined in the Security Agreement) and the Maker will have no personal liability for any deficiency.[40]

WITH RESPECT TO INTEREST:

The Maker will pay a total of $3,990 in 24 equal monthly interest payments commencing one year from the date of this Promissory Note. All other interest will be paid to the Company from the remainder, after payment of management fees in accordance with the Management Agreement, of the Maker's share of the proceeds realized from the sale or other income derived from the animals in the Maker's Herd. In the event such proceeds shall be insufficient to pay such accumulated interest, any deficiency will be carried forward and charged against the remainder of the Maker's share of the proceeds realized from future sales. Interest will be paid by the Maker in an amount sufficient to cover the estimated interest payable as of the end of the calendar year in which cattle income is realized. [Fn. ref. omitted.]

The Maker has no personal liability of any kind whatsoever for the interest payments referred to above and in the event of a default in the payment of such interest the Company will look only to the collateral (as that term is defined in the Security Agreement) and the Maker has no personal liability for any deficiency in interest payments.

WITH RESPECT TO PRINCIPAL AND INTEREST:

Any unpaid balance of principal and interest will be due twenty (20) years from the date hereof.

Grodt & McKay executed an identical promissory note for $58,000 except for the first sentence of the first paragraph under the "With Respect to Interest" section, which provided:

The Maker will pay $2,030.00 commencing six months after January 1 of the year following the date of this Promissory Note; and every six months there-

---

40. [9] The memorandum specifically states that the notes will be recourse and the herd owner will be personally liable for the entire unpaid balance thereof upon maturity. It may be that the notes were made nonrecourse for petitioners because they were corporations, and, during 1976, corporations such as petitioners were not subject to the at-risk provisions of § 465. Testimony in this case also indicates that, in 1978, Davis Equipment and Cattle Co. amended Davis Equipment's note to conform with changes made to § 465.

after until four interest payments of like amount have been received by holder of the note.

The security agreements provide for assignments from petitioners to Cattle Co. of their interests in their herds to secure petitioners' payment and performance of all obligations to Cattle Co. required under the sales agreements, the promissory notes, and the management agreements.

The final agreements rounding out Cattle Co.'s planned cattle-breeding program were management agreements. In these agreements, Cattle Co. agreed to "breed, care for, manage, feed, transport and provide whatever is necessary, including, without limitation, medical services and facilities to the" herds. Cattle Co. also agreed to cull the herds periodically, and to sell most breeding cows by their 10th birthday. The management agreement also provided the following guaranty regarding the live-calf birth rate of cows in Cattle Co.'s charge:

> 5. The Company agrees that, commencing with the fiscal year (January 1 to December 31) starting on the first January 1 to follow the signing of this Agreement, if for any reason whatsoever the Breeding Herd shall have less than an 80% annual live calf birth rate and if such deficiency shall not have been offset by calves born from the date of entry into a Program in excess of the 80% minimum for all previous fiscal years, then the Company shall promptly transfer to Owner and add to Owner's Herd a sufficient number of animals comparable to the progeny of other herds managed by the Company necessary to make up such net deficiency. The animals so transferred to make up any deficiency shall be approximately 50% heifer calves and 50% bull calves. Progeny in excess of 80% shall be retained by the Company.

> 6. Beginning with the 1977 calf crop (i.e. calves born during the fiscal year commencing January 1, 1977), the Company may retain from each fiscal year's calf crop sufficient heifer calves to be ultimately added as replacements to the Breeding Herd. The Breeding Herd will consist of not less than five animals at all times, except during liquidation.

The management agreements, like the sales agreements, recite that Cattle Co. will artificially inseminate the cows in the breeding herds at no additional cost to petitioners.

Petitioners agreed to pay Cattle Co. $3,000 per year per unit for its services during the first 3 years the management agreements are in effect. After that time, and until the interest and principal due under the promissory notes is paid, Cattle Co. is to receive as management fees an amount equal to "25 percent of all net proceeds (gross sales price less commissions, sales costs and brokerage fees) derived from" petitioners' herds. The remaining 75 percent of the net proceeds is to be applied against the outstanding interest and principal due on the notes. Once all interest and principal is paid, Cattle Co. is to receive as management fees 75 percent of all net proceeds from petitioners' herds, and petitioners will receive 25 percent of the net proceeds.

Under the management agreements, Cattle Co. has full control over all sales of animals for which full payment is received in less than 24 months. On sales extending credit for 24 months or more, Cattle Co. must obtain petitioners' consent, which consent cannot be unreasonably withheld. Cattle Co. has the obligation to transmit semiannual accounting reports to petitioners and semiannual reports providing the following information regarding each animal in petitioners' herds: ear tattoo and ear tag numbers, name, sex, date of birth, registration number, breeding, calving, and progeny information. Cattle Co. further agreed to keep extensive herd records at their offices which would be available to petitioners. These records were to include Black Angus registration certificates on all herd animals, sales and breeding information, and other records related to the cattle-breeding program.

Other pertinent provisions of the management agreements provided:

14. The Company agrees to forthwith replace any animal in the Breeding Herd which shall, prior to its tenth (10th) birthday, die or be lost by theft or disappearance. All substitutions shall be of comparable quality for the animal for which they are substituted.

15. Subject to the express provisions contained herein and as long as either this Agreement is in effect or the Note remains unpaid, the Company shall have full control of the matters set forth in Section 7 hereof [relating to the sale of animals and prices therefor, the retention of progeny, the incorporation of progeny in the breeding program, and the selling, culling or replacing of animals in the herd] and the location, maintenance, expansion, breeding and culling of the Herd which constitutes the collateral security for such Note. The Company will also retain the right to determine the most opportune time for sales from the Herd and the right to make such sales. Upon any default by the Company pursuant to the provisions of Section 19 below [relating to federal bankruptcy and reorganization, assignment for the benefit of creditors, and voluntary receivership, liquidation or reorganization under state law] and the termination of this Agreement pursuant thereto, or upon payment of the Note in full, Owner shall have the right to enter into any management agreement with respect to the Herd which Owner, in his sole judgment or discretion, may decide.

16. Either the Company or the Owner shall have the option to cause the liquidation of the Herd by giving written notice to the other at any time after the unpaid principal balance due on the Note has been reduced to $13,125 or less; provided, however, that the Company shall have such option to cause the liquidation of the Herd at any time before the principal balance of the Note has been reduced to $13,125 provided that the net proceeds of such liquidation shall at least equal three times the then remaining principal balance due on the note.

17. This Agreement shall terminate when the liquidation of the Herd has been completed and all net proceeds therefrom have been distributed as provided herein; provided, however, that the Company shall have the option to sooner terminate this Agreement by giving written notice to Owner at any time after

the Note has been paid in full or after failure to cure any default in the payment thereof within 30 days after written notice of such default. The Company also has the right to terminate this Agreement upon Owner's default in payment of the management fees provided for in Section 8 hereof.

18. In the event of termination by the Company, the Company will give the Owner notice of such termination and the Owner will then have 10 days to advise the Company of his or its desire that the Company not liquidate the Herd. The Owner must then, at his or its own expense and within 30 days of the date of the Company's notice, remove his or its Herd and pay the Company the percentage of the Herd value as determined in accordance with Section 11 of the Sales Agreement, together with any unpaid management fees and unpaid principal and interest due on the Note calculated to the date of payment or, in the event a Note is not executed, payment in full of the purchase price and interest to date.

19. In the event the Company shall file a voluntary petition in bankruptcy, whether federal or state, or petition for any form of reorganization under the Bankruptcy Act of the United States or of any state, or make an assignment for the benefit of creditors, or voluntarily submit to any procedure for receivership, liquidation or reorganization under state law, or be the subject of an involuntary petition of bankruptcy which is not discharged within 90 days after being filed, Owner shall have the option to (1) remove the Herd from the Company's care, possession and control, and all further obligations of Owner to the Company under this Management Agreement shall promptly terminate or (2) in full satisfaction of all of his remaining obligations to the Company, he may assign all of his right, title and interest in the cattle to the Company.[41]

The memorandum also included an extensive explanation of expected tax consequences concluding, but not guaranteeing, that an investor qualified for an investment credit and depreciation on the herd using a basis of $30,000. In addition, the memorandum indicated that investors could deduct the management fees and interest expenses, and that the profits realized from the sale of cattle would be taxed as capital gains (subject to the recapture provisions of section 1245). The memorandum advised potential investors that substantial expenses in excess of income were expected in the early years of the investment and that they should be prepared to retain their herds for at least 10 to 15 years. The memorandum further notified petitioners that Cattle Co. might enter into sales transactions with its officers and principals. Finally, the memorandum, as well as several of the agreements, warned investors that the offerings were not registered and that Federal and State securities regulations prohibited the transfer of an investor's rights unless registered or unless an exemption was available.[42]

---

41. [11] In addition to the agreements already described, both petitioners also executed subscription agreements on Dec. 9, 1976, in which they acknowledged that they had either a net worth of at least $50,000 and taxable income subject to an income tax rate of at least 40 percent, or a net worth of at least $100,000.

42. [12] The memorandum indicated that the expected cost of each cow in each investor's herd was between $1,000 and $1,500, that the value of the warranties which went with the cows was $15,000,

Cattle Co. was incorporated on December 30, 1976,[43] and has its principal place of business in Des Moines, Iowa. Alfred T. Zimmerman is a director, chairman of the board, vice president, and secretary-treasurer of Cattle Co. John R. Hunter is a director and president of Cattle Co.[44] As of December 30, 1976, Zimmerman and Hunter each owned 50 percent of the outstanding stock of Cattle Co.[45] Hunter transferred approximately 50 Angus and Maine Anjou *commercial* cattle to Cattle Co. as his capital contribution. Cattle Co.'s unaudited balance sheet dated December 30, 1976, lists the following:

BALANCE SHEET

Assets		
Cash		$2,000
Cattle (approximate market value)		50,000
Total assets		52,000
Liabilities and equity		
Liabilities		0
Capital stock—	Shares outstanding	Amount
Issued for cash	10	$1
Issued for cattle	190	19
Additional paid-in capital	51,980	52,000
Total liabilities and equity		52,000[46]

and that a portion of the balance represented profit to Cattle Co. The memorandum also describes the purchase price to investors as including the "raising, breeding and maintaining the animals prior to sale, investigation and inspection of cattle in order to obtain quality animals, sales commissions, transportation and insurance for purchased animals, veterinarian fees, costs of this offering, financing expenses, overhead charges for supervisory and management staffs and recordation of registration fees of animals with the appropriate breeding associations."

43. [13] Cattle Co.'s incorporation on Dec. 30, 1976, directly conflicts with representations made in the memorandum and agreements implying that Cattle Co. was already in existence on Dec. 8, 1976—the date of the memorandum. In addition, both petitioners believed that Cattle Co. existed at the time they executed the documents described above.

44. [14] Both Grodt and Davis knew Zimmerman prior to their transactions with Cattle Co. Grodt has known Zimmerman for roughly 25 years and they are associates in Centurion Financial Management, an apparently unrelated business. Zimmerman had been an adviser to Davis on pension and profit-sharing plans. Grodt also knew Hunter personally and professionally prior to his investment with Cattle Co. There were, however, no familial or significant personal relationships between petitioners' principals and Cattle Co.'s principals.

45. [15] The record contains no evidence concerning the stock ownership of Cattle Co. subsequent to the date of its incorporation.

46. [16] There is no explanation of how the contributed cattle was valued, whether the 50 head of cattle contributed by Hunter constituted the total number of cows contributed, or who paid the initial $2,000 to Cattle Co.

Grodt & McKay's check for $2,000 and Davis Equipment's check for $1,500 as their downpayments on the units were dated December 30, 1976. Cattle Co. owned no *purebred* Angus cows on either December 9 or 11, 1976 (the dates petitioners executed the agreements), or December 30, 1976 (the date on petitioners' checks for the downpayments). Cattle Co. deposited petitioners' checks in its account on January 4, 1977.

On February 3, 1977, Cattle Co. purchased nine purebred Angus heifers and one bull for $5,600 (an average price of $560 per head). On February 9, 1977, Cattle Co. purchased four purebred Angus heifers for $1,820 (an average price of $455 per head). And on March 18, 1977, Cattle Co. purchased one heifer and one cow (both purebred) from Hunter for $1,235.

Cattle Co.'s records indicate that the nine cows purchased on February 3, 1977, were originally designated as part of the Grodt & McKay basic herd. At some later time, Cattle Co. changed this designation so that only six of the cows purchased on February 3, 1977, were part of the Grodt & McKay basic herd. Cattle Co. then designated three of the cows purchased on February 9, 1977, as part of the Grodt & McKay basic herd. The 10th cow designated as part of the Grodt & McKay basic herd was born on April 9, 1977, and was not a registered purebred. Of the cattle eventually designated as the Grodt & McKay basic herd, only five were of breeding age when purchased by Cattle Co. in February 1977, four became of breeding age during 1977, and one became of breeding age in 1978.

In 1977, three female calves and one male calf were born to the Grodt & McKay basic herd, of which the three females were purebreds. In 1978, three female calves and five male calves were born to the Grodt & McKay basic herd, of which all of the females and one of the males were purebreds. In 1979, five male calves and one female calf were born to the Grodt & McKay basic herd, none of which were purebreds. In 1979, there were also two female calves born to the Grodt & McKay herd, exclusive of the basic herd, both of which were purebreds. In May or June 1980, one of the cows in the Grodt & McKay basic herd died, but it had not been replaced by the time of the trial in this case (October 1980). One of the cows in the Grodt & McKay basic herd has never borne a calf.

Cattle Co.'s records indicate that three of the cattle purchased on February 3, 1977, and originally designated as part of the Grodt & McKay basic herd were eventually designated as part of the Davis Equipment basic herd. One of the cattle purchased on February 9, 1977, and one of the cows purchased from Hunter on March 18, 1977, were designated as the remainder of the Davis Equipment basic herd. None of the cattle designated as the Davis Equipment basic herd were of breeding age when purchased by Cattle Co. in February and March 1977.

There were no calves born to the Davis Equipment basic herd in 1977. In 1978, three female calves were born to the Davis Equipment basic herd, two of which were purebreds.[47] In 1979, three female calves and one male calf were born to the Davis Equipment basic herd, two of which were purebreds.

---

47. [17] One of these purebred calves was transferred to the Grodt & McKay herd.

The cattle comprising petitioners' herds had an average value as of January 1, 1977, of less than $600 per head. The average sales price for purebred Black Angus cows between October 1, 1975, and September 30, 1976, was $537; between October 1, 1976, and September 30, 1977, it was $542; between October 1, 1977, and September 30, 1978, it was $703; and between October 1, 1978, and September 30, 1979, it was $1,096.

Petitioners made the following payments to Cattle Co. under the terms of the agreements:

Payment	Grodt & McKay	Davis Equipment
Downpayment	$2,000	$1,500
Management fees		
1977	$6,000	$3,000
1978	$6,000	$3,000
1979	$6,000	$3,000
Interest		
1977	$4,060	$1,995
1978	$4,060	$1,995
Total	$28,120	$14,490

Cattle Co. issued various reports (in the form of letters from Zimmerman to petitioners) purporting to comply with its obligations under the management agreements. These reports were inaccurate, inconsistent from one year to the next, and varied from the information found in Cattle Co.'s books and records. Neither petitioner sufficiently examined these reports to determine whether Cattle Co. was complying with its warranties. At the time of trial, petitioners' herds were no better than average *commercial* herds. Over the years Cattle Co. has sold some cattle from each petitioner's herd, but it did not submit records from these sales to petitioners as required by the agreements. The net profits from these sales have been used to reduce petitioners' indebtedness to Cattle Co.

When petitioners entered the agreements with Cattle Co., they were both fully aware that Cattle Co.'s cost of the cows to be placed in their herds would be significantly less than the $6,000-per-head price they were paying. Petitioners attributed the difference to Cattle Co.'s warranties and management services. Both petitioners were in financial positions to seek investment opportunities, but they failed to establish that they had any reasonable purpose for entering into the cattle-breeding activities other than the tax benefits they anticipated.

Petitioners did not supervise their investments with Cattle Co. in a prudent business manner. Neither petitioner has requested that Cattle Co. make any transfers to its herd to meet the requirements of the various warranties, and there is no evidence that any such transfers (other than the transfer mentioned in note 17 *supra*) have been made. Grodt saw the herd record sheets, but he did not check to see whether any of the cows in the Grodt & McKay basic herd were nonbreeders. In addition,

Grodt did not know that one of the cows in the Grodt & McKay basic herd was not a purebred and that one was not born until April 7, 1977. Davis, on the other hand, never physically inspected the Davis Equipment herd until the spring of 1978. Davis has never inspected the herd record sheets and has never seen complete records of the sales from the Davis Equipment herd.

During 1977 and 1978, Hunter managed petitioners' herds. In 1979 and 1980, Cattle Co. contracted with Dennis Ory on an annual basis to feed and care for all of the cattle in petitioners' herds. Ory does the recordkeeping, furnishes labor, selects cattle for Cattle Co., manages the breeding, and pays for all direct maintenance expense of the cattle such as feed and veterinarian costs. Ory was compensated for these services in the amount of $250 per head in 1979, and $260 per head in 1980. Cattle Co. paid for semen and the certificate attesting to the donor-bull's quality whenever cattle were artificially inseminated. Such semen costs, including certification, were between $100 and $150 per insemination. Cattle Co. also furnished some of the necessary summer pasture land.

On its 1976 Federal income tax return, Grodt & McKay claimed a $786.68 investment tax credit based on its purchase of the two units of cattle for $60,000. On its 1977 income tax return, Grodt & McKay took deductions for depreciation of $7,500, management fees of $6,000, and interest of $4,060, all attributable to its herd of cattle. Davis Equipment claimed a depreciation deduction of $357.14 on its 1976 tax return, based on its herd of cattle. On its 1977 tax return, Davis Equipment claimed deductions for depreciation of $4,286, management fees of $3,000, interest of $1,995, and fees to the Angus Association of $20, all attributable to its herd of cattle.[48]

Respondent disallowed all of petitioners' investment tax credits and depreciation deductions on the primary basis that the benefits and burdens of ownership of the cattle had not been transferred to petitioners. Alternatively, respondent determined that petitioners were not entitled to the depreciation deductions because they had failed to establish that they used the cattle in a trade or business or in the production of income, or that the cattle-breeding activity was entered into for profit. As a second alternative, respondent limited petitioners' depreciation deductions to amounts calculated using a fair market value for the cattle of $800 per head.

Respondent disallowed petitioners' management fees deduction on the primary ground that petitioners did not establish that the fees were ordinary and necessary expenses incurred in business or for the production of income, or that they were incurred in connection with an activity entered into for profit. Alternatively, respondent determined that the management fees should be limited to a reasonable amount — $500 per head per year for Grodt & McKay's herd, and $250 per head per year for Davis Equipment's herd.

---

48. [18] In his notice of deficiency, respondent made adjustments in Davis Equipment's claimed investment tax credit. It is not clear, however, whether any part of the adjustments is attributable to an investment tax credit claimed on the cattle. To the extent that it is, our decision regarding Grodt & McKay's investment tax credit also applies to Davis Equipment.

Respondent disallowed petitioners' interest expense deductions on the primary ground that it had not been shown that the assets purchased had a fair market value equal to or exceeding the face amount of the note. Alternatively, respondent disallowed the interest deductions on the ground that the note was not a bona fide indebtedness.

Finally, respondent disallowed Davis Equipment's $20 Angus Association fee because it was not an ordinary and necessary business expense.

* * *

ANALYSIS

The first issue for decision is whether petitioners' transactions with Cattle Co. were bona fide arm's-length sales for Federal income tax purposes, or whether they lacked the commercial, legal, and economic substance of sales. Respondent contends that the transactions were shams devoid of commercial, legal, and economic substance. Petitioners, on the other hand, assert that the transactions were bona fide cattle sales and should be treated accordingly. We agree with respondent that the transactions do not have the economic substance of sales.

A taxpayer's use of a device to form an illusion of reality and thereby create or inflate tax benefits is not a novel problem. It is well settled that the economic substance of transactions, rather than their form, governs for tax purposes. *Gregory v. Helvering*, 293 U.S. 465 (1935). Recently, in *Frank Lyon Co. v. U.s.*, 435 U.S. 561 (1978), the Supreme Court summarized the principles underlying this doctrine:

> This Court, almost 50 years ago, observed that "taxation is not so much concerned with the refinements of title as it is with actual command over the property taxed — the actual benefit for which the tax is paid." *Corliss v. Bowers*, 281 U.S. 376, 378 (1930). In a number of cases, the Court has refused to permit the transfer of formal legal title to shift the incidence of taxation attributable to ownership of property where the transferor continues to retain significant control over the property transferred. E.g., *Comm'r v. Sunnen*, 333 U.S. 591 (1948); *Helvering v. Clifford*, 309 U.S. 331 (1940). In applying this doctrine of substance over form, the Court has looked to the objective economic realities of a transaction rather than to the particular form the parties employed. The Court has never regarded "the simple expedient of drawing up papers," *Comm'r v. Tower*, 327 U.S. 280, 291 (1946), as controlling for tax purposes when the objective economic realities are to the contrary. "In the field of taxation, administrators of the laws and the courts are concerned with substance and realities, and formal written documents are not rigidly binding." *Helvering v. Lazarus & Co.*, 308 U.S., at 255. *See also Comm'r v. P. G. Lake, Inc.*, 356 U.S. 260, 266–267 (1958); *Comm'r v. Court Holding Co.*, 324 U.S. 331, 334 (1945). Nor is the parties' desire to achieve a particular tax result necessarily relevant. *Comm'r v. Duberstein*, 363 U.S. 278, 286 (1960).

However, under the circumstances in *Frank Lyon Co.*, the Supreme Court found that the substance of the challenged transactions were as structured, noting that where—

> [T]here is a genuine multiple-party transaction with economic substance which is compelled or encouraged by business or regulatory realities, is imbued with tax-independent considerations, and is not shaped solely by tax-avoidance features that have meaningless labels attached, the Government should honor the allocation of rights and duties effectuated by the parties.

Bearing these fundamental precepts in mind, we now must examine the transactions before us to determine whether they amount to sales of cattle.

The term "sale" is given its ordinary meaning for Federal income tax purposes and is generally defined as a transfer of property for money or a promise to pay money. *Comm'r v. Brown*, 380 U.S. 563, 570–571 (1965). The key to deciding whether petitioners' transactions with Cattle Co. are sales is to determine whether the benefits and burdens of ownership have passed from Cattle Co. to petitioners. This is a question of fact which must be ascertained from the intention of the parties as evidenced by the written agreements read in light of the attending facts and circumstances. *Haggard v. Comm'r*, 24 T.C. 1124, 1129 (1955), *affd.* 241 F.2d 288 (9th Cir. 1956).[49] Some of the factors which have been considered by courts in making this determination are: (1) Whether legal title passes (*Comm'r v. Segall*, 114 F.2d 706, 709 (6th Cir. 1940), *cert. denied* 313 U.S. 562 (1941); *Oesterreich v. Comm'r*, 226 F.2d 798, 802 (9th Cir. 1955)); (2) how the parties treat the transaction (*Oesterreich v. Comm'r*, *supra* at 803); (3) whether an equity was acquired in the property (*Haggard v. Comm'r*, 241 F.2d 288, 289 (9th Cir. 1956); *Oesterreich v. Comm'r*, *supra* at 803; *see Mathews v. Comm'r*, 61 T.C. 12, 21–23 (1973), *revd.* 520 F.2d 323 (5th Cir. 1975), *cert. denied* 424 U.S. 967 (1976)); (4) whether the contract creates a present obligation on the seller to execute and deliver a deed and a present obligation on the purchaser to make payments (*Wiseman v. Scruggs*, 281 F.2d 900, 902 (10th Cir. 1960)); (5) whether the right of possession is vested in the purchaser (*Wiseman v. Scruggs*, *supra* at 902; *Comm'r v. Segall*, *supra* at 709); (6) which party pays the property taxes (*Harmston v. Comm'r*, 61 T.C. 216, 229 (1973), *affd.* 528 F.2d 55 (9th Cir. 1976)); (7) which party bears the risk of loss or damage to the property (*Harmston v. Comm'r*, *supra* at 230); and (8) which party receives the profits from the operation and sale of the property (*Harmston v. Comm'r*, *supra* at 230). *See generally Estate of Franklin v. Comm'r*, 64 T.C. 752 (1975), *affd. on other grounds* 544 F.2d 1045 (9th Cir. 1976). Using the above criteria as guideposts, we conclude that Cattle Co. did not sell the cattle to petitioners.

Unfortunately, the record in the present case is inadequate to determine whether petitioners or Cattle Co. held legal title to the cattle in petitioners' herds. The evidence does establish, however, that petitioners allowed Cattle Co. to represent itself as record owner of the cattle in their herds with the American Angus Association, even though

---

49. [19] *See also* Midwest Metal Stamping Co. v. Comm'r, T.C. Memo. 1965-279.

the sales agreements call for the registration of the cows in the name of Cattle Co. *for the benefit of petitioners*. In fairness, it should be noted that the herd record sheets maintained by Cattle Co. do list petitioners as the owners of the cattle in their herds. The record does not disclose, however, whether the registration certificates are readily available to the public or relied on in the industry as a means of ascertaining legal ownership. Under the terms of the agreements, petitioners had the right to inspect Cattle Co.'s records and the registration certificates (which were kept as a part of Cattle Co.'s records). Although Grodt inspected the records on behalf of Grodt & McKay, he apparently made no demand on Cattle Co. to correct the registration certificates to show that Cattle Co. held title for the benefit of Grodt & McKay. Davis, on the other hand, did not even bother to inspect the records for Davis Equipment. We find that petitioners treated Cattle Co. as the record owner and consented to its representation of that status to third parties.

Petitioners did not acquire any equity in the cattle either at the time they purportedly purchased the cattle, or subsequently when Cattle Co. actually acquired the cattle finally designated as part of petitioners' basic herds. Petitioners ostensibly paid $6,000 per head for cows they knew were worth far less and which we find had a fair market value not in excess of $600 per head. Petitioners explained that they were purchasing far more than just the cows. They contend that they were also purchasing warranties and guaranties which went along with the cows, the expertise and assistance of Cattle Co. in their cattle-breeding endeavors, and the various management services rendered by Cattle Co. Petitioners introduced extensive evidence from purported experts to urge the conclusion that the fair market value of each cow in light of these additional considerations was approximately equal to the ostensible purchase price of $6,000 per head. We found this evidence and petitioners' explanation unsatisfactory.

Petitioners maintain that in determining a fair market value for the cattle we cannot look at the various agreements in isolation, but rather must view them in total as constituting the entire purchase. We agree with petitioners that any analysis of the transactions in this case must consider all of the agreements together. When we do so, petitioners' cause is hardly advanced.

Based on the actual prices paid by Cattle Co. for the cows in petitioners' herds, and on the average sales prices of similar cows during the period when Cattle Co. made these purchases, we have found that the fair market value of the cattle was $600 per head. In addition, since the standard practice in the industry when selling breeding cattle is to include a nonbreeder warranty, that warranty adds nothing to the established fair market value of petitioners' cattle. In the same fashion, the warranty that the cows are purebreds does not add any value to the cattle since the average prices relied upon were also for purebred cattle.

To the extent petitioners contend that the fair market value of the cattle should include the costs of management services, artificial insemination, and insurance against all risks of death or other loss of the cows, we cannot agree. These expenses are the period expenses of maintaining, using, and protecting the cattle. Under the circumstances of this case, there is no reason to include the cost of these items as a component of the cost of the cattle.[50]

There remains for consideration only the 80-percent live calf birth rate warranty.[51] We need not here decide whether a warranty of this type is a proper component of cost, since this warranty, plus the initial $600 fair market value for each cow, does not begin to equal $6,000.

On the evidence introduced in this case, it is very difficult to determine whether the 80-percent live calf birth rate warranty had any substantial value. Respondent introduced evidence tending to establish that an 80-percent live calf birth rate is the industry average, whereas petitioners introduced evidence that the average is only 70 percent. Rather than rely on questionable evidence from both sides to determine what the industry average actually is, we will assume the industry average is 70 percent. Petitioners bear the burden of proving that, based on an industry average of 70 percent, the value per cow of the 80-percent live calf birth rate is equal to $5,400 ($6,000 less $600). Petitioners made numerous calculations attempting to establish this, but these calculations were not persuasive.[52] We therefore hold that this warranty had only minimal value.

Petitioners have failed to establish that the fair market value of the cattle was at least approximately equal to the purchase price. Since a normal attribute of a true arm's-length sale is a purchase price at least approximately equal to fair market value, the totally disproportionate purchase price in this instance strongly militates against

---

50. [20] Assuming the transactions should be treated as structured by petitioners, these types of costs are more properly characterized as management expenses which were more than amply paid for under the management agreements. Moreover, if petitioners did view the $6,000 price per cow as including these costs, it was incumbent on petitioners to establish what portion of the price is so allocable to these items. Petitioners made no attempt to make an allocation.

51. [21] Our analysis here will not focus on the fact that Cattle Co. failed to live up to most of its warranties and promises. Rather, we find that at the time petitioners executed the agreements, they reasonably expected Cattle Co. to meet its obligations.

52. [22] The agreements, themselves, provide Cattle Co. with a convenient method of greatly reducing, if not entirely eliminating, any risks it has under the 80-percent live calf birth rate warranty. The warranty covers all cows in the breeding herds. A heifer born into the herds is not considered a part of the breeding herds until she reaches the age of 24 months. However, an Angus heifer reaches breeding age between 18 and 20 months. Thus, Cattle Co. has between 4 and 6 months to attempt to breed the heifer before that heifer is covered by the warranty. If it is apparent to Cattle Co. that the heifer will not breed, or has a low tendency to breed, Cattle Co. can cull the heifer from the herd before it joins the breeding herds and thus reduce its present and future obligations under the warranty. Cattle Co. has the unfettered discretion to cull the herds periodically. If a cow which is part of the breeding herds fails to become impregnated, there is only one limitation on Cattle Co.'s ability to cull that cow from the breeding herds, namely, that each breeding herd never consist of fewer than five animals. Thus, Cattle Co.'s promise, albeit on the surface a somewhat valuable warranty, is worth little. Even if Cattle Co.'s ability to cull cows from the herds is subject to an implied reasonableness standard, it is difficult to imagine how the culling of a nonbreeder from breeding herds of cattle is anything but reasonable.

petitioners' contention that a true sale has taken place. *Estate of Franklin v. Comm'r*, 544 F.2d 1045 (9th Cir. 1976), *affg. on different grounds* 64 T.C. 752 (1976).[53]

Additionally, the agreements are clear that petitioners have no right to possess the cattle or to exercise any real control or dominion over them. Cattle Co. has complete control over the sale of animals, the sales price,[54] retention of progeny, the incorporation of progeny into the breeding herds, the culling and replacing of herd animals, and the location, maintenance, expansion, and breeding (including artificial insemination) of the herds. Petitioners' only rights with respect to the possession, control, or dominion of the herds are extremely limited and, as a practical matter, valueless.

Petitioners have the right to terminate the management agreements on 30 days' notice, to cause the liquidation of the herds when the note balances are $13,125 or less, and, under certain circumstances,[55] to remove their herds from Cattle Co.'s "care, possession and control" or to assign all their interests in the cattle back to Cattle Co. To acquire actual possession of the cattle, however, petitioners must fully pay off their notes and they must release Cattle Co. from all obligations under the agreements. Petitioners must also pay additional management fees equal to one-half the value of their progeny or the herds. If, however, petitioners exercise the right to take possession of their cattle during 1977, 1978, or 1979, the purchase price is reduced $20,000, $15,000, or $7,500 per unit, respectively.

These provisions, while ostensibly giving petitioners rights to the possession, control, and dominion over their cattle, are mere facades without any substance. For example, during 1977 each petitioner could obtain possession of each unit of cattle by paying $10,000, less the downpayment, and by agreeing to release Cattle Co. from all of its obligations. Assuming the cattle did not have any progeny at the time petitioners exercised this right, they would be paying a total of $10,000 for cattle with a maximum fair market value of $3,000 ($600 for each of five cows). A purported right to possession, control, and dominion, when burdened by a cumbersome cost which no reasonable person would pay is a hollow right indeed.[56] A true sale for tax purposes must provide the purchaser with more.

---

53. [23] In *Narver v. Comm'r*, 75 T.C. 53, 98 (1980), on appeal (9th Cir., Jan. 15, 1981), we adopted the analysis of Estate of Franklin v. Comm'r, 544 F.2d 1045, *affg. on different grounds* 64 T.C. 752 (1975).

54. [24] The one exception to this is that Cattle Co. must obtain petitioners' consents for any sales for which it is extending credit for 24 months or more. Petitioners' consents, however, may not be unreasonably withheld.

55. [25] E.g., Cattle Co.'s liquidation, bankruptcy, receivership, etc.

56. [26] This situation continues at least until the value of petitioners' herds are equal to twice the outstanding balances on their notes—a point in time almost entirely controlled by Cattle Co. because it has full control over sales and sales prices. Once this point is reached, it is to the advantage of Cattle Co.'s principals to liquidate the herd by having Cattle Co. sell it to themselves. Since this will produce no possessory interest in petitioners, it is highly unlikely that the notes will be paid off prior to a decision by Cattle Co. to liquidate the herds.

Continuing our analysis, we find that under the terms of the agreements, Cattle Co. assumed all of these risks with respect to the cattle in petitioners' herds. Petitioners' risks in this regard are only that Cattle Co. might not make good on its promises to assume these risks. This is not the risk normally associated with ownership for tax purposes.

Finally, we must examine the allocation of the profits from sales. Here, Cattle Co. and petitioners have used labels to create the appearance that petitioners are receiving a benefit from the net profits from sales of cattle. In fact, until the amount of net proceeds from each petitioner's herd is equal to 133 percent[57] of the amount of each petitioner's promissory note plus interest, 100 percent of the profits go to Cattle Co. These funds are labeled as management fees and principal and interest payments on the promissory notes. The labels, however, are not controlling. Only after the principal amount of the note is retired will petitioners ever receive any cash, and even then they will be entitled to only 25 percent of the net proceeds. This is merely a not very realistic chance to acquire a profits interest in the future if the value of the herds greatly increases. We conclude that this allocation of speculative future profits is inadequate to support a sale for Federal tax purposes.

In short, when the various agreements are probed beneath their labels and are considered in the context of the surrounding facts and circumstances, it strains credulity and offends logic to find that a true sale, to be recognized for tax purposes, had taken place. We must conclude the contrary.

The next question for decision is how should the transactions be treated for Federal income tax purposes. Respondent maintains that since the transactions are not sales it follows, ipso facto, that the transactions are shams having no economic, legal, or commercial effect and should be disregarded for Federal tax purposes.[58] While we disagree with respondent's premise that any transaction which purports to be a sale, but which is not, is necessarily a sham (*see Estate of Franklin v. Comm'r*, 64 T.C. 752 (1975), *affd. on different grounds* 544 F.2d 1045 (9th Cir. 1976) (purported sales were not sales but options)),[59] we do find that under the circumstances of this case the transactions between petitioners and Cattle Co. should be entirely disregarded for tax purposes.

The courts have, in appropriate circumstances, disregarded for Federal tax purposes transactions entered into without any economic, commercial, or legal purpose other than the hoped-for favorable tax consequences flowing therefrom. *Knetsch v. U.S.*, 364 U.S. 361 (1960); *Gregory v. Helvering*, 293 U.S. 465 (1935); *Estate of Franklin v.*

---

57. [28] Since the net proceeds from sales will be allocated one-quarter to management fees and three-quarters to principal, plus interest, sales must produce 133 percent of the total principal, plus interest, to retire the note.

58. [29] Some support for this result can be found in the language of *Narver v. Comm'r, supra*, and the Ninth Circuit's opinion in *Estate of Franklin v. Comm'r, supra*. See *Hager v. Comm'r*, 76 T.C. 759, 775 n. 8 (1981).

59. [30] *See also* 1 B. Bittker, Federal Taxation of Income, Estates and Gifts, par. 4.4, at 4–56 (1981).

Comm'r, supra; Goldstein v. Comm'r, 364 F.2d 734 (2d Cir. 1966), *cert. denied* 385 U.S. 1005 (1967); *Diggs v. Comm'r,* 281 F.2d 326 (2d Cir. 1960), *cert. denied* 364 U.S. 908 (1960); *Derr v. Comm'r,* 77 T.C. 707 (1981); *Hager v. Comm'r,* 76 T.C. 759 (1981); *Narver v. Comm'r,* 75 T.C. 53 (1980), *on appeal* (9th Cir., Jan. 15, 1981); *Beck v. Comm'r,* 74 T.C. 1534 (1980); *Milbrew v. Comm'r,* T.C. Memo. 1981-610.[60] While we do not here propose to draw precise lines of demarcation between valid and invalid tax shelters, the facts of this case are so far over the line that it is appropriate to disregard the transactions for tax purposes.

Analysis of the transactions involved reveals only attempted tax benefits, not any realistic possibility of economic reward. The agreements make clear that none of the profits from the cattle-breeding activities will actually flow to petitioners until such time as the principal amounts of the notes are paid in full. Prior to this time, if the transactions are treated as structured and given the tax consequences explained in the memorandum and anticipated by petitioners, the only benefits petitioners can expect from the transactions are tax benefits. Petitioners hoped to be entitled to investment tax credits and depreciation deductions based on a cost of $30,000 per unit. They also hoped to deduct the amounts designated as management fees and interest which were paid during the first 3 years to Cattle Co. During the time prior to complete payment of the note, they hoped that the net proceeds from sales of cattle would be taxed as capital gains.

This tax treatment is not basically different from the tax benefits which might be available under valid tax shelter arrangements (e.g., depreciable real estate). Favorable tax consequences alone are no reason to ignore transactions for tax purposes. However, where there is no substance to the transactions aside from the hoped-for tax consequences, a different question is presented.

Grodt and Davis gave extensive testimony regarding their alleged profit motives for executing the agreements. They contend they sought the profits which might arise from a successful cattle-breeding activity, and they relied entirely on Cattle Company and its officers to carry on the venture. Petitioners also testified that they anticipated that the notes would be paid in full. Despite the testimony of Grodt and Davis, we do not believe petitioners ever expected any economic gain from the cattle-breeding activities.

While investors may leave the conduct of business to others, the behavior of Grodt and Davis in this instance is indicative of the lack of business substance to this transaction. Both Grodt and Davis were experienced businessmen. Yet, neither ever carefully reviewed any of Cattle Co.'s books and records or the "reports" sent to them by Cattle Co. Neither sought to have Cattle Co. meet its obligations under the agreements. In sum, petitioners appeared completely indifferent to the success or failure of the venture.

Petitioners have also not convinced us that the notes will ever be fully retired. On brief, petitioners made elaborate calculations of increases in the value of their herds.

---

60. [31] These cases represent merely a sampling of the enormous number of cases in which courts have concluded that the facts do not support the tax consequences requested by taxpayers.

These calculations, however, were unpersuasive. Moreover, under the terms of the agreements, themselves, there is little realistic hope that the notes will ever be fully paid prior to a decision by Cattle Co. to liquidate the herd. Any liquidation of the herd prior to the time the values of the herds are equal to twice the outstanding balance of the notes will give 100 percent of the proceeds to Cattle Co. After that, Cattle Co. will have to share any proceeds with petitioners until theoretically petitioners reach a maximum share of 25 percent. However, the memorandum specifically warned petitioners that Cattle Co. might enter into sales transactions with its officers (Zimmerman and Hunter). Thus, if the cattle-breeding activity were successful, Cattle Co. could liquidate the herds by selling them to Zimmerman and Hunter when the value of the cattle exceeded twice the outstanding balance of the notes.[61] If, as should be expected, the liquidations take the shape of a sale to Cattle Co.'s principals, they will effectively eliminate any prospect for profit to petitioners and maximize the profits to Cattle Co. and its principals. In light of this very real probability, petitioners, who were experienced businessmen, could not have harbored any serious expectation of profit.

HOLDING

In summary, we hold that, under the factual circumstances of this case, where petitioners have gone to great lengths to clothe in "sales" garb transactions which are not sales, and where petitioners' only real expectations of profit rest on the hoped-for tax benefits, the transactions do not have sufficient substance apart from tax manipulation to be recognized for tax purposes.

Buono v. Commissioner

United States Tax Court
74 T.C. 187 (1980)

FACTS

* * *

In 1973, a corporation known as the Marlboro Improvement Corp. (referred to hereinafter as Marlboro Improvement) sold some real property which gave rise to recognizable gain. During 1973, each of the male petitioners were shareholders of Marlboro Improvement, a corporation which had elected to be treated as a small business corporation under subchapter S of the Internal Revenue Code. Each shareholder reported his aliquot share of the net proceeds from the sale on his 1973 tax return as gain from the sale of a capital asset.

In 1967, petitioner Henry Traphagen learned that a neighbor, Kenneth V. Hayes, was interested in selling a large tract of farmland. With the exception of a 1-acre portion

---

61. [32] While Cattle Co. is somewhat restricted in its power to liquidate before the notes are reduced to $13,125, the company's power to control the culling of the herd and sale of the cattle does not present it with any inseparable obstacle to the shift of any gains to itself and its owners and away from its purported investor.

which was to be retained for a personal residence, Hayes wanted to dispose of the entire tract as he had recently retired from farming. The property was located in the township of Marlboro, Monmouth County, N.J. (referred to hereinafter as Marlboro or the town), about a half mile from Traphagen's residence, and consisted of approximately 130 acres.

Traphagen believed that acquisition of this property would present a good opportunity for financial gain. Up until that time, there had been minimal residential development in Marlboro because many residents wanted to preserve the town's rural atmosphere. Traphagen felt that a significant market for the sale of residential property had resulted from the town's antidevelopment climate. For example, he was aware that Monmouth Heights, a successful residential development having over 300 homes, had been built approximately one-third of a mile from Hayes's tract.

Traphagen also realized that property which had been approved for subdivision was significantly higher in value than raw land. In this context, approval of a subdivision plan means that the local municipality has authorized the respective sizes for each building lot within a tract as well as the layout for streets, sewers, sidewalks, and any commercial areas. As a consequence, developers of residential housing are generally willing to pay a premium for land which has already obtained subdivision approval.

At the time, the zoning ordinance of Marlboro Township provided for 4 0/30 or three-quarter-acre zoning. Under this ordinance, 40 single-family residences could be built per 30 acres of land. In other words, each building lot was required to contain three-quarters of an acre of land. During the negotiations with Hayes, Traphagen informally approached the Marlboro Planning Board to ascertain whether an application for subdivision approval pursuant to the 4 0/30 zoning ordinance would encounter any difficulty. Members of the planning board informed Traphagen that he would not have any problems in processing an application under the current zoning ordinance.

Hayes and Traphagen agreed to a purchase price of $2,200 an acre. After this final price was negotiated, Traphagen contacted a longtime friend, petitioner John Fiorino, and asked him if he would be interested in jointly purchasing Hayes's property as Traphagen felt that the transaction was too large to handle alone. Fiorino agreed to join Traphagen in this venture.

A contract for purchase of the property was executed on December 11, 1967, with both Traphagen and Fiorino as parties thereto. The total net purchase price was $270,600. Hayes received $20,000 on the signing of the contract with an additional $30,000 due on April 30, 1968. The balance of the purchase price was to be financed by a purchase-money mortgage held by Hayes. No principal payments were due until 4 years after the closing date. Interest on the mortgage was set at 6 percent and due quarterly.

Soon after the purchase contract was executed, Fiorino and Traphagen sought other investors to join them. Both realized that the transaction, with all of its attendant financial burdens, was too large for them to manage by themselves. The additional people who entered into the transaction comprise the remaining petitioners in this case. All were personal friends of either Fiorino or Traphagen (or both).

The petitioners agreed that a corporation would be formed to hold the property with each petitioner being entitled to a percentage interest commensurate with his respective capital contribution. Accordingly, Marlboro Improvement was formed on June 19, 1968, under the laws of New Jersey with Traphagen, Fiorino, and petitioner Francis A. Miller listed as the incorporators.

* * *

In addition, Marlboro Improvement elected to be taxed as a small business corporation under the provisions of subchapter S, subtitle A, of the Internal Revenue Code.

On June 19, 1968, Hayes transferred the property to Marlboro Improvement by deed. The final purchase price was $286,374. As the corporation was credited with a $50,000 downpayment, the amount of the purchase-money mortgage was $236,374.

The petitioners, generally, were in agreement that the property would be held for about 1 1/2 years. They intended to sell the entire tract intact as there were no plans to develop the property and dispose of it in separate lots. However, as it was apparent that an approved subdivision plan would significantly enhance the property's marketability and value, soon after the property was acquired, Marlboro Improvement undertook the preliminary steps needed to process a subdivision application.

In connection with its subdivision application, Marlboro Improvement was required to submit a plan setting forth the boundaries of the respective lots as well as the street plans for the tract. Marlboro Improvement retained engineers to draft a map (or sketch plat) showing the division of land into the respective lots, the street layout, and the proposed location of water and sewer lines. In order to prepare the map, the engineers took numerous topographical surveys of the land.

On December 3, 1968, Marlboro Improvement applied to the Marlboro Planning Board for a classification of its proposed subdivision. The details of the subdivision were set forth on the sketch plat it submitted with its application. On December 23, 1968, the application was classified as a "major" subdivision (since the property would eventually be developed residentially).

The subdivision plan which was submitted to the planning board proposed a division of the entire tract, with the exception of a 15-acre portion, into three-quarter-acre residential lots. The 15-acre portion was reserved for a shopping center, since that portion of the tract had already been zoned commercially under the town's zoning ordinance.[62]

* * *

The final workshop meeting occurred sometime in the early part of July 1969, about 1 week before Marlboro's application for preliminary approval was to be formally heard. At this meeting, the planning board informally agreed to approve Marlboro's subdivision. Consequently, Traphagen and the other petitioners anticipated that the

---

62. [6] Mr. Hayes was able to farm this land since he was paying taxes to maintain an agricultural assessment.

planning board would automatically vote in favor of approving Marlboro Improvement's subdivision plan at the formal application hearing.

The next week at the regular planning board meeting, the expectations for routine approval were not realized. The planning board proposed a resolution that the township of Marlboro amend its zoning ordinance to provide for 2-acre residential zoning for the entire town. Pursuant to this proposed amendment, every residential lot would have to consist of a minimum of 2 acres. The planning board failed to act on Marlboro Improvement's application and deferred consideration thereon until its next regular meeting.

On or about July 14, 1969, the Marlboro Township Council abided by the planning board's proposal and adopted an ordinance, effective August 18, 1969, changing the town's residential zoning requirements to 2 acres.

After the amendment was passed, the planning board conducted its next meeting. The corporation's subdivision application was routinely denied since it no longer conformed with the town's zoning requirements.

* * *

Submission of a conforming subdivision plan was not, however, viewed as a viable alternative since a residential tract with larger lot sizes was not considered readily salable. Petitioners felt that they had no option other than to seek legal redress for their grievances. As a result, litigation ensued between Marlboro Improvement and the town over the zoning amendment. Finally, in April of 1972, Marlboro Improvement and the town agreed to a settlement. Pursuant to this settlement (as evidenced by a consent judgment), Marlboro Improvement was granted the right to file and obtain approval for a subdivision plan based on half-acre zoning (the town had recently amended its zoning ordinance in contemplation of the settlement). Every building lot was required to consist of at least one-half acre. In addition, Marlboro Improvement agreed to dedicate 70 acres to the town; a 15-acre portion of the tract was to retain its commercial zoning.

Marlboro Improvement subsequently applied to the Marlboro Planning Board for approval of its revised sketch plat. The subdivision map consisted of 79 half-acre residential lots, a 15-acre area for future development as a shopping center, and a 70.6-acre residual area to be dedicated to the town. The subdivision application was given final approval on November 9, 1972, in a resolution by the Marlboro Township Council.

The portion of the property which had been subdivided into 79 half-acre lots was sold to Fairfield Manor, Inc. (Fairfield). Fairfield, a development company, had learned that Marlboro Improvement was in the process of making its revised subdivision application. A Fairfield developer had spoken to Mrs. Traphagen one day while paying a water bill and she informed him about the property which Marlboro Improvement held.

A contract to sell the property to Fairfield was executed on November 3, 1972. The 79-lot tract was deeded to Fairfield on January 25, 1973, for a total purchase price of $513,500.

The 130-acre tract acquired from Hayes in 1968 is the only property Marlboro Improvement has ever owned. With respect to the 79-lot portion sold to Fairfield, the corporation did not engage in any advertising, solicitation, sales promotion, or other marketing techniques. The only other realty transactions which Marlboro Improvement had any involvement with were a condemnation by the State of New Jersey of a 2 1/2-acre portion and the subsequent sale of the remaining 15-acre shopping center lot.

During this same approximate time period, the corporation was involved in negotiations over a condemnation award. The State of New Jersey had condemned 2 1/2 acres of the tract in order that a new State highway, Route 18, could be constructed. The proposed highway cut through the lower portion of the tract and would isolate about 5 acres. Eventually, in 1972, the State of New Jersey paid Marlboro Improvement $29,000 for the 2 1/2 acres it condemned.[63]

The 15-acre lot had originally been zoned commercially for future development as a shopping center. After the sale to Fairfield, this was the only land Marlboro Improvement held. The town, however, had second thoughts about permitting the development of the 15-acre lot into a shopping center. As a result, Marlboro Improvement applied for a zoning variance on June 15, 1976. The planning board, on November 3, 1976, approved the application by Marlboro Improvement for a zoning variance and allowed it to obtain residential zoning for the 15 acres. That portion was subsequently subdivided into 30 residential lots and sold.

During the period from the acquisition of Hayes's property until the eventual sale to Fairfield, Marlboro Improvement incurred various expenses totaling over $100,000. In addition to the engineering fees, there was a $3,000 fee incurred in connection with the subdivision application. A major portion of the expenses Marlboro Improvement paid was attributable to interest and local taxes, which petitioner Ben Roberts, Marlboro Improvement's accountant, estimated at $5,000 per quarter during the period Marlboro Improvement held the property.

During the period from acquisition until sale, the value of raw land in the vicinity of Marlboro Township increased at a rate of 5 to 10 percent per year.

The petitioners in this case have varying backgrounds, with some of them having previously engaged in real estate activities. Traphagen, between 1967 and 1973, was employed for over 30 years as a tool and die maker.

* * *

Prior to his residence in Marlboro, Traphagen lived in Matawan Township.... his familiarity with zoning procedures was derived from his service as a member of the Matawan Planning Board. At one time, he was involved in selling residences and he still maintains a salesman's license. However, the last commission he derived from selling a home was approximately 10 years ago in 1970.

---

63. [8] Most of this award was paid to Hayes since Marlboro Improvement was in arrears on its first principal payment ($25,000).

John Fiorino is a licensed real estate and insurance broker and an appraiser of residential land. He is the owner of Van's Agency, a real estate agency where Traphagen was once employed for a short time. The business premises of Van's Agency were used for conducting Marlboro Improvement's affairs.

* * *

Francis Miller is an industrial real estate broker involved in the sale and leasing of factories, warehouses, office space, and industrial land.... Miller was a partner with Fiorino in Van's Agency. Most of their business involved the resale of residential homes in Matawan, N.J. Miller left Van's Agency in 1969. He never had any previous involvement in a residential real estate venture.

Ben Roberts is a certified public accountant who learned of this venture from Traphagen. He was treasurer of Marlboro Improvement and was responsible for the corporation's books and records, including its tax returns.

George V. Buono is a school principal and has been so employed since 1961. He first learned of Hayes's tract from Fiorino.

Thomas F. Kane is in the securities business. Miller first informed him of the property. He sold his interest in the corporation after the property was sold to Fiorino and Traphagen in 1973.

With the exception of Traphagen and Fiorino, all of the petitioners were passive investors in the transaction. Each contributed their proportionate initial capital outlay and made such additional contributions as were necessary. Traphagen and Fiorino were actively involved in Marlboro Improvement's affairs, particularly with respect to obtaining subdivision approval and the lawsuit with the town. As a consequence, after the sale to Fairfield, the corporation voted them $25,675 for services they rendered on its behalf.

ANALYSIS

This Court has previously held that "there is nothing unique or improper about a corporation engaging in exclusively investment activity," including under this rubric a subchapter S corporation. *Howell v. Comm'r*, 57 T.C. 546, 553 (1972). We make this observation at the outset, notwithstanding the fact that neither party has argued the point or indeed even brought the Howell case to the attention of the Court, because it has been black letter law ever since *Moline Properties, Inc. v. Comm'r*, 319 U.S. 436 (1943), that a corporation is, almost by definition, an entity engaged in "business activity." Without Howell, one might have erroneously assumed that a corporation's inherent nature foreclosed any further inquiry into the question before us.

* * *

We found as a fact in Howell that the corporation "at no time subdivided the tract," notwithstanding the fact that the corporation sold off three separate parcels. This is apparently permissible in Georgia although it would not be in New Jersey, where the tract sub judice is located. N.J. Stat. Ann. §§. 40:55-1.2, 40:55-1.18, 40:55-1.23 (West

1967) (repealed 1975; current version at §§. 40:55D-37, 40:55D-54, 40:55D-55 (West Supp. 1979)).[64]

In the case before us, petitioners are, in effect, asking us to go one step beyond Howell, where the corporation remained an investor vis-a-vis dealer when it merely disposed, in a single sale, of most of its empty land. We are here asked to confirm capital gains treatment to Marlboro Improvement where it disposed, in a single sale, of most of its empty land, but only after obtaining subdivision approval for half-acre building lots.

Respondent's first argument for denying capital gain treatment is based on the contention that the property Marlboro Improvement sold to Fairfield was "property held by the taxpayer primarily for sale to customers in the ordinary course of (its) trade or business." (§ 1221(1).) In this regard, respondent asserts that the corporation was in the business of packaging a product, i.e., subdivided property, for sale to builders of residential homes. According to the respondent, the gain from the sale of this "package" is primarily due to the activities which Marlboro Improvement undertook in obtaining approval of its subdivision application and not to market appreciation accruing over a substantial period of time. In such a case, respondent maintains that any gains must be treated as ordinary income since the policies underlying the capital gain provisions are lacking.[65]

Petitioners, on the other hand, argue that the Hayes's tract was acquired and has consistently been held solely for investment purposes and that Marlboro Improvement was never in the business of selling real estate. Petitioners urge that ordinary income treatment should not result since the property was merely subdivided (i.e., approved by the township of Marlboro to be sold in separate lots) and sold intact. Given the presence of only a single conveyance, petitioners claim that Marlboro Improvement's activities lack sufficient continuity and frequency to constitute a trade or business under § 1221(1). In other words, merely obtaining approval for a subdivision plan cannot, in the case of an isolated sale of a single piece of land, constitute a business which a subsequent sale would be in the ordinary course thereof.

Many courts, including this one, have relied on a group of certain key factors to determine whether property is excluded from the § 1221 capital asset definition. Although we are mindful that specific factors or their combination are not necessarily controlling, resort to these classic factors provides us at least with a starting point for

---

64. [11] In other words, it would have been necessary for Marlboro Improvement, the subch. S corporation in the case before us, to have obtained some subdivision approval before doing what the Howell subch. S corporation did.

65. [12] *See, e.g., Malat v. Riddell,* 383 U.S. 569, 572 (1966), where the Supreme Court commented about § 1221(1) as follows: "The purpose of the statutory provision with which we deal is to differentiate between the 'profits and losses arising from everyday operation of a business' on the one hand (*Corn Products Refining Co. v. Comm'r,* 350 U.S. 46, 52), and 'the realization of appreciation in value accrued over a substantial period of time' on the other. (*Comm'r v. Gillette Motor Transport, Inc.,* 364 U.S. 130, 134.)"

our analysis.[66] For example, in determining whether property is held primarily for sale to customers in the ordinary course of business, the following factors have been considered: The nature and purpose of the acquisition of the property and the duration of the ownership; the extent and nature of the taxpayer's efforts to sell the property; the number, extent, continuity, and substantiality of the sales; the extent of subdividing, developing, and advertising to increase sales; the use of a business office for the sale of the property; the character and degree of supervision or control exercised by the taxpayer over the representative selling the property; and the time and effort the taxpayer habitually devoted to the sale. *U.S. v. Winthrop*, 417 F.2d 905, 910 (5th Cir. 1969); *Kaltreider v. Comm'r*, 255 F.2d 833 (3d Cir. 1958), *affg.* 28 T.C. 121 (1957); *Howell v. Comm'r, supra*.

Here, there is little dispute concerning Marlboro Improvement's purpose for acquiring Hayes's tract. The petitioners testified that they intended to hold the property for approximately 1 1/2 years and then resell it at a profit. It is evident that petitioners intended ab initio to resell the property as soon as the subdivision plan had been approved. But even though Marlboro Improvement may have held the property at all times for sale to customers, our analysis cannot end here. Satisfying the "held for sale to customers" requirement of § 1221(1) does not resolve the issue at hand. We must also determine whether Marlboro Improvement's activities constituted a trade or business since the sale to Fairfield must have been made in the ordinary course thereof. *U.S. v. Winthrop*, supra at 911; *Bynum v. Comm'r*, 46 T.C. 295, 302 (1966) (concurring opinion by Judge Tannenwald).

We are convinced that Marlboro Improvement did not hold the tract "for sale to customers in the ordinary course of a trade or business" for purposes of § 1221(1). As we held in *Howell v. Comm'r*, supra at 555, even though the property may have been acquired with the ultimate intention of reselling, this does not result in a determination that the property was held primarily for sale in the ordinary course of business.

Our determination here is based on considerations which relate primarily to a lack of frequent and substantial sales activity. In the context of this case, we consider the lack of frequent sales to be the most important objective factor for purposes of characterizing the gain petitioners received. *Biedenharn Realty Co. v. U. S.*, 526 F.2d 409 (5th Cir. 1976);[67] *Gamble v. Comm'r*, 68 T.C. 800, 812 (1977).

All of the evidence demonstrates the isolated nature of the transaction. Hayes's tract has been the only property Marlboro Improvement acquired. Related to this is a lack of improvements, construction, or sale of the tract in individual lots. The solitary nature of the acquisition and the single sale to Fairfield, by definition, precludes

---

66. [13] It is readily apparent that any one case can be sui generis since its particular outcome may result from its own peculiar facts. *See Thompson v. Comm'r*, 322 F.2d 122, 127 (5th Cir. 1963), *affg. in part and revg. in part* 38 T.C. 153 (1962).

67. [14] The Fifth Circuit has recently emphasized in *Suburban Realty Co. v. U.S.*, 615 F.2d 171, 178 (5th Cir. 1980), that the frequency and substantiality of sales is the most important factor for determining whether the taxpayer is engaged in the real estate business.

a finding that Marlboro Improvement was engaged in substantial and frequent real estate sales over an extended period of time. The only other dispositions of property consisted of the condemnation by New Jersey for Route 18 and the subsequent sale of the shopping center portion after the township of Marlboro retreated from its plan to permit the development of that area commercially. Both of these dispositions, which resulted solely from the mandates of State and local governments, were essentially involuntary and do not add anything of significance for purposes of analyzing the frequency and substantiality of Marlboro Improvement's sales.

In our view, Marlboro Improvement's efforts in obtaining subdivision approval and selling the major parcel as a single tract, coupled with two separate dispositions of the highway and shopping center parcels, do not put the corporation in a trade or business. Admittedly, subdivision of the tract into half-acre building lots takes us in the direction of the indistinct line of demarcation between investment and dealership. It may confidently be expected that eventually another case will present us with a fact situation where the taxpayer not only subdivides, but also physically lays out streets and puts in utilities before disposing of the tract in one single transaction. That decision, of course, is for another day.[68]

* * *

The crucial fact, which we believe petitioners have established by wholly convincing evidence, is that their intention was at all times to sell the unimproved property as a single tract. The major subdivision which they were reluctantly required to undertake—and successfully accomplished after encountering massive aggravating obstacles—placed the gloss on the tract which made it salable.

As the Third Circuit (the court to which this case would be appealed) has held in *Jersey Land & Development Corp. v. U.S.*, 539 F.2d 311 (3d Cir. 1976), the ultimate issue in a dealer versus investor case is "a taxpayer's motivation in holding a particular piece of property." We have found that petitioners' intention was at all times to sell the unimproved property as a single tract, and in our view this puts Marlboro Improvement in the investor category.

We are not unmindful that the Third Circuit found ordinary income rather than capital gain in *Jersey Land & Development Corp. v. U.S.*, *supra*. Nevertheless, we believe the facts in the case before us to be sufficiently different to justify a result different from that in *Jersey Land & Development Corp. v. U.S.*, *supra*. In that case, the taxpayer corporation was a sister corporation of a trucking company which required expanded facilities. Taxpayer entered into a lease-option agreement with the township of North Bergen, N.J., covering approximately 97 acres of marshland in

---

68. [16] The Sixth Circuit recently upheld a District Court determination that sales proceeds were taxable as capital gain in a case where the property was subdivided, improved by the addition of gravel roads, and disposed of in lots (in a 17-year period, 87 lots were disposed of in 45 separate sales). *Gartrell v. U.S.*, 619 F.2d 1150 (6th Cir. 1980).

the township. Taxpayer's option was contingent upon its filling and grading the tract. Taxpayer was required to fill and grade at least 25 acres during the first year of the lease and at least 10 acres in each subsequent year. Upon completion of the filling and grading of any 5-acre segment, taxpayer could exercise its option to purchase that segment.

About halfway through the lease term, the trucking company was sold to an unrelated business, but the taxpayer continued grading, filling, and acquiring segments of the land. Significantly, shortly after the trucking company was sold, the taxpayer commenced selling segments of the unimproved land, and within 7 years it had sold approximately 40 of its 75 acres at a considerable profit in six separate transactions. Finally, the Circuit Court found it extremely significant that a number of the trucking company's other corporations acquired, improved, and resold marshland properties during the same general time frame as Jersey Land so operated. The court, accordingly, concluded that the taxpayer's acquisition, improvement, and sale of the property, which was part of a pattern of similar activities carried on by associated corporations, established that the taxpayer held the tract primarily for sale in the ordinary course of its business, resulting in ordinary income rather than capital gain.

Some of the facts that distinguish the case before us from those in Jersey Land are: Marlboro Improvement acquired the tract in a single transaction, rather than piecemeal over an extended period — a fact connoting commercial activity; Marlboro Improvement did nothing comparable to grading and filling by way of improvement; in fact, it made no improvements notwithstanding respondent's efforts to characterize subdivision as an "improvement," a concept not generally recognized in the real estate world; the subdivision became a necessity by reason of the exigencies of the real estate market as they existed in 1973 and the years immediately preceding, whereas the grading and filling by Jersey Land, at least after its trucking company sibling was sold, was entirely voluntary and part of a continuing program to improve the land and, as the Circuit Court concluded, to market the land piecemeal; Marlboro Improvement was in no way related to any other corporation and was by no stretch of the imagination part of a pattern of business activities carried on by associated corporations.

Thus, while questions in the dealer-investor area are rarely wholly free from doubt, we believe petitioners' facts are distinguishable from those of Jersey Land. There is simply lacking here the continuing commercial activity which tainted the taxpayer's claim of investment for capital gains in Jersey Land & Development.

In view of the fact that Marlboro Improvement's activities do not fall within the general fact pattern of cases which have found ordinary income — i.e., subdivision in conjunction with improvements and lot sales — respondent argues that the activities in connection with obtaining approval for the subdivision plan, alone, constitute a trade or business for purposes of section 1221(1). Respondent's position is that the factors which courts have traditionally utilized in this area are only useful in determining whether a taxpayer is a "dealer" in real estate and that the concept of a trade or business in § 1221(1) is broader and not necessarily synonymous with the word "dealer."[69]

To buttress this argument, respondent has directed our attention to several cases that have discussed the role which nonmarket appreciation plays in determining the character of gain on the sale of property. Respondent indicates that any appreciation of the property could not have exceeded 10 percent for any one year during Marlboro Improvement's holding period.[70] Accordingly, respondent contends the bulk of the gain realized on the sale to Fairfield is attributable to Marlboro Improvement's obtaining approval for its subdivision plan and thus urges that capital gain treatment should be denied since the property's appreciation did not accrue over a substantial period of time, citing *Comm'r v. Gillette Motor Co.*, 364 U.S. 130 (1960). The underlying premise of this argument is that any activity of the taxpayer which gives rise to substantial appreciation must be deemed a trade or business under § 1221(1).

The Fifth Circuit in *U.S. v. Winthrop*, 417 F.2d at 909, refused to adopt a per se rule denying capital gain treatment whenever the "efforts" of the taxpayer resulted in the property's appreciation. In rejecting what it perceived as an overly broad interpretation of the Corn Products doctrine, the court stated:

> Indeed, the cases are many where taxpayer efforts have contributed to value and have been accorded capital gains treatment.... We therefore conclude that this blanket interdiction of capital gains treatment where there has been any laying on of hands is belied by the past decisions of this court.[71]

Petitioners, through Marlboro Improvement, merely subdivided the land in order to make it more marketable and enhance its value. Indeed, many cases have allowed capital gains treatment for taxpayers who subdivided their property even though improvements were made thereto and even though sales were effected by numerous dispositions of individual lots....

The cases which respondent has cited as authority for a blanket "taxpayer efforts" rule fail to lend support for such a proposition. Although the appreciation at issue in each of the cases was attributable mainly to the efforts of the taxpayer, such a factor supported a finding that the substantiality and frequency of the activities in question were sufficient to put the taxpayer in the real estate business. In other words, the fact that a taxpayer's activities contributed to the property's appreciation did not acquire significance independent of the question whether these activities constituted a trade or business under § 1221(1). That question should not be resolved by examining only whether the property's appreciation is due mainly to the taxpayer's efforts. Rather,

---

69. [18] For a discussion regarding dealers, *see Kemon v. Comm'r*, 16 T.C. 1026, 1032–1033 (1951).

70. [20] This is based on the testimony of John Brody, a real estate appraiser familiar with property located in the Marlboro area. He estimated that during the late 1960's and early 1970's, the real estate in Marlboro Township increased in value between 5 and 10 percent each year.

71. [22] The Winthrop court ultimately held for the Commissioner, but on different grounds.

the focus of the inquiry is whether the taxpayer's activities rise to the level of a trade or business.[72]

In an area of the tax law which is essentially factual, we cannot adhere to a blanket rule that any activity which results in appreciation necessarily constitutes a §1221(1) business. Accordingly, we conclude that Marlboro Improvement did not hold the portion of land sold to Fairfield as property to be sold to customers in the ordinary course of a trade or business under section 1221(1).

We now turn to the respondent's second argument for taxing petitioners' sales proceeds as ordinary income. Respondent argues that petitioners are not entitled to report the income from the sale to Fairfield as capital gain because of the provisions of §1.1375-1(d), Income Tax Regs., which reads in part as follows:

> (d) Level for determining character of gain. Ordinarily, for purposes of determining whether gain on the sale or exchange of an asset by an electing small business corporation is capital gain, the character of the asset is determined at the corporate level. However, if an electing small business corporation is availed of by any shareholder or group of shareholders owning a substantial portion of the stock of such corporation for the purpose of selling property which in the hands of such shareholder or shareholders would not have been an asset, gain from the sale which would be capital gain, then the gain on the sale of such property by the corporation shall not be treated as a capital gain....

Respondent points out that three of Marlboro Improvement's shareholders, Miller, Traphagen, and Fiorino, engaged in real estate activities and possessed sales licenses. Respondent maintains that the subject property would not be a capital asset in their hands by virtue of such activities. Since they owned 55 percent of the stock of Marlboro Improvement, admittedly a substantial portion, respondent concludes that, under the regulation, Marlboro Improvement's sale of the property cannot be treated as capital gain.

The flaw in respondent's argument is his assertion that the property would not have been a capital asset in the hands of any of the three shareholders. On the basis of the facts presented, we find that the property would have been a capital asset in the hands of any of Miller, Traphagen, or Fiorino.

Fiorino presents the most likely choice for dealer status: he is a licensed real estate broker and appraiser of residential realty. However, the fact that a taxpayer is a broker does not require a determination that he is in the business of buying and selling real estate for his own account (in other words, a dealer). *Howell v. Comm'r*, supra.

A broker is, in effect, a middleman or go-between who brings buyers and sellers together and who receives compensation for such efforts in the form of commissions.

---

72. [25] The fact that a substantial amount of appreciation is due to the taxpayer's activities is, of course, a significant factor to consider in making this determination. However, such does not, standing alone, necessarily require a finding that the taxpayer's property is excluded from the capital asset definition by §1221(1).

Brokerage activities necessarily relate to property owned by others. *Thomas v. Comm'r*, 254 F.2d 233, 236–237 (5th Cir. 1958). The activities of a dealer, on the other hand, more closely resemble those performed by a merchant or retailer of goods. A dealer is a person who buys and sells property as stock in trade for his own account. *Thomas v. Comm'r*, supra.

Although a taxpayer can be both a broker and a dealer, *Tomlinson v. Dwelle*, 318 F.2d 60 (5th Cir. 1963), the two terms are not synonymous. Thus, it is clear that Fiorino's brokerage activities do not mandate a finding that Marlboro Improvement should be accorded dealer status.

In the instant case, there is no evidence that Fiorino bought and sold property on his own account and in such an extensive manner as to constitute a separate business as a dealer. It is also clear that the property would have been a capital asset in the hands of both Miller and Traphagen. Miller merely possessed a broker's license and, moreover, his real estate activities involved a different genre, namely, industrial real estate. Traphagen's connection with the real estate business was attenuated at best: he possessed a broker's license and his last sale occurred approximately in 1970.

As regulation § 1.1375-1(d) itself indicates, the character of an asset is normally determined at the corporate level. Moreover, as we have already noted, corporations are almost universally accorded recognition as separate viable entities under the tax law. *Moline Properties, Inc. v. Comm'r*, supra. We simply do not perceive the case at hand to be the type of abuse situation which respondent's regulation was intended to ameliorate. Since we consider the regulation inapplicable here, we expressly leave open the question of its validity.

HOLDING

Accordingly, we hold that petitioners were entitled to report the income from the tract sale as capital gain.

Gangi v. Commissioner

United States Tax Court
54 T.C.M. (CCH) 1048 (1987)

MEMORANDUM FINDINGS OF FACT AND OPINION

CLAPP, JUDGE:

Respondent determined deficiencies in petitioners' Federal income taxes as follows:

	Year	Amount
Charles R. Gangi and Mary C. Gangi docket No. 38613-84	1979	$202,845
	1980	7,961
		$210,806
Carl R. Maginn and Charlotte R. Maginn docket No. 38614-84	1979	$118,691
	1980	29,488
		$148,179

These cases were consolidated for trial, briefing and opinion. The sole issue for determination is whether petitioners realized capital gain or ordinary income from the sale as condominium units of a building previously held for rental of apartments.

FINDINGS OF FACT

Some of the facts have been stipulated and are so found. The stipulation of facts and the attached exhibits are incorporated by reference.

Petitioners Charles R. Gangi and Mary C. Gangi ("Gangi or Gangis") resided in Glendale, California, when they filed their petition. Petitioners Carl R. Maginn and Charlotte R. Maginn ("Maginn or Maginns") resided in Glendale, California, when they filed their petition. Each of the petitioners was separately in the business of constructing and selling single family homes and in some cases apartment buildings. From time to time, Gangi and Maginn independently constructed or purchased property which each held as rental property for investment. None of such property is at issue in this case.

In 1970, Maginn and Gangi formed a partnership. This was the first time that they did business together. The partnership constructed a 36-unit apartment building in Glendale, California ("building") which was completed in November 1970. The building was the partnership's only asset.

The partnership constructed the building in a superior manner, using top quality materials more commonly found in the construction of single family homes. They intended to keep the building as a retirement investment and therefore wanted it to remain in good condition for a number of years.

From November 1970 to August 1978, the property was held solely as rental property. The partnership hired a resident property manager to handle the daily operations of the building, and consequently, the building did not require much daily supervision from Gangi or Maginn. Petitioners' role with respect to the operation was that of general manager, and Gangi and Maginn switched off every other year in that position.

The cost to the partnership for the construction of the building was $666,083 of which $559,388 was allocable to the building and $106,695 to the land. The annual gross income from the building to the partnership was $113,389 in 1976, $116,293 in 1977 and $82,852 in 1978. The net rental income before depreciation and payments to the general partners was $47,664 in 1976, $44,311 in 1977 and $1,598 in 1978.

In June 1977, Maginn and Gangi no longer wished to remain partners and contemplated selling their building and liquidating their investment. They determined that converting the building to condominium units and listing them for sale would be the most profitable way to liquidate their investment. The building was not generating enough rental income to justify its sale as a rental building from an economic perspective.

From June 1977 to August 1978, conversion engineering and legal work to convert the 36-unit apartment building to 36 condominium units was authorized and completed. In connection with the conversion of the building, the partnership incurred expenses totalling $29,220.51.

These expenses included:

Designs, plans and maps	$1,385.33
Engineering costs	7,605.62
Fees and permits	350.00
Title and legal fees	3,922.00
Dept. of Real Estate	100.00
Bonds	1,010.00
Expense for model	3,987.90
Brochures	859.66
Acceptance fee (bank charge)	10,000.00
Total	$29,220.51

An additional $100,163.93 in expenses, which would have been incurred by the partnership whether the building was sold as a whole, prior to conversion, or as condominium units, are itemized as follows:

Hardware, lumber, misc.	$15,048.09
Painting	4,319.73
First floor paving	1,250.00
Labor, misc.	28,675.15
Fixtures	709.03
Flooring/carpeting	32,036.35
Masonry art	3,500.00
Ms. Kay Interior	6,859.48
Landscaping	1,664.10
Awning	1,102.00
Commission	5,000.00
Total	$100,163.93

No structural changes were made to the units themselves and no work was done to the building that would require a building permit.

Beginning in September 1978, the units were listed for sale pursuant to an exclusive listing agreement with an independent real estate company, Greg Gangi Realty. Greg Gangi Realty was owned by Sal Gangi, Gangi's brother and John Greg, a longtime builder and real estate broker from the Glendale area. John Greg is unrelated to either Gangi or Maginn. The partnership interviewed other real estate companies but contracted with Greg Gangi Realty based on their low 1 3/4 percent commission and their prior activity in the relatively new condo market.

The sale of the units was advertised in the Glendale News Press. Sales brochures advertising the units were also printed. The real estate company used one of the units as a model unit and placed a salesperson there during normal business hours to market and sell the units. Neither Gangi or Maginn ever carried on any selling activities. During 1979, the partnership sold 26 of the 36 individual condominium units to 26 different purchasers for a total gross sales price of $1,716,295. In late 1979, four units each were distributed to Gangi and Maginn. The final two units were sold by the partnership in individual transactions to two unrelated buyers in March 1980 for a total gross sales price of $143,000.

In November 1979, Gangi sold three of his four condominium units for a gross sales price of $255,000. The fourth unit was held as rental property in 1979 and 1980. All four of Maginn's units were held as rental property in 1979 and 1980.

The partnership was liquidated in March 1980 after the sale of the last condo on March 21, 1980. Gangi and Maginn never constructed or acquired another rental apartment building which was converted into condominium units for sale, other than the property in question. Gangi and Maginn never carried on business activities with each other after the liquidation of the partnership.

Gangi reported a long-term capital gain of $379,172 on his 1979 tax return, representing his share of the partnership's long-term capital gain. The remainder of the partnership's long-term capital gain, $379,172, was reported on Maginns' 1979 return. Each petitioner also reported his allocable share of the $85,515 ordinary income on his respective 1979 returns. On the 1980 tax returns, the partnership reported a long-term capital gain of $101,089 from the sale of the remaining condominium units, and Gangi and Maginn reported $19,818 and $81,271, respectively, of the $101,089 capital gains on their 1980 tax returns.

OPINION

The sole issue is whether Gangi and Maginn realized capital gain or ordinary income from the sale of the condominium units. If the partnership held the units primarily for sale to customers in the ordinary course of its trade or business pursuant to section 1221(1) or 1231(b)(1)(B),[73] any gain realized on their sale will be taxed as ordinary income. If the partnership held the units for investment, the resulting gain will be capital gain. *Malat v. Riddell*, 383 U.S. 569, 572 (1966).

For realization of ordinary income, the property must first be held primarily for sale, and second, for sale in the ordinary course of business. *Howell v. Commissioner*, 57 T.C. 546, 555 (1972).

The word primarily has been interpreted to mean "principally" or "of first importance." *Malat v. Riddell, supra*. In determining this issue, we have considered cases interpreting section 1221(1) to be authority for section 1231(b)(1)(B) cases. *Cottle v. Commissioner*, 89 T.C. ___ (1987) (slip opinion at 30–31). Finally, we must construe

---

73. [1] Unless otherwise indicated, all section references are to the Internal Revenue Code of 1954, as amended and in effect during the taxable years in question, and all Rule references are to the Tax Court Rules of Practice and Procedure.

the statute providing capital gains treatment narrowly, as it is a relief provision and an exception to the normal tax rates. *Commissioner v. P. G. Lake, Inc.*, 356 U.S. 260, 265 (1958); *Corn Products Co. v. Commissioner*, 350 U.S. 46, 52 (1955).

In the instant case, respondent argues that converting the 36-unit apartment building into individual units and the subsequent sale of the units constituted a shift from an investment/rental operation to sale in the ordinary course of business, and that this resulted in Gangi and Maginn realizing ordinary income in 1979 and 1980.

Petitioners counter that their primary intention in converting the building and selling the units was to liquidate their investment and terminate the business, a business decision necessitated by the Glendale real estate market and a desire by Gangi and Maginn to go their separate ways. Petitioners, accordingly, seek long-term capital gain treatment for any sales proceeds from the units. They bear the burden of proving that they dealt with the units as investors and not as dealers. *Welch v. Helvering*, 290 U.S. 111 (1933); Rule 142(a). Neither party argues that it is impermissible for people in the business of selling real estate to have separate designated investments that do not fall into the ordinary income category. *Maddux Construction Co. v. Commissioner*, 54 T.C. 1278, 1284 (1970).

We conclude that Gangi and Maginn did not hold the building "primarily" for sale to customers in the ordinary course of business. They purchased the land and built the building as a retirement investment, and for 8 to 9 years rented the units in accordance with their initial investment motive. When for business and personal reasons they determined it was in their best interest to sell, a business judgment was made to convert the building to condominiums. This decision was made in connection with their investment in real estate, and not in the ordinary course of a business. While we are aware that the purpose for which a taxpayer originally holds the property is not determinative of how the gain from a subsequent sale will be treated for tax purposes, it is nevertheless an important factor to be considered. *Jersey Land and Development Corp. v. United States*, 539 F.2d 311, 315 (3d Cir. 1976); *Ehrman v. Commissioner*, 120 F.2d 607, 610 (9th Cir. 1941); *Daugherty v. Commissioner*, 78 T.C. 623, 629 (1982); *Biedermann v. Commissioner*, 68 T.C. 1, 11 (1977). Thus, while we concede that Gangi and Maginn "sold" the condominium units, we do not think that this activity rises to the level of holding property "primarily" for sale to customers. Petitioners' original intent is relevant for our purposes under all the facts and circumstances.

Based on the law as articulated by the Ninth Circuit, the circuit to which this case is appealable, see *Golsen v. Commissioner*, 54 T.C. 742 (1970), affd. 445 F.2d 985 (10th Cir. 1971), cert. denied 404 U.S. 940 (1971), we also determine that Gangi and Maginn were not selling units in the ordinary course of their trade or business. In determining this issue, no one factor is controlling, each case turns on its own particular set of facts and circumstances. *Parkside, Inc. v. Commissioner*, 571 F.2d 1092, 1096 (9th Cir. 1977); *Austin v. Commissioner*, 263 F.2d 460, 462 (9th Cir. 1959). Courts have, however, considered the following factors more heavily to determine this issue:

the nature of the acquisition of the property, the frequency and continuity of sales over an extended period, the nature and the extent of the taxpayer's business, the activity of the seller about the property, and the extent and substantiality of the transactions. *Redwood Empire S & L Assoc. v. Commissioner*, 628 F.2d 516, 517 (9th Cir. 1980).

See *Parkside v. Commissioner, supra* at 1096; *Austin v. Commissioner, supra* at 462. For purposes of our discussion, we will discuss only those factors we find relevant.

Respondent urges us to conclude that Gangi and Maginn sold the units in the ordinary course of their trade or business based on the above list of factors. Respondent points to petitioners' activities in connection with the conversion including the substantial sales, the advertising to increase the sales, the model condominium unit, and the overall involvement of the partnership with the conversion process.

Specifically, respondent notes that 1) the partnership sold twenty-six units to twenty-six different purchasers during 1979 and two units to two purchasers in 1980; 2) the partnership expended $129,384.44 to convert the building into condominium units; 3) the partnership advertised the sale of the condominium units in a local newspaper; 4) the partnership opened a model unit 6 days a week from noon to 5 p.m. to facilitize the sales; and, finally, 6) that the partnership received more money as a result of the conversion of the building into condominium units than it would have received had the building been sold intact. Respondent, thus, argues that Gangi and Maginn's efforts to sell the units rise to the level of producing sales in the ordinary course of a trade or business.

Petitioners view the transaction differently. In 1970, Gangi and Maginn formed a partnership, which constructed the building for investment purposes. From November 1970 to August 1978, the property was held solely as rental property. In June 1977, petitioners no longer wished to remain as partners, and they concluded that a conversion to condominiums would be the most profitable way for them to liquidate their investment. Maginn testified that the Glendale real estate market for rental real property had declined. Moreover, the building was "showing a relatively poor return * * *." Confronted with the desire to terminate the partnership and a poor market to sell rental real estate, they decided the additional expenditures to convert the building were worthwhile.

Two cases in particular lead us to the result that petitioners are entitled to capital gain treatment on their gains from the sale of the condominium units.

In *Heller Trust v. Commissioner*, 382 F.2d 675, 680 (9th Cir. 1967), the court held that where the facts clearly indicated that the taxpayer held his property as rental/investment property and that "this purpose continued until shortly before the time of a sale, and that the sale is prompted by a liquidation intent, the taxpayer should not lose the benefits provided for by the capital gain provisions."

In *Heller*, the taxpayer sold 169 duplexes (which formerly had been rented) between the years 1955 and 1958. He hired a staff, advertised the sale and opened a model unit in connection with the sales. The Ninth Circuit noted that the situation had changed between the time the taxpayer originally acquired the investment and the time the duplexes were sold. There was a decline in the taxpayer's health and in the economic conditions of the area in general.

The court commented that if it followed the lower court's treatment of the duplexes as being for sale in the ordinary course of business, the court could not conceive of "how persons with an investment such as we have here could bring themselves within the purview of the capital gains provisions of the statute where * * * they had to abandon a disappointing investment by means of a series of sales." The court stated that they did not "believe that such a harsh treatment is warranted under the applicable law and the facts of this case." *Heller v. Commissioner, supra* at 680.

We find that petitioners' motives were equally as strong for abandoning their investment. Just as declining health is unanticipated, so is the disintegration of a business relationship between two partners. Moreover, from the testimony of Maginn, it is evident that there was a decline in interest for rental buildings in the Glendale real estate market at the time Gangi and Maginn decided to terminate the partnership, and sell the building.

Respondent argues, however, that the Ninth Circuit decided as it did in *Heller* because the taxpayer "apparently" fell within the "liquidation niche" articulated in *Biedenharn Realty Co. v. United States*, 526 F.2d 409, 416 (5th Cir. 1976).[74] We do not find respondent's argument persuasive. In the first place, *Biedenharn* was decided 9 years after *Heller*, so the Ninth Circuit could not have considered *Biedenharn* in reaching its decision. Furthermore, to the extent that the Ninth Circuit carved out a "niche" in *Heller*, it is a much broader "niche" than the "externally induced factor" rule articulated in *Biedenharn*.

We conclude, based on the facts and circumstances of this case, that petitioners fall within *Heller*'s framework. Moreover, it is likely they might fall within the *Biedenharn* niche as well, although we do not have to find this to decide for petitioners on this issue. *Heller* is sufficient for our purposes.

---

74. [2] In *Biedenharn*, the Fifth Circuit considered the issue of whether a taxpayer's prior investment intent will endure and control despite substantial sales activity, and the court stated that:

> We reject the Government's sweeping contention that prior investment intent is always irrelevant. *There will be instances where an initial investment purpose endures in controlling fashion not withstanding continuing sales activity.* We doubt that this aperture, where an active subdivider and improver receives capital gains, is very wide; yet we believe it exists. *We would most generally find such an opening where the change from investment holding to sales activity results from unanticipated, externally induced factors which make impossible the continued pre-existing use of the reality.* * * * Acts of God, condemnation of part of one's property, new and unfavorable zoning regulations, or *other events forcing alteration of taxpayer's plans* create situations making possible subdivision and improvement as a part of a capital gains disposition. [*Biedenharn Realty Co. v. United States, supra* at 421–422.] [Emphasis added.]

Only a limited number of cases have found the liquidation "niche" available to taxpayers as a means to retain capital gains treatment. See, e.g., *Barrios Estate v. Commissioner*, 265 F.2d 517 (5th Cir. 1959); *Erfurth v. Commissioner*, T.C.Memo 1987-232.

We also note *Parkside, Inc. v. Commissioner*, 571 F.2d 1092 (9th Cir. 1977). In *Parkside*, the Ninth Circuit contemplated whether income from the sale of certain duplexes constituted personal holding company income to the seller-corporations under section 543(b)(3).[75] The Court then turned to section 1221(1) cases for guidance as no cases directly interpreted 543(b)(3). In *Parkside*, the corporate taxpayers held 47 duplex houses for rent. In light of the fact that expenses were continuously larger than receipts, the taxpayers decided to sell the duplexes rather than to continue to rent them unprofitably. In order to maximize income, it was further decided to sell the duplexes individually rather than as a block. In order to avoid sales difficulties, the taxpayers devised a unique set of criteria for potential purchasers including employment, credit and residence specifications. The duplexes were then advertised for sale. Eventually, a succession of real estate agents was hired who ultimately sold all 47 of the duplexes from January 1965 to October 1966. In connection with the sales, the taxpayer incurred at least $50,000 in brokerage fees. The duplexes were sold "as is"; there was no subdivision or improvements. From the date of the sales to the date of trial, the taxpayers acquired no additional real property. Based on these activities, the taxpayers asserted that the duplexes were held primarily for sale in the ordinary course of business and that such income was not personal holding company income. The Ninth Circuit held that the duplexes were held in the ordinary course of business, reversing this Court's opinion to the contrary.

Respondent argues that under *Parkside*, petitioners must recognize ordinary income as they were even more involved with the conversion than the taxpayers in Parkside were with the sale of their duplexes. Respondent dwells on the fact that the partnership spent substantial sums on improvements prior to the conversion and on the conversion itself. Moreover, they find the model unit to be a "crucial" feature of the sales process, along with the advertisements in the local paper and the printed sales brochures.

We read the facts differently. In *Parkside*, the taxpayer argued for ordinary income treatment and testified that the primary holding purpose was for sale in the ordinary course of business. Gangi and Maginn, on the other hand, held the building primarily for rental. Their primary purpose was to liquidate an investment which they held for 8 years as rental property. Moreover, in *Parkside*, the Ninth Circuit noted the "substantial commitment" of the taxpayer to sales and commented on the "substantial advertising of the sales venture; and the substantial sums expended for brokerage commissions." *Parkside v. Commissioner, supra* at 1096. Both factors are lacking here. Gangi and Maginn placed advertisements in only one newspaper, the Glendale News Press. The extent of the partnership's advertising to promote the sales totalled $4,437.

---

75. [3] The Internal Revenue Code treats interest on debts owed to the corporation, to the extent such debts represent the price for which real property held primarily for sale to customers in the ordinary course of [the taxpayer-corporation's] trade or business was sold or exchanged * * * [,] section 543(b)(3), as "rent" which, in turn, is generally excluded from personal holding company income where it constitutes 50 percent or more of taxpayer's adjusted ordinary gross income, section 543(a)(2)(A). [*Parkside v. Commissioner, supra* at 1094.]

This amount is minimal compared to the gross sales price of the units of $2,114,295. Moreover, petitioners paid a low brokerage commission of 1 3/4 percent. Unlike the taxpayer in *Parkside*, Gangi and Maginn were not substantially involved with the sales end of the condominiums.

It must also be noted that the majority of the improvements made to the building prior to sale consisted of maintenance such as painting and carpeting that would have been necessary even if petitioners continued to hold the building as rental/investment property.[76] No structural changes were made to the units themselves and no state or local permits were required prior to the conversion. We do not find that these activities rise to the level of being in the ordinary trade or business of holding condominium units for sale to customers. See *Austin v. Commissioner*, 263 F.2d 460 (9th Cir. 1959).

The Ninth Circuit in *Parkside* stated that the fact "That sales take place in the course of a 'liquidation' neither automatically compels nor forecloses a finding that property was held primarily for sale in the ordinary course of a trade or business," and cautioned that their opinion does not "establish * * * a precise balance of factors as a rule of law for all cases of this type. In the final analysis, each case must be decided upon its own facts. This is especially so in tax matters." *Parkside v. Commissioner, supra* at 1096.

Based on the facts and circumstances of the instant case, we find for petitioners and hold they are entitled to capital gains treatment.

Decision will be entered under Rule 155.

Priv. Ltr. Rul. 83-38-114

June 23, 1983

Dear Mr. * * *

This is in reply to your request for a ruling regarding the conversion of a building into condominium units and the donation of two of the condominium units to a charitable foundation.

The Company operates a department store in the downtown area of the City and it owns the fee interest in the store property. The Company plans to convert the store building into several condominiums units. Each unit will consist of one or more floors (or portions thereof) of the building and an undivided interest in the common areas.

The Company intends to donate and convey the fee interest in two of the condominium units to the Foundation. The Foundation is in the process of incorporation and will take the necessary steps to be recognized as an organization described in section 501(c)(3) of the Internal Revenue Code and section 170(c).

---

76. [4] Petitioners point out that the total expense of the maintenance and cosmetic improvements made prior to sale was $100,163.93 which is not substantial (4.7%) compared to the gross sales price of $2,114,295 realized from the sale of 31 of the 36 units.

The condominium units retained by the Company will be used in its retail operations or leased to third parties.

Section 170(a) of the Code provides, subject to certain limitations, a deduction for contributions and gifts to or for the use of organizations described in section 170(c), payment of which is made within the taxable year.

Section 170(f)(3)(A) of the Code provides, in general, that a deduction is denied in the case of a contribution of a partial interest in property.

Section 170(f)(3)(B)(ii) of the Code provides that the general rule in section 170(f)(3)(A) does not apply to a taxpayer's contribution of an undivided portion of the taxpayer's entire interest in property.

The conversion of a commercial or residential building into condominium units is analogous to the subdivision of real property into lots. See Rev. Rul. 79-276, 1979-2 C.B. 200. The result of such a conversion is the creation of separate units. Under the law of the state in which the condominium units will be formed, the owner of each unit has a fee interest in the unit and an undivided interest in all common areas.

Accordingly, we conclude that the contribution of the condominium units to an organization described in section 170(c) of the Code is deductible under section 170(a), subject to the limitations provided in section 170.

The conversion of an existing building into condominium units usually changes the tax status of the building from property used in a trade or business or held for investment to property held primarily for sale. As a result, the income from the sale of the individual condominium units is usually ordinary income rather than capital gain. In this respect, you should note that section 170(e)(1)(A) of the Code provides that the amount of any charitable contribution of property will be reduced by the amount of gain that would not have been long-term capital gain if the property contributed had been sold by the taxpayer at its fair market value (determined at the time of the contribution).

This ruling is directed only to the taxpayer who requested it. Section 6110(j)(3) of the Code provides that it may not be used or cited as precedent.

Except as specifically ruled upon above, no opinion is expressed as to the federal income tax consequences of the transaction described above under any other provision of the Internal Revenue Code.

In accordance with section 9.21 of Rev. Proc. 83-1, 1983-1 I.R.B. 16, a copy of this letter should be attached to any return that is relevant to the transaction described in this letter. We are enclosing a copy for that purpose.

In accordance with the power of attorney on file, we are sending a copy of this letter to your authorized representative.

Sincerely yours,

Anthony Manzanares, Jr.

Chief

Individual Income Tax Branch

Chapter 8

Tax Planning for Real Estate Ownership and Subdivision

I. Commentary

The manner in which property owners hold property may affect the character of the gain or loss recognized on the disposition of the property. For example, if a property owner holds property as inventory, the property will probably be inventory, even if the property owner does not expend efforts to develop, market, or sell it. The question often arises whether a dealer can own property for investment. The concern is that any property a dealer holds may be deemed to be inventory. To avoid that possibility, attorneys must consider whether property-ownership structures help preserve investment aspects of some property that a dealer owns. Attorneys should also help property owners understand the legal risks that property ownership presents. Two general ownership structures are available to property owners that may help preserve the property's classification and reduce risks—(1) a single-entity ownership structure and (2) a multiple-entity ownership structure. Attorneys can also help property owners plan to avoid the loss of long-term capital gains on the transition from investment to development purpose by using a multiple-entity ownership-development structure.

A. Single-Entity Ownership Structure

Under the single-entity ownership structure, the property owner holds all property in a single legal entity. When advising clients with respect to such structures, attorneys must be familiar with measures that owners must take to ensure that property retains the classification that the owner intends it to have. Attorneys must consider the extent to which bookkeeping, activities conducted with respect to the property, and other aspects of property ownership affect the property's classification. Case law will help attorneys provide advice with respect to these matters.[1]

Attorneys must also consider the legal issues that may arise under the single-entity ownership structure. If a single entity owns several pieces of property, a liability that

---

1. *See, e.g.*, Municipal Bond Corp. v. Commissioner, 341 F.2d 683 (8th Cir. 1965); Wood v. Commissioner, 276 F.2d 586 (5th Cir. 1960).

arises with respect to a single piece of property may attach to all property under common legal ownership. If an attorney recommends that a single entity own multiple pieces of property, the attorney should be prepared to advise clients about how they might reduce the risks associated with the single-owner structure.

B. Multiple-Entity Ownership Structure

To avoid potential tax complexities and risks associated with the single-entity ownership structure, some attorneys advise clients to consider forming separate legal entities to own separate pieces of property. To properly advise clients with respect to the multiple-entity ownership structure, attorneys must be familiar with relevant case law that considers whether the activities of commonly controlled multiple entities are separate for tax purposes.[2] Attorneys must consider whether separate legal ownership is sufficient to separate the activities of the various legal entities or whether the various entities must also be separate for tax purposes. Recall that a single-member limited liability company can be disregarded for tax purposes.[3] Attorneys must consider whether disregarded entities will help the property owners establish their holding intent for asset-classification purposes. If not, the attorneys should ensure that the separate legal entities are not disregarded for tax purposes. Even if the various legal entities are separate tax entities, attorneys must structure the ownership to ensure that activities of one entity are not imputed to other entities or the entity owners.

Often attorneys must change the ownership arrangement to ensure that property is held in the best structure. Attorneys must think carefully about what entities they must form and how they must move property to obtain the most favorable structure. The movement of property can have significant legal and tax consequences. Legal consequences concern the documentation of the needed transactions and may derive from the movement of legal title to the property. Attorneys must be familiar with the tax consequences of any restructuring that may occur, including whether movement of property will trigger gain, affect the property's basis or the basis the owners have in their entity interests, or change the property's holding period.[4]

C. Veil Piercing

Regardless of the structure the property owners choose, attorneys should help them understand the potential for veil piercing and take measures to prevent veil piercing. The veil-piercing doctrine allows courts to disregard the legal structure of an entity and impose liability on the members of the entity in certain circumstances. The veil-piercing doctrine originated in corporate law, but some courts apply it to

---

2. *See, e.g.,* Riddell v. Scales, 406 F.2d 210 (9th Cir. 1969); Municipal Bond Corp. v. Commissioner, 341 F.2d 683 (8th Cir. 1965); Kaltreider v. Commissioner, 255 F.2d 833 (3d Cir. 1958); Burgher v. Campbell, 244 F.2d 863 (5th Cir. 1957); Boyer v. Commissioner, 58 T.C. 316 (1972).

3. *See supra* Chapter 4.

4. *See* I.R.C. §§ 705, 721, 722, 723, 731, 1223. *But see* I.R.C. §§ 724(b) (applying special rules to contributions of inventory), 751(d) (defining inventory).

limited liability companies.[5] If the property owners choose the multiple-entity structure to hold their property, multiple related parties will engage in several transactions. The multiple-entity ownership structure and related party transactions could subject the entities' separateness to close scrutiny, should a dispute arise with a third party that interacts with one of the legal entities. To help ensure that courts will respect the entities, attorneys must be familiar with the factors that courts consider when deciding veil-piercing cases and they must ensure that the transactions and entities reflect the formalities that will preserve the entities' separate status. Thus, attorneys must properly form all entities, properly document all transactions between the entities and owners, ensure that all transactions have legal substance, and encourage their clients to observe the formalities of owning and managing a legal entity.

D. Separating Investment and Development Functions

Property owners may hold property for investment and later decide to subdivide and develop the property. If the property becomes inventory prior to disposition, all gain the property owner recognizes on the disposition of the property will be subject to ordinary income rates.[6] Thus, property owners may wish to separate the investment function from the developer and dealer activities to recognize as long-term capital gain any portion of the gain attributable to the period for which they held the property for investment.

To separate the investment and development functions, attorneys may consider advising property owners to form separate entities to perform the various functions. Under such a structure, one legal entity would hold property for investment and one would perform all of the development activities.[7] The developer entity would acquire the property from the investor entity when the time was ripe for development. If the arrangement is structured appropriately, the investor entity would recognize long-term capital gain on the transfer to the developer entity.

Often the developer entity will not have sufficient funds to acquire property. The question therefore is whether the developer can issue a note to acquire the property from the investor entity. If the transaction is not structured properly, the transfer to the developer entity may be a contribution instead of a sale. If the transfer is a contribution, the developer entity will generally take the basis the investor entity had in the property.[8] The investor entity will then recognize the full amount of the gain, all of which would be subject to ordinary income rates. The attorney's challenge is to ensure that the transfer to the developer entity is a valid sale for income tax purposes. Several cases address structures that separate investment and development functions. Those cases will guide attorneys who structure such transactions.

---

5. *See, e.g.,* Kaycee Land & Livestock v. Flahive, 46 P.3d 323 (Wyo. 2002).

6. *See supra* Chapter 2.

7. *See* Bramblett v. Commissioner, 960 F.2d 526 (5th Cir. 1992); Bradshaw v. United States, 683 F.2d 365 (Ct. Cl. 1982); Boyer v. Commissioner, 58 T.C. 316 (1972).

8. *See* I.R.C. §§ 362(a), 723.

1. Significance of Related-Party Developer

The tax benefit of separating the investment function from the development function will be lost in part if the property owners must pay dividends tax on the distribution of gain proceeds from the developer entity. To avoid tax on distributions, the property owners will most likely prefer that the developer entity be a pass-through entity. Thus, they will prefer that the developer entity be either a tax partnership or an S corporation. If the developer entity is a tax partnership, the gain on the sale from the investment entity to the developer entity will be ordinary income, if the two entities are related.[9] Consequently, separating the investment and development function will be effective only if the two entities are not related or the developer entity is an S corporation.

Transactions between related parties are often subject to close scrutiny because they may not be arm's-length. Therefore, attorneys that recommend related-party structures must ensure that the transaction represents an arm's-length transaction. Furthermore, if the developer entity decides to issue a note for the property, the note must be bona fide indebtedness of the developer entity. Special rules also often apply to transactions between related parties. For example, a transfer to a related party may lose installment-sale treatment if the related party subsequently disposes of the transferred property, and the transactions are tax motivated.[10] If the related party subsequently transfers only a portion of the property, however, the transfer may trigger only partial recognition of the deferred gain.[11] Attorneys must consider the ramifications of such rules and carefully advise clients with respect to issues that may arise if the parties are related.

Two other rules apply to transfers of depreciable property to a related party, which can deny capital gain treatment on the sale and deny gain deferral under the installment method. The first rule treats as ordinary income any gain recognized on the sale of property to a related party if the property is subject to depreciation in the hands of a related party purchaser.[12] The second rule denies deferral under the installment method for property subject to depreciation in the hands of the related party purchaser.[13] A non-tax-avoidance exception applies to the second rule.[14]

To avoid the challenges that arise if the investor and developer entities are related, some property owners may prefer to sell investment property to an unrelated developer. Working with an unrelated developer will have non-tax costs. The owners

---

9. *See* I.R.C. § 707(b).

10. *See* I.R.C. § 453(e)(1) (accelerating gain recognition), (2) (limiting the application of the rule generally to subsequent transfers that occur within two years after the first transfer), (7) (providing an exception to the general rules for transfers that are not tax motivated); Tecumseh Corrugated Box Co. v. Commissioner, 932 F.2d 526 (6th Cir. 1991).

11. *See* I.R.C. § 453(e)(3).

12. *See* I.RC. § 1239(a).

13. *See* I.R.C. § 453(f)(7), (g)(1).

14. *See* I.R.C. § 453(g)(2). For an in-depth discussion of these rules, see Bradley T. Borden & Matthew E. Rappaport, *Accounting for Pre-Transfer Development in* Bramblett *Transactions*, 41 REAL EST. TAX'N 162 (3d Quarter, 2014).

of the investor entity must give up control of the developer entity or restructure their ownership of the developer entity to ensure that the entities are not related for tax purposes.[15] The owners of the investor entity would probably like to participate in some of the gain realized from the development function. If the two entities are not related, however, the owners of the investment entity may have to share gain from development with one or more unrelated persons. If the arrangement gives the owners of the investor entity too much control or too many rights in the developer entity, the IRS and courts may deem the two entities to be related. The owners of the investor entity will give up some control and some rights in the developer entity if the two entities are truly unrelated for tax purposes. The tradeoff is that the property owners gain more certainty with respect to tax consequences in exchange for forfeiting economic and legal rights. Tax advisors must help clients weigh these matters.

2. Gain from Installment Sales

Section 453 allows taxpayers to defer gain using the installment method. If the developer issues a note to the investment entity in exchange for property, the transaction might qualify for the installment method. Transactional tax attorneys must know how to determine the timing and amount of gain recognition under the installment method, as defined in the Internal Revenue Code and regulations.[16] They also must consider whether one of the exceptions to the installment method apply to a particular sale.[17]

Under the installment method, the seller of property recognizes an amount of gain on the receipt of a payment equal to the amount of the payment multiplied by the gross profit and divided by the contract price (the "gross profit ratio"[18]).[19] "Gross profit" is the "selling price" minus the adjusted basis of the property.[20] "Contract price" generally means selling price reduced by qualifying indebtedness.[21] As a result of these rules, the seller of property generally should recover a portion of the property's adjusted basis on the receipt of each payment, as the following example illustrates.

Assume Eva transfers a piece of property with a $50,000 adjusted basis and subject to no liabilities to an unrelated purchaser in exchange for $50,000 of cash and a $100,000 note. Eva thus realizes $100,000 of gain on the transfer ($150,000 amount realized minus $50,000 adjusted basis).[22] The note provides that the purchaser will pay $60,000 the following year and $40,000 the year after that. Assuming the installment method applies to this transaction, Eva would recognize gain on the receipts of the initial payment

---

15. *See* I.R.C. §§ 267(b), 707(b) (defining related parties).

16. *See* I.R.C. § 453; Treas. Reg. § 15a.453-1(b). A taxpayer may elect out of the installment sale treatment. *See* I.R.C. § 453(d).

17. *See, e.g.,* I.R.C. § 453(b).

18. *See* Treas. Reg. § 15a.453-1(b)(2)(i).

19. *See* I.R.C. § 453(c); Treas. Reg. 15a.453-1(b)(3) (defining payment).

20. *See* Treas. Reg. § 15a.453-1(b)(2)(v).

21. *See* Treas. Reg. § 15a.453-1(b)(2)(ii).

22. *See* I.R.C. § 1001(a).

and the installment payments. The gain she recognizes will equal the amount of the payment received multiplied by the gross profit ratio. Eva will have $100,000 gross profit equal to her $150,000 selling price minus the $50,000 adjusted basis. Her contract price will be the $150,000 selling price. Consequently, Eva's profit ratio will be 2/3 ($100,000/$150,000), so she must recognize gain equal to two-thirds of every payment she receives. She will recognize the total $100,000 of realized gain as follows.

Computation of Gain Recognized under Installment Method

Payment	x Gross Profit Ratio	= Gain Recognized
$50,000 initial payment	x 2/3	= $33,333
$60,000 first installment	x 2/3	= $40,000
$40,000 second installment	x 2/3	= $26,667
Total Gain Recognized		$100,000

The installment method applies to defer gain realized on the disposition of property, so the character of gain recognized under the installment method should be the same as the character of gain that the seller would have recognized on a taxable disposition of the property. If the property has unrecaptured section 1250 gain and adjusted net capital gain, the seller recognizes the unrecaptured section 1250 gain before recognizing the adjusted net capital gain.[23] If the recipient of the installment note later sells it, the gain or loss recognized on that sale generally will be the difference between the amount realized and the note's adjusted basis.[24] The character of such gain or loss shall reflect the character of gain or loss realized on the original transfer in exchange for the note.[25] The character of the gain follows the note, if the recipient of the note later transfers it in a tax-free distribution or contribution.[26]

If the face amount of an installment note exceeds $5,000,000, then a person who reports gain on the sale of property under the installment method may be required to pay interest on the amount of tax deferred under the installment method.[27] This interest charge applies if the sales price of the property exceeds $150,000, the installment applies to the sale, the amount of the obligation received is outstanding at the

---

23. *See* Treas. Reg. § 1.453-12(a).
24. *See* Treas. Reg. § 1.453-9(b).
25. *See* Treas. Reg. § 1.453-9(a).
26. *See* Treas. Reg. § 1.453-9(c)(2), (3).
27. *See* I.R.C. § 453A(a)(1), (b).

close of the taxable year, and face amount of the obligation is at least $5,000,000.[28] The interest charge, which is an addition to tax but might be deductible as interest,[29] is based upon a percentage of the deferred tax liability multiplied by the underpayment rate.[30] The following example illustrates the computation of the interest on the deferred tax liability.

Earlier this year, Nisha sold Office Building (property she held for use in business for more than one year) for $50,000,000 when it had an adjusted basis of $30,000,000. As consideration, she received $10,000,000 of cash and a $40,000,000 note payable in equal annual installments over ten years. Nisha's gain realized on this transaction is $20,000,000 ($50,000,000 amount realized – $30,000,000 adjusted basis). Because at least one payment on the note will be made in a subsequent tax year, the transaction qualifies for installment sale treatment. The gross profit ratio for the installment method is 40% ($20,000,000 gross profit ÷ $50,000,000 contract price), so Nisha will recognize $4,000,000 of gain on the disposition and defer and the remaining $16,000,000 of gain. The sales price of this transaction is greater than $150,000, and the face amount of the outstanding obligation received is greater than $5,000,000 at the end of the year (the entire amount of the note is still outstanding at the end of Nisha's taxable year), so Nisha must pay interest on the deferred tax liability.

The interest on the deferred tax liability equals the "applicable percentage" of the "deferred tax liability" multiplied by the "underpayment rate."[31] The applicable percentage is the excess of the outstanding obligation ($40,000,000) over $5,000,000 ($35,000,000) divided by the outstanding amount of the obligation ($40,000,000), which in this case is 87.5% ($35,000,000 ÷ $40,000,000). The deferred tax liability is the amount of gain that has not been recognized ($16,000,000) multiplied by the maximum rate of tax.[32] The maximum tax rate is the rate that applies to long-term capital gain, if the gain will be long-term capital gain.[33] Office Building appears to be depreciable property, so some of the deferred gain could be unrecaptured section 1250 gain.[34] Assume that $3,000,000 of the deferred gain is unrecaptured section 1250 gain taxed at 25% ($750,000 deferred tax liability), and the remaining $13,000,000 of deferred gain is regular long-term capital gain taxed at 20% ($2,600,000 deferred tax liability). Nisha's deferred tax liability at the end of the tax

---

28. *See* I.R.C. § 453A(b).

29. *See* I.R.C. § 453A(c)(1), (5). Because section 453A(c)(1) treats the interest as an addition to tax, the deductibility of the interest will be subject to the limits on personal interest. *See* I.R.C. § 163(h). Personal interest appears to include the interest paid under section 453A. *See* Treas. Reg. § 1.163-9T(b)(2)(i). Consequently, the deduction for the interest on the deferred tax appears to be available only to corporations.

30. *See* I.R.C. § 453A(c)(2).

31. *See* I.R.C. § 453A(c)(2).

32. *See* I.R.C. § 453A(c)(3).

33. *See* I.R.C. § 453A(c)(3) (flush language).

34. A person reporting gain under the installment method recognizes unrecaptured section 1250 gain before recognizing regular long-term capital gain. *See* Treas. Reg. § 1.453-12(a).

year is $3,350,000. That amount multiplied by the 87.5% applicable percentage is $2,931,250, which Nisha will multiply by the underpayment rate to determine the interest she owes.

The underpayment rate is the Federal short-term rate plus three percentage points.[35] Assuming the Federal short-term rate is 1% at the end of the year,[36] the underpayment rate will be 4%. Consequently, Nisha will owe $117,250 of interest on the tax liability she defers under the installment method, and, as an individual, she will not be able to deduct the interest payment. That is not an insignificant amount, and Nisha must consider how it affects the benefits of gain deferral. Furthermore, she will have to pay interest at the end of each year on the applicable percentage of the amount deferred tax liability that is outstanding on the note at the end of each such year.

II. Primary Legal Authority

Bramblett v. Commissioner

United States Court of Appeals, Fifth Circuit
960 F.2d 526 (1992)

FACTS

On May 16, 1979, William Baker, Richard Bramblett, Robert Walker, and John Sexton formed the Mesquite East Joint Venture. Baker, Bramblett, Walker, and Sexton had respective 50%, 22%, 18%, and 10% interests in the joint venture. The stated purpose of the joint venture was to acquire vacant land for investment purposes. On June 4, 1979, the same four individuals formed Town East Development Company, a Texas corporation, for the purpose of developing and selling real estate in the Mesquite, Texas area. The shareholders' interests in Town East mirrored their interests in Mesquite East.

In late 1979 and early 1980, Mesquite East acquired 180.06 acres of land from Bramco, a corporation of which Bramblett was the sole shareholder. Also, in late 1979, Mesquite East acquired 84.5 acres of land from an unrelated third party, bringing its acquisitions to a total of 264.56 acres. Subsequent to its acquisition of the property and prior to the sale at issue here, Mesquite East made four separate sales of its acquired land. In three of the four instances, Mesquite East initially sold the property to Town East, which then developed it and sold it to third parties. In each of these instances, prior to the time Town East purchased the property from Mesquite East, it already had a binding sales agreement with the third party. In the fourth transaction, Mesquite East sold property directly to Langston/R & B Financial Joint Venture No. 1. Mesquite East's gross profit on these four transactions was $68,394.80 and it reported this amount as ordinary income on its 1981 partnership tax return.

---

35. *See* I.R.C. §§ 453A(c)(2)(B), 6621(a)(2).

36. The Federal short-term rate is the rate that applies to the month with or within which the taxpayer's taxable year ends. *See* I.R.C. § 453A(c)(2)(B).

Following these transactions, Town East still owned 121 acres. In 1982, Baker, acting as trustee, entered into five contingent contracts of sale for portions of this property. Mesquite East consulted its attorneys and accountants seeking advice on how to structure the transactions to avoid ordinary income tax on the sale. In December 1982, Mesquite East sold the property to Town East in exchange for two promissory notes totaling $9,830,000.00, the amount an appraiser determined to be the fair market value of the land. The notes provided for an interest rate of twelve percent per annum on the unpaid balance and an annual principle payment of $1.5 million. Town East proceeded to develop the property and sold most of it to unrelated third parties in eight different transactions. Town East made no payments on the notes until after the property had been sold to third parties. Town East paid the entire principal amount by the end of 1984, but it did not make the required interest payments.

Mesquite East characterized its profits from this sale as long-term capital gain on its 1983 and 1984 partnership tax returns. On audit, the Commissioner of Internal Revenue determined that the profits constituted ordinary income and asserted deficiencies in income tax attributable to the taxpayers' distributive share of the gain realized on the sale.

The Brambletts petitioned the tax court for a redetermination of the asserted deficiencies. The tax court upheld the deficiencies, finding that the sale of land was the business of Mesquite East, and that, therefore, the profits were ordinary income. The tax court stated that this was true whether the business was conducted directly or through Town East. The tax court noted that the businessmen were owners in proportionate shares of the joint venture and the corporation, that the corporation was formed less than a month after the joint venture, that the corporation routinely entered into contracts of sale to third parties before buying the property from the joint venture, that the corporation made no payments to the joint venture until funds were received from third parties, that the corporation did not make the required interest payments and that the corporation only developed land that it bought from the joint venture. The court further stated that its opinion was consistent with *Moline Properties, Inc. v. Comm'r*, 319 U.S. 436 (1943), because the joint venture and the corporation were treated as separate entities for tax purposes; sales of the property by the corporation were taxed to the corporation and sales of the property by the partnership were taxed to the partnership. The tax court recognized that whether the corporation was an agent of the partnership must be determined by the standards set forth in *Commissioner v. Bollinger*, 485 U.S. 340 (1988). The court then stated that "[t]he point to be made here, however, is that evidence of the corporation's activities and their correlation with activities of the joint venture is proof of the nature of the business of the joint venture.... [T]he totality of the evidence supports the conclusion that the business of the joint venture was the sale of land and that the resulting gains should be taxed as ordinary income." The Brambletts now appeal the decision of the tax court.

On appeal, the Brambletts argue that Town East was not the agent of Mesquite East, and that, therefore, its activities cannot be attributed to Mesquite East. They further argue that Mesquite East itself was not in the business of selling property, making the tax court's determination that the profits are ordinary income incorrect. The commissioner argues that under the well-known principle of "substance over form," the business of Town East, selling property, can be attributed to Mesquite East, making its profits ordinary income.

ANALYSIS

In order to qualify for favorable treatment as long-term capital gain under Section 1202 of the Internal Revenue Code of 1954, the gain must arise from the sale or exchange of a "capital asset" held more than one year. 26 U.S.C. § 1222(3). "[P]roperty held by the taxpayer primarily for sale to customers in the ordinary course of his trade or business" cannot be a capital asset. 26 U.S.C. § 1221(1). It is well settled that the definition of a capital asset is to be construed narrowly. *Corn Products Refining Co. v. Comm'r*, 350 U.S. 46, 52 (1955). The determination of whether Mesquite East was directly involved in the business of selling land is a factual determination, to be reversed only if clearly erroneous. *Byram v. U.S.*, 705 F.2d 1418, 1423–24 (5th Cir.1983).

The tax court's opinion is in some respects, not very clear. At one point, the court stated that the facts support the conclusion that Mesquite East was in the business of selling land, directly or through Town East. Later, the court mentioned the agency principle, but did not specifically hold that Town East was the agent of Mesquite East. Finally, the court stated that the totality of evidence supports the conclusion that the business of the joint venture was the sale of land. The commissioner argues that what the tax court meant, was that under the substance over form principle, the activities of Town East can be attributed to Mesquite East.

This court can affirm a lower court's decision if there are any grounds in the record to support the judgment. *Mangaroo v. Nelson*, 864 F.2d 1202, 1204 n. 2 (5th Cir.1989); *Watts v. Graves*, 720 F.2d 1416, 1419 (5th Cir.1983). Therefore, we can affirm the decision of the tax court on one of three alternative grounds: (1) that the tax court was not clearly erroneous in finding that Mesquite East was directly in the business of selling land; (2) that Town East was the agent of Mesquite East; or (3) that the activities of Town East and their relationship to Mesquite East support the conclusion that Mesquite East was in the business of selling land.

The tax court held that Mesquite East was in the business of selling land, either directly or through Town East. This court has developed a framework to be used in determining whether sales of land are considered sales of a capital asset or sales of property held primarily for sale to customers in the ordinary course of a taxpayer's business. *Suburban Realty Co. v. U.S.*, 615 F.2d 171 (5th Cir.1980), *cert. denied*, 449 U.S. 920 (1980); *Biedenharn Realty Co. v. U.S.*, 526 F.2d 409 (5th Cir.1976), *cert. denied*, 429 U.S. 819 (1976); *U.S. v. Winthrop*, 417 F.2d 905 (5th Cir.1969). Three principal questions must be considered:

(1) Was the taxpayer engaged in a trade or business, and if so, what business?

(2) Was the taxpayer holding the property primarily for sale in that business?

(3) Were the sales contemplated by the taxpayer "ordinary" in the course of that business?

Suburban Realty, 615 F.2d at 178. Seven factors which should be considered when answering these three questions are: (1) the nature and purpose of the acquisition of the property and the duration of the ownership; (2) the extent and nature of the taxpayer's efforts to sell the property; (3) the number, extent, continuity and substantiality of the sales; (4) the extent of subdividing, developing, and advertising to increase sales; (5) the use of a business office for the sale of the property; (6) the character and degree of supervision or control exercised by the taxpayer over any representative selling the property; and (7) the time and effort the taxpayer habitually devoted to the sales. *Id.* at 178; *Biedenharn*, 526 F.2d at 415; *Winthrop*, 417 F.2d at 910. The frequency and substantiality of sales is the most important factor. *Suburban Realty*, 615 F.2d at 178; *Biedenharn*, 526 F.2d at 416.

A review of these factors indicates that any finding by the tax court that Mesquite East was directly in the business of selling land is clearly erroneous. Mesquite East did not sell land frequently and the only substantial sale was the sale at issue. It conducted a total of five sales over a three-year period; two in 1979, one in 1980, one in 1981, and the one at issue in 1982. As a result of the first four transactions, Mesquite East made a profit of $68,394.80. On the sale at issue, Mesquite East made a profit of over seven million dollars. This record of frequency does not rise to the level necessary to reach the conclusion that the taxpayer held the property for sale rather than for investment. *Suburban Realty*, 615 F.2d at 174 (taxpayer made 244 sales over a thirty-two year period); *Biedenharn*, 526 F.2d at 411–412 (during thirty-one year period, taxpayer sold 208 lots and twelve individual parcels from subdivision in question; 477 lots were sold from other properties); *Winthrop*, 417 F.2d at 907 (taxpayer sold 456 lots over a nineteen-year period).

In *Byram*, this court affirmed the district court's finding that even though taxpayer made twenty-two sales over a three-year period, netting $3.4 million, he did not hold the property in question for sale:

Though these amounts are substantial by anyone's yardstick, the district court did not clearly err in determining that 22 such sales in three years were not sufficiently frequent or continuous to compel an inference of intent to hold the property for sale rather than investment. This is particularly true in a case where the other factors weigh so heavily in favor of the taxpayer. "Substantial and frequent sales activity, standing alone, has never been held to automatically trigger ordinary income treatment." *Byram*, 705 F.2d at 1425. In *Byram*, the taxpayer did not initiate the sales, he did not maintain an office, he did not develop the property and he did not devote a great deal of time to the transactions. *Id.* at 1424. The taxpayer held the property for six to nine months. In the case at hand, all of the other factors also weigh heavily in favor of the taxpayers. The stated purpose of Mesquite East was to acquire the property for investment purposes. It sought advice as to how to structure the transaction to preserve its investment purpose. Mesquite East held the property in question for over three years. Mesquite East did not advertise or hire brokers, it did not develop the property and it did not maintain an office. The partners did not spend more than a minimal amount of time on the activities of Mesquite East. In the light of the fact that all of these factors weigh so heavily in favor of the taxpayers, and in the light of the fact that Mesquite East made only one substantial sale and four insubstantial sales over a three-year period, any finding by the tax court that Mesquite East was directly in the business of selling land is clearly erroneous. Therefore, we cannot affirm the tax court's decision on this ground.

It is not clear from the tax court's opinion whether the court found that Town East was the agent of Mesquite East, and that therefore, Mesquite East was in the business of selling land through Town East, or whether it attributed the activities of Town East to Mesquite East based on a "substance over form" principle.[37]

National Carbide and *Bollinger* set forth the standards for determining when a corporation is an agent of its shareholders. In *National Carbide*, the Court addressed whether three wholly owned subsidiaries of a corporation were agents of the parent corporation. The subsidiaries argued that since they were the agents of the parent, the income from their activities was really the parent's income. *National Carbide*, 336 U.S. 422, 424 (1949). The Court held that the fact that the subsidiaries were completely owned and controlled by the parent was not enough to support the conclusion that they were the parent's agents. *Id.* 336 U.S. at 429.

Whether the corporation operates in the name and for the account of the principal, binds the principal by its actions, transmits money received to the principal, and whether the receipt of income is attributable to the services of the employees of the principle and to assets belonging to the principal are some of the relevant considerations in determining whether a true agency exists. If the corporation is a true agent, its relations with its principal must not be dependent upon the fact that it is owned by the principal, if such is the case. Its business purpose must be the carrying on of the normal duties of an agent.

The Supreme Court held that the subsidiaries were not agents of the corporation simply when the business arrangement arose because of ownership and domination by the parent. The Court acknowledged that the arrangement would not have been the same if third parties owned the subsidiaries.

---

37. [1] The Brambletts argue that Town East was not the agent of Mesquite East and that the tax court incorrectly applied agency law. The commissioner argues that the tax court did not rely on agency principles at all. The commissioner also contends that agency principles should not apply in this case. He argues that in *National Carbide Corp. v. Comm'r*, 336 U.S. 422 (1949), and *Comm'r v. Bollinger*, 485 U.S. 340 (1988), the Court addressed the issue of whether the corporation could be viewed as holding the property as an agent for its shareholders, and consequently whether it should be taxed on any income received as a result of that property. In the case at hand, the commissioner argues that it is clear that Town East was a bona fide corporation and that its sales income was properly taxable to it. He argues that what is at issue in this case is the character of the gain on Mesquite East's sale to Town East. We do not reach the issue of what the tax effect would be if Town East were the agent of Mesquite East; we only hold that under National Carbide and Bollinger, Town East was not the agent of Mesquite East.

The Supreme Court again addressed the agency question in *Bollinger*. There, several partnerships were formed to develop apartment complexes, and in each instance, the partnership entered into an agreement with the same corporation, which was wholly owned by Bollinger. The agreements provided that the corporation would hold title to the properties as the partnerships' agent, but that the partnerships would have sole control, responsibility and ownership of the complexes. The partnerships reported the income and losses generated by the complexes on their tax returns, and the partners reported their distributive share. The Commissioner disallowed the losses, arguing that the *National Carbide* test had not been met and that since the corporation was not the agent of the partnerships, it should not be ignored for tax purposes. The Commissioner argued that in order for the fifth *National Carbide* factor—that the corporate agent's relations with the principal not be dependent on the fact that it is owned by the principal—to be satisfied, there must be an arm's length agreement between the two which includes the payment of a fee for agency services. The Supreme Court noted that the fifth factor was abstract and refused to hold that it required an arm's length agreement plus an agency fee. Instead, the Court held that the agency relationship was proved and tax-avoiding manipulation avoided when:

> [T]he fact that the corporation is acting as agent for its shareholders with respect to a particular asset is set forth in a written agreement at the time the asset is acquired, the corporation functions as agent and not principal with respect to the asset for all purposes, and the corporation is held out as the agent and not the principal in all dealings with third parties relating to the asset.

An analysis of the *National Carbide* factors does not lead to the conclusion that Town East was the agent of Mesquite East. There is no evidence that Town East ever acted in the name of or for the account of Mesquite East. Town East did not have authority to bind Mesquite East. Town East did transfer money to Mesquite East, but it was the amount of the agreed upon fair market value of the property at the time of the sale. Town East realized a profit from its development that was much larger than a typical agency fee. The receipt of income by Town East was not attributable to the services of employees of Mesquite East or assets belonging to the joint venture. None of the first four factors support the conclusion that Town East was the agent of Mesquite East. Under the fifth factor, common ownership of both entities is not enough to prove an agency relationship. The sixth factor requires the business purpose of the agent to be the carrying on of normal agent duties. It is clear that Town East was not carrying on the normal duties of an agent; it was not selling or developing the property on behalf of Mesquite East because Town East retained all of the profit from development. Thus, under the standards set forth in *National Carbide*, Town East was not an agent of Mesquite East. Nor are there any other factors, such as those in *Bollinger*, that indicate that Town East was the agent of Mesquite East. Therefore, we cannot affirm the tax court's decision on the grounds that Town East was the agent of Mesquite East.

The Commissioner argues that the tax court correctly attributed the activities of Town East to Mesquite East. He further argues that the well known principle of substance over form supports this attribution. The Supreme Court recently stated that in applying the principle of substance over form:

> [T]he Court has looked to the objective economic realities of a transaction, rather than to the particular form the parties employed. The Court has never regarded "the simple expedient drawing up of papers," as controlling for tax purposes when the objective economic realities are to the contrary. "In the field of taxation, administrators of the laws and the courts are concerned with substance and realities, and formal rigid documents are not rigidly binding." Nor is the parties' desire to achieve a particular tax result necessarily relevant.

The Supreme Court further stated, however, that in cases where the form chosen by the taxpayer has a genuine economic substance, "is compelled or encouraged by business or regulatory realities, is imbued with tax-independent considerations, and is not shaped solely by tax-avoidance features," the government should honor the tax consequences effectuated by the taxpayer.

The Commissioner argues that when determining what the partnership's purpose was for holding the land, the tax court correctly looked to the economic substance of the transactions as a whole and attributed the activity of Town East to Mesquite East. We disagree. The business of a corporation is not ordinarily attributable to its shareholders. Neither the tax court nor the Commissioner argue that Town East is a sham corporation whose corporate shield can be pierced. Indeed, the tax court recognized and the Commissioner contends that both are separate taxable entities. Moreover, there was clearly at least one major independent business reason to form the corporation and have it develop the land and sell it — that reason being to insulate the partnership and the partners from unlimited liability from a multitude of sources. Furthermore, there is no substantial evidence that the transaction was not an arm's length transaction or that business and legal formalities were not observed. Finally, the partnership bought the real estate as an investment, hoping its value would appreciate.[38] The partnership, however, bore the risk that the land would not appreciate. Therefore, the tax court erred in finding that the activity of Town East can be attributed to Mesquite East and, consequently, that Mesquite East was in the business of selling land. Mesquite East held the land as an investment and is therefore entitled to capital gains treatment on the gain realized by the sale.

OPINION

Thus, we conclude. Any finding by the tax court that Mesquite East was directly in the business of selling land is clearly erroneous. Neither the frequency nor the substantiality of the sales made by Mesquite East supports the conclusion that Mesquite

---

38. [2] The main objective of the § 1221(1) exclusion is to distinguish between business and investment, and to disallow capital gains treatment on the everyday profits of the business and commercial world. A taxpayer who sells a parcel of undeveloped land bought as an investment is clearly entitled to capital gains treatment on the gain realized by the sale. Stanley S. Surrey, *Definitional Problems in Capital Gains Taxation*, 69 Harv. L. Rev. 985, 990 (1956).

East was directly in the business of selling land. The tax court's opinion cannot be affirmed on the grounds that Town East was the agent of Mesquite East. An analysis of the *National Carbide* factors compels the conclusion that Town East was not acting as the agent of Mesquite East and there are no other factors, such as those in *Bollinger*, that support that conclusion. Finally, the activities of Town East may not be attributed to Mesquite East when determining whether Mesquite East was in the business of selling land. The corporation is not a sham; there was at least one major independent reason to form the corporation. Furthermore, the partners did invest in a capital asset in the sense that they bore the risk that the land would not appreciate. Therefore, the partnership held the land as a capital asset and is entitled to capital gains treatment. The decision of the tax court is ... reversed

Tecumseh Corrugated Box Co. v. Commissioner

United States Court of Appeals, Sixth Circuit

932 F.2d 526 (1991)

OPINION

RALPH B. GUY, JR., CIRCUIT JUDGE.

Petitioner, Tecumseh Corrugated Box Company (petitioner, taxpayer, or Tecumseh), appeals from a Tax Court decision finding in favor of respondent, Commissioner of Internal Revenue (respondent or Commissioner). The Tax Court held that petitioner could not use the installment method to account for capital gains resulting from the sale of its properties. 94 T.C. 360.

Petitioner argues that the Tax Court erred because the sale of one of its properties took place under the threat of condemnation. Thus, petitioner was still entitled to account for its capital gains on an installment basis. Additionally, petitioner argues that because the purpose of its transactions was to resolve its labor problems, rather than to avoid paying taxes, it should be excepted from the general rule precluding installment write offs. We find petitioner's arguments without merit and, accordingly, affirm.

I.

Tecumseh was a corporation with its principal place of business in Tecumseh, Michigan, at the time it filed its petition. Its stockholders and their corresponding percentages of ownership of Tecumseh during the years in issue were as follows: J.J. Robideau Living Trust (7.95%), G.E. Robideau Living Trust (.70%), J.A. Robideau Living Trust (13.49%), Margaret A. Robideau (13.49%), Jeffrey T. Robideau (13.49%), J.J. Robideau Irrevocable Trust Number One (39.09%), J.J. Robideau Irrevocable Trust # 2 (9.79%), and The Robideau Foundation (2%).

We adopt the Tax Court's statement of the facts as set forth below. From its inception in 1963, Tecumseh has been engaged in the manufacturing and selling of corrugated containers. Between 1972 and 1985, petitioner conducted paper milling and box manufacturing operations at its Jaite Mill plant located near Cleveland, Ohio. The paper mill manufactured cardboard from pulp and other raw materials. This cardboard was sold to petitioner's other divisions and other box fabricators. The box operation produced boxes for sale.

The paper mill, which was constructed in 1905, was the anchor of the Jaite Mill Historic District. This mill, which originally produced paper sacks from rags and rope, recycled cardboard boxes into high quality kraft paper. Tecumseh's other divisions molded the paper and used it for the middle layer of the corrugated cardboard boxes that it manufactured.

In 1979, the machinery and equipment comprising the Jaite Mill plant were entered in the National Register of Historic Places by the Heritage Conservation and Recreation Service, United States Department of the Interior. None of petitioner's box plant equipment had any historical significance.

On December 27, 1974, Congress enacted Public Law 93-555 (the Act), which formally established the Cuyahoga Valley National Recreation Area (Cuyahoga). 16 U.S.C. §460ff. Tecumseh's Jaite Mill plant, including the box plant and certain other properties, was located within the boundaries of Cuyahoga.

Congress originally appropriated $34,500,000 for the acquisition of lands within Cuyahoga but ultimately increased the appropriation to $70,100,000. *See* 16 U.S.C. §460ff-5(a). The funds appropriated by Congress were not earmarked to purchase any specific properties. Rather, the Secretary of the Interior established an acquisition plan that indicated the order in which property would be acquired with the appropriated funds. 16 U.S.C. §460ff-2(a).

Petitioner was aware of the Act and, at various meetings of its board of directors, discussed the possibility that its property would be condemned. As early as May 1974, petitioner was aware of the possibility that the Jaite Mill and Cleveland box plants and surrounding property would be acquired by the National Park Service for Cuyahoga. In May 1974, petitioner retained Ernest Genovese (Genovese), a local attorney, to advise petitioner regarding the possible acquisition of its real estate by the National Park Service.

In 1975, petitioner was contacted by William Birdsell (Birdsell), Park Superintendent of Cuyahoga. Birdsell informed petitioner of the government's plan to acquire properties owned by petitioner in and around Cuyahoga, including the Jaite Mill and Cleveland box plants. Petitioner was also advised by the Army Corps of Engineers that the plan projected acquisition of the Jaite Mill and Cleveland box plants for 1980, the last year of acquisition.

The National Park Service established a priority list with respect to the order in which properties would be acquired. Petitioner knew that its properties were assigned a low priority in connection with the acquisition plan. Petitioner was also aware that acquisition of its properties was dependent upon congressional appropriations and that delays due to lack of funding could occur.

Petitioner was anxious to sell its Jaite Mill and Cleveland box plants. As early as 1975, petitioner looked for prospective purchasers for the Jaite Mill plant, but those contacted were not interested.

Beginning in 1975, Genovese attempted to get the National Park Service to acquire petitioner's properties earlier than scheduled. In July 1976, Genovese contacted United States Congressman John F. Seiberling for assistance. Congressman Seiberling reviewed the reasons given by the National Park Service for delayed acquisition of petitioner's properties and concurred with its position.

By letter dated December 15, 1977, Genovese attempted to persuade the National Park Service to provide for an early acquisition of Tecumseh's properties due to the economic hardship of retaining the properties. Title 16 U.S.C. § 460ff-1(g) provides:

> In exercising his authority to acquire property [for the Cuyahoga Valley National Recreation Area], the Secretary shall give prompt and careful consideration to any offer made by an individual owning property within the recreation area to sell such property, if such individual notifies the Secretary that the continued ownership of such property is causing, or would result in, undue hardship.

In January 1978, appraisers and land acquisition officers for the National Park Service made a preliminary inspection of petitioner's property prior to requesting bids for an appraisal. The appraisal was never ordered.

In March 1978, Tecumseh purchased land in Twinsburg, Ohio, with the intent of constructing a new building to replace the Cleveland box plant that was to be acquired by the National Park Service. During March, April, and May 1978, Genovese, on behalf of petitioner, vigorously attempted to get the National Park Service to acquire its properties as soon as possible.

In early 1978, Tecumseh retained counsel for a review and determination of the potential tax effects of the sale of its properties to the federal government. Specifically, petitioner requested advice on whether it could defer realizing income for federal income tax purposes from the receipt of the proceeds from the sale of its properties. Petitioner's tax counsel suggested that petitioner obtain a private letter ruling for a determination of the possibility of electing to defer the realization of gain pursuant to section 1033, which allows deferral when properties are condemned. Petitioner did not pursue counsel's advice.

By letter dated June 26, 1978, Park Superintendent Birdsell advised Genovese that, "[a]s discussed with you previously, our plans have not changed; when acquisition of this property will occur has not been finalized. However, it is unlikely that acquisition will take place before late in fiscal year 1980 (fiscal year 1980 begins October 1, 1979)."

In early 1979, the National Park Service developed a proposal to divide petitioner's properties into five parcels. According to the terms of this proposal, the National Park Service would purchase the four small, unimproved parcels but not the more expensive parcel containing the Jaite Mill and Cleveland box plants. Petitioner objected to the acquisition of anything other than the entire property and declined the National Park Service's proposal in 1979 and again in 1981. By July 1979, petitioner was aware that its properties were not scheduled to be purchased in 1980. By April 1980, petitioner was aware that the government had halted all purchases of property for Cuyahoga because it lacked funds.

In a letter to Genovese dated November 7, 1979, James J. Robideau (Robideau), Tecumseh's president, explained that petitioner was having serious labor problems due to the uncertainty of acquisition by the National Park Service. These labor problems included high employee turnover, defective products, serious absenteeism, and unfavorable contract terms. Robideau also noted that regular, long-standing customers were beginning to turn elsewhere.

In December 1980, the Ohio Environmental Protection Agency (Ohio EPA) cited petitioner for violations with respect to the oil-fired boiler system and waste water treatment facilities at the Jaite Mill plant. Petitioner installed new gas-fired boilers in response to the Ohio EPA's actions. To settle the matter with the Ohio EPA, petitioner signed a consent decree and paid a $4,500 fine.

By September 1981, the uncertainty of the acquisition was impeding petitioner's ability to negotiate contracts of any duration with regular and potential customers. Due to these circumstances, petitioner intended to claim hardship again in an attempt to expedite the acquisition of its property by the National Park Service. In a letter dated November 4, 1981, the National Park Service confirmed its agreement to an acquisition strategy for petitioner's properties. Pursuant to this strategy, the government intended to subdivide petitioner's property into five parcels and to purchase the four unimproved parcels "on a one-per-year" basis "as soon as funds are available and the required surveys and appraisals are completed." Acquisition of the fifth parcel, which included the mill and associated structures, would be "postponed until appropriations for that purpose are available." The property was to be divided in order to facilitate government acquisition of the smaller, less expensive parcels.

By letter dated July 20, 1982, petitioner was advised that the National Park Service was ordering appraisals of the four small, unimproved parcels. These appraisals were in fact ordered. Because of continued economic problems during 1982, petitioner weighed the possibility of continuing the operations at the Jaite Mill facilities versus the cost of shutting down the paper mill and box plant.

In early 1983, petitioner began negotiating with the National Park Service with respect to the piecemeal acquisition strategy. By March 16, 1983, petitioner and the National Park Service had agreed that the four small parcels would be purchased in 1983. On the same date, petitioner and the National Park Service reached an agreement in principle that the remaining parcel containing the paper mill and box plant would be purchased in 1984, if funds were available.

In May 1983, Tecumseh began soliciting preliminary figures for construction of a replacement facility for the box plant on property it already owned in Twinsburg, Ohio. Also in May 1983, Tecumseh ordered an appraisal of the four small parcels by S.M. Dix & Associates, Inc. (Dix). In July 1983, National Park Service personnel toured the paper mill and box plant in preparation for the acquisition.

Prior to September 1, 1983, the National Park Service offered to purchase the four small parcels for a total price of $219,500. Despite Genovese's recommendation to accept this offer, petitioner rejected the offer and made no counter offer. Petitioner, however, took action intended to force immediate condemnation of its properties. It executed a topsoil removal agreement with a commercial topsoil marketing company. Removal of topsoil would have required clear-cutting trees and other vegetation, causing extensive damage to the land. The Act prohibits removal of topsoil and cutting of timber to the detriment of the land. *See* 16 U.S.C. § 460ff-1(c); 16 U.S.C. § 460ff-3.

On September 15, 1983, the National Park Service petitioned Congress to authorize a declaration of taking of the four small, unimproved parcels to prevent removal of the topsoil and timber. Congress, however, denied the National Park Service the authority to file the requested declaration of taking.

Prior to September 17, 1983, petitioner was visited by an Ohio EPA inspector and received another citation regarding the paper mill operation. On September 17, 1983, Genovese met with Congressman Seiberling and representatives of the National Park Service. The results of this meeting were reported to petitioner's board of directors on September 2, 1983, and recorded in the corporate minutes as follows:

(a.) The Chairman and the Appropriation committee will introduce a special bill for the purchase of the property, stressing the fact that they needed to buy the land first.

(b.) That the agreement will be in writing and the Park Authority would do the following:

   (1) Will provide [petitioner] with a time table (approximately 6 months)

   (2) Put in motion a request to receive appraisals (30 days)

   (3) An additional 30 days to pick the appraisal

   (4) 120 days to get all the numbers together

   (5) 30 days to make recommendation to Congress

   (6) They would write the [Ohio] EPA and inform them that they are going to buy the land within sixty (60) days, providing [petitioner] agreed to sell the land right now.

On September 22, 1983, Tecumseh agreed to sell to the United States Department of the Interior the four small, unimproved parcels of land for a total price of $235,375. On the advice of Genovese, petitioner considered the sale an involuntary conversion. As of November 22, 1983, petitioner considered that the four small, unimproved parcels had been sold to the government, although payment had not yet been received. As of that date, petitioner also anticipated that its remaining property would be sold by June 1984.

Petitioner's labor problems were caused by employee uncertainty over the purchase of the plant by the National Park Service. Due to these continuing labor problems, petitioner consulted with Donald Lansky (Lansky), labor counsel, on potential methods to circumvent or eliminate the labor union and its collective bargaining agreement. In a memorandum from Lansky dated January 19, 1984, petitioner received advice concerning the basic principles of successorship and alter ego employers to be considered in evaluating the risks and methods of structuring the sale of a family business. The memorandum noted:

> Normally, where assets are purchased, the issue is whether the buyer is a "successor employer" who is obligated to bargain with the seller's union(s). ... The determination of the successorship issue is based on whether the identity of the employing enterprise remains intact. The result of being a successor is that the buyer is then required to recognize and bargain with the union that had represented the predecessor's employees....

> * * *

> ... The NLRB will find alter ego status "where the two enterprises 'have substantially identical' management, business purpose, operation, equipment, customers and supervision, as well as ownership...."

> The threshold question to be determined in alter ego cases is whether there is common ownership or control. In this respect, the existence of a family relationship between the new and old owners has been considered by the NLRB as an important factor in finding common ownership and in denying the existence of an arm's length transaction on the sale....

> ... To avoid the risks of being considered an alter ego, it is, therefore, imperative to maximize the differences between the new and old entities. In this respect, it may be helpful to have a complete cessation of operations of the existing company before the new entity is established to take over. Even here, however, where this is a mask for avoiding labor law obligations, the NLRB will not treat the transaction as being at "arm's length."

Despite this advice, petitioner did not restructure its operations with new lines of production, injection of capital and equipment, and changes in management or supervision. Petitioner was subsequently advised by different labor counsel that it could not avoid or eliminate the collective bargaining unit by structuring a sale of its property to another related entity.

By letter dated February 8, 1984, the National Park Service advised petitioner that it had advertised for the services of an appraiser to appraise petitioner's remaining property. The advertisement projected awarding the contract for appraisal by April 1, 1984, with a 120-day delivery schedule. At that time, the parties understood that a written appraisal would be delivered in August 1984.

Petitioner transferred the four small, unimproved parcels of land to the United States by warranty deed dated February 17, 1984, for $235,375.

After the February 1984 sale, petitioner still owned Tract No. 107-117, which contained the Jaite Mill plant, consisting of 59.59 acres of land. Prior to September 1983, all of the tracts were included in one large parcel of land owned by petitioner. The five tracts were interdependent, and the government intended to acquire all of them.

By letter dated March 16, 1984, the Ohio EPA gave petitioner an extension allowing it to operate the Jaite Mill plant until September 15, 1984, without curing its waste water violations. Subsequently, the Ohio EPA agreed to allow petitioner to operate the paper mill until November 15, 1984. Petitioner agreed to close permanently its paper mill operations at that time unless all its pollution problems were corrected. The Ohio EPA's extension was based on its understanding that the National Park Service would deliver an appraisal of petitioner's property by September 1, 1984, and would complete the purchase of petitioner's property no later than January 1, 1985.

Petitioner retained Dix to provide an appraisal of its remaining property for sale to the government. On May 22, 1984, appraisers from Dix conducted an inspection of petitioner's real and personal property within Cuyahoga. On July 13, 1984, the appraiser retained by the United States, Keystone Appraisal Company (Keystone), also inspected petitioner's Cuyahoga property. The appraisers from Keystone were accompanied by representatives of petitioner during their inspection of petitioner's property.

On May 31, 1984, petitioner entered into a land contract (the first disposition) to sell its remaining properties within Cuyahoga, including buildings, machinery, equipment, and trade fixtures, to the James J. Robideau Irrevocable Trust Number One and the James J. Robideau Irrevocable Trust Number Two (the Trusts). The Trusts were also shareholders in Tecumseh. As of May 31, 1984, petitioner did not have a written appraisal of its property. Under the terms of the contract, petitioner as seller and the Trusts as purchaser agreed:

> (k) That the full consideration for the sale of the land to the Purchaser shall be the price at which the property is finally acquired by the United States Department of the Interior, National Park Services, Cuyahoga Valley National Recreation Area, of which the sum of Ten Thousand Dollars ($10,000) will be paid to the Seller at the time that such price is so determined. The balance of such purchase price shall be paid to the Seller with interest thereon from the date hereof at the rate of nine percent (9%) per annum while Purchaser is not in default, and at the rate of nine percent (9%) per annum during the period of any default in payment. Such additional purchase price shall be paid over a period of fifteen (15) years, in equal annual installments including interest at the aforesaid rate of nine percent (9%) per annum, commencing on the anniversary date hereof and annually thereafter until paid in full; such payments to be applied first upon interest and then the balance on principal. Provided, however, the Purchaser shall have the right to prepay all or any part of the unpaid principal balance with accrued interest at any time without penalty.

> * * *

> (n) In the event that there arises any Federal and/or State income tax liability to the Seller due to any subsequent disposition of the subject property by the Purchaser, Purchaser agree [sic] to make, in addition to any other re-

quired payments, a payment to Seller sufficient to cover said tax liability, and any interest and penalty thereon. Payment shall be made by Purchaser within the time limit specified by the appropriate taxing authority for payment of any such tax liability of the Seller.

(o) In addition to the land described in Paragraph 1, the herein contemplated sale shall include all machinery, equipment and trade fixtures located in, on, attached or appurtenant to the said land, buildings and improvements thereto, and all of the oil, gas and other minerals, and the constituents thereof, owned by the Seller in and under the said land, or wheresoever located....

Contemporaneously with execution of the land contract on May 31, 1984, the Trusts executed an assignment of the land contract to the JMJ Development Company (the partnership) for "the full consideration of One Dollar ($1.00) and no other consideration." The partnership, as assignee, agreed to assume and to pay the indebtedness under the land contract. Also on May 31, 1984, the partnership filed for recording a memorandum of land contract with the Summit County, Ohio, Registrar of Deeds.

The partnership was formed on June 5, 1980, retroactively effective as of November 30, 1979, by the J.J. Robideau Irrevocable Trust Number One and the James J. Robideau Irrevocable Trust Number Two. The James J. Robideau Irrevocable Trust Number One owned an 80-percent interest in the capital of the partnership, and the James J. Robideau Irrevocable Trust Number Two owned a 20-percent interest in the capital of the partnership.

By lease dated June 28, 1982, the partnership held oil and gas rights under the Jaite Mill and Cleveland box plants and surrounding property. The partnership agreement provides that distributions to the partners of net operating profits of the partnership shall be made at such times as the partners shall reasonably agree.

Pursuant to a lease dated May 31, 1984, the partnership leased the property, machinery, and equipment back to petitioner. On its U.S. Partnership Return of Income, the partnership reported gross rental income of $121,855 and $614,463 for 1984 and 1985, respectively.

By letter dated September 20, 1984, Genovese again attempted to persuade Congressman Seiberling that petitioner was suffering a severe hardship due to the delay by the National Park Service in acquiring the property. Genovese referred to petitioner as the owner of the property; the partnership was not mentioned.

Genovese represented both petitioner and the partnership in connection with the sale of the property. By letter dated November 13, 1984, Genovese, on behalf of petitioner, advised the National Park Service that "my client, Tecumseh Corrugated Box Company, is prepared to sell all of its assets ... for the sum of $4,500,000.00, payable $2,000,000.00 this year, and the balance of $2,500,000.00 when the funds are available for said acquisition." Sale of the property to the National Park Service was approved by Robideau, as petitioner's president, and by petitioner's board of directors.

By letter dated November 27, 1984, J.W. Blanton, Jr. (Blanton), Land Resource Officer, Cuyahoga Valley Land Acquisition Office, National Park Service, notified

Genovese that petitioner's offer was acceptable subject to an approved appraisal of not less than $4,500,000. Blanton also enclosed a corporate offer to sell real property requiring the signatures of all principals, including corporate officers of petitioner and the partnership. The National Park Service also required a corporate resolution by petitioner authorizing its officers to sell the property to the United States.

As of December 1984, petitioner considered the remaining parcel of improved real estate as sold to the federal government. (The parties consistently refer to the sale as "the December 1984 sale," although title did not pass until January 1985.) By corporate warranty deed dated January 16, 1985, petitioner and the partnership, as grantors, transferred title to the property to the United States (the second disposition) for the total sum of $4,500,000, with $2,000,000 payable at closing and $2,500,000 payable on or before December 1, 1985.

After the property was acquired by the United States, the paper mill operation was discontinued and only the box plant was continued in operation. By December 1984, petitioner was operating its box plant in new quarters. Approximately $1,460,000 was expended to construct a building to replace the operations performed at the box manufacturing business. The employees of the box plant continued the same union representation.

At the time of the first disposition of the property on May 31, 1984, to the Trusts, petitioner, for accounting purposes, entered the sale of the property as a land contract receivable of $2,000,000 from the partnership. Subsequently, an adjusting journal entry was recorded on petitioner's books and records for the fiscal year ending October 31, 1984, to reflect an additional land contract receivable from the partnership.

In the notes to its financial statements for the fiscal year ending October 31, 1984, petitioner disclosed the land contract and lease as follows:

NOTE 6: RELATED PARTY TRANSACTIONS

The Company is leasing or renting trailers, automobiles, computer equipment, and a maintenance facility from a corporation owned and operated by the immediate family of the President and major stockholder of the Company. The current monthly charge under these arrangements is $19,279. The total payments to this related party during the year amounted to $218,795. These leasing arrangements are classified as operating leases.

The Company has two land contracts receivable from a partnership whose partners are irrevocable trusts created for the benefit of the children of the President of the Company. The land contracts receivable are payable over the next six to fifteen years with interest at six to eleven percent per annum.

* * *

NOTE 9: EXTRAORDINARY ITEM

The Company sold its Jaite facility and equipment on May 31, 1984 to a partnership whose partners are irrevocable trusts as discussed in note 6. The total selling price of $4,050,000 [sic] is contingent upon the subsequent sale of the property by the partnership to the United States Department of the Interior. The amount has been reported as an extraordinary item since it is of an unusual nature and is not expected to occur again. The amount has been reported at the net of the applicable income taxes of $1,433,604.

The partnership received payments from the United States in the amounts of $2,000,000 and $2,500,000 on January 18, 1985, and May 3, 1985, respectively. On its 1985 federal income tax return, the partnership reported a sale of the property on January 16, 1985, and reported a gain of $251,667. The gain reported by the partnership was equal to the depreciation on the property, machinery, and equipment claimed from May 31, 1984, through January 16, 1985.

On its 1985 income tax return, petitioner reported principal payments of $136,884 received from the partnership. Also on its 1985 income tax return, petitioner reported a net long-term capital loss of $14,950. Petitioner elected to carryback the net capital loss to its fiscal year ending October 31, 1985, and claimed a $4,186 decrease in tax.

NOTE 9: EXTRAORDINARY ITEM-DISCONTINUED OPERATIONS

In December of 1984 the Jaite Mill was sold to the National Park Service and at that time all paper mill operations ceased. The Jaite Mill Division had been a part of the corporation for seventeen years. The loss of $46,246 reflects the operations loss for approximately one and one half months of this current fiscal year plus expenses connected with closing the operation.

Subject to the availability of funds, the National Park Service is supposed to acquire every piece of land designated for Cuyahoga. As of the trial date in June 1989, however, there were numerous parcels of land within Cuyahoga that still had not been acquired by the National Park Service.

As a result of petitioner's transactions, the Commissioner determined that the taxpayer was required to recognize all of its gain from the sale in 1985, the year in which the government paid the entire sales price to the trusts/partnership, even though the taxpayer had elected to recognize its gain in installments. The petitioner argued that its transactions fell within an exception to the Internal Revenue Code. The Tax Court ruled in favor of the Commissioner.

Petitioner appealed.

II.

Generally, the entire amount of gain from the sale of a property is taxed within the year of sale. 26 U.S.C. § 451. Title 26 U.S.C. § 453 provides, however, that certain sales may be accounted for in installments. 26 U.S.C. § 453(a).[39] Such sales, called "installment sales," occur "where at least 1 payment is to be received after the close of the taxable year in which the disposition occurs." 26 U.S.C. § 453(b)(1). In an installment sale, "the income recognized for any taxable year from a disposition is that

---

39. [1] Specifically, 26 U.S.C. § 453(a) provides that "income from an installment sale shall be taken into account ... under the installment method."

proportion of the payments received in that year which the gross profit (realized or to be realized when payment is completed) bears to the total contract price." 26 U.S.C. § 453(c). "Thus, the installment method alleviates possible liquidity problems which might arise from bunching of gain in the year of sale when a portion of the selling price has not been actually received." S.Rep. No. 1000, 96th Cong., 2d Sess. 7 (1980) U.S.Code Cong. & Admin.News 1980, pp. 4696, 4701.

Section 453 is not without exceptions, however. In particular, section 453(e)(1) provides:

(e) Second dispositions by related persons. —

(1) In general. — If—

(A) any person disposes of property to a related person (hereinafter in this subsection referred to as the "first disposition"), and

(B) before the person making the first disposition receives all payments with respect to such disposition, the related person disposes of the property (hereinafter in this subsection referred to as the "second disposition"), then, for purposes of this section, the amount realized with respect to such second disposition shall be treated as received at the time of the second disposition by the person making the first disposition.

26 U.S.C. § 453(e)(1).[40] As the Senate Finance Committee explained in a report discussing the 1980 amendments to the provision, "the amount realized upon certain resales by the related party installment purchaser will trigger recognition of gain by the initial seller, based on his gross profit ratio, only to the extent the amount realized from the second disposition exceeds actual payments made under the installment sale." S.Rep. No. 1000, 96th Cong., 2d Sess. 14-15 (1980) U.S.Code Cong. & Admin.News 1980, pp. 4696, 4709. The change in legislation was prompted by "intra-family transfers of appreciated property [leading] to unwarranted tax avoidance by allowing the realization of appreciation within a related group without the current payment of income tax." Id. at 14. U.S.Code Cong. & Admin.News 1980, pp. 4696, 4709.

Section 453(e)(1), an exception to section 453(a), also has exceptions. Section 453(e)(6)(B) provides that involuntary conversions are not treated as second dispositions for the purposes of section 453(e)(1) and, thus, the first party disposing of the property can still account for capital gains on an installment basis. The specific language of 26 U.S.C. § 453(e)(6)(B) is as follows: "A compulsory or involuntary conversion (within the meaning of section 1033) and any transfer thereafter shall not be

---

40. [2] Title 28 U.S.C. § 453(f)(1) defines the term "related person" as follows:

(1) **Related person.**—Except for purposes of subsection (g) and (h), the term "related person" means—

(A) a person whose stock would be attributed under section 318(a) (other than paragraph (4) thereof) to the person first disposing of the property, or

(B) a person who bears a relationship described in section 267(b) to the person first disposing of the property.

treated as a second disposition if the first disposition occurred before the threat or imminence of the conversion." Section 1033 addresses the ways in which property can be involuntarily converted: "If property (as a result of its destruction in whole or in part, [through] theft, seizure, or requisition or condemnation or threat or imminence thereof) is compulsorily or involuntarily converted ... [,]" then various Internal Revenue Code provisions are triggered. 26 U.S.C. § 1033.

Petitioner acknowledges that the James J. Robideau Irrevocable Trust Number One, the James J. Robideau Irrevocable Trust Number Two, and JMJ Development Company are "related persons" within the meaning of sections 453(e)(1) and 453(f)(1). Thus, barring the application of some exception, petitioner would not be permitted to treat the sale of the Jaite Mill property under the installment method.

Petitioner argues, however, that one of the exceptions to 453(e)(1) applies, namely, section 453(e)(6). Petitioner argues that the sale of the property by the JMJ partnership in December of 1984 occurred under threat or imminence of condemnation by the federal government as part of the federal government's plan to acquire land for the Cuyahoga Valley National Recreation Area. We disagree and find, as respondent argues, that the sale was voluntary.

From the outset, we note that any factors indicating the government's intent to condemn which occurred *before* the first sale are discounted entirely for the purposes of section 453(e)(6)(B). The statute expressly provides that, before an exception for condemnation applies, "the first disposition [must have] occurred *before* the threat or imminence of the conversion." 26 U.S.C. § 453(e)(6)(B) (emphasis added). The first sale took place in May of 1984 and the second sale took place in December of 1984, although the Tax Court points out that the second sale was not recorded until January of 1985.

The Act providing for the creation of the Cuyahoga Valley National Recreation Area specifically enumerates the ways in which the Secretary of the Interior can acquire lands. The Secretary "may acquire lands, improvements, waters, or interest therein by donation, purchase with donated or appropriated funds, exchange, or transfer." 16 U.S.C. § 460ff-1(b). Condemnation is not listed as an option.

Even if we were to accept, *arguendo,* that the Secretary, via Congress, was empowered to condemn petitioner's property, the Secretary's only attempt at condemnation failed. When the petitioner sought to expedite the federal government's acquisition of his property, he negotiated an agreement to remove the topsoil from his property, an action clearly incompatible with any ultimate use of the property as a recreation area. The Secretary then petitioned Congress to authorize a taking of petitioner's land, but Congress denied the Secretary authority to do so. Because the Act did not explicitly provide the Secretary of the Interior with the power to condemn and because the Secretary's only attempt to condemn petitioner's property failed, we find that the Secretary, on his own, could not condemn petitioner's property. Thus, petitioner's argument, that the second disposition of his property, *i.e.,* the purchase by the federal government from the JMJ partnership was made under a threat of condemnation, is fundamentally flawed.

Even though the Secretary of the Interior could not have condemned petitioner's property under these circumstances, we will, nonetheless, address petitioner's arguments that condemnation of his property was threatened or imminent. The Tax Court has been liberal in defining the phrase "threat of condemnation" as employed in 26 U.S.C. § 1033. *Rainier Co. v. Commissioner,* 61 T.C. 68, 76 (1973), *rev'd on other grounds,* 538 F.2d 338 (9th Cir.1975). A threat of condemnation exists "if the taxpayer might reasonably believe from representations of government agents and from surrounding circumstances that condemnation was likely to take place if he did not sell his property." *Id.*

Petitioner does not argue, at least directly, that government agents told him that his property would be condemned if he did not sell it. Petitioner does, however, make an oblique reference to testimony at trial by a government's witness, Blanton, implying that the government had somehow indicated that it would condemn petitioner's land if it was necessary. Petitioner contends that Blanton "testified that taking and condemnation were available to the Government as methods of acquiring Petitioner's land and that he had discussed this possibility with [petitioner's attorney]." Review of Blanton's testimony reveals that he discussed the taking of petitioner's land in response to petitioner's attempt to execute a topsoil agreement and not in regard to the petitioner's land as a whole. More importantly, the Secretary's attempt to take the land, as referred to by Blanton and discussed earlier, took place in 1983. Because the first disposition of petitioner's land took place in 1984, any impression petitioner may have had regarding a potential threat of condemnation by the government was created *before* the first transaction. Thus, Blanton's threat, if indeed it can be called a threat, militates against applying the "threat of condemnation" exception to the current case.

Moreover, plaintiff points to no other direct evidence that any government representative ever suggested that petitioner's land would ultimately be condemned by the government. This is particularly significant because, in *Rainier,* one of the factors that militated against finding the existence of a threat of condemnation was the fact that "no one actually stated that the land would be condemned if petitioner did not cooperate." *Id.* at 76.

Furthermore, explicit and direct statements regarding condemnation supported the decisions in the only two cases finding the existence of a threat of condemnation. The most straightforward case is *Maixner v. Commissioner,* 33 T.C. 191 (1959). In *Maixner,* the petitioners refused to execute an agreement with an agent for Minnesota's Department of Highways, which would have permitted the removal of gravel from their property. The agent "advised the [petitioners] that if they would not agree to the terms of his offer he would have the gravel deposits condemned." *Id.* at 193. The court held that "it was reasonable for petitioners to infer that [the agent] spoke with sufficient authority to make it likely that his threats could and would be carried out if petitioners did not execute the agreements he presented." *Id.* at 195.

In *S. & B. Realty Co. v. Commissioner,* 54 T.C. 863 (1970), the other case finding condemnation, the taxpayer had been told by authorities on two occasions that one of the actions available to the urban renewal agency was to condemn petitioner's property. Although the renewal agency provided the taxpayer with three options, which would have avoided condemnation, the court held that "[t]here was certainly 'an indication of something impending' which was undesirable.... In our opinion, had it not been for this sword of Damocles petitioner would not have sold his property." *Id.* at 870. The court continued: "The crucial factor is that the petitioner was compelled by this impending consequence to take evasive action." *Id.* The court then addressed the purposes of the statutory provision:

> When Congress enacted [the predecessors of 1033,] it obviously intended to grant a measure of tax relief to those who were, compelled by the specified circumstances, to convert their property into cash. This intended relief should not be abrogated merely because the omnipotent, condemning authority affords the taxpayer the opportunity to retain his property by making an additional investment. Such an opportunity neither assuages the compulsion nor contravenes the intent of Congress.

Id. at 871. Additionally, petitioner points to the following circumstantial factors, arguing that they indicate the threat or imminence of a threat of condemnation:

1) Petitioner was aware of the government's power to condemn and that his property was within the boundaries of the recreation area.

2) Although the government had not previously had the funding to acquire petitioner's land, as of December of 1984, Congress had appropriated the required funds.

3) The government appraised and made an offer for the property.

4) Petitioner relied on the advice of its condemnation attorney that the government would be condemning petitioner's property.

We will address the factors set forth by petitioner in turn.

First, the fact that petitioner was aware that the government had condemnation authority and that petitioner's land fell within the boundaries of the proposed recreation area is irrelevant. Petitioner was aware of this *before* it sold its property to the JMJ partnership and, thus, the section 453(e)(6)(B) exception cannot apply.

Second, the availability of funds to purchase petitioner's property does not create a legitimate expectation of condemnation. While the unavailability of adequate funding can be used to find the non-existence of a threat of condemnation, the converse is not true. Under petitioner's reasoning, *any* availability of funding could create a threat of condemnation. Rather, the availability of funding is merely a prerequisite to a purchase and does not even suggest that condemnation is the method through which the government will ultimately acquire the property. In *Rainier,* although the City of Seattle did not initially have the funds to purchase the petitioner's baseball stadium, the city ultimately acquired the money to purchase the property. Indeed, the City of Seattle would have been entirely unable to purchase the stadium without sufficient funds.

Petitioner's third argument, that the government's appraisal and offer to purchase petitioner's land constituted an imminent threat of condemnation, is equally without basis. Again, the circumstances petitioner relies on for support are simply the usual prerequisites to the purchase of any property. In *Rainier*, the City of Seattle also appraised the land it subsequently purchased, but the *Rainier* court did not hold that appraisals somehow signified that the City of Seattle was making preparations to condemn the petitioner's land. Rather, the appraisals provided benchmarks for the appropriate market price of the property. *Rainier*, 61 T.C. at 73.

In light of petitioner's unsuccessful attempts to accelerate the acquisition process and petitioner's other arguments offered to support a finding of condemnation, the *Rainier* court's holding is particularly on point. In *Rainier*, the Tax Court ultimately held that "[a] realistic view of the negotiations between petitioner and the City appears to be that the City was merely enlisting the cooperation of petitioner with the knowledge that such cooperation probably would be forthcoming. Petitioner had been trying to interest the City and County in its stadium for over a year...." *Id.* at 76. Additionally, in the current case, the petitioner had tried unsuccessfully to sell his property as early as 1975.

Finally, petitioner's argument that it relied on its attorney's advice that condemnation was imminent is equally without merit. When asked if he thought that the government was going to condemn his property, Tecumseh's president responded with the following: "No, I can't say that I—I did, not during my lifetime." Thus, it appears that petitioner's president did not rely on his attorney's legal advice.

III.

Petitioner also argues that because the principal purpose of the first disposition of its property was to circumvent the collective bargaining agreement at its Jaite Mill plant and not to avoid paying taxes, it should be permitted to account for its capital gains using the installment method. The respondent does not agree that labor problems prompted the first disposition of petitioner's property. Further, the respondent argues that, even accepting petitioner's argument as to the purpose of the first disposition, because tax avoidance was at least *one* of petitioner's reasons for the first disposition, petitioner should not have been able to use the installment method. We agree with respondent. Tax avoidance does not have to be the exclusive reason for petitioner's action to fall within the provision disallowing the use of the installment method. We find that tax avoidance was at least one of the motivations for petitioner's disposition of his property.

Title 26 U.S.C. §453(e)(7) provides the following:

This subsection [453(e)] shall not apply to a second disposition (and any transfer thereafter) if it is established to the satisfaction of the Secretary [of Internal Revenue] that neither the first disposition nor the second disposition had as one of its principal purposes the avoidance of Federal income tax.

We note that neither the parties nor the Tax Court has relied on any cases interpreting this provision, and we are also unable to find any cases directly on this issue. Thus, we will review the legislative history concerning this provision as well as cases interpreting similar provisions of the Internal Revenue Code.

The Senate Finance Committee Report on this provision summarized it as follows: "[T]he resale rules will not apply in any case where it is established to the satisfaction of the Internal Revenue Service that none of the dispositions had as one of its principal purposes the avoidance of Federal income taxes." S.Rep. No. 1000, 96th Cong., 2d Sess. 16 (1980) U.S.Code Cong. & Admin.News 1980, pp. 4696, 4710. The Senate Report acknowledged that 453(e)(7) "put[s] [the] taxpayer at a disadvantage if he or she should seek a court ruling on the merits of the issue." *Id.* at 17. Thus, the Committee "accept[ed] the ... legislation only with the specific understanding that ... [t]he Commissioner shall treat taxpayers fairly and equitably in light of all the facts and circumstances of each particular case in a manner consistent with the remedial intent of the preceding sections...." *Id.* at 17–18. Even exercising the caution the Senate advised in interpreting this provision, petitioner's argument fails.

The Senate Report advised that the non-tax exception should be limited to "exceptional cases" and "would not apply if the resale terms would permit significant deferral of recognition of gain from the initial sale when proceeds from the resale are being collected sooner." *Id.* at 16. The circumstances of petitioner's transaction do not present an exceptional case. Indeed, petitioner's transaction falls precisely within the category of transactions specifically exempted from the non-tax avoidance provision. Because the federal government paid the JMJ partnership for the property in full in 1985, although in two installments, JMJ was able to collect the proceeds from the resale in full, while petitioner was still accounting for the sale using the installment method. This arrangement resulted in the deferral of the realization of capital gains by petitioner, and, thus, its purpose was for tax avoidance.

Further, the Senate Report provides illustrative examples of appropriate uses for the exception: "[I]t is anticipated that the regulations and rulings under the nontax avoidance exception will deal with certain tax-free transfers which normally would not be treated as a second dispos[it]ion of the property, e.g., charitable transfers, like-kind exchanges, gift transfers, and transfers to a controlled corporation or a partnership." *Id.* Petitioner's disposition of his property does not bear resemblance to any examples of non-tax avoidance set forth by the Senate Finance Committee.

Moreover, in addition to the legislative history of section 453(e)(7), case law analyzing analogous provisions does not support petitioner's argument. Title 26 U.S.C. § 306(b)(4) concerns the disposition of stock and provides that gains shall not be realized if the transaction "was not in pursuance of a plan having as one of its principal purposes the avoidance of Federal income tax." In *Pescosolido v. Commissioner,* 883 F.2d 187 (1st Cir.1989), the First Circuit held that a taxpayer's charitable donations of stock did not negate tax avoidance as a principal purpose for the transaction and, thus, the transaction did not fall within the ambit of section 306(b)(4). The taxpayer in *Pescosolido* argued that he consolidated several companies in which he was the sole owner with another company in which he was the principal shareholder "to permit him to retain control of and participate in the future growth" of the resulting company as well as "to 'freeze' the value of a portion of his equity stake in the corporation for estate planning purposes." *Id.* at 189. Additionally, the taxpayer argued that "he did not have the tax consequences of his charitable donations in mind at the time he made them." *Id.* at 190. The First Circuit stated that the Tax Court was free to disregard self-serving statements made by the taxpayer. *Id.* The First Circuit ultimately held that even though they did not doubt the sincerity of the taxpayer's motivations in his disposition of the stock, *id.* at 190, the Tax Court was not clearly erroneous in finding that avoidance of federal income tax was one of the principal purposes of the disposition. *Id.* at 189.

Applying the *Pescosolido* court's analysis to the current case, we find that the Tax Court did not err in finding that one of the purposes of petitioner's disposition of property was to avoid taxes. Even granting, as the *Pescosolido* court did, petitioner's contention that labor difficulties motivated petitioner's actions, we nonetheless find that tax avoidance was a principal consequence of petitioner's actions.

Finally, our conclusion is further supported by the Third Circuit's decision in *Fireoved v. United States,* 462 F.2d 1281 (3d Cir.1972). In *Fireoved,* also a section 306 case, the district court "found that although one of the purposes involved in the issuance of the preferred stock dividend may have been business related, another principal purpose was the avoidance of Federal income tax." *Id.* at 1287. Because "'one of the principal purposes' was motivated by 'tax avoidance[,]'" the Third Circuit held that "the district court did not err in refusing to apply the exception created by section 306(b)(4)(A)." *Id.*

AFFIRMED.

Riddell v. Scales

United States Court of Appeals, Ninth Circuit
406 F.2d 210 (1969)

FACTS

The pertinent facts are not in dispute. On April 9, 1953, Kearney Park Development Corp. ("Kearney Park") contracted to buy certain unimproved realty located near Miramar Naval Air Station in San Diego, California. As part of the purchase price Kearney Park gave one note for $80,000 and a second note for $553,750, each of which was secured by a deed of trust. At the time of the purchase, the land was subject to a prior improvement lien. By 1955 the notes were in default, and the improvement bond payments and the taxes were delinquent. During the same year news was released that the Navy might acquire the land to expand the Miramar flight pattern. In 1956 a real estate dealer, B. B. Margolis, and the taxpayers in this case bought the $80,000 note for $30,000 and the $553,750 note for $270,000 and placed the notes in two simple holding trusts. The trust declaration provided that the trustors, representing sixty per cent of the beneficial ownership, could instruct the trustee to dispose of the corpus or could enter into agreements with the owner of the security to participate in any gain realized from the sale of the property.

On June 15, 1956, Margolis and the taxpayers, acting through the trust, agreed with Kearney Park to postpone payment of the notes and to waive all past defaults and to pay the delinquent installments on the improvement bonds and the taxes. The parties further agreed that upon the sale or condemnation of the land, the proceeds would be disbursed in the following order: (1) to pay off the bonds and the taxes; (2) to pay principal and interest on the notes; (3) to reimburse the trusts for advancements; (4) to pay Kearney Park its original investment in the land; and (5) to divide the balance equally between Kearney Park and the trusts. The trusts' right to share in the gain on sale or other disposition of the land was secured by a further deed of trust.

In March 1958 Kearney Park and the trusts entered an agreement to sell a portion of the land to the Navy. In April 1958 Margolis sold his beneficial interest in the trusts to one of the taxpayers. The sale to the Navy was ultimately completed, and the proceeds were distributed to the taxpayers in accordance with their agreement. The assets distributed include the principal and interest collected on the notes, the trusts' share of the purchase price of the land, and an undivided interest in the unsold portion of the land.

In *Margolis v. Comm'r*, 337 F.2d 1001, 1008–1009 (9th Cir. 1964), modified 339 F.2d 537 (1964), this court considered the tax consequences to Margolis of these transactions. Margolis' beneficial interests in the trusts represented two distinct rights: (1) his right to payment of principal and interest due on the notes and (2) his right to share in any gain realized upon the sale or other disposition of the land. We held that to the extent that Margolis' share in the unpaid principal of the notes exceeded his basis, the sum attributable to his interest in the notes received upon his disposition of his beneficial interest in the trusts was capital gain. However, insofar as his sale of his beneficial interest in the trusts was attributable to his interest in the gain on sale of the land, the gain realized was ordinary income, rather than capital gain, because Margolis was individually in the business of buying and selling real estate.

Both the taxpayers and the Government rely on the Margolis decision and accept its division of the taxpayers' interests in the trusts into two distinct rights. We are called upon to decide whether and to what extent the tax consequences of the transactions to the present taxpayers differ from those to Margolis.

ANALYSIS

The District Court held that the profit realized from the payment in full of the notes purchased by the taxpayers at a discount was capital gain except for that portion of the payment representing interest. We do not agree. Capital gains treatment is available only when there has been a technical sale or exchange of a capital asset. (26 U.S.C. §1222.) Margolis met this requirement by selling his beneficial interest in the trusts, including his interest in the notes. The present taxpayers neither sold nor exchanged their interests in the notes; they held the notes until they were paid by the maker. "It is well settled that where a note is paid by or on behalf of the maker in satisfaction of the maker's liability thereon, a sale or exchange of property ... does not result." (*Lee v. Comm'r*, 119 F.2d 946, 948 (7th Cir. 1941); *see Fairbanks v. U.S.*, 306 U.S. 436 (1939); *Phillips v. Frank*, 295 F.2d 629, 633 (9th Cir. 1961), §1232 of

26 U.S.C., which makes the retirement of certain indebtedness an exchange, does not apply to the taxpayers' notes.

The Government admits that the taxpayers' receipt through the trusts of a share of the gain realized upon the sale of the land by Kearney Park to the Navy was gain from the sale or exchange of property. It contends, however, that the taxpayers' interests in the land were not capital assets because the taxpayers held the land primarily for sale to customers in the ordinary course of business within the meaning of 26 U.S.C. § 1221(1). The Government's contention rests solely upon the taxpayers' association with Margolis, who was a real estate dealer, in a joint venture concerning the real property in issue. It is undisputed that the taxpayers were not otherwise engaged in the business of buying and selling land on their own account. We reject the Government's contentions.

Margolis' intent and purpose to hold his equitable interest in the land for sale in the ordinary course of his business cannot be imputed to the present taxpayers. "Not all participants in a joint venture need have the same intent and purpose. For some it may be just a step in carrying on their business; for others it may be merely a single opportune investment with a view of ultimate profit but unrelated to any business of the participant." (*U.S. v. Rosebrook*, 318 F.2d 316, 319 (9th Cir. 1963).) The present taxpayers did not become real estate dealers solely because they were associated in a joint venture with a real estate dealer.

The alternative contention of the Government is that the taxpayers became real estate dealers by embarking upon the joint venture with respect to the very parcel of land in issue. The Government says:

> Where two or more individuals combine in a joint enterprise for their mutual benefit, with an understanding that they are to share in the profits or losses, each is to have a voice in the management, and the venture acquires property and holds it for sale to customers in the ordinary course of business of such venture, the profits are clearly taxable as ordinary income rather than as capital gains.

Luckey v. Comm'r, 334 F.2d 719 (9th Cir. 1964); *Brady v. Comm'r*, 25 T.C. 682 (1955); *see also Bauschard v. Comm'r*, 279 F.2d 115 (6th Cir. 1960).

The cases relied upon by the Government do not support the broad proposition for which they are cited. In those cases the taxpayers entered a joint venture to acquire, subdivide, and sell real property. The joint venture in each instance was itself conducting an active real estate business. None of these cases stands for the principle that every joint venture which has as its object the acquisition and sale of a parcel of property as a speculative investment conducts a real estate business.

Taxpayers who are not themselves engaged in the business of dealing in real property can form a joint venture for the purpose of acquiring and disposing of a parcel of property as an investment without thereby becoming real estate dealers. Their venture is not a trade or business within the meaning of 26 U.S.C. § 1221(1). (*Comm'r v. Williams*, 256 F.2d 152, 155 (5th Cir. 1956)). In the present case the operations of the joint venturers were restricted to those necessary to the realization of a profit on a speculative investment by the taxpayers. The land was neither subdivided nor developed by the joint venture. The trustee representing the joint venturers merely negotiated the agreement with Kearney Park, assisted in the completion of the sale to the Navy, and distributed the amount realized on the transactions to the beneficiaries of the trust.

OPINION

The District Court's decision that the gain realized from the sale of the land was as to these taxpayers capital gain and not ordinary income is correct.

Municipal Bond Corporation v. Commissioner
United States Court of Appeals, Eighth Circuit
341 F.2d 683 (1965)

FACTS

Taxpayer is a corporation incorporated under the laws of Missouri on October 23, 1924. It files its income tax returns on a calendar year basis. Returns for the years here involved were timely filed with the Collector at Kansas City, Missouri. All real estate sales here involved were reported and tax was paid thereon on the basis that taxpayer was entitled to report the gain as capital gains.

Charles F. Curry has since incorporation been president, director and chief executive officer of the taxpayer. He obtained a controlling stock interest in 1939 and during the taxable years here involved he owned 2063 of the 2310 shares of corporate stock outstanding. The balance of the stock was at least largely owned by members of Mr. Curry's immediate family and nominees.

Taxpayer on December 31, 1945, held fifteen parcels of real estate with a cost of $39,350. On December 21, 1953, it owned twenty-five parcels with a cost of $222,620, and on December 31, 1958, it owned nineteen properties with a cost of $230,311. Taxpayer made nineteen sales of real estate in the involved years. During such period it purchased six additional properties. The Tax Court found, "Petitioner never at any time maintained a sales force or regularly engaged in sales activities. Many of its sales resulted from inquiries made by prospective purchasers." 41 T.C. 20, 22.

The rentals for the years 1954 to 1958 ran from $25,215 to $27,586. The Tax Court found on an overall basis taxpayer's gains from real estate and from rentals were about equal. The average holding period of the properties was four and one-half years.

Taxpayer individually or with members of his immediate family owned a controlling or substantial interest in eight other corporations. Some of these corporations held real estate for rental and investment and others held real estate for resale to customers. One of the corporations was a real estate sales and management agency. Each of the corporations served a legitimate business purpose. It is not here contended that any of such corporations is only a shell or a sham, nor is it contended that the corporate veil of such corporations should be pierced.

ANALYSIS

The Tax Court upheld the Commissioner's contention that all gains on sales of real estate during the 1954–58 period as well as installments collected in such years on prior sales were taxable as ordinary income. If capital gains treatment is not available, the correctness of the deficiency determination is not questioned. The principal question here presented as stated by the Commissioner is:

> 1. Whether the Tax Court correctly held that the gains from the sale of certain real estate by the taxpayer during the tax years 1954 through 1958, inclusive, and the gains from the sale of certain real estate in prior years, installment payments from which were received during the tax years here involved, were gains from the sale of real estate held primarily for sale to customers in the ordinary course of taxpayer's trade or business within the meaning of Sections 1221 and 1231 of the Internal Revenue Code of 1954, with the result that such gains are taxable as ordinary income rather than as capital gain.

The pertinent provisions of the Internal Revenue Code of 1954 here involved are: § 1221 [definition of capital asset] ... and § 1231(b) [definition of property used in the trade or business].... The corresponding 1939 code provisions are found in § 117(a) and (j), I.R.C.1939.

The Tax Court held that the sales here in controversy did not constitute sales of capital assets within the meaning of the statutes just quoted, upon the ground that such sales came within the exclusion of such statutes since the subject matter of the sale constituted "property held by the taxpayer primarily for sale to customers in the ordinary course of his trade or business."

It is conceded that all real estate sold was held more than six months and it is clear that the real estate was held by the taxpayer in its trade or business. Thus, the crucial question presented is whether the Tax Court's determination that the real estate sold was primarily held for sales to customers in the ordinary course of taxpayer's trade or business is clearly erroneous.

It is quite true that the clearly erroneous standard of Fed. R. Civ. P. 52(a) applies to findings of fact made by the Tax Court. However, it is equally clear that findings of fact induced by an erroneous view of the law are not binding upon this court. *Greenspon v. Comm'r*, 229 F.2d 947, 949 (8th Cir. 1956); *Marcella v. Comm'r*, 222 F.2d 878, 881 (8th Cir. 1955).

Taxpayer contends that the Tax Court erroneously interpreted the meaning of the word "primarily" as used in §§ 1221 and 1231 and in support thereof points to the portion of the Tax Court's opinion reading:

> The term "primarily" as used in the statute has been construed to mean "substantial." *Rollingwood Corp. v. Comm'r*, 190 F.2d 263 (9th Cir. 1951); *Harrah v. Comm'r*, 30 T.C. 1236 (1958); *American Can Co. v. Comm'r*, 37 T.C. 198 (1963). This construction permits recognition of the dual purpose concept inherent in some types of business operations. In petitioner's real estate operations, its dual purpose is obvious. Petitioner acquired and held real estate

for the dual purpose of both investment and sale to the public. And while the sales purpose, in some instances, may not have been predominant over the investment purpose, it was, nevertheless, substantial throughout the entire period under review. Petitioner's gains from the sale of properties in some years exceeded its gains from all other sources. They were substantial in each of the years involved. On an overall basis the gains from real estate sales and from rentals, petitioner's two principal sources of income, were about equal.

41 T.C. 23, 29.

While the cases cited by the Tax Court in the foregoing quotation lend some support to interpreting the word "primarily" found in the statutes as the equivalent of "substantial," we reject such interpretation.

In *U.S. v. Bennett*, 186 F.2d 407, 411 (5th Cir. 1951), the court, in interpreting the statutes we are here considering determined that gains from sales of cattle culled from a breeding herd were entitled to capital gains treatment, stated:

If the statute had been intended to mean what the collector contends for, the word "primarily" would not have been in it. Since "primarily" is in the statute, it seems clear to us that to hold, as the collector contends, that the main, the first, purpose of the keeping of these breeder cattle was for sale, does complete violence to the statute and to its purpose and intent.

In *Albright v. U.S.*, 173 F.2d 339, 344 (8th Cir. 1949), we found that a capital gain was derived from selling culls from a dairy herd on a consistent basis. We said, "A dairy farmer is not primarily engaged in the sale of beef cattle. His herd is not held primarily for sale in the ordinary course of his business. Such sales as he makes are incidental to his business and are required for its economical and successful management."

In *W.R. Stephens Co. v. Comm'r*, 199 F.2d 665, 669 (8th Cir. 1952), we held automobiles assigned to a dealer for his use were held primarily for sale to customers in the ordinary course of business. We discussed the Bennett and Albright cases, supra, stating:

In those cases it was held, in substance, that livestock acquired by a stock breeder and held for breeding purposes, and not sold until its usefulness for such purposes had passed, was not held "primarily for sale to customers in the ordinary course of his trade or business." In those cases, while it appeared that the taxpayer would eventually sell his breeding stock when it ceased to be such, it was shown that his main objective in acquiring and holding the stock was for breeding purposes and not for the purpose of sale.

In *Greenspon v. Comm'r*, 229 F.2d 947 (8th Cir. 1956), and *Dillon v. Comm'r*, 213 F.2d 218 (8th Cir. 1954), we rejected as clearly erroneous the court's determination that the property sold was held primarily for sale to customers in the ordinary course of business.

Gotfredson v. U.S., 303 F.2d 464, 468 (6th Cir. 1962), involved the issue of capital gain treatment with respect to sales from a dairy herd. The trial court instructed that cattle could be held for a dual purpose of carrying on the dairy business and for sale to customers and that if they were held for such dual purpose, the finding should be for the Government. The court reversed, stating: "The trial court in instructing the jury with regard to 'dual purpose' took away from the jury the issue concerning the essential primary purpose for which the appellants herein held the cattle."

The Commissioner, relying upon *Corn Products Refining Co. v. Comm'r*, 350 U.S. 46, 52 (1955), urges that the definition of a capital asset must be narrowly applied and its exclusions interpreted broadly. The case so holds. The case does not go to the extent of holding that the plain meaning of unambiguous words used in the statute must be disregarded or distorted. In *Hanover Bank v. Comm'r*, 369 U.S. 672, (1962), the court quotes and follows the teaching of *Crane v. Comm'r*, 331 U.S. 1, 6 (1947), reading, "A firmly established principle of statutory interpretation is that 'the words of statutes—including revenue acts—should be interpreted where possible in their ordinary, everyday senses.'" And then goes on to say:

> The statute in issue here, in plain and ordinary language, evidences a clear congressional intent to allow amortization with reference to any call date named in the indenture. Under such circumstances we are not at liberty, notwithstanding the apparent tax-saving windfall bestowed upon taxpayers, to add to or alter the words employed to effect a purpose which does not appear on the face of the statute.

We followed this principle in *U.S. v. Martin*, 337 F.2d 171, 174 (8th Cir. 1964).

In *Yunker v. Comm'r*, 256 F.2d 130, 133 (6th Cir. 1958), the court, in dealing with the interpretation of the statutes we are here considering but with respect to different words thereof, states:

> With respect to the interpretation of the statute, the words and phrases, "trade or business," "ordinary" and "customers" are to be construed in their ordinary and not in an artificially created meaning. *Higgins v. Comm'r*, 312 U.S. 212 (1941). To be engaged in the real estate business means to be engaged in that business 'in the sense that term usually implies.

Dillon v. Comm'r, 213 F.2d 218, 220 (8th Cir. 1954).

* * *

The word "primarily" is unambiguous and has a well-recognized and understood meaning. It has been construed in various types of cases of federal and state courts as meaning "of first importance or principally." *Benitez v. Bank of Nova Scotia*, 125 F.2d 523 (1st Cir. 1942) (whether primarily engaged in production of poultry so as to be entitled to file bankruptcy as a farmer).

* * *

We find nothing in the statutes as a whole which manifests any intent on the part of Congress to give the word "primarily" any meaning different from its plain, usual and well-understood meaning. It must be assumed that Congress placed such word in the statute for a purpose. The Tax Court, in the interpretation which it made, is reading the word "primarily" out of the statute. In so doing the court misinterpreted the statute.

Taxpayer also complains that the Tax Court erred in limiting consideration of the taxpayer's purpose of holding the real estate to circumstances existing at the time of sale. The Tax Court did make an ultimate finding reading: "The properties sold by petitioner during the years in question were, at the time of sale, held by petitioner primarily for sale in the ordinary course of its trade or business." (Emphasis added.) 41 T.C. 20, 28. In *U.S. v. Cook*, 270 F.2d 725, 729 (8th Cir. 1959), which involves the question of whether taxpayer was entitled to capital gain treatment on pelts from minks culled from a herd, we said:

> We think the critical period for characterization of the property goes further back than the time of disposition. The property is properly characterized at the time it is acquired for use by the taxpayers in their trade or business and during the period it is so used. *McDonald v. Comm'r*, 214 F.2d 341, 343 (2d Cir. 1954). There is no requirement in the statute that the property be used in the trade or business of the taxpayer right up to and including the date of sale or exchange. The statute contemplates and the regulations provide for a reasonable time for disposition after the necessary termination of the property's intended use.

3B Mertens Law of Federal Income Taxation, § 22.138, pp. 628–29, states:

> If the taxpayer's situation is examined at the very moment the property is sold, it will invariably be found that there was an intent to sell, but such a literal approach would nullify the statutory provisions conferring capital gain or loss treatment, and would seem to go beyond the legislative intent behind the exclusion involved.

Doubtless the purpose for which the property was acquired, the purpose for which it was held, as well as the motive at the time of sale and the method of sale are among the factors to be considered in resolving the issue. Ordinarily, no one factor is conclusive and the question of intention or purpose is largely one of fact. *Broughton v. Comm'r*, 333 F.2d 492, 495 (6th Cir. 1964); *Frankenstein v. Comm'r*, 272 F.2d 135 (7th Cir. 1959).

The Commissioner insists the Tax Court's decision is not based upon the challenged finding above set out but that proper consideration has been given to all relative factors. There is support in the opinion as a whole for such contention. We would be reluctant to reverse upon the "time of sale" asserted error standing alone. However, inasmuch as this case is to be remanded, we emphasize that the Tax Court in making its findings should not limit its consideration solely to circumstances existing at the time of sale.

A full and careful consideration of the Tax Court's findings and opinion as a whole, convinces us that at least with respect to some of the property sold the Court's decision may be predicated upon its erroneous interpretation of the word "primarily".

We also observe the taxpayer's purpose of holding property may vary with respect to different tracts. Upon the capital gain issue, purpose or intention must be determined with respect to each tract and such purpose may vary with respect to the different tracts. *Margolis v. Comm'r*, 337 F.2d 1001 (9th Cir. 1964); *Wood v. Comm'r*, 276 F.2d 586, 590 (5th Cir. 1960); 3B Mertens Law of Federal Income Taxation § 22.139.

It is the function of the Tax Court, not this court, to find the facts. However, such findings must be based upon proper legal standards. We shall cite a few excerpts from the Tax Court opinion for the purpose of showing that the Court's findings were induced by failing to give the word "primarily" its proper interpretation:

> One property was sold to a church of which Mr. Curry was a member. As to this, the Tax Court found, "Officials of the church selected the site and requested Curry to arrange for its purchase from petitioner. The property had not previously been offered for sale by petitioner." 41 T.C. 20, 25.

With respect to the sale of a property to Kansas City Power & Light Co., the Court states:

> The sale of property and right-of-way to Kansas City Power & Light Co. was initiated by representatives of the company. Petitioner made the sale reluctantly and with knowledge of the power of the utility to acquire the property by condemnation. 41 T.C. 20, 26.

Another tract was sold to the school district for school purposes. The purchase was instigated by the school board which had a right to condemn.

A tract adjoining American Red Cross property was sold to the Red Cross. As to this, the court said: "Petitioner had never previously offered the property for sale or contemplated selling it. During petitioner's ownership of the property, 1947–54, it had produced rentals of $5,830." 41 T.C. 20, 25.

Speaking of a number of relevant sales, the Tax Court observes: "The low cost rental properties which comprised a substantial portion of petitioner's real estate holdings were usually sold when they required extensive repairs or when the sale values exceeded the rental values. Undeniably, they were held for sale after they were deemed unsuitable for rental." 41 T.C. 20, 29. This last situation would appear to resemble the sale of culls from the livestock herds in the cases hereinabove discussed.

Taxpayer about 1940 had acquired a 240 acre tract called Blue Valley by purchase of tax certificates from which tax deed was acquired, and later to clear title a deed from the former owner was obtained. The total cost of this property was about $80 an acre. Eighty-seven acres of this land adjoined the Frisco Railroad. The Tax Court recites that the taxpayer envisioned developing this land as a commercial park in which it might construct buildings for lease or sale to industries and that it sought help in financing such projects from the railroad, and other institutions. Later, after extended negotiations, an arrangement was worked out whereby the railroad leased the land for ten years with option to renew for 89 years at an annual rental of $100 an acre, with an option to the railroad to purchase any part at $4,000 per acre. The option was placed in the lease at the insistence of the railroad and the option price was at a figure in excess of the market value. Several of the sales here involved resulted from the railroad exercising its option to purchase portions of the tract.

We again call attention to the portion of the Tax Court's opinion heretofore quoted wherein it stated, "And while the sales purpose, in some instances, may not have been predominant over the investment purpose, it was, nevertheless, substantial throughout the entire period under review." 41 T.C. 20, 29. This statement in and of itself leads us to believe that the Tax Court did not base its findings and decision on a determination of the primary or predominant purpose of taxpayer in acquiring and holding the various properties.

OPINION

No purpose will be served in attempting to analyze the evidence with respect to all the properties here involved. We express here no view as to the facts but remand the case to the Tax Court for findings based upon the standards hereinabove set forth with respect to each property.

Taxpayer urges that the Tax Court erred in admitting evidence over its objection and denying its motion to strike with respect to evidence offered as to activities of other corporations in which Mr. Curry had a substantial interest. Some of such evidence was doubtless proper and other portions of the evidence might well have been properly excluded. We do not believe prejudicial error has here been established. We have repeatedly held that in cases tried to a court without a jury prejudicial error in receiving incompetent evidence will not be found unless it is affirmatively shown that such evidence induced the court to make a finding which would not otherwise have been made. *Lessmann v. Commissioner*, 327 F.2d 990, 996–97 (8th Cir. 1964), and cases there cited.

We do observe that under the record here it appears that taxpayer is a separate and distinct corporate entity and no basis has been shown for piercing the corporate veil. Hence, it is our view that the operations of the other corporations would have no probative force in establishing taxpayer's purpose of holding real estate except to the extent that it might be shown that the other corporations were acting as an agent for the taxpayer. *See Frank v. Comm'r*, 321 F.2d 143, 150 (8th Cir. 1963); *Kaltreider v. Comm'r*, 255 F.2d 833, 838 (3d Cir. 1958).

In the Tax Court, taxpayer with respect to installments on sales made in prior years urged that the Commissioner is estopped from changing his position. The Commissioner had accepted capital gain treatment of the installment sales in prior years. The Tax Court properly rejected the estoppel defense and taxpayer is not asserting error here with respect to such ruling. The taxpayer however does insist that upon the basis of the facts, it is entitled to capital gain treatment on the sale installments collected in the involved years, and in our view is entitled to have a fact determination made with respect to the installment sales.

Wood v. Commissioner

United States Court of Appeals, Fifth Circuit

276 F.2d 586 (1960)

FACTS

The taxpayer is a resident of Lubbock, Texas. Early in 1945, after being in the printing business for twenty years, his doctors advised him to get out of business for reasons of health. This he did promptly, selling his business and his residence. He and his wife moved to a hotel. Wood had been active in religious pursuits for many years and, upon selling his business, he announced it to be his intention to devote the rest of his life to religious endeavors. He invested the proceeds from the sale of his business in Government bonds. In October of 1945, he was telling one of his long-time friends, an investment counselor, of the sale of his business and the investment of the proceeds. The friend suggested that Government bonds afforded no protection against inflation and recommended that at least a part of his investment should be in common stocks or real estate. Following the suggestion of his friend, Wood decided to take his money out of the Governments and invest it in real estate strategically located on the outskirts of Lubbock. In a letter to his bookkeeper, Wood declared his intention to hold these properties and derive income from them during his life and leave them to his wife. Like statements were made to others. About this time Wood rented an office on the door of which was the caption "William C. Wood, Investments." His telephone listing was under "Listed Investments." He was not licensed as a real estate broker and did not act for others in real estate transactions unless his activity with respect to the Woodlawn subdivision, which is hereafter discussed, could be so designated.

Wood's first venture into real estate ownership was the purchase in November of 1945, of the so-called Merrill tract. The purchase price was $40,000, of which half was paid in cash and the balance was represented by promissory notes. This land was on the outskirts of Lubbock. Railroad trackage ran along the length of the property. The tract had been platted and the lots had been listed for sale with several real estate brokers by those from whom the taxpayer bought it. The taxpayer removed an old building and did other clearing. He arranged for additional trackage. He cancelled the listings of the lots in the tract which had been made by his predecessors in title. Wood had the land replatted into odd-shaped lots of different sizes with each lot having railway trackage. These things being done, the taxpayer was ready to enter into long-term leases of the several lots to tenants needing sites for industrial purposes.

Of a similar character was the so-called Nelson-Brown Addition. This too was a subdivision in a section of Lubbock suitable for industrial development. By three separate purchases, in April, 1947, January, 1950, and October, 1951, Wood acquired most of the subdivision. At his own expense, Wood arranged for railroad trackage to be brought into the property. As in the case of the Merrill tract the taxpayer did not acquire the Nelson-Brown land for the purpose of selling it. He intended to make long-term leases and, to this end, he asked Cox and Murfee to find tenants.

The efforts made to make leases on the land in the two tracts were quite extensive and intensive. A brochure was prepared to show the attractive features of the properties as industrial sites, in which it was asserted that attractive leases could be arranged. The brochure stated, "Properties Shown are Not for Sale." The brochure was widely distributed. Interest was developed by the brochures and otherwise. One lease was made. It contained an option to purchase which was subsequently exercised. Most of those who were interested were unwilling to make leases, usually because of the necessity of having fee ownership in order to finance the construction of improvements. Wood was unwilling to erect any improvements on the property, because he could have done so only with borrowed capital, and it was his desire to leave the property to his wife without encumbrance. When some of the interested prospects were unwilling to enter into leases but offered to buy sites, these offers were submitted by Cox or Murfee to Wood and, from time to time sales were made. During the years involved in this proceeding seven sales were made of land in the Merrill tract; two in 1949, two in 1950, and three in 1951. No sales were made in 1948, 1952 or 1953. Sales of land in the Nelson-Brown tract followed pretty much the same pattern. Two sales were made in each of the years 1949, 1950, 1951 and 1953; none in 1948 or 1952. During the period the activity was directed toward not making sales but to the making of leases. As the Tax Court pointed out in its opinion:

> Wood believed that he could lease Nelson-Brown and Merrill as industrial properties when he made his original investments in those properties. He attempted to promote the city of Lubbock, through Chamber of Commerce activities. He was made president of the local chamber in 1950 and also worked for four years in a special group of the chamber designed to promote the city. He believed that the Chamber of Commerce could attract firms to Lubbock that would lease properties.

Although Cox became convinced that the likelihood of obtaining lessees in substantial numbers was remote, he was unable to convince Wood that this was so. Throughout all of the tax years and to and at the time of the trial before the Tax Court Wood believed that these properties could be leased for industrial purposes. The Tax Court concluded that while these properties were offered for lease, and not for sale, the taxpayer was willing to have them sold, and the properties were for sale in fact. The gains made on the sales from these two tracts were determined to be ordinary income.

Early in 1946 Wood bought an 80-acre tract just west of the Lubbock city limits. This land was then planted in cotton but Wood believed that eventually it would be good property. Wood promised Murfee the exclusive selling rights if the property was put on the market. Prior to this purchase the taxpayer had agreed to sell each of four friends ten acres in the east half of the tract purchased. He agreed with his friends that he would not market his land until theirs had been sold. With one of them, T. E. Bucker, the taxpayer agreed to repurchase any part of his parcel remaining unsold at any time. His associates desired to sell their lands as soon as possible and, upon their insistence, Wood agreed to the subdividing, platting and dedication of the entire eighty acres. The subdivision was called Woodlawn. The lots of the others moved slowly, due in part to the absence of utilities. In August of 1946 Buckner, with about three-fourths of his ten acres unsold, called upon Wood to repurchase it. To effect this repurchase Wood was required to borrow from his bank.

In February of 1947 the taxpayer was informed that the Lubbock School District would put a school on the west side of Woodlawn. He sold the school district seven and a half acres. Water, sewer and electric lines were then extended throughout Woodlawn.

Needing funds to repay the bank the money borrowed for the repurchase of the Buckner lots, Wood authorized Murfee to sell these lots and they were disposed of before the last of August, 1947. The lots of the others in the east half of the subdivision had been sold and there was a demand for those of the taxpayer. Without the knowledge of Wood, his lots in Woodlawn were advertised for sale by Murfee. Although he did not personally participate in any sales activity, the taxpayer realized that the subdivision had reached the near maximum of its development potential and he acquiesced, without objection, in the sales arranged by Murfee and did what was required of him in the closing of sales. In the last half of 1947 there were 19 sales of Woodlawn lots, in 1948 there were 47 such sales, in 1949 eight sales were effected, and in the first half of 1950 seven sales exhausted the taxpayer's Woodlawn property. Such of these lots as were sold during the tax years of 1948 through 1950 were found by the Tax Court to have been held primarily for sale of customers in the ordinary course of the taxpayer's trade or business.

The taxpayer contends that both the industrial and residential properties were capital assets, and the profits from the sales of these properties were capital gains, subject to federal income taxation as such rather than as ordinary income as held by the Tax Court.

ANALYSIS

This Court, on former occasions, has considered and discussed all of the questions presented here.... Repetition would serve no useful purpose. We therefore consider this case in the light of the established tests and, in so doing, we find ourselves in agreement with the conclusion of the Tax Court with respect to the residential or Woodlawn tract. The Tax Court did not separately consider the residential and the industrial property. We think it is necessary to do so.

The residential tract, or that portion of it retained or reacquired by the taxpayer, was purchased for the purpose of ultimate resale after an enhancement in value. That enhancement was fully realized soon after the school was erected in the subdivison. Wood financed and supervised the platting and subdividing of the tract. He acquiesced in the sales promotion and advertising by the agent. Over the period of thirty-five months, eighty-one sales were made with the result that all of the taxpayer's lots in Woodlawn were disposed of. We are aware of the decisions holding that various factors here present did not require a determination that property was held primarily for sale to customers in the ordinary course of trade or business. But each case must be decided on its own peculiar facts. *Smith v. Dunn, supra.* Specific factors, or combinations of them are not necessarily controlling. *Smith v. Comm'r, supra.* The Tax Court's holding as to the Woodlawn property is correct and is affirmed.

There was a very considerable difference in the taxpayer's purposes and activity with respect to the industrial Merrill and Nelson-Brown properties on the one hand, and the residential Woodlawn development on the other. These differences, we think, require a different treatment, for tax purposes, of the profits resulting from sales. The Tax Court reached the conclusion that, "The industrial lots were not held for leasing in the ordinary course of business and do not qualify as property within the ambit of § 117(j), and we do not understand the petitioner to contend otherwise." The contrary is vigorously asserted and we think is maintained. We do not think there is substantial evidence to support the Tax Court's finding. The industrial sites were purchased for leasing and there was never any departure or deviation from this intention as the primary purpose. Sales were made to get funds to make payments on the property, and sales were made of some lots in order that the remainder might be made attractive to prospective tenants. These sales were in furtherance of Wood's primary purpose of leasing these tracts. It may be that this purpose was difficult, or perhaps impossible, of accomplishment, but nevertheless it was a purpose in which Wood was sincere and steadfast. It is our decision that he was entitled to capital gains treatment on the profits realized from the sales of the industrial sites.

It will not be questioned that a property owner may hold some of it for sale to customers in the ordinary course of business and hold the remainder as capital assets. *See Foran v. Comm'r*, 165 F.2d 705 (5th Cir. 1948); *Wood v. Comm'r*, 197 F.2d 859 (5th Cir. 1952).

* * *

Kaltreider v. Commissioner

United States Court of Appeals, Third Circuit
255 F.2d 833 (1958)

FACTS

In 1936, Walter H. and Irene C. Kaltreider ("taxpayers"), husband and wife, purchased twenty-seven acres of farmland located on the outskirts of York, Pennsylvania, for $9,500.00. In 1938 they built their residence on a part of that land and continued to use the property exclusively for farming for a number of years.

On October 21, 1947, taxpayers, together with their son, Walter H. Kaltreider, Jr., a graduate engineer, organized Kaltreider Construction Inc. ("Corporation") under the laws of Pennsylvania to carry on a building and construction business.

The capital of Corporation was initially contributed by taxpayers and their son and, with the exception of twenty-five shares issued to each of taxpayers' two grandchildren on December 25, 1952, all outstanding stock has been held by them since the incorporation.

During 1951 and 1952, the taxable years in issue, taxpayers' son served as president of Corporation. The taxpayers, husband and wife, acted as treasurer and secretary respectively. Throughout this period Corporation was engaged in the construction of homes, garages, schoolhouses, and freight truck terminals.

During 1948 taxpayers developed a seven-acre tract of their twenty-seven acre farm and subdivided it into fifteen lots; Corporation constructed homes on eleven of them. In 1952 the taxpayers developed a second seven-acre tract of their farm and subdivided it into thirteen lots; Corporation constructed homes on seven of them.

Two of the homes were sold in 1949, and four in 1950, at a profit. In their joint income tax returns for the years 1949 and 1950, taxpayers treated the profits as ordinary income. On the first page of their tax returns the taxpayers listed their occupation as "Contractor" while in Schedule "C" of the tax returns, in which they specifically reported the profits, they listed the "nature of (their) business" as "Real Estate".

Five of the homes and the four remaining vacant lots[41] in the 1948 development were sold at a profit by taxpayers in 1951, the first of the two taxable years in issue. In their 1951 tax return taxpayers made allocation of sales price, costs, and gross profits between houses and lots. The profits allocated to sales of houses ($350.00) was reported as ordinary income in Schedule "C" and one half ($10,478.90) of the profit allocated to sale of the lots was reported as long-term capital gain in Schedule "D".

The allocation procedure established by taxpayers in their 1951 tax return was pursued in their 1952 tax return with respect to the seven homes which were built and sold that year. Profit allocated to sale of houses ($5,150) was reported as ordinary income in Schedule "C" and one-half ($6,744.50) of the profit allocated to sale of the lots on which the houses were built was reported as a long-term capital gain in Schedule "D".

On the first page of their 1951 and 1952 tax returns taxpayers listed their occupation as "Contractor". On Schedule "C" of the 1951 return taxpayers stated the nature of their business to be "Sale of Homes"; on Schedule "C" of their 1952 return it was stated to be "Contractor" and their principal product was described as "Homes".

Taxpayers' tax returns for the years 1949 to 1952, inclusive, were prepared by their accountant, John Cusma, from memoranda which they supplied him. He also prepared their declarations of estimated tax—except for the year 1952 when he failed to do so. His failure, he testified, "was purely an error on my part; he (taxpayers) had nothing to do with it."

Cusma was also Corporation's auditor and prepared its tax returns for the taxable years here involved. He had been engaged as a public accountant in York, Pennsylvania

---

41. [7] The lots were sold to Corporation.

since 1944. Prior to that time he was an investigator for the United States Department of Labor.

At the request of one of taxpayers' attorneys Cusma prepared amended returns for both taxpayers and Corporation in which profit allocated to the sale of houses that year in taxpayers' original 1952 return was eliminated and included instead in Corporation's return.

On the score of the taxpayers' activities in general during the taxable years involved and the period beginning with the launching of the development in 1948 these facts may be added to those already stated:

> Taxpayers were not licensed real estate brokers nor did they hold themselves out to be such; they did not list the lots in their two developments with any real estate agents; they placed no signs on the lots, nor did they advertise in newspapers. Contracts for sales of the houses in their developments were made either in the name of Corporation or Corporation and taxpayers jointly; never by taxpayers alone. With respect to the transfer of title to the houses following their sale all such transfers by deed were made by taxpayers since they were the title holders of the lots and the houses built upon them.

During the years 1949 to 1952, inclusive, taxpayers were not engaged in farming, as evidenced by their own tax returns for those years.

On the facts as stated the Tax Court made the following finding of fact:

> During the years in issue, the petitioners (taxpayers) were engaged in the business of subdividing, improving and selling real estate. The lots sold by them during the taxable years under consideration constituted property held primarily for sale to customers in the ordinary course of their trade or business.

In its Opinion the Tax Court, in support of its finding, stated:

> In 1948 and again in 1952, one of the tax years in issue, the petitioners (taxpayers) incurred considerable expense in subdividing the acreage in question into some 28 lots for residential purposes. They then caused their closely held family corporation to construct houses on 18 of those lots; 12 of which were sold to individual purchasers during the taxable years under consideration. The record does not disclose what motives underlay the original purchase of the 27-acre tract. However, even were we to make the gratuitous assumption that petitioners (taxpayers) acquired the land solely for investment purposes, nothing of merit would be added to their case. When they embarked upon the development, construction, and sales program which we have outlined, they acquired the status of "dealers" in relation to the property in issue and thereupon became engaged in the real estate business.... With respect to the part which Corporation played in constructing the houses, and the taxpayers' contention that under its arrangement with Corporation the latter was to receive that portion of the purchase price allocable to the house while taxpayers received only that portion allocable to the land, the

Tax Court determined that " ... whatever was done here by the Corporation was done at the instance and for the benefit of the petitioners (taxpayers) as their agent." In connection with this last statement the Tax Court said: " ... It is an accepted principle of law that one may conduct a business through agents, and that because others may bear the burdens of management, the business is none the less his."

Taxpayers' position here may be summed up as follows:

Their property was acquired for residential and investment purposes; they actually farmed it for several years; they were not real estate brokers nor did they hold themselves out as such; they did not list or advertise their property, or any of it, for sale; the costs of construction of the houses were borne by Corporation and taxpayers were only paid for the land; Corporation "found purchasers for the homes" and sold them; taxpayers under their arrangement with Corporation sold the land only to one customer, Corporation.

The Commissioner's position is that the Tax Court's determination is amply sustained by the record; that it is further supported by the fact that "taxpayers declared themselves to be in the business of selling real estate (and homes) by their statement contained in Schedule "C" of their income tax returns for the taxable years now on review", and "Similar statements ... in Schedule 'C' of taxpayers' 1949 and 1950 income tax returns."

ANALYSIS

With respect to the Tax Court's findings that (1) taxpayers were in the real estate business and the properties sold by them "constituted property held primarily for sale to customers in the ordinary course of their trade or business", and (2) taxpayers' failure to file the required declaration of estimated tax for 1952 was not due to "reasonable cause", it is well-settled that such findings are "in the nature of an ultimate finding of fact and since such finding is but a legal inference from other facts it is subject to review free of the restraining impact of the so-called 'clearly erroneous' rule applicable to ordinary findings of fact by the trial court...."[42]

On review of the record we are of the opinion that there is an abundance of evidence to support both of the Tax Court's findings and its Decision.

As to the finding with respect to the nature of taxpayers' business, these principles are well-settled: "There, is no fixed formula or rule of thumb" for determining whether property is held primarily for sale to customers in the ordinary course of the taxpayer's business and "Each case must, in the last analysis, rest upon its own facts."[43] No single factor or test is dispositive.[44] Factors considered are: (1) the purpose for which the property was acquired; (2) the purpose for which it was held; (3) improvements, and their extent, made to the property by taxpayer; (4) frequency, num-

---

42. [10] Philber Equipment Corporation v. Comm'r, 237 F.2d 129, 131 (3d Cir. 1956); Curtis Company v. Comm'r, 232 F.2d 167, 168 (3d Cir. 1956).

43. [11] Mauldin v. Comm'r, 195 F.2d 714, 716 (10th Cir. 1952); Pool v. Comm'r, 251 F.2d 233, 236 (9 Cir., 1957).

44. [12] Gamble v. Comm'r, 242 F.2d 586, 590 (5th Cir. 1957).

ber and continuity of sales; (5) the extent and substantiality of the transactions; (6) the nature and extent of taxpayer's business; (7) the extent of advertising to promote sales, or the lack of such advertising; and (8) listing of the property for sale directly or through brokers.[45]

In considering the activities of the taxpayer the rule is settled that a person may engage in business via an agent, and the sales activities of an agent for the benefit of the principal will be imputed to the principal.[46]

In evaluating the foregoing factors for the purpose of determining whether gain was derived from the sale of capital assets or represented ordinary income we must keep in mind the teaching that the term "capital assets" as used in § 117 must be "construed narrowly."[47]

In the instant case these critical factors sustain the Tax Court's determination of fact and law that the properties sold by taxpayers in 1951 and 1952 were held by them primarily for sale to customers in the ordinary course of business within the meaning of § 117(a) and (j):

Taxpayers paid $9,500 for their twenty-seven acre farm in 1936. While they farmed the land for several years thereafter, they had ceased farming in 1948 when they launched upon the initial seven-acre subdivision and development and did not thereafter resume farming operations. Taxpayer Walter H. Kaltreider, Sr. was in the cigar business from 1944 to 1949. The cost of the 1948 and 1952 developments (involving altogether fourteen acres) totaled $18,263; almost twice the $9,500 cost of the twenty-seven acre farm, and more than three times the $4,926 original cost of the acreage improved. The development and subdivision, in addition to surveying, involved extensive improvements, such as grading, fencing and stone surfacing. In addition to the development costs, taxpayers caused their family-owned corporation, in which they owned two-thirds of the stock in 1951 and more than sixty per cent in 1952, to

---

45. [13] Cases cited in notes 11 and 12; also Di Lisio v. Vidal, 233 F.2d 909 (10th Cir. 1956); Cohn v. Comm'r, 226 F.2d 22 (9th Cir. 1955); Friend v. Comm'r, 198 F.2d 285 (10th Cir. 1952); Rollingwood Corp. v. Comm'r, 190 F.2d 263 (9th Cir. 1951).

46. [14] Achong v. Comm'r, 246 F.2d 445, 447 (9th Cir. 1957).

47. [15] Corn Products Refining Co. v. Comm'r, 350 U.S. 46 (1955), rehearing denied, 350 U.S. 943. It is there stated 350 U.S. at 52: 'But the capital-asset provision of § 117 must not be so broadly applied as to defeat rather than further the purpose of Congress. Burnet v. Harmel, 287 U.S. 103 (1932). Congress intended that profits and losses arising from the everyday operation of a business be considered as ordinary income or loss rather than capital gain or loss. The preferential treatment provided by 117 applies to transactions in property which are not the normal source of business income. It was intended to 'relieve the taxpayer from ... excessive tax burdens on gains resulting from a conversion of capital investments, and to remove the deterrent, effect of those burdens on such conversions.' Burnet v. Harmel, 287 U.S. at 106. Since this section is an exception from the normal tax requirements of the Internal Revenue Code, the definition of a capital asset must be narrowly applied and its exclusions interpreted broadly. This is necessary to effectuate the basic congressional purpose. This Court has always construed narrowly the term 'capital assets' in 117. See Hort v. Comm'r, 313 U.S. 28 (1941); Kieselbach v. Comm'r, 317 U.S. 399 (1943).' See also Simonsen Industries, Inc., v. Comm'r, 243 F.2d 407, 409 (7th Cir. 1957); Pool v. Comm'r, cited Note 11.

expend $274,221 on the construction of eighteen homes, twelve of which were sold during 1951 and 1952, the tax years under review. Taxpayers sold $43,241[48] stock in February, 1949. The cost of the construction of the two homes sold in 1949 (the first of the eighteen homes built on the two developments) was $36,700. The taxpayers in each instance executed, as grantors, the deeds which conveyed title to the individual purchasers of the eighteen homes which were built and sold. They also executed the deeds, as grantors, conveying title to the four vacant lots sold to Corporation in 1951. Corporation acted as taxpayers' agent in constructing the eighteen homes, advertising them for sale and in negotiating their sales. In many instances taxpayers were directly paid the consideration received on the sale of the homes. In 1949 and 1950 income tax returns they reported the profits made on the sale of the homes as ordinary income and described themselves as being in the real estate business and as "Contractors". In their 1951 and 1952 tax returns they respectively listed themselves as "Contractors" and their business as being "Sales of Homes" and "Homes".

It is settled that statements of this nature (self-description of business or occupation) constitute evidence of taxpayers' business.

There remains for disposition taxpayers' contention that the Tax Court erred in sustaining the Commissioner's imposition of penalties for failure to file a declaration of estimated tax in 1952 as required by §294(d)(1)(A), and for substantial underestimation of tax due for 1952 under §294(d)(2).

As earlier stated, taxpayers urged, in the Tax Court, that they had relied solely on their accountant to file the 1952 declaration; he failed to do so and therefore their failure to file was due to reasonable cause and not willful neglect. We agree with the Tax Court that proof had not been presented that the accountant was qualified to advise taxpayers' concerning tax matters or that their reliance was well-placed.

The penalty for substantial underestimation of estimated tax under §294(d)(2) is not subject to a reasonable cause limitation nor indeed to any other defense. Where no declaration of estimated tax is filed the estimate is considered to be zero and the penalty mandatory.

Burgher v. Campbell

United States Court of Appeals, Fifth Circuit
244 F.2d 863 (1957)

FACTS

In 55 separate findings of fact the trial court separated into two categories the lands sold by the taxpayers during the years in controversy. The findings that part of the land was held by taxpayers for investment resulted in a conclusion by the court that the gains from their sale should have been taxed at capital gains rates and thus resulted in a judgment for a refund of the taxes illegally collected as on ordinary income. The findings that part of the lands were held primarily for sale to customers

---

48. [16] The total paid-in capital of Corporation was $50,000.

in the ordinary course of trade or business when sold resulted in a conclusion by the court that taxes exacted by the Director of Internal Revenue on the ordinary income basis were legally collected.

ANALYSIS

Neither the Government nor taxpayers are in doubt as to the applicable law in such cases. They both cite the same authorities. *Smith v. Comm'r*, 232 F.2d 142 (5th Cir. 1956); *Ross v. Comm'r*, 227 F.2d 265 (5th Cir. 1955); *Smith v. Dunn*, 224 F.2d 353 (5th Cir. 1955); *Goldberg v. Comm'r*, 223 F.2d 709 (5th Cir. 1955), to mention only a few.

It cannot be seriously contended by taxpayers that the trial court reached its ultimate conclusions by applying incorrect principles of law or that there was no substantial evidence on which the trial court might properly draw the inference that Mr. Burgher, who had spent his entire business life in one phase or another of the real estate business and who had bought and sold real estate for his own account before 1942 and had admittedly done so after the tax years here in question, selling some of the lots in the very tracts here in issue, did hold the Shaughnessy tracts as a developer of real estate. We need not recite all the facts pro and con, since we, of course, do not reverse the judgment of a trial court in a case such as this even under the theory announced in *Galena Oaks Corporation v. Scofield*, 218 F.2d 217 (5th Cir. 1954), unless we are convinced that the judgment was clearly erroneous. We do, however, point to the fact that part of this land was sold to a wholly owned corporation a little over two years after it was acquired and was by it subdivided and sold to the public. Such action was consistent with a holding by the taxpayers for sale rather than for investment. The fact that it was sold in a raw state in a tract of 41 acres in not decisive. The question is whether it was held for sale at the time. Neither is it decisive that the customer to which it was sold was a wholly owned corporation. The fact that Mr. Burgher with all of his buying and selling history bought the land in 1945 and sold it in 1947 to a corporation controlled by him and which immediately subdivided and sold lots from it, is ample evidence on which the court could find that it was bought in 1945 for that purpose. There is the further fact that Mr. Burgher got back some of the lots himself and later sold them, admittedly in the ordinary course of his real estate business. The trial court was not required to accept the theory advanced by the taxpayer that this particular property for these particular years was held for investment rather than for sale when it was actually sold so soon after its acquisition. The sale of other parts of the Shaughnessy tract and of the Parnell tract, bought in 1946, part to an individual and part to the City of Dallas for a park, could reasonably be identified by the trial court with the business of the taxpayers.

HOLDING

We conclude that the findings of fact necessary to support the court's conclusion that the property sold was held primarily for sale to customers in the ordinary course of taxpayers' business are supported by substantial evidence and are not clearly erroneous and the judgment must be affirmed.

Bradshaw v. United States

United States Court of Claims

683 F.2d 365 (1982)

FACTS

On January 6, 1961, Thomas E. Swift (Thomas) purchased a tract of land, consisting of approximately 200 acres, in Dalton, Whitfield County, Georgia, for $60,000. Two dispositions of property out of this 200 acres were made by Thomas in the summer of 1968. The consolidated cases herein concern one of these dispositions, the transfer of 40.427 acres, subsequently known as Castlewood Subdivision (the subdivision), to Castlewood on July 29, 1968. The conservative fair market value of the subdivision on the date of transfer was $250,000. Thomas' adjusted basis in this portion of the property was $8,538. In exchange for the transfer, Thomas received from Castlewood five promissory notes (the Castlewood notes), each in the principal amount of $50,000 and bearing interest at the rate of 4 percent per annum. The first note matured on January 29, 1971, with each successive note maturing at 1-year intervals. Thomas received no down payment for the transfer, and no security or other collateral was taken for the purchase price. He elected to report his gain from the transaction on the installment method pursuant to section 453(b).

At the time of transfer, various opportunities were available to Thomas to dispose of the subdivision, including sale to third parties. While he had not developed property himself, Thomas was highly expert in real estate matters in the Dalton area. Based upon this knowledge, including knowledge of sales of other real estate in the vicinity of the subdivision, Thomas evaluated the prospects for the development of the subdivision to be bright, whether such development was undertaken by himself, by a corporation that he might organize, or by a third party. He considered the alternative opportunities available to him to dispose of the property and decided to develop the property himself through a corporation rather than sell it to a third party.[49]

Consequently, Castlewood was organized and incorporated on July 29, 1968, under the laws of the State of Georgia, to obtain, subdivide, develop and sell lots in the subdivision. On July 29, 1968, Castlewood issued its Certificate No. 1, representing 50 shares of common stock, to Thomas in exchange for the transfer to the corporation of an automobile valued at $4,500. At all times relevant herein, Thomas was the sole shareholder of Castlewood and was responsible for conducting its business affairs.

---

49. [5] It is admitted that Thomas was aware of the different tax consequences that would attach to a sale of the subdivision, as opposed to a capital contribution of the property, to the corporation he might organize. In utilizing a corporate form to obtain the property, he sought to realize his accumulated gain in the property through the date of transfer, and by using a corporation to develop and sell lots from the property, he sought to limit his personal liability in order to insulate other non-corporate businesses in which he was involved.

His expertise was available to and utilized by the corporation in its development of the subdivision, enabling it to minimize development costs and thus increase profits.

The expected source of income and anticipated profit of Castlewood, and the expected source of payment of the five notes, with interest, was from the sale of the lots in the subdivision. At the time of the transfer to the corporation, Thomas anticipated that when developed, lots from the subdivision could be sold at a profit by the corporation and that the amount of such profit would increase over time. He had a plan for the development of the property which was timed so as to take full advantage of the opportunities for profit. He further anticipated that the development of the property would succeed and yield a profit to the corporation in the range between $100,000 and $150,000. He expected a positive cash flow to the corporation within about a year and a half, thereby providing sufficient funds to pay the first of the notes, due in January of 1971, and that the corporation could in the regular course of its business pay the five notes as they came due.

Because of the growing character of, and need for housing in, the Dalton, Georgia area, the value of the subdivision was, at all times relevant herein, increasing. In fact, the character and location of the subdivision was such that the property could reasonably be anticipated to be readily marketable at its development. If, however, the subdivision had not been developed, or if the development process had been slowed, Castlewood could have borrowed the money against the property to pay off the notes.

Prior to the creation of Castlewood and the transfer of the property thereto, Thomas estimated that development costs for the subdivision would be approximately $50,000. He anticipated that he would have a ready source of funds from C & S Concrete Products Company (C&S) to meet these development expenses. C&S was a partnership formed by Thomas, which was engaged in the manufacture of concrete products used in the building trade. At all times relevant herein, C&S was wholly owned directly or beneficially by Thomas, his wife, Frances, and their three children, Jolana, Lori and Stephen. Thomas' drawing account on C&S was, in essence, his personal bank account. Thomas had no personal bank account, and when using funds from his drawing account at C&S, he was in effect using his own personal funds.

As expected, the corporation's development expenses were primarily funded through advances from the partnership, totaling $34,116.10, at various times from August 31, 1968 through August 10, 1970.[50] These advances were treated as interest-free loans by both parties and were charged to an open account on the books of C&S. The partnership took no collateral or other security interest. The loans were repaid in four installments over an 8-year period.

---

50. [7] Castlewood also borrowed $521.94, interest free, from Thomas in November 1968 for the payment of the 1968 real estate taxes on the subdivision. This amount was repaid in full on September 18, 1972.

Castlewood subdivided the subdivision into two tracts. Tract I consisted of 26 lots. Tract II consisted of eight lots. Each lot averaged approximately one acre. Lots were not formally offered for sale nor were any lots sold during the corporation's first two fiscal years (ended July 31, 1969, and July 31, 1970). Thomas was contacted by parties wishing to purchase lots before the development was completed, but before commencing the development, he had decided that no lots would be sold until all of the planned development activities had been completed. This was because, among other reasons, he did not want anyone coming onto the property and cutting up the roads that he had put in, to install subsequent improvements such as water lines. All of the improvements made by Castlewood were completed before any of the lots were sold or offered for sale.[51] Except for paving on two lots and surveying, the eight lots in Tract II were essentially undeveloped. From August 1970 to April 1973, Castlewood sold 16 lots in Tract I and two lots in Tract II for an aggregate sales price of $239,880. It did not advertise the sale of these lots, use realtors, or pay sales commissions. The property sold had an allocated land cost (of the $250,000 purchase price) and development cost of $159,378.39, yielding a net return to the corporation of $80,501.11. Castlewood reported sales of lots on its federal income tax returns for the fiscal years ended July 31, 1971, July 31, 1972, and July 31, 1973.

Subsequent to its 1973 fiscal year, Castlewood, upon the advice of its accountant, decided to cease selling lots in the subdivision as a result of the position taken by the Commissioner of Internal Revenue (Commissioner) on audit. During the period when no sales were made, both Thomas and his son Stephen were contacted by parties seeking to purchase lots. Castlewood reported no income from operations for its remaining fiscal years and was liquidated on September 23, 1976.[52] Castlewood never paid any salaries or declared or paid any dividends.

On December 21, 1970, prior to the time that the first Castlewood note became due, Thomas organized and incorporated SJL. This corporation was formed by Thomas as part of his estate planning and was established in order to provide funds and opportunities for dealings in and the development of real estate and related activities by his children.[53] Its formation in December of 1970 was precipitated by the fact that the first Castlewood note was due in January of 1971. On December 28, 1970, Thomas transferred to SJL the five Castlewood notes in exchange for all of the stock of SJL in a transaction qualifying for nonrecognition of gain under section 351. On December

---

51. [8] Improvements included paved streets, sewers and utilities. Castlewood did not construct residences on the lots; this was done or arranged by the purchaser of each lot.

52. [10] Subsequent to the liquidation, Thomas' estate sold all but three of the lots remaining in Tract I and all but four of the lots remaining in Tract II for a total sales price of $170,000. This property had an allocable land cost (of the $250,000 purchase price) and development cost of $75,239.43, yielding a net return, over the corporation's original cost, of $94,760.57.

53. [11] SJL, at various times, considered various real estate transactions, but never invested in nor acquired real estate or options for real estate, or otherwise consummated any transactions or engaged in any business with third parties as a result of considering those transactions.

29, 1970, and January 4, 1971, he made equal gifts of all of the stock of SJL to his wife and three children, so that after the gifts each owned one-fourth of the corporation.

On or about January 19, 1971, SJL filed an election under section 1372(a) for status as a small business corporation (subchapter S corporation). This election was accepted by the Commissioner on February 1, 1971.

The note due January 29, 1971, was paid by Castlewood as due, together with $5,000 interest, to SJL. The note due January 29, 1972, was paid on January 31, 1972, together with $7,000 interest. The note due January 29, 1973, was paid on February 14, 1973, together with $9,000 interest.[54] The funds needed by Castlewood to repay the notes, plus interest, were generated solely from the sales of lots in the subdivision. Castlewood deducted the interest payments made to SJL on its relevant corporate income tax returns. On its subchapter S income tax returns for the 1971, 1972 and 1973 fiscal years, SJL reported the payments it received from Castlewood as long-term capital gain to the extent the principal of each note exceeded its adjusted basis in the note. Consistent with its subchapter S status, SJL paid no tax on this income or on the interest income received from Castlewood. Rather, the shareholders, Frances, Jolana, Lori and Stephen, reported and paid taxes on their allocable share of the long-term capital gain and interest income received by SJL.

On May 14, 1971, SJL distributed $4,000 to Jolana, Lori and Stephen and $2,000 to Frances. On January 31, 1972, SJL distributed $23,000 to Jolana, Lori and Stephen and $25,000 to Frances.

By statutory notice of deficiency dated September 20, 1976, the Commissioner determined that additional income tax was due from Castlewood for its 1971 and 1972 tax years, for the reason that the transfer of the subdivision to that corporation by Thomas was not a sale, as treated by the corporation on its tax returns, but rather a transfer of property solely in exchange for stock or securities within the meaning of section 351. Thus, he concluded that, pursuant to section 362, Castlewood's pre-development basis in the property was equal to that of the transferor immediately before the transfer, or $8,538. This, in turn, increased Castlewood's taxable income on sales of lots. Additionally, the Commissioner concluded that no debtor-creditor relationship was established between Castlewood and Thomas, thereby disallowing certain deductions of interest paid to SJL on the notes taken for the purchase price of the property.

---

54. [12] During its 1971, 1972 and 1973 fiscal years, SJL had no receipts other than the payments on the notes from Castlewood, including interest. Subsequent to its 1973 fiscal year, Castlewood decided, on the advice of its accountant, to postpone payment of the final two notes held by SJL. This decision was based on the uncertain tax effect of payment resulting from the positions taken by the Commissioner on audit. SJL has never made demand for payment or attempted to collect the final two notes, but rather agreed to extend the time for payment, pursuant to the advice of its accountant, based upon the uncertainty of the tax treatment which would be accorded it, as payee, upon the payment of any amount with respect to the notes. No written agreements evidenced this extension, and no interest or advance interest was paid in connection with this extension.

By statutory notice of deficiency dated September 20, 1976, the Commissioner determined that additional income tax was due from each of Jolana, Lori and Stephen for their 1972 tax years and from Frances for her 1971 and 1972 tax years. The Commissioner concluded that SJL no longer qualified as a subchapter S corporation because more than 20 percent of its gross receipts (amounts received as payment on the Castlewood notes) constituted passive investment income within the meaning of § 1372(e)(5). Accordingly, the distributions made by SJL to each shareholder,[55] and reported as interest income and long-term capital gain, were actually taxable as dividends, due to the termination of SJL's subchapter S status.[56]

Assessments of tax and interest were made on February 9, 1977, which were promptly paid. Claims for refund were formally denied on July 6, 1977. Each plaintiff filed a timely petition with this court on September 26, 1977.

ANALYSIS

The first question concerns the proper tax treatment of Thomas' transfer of the subdivision to Castlewood in exchange for the five $50,000 promissory notes. If the transfer is treated as a sale, as plaintiff contends, then Castlewood's adjusted basis for its sales of the lots from the subdivision property would include the $250,000 purchase price (a cost basis), it would be allowed deductions of the interest paid on the notes and its taxable income would be generally as shown on its returns for the years in issue. However, if, as defendant claims, the transfer was not a sale but was either a transfer under § 351[57] or a contribution to the corporation's capital, then Castlewood's adjusted basis in the lots sold would be reduced to Thomas' original basis (a carryover basis) pursuant to § 362, it would be denied deductions of the interest paid on the notes and its taxable income would be generally as shown on the notice of deficiency issued with respect to it.

The sale versus capital contribution problem arises from a situation which often confronts taxpayers with holdings in undeveloped real estate. It is not uncommon for a landowner with a large tract of land suitable for development to want to freeze as capital gain the appreciation in the value of the property that has accrued during its ownership. While an outright sale of the property achieves this result, it also de-

---

55. [13] Only the January 31, 1972 distribution is in issue for Jolana, Lori and Stephen. As to Frances, the May 14, 1971 distribution is in issue with respect to her fiscal year ended June 30, 1971, and the January 31, 1972 distribution is in issue with respect to her fiscal year ended June 30, 1972.

56. [14] A notice of deficiency was also issued to SJL for its taxable years ended November 30, 1971, and November 30, 1972. However, SJL is not a party to the proceedings in this court. Instead, SJL filed a petition in the United States Tax Court for a redetermination of its tax liability for those years, due to an inadequacy of funds to pay the deficiencies asserted against it.

57. [15] Section 351 provides in pertinent part:

(a) General Rule. — No gain or loss shall be recognized if property is transferred to a corporation by one or more persons solely in exchange for stock or securities in such corporation and immediately after the exchange such person or persons are in control (as defined in section 368(c)) of the corporation. For purposes of this section, stock or securities issued for services shall not be considered as issued in return for property.

prives the landowner of any participation in the profits to be reaped from its ultimate development. On the other hand, if the landowner develops and sells the property himself, he runs the risk of being treated as a dealer of the property and any gain generated through sales, including the gain associated with the land's appreciation in value while undeveloped, is taxable to him at ordinary income rates....

In the face of such a dilemma, taxpayers have devised an apparently viable solution. By selling the real property to a controlled corporation, they can realize their capital gain on the appreciation which has accrued during their ownership and, at the same time, preserve their opportunity to later participate in the developmental profits as shareholders of the development corporation. Moreover, the corporation obtains a cost basis in the real property, thereby reducing the amount of ordinary income to be received from subsequent sales.

Not unexpectedly, the Commissioner has repeatedly challenged the characterization of such a transaction as a sale, instead maintaining that the transfer is, in reality, a capital contribution and that the transferee corporation is only entitled to a carryover basis for the property....

Although often litigated, the courts which have considered the sale versus § 351/capital contribution question have not always been careful to distinguish between these two separate arguments. Indeed, it is understandable that the analyses of these prior cases have been fraught with overlap, for both propositions require an examination of substantially the same criteria. However, since a decision for plaintiff on the capital contribution question does not necessarily dispose of the § 351 question,[58] our discussion proceeds in two stages. Initially, we consider the "sale" versus "capital contribution" distinction. Thereafter, we address defendant's contention that § 351 applies to the subject transaction because the Castlewood notes constituted "stock or securities" within the intendment of the statute.

The proper characterization of a transaction, as a "sale" or a "capital contribution," is a question of fact to be decided as of the time of the transfer on the basis of all of the objective evidence. *Gooding Amusement Co. v. Comm'r*, 236 F.2d 159, 165 (6th Cir. 1956), cert. denied, 352 U.S. 1031 (1957). While the form of the transaction is relevant, we are required to examine all of the pertinent factors in order to determine whether the substance of the transaction complies with its form. *Gregory v. Helvering*, 293 U.S. 465, 469–70 (1935). The essential nature of the transaction is to be determined from a consideration of all of the surrounding circumstances. *Piedmont Corp. v. Comm'r*, 388 F.2d 886, 889 (4th Cir. 1968).

In this case, the objective evidence points to a sale. First, and foremost, the price paid for the subdivision reflected its actual fair market value. Since it has been stip-

---

58. [17] Application of § 351 is mandatory if all of the conditions precedent therefore are satisfied. *Pocatello Coca-Cola Bottling Co. v. U.S.*, 139 F. Supp. 912, 915 (D. Idaho 1956).

ulated that the value of the subdivision was $250,000, the very amount for which it was sold to Castlewood, the transfer cannot be considered a "pretextuous device" to divert the earnings and profits of the corporation, otherwise taxable as ordinary income, into sales proceeds taxable as capital gain. *Piedmont Corp. v. Comm'r*, 388 F.2d 886, 889 (4th Cir. 1968). The sales price did not constitute an inflated value for the property, and, thus, did not represent an attempt to transfer to Thomas any subsequent capital increment in the value of the property, nor any of the gain from its development. In this respect, the transfer was clearly a sale.

Additionally, the various formalities of a sale were strictly observed. The five instruments involved constituted negotiable instruments in the form of "notes" under Georgia law, Ga. Code Ann. § 109A-3-104 (1979), contained an unqualified obligation to pay the principal amount, with fixed maturity dates ranging from two and one-half to six and one-half years after the date of sale and bore a reasonable rate of interest. The notes were not subordinated to general corporate creditors and contained a means for collection at maturity, which was never utilized as the principal and interest were always paid as due until the Commissioner challenged the tax treatment of those payments. On these bases, the notes contained all of the traditional elements of sales-generated debt.

Even so, defendant asks that upon consideration of the economic substance of the transfer, the transaction be recast as a capital contribution. This is so, we are told, because Congress has dictated that no tax consequences shall attach to a transaction where direct ownership of property is changed into indirect ownership through a proprietary interest in a corporation. Thus, where the circumstances of a purported sale demonstrate that the transferor, in fact, retained a continuing interest in the property transferred, the transaction is more appropriately characterized as a capital contribution.

Defendant calls our attention to an alleged factual pattern to be discerned in those instances where it has been determined that the economic substance of a purported sale was actually a contribution to capital. In such cases, it is claimed, a newly formed, inadequately capitalized corporation received assets which were essential to its purpose, and which required at the outset substantial improvements to convert them into income-producing property. Whereas, in those cases holding that the transaction resulted in a sale, the transfer involved proven, income-producing assets. Defendant submits that the distinction drawn in these cases turns on the nature and degree of risk inherent in the transfer of unproven assets and that in such instances, because of the high degree of risk, the transferor is likely to have retained a continuing interest in the property transferred.

In the present case, defendant maintains, unproven real property was transferred to an untried, undercapitalized business in return for notes, which were to be satisfied from the proceeds expected to be generated through the sale of lots. From this, defendant urges that we conclude that the notes represented a continuing interest in the corporate business, for repayment was totally dependent upon the success of the enterprise.

We cannot quarrel with the policies underlying § 351, nor with its intended scope. However, even accepting defendant's premise that the prior cases can be meaningfully differentiated along the lines suggested, we are unable to agree with the conclusion defendant draws in this case. Rephrasing defendant's position, we are asked to find that the degree of risk herein was of the type normally associated with a capital contribution. Thus stated, the salient inquiry is whether the notes occupied the position of equity, the assets and prospects of the business being unable to assure payment of the debt according to its terms.

Admittedly, the stipulated facts show Castlewood to have been a "thin" corporation. Its initial capitalization consisted entirely of an automobile valued at $4,500. The corporation then issued five notes, each in the face amount of $50,000, in consideration for the subdivision property. While an additional $3,200 was contributed to Castlewood 4 months later, in practical terms it had no funds of its own with which to conduct business, instead relying on advances totalling over $34,000 from C&S to develop the property. It cannot be refuted that Castlewood had a very high ratio of debt to equity. But the mere fact that a corporation is or is not thinly capitalized does not, per se, control the character of the transaction....

The facts reveal that in addition to its formal capitalization, Castlewood anticipated having access to, did have access to, and utilized funds in the form of loans from C&S, the partnership owned by Thomas and his family, which served as Thomas' personal bank account. Castlewood also had access to an important resource in the expertise Thomas brought to the business, which allowed the corporation to minimize its development expenses. *See Murphy Logging Co. v. U.S.*, 378 F.2d 222, 224 (9th Cir. 1967). Given these resources, which were certainly adequate to finance the level of development activities undertaken, and the absence of any need to employ advertising or to use realtors, there was little reason for the corporation to maintain a large surplus of liquid capital. Under the circumstances, we cannot say that undercapitalization is fatal to plaintiff's position.

Integrally related to this discussion, as defendant recognizes, is the nature or quality of the risk assumed by the transferor. However, unlike defendant, we do not find the fact that what was sold to Castlewood was unimproved real estate to be necessarily indicative of a high degree of risk. Concomitantly, nor do we view repayment of the Castlewood notes to have been dependent upon the success of the business. Under the stipulated facts of this case, at the time of transfer, because of the character and location of the subdivision, there was a reasonable anticipation that the development of the property would succeed and yield a profit. And, as planned, the subdivision was developed, a cash flow generated and the notes paid, with interest, as due. While repayment from the receipts of the business was a logical necessity, repayment from the profits was not. A successful enterprise herein would have been one which realized a profit from its developmental activities, that is, one which generated income over and above the value of the property as purchased. And while that occurred, it was not from that success that the notes were paid, but from the value of the property which was there from the date of sale. It is of prime importance that the property was, at all times, saleable in its undeveloped condition.[59] At the time of transfer, there existed contemporaneous opportunities to sell the property to third parties. In fact, a portion of the original tract had been sold, undeveloped, to a third party immediately before the sale to Castlewood. The record does not support defendant's conclusion that the property required extensive improvements in order to convert it into an income-producing asset, or even to generate a cash flow. Although lots were not sold until development was finished, this was merely by design. Prospective purchasers had sought to buy lots before development was complete and, once sales were commenced, lots were sold undeveloped. Moreover, at all times the value of the property was increasing, irrespective of its development, and, if necessary, the corporation could have borrowed the money against the property to pay off the notes. Clearly, it was always within Castlewood's ability to make payment as required. To be sure, as with any new venture, there was some risk of loss; but the evidence manifests that such risk was significantly reduced in this case. From the beginning, there existed a reasonable assurance of repayment of the notes regardless of the success of the business. To us, this is further indicia that the notes were debt, not equity. The facts just do not support the inference that, in holding the Castlewood notes, Thomas was assuming the risk of loss normally associated with equity participation.

We are referred by defendant to, among others, *Burr Oaks Corp. v. Comm'r*, 365 F.2d 24 (7th Cir. 1966), *cert. denied*, 385 U.S. 1007 (1967), and *Aqualane Shores, Inc. v. Comm'r*, 269 F.2d 116 (5th Cir. 1959), two of the leading decisions to hold a purported sale to be a contribution to capital. In Burr Oaks, undeveloped land, intended for subdivision, was transferred to a newly formed corporation for more than twice its fair market value. In exchange therefor, the transferors received back 2-year promissory notes. Development costs ran extremely high and sales of lots were, at best, slow. Consequently, the notes were only partially paid at maturity and new notes were given for the unpaid balance. Moreover, some of the property was eventually retransferred to the noteholders at little or no cost. On these facts, the Seventh Circuit had no difficulty affirming the decision of the Tax Court, finding a strong inference that the transfer was an equity contribution where "payment to the transferors (was) dependent on the success of an untried undercapitalized business with uncertain prospects." 365 F.2d at 27. In Aqualane Shores, the land transferred to the development corporation was mangrove swamp. Thus, vast improvements were essential to its successful development, which, even then, was highly speculative. With its only source of revenue being the sale of lots, the corporation was forced to borrow substantial amounts of money in order to put the land in marketable condition. No payments on the notes taken back for the land

---

59. [19] Defendant makes the argument that if a creditor looks to the liquidation of the corporation's assets for payment, such is an indication that the true nature of his holding is that of a proprietary interest in the business. While this may be true in some instances, it is not necessarily so where the asset is readily marketable in its raw form. In the common situation, the asset must produce income for the creditor to be paid. Consequently, liquidation of the asset destroys the business. However, in this case, liquidation of the subdivision fulfilled the purpose of the business. Thus, repayment was part of the natural disposition of the asset.

were made for 4 years after maturity. On this basis, payment of the obligations to the transferors was deemed to be dependent upon and at the risk of the success of the venture, and the transfer subject to §112(b)(5), the predecessor to §351.269 F.2d at 119–20.

The evidentiary basis of the present case, as previously set forth, contrasts sharply with these decisions. Unlike either case, the prospects for financial success were bright, such success was realized, and the corporation was always able to meet its obligations as they matured. Moreover, the promise of repayment was never in jeopardy, for the properties' self-liquidating potential guaranteed that repayment of the notes would not be subject to the fortunes of the business. In all major respects, the present case is more analogous to *Piedmont Corp. v. Comm'r*, 388 F.2d 886 (4th Cir. 1968), than to either Burr Oaks or Aqualane Shores.[60] Piedmont involved successive transfers of options to purchase real property to a controlled corporation in exchange for unsecured promissory notes. The Fourth Circuit considered Burr Oaks and Aqualane Shores, but found both to be distinguishable. In reversing the decision of the Tax Court that the transfers were in effect a contribution to capital, the following were held to be determinative: (1) the facts[61] indicated "some degree of certainty to the financial success of the venture"; (2) "a fair purchase price was paid"; (3) the corporation "paid the interest and installments of principal when due, promptly and regularly"; and (4) the corporation "did not retransfer any portion of any option, or any land which it acquired by exercise of an option" to the note holders. Thereupon, the court concluded that "an evidentiary basis to disregard the purported sales as bona fide sales (was) lacking." 388 F.2d at 890–91.

These same factors appear in this case[62] and, accordingly, we choose to be guided in our deliberations by Piedmont, rather than by Burr Oaks or Aqualane Shores. As supported by the record and confirmed by Piedmont, the transfer was in substance, as well as in form, a sale and not a capital contribution.

Defendant's remaining contention is that, notwithstanding a determination that the Castlewood notes were valid debt, the subject transaction falls within the literal

---

60. [21] The only colorable distinction between Piedmont and the present case is that in Piedmont the transferee corporation had been organized several years before the contested transfer, but until that time had remained dormant with nominal assets. Inasmuch as §351 and §362(a) apply equally to existing, as well as to newly formed, corporations, we find this difference to be without significance.

61. [24] These facts were that negotiations for purchase by third parties had begun before the corporation obtained title to the land and that the land was adjacent to a shopping center in the course of development.

62. [25] The facts in the instant case which indicated "some degree of certainty to the financial success of the venture" were that there was a reasonable expectation of profit to the corporation over and above its costs, that the property was reasonably anticipated to be readily marketable at its development and that the opportunity for sale to third parties had existed at the time of the decision to make the sale to the corporation.

provisions of section 351. The specific requirement in issue is whether the notes were "securities" within the meaning of the statute.[63]

A transferor has received a security if the instrument taken back in the exchange represents a continuing proprietary interest in the transferee corporation. *Le Tulle v. Scofield*, 308 U.S. 415, 420 (1940); *Pinellas Ice Co. v. Comm'r*, 287 U.S. 462, 470 (1933). The test as to the "securities" status of debt obligations is set forth in *Camp Wolters Enterprises, Inc. v. Comm'r*, 22 T.C. 737 (1954), aff'd, 230 F.2d 555 (5th Cir. 1956), cert. denied, 352 U.S. 826 (1956):

> The test as to whether notes are securities is not a mechanical determination of the time period of the note. Though time is an important factor, the controlling consideration is an overall evaluation of the nature of the debt, degree of participation and continuing interest compared with similarity of the note to a cash payment, the purpose of the advances, etc.

22 T.C. at 751.

Defendant contends that the present case is not materially different from the situation in *United States v. Hertwig*, 398 F.2d 452 (5th Cir. 1968); see also *Dennis v. Comm'r*, 473 F.2d 274 (5th Cir. 1973). In *Hertwig*, on the day that the corporation was formed, the promoters transferred $10,000 cash in exchange for stock, and patents worth $3,000,000 in exchange for unsecured promissory notes. The patents were the primary assets of the corporation. The notes were not subordinated and the promoters did not waive any of their rights to enforce the terms of the notes. It was stipulated that the price of $3,000,000 was reasonable and that the parties had a reasonable expectation that the notes would be paid. From this evidence, the Fifth Circuit held that the notes were "securities" within the meaning of the statute, since the promoters had retained a continuing proprietary interest in the success of the venture. 398 F.2d at 455.

Notwithstanding these factual similarities with the present case, we are not moved to characterize the Castlewood notes as § 351 "securities." To us, the critical distinction in *Hertwig* is that upon receiving the patents, the corporation therein then licensed two companies controlled by the transferor-promoters to use the inventions covered by the patents in return for an agreed royalty and also agreed to act as the sales agent for the licensees on a commission basis. In other words, payment of the notes was dependent upon the receipt of royalties and commissions from the licensees. It is readily apparent that the successful exploitation of the patents became necessary to satisfaction of the notes, thereby increasing the risk assumed by the note holders. The extent of this risk is graphically illustrated by the fact that interest payments on the notes were discontinued only one year after issuance and further by the fact that

---

63. [26] Inasmuch as Thomas was, at all times relevant herein, the sole shareholder of Castlewood, the control requirement, as defined in § 368(c), was satisfied. While on brief defendant also maintained that the Castlewood notes could be considered "stock" within the meaning of § 351, our determination that the notes did not constitute an equity investment in the corporation precludes this possibility.

the actual principal payments made to the note holders fell far short of the amounts required to be paid, due largely to the inability of the licensees to pay the royalties and commissions owed to the corporation. 398 F.2d at 453–54. Clearly, these transferor-note holders had a continuing proprietary stake in the business, for their ultimate payment was utterly contingent upon the profitable use of the patents.[64]

We have already given our reasons as to why the Castlewood notes did not constitute a continuing proprietary interest in Castlewood and we will not repeat them here. It is sufficient to say that the degree of risk represented by these notes was insubstantial in comparison to that existing in *Hertwig*. Our evaluation of the Castlewood notes convinces us that they were not "securities" within § 351.

* * *

Boyer v. Commissioner

United States Tax Court
58 T.C. 316 (1972)

FACTS

Some of the facts have been stipulated and are found accordingly. The stipulation of facts, together with the exhibits attached thereto, are incorporated herein by this reference.

Charles W. Brooks (hereinafter sometimes referred to as Brooks) and Jewel Brooks, husband and wife, resided in Medford, Oreg., when they filed the petition herein. During the calendar years 1966 through 1968 they filed joint income tax returns with the district director of internal revenue, Portland, Oreg.

Robert A. Boyer (hereinafter sometimes referred to as Boyer) and Marjorie A. Boyer, husband and wife, resided in Medford, Oreg., when they filed the petition herein. For the calendar years 1966 through 1968, they filed joint income tax returns with the district director of internal revenue, Portland, Oreg.

B Investments Co., Inc. (hereinafter sometimes referred to as B Investments), is a corporation organized under the laws of the State of Oregon, with its principal place of business located at Medford, Oreg., when it filed the petition herein. It filed its corporate income tax returns for the years 1966 through 1968 with the district director of internal revenue, Portland, Oreg.

On April 4, 1966, Brooks and Boyer entered into an earnest-money agreement with O. Gordon Hudson and wife, Ralph Thompsen and wife, and Joe Hearin and wife for the purchase of a parcel of land located in the city of Medford, Oreg. The exact size of the parcel was undetermined but it was estimated to contain between

---

64. [27] Moreover, it is obvious that the patents were assigned to the intermediate corporation before being transferred to the licensees solely in an attempt to convert the amounts to be received through exploitation of the patents from ordinary income to capital gain. *See* Dennis v. Comm'r, 473 F.2d 274, 278, 281–85 (5th Cir. 1973). Such a motive further distinguishes *Hertwig* from the present case.

25 and 30 acres. The earnest-money agreement stated the purchase price to be $6,000 an acre, but if the total exceeded $150,000 the purchasers could limit the purchase to 25 acres. The purchase price was to be paid $15,000 down and the balance not later than October 1, 1966. The agreement also recited that it was understood that the purchasers were entering into the agreement for the purpose of subdividing the property and selling lots in the subdivision and provided for a refund of the down-payment if approval of the subdivision could not be obtained.

On May 25, 1966, the sellers conveyed 12.5 acres to Brooks and Boyer by warranty deed, and petitioners paid an additional $60,000 on the purchase price. Petitioners had begun surveying and platting this land, identifying it as Country Club Meadows Tract I (hereinafter sometimes referred to as tract I). On June 7, 1966, an additional 12.5 acres, tract II, were conveyed to Brooks and Boyer, which were designated Country Club Meadows Tract II. The final contiguous parcel, 8.325 acres of Country Club Meadows, which did not constitute a part of either tract I or tract II, was conveyed to petitioners on July 2, 1968. A later survey of the entire purchase determined the total amount of land to be approximately 33 acres.

B Developers, Inc., an Oregon corporation with its principal office located in Medford, Oreg., was chartered on May 11, 1966. The initial capital in the corporation consisted of $25,000 subscribed and paid in cash equally by petitioners Brooks, Boyer, and B Investments, who were the only shareholders. Each shareholder owned 83 1/2 shares of the corporation stock which had a par value of $100 per share. In addition to the initial paid-in capital, at its inception B Developers obtained an unsecured $45,000 loan at 7-percent interest from B Investments. B Developers, Inc., reported its income on the basis of a fiscal year ending March 31.

Under date of May 12, 1966, Brooks and Boyer entered into a land sales contract with B Developers whereby they agreed to sell tract I to the corporation at a price of $12,000 an acre, for a total purchase price of $160,000. The agreement provided that B Developers was to pay $25,000 upon execution of the agreement with the remaining balance of $135,000 to be paid in monthly installments of not less than $2,000. As purchaser, B Developers was also required to get approval of the proposed subdivision plan before the transaction could be completed. Legal title to the property was to remain in the names of Brooks and Boyer with the provision that they would convey title to any portion of tract I to B Developers upon its payment of $13,500 an acre for the released land. During the years in question, as a lot was sold, Brooks and Boyer would convey title to the lot through B Developers to the ultimate residential purchaser. Petitioners Brooks and Boyer reported the income from the tract I sale on an installment basis and all gain was reported as short-term capital gain.

In April of 1968, Brooks and Boyer entered into an agreement with B Developers to sell it an additional 9.96 acres of tract II for $100,000, or $10,000 an acre. By purported terms of the agreement, B Developers was to make a $3,000 downpayment with $55,000 due in 3 months. The remaining balance, $42,000, was subject to negotiation between the parties. Again the two vendors kept legal title to the property and the supposed contract contained a provision for release of the lands to the corporation as payment was made therefor. The 1968 income tax returns of Brooks and Boyer indicated their receipt of $50,000 each from B Developers for the purchase of tract II, the gain therefrom being reported as long-term capital gain.

On June 27, 1966, B Developers and Brooks and Boyer and their wives executed a note payable to Commonwealth, Inc., for $191,000 secured by a mortgage on tract I. The money was borrowed to develop tract I by installation of streets, sewers, and other improvements. Subsequently, improvements were made to tract I at a cost of $120,537.49. Charles W. Brooks supervised performance of the contracts for construction of the streets, sewers, and other improvements as an officer of B Developers, but he received no salary for this particular work. A schedule was drafted to indicate the description of tract I lots, the asking price for each lot, and its cost. The projected asking price for all the lots totaled $339,050 and the projected cost totaled $280,537.49. By the end of its fiscal year, March 31, 1970, B Developers had sold all but 7 or 8 of the 42 lots in tract I, most of them for a price less than the projected asking price, and had experienced a loss on its residential development operations in each of the years 1966, 1967, and 1968.[65]

Also, following the contract for sale of tract II in June of 1968, B Developers and Brooks and Boyer, together with their wives, mortgaged tract II with the United States National Bank of Oregon to secure a $152,500 loan for B Developers, ostensibly for improvement of this second parcel. The settlement statement relative to this loan indicates the proceeds were disbursed $83,667.77 to settle the corporation's obligation to Commonwealth, Inc., under the prior $191,000 loan, $55,197.90 to petitioners Brooks and Boyer as sellers, $10,802.93 to B Developers, and the balance for payment of costs. During the years in question, improvements were made to tract II at a cost of $84,884.74. A schedule drafted to indicate the description of tract II lots, their asking prices and costs, reflects a total asking price of $258,250 and total costs of $184,884.74. All of the 31 lots in tract II except 3 were either sold or under option to sell by the end of B Developers' fiscal year ending March 31, 1970. However, this development activity also generated an annual operating loss. The lots of tract II consistently sold for between $1,500 and $2,000 less than the asking price Brooks and Boyer had set, purportedly with the advice and approval of B Investments.

Throughout the development and sale of both tract I and tract II B Developers' land sales division had no employees for subdividing, construction, or sales of the lots in Country Club Meadows. Attendantly, Brooks and Boyer had not at any time, in their individual capacities, engaged in subdividing, developing, advertising, pro-

---

65. [4] These annual losses arose from the fact that the small gross profit experienced on the sales of the lots were insufficient to meet even the annual interest obligations of the corporation due on its loan from B Investments, the loans secured by mortgages on tract I and tract II, and the outstanding balance of the purchase prices on tract I and tract II owed to Brooks and Boyer.

motion, or any activity leading to sale of any lots in either tract I or tract II.[66] Most of the lots were sold to contractors who build houses on them for ultimate purchasers.

From 1966 through 1969 Robert A. Boyer was self-employed as a practicing attorney with his offices in Medford, Oreg. Petitioner Charles W. Brooks was also self-employed at all relevant times herein as owner of a restaurant and Brooks Construction Co.

Both petitioners have, throughout the years, engaged in numerous passive real estate investment activities. During the years in question Boyer was a partner in seven or eight partnerships which were involved in the holding or use of land.[67] Petitioner Brooks, in addition to his various land partnerships with Boyer, was a partner in a venture to construct the Tiki Lodge Motel in 1966, the motel being subsequently operated for a short period and sold at a gain. Brooks Construction Co. also built two brick office buildings in 1965 which Brooks held and rented until 1967, when he sold them for no gain. Neither Brooks nor Boyer owned any interest in B Investments, however, nor was either individual an officer or employee of the corporation.

Brooks, Boyer and B Investments Co., Inc., is a partnership which was organized on March 1, 1966. The partnership is composed of petitioners Brooks, Boyer, and B Investments, each as owner of a one-third interest in the partnership. The records of the partnership are maintained on the basis of cash receipts and disbursements.

On March 1, 1966, the partnership purchased the Fluhrer Building for a lump-sum price of $224,078.85. For the 4 months following the purchase date it collected all rents and paid all the expenses of the Fluhrer Building, reflecting all revenues and expenditures on its records. However, by a written lease agreement dated June 30, 1966, the partnership leased the office building to B Developers for a term of 10 years at a gross rental of $15,000 a year. The agreement provided that the real property taxes were to be paid by the partnership while B Developers was responsible for the

---

66. [6] Brooks Construction Co., owned by Charles W. Brooks, did build two houses at cost on tract I lots as a means of stimulating the subdivision's lot sales.

67. [7] The partnerships were as follows:
 1. Boyer, Brooks, Brooks and Brooks partnership owned a resort lodge.
 2. Brooks, Brooks and Boyer partnership owned various parcels of unimproved land in Curry County and Jackson County, Oreg.
 3. Dynamic Enterprises partnership owned a ranch, a five-eighths interest in 73 acres located in the city of Ashland, Oreg., and a nine-sixteenths interest in another 365-acre ranch.
 4. Boyer had a partnership with two Ashland attorneys which held a lease on an interchange site of an interstate highway subleased to an oil company and a motel. The partnership also owned a pancake house restaurant and a service station in Roseburg, Oreg.
 5. Boyer and Bashaw partnership owned unimproved property in Jacksonville, Oreg.
 6. Boyer and Sterton partnership was formed in 1967 to purchase and renovate the Queen Building in Medford, Oreg.
 7. The Boyer and Brooks partnership, which purportedly sold Country Club Meadows to B Developers and which owned two or more other pieces of property, was another of petitioners' activities.
 8. Brooks, Boyer, and B Investments partnership owned the Fluhrer Building in Medford, Oreg., leased to B Developers.

payment of the fire insurance on the building. Boyer testified that the full amount of the annual rent was payable at the end of each year of the lease.

From July 1, 1966, B Developers collected all rents from the Fluhrer Building and paid its operating expenses. Carl Bismark, who manages B Investments and is vice president of B Developers, was chosen to manage the office building for B Developers at a salary of $400 a month.

During the first year of the rental term, July 1, 1966, to June 30, 1967, B Developers did not make any rental payments to the partnership as required by the lease. During the second year two rental payments were made—the first in the amount of $5,000 made on November 15, 1967, and the second in the amount of $15,000 made on February 29, 1968. On December 30, 1968, in the third year of the lease, B Developers paid the real estate taxes on the building in the amount of $3,722.25. Two months later, in February of 1969, the Fluhrer Building was destroyed by fire.

For the fiscal years ending March 31, 1967, 1968, and 1969, B Developers collected rents from the Fluhrer Building tenants in the amounts of $31,768.93, $43,883.82, and $38,901.82, respectively. The operating expenses and salaries paid for maintenance of the building during those years were approximately $15,750, $23,500, and $21,000, respectively.

When B Developers leased the building from the partnership in 1966 it was in disrepair and it was not fully occupied. In the course of the first year's operations under the lease, B Developers spent $11,705.12 to improve the appearance of the building and to refinish some of the offices for its new tenants. Additionally, the corporation aggressively sought new tenants to rent the unoccupied offices. The reason the rental payments were not made by B Developers to the partnership for its first year under the lease was because the corporation's current rental receipts from its tenants were used to fund the improvements to the Fluhrer Building in lieu of borrowed money and the corporation was also in a tight cash position because of its real estate development activities.

The partnership included in its income for its calendar years 1966, 1967, and 1968 only the actual amounts it received or constructively received as rental during those years, being zero for 1966, $5,000 in 1967, and $18,722.25 in 1968. It deducted taxes and depreciation on its partnership returns for those years. The partners, petitioners herein, reported their respective shares of the partnership income or loss on their individual returns. Respondent determined that the full amount of the rental payments due from B Developers to the partnership should be allocated to the partnership in each of these years, resulting in additional income of $7,500 to the partnership in 1966, $10,000 in 1967, and an overpayment of $3,722.25 in 1968. The resulting adjustments in the taxable incomes of the partners give rise to the second issue we must decide.

ANALYSIS

The first issue is whether Brooks and Boyer are entitled to treat their profit from the sale of tract II to B Developers as capital gain or ordinary income. To decide this issue we must determine whether tract II was property held by them primarily for sale to customers in the ordinary course of their trade or business, within the meaning of § 1221,[68] when they sold that property. The question is entirely a factual one and requires an objective rather than a subjective approach. *Kelley v. Comm'r*, 281 F.2d 527 (9th Cir., 1960); *Bauschard v. Comm'r*, 279 F.2d 115 (6th Cir. 1960); *Pointer v. Comm'r*, 48 T.C. 906 (1967), *affd.* 419 F.2d 213 (9th Cir. 1969); *Bynum v. Comm'r*, 46 T.C. 295 (1966); *Oace v. Comm'r*, 39 T.C. 743 (1963).

With regard to the first issue, petitioners Brooks and Boyer premise their position upon the separateness, for tax purposes, of B Developers and themselves. They contend that all transactions involving the real property conveyed by them to B Developers were conducted by the corporation alone, and that as a result they were not individually engaged in the real estate business. Furthermore, petitioners emphasize that they were engaged in no sales or promotional activities with respect to tract II lots, they retained title to the property only as security for the purchase price due, and B Investments owned one-third of the equity interest in B Developers and had complete veto power over all real estate transactions between B Developers and Brooks and Boyer.

Respondent on the other hand, places considerable reliance on the fact Brooks and Boyer participated in the development of the land, in setting prices on the lots, and in obtaining financing so B Developers could proceed with its improvement plans. Respondent contends both petitioners bought the property with an initial intent to subdivide and develop it, and they carried out their plan with the use of B Developers, the plan being to sell tracts I and II to the corporation at artificially high prices, thus prematurely squeezing out all potential gain from the finished operation at capital gains rates. Thus, respondent argues B Developers acted as a conduit or agent in completing the development and sale of the property for Brooks and Boyer.

A compendium of the circumstances and facts surrounding the 4-year development and sale of tracts I and II of Country Club Meadows clearly indicates respondent was correct in his determination with regard to Brooks and Boyer. We believe the evidence presented in the record as a whole supports his position that B Developers acted as an agent or alter ego for both petitioners when it subdivided and sold tract II lots in Country Club Meadows. Certainly, the evidence is insufficient to prove error in respondent's determination. Consequently, the activities of B Developers with regard to Country Club Meadows are attributable to Brooks and Boyer making them real estate developers or dealers and, as such, their profits from the sale of

---

68. [9] Pertinent parts of 1221 provide:

   For purposes of this subtitle, the term "capital asset" means property held by the taxpayer (whether or not connected with his trade or business), but does not include—

   (1) stock in trade of the taxpayer or other property of a kind which would properly be included in the inventory of the taxpayer if on hand at the close of the taxable year, or property held by the taxpayer primarily for sale to customers in the ordinary course of his trade or business;

tract II are taxable as ordinary income. *See Johnson v. United States*, 188 F.Supp. 939 (N.D. Cal. 1960).

Petitioners argue that their investments in real estate were all personal and passive and did not constitute the business of dealing in real estate. Those passive real estate partnerships, however, are not of primary concern here. We are more concerned with their activities and objectives relative to the Country Club Meadows acreage which they bought and sold to B Developers shortly thereafter for about twice the price they paid for it. Their dominance over B Developers and their dealings with it lead us to believe there was not a true arm's-length relationship in the entire Country Club Meadows development venture. A hand-in-glove operation, such as this, where a few shareholders control a corporation and act as its executive officers, will always draw our close scrutiny, and the burden is on the taxpayer to prove the existence of two separate bona fide interests. *Cf. Darco Realty Corp. v. Comm'r*, 301 F.2d 190 (2d Cir. 1962), *aff'g* a Memorandum Opinion of this Court; *Kaltreider v. Comm'r*, 255 F.2d 833 (3rd Cir. 1958), *aff'g* 28 T.C. 121 (1957).

We are convinced that Brooks and Boyer intended from the outset to subdivide and develop the Country Club Meadows property and that the formation of B Developers and sale to it of tract I for twice the price they paid for it immediately after they had acquired the land was part of a preconceived plan to insulate Brooks and Boyer from the real estate development business so they could siphon off most if not all of the profits from the Country Club Meadows project at capital gains rates. We also believe this plan carried through the transfer and development of tract II and the sale of lots therefrom. This conviction is supported by the earnest-money agreement with the original owners of the land which recited that the buyers intended to subdivide and sell the land and Boyer's attempts to get the land rezoned for residential use; by evidence that Brooks and Boyer set the price on the sale to the corporation and that the corporation actually lost money on the development and sale of both tracts I and II because of the artificially inflated price it paid for the property and the interest due on the sizable amounts it had to borrow to buy the property and develop it; by evidence that Brooks and Boyer controlled the operations of the corporation and apparently were the only individuals who participated in the development of the property, B Developers having no other employees working on the development; and evidence that Brooks and Boyer arranged financing for the corporation by cosigning the notes evidencing the loans, a part of the proceeds of which were used to pay them the purchase price of the property. *See Kaltreider v. Comm'r, supra; Pointer, supra; Browne v. U.S.*, 356 F.2d 545 (Ct. Cl. 1966).

Petitioners contend that B Investments, as a one-third owner and substantial creditor of B Developers, had absolute veto power over all of B Developers' real estate activities. We are not at all persuaded that this unique power ever really existed; and certainly there is no evidence that it was ever exercised. Carl Bismark, as representative of B Investments, is alleged to have participated in the affairs of B Developers. However, we find only one document in evidence bearing his signature. No written evidence was produced to substantiate the existence of the claimed veto power of B

Investments. Neither Bismark nor any other representative of B Investments took the witness stand during the trial to substantiate Boyer's testimony in this regard. This fact was unmentioned and unexplained at the trial and gives rise to the assumption that had such testimony been offered it would have been unfavorable to petitioners. *Wichita Terminal Elevator Co. v. Comm'r*, 6 T.C. 1158 (1946), *affd.* 162 F.2d 513 (10th Cir. 1947). We are also somewhat mystified as to why Brooks and Boyer were paid the purchase price of the property while no payments had been made on the $45,000 loan made by B Investments to B Developers up to the time of the trial.

Another factor we feel compelled to mention is the lack of solid evidence in the record to establish the sale of tract II to B Developers. No formally executed and recorded land sales contract for tract II was offered in evidence as was offered with respect to the sale of tract I. Instead, we are asked to accept that there was such a sale on the basis of Boyer's testimony and an unacknowledged and unrecorded carbon copy of an earnest-money agreement between Brooks and Boyer as individual sellers and as purchasers for the benefit of B Developers. This evidence is not persuasive in light of the close relationship between petitioners and the corporation.

The rule is settled that a person may engage in a business via an agent and the activities of the agent for the benefit of the principal will be imputed to the principal. *Kaltreider v. Comm'r, supra*; *Achong v. Comm'r*, 246 F.2d 445 (9th Cir. 1957). In our opinion that rule is appropriately used here, *Bauschard v. Comm'r*, 31 T.C. 910 (1959), *affd.* 279 F.2d 115 (6th Cir. 1960). Had petitioners truly intended that the corporation develop this property as an independent business venture, the property would have either been acquired by the corporation in the first instance or it would have been transferred to the corporation at a price which would have permitted the corporation to make a profit on the venture. Instead, it is our conclusion that the controlled corporation was simply used by Brooks and Boyer to develop the land for them so they could take the profits of the venture out as capital gain. Looking through the form of the arrangements to the substance we find that Brooks and Boyer were real estate dealers with respect to tract II and that their gain on the sale of this property was ordinary income. Compare *Royce W. Brown*, 54 T.C. 1475 (1970), *affd.* 448 F.2d 514 (10th Cir. 1971).

* * *

Kaycee Land & Livestock v. Flahive

Wyoming Supreme Court
46 P.3d 323 (2002)

FACTS

In a W.R.A.P. 11 certification of a question of law, we rely entirely upon the factual determinations made in the trial court. *Allhusen v. State By and Through Wyoming Mental Health Professions Licensing Board*, 898 P.2d 878, 881 (Wyo.1995). The district court submitted the following statement of facts in its order certifying the question of law:

1. Flahive Oil & Gas is a Wyoming Limited Liability Company with no assets at this time.

2. [Kaycee Land and Livestock] entered into a contract with Flahive Oil & Gas LLC allowing Flahive Oil & Gas to use the surface of its real property.

3. Roger Flahive is and was the managing member of Flahive Oil & Gas at all relevant times.

4. [Kaycee Land and Livestock] alleges that Flahive Oil & Gas caused environmental contamination to its real property located in Johnson County, Wyoming.

5. [Kaycee Land and Livestock] seeks to pierce the LLC veil and disregard the L[L]C entity of Flahive Oil & Gas Limited Liability Company and hold Roger Flahive individually liable for the contamination.

6. There is no allegation of fraud.

ANALYSIS

The question presented is limited to whether, in the absence of fraud, the remedy of piercing the veil is available against a company formed under the Wyoming Limited Liability Company Act (Wyo. Stat. Ann. §§ 17-15-101 to -144 (LexisNexis 2001)). To answer this question, we must first examine the development of the doctrine within Wyoming's corporate context. As a general rule, a corporation is a separate entity distinct from the individuals comprising it. *Opal Mercantile v. Tamblyn*, 616 P.2d 776, 778 (Wyo.1980). Wyoming statutes governing corporations do not address the circumstances under which the veil can be pierced. However, since 1932, this court has espoused the concept that a corporation's legal entity will be disregarded whenever the recognition thereof in a particular case will lead to injustice. *See Caldwell v. Roach*, 12 P.2d 376, 380 (Wyo. 1932). In *Miles v. CEC Homes, Inc.*, 753 P.2d 1021, 1023 (Wyo.1988) (quoting *Amfac Mechanical Supply Co. v. Federer*, 645 P.2d 73, 77 (Wyo.1982)), this court summarized the circumstances under which the corporate veil would be pierced pursuant to Wyoming law:

> Before a corporation's acts and obligations can be legally recognized as those of a particular person, and vice versa, it must be made to appear that the corporation is not only influenced and governed by that person, but that there is such a unity of interest and ownership that the individuality, or separateness, of such person and corporation has ceased, and that the facts are such that an adherence to the fiction of the separate existence of the corporation would, under the particular circumstances, sanction a fraud or promote injustice. Quoting *Arnold v. Browne*, 27 Cal.App.3d 386, (1972) (overruled on other grounds).

We provided the following factors to be considered in determining whether a corporate entity may be disregarded:

> Among the possible factors pertinent to the trial court's determination are: commingling of funds and other assets, failure to segregate funds of the separate entities, and the unauthorized diversion of corporate funds or assets

to other than corporate uses; the treatment by an individual of the assets of the corporation as his own; the failure to obtain authority to issue or subscribe to stock; the holding out by an individual that he is personally liable for the debts of the corporation; the failure to maintain minutes or adequate corporate records and the confusion of the records of the separate entities; the identical equitable ownership in the two entities; the identification of the equitable owners thereof with the domination and control of the two entities; identification of the directors and officers of the two entities in the responsible supervision and management; the failure to adequately capitalize a corporation; the absence of corporate assets, and undercapitalization; the use of a corporation as a mere shell, instrumentality or conduit for a single venture or the business of an individual or another corporation; the concealment and misrepresentation of the identity of the responsible ownership, management and financial interest or concealment of personal business activities; the disregard of legal formalities and the failure to maintain arm's length relationships among related entities; the use of the corporate entity to procure labor, services or merchandise for another person or entity; the diversion of assets from a corporation by or to a stockholder or other person or entity, to the detriment of creditors, or the manipulation of assets and liabilities between entities so as to concentrate the assets in one and the liabilities in another; the contracting with another with intent to avoid performance by use of a corporation as a subterfuge of illegal transactions; and the formation and use of a corporation to transfer to it the existing liability of another person or entity [citation]. 645 P.2d at 77–78 (quoting *Arnold v. Browne, supra,* 103 Cal. Rptr. at 781–82).

Miles, 753 P.2d at 1023–24.

Wyoming courts, as well as courts across the country, have typically utilized a fact driven inquiry to determine whether circumstances justify a decision to pierce a corporate veil. *Opal Mercantile,* 616 P.2d at 778. This case comes to us as a certified question in the abstract with little factual context, and we are asked to broadly pronounce that there are no circumstances under which this court will look through a failed attempt to create a separate LLC entity and prevent injustice. We simply cannot reach that conclusion and believe it is improvident for this court to prohibit this remedy from applying to any unforeseen circumstance that may exist in the future.

We have long recognized that piercing the corporate veil is an equitable doctrine. *State ex rel. Christensen v. Nugget Coal Co.,*144 P.2d 944, 952 (Wyo. 1944). The concept of piercing the corporate veil is a judicially created remedy for situations where corporations have not been operated as separate entities as contemplated by statute and, therefore, are not entitled to be treated as such. The determination of whether the doctrine applies centers on whether there is an element of injustice, fundamental unfairness, or inequity. The concept developed through common law and is absent from the statutes governing corporate organization. *See* Wyo. Stat. Ann. §§ 17-16-101 to -1803 (LexisNexis 2001). Appellee Roger Flahive suggests that, by the adoption of

§ 17-16-622(b)—a provision from the revised Model Business Corporation Act—
the Wyoming legislature intended to explicitly authorize piercing in the corporate
context and, by inference, prevent its application in the LLC context. A careful review
of the statutory language and legislative history leads to a different conclusion. § 17-
16-622(b) reads: "Unless otherwise provided in the articles of incorporation, a shareholder of a corporation is not personally liable for the acts or debts of the corporation
except that he may become personally liable by reason of his own acts or conduct."
Mr. Flahive contrasts that language with the LLC statute which simply states the underlying principle of limited liability for individual members and managers. Wyo.
Stat. Ann. § 17-15-113 (LexisNexis 2001). § 17-15-113 provides:

> Neither the members of a limited liability company nor the managers of a
> limited liability company managed by a manager or managers are liable under
> a judgment, decree or order of a court, or in any other manner, for a debt,
> obligation or liability of the limited liability company.

However, we agree with Commentator Gelb that: "It is difficult to read statutory
§ 17-15-113 as intended to preclude courts from deciding to disregard the veil of an
improperly used LLC." Harvey Gelb, *Liabilities of Members and Managers of Wyoming
Limited Liability Companies*, 31 Land & Water L. Rev. 133 at 142 (1996).

Section 17-16-622—the statute relied upon by Mr. Flahive as indicating legislative
intent to allow piercing of the corporate veil—when considered in the context of
its legislative history, provides no support for the conclusion that the legislature intended in any way to limit application of the common-law doctrine to LLCs. As
previously explained, § 17-16-622 was adopted from the revised Model Business
Corporation Act, and the comments therein clarify that subsection (b) "sets forth
the basic rule of nonliability of shareholders for corporate acts or debts that underlies
modern corporation law" and "recognizes that such liability may be assumed voluntarily or by other conduct." 1 Model Bus. Corp. Act Ann. § 6.22 at 6–94 to 6–
95 (Supp. 1997). This provision was added in 1984 and was not intended to "treat
exhaustively the statutory bases for imposing liability on shareholders." *Id.* at 6–96,
144 P.2d 944. The official comments in the revised Model Business Corporation
Act specifically recognize the separate existence of the common law by stating:
"Shareholders may also become liable for corporate obligations by their voluntary
actions or by other conduct under the common law doctrine of 'piercing the corporate veil.'" *Id.*

We note that Wyoming was the first state to enact LLC statutes. Many years passed
before the Internal Revenue Service's approval of taxation of LLCs as partnerships
led to other states adopting LLC legislation and the broad usage of this form for business organizations. William D. Bagley, *The History of the LLC in the USA*, Limited
Liability Company Reporter 94-302 (May/June 1994); *see also* Karin Schwindt, *Limited
Liability Companies: Issues in Member Liability*, 44 UCLA L. Rev. 1541, 1543 (1997).
Wyoming's statute is very short and establishes only minimal requirements for creating
and operating LLCs. It seems highly unlikely that the Wyoming legislature gave any
consideration to whether the common-law doctrine of piercing the veil should apply

to the liability limitation granted by that fledgling statute. It is true that some other states have adopted specific legislation extending the doctrine to LLCs while Wyoming has not. However, that situation seems more attributable to the fact that Wyoming was a pioneer in the LLC arena and states which adopted LLC statutes much later had the benefit of years of practical experience during which this issue was likely raised.

Mr. Flahive insists that, if the legislature intended for liability to be asserted against the members of an LLC, it could have added similar language to the LLC chapter at the same time it adopted provisions of the revised Model Business Corporation Act. However, adoption of those amendments in 1989, twelve years after the enactment of the LLC statutes, while remaining silent on the issue of piercing the veil in the LLC statutes, is far too attenuated to indicate a clear legislative intent to restrict application of the common law to LLCs. It stands to reason that, because it is an equitable doctrine, "[t]he paucity of statutory authority for LCC piercing should not be considered a barrier to its application." Schwindt, *supra* at 1552. Lack of explicit statutory language should not be considered an indication of the legislature's desire to make LLC members impermeable. *Id.* at 1555, 144 P.2d 944; Robert B. Thompson, *The Limits of Liability in the New Limited Liability Entities*, 32 Wake Forest L. Rev. 1, 19 (1997). Moreover,

> It is not to be presumed that the legislature intended to abrogate or modify a rule of the common law by the enactment of a statute upon the same subject; it is rather to be presumed that no change in the common law was intended unless the language employed clearly indicates such an intention.... The rules of common law are not to be changed by doubtful implication, nor overturned except by clear and unambiguous language. *McKinney v. McKinney*, [59 Wyo. 204,] 135 P.2d [940,] 942 [(1943)], quoting from 25 R.C.L. 1054, §280.

Allstate Insurance Company v. Wyoming Insurance Department, 672 P.2d 810, 824 (Wyo.1983).

With the dearth of legislative consideration on this issue in Wyoming, we are left to determine whether applying the well established common law to LLCs somehow runs counter to what the legislature would have intended had it considered the issue. In that regard, it is instructive that: "Every state that has enacted LLC piercing legislation has chosen to follow corporate law standards and not develop a separate LLC standard." Philip P. Whynott, The Limited Liability Company §11:140 at 11-5 (3d ed.1999). Statutes which create corporations and LLCs have the same basic purpose —to limit the liability of individual investors with a corresponding benefit to economic development. Eric Fox, *Piercing the Veil of Limited Liability Companies*, 62 Geo. Wash. L. Rev. 1143, 1145–46 (1994). Statutes created the legal fiction of the corporation being a completely separate entity which could act independently from individual persons. If the corporation were created and operated in conformance with the statutory requirements, the law would treat it as a separate entity and shelter the individual shareholders from any liability caused by corporate action, thereby encouraging investment. However, courts throughout the country have consistently recognized certain unjust circumstances can arise if immunity from liability shelters those who have failed to operate a corporation as a separate entity. Consequently, when corporations fail to follow the statutorily mandated formalities, co-mingle funds, or ignore the restrictions in their articles of incorporation regarding separate treatment of corporate property, the courts deem it appropriate to disregard the separate identity and do not permit shareholders to be sheltered from liability to third parties for damages caused by the corporations' acts.

We can discern no reason, in either law or policy, to treat LLCs differently than we treat corporations. If the members and officers of an LLC fail to treat it as a separate entity as contemplated by statute, they should not enjoy immunity from individual liability for the LLC's acts that cause damage to third parties. Most, if not all, of the expert LLC commentators have concluded the doctrine of piercing the veil should apply to LLCs. *See generally* Fox, *supra*; Gelb, *supra*; Robert G. Lang, Note, *Utah's Limited Liability Company Act: Viable Alternative or Trap for the Unwary?*, 1993 Utah L. Rev. 941, 966 (1993) (Part 2); Stephen B. Presser, Piercing the Corporate Veil § 4.01[2] (2002); Ann M. Seward & Laura Stubberud, *The Limits of Limited Liability—Part Two*, Limited Liability Company Reporter 94-109 (Jan./Feb. 1994); Schwindt, *supra*. It also appears that most courts faced with a similar situation—LLC statutes which are silent and facts which suggest the LLC veil should be pierced—have had little trouble concluding the common law should be applied and the factors weighed accordingly. *See, e.g., Hollowell v. Orleans Regional Hospital*, No. Civ. A. 95-4029, 1998 WL 283298 (E.D. La. May 29, 1998); *Ditty v. CheckRite, Ltd., Inc.*, 973 F. Supp. 1320 (D. Utah 1997); *Tom Thumb Food Markets, Inc. v. TLH Properties, LLC*, No. C9-98-1277, 1999 WL 31168 (Minn. Ct. App. Jan.26, 1999).

Certainly, the various factors which would justify piercing an LLC veil would not be identical to the corporate situation for the obvious reason that many of the organizational formalities applicable to corporations do not apply to LLCs. The LLC's operation is intended to be much more flexible than a corporation's. Factors relevant to determining when to pierce the corporate veil have developed over time in a multitude of cases. It would be inadvisable in this case, which lacks a complete factual context, to attempt to articulate all the possible factors to be applied to LLCs in Wyoming in the future. For guidance, we direct attention to commentators who have opined on the appropriate factors to be applied in the LLC context. Fox, *supra*; Gelb, *supra*; Curtis J. Braukmann, Comment, *Limited Liability Companies*, 39 U. Kan. L. Rev. 967 (1991); Presser, *supra*; Seward & Stubberud, *supra*; Larry E. Ribstein & Robert R. Keatinge, *Members' Limited Liability*, Limited Liability Companies § 12.03 (1999); Robert R. Keating et al., *The Limited Liability Company: A Study of the Emerging Entity*, 47 The Business Lawyer 375 (1992).

The certified question presents an interesting internal inconsistency. It begins, "In the absence of fraud," thereby presenting the assumption that a court may pierce an LLC's veil in a case of fraud. Thus, the certified question assumes that, when fraud is found, the courts are able to disregard the LLC entity despite the statutory framework which supposedly precludes such a result. Either the courts continue to possess the equitable power to take such action or they do not. Certainly, nothing in the statutes suggests the legislature gave such careful consideration and delineated the specific circumstances under which the courts can act in this arena. If the assumption is correct, individual LLC members can be held personally liable for damages to innocent third parties when the LLC has committed fraud. Yet, when the LLC has caused damage and has inadequate capitalization, co-mingled funds, diverted assets, or used the LLC as a mere shell, individual members are immune from liability. Legislative silence cannot be stretched to condone such an illogical result.

In *Amfac Mechanical Supply Co.*, this court clarified that a showing of fraud or an intent to defraud is not necessary to disregard a corporate entity. 645 P.2d at 79. We clearly stated: "Fraud is, of course, a matter of concern in suits to disregard corporate fictions, but it is not a prerequisite to such a result." *Id.* Other courts have echoed this view: "Liability on the basis of fraud, however, does not encompass the entire spectrum of cases in which the veil was pierced in the interest of equity." Fox, *supra* at 1169. Thus, even absent fraud, courts have the power to impose liability on corporate shareholders. *Id.* at 1170. This same logic should naturally be extended to the LLC context. We have made clear that: "Each case involving the disregard of the separate entity doctrine must be governed by the special facts of that case." *Opal Mercantile*, 616 P.2d at 778. Determinations of fact are within the trier of fact's province. *Id.* The district court must complete a fact intensive inquiry and exercise its equitable powers to determine whether piercing the veil is appropriate under the circumstances presented in this case.

OPINION

No reason exists in law or equity for treating an LLC differently than a corporation is treated when considering whether to disregard the legal entity. We conclude the equitable remedy of piercing the veil is an available remedy under the Wyoming Limited Liability Company Act.

Chapter 9

Accounting for Real Estate Improvements

I. Commentary

Property owners incur various costs to improve property. They must determine which of those costs they can deduct when paid and which they must capitalize. People in the real estate industry place construction and subdivision costs into two categories: hard costs and soft costs. Hard costs would include items such as materials and construction labor costs; soft costs would include items such as overhead. Tax law, on the other hand, places construction and subdivision costs in two different categories—direct costs and indirect costs—and generally requires taxpayers to capitalize such costs under the uniform capitalization rules (UCR).[1] If the costs are incurred as part of a long-term contract, property owners generally must account for costs to improve the property using the percentage of completion method (PCM).[2]

The first step in determining how to account for costs related to property is determining whether the property owner must capitalize the costs under section 263A or account for them using the percentage of completion method in section 460. Section 263A applies to a property only if section 460 does not.[3] Section 460 applies to any long-term contract, which is defined as "any contract for the manufacture, building, installation, or construction of property if such contract is not completed within the taxable year in which the contract is entered into."[4] Thus, a property owner who contracts to build and sell property would often come within the rules in section 460. On the other hand, a property owner who improves property and then sells it would not appear to come within section 460. The general significance of coming within the definition of long-term contract is that a property owner constructs im-

---

1. *See* I.R.C. §263A(a)(2); Treas. Reg. §1.263A-1(e) (identifying direct and indirect costs). Taxpayers who improve or subdivide real property may not use inventory accounting, so they must capitalize the costs. *See* Homes by Ayres v. Commissioner, 795 F.2d 832 (9th Cir. 1986); Von-Lusk v. Commissioner, 104 T.C. 207 (1995).

2. *See* I.R.C. §460(a).

3. *See* I.R.C. §263A(c)(4). Contract work done to subdivide real property comes within the definition of building, installation, or construction. *See* Treas. Reg. §1.460-3(a).

4. *See* I.R.C. §460(a), (f).

provements under a longer-term contract generally must use the PCM to account for income and costs associated with the contract.[5]

Two significant exceptions apply to the general rule for long-term construction contracts. Property owners are not required to use the PCM for home construction contracts and small construction contracts (i.e., exempt construction contracts).[6] In fact, section 263A applies to certain home construction contracts.[7] Otherwise, one of the exempt contract methods applies to exempt construction contracts.[8] The exempt contract methods include the PCM, the exempt-contract percentage-of-completion method (EPCM), and the completed-contract method (CCM).[9] The specifics of each of these methods is beyond the scope of this book, but a general overview of each is in order. Tax advisors must be aware that various methods are available for exempt construction contracts and be mindful that one method may generate better tax results than the others.

The difference between the various methods is generally the taxable year in which the property owner will recognize income. Under the PCM, the property owner recognizes a portion of the total contract price as gross income as the taxpayer incurs allocable contract costs.[10] Under the PCM, the property owner determines the percentage of completion by comparing allocable contract costs incurred with estimated total allocable contract costs.[11] The EPCM, on the other hand, allows a property owner to use any method of cost comparison or to compare work performed on the contract to total estimated work to be performed.[12] Finally, the CCM allows a property owner to take gross contract price and all allocable contract costs incurred into account in the contract completion year.[13]

Under both section 263A and section 460, property owners must determine how to properly allocate direct and indirect costs to real estate improvements. Allocating indirect costs to a project is different from the section 460 allocation of income and costs to certain periods. Allocating indirect costs requires the property owner to determine which indirect costs should be allocated to a project. After making such determinations under section 460, the accounting method would determine the period to which such costs are allocated.

The rules governing the allocation of costs are complex. The specifics of the allocation rules are beyond the scope of this book, but a general understanding of the rules is important. Consider the allocation rules under section 263A and section 460

5. *See* I.R.C. §460(a).
6. *See* I.R.C. §460(e)(1); Howard Hughes Company, L.L.C. v. Commissioner, 805 F.3d 175 (2015).
7. *See id.* (flush language).
8. *See* Treas. Reg. §1.460-4(c).
9. *See id.* (implying that other methods are also permissible).
10. *See* Treas. Reg. §1.460-4(b)(1).
11. *See id.*
12. *See* Treas. Reg. §1.460-4(c)(2)(i).
13. *See* Treas. Reg. §1.460-4(d)(1).

in turn. The section 263A allocation rules generally apply to property owners who produce property (whether for use in a trade or business or for investment) and property owners who acquire section 1221(a)(1) property.[14] The allocation begins with a two-step process. First, property owners must allocate costs to resale or production activities.[15] Second, they must allocate those costs to specific items of property produced, acquired for resale, or on hand at the end of the taxable year.[16] The regulations list costs and cost allocation methods that property owners generally must use to allocate indirect costs under section 263A.[17] The regulations specifically address how property owners that are part of a complex ownership structure must allocate some of the indirect costs incurred with respect to the property.[18]

Section 460 has its own set of cost-allocation rules.[19] In fact, the cost-allocation rules that apply depend upon the method of accounting that applies to a particular long-term contract.[20] If the long-term contract is subject to the PCM, the general cost-allocation rules under section 263A, with some minor modifications, or a simplified cost-to-cost method would apply.[21] If the long-term contract is subject to the PCCM, the general cost-allocation rules under section 263A, with minor modifications, would apply.[22] If the long-term contract is subject to the CCM, the section 263A cost-allocation rules apply, or the property owner may elect to use rules under the section 460 regulations that define indirect costs differently and may exclude some costs that section 263A includes.[23] Exempt construction contracts that use either the PCM or CCM are not subject to the cost-allocation rules in the section 460 regulations, so they would be subject to the general rules in section 451, which are beyond the scope of this book.[24]

---

14. *See* Treas. Reg. § 1.263A-1(a)(3). Those rules are subject to some exceptions, which generally do not apply in the real estate context. *See* Treas. Reg. § 1.263A-1(b).

15. *See* Treas. Reg. § 1.263A-1(c)(1). Allocable costs only include those that would give rise to a deduction, but for section 263A. *See* Treas. Reg. § 1.263A-1(c)(2). Property owners recover 263A costs through depreciation or by an adjustment to basis. *See* Treas. Reg. § 1.263A-1(c)(4).

16. *See id.*

17. *See* Treas. Reg. § 1.263A-1(e)(3) (identifying examples of indirect costs); Treas. Reg. § 1.263A-1(f) (identifying cost allocations methods). Property owners may qualify for simplified production method under Treas. Reg. § 1.263A-2 or the simplified production method under Treas. Reg. § 1.263A-3. A reseller that produces property must capitalize both the costs associated with reselling and those associated with production. *See* Treas. Reg. § 1.263A-3(a)(2). If a property owner engages in both production and resale activities, the property owner may elect the simplified production method, but not the simplified resale method. *See* Treas. Reg. § 1.263A-3(a)(4).

18. *See* Treas. Reg. § 1.263A-1(e)(4), -1(j).

19. *See* I.R.C. § 460(c)(1) (providing generally that the section 451 allocation rules apply to long-term contracts); I.R.C. § 460(b)(3) (providing that Treasury may prescribe simplified cost-allocation rules for long-term contracts).

20. *See* Treas. Reg. § 1.460-5(a).

21. *See* Treas. Reg. § 1.460-5(b) (adopting the allocation rules in Treas. Reg. § 1.263A-1(e) through (h); Treas. Reg. § 1.460-5(c) (allowing property owners to elect the simplified cost-to-cost method).

22. *See* Treas. Reg. § 1.460-5(e).

23. *See* Treas. Reg. § 1.460-5(d).

24. *See* Treas. Reg. § 1.460-5(a); I.R.C. § 460(c)(1).

Separate rules apply to the allocation of interest to both long-term contracts and property subject to section 263A.[25] The rules governing long-term contracts generally defer to section 263A to determine the allocation of interest.[26] Under section 263A, a property owner must allocate interest costs paid or incurred during the construction period that are allocable to property produced by the property owner that has a long useful life and meets production period requirements.[27] The regulations provide detail for applying the general rules in the statute.[28]

II. Primary Legal Authority

Howard Hughes Company, L.L.C. v. Commissioner

United States Court of Appeals, Fifth Circuit

805 F.3d 175 (2015)

OPINION

KING, CIRCUIT JUDGE:

Petitioners-Appellants used the completed contract method of accounting in computing their gains from sales of property under long-term construction contracts. The Internal Revenue Service challenged the method of accounting, arguing that the contracts at issue do not qualify as home construction contracts and that Petitioners–Appellants should therefore have used the percentage of completion method in computing their gains. The Tax Court sided with the Internal Revenue Service. We AFFIRM.

I. FACTUAL AND PROCEDURAL BACKGROUND

Petitioners The Howard Hughes Company, LLC (THHC) and Howard Hughes Properties, Inc. (HHPI) are subsidiaries of the Howard Hughes Corp., an entity involved in selling and developing commercial and residential real estate. Among the real estate holdings originally owned by Howard Hughes Corp. is a 22,500-acre plot of land west of downtown Las Vegas, Nevada, known as Summerlin. In the 1980s this land was selected for development and was divided into three geographic regions: Summerlin North, Summerlin South, and Summerlin West.[29] Each of the Summerlin geographical regions was further divided into villages, which were then divided into parcels or neighborhoods containing individual lots. Petitioners intended to develop

---

25. *See* I.R.C. §§ 460(c)(3), 263A(f).

26. *See* I.R.C. § 460(d)(3)(A) (adding some rules that would specifically apply to long-term contracts).

27. *See* I.R.C. § 263A(f).

28. *See* Treas. Reg. § 1.263A-8. *See also* Treas. Reg. § 1.460-5(b)(2)(v) (providing rules for allocating interest costs to long-term contracts).

29. [1] As of today, THHC owns Summerlin West and HHPI owns Summerlin North and Summerlin South, excluding any tracts of land within each region that have been sold to third parties. Since its development, Summerlin has grown into a residential community with approximately 100,000 residents living in 40,000 homes as of 2010.

Summerlin as a large master-planned residential community. To secure the rights to develop Summerlin, Petitioners reached master development agreements (MDAs) with the City of Las Vegas and Clark County, which required Petitioners to submit village development plans for municipal approval.

Petitioners generated revenue from their holdings in Summerlin by selling property within the community to commercial builders or individual buyers who would then construct homes on the property. The first land sales in Summerlin North took place approximately in 1986, in Summerlin South in 1998, and in Summerlin West in 2000.[30] Petitioners' sales generally fell into one of four categories: pad sales, finished lot sales, custom lot sales, or bulk sales. In a pad sale, Petitioners would construct all the infrastructure in a village up to a parcel boundary and then sell a parcel to a homebuilder who would be responsible for any subdivision of the parcel, infrastructure in the parcel, and any construction therein. In a finished lot sale, Petitioners divided the parcels into lots, constructed the village and parcel infrastructure up to the individual lot lines, and then sold neighborhoods to buyers. For both pad sales and finished lots sales, Petitioners reached building development agreements (BDAs) that required the buyers–builders to do further development work on the property. In custom lot sales, Petitioners sold individual lots to buyers who were contractually bound to build residential dwelling units. And in bulk sales, Petitioners sold entire villages to buyers who would then subdivide the villages into parcels and be responsible for all of the infrastructure improvements within the villages.

Under the land sale contracts and MDAs, Petitioners were obligated to construct infrastructure and other common improvements in Summerlin. The MDAs Petitioners signed with municipal authorities required the construction of parks, roadways, fire stations, flooding facilities, and other infrastructure. And the BDAs required Petitioners to construct roads and utility infrastructure such as water and sewer systems up to the line of the lots sold to homebuilders, who would then assume responsibility for completing the infrastructure on their lots.[31] Important to this case, Petitioners did not build homes, perform any home construction work, or make improvements within the boundaries of any lots in Summerlin.

For the tax years at issue (2007 and 2008), Petitioners used the "completed contract method" of accounting in computing gain for tax purposes from their long-term contracts for the sale of residential property in Summerlin West and South. By using this method, Petitioners deferred reporting income on a contract for the sale of land until the contract was "complete," i.e., until the year in which Petitioners' incurred costs reached 95% of

---

30. [2] The tax deficiencies at issue here, however, only relate to contracts involving Summerlin South and Summerlin West.

31. [3] The costs attributable to these common improvement activities that were incurred by Petitioners exceeded 10% of the various total contract prices. Under an operative Treasury Regulation, a contract cannot be a construction contact "if the contract includes the provision of land by the taxpayer and the estimated total allocable contract costs, as defined in paragraph (b)(3) of this section, attributable to the taxpayer's construction activities are less than 10 percent of the contract's total contract price." Treas. Reg. § 1.460–1(b)(2)(ii).

their estimated contract costs.[32] *See* Treas. Reg. §1.460–1(c)(3)(A). This is in contrast to the general method of reporting income for tax purposes under long-term contracts, the "percentage of completion" method. The percentage of completion method requires a taxpayer to recognize gain or loss annually in proportion to the progress the taxpayer has made during the year toward completing the contract, determined by comparing costs allocated and incurred before the end of the year to the estimated contract costs.[33] Petitioners claimed that they were entitled to use the completed contract method because their contracts were "home construction contracts" under I.R.C. §460(e)(1).

Respondent, the Commissioner of Internal Revenue (the Commissioner), disagreed with Petitioners' method of accounting and issued notices of deficiency for the 2007 and 2008 tax years, changing the method of accounting as the Commissioner is authorized to do under I.R.C. §446(b). The Commissioner asserted that Petitioners were required to use the percentage of completion method to report gains or losses under their contracts. As a result of this change in the method of accounting, the Commissioner increased Petitioners' taxable income for 2007 and 2008 as follows:

Petitioner	2007	2008	Total
THHC	$209,875,725	$19,399,420	$229,275,145
HHPI	$156,303,168	$37,192,046	$193,495,214

Petitioners challenged the deficiencies[34] in the United States Tax Court. The Tax Court held that Petitioners' contracts were long-term contracts within I.R.C. §460 but were

---

32. [4] As noted by one treatise:

Under the completed contract method, the taxpayer does not report income until the tax year in which the contract is completed and accepted.... Expenses allocable to the contract are deductible in the year in which the contract is completed. Expenses not allocated to the contract (i.e., period costs) are deductible in the year in which they are paid or incurred, depending on the method of accounting employed.

U.S. *Master Tax Guide* ¶1552 (96th ed.2013).

33. [5] More specifically:

Under the percentage-of-completion method, gross income is reported annually according to the percentage of the contract completed in that year. The completion percentage must be determined by comparing costs allocated and incurred before the end of the tax year with the estimated total contract costs (cost-to-cost method or simplified cost-to-cost method). Thus, for a particular tax year, the taxpayer includes a portion of the total contract price in gross income as the taxpayer incurs allocable contract costs for the year. Any contract income that has not been included in the taxpayer's gross income by the end of the tax year in which the contract is completed is included in gross income for the following tax year.

U.S. Master Tax Guide ¶1552.

34. [6] Other adjustments by the Commissioner, when added to the increases in Petitioners' taxable income, resulted in the Commissioner assessing the following total deficiencies against Petitioners:

Petitioner	2007	2008
THHC	$73,456,504	$6,789,797
HHPI	$50,633,554	$13,228,620

not "home construction contracts" under I.R.C. § 460(e)(6)(A) that would permit the use of the completed contract method. *Howard Hughes Co., LLC v. Comm'r*, 142 T.C. 355, 2014 WL 10077466, at *14–25 (T.C. June 2, 2014).

Interpreting the "home construction contracts" exception in I.R.C. § 460(e)(6)(A) and its accompanying regulations, the Tax Court based its reasoning on three points. First, provisions of the Internal Revenue Code permitting the deferral of income (such as § 460(e)(6)(A)) are to be "strictly construed." *Id.* at *18. Second, Petitioners' costs do not come within subsection (i) of § 460(e)(6)(A), which requires that costs be incurred "with respect to" dwelling units. According to the Tax Court, Petitioners did not engage in any activities "attributable to the construction of the dwelling units" because they did not intend to build dwelling units and their costs did not have a sufficient causal nexus to the construction of dwelling units. *Id.* at *21. The lack of any home construction activity on the part of Petitioners was particularly important to the Tax Court. Apart from the statutory text, the court pointed to the legislative history of the Technical and Miscellaneous Revenue Act of 1988 (TAMRA), which gave birth to § 460(e)(6)(A) and which suggested that the home construction contract exception to the use of the percentage of completion method was specifically directed toward taxpayers involved in building homes. *Id.* at *21–22.

Third, Petitioners' costs did not come within subsection (ii) of § 460(e)(6)(A) as the costs were not incurred for improvements "on the site of such dwelling units," a phrase which the court interpreted to mean "the individual lot." *Id.* The Tax Court also rejected Petitioners' arguments that their common improvement costs came within subsection (ii) because of a regulation that counted common improvement costs towards home constructions costs.[35] According to the court, the regulation required the taxpayer to "at some point incur some construction cost with respect to the dwelling unit to include these costs in the dwelling unit cost," but "[Petitioners] ha[d] no dwelling unit costs in which to include the common improvement costs."

---

35. [7] The regulation states:

(2) Home construction contract—(i) In general. A long-term construction contract is a home construction contract if a taxpayer (including a subcontractor working for a general contractor) reasonably expects to attribute 80 percent or more of the estimated total allocable contract costs (including the cost of land, materials, and services), determined as of the close of the contracting year, to the construction of—

(A) Dwelling units, as defined in section 168(e)(2)(A)(ii)(I), contained in buildings containing 4 or fewer dwelling units (including buildings with 4 or fewer dwelling units that also have commercial units); and

(B) Improvements to real property directly related to, and located at the site of, the dwelling units.

(ii) Townhouses and rowhouses. Each townhouse or rowhouse is a separate building.

(iii) Common improvements. A taxpayer includes in the cost of the dwelling units their allocable share of the cost that the taxpayer reasonably expects to incur for any common improvements (e.g., sewers, roads, clubhouses) that benefit the dwelling units and that the taxpayer is contractually obligated, or required by law, to construct within the tract or tracts of land that contain the dwelling units.

Treas. Reg. § 1.460–3(b)(2).

Id. at *23.[36] The court concluded its opinion by "draw[ing] a bright line," under which a "contract [could] qualify as a home construction contract only if the taxpayer builds, constructs, reconstructs, rehabilitates, or installs integral components to dwelling units or real property improvements directly related to and located on the site of such dwelling units." *Id.* at *25. It held that this rule was necessary to keep costs that were attenuated to home construction from being the basis for the completed contract method of accounting. *Id.*

The Tax Court issued its consolidated decision on June 2, 2014, and entered decisions finally disposing of Petitioners' claims on September 15, 2014. Petitioners then timely appealed the decision of the Tax Court. We have jurisdiction under I.R.C. §7482(a)(1).

II. STANDARD OF REVIEW

"In reviewing Tax Court decisions, we apply the same standard as applied to district court determinations." *Rodriguez v. Comm'r,* 722 F.3d 306, 308 (5th Cir.2013). Because this case presents a question of statutory interpretation, an issue of law, "the proper standard of review is *de novo.*" *BMC Software, Inc. v. Comm'r,* 780 F.3d 669, 674 (5th Cir.2015).

III. THE HOME CONSTRUCTION CONTRACTS EXCEPTION

The case before us concerns a matter of statutory interpretation of the Internal Revenue Code. In particular, the issue is whether or not Petitioners' contracts were "home construction contracts" within the meaning of I.R.C. §460(e)(6)(A), thereby making Petitioners eligible to use the completed contract method of accounting. Our statutory analysis here is guided by two principles. The first is that in deciding "question[s] of statutory interpretation, we begin, of course, with the words of the statute." *Phillips v. Marine Concrete Structures, Inc.,* 895 F.2d 1033, 1035 (5th Cir.1990) (en banc). This entails not only looking to language of the statute, but also "follow[ing] 'the cardinal rule that statutory language must be read in context.'" *Hibbs v. Winn,* 542 U.S. 88, 101, 124 S.Ct. 2276, 159 L.Ed.2d 172 (2004) (quoting *Gen. Dynamics Land Sys. Inc. v. Cline,* 540 U.S. 581, 596, 124 S.Ct. 1236, 157 L.Ed.2d 1094 (2004)). The second is "the well settled principle that statutes granting tax exemptions or deferments must be strictly construed." *Elam v. Comm'r,* 477 F.2d 1333, 1335 (6th Cir.1973); *see also United States v. Centennial Sav. Bank FSB,* 499 U.S. 573, 583, 111 S.Ct. 1512, 113 L.Ed.2d 608 (1991) ("[T]ax-exemption and -deferral provisions are to be construed narrowly."). As we conclude today, the Tax Court faithfully applied both these precepts in holding that Petitioners' contracts were not "home construction contracts."

---

36. [8] The Tax Court noted that regulations proposed in 2008, but not yet adopted by the Treasury Department, would have allowed for common improvement costs to come within "home construction costs" even if a contract did not provide for the construction of a dwelling unit. *Id.* at *24 n.19. However, the court declined to attach any importance to the regulations and added that they supported the view that common improvement costs were not covered by the statute and existing regulations. *Id.*

A.

The "home construction contract" exception is part of a broader statutory provision, I.R.C. § 460, covering how taxpayers must report income on long-term contracts. Section 460 was first enacted as part of the Tax Reform Act of 1986 in response to the latitude taxpayers had previously enjoyed in choosing a method of accounting for long-term contracts. *See* Staff of the Joint Comm. on Tax'n, 99th Cong., General Explanation of the Tax Reform Act of 1986 527 (Comm. Print 1987) ("Congress believed that the completed contract method of accounting for long-term contracts permitted an unwarranted deferral of income from those contracts."). The provision removed this latitude and instead required taxpayers to account for long-term contracts using the percentage of completion method. *See* I.R.C. § 460(a).

While § 460 generally prohibits the use of the completed contract method, there are two exceptions found in I.R.C. § 460(e)(1) that allow the use of this method.[37] The first (not at issue here) is an exception for long-term construction contracts expected to be completed within two years of the commencement date, if performed by taxpayers whose annual gross receipts averaged $10 million or less for the three preceding taxable years. I.R.C. § 460(e)(1)(B). The second is the exception for "home construction contracts" at issue today. I.R.C. § 460(e)(1)(A). The exception was added in 1988 under the TAMRA. Pub. L. No. 100–647, § 5041, 102 Stat. 3342, 3673. Although it is unclear precisely why the exception was added, statements surrounding its enactment suggest that Congress was concerned about problems that homebuilders had experienced in using the percentage of completion method.[38]

The term "home construction contract" is defined in the statute under § 460(e)(6)(A).

---

37. [9] This provision, in full, states:

(1) In general.—Subsections (a), (b), and (c)(1) and (2) [detailing the percentage of completion method of accounting] shall not apply to—

(A) any home construction contract, or

(B) any other construction contract entered into by a taxpayer—

(i) who estimates (at the time such contract is entered into) that such contract will be completed within the 2–year period beginning on the contract commencement date of such contract, and

(ii) whose average annual gross receipts for the 3 taxable years preceding the taxable year in which such contract is entered into do not exceed $10,000,000.

In the case of a home construction contract with respect to which the requirements of clauses (i) and (ii) of subparagraph (B) are not met, section 263A shall apply notwithstanding subsection (c)(4) thereof.

I.R.C. § 460(e)(1).

38. [10] In particular, Senator Dennis DeConcini noted that "homebuilders receive very small down payments and usually incur significant costs to develop the land and finish the home before receiving the final payment," and that "[t]he homebuilder does not receive progress payments," making it difficult for homebuilders to recognize income throughout the contract under the percentage of completion method. 134 Cong. Rec. 29,962 (1988). When the provision emerged from the conference report, Representative William Archer, Jr. stated in support of it: "I was particularly pleased that we changed the 'completed contract method of accounting' provisions under current law to exempt single family residential construction—thereby reducing the cost of homes." 134 Cong. Rec. 33,112 (1988).

That provision qualifies a contract as a home construction contract if:

> 80 percent or more of the estimated total contract costs (as of the close of the taxable year in which the contract was entered into) are reasonably expected to be attributable to activities referred to in paragraph 4 [building, construction, reconstruction, rehabilitation, or integral component installation] with respect to—
>
>> (i) dwelling units (as defined in section 168(e)(2)(A)(ii)) contained in buildings containing 4 or fewer dwelling units (as so defined) and
>>
>> (ii) improvements to real property directly related to such dwelling units and located on the site of such dwelling units.

I.R.C. § 460(e)(6)(A).

As the Tax Court recognized, this statute creates an "80% test" that allows a contract to qualify as a "home construction contract" if 80% of its costs come from construction activities directed toward subsections (i) and (ii) of the statute. *Howard Hughes Co.*, 142 T.C. 355, 2014 WL 10077466, at *19. Our analysis next turns to whether Petitioners come within either subsection.

B.

Subsection (i) of § 460(e)(6)(A) states that construction activities satisfy the 80% test if they "are reasonably expected to be attributable to activities referred to in paragraph (4) with respect to ... dwelling units." The Tax Court held that this subsection applies "only if the taxpayer builds, constructs, reconstructs, rehabilitates, or installs integral components to dwelling units." *Id.* at *25. A plain reading of the statute supports the Tax Court's holding. Subsection (i) refers to "activities ... with respect to ... dwelling units." Since a dwelling unit is "a house or apartment used to provide living accommodations," I.R.C. § 168(e)(2)(A)(ii)(I), this necessarily means that a taxpayer seeking to use the completed contract method must be engaged in construction, reconstruction, rehabilitation, or installation of an integral component of a home or apartment. This reading is further supported by the definition of "activities" in subsection § 460(e)(4) as "building, construction, reconstruction, or rehabilitation of, or the installation of any integral component to, or improvements of, real property." Petitioners argue that this reading imposes a "homebuilder requirement," turning the eligibility of using the completed contract method on the identity of the taxpayer rather than on the costs incurred. This is incorrect. While homebuilders certainly come within subsection (i), the activities listed in § 460(e)(4) can encompass subcontractors so long as their costs come from work done on a dwelling unit. Because "the costs [P]etitioners incur[red] [we]re not the actual homes' structural, physical construction costs," or were not related to work on dwelling units, Petitioners do not come within subsection (i). *Howard Hughes Co.*, 142 T.C. 355, 2014 WL 10077466, at *23.

As an alternative, Petitioners argue that the phrase "with respect to" in the statute only requires some causal relationship between the dwelling units and construction costs incurred. Petitioners argue that their work satisfies this causal relationship since the common improvements and community infrastructure in Summerlin would not have been built by Petitioners but "for the contractually required construction of dwelling units." The Tax Court squarely rejected this reading, however. It noted that "Petitioners' interpretation of the statute would make any construction cost tangentially related to a dwelling unit … a cost to be counted in determining whether a contract is a home construction contract." *Id.* at *21. The Tax Court correctly recognized that this interpretation could not be harmonized with the narrow exceptions to the percentage of completion method for long-term contracts provided by Congress and the principle that tax deferments are to be strictly construed.

Furthermore, if construction costs need only have some causal relationship with a dwelling unit to come within subsection (i), then costs from "improvements to real property directly related to such dwelling units and located on the site of such dwelling units" should also come within subsection (i). However, Congress has separately codified those costs in subsection (ii). And in statutory interpretation we generally follow "the rule against superfluities, [which] instructs courts to interpret a statute to effectuate all its provisions, so that no part is rendered superfluous." *Hibbs,* 542 U.S. at 89, 124 S.Ct. 2276. We cannot accept Petitioners' broad reading of "with respect to" as it would render subsection (ii) superfluous.

C.

Petitioners next argue that their construction contracts fall within subsection (ii) of § 460(e)(6)(A). The Tax Court correctly rejected that argument because Petitioners' construction activities for common improvements were not "located on the site of such dwelling units." The court held that the word "site" in the statute meant a single site of a building otherwise described as a "lot." *Howard Hughes Co.,* 142 T.C. 355, 2014 WL 10077466, at *22. Because Petitioners never made improvements on the lots where homes were built, the Tax Court concluded that Petitioners' construction activities did not come within the plain language of the statute. Petitioners argue here, as they did below, that the word "located on the site" refers to "construction that occurs in the residential subdivision" or "at least the entire village." In particular, Petitioners point to the fact that the term "site" is used in the singular, implying that a single "site" will include many "dwelling units." But the Tax Court's construction of the word "site" takes into account that a single "site" will include "dwelling units," and it is consistent with the statute. As the Tax Court observed, subsection (i) of the statute allows "a construction contract for a building with four or fewer dwelling units to still be considered a home construction contract." *Id.* at *22. A single "site" of "a building" (otherwise known as a "lot") would thus include "dwelling units," plural, because subsection (i) contemplates that buildings can include more than one dwelling unit. Petitioners' contrary reading of "site" is far too broad[39] and conflicts

---

39. [11] While Petitioners state that "site" can mean a subdivision or a village, they offer no limiting definition of the term. Under Petitioners' definition, "site" could mean a location even broader than a village.

with the principle that statutes granting tax deferments are construed narrowly. Petitioners do not fall within the plain language of subsection (ii).

Apart from the statutory text, Petitioners argue that they qualify for the tax deferment contemplated by the statute as the result of a Treasury regulation that flows from subsection (ii). That regulation states:

> A taxpayer includes in the cost of the dwelling units their allocable share of the cost that the taxpayer reasonably expects to incur for any common improvements (e.g., sewers, roads, clubhouses) that benefit the dwelling units and that the taxpayer is contractually obligated, or required by law, to construct within the tract or tracts of land that contain the dwelling units.

Treas. Reg. § 1.460–3(b)(2)(iii). Petitioners argue that this regulation allows them to count their common improvement costs in the 80% test since it directly refers to the type of "common improvements" they constructed. Furthermore, Petitioners argue that the regulations show that the term "site" has a broader meaning than the Tax Court's interpretation. This is because § 1.460–3(b)(2)(iii) uses the phrase "tracts of land that contain the dwelling units" and another regulation uses the phrase "*at* the site of [] the dwelling units," Treas. Reg. § 1.460–3(b)(2)(i)(B), instead of the statutory phrase "*on* the site of such dwelling units."

Petitioners' arguments are unpersuasive. The Commissioner repeatedly rejected Petitioners' reading of the regulation at oral argument, in the briefing, and in previous internal memoranda. *See* I.R.S. Tech. Adv. Mem. 200552012, 2005 WL 3561182 (Dec. 30, 2005).[40] Assuming, *arguendo*, that the regulation does construe § 460(e)(6)(A)(ii), the Tax Court concluded that Petitioners do not come within this regulation. Section 1.460–3(b)(2)(iii) allows a taxpayer to "include in *the cost of the dwelling units* ... any common improvements." Treas. Reg. § 1.460–3(b)(2)(iii) (emphasis added). The Tax Court noted that this meant that "the taxpayer must [have] at some point incur [red] some construction cost with respect to the dwelling unit to include [common improvement] costs in the dwelling unit cost." *Howard Hughes Co.*, 142 T.C. 355, 2014 WL 10077466, at *23. However, "Petitioners ha[d] no dwelling unit costs in which to include the common improvement costs." *Id.*

Petitioners argue that the Tax Court improperly inferred a prohibition from an affirmative regulation and that the Tax Court unfairly imputed a requirement to incur

---

40. [12] The Commissioner asserted in the briefing and admitted at oral argument that this regulation is not derived from the language of § 460(e)(6)(A) but is instead derived from a general grant of rulemaking authority under § 460(h). The Commissioner argued that the regulation was promulgated to remedy a gap in the statute. It was previously thought that § 460(e)(6)(A) would not allow "a builder of a planned community ... [to] us[e] the completed contract method of accounting based on common improvement costs, if the allocable share of those costs exceed[ed] 20 percent of the total allocable costs of a contract for the sale of a house within a community." The ensuing regulation was designed, according to the Commissioner, to address this issue. The Commissioner's reading of the regulation as having no basis in § 460(e)(6)(A) may be problematic. However, we need not decide that or delve into the issue any deeper because Petitioners do not come within the regulation even if it does modify § 460(e)(6)(A)(ii).

dwelling unit costs from § 460(e)(6)(A)(i), when the regulation only modifies § 460(e)(6)(A)(ii). The Tax Court properly interpreted the plain language of the regulation. The regulation sets out how common improvement costs can be eligible for inclusion in the 80% test, and Petitioners' costs are not eligible under the plain terms of the regulation.[41] As the Tax Court noted, the plain text refers to the "costs of the dwelling units," meaning that there must be dwelling unit costs before taxpayers can count their common improvement costs towards the 80% test.

Finally, Petitioners point to regulations proposed in 2008 (but not yet adopted) providing that taxpayers can meet the 80% test with "a contract for the construction of common improvements ... even if the contract is not for the construction of any dwelling unit." 73 Fed. Reg. 45,180, 45,180 (Aug. 4, 2008); *see also* Prop. Treas. Reg. § 1.460–3(b)(2) (2008). Petitioners argue that these regulations "refute the Tax Court's interpretation of the statute" and show that the statute does not limit the statute to "only those taxpayers with direct dwelling-unit-construction costs." But we have noted that "proposed regulations are entitled to no deference until final." *Matter of Appletree Markets, Inc.,* 19 F.3d 969, 973 (5th Cir.1994); *see also id.* ("To give effect to regulations that have merely been proposed would upset the balance of powers among the constitutional branches."). We attach no weight to the proposed regulations.[42] Petitioners' construction costs do not fall within § 460(e)(6)(A)(ii).

IV. CONCLUSION

Petitioners' contracts are not "home construction contracts" under I.R.C. § 460(e)(6)(A). We AFFIRM.

Homes by Ayres v. Commissioner

United States Court of Appeals, Ninth Circuit
795 F.2d 832 (1986)

FACTS

Taxpayers engage in the construction and sale of large-scale tract housing developments. A typical development consists of 150 houses built in three "phases." For the years in question, taxpayers used an accrual method of accounting to compute their gross income from the sale of houses. Taxpayers capitalized into accounts they characterized as "inventories" the cost of their land held for development and sale,

---

41. [13] Like any measure defining the eligibility for a particular benefit, this regulation will necessarily be exclusory or "prohibitive" in applications where an entity does not meet the eligibility criteria.

42. [14] The proposed regulations, if anything, undermine Petitioners' position that the statute includes common improvement costs in the 80% test without dwelling unit construction. The preamble to the proposed regulations states that they "expand the types of contracts eligible for the home construction contract exemption." 73 Fed.Reg. 45,180, 45,180 (Aug. 4, 2008). This passage suggests the proposed regulations are beyond the scope of § 460(e)(6)(A). But, as Petitioners note elsewhere in their briefing, regulations cannot "expand the universe of qualifying costs."

the cost of offsite improvements, and the direct and indirect costs of onsite work-in-process and completed houses.

Taxpayers accounted for their construction costs by accumulating costs for each phase of a subdivision. These costs included direct costs, such as labor, materials, and permits, and indirect costs, such as overhead, payroll taxes, and vehicle operation costs. In the pre-LIFO years, taxpayers would accumulate all direct and indirect costs for the year and then allocate them according to one of three methods to determine the cost of the houses sold in each phase.

One technique for allocating the pool of capitalized costs is the "relative sales value method." This method determines cost of houses sold by multiplying total capitalized costs (costs already incurred plus estimated costs of completion) by the ratio of the selling prices of the houses sold to the estimated selling prices of all houses in the phase. Another technique for cost allocation, called "average cost method," calls for multiplying total capitalized costs by the ratio of the total number of houses sold to the aggregate number of houses to be sold in a phase. Finally, the "square footage method" allocates costs by multiplying total capitalized costs by the ratio of the aggregate square footage of houses sold to the aggregate square footage of all houses to be sold in a phase. All three of these methods comport with generally accepted accounting principles and the IRS admits that they accurately reflect income.

Taxpayers filed an application (Form 970) to use a LIFO inventory method with their returns for the fiscal years 1976, 1977, and 1978. They used LIFO methods with respect to all onsite costs (work-in-process and completed houses) and excluded offsite costs and land held for development from LIFO treatment. Application of the LIFO method was identical to the pre-LIFO accounting method except that an additional computational step was added that resulted in a higher cost of homes sold and therefore less income. LIFO results in lower net income in high inflation years, such as the late 1970's, because the recently inventoried, higher priced goods are offset against current sales. The IRS disallowed the LIFO inventory pricing and asserted deficiencies based on taxpayers' pre-LIFO methods. The Tax Court held that under 26 U.S.C. §471 (Internal Revenue Code of 1954, as amended, hereafter cited as "I.R.C."), tract home builders could not adopt inventory accounting methods for tax purposes and therefore disallowed LIFO inventory treatment for taxpayers.

ANALYSIS

Whenever a taxpayer changes accounting methods, the consent of the Commissioner must be obtained. I.R.C. §446(e). "The Commissioner has broad powers in determining whether accounting methods used by a taxpayer clearly reflect income...." *Comm'r v. Hansen*, 360 U.S. 446, 467 (1959). If the Commissioner determines that a particular accounting method does not clearly reflect income, he may compute taxable income under an accounting method which, in his opinion, does reflect income clearly. I.R.C. §446(b).

An exception exists to the general rule that the Commissioner must consent to a change in taxpayer's accounting methods. Taxpayers who regularly keep inventories may convert to LIFO without the Commissioner's approval. Treas. Reg. § 1.472-1(a). The Commissioner's discretion as to an election of LIFO by a taxpayer who regularly keeps inventories "is far more circumscribed than in the case of changes of accounting method generally." *Peninsula Steel Products & Equipment Co. v. Comm'r*, 78 T.C. 1029, 1055 (1982) (footnote omitted); *accord RECO Industries v. Comm'r*, 83 T.C. 912, 929–30 (1984). In this case, taxpayers argue that they maintained inventories in the pre-LIFO years and that therefore they were entitled to convert to a LIFO method as a matter of right under Treas. Reg. § 1.472-1(a). We agree with the Tax Court's holding that tract home developers, as a matter of law, cannot maintain inventories for tax purposes and therefore taxpayers needed the Commissioner's consent prior to changing accounting methods.

Section 471 provides in part that "[w]henever in the opinion of the Secretary the use of inventories is necessary in order clearly to determine the income of any taxpayer, inventories shall be taken by such taxpayer on such basis as the Secretary may pre-scribe...." The Commissioner, as the Secretary's delegate, has promulgated regulations under section 471 which specify when inventory accounting is appropriate for tax purposes. Treasury Regulation § 1.471-1 states that: "In order to reflect taxable income correctly, inventories ... are necessary in every case in which the production, purchase, or sale of merchandise is an income-producing factor." Further regulations under section 471 permit certain taxpayers to take inventories such as securities dealers,[43] farmers,[44] and miners.[45]

Taxpayers argue that section 471 does not limit inventory accounting for tax pur-poses to cases involving "merchandise" or one of the other exceptions listed in the regulations. In effect, the taxpayers position is that section 471 and the accompanying regulations do not create an exclusive list of situations in which inventory accounting is permissible. Taxpayers contend that inventory accounting might be appropriate for other taxpayers so long as inventories clearly reflect income. The taxpayers thus conclude that we should remand this case to the Tax Court to determine whether taxpayers used an inventory method.

We reject taxpayers' interpretation of section 471. The Commissioner has discretion under section 471 to specify when inventories are necessary to reflect income correctly. *W.C. & A.N. Miller Development Co. v. Comm'r*, 81 T.C. 619, 627 (1983). The Com-missioner requires inventories for taxpayers which produce or sell merchandise under Treas. Reg. § 1.471-1. All other uses of inventory accounting for tax purposes are per-missive. We believe that the Treasury implicitly rejected taxpayers' construction of section 471 when it promulgated Treas. Reg. §§ 1.471-5, 1.471-6 and 1.471-7 in 1960. For example, Treas. Reg. § 1.471-6 states, "[a] farmer may make his return upon an inventory method instead of the cash receipts and disbursements method." Had the Treasury interpreted section 471 to permit all taxpayers to choose the inventory

---

43. [1] Treas. Reg. § 1.471-5.

44. [2] Treas. Reg. § 1.471-6.

45. [3] Treas. Reg. § 1.471-7.

method of accounting, it would not have granted farmers permission to do so. See also Treas. Reg. § 1.472-1 ("Any taxpayer *permitted* or required to take inventories pursuant to the provisions of section 471....") (emphasis added).

The Commissioner has consistently maintained that real property cannot be inventoried for tax purposes. *W.C. & A.N. Miller Development Co. v. Comm'r*, 81 T.C. 619, 628–29 (citing *Atlantic Coast Realty Co. v. Comm'r*, 11 B.T.A. 416 (1928)); see also Rev. Rul. 69-536, 1969-2 C.B. 109. In *Miller*, the Tax Court specifically held that taxpayers who mass produce tract homes on subdivided lots may not inventory the costs of developing those homes. 81 T.C. at 628–29. "It has consistently been held that the costs of improvements to subdivided real estate held for sale are capital expenditures, allocable to the basis of the taxpayer in the various unsold lots." *Id.* at 632; see I.R.C. § 263(a); Treas. Reg. §§ 1.263(a)-1(a)(1), 1.263(a)-2(a) & 1.263(a)-2(d). Gain from the sale of property is defined as "the excess of the amount realized therefrom over the adjusted basis." I.R.C. § 1001(a). Section 1012 states that the basis of property is its cost, with some exceptions not relevant to this case. When subdivided lots are sold, "the cost or other basis of the entire property shall be equitably apportioned among the several parts, and the gain realized or loss sustained on the part of the entire property sold is the difference between the selling price and the cost or other basis allocated to such part." Treas. Reg. § 1.61-6(a). Finally, basis in real estate must be adjusted to reflect the cost of improvements. Treas. Reg. § 1.1016-2(a). Although taxpayers allocate their accumulated costs in a way which resembles an inventory method, there is no basis under the Code or established precedent for the contention that tract homes may be inventoried.[46]

Taxpayers acknowledge that the Commissioner and the courts have refused to allow inventory accounting methods with real estate. They attempt to distinguish these earlier precedents on the ground that financial accounting techniques have changed sufficiently to warrant inventory treatment for tract home developers. In *Atlantic Coast*, the Board of Tax Appeals reasoned in 1928 that valuation problems prevented using inventory accounting methods for real estate. 11 B.T.A. at 419–20. Taxpayers presented expert evidence in the Tax Court that current financial accounting standards allow for real property to be inventoried. However, *Atlantic Coast* also denied inventory treatment on the ground that real estate should receive different

---

46. [4] The remedy sought by the taxpayers here, remand to the Tax Court to determine specifically if the taxpayers were using an inventory system during the pre-LIFO years, would be superfluous because the Tax Court already rejected "'petitioner's contention that capitalization is an inventory method.'" Accordingly, the Tax Court held that Miller prohibited home developers from taking inventories and thereby adopting LIFO inventory methods. In reaching this conclusion, the Tax Court stated that this case is "substantially similar" to *Miller* on its facts. Taxpayers argue that in *Miller* the taxpayer failed to prove that an inventory system was in use and therefore the Tax Court incorrectly relied on *Miller*. The "job cost" accumulation method used in *Miller*, however, bears a close resemblance to the techniques employed by taxpayers. Both methods are capitalization techniques, though admittedly the taxpayers' method is more sophisticated. Taxpayers' own expert witness stated that taxpayers in effect used a "job cost inventory cost accumulation" method. Adding the label "inventory" amounts to nothing more than an attempt by taxpayers to realize substantial tax savings through a LIFO method.

tax accounting because of its unique attributes. *Id.* at 420 (real estate value established "only by identifying each parcel in question"). The fact that financial accounting standards have progressed does not mean that taxpayers have a right to inventory accounting methods for tax purposes. Tax and financial accounting methods frequently diverge. *Thor Power*, 439 U.S. at 541. The Commissioner has broad discretion over accounting techniques and, as a matter of law, real estate cannot be inventoried until he changes his position or Congress changes the law.[47]

The Tax Court correctly concluded that section 471 generally prohibits the taking of inventories for property other than merchandise. Property other than merchandise can be inventoried only if the regulations to section 471 expressly provide for inventory accounting or the Commissioner consents to the use of inventories. The Commissioner has never consented, either in a regulation or a revenue ruling, to inventory accounting for real estate or real estate developments.

Von-Lusk v. Commissioner

United States Tax Court
104 T.C. 207 (1995)

OPINION

This case involves the Commissioner's determination that certain expenses deducted in Von-Lusk's returns for 1988, 1989, and 1990, were not deductible but instead were to be capitalized under section 263A.[48]

Von-Lusk (also referred to as "the Partnership") is a California limited partnership. Petitioner, the Lusk Company, is an S corporation and was the tax matters partner of Von-Lusk for 1988, 1989, and 1990. On the date the petition was filed in this case, the principal place of business for both the Partnership and the Lusk Company was in Irvine, California.

Von-Lusk filed a U.S. Partnership Return of Income (Form 1065) for each of the calendar years 1988, 1989, and 1990. On December 14, 1992, the Commissioner issued Notices of Final Partnership Administrative Adjustment (FPAA) to Von-Lusk for those years in which deductions claimed on the returns for each of the years were disallowed as follows:

---

47. [5] Taxpayers contend that even if inventories are limited to "merchandise," tract homes constitute merchandise under section 471. The Tax Court has held that merchandise does not include real property. *Miller*, 81 T.C. at 630. This conclusion is supported by accounting literature which defines merchandise as tangible personal property. Statement 1, A.R.B. No. 43., ch. 4, reprinted in 4 A.I.C.P.A. Professional Standards, AC § 5121.03 (CCH 1979); W. Meigs, C. Johnson & R. Meigs, Accounting: The Basis for Business Decisions 405 (6th ed. 1984). Finally, common usage of the term merchandise excludes real estate and improvements to real estate. Webster's Ninth New Collegiate Dictionary (1983). While taxpayers correctly note that terms are not static in the law, we fail to see an adequate justification for expanding merchandise beyond its current legal, accounting, and common definitions.

48. [1] Unless otherwise indicated, all section references are to the Internal Revenue Code in effect for the years at issue, and all Rule references are to the Tax Court Rules of Practice and Procedure.

Partnership Item	1988	1989	1990
Interest expense	$190,761	$352,150	$457,659
Taxes	206,377	229,845	211,903
Other deductions	110,725	201,443	187,797

After the initial pleadings in this Court, the Commissioner filed an amendment to answer, in which the Commissioner conceded the foregoing interest expense deductions. The adjustments in the FPAAs for taxes and other deductions remain at issue. The explanation of adjustments in the FPAAs stated that "The deduction for taxes is not allowed because the partnership has not established that the amounts claimed were not capital in nature." It went on to state that "The deduction for other expenses is not allowed because the partnership has not substantiated that the amounts claimed were ordinary and necessary expenses paid or incurred by the partnership during the taxable year in carrying on a trade or business or an activity engaged in for profit or that the amounts claimed were not capital in nature."

Von-Lusk was formed in 1966 with the stated purpose of managing, holding, and developing for investment approximately 278 acres of raw land (the Property), which was contributed to the Partnership by its partners in 1966. Prior to the transfer, the general and limited partners (collectively) each owned an undivided one-half interest in the Property. The general partner (The Lusk Company) and the limited partners collectively (various members of the Von der Ahe family) each own a 50-percent interest in the Partnership.

The Lusk Company is a residential and commercial real estate development company. The Lusk Company is the general partner in more than 40 general and limited partnerships in California (the Lusk partnerships). The Lusk partnerships invest in and develop real estate, own and rent apartments, commercial buildings and industrial buildings, and own and operate a livestock ranch and farm.

The Lusk Company, as general partner and managing partner of real estate development partnerships, engages the services of many contractors, lobbyists, various engineers, architects, and others to perform services for these partnerships. These independent contractors, on behalf of the Lusk partnerships, meet with government officials, obtain building permits and zoning variances, negotiate permit fees, perform engineering and feasibility studies, and draft architectural plans. The contractors bill the Lusk partnerships that benefit from their work for the cost of their services. During 1988, 1989, and 1990, Von-Lusk incurred independent contractor costs of $17,912, $62,611, and $88,848, respectively. Von-Lusk claimed these amounts on its returns for such years under the caption "other deductions" as consultants, advertising, insurance, market research, off premise sales, and other costs.

Service Mortgage Company is a California corporation and an affiliate of The Lusk Company. Service Mortgage Company provides management services for The Lusk Company and the Lusk partnerships. Service Mortgage Company employs executives, project managers, secretaries, and accountants. These employees monitor the Lusk partnership projects and review and direct the work of the contractors discussed above. Service Mortgage Company bills the cost of their employees to the Lusk partnerships that benefit from the work.

When Service Mortgage Company bills a Lusk partnership other than a partnership engaged in property management or rental activities, the amount is charged to a "work in progress" account for that particular partnership. Service Mortgage Company includes a mark-up for overhead and facilities costs in the wages charged to "work in progress" accounts. The Lusk partnerships that own and operate rental property are charged for time spent by Service Mortgage Company's administrative personnel. These charges are deducted by the Lusk partnerships as period costs.

During 1988, 1989, and 1990, Service Mortgage Company billed Von-Lusk in the amounts of $92,813, $138,822, and $98,949, respectively. These amounts include the wages, payroll taxes, and fringe benefits of Service Mortgage Company's administrative personnel and the overhead mark-up described above. The overhead mark-up represents approximately 40 percent of the total amount billed. The wages, payroll taxes, and fringe benefits of Service Mortgage Company's administrative personnel represent approximately 60 percent of the total amount billed. Accordingly, during 1988, 1989, and 1990, Service Mortgage Company billed Von-Lusk approximately $37,125, $55,529, and $39,580, respectively, for overhead and $55,688, $83,293, and $59,369, respectively, for the wages, payroll taxes, and fringe benefits of Service Mortgage Company's administrative personnel. Von-Lusk deducted the amounts it paid to Service Mortgage Company during the years 1988, 1989, and 1990, on its tax returns for those years under the caption "other deductions—wages and salaries".

The "other deductions" claimed on Von-Lusk's tax returns for the years 1988, 1989, and 1990, consist of the following costs:

Other Deductions	1988	1989	1990
Consultants	$13,563	$49,750	$74,644
Advertising	475	3,875	0
Insurance	711	905	916
Wages & salaries	92,813	138,822	98,949
Market research	500	1,625	6,934
Off premise sales	2,516	3,837	5,514
Other costs	147	2,619	840
TOTAL	$110,725	$201,433	$187,797

The deductions for "Advertising", "Market Research", and "Off Premise Sales" refer to costs incurred to advise Von-Lusk as to the appropriateness of product mix and pricing for the Property. Von-Lusk did not engage in active sales efforts during 1988, 1989, and 1990. On its returns for the years 1988, 1989, and 1990, Von-Lusk deducted real property taxes incurred and paid in the amounts of $206,377, $229,845, and

$211,303, respectively. Von-Lusk also deducted $600 in 1990 for a California franchise tax shown to be due on its California franchise tax return.

The Property is located in San Bernardino County, California, in an area called Chino Hills. Chino Hills was incorporated on December 1, 1991. Prior to this date, development was controlled by the San Bernardino County Planning Commission and Board of Supervisors.

In August 1982, the San Bernardino County Board of Supervisors approved the Chino Hills Specific Plan, which provided for 2,779 dwelling units on the Property. In 1985, Von-Lusk agreed to the inclusion of the Property in Chino Hills Assessment District No. 85-1, which is a special assessment district that was formed to provide for the acquisition and construction of certain public improvements within the district. Without further elaboration or explanation the parties have stipulated that "This special assessment increased Von-Lusk's property taxes by over $200,000 per year."

In 1985, Von-Lusk submitted a preliminary development plan for the Property to the San Bernardino County Board of Supervisors. In January 1986, the San Bernardino County Board of Supervisors approved the preliminary development plan for the Property (also referred to as the Lusk Los Serranos property and/or Fairfield Ranch). The approved Lusk Los Serranos Preliminary Development Plan provided for 1,444 dwelling units on the Property. The Chino Hills Specific Plan (referred to above) had provided for 2,779 dwelling units on the Property.

The San Bernardino County Board of Supervisors set a development fee of $31,680,600 for the Property. The County did not reduce the development fee when it approved the Preliminary Development Plan. The Preliminary Development Plan allowed 1335 fewer units than the Chino Hills Specific Plan. On a per unit basis, this increased the development fee from $11,400 per unit to $21,940 per unit. During 1988, 1989, and 1990, Von-Lusk pursued an appeal in an attempt to reduce the development fee.

In January 1986, the San Bernardino County Board of Supervisors informed Von-Lusk that it would not approve a final development plan and tract map for the Property unless certain conditions were met. In 1987, in response to an application filed by Von-Lusk, the Property was removed from the agricultural preserve and zoned for residential development. The rezoning was done in accordance with the Chino Hills Specific Plan and constituted a rezoning of the Property for future use. The Property was used by tenant farmers to raise grass and grains during the years 1988, 1989, and 1990.

On September 22, 1988, Von-Lusk submitted tentative tract maps to the San Bernardino County Board of Supervisors. On May 18, 1989, the County approved the tentative tract maps, subject to certain conditions. Condition No. 70 provides:

> no map shall be recorded for any phase of this tract until all necessary contracts have been approved and executed for the construction of Soquel Canyon Parkway from El Prado Road/Central Avenue to its planned connection with lower Carbon Canyon Road or an alternative highway in Orange County and

no building permits shall be issued until 90 days prior to the projected completion of the parkway.

During 1988, 1989, and 1990, no agreement was reached between San Bernardino County and Orange County as to the location of the Soquel Canyon Parkway connection, no funding issues for the highway were approved, and no physical activities were commenced in connection with the construction of the highway.

Condition No. 125 also imposed by the San Bernardino County Board of Supervisors as a condition for approval of the tentative tract map required Von-Lusk to design, construct, and finance a six-lane addition to Soquel Canyon Parkway from the Corona Expressway interchange east to Chino Creek, a six-lane bridge at Chino Creek, a six-lane section of Soquel Canyon Parkway from the Chino Creek Bridge east to the El Prado Road/Central Avenue intersection, and a one-half width section of Central Avenue from the Corona Expressway east to the Chino Creek.

Von-Lusk appealed Condition No. 70 and several other conditions. This appeal was pending during the years 1988, 1989, and 1990. During those years Von-Lusk could not obtain building permits for the Property because Condition No. 70 had not been met. During the years 1988, 1989, and 1990, Von-Lusk did not make any physical improvements to the Property and the Property continued to be used by tenant farmers to raise grass and grains.

The parties stipulated that on August 6, 1993, section 1.263A-1 through 1.263A-6, Income Tax Regs., was adopted, and that these regulations apply to costs incurred in taxable years beginning after December 31, 1993. Accordingly, the parties agreed that neither party would argue that the facts contained in the stipulation of facts cause section 1.263A-2(a)(3)(ii), Income Tax Regs., to apply to the Property.

No controversy is before us as to whether Von-Lusk was engaged in an activity for profit, or whether the expenditures at issue were properly made in pursuit of a business profit. Both parties have limited their argument to, and our opinion deals exclusively with, whether the expenditures at issue should have been capitalized under section 263A or were properly deducted, as claimed by petitioner.

The general rule of section 263A is found in section 263A(a)....

* * *

Subsection (b) describes the property to which section 263A applies. Briefly stated, section 263A applies to (1) property produced by the taxpayer and (2) property acquired for resale. The parties agree that the property at issue was not acquired by Von-Lusk for resale, as contemplated by the statute. Therefore, for section 263A to be applicable, the property must be "produced by the taxpayer."

Section 263A(g)(1) states that "The term 'produce' includes construct, build, install, manufacture, develop, or improve." The term produce is given further explanation in section 1.263A-1T(a)(5)(ii), Temporary Income Tax Regs., 52 Fed. Reg. 10061 (Mar. 30, 1987), which states that "For purposes of this section, the term 'produce' includes construct, build, install, manufacture, develop, improve, create, raise or grow."

If Von-Lusk's activities fall within the description "construct, build, install, manufacture, develop, improve, create, raise or grow", then Von-Lusk "produced" the property. If Von-Lusk "produced" the property, then section 263A applies. If section 263A applies then the direct and a proper share of the indirect costs of the property are to be capitalized.

Section 263A is a relatively new addition to the Internal Revenue Code, having been added by section 803 of the Tax Reform Act of 1986, Pub. L. 99-514, 100 Stat. 2085, 2350. The statute itself does not provide a comprehensive definition of "produce". Rather, it merely lists a series of examples of activities which are included in the term "produce". Sec. 263A(g)(1). The Commissioner's regulations quoted above follow this path, choosing merely to add to the statutory list of examples rather than setting forth a comprehensive definition.

It falls on us then to determine whether Von-Lusk's activities come within the word "produce" as used by Congress in section 263A. To the extent that the legislative history accompanying section 263A furnishes some guide as to what activities Congress meant to include within the term "produce", it may be found in the reasons behind the development of section 263A. As the Senate Finance Committee stated:

> The committee believes that the present-law rules regarding the capitalization of costs incurred in producing property are deficient in two respects. First, the existing rules may allow costs that are in reality costs of *producing*, acquiring, or *carrying* property to be deducted currently, rather than capitalized into the basis of the property and recovered when the property is sold or as it is used by the taxpayer. This produces a mismatching of expenses and the related income and an unwarranted deferral of taxes. Second, different capitalization rules may apply under present law depending on the nature of the property and its intended use. These differences may create distortions in the allocation of economic resources and the manner in which certain economic activity is organized.

> The committee believes that, in order to more accurately reflect income and make the income tax system more neutral, a single, comprehensive set of rules should govern the capitalization of costs of producing, acquiring, and holding property, including interest expense, subject to appropriate exceptions where application of the rules might be unduly burdensome. [Emphasis added.]

S. Rept. 99-313 (1986), 1986-3 (Vol. 3) C.B. 140. For virtually identical language, *see* H. Rept. 99-426 (1985), 1986-3 (Vol. 2) C.B. 625; Staff of the Joint Comm. on Taxation, General Explanation of the Tax Reform Act of 1986 (J. Comm. Print 1987, 508–509).

Two purposes behind the enactment of section 263A can be gathered from this legislative history. First, Congress expected that a single set of comprehensive rules would be applied to determine whether to capitalize costs. Second, Congress expected those rules to be applied from the acquisition of property, through the time of production, until the time of disposition. To give full effect to this Congressional purpose a broad definition of "produce" is necessary.

We must determine whether the activities engaged in by Von-Lusk properly fit within a broad definition of "produce". Von-Lusk deducted as "other expenses", under the headings consultants, advertising, insurance, market research, off premise sales, and other costs, amounts paid for the services of independent contractors. The functions performed by these independent contractors included meeting with government officials, obtaining building permits and zoning variances, negotiating permit fees, performing engineering and feasibility studies, and drafting architectural plans. Von-Lusk deducted under "other deductions-wages & salaries" amounts paid to Service Mortgage Company. The amounts paid Service Mortgage Company represented compensation for services provided by Service Mortgage Company in reviewing and directing the work of the contractors discussed above.

While the pursuit of building permits and zoning variances, negotiating permit fees and similar activities may not readily spring to mind as examples of production activity, we think that upon reflection they are properly classifiable as such. Such activities are ancillary to actual physical work on the land and are as much a part of a development project as digging a foundation or completing a structure's frame. The project cannot move forward if these steps are not taken.

Von-Lusk took purposeful steps to begin the development of the Property. Petitioner attempts to place weight on the fact that Von-Lusk was formed with the stated purpose of managing, holding, and developing the Property for investment. Petitioner claims Von-Lusk's activities never went beyond managing and holding. The stipulated facts indicate otherwise. Meeting with government officials, obtaining building permits and zoning variances, negotiating permit fees, performing engineering and feasibility studies, drafting architectural plans, and appealing development conditions go beyond managing and holding. These activities represent the first steps of development.

Having determined that Von-Lusk's activities represented the first steps in the development of the Property, it then follows that Von-Lusk produced the property, as contemplated by Congress. As such, section 263A applies to the Property, and Von-Lusk must capitalize the direct and a proper share of the indirect costs of the property.

We note that petitioner made no argument as to whether the costs at issue represented direct or indirect costs of the Property. Petitioner contended only that section 263A does not apply to the Property. Although we may treat this issue as conceded, see Rule 142(a), we consider it briefly below.

Section 263A(a)(2) states that the costs described in this paragraph with respect to any property are (A) the direct costs of such property, and (B) such property's proper share of those indirect costs (including taxes) part or all of which are allocable to such property. Section 1.263A-1T(b)(2)(i), Temporary Income Tax Regs., 52 Fed. Reg. 10061-10062, states: "Direct material costs and direct labor costs must be capitalized with respect to a production or resale activity.... 'Direct labor costs' include the cost of labor that can be identified or associated with a particular activity." The costs deducted under "other deductions" pertained to the cost of various professionals. As such they represent the cost of labor which can be identified or associated with a particular activity.

The fact that the services of these professionals were arranged by the Lusk Company or performed by Service Mortgage Company does not take them out from under section 263A. While they may, therefore, become indirect costs, they remain "costs that directly benefit or are incurred by reason of the performance of a production or resale activity". Sec. 1.263A-1T(b)(2)(ii), Temporary Income Tax Regs. They still must be capitalized. While only the "proper share" of the indirect costs are to be capitalized, petitioner offered no proof or argument that any of these costs did not relate to the activities that we have determined to be part of the development of the property.

The property taxes paid by Von-Lusk must also be capitalized. Taxes otherwise allowable as a deduction are specifically listed as an example of indirect costs. Sec. 263A(a)(2)(B); sec. 1.263A-1T(b)(2)(iii)(I), Temporary Income Tax Regs.

Petitioner states in its brief "With respect to the terms used to define 'produce' it would seem to be a logical conclusion that the physical appearance of raw land would be altered to some degree." Petitioner attempts to use the fact that no physical change occurred on the Property to argue that there was no production. However, section 263A contains no requirement that there be a physical change. To read such a requirement into the statute would, in our judgment, subvert the purpose of Congress in enacting a broad set of uniform rules. In our opinion, Congress meant to include in the costs to be capitalized the preliminary, nonphysical steps of development at issue here.

Petitioner's argument is similar to one rejected by this Court in *Louisiana Land & Exploration Co. v. Comm'r*, 7 T.C. 507 (1946), *affd.* 161 F.2d 842 (5th Cir.1947). There the taxpayer attempted to deduct amounts expended for a geophysical survey of property under lease to the taxpayer. The Commissioner argued that those amounts should be capitalized under section 24(a)(2) of the Internal Revenue Code of 1939 (the forerunner of section 263). Section 24(a)(2) prohibited the deduction of amounts paid for permanent improvements or betterments made to increase the value of any property or estate.

The taxpayer argued "the geophysical survey was not an improvement or betterment of its property, because it added nothing tangible thereto, and that it did not and could not increase the value of the property". *Louisiana Land & Exploration Co. v. Comm'r, supra* at 514. The Court rejected this argument. In language especially pertinent to the present case, the Court stated:

> Under these circumstances it seems abundantly clear that the survey was the first step in the over-all development for oil of these tracts of land and that the benefit derived from the expenditure was to be enjoyed by petitioner in its business during the entire useful life of the asset being developed.... It is well settled that development expenses such as the platting, mapping, and subdividing of a tract of land held for sale must be capitalized and treated as an adjustment of the taxpayer's basis for such property..., and we are un-

able to perceive any significant difference between such expenses and the one involved here. [Id. at 516; citations omitted.]

The Court rejected a requirement of physical change for capitalization. The result there reached is even more strongly called for in the present case. In Louisiana Land & Exploration Co., supra, the Court dealt with the precursor of section 263, whereas here the controlling provisions are in section 263A. And the legislative history of section 263A discloses that Congress was concerned with broadening, not narrowing, the scope of section 263 so as to avoid a "mismatching of expenses and the related income", and sought to provide for a more accurate reflection of income. See supra at 12.

Petitioner next argues that the property could not be "produced" until the "production period" began. The "production period" is defined in section 263A(f)(4)(B) as beginning on the date on which production of the property begins, and ending on the date on which the property is ready to be placed in service or is ready to be held for sale. Petitioner relies upon the following explanation of the term "production period" in I.R.S. 1988-2 C.B. 422, Notice 88–99.

For purposes of the interest capitalization rules, the production period of real property generally begins when physical activity is first performed upon the property (e.g., the grading or clearing of land, the excavation of foundations or lines for utilities, the performance of mechanical activities such as plumbing or electrical work upon a building that is being rehabilitated or improved, or any other work relating to the construction or improvement of real property).

* * *

Petitioner argues that since no physical activity was performed on the Property, the production period did not begin for purposes of the interest capitalization rules, and that it therefore did not "produce" the property.

While petitioner's argument does have a superficial appeal, it does not survive close scrutiny. Subsection (f) of section 263A provides special rules for the allocation of interest to property produced by the taxpayer. It has no effect on the costs here at issue. Indeed, the narrow scope of subsection (f) is reflected in the Commissioner's concession as to the deductibility of the interest items for each of the 3 years at issue. To read the requirements of subsection (f) as applying to all costs would change the special rule to a general rule. Put differently, if no costs were to be capitalized until the beginning of the "production period," then section 263A(f)(1)(A) would be superfluous. Such a construction "offends the well-settled rule of statutory construction that all parts of a statute, if at all possible, are to be given effect." *Weinberger v. Hynson, Westcott & Dunning, Inc.*, 412 U.S. 609, 633 (1973). *See also Phillips Petroleum Co. v. Comm'r*, 101 T.C. 78, 97 (1993) (all parts of a statute must be read together, and each part should be given its full effect).

Petitioner next argues for a consistency requirement between section 263A and section 312(n)(1). Section 312(n)(1) requires an adjustment to the earnings and profits account for construction period carrying charges. It imposes a capitalization requirement for interest, property taxes, and similar carrying charges incurred during the construction period. The term "construction period" is given the same meaning as the term "production period" under section 263A(f)(4)(B). Sec. 312(n)(1)(C).

Because the costs at issue were not incurred during the section 263A(f)(4)(B) production period, they were not incurred during the "construction period" and are, therefore, not required to be capitalized under section 312(n)(1). Petitioner argues that, in the interest of consistency, we should not require capitalization under section 263A. We disagree.

Section 312(n)(1) applies to costs that are otherwise deductible. Section 312(n)(1)(B) includes construction period carrying charges "to the extent such interest, taxes, or charges are attributable to the construction period for such property and would be allowable as a deduction in determining taxable income under this chapter for the taxable year in which paid or incurred." If costs must be capitalized under other provisions of the Internal Revenue Code, then section 312(n)(1) is not applicable. Earnings and profits will be accurately reflected through the taxpayer's decreased deductions and increased income.

The final argument made by petitioner is that some of these costs are specifically excluded from capitalization under section 1.263A-1T(b)(2)(v)(A), Temporary Income Tax Regs., 52 Fed. Reg. 10063. The costs excluded by that regulation are marketing, selling, advertising, and distribution expenses. Petitioner uses this regulation to argue that the advertising, market research, and off premise sales expenses are not capital expenditures.

Petitioner stipulated that those expenditures "refer to costs incurred to advise Von-Lusk as to the appropriateness of product mix and pricing for the Property. Von-Lusk did not engage in active sales efforts during 1988, 1989 and 1990." As such, these expenses are not of the type contemplated by the above cited regulation. The label applied by petitioner is irrelevant.

We are aware that conditions imposed on Von-Lusk by local government authorities made the delay of this project unavoidable and the continued pursuit of the project so financially unattractive as to possibly preclude going forward with it. That does not change our view that steps were taken to begin the development of the Property. The result of those steps is that Von-Lusk came under the rule of section 263A.[49]

In the light of our conclusion above that the deductions in controversy must be capitalized, it is unnecessary to consider the Commissioner's alternative argument that the "other expenses," if not required to be capitalized by section 263A should be capitalized under section 263.

---

49. [2] We are aware of the opinion in *Hustead v. Comm'r*, T.C. Memo. 1994-374, which contains some dicta as to the scope of the term "produce" in respect of certain expenditures for activities that were less extensive than and were quite unlike the expenditures involved herein. The case also considered whether the property was held by the taxpayer primarily for sale to customers in the ordinary course of trade or business so as to bring sec. 263A(b)(2) into play in the circumstances there before the Court. The Court ultimately by-passed the applicability of sec. 263A, and held the expenditures nondeductible by reason of sec. 263.

Chapter 10

Principles of Section 1031
Gain and Loss Deferral

I. Commentary

The primary gain deferral provision for real-estate investors is section 1031. That provision requires property owners to defer gain or loss recognition on the exchange of certain like-kind properties.[1] In concept, section 1031 is fairly simple, but in application, it becomes somewhat complicated. Because section 1031 provides non-recognition of gain, it is part of many real estate transactions.

To qualify for section 1031 nonrecognition, a transaction must come within the section 1031 definition of exchange, the properties in the exchange must be business-use or investment property, and the property received in the exchange (the replacement property) must be like kind to the transferred property (the relinquished property).[2] The transaction must also avoid the pitfalls of the related-party-exchange rules.[3] Section 1031 is not an elective provision, so if a property owner exchanges loss property as part of a section 1031 exchange, the loss will be deferred.

A. Exchange Requirement

An exchange is "a reciprocal transfer of property, as distinguished from a transfer of property for money consideration only."[4] Legislative history and case law reveal that a transaction does not qualify for complete nonrecognition under section 1031 if the party attempting the exchange actually or constructively receives money or other non-like-kind property (i.e., boot).[5] Thus, if a transaction is not a direct exchange, the attorney must help the property owner structure the transaction to avoid the actual or constructive receipt of money or non-like-kind property.[6] Because courts

---

1. *See* Redwing Carriers, Inc. v. Tomlinson, 399 F.2d 652 (5th Cir. 1968).
2. *See* I.R.C. § 1031(a)(1).
3. *See* I.R.C. § 1031(f).
4. *See* Treas. Reg. § 1.1002-1(d).
5. *See* Carlton v. United States, 385 F.2d 238 (5th Cir. 1967); Halpern v. United States, 286 F. Supp. 255 (N.D. Ga. 1968).
6. *See infra* Chapters 11–13, 15–17.

should strictly construe the aspects of section 1031,[7] attorneys must carefully follow structures that courts and the IRS have approved.

B. Holding and Use Requirement

Section 1031 also requires the person doing the exchange to hold the relinquished property for productive use in a trade or business or for investment and that the same person acquire the replacement property to hold for productive use in a trade or business or for investment.[8] Thus, exchanges of personal-use property and inventory will not qualify for section 1031 nonrecognition. In fact, section 1031 specifically excludes "stock in trade or other property held primarily for sale" from nonrecognition treatment.[9] Notice that the exclusion in section 1031 differs from the definition of dealer property.[10] Consequently, a property could be a capital asset and still not qualify for section 1031 nonrecognition.[11]

Another aspect of the holding and use requirement is that the tax person that disposes of the relinquished property must acquire the replacement property. Thus, if a tax partnership disposes of relinquished property, the same tax partnership must acquire the replacement property. Satisfying this aspect of the holding and use requirement can be difficult if some form of ownership transaction occurs while the exchange is pending. For example, an individual may dispose of relinquished property and wish to include another investor in the acquisition of a larger replacement property. If the individual and other investor form a partnership to acquire the replacement property, the transaction will fail to satisfy the holding and use requirements because one tax person (the individual) transferred property and another tax person (the new partnership) acquired property. Advisors must carefully monitor changes of ownership that occur in proximity to an exchange to ensure that such proximate transactions do not disqualify the intended exchange from section 1031 nonrecognition.[12]

C. Like-Kind Property Requirement

For a transaction to qualify for section 1031 nonrecognition, the exchange properties must be like kind. The like-kind property requirement has reference to the nature and character of the property, not its grade or quality.[13] Thus, city real estate can be like kind a ranch or farm, improved real property can be like kind to unim-

---

7. *See* Treas. Reg. § 1.1002-1(b).

8. *See* I.R.C. § 1031(a)(1).

9. *See* I.R.C. § 1031(a)(2)(A).

10. *See* I.R.C. § 1221(a)(1); Land Dynamics v. Commissioner, 37 T.C.M. (CCH) 1119 (1978).

11. *See* Black v. Commissioner, 35 T.C. 90 (1960).

12. *See infra* Chapter 17.

13. *See* Treas. Reg. § 1.1031(a)-1(b).

proved real property, and a leasehold with 30 years or more to run can be like kind to other real property.[14]

D. Computing Gain and Loss Deferral

Section 1031 is a gain-deferral provision, meaning that the basis an exchanger had in relinquished property will determine the basis the exchanger takes in the replacement property. If the exchanger later transfers the replacement property in a taxable transaction, the exchanger will recognize the deferred gain or loss.[15] If the exchanger receives money or non-like-kind property as part of the exchange, the exchanger will recognize gain (but not loss) on the exchange, and special rules apply to determine the basis the exchanger takes in the replacement property.[16] The tax rates that apply to the deferred gain or loss will depend in part on the holding period the exchanger takes in the replacement property.[17] A basic examples illustrates the fundamental concepts of gain deferral.

Janae owns Office for use in her business. She purchased Office several years ago and it now has an adjusted basis of $1,250,000 and is subject to no debt. Janae exchanges Office for Apartment, which Janae will hold for investment, worth $3,750,000 and $250,000 of cash. Janae realizes $2,750,000 of gain on this exchange ($4,000,000 amount realized – $1,250,000 adjusted basis).[18] Under section 1031(b), Janae must recognize the realized gain to the extent of the $250,000 of non-like-kind property (i.e., boot) she receives. Consequently, Janae defers $2,500,000 of realized gain. The gain is deferred through the adjusted basis that Janae takes in Apartment. Under section 1031(d), Janae takes a basis in Apartment equal to the $1,250,000 adjusted basis she had in Office, decreased by the $250,000 of boot she received, and increased by the $250,000 of gain she recognized. Under section 1223(1), her holding period in Apartment will include the holding period she had in Office. Because Janae held Office for use in her business,

---

14. *See* Treas. Reg. § 1.1031(a)-1(c). Although the definition of like-kind real property is fairly broad, advisors must be careful about making blanket statements regarding the definition because there are numerous exceptions to the general rule that all real property is like kind. *See, e.g.,* Wiechens v. U.S., 228 F. Supp. 2d 1080 (D. Ariz. 2002); Kelly E. Alton & Louis S. Weller, *Does State Law Really Determine Whether Property Is Real Estate for Section 1031 Purposes?*, 32 Real Est. Tax'n 30 (4th Quarter 2004) (positing the question of whether property that crosses state lines and classified differently in two states is like kind); Bradley T. Borden, *The Whole Truth About Using Partial Real Estate Transactions in Section 1031 Exchanges*, 31 Real Est. Tax'n 19 (4th Quarter 2003) (analyzing cases and rulings that consider whether partial interests in real property are like kind to other real property).

15. One way to check the accuracy of the amount of basis assigned to the replacement property is to imagine a hypothetical sale of the replacement property for its fair market value immediately following the exchange. If the gain or loss recognized on that hypothetical sale triggers recognition of all of the deferred gain or loss, the amount assigned to the basis of the replacement property should be correct.

16. *See* I.R.C. § 1031(b), (d); Treas. Reg. §§ 1.1031(b)-1, 1.1031(d)-1.

17. *See* I.R.C. § 1223(1).

18. *See* I.R.C. § 1001(a); *supra* Chapter 2.

the gain she recognizes will be section 1231 gain. If that gain is long-term capital gain, the rules in section 1(h) will determine the rates that apply to the gain.[19]

Computation of Section 1031(b) Gain and Basis in Replacement Property

Amount Realized		
FMV of Apartment	$3,750,000	
Cash	$250,000	
Total Amount Realized		$4,000,000
Adjusted Basis		($1,250,000)
Gain Realized		$2,750,000
Gain Recognized		$250,000
Basis in Apartment		
Adjusted Basis of Office		$1,2500,000
Boot Received		($250,000)
Gain Recognized		$250,000
Basis		$1,250,000

Special rules apply to exchanges of encumbered property.[20] Tax attorneys must thoroughly understand the rules governing exchanges of encumbered property and be prepared to explain the rules to clients because property owners often view the economics of the transaction differently from the tax rules. Tax attorneys often must explain to clients how transactions must be structured to avoid gain recognition on the exchange of encumbered property. As a general matter, section 1031 treats debt relief as boot received,[21] but cash paid and liability assumed can offset liability relief.[22] An example helps illustrate the application of the debt-boot rules, and the examples in the regulations provide additional insight into various scenarios.[23] Because the rules can be counterintuitive, a person should always track through the regulations when considering the tax consequences of exchanges of encumbered property.

Rosa owns raw land for investment. It is worth $2,000,000, has $450,000 adjusted basis, and is subject to a $575,000 liability. If Rosa transfers the raw land for $1,425,000 of like-kind property, section 1031(d) will treat her as receiving $575,000 of boot. She can avoid that result by acquiring like-kind property worth $2,000,000, which will require her to invest an additional $575,000 of cash in the replacement property or to assume $575,000 liability as part of the acquisition of the replacement property.[24]

---

19. *See supra* Chapter 2.
20. *See* I.R.C. § 1031(d); Treas. Reg. § 1.1031(d)-2.
21. *See* I.R.C. § 1031(d).
22. *See* Treas. Reg. § 1.1031(d)-2.
23. *See id.*
24. *See* Treas. Reg. § 1.1031(d)-2, Example (2).

Her basis in the replacement property will equal the $450,000 basis she had in the raw land, decreased by the $575,000 of money she is deemed to receive if she acquires replacement property worth $1,425,000, and increased by the amount of gain she recognizes. If she acquires replacement property worth $2,000,000, her basis in the replacement property will be the $450,000 adjusted basis she had in the raw land, increased by the amount of cash she pays and liability she assumes, and decreased by the liability from which she is relieved.[25]

When a person transfers property subject to a liability, the purchaser could take the property subject to the liability. In such situations, the transferor would receive cash proceeds equal to the difference between the property's value and the amount of the outstanding liability. Purchasers do not, however typically take property subject to liability. Instead, at closing, a portion of the purchaser's proceeds go to pay down the transferor's liability, and the transferor will receive the net proceeds. When a person transfers property subject to a liability as part of a section 1031 exchange, the law generally treats the payment of the liability at closing the same way it treats liability assumed by the purchaser.[26] Consequently, when discussing section 1031 exchanges, people often simply say that a person is transferring property subject to a liability in either type of situation.

II. Primary Legal Authority

Redwing Carriers, Inc. v. Tomlinson

United States Court of Appeals, Fifth Circuit
399 F.2d 652 (1968)

FACTS

The following facts were substantially stipulated, and the district court's findings on the few disputed fact questions were not clearly erroneous. Redwing is a Florida corporation engaged in the business of hauling bulk commodities as a common carrier, subject to regulation by the Interstate Commerce Commission. Trucksales, Inc., a Florida corporation engaged in the business of selling trucks, parts and equipment, is a wholly-owned subsidiary of Redwing. During the years in question Trucksales was a franchised dealer for G.M.C. trucks. Charles E. Mendez, as president and chairman of the board of both Redwing and Trucksales, was the moving force behind the transactions in question.

During 1958 Trucksales purchased twenty-eight new G.M.C. diesel tractor trucks from G.M.C. for cash. At or about the same time Redwing transferred title to twenty-seven used trucks to G.M.C. for cash. In 1959 and 1961 essentially identical transactions involving thirty-six and fourteen trucks, respectively, were executed. Also during 1959 transactions in like form were executed with White Motor Company.

---

25. *See* Treas. Reg. § 1.1031(d)-2.
26. *See, e.g.,* Barker v. Comm'r, 74 T.C. 555 (1980).

Because it is an extremely profitable trucking concern, Redwing is considered a prestige account by both G.M.C. and White Motor Company. Thus Mendez, who handled all negotiations in these transactions, was in a strong bargaining position and was able to insist upon casting these purchases of new equipment and trade-ins in the form of separate purchases of the new and sales of the old.

Mendez did not specify which corporation he was representing at any time to either White or G.M.C., and it made no difference to the manufacturers whether they were dealing with Redwing or with Trucksales. Both Redwing and Trucksales used the same Tampa address on the checks used in these transactions, even though Trucksales is located in Fort Lauderdale and even though it used a Fort Lauderdale bank account for all of its other business activities. Most of the trucks involved were delivered by White and G.M.C. directly to Redwing in Tampa, despite the fact that they were ostensibly being sold to Trucksales in Fort Lauderdale for resale to Redwing.

In addition to the above indicia of transactional unity, the district court found a definite contractual interdependency between the sale of new trucks and the trade-in of old trucks. In its findings of fact the court noted: "There would have been no purchase by plaintiffs of new trucks or tractors without concurrent and binding agreements to purchase plaintiff's used equipment."[27]

The district court further found that G.M.C. viewed these transactions as trade-ins which were occasioned by the purchase of new equipment and that the form of selling the old and purchasing the new was arranged solely on Mendez' insistence. A G.M.C. executive testified that the price which G.M.C. paid for the used trucks was in excess of their fair market value and that G.M.C. would be able to calculate a profit only by viewing the purchases of used trucks and sales of new trucks as one transaction.[28]

It is apparent that Mendez sculptured these transactions so as to achieve the best possible tax results for Redwing. Instead of obtaining customary discounts from the retail price of the new trucks, Mendez would insist that the manufacturers add the discount amount to the price of the used trucks being repurchased. The gain of the trade-in price over the depreciated basis of the used trucks would be recognized at capital gains rates, and the basis of the new trucks for depreciation purposes would be inflated. As a result, Redwing's depreciation deductions from ordinary income would also be inflated, resulting in considerable tax savings.[29]

---

27. [4] This finding of fact was in fact substantiated by the testimony of Charles E. Mendez: "Q. Mr. Mendez, when you negotiated these ideals with White and General Motors Corporation for the purchase of new equipment, did you insist that they agree to take your old equipment as a part of each of these deals? A. Well, I was buying a certain number of trucks, and I was selling a certain number of trucks. Q. But as a part of the agreement to buy the new trucks, did you insist that they take these used trucks? A. Well, it was part of the deal. Sure. Q. It was part of the deal? A. Yes, sir."

28. [5] We take judicial notice of the fact that General Motors Corporation is not a non-profit corporation and that it does not consciously sell and buy trucks except for the purpose of making a profit.

29. [6] In 1962 the Internal Revenue Code was amended by the addition of § 1245, the depreciation recapture provision, to make it no longer desirable to handle transactions in this manner. In essence, § 1245 withdraws capital gains treatment from gains on the disposition of depreciable personal property

As is obvious from the above facts, these Mendez-dominated transactions were severable in form only. On substance, the sale was in bondage to the purchase and the purchase indissolubly dependent upon the sale. If Redwing had not carried out the agreement to buy the new trucks, the auto makers would have had no juristic obligation to purchase the used trucks. The buying and selling were synchronous parts meshed into the same transaction and not independent transactions.

ANALYSIS

Section 1031 requires the non-recognition of gain or loss in transactions when in theory the taxpayer may have realized gain or loss, but in substance his economic interest in the property has remained virtually unchanged by the transaction. *Century Electric Co. v. Comm'r*, 192 F.2d 155, 159 (8th Cir. 1951), *cert. den.*, 342 U.S. 954 (1952). Compare *Trenton Cotton Oil Co. v. Comm'r*, 147 F.2d 33, 36 (6th Cir. 1945).[30] With its paper armor crumpled, Redwing's transactions are brought directly within the ambit of § 1031, and, more specifically, within that of Treas. Reg. § 1.1031(a)-1(c):

> (c) No gain or loss is recognized if (1) a taxpayer exchanges property held for productive use in his trade or business, together with cash for other property of like kind for the same use such as a truck for a new truck or a passenger automobile for a new passenger automobile to be used for a like purpose; ...

Because of the expertise of Internal Revenue Service in interpreting the Internal Revenue Code which it is charged with administering, Treasury regulations come to us with great persuasive force. *South Texas Land Co. v. Comm'r*, 333 U.S. 496, 501 (1947); *U.S. v. D.I. Operating Co.*, 362 F.2d 305, 308 (9th Cir. 1966), *cert. den.*, 385 U.S. 1024 (1967); *cf. Estate of Willett v. Comm'r*, 365 F.2d 760 (5th Cir. 1966); *Whirlwind Mfg. Co. v. U.S.*, 344 F.2d 153 (5th Cir. 1965). When, as here, the regulation has long continued without substantial change, applying to unamended or substantially reenacted states, the regulation is deemed to have the effect of law. *U.S. v. Correll*, 389 U.S. 299 (1967); *Fribourg Nav. Co. v. Comm'r*, 383 U.S. 272, 283 (1966). In *Vitter v. U.S.*, 279 F.2d 445 (5th Cir. 1960), cert. den., 364 U.S. 928 (1960), Judge Brown, speaking for our Court, articulated this rule of construction as follows:

> When a Treasury Regulation interprets a section of the Code and the Regulation remains in effect and unchanged for a long period of time, re-enactment of the statute without change is presumed to show congressional approval of the Regulation which thereby acquires the force and effect of law ... (numerous cases cited). 279 F.2d at 450 (at fn. 9).

---

and certain other tangible property (exclusive of buildings and their structural components) to the extent that depreciation had been deducted for such property by the seller in previous years. It permits only the excess of the sales price over the original cost to be treated as a capital gain and requires that the remainder be treated as ordinary income. *See* Mertens, Federal Income Taxation, Code Commentary § 1245.

30. [7] As for Redwing's contention that the provisions of § 1031 are taxpayer elective, *see* U.S. v. Vardine, 305 F.2d 60,66 (2d Cir. 1962), where this contention was definitively answered as follows: "(Section) 1031 and its predecessor are mandatory, and not optional; a taxpayer cannot elect not to use them."

The relevant part of Treas. Reg. § 1.1031(a)-1(c), as well as Section 1031(a) of the Internal Revenue Code, is identical to its predecessor under the 1939 Code.[31] Despite extensive changes in the Internal Revenue Code in 1954, no change was made in what is now § 1031(a). Further amendments were made to other parts of § 1031 in 1958 and 1959, but § 1031(a) was left untouched. It is reasonable to assume, therefore, that Congress knew and approved of the application of § 1031(a) to trade-ins of trucks.

The Treasury's interpretation of § 1031(a) was also manifested in Revenue Ruling 61-119, 1961-1 Cum.Bull. 395. This Ruling bears directly on the exact question at bar:

> Where a taxpayer sells old equipment used in his trade or business to a dealer and purchases new equipment of like kind from the dealer under circumstances which indicate that the sale and the purchase are reciprocal and mutually dependent transactions, the sale and purchase is an exchange of property within the meaning of section 1031 of the Internal Revenue Code of 1954, even though the sale and purchase are accomplished by separately executed contracts and are treated as unrelated transactions by the taxpayer and the dealer for record keeping purposes.

The district court in its conclusions of law relied heavily on that Ruling, and we agree. Although the Ruling does not have the force and effect of law, we find it to be a persuasive interpretation of the Code and Regulations. See 3 Mertens, Federal Income Taxation §§ 20.31 and 20.165 (at p. 724).

Despite Redwing's arguments to the contrary, Revenue Ruling 61-119 is founded upon well established principles of tax law. Both the Supreme Court and our Court have on numerous occasions stated that when the realities of a transaction differ from its paper shell, the Internal Revenue Service and the courts may open the shell and look inside to determine the substance of the transaction. *Comm'r v. Court Holding Co.*, 324 U.S. 331, 334 (1944); *Higgins v. Smith*, 308 U.S. 473, 477 (1939); *Helvering v. F. & R Lazarus Co.*, 308 U.S. 252, 256 (1939); *Gregory v. Helvering*, 293 U.S. 465 (1934); *U.S. v. Henderson*, 375 F.2d 36, 40 (5th Cir. 1967), cert. den., 389 U.S. 953 (1967); *Kinney v. U.S.*, 358 F.2d 738, 739 (5th Cir. 1966); *Willow Terrace Development Co. v. Comm'r*, 345 F.2d 933, 936 (5th Cir. 1965), cert. den., 382 U.S. 938 (1965); *Cobb v. Callan Court Co.*, 274 F.2d 532, 539 (5th Cir. 1960). *See also Coastal Terminals, Inc. v. U.S.*, 207 F. Supp. 560, 562 (D.C.S.C. 1962), aff'd 320 F.2d 333 (4th Cir. 1963), wherein this rule was applied in a Section 1031 case.

In *Blackstone Realty Co. v. Comm'r*, 398 F.2d 991, 996, (5th Cir. 1968), we said:

> Our income tax law is premised on fact and not fiction. A transaction is analyzed for its pragmatic realities. Although a taxpayer is free to negotiate a contract with an intent to avoid or minimize taxes, such benefit cannot be awarded to Blackstone Realty in the absence of negotiations for prices and

---

31. [8] The predecessor of § 1031 in 1939 Code was § 112(b)(1). The regulation under that section is found in Regs. 19.112(b) (1)-1 (Aug. 23, 1939) and later in Regs. 118 § 39.112(b)(1)-1(b) (1953).

values. The intention to avoid or minimize taxes, beneficent as it is, cannot be employed where the end product is a mere subterfuge. *Martin v. Comm'r*, 294 F.2d 282 (6th Cir. 1967); *MacRae v. Comm'r*, 294 F.2d 56 (9th Cir. 1961), *cert. den.*, 368 U.S. 955 (1962); *Trousdale v. Comm'r*, 219 F.2d 563 (9th Cir. 1955). *Cf. Reef Corporation v. Comm'r*, 368 F.2d 125 (5th Cir. 1966), cert. den., 386 U.S. 1018 (1967); *General Guaranty Mortgage Co., Inc. v. Tomlinson*, 335 F.2d 518 (5th Cir. 1964).

See also Comm'r v. Tower, 327 U.S. 280, 288–289 (1945); *Particelli v. Comm'r*, 212 F.2d 498, 500 (9th Cir. 1954); *Gyro Engineering Corp. v. U.S.*, 276 F. Supp. 454, 465 (C.D. Calif. 1967).

Equally well established is the corollary that an integrated transaction may not be separated into its components for the purposes of taxation by either the Internal Revenue Service or the taxpayer. *Roebling Securities Corp. v. U.S.*, 176 F. Supp. 844, 847 (D.C.N.J. 1959). In *Kanawha Gas & Utilities Co. v. Comm'r*, 214 F.2d 685, 691 (5th Cir. 1954), our Court through Judge Rives said:

In determining the incidence of taxation, we must look through form and search out the substance of a transaction.... (cases cited) This basic concept of tax law is particularly pertinent to cases involving a series of transactions designed and executed as parts of a unitary plan to achieve an intended result. Such plans will be viewed as a whole regardless of whether the effect of so doing is imposition of or relief from taxation. The series of closely related steps in such a plan are merely the means by which to carry out the plan and will not be separated.

See also Jacobs v. Comm'r, 224 F.2d 412 (9th Cir. 1955); *Century Electric Co. v. Comm'r*, 192 F.2d 155 (8th Cir. 1951), *cert. den.*, 342 U.S. 954 (1952); *Mather v. Comm'r*, 149 F.2d 393 (6th Cir. 1945); *Comm'r v. Ashland Oil & Refining*, 99 F.2d 588, 591 (6th Cir. 1938), cert. den., 306 U.S. 661 (1939); *Kinney v. U.S.*, 228 F. Supp. 656, 661 (W.D. La. 1964), aff'd 358 F.2d 738 (5th Cir. 1966).

The above cases show quite clearly that a tax-free exchange cannot be transformed into two sales by the arbitrary separation of time and exchange of cash. *See Comm'r v. North Shore Bus Co.*, 143 F.2d 114 (2d Cir. 1944), which held that a trade-in of used busses in connection with a purchase of new ones was an exchange governed by the predecessor of Section 1031 despite the taxpayer's receipt of cash from the seller in order to pay off the mortgage on the used busses. *See also National Outdoor Advertising Bureau v. Helvering*, 89 F.2d 878, 890 (2d Cir. 1937), reversing on other grounds, 32 B.T.A. 1025 (1935); *Graves, Cox and Co.*, 27 B.T.A. 546 (1933); *Joseph J. Vidmar*, 11 T.C.M. (CCH) 854 (1952).

The appellant attempts to bolster its defenses, however, with a decision from our Court, *Carlton v. U.S.*, 385 F.2d 238 (5th Cir. 1967). In that case the taxpayer had sold ranch property to a purchasing corporation for cash. As part of this sale, the purchaser had assigned to the taxpayer contracts to purchase two similar tracts of land, which purchases the taxpayer had immediately consummated. Although it was stipulated that both the taxpayer and the purchaser had intended to effect an exchange—indeed that they had performed the three-way transaction merely to avoid unnecessary duplication in title transfer—we refused to accept the taxpayer's classification of the overall transaction as a tax-free exchange under Section 1031.

The appellant would have us follow Carlton here as if that case had ignored transactional substance and instead had viewed the whole only as an aggregate of separate, unrelated transfers. On the contrary, in that case we gave weight to the various individual transfers only because they were separate and unrelated. In Carlton we were reviewing a three-way transaction in which the taxpayer had received, in return for property, cash which was not restricted in use to the purchase of like property. The most that could be said for the transactional relationship in Carlton was that the sale for cash between the taxpayer and a purchaser had been complementary with the later purchase of like property between the taxpayer and a seller. In the case at bar, however, there were only two parties to each exchange of trucks (ignoring intracorporate fictional distinctions), and the alleged "sale" and "trade-in sales," instead of being separate, were related by contractual interdependency.

In Carlton both the transfers of land and the interparty obligations were severable and, in fact, severed. Here we find, as did the district court, the same transactional twining from beginning to end. Carlton, then, is clearly distinguishable and certainly does not stand as an obstacle to the pertinent tax considerations which we have discussed supra.[32]

OPINION

Taxation is transactional and not uniform. Our tax laws are not so supple that scraps of paper, regardless of their calligraphy, can transmute trade-ins into sales. Although Redwing's transfers may have been paper sales, they were actual exchanges. A taxpayer may engineer his transactions to minimize taxes, but he cannot make a transaction appear to be what it is not. Documents record transactions, but they do not always become the sole criteria for transactional analysis.

---

32. [9] *Carlton* is distinguishable on one ground other than those which have been previously discussed. *Carlton* involved the taxpayer's, not the Commissioner's, contention that documentary form was irrelevant in light of the "substance" of the transaction. In such circumstances the Commissioner's evidentiary problems became paramount because of the lack of insider information to prove or disprove true "substance." Moreover, since "substance" considerations can often be viewed effectively only from hindsight, the neglect of "form" could engender post-transactional tax planning on the part of many taxpayers. On the other hand, when as here the taxpayer insists that we abide by his forms and the Commissioner attempts to convince us otherwise, there is little danger, should we reject form, of our having been misled by insider reconstruction of a transaction after its effects have been determined. We, therefore, read *Carlton* as teaching that although a taxpayer's own documents are not conclusive, they normally override any conflicting subjective considerations advanced by that taxpayer. Especially in light of the above distinction, we see no need in comparing Carlton with preceding cases through obiter dicta for a determination of whether the vital missing ingredient there was (1) the lack per se of a two-party exchange of ownership rights in like property or merely (2) the failure of the cash transfer to be contractually intertwined to the immediate purchase of like property.

Carlton v. United States

United States Court of Appeals, Fifth Circuit

385 F.2d 238 (1967)

FACTS

This is an appeal from a judgment of the United States District Court for the Southern District of Florida denying the claim of the appellants for a refund of income taxes and interest paid after a deficiency was assessed by the Internal Revenue Service for the tax year 1959. In their joint return for 1959, the appellants did not recognize the gain realized on the transfer of several parcels of real property but treated the transfers as an exchange of property under 1031 of the I.R.C. of 1954. The I.R.S. asserted that the transfers constituted a sale and not an exchange and assessed a deficiency of $34,337.63 together with interest. The appellants paid the deficiency assessed, and filed a timely claim for refund. The claim was disallowed by the District Director of Internal Revenue and this suit followed. The district court concluded that the transfers constituted a sale and repurchase and rendered judgment for the Government. We affirm.

The facts of the case are fully stipulated. During the year 1959 and for several years prior thereto the appellants had been engaged in the ranching business. In connection with that business they owned a tract of land in Saint Lucie County, Florida, (ranch property) having a basis of $8,918.91. On October 18, 1958, they executed a contract with General Development Corporation (General) which gave General an option to acquire the ranch property for $250.00 an acre. General paid the appellants $50,000 deposit which was to be credited to the total purchase price should General exercise its option. The contract also provided that the appellant could require General, by notifying it in writing, to acquire such other land as designated by the appellants for the purpose of exchange in lieu of a cash payment or mortgage. General's obligation to supply funds for any down payment which might be needed to bind any contracts to purchase other land for exchange was not to exceed the $50,000 advanced at the time the option was executed. In the event such an exchange could not be effected, General was to pay for the ranch property by cash and a mortgage securing the balance of the purchase price. From the outset of negotiations with General, the appellants desired to continue ranching operations and intended to exchange the ranch property for other property suitable for ranching. They also desired an exchange as opposed to a sale in order to obtain the tax benefits incident to an exchange under § 1031. At all times General desired simply to purchase the ranch property.

Following the execution of the option contract with General, Thad Carlton (Carlton) found two suitable parcels of land, one in Gladen County, Florida (Lyons), and one in Hendry County, Florida (Fernandez). He conducted all the negotiations for the acquisition of these lands and paid the deposit for each by a cashier's check issued by his bank. The total deposit on both pieces of property did not exceed the fifty thousand dollars paid by General. When the negotiations to acquire the Lyons and Fernandez properties were complete, Carlton notified General in writing that he would require it to purchase these lands for the purpose of exchanging them for his ranch property, and the actual agreements of sale were executed by General.[33] On May 11, 1959 General exercised its option to acquire the ranch property and arrangements were made to close the entire transaction around August 1, 1959. The closing of the several transactions actually occurred on August 3rd and 4th and in closing the appellants deviated from the original plan which resulted in the tax problem here in issue.

In order to avoid unnecessary duplication in title transfer, a procedure was adopted whereby title to the Lyons and Fernandez properties would be conveyed directly to the appellants instead of to General and then to the appellants. To accomplish this result, General, on August 3rd, assigned to the appellants its contracts to purchase the two pieces of property and paid the appellants, by check, the total amount it would have been required to pay if it had actually first purchased the Lyons and Fernandez property in its own name and then conveyed the land to the appellants. Later that same day Carlton took the assignment of the contracts to purchase and purchased the Lyons property, using his personal check to close the sale. On August 4 he purchased the Fernandez property in a similar manner. At the time Carlton issued these checks, the balance in his checking account was too small to cover them, but he deposited the check received from General when the transaction with it was closed to meet these outstanding checks. This check was the balance of the cash purchase price and was in addition to the $50,000.00 paid when the option was executed.

The district court held that on the basis of these facts the transfers constituted a sale and repurchase. The court concluded that because General never acquired the legal title to the Lyons and Fernandez property, it could not have exchanged those properties for the ranch property. Rather, the court found that the appellants sold the ranch property to General and applied the cash thereby acquired to the purchase of the Lyons and Fernandez properties. The court also noted that Carlton was the active party in arranging the acquisition of the Lyons and Fernandez tracts and that he was personally liable on the notes and mortgages involved in such acquisitions. The appellants contend on this appeal that the district court erred in focusing on one aspect of a continuing transaction. They assert that the procedure adopted must be viewed as a single unitary transaction through which they intended to exchange properties, and which resulted in their acquiring property suitable for ranching and relinquishing their rights to like property. They insist that intent is the essential element which distinguishes a sale from an exchange. Since the Government has stipulated that an exchange was intended, and since the net result of the transaction was an exchange of ranching properties, they conclude, the transfers must be considered an exchange.

---

33. [2] At the insistence of the vendor, Carlton endorsed the note involved in the acquisition of the Lyons property. The exercise of this option by the appellants obligated General to effect an exchange and thereafter General could no longer purchase the ranch property but was obligated to make an exchange.

Section 1031 of the I.R.C. of 1954, 26 U.S.C. § 1031 (1964) provides, in pertinent part, that the gain realized on the exchange of property of like kind held for productive use or investment shall not be recognized except to the extent that "boot" or cash is actually received. There is little doubt that the ranch property and the Lyons and Fernandez properties are of like kind, and that the properties were held by the appellants for productive use. The only question presented here is whether the transfer of the properties constituted a sale or an exchange.

Both parties agree that had the appellants followed the original plan, whereby General would have acquired the legal title to the Lyons and Fernandez properties and then transferred the title to such properties to the appellants for their ranch property, the appellants would have been entitled to postpone the recognition of the gain pursuant to § 1031. However, instead of receiving the title to the Lyons and Fernandez properties from General for their ranch property, the appellants received cash and an assignment of General's contract rights to those properties. Thus, the ultimate question becomes whether the receipt of cash by the appellants upon transferring their ranch property to General transformed the intended exchange into a sale. The Government asserts that it does, and under the facts and in the circumstances of this case, we agree.

ANALYSIS

Section 1031 was designed to postpone the recognition of gain or loss where property used in a business is exchanged for other property in the course of the continuing operation of a business. In those circumstances, the taxpayer has not received any gain or suffered any loss in a general and economic sense. Nor has the exchange of property resulted in the termination of one venture and assumption of another. The business venture operated before the exchange continues after the exchange without any real economic change or alteration, and without realization of any cash or readily liquefiable asset. *Jordan Marsh Co. v. Comm'r*, 269 F.2d 453 (2d Cir. 1959); *cf. Portland Oil Co. v. Comm'r*, 109 F.2d 479 (1st Cir. 1940) cert. den., 310 U.S. 650. The statute specifically limits the nonrecognition of gain or loss to exchanges of property, and it is well settled that a sale and repurchase do not qualify for nonrecognition treatment under the section. *Coleman v. Comm'r*, 180 F.2d 758 (8th Cir. 1950); *Rogers v. Comm'r*, 44 T.C. 126 (1965) aff'd 377 F.2d 534 (9th Cir. 1965); *Cowden v. Comm'r*, 65,278 P-H Memo TC (1965); see generally 3 Mertens, Federal Income Taxation §§ 20.16–20.31 (1967). Thus, even though the appellants continued their ranching business after the transaction here in question, that does not control the tax consequences of the transfers. Rather, it is essential that the transfers constituted an exchange and not a sale and repurchase if the tax benefits of § 1031 are to be applicable.

The appellants contend that the entire transaction must be viewed as a whole in determining whether a sale or an exchange has occurred. They argue that the transfer of the ranch property to General for the cash and assignments was part of a single unitary plan designed and intended to effect an exchange of their ranch property for other property suitable for ranching. Thus, they conclude, the transfers of property should be construed to be an exchange.

While it is true that the incidence of taxation is to be determined by viewing the entire transaction as a whole, *Kanawaha Gas & Util. Co. v. Comm'r*, 214 F.2d 685 (5th Cir. 1954), that rule does not permit us to close our eyes to the realities of the transaction and merely look at the beginning and end of a transaction without observing the steps taken to reach that end. *Comm'r v. Court Holding Co.*, 324 U.S. 331 (1945). The requirement is that the transaction be viewed in its entirety in order to determine its reality and substance, for it is the substance of the transaction which decides the incidence of taxation. *Century Elec. Co. v. Comm'r*, 192 F.2d 155, 159 (8th Cir. 1951). In the instant case, while elaborate plans were laid to exchange property, the substance of the transaction was that the appellants received cash for the deed to their ranch property and not another parcel of land.[34] The very essence of an exchange is the transfer of property between owners, while the mark of a sale is the receipt of cash for the property. *See Mercantile Trust Co. v. Comm'r*, 32 B.T.A. 82 (1935); *Coastal Terminals, Inc. v. U.S.*, 320 F.2d 333 (4th Cir. 1963); *Alderson v. Comm'r*, 317 F.2d 790 (9th Cir. 1963); *Allegheny County Auto Mart, Inc. v. Comm'r*, 39 T.C. 615 (1953), aff'd 208 F.2d 693 (3rd Cir. 1953); *W. D. Haden Co. v. Comm'r*, 165 F.2d 588, 590 (5th Cir. 1948); *Trenton Cotton Oil Co. v. Comm'r*, 147 F.2d 33, 36 (6th Cir. 1945); *see generally* 3 Mertens, *supra* at § 20.28. Where, as here, there is an immediate repurchase of other property with the proceeds of the sale, that distinction between a

---

34. [4] While the characterization by a taxpayer of the nature of a transaction is not determinative, what the taxpayer said and did during the course of the transaction may shed some light on what was actually done. Although not of controlling importance, the following stipulated facts shed some light on what the taxpayer did in this case: "Simultaneously with the forwarding of the executed copies of the aforementioned contract to General on September 27, 1958, Plaintiffs entered into an agreement with two real estate brokers who were instrumental in negotiating the options. The agreement obligated Plaintiffs to pay stipulated commissions to said brokers in the event that the options were exercised and 'the transactions of sale and purchase ... closed.'" On January 4, 1959, Decedent physically inspected the Lyons property, and then advised the representatives of the Lyons Estate that he was working out a final schedule with General in order to determine the amount of time "I will need to close the purchase." Decedent (Carlton) reiterated an earlier statement that "it was his intention to close the purchase of the Lyons property, ... irrespective of whether or not General Development Corporation elects to exercise its option to purchase my property. I cannot well afford to forfeit the $32,500.00 payment, if it can possibly be avoided." On May 14, 1959, after receipt of the aforementioned election by General, Decedent requested the Estate to update the abstracts on its property and have them sent to him. On the same date, he requested permission from the Estate to clean up the premises of the Lyons property and to begin construction of two houses and a barn on them on or about June 1, 1959, in order to have the construction completed at the time of closing, when he desired to move his ranching operation there. Decedent promised to prohibit any liens from attaching to the premises, and stated that the sale of his property to General "will be closed at the same time I close my purchase with you." On June 2, 1959, the following endorsement was added to this contract over the signature of Decedent, as required by Mr. and Mrs. Fernandez: "I accept and agree to the provisions of the foregoing, and I further agree with the sellers, that when the property is conveyed to me, I will assume the mortgage and be personally responsible for its payment. I further agree that sellers shall have 90 days from date of closing to remove their cattle from the property." The closing of the transaction involving the sale from Plaintiffs to General was held in Miami as scheduled on August 3, 1959. The amount shown on the closing statement as "cash to close" was paid by General by means of a cashier's check in the amount of $199,797.78 payable to Plaintiffs. On the same date, General issued its ten-year, interest-bearing, installment promissory note, in the amount of $952,143.00 to Plaintiffs.

sale and exchange is crucial. Further, General was never in a position to exchange properties with the appellants because it never acquired the legal title to either the Lyons or the Fernandez property. Indeed, General was not personally obligated on either the notes or mortgages involved in these transaction. Thus it never had any property of like kind to exchange. Finally, it cannot be said that General paid for the Lyons and Fernandez properties and merely had the properties deeded directly to the appellants.[35] The money received from General by the appellants for the ranch property was not earmarked by General to be used in purchasing the Lyons or Fernandez properties. It was unrestricted and could be used by the appellants as they pleased. The fact that they did use it to pay for the Lyons and Fernandez properties does not alter the fact that their use of the money was unfettered and unrestrained. It is an inescapable fact that the money received by appellants from General was money paid to them for a conveyance of their land. As a result, the separate transaction between General and the appellants must be construed to be a sale, and the transactions between the appellants and Lyons and Fernandez as a purchase of other property. *Trenton Cotton Oil Co. v. Comm'r*, supra; *Spalding v. Comm'r*, 7 B.T.A. 588 (1927); *Rogers v. Comm'r, supra*; 3 Mertens, *supra* § 20.28 at pp. 94–5.

The appellants' intention and desire to execute an exchange does not alter the reality and substance of the situation. It is well established that the intention of a taxpayer to avail himself of the advantages of a particular provision of the tax laws does not determine the tax consequences of his action, *Comm'r. v. Duberstein*, 363 U.S. 278 (1960), but what was actually done is determinative of the tax treatment. *Weiss v. Stearn*, 265 U.S. 242 (1924). Thus, the intention of the appellants to effect an exchange does not convert the transfer of property for cash into an exchange. The cases on which the appellants rely in support of their assertion that intent determines whether a transfer is a sale or exchange are factually distinguishable and inapposite.[36] They deal with the question of whether certain transfers between corporations and their stockholders are sales, exchanges for corporate stock, or capital investments. The sections under which they were decided and the problems they present are far different from the subject matter with which § 1031 is concerned.

OPINION

Therefore, we are compelled to conclude that the transfer of the ranch property to General constituted a sale, and rendered the nonrecognition of gain provisions of § 1031 inapplicable. Considering how close the appellants came to satisfying the requirements of that section and the stipulation that an exchange was intended, this result is obviously harsh. But there is no equity in tax law. *Henderson Clay Products v. U.S.*, 324 F.2d 7, 12 (5th Cir. 1962), and such must the result be if the limitation in § 1031 to exchanges is to have any meaning.

---

35. [5] For a similar situation in which such a transfer was held to be an exchange, *see* W. D. Haden Co. v. Comm'r, *supra*.

36. [6] The appellants cite *Sarkes Tarzian, Inc. v. U.S.*, 240 F.2d 467 (7th Cir. 1957); *Rowan v. U.S.*, 219 F.2d 51 (5th Cir. 1955); *Kimbell-Diamond Milling Co. v. Comm'r.*, 187 F.2d 718 (5th Cir. 1951).

Wiechens v. United States

United States District Court, District of Arizona

228 F. Supp. 2d 1080 (2002)

FACTS

Plaintiff Donald Wiechens, a single man, and Plaintiffs Gary and Deborah Wiechens, husband and wife ("Plaintiffs"), are partners in the Wiechens Properties Limited Partnership, an Arizona limited partnership (the "Partnership"). (Compl. at ¶ 1.) The Partnership owns land within the boundaries of the Harquahala Valley Irrigation District ("HVID"). (Compl. at ¶ 9.) The HVID is an Arizona municipal corporation that was formed in 1964 for the purpose of establishing a local water distribution system in and about Harquahala Valley, Arizona. (Def.'s Mem. in Supp. of Mot. for Summ. J. at p.2.).

Although Plaintiffs and Defendant United States of America ("Defendant") disagree about the origin and duration, it is undisputed that the Partnership obtained the right to receive Colorado river water on an annual basis to irrigate its land that was located within the boundaries of the HVID ("water rights"). (Def.'s Resp. to Pls.' Mot. for Summ. J. at pp.4–5.) In December 1992, the HVID and the United States Department of Interior ("Department of Interior") entered into a contract whereby the HVID landowners were allowed to sell their water rights back to the government without an accompanying sale of the land. (Pls.' Mot. for Partial Summ. J. at pp.1–2.).

The Partnership opted to retain its land within the boundaries of the HVID, but to exchange its water rights for an interest in farm land. (*Id.* at p.2.) The Partnership initially assigned its water rights to Yuma Title & Trust Company ("Yuma Title"). (Def.'s Mem. in Supp. of Mot. for Summ. J. at p.3.) Yuma Title, in turn, relinquished the Partnership's water rights to the HVID, which sold all the water rights it received from the HVID landowners to the Department of Interior. (Pls.' Mot. for Partial Summ. J. at p.2.) After paying expenses, HVID agreed to pay the district landowners approximately $24,000,000, prorated to the acreage owned by each, for their water rights. (*Id.* at p.2.).

The HVID paid Yuma Title $495,924.99 for the Partnership's relinquished water rights. (Def.'s Statement of Facts in Support of Motion for Summary Judgment ("Def.'s SOF") at ¶¶ 4–7.) The HVID also paid Donald Wiechens, the Partnership's general partner, $34,022.88 for the Partnership's relinquished water rights. (Def.'s SOF at ¶¶ 4–7.) Yuma Title then transferred the $495,924.99 to a third-party, Blohm's Farms, Inc., in exchange for the transfer of title to approximately 160 acres of certain farm land to the Partnership. (Def.'s SOF at ¶ 8; Pls.' Mot. for Partial Summ. J. at p.2.) The total consideration for conveyance of the Blohm's Farms land to the Partnership was $567,810. (Def.'s SOF at ¶ 9.) Plaintiffs maintain that they did not report any resulting income from the above transactions to the Internal Revenue Service ("IRS") because they believed the transactions qualified for non-recognition tax treatment under 26 U.S.C. § 1031. (Pls.' Mot. for Partial Summ. J. at p.2.).

On November 3, 1997, the IRS made assessments against Plaintiff Donald Wiechens, for tax in the amount of $101,395.00 and for interest in the amount of

$37,277.64 with respect to the 1993 tax year. (Def.'s Mem. in Supp. of Mot. for Summ. J. at pp. 1–2.) On November 10, 1997, the IRS made assessments against Plaintiffs Gary and Deborah Wiechens for tax in the amount of $97,986.00 and for interest in the amount of $36,255.80 with respect to the 1993 tax year. (*Id.*) Plaintiffs made payments with respect to their 1993 tax returns. (*Id.*).

Plaintiffs initiated this tax refund action with a complaint filed in the United States District Court for the District of Arizona on September 28, 2000. Both Plaintiffs and Defendant have filed motions for summary judgment. Plaintiffs contend that its water rights constitute an interest in real property, that the properties exchanged were of "like-kind" and, therefore, that the exchange qualifies for non-recognition treatment and any gain realized is not taxable. (Pls.' Mot. for Partial Summ. J. at p.5.) Defendant claims that Plaintiffs' exchange of water rights for farm land was not an exchange of "like-kind" properties under 26 U.S.C. § 1031 and, therefore, that Plaintiffs' transaction does not qualify for non-recognition treatment and is taxable. (Def.'s Mem. in Supp. of Mot. for Summ. J. at p.2.).

ANALYSIS

A court must grant summary judgment if the pleadings and supporting documents, viewed in the light most favorable to the nonmoving party, "show that there is no genuine issue as to any material fact and that the moving party is entitled to judgment as a matter of law." Fed. R. Civ. P. 56(c) (1995); *see also Celotex Corp. v. Catrett*, 477 U.S. 317, 322–23 (1986); *Jesinger v. Nevada Federal Credit Union*, 24 F.3d 1127, 1130 (9th Cir. 1994). Substantive law determines which facts are material. *See Anderson v. Liberty Lobby*, 477 U.S. 242, 248 (1986); *see also Jesinger*, 24 F.3d at 1130. "Only disputes over facts that might affect the outcome of the suit under the governing law will properly preclude the entry of summary judgment." *Anderson*, 477 U.S. at 248. The dispute must also be genuine, that is, the evidence must be "such that a reasonable jury could return a verdict for the nonmoving party." *Id.; see also Jesinger*, 24 F.3d at 1130.

A principal purpose of summary judgment is "to isolate and dispose of factually unsupported claims." *Celotex*, 477 U.S. at 323–24. Summary judgment is appropriate against a party who "fails to make a showing sufficient to establish the existence of an element essential to that party's case, and on which that party will bear the burden of proof at trial." *Id.* at 322; *see also Citadel Holding Corp. v. Roven*, 26 F.3d 960, 964 (9th Cir. 1994). The moving party need not disprove matters on which the opponent has the burden of proof at trial. *See Celotex*, 477 U.S. at 317. The party opposing summary judgment "may not rest upon the mere allegations or denials of [the party's] pleadings, but ... must set forth specific facts showing that there is a genuine issue for trial." Fed. R. Civ. P. 56(e); *see Matsushita Elec. Indus. Co. v. Zenith Radio*, 475 U.S. 574, 585–88 (1986); *Brinson v. Linda Rose Joint Venture*, 53 F.3d 1044, 1049 (9th Cir. 1995).

I. The Partnership's water rights constitute an interest in real property.

Plaintiffs, in their motion for partial summary judgment, assert that the facts of this case are undisputed and maintain that the only issue for the Court to resolve is if the Partnership's water rights constitute an interest in real property. Plaintiffs contend that the Partnership's water rights are an interest in real property and, as a result, argue that the exchange of its water rights for farm land qualifies as a "like-kind" exchange subject to non-recognition treatment under 26 U.S.C. § 1031. For the purposes of the Motion for Summary Judgment, Defendant, does not dispute Plaintiffs' assertion that the Partnership's water rights constitute an interest in real property, but Defendant challenges Plaintiffs' argument that the exchanged water rights and farm land are "like-kind" property.

Plaintiffs argue that Arizona courts have concluded that water rights are interests in real property. Plaintiffs support this contention by citing *Paloma Investment Limited Partnership v. Jenkins*, 978 P.2d 110 (1998), in which the Arizona court stated "[i]n general, water rights are property rights. *In the Matter of the Rights to the Use of the Gila River*, 830 P.2d 442, 447 (1992). Those rights are interests in real property. *See* 93 C.J.S. Waters § 1 (1956)." The Court agrees with Plaintiffs' assertion that based on the *Paloma* decision, as well as later Arizona decisions, the Partnership's water rights do constitute an interest in real property. However, further analysis is required to determine if the Partnership's exchange satisfies the requirements for non-recognition status under 26 U.S.C. § 1031.

II. The Partnership's water rights originated with the November 18, 1983 water service subcontract and are limited.

Plaintiffs and Defendant dispute the origin and duration of the Partnership's water rights. Plaintiffs assert that the Partnership's water rights were perpetual, that the water rights originated from the United States Supreme Court decision in *State of Arizona v. State of California*, 373 U.S. 546 (1963), and that the water rights were definitively established by a later Department of Interior water allocation notice, 48 Fed. Reg. 12446 (Mar. 24, 1983). (Pls.' Resp. to Def.'s Mot. for Summ. J. at p.4.) Defendant, on the other hand, contends that neither the Supreme Court's decision in *Arizona v. California*, nor the March 24, 1983 Department of Interior water allocation notice entitled the Partnership or the other HVID landowners to perpetual water rights. Rather, Defendant argues that the HVID landowners became entitled to limited water rights by virtue of a November 18, 1983 water service subcontract ("Subcontract") between the Department of Interior, the Central Arizona Project ("CAP") Water District and the HVID. (Def.'s Corrected Reply to Pls.' Resp. to Def.'s Mot. for Summ. J. at p.2.).

The background and disposition of the HVID landowners' water rights were recently examined by the Tax Court in *Gladden v. Commissioner*, 112 T.C. 209 (1999). The *Gladden* court stated that the *Arizona v. California* decision entitled the State of Arizona, but not individual parties, to an annual claim of 2.8 million acre-feet of Colorado River water. *Id* at 210. Further, the court stated that the HVID was formed for the purpose of establishing a local water distribution system in and about the Harquahala Valley, and that irrigation districts may purchase or acquire water rights for irrigation purposes. *Id.* at 211. Additionally, the *Gladden* court determined that the March 24, 1983 Department of Interior notice initially allocated 7.67 percent of non-Indian agricultural lower Colorado River water for redistribution to the HVID, but not to individual landowners, for the purpose of irrigating farmland located within the geographic boundaries of the HVID water district. *Id.* at 211–12. The *Gladden* court further stated that a November 18, 1983 Subcontract between the Department of Interior, the CAP Water District and the HVID established delivery of allocated Colorado River water by the CAP Water District to the HVID for a 50-year period. *Id.* at 212. Notably, the *Gladden* court determined that individual landowners, such as the Partnership, although not named in the November 18, 1983 Subcontract, became entitled to receive an allocation of Colorado River water from the Subcontract only if the individual's land qualified as "eligible land" pursuant to the Subcontract. *Id.* at 212. Specifically, the *Gladden* court stated "under the Subcontract, the [landowner] was entitled to receive each year from [the HVID] a specified quantity of Colorado River water." *Id.* Throughout the remainder of the *Gladden* court's opinion and discussion of the HVID landowners' water rights, the court refers to the HVID landowners' water rights as being derived from the Subcontract. *See id.* at 213–16, 222–23.

On appeal, the Ninth Circuit did not dispute the *Gladden* court's determination of the origin and duration of the HVID landowners' water rights. The Ninth Circuit stated "[i]n 1983, [the HVID] obtained the right to take Colorado River water for redistribution within its boundaries and the [individual landowners] in turn obtained water rights from [the HVID]." *Gladden v. Comm'r*, 262 F.3d 851, 852 (9th Cir.2001).

Although Plaintiffs claim that the March 24, 1983 Department of Interior notice established the Partnership's water rights, the Court disagrees. First, the Court notes that when the Partnership acquired its interest in land, and thereafter until 1983, the Partnership did not have vested property rights in Colorado River water. In 1983, the Partnership acquired Colorado River water rights separately from any acquisition or sale of its ownership interest in the land.

Secondly, it is apparent to the Court that the Partnership's water rights originated from the November 18, 1983 Subcontract and that the rights were limited. The March 24, 1983 notice did not allocate water rights to individual landowners but, instead, specifically states that "[a] final allocation of CAP water and a contract with the [Department of Interior] Secretary for delivery of water is required...." (1983 WL 133337 (F.R.) at p.12450.) The December 1, 1992, Master Agreement for the relinquishment of CAP water between the parties further supports the Court's view by stating, "[u]nder a decision promulgated in ... the Federal Register, dated March 24, 1983, the Secretary allocated to the HVID certain CAP water. Thereafter, the HVID executed the [November 18, 1983] Water Service Subcontract under which it is entitled to CAP water with an agricultural priority." (Master Agreement for the Relinquishment of Central Arizona Project Water at ¶ 3.3.)

The March 24, 1983 notice and the November 18, 1983 Subcontract also place many limitations on the water rights. For example, both documents limit the HVID to 7.67 percent of the total supply of agricultural water available for delivery from CAP. The documents provide that the CAP water may only be used for irrigation.

The documents also stipulate that during water shortages, all municipal, industrial, and Indian uses of the water have priority over non-Indian irrigation uses. Finally, the November 18, 1983 Subcontract, under which the Partnership's water rights derived, is limited to a 50-year period. Based on these factors, the Court agrees with the finding of the *Gladden* Tax Court and the Ninth Circuit's affirmation that the water rights at issue originated from the November 18, 1983 Subcontract. Thus, the Partnership's water rights are limited in quantity, priority, and to a 50-year duration.

III. The Partnership's exchange of water rights for farm land was not an exchange of "like-kind" properties under 26 U.S.C. § 1031.

Typically, taxpayers must recognize gain or loss upon the sale or exchange of property. 26 U.S.C. § 1001. Therefore, as a general rule, a transfer of property in exchange for money or other property is taxable. An exception, however, provides that no gain or loss shall be recognized upon an exchange of like-kind properties. 26 U.S.C. § 1031(a). Treasury Regulations explain the "like-kind" property requirement as follows:

> As used in § 1031(a), the words "like-kind" have reference to the nature or character of the property and not to its grade or quality. One kind or class of property may not, under that section, be exchanged for property of a different kind or class.

Treas. Reg., 26 C.F.R. § 1.1031(a)-1(a)(2)(b). The elements of proof to establish that a property transfer qualifies as a like-kind exchange are as follows: (1) there must be an exchange, (2) the properties exchanged must be of a like-kind, and (3) the property transferred and the property received must be held by the taxpayer either for use in a trade or business, or for investment. 26 U.S.C. § 1031(a).

Plaintiffs contend that because the Partnership's water rights constitute an interest in real property, its exchange of the water rights for farm land qualifies as a like-kind exchange and is not taxable. However, Defendant counters that, "not every exchange of real property interests meets the section 1031 like-kind requirement." *Smalley v. Commissioner*, 116 T.C. 450 (2001). Defendant contends that a 1955 IRS Revenue Ruling (Rev.Rul.55-749) discussed the tax consequences of an exchange of water rights for a fee simple interest in land. Revenue Ruling 55-749 clearly advises that water rights of a limited amount or duration are not sufficiently similar under § 1031 to a fee simple interest in land. The Court is persuaded by the argument that an exchange of non-perpetual water rights, such as the Partnership's, for a fee simple interest in land does not satisfy § 1031.

Plaintiffs also contend, however, that even if the Partnership's water rights are limited to a 50-year duration, the water rights should still be considered of a like-kind with the fee simple interest in the farm land. To support this argument, Plaintiffs reference Treasury Regulation § 1.1031(a)-1(a)(2)(c), which sets forth examples of exchanges of properties that are of a like-kind. 26 C.F.R. § 1.1031(a)-1(a)(2)(c). One example, on which Plaintiffs rely, is the exchange of a leasehold of a fee with 30 years or more to run for real estate. *Id.* Plaintiffs argue that the Partnership's water rights, which the Court views as limited to a 50-year duration, are equivalent to the leasehold of a fee for 30 years or more and, therefore, constitute a like-kind exchange.

The Court agrees with Defendant's argument that equating the Partnership's water rights to a leasehold of a fee for 30 years or more is inappropriate. As the Tax Court stated in *Koch v. Commissioner*, 71 T.C. 54, 65 (1978), application of § 1031 "requires a comparison of the exchanged properties to ascertain whether the nature and character of the transferred rights in and to the respective properties are substantially alike." Factors to be considered in this analysis include "the respective interests in the physical properties, the nature of the title conveyed, the rights of the parties, [and] the duration [of the interests]." *Id.* The documentary evidence presented by the parties, as previously discussed, establish that the Partnership's water rights were narrowly restricted, unlike a fee simple interest in land. Although the Court agrees with Plaintiffs, that the Partnership's water rights constitute an interest in real property, the Court finds that the Partnership's water rights were limited in priority, quantity, and duration, and they were not sufficiently similar to the fee simple interest that it acquired in the Farm Land to qualify as like-kind property.

Halpern v. United States

United States District Court, Northern District of Georgia
286 F. Supp. 255 (1968)

FACTS

The facts in this action by a taxpayer seeking a refund of taxes paid are fully set forth in a stipulation by the parties. There being no conflict between the evidence and the stipulation, the latter is hereby incorporated in this order.

For convenience, however, the substance of the facts as they appear to the court may be briefly stated. At the outset of the transactions in question, plaintiff owned an equity in the Verbena property of $32,000 and had $14,000 in cash. Chennault owned an equity in the Wadley property of $15,000 and had $17,000 cash. Kidd and Smith together had an equity in the Hollywood property worth $19,000. Bartlett had an equity in the Gordon property worth $77,000. At the end of the transactions, plaintiff's assets of $46,000 had been transmuted into the Wadley equity ($15,000), the Hollywood equity ($19,000), and $12,000 worth of equity in the Gordon property. Chennault's $32,000 worth of assets had been wholly transmuted into the Verbena equity; Kidd and Smith had $19,000 in cash; Bartlett had $12,000 in cash, and plaintiff's note for $65,000. (Plaintiff's mortgage on the Verbena property of $38,700 and Chennault's mortgage on the Wadley property of $25,800 had each been assumed by the new owners of the properties.)

ANALYSIS

The taxpayer contends that the series of transactions which brought about these changes in position was designed and executed so as to make the transaction a unitary one and thus a tax-free exchange (for Halpern) of like property within the scope of

Internal Revenue Code of 1954 § 1031(a). The Government, on the other hand, contends that the plaintiff exchanged his Verbena property solely for the Wadley property of Chennault plus a cash 'boot' paid by Chennault, which the plaintiff promptly reinvested in the Hollywood and Gordon properties. If this latter contention is so, then plaintiff's profits from the Verbena-Wadley transfer are taxable under the provision of § 1031(b) as an exchange not wholly in kind.

These profits are calculated as the decrease in mortgages payable by plaintiff ($13,000), plus the difference between the sum of the fair market value of the Wadley property ($40,000) and the cash received by plaintiff ($17,000), and plaintiff's basis in the Verbena property of $48,000, or a total difference of $9,000. The gain realized by plaintiff is thus approximately $22,000 ($13,000 $9,000), which when taxed at 50%, results in the $10,740.67 in dispute here.

Both sides have cited and distinguished numerous cases attempting to show that the facts in this case are or are not similar to those in some other case before some other court. These cases have been carefully studied, and it would appear that regardless of the details of the transactions involved (which inevitably vary from case to case), certain principles have been relatively consistently applied.

It is clear, for instance, that it is legally irrelevant that the taxpayer-plaintiff intended to devise a transaction which would bring him within the letter of the statute. Intent to avoid a tax is not determinative of no liability, just as a lack of intent cannot operate to create a liability if the taxpayer is otherwise entitled to favorable treatment. *Comm'r v. Duberstein*, 363 U.S. 278 (1960); *Carlton v. U.S.*, 385 F.2d 238 (5th Cir. 1966).

Equally irrelevant is plaintiff's contention that plaintiff signed the contracts to purchase the Hollywood and Gordon properties as some sort of accommodation to Chennault, and in accord with the agreement between plaintiff and Chennault executed on May 6, 1961. That agreement did not require and at no time in the course of the transaction did Chennault acquire any legal interest in either of the two properties in which the profits realized by the plaintiff from the original two-party exchange were subsequently invested. Chennault's only role in these transactions, even by the terms of the May 6 agreement, was to "arrange to secure the conveyance to Halpern by warranty deed of the parcels of (Gordon Road and Hollywood Road) property." The agreement provided further that the "conveyances to Halpern of the parcels (Wadley, Gordon and Hollywood) shall be in consideration of the conveyance to Chennault by Halpern of the (Verbena) property...." There is no evidence that Chennault "arranged" the transfer of the Gordon and Hollywood properties[37] or that these

---

37. [3] Indeed, this is belied by the plaintiff's own deposition, which states, "Now the reason for me going out there (to the Gordon and Hollywood properties) instead of Chennault, now he's a colored fellow and he—and these two areas were predominantly white. And six years ago it was just not a very healthy thing for a colored person to go into a white area and buy property." This would suggest that Chennault was hardly in a position to "arrange" these transfers.

clauses are anything more than a transparent self-serving attempt to create some apparent link between Chennault and the properties Halpern intended to acquire.

Two more of plaintiff's remaining contentions are likewise of no great weight. It is conceded by the Government that all of the real property involved in these transactions is of "like kind" as required by the statute. However, it is not enough that the property be of "like kind", as required by § 1031(a). There must be an exchange of like property. Similarly, it is not controlling that the Government has treated part of the Verbena-Wadley exchange as an exchange of like property within the ambit of § 1031(b). The question is whether the Hollywood and Gordon properties were exchanged, rather than merely purchased by plaintiff. Only if plaintiff assumes the only point in question (whether the transaction was a single or severable one) does the Government's treatment of the Verbena-Wadley exchange have any significance.

Therefore, the sole question remaining is really whether the transfer of the Hollywood and Gordon properties was an integral part of the Wadley-Verbena transfer or whether it was in fact a reinvestment of the profits resulting from the Wadley-Verbena transfer. Central to this question, in the court's view of the problem, is the fact that at no time in either the planning or execution of the transaction did Chennault ever acquire even an equitable title to the Hollywood or Gordon properties. Nor were the contracts with the owners of the Hollywood and Gordon properties, which were separately negotiated by the plaintiff, dependent in any way on the consummation of the transaction with Chennault. The facts show that the transaction with Chennault was not at all dependent on the Hollywood and Gordon transactions, although the agreement purports to make it so. When the owner of the Gordon property discovered she could not deliver a warranty deed on June 1, 1961, the transfer with Chennault was consummated regardless and the Gordon property was finally transferred to Halpern in a completely separate title closing on September 19, 1961. There is no indication that Chennault or the owner of the Hollywood property made their part in the transaction contingent in any way upon Halpern's being able to complete his deal with Mrs. Bartlett for the Gordon property. In all the cases relied on by plaintiff in which a third party's property was received by the plaintiff, the title to that property first passed through the second party who was the primary exchange partner. *See Coastal Terminals, Inc. v. U.S.*, 320 F.2d 333 (4th Cir. 1963); *Alderson v. Comm'r*, 317 F.2d 790 (9th Cir. 1963); *J. H. Baird Publishing Co. v. Comm'r.*, 39 T.C. 608 (1962). In effect, the exchange in each of these cases was between two parties, one of whom had, in his own manner, previously acquired property which was to be subsequently exchanged with that of the taxpayer. Nor is plaintiff's situation comparable to the true three-party transaction described in Rev. Rul. 57-244, in which the participation of each party is essential to the contract and the failure of any one element of the exchange would cause the entire contract to be unenforceable. *Cf., W. D. Haden Co. v. Comm'r.*, 165 F.2d 588(2) (5th Cir. 1948).[38] Rather than the triangular relationship

---

38. [4] Note that in Haden the court restated the rule that a party (corresponding to Chennault here) could bind himself to exchange property he did not own but could acquire. But in Haden, the

envisioned in Rev. Rul. 57-244, the present case is one in which the taxpayer is separately obligated to each of the other two parties, who have no mutual obligations between themselves. Mere simultaneity of execution cannot make separate contracts an indivisible whole, regardless of the naked intention of one of the parties.

The fact that plaintiff never actually received in hand the cash resulting from the exchange with Chennault is not critical. While the receipt of cash may require a conclusion that a particular transaction is a sale (*see Carlton v. U.S.*, supra), the failure to actually receive the cash does not automatically require a corollary finding that a transaction is an exchange. In the present case, Lawyers Title Insurance Company was clearly acting as a mere temporary depository of the surplus funds resulting from the Verbena-Wadley exchange. On receipt of them, it was to pay to the owners of the Gordon and Hollywood properties the amounts stipulated if Halpern approved the title he was to receive. If he did not accept the title within six months, then the money could be used for the purchase of such other property as Halpern directed. But if Halpern after six months had called for the money to be paid to him in cash, it is difficult to see who would have had the standing to object. Certainly Halpern received a constructive right to receipt of the money when it was paid to Lawyers Title under these circumstances, and its failure to actually come to rest in his hands need not detain us.

Much of the decision in *Carlton v. U.S.*, supra, seems directly applicable to the present case. "The requirement is that the transaction be viewed in its entirety in order to determine its reality and substance, for it is the substance of the transaction which decides the incidence of taxation. In the instant case, while elaborate plans were laid to exchange property, the substance of the transaction was that the appellants received cash for the deed … and not another parcel of land.… Further, General (read "Chennault") was never in a position to exchange properties with the appellants because it never acquired the legal title to either the Lyons (read "Hollywood") or the Fernandez (read "Gordon") property.… The money received from General by the appellants for the ranch (read "Verbena") property was not earmarked by General to be used in purchasing the Lyons or Fernandez properties. It was unrestricted and could be used by the appellants as they pleased. The fact that they did use it to pay for the Lyons and Fernandez properties does not alter the fact that their use of the money was unfettered and unrestrained. It is an unescapable fact that the money received by appellants from General was money paid to them for a conveyance of their land. As a result, the separate transaction between General and the appellants must be construed to be a sale, and the transactions between the appellants and Lyons and Fernandez as a purchase of other property.… Considering how close the appellants came to satisfying the requirements of that section (§ 1031) and the stipulation that an exchange was intended, this result is obviously harsh. But there is no equity in tax law." 385 F.2d 238 at 241–243.

Therefore, judgment is rendered for the defendant.

---

second party had a valid contract to acquire the property in question, which is not the case as between Chennault and the other parties here, Smith-Kidd and Bartlett.

Barker v. Commissioner

United States Tax Court

74 T.C. 555 (1980)

OPINION

Nims, Judge:

Respondent determined a deficiency in taxes of $160 for the year 1973 and $4,824 for the year 1974. After concessions by the parties, there are two issues remaining for our decision:

(1) Should petitioner have recognized gain in 1974 on a transaction in which she disposed of her Demion property and acquired the Casa El Camino property?

(2) Did the buildings located on the petitioner's Casa El Camino property have a useful life of 30 years at the time such property was acquired by petitioner, as determined by respondent?

FINDINGS OF FACT

Most of the facts were fully stipulated and are found accordingly. The stipulation of facts and the exhibits attached thereto are incorporated by this reference.

The residence of the petitioner at the time the petition was filed in this case was Oceanside, Calif.

In June 1971, the petitioner acquired from Covington Bros., Inc., a parcel of real property, consisting of a four-plex residential building located at 18551 Demion Way, Huntington Beach, Calif. (the Demion property), along with personal property, consisting of furnishings related to the property. Covington Bros., Inc., was a California corporation in the business of buying and selling real estate. The Demion property was held by the petitioner primarily for rent to tenants.

In the spring of 1974, Mr. and Mrs. Goodyear contacted petitioner to inquire about purchasing the Demion property. Petitioner spoke to her accountant, Richard A. Harrison, about setting up a tax-free exchange to dispose of the property. After the contact by the Goodyears, petitioner contacted Covington Bros. and arrangements were made to effect an exchange through Covington Bros. and Grover Escrow Corp. Grover Escrow was handling three parcels of property, lots 15, 16, and 17 of the Casa El Camino subdivision, which were sought by petitioner. Petitioner then told the Goodyears that she would make the Demion property available to them but that the transaction would have to be done as an exchange through Grover Escrow.

To effect these transactions as an exchange, the parties entered into a series of contractual arrangements which took the form of escrow agreements. The intent of the parties was to structure a simultaneous transaction through these escrow agreements and escrow accounts by which Covington Bros. would acquire the Casa El Camino lots and exchange the lots for petitioner's Demion property which Covington Bros. would then sell to Virginia Goodyear. The parties to the various agreements are set forth below:

Escrow No. —	Seller	Buyer	Property
4-2863-01	Barker	Covington	Demion
4-2864-01	Barker	Goodyear	Demion
4-2861-01	Covington	Barker	Casa El Camino No. 15
4-2862-01	Covington	Barker	Casa El Camino No. 17
4-2906-01	Covington	Barker & Bear	Casa El Camino No. 16

Escrow No. 4-2863-01, dated April 15, 1974, was established for the transfer of the Demion property from petitioner to Covington Bros. It listed Covington Bros. as the purchaser and petitioner as the seller. The escrow agreement provided, in pertinent part, as follows:

> In order to effect an exchange I (Covington Bros.) will hand you (Grover Escrow) a deed to real property (Casa El Camino) described in escrows 4-2861-01 and 4-2862-01 in which, for the purpose of this escrow I have an equity of $17,000.00 and will take title subject to the existing encumbrances.

> We, the undersigned buyers (Covington Bros.) agree to accept a deed to real property (Demion) described in this escrow, and we agree to execute a deed affecting this property in favor of and these transactions are to file concurrently herewith.

> In the event the equity of the seller, Earlene T. Barker, is greater than $17,000.00, said overage is to be paid to her at the consummation of these transactions, after payment of necessary incurred costs in said escrows and the property conveyed herein.

> We, the purchasers herein are not to be at any costs in this transaction, nor in the transactions affecting the transfer of title to the ____. All costs relating to seller for this transaction is to be paid by Earlene T. Barker.

> This escrow involves an exchange of property as set forth herein in escrow 4-2861-01 and 4-2862-01 at Grover Escrow Corporation.

> In connection with all documents in these escrows, which are to record concurrently you are instructed to transfer and/or accept funds and/or equities to comply with terms and conditions contained herein.

> Escrow 4-2863-01, 4-2861-01 and 4-2862-01 shall be considered as exchange escrows between parties and any wording therein contrary is to be considered null and void.

> The successful closing of this transaction is contingent upon the concurrent recording of Escrow 4-2861-01, 4-2862-01 and 4-2864-01.

Escrow No. 4-2864-01, dated April 15, 1974, was established for the transfer of the Demion property to Virginia Goodyear. It listed petitioner as the seller and Virginia Goodyear as the buyer. The escrow agreement provided, in pertinent part, as follows:

Prior to June 3, 1974, I (Goodyear) will hand you (Grover Escrow) $17,000.00 and do hand you now the sum of $300.00 and have handed the seller (Barker) the sum of $200.00 to be deposited into escrow and will cause to be handed you by means of a new conventional loan to file the sum of $68,500.00, making a total consideration in this transaction of $85,700.00 * * *

The successful closing of escrow is subject to buyer (Goodyear) obtaining and qualifying for a new conventional loan to file in favor of Allstate Savings and Loan Association in the principal sum of $68,500.00. Buyers execution of loan documents shall be deemed his approval of all terms and conditions contained therein. You are authorized and instructed to comply with the instructions of the lender of the first trust deed to file and loan funds to be credited herein.

Seller (Barker) to present to escrow, prior to the close, a rental schedule for the purpose of prorations; security money, to be credited the buyer and debited the seller.

Buyer (Goodyear) to pay all costs for the new loan to file. All remaining costs to be paid as follows: Buyer to pay up to but not exceeding the sum of $200.00 with the balance of the costs to be paid for by the seller. Costs of the seller will be paid by the seller in escrow 4-2863-01, which is for the purpose of effecting an exchange.

The successful closing of escrow is contingent upon the concurrent recordings of escrow 4-2863-01, 4-2861-01 and 4-2862-01.

Seller named herein agrees to provide a termite clearance covering subject property from a licensed termite control service which shows no visible signs of termites, dry rot and/or fungus in all accessible area. You are hereby authorized and instructed to pay for this report and any corrective work required, from the net proceeds due seller in this transaction.

Entered as a memorandum only and you as escrow holder are not to be concerned or held liable and/or responsible for same: All heating, plumbing and electrical appliances to be in good working order at the close of escrow.

In the event of cancellation by buyer, buyer understands the $500.00 on deposit is non-refundable.

Three escrows (Nos. 4-2862-01, 4-2861-01, and 4-2906-01) were established for the transfer of the Casa El Camino property (lots 15, 16, and 17) from Covington Bros. to petitioner. Each escrow agreement listed Covington Bros. as the seller and petitioner as the buyer (Jim B. Bears was also a buyer in escrow No. 4-2906-01).

Escrow Nos. 4-2861-01 and 4-2862-01 for lots 15 and 17, dated April 15, 1974, provided in pertinent part as follows:

In order to effect an exchange I (Barker) will hand you (Grover Escrow) a deed to real property described in escrow 4-2863-01 in which I have an equity of $17,000.00, $8500.00 to be applied to escrow 4-2861-01 and $8500.00

to be applied to escrow 4-2862-01 and will execute the necessary papers to reflect a loan of $67,900.00 and will also execute a second purchase money trust deed in favor of seller (Covington Bros.) in the sum of $8500.00, making a total consideration in this transaction of $84,900.00.

This escrow involves an exchange of property (Demion) as set forth herein in escrow 4-2861-01 and 4-2863-01 at Grover Escrow Corporation.

In connection with all documents in these escrows, which are to record concurrently, you are instructed to transfer and/or accept funds and/or equities to comply with the terms and conditions contained herein. Funds needed to cover purchasers (Barker) closing costs incurred in this transaction to be transferred from funds due seller (Covington Bros.) in escrow 4-2863-01. Escrows 4-2861-01, 4-2862-01 and 4-2863-01 shall be considered as exchange escrows between parties and any wording therein contrary is to be considered null and void.

Successful closing of this transaction is contingent upon concurrent recording of escrow 4-2864-01.

In the event of cancellation, buyer (Barker) to pay a $50.00 cancellation fee to the seller (Covington Bros.), plus any additional costs incurred.

Escrow No. 4-2906-01, for lot 16 dated April 23, 1974, provided, in pertinent part, as follows:

In order to effect an exchange I (Barker) will hand you (Grover Escrow) a deed to real property (Demion) described in escrow 4-2863-01 in which I have an equity of $17,000.00, $8500.00 to be applied to escrow 4-2861-01 and $8500.00 to be applied to escrow 4-2862-01 and any overage in the equity to be applied to escrow 4-2906-01 and will execute the necessary papers to reflect a loan of $67,900.00 and will also execute a second purchase money trust deed in favor of seller in the sum of $8500.00, making a total consideration in this transaction of $84,900.00. Any shortage in equity to be adjusted in the cash through escrow.

The rest of the agreement contained the same terms as the escrow agreements for lots 15 and 17.

Closing was on or about June 10, 1974. After the terms of the escrow agreements were carried out, Virginia Goodyear ended up with title to the Demion property and petitioner ended up with title to the Casa El Camino lots. Documents recorded at the Orange County, Calif., Hall of Records show that the Demion property was first deeded to Covington Bros. and then from Covington Bros. to Goodyear.

Total consideration paid by Virginia Goodyear was $85,700, which included $17,200 cash plus the $68,500 proceeds of a new trust deed taken out by Goodyear on the Demion property.

The proceeds from the sale of the Demion property were applied to satisfy an existing first trust deed on the property of $54,968.17 and a second trust deed on the property of $7,320.62. After other expenses incidental to the sale were satisfied, a total of $20,825.41 was credited on June 10, 1974, to a new escrow account numbered 4-2863-01.

Lots 15, 16, and 17 of the Casa El Camino property were acquired by petitioner on or about June 10, 1974, pursuant to the above escrow agreements. (Lot 16 was acquired by petitioner in a joint venture with Jim B. Bears.)

The consideration for lot 15 of the Casa El Camino property, along with expenses incidental to the acquisition of this property, were paid by means of petitioner's assuming a first trust deed on the property of $67,900, and executing a second trust deed on the property of $8,500 in favor of Covington Bros., and by a transfer of cash from escrow account 4-2863-01 in the amount of $8,756.58 and by petitioner's payment of $300 in cash.

The consideration for lot 17 of the Casa El Camino property, along with expenses incidental to the acquisition of this property, were paid by petitioner's assuming a first trust deed on the property of $67,900, executing a second trust deed in favor of the sellers of $8,500, and by a transfer of cash from escrow account 4-2863-01 in the amount of $8,827.54 and the payment of $300 in cash.

The consideration for lot 16 of the Casa El Camino property was paid by petitioner's and Jim B. Bears' assuming a first trust deed on the property of $67,900, executing a second trust deed on the property in favor of the sellers in the amount of $8,500, and by a transfer of cash from escrow account 4-2863-01 in the amount of $3,191.19 and the payment of cash.

Petitioner incurred expenses of $1,802.18 in disposing of the Demion property. (On brief, respondent conceded that this amount should be added to petitioner's basis in the Demion property.)

In the notice of deficiency, respondent determined that petitioner's disposition of the Demion property was a taxable event. Respondent also determined that the useful life of the Casa El Camino buildings was 30 years and thus disallowed a portion of the depreciation petitioner claimed on the Casa El Camino property on her 1974 income tax return.

OPINION

This case involves another variant of the multiple-party, like-kind exchange by which the taxpayer, as in this case, seeks to terminate one real estate investment and acquire another real estate investment without recognizing gain. The statutory provision for nonrecognition treatment is section 1031.[39] The touchstone of section 1031, at least in this context, is the requirement that there be an exchange of like-kind business or investment properties, as distinguished from a cash sale of property by the taxpayer and a reinvestment of the proceeds in other property.

---

39. [9] All statutory references are to the Internal Revenue Code of 1954, as in effect during the years in issue, except as otherwise expressly indicated.

The "exchange" requirement poses an analytical problem because it runs headlong into the familiar tax law maxim that the substance of a transaction controls over form. In a sense, the substance of a transaction in which the taxpayer sells property and immediately reinvests the proceeds in like-kind property is not much different from the substance of a transaction in which two parcels are exchanged without cash. *Bell Lines, Inc. v. United States*, 480 F.2d 710, 711 (4th Cir. 1973). Yet, if the exchange requirement is to have any significance at all, the perhaps formalistic difference between the two types of transactions must, at least on occasion, engender different results. *Accord, Starker v. United States*, 602 F.2d 1341, 1352 (9th Cir. 1979).

The line between an exchange on the one hand and a nonqualifying sale and reinvestment on the other becomes even less distinct when the person who owns the property sought by the taxpayer is not the same person who wants to acquire the taxpayer's property. This means that multiple parties must be involved in the transaction. In that type of case, a like-kind exchange can be effected only if the person with whom the taxpayer exchanges the property first purchases the property wanted by the taxpayer. This interjection of cash, especially when the person who purchases the property desired by the taxpayer either uses money advanced by the taxpayer or appears to be acting as his agent, or both, makes the analysis that much more difficult.

In the instant case, petitioner faced just such a problem. Virginia Goodyear wanted to acquire petitioner's Demion property, and an unidentified third party owned the Casa El Camino property that petitioner sought to acquire. To effect the exchange, petitioner brought in a fourth party, Covington Bros., Inc., who, in a simultaneous transaction, was supposed to acquire both properties and transfer the Casa El Camino property to petitioner in return for the Demion property and the Demion property to Goodyear for the cash. This cash and the proceeds of new mortgages taken out by petitioner on the Casa El Camino property was used to compensate the ex-owners of the Casa El Camino property. The contractual arrangements took the form of escrow agreements and the dollars were evened out through escrow accounts.

Petitioner contends that the parties successfully completed a like-kind exchange; respondent contends otherwise, maintaining that petitioner sold the Demion property and reinvested the proceeds in the Casa El Camino property, all of which amounted to a taxable transaction.

We begin by observing that there is nothing inherent in a multiple-party exchange that necessarily acts as a bar to section 1031 treatment. Thus, it is not a bar to section 1031 treatment that the person who desires the taxpayer's property acquires and holds another piece of property only temporarily before exchanging it with the taxpayer. *Mercantile Trust Co. of Baltimore v. Commissioner*, 32 B.T.A. 82 (1935); *Alderson v. Commissioner*, 317 F.2d 790 (9th Cir. 1963), revg. 38 T.C. 215 (1962); *Starker v. United States, supra*; Rev. Rul. 75-291, 1975-2 C.B. 332.[40] Similarly, it is not fatal to

---

40. [10] In Rev. Rul. 75-291, 1975-2 C.B. 332, the Commissioner suggests as a caveat to its acceptance of temporary ownership those situations where the person purchasing the property for exchange with the taxpayer was actually acting as the agent for the taxpayer in making the purchase.

section 1031 treatment that the person with whom the taxpayer exchanges his property immediately sells the newly acquired property. *W.D. Haden Co. v. Commissioner*, 165 F.2d 588 (5th Cir. 1948); *Mays v. Campbell*, 246 F. Supp. 375 (N.D. Tex. 1965).

Difficulties arise, however, when the transaction falls short of the paradigm in which transitory ownership is the only feature distinguishing the transaction from two-party exchanges. Still, the courts (and by and large the Commissioner), in reviewing these transactions, have evinced awareness of business and economic exigencies.

Often the taxpayer and a prospective purchaser will enter into an exchange agreement before acceptable like-kind property has been located. In *Alderson v. Commissioner, supra*, as in *Biggs v. Commissioner*, 69 T.C. 905 (1978), on appeal (5th Cir., Oct. 23, 1978), the court approved tax-free exchange treatment since the properties were designated before the date set for transfer of taxpayer's property even though the to-be-received properties had not been identified as of the date of the agreement.[41] This aspect of *Alderson* was approved in Rev. Rul. 77-297, 1977-2 C.B. 304, in which the Commissioner also allowed the taxpayer to search for and select the property to be received by him in the exchange. In fact, in *Alderson*, the Ninth Circuit was also satisfied even though originally the taxpayer negotiated a sale and only later amended the escrow agreement to provide for a "three corner" exchange in lieu of a cash sale. *See also Coupe v. Commissioner*, 52 T.C. 394 (1969). Rev. Rul. 77-297 also cited this aspect of *Alderson* with approval.

In *W.D. Haden Co. v. Commissioner*, 165 F.2d 588 (5th Cir. 1948), an individual purchased property from a third party with the intent of exchanging this property for property held by the taxpayer, but the individual never acquired legal title to the property. Despite this, the court sanctioned tax-free exchange treatment, holding that the buyer may direct the third party to deed this property directly to the taxpayer so long as the cash paid to the third party is transferred directly from the buyer to the third party and not through the taxpayer. *See also Biggs v. Commissioner*, 69 T.C. 905 (1978), where this Court sustained tax-free exchange treatment, again notwithstanding the fact that the exchanging party did not obtain legal title to the property to be exchanged.

In *124 Front Street, Inc. v. Commissioner*, 65 T.C. 6 (1975), section 1031 treatment was in order for a taxpayer where a corporation advanced funds to the taxpayer to permit him to exercise an option he held on property. The taxpayer then exchanged the newly acquired property for property held by the corporation. In *Biggs v. Commissioner, supra*, a similar result ensued where the taxpayer advanced funds to a fourth party to enable it to purchase the sought property (the taxpayer ultimately recovering his funds when the several titles closed).

Notwithstanding those deviations from the standard multiple-party exchanges which have received judicial approval, at some point the confluence of some sufficient number of deviations will bring about a taxable result. Whether the cause be eco-

---

41. [11] In *Starker v. United States*, 602 F.2d 1341 (9th Cir. 1979), the Ninth Circuit approved tax-free exchange treatment even though the properties were not even selected until some time after the taxpayer had "exchanged" his property.

nomic and business reality or poor tax planning, prior cases make clear that taxpayers who stray too far run the risk of having their transactions characterized as a sale and reinvestment.

For example, in *Carlton v. United States*, 385 F.2d 238 (5th Cir. 1967), the parties intended to enter into an *Alderson* like-kind exchange (i.e., the person who wanted the taxpayer's property was to temporarily acquire and hold the property wanted by the taxpayer), but to avoid unnecessary duplication in the transfer of money and titles, the third party conveyed his property directly to the taxpayer, and the buyer paid money to the taxpayer, intending that the taxpayer pay this money to the third party. Focusing on the taxpayer's receipt of cash rather than real property, the court held that the transaction was a sale.

In *Rogers v. Commissioner*, 44 T.C. 126 (1965), affd. per curiam 377 F.2d 534 (9th Cir. 1967), the taxpayer granted a purchase option to Standard Oil Co. of California prior to his agreement with third parties to exchange the property subject to the outstanding option. Standard Oil exercised its option and paid the purchase price into escrow just before the exchange was completed. Therefore, the taxpayer was held to have sold his property before the exchange took place, and section 1031 treatment was denied.

It is against this background that the present four-party, like-kind exchange must be analyzed. At the outset, we note that this transaction is earmarked by several factors characteristic of section 1031 exchanges. It is clear that the parties intended that there would be an exchange of the properties. While intent alone is not sufficient (*Carlton v. United States*, 385 F.2d 238 (5th Cir. 1967)), it is relevant to a determination of what transpired. *Biggs v. Commissioner, supra* at 915.

Consonant with this intent, the essence of the agreements among the parties was that petitioner would exchange the Demion property for the Casa El Camino property rather than have petitioner sell the Demion property and reinvest the proceeds. This was accomplished through contractual arrangements which were such that petitioner did not, or could not, obtain actual or constructive receipt of the cash proceeds from the sale of the Demion property to Goodyear.

Each of the contractual arrangements between the parties was a mutually interdependent part of an integrated plan; each transaction was contingent upon the successful completion of the other transactions; and the transactions were to be completed simultaneously. Under the agreements, moneys paid into escrow were earmarked for the Casa El Camino property; petitioner had no option of taking cash in lieu of this property. Finally, title passage was consistent with the idea that this was an exchange of properties. Title for the Demion property passed from the petitioner to Covington Bros. and then to Goodyear; conversely, title for the Casa El Camino property passed from the initial owner to Covington Bros. and then to petitioner.

There are, however, two features of this transaction which could be construed as suspect under section 1031: Covington Bros.' transitory ownership of the properties and the possibility that petitioner could have received cash rather than real estate.

At first blush, the transitory nature of Covington Bros.' ownership of the Demion property on the one hand and the Casa El Camino property on the other seems to lend itself to a step-transaction argument; that is, Covington Bros.' ownership of the properties could be viewed as nothing more than an unnecessary and formalistic step of no legal or economic significance which should be ignored in determining the character of the transaction for tax purposes. But, as indicated above, the Commissioner accedes to transitory ownership in the three-party context (Rev. Rul. 77-297, *supra*), and we can perceive no reason why the four-party context should be treated any differently. In other four-party exchanges previously considered by the courts and decided in favor of the taxpayer, the fourth party has held title to the properties for no longer than a transitory period. We do not understand respondent's attack on four-party exchanges to be so broad-based that he thinks none qualify for section 1031 treatment. *See Coupe v. Commissioner, supra; Biggs v. Commissioner, supra.*[42] Indeed, respondent has not made such an argument here. To the complaint that this treatment places undue emphasis on a formalistic step of no substance, we repeat what we have already said: that the conceptual distinction between an exchange qualifying for section 1031 on the one hand and a sale and reinvestment on the other is largely one of form.

Respondent has chosen to focus his attack on those attributes of this transaction which depart from the standard four-party exchange. Respondent's basic contention is that the agreement providing for the transfer of the Demion property from petitioner to Goodyear is separate and distinct from the agreement providing for the transfer of the Casa El Camino property to petitioner. Respondent's view has it that escrow No. 4-2864-01 between petitioner as seller and Goodyear as buyer obligated petitioner to sell the Demion property to Goodyear upon payment of an appropriate amount of cash into escrow. He contends that petitioner could have taken the cash by paying a $50 penalty, plus costs, after transferring the Demion property to Goodyear and withdrawing from the agreements calling for her to acquire the Casa El Camino property. And respondent views the provision for simultaneous escrow closings on the Demion and Casa El Camino properties as an artifice through which petitioner avoids cash passing through her hands. Respondent draws the conclusion that the transactions should be characterized as a sale and reinvestment of funds which does not qualify as a section 1031 exchange.

The basic weakness in respondent's position is that it treats too cavalierly the language in the escrow agreements providing that the successful closing of each transaction is contingent upon the successful closing of all the other transactions. The

---

42. [12] There is no evidence, and respondent has not argued, here, that Covington Bros. was the agent of petitioner, and thus petitioner, through her agent, has purchased the Casa El Camino property. *Cf. Coupe v. Commissioner,* 52 T.C. 394 (1969); *J.H. Baird Publishing Co. v. Commissioner,* 39 T.C. 608 (1962). *But see Biggs v. Commissioner,* 69 T.C. 905 (1978), where this Court sustained a four-party, like-kind exchange after explicitly noting that no finding had been made that the fourth party was acting as the agent of the purchaser of the taxpayer's property, rather than as the taxpayer's agent. 69 T.C. at 917.

mutual interdependence of the Demion and Casa El Camino transfers could not have been made more explicit.[43]

In this context, the fact that the escrow agreement (No. 4-2864-01) providing for the transfer of the Demion property to Goodyear listed Barker rather than Covington as "seller" takes on less significance.[44] Indeed, there is plenty of evidence that Goodyear received the property from Covington Bros. rather than Barker. There was a separate escrow agreement providing for the transfer of the Demion property from Barker to Covington Bros. The escrow ledger for escrow account No. 4-2864-01 listed Covington Bros. as the seller rather than Barker. And at the Hall of Records there was recorded the passage of title from Barker to Covington to Goodyear.

In short, it seems clear that the listing of Barker as seller of the Demion property rather than Covington Bros. was the result of a mistake or sloppiness or both. It is certainly at odds with both the contractual agreements among the parties and the way in which these agreements were carried out. We decline respondent's invitation to find that Goodyear received the Demion property directly from petitioner rather than through Covington Bros.

Respondent has also made too much out of the contract cancellation clause in contending that petitioner had the option of taking either cash or property at the time of the exchange. It is true that petitioner's agreement with Covington Bros. regarding the Casa El Camino property provided that "In the event of cancellation, buyer [is] to pay a $50.00 cancellation fee to the seller, plus any additional costs incurred." But that does not mean that petitioner could simply see the transfer of the Demion property through, then withdraw from the Casa El Camino agreements by paying the penalty, and thereby accomplish the receipt of cash proceeds, as respondent insists. Rather, the mutually interdependent nature of the escrow agreements was such that the cancellation of the agreements was explicitly designed to render the others ineffective if petitioner attempted to take the course suggested by respondent.[45]

---

43. [13] We emphasize the contractual interdependence of the transfers, not because contractual interdependence is required in a multiple-party exchange, but because it highlights the exchange character of this transaction. In *Biggs v. Commissioner*, 69 T.C. 905 (1978), the Court sustained tax-free exchange treatment, even though there was no contractual interdependence between the transfers of property, because there was mutual dependence; i.e., an integrated plan intended to effect an exchange of like-kind properties. 69 T.C. at 914–915. Contractual interdependence also helps bolster a taxpayer's case when, as here, there is something in one of the agreements inconsistent with exchange treatment.

44. [14] Respondent does not argue that the use of the terms "buyer" and "seller" in the escrow agreements, rather than "transferor" and "transferee," in and of itself means that a sale occurred. Rather, respondent's concern is that escrow No. 4-2864-01 seems to provide for a direct transfer of the Demion property from Barker to Goodyear, which is inconsistent with petitioner's argument that the property was transferred from Barker to Covington and then to Goodyear.

45. [15] If the original agreements were canceled, petitioner could presumably have entered into an entirely new agreement with Goodyear to sell the Demion property directly to Goodyear (for cash), but the possibility of receiving cash by canceling one transaction and entering into an entirely new transaction would not, in and of itself, affect the efficacy of a like-kind exchange.

Under the Commissioner's administrative position, an exchange can be effected through an escrow account as long as the taxpayer cannot obtain use of the escrow moneys. Rev. Rul. 77-297, *supra*. Since the money paid into escrow here was earmarked for the Casa El Camino property and could never be made available to petitioner under the terms of the escrow agreements, this transaction meets that measure.[46]

Accordingly, we find respondent's contentions without merit and we hold that the transaction in the instant case falls within the ambit of section 1031.

Respondent has an alternative argument which must be addressed since we have found that the transaction qualifies as a like-kind exchange under section 1031. As part of the transaction, and simultaneously with the exchange of the properties, petitioner's mortgage on the Demion property was satisfied, and Goodyear took out a new mortgage on that property. Respondent characterizes the mortgage payment as cash boot to petitioner and contends that section 1031(b)[47] requires petitioner to recognize realized gain up to the amount of the cash used to satisfy the mortgage. To analyze this issue, we must explore the boot and boot-netting rules under section 1031(b).

Money or property other than "like-kind" property received in a section 1031 exchange is taxed as boot under section 1031(b). Furthermore, where property transferred by a taxpayer is subject to a mortgage, the amount of the mortgage is treated as boot received by the taxpayer. Sec. 1.1031(b)-1(c), Income Tax Regs.; *Allen v. Commissioner*, 10 T.C. 413 (1948). The presence of boot in a like-kind exchange does not disqualify the transaction from section 1031 tax-free treatment. Under section 1031(b), gain is recognized on the transaction, but only in an amount not in excess of the boot received.[48]

Section 1031(b) speaks in terms of boot received but does not mention boot given.[49] However, the regulations under section 1031 allow the netting of boot in some sit-

---

46. [16] We note that this case is appealable to the Ninth Circuit. In *Starker v. United States*, 602 F.2d 1341 (9th Cir. 1979), the Ninth Circuit found that a transaction qualified as a sec. 1031 exchange even though the agreement permitted the taxpayer to receive cash, rather than property, in exchange for his property, so long as he never received cash and ended up with property.

47. [17] Sec. 1031(b) provides as follows:

(b) GAIN FROM EXCHANGES NOT SOLELY IN KIND.—If an exchange would be within the provisions of subsection (a), of section 1035(a), of section 1036(a), or of section 1037(a), if it were not for the fact that the property received in exchange consists not only of property permitted by such provisions to be received without the recognition of gain, but also of other property or money, then the gain, if any, to the recipient shall be recognized, but in an amount not in excess of the sum of such money and the fair market value of such other property.

48. [18] This rule can be illustrated as follows: If A exchanges property worth $5,000 and subject to a mortgage of $3,000 for property worth $2,000, A has received $3,000 boot and he must recognize gain realized up to that $3,000.

49. [19] For purposes of this opinion, we adopt the following terminology: A taxpayer who assumes a liability or accepts property subject to a liability gives boot, and a taxpayer whose liability is assumed or who transfers property subject to a liability receives boot.

uations. When there are mortgages on both sides of the exchange, the mortgages are netted and the difference becomes, for the purpose of determining how much gain is to be recognized, the "money or other property" received by the party transferring the property with the larger mortgage. Sec. 1.1031(b)-1(c) and sec. 1.1031(d)-2, examples (1) and (2), Income Tax Regs.

The regulations have limits on netting of boot when the boot on one or both sides of the transaction consists of something other than reciprocal liabilities. While a taxpayer who receives boot by surrendering mortgaged property can offset the boot by any boot given, including cash, a taxpayer who receives consideration in the form of cash to compensate for a difference in net values in the properties (fair market value less mortgage) cannot offset the cash boot by boot given by virtue of receiving mortgaged property. Sec. 1.1031(d)-2, examples (1) and (2), Income Tax Regs.[50]

Thus, a taxpayer who receives cash consideration to compensate for a difference in net values must recognize gain realized to the extent of the sum of cash received and the net difference in favor of himself between the mortgage on the property transferred and the mortgage on the property received. *Allen v. Commissioner*, 10 T.C. 413 (1948). Furthermore, he cannot offset the cash boot received by the net of mortgages even if the property he receives has a larger mortgage. Conversely, a taxpayer who pays cash boot can use the cash paid to offset the net difference where the mortgage on the property transferred exceeds the mortgage on the property received.[51]

In the instant case, if petitioner had simply exchanged the Demion property for the Casa El Camino property (and paid money as she did to compensate for the larger net value (fair market value less mortgage) of the Casa El Camino property over the Demion property), it is clear that no gain would be recognized to petitioner under section 1031(b). Petitioner would be viewed as simply having moved her equity in the Demion property (which was subject to mortgages of $62,288.79) to the Casa El Camino property, which was subject to a larger liability, a classic case of no net boot to petitioner under the section 1031 regulations. Any gain realized by petitioner under this posture of the case need not be recognized since she received no cash or net cash

---

50. [20] This rule was applied in *Coleman v. Commissioner*, 180 F.2d 758 (8th Cir. 1950), and was made a part of the regulations in 1956. T.D. 6210 (Nov. 6, 1956), 1956-2 C.B. 508, 513.

51. [21] S. Surrey, W. Warren, P. McDaniel & H. Ault, Federal Income Taxation, Cases and Materials, pp. 873–874 (1972), contains the following illustrative example which we have paraphrased:

> If A exchanged property worth $55,000 but subject to a $20,000 mortgage for B's property worth $65,000 but subject to a $40,000 mortgage and $10,000 cash, A would recognize gain (to extent realized) only to the extent of the $10,000 cash received plus the net of mortgages if the net was favorable to A. Since A is taking subject to a $40,000 mortgage while being relieved of a $20,000 mortgage, the net of mortgages does not result in any boot to A. Thus, gain is recognized to the extent of the $10,000 cash. (Note, however, that if cash and mortgages were netted together, there would be no net boot to A. However, cash received cannot be netted against mortgages.)

As for B, gain will be recognized only to the extent of $10,000 (the net of the $40,000 mortgage less the $20,000 mortgage and the $10,000 cash) since the cash transferred may be subtracted from the net of mortgages to reduce boot.

equivalent. This result would obtain even if Goodyear then immediately paid off the liability on the Demion property.

This case does not exactly parallel the above scenario, however, because in reality the mortgage on the Demion property was not paid off by Goodyear after the exchange but was paid off contemporaneously with the exchange. On the facts of this case, and for reasons developed infra, this distinction is not critical.

A taxpayer is not allowed to offset cash received by boot given in a case where the taxpayer has received two distinct assets—like-kind property (albeit mortgaged) and cash—and the taxpayer has an unfettered right to do with the cash as he pleases. *Coleman v. Commissioner*, 180 F.2d 758 (8th Cir. 1950). In that type of case, the taxpayer can exit the transaction with non-like-kind property—the cash. It seems appropriate to trigger the recognition of gain in those circumstances.

But when liabilities are paid off contemporaneously with the exchange, the taxpayer does not obtain dominion and control over the cash, and the taxpayer's net investment in the new like-kind property is no less than his net investment in the old. Indeed, in the instant case, the net effect mandated by the interdependent contractual arrangements among the parties was not simply to maintain petitioner's investment at the same level; her investment—now transferred to the Casa El Camino property—was actually increased since she paid additional money as part of the acquisition price of the Casa El Camino property. Moreover, the agreements among the parties were such that petitioner never received (nor did she ever have the option to receive) non-like-kind property, i.e., unfettered cash. Conceptually, then, there is no reason that boot-netting should not be permitted in such situations, and we think it proper to allow it. It follows under this approach that petitioner will be permitted to offset the Demion and Casa El Camino liabilities in determining net boot.

Respondent would answer that we have framed the issue incorrectly and that this contemporaneous transaction should be analyzed as if petitioner received the cash and paid off the liability on the Demion property prior to transferring that property. Even if we were convinced this characterization were appropriate, we think the same result would obtain. It is significant in this regard that the cash in the instant case was used to satisfy the liability on the property that the petitioner transferred (the Demion property) and that the petitioner was contractually bound to use the cash for that purpose. Under no circumstance would petitioner have been able to come away from the transaction with non-like-kind property in the form of cash. Moreover, the receipt of cash and satisfaction of the liability on the Demion property did not compensate petitioner for a larger net value (fair market value less mortgage) of the Demion property over the Casa El Camino property. The payment, standing alone, also would not enhance petitioner's wealth at all—prior to the exchange, to the extent one liability has been satisfied, petitioner has a corresponding obligation to the payor of the cash. In a sense, petitioner was little more than a conduit for the moneys used to pay off the mortgage on the Demion property, and she had no option to put the moneys to other use. Under this approach, since petitioner does not really benefit until the properties are exchanged, we would still find that petitioner could offset all boot received by boot given.

In essence, this is the thrust of *Commissioner v. North Shore Bus Co.*, 143 F.2d 114 (2d Cir. 1944), affg. a Tax Court Memorandum Opinion, the reasoning of which we adopt in this case. That case involved an exchange of old buses for new buses. Prior to transferring the old buses, the taxpayer received a sum of cash from the owner of the new buses to pay off an outstanding mortgage on the old buses. Taxpayer was obligated under the contract to use the cash for that purpose. The Second Circuit refused to characterize the payment as cash boot. Rather, it viewed the transaction as one in which the taxpayer either simply changed creditors (from the bank to the bus company) or acted as a conduit for the funds.

Accordingly, we hold that boot-netting is permissible in a case where, contemporaneously with the exchange of properties and where clearly required by the contractual arrangement between the parties, cash is advanced by the transferee (in this case, Goodyear through Covington Bros.) to enable the transferor-taxpayer (petitioner) to pay off a mortgage on the property to be transferred by the taxpayer (here, the Demion property). Since these criteria have been met, we find that the exchange in this case was completely tax free to petitioner.

We hasten to add that there is nothing in this analysis that is inconsistent with, or casts doubt upon, the regulations under section 1031 or the holding in Coleman v. Commissioner, supra. The boot-netting precept stated earlier, that cash consideration received cannot be offset by liabilities assumed, does not appear in the regulations as a broadly stated principle; rather, the rule arises in the context of regulation examples under sec. 1.1031(d)-2, Income Tax Regs. There are factual differences between the regulation examples and this case that go to the essence of the boot-netting principles.

In *Coleman* and in those examples, the cash was paid to the taxpayer to compensate him for a difference in net values (fair market value less mortgage) in the properties exchanged and to enable him to pay off (or to compensate him for assuming) the mortgage on the property he was to receive. Where cash boot is paid to account for differences in net values in the properties, the taxpayer has received non-like-kind property—the cash—which he is free to dispose of as he wishes. He may, but need not, use the money to pay off the mortgage on the property he has received. This is the key factor which distinguishes *Coleman* and the examples in the regulations from the case before us.

The second issue concerns the useful life of the buildings on the Casa El Camino lots. Each of these buildings was new. Respondent determined that the useful life for these buildings was 30 years and adjusted the depreciation deduction accordingly. At trial, petitioner introduced no evidence regarding the useful life of these buildings. Accordingly, respondent's determination is sustained. Rule 142(a), Tax Court Rules of Practice and Procedure.

Decision will be entered under Rule 155.

Black v. Commissioner

United States Tax Court

35 T.C. 90 (1960)

FACTS

Petitioner is a single person, and a resident of Phoenix, Arizona. She filed an individual income tax return and two amended returns for the year 1955 with the district director of internal revenue for Arizona.

Prior to July 29, 1955, and from 1940, petitioner owned 200 acres of unimproved desert land situated in Maricopa County, Arizona. She was not employed. She resided in a rented "court" at 2627 North Central Avenue in Phoenix.

On July 29, 1955, petitioner, as seller, and Philo C. Carter, a real estate broker of Glendale, Arizona, as buyer, entered into escrow agreement No. 9248, upon the closing of which she would exchange her desert land for a total consideration of $19,500, to consist of residential property at a value of $7,500, a purchase money mortgage in the amount of $11,000, and $1,000 in cash. On the same date, Carter, as seller, and petitioner, as buyer, entered into escrow agreement No. 9247, upon the closing of which petitioner would acquire the residential property as a stated value of $7,500 as a "credit by trade" of the property covered by escrow agreement No. 9248. The closing under each escrow agreement was contingent on the concurrent closing of the other. The cost to petitioner of the desert land was $2,035 and her cost in making the exchange was $147.91, resulting in a net gain to her of $17,317.09.

Under escrow agreement No. 9248 covering transfer by petitioner of the desert property, the $11,000 purchase money mortgage was payable as follows:

> In annual installments of $2,200.00 or more on or before the 1st of September
> of each and every year, beginning 9/1/56, with interest on all unpaid principal
> at the rate of 5% per annum from 9/1/55, payable annually and in addition
> to the payments of principal.

On August 10, 1955, Carter authorized and directed the escrow agent to show Arizona Rochester Development Corporation, an Arizona corporation, as nominee. Petitioner had no dealings with that corporation.

The escrows were closed on an undetermined date, probably between August 10 and August 31, 1955. At some undetermined time, either prior to or shortly after the closing of the escrows, the persons who had been occupying the residence vacated it. It appeared to petitioner that the property "needed fixing up," and she wanted to do the work herself. The property was situated about 6 miles from where she was living and to reach it she was required to go by public transportation, make a transfer, and then walk about a mile and a half. The trips back and forth would absorb some substantial portion of the time she desired to devote to the work, and it was more economical as well as more convenient for her to live on the property. Accordingly, on or about August 31, 1956, she moved into the house and had her mailing address changed to that location. Included in the work done was the painting of the outside of the house, which took considerable time. When she had completed the work she listed the property for sale with a real estate agent. She was living in the residence when it was sold in April 1956. She received $7,500 for the property. At all times after acquisition of the property she had held it primarily for sale.

In her original income tax return for 1955, filed on April 16, 1956, petitioner listed her address as 3214 West Northview Avenue, Phoenix, which was the address of the property in question. The only income reported was in the amount of $5,926.04, which was shown as long-term capital gain realized from the disposition of her desert property. Attached to the return was a computation reflecting $17,317.09 as the amount of gain realized, $11,852.09 as the amount of the gain to be recognized, and $5,926.04 as "long-term" gain, the amount taken into account for tax purposes. The $11,852.09 represented the mortgage of $11,000 and cash of $852.09 ($1,000 cash received less $147.91, cost of the exchange). At the bottom of the computation sheet was the following reference: "per Sec. 351, 356, 371, 1031, I.R.C.-1954," followed by "Sec. 112-c I.R.C.-1939." With a standard deduction in the amount of $592.60 and a personal exemption of $600, the taxable income reported was shown as $4,733.44, and the tax thereon as $1,030.69.

On June 15, 1956, petitioner filed an amended return for 1955. At that time, her address was given as 4136 North 19th Street, Phoenix. In a computation attached to the return, the market value of the $11,000 mortgage was stated to be $8,800, which resulted in a showing that there was realized a gain of $15,117.09, a recognized gain of $9,652.09, and a taxable "long-term" gain of $4,826.05. The tax liability was reported as $783, and an overpayment of the tax was shown as $247.69.

On October 2, 1956, petitioner filed a second amended return for 1955. In this return, she was shown to have elected to report the gain from the sale or exchange on the installment basis, the basis therefor being that the $11,000 was payable at the rate of $2,200 per year for 5 years, commencing September 1, 1956. The computation showed a realization of long-term capital gain of $1,000, an exclusion of long-term capital gain of $500 and income of long-term capital of $500, resulting in the reporting of "No Tax" due and an overpayment, described as "Paid on original return," of $40, refund of which was requested.

Respondent determined that the long-term capital gain to be recognized from the exchange was $17,317.09, and not $11,852.09, as reported by petitioner.

At the time of the exchange petitioner acquired the new property as other property to be held primarily for sale.

ANALYSIS

The question presented is whether upon the disposition by petitioner of her desert property the gain realized to the extent of the fair market value of the residential property received in exchange is not, § section 1031(b) of the Internal Revenue Code of 1954, to be recognized. Respondent has determined that the exchange does not meet the statutory requirements for nonrecognition of the gain in question. Both parties have accepted $7,500 as the fair market value of the residential property received.

In §1031(a) of the Code, it is provided that "(n)o gain or loss shall be recognized if property held for productive use in trade or business or for investment (not including stock in trade or other property held primarily for sale ...) is exchanged solely for property of a like kind to be held either for productive use in trade or business or for investment." If, however, the property received in exchange includes money or property other than property permitted under subsection (a) to be received without recognition of gain, then under subsection (b) the gain is to be recognized to the extent of "the sum of such money and the fair market value of such other property."

According to §1.1002-1(b) of the Income Tax Regulations, exceptions to the general rule, including the exceptions provided in §1031 of the Code, "are strictly construed and do not extend either beyond the words or the underlying assumptions and purposes of the exception." According to subsection (c) of that section, "(t)he underlying assumption of these exceptions is that the new property is substantially a continuation of the old investment still unliquidated."

Similar language has been used in regulations extending back to those promulgated under the Revenue Act of 1934.

With respect to the exception provided in §1031 of the Code, the definition of "like kind" is stated in section 1.1031(a)-1(b) of the Income Tax Regulations, as follows:

> As used in section 1031(a), the words "like kind" have reference to the nature or character of the property and not to its grade or quality. One kind or class of property may not, under that section, be exchanged for property of a different kind or class. The fact that any real estate involved is improved or unimproved is not material, for that fact relates only to the grade or quality of the property and not to its kind or class. Unproductive real estate held by one other than a dealer for future use or future realization of the increment in value is held for investment and not primarily for sale.

"Like kind" has been similarly defined in prior regulations, extending back to the Revenue Act of 1924. Regs. 118, §39.112(b)(1)-1; Regs. 111, §29.112(b)(1)-1; Regs. 103, §19.112(b)(1)-1; Regs. 101, art. 112(b)(1)-1; Regs. 94, art. 112(b)(1)-1; Regs. 86, art. 112(b)(1)-1; Regs. 77, art. 572 (§112, 1932 Act); Regs. 69, art. 1572(a) (§203, 1926 Act); Regs. 65, art. 1572(a) (§203, 1924 Act).

That the desert land was held for investment appears to be accepted by both parties, and according to the regulations there is an underlying assumption that residential property received in exchange was substantially a continuation of the old investment still unliquidated. That is not to say, however, that the exceptions are not to be given full force and effect even though they are to be strictly construed and do not extend either beyond the words or the underlying assumptions and purposes of the exceptions. Our inquiry accordingly must be directed to the exceptions, and to whether or not the residential property is covered thereby.

Admittedly, the desert property, the property exchanged, was not property held for productive use, and though at the trial there was some reference to a possible holding of the residential property for rent, the petitioner makes no claim that it was ever so held, but rather, contends that within the meaning of the statute it was property of a like kind to be held for investment.

From a reading of the wording of the exception, it is apparent, we think, that if the exception did cover the property in question it was because it was either stock in trade or other property held primarily for sale. On the facts here, we may pass the stock-in-trade category without any detailed discussion, since it is patent on the record before us that petitioner was not engaged in a business of buying and selling real estate or in any other business during the pertinent period, and thus the residential property acquired could not have been, as to her, stock in trade. We are of the view, however, that on the evidence the property when acquired was 'to be held' and was in fact held by petitioner primarily for sale. It was petitioner's testimony that she accepted Carter's offer for her desert property which called for part payment in the residential property because she thought it was the best "deal" she could get. And while on direct testimony she did testify that in acquiring the property she was undecided whether to rent, sell, or just hold it and after acquiring it she had thought of renting it, she later testified on cross-examination that she was at all times attempting to sell the property and when she had finished her painting and other work she placed it in the hands of a real estate agent for sale, the sale being effected very shortly while she was still residing in the house. We are accordingly convinced that petitioner did not acquire the property to be held as an unliquidated continuation of the old property and for investment, but that at all times it was held primarily for sale, and we hold that the gain represented thereby falls within the exception to § 1031(a) and must be recognized.

To support her position that the property was not held primarily for sale within the meaning of § 1031(a), petitioner cites and relies on *Loughborough Development Corporation*, 29 B.T.A. 95 (1933), and *Atlantic Coast Realty Co.*, 11 B.T.A. 416 (1928). Neither case is in point. In the Atlantic Coast Realty case, the question was whether a corporation engaged in buying and selling land was entitled to have its income determined by the use of inventories. The question here and the applicable statutory provision are wholly different.

In Loughborough Development Corporation, the question was whether gain from the sale of real estate by a corporation which under its charter was authorized to engage in the real estate business was capital gain under the capital gains provisions of the statute or ordinary income, the basis for the latter being that the gain on the real estate was on the sale of property "held by the taxpayer primarily for sale to customers in the ordinary course of his trade or business." It was there found on the evidence that the property sold had not been so held, and it was held that it made no difference that the taxpayer was authorized by its charter to engage in the business of buying and selling real estate and that the particular real estate was not brought within the exception to the capital gains statute if in fact the real estate was not held primarily for sale to customers in the ordinary course of the taxpayer's business.

In the instant case, we are dealing with an entirely different statute, namely, § 1031, and as to that section the words "for sale to customers in the ordinary course of" the taxpayer's trade or business are quite conspicuous by their absence. For the exception in § 1031 to apply, there is no requirement that the taxpayer be conducting a trade or business, or that the property in question be held "for sale to customers in the ordinary course of" a trade or business carried on by the taxpayer. There can be no question, we think, that had it been intended that the scope of the exception in § 1031 should be so limited, language comparable to that used in the capital gains provisions, and which was in question in Loughborough Development Corporation, would likewise have been used in § 1031. The only requirement for applicability of the exception in § 1031 is that the property received in exchange be "held primarily for sale." The record shows that the residence was so held, and we accordingly hold that the non-recognition-of-gain provisions of that section does not apply.

Land Dynamics v. Commissioner

United States Tax Court

37 T.C.M. (CCH) 1119 (1978)

FACTS

Some of the facts have been stipulated and are so found. The stipulation of facts, together with the exhibits attached thereto, are incorporated herein by this reference.

At the time of filing the petition herein petitioner, Land Dynamics, formerly known as Bonanza Enterprises and successor-in-interest to Bonadelle Enterprises, Bonadelle Ranchos, J.P.B. Homes, Bonadelle Land Company, J.P.B. Land Company, Bonadelle Construction Company, P. and J. Construction Company, Bonadelle Land Sales, Bonadelle Development Company and Bonadelle Homes, Inc., pursuant to a reorganization effective September 1970, was organized under the laws of the State of California with its principal place of business in Fresno, California.

During the taxable years ended February, 1969, February, 1970, February, 1971 and July 31, 1971, Bonadelle Ranchos was a California corporation and filed corporate income tax returns for said years. It was engaged in the business of real estate development and sales.

In the calendar year 1966, Bonadelle Ranchos acquired 60 acres of realty (hereinafter referred to as the Arbelbide parcel) in Fresno, California. At date of acquisition said parcel was raw land and up to and including its fiscal year ended February 28, 1970, Bonadelle Ranchos developed the parcel into an orange grove and harvested a single crop from said grove.

During the fiscal year ended February 28, 1970, Bonadelle Ranchos exchanged the Arbelbide property (which now consisted of orange trees, building and pipeline) for property consisting of 1,315 acres of grassland in the County of Tulare, State of California (hereinafter referred to as the Tulare property).

Petitioner did not subdivide either the Arbelbide or the Tulare properties. The Tulare property was sold, in its entirety, to one purchaser during the taxable year ended December 31, 1971. Additionally, such property was not offered for sale until its actual sale in 1971.

The exchange of the Arbelbide property for the Tulare property was entered on the books and records of Bonadelle Ranchos as a tax-free exchange at the time that the transaction occurred.

Respondent in his notice of deficiency, dated December 12, 1975, determined that the exchange did not qualify as a nontaxable exchange under § 1031(a) inasmuch as there was "an exchange of investment property for property held primarily for sale in a trade or business." Respondent then allocated the $110,721 gain realized on the exchange between § 1245 gain ($6,827) and § 1231 gain ($103,894).

ANALYSIS

The parties agree upon the law applicable herein, to wit: Under § 1031(a) no gain or loss is recognized when property held for the productive use in a trade or business or for investment, is exchanged solely for property of a like kind which is also held either for the productive use in a trade or business or for investment. If, however, the property received in the exchange includes money or property other than property permitted under subsection (a) then gain is recognized to the extent of the sum of money and the fair market value of such other property. Section 1031(b). Property not qualifying under subsection (a) includes "property held primarily for sale." Moreover there is no requirement that the property be held primarily "for sale to customers in the ordinary course of" a trade or business carried on by taxpayer, but only that the property be "held primarily for sale." *Woodbury v. Comm'r*, 49 T.C. 180, 197 (1967); 3 Mertens Law of Federal Income Taxation, sec. 20.26, p. 96 (1972 rev.). Finally, the parties agree that the term "primarily" means "of first importance, or principally." See *Malat v. Riddell*, 383 U.S. 569, 572 (1966).

As previously stated respondent in his notice of deficiency determined the exchange did not qualify under § 1031 inasmuch as there was an exchange of investment property (Arbelbide) for property held primarily for sale in a trade or business (Tulare). Consequently, the issue is narrowly drawn and our focus is solely upon the characterization of the Tulare property received and held by petitioner.

Moreover as previously stated petitioner is in the business of real estate development and sales. A preliminary prospectus prepared in 1972 for the sale of additional shares of petitioner's common stock stated, particularly, that petitioner is primarily engaged in the business of (1) on-site construction and sale of moderately priced single family homes; (2) the acquisition, subdivision and sale of land for recreational and second-home sites; (3) the acquisition, development and sale of agriculture properties; and (4) the purchase and sale of residential and commercial land. In connection with the recreational land developments parcels of land, customarily mountain or foothill properties, are acquired by petitioner. If because of the topography or other reasons the land is not suitable for recreational or second homesite subdivisions, it is sold in bulk. The Tulare property sold prior to the prospective date, was one of these bulk sales sold prior to December 31, 1971. Additionally the prospectus provided that petitioner:

> [A]cquires land for use in its real estate programs and not for investment.
> Its land acquisition policy is to acquire sites which are suitable for residential

development within a period of three to five years, sites which are suitable for recreational development within two to three years, and sites which are suitable for agricultural development and sale within one to three years.

Therefore based on the above respondent contends on brief that, if one assumes petitioner acquired Tulare without knowledge that it could not be subdivided, then the primary purpose for acquisition was subdivision for sale. Alternatively, if petitioner had knowledge that the property could not be subdivided, then the property was acquired solely for bulk sale. In either event, the acquisition of Tulare falls outside § 1031(a).

Petitioner replies that there are exceptions to its general policy of not acquiring land for investment purposes. It relies upon the testimony of its officer and general counsel in support thereof. The general counsel was employed by petitioner in November of 1971 and was involved in the preparation, accuracy and filing of the prospectus. However, we note that he had no personal knowledge of the Arbelbide-Tulare exchange and testified that he didn't "know whether it was an exception or not" to the corporation's policy of not acquiring land for investment.

Also petitioner contends that, if the Tulare property, grazing land, was not suitable for development and sale as recreational land development property, then it could not be held for sale for that purpose, i.e.: it was not part of petitioner's inventory of recreational land. It simply was grassland and was not listed or offered for sale prior to its sale in 1971, two years after its acquisition.

We recognize that it is well established that petitioner, a dealer in land, may also acquire and hold real property for investment purposes. *Maddux Construction Co. v. Comm'r*, 54 T.C. 1278, 1286 (1970). "(A) subsequent sale is not conclusive on the question of the primary purpose in acquiring and holding real estate." *Municipal Bond Corporation v. Comm'r*, 382 F.2d 184, 188 (8th Cir. 1967). However the fact that land was held for many years does not establish an intention to hold the property for investment rather than sale. *Stockton Harbor Indus. Co. v. Comm'r*, 216 F.2d 638, 655 (9th Cir. 1954), *affg.* a Memorandum Opinion of this Court, cert. denied 349 U.S. 904 (1955). In short, petitioner has been active as a dealer in the purchase and sale of realty. It has the burden of proving that "when ... (it) dealt with the parcels of land (involved herein) ... (it) was wearing the hat of an investor rather than that of a dealer." *Pritchett v. Comm'r*, 63 T.C. 149, 164 (1974).

Herein petitioner has not submitted one iota of evidence to prove its investor status in connection with its holding of the Tulare property. Based upon the record presented we only can draw negative inferences and conclude that the exchange does not qualify under § 1031(a).

Chapter 11

Structuring Gain-Deferral Transactions

I. Commentary

If an exchange will satisfy the like-kind property requirement and the holding and use requirement, often the challenge will be to ensure that the transaction satisfies the exchange requirement. Property owners often agree to sell relinquished property to one buyer and acquire like-kind property from a different seller. Case law provides that if the property owner does not actually or constructively receive cash or non-like-kind property, a multiple-party exchange can qualify for section 1031 nonrecognition.[1] Time might pass between the disposition of the relinquished property and the acquisition of the replacement property. Section 1031 allows deferred exchanges. An exchange may qualify for section 1031 nonrecognition if the exchanger identifies replacement property within 45 days after the transfer of the relinquished property and acquires replacement property within 180 days after the transfer of the relinquished property.[2] Thus, exchangers may do deferred multiple-party exchanges.

The deferred multiple-party exchange presents many challenges. First, the exchanger will want some assurance that the exchange proceeds are secure while the exchange is pending. The exchanger may wish to control the proceeds held by the facilitator, but too much control by the exchanger would put the exchanger in actual or constructive receipt of them and cause the transaction to fail the exchange requirement.

---

1. *See, e.g.*, Biggs v. Commissioner, 632 F.2d 1171 (5th Cir. 1980); Starker v. United States, 602 F.2d 1341 (9th Cir. 1979); Mercantile Trust Co. v. Commissioner, 32 B.T.A. 82 (1935).

2. *See* I.R.C. § 1031(a)(3). The 180-day exchange period may be shortened if the exchanger's tax return due date (for the year the relinquished property was transferred) is before the end of the 180-day period. *Id. See also* Treas. Reg. § 1.1031(k)-1(b)-(d). Taxpayers may identify more than one replacement property under the 3-property rule and the 200-percent rule. *See* Treas. Reg. § 1.1031(k)-1(c)(4).

Treasury has published safe harbors that help exchangers accomplish section 1031 exchanges with some assurance that they will not be in actual or constructive receipt of exchange proceeds.[3] The three most prevalent safe harbors are the qualified intermediary, the qualified trust, and the qualified escrow account. Each safe harbor has several requirements that an exchanger must satisfy to obtain the certainty the safe harbors afford. The examples in the regulations illustrate the type of structures taxpayers may utilize with the safe harbors.[4]

Second, the party that facilitates the exchange often will prefer not to enter the chain of title of any of the exchange properties. Courts have held that a multiple-party transaction can satisfy the exchange requirement even if the facilitator does not take legal title to the exchange properties.[5] The qualified intermediary safe harbor regulations provide strict rules for direct-deed transfers that, if followed, will help the exchanger accomplish a reciprocal transfer for tax purposes in a multiple-party exchange.[6] Attorneys must carefully read the safe-harbor rules to suss out the requirements that govern direct-deeding.

Third, related-party-exchange rules may apply to multiple-party exchanges. Direct and indirect exchanges with related parties can qualify for section 1031 nonrecognition, but they are subject to special rules.[7] Parties to a direct related-party exchange generally must hold the exchange properties for two years following the exchange for the exchange to qualify for nonrecognition.[8] The rules governing indirect related-party exchanges are more complicated.[9] Attorneys must be aware of those rules if related parties are part of an indirect exchange and consider whether they may help the exchanger plan to avoid the negative consequences that may derive from a related-party exchange. When examining the authorities that have addressed related-party exchanges, attorneys should consider whether the application of the rules governing related-party exchanges depends upon whether the exchanger acquires property from a related party or transfers property to a related party. Also consider how the purposes (i.e., to prevent basis-shifting and cashing-out) of the rules governing related-party exchanges may affect when the rules apply.

---

3. See Treas. Reg. § 1.1031(k)-1(g). Chapter 12 provides more opportunity to consider ways to help protect exchange proceeds.

4. *See* Treas. Reg. § 1.1031(k)-1(g)(8).

5. *See* Biggs v. Commissioner, 632 F.2d 1171 (5th Cir. 1980); Coastal Terminals, Inc. v. United States, 320 F.2d 333 (4th Cir. 1963).

6. *But see* Treas. Reg. § 1.1031(k)-1(g)(4) (enumerating the requirement that a qualified intermediary must acquire and transfer the relinquished and replacement properties).

7. *See* I.R.C. § 1031(f).

8. *See* I.R.C. § 1031(f).

9. *See, e.g.*, Teruya Bros., Ltd. v. Comm'r, 580 F.3d 1038 (9th Cir. 2009); Rev. Rul. 2002-83, 2002-2 C.B. 927; Priv. Ltr. Rul. 2007-09-036 (Nov. 28, 2006).

II. Primary Legal Authority

Teruya Brothers, Ltd. v. Commissioner

United States Court of Appeals, Ninth Circuit

580 F.3d 1038 (2009)

FACTS

Teruya Brothers, Ltd. ("Teruya") is a Hawaii corporation involved in, among other things, the purchase and development of residential and commercial real estate. This appeal concerns the tax treatment of real estate transactions involving two of Teruya's properties, the Ocean Vista condominium complex ("Ocean Vista"), and the Royal Towers Apartment building ("Royal Towers").

Teruya owned a fee simple interest in a parcel of land underlying the Ocean Vista complex in Honolulu, Hawaii. Golden Century Investments Company ("Golden") held a long-term lease on the land, and the Association of Apartment Owners of Ocean Vista ("the Association") held a sublease on the property.

In March 1993, the Association wrote to Teruya, inquiring about the possibility of purchasing Ocean Vista. Teruya responded that it was not interested in selling, though it later told Golden, which was also interested in the property, that it might part with the land through a like-kind exchange.

Following a series of negotiations, Golden sent a letter of intent to purchase Ocean Vista from Teruya for $1,468,500. It also offered its cooperation "so that Teruya can effectuate a [§] 1031 tax deferred exchange of Teruya's [i]nterests." The letter of intent was later amended to state, "It is understood and agreed that Teruya's obligation to sell Teruya's interests to [Golden] is conditioned upon Teruya consummating a [§] 1031 tax deferred exchange of Teruya's [i]nterests."

In June 1994, Teruya proposed purchasing real property known as Kupuohi II from Times Super Market, Ltd. ("Times"), a company in which it owned 62.5% of the common shares. The proposal stated that "The purchase will be subject to a [§] 1031 four party exchange," and allowed Teruya to cancel the proposed purchase "should the Ocean Vista transaction fail to proceed according to present plans." Times agreed to sell Kupuohi II for $2,828,000.

On April 3, 1995, the Association made a formal offer to purchase Ocean Vista for $1,468,500,[10] which Teruya accepted. The parties' contract provided that "Teruya may, in its sole discretion, structure this transaction as a tax-deferred exchange pursuant to § 1031 of the Internal Revenue Code." The contract also included as a condition precedent to the sale that "Teruya shall be in a position to close on its exchange replacement properties."

---

10. [2] Teruya, Golden, and the Association had executed an Assignment, Assumption, and Release which substituted the Association for Golden.

In August, T.G. Exchange, Inc. ("TGE") contracted to act as an "exchange party to complete the exchange" of Ocean Vista. TGE would convey Ocean Vista to the Association, and then acquire replacement property for Teruya with the Ocean Vista sale proceeds, all with the stated purpose of qualifying the exchange under 26 U.S.C. § 1031. Teruya agreed to identify suitable replacement property, and to provide any funds in excess of the Ocean Vista sale proceeds needed to purchase the replacement property. The parties agreed that if Teruya could not locate suitable replacement property, the contract between Teruya and TGE would be terminated.

On September 1, 1995, per the agreement, TGE sold Ocean Vista to the Association for $1,468,500. That same day, TGE used the proceeds from the Ocean Vista sale along with an additional $1,366,056 from Teruya to purchase Kupuohi II from Times for $2,828,000.[11] TGE then transferred Kupuohi II to Teruya.

Teruya's basis in Ocean Vista was $93,270, but it deferred recognizing gain on its $1,345,169 in post-expense profits under the like-kind exchange provisions of 26 U.S.C. § 1031. Times had a basis in Kupuohi II of $1,475, 361, and realized and recognized a $1,352,639 gain on the property's sale. Times paid no tax on this gain, however, because it had a large net operating loss for the tax year in question.

In sum, before the transaction Teruya owned Ocean Vista and Times owned Kupuohi II. After the exchange, Teruya owned Kupuohi II, the Association owned Ocean Vista, and Times had the cash from the sale of Ocean Vista (along with additional funds from Teruya).

The Royal Towers exchange substantially mirrored the Ocean Vista transaction.

In 1994 Teruya owned a fee simple interest in Royal Towers, an apartment complex in Honolulu, Hawaii. Late that year, Teruya agreed to sell Royal Towers to Savio Development Company ("Savio") for $13.5 million (later negotiated down to $11,932,000). As with the Ocean Vista transaction, this agreement was expressly conditioned on Teruya successfully completing a § 1031 exchange.

Anticipating that Royal Towers would soon be sold, in September 1994 Teruya sent Times a letter of intent to purchase two pieces of land known respectively as Kupuohi I and Kaahumanu. The letter was materially identical to the one Teruya sent to Times regarding Kupuohi II, and stated that "[t]he purchase will be subject to a [§] 1031 four party exchange," and that Teruya could cancel the proposed purchase "should the sale of the Royal Towers apartment fail to proceed according to present plans." Both companies' boards of directors approved the two properties' sale in early 1995, with Kupuohi I to be sold for $8,900,000, and Kaahumanu for $3,730,000.

In August 1995, Teruya contracted with TGE in order to qualify the exchange under § 1031. Similar to its agreement concerning the Ocean Vista exchange (which would be signed two days later), TGE would convey Royal Towers to Saito, acquiring re-

---

11. [3] As the Tax Court noted below, some of the numbers in the parties' stipulation of facts yield computational inconsistencies. Where the Tax Court made express findings as to the correct figures, we adopt and incorporate those determinations. As the precise numbers involved are not relevant to this appeal, we otherwise leave in place the parties' stipulated figures without further notation.

placement property for Teruya with the Royal Tower sale proceeds. Teruya agreed to identify suitable replacement property, and to provide any funds in excess of the Royal Towers sale proceeds needed to purchase the replacement property. The parties agreed that if Teruya could not locate suitable replacement property, the agreement between Teruya and TGE would be terminated.

TGE sold Royal Towers to Saito on August 24, 1995 for $11,932,000. Also on August 24, TGE used the proceeds from the Royal Towers sale along with $724,554 in additional funds from Teruya to purchase Kupuohi I and Kaahumanu from Times for $8,900,000 and $3,730,000, respectively. TGE then transferred the two properties to Teruya.

Teruya's basis in Royal Towers was $670,506, but it deferred the recognition of its $10,700,878 in post-expenses profits under 26 U.S.C. § 1031. Times had a basis in Kaahumanu of $1,502,960, and realized and recognized a $2,227,040 gain on the property's sale. Just as with Kupuohi II, though, Times paid no tax on this gain because it had a large net operating loss for the tax year in question.

Times had a basis in Kupuohi I of $15,602,152, and realized a capital loss of $6,453,372 on its sale. It did not recognize this loss, however, because 26 U.S.C. § 267 prohibits the recognition of losses from sales and exchanges of property between "related parties."[12]

In sum, before the exchanges Teruya owned Royal Towers and Times owned Kupuohi I and Kaahumanu. Afterwards, Teruya owned Kupuohi I and Kaahumanu, Savio owned Royal Towers, and Times held the cash from the sale of Royal Towers to Savio (along with additional funds from Teruya).

On its corporate income tax return for the taxable year ending March 31, 1996, Teruya, pursuant to 26 U.S.C. § 1031, deferred gain of $1,345,169 from the Ocean Vista transaction, and $10,700,878 from the Royal Towers transaction.

Rejecting Teruya's treatment of the exchanges, the IRS issued Teruya a notice of deficiency of $4,144,359 for the tax year ending March 31, 1996. Teruya petitioned the Tax Court for a redetermination. The Tax Court considered the petition on the basis of stipulated facts, and it affirmed the IRS's non-recognition treatment in a published opinion. See *Teruya Bros., Ltd. & Subsidiaries v. Comm'r*, 124 T.C. 45 (2005). This timely appeal followed.

ANALYSIS

26 U.S.C. § 1031(a)(1) is a well-worn exception to the general rule that taxpayers must recognize gains or losses realized from the disposition of property in the year of realization. See 26 U.S.C. § 1001(c). Rather, in a so-called "section 1031" exchange, gain realized on the exchange of like-kind property held for productive business use or investment need not be recognized until the acquired property is finally disposed

---

12. [4] The definition of "related person" is drawn from 26 U.S.C. §§ 267(b) and 707(b)(1), and includes, *inter alia*, family members, partnerships, and entities over which the taxpayer has control (or which control the taxpayer). See 26 U.S.C. § 1031(f)(3). Teruya has stipulated that at all times relevant to this litigation it and Times were "related parties."

of. To preserve the appropriate tax consequences, the taxpayer retains his original basis in the newly acquired property. *Id.* at § 1031(d).

The concept behind this exception derives from the assumption that when an investor exchanges a piece of property for another of like-kind, he is merely continuing an ongoing investment, rather than ridding himself of one investment to obtain another. *See Starker v. United States*, 602 F.2d 1341, 1352 (9th Cir.1979) ("The legislative history [of § 1031] reveals that the provision was designed to avoid the imposition of a tax on those who do not 'cash in' on their investments in trade or business property."). "In effect, the nonrecognition provisions further defer tax consequences when, notwithstanding an exchange, the taxpayer maintains a continuing interest in similar property." 2 BORIS BITTKER & LAWRENCE LOKKEN, FEDERAL TAXATION OF INCOME, ESTATES AND GIFTS, (3d ed.2000), ¶ 44.1.1.

Before 1989, taxpayers acting in concert could lawfully use § 1031 to defer the recognition of gain or accelerate the recognition of loss even as they cashed out of their investments, as indicated by the following example:

> [A]ssume *T* owns Blackacre, which is worth $100 and has a basis of $20, and her wholly owned corporation, *C* Corp., owns like kind property (Whiteacre), which is also worth $100 but has a basis of $140; *T* and *C* swap, and *C* immediately sells Blackacre to an unrelated person. If *T* had sold Blackacre, she would have recognized gain of $80, but *C*, whose $140 basis for Whiteacre becomes its basis for Blackacre, recognizes loss of $40.... [T]he presale exchange ... [has] the effect of deferring recognition of *T*'s potential gain and accelerating recognition of *C*'s $40 loss.

Id. ¶ 44.2.8.

Congress enacted § 1031(f) in 1989, largely eliminating what it considered to be a tax loophole contained in the section. *See* Omnibus Budget Reconciliation Act of 1989, Pub. L. No. 101-239, § 7601, 103 Stat. 2106 (1989). Section 1031(f)(1) largely precludes the nonrecognition treatment of gain or loss when a taxpayer exchanges like-kind property with a related person, and when either party then disposes of the exchanged property within two years.

Congress also included § 1031(f)(4), which provides that a taxpayer may not claim nonrecognition treatment under § 1031 for "any exchange which is part of a transaction (or series of transactions) structured to avoid the purposes of [§ 1031(f)]."

Section 1031(f) includes several exceptions, as well. As relevant here, exchanges that otherwise run afoul of § 1031(f)(1)'s requirements may still qualify for nonrecognition treatment where "it is established to the satisfaction of the Secretary that neither the exchange nor [the subsequent property] disposition had as one of its principal purposes the avoidance of Federal income tax." § 1031(f)(2)(C).[13]

---

13. [6] Nonrecognition treatment is also accorded to otherwise improper like kind exchanges where the property is disposed of after the taxpayer's or related party's death, or in a compulsory or involuntary conversion. *See* § 1031(f)(2)(A)-(B).

We review the Tax Court's conclusions of law and interpretations of the tax code de novo. *Westpac Pac. Food v. Comm'r*, 451 F.3d 970, 974 (9th Cir.2006). We review the Tax Court's factual findings, including factual inferences drawn from a stipulated record, for clear error. *Smith v. Comm'r*, 300 F.3d 1023, 1028 (9th Cir.2002).

In conducting our analysis, we are mindful of the fact that tax classifications "turn on 'the objective economic realities of a transaction rather than … the particular form the parties employed." *Boulware v. U.S.*, 552 U.S. 421 (2008) (quoting *Frank Lyon Co. v. U.S.*, 435 U.S. 561, 573 (1978)). Exceptions to the general rule requiring the recognition of all gains and losses on property dispositions are to be "strictly construed and do not extend either beyond the words or the underlying assumptions and purposes of the exception." 26 CFR 1.1002-1(b). Thus, "[n]onrecognition is accorded by the Code only if the exchange is one which satisfies both (1) the specific description in the Code of an excepted exchange, and (2) the underlying purpose for which such exchange is excepted from the general rule." *Id.*[14]

As an initial matter, the government quite properly concedes that the Ocean Vista and Royal Towers transactions both qualify as like-kind exchanges under § 1031(a)(1). Indeed, although significantly more complex than "traditional" two-party transactions, four-party like-kind exchanges like those utilized here have existed for nearly as long as the § 1031 exception itself. *See, e.g., Mercantile Trust Co. v. Comm'r*, 32 B.T.A. 82 (1935). The Tax Court has succinctly described such exchanges' general form:

> Involved in this type of exchange is a taxpayer desiring to exchange property, a prospective purchaser of the taxpayer's property, a prospective seller of the property the taxpayer wishes to receive in exchange, and a fourth party. In a simultaneously executed transaction (usually done through escrow) the fourth party receives the taxpayer's property and sells that property to the prospective purchaser. With the funds he receives, he purchases the prospective seller's property and then transfers that property to the taxpayer. When the smoke has cleared, the taxpayer has exchanged his property in a so-called 1031 transaction, the prospective purchaser has the taxpayer's property, the prospective seller has cash, and the fourth party, with the exception of agreed compensation, nothing.

Coupe v. Comm'r, 52 T.C. 394, 405, 1969 WL 1553 (1969) (citing *Mercantile Trust*, 32 B.T.A. 82). Applying this framework to our case, Teruya is the taxpayer, Times the prospective seller, the Association and Saito each prospective purchasers, and TGE the "fourth party," or qualified intermediary.[15]

---

14. [7] The examination in this case began before the July 22, 1998 effective date of 26 U.S.C. § 7491, so that section's burden-shifting rules do not apply here. *See* Internal Revenue Service Restructuring and Reform Act of 1998, Pub L. No. 105-206, Title III, § 3001(a), 112 Stat. 685, 726–27 (1998).

15. [8] A qualified intermediary is a person, not the taxpayer or one closely related to him, who "[e]nters into a written agreement with the taxpayer … and, as required by the exchange agreement, acquires the relinquished property from the taxpayer, transfers the relinquished property, acquires

The government also does not argue that § 1031(f)(1)'s restrictions on direct exchanges between related parties encompass these indirect transactions. For like-kind exchanges conducted through a qualified intermediary, as these were, "the qualified intermediary is not considered the agent of the taxpayer for purposes of section 1031(a)." 26 C.F.R. § 1.1031(k)-1(g)(4)(i). Teruya, therefore, may be said to have exchanged properties with TGE, not "with a related person," as required to implicate § 1031(f)(1).

Thus, these exchanges may only be denied nonrecognition treatment if they were "part of a transaction (or series of transactions) structured to avoid the purposes of [§ 1031(f)]." § 1031(f)(4).

The first step in determining whether these transactions were structured to avoid § 1031(f)'s purposes is, of course, identifying what those purposes are. To discern a statute's purposes, "we look first to the language of the statute and second to its legislative history." *In re Stringer*, 847 F.2d 549, 551 (9th Cir.1988). In this case, though, the statute's text provides precious few clues as to Congress's intent. Section 1031(f)'s existence alone tells us that Congress wanted to limit the ability of related parties to claim nonrecognition treatment for § 1031 exchanges. But, given that Teruya's exchanges are not expressly covered under § 1031(f)(1), it would beg the question to conclude from the statute's text alone that Congress wanted to deny these transactions nonrecognition treatment.

Accordingly, we turn to § 1031(f)'s legislative history.

The House Report accompanying § 1031(f) establishes that one of Congress's primary concerns in passing this legislation was its belief "that the 'like-kind' standard as applied to exchanges of property [wa]s too broad." H.R. Rep. No. 101-247, pt. 6, at 1340 (1989). "Under present law, taxpayers have been granted nonrecognition treatment ... in circumstances where they have significantly changed their investment as a result of the exchange or conversion." *Id*. Instead, the committee felt "it is appropriate to accord nonrecognition treatment only to exchanges and conversions where a taxpayer can be viewed as merely continuing his investment." *Id*.

Congress also wanted to prevent related parties from taking advantage of § 1031(d)'s basis-shifting provisions to avoid gains or accelerate losses on cashed-out investments. The House committee wrote:

> Because a like-kind exchange results in the substitution of the basis of the exchanged property for the property received, related parties have engaged in like-kind exchanges of high basis property for low basis property in anticipation of the sale of the low basis property in order to reduce or avoid the recognition of gain on the subsequent sale. Basis shifting also can be used to accelerate a loss on retained property. The committee believes that if a related party exchange is followed shortly thereafter by a disposition of the property, the related parties have, in effect, 'cashed out' of the investment, and the original exchange should not be accorded nonrecognition treatment.

---

the replacement property, and transfers the replacement property to the taxpayer." 26 C.F.R. § 1.1031(k)-1(g)(4)(iii).

Id.

Finally, the House committee offered an example of a transaction it intended § 1031(f)(4) to cover:

> [I]f a taxpayer, pursuant to a prearranged plan, transfers property to an unrelated party who then exchanges the property with a party related to the taxpayer within 2 years of the previous transfer in a transaction otherwise qualifying under section 1031, the related party will not be entitled to nonrecognition treatment under section 1031.

Id. at 1341.

With this legislative background in mind, we conclude that the Tax Court did not err in determining that the transactions were structured to avoid the purposes of § 1031(f)(4). Under the guise of a like-kind exchange, the transactions allowed related parties to receive nonrecognition treatment while cashing out of investments using § 1031's basis-shifting provisions. Precluding this type of tax result was one of Congress's primary aims in enacting § 1031(f)(4).

We first reject Teruya's contention that the economic consequences of these transactions to Times are irrelevant to our inquiry, and that Teruya's continued investment in real property is dispositive. Section 1031(f)(1)(C)(i) disallows nonrecognition treatment if the related party disposes of exchanged property within two years, regardless of whether the taxpayer does as well. Thus, examining the taxpayer and related party's economic position in aggregate is often the only way to tell if § 1031(f) applies. Moreover, Congress's concern about related taxpayers acting in concert, as well as the House Report's admonition that exchanges should not be accorded nonrecognition treatment where "the related *parties* have, in effect, 'cashed out' of the investment," H.R. Rep. No. 101-247, pt. 6, at 1340 (emphasis added), confirm that the taxpayer and the related party should be treated as an economic unit in this inquiry. Taxpayers cannot escape § 1031(f) simply by hiding the benefits of improper like-kind exchanges with a related party.

Here, the changing economic positions of Teruya and Times readily show that the related parties used these exchanges to cash out of an investment in low-basis real property. Before the exchanges, Teruya owned Ocean Vista and Royal Towers, and Times owned Kupuohi I, Kupuohi II, and Kaahumanu. After the exchanges, Ocean Vista and Royal Towers had been sold, Teruya owned Kupuohi I, Kupuohi II, and Kaahumanu, and Times now had the cash from the Ocean Vista and Royal Towers sale (along with boot from Teruya). All in all, Teruya and Times decreased their investment in real property by approximately $13.4 million, and increased their cash position by the same amount. By allowing Teruya and Times to cash out of a significant investment in real property under the guise of a non-taxable like-kind exchange, these transactions were undoubtedly structured in contravention of Congress's desire that nonrecognition treatment only apply to transactions "where a taxpayer can be viewed as merely continuing his investment." *See* H.R. Rep. No. 101-247, pt. 6, at 1340.

Indeed, as Teruya could have achieved the same property dispositions through far simpler means, it appears that these transactions took their peculiar structure for no purpose except to avoid § 1031(f). Teruya could have exchanged its properties directly with Times, followed by Times selling Ocean Vista and Royal Towers to the third-party purchasers. There was no need to use (and pay) a qualified intermediary. The rub, of course, is that Teruya couldn't have done this tax free, as direct exchanges between related parties are ineligible for nonrecognition treatment when the exchanged property is sold within two years. Instead, Teruya employed TGE, whose presence ensured that Teruya was technically exchanging properties with the qualified intermediary, not with its related party. TGE's involvement in these transactions thus served no purpose besides rendering simple—but tax disadvantageous—transactions more complex in order to avoid § 1031(f)'s restrictions.[16]

Our initial conclusion that these transactions were structured to avoid § 1031(f)'s purposes does not end our inquiry, for Teruya argues, and the Tax Court held below, that § 1031(f)(2) provides an additional limitation on § 1031(f)(4)'s scope.

As discussed previously, § 1031(f)(2) establishes several circumstances where a related party exchange may still qualify for nonrecognition treatment despite technically violating § 1031(f)(1). The broadest of these exceptions, § 1031(f)(2)(C), allows otherwise improper exchanges to earn nonrecognition treatment where "it is established to the satisfaction of the Secretary that neither the exchange nor [the subsequent] disposition had as one of its principal purposes the avoidance of Federal income tax."

By their plain language, § 1031(f)(2)'s exceptions only apply to exchanges that violate § 1031(f)(1), which, as discussed above, these exchanges do not. Still, the Tax Court held below that "[b]ecause [§ 1031(f)(2)] is subsumed within the purposes of § 1031(f), any inquiry into whether a transaction is structured to avoid the purposes of section § 1031(f) should also take this exception into consideration." *Teruya Brothers*, 124 T.C. at 53. We agree. Section 1031(f)(4) denies nonrecognition treatment only to those transactions that violate § 1031(f)(1)'s purposes. As transactions falling within § 1031(f)(2)'s exceptions by their very nature do not violate those purposes, § 1031(f)(2) must independently limit § 1031(f)(4)'s scope. In other words, a transaction does not violate § 1031(f)(4) if the taxpayer can establish "to the satisfaction

---

16. [9] We do not imply that taxpayers are precluded from using a qualified intermediary to facilitate a like-kind exchange with a related party. Qualified intermediaries may provide legitimate services to facilitate complex (but permissible) exchanges, such as by assisting with escrow. However, given the facts of this case, we conclude that the Tax Court did not clearly err in inferring that the qualified intermediary was interposed in this case in an attempt to circumvent the § 1031(f)(1) limitations. The government argues that every deferred exchange between related parties involving a qualified intermediary should be recast as a direct exchange between the related parties. Under that analysis, the government argues, if § 1031(f)(1) would preclude nonrecognition treatment for the recast transaction, then the deferred exchange should be deemed to have been structured to avoid the purposes of § 1031(f). The Tax Court properly rejected that mechanical theory as inconsistent with the structure of the statute.

of the Secretary" that the transaction did not have "as one of its principal purposes the avoidance of Federal income tax."

Despite our determination that § 1031(f)(2) independently limits § 1031(f)(4), we conclude that the record supports the Tax Court's determination that the improper avoidance of federal income tax was one of the principal purposes behind these exchanges. We therefore affirm the Tax Court's denial of nonrecognition treatment to Teruya.[17]

The Tax Court's conclusion that these transactions were structured for unwarranted tax avoidance purposes is supported by an examination of the tax consequences of the Royal Towers exchange. Had Teruya sold Royal Towers directly to Saito, it would have had to recognize nearly $11 million in gain. Because the transaction was presented as a like-kind exchange, however, only Times, which sold Kupuohi I and Kaahumanu to TGE, had to recognize any profit. However, Kaahumanu had a much higher basis than Royal Towers (relative to its fair market value), and Kupuohi I's basis far exceeded its fair market value. Thus, Times recognized only $2.2 million in gain on the transaction, far less than Teruya would have faced from the direct sale of Royal Towers. Moreover, Times paid no tax on even this smaller gain, as it was able to carry over net operating losses from previous years. Similarly, in the Ocean Vista transaction, though Times recognized gain virtually identical to that which Teruya deferred, Times paid no tax due to its net operating losses. Thus, the Teruya/Times economic unit achieved far more advantageous tax consequences by employing this unique structure than it would have had Teruya simply sold its properties to the third-party buyers itself.[18]

Teruya contends that it did not have an improper tax avoidance purpose because it never had any fixed right to cash at the time of these transactions; indeed, the exchanges could only have been completed as § 1031(a) like-kind exchanges. But this argument misses the point. Teruya's undisputed intent to complete successfully a like-kind exchange—perhaps germane to whether the transactions were exchanges or sales under § 1031(a)—is irrelevant to whether these transactions were structured to avoid § 1031(f)'s purposes. Moreover, by focusing only on its own continued investment in like-kind property, Teruya ignores the crucial tax consequences of these exchanges to its related party, Times.[19]

---

17. [11] In other contexts involving similar language, courts have disagreed on the standard to apply in reviewing whether a taxpayer has established a fact "to the satisfaction of the Secretary." *Compare* R.E. Dietz Corp. v. U.S., 939 F.2d 1, 5 (2d Cir.1991) (applying arbitrary and capricious standard), *with* Schoneberger v. Comm'r, 74 T.C. 1016, 1024, 1980 WL 4584 (1980) (applying "strong proof" standard). We need not decide the appropriate standard to apply, nor do we interpret the precise contours in this context of the phrase "to the satisfaction of the Secretary."

18. [12] Theoretically, the tax price to Times from reducing its net operating losses may have equaled or even exceeded the tax Teruya deferred, particularly in the Ocean Vista transaction. *See generally* Kelly Alton et al., *Related-Party Like-Kind Exchanges*, 115 TAX NOTES 467, at 26–27 (2007). We need not determine whether this possibility would evince a non-tax avoidance purpose, as Teruya has not argued the point on appeal.

19. [13] The Conference Committee Report to § 1031(f) suggests several kinds of transactions between related parties that "generally" will not have unwarranted tax avoidance as a principal purpose,

HOLDING

For the aforementioned reasons, we affirm the Tax Court's determination that these exchanges were structured to avoid the purposes of § 1031(f), and thus violate § 1031(f)(4).

Biggs v. Commissioner

United States Court of Appeals, Fifth Circuit
632 F.2d 1171 (1980)

FACTS

The numerous transactions which form the subject of this suit are somewhat confusing and each detail is of potential significance. Thus, it will be necessary to recount with particularity the facts as found by the Tax Court.

Biggs owned two parcels of land located in St. Martin's Neck, Worcester County, Maryland (hereinafter referred to as the "Maryland property"). Sometime before October 23, 1968, Biggs listed this property for sale with a realtor. The realtor advised Biggs that he had a client, Shepard G. Powell, who was interested in purchasing the property.

Biggs and Powell met on October 23, 1968 to discuss Powell's possible acquisition of the Maryland property. Biggs insisted from the outset that he receive real property of like kind as part of the consideration for the transfer. Both men understood that Biggs would locate the property he wished to receive in exchange, and Powell agreed to cooperate in the exchange arrangements to the extent that his own interests were not impaired.

On October 25, 1968, Biggs and Powell signed a memorandum of intent which provided, in pertinent part, the following:

I. PURCHASE PRICE: $900,000 NET to SELLERS.

    c. $25,000.00 down payment at signing of contract, ...

    d. $75,000.00 additional payment at time of settlement, which shall be within ninety (90) days after contract signing, making total cash payments of $100,000.00.

II. MORTGAGE:

    a. Balance of $800,000.00 secured by a first mortgage on Real Estate to SELLERS at a 4% interest rate; 10 year term.

The memorandum contained no mention of the contemplated exchange of properties. Upon learning of this omission, Biggs' attorney, W. Edgar Porter, told Powell

---

such as exchanges that do not involve basis shifting. *See* 101 H.R. Conf. Rep. No. 386, at 614. Teruya has not argued that its exchanges fall within these exceptions.

that the memorandum of intent did not comport with his understanding of the proposed transaction. Powell agreed to have his attorney meet with Porter to work out the terms of a written exchange agreement.

Biggs began his search for suitable exchange property by advising John Thatcher, a Maryland real estate broker, of the desired specifications. Subsequently, Biggs was contacted by another realtor, John A. Davis, who had in his inventory four parcels of land located in Accomack County, Virginia, collectively known as Myrtle Grove Farm (hereinafter referred to as "the Virginia property"). Biggs inspected the property, found it suitable, and instructed Davis to draft contracts of sale.

As initially drawn, the contracts named Biggs as the buyer of the Virginia property. However, at Porter's suggestion, they were modified to describe the purchaser as "Franklin B. Biggs (acting as agent for syndicate)." The contracts were executed on October 29th and 30th, 1968, and contained the following terms:

Paid on execution of contract	$13,900.00
Balance due at settlement	115,655.14
Indebtedness created or assumed	142,544.86
Total—Gross Sales Price	$272,100.00

Upon signing the contracts, Biggs paid $13,900.00 to the sellers of the Virginia property.

Because Powell was either unable or unwilling to take title to the Virginia property, Biggs arranged for the title to be transferred to Shore Title Company, Inc. (hereinafter referred to as "Shore"), a Maryland corporation owned and controlled by Porter and certain members of his family. However, it was not until December 26, 1968 that the purchase was authorized by Shore's board of directors. On January 9, 1969, prior to the transfer to Shore, Biggs and Shore entered into the following agreement with respect to the Virginia property:

1. At any time hereafter that either party hereto requests the other party to do so, Shore Title Co., Inc. will and hereby agrees to convey unto the said Franklin B. Biggs, or his nominee, all of the above mentioned property, for exactly the same price said Shore Title Co., Inc. has paid for it, plus any and all costs, expenses, advances or payments which Shore Title Co., Inc. has paid or will be bound in the future to pay, over and above said purchase price to Shore Title Co., Inc., in order for Shore Title Co., Inc., to acquire or hold title to said property; and it (is) further agreed that at that time, i.e.,—when Shore Title Co., Inc. conveys said property under this paragraph and its provisions, the said Franklin B. Biggs, or his nominee will simultaneously release or cause Shore Title Co., Inc. to be released from any and all obligations which the latter has created, assumed or become bound upon in its acquisition and holding of title to said property.

2. All costs for acquiring or holding title to said property by both the said Shore Title Co., Inc. and Franklin B. Biggs, or his nominee shall be paid by the said Franklin B. Biggs, or his nominee at the time of transfer of title under paragraph numbered 1 hereof.

On or about the same date, the contracts for the sale of the Virginia property were closed. Warranty deeds evidencing legal title were delivered to Shore by the sellers. Biggs advanced to Shore the $115,655.14 due at settlement and, by a bond secured by a deed of trust on the property, Shore agreed to repay Biggs. Shore also assumed liabilities totalling $142,544.86 which were secured by deeds of trust in favor of the sellers and another mortgagee. Biggs paid Thatcher's finder's fee and all of the closing costs.

On February 26, 1969, Shore and Powell signed an agreement for the sale by Shore of the Virginia property to Powell or his assigns. Payment of the purchase price was arranged as follows:

Upon execution of the agreement	$100.00

Vendee assumed and covenanted to pay the following promissory notes, all secured by deeds of trust on Virginia property:

To Shore Savings & Loan Association	58,469.86
To those from whom Shore acquired the Virginia property	84,075.00
To Franklin B. Biggs	115,655.14
Balance due at settlement	13,900.00
Total purchase price	272,200.00

The next day, February 27, 1969, Biggs and Powell executed a contract which provided that Biggs would sell the Maryland property to Powell or his assigns upon the following terms:

Cash, upon execution	$25,000.00
Cash, at settlement	75,000.00
First mortgage note receivable from Mr. Powell	800,000.00
Total	$900,000.00

The contract further stated:

Sellers and Purchaser acknowledge the existence of a Contract of Sale dated February 26th, 1969, between Shore Title Co., Inc., Vendor-Seller, and Shepard G. Powell or Assigns, Vendee-Purchaser, copy of which is attached hereto and made a part hereof, whereby that Vendor has contracted to sell and that Vendee has agreed to buy from that Vendor at and for the purchase price of Two Hundred Seventy Two Thousand Two Hundred Dollars ($272,200.00) ... (the Virginia property). As a further consideration for the making of this

Contract of Sale ... for the sale and purchase ... of ... (the Maryland property) the said Shepard G. Powell or Assigns, for the sum of One Hundred Dollars ($100.00) in cash, in hand paid, receipt whereof is hereby acknowledged, does hereby bargain, sell, set over and transfer unto said Franklin B. Biggs all of the right, title and interest of the said Shepard G. Powell or Assigns in and to said Virginia property and said Contract of Sale relating thereto, upon condition that the said Franklin B. Biggs assumes and covenants to pay (which he hereby does) all of the obligations assumed by the said Shepard G. Powell under the aforesaid Contract of Sale between him and Shore Title Co., Inc.; and said Franklin B. Biggs hereby agrees to hold Shepard G. Powell or Assigns harmless from any liability under any and all of said obligations on said Virginia property, and the said Shepard G. Powell and said Franklin B. Biggs do hereby jointly and separately agree to execute and deliver any and all necessary papers to effect delivery of title to said Virginia property to said Franklin B. Biggs and to relieve said Shepard G. Powell from any and all obligations assumed by him thereon.

On the same date, Powell and his wife assigned their contractual right to acquire the Maryland property to Samuel Lessans and Maurice Lessans. The Lessanses, in turn, sold and assigned their rights to acquire the Maryland property to Ocean View Corporation (hereinafter referred to as "Ocean View") a Maryland corporation, for $1,300,000.00 by an agreement dated May 22, 1969. The purchase price was comprised of $150,000.00 to be paid into escrow at the time the contract was signed, an $800,000.00 note executed by Ocean View in favor of Biggs at the time of settlement, a $250,000.00 note from Ocean View to the Lessanses, and a $100,000.00 note from Ocean View to the real estate agents at closing.

Ocean View was incorporated on May 21, 1969. At the first meeting of its board of directors, the corporation was authorized to acquire the Maryland property and, also, to quit-claim any interest it might have in the Virginia property. It is undisputed, though, that neither the Lessanses nor Ocean View had any interest whatsoever in that property.

On May 24, 1969, Shore executed a deed conveying all of its right, title and interest in the Virginia property to Biggs. Powell and his wife, the Lessanses and Ocean View all joined in executing the deed as grantors, despite their apparent lack of any cognizable interest in the property. This instrument provided that:

> [T]he said Shore Title Co., Inc., a Maryland corporation, executes this deed to the Grantee herein for the purpose of conveying the ... Virginia property hereinafter described by good and marketable title, subject to the assumption by the Grantee herein of the obligations hereinafter referred to, and all of the other Grantors herein join in the execution of this deed for the purpose of releasing and quit-claiming any interest in and to the property described herein and for the purpose of thereby requesting Shore Title Co., Inc. to convey said property to the Grantee herein in the manner herein set out....

By the same deed, Biggs agreed to assume and pay the notes in favor of the mortgagee and the owners from whom Shore had acquired the Virginia property, in the total sum of $142,544.86. On May 29, 1969, Biggs executed a deed of release in favor of Shore indicating payment in full of the $115,655.14 bond.

On May 26, 1969, Biggs and his wife, Powell and his wife and the Lessanses sold the Maryland property to Ocean View. Contemporaneously, Ocean View executed a mortgage in the face amount of $800,000.00 in favor of Biggs. Also on this date, all of the contracts were closed. Ocean View received the deed to the Maryland property and Biggs accepted title to the Virginia property.

Biggs reported his gain from the sale of the Maryland property on his 1969 federal income tax return as follows:[20]

Selling price of Maryland property	$900,000.00	100.00%
Exchange — Virginia Property	298,380.75	33.15%
Boot	$601,619.25	66.85%
Selling price Maryland property	$900,000.00	
Basis-date of Exchange	186,312.80	
Gain	$713,687.20	
Not recognized-exchange (Sec. 1031 I.R.C.)	236,587.31	
33.15%		
Taxable gain	$477,099.89	53.011%

Biggs elected to report the transaction under the installment sales provision of § 453 of the Code. The Commissioner issued a notice of deficiency based upon his determination that there was no exchange of like-kind properties within the meaning of § 1031. The Tax Court disagreed, and ruled in favor of Biggs.

ANALYSIS

Section 1031 provides, in pertinent part, that the gain realized on the exchange of like-kind property held for productive use or investment shall be recognized only to the extent that "boot" or cash is received as additional consideration. The Commissioner does not deny that Biggs fully intended to carry out an exchange that would pass muster under § 1031. It was undoubtedly for this purpose that Biggs insisted from the beginning of his negotiations with Powell that he receive property of like kind as part of the consideration for the transfer of the Maryland property. Cf. *Alderson v. Comm'r*, 317 F.2d 790 (9th Cir. 1963). However, as this court made clear in

---

20. [1] Biggs admits that, even if the transaction qualifies as a § 1031 exchange, he used an incorrect method to calculate the gain to be recognized.

Carlton v. U.S., 385 F.2d 238 (5th Cir. 1967), the mere intent to effect a § 1031 exchange is not dispositive. Indeed, the Commissioner's primary contention is that, under the authority of our holding in Carlton, Biggs failed to accomplish an exchange because the purchaser, Powell, never held title to the Virginia property.

The facts on which Carlton was decided parallel those which we now consider in several respects. Carlton, the taxpayer, wished to trade a tract of ranch land for other property of a similar character in order to obtain the tax benefits afforded by s 1031. This intent was made explicit in the negotiations and resulting option contract entered into by Carlton and General, a corporation which desired to purchase the ranch property. Carlton proceeded to locate two parcels of suitable exchange property, negotiate for the acquisition of this property, and pay a deposit on each parcel. General executed the actual agreements of sale and then assigned its contract rights to purchase the exchange property to the taxpayer. However, the crucial factor which distinguishes Carlton from the instant case is that General actually paid cash for the ranch property which Carlton then used two days later to purchase the exchange property. A panel of this court held that the receipt of cash transformed the intended exchange into a sale:

> [W]hile elaborate plans were laid to exchange property, the substance of the transaction was that the appellants received cash for the deed to their ranch property and not another parcel of land. The very essence of an exchange is the transfer of property between owners, while the mark of a sale is the receipt of cash for the property.

385 F.2d at 242 (footnote and citations omitted).

Although the payment and receipt of cash was the determinative factor, the court went on to cite additional reasons to support its holding of a sale, rather than an exchange:

> Further, General was never in a position to exchange properties with the appellants because it never acquired the legal title to either the Lyons or the Fernandez property. Indeed, General was not personally obligated on either the notes or mortgages involved in these transactions. Thus it never had any property of like kind to exchange. Finally, it cannot be said that General paid for the Lyons and Fernandez properties and merely had the properties deeded directly to the appellants. The money received from General by the appellants for the ranch property was not earmarked by General to be used in purchasing the Lyons or Fernandez properties. It was unrestricted and could be used by the appellants as they pleased.

385 F.2d at 242–243. The Commissioner maintains that this language in Carlton establishes as an absolute prerequisite to a § 1031 exchange that the purchaser have title to the exchange property. We do not agree with this interpretation. The Carlton decision was based on the aggregate circumstances discussed therein and, as we have noted, the most significant of these was the receipt of cash by the taxpayer. In the present case, the transfer of the Maryland property and the receipt of the Virginia

property occurred simultaneously, and the cash paid to Biggs at the closing constituted "boot." Also in contrast to the facts found in Carlton, Powell, as contract purchaser, did "assume[] and covenant[] to pay ... promissory notes, all secured by deeds of trust on the Virginia property," plus the balance due at settlement. We cannot ignore the legal obligations and risks inherent in this contractual language, even though Powell was subject to such risks only for a short period of time. Also, the unrestricted use of funds which was a problem in Carlton is of no concern here because Biggs received cash only upon the closing of all transactions.

Thus, we are left with the sole consideration that Powell never acquired legal title to the Virginia property. Yet, if we were to decide, as the Commissioner urges, that this factor alone precludes a § 1031 exchange, we would contravene the earlier precedent established by this court in *W.D. Haden Co. v. Comm'r*, 165 F.2d 588 (5th Cir. 1948). Haden also involved a multi-party exchange in which the purchaser, Goodwin, never held title to the exchange property. However, since Goodwin had contracted to purchase the property, the court held that the taxpayer had effected a like-kind exchange, stating that the purchaser "could bind himself to exchange property he did not own but could acquire." 165 F.2d at 590.

Our resolution of the title issue is also tangentially supported by language contained in the Ninth Circuit's recent opinion in *Starker v. U.S.*, 602 F.2d 1341 (9th Cir. 1979). Briefly stated, the Starker facts involved a transfer of the taxpayer's real property to the purchaser, Crown Zellerbach Corp., in exchange for the corporation's promise to acquire other real property in the future and convey it to the taxpayer. The government argued that this arrangement did not qualify for § 1031 treatment because the transfers were not simultaneous and, alternatively, the contract right received by the taxpayer was personal property and, hence, not like-kind to the real property he had conveyed. The Ninth Circuit disagreed and, in response to the latter argument, stated:

> This is true, but the short answer to this statement is that title to real property, like a contract right to purchase real property, is nothing more than a bundle of potential causes of action: for trespass, to quiet title, for interference with quiet enjoyment, and so on. The bundle of rights associated with ownership is obviously not excluded from section 1031; a contractual right to assume the rights of ownership should not, we believe, be treated as any different than the ownership rights themselves. Even if the contract right includes the possibility of the taxpayer receiving something other than ownership of like-kind property, we hold that it is still of a like kind with ownership for tax purposes when the taxpayer prefers property to cash before and throughout the executory period, and only like-kind property is ultimately received.

602 F.2d at 1355. Of course, we need not, and do not, express either acceptance or disapproval of the ultimate holding in Starker. However, the Ninth Circuit's discussion of the title versus right-to-purchase problem is, we believe, consistent with our own analysis.

We must also reject the Commissioner's assertions that the Tax Court applied the so-called "step-transaction doctrine" incorrectly, and that the transactions which occurred here were in substance a sale for cash of the Maryland property and an unrelated purchase of the Virginia property. The step-transaction doctrine was articulated in *Redwing Carriers, Inc. v. Tomlinson*, 399 F.2d 652 (5th Cir. 1968):

> [A]n integrated transaction may not be separated into its components for the purposes of taxation by either the Internal Revenue Service or the taxpayer. (Citation omitted.) In *Kanawha Gas and Utilities Co. v. Comm'r*, 214 F.2d 685, 691 (5th Cir. 1954), our Court through Judge Rives said:
>
> > In determining the incidence of taxation, we must look through form and search out the substance of a transaction.... (cases cited) This basic concept of tax law is particularly pertinent to cases involving a series of transactions designed and executed as parts of a unitary plan to achieve an intended result. Such plans will be viewed as a whole regardless of whether the effect of so doing is imposition of or relief from taxation. The series of closely related steps in such a plan are merely the means by which to carry out the plan and will not be separated.

399 F.2d at 658. The Tax Court found that the many transactions leading to the ultimate transfers of the Maryland and Virginia properties were part of a single, integrated plan, the substantive result of which was a like-kind exchange. This finding is amply supported by the evidence. Biggs insisted at all times that he receive like-kind property as part of the consideration for the transfer of the Maryland property. Powell agreed to this arrangement and assured Biggs of his cooperation. Biggs was careful not to contract for the sale of the Maryland property until Powell had obtained an interest in the Virginia land. When he and Powell did enter into an agreement of sale on February 26, 1969, the exchange was made an express condition of the contract. Biggs also avoided the step which was fatal to the taxpayer's intended exchange in Carlton; i.e., he did not receive any cash prior to the simultaneous closings of the properties on May 26, 1969. Under these circumstances, the Tax Court correctly determined that all transactions were interdependent and that they culminated in an exchange rather than a sale and separate purchase.

Finally, we examine the Commissioner's claim that Shore was serving as an agent for Biggs throughout the transactions, and that the accomplishment of the intended exchange was thereby precluded.[21] Admittedly, the exchange would have been meaningless if Shore, acting as Biggs' agent, acquired title to the Virginia property and then executed the deed conveying title to Biggs. For, in essence, Biggs would have merely effected an exchange with himself. Cf. *Coupe v. C.I.R.*, 52 T.C. 394 (1969).

---

21. [4] In advancing this argument, the Commissioner does not seem to focus on Shore's purported status as Biggs' agent, but rather on the fact that Shore was not Powell's agent for purposes of accepting title to the Virginia property. However, our disposition of the title question renders the absence of a principal-agent relationship between Powell and Shore irrelevant.

However, while the Tax Court refused to find, in contrast to its decision in Coupe, that Shore acted as an agent for the purchaser, Powell, it also specifically determined that Shore was not an agent of Biggs. Rather, Shore accepted title to the Virginia property, albeit at Biggs' request, merely in order to facilitate the exchange. We believe that this is an accurate characterization of Shore's role in the transactions. Consequently, we reject the Commissioner's agency notion also.

OPINION

Undoubtedly, the exchange of the Maryland and Virginia properties could have been more artfully accomplished and with a greater economy of steps. However, we must conclude on the facts before us that the taxpayer ultimately achieved the intended result. Accordingly, the decision of the Tax Court is affirmed.

Starker v. United States

United States Court of Appeals, Ninth Circuit
602 F.2d 1341 (1979)

FACTS

On April 1, 1967, T.J. Starker and his son and daughter-in-law, Bruce and Elizabeth Starker, entered into a "land exchange agreement" with Crown Zellerbach Corporation (Crown). The agreement provided that the three Starkers would convey to Crown all their interests in 1,843 acres of timberland in Columbia County, Oregon. In consideration for this transfer, Crown agreed to acquire and deed over to the Starkers other real property in Washington and Oregon. Crown agreed to provide the Starkers suitable real property within five years or pay any outstanding balance in cash. As part of the contract, Crown agreed to add to the Starkers' credit each year a "growth factor", equal to six per cent of the outstanding balance.

On May 31, 1967, the Starkers deeded their timberland to Crown. Crown entered "exchange value credits" in its books: for T.J. Starker's interest, a credit of $1,502,500; and for Bruce and Elizabeth's interest, a credit of $73,000.

Within four months, Bruce and Elizabeth found three suitable parcels, and Crown purchased and conveyed them pursuant to the contract. No "growth factor" was added because a year had not expired, and no cash was transferred to Bruce and Elizabeth because the agreed value of the property they received was $73,000, the same as their credit.

Closing the transaction with T.J. Starker, whose credit balance was larger, took longer. Beginning in July 1967 and continuing through May 1969, Crown purchased 12 parcels selected by T.J. Starker. Of these 12, Crown purchased 9 from third parties, and then conveyed them to T.J. Starker. Two more of the 12 (the Timian and Bi-Mart properties) were transferred to Crown by third parties, and then conveyed by Crown at T.J. Starker's direction to his daughter, Jean Roth. The twelfth parcel (the Booth property) involved a third party's contract to purchase. Crown purchased that contract right and reassigned it to T.J. Starker.

The first of the transfers from Crown to T.J. Starker or his daughter was on September 5, 1967; the twelfth and last was on May 21, 1969. By 1969, T.J. Starker's credit balance had increased from $1,502,500 to $1,577,387.91, by means of the 6 per cent "growth factor". The land transferred by Crown to T.J. Starker and Roth was valued by the parties at exactly $1,577,387.91. Therefore, no cash was paid to T.J. Starker, and his balance was reduced to zero.

In their income tax returns for 1967, the three Starkers all reported no gain on the transactions, although their bases in the properties they relinquished were smaller than the market value of the properties they received. They claimed that the transactions were entitled to nonrecognition treatment under section 1031 of the Internal Revenue Code (I.R.C. § 1031).

* * *

The Internal Revenue Service disagreed, and assessed deficiencies of $35,248.41 against Bruce and Elizabeth Starker and $300,930.31 plus interest against T.J. Starker. The Starkers paid the deficiencies, filed claims for refunds, and when those claims were denied, filed two actions for refunds in the United States District Court in Oregon.

In the first of the two cases, *Bruce Starker v. U.S.* (Starker I), 75-1 U.S. Tax Cas. (CCH) P 8443 (D.Or.1975), the trial court held that this court's decision in *Alderson v. Comm'r*, 317 F.2d 790 (9th Cir. 1963), compelled a decision for the taxpayers. Bruce and Elizabeth Starker recovered the claimed refund. The government appealed, but voluntarily dismissed the appeal, and the judgment for Bruce and Elizabeth Starker became final.

The government, however, did not capitulate in *T.J. Starker v. U.S.* (Starker II), the present case. The government continued to assert that T.J. Starker was not entitled to section 1031 nonrecognition. According to the government, T.J. Starker was liable not only for a tax on his capital gain, but also for a tax on the 6 per cent "growth factor" as ordinary income (interest or its equivalent).

The same trial judge who heard Starker I also heard Starker II. Recognizing that "many of the transfers here are identical to those in Starker I", the court rejected T.J. Starker's collateral-estoppel argument and found for the government. The judge said:

> I have reconsidered my opinion in Starker I. I now conclude that I was mistaken in my holding as well in my earlier reading of Alderson. Even if Alderson can be interpreted as contended by plaintiff, I think that to do so would be improper. It would merely sanction a tax avoidance scheme and not carry out the purposes of s 1031. *T.J. Starker v. U.S.*, 432 F. Supp. 864, 868, 77-2 U.S. Tax Cas. (CCH) P 9512 (D.Or.1977).

Judgment was entered for the government on both the nonrecognition and ordinary income (interest) issues, and this appeal followed.

T.J. Starker asserts that the district court erred in holding that: (a) his real estate transactions did not qualify for nonrecognition under I.R.C. § 1031; (b) the government was not collaterally estopped from litigating that issue; and (c) the transactions caused him to have ordinary income for interest, in addition to a capital gain.

* * *

ANALYSIS

In order for collateral estoppel to apply, the issue to be foreclosed in the second litigation must have been litigated and decided in the first case. The government argues that the legal question presented in T.J. Starker is different than that in Bruce Starker. According to the government, Bruce Starker merely decided that the term "exchange" in § 1031 does not require a simultaneous exchange of title or beneficial ownership. By contrast, it argues, T.J. Starker presents the question whether the lack of a simultaneous exchange and the possibility of the taxpayer's receiving cash render the consideration given the taxpayer something other than "property of a like kind".

* * *

As to Timian, Bi-Mart, and Booth properties, the facts of Starker I are so different from those of this case that the entire issue of the applicability of § 1031 to them was properly before the district court in Starker II. The court therefore correctly went to the merits of the litigants' arguments as they pertained to these parcels. We now turn to those arguments.

As with the other nine parcels T.J. Starker received, none of these three properties was deeded to him at or near the time he deeded his timberland to Crown. T.J. Starker admits that he received no interest in these properties until a substantial time after he conveyed away title to his property. Thus, the question whether § 1031 requires simultaneity of deed transfers is presented as to all three. In addition, each of these parcels presents its own peculiar issues because of the differing circumstances surrounding their transfers.

Timian and Bi-Mart Properties

The Timian property is a residence. Legal title to it was conveyed by Crown at T.J. Starker's request to his daughter, Jean Roth, in 1967. T.J. Starker lives in this residence, and pays rent on it to his daughter. The United States argues that since T.J. Starker never held legal title to this property, he cannot be said to have exchanged his timberland for it. Furthermore, the government contends, because the property became the taxpayer's personal residence, it is neither property "held for investment" nor of a like kind with such property under the meaning of the Code. On the other hand, the taxpayer argues that there was, in economic reality, a transfer of title to him, followed by a gift by him to his daughter.

The Bi-Mart property, a commercial building, was conveyed by Crown to Roth in 1968. The government raises the same issue with regard to the Bi-Mart property: since T.J. Starker never had title, he did not effect an exchange. T.J. Starker points out, however, that he expended substantial time and money in improving and maintaining the structure in the three months prior to the conveyance of the property to his daughter, and he emphasizes that he controlled and commanded its transfer to her.

We begin our analysis of the proper treatment of the receipt of these two properties with a consideration of the Timian residence. T.J. Starker asserts that the question whether such property can be held "for investment" is unsettled. We disagree. It has long been the rule that use of property solely as a personal residence is antithetical to its being held for investment. Losses on the sale or exchange of such property cannot be deducted for this reason, despite the general rule that losses from transactions involving trade or investment properties are deductible. Treas. Regs. § 1.165-9(a); *See Shields v. Comm'r*, 1978-120 T.C.M. (CCH) Dec. 35,064(M). A similar rule must obtain in construing the term "held for investment" in section 1031. 3 J. Mertens, Law of Federal Income Taxation § 20.26 (1972); See *Boesel v. Comm'r*, 65 T.C. 378, 389 (1975); Rev. Rul. 59-229, 1959-2 Cum.Bull. 180. Thus, nonrecognition treatment cannot be given to the receipt of the Timian parcel.

Moreover, T.J. Starker cannot be said to have received the Timian or Bi-Mart properties in exchange for his interest in the Columbia County timberland because title to the Timian and Bi-Mart properties was transferred by Crown directly to someone else, his daughter. Under an analogous nonrecognition provision, section 1034 of the Code, the key to receiving nonrecognition treatment is maintaining continuity of title. Under section 1034, if title shifts from the taxpayer to someone other than the taxpayer's spouse, nonrecognition is denied. *Marcello v. Comm'r*, 380 F.2d 499 (5th Cir. 1967); *Boesel v. Comm'r, supra*, we find similar reasoning compelling here. Although in some cases a father and his daughter may be seen as having an identity of economic interests (*Cf. McWilliams v. Comm'r*, 331 U.S. 694, 699 (1947)), that unity is not sufficient to make transfer of title to one the same as transfer of title to the other. T.J. Starker has not shown that he has any legally cognizable interest in the Timian or Bi-Mart properties that would entitle him to prevent Jean Roth from exercising full ownership rights. In case of a disagreement about the use or enjoyment of these properties, her wishes, not his, would prevail. In these circumstances, T.J. Starker cannot be said to have "exchanged" properties under § 1031, because he never received any property ownership himself.

Booth Property

The Booth property is a commercial parcel, title to which has never been conveyed to T.J. Starker. The transfer of this property to him was achieved in 1968 by Crown's acquiring third parties' contract right to purchase the property, and then reassigning the right to T.J. Starker. In addition to emphasizing the lack of simultaneity in the transfers, the government points here to the total lack of deed transfer.

An examination of the record reveals that legal title had not passed by deed to T.J. Starker by the time of the trial. He continued to hold the third-party purchasers' rights under a 1965 sales agreement on the Booth land. That agreement notes that one of the original transferors holds a life interest in the property, and that legal title shall not pass until that life interest expires. In the meantime, the purchasers are entitled to possession, but they are subject to certain restrictions. For example, they are prohibited from removing improvements and are required to keep buildings and fences in good repair. Under the agreement, a substantial portion of the purchase price must be invested, with a fixed return to be paid to the purchaser of the life interest. Should any of these conditions fail, the agreement provides, the sellers may elect, Inter alia, to void the contract.

Despite these contingencies, we believe that what T.J. Starker received in 1968 was the equivalent of a fee interest for purposes of § 1031. Under Treas. Regs. § 1.1031(a)-1(c), a leasehold interest of 30 years or more is the equivalent of a fee interest for purposes of determining whether the properties exchanged are of a like kind. Under the assigned purchase rights, Starker had at least the rights of a long-term lessee, plus an equitable fee subject to conditions precedent. If the seller's life interest lasted longer than 30 years, the leasehold interest would be the equivalent of a fee; the fact that the leasehold might ripen into a fee at some earlier point should not alter this result. Thus, we hold that what T.J. Starker received in 1968 was the equivalent of a fee.

This does not solve the riddle of the proper treatment of the Booth parcel, however. Since the taxpayer did not receive the fee equivalent at the same time that he gave up his interest in the timberland, the same issue is presented as with the nine parcels on which the government was estopped, namely, whether simultaneity of transfer is required for nonrecognition treatment under § 1031.

The government's argument that simultaneity is required begins with Treas. Reg. § 1.1002-1(b). That regulation provides that all exceptions to the general rule that gains and losses are recognized must be construed narrowly:

> ... Nonrecognition is accorded by the Code only if the exchange is one which satisfies both (1) the specific description in the Code of an excepted exchange, and (2) the underlying purpose for which such exchange is excepted from the general rule.

There are two problems, however, with applying this regulation to § 1031.

First, the "underlying purpose" of § 1031 is not entirely clear. The legislative history reveals that the provision was designed to avoid the imposition of a tax on those who do not "cash in" on their investments in trade or business property. Congress appeared to be concerned that taxpayers would not have the cash to pay a tax on the capital gain if the exchange triggered recognition. This does not explain the precise limits of § 1031, however; if those taxpayers sell their property for cash and reinvest that cash in like-kind property, they cannot enjoy the section's benefits, even if the reinvestment takes place just a few days after the sale. Thus, some taxpayers with liquidity problems resulting from a replacement of their business property are not covered by the section. The liquidity rationale must therefore be limited.

Another apparent consideration of the drafters of the section was the difficulty of valuing property exchanged for the purpose of measuring gain or loss. Section 1031(a) permits the taxpayer to transfer the basis of the property he or she gives up to the property he or she receives, thus deferring the valuation problem, as well as the tax, until the property received is sold or otherwise disposed of in a transaction in which gain or loss is recognized.

But this valuation rationale also has its limits. So long as a single dollar in cash or other non-like-kind property ("boot") is received by the taxpayer along with like-kind property, valuation of both properties in the exchange becomes necessary. In that case, the taxpayer is liable for the gain realized, with the maximum liability being on the amount of cash or other "boot" received, under I.R.C. § 1031(b). To compute the gain realized, one must place a value on the like-kind property received. Moreover, the nonrecognition provision applies only to like-kind exchanges, and not to other exchanges in which valuation is just as difficult. Therefore, valuation problems cannot be seen as the controlling consideration in the enactment of § 1031.

In addition to the elusive purpose of the section, there is a second sound reason to question the applicability of Treas. Regs. § 1.1002-1: the long line of cases liberally construing § 1031. If the regulation purports to read into § 1031 a complex web of formal and substantive requirements, precedent indicates decisively that the regulation has been rejected. *See Biggs v. Comm'r,* 69 T.C. 905, 913–14 (1978).[22] We therefore analyze the Booth transaction with the courts' permissive attitude toward § 1031 in mind.

In *Biggs,* the Tax Court took this liberal treatment even further. It found that a "four corner" exchange qualified for § 1031 nonrecognition. The party to whom the taxpayer was deeding his property (the "second party") did not want to take title to the property the taxpayer ultimately desired. As a result, the taxpayer advanced money to a syndicate, which bought the desired property from a fourth party and transferred it directly to the taxpayer. The taxpayer then transferred his original property to the second party, and got back his cash advance to the syndicate, ultimately out of the pocket of the second party. Since the various transfers were all part of a single overall plan, the Tax Court found that § 1031 had been satisfied. *See also Coupe v. Comm'r,* 52 T.C. 394 (1969) (similar "four corner" exchange qualifies under section 1031).

Two features of the Booth deal make it most likely to trigger recognition of gain: the likelihood that the taxpayer would receive cash instead of real estate, and the time gap in the transfers of the equivalents of fee title.

In assessing whether the possibility that T.J. Starker might receive cash makes § 1031 inapplicable, an important case is *Alderson v. Comm'r,* 317 F.2d 790 (9th Cir.

---

22. [10] For example, courts have held that "three corner" exchanges qualify for § 1031 nonrecognition treatment. In *Biggs,* 69 T.C. 905 (1978), the court described these transactions and summarized the ease with which a taxpayer can use them to qualify for nonrecognition treatment:

… In such a transaction, the taxpayer desires to exchange, rather than to sell, his property. However, the potential buyer of the taxpayer's property owns no property the taxpayer wishes to receive in exchange. Therefore, the buyer purchases other suitable property from a third party and then exchanges it for the property held by the taxpayer.

In numerous cases, this type of transaction has been held to constitute an exchange within the meaning of § 1031. *E.g., Alderson v. Comm'r,* 317 F.2d 790 (9th Cir. 1963); (other citations omitted). In so holding, the courts have permitted taxpayers great latitude in structuring transactions. Thus, it is immaterial that the exchange was motivated by a wish to reduce taxes. *Mercantile Trust Co. v. Comm'r,* (32 B.T.A. 82,) 87 ((1935)). The taxpayer can locate suitable property to be received in exchange and can enter into negotiations for the acquisition of such property. *Coastal Terminals, Inc. v. U.S.,* 320 F.2d 333, 338 (4th Cir. 1963); *Alderson v. Comm'r,* 317 F.2d at 793; *Coupe v. Comm'r,* 52 T.C. (394,) 397–98 ((1969)). Moreover, the taxpayer can oversee improvements on the land to be acquired (*J. H. Baird Publishing Co. v. Comm'r,* 39 T.C. (608,) 611 ((1962))) and can even advance money toward the purchase price of the property to be accepted by exchange (*124 Front Street, Inc. v. Comm'r,* 65 T.C. 6, 15–18 (1975)). Provided the final result is an exchange of property for other property of a like kind, the transaction will qualify under section 1031." *Biggs v. Comm'r,* 69 T.C. at 913–14.

1963). There, this court held that a "three corner" exchange qualified for nonrecognition treatment. The taxpayer and Alloy entered into an agreement for the simple cash sale of the taxpayer's property, but later amended the agreement to provide that Alloy would purchase another parcel to effect a swap with the taxpayer. This amendment did not totally eradicate the possibility that the cash transaction would take place; it provided, in the words of the court, that "if the exchange was not effected by September 11, 1957, the original escrow re the purchase for cash would be carried out." 317 F.2d at 791. The exchange was effected when reciprocal deeds were recorded. Said the court:

> True, the intermediate acts of the parties could have hewn closer to and have more precisely depicted the ultimate desired result, but what actually occurred on September 3 or 4, 1957, was an exchange of deeds between the petitioners and Alloy which effected an exchange of the Buena Park property for the Salinas property. *Alderson v. Comm'r*, 317 F.2d at 793.

The court stressed that, although at the time the contract was amended there was a possibility that a cash sale would take place, there was from the outset no intention on the part of the taxpayer to sell his property for cash if it could be exchanged for other property of a like kind. Thus, *Alderson* followed *Mercantile Trust Co. v. Comm'r*, 32 B.T.A. 82 (1935), a case in which the taxpayer could have required the other party to the exchange to pay cash if that other party was unable to purchase an identified parcel that the taxpayer desired. In Mercantile Trust, the taxpayer succeeded in getting nonrecognition treatment by virtue of its intention to get other property, rather than cash, if possible.

Coastal Terminals, Inc. v. U.S., 320 F.2d 333 (4th Cir. 1963), held similarly. There, a "three corner" exchange was effected, with both the taxpayer and the other party to the exchange maintaining until the closing the option to cancel the exchange and bring about a cash sale instead. Citing Alderson with approval, the court noted that the taxpayer intended to sell the property for cash only if it was unable to locate a suitable piece of property to take in exchange. Because an exchange took place, nonrecognition treatment was granted.

The Fifth Circuit has indicated its agreement with this approach in *Carlton v. U.S.*, 385 F.2d 238 (5th Cir. 1967). There, the taxpayers gave General an option to purchase their property for cash, but maintained the right to require General to acquire land and transfer it to them in lieu of cash. From the outset, the taxpayers intended to get suitable property, and not cash, in return. As it turned out, at the closing, General transferred to the taxpayers a contract right to purchase two parcels, and enough cash to purchase them, in exchange for the taxpayers' land. Because of the form of payment, § 1031 was held not to apply. But the court noted that the government agreed that had the taxpayers followed the original plan, with General acquiring title and then transferring it to the taxpayers, the section would have applied.

Thus, the mere possibility at the time of agreement that a cash sale might occur does not prevent the application of § 1031. Even in cases such as Coastal Terminals, where the taxpayers had the contract right to opt for cash rather than property, a preference by the taxpayers for like-kind property rather than cash has guaranteed nonrecognition despite the possibility of a cash transaction.[23]

In this case, the taxpayer claims he intended from the very outset of the transaction to get nothing but like-kind property, and no evidence to the contrary appears on the record. Moreover, the taxpayer never handled any cash in the course of the transactions. Hence, the Alderson line of cases would seem to control.

The government contends, however, that Alderson and other precedents of its type are distinguishable. It points out that in those cases, there may have been a possibility of a receipt of cash at the time of the exchange Agreement, but there was no possibility of receiving cash at the time the taxpayer Transferred the property pursuant to the agreement. This difference in timing, says the commissioner, renders the Alderson line of cases inapplicable.

At least one appellate decision indicates, however, that title may not have to be exchanged simultaneously in order for section 1031 to apply. In *Redwing Carriers, Inc. v. Tomlinson*, 399 F.2d 652 (5th Cir. 1968), the government argued successfully that mutual transfers of trucks that occurred "at or about" the same time were in fact an "exchange" under § 1031. In Redwing Carriers, the taxpayer was attempting to deduct a loss in the purchase of new trucks to replace old trucks; the government disallowed recognition of the loss on the ground that § 1031(c) applied. To keep its replacement transactions outside the scope of the section, a parent corporation transferred its old trucks to a subsidiary, bought new trucks for cash, and had the subsidiary sell the old trucks to the manufacturer for cash. The court viewed the transactions as a whole, and disallowed the loss under § 1031. Some lack of simultaneity was apparently "tolerated" by the commissioner and the court. As the court explained, the transfers to the subsidiary by the parent and to the parent by the manufacturer took place "at or about" the same time. 399 F.2d at 655. Nonetheless, the government urges this court to distinguish Redwing Carriers, and Alderson and its kin, on the ground that the transfers of title in T.J. Starker's case were separated by a "substantial" period of time. We decline to draw this line.

The government also argues that the contract right to receive property or cash was not "like" title to property, because it was like cash. It asks us to impose a "cash equivalency" test to determine whether § 1031 applies. One flaw in this argument is

---

23. [11] Of course, a mere intent to avoid taxation of the transaction is not sufficient. For example, in *Smith v. Comm'r*, 537 F.2d 972 (8th Cir. 1976), the taxpayer bought a parcel of Custer County land. Shortly thereafter, he decided to sever a cotenancy on other land with his brother. He conveyed the Custer County land to his brother for cash, and then his brother transferred the Custer County land back to him in exchange for the taxpayer's share of the cotenancy. The net result of the three transfers was that the taxpayer gave up his share of the cotenancy, and got the Custer County property. His brother gave up cash, and the former owner of the Custer County land got cash. Nevertheless, because the taxpayer purchased the Custer parcel before deciding to make an exchange with his brother, the court refused to view all the exchanges as a whole. The formal transfers of cash to and from the taxpayer's hands defeated the attempt to fit the exchanges within section 1031.

that title to land is no more or less equivalent to cash than a contract right to buy land. The central concept of § 1031 is that an exchange of business or investment assets does not trigger recognition of gain or loss, because the taxpayer in entering into such a transaction does not "cash in" or "close out" his or her investment. To impose a tax on the event of a deed transfer upon a signing of an exchange agreement could bring about the very result § 1031 was designed to prevent: "the inequity ... of forcing a taxpayer to recognize a paper gain which was still tied up in a continuing investment of the same sort." *Jordan Marsh Co. v. Comm'r*, 269 F.2d 453, 456 (2d Cir. 1959).

Against this background, the government offers the explanation that a contract right to land is a "chose in action", and thus personal property instead of real property. This is true, but the short answer to this statement is that title to real property, like a contract right to purchase real property, is nothing more than a bundle of potential causes of action: for trespass, to quiet title, for interference with quiet enjoyment, and so on. The bundle of rights associated with ownership is obviously not excluded from § 1031; a contractual right to assume the rights of ownership should not, we believe, be treated as any different than the ownership rights themselves. Even if the contract right includes the possibility of the taxpayer receiving something other than ownership of like-kind property, we hold that it is still of a like kind with ownership for tax purposes when the taxpayer prefers property to cash before and throughout the executory period, and only like-kind property is ultimately received.

The metaphysical discussion in the briefs and authorities about whether the "steps" of the transactions should be "collapsed", and the truism that "substance" should prevail over "form", are not helpful to the resolution of this case. At best, these words describe results, not reasons. A proper decision can be reached only by considering the purposes of the statute and analyzing its application to particular facts under existing precedent. Here, the statute's purposes are somewhat cloudy, and the precedents are not easy to reconcile. But the weight of authority leans in T.J. Starker's favor, and we conclude that the district court was right in Starker I, and wrong in Starker II. Thus, on the merits, the transfer of the timberland to Crown triggered a like-kind exchange with respect to the Booth property.

SIX PER CENT "GROWTH FACTOR"

The next issue presented is whether the 6 per cent "growth factor" received by T.J. Starker was properly treated as capital gain or as ordinary income. The government successfully argued below that this amount should be treated as ordinary income because it was disguised interest. The taxpayer, on the other hand, contends that the 6 per cent "growth" provision merely compensated him for timber growth on the Columbia County property he conveyed to Crown.

The taxpayer's argument is not without some biological merit, but he was entitled to the 6 per cent regardless of the actual fate of the timber on the property. He retained no ownership rights in the timber, and bore no risk of loss, after he conveyed title to Crown.[24] We agree with the government that the taxpayer is essentially arguing "that he conveyed $1,502,500 to a stranger for an indefinite period of time (up to five years) without any interest." The 6 per cent "growth factor" was "compensation for the use or forbearance of money", that is, for the use of the unpaid amounts owed to Starker by Crown. Therefore, it was disguised interest. See *United States v. Midland-Ross Corp.*, 381 U.S. 54, 57 (1965); *Deputy v. duPont*, 308 U.S. 488, 497–98 (1940).

TIMING OF INCLUSION

Our final task, having characterized the proper nature of T.J. Starker's receipts, is to decide in which years they are includable in income. The Timian and Bi-Mart properties do not qualify for nonrecognition treatment, while the other 10 properties received do qualify. In this situation, we believe the proper result is to treat T.J. Starker's rights in his contract with Crown, insofar as they resulted in the receipt of the Timian and Bi-Mart properties, as "boot", received in 1967 when the contract was made. We hold that section 1031(b) requires T.J. Starker to recognize his gain on the transaction with Crown in 1967, to the extent of the fair market values of the Timian and Bi-Mart properties as of the dates on which title to those properties passed to his appointee.

We realize that this decision leaves the treatment of an alleged exchange open until the eventual receipt of consideration by the taxpayer. Some administrative difficulties may surface as a result. Our role, however, is not necessarily to facilitate administration. It is to divine the meaning of the statute in a manner as consistent as possible with the intent of Congress and the prior holdings of the courts. If our holding today adds a degree of uncertainty to this area, Congress can clarify its meaning.

As to the disguised interest, the district court erred in holding T.J. Starker liable for ordinary income in 1967. As a taxpayer reporting on the cash method, T.J. Starker was not liable for taxes on interest income until that interest was received. Although receipt may be actual or constructive, Crown's liability for the "growth factor" did not commence until after 1967 had expired. Had suitable properties been found for T.J. Starker in 1967 (as was the case with Bruce and Elizabeth), Crown would have owed T.J. Starker no "growth factor" at all. Therefore, the government should not have assessed an ordinary income tax on the "growth factor" in 1967. The proper years of inclusion would have been those in which the taxpayer received the interest. To the extent T.J. Starker paid the ordinary tax for 1967, he was entitled to his refund.

---

24. [13] Starker and Crown, as sophisticated managers of timberlands, presumably knew about fire, blowdown, bugkill, government regulations, and other risks that ordinarily pass with title unless otherwise allocated in transactions spread over time.

Mercantile Trust Co. v. Commissioner

United States Board of Tax Appeals

32 B.T.A. 82 (1935)

FACTS

Petitioners assign as error, the respondent's determination that they sold certain real estate, theretofore held for investment. Petitioners allege that such property was exchanged for cash and like property to be held for investment. In the alternative, if the transaction is held to be a sale and purchase and not an exchange, petitioners assign error in respondent's determination of the March 1, 1913, value of the property, disposition of which was made in that transaction.

The stipulation of facts pertinent to the first issue, including the agreements, deeds, checks, and papers executed by the several parties to the 1929 transaction in controversy, is included herein by reference.

Petitioners are the duly constituted trustees of the estate of Charles D. Fisher, who died testate in 1905. On and before March 7, 1929, as trustees of the Fisher estate, they held title to two parcels of real estate known as 114-116 East Baltimore Street, Baltimore, Maryland, hereinafter referred to as the Baltimore Street property. Such properties were contiguous to the property known as the Emerson Hotel and were leased to and occupied by a restaurant. At the same time the estate of Annie E. O. Wylie owned real estate known as 223 West Lexington Street, Baltimore, Maryland (hereinafter referred to as the Lexington Street property), which was rented under a long term lease to F. W. Woolworth & Co.

On March 7, 1929, petitioners, as trustees of the Fisher estate, entered into a written contract with the Title Guarantee & Trust Co. (hereinafter referred to as the Title Co.) under the terms of which petitioners agreed with the Title Co. to exchange the Baltimore Street properties, as an entirety in fee simple, for the Lexington Street property in fee simple, subject to the outstanding lease thereon, and $33,000 in cash. The agreement further provided that in the event the Title Co. could not obtain ownership of the Lexington Street property by purchase, the petitioners could require the Title Co. to pay $300,000 cash for the Baltimore Street properties in lieu of the above mentioned exchange. The Title Co. paid $4,000 to petitioners at the execution of this contract, which sum was to be credited to the Title Co. upon consummation of the transaction.

On March 11, 1929, the Title Co. entered into a written contract with the trustee of the Wylie estate for the purchase of the Lexington Street property for a price of $267,000 cash. The Title Co. paid that trustee, at the execution of this contract, $1,000 to be credited to the Title Co. upon consummation of that transaction.

On March 11, 1929, the Title Co. entered into a written contract for the sale of the Baltimore Street property to the Emerson Hotel Co. for a price of $300,000 cash. The Emerson Hotel Co. paid the Title Co. $5,000 upon execution of this contract, which was to be credited to the Emerson Hotel Co. upon consummation of this transaction.

On April 15, 1929, the parties to the several contracts simultaneously executed the following deeds of conveyance. The trustee of the Wylie estate deeded to the Title Co. the Lexington Street property. The Title Co. deeded to the petitioners, as trustees of the Fisher estate, the Lexington Street property. The petitioners, as trustees of the Fisher estate, deeded to the Title Co., the Baltimore Street property. The Title Co. deeded to the Emerson Hotel Co. the Baltimore Street property.

On the same date, April 15, 1929, pursuant to the contracts and deeds, the following cash payments were made. The Emerson Hotel Co. issued its check payable to the Title Co. in the sum of $294,416.67 representing the agreed purchase price of $300,000 for the Baltimore Street property less adjustments for the $5,000 paid by Emerson Hotel Co. upon execution of the contract of sale and rent for a half month. Such check was deposited in the Title Co.'s bank account. The Title Co. issued its check payable to the trustee of the Wylie estate in the sum of $265,478.42 representing the agreed purchase price of $267,000 for the Lexington Street property, less adjustments for the $1,000 paid by the Title Co. upon execution of the contract of sale and rent for a half month. The Title Co. issued its check payable to the petitioner, Mercantile Trust Co., trustee of the Fisher estate, in the sum of $28,938.25 representing that part of agreed purchase price to be paid in cash (in addition to the deed to the Lexington Street property) for the Baltimore Street property, that is, $33,000 less adjustments for the $4,000 paid by the Title Co. upon the execution of the contract and rent for a half month. The petitioners paid commissions and title fees amounting to $8,573.10, leaving the sum of $24,426.90 as the net cash received on the transaction.

In their return for the Fisher estate for 1929, the petitioners reported a capital gain of $24,426.90 as representing the net cash received on a transaction which was an exchange of real property for other like property, held for investment.

The respondent disregarded the form of the transaction and determined that petitioners sold the Baltimore Street property to the Emerson Hotel Co. for $300,000 cash and then purchased the Lexington Street property in two separate transactions. He computed a capital net gain of $179,621.10 as follows:

Sales Price Baltimore Street property		$300,000.00
Less Commission and Title Fee		8,573.10
		$291,426.90
Fair Market Value on March 1, 1913	$125,000.00	
Less depreciation on value of building	13,194.20	
$41,000 at 2% for 15 years		111,805,80
and 10 months		
Capital net gain		$179,621.10
Capital net gain reported		24,426.90
Increase		$155,194.20

Respondent contends that while there is no imputation of fraud, "because no deception was practiced and means legal in themselves were used", the proposed exchange was a sham device for tax avoidance. He further contends that the Title Co. acted purely as an agent or dummy and not as a principal for the purchase and sale of either of the properties; that the governing factor in the transaction was a sale of the Baltimore Street property by petitioners to the Emerson Hotel Co. because the latter desired it, while petitioners objected to the realization of a large taxable profit; that the transaction was carried out in the form above outlined to prevent a straight sale of the Baltimore Street property by petitioners to the Emerson Hotel Co. for cash; that the whole device was so essentially fictitious, the form should be disregarded and the transaction held to be a sale of the Baltimore Street property by petitioners for cash and then, in a separate transaction, a purchase of the Lexington Street property by petitioners for cash.

Respondent argues that the Emerson Hotel Co. was the moving party and the Title Co. was its agent in acquiring petitioners' Baltimore Street property. This may be true. But even if it were, respondent's position is not helped thereby.

ANALYSIS

If the Title Co. were acting as agent for the Emerson Hotel Co., then clearly it purchased the Lexington Street property on behalf of the Emerson Hotel Co. and, pursuant to its agreement with petitioners, but acting for the Emerson Hotel Co., exchanged the Lexington Street property plus $33,000 for the Baltimore Street property. Certainly, the Title Co. as agent for the Emerson Hotel Co. did not purchase the Baltimore Street property for $300,000 cash as contended by respondent.

In our opinion, the respondent's position cannot be sustained unless the Title Co. represented the petitioners as their agent, both in the transfer of the Baltimore Street property to the Emerson Hotel Co., and in the purchase of the Lexington Street property. The record, however, conclusively contradicts the existence of that status in either transaction. Petitioners' only contract disclosed here was with the Title Co. alone. It was enforceable against that company as principal. In the event the Title Co. had not been able to secure title to the Lexington Street property, and thus comply with the exchange provisions of the contract, petitioners could have compelled the Title Co., individually, to pay $300,000 to petitioners for the Baltimore Street property. The Title Co. was the party acquiring the Baltimore Street property. The consideration was to be paid by the Title Co. and the latter did, in fact, pay to the petitioners, in its own behalf, $4,000 upon the execution of that contract. The balance due under the exchange provisions of the contract upon its consummation, namely, the remainder of the cash consideration and the transfer of title to the Lexington Street property, was received by the petitioners from the Title Co. in the performance of the individual obligation of that company.

It may be true, as urged by respondent, that the Emerson Hotel Co. desired the Baltimore Street property and was willing to pay a price which would have netted petitioners a large profit. In any event petitioners could have sold that property for cash, thus incurring a tax liability, and then invested the proceeds in other property as an investment, or, they could have effected an exchange of this investment property for property of a like kind and thus avoided tax liability by postponing the realization of recognized gain as provided by § 112(b)(1) and (c)(1) of the Revenue Act of 1928.[25]

Respondent admits that the transaction was carried out in a legal manner, and that no fraud was perpetrated. We cannot find that it was a mere device, essentially fictitious. The several agreements and deeds executed, and the cash payments made by the four interested parties were not simulated transactions. They were intended to and did constitute juristic facts—not fictions. The agreements created fixed liabilities. The deeds transferred legal title. The cash payments were real. Petitioners actually conveyed the Baltimore Street property to the Title Co. They likewise received from that company, in exchange, the Lexington Street property and $33,000. These real transactions must here be given their normal effect. So, our single inquiry is whether these facts bring the petitioners in the pending transaction within the scope of the quoted statutory provisions. *Gregory v. Helvering*, 293 U.S. 465 (1935); *Royal Marcher*, 32 B.T.A. 76 (1935).

The obvious purpose and effect of these provisions, as well as their predecessors, in the Revenue Act of 1921, § 202(c)(1),[26] (d)(1),[27] and (e),[28] and the amendment of the Act of March 4, 1923, was to permit the postponement of recognition of taxable gain or loss upon an exchange there described until the disposition of the property

---

25. [1] SEC. 112(b)(1) PROPERTY HELD FOR PRODUCTIVE USE OR INVESTMENT.—No gain or loss shall be recognized if property held for productive use in trade or business or for investment (not including stock in trade or other property held primarily for sale, nor stocks, bonds, notes, choses in action, certificates of trust or beneficial interest, or other securities or evidences of indebtedness or interest) is exchanged solely for property of a like kind to be held either for productive use in trade or business or for investment.... (c)(1) If an exchange would be within the provisions of subsection (b)(1), (2), (3), or (5) of this section if it were not for the fact that the property received in exchange consists not only of property permitted by such paragraph to be received without the recognition of gain, but also of other property or money, then the gain, if any, to the recipient shall be recognized, but in an amount not in excess of the sum of such money and the fair market value of such other property.

26. [2] SEC. 202(c)(1) When any such property held for investment, or for productive use in trade or business (not including stock-in-trade or other property held primarily for sale), in exchanged for property of a like kind or use.

27. [3] SEC. 202(d)(1) Where property is exchanged for other property and no gain or loss is recognized under the provisions of subdivision (c), the property received shall, for the purposes of this section, be treated as taking the place of the property exchanged therefor, except as provided in subdivision (e).

28. [4] SEC. 202(e) Where property is exchanged for other property which has no readily realizable market value, together with money or other property which has a readily realizable market value, then the money or the fair market value of the property having such readily market value received in exchange shall be applied against and reduce the basis, provided in this section, of the property exchanged, and if in excess of such basis, shall be taxable to the extent of the excess; but when property is exchanged for property specified in paragraphs (1), (2), and (3) of subdivision (c) as received in exchange, together with money or other property of a readily realizable market value other than that specified in such paragraphs, the money or the fair market value of such other property received in exchange shall be applied against and reduce the basis, provided in this section, of the property exchanged, and if in excess of such basis, shall be taxable to the extent of the excess.

received in the exchange. In the ultimate analysis of the present transaction, this was all petitioners intended or accomplished.

The present exchange was not connected with a corporate reorganization. Neither in the last-quoted provisions nor in their successors, here applicable, does there appear any express or implied indication of a legislative intent to premise the nonrecognition of gain or loss there provided upon any other condition than that stated specifically therein. Compare *Gregory v. Helvering, supra*, which construed subsections (g) and (i)(1)(B) of the same section (112) and Revenue Act (1928) here under consideration. Nonrecognition of gain or loss does not depend here upon the impossibility of a sale of the property by the taxpayer. The only condition precedent to that nonrecognition is the actual exchange of property held for investment for like property to be held for investment, with or without so-called "boot." Cf. *John S. Garvan*, 23 B.T.A. 817 (1931); *George E. Hamilton*, 30 B.T.A. 160 (1934); *Loughborough Development Corporation*, 29 B.T.A. 95 (1933); *W.H. Hartman Co.*, 20 B.T.A. 302 (1930); *Sarther Grocery Co.*, 22 B.T.A. 1273 (1931).

In the cited case of *Gregory v. Helvering*, supra, the Supreme Court determined the taxable status of the questioned transaction "by what actually occurred"—the receipt of the taxed stock by the taxpayer. To sustain respondent upon the present record, we would be compelled to ignore the exchange that actually occurred, and tax, as received by the taxpayers, money never, in fact, received by or for them, in a sale that did not occur. We cannot here thus substitute fiction for fact.

If petitioners' present alternative agreements to exchange or sell had been with the trustee of the Wylie estate and the Emerson Hotel Co., separately, clearly it could not be said that an actual exchange of petitioners' investment property with the former party was an actual sale of it to the latter, merely because petitioners exchanged rather than sold the property for the purpose of postponing or avoiding income taxes. Since such agreements were with the same party, the Title Co., this admitted purpose does not convert petitioners' actual nontaxable exchange into a taxable sale. *Gregory v. Helvering, supra; Bullen v. Wisconsin*, 240 U.S. 625 (1916).

The above mentioned agreement of March 7 evidenced an intention to exchange the Baltimore Street property, if certain conditions were met, and to sell it, if those conditions were not met. Those conditions were met. The property was, in fact, exchanged. That fact is controlling here. *United States v. Phellis*, 257 U.S. 156 (1921); *Sarther Grocery Co., supra*.

We conclude that the petitioners exchanged real property held for investment, for like property to be held for investment, plus $24,426.90 net cash. So, pursuant to § 112(b)(1) and (c)(1), supra, the recognized gain does not exceed the amount of cash received by them in the exchange. Cf. *George E. Hamilton, supra; Loughborough Development Corporation, supra; W.H. Hartman Co., supra*.

Revenue Ruling 2002-83

2002-2 C.B. 927

ISSUE

Under the facts described below, is a taxpayer who transfers relinquished property to a qualified intermediary in exchange for replacement property formerly owned by a related party entitled to nonrecognition treatment under § 1031(a) of the Internal Revenue Code if, as part of the transaction, the related party receives cash or other non-like-kind property for the replacement property?

FACTS

Individual A owns real property (Property 1) with a fair market value of $150x and an adjusted basis of $50x. Individual B owns real property (Property 2) with a fair market value of $150x and an adjusted basis of $150x. Both Property 1 and Property 2 are held for investment within the meaning of § 1031(a). A and B are related persons within the meaning of § 267(b).

C, an individual unrelated to A and B, wishes to acquire Property 1 from A. A enters into an agreement for the transfers of Property 1 and Property 2 with B, C, and a qualified intermediary (QI). QI is unrelated to A and B.

Pursuant to their agreement, on January 6, 2003, A transfers Property 1 to QI and QI transfers Property 1 to C for $150x. On January 13, 2003, QI acquires Property 2 from B, pays B the $150x sale proceeds from QI's sale of Property 1, and transfers Property 2 to A.

ANALYSIS

Section 1031(a)(1) provides that no gain or loss shall be recognized on the exchange of property held for productive use in a trade or business or for investment if the property is exchanged solely for property of a like kind that is to be held either for productive use in a trade or business or for investment. Under § 1031(d), the basis of property acquired in a § 1031 exchange is the same as the basis of the property exchanged, decreased by any money the taxpayer receives and increased by any gain the taxpayer recognizes.

Section 1031 and the regulations thereunder allow for deferred exchanges of property. Under § 1031(a)(3) and § 1.1031(k)-1(b) of the Income Tax Regulations, however, the property to be received by a taxpayer in the exchange (replacement property) must be: (i) identified within 45 days of the transfer of the property relinquished in the exchange (relinquished property) and (ii) received by the earlier of 180 days after the transfer of the relinquished property or the due date (including extensions) of the transferor's tax return for the taxable year in which the relinquished property is transferred.

Section 1.1031(k)-1(g)(4) allows taxpayers to use a qualified intermediary to facilitate a like-kind exchange. In the case of a transfer of relinquished property involving a qualified intermediary, the taxpayer's transfer of relinquished property to a qualified intermediary and subsequent receipt of like-kind replacement property from the qualified intermediary is treated as an exchange with the qualified intermediary.

Section 1031(f) provides special rules for property exchanges between related parties. Under § 1031(f)(1), a taxpayer exchanging like-kind property with a related person cannot use the nonrecognition provisions of § 1031 if, within 2 years of the date of the last transfer, either the related person disposes of the relinquished property or the taxpayer disposes of the replacement property. The taxpayer takes any gain or loss into account in the taxable year in which the disposition occurs. For purposes of § 1031(f), the term "related person" means any person bearing a relationship to the taxpayer described in § 267(b) or 707(b)(1).

Section 1031(f) is intended to deny nonrecognition treatment for transactions in which related parties make like-kind exchanges of high basis property for low basis property in anticipation of the sale of the low basis property. The legislative history underlying § 1031(f) states that "if a related party exchange is followed shortly thereafter by a disposition of the property, the related parties have, in effect, 'cashed out' of the investment, and the original exchange should not be accorded nonrecognition treatment." H.R. Rep. No. 247, 101st Cong. 1st Sess. 1340 (1989).

To prevent related parties from circumventing the rules of § 1031(f)(1), § 1031(f)(4) provides that the nonrecognition provisions of § 1031 do not apply to any exchange that is part of a transaction (or a series of transactions) structured to avoid the purposes of § 1031(f)(1). The legislative history underlying § 1031(f)(4) provides:

> If a taxpayer, pursuant to a pre-arranged plan, transfers property to an unrelated party who then exchanges the property with a party related to the taxpayer within 2 years of the previous transfer in a transaction otherwise qualifying under section 1031, the related party will not be entitled to nonrecognition treatment under section 1031. *Id.* at 1341.

Accordingly, under § 1031(f)(4), if an unrelated third party is used to circumvent the purposes of the related party rule in § 1031(f), the nonrecognition provisions of § 1031 do not apply to the transaction.

In the present case, A is using QI to circumvent the purposes of § 1031(f) in the same way that the unrelated party was used to circumvent the purposes of § 1031(f) in the legislative history example. Absent § 1031(f)(1), A could have engaged in a like-kind exchange of Property 1 for Property 2 with B, and B could have sold Property 1 to C. Under § 1031(f)(1), however, the non-recognition provisions of § 1031(a) do not apply to that exchange because A and B are related parties and B sells the replacement property within 2 years of the exchange.

Accordingly, to avoid the application of § 1031(f)(1), A transfers low-basis Property 1 to QI who sells it to C for cash. QI acquires the high-basis replacement property from B and pays B the cash received from C. Thus, A engages in a like-kind exchange with QI, an unrelated third party, instead of B. However, the end result of the transaction is the same as if A had exchanged property with B followed by a sale from B to C. This series of transactions allows A to effectively cash out of the investment in Property 1 without the recognition of gain.

A's exchange of property with QI, therefore, is part of a transaction structured to avoid the purposes of § 1031(f) and, under § 1031(f)(4), the non-recognition provisions of § 1031 do not apply to the exchange between A and QI. A's exchange of Property 1 for Property 2 is treated as a taxable transaction. Under § 1001(a), A has gain of $100x, the difference between A's amount realized on the exchange ($150x, the fair market value of Property 2) and A's adjusted basis in the property exchanged ($50x).

HOLDING

Under the facts described above, a taxpayer who transfers relinquished property to a qualified intermediary in exchange for replacement property formerly owned by a related party is not entitled to nonrecognition treatment under § 1031(a) of the Internal Revenue Code if, as part of the transaction, the related party receives cash or other non-like-kind property for the replacement property.

Priv. Ltr. Rul. 2007-09-036

(Nov. 28, 2006)

FACTS

Taxpayer is a State A limited liability company (LLC) that is taxed as a partnership. Taxpayer is an affiliate of Parent REIT, a publicly held real estate investment trust (REIT) organized in State B that elected to be taxed as a REIT beginning with its taxable year ended on Date C.

Parent REIT is the sole general partner and 90 percent owner of Operating Partnership, a State A limited partnership that is classified as a partnership for federal income tax purposes. Operating Partnership owns a 99 percent interest in Taxpayer and is the managing member. Operating Partnership also is sole owner of various entities that have each filed an election under § 856(l)(1) to be treated as a taxable REIT subsidiary of Taxpayer.

Taxpayer owns multiple parcels of real property through separate LLC's and partnerships. Taxpayer owns all of Property D LLC, a disregarded entity that owns Property D, an office and retail property. Taxpayer has owned and held Property D for more than two years in its business of leasing space to tenants.

Taxpayer proposes the following transaction:

1) Taxpayer will agree to transfer all its membership interest in Property D LLC to a taxable REIT subsidiary (Buyer TRS) for an amount of cash equal to its fair market value (Sale Agreement).

2) Taxpayer will enter into an agreement with an unrelated party to act as a qualified intermediary (QI) (as defined in § 1.1031(k)-1(g)(4) of the Income Tax Regulations) in the Taxpayer's exchange. The QI will not be a "disqualified person" with respect to Taxpayer within the meaning of § 1.1031(k)-1(k).

3) Taxpayer will assign to QI its rights to receive all proceeds payable by Buyer TRS in the Sales Agreement.

4) Buyer TRS will pay the price stated in the Sale Agreement to QI and Taxpayer will convey its interest in Property D LLC to Buyer TRS.

5) Taxpayer will identify a limited number of replacement properties to QI within 45 days after the transfer of its interest in Property D LLC to Buyer TRS in compliance with § 1.1031(k)-1(b) and (c).

6) Taxpayer will direct QI to acquire and transfer to Taxpayer one or more of the designated replacement properties within 180 days after Taxpayer's transfer of its interest in Property D LLC.

Buyer TRS anticipates selling some or all of the property it acquired from Taxpayer within two years from the date of its acquisition by Buyer TRS. Taxpayer and Buyer TRS are related within the meaning of § 1031(f)(3).

ANALYSIS

Section 1031(a)(1) generally provides that no gain or loss shall be recognized on the exchange of property held for productive use in a trade or business or for investment if such property is exchanged solely for property of like kind which is to be held either for productive use in a trade or business or for investment.

Section 1031(f) sets forth special rules for exchanges between related persons. Section 1031(f)(1) provides that if (A) a taxpayer exchanges property with a related person; (B) there is nonrecognition of gain or loss to the taxpayer in accordance with § 1031 with respect to the exchange; and (C) within 2 years of the date of the last transfer that was part of the exchange either the taxpayer or the related person disposes of the property received in the exchange, then there is no nonrecognition of gain or loss in the exchange. In other words, the gain or loss that was deferred under § 1031 must be recognized. Any gain or loss the taxpayer is required to recognize by reason of § 1031(f)(1) is taken into account as of the date of the disposition of the property received in the exchange (the second disposition).

Section 1031(f)(4) provides that § 1031 shall not apply to any exchange that is part of a transaction, or series of transactions, structured to avoid the purposes of § 1031(f). Thus, if a transaction is set up to avoid the restrictions on exchanges between related persons, § 1031(f)(4) operates to prevent nonrecognition of the gain or loss on the exchange.

In the present case, § 1031(f)(1) is not applicable to currently tax Taxpayer's disposition of Property D because Taxpayer is exchanging property with a QI that is not a related person.[29] However, § 1031(f)(4) provides that § 1031 shall not apply to any exchange that is part of a transaction, or series of transactions, structured to avoid the purposes of § 1031(f). Thus, § 1031 will not apply if Taxpayer's exchange is struc-

---

29. [1] Although Taxpayer transferred its interest in Property D LLC, a disregarded entity, the sale of such interest is treated as a sale of the assets of the disregarded entity for federal income tax purposes. Rev. Rul. 99-5, 1999-1 C.B. 434.

tured to avoid the "purposes" of § 1031(f). Both the Ways and Means Committee Report and the Senate Finance Committee Print describe the policy concern that led to enactment of § 1031(f):

> Because a like-kind exchange results in the substitution of the basis of the exchanged property for the property received, related parties have engaged in like-kind exchanges of high basis property for low basis property in anticipation of the sale of the low basis property in order to reduce or avoid the recognition of gain on the subsequent sale. Basis shifting also can be used to accelerate a loss on retained property. The committee believes that if a related party exchange is followed shortly thereafter by a disposition of the property, the related parties have, in effect, "cashed out" of the investment, and the original exchange should not be accorded nonrecognition treatment.

H.R. Rep. No. 247, 101st Cong. 1st Sess. 1340 (1989); S. Print No. 56, at 151. The Committee Reports also included the following example of when § 1031(f)(4) applies:

> If a taxpayer, pursuant to a pre-arranged plan, transfers property to an unrelated party who then exchanges the property with a party related to the taxpayer within 2 years of the previous transfer in a transaction otherwise qualifying under § 1031, the related party will not be entitled to nonrecognition treatment under § 1031.

H.R. Rep. No. 247, at 1341; S. Print No. 56, at 152.

In Rev. Rul. 2002-83, the Service discussed and applied § 1031(f)(4) to the following facts:

> Individual A owns real property (Property 1) with a fair market value of $150x and an adjusted basis of $50x. Individual B owns real property (Property 2) with a fair market value of $150x and an adjusted basis of $150x. Both Property 1 and Property 2 are held for investment within the meaning of § 1031(a). A and B are related persons within the meaning of § 267(b). C, an individual unrelated to A and B, wishes to acquire Property 1 from A. A enters into an agreement for the transfers of Property 1 and Property 2 with B, C, and a qualified intermediary (QI). QI is unrelated to A and B. Pursuant to their agreement, on January 6, 2003, A transfers Property 1 to QI and QI transfers Property 1 to C for $150x. On January 13, 2003, QI acquires Property 2 from B, pays B the $150x sale proceeds from QI's sale of Property 1, and transfers Property 2 to A.

In analyzing these facts under § 1031(f)(4), the Service quoted the legislative history cited above for the proposition that § 1031(f)(4) is intended to apply to situations in which related parties effectuate like-kind exchanges of high basis property for low basis property in anticipation of the sale of the low basis property. In such case, the original exchange should not be accorded nonrecognition treatment. Under the facts in the revenue ruling, A and B were attempting to sell Property 1 to an unrelated party while using the substituted basis rule of § 1031(d) to reduce the gain on such sale from $100x to $0. This allowed the parties to "cash out" of their investment in

Property 1 without the recognition of gain. The Service concluded that the transaction was structured to avoid the purposes of § 1031(f) and, therefore, A had gain of $100x on its transfer of Property 1.

In the present case, Taxpayer and Buyer TRS are not exchanging properties either directly or through the QI. Buyer TRS did not own, prior to the exchange, any property that Taxpayer will acquire in the exchange. Rather, prior to the exchange, Taxpayer owns Property D and Buyer TRS, the related person, will acquire Property D by purchasing it for a fair market value price from the QI. Thus, because there is no transaction, or series of transactions, structured to avoid the purposes of § 1031(f), § 1031(f)(4) is not applicable. In addition, because § 1031(f)(1) and § 1031(f)(4) are not applicable, the restriction contained in § 1031(f)(1)(C) on disposition of the relinquished property or the replacement property within two years of acquisition does not apply.

OPINION

Based on the facts and representations submitted by Taxpayer, we rule that § 1031(f) will not apply to trigger recognition of any gain realized when Taxpayer (i) transfers the relinquished property to Buyer TRS, a related person, for cash consideration received by the QI, (ii) acquires like-kind replacement property from an unrelated person through the QI, and (iii) Buyer TRS disposes of some or all of Taxpayer's relinquished property within two years of the acquisition.

DISCLAIMERS

These rulings relate only to the application of § 1031(f) to the exchanges described above. No opinion is expressed regarding whether the other requirements of § 1031 have been satisfied. In addition, no opinion is expressed regarding whether Parent REIT qualifies as a REIT for federal income tax purposes. Finally, except as specifically provided above, no opinion is expressed as to the federal tax treatment of the transaction under any other provisions of the Internal Revenue Code and the Income Tax Regulations that may be applicable or under any other general principles of federal income taxation.

The rulings contained in this letter are based upon information and representations submitted by the taxpayer and accompanied by a penalty of perjury statement executed by an appropriate party. While this office has not verified any of the material submitted in support of the request for rulings, it is subject to verification on examination. This ruling is directed only to the taxpayers requesting it. Section 6110(k)(3) of the Code provides that it may not be used or cited as precedent.

A copy of this letter must be attached to any income tax return to which it is relevant. We enclose a copy of the letter for this purpose. Also enclosed is a copy of the letter showing the deletions proposed to be made when it is disclosed under § 6110. In accordance with the Power of Attorney on file with this office, a copy of this letter is being sent to your authorized representative.

This ruling is directed only to Taxpayer. Section 6110 (k)(3) provides that it may not be cited as precedent.... This document may not be used or cited as precedent. Section 6110(j)(3) of the Internal Revenue Code.

Chapter 12

Safeguarding Exchange Proceeds

I. Commentary

To competently advise property owners with respect to deferred multiple-party exchanges, attorneys must be familiar with each of the safe harbors. The safe harbors do not, however, guarantee that exchange proceeds will be safe.[1] In fact, several qualified intermediaries have lost exchange proceeds they held, either through mismanagement or theft.[2] Exchangers who cannot complete an exchange due to qualified intermediary misbehavior lose the tax benefit of the exchange and may lose their exchange proceeds.[3] Attorneys must, therefore, be aware of the risk associated with hiring a qualified intermediary and consider ways to minimize the risk. The operations and investment practices of qualified intermediaries are not transparent, so they make unverifiable claims about their practices. Consequently, due diligence often will not uncover bad behavior by companies that may enjoy strong public reputations.

Some attorneys may suggest that exchangers can minimize their risks of hiring a qualified intermediary by using a combination of safe harbors (such as a qualified intermediary and qualified escrow account or qualified trust).[4] Such combinations may raise the cost of the exchange and dissuade exchangers from choosing such alternatives. The effect of combined safe harbors may be to keep exchange proceeds out of the bankruptcy estate of a failed qualified intermediary, but the time it takes to retrieve the proceeds may push the transaction beyond the section 1031 time limits and disqualify the intended exchange from section 1031 nonrecognition. Furthermore, reports related to qualified intermediary collapses suggest that eventually exchangers typically recover most, if not all, of their exchange proceeds from the bankruptcy

---

1. *See* Millard Refrigerated Servs. v. LandAmerica 1031 Exch. Servs. (*In re* LandAmerica Fin. Group, Inc.), 412 B.R. 800 (E.D. Va. 2009). *But see* Joint Motion Pursuant to Rule 9019, Case 08-03149-KRH, Doc. 39 (Bankr. E.D. Va. Feb. 19, 2009) (approving the settlement regarding funds held in a qualified escrow account).

2. *See* Bradley T. Borden, *Section 1031 Qualified Intermediaries in the New Economy*, 27 J. Tax'n Inv. 86 (2009).

3. The IRS provides a safe harbor method for reporting gain or loss for exchangers who lose exchange proceeds at the fault of the qualified intermediary. *See* Rev. Proc. 2010-14, 2010-12 I.R.B. 456.

4. *See* Treas. Reg. § 1.1031(k)-1(g).

estate of the failed qualified intermediary.[5] In fact, the vast majority of exchanges that intermediaries facilitate take advantage of only the qualified intermediary safe harbor. Instead, some exchangers rely solely on the qualified intermediary safe harbor, but insist that the intermediary use an account that requires the signature of both the qualified intermediary and the exchanger for any withdrawals to be made. Attorneys who assist exchangers with such arrangements must ensure that they satisfy the safe harbor requirements.[6]

Many exchangers, particularly those with lower-value properties, choose not to hire tax advisors when they do section 1031 exchanges. Instead, they often rely upon exchange facilitators for advice regarding their exchanges. Most exchange facilitators provide in their form documents that they do not provide legal and tax advice, but that may not stop them from doing so. Furthermore, if an exchanger is not otherwise receiving tax advice, exchange facilitators will often feel pressure or a sense of obligation to provide advice. Facilitators who provide tax advice and oversee an exchange owe a duty of care to exchangers, which exposes facilitators to liability for negligence if they fail to fulfill that duty.[7]

II. Primary Legal Authority

Millard Refrigerated Services, Inc. v. LandAmerica 1031 Exchange Services, Inc.

United States Bankruptcy Court, Eastern District of Virginia
412 B.R. 800 (2009)

FACTS

This case is one of over 85 adversary proceedings that have been brought, so far, by former customers of LES in connection with its Chapter 11 bankruptcy case. Each of these former customers asserts that money deposited into the bank accounts of LES to facilitate like-kind exchanges was held in trust for its benefit and should be returned to it. As of the Petition Date, the Debtor had approximately 450 uncompleted exchange transactions. Each of these uncompleted exchange transactions was governed by a separate exchange agreement executed by LES and its former customer.

The Debtor identified two primary types of exchange agreements that LES utilized in the course of its operations: (a) agreements that included language contemplating that the applicable exchange funds would be placed into an account or sub-account associated with the relevant customer's name (the "Segregated Account Agreements"); and (b) agreements that did not include this "segregation" language (the "Commingled Account Agreements"). Approximately 50 of the uncompleted

---

5. *See* Bradley T. Borden, Paul L.B. McKenney & David Shechtman, *Like-Kind Exchanges and Qualified Intermediaries*, 124 TAX NOTES 55 (July 6, 2009).

6. *See* Treas. Reg. § 1.1031(k)-1(g)(4), (6).

7. *See, e.g.*, Kreisers, Inc. v. First Dakota Ltd. P'ship, 852 N.W.2d 413 (S.D. 2014).

exchange transactions involved Segregated Account Agreements while the remaining approximately 400 of the uncompleted exchange transactions involved Commingled Account Agreements.

The Court entered a protocol order on January 16, 2009, wherein the Court stayed the litigation in all but five of the over 85 adversary proceedings (the "Protocol Order"). Each of the five select cases, which were allowed to proceed on an expedited basis, presented legal and factual issues that were common to certain of the other adversary proceedings. Three of the select cases were representative of customers who had Commingled Account Agreements: those with type A agreements, those with type B agreements, and customers with hybrid agreements under which both cash and non-cash proceeds were transferred to LES.[8] Two of the select cases were representative of customers who had Segregated Account Agreements: customers with escrow account agreements and customers with segregated exchange agreements. The Millard adversary proceeding currently before the Court is the adversary proceeding selected to be the representative case for customers with segregated exchange agreements.

By Order entered February 10, 2009, the Court divided the litigation involving the five select cases into phases and limited the scope of the first phase to tracing of exchange funds, contractual interpretation of the exchange agreements, the existence of an express trust and the existence of a resulting trust. In the Millard adversary proceeding, the case presently before the Court, hearing was conducted on the cross motions for partial summary judgment on April 7, 2009, at which counsel for Millard, counsel for the LFG Committee, counsel for the LES Committee, and counsel for the Debtor all presented argument. Pursuant to the terms of the Court's Protocol Order, all of the parties to the stayed adversary proceedings were permitted to file amicus briefs advocating their respective positions in this case.

This Memorandum Opinion sets forth the Court's findings of fact and conclusions of law pursuant to Rule 7052 of the Federal Rules of Bankruptcy Procedure.[9] The Court has subject matter jurisdiction over this adversary proceeding pursuant to 28 U.S.C. §§ 157(a) and 1334 and the General Order of Reference from the United States District Court for the Eastern District of Virginia dated August 15, 1984. This is a core proceeding under 28 U.S.C. §§ 157(b)(2)(A), (M) and (O), in which final orders

---

8. [1] As defined by the parties, Commingled Type A Cases generally involve the wire transfer of exchange funds to a general LES account at SunTrust Bank; Commingled Type B Cases generally involve the deposit by LES of exchange funds into a LES account at SunTrust Bank. (Joint Motion of Debtor and LES Committee for Order Establishing Scheduling Protocol, ¶ 8.) Another distinction between Type A and Type B Cases can be found in Section 3(a) of the respective Exchange Agreements. The Type A agreements state that interest will be computed from the first business day following LES' receipt of funds in the account "it maintains at SunTrust Bank for the purpose of collecting taxpayers' exchange funds." The use of the plural possessive "taxpayers'" suggests that the funds of multiple customers are being deposited into the same SunTrust account. The Type B agreements state that interest will be computed after receipt "in an account maintained at SunTrust Bank" without reference to other "taxpayers." The hybrid agreements are otherwise Type B agreements.

9. [3] Findings of fact shall be construed as conclusions of law and conclusions of law shall be construed as findings of fact when appropriate. See Fed. R. Bankr. P. 7052.

or judgments may be entered by a bankruptcy judge. Venue is appropriate in this Court pursuant to 28 U.S.C. § 1409(a).

Millard contends that it is entitled to partial summary judgment with respect to Count I (Declaratory Relief) and Count II (Injunctive Relief) of its Complaint against LES because its exchange funds were held in three segregated sub-accounts of LES established and maintained for the benefit of Millard. Millard contends that the exchange funds held in the segregated accounts are held in trust and, therefore, are not property of the Debtor pursuant to 11 U.S.C. § 541(d). Thus, it argues that the exchange funds should be turned over to Millard in their entirety, outside of the bankruptcy pro rata distribution system.

The Committees and the Debtor counter that the exchange funds were held by LES pursuant to the terms of exchange agreements executed by Millard and LES. The three exchange agreements at issue here, they argue, set forth the complete agreement and understanding of the parties plainly and unambiguously. The Committees point out that under the terms and provisions of the exchange agreements, Millard disclaimed all "right, title and interest" in and to the exchange funds and provided LES with exclusive rights of "dominion, control and use" with respect to the exchange funds. From this they argue that it was the clear intention of the parties not to create a trust arrangement. The Committees and the Debtor assert that Millard vested LES with full authority over the exchange funds and, in so doing, Millard transferred clearly more than bare legal title to the exchange funds. They conclude that the contractual relationship established between Millard and LES was not one of trustee and beneficiary; rather, they assert that the relationship was, and continues to be, one of debtor and creditor. Thus, they argue that while the Debtor may be contractually obligated to perform the exchange transactions on Millard's behalf, its failure to do so would render it liable only for the breach of its contract and under no other theory of liability. They argue that Millard should receive the same pro rata treatment as all of the other former exchange customers of LES.[10]

The material facts are not in dispute. Millard is a Georgia corporation engaged in the refrigerated warehouse and distribution business. It maintains 35 locations throughout the country. LES is a wholly owned subsidiary of LandAmerica Financial Group, Inc. ("LFG"). On November 24, 2008, LES ceased doing business as a qualified intermediary for like-kind exchanges. On November 26, 2008 (the "Petition Date"), LES filed, along with LFG, a petition for relief under Chapter 11 of the United States

---

10. [4] In the ordinary course of its business, LES invested certain of the exchange funds it received from its former customers. Some of the invested exchange funds received by LES are now held in the form of illiquid auction rate securities as a result of the unprecedented, rapid economic decline experienced in the latter part of 2008 that left the credit markets frozen. As a consequence, LES does not have the ability from a liquidity standpoint to fund all of the exchanges it is contractually obligated to complete within the time parameters that § 1031 of the Internal Revenue Code requires. To permit one group of exchangers to recover their exchange funds under a trust theory necessarily reduces the amount of liquid funds available for distribution to other exchange creditors and impacts all of the other exchange creditors adversely, whether similarly situated or otherwise.

Bankruptcy Code in this Court. The LES Committee and the LFG Committee both are statutory committees appointed in the respective bankruptcy cases of LES and LFG. The Committees were each granted leave to intervene in this action.

Prior to the Petition Date, LES was a qualified intermediary for like-kind exchanges consummated by taxpayers pursuant to § 1031 of the Internal Revenue Code, 26 U.S.C. § 1031 ("1031 Exchange"). A 1031 Exchange allows a taxpayer to defer the payment of tax that otherwise would be due upon the realization of a gain on the disposition of business or investment property. *Id.* In the typical transaction, an exchanger such as Millard assigns its rights as seller under a purchase agreement for the disposition of business or investment property to a qualified intermediary such as LES. The purchaser of the relinquished property transfers the net sales proceeds directly to the qualified intermediary.

Under § 1031, the exchanger must identify like-kind replacement property within 45 days. The exchanger has 180 days to close on the replacement property. *Id.* The qualified intermediary purchases the replacement property and then transfers the replacement property to the exchanger. In the event that the replacement property is not identified or the closing is not completed within the specified time periods, then the qualified intermediary pays an amount equal to the net sales proceeds it realized from the sale of the relinquished property to the exchanger. This series of transactions is governed by a written exchange agreement executed by the exchanger and the qualified intermediary.[11]

Beginning in 1992, LES maintained a general, multipurpose checking account at SunTrust Bank, Inc. ("SunTrust"). This checking account was titled in LES' own name, bearing an account number with the last four digits "3318." LES used this account as its general operating account. The SunTrust account received cash (i) in the form of certain customers' exchange funds, (ii) in the form of service fees charged to customers, (iii) in the form of interest, and (iv) in the form of returns on LES' investment of the cash it received. LES disbursed funds from the SunTrust account to pay its expenses, to pay dividends to LFG, to make investments in other investment

---

11. [6] The treasury regulations governing § 1031 Exchanges make clear that the taxpayer must abrogate all control over the exchange funds until the exchange is completed. "If the taxpayer actually or constructively receives money or property in the full amount of the consideration for the relinquished property before the taxpayer actually receives like-kind replacement property, the transaction will constitute a sale and not a deferred exchange, even though the taxpayer may ultimately receive like-kind replacement property." Treas. Reg. § 1.1031(k)-1(f). However, the abrogation of control required by the treasury regulations does not require the taxpayer to relinquish all right, title and interest to the exchange funds as the parties to these Exchange Agreements (as hereinafter defined) contracted for Millard to do. *See* DeGroot v. Exchanged Titles, Inc., 159 B.R. 303, 306 (Bankr. C.D. Cal. March 27, 1993) ("for the purpose of the exchange ... there was no need for [the accommodator] to acquire 'real' interest in the ... property ... to make the exchange qualify under the statute.... ' ") (citation omitted); Cook v. Garcia, No. 96-55285, 1997 U.S. App. LEXIS 5980, 1997 WL 143827, at *1 (9th Cir.1997) ("A taxpayer need not abandon all equitable interests in the proceeds ... for a transaction to qualify as a non-taxable event under section 1031."). This negates Millard's argument that the disclaimers contained in Section 2 of the Exchange Agreements were included only because the treasury regulations required them to be included.

vehicles, and to purchase replacement property for customers who had not insisted that their exchange funds be deposited in segregated accounts.

LES used funds in the SunTrust account to invest in a variety of short-term investments, including money market mutual funds, short-term bonds, certificates of deposit, floating rate notes, and auction rate securities.[12] The auction rate securities were held in a brokerage investment account at SmithBarney and SunTrust Robinson Humphrey. Each evening, the aggregate cash balance in the SunTrust account was swept out into an LES overnight investment account and then returned to the SunTrust account the following morning. The SunTrust account is referred to as the commingled account of LES (the "Commingled Account").

Treasury Regulation Section 1.468B-6, 26 C.F.R. § 1.468B-6,[13] establishes rules concerning the taxation of exchange funds held by exchange facilitators. The default rule established by the treasury regulation is that where the exchange funds exceed $2 million, they will be treated for tax purposes as a loan from the taxpayer to the qualified intermediary. Treas. Reg. § 1.468B-6(c)(1); Treas. Reg. § 1.7872-5(b)(16). There are, however, four safe harbor exceptions to this default rule. One of those safe harbors provides that if a qualified intermediary holds the exchange funds in a segregated account established under the taxpayer's name and identification number, then the qualified intermediary need not take into account items of income, deduction, and credit attributable to the exchange funds. Treas. Reg. § 1.468B-6(c)(2)(i)–(ii). Under this exception exchange funds held in sub-accounts are treated as separate accounts even though they may be linked to a master account. Treas. Reg. § 1.468B-6(c)(2)(ii).

LES entered into an exchange management control account agreement with Citibank, N.A. ("Citibank") in August 2008. This management control account agreement permitted LES to open segregated client sub-accounts (the "Segregated Accounts") under one or more control accounts. Millard and LES entered into three substantially identical exchange agreements on October 21, 2008 (the "Exchange Agreements"), with LES acting as qualified intermediary. Previously, prior to 2006, Millard had successfully completed two 1031 Exchange transactions with a different qualified intermediary known as Apex Property Exchange, Inc. In connection with those earlier exchange transactions, Millard had specifically negotiated for the exchange funds to be held in segregated sub-accounts associated with Millard's name and taxpayer identification number. Consistent with those previous transactions, Millard discussed with LES the use of the Segregated Accounts for the 2008 1031 Exchange transactions; and ultimately, the parties agreed that the proceeds of the sales of Millard's Relinquished Properties would be placed in the Segregated Accounts maintained by LES at Citibank.[14]

---

12. [7] See note 4 [*supra*] regarding LES' investments in auction rate securities.

13. [8] All subsequent references to Treasury Regulations may be found in Title 26 of the Code of Federal Regulations in correspondingly numbered sections.

14. [10] *See* Treas. Reg. § 1.1031(k)-1(g)(4)(i). The language of this section says that the "determination of whether the taxpayer is in actual or constructive receipt of money or other property before the taxpayer actually receives like-kind replacement property is made as if the qualified inter-

Pursuant to the three Exchange Agreements dated October 21, 2008, Millard assigned to LES its rights as seller under purchase agreements for three separate properties (the "Relinquished Properties"). The net sale proceeds from the sale of Millard's Relinquished Properties (the "Exchange Funds") were transferred by the closing agents directly to the LES master account at Citibank. The Exchange Funds were then moved from the master account into the separate sub-accounts, i.e. the Segregated Accounts, associated with Millard's name and Millard's taxpayer identification number. The Exchange Funds were never held in the Commingled Account. The Segregated Accounts were in the name of and were controlled by LES. Only LES had the ability to direct the disbursement or withdrawal of the Exchange Funds. LES was the only signatory on the Segregated Accounts. Only LES had direct control of movement within or between the master account and the sub-accounts. The parties agreed in the Exchange Agreements that LES could earn interest or other fees on the Exchange Funds through its maintenance of the master account and the Segregated Accounts.

Section 2 of each of the Exchange Agreements provides in pertinent part:

> (c) Subject to the investment protocol described in Paragraph 3 below, LES shall have sole and exclusive possession, dominion, control and use of all Exchange Funds, including interest, if any, earned on the Exchange Funds.... This agreement i) expressly limits the Taxpayer's[15] rights to receive, pledge, borrow or otherwise obtain the benefits of money or other property held by the qualified intermediary.... Taxpayer shall have no right, title, or interest in or to the Exchange Funds or any earnings thereon and Taxpayer shall have no right, power, or option to demand, call for, receive, pledge, borrow or otherwise obtain the benefits of any of the Exchange Funds....

Section 3 of each of the Exchange Agreements (to which Section 2 was expressly subject) requires LES to place the Exchange Funds in Segregated Accounts. It further provides that all earnings on the Exchange Funds were payable to Millard.[16] Section 3 does not restrict the ability of LES to pledge, encumber, borrow, or otherwise receive the benefits of the Exchange Funds placed in the Segregated Accounts. Section 4 of

---

mediary is not the agent of the taxpayer." This suggests that the intent of the Internal Revenue Service is to treat the funds as NOT those of the taxpayer.

15. [11] Under the terms of the Exchange Agreements, Millard is defined as "Taxpayer."

16. [12] Millard argues that the use of an apostrophe "s" in the phrase "Taxpayer's Exchange Funds," as that phrase is used in Section 3 of the Exchange Agreements, connotes that the funds in the Segregated Accounts belong to Millard, the taxpayer. But this forced interpretation of Section 3 proves too much. If the Court were to adopt this interpretation, then more than just the beneficial interest in the Exchange Funds would remain with the taxpayer and the transaction would not pass IRS regulatory scrutiny for a 1031 Exchange. This forced interpretation would also require the Court to ignore completely the unambiguous language in Section 2 that LES shall have sole and exclusive possession, dominion, control and use of the Exchange Funds and that Millard shall have no right, title, or interest in or to the Exchange Funds. If the alternate interpretation that Millard now advances was truly what the parties intended, there were better ways to evidence that intent than through the use of an apostrophe "s" in an isolated phrase contained in Section 3 of the parties' Exchange Agreement.

each of the Exchange Agreements sets forth the procedures for Millard to identify the Replacement Property. Section 5 of each of the Exchange Agreements sets forth the terms under which LES will acquire the Replacement Property and transfer it to Millard. Section 6 of each of the Exchange Agreements makes clear that the sole purpose of the Exchange Agreements is to facilitate Millard's exchange of the Relinquished Properties for the Replacement Properties. Section 6(c) of each of the Exchange Agreements expressly limits the duties and obligations of LES. That section provides:

> LES shall only be obligated to act as an intermediary in accordance with the terms and conditions of this Exchange Agreement and shall not be bound by any other contract or agreement, whether or not LES has knowledge of any such contract or agreement or of its terms or conditions. LES has undertaken to perform only such duties as are expressly set forth herein, and no additional duties or obligations shall be implied hereunder or by operation of law or otherwise.

Each of the Exchange Agreements contains an integration (or merger) clause in Section 11 providing that "[t]his Exchange Agreement contains the entire understanding between and among the parties hereto."

ANALYSIS

* * *

Section 541 of the Bankruptcy Code provides for the creation of a bankruptcy estate upon the filing of a bankruptcy petition.[17] Property included within that estate is defined very broadly to include every interest that a debtor has in property as of the commencement of the bankruptcy case, wherever located and by whomever held. *United States v. Whiting Pools, Inc.*, 462 U.S. 198, 204–05 (1983) ("The House and Senate Reports on the Bankruptcy Code indicate that § 541(a)(1)'s scope is broad."); *Grochal v. Ocean Tech. Servs. Corp. (In re Baltimore Marine Indus.)*, 476 F.3d 238, 240 (4th Cir. 2007) ("Section 541 of the Bankruptcy Code governs the composition of the bankruptcy estate and provides a broad definition of 'property of the estate.'").

In line with the broad definition of "property of the estate," money held in a bank account in the name of a debtor is presumed to be property of the bankruptcy estate. *See, e.g., In re Amdura Corp.*, 75 F.3d 1447, 1451 (10th Cir. 1996) ("We presume that deposits in a bank to the credit of a bankruptcy debtor belong to the entity in whose name the account is established."); *Boyer v. Carlton, Fields, Ward, Emmanuel, Smith & Cutler, P.A. (In re U.S.A. Diversified Prods., Inc.)*, 100 F.3d 53, 55 (7th Cir. 1996) ("Property of the debtor is defined to include all legal or equitable interests of the debtor ... and obviously that includes the interest that a depositor has in the money

---

17. [14] Section 541 of the Bankruptcy Code provides in pertinent part:

    (a) The commencement of a case under § 301, 302, or 303 of this title creates an estate. Such estate is comprised of all the following property, wherever located and by whomever held:

        (1) Except as provided in subsections (b) and (c)(2) of this section, all legal or equitable interests of the debtor in property as of the commencement of the case.

in his account, more precisely the money owed him by the bank by virtue of the account.") (internal quotations omitted); *Asurion Ins. Servs., Inc. v. Amp'd Mobile, Inc. (In re Amp'd Mobile, Inc.)*, 377 B.R. 478, 483 (Bankr. D. Del. 2007) ("Property held by a debtor is presumed to be property of the estate."); *Sousa v. Bank of Newport*, 170 B.R. 492, 494 (D.R.I. 1994) (the bankruptcy estate "includes funds held in a checking or savings account"); *Stratton v. Equitable Bank, N.A.*, 104 B.R. 713, 726 (D.Md.1989) (funds deposited in an account owned and controlled by the debtor become the debtor's property).[18]

In this case, the facts mandate a presumption that the Exchange Funds are the property of the LES bankruptcy estate. The Exchange Funds were derived from the proceeds of the sale of the Relinquished Properties that Millard had assigned to LES. The Exchange Funds were transferred from the third party purchasers of these Relinquished Properties directly into the bank account of LES by the closing agents. The transferred funds remained in the bank accounts of LES through the Petition Date. Millard never had any ability to withdraw the funds. The accounts were under the complete control of LES. Only LES had the ability to disburse or withdraw the funds. As LES maintained the exchange funds in bank accounts in its name and under its control, the money is presumably property of the LES bankruptcy estate. *Boyer v. Carlton, Fields, Ward, Emmanuel, Smith & Cutler, P.A. (In re USA Diversified Products, Inc.)*, 100 F.3d 53, 55 (7th Cir.1996) (estate property "includes the interest that a depositor has in the money in its account"); *Elsaesser v. Gale (In re Salt Lake City R.V., Inc.)*, No. 95-03264-7, 1999 WL 33486709, at 4 (Bankr. D. Idaho, March 17, 1999) ("[m]oney in a bank account under the debtor's control presumptively constitutes property of the debtor's estate....").

To rebut this presumption that the funds are property of the bankruptcy estate of LES, Millard must show that it retained some right to the funds. Any such right to the funds must be established as an interest in property recognized under state law.[19] *Butner v. United States*, 440 U.S. 48, 55 (1979). Millard contends that LES was temporarily holding the Exchange Funds on its behalf solely for the purpose of facilitating the exchange of the Relinquished Properties for the Replacement Properties. Millard maintains that it never parted with its equitable interest in the ownership of the Exchange Funds[20] and that LES was holding the Exchange Funds in trust for Millard's

---

18. [15] *See* Collier on Bankruptcy ¶ 541.09 (Alan N. Resnick & Henry J. Sommer, eds., 15th ed. Rev.2008) ("deposits in the debtor's bank account become property of the estate under § 541(a)(1)").

19. [16] One of Millard's alternative arguments is that LES was acting as a mere conduit for its Exchange Funds; and, as such, the funds are excluded from the LES bankruptcy estate pursuant to § 541(d) of the Bankruptcy Code as a matter of federal common law. In support, it cites City of Springfield, Mass. v. Ostrander (In re LAN Tamers), 329 F.3d 204 (1st Cir. 2003); T & B Scottdale Contractors, Inc. v. United States, 866 F.2d 1372 (11th Cir. 1989). In those cases cited by Millard in support of this position, the funds originated from a Federal program and were earmarked for a specific statutory purpose. That is not the case here where the Exchange Funds represent the net proceeds of third party purchasers' acquisitions of Relinquished Properties.

20. [17] Legal title to property and the equitable interest in property are separate property interests. *See, e.g.*, In re Halabi, 184 F.3d 1335, 1337 (11th Cir. 1999).

benefit. Therefore, it asserts, although the Exchange Funds may have been held in the bank accounts of LES, they did not become property of the LES bankruptcy estate. 11 U.S.C. § 541(d).[21] Millard points to the fact that under the Exchange Agreements LES was required to place the Exchange Funds in segregated sub-accounts associated with Millard's name and taxpayer identification number.[22] Millard also points to the fact that nothing in the Exchange Agreements imposes on LES any risk of loss commonly associated with ownership. These facts, together with the fact that Millard retained the benefits of accrued interest, are strong indicia, Millard argues, that it never parted with its equitable ownership interest in the Exchange Funds. Millard concludes, therefore, that LES holds the funds in trust for its benefit.

Whether property in the possession of the Debtor is held in trust for Millard is a question of state law. *Butner*, 440 U.S. at 55, 99. While federal law creates the bankruptcy estate, state law defines the scope and existence of the debtor's interest in property. *Raleigh v. Ill. Dept. of Revenue*, 530 U.S. 15, 20 (2000) ("The 'basic federal rule' in bankruptcy is that state law governs the substance of claims, Congress having 'generally left the determination of property rights in the assets of the bankrupt's estate to state law.'") (quoting *Butner*, 440 U.S. at 57). LES and Millard agreed that the Exchange Agreements would be governed by Virginia law.[23] That contractual choice of law provision is determinative of the law to be applied in this case. *See Holmes Envtl., Inc. v. Suntrust Banks, Inc. (In re Holmes Envtl., Inc.)*, 287 B.R. 363, 374 (Bankr.E.D.Va.2002) (*citing Tate v. Hain*, 181 Va. 402, 410 (1943)).

Under the terms of the Court's February 10, 2009, order, the question to be resolved at this stage of the litigation is whether the Exchange Funds are excluded from property of LES' bankruptcy estate because of the existence of either an express trust or a resulting trust. The Court will look to the law of the Commonwealth of Virginia for its analysis of these two issues. Millard bears the burden of proving the existence of a trust. *See Page v. Page*, 132 Va. 63 (1922) (party seeking to establish a trust has the burden of proving its existence); *Chiasson v. J. Louis Matherne & Assocs. (In re Oxford Mgmt., Inc.)*, 4 F.3d 1329, 1335 (5th Cir. 1993) ("When the property of an estate is

---

21. [18] Section 541(d) of the Bankruptcy Code creates a limitation on the otherwise broad definition of property of the estate. That section provides in pertinent part that: "property in which the debtor holds, as of the commencement of the case, only legal title and not an equitable interest ... becomes property of the estate under sub-section (a)(1) or (2) of this section only to the extent of the debtor's legal title to such property, but not to the extent of any equitable interest in such property that the debtor does not hold."

22. [19] Nothing in the Exchange Agreements, however, prohibited LES from investing the Exchange Funds that were placed into the Segregated Accounts (indeed LES was indemnified in the event it chose not to do so), from transferring the Exchange Funds out of the Segregated Accounts, from encumbering or pledging the Segregated Accounts for its own use, or from otherwise obtaining the benefits of the Exchange Funds. In fact, the funds in the Segregated Accounts were entirely and completely vulnerable to attachment and levy by third party creditors of LES.

23. [20] Section 11 of the Exchange Agreements provides that "[t]his Exchange Agreement shall be governed by and construed in accordance with the applicable laws of the Commonwealth of Virginia without regard to the conflict of laws provisions thereof...."

alleged to be held in trust, the burden of establishing the trust's existence rests with the claimants.").

Under Virginia law, an express trust is created only where there is "an affirmative intention to create it." *Peal v. Luther*, 199 Va. 35, 37 (1957); *Leonard v. Counts*, 221 Va. 582, 588 (1980) (an express trust is "based on the declared intention of the trustor."). The affirmative intention to create a trust may be established by "either express language to that effect or circumstances which show with reasonable certainty that a trust was intended to be created." *Woods v. Stull*, 182 Va. 888, 902 (1944); *Rivera v. Nedrich*, 259 Va. 1, 6 (1999).

There is no express language in the Exchange Agreements that creates a trust. The words "trust," "trustee," or "beneficiary" do not appear anywhere in the Exchange Agreements. Given the omission of any language normally associated with the creation of a trust, Millard must demonstrate with "reasonable certainty" circumstances that show both parties to the Exchange Agreement nevertheless intended to create a trust. *Woods v. Stull*, 182 Va. at 902.

The Court thus turns to an examination of whether Millard has demonstrated the parties' intent to create a trust despite the absence of express language to do so. Although formal or technical words are not necessary to create a trust, the fact that the Exchange Agreements make no mention of a "trust" is significant in determining whether a trust was intended. *See In re Estate of Vallery*, 883 P.2d 24, 27 (Colo.App.1993). Here, not only is there an absence of any language that the parties intended to create a trust, but there is language in the Exchange Agreements that actually evidences an intent *not* to do so. Millard, in the Exchange Agreements, conveyed exclusive possession, dominion,[24] control and use of the Exchange Funds to LES. It also disclaimed any right, title or interest in and to the Exchange Funds. That conveyance combined with that disclaimer is inconsistent with the establishment of a trust. Under a trustee-beneficiary relationship, the trustee holds legal title in the trust property and the beneficiary holds an equitable interest in the trust property. *Kubota Tractor Corp. v. Strack*, Case No. 4:06cv145, 2007 U.S. Dist. LEXIS 9803, 2007 WL 517492, at 4 (E.D. Va. 2007) (citing *Broaddus v. Gresham*, 181 Va. 725, 731 (1943)) (reversed on other grounds, *Kubota Tractor Corp. v. Strack (In re Strack)*, 524 F.3d 493 (4th Cir. 2008)). However, Millard relinquished *any and all* interests in the property, including the equitable interest that a beneficiary of a trust would retain in trust property. Millard expressly disclaimed the equitable interest that it now asks this Court to find that it otherwise somehow retained.

Further evidence that the parties did not intend the Exchange Agreements to create a trust can be found in the parties' agreement to limit the duties of LES to those expressly contained in the Exchange Agreements. A trust necessarily requires the establishment of fiduciary duties. *See Restatement (3d) of Trusts § 2* (2003) (stating that a

---

24. [21] "Dominion" has been defined by one court as "perfect control in right of ownership, and indicates that it was the intention to make the instrument as effectual as a conveyance as it was possible for the parties to make it." Baker v. Westcott, 73 Tex. 129 (1889).

trust is a fiduciary relationship with respect to property); *In re Nova Real Estate Inv. Trust*, 23 B.R. 62, 66 (Bankr.E.D.Va.1982) ("A trust involves a duty of the fiduciary to deal with particular property for the benefit of another.").[25] Fiduciary duties create a special relationship of trust and good faith that goes beyond the duties set forth in an ordinary contract between commercial parties. *See Balbir Brar Associates v. Consol. Trading Servs. Corp.*, At Law No. 137795, 1996 WL 1065615 at 5 (Va. Cir. Ct. 1996) (distinguishing between contract duties and fiduciary duties).

The parties to the Exchange Agreements acknowledged that LES was not undertaking any duties not expressly set forth in the Exchange Agreements (i.e. the contract duties) including any implied duties or any duties imposed by operation of law. This limitation on the scope of LES' duties eliminates any argument that LES had a duty to act as a fiduciary for Millard. *Metric Constructors, Inc. v. Bank of Tokyo-Mitsubishi, Ltd.*, Case No. 99-2330, 2000 U.S. App. LEXIS 23185, 2000 WL 1288317, at 4 (4th Cir. Sept.13, 2000) (holding that no fiduciary duties existed where the plaintiff "expressly consented (in the Consent Agreement) to the [defendants'] disclaimer of any fiduciary relationship toward it"). The Exchange Agreements provide that LES was acting in the narrow capacity as an exchange facilitator. The parties agreed that LES assumed no duties not expressly set forth in the Exchange Agreements including fiduciary duties and none can be implied or imposed by operation of law. LES merely had the contractual duty to effect the exchanges. The unambiguous language of the Exchange Agreements makes clear that the parties intended their relationship to be one of contract obligor and obligee.

The Exchange Agreements were integrated contracts. *See Robinette v. Robinette*, 4 Va. App. 123 (1987); *see also Lisk v. Criswell (In re Criswell)*, 52 B.R. 184, 197 (Bankr.E.D.Va.1985) (holding that an integrated agreement containing a merger clause precluded parties from claiming any reliance on "terms, conditions, statements, warranties, or representations not contained [in the integrated agreement]"). Millard cannot utilize extrinsic evidence to modify or alter the contracts' plain statements (i) that Millard had no interest, including any equitable interest, in or to the Exchange Funds and (ii) that LES owed to Millard no duty, including any fiduciary duty, not expressly set forth in the Exchange Agreements. *Robinette v. Robinette*, 4 Va. App. at 128 (holding that a party cannot introduce parol evidence to show the existence of a trust if it would defeat or contradict the terms of an express agreement). The objective language of the Exchange Agreements precludes consideration of any subjective belief that the parties may have had regarding the relationship between them. *Boone v. U.S. Attorney*, Case No. 7:06VA00006, 2006 U.S. Dist. LEXIS 22161, 2006 WL 1075010, at 3 (W.D. Va. Apr.21, 2006) ("Boone may have had a subjective intent to

---

25. [22] A trustee has a fiduciary obligation to act for the benefit of the trust beneficiary. *See* Continental Cas. Co. v. Powell, 83 F.2d 652, 654 (4th Cir. 1936) ("There is a fiduciary relation between trustee and beneficiary; there is not a fiduciary relation between debtor and creditor.") (internal citations omitted); Caldwell v. Hanes (In re Hanes), 214 B.R. 786, 812 (Bankr. E.D. Va. 1997) ("The trustee ... is a fiduciary of the trust beneficiaries.") (internal citations omitted).

the contrary, but it is the objective manifestation of intent, as shown by the words used in the agreement, that governs.").[26]

Millard argues that the intent of the parties to create a trust can be gleaned from the requirement set forth in the Exchange Agreements that the Exchange Funds were required to be held in segregated sub-accounts, but this argument fails. The requirement of Segregated Accounts may provide evidence on the traceability of the funds, but that alone does not create a trust.

In order to establish such a right as trust beneficiary, a claimant must make two showings: first the claimant must prove the existence and legal source of a trust relationship; second, the claimant must identify the trust fund or property and, where the trust fund has been commingled with general property of the bankrupt, sufficiently trace the property or funds—the res. *Conn. Gen. Life Ins. Co. v. Universal Ins. Co.*, 838 F.2d 612, 618 (1st Cir.1988). *See also Southwest State Bank v. Ellis*, 310 B.R. 762, 764 (Bankr.W.D.Okla.2004) (holding that agreement to segregate and not commingle proceeds from the sale of borrower's collateral cannot create a trust in lender's favor under "fiduciary capacity" exception to discharge under § 523(a)(4)); *Barclay's Amer./ Bus. Credit, Inc. v. Long (In re Long)*, 44 B.R. 300, 305 (Bankr.D.Minn.1983) (holding that "existence of a collateral account, into which proceeds from receivables were to be deposited in order to segregate the money" did not "create a fiduciary relationship where the substance of the relationship between the parties was that of creditor/debtor"); *cf. Kubota Tractor Corp. v. Strack (In re Strack)*, 524 F.3d 493 (4th Cir.2008) (holding that proceeds from the sale of collateral were held in trust where the agreement between the parties created an express trust in the sales proceeds).[27] The fact that the Exchange Funds were required to be placed in segregated sub-accounts provides only half of the equation. Segregation alone is insufficient to prove the parties' affirmative intention to create an express trust.[28]

---

26. [23] Millard argues that post-contractual conduct is competent to alter or contradict the express terms of an integrated contract. However, the cases cited by Millard apply to subsequent parol *agreements* between the parties—not just the parties' conduct. *See* Piedmont Mt. Airy Guano Co. v. Buchanan, 146 Va. 617, 131 S.E. 793 (1926); Centex Constr. v. Acstar Ins. Co., 448 F.Supp.2d 697, 712 (E.D. Va., 2006). No post-execution agreements between LES and Millard have been alleged in this case. Furthermore, whether a trust was created is to be determined at the time of the transfer of the property.

27. [24] Millard argues that *Strack* stands for the proposition that a segregation provision in an agreement demonstrates with reasonable certainty the intent to establish an express trust. However, the plain language of the agreement in *Strack* required the debtor to "hold the same in trust." In re Strack, 524 F.3d, at 495–96.

28. [25] The requirement for segregated accounts in the Exchange Agreements reflects the desire of the parties to satisfy one of the safe harbors offered by the Treasury Regulations in order to obtain favorable tax treatment. It does not, without more, evidence an intention to establish an express trust. Treasury Regulation section 1.468B-6 requires that any exchange funds exceeding $2 million must be maintained by a qualified intermediary in a separately identified account with all earnings on the account going to the exchanger or in a commingled account with earnings on the account disbursed pro rata to the commingled exchangers. See Treas. Reg. § 1.468B-6 (2008). Failure to do so results in treatment of the exchange funds as a loan to the qualified intermediary for tax purposes. *See id.* The

Finally, the intention of the parties not to create an express trust can be gleaned from their decision to use the qualified intermediary option from among the four safe harbor options available within the Treasury Regulations. Qualified intermediaries are not the only means for effectuating like-kind exchange transactions under § 1031. Treasury Regulation § 1.1031(k)-1(g), which addresses the delivery of funds to third-parties in connection with a 1031 Exchange, provides, in pertinent part, as follows:

Safe harbors—

(1) In general. Paragraphs (g)(2) through (g)(5) of this section set forth four safe harbors the use of which will result in a determination that the taxpayer is not in actual or constructive receipt of money or other property for purposes of section 1031 and this section....

(2) Security or guarantee arrangements....

(3) Qualified escrow accounts and qualified trusts....

(4) Qualified Intermediaries....

(5) Interest and Growth Factors

Treas. Reg. § 1.1031(k)-1(g). These safe harbors are not mutually exclusive. *See* 26 Treas. Reg. § 1.1031(k)-1(g)(1) ("More than one safe harbor can be used in the same deferred exchange, but the terms and conditions of each must be separately satisfied."). Millard and LES had the option to utilize a "qualified escrow" or to establish a "qualified trust" pursuant to subsection (g)(3) of the Treasury Regulation. The qualified trust option requires a written trust agreement. 26 C.F.R. § 1.1031(k)-1(g)(iii)(B). Instead of using either of these available options, the parties chose the "qualified intermediary" safe harbor. The Exchange Agreements specifically state that: "LES and Taxpayer acknowledge and agree that this Exchange Agreement is intended to satisfy the safe harbor provisions of § 1.1031(k)-1(g)(4) of the Regulations." Exchange Agreement at ¶ 6(a). The parties did not in addition separately satisfy the terms and conditions of the Treasury Regulations for the creation of either a qualified escrow or a qualified trust. As the LES Committee points out in its brief, the parties' decision to eschew the escrow and trust provisions of the tax code in favor of a different safe harbor evidences that there was no intention to create a trust relationship. The Court thus finds that no express trust was created in any of the three 1031 Exchange transactions at issue.

As the Court has found that the parties to the Exchange Agreements did not intend to create an express trust, Millard is not now entitled to the imposition of a resulting trust. In Virginia a resulting trust is "an indirect trust that arises from the parties' intent or from the nature of the transaction and does not require an express declaration of trust." *1924 Leonard Rd., L.L.C. v. Van Roekel*, 272 Va. 543, 552 (2006) (citing *Tiller*

Exchange Agreements' Segregated Accounts were set up as required in the Treasury Regulations, thus contradicting Millard's argument that the Segregated Accounts were indicative necessarily of an intention to create a trust relationship.

v. Owen, 243 Va. 176, 180 (1992); *Salyer v. Salyer*, 216 Va. 521, 525, 219 S.E.2d 889, 893 (1975)). The party seeking to establish such a trust must do so by clear and convincing evidence. *Id.* (citing *Leonard v. Counts*, 221 Va. 582, 589 (1980)).

"For a resulting trust to arise, the alleged beneficiary must pay for the property, or assume payment of all or part of the purchase money before or at the time of purchase, and have legal title conveyed to another without any mention of a trust in the conveyance." *1924 Leonard Rd.*, 272 Va. at 552 (citing *Morris v. Morris*, 248 Va. 590, 593 (1994)). *See also Tiller*, 243 Va. at 180; *Leonard*, 221 Va. at 588 (1980). In *Morris*, the Supreme Court of Virginia quoted its prior opinion in *Kellow v. Bumgardner*, 196 Va. 247 (1954):

> The existence of a resulting trust thus depends upon an equitable presumption of intention, based upon the natural precept that one who advances the purchase money for real property is entitled to its benefits. Therefore, after it has been shown that payment of all or a part of the purchase price for property has been paid by one person and title thereto has been placed in the name of another, the factor which will determine whether the title is to be impressed with a trust in favor of the payor is the intention of the party providing the purchase money. If no evidence of intention is available, then the presumed intention will stand; *but if there is evidence that the person who provided the money had some intention other than to secure the benefits for himself, the presumed intention fails and no resulting trust will be recognized.*

Morris, 248 Va. at 593, (quoting *Kellow*, 196 Va. at 255, 83 S.E.2d at 396) (emphasis added).

Millard argues that a trust was found to exist in each of the few reported cases that dealt with like-kind exchange transactions utilizing segregated accounts.[29] In those cases, the courts were compelled to discern the intent of the parties from the circumstances surrounding their conduct, and the courts imposed resulting trusts.[30] In none of those cases was it found, however, that the parties had entered into a fully integrated agreement that evidenced an intention not to create a trust. In this case, the parties' intentions are readily discernible from the Exchange Agreements themselves. The Court need not divine the intent of the parties from the surrounding circumstances. Millard and LES were each experienced, sophisticated parties to complex documented commercial transactions. They were separately represented by capable counsel and experienced financial professionals.[31] If the parties had wanted to create a trust, they

---

29. [26] *See* Taxel v. Surnow (In re San Diego Realty Exchange, Inc.), No. 92-56526, 1994 U.S. App. LEXIS 10317, 1994 WL 161646 (9th Cir. May 2, 1994); Siegel v. Boston (In re Sale Guaranty Corp.), 220 B.R. 660 (9th Cir. BAP 1998).

30. [27] In *Cook v. 1031 Exch. Corp.*, 29 Va. Cir. 302, 1992 WL 885015 (Va. Cir. Ct. 1992), another case upon which Millard relies, the court found that the parties stipulated that the funds were held in trust.

31. [28] Consistent therewith, Section 11 of the Exchange Agreements provides that: "Each party hereto and their legal counsel have reviewed this Exchange Agreement and have had an opportunity to revise (or request revision of) this Exchange Agreement and, therefore, any usual rules of con-

certainly were capable of doing so. They did not. A resulting trust cannot be imposed in the face of Exchange Agreements that demonstrate clearly a contrary intent. The Court thus finds that no resulting trust was created in any of the three § 1031 Exchange transactions at issue. This result obtains without regard to the considerable hurdle that Millard would otherwise have to overcome that a resulting trust must be established through clear and convincing evidence.

CONCLUSION

The Exchange Funds are not excluded from property of the estate pursuant to 11 U.S.C. § 541(d) because of the existence of an express trust or as a result of the imposition of a resulting trust. The plain, unambiguous language of the Exchange Agreements clearly establishes that it was not the intent of LES or Millard to create an express trust. As the Exchange Agreements were integrated contracts, Millard cannot use parol evidence to prove the existence of an express trust. Given the parties' clear intent in the Exchange Agreements not to create an express trust, it is inappropriate for the court to impose a resulting trust upon them. This is especially the case where the parties are sophisticated, as they are here, and where the parties have included a merger clause in their agreement. Therefore, the Court will deny Millard's motion for partial summary judgment and grant partial summary judgment in favor of the Committees against Millard. The Court will dismiss Millard's requested relief for declaratory judgment and injunctive relief as set forth in Counts I and II of its Complaint. A separate order shall issue.

Kreisers Inc. v. First Dakota Title Limited Partnership

Supreme Court of South Dakota
852 N.W.2d 413 (2014)

OPINION

GILBERTSON, CHIEF JUSTICE.

Kreisers Inc. hired First Dakota Title to assist it with a like-kind property exchange in order to receive tax deferred benefits under 26 U.S.C. § 1031. After a partial failure of that exchange, Kreisers sued First Dakota for negligence and negligent misrepresentation. The circuit court determined that First Dakota was negligent in assisting Kreisers with the exchange. First Dakota appeals. We affirm.

FACTS AND PROCEDURAL HISTORY

Kreisers Inc. is a Subchapter S corporation that distributes and sells medical supplies. Its principal office is located in Sioux Falls, South Dakota. In 2006, Kreisers owned real property (hereinafter "relinquished property") located on South Minnesota Avenue in Sioux Falls. Kreisers moved its business from the relinquished property in 2001, and placed the property on the market for sale in 2005. Around the time Kreisers placed the relinquished property on the market, it sought to acquire replacement

---

struction requiring that ambiguities are to be resolved against a particular party shall not be applicable in the construction and interpretation of this Exchange Agreement."

property for warehouse services. Kreisers retained Dan Tunge to market the relinquished property and to assist with locating and acquiring replacement property. Tunge was informed that Kreisers was interested in pursuing a possible like-kind property exchange under 26 U.S.C. § 1031.[32]

In October 2006, Kreisers accepted an offer to sell the relinquished property to Urology Specialists Chartered for $765,000. Philip Johnson, an accountant and the eventual Chief Financial Officer of Kreisers, was already contemplating a like-kind exchange at this time; however, he knew little about § 1031 exchanges. Accordingly, officers from Kreisers met with MSM McGladrey, Inc., an accounting firm that performed regulation accounting and tax services for Kreisers and some of its shareholders. Following the meeting, Jason Zanderson and Tracy Peterson of McGladrey sent Johnson a memo on October 20, 2006, regarding like-kind exchanges of property. The memo discussed a new building to be constructed on replacement property as part of the like-kind exchange.

Prior to receiving the offer from Urology Specialists, Tunge had located possible replacement property in the Sioux Falls Industrial Park in the northeast part of Sioux Falls. Kreisers hoped to construct a new warehouse facility on the replacement property. On October 20, 2006, Kreisers entered into a purchase agreement with the Sioux Falls Development Foundation, Inc. to purchase the replacement property for $356,160.

Following the agreement to purchase the replacement property, Kreisers began preliminary work on developing plans for the construction of a new warehouse to be built on the replacement property. In March 2007, Kreisers selected Peska Construction as the contractor. A final contract between the parties was executed in May 2007. Peska Construction was informed of the § 1031 exchange and of the requisite time constraints for completing such an exchange.

On February 28, 2007, Urology Specialists assigned its purchase agreement with Kreisers to Brenkevco Properties LLC by written agreement. Shortly after the signing of the Brenkevco agreement, Tunge recommended that Johnson contact James Rogers of First Dakota Title regarding the possibility of First Dakota assisting Kreisers with a § 1031 exchange. Rogers, who is an attorney, was the manager of the title department at First Dakota. First Dakota advertised that it could provide § 1031 tax deferred exchange services. It did not advertise any limits on the types of § 1031 services it provided.

Sometime in early March 2007, Johnson called Rogers. The conversation was brief, lasting about three to four minutes. Johnson informed Rogers that Kreisers was working with McGladrey on a § 1031 exchange. Rogers testified that he recalled discussing

---

32. [1] § 1031 provides in part:

No gain or loss shall be recognized on the exchange of property held for productive use in a trade or business or for investment if such property is exchanged solely for property of like kind which is to be held either for productive use in a trade or business or for investment.

a § 1031 exchange with Johnson, but did not remember the specifics of the conversation. Rogers told Johnson that First Dakota performed § 1031 exchange services. Rogers did not rely on a checklist of information and did not recall asking Johnson many questions. First Dakota had no written protocol or procedures to guide its employees in connection with § 1031 exchanges. There is no evidence that Johnson and Rogers discussed an improvement (or construction) § 1031 exchange. Johnson testified that he told Rogers to call Zanderson of McGladrey. Rogers did not call Zanderson, and Johnson did not instruct Zanderson to call Rogers.

A closing date was set for both the replacement property and the relinquished property. To comply with § 1031, closing on the relinquished property occurred first. First Dakota agreed to act as the closing agent and to provide § 1031 exchange services. Rogers was charged with assembling the necessary information for a § 1031 exchange, which included preparing documents that had been created by Attorney Sam Assam, who was retained by First Dakota to draft a series of form documents for § 1031 exchanges. After preparing the documents, Rogers sent them back to Assam for review.

Assam's documents were only meant for forward § 1031 exchanges as it was First Dakota's policy to only handle forward or delayed exchanges. In a forward exchange, First Dakota would act as a "qualified intermediary." It would take an assignment of the purchase agreement from the seller of property and act as a seller for purposes of facilitating a § 1031 exchange. It would then receive the sale proceeds from the purchaser of the relinquished property following closing and agree to hold and use those proceeds to purchase replacement property for the seller at a later closing. First Dakota, as a matter of policy, did not handle construction exchanges, although they did not advertise this restriction.[33]

Rogers did not ask whether Kreisers intended a construction exchange instead of a forward exchange. Although it was normally his practice to contact a client's attorney or accountant to discuss the details of a § 1031 exchange, Assam did not do so in this case. Assam reviewed the documents, but did not discuss with Kreisers or Rogers whether something other than a forward exchange was contemplated.

Kreisers closed on the relinquished property at the office of First Dakota on April 16, 2007. The closing was conducted in phases with the buyer and seller meeting separately to execute the necessary documents. David H. Larson, President of Kreisers, and Johnson represented Kreisers at the closing. The closing agent for First Dakota was Sue Reiff. Tunge was also present.

At closing, First Dakota provided Kreisers with the closing documents, including the § 1031 documents that had been prepared by Rogers and reviewed by Assam. Reiff briefly summarized each document for Larson and Johnson while Larson signed the documents. Johnson testified that he talked about the warehouse construction

---

33. [2] It is undisputed that a construction exchange is slightly more complex than a forward exchange. A construction exchange requires the parties to designate the improvements that will be made to the replacement property. Those improvements must be then made within 180 days.

project at the closing. Larson did not recall any such conversation. Reiff stated that she had no independent recollection of the closing, but testified that if there was any indication that Kreisers intended a construction exchange, rather than a forward exchange, she would have stopped the closing to obtain additional guidance because of First Dakota's policy of not handling construction exchanges.[34] Reiff told Larson and Johnson that she would fill in the property description on the form required to designate the replacement property. Larson signed the blank description form. Reiff later completed the designation of replacement property by describing the replacement property that was to be purchased from the Foundation. Reiff never sent the completed form to Kreisers.

Kreisers closed on the replacement property at First Dakota on April 19, 2007. Mary Olson handled the closing for First Dakota on April 19. Once again, First Dakota acted as both the closing agent and the qualified intermediary for the § 1031 exchange; and both the buyer and the seller met separately with First Dakota. Larson and Johnson represented Kreisers at the closing. The closing lasted about five minutes. There was no discussion regarding a construction exchange. There is no evidence that Kreisers read the closing documents or that their attorneys reviewed the documents.

The Foundation delivered a warranty deed dated April 20, 2007, to First Dakota conveying title to the replacement property. The deed was recorded by First Dakota on April 25. Kreisers was not provided a copy of the deed at closing. The deed and final owner's policy of title insurance were not mailed to Kreisers until July 1, 2007.

Following closing, First Dakota held the excess proceeds of $328,733.87, which represented the difference between the net cash received from the sale of the relinquished property and the amounts paid by Kreisers for closing costs and the purchase of the replacement property. Kreisers had 45 days from the closing of the relinquished property to designate replacement property. First Dakota knew that Kreisers had designated the property from the Foundation as replacement property.

On or around June 30, 2007, and after the expiration of the 45 days, Peska submitted to Kreisers its first request for payment for its construction of the warehouse on the replacement property. Johnson instructed First Dakota to pay Peska from the excess proceeds still retained by First Dakota. Rogers informed Johnson that Kreisers's § 1031 exchange was not qualified as a construction exchange. Johnson contacted Zanderson at McGladrey to see if anything could be done to salvage the tax deferral on the remaining funds. Rogers spoke with Mark Wahlstrom, the President of First Dakota. Wahlstrom instructed Rogers to contact a § 1031 expert to see if the deferral could be salvaged. Rogers contacted Chris Moran of Dakota Homestead Title Insurance Company. Ultimately, no construction proceeds were disbursed by First Dakota to Peska, and the remaining funds on deposit were paid to Kreisers on August 27, 2007. As a result, the amount of proceeds from the sale of the relinquished property used to purchase the replacement property qualified for tax deferral. However, the remain-

---

34. [3] Tunge did not testify at trial.

ing proceeds that were ultimately paid to Kreisers by First Dakota did not qualify for tax deferral, and therefore, were subject to various taxes. The recognized gain for tax purposes was $317,087.

In light of the partial failure of the like-kind exchange, Kreisers sued First Dakota for monetary damages, alleging claims of negligence and negligent misrepresentation against First Dakota. First Dakota asserted that Kreisers was contributorily negligent. The case was tried by a court trial on September 11–13, 2012. The court rejected Kreisers's negligent misrepresentation claim. However, the circuit court determined that First Dakota was negligent in the performance of its duties and that Kreisers was not contributorily negligent. Kreisers was awarded $119,704, plus prejudgment interest, which represented Kreisers's additional tax liability of $172,804 minus certain offsets for tax savings.

On appeal, First Dakota alleges that the circuit court erred because it applied tort law instead of the contract signed by the parties. Similarly, First Dakota argues that the circuit court erred in concluding that First Dakota had a common law duty beyond the contract entered between First Dakota and Kreisers. Finally, First Dakota claims that Kreisers was contributorily negligent.

Kreisers also filed a notice of appeal in this case. Kreisers argues that the circuit court erred in concluding that First Dakota was not guilty of negligent misrepresentation. Additionally, Kreisers asserts that the circuit court erred in its calculation of damages when it applied certain tax offsets.

ANALYSIS AND DECISION

1. Whether the circuit court erred in applying negligence principles rather than the contractual documents.

First Dakota argues that the circuit court erred in applying tort law rather than contract law to determine what duty First Dakota owed Kreisers. First Dakota asserts that under *Fisher Sand & Gravel Co. v. South Dakota Department of Transportation,* 1997 S.D. 8, 558 N.W.2d 864, Kreisers and First Dakota had no relationship outside of the contract formed by the closing documents. First Dakota maintains that the contractual documents set forth the duties of the parties with respect to the transaction. Whether a duty exists in a negligence action is a question of law that we review de novo. *Patitucci v. City of Hill City,* 2013 S.D. 62, ¶9, 836 N.W.2d 623, 626 (citation omitted).

"Tort liability requires 'a breach of a legal duty independent of contract.'" *Schipporeit v. Khan,* 2009 S.D. 96, ¶7, 775 N.W.2d 503, 505 (quoting *Grynberg v. Citation Oil & Gas Corp.,* 1997 S.D. 121, ¶18, 573 N.W.2d 493, 500). "This independent legal duty must arise 'from extraneous circumstances, not constituting elements of the contract.'" *Id.* (quoting *Grynberg,* 1997 S.D. 121, ¶18, 573 N.W.2d at 500). In contrast, "negligence that consists merely in the breach of a contract will not afford grounds for a tort action by third parties and is limited under a breach of contract cause of action to the party to the contract or for whose benefit the contract was made." *Fisher Sand & Gravel Co.,* 1997 S.D. 8, ¶15, 558 N.W.2d at 868.

The circuit court determined that First Dakota owed Kreisers a common law duty of care that arose when First Dakota held itself out as being qualified to handle § 1031 exchanges. First Dakota agreed to provide these services prior to signing any contract with Kreisers. Therefore, the circuit court concluded that First Dakota had a common law duty to exercise reasonable and proper care in the handling of the § 1031 exchange, including the drafting of the closing documents.

In an attempt to distinguish the circuit court's decision, First Dakota relies on *Fisher Sand & Gravel Co.*, where this Court rejected a negligence claim against the South Dakota Department of Transportation (DOT). 1997 S.D. 8, ¶ 16, 558 N.W.2d at 868. *Fisher Sand & Gravel Co.* involved a breach of contract claim and a negligence claim brought by Fisher, a supplier of aggregate, against DOT. DOT had accepted a bid for a concrete paving project, with Fisher acting as a subcontractor on the project. However, DOT required Fisher to obtain sand from a different source than was Fisher's custom, which resulted in a "mark up" in the cost of Fisher's performance. *Id.* ¶ 6, 558 N.W.2d at 866. In rejecting Fisher's negligence claim, we noted that Fisher failed to show "that DOT breached any duties, rights, or obligations independent of those imposed upon them under the contract." *Id.* ¶ 18, 558 N.W.2d at 869. We stated that "[o]utside of the contract there was no relationship between [Fisher and DOT]." *Id.* ¶ 13, 558 N.W.2d at 867.

However, we also observed in *Fisher Sand & Gravel Co.* that "[i]f the relationship of the parties is such as to support a cause of action in tort, that cause of action is not to be denied because the parties happened also to have made a contract." *Id.* ¶ 19, 558 N.W.2d at 869 (quoting *Redgrave v. Boston Symphony Orchestra, Inc.*, 557 F.Supp. 230, 238 (D.Mass.1983)). Furthermore, "it is generally recognized that one who undertakes to provide professional services has a duty to the person for whom the services are performed to use such skill and care ordinarily exercised by others in the same profession." *Limpert v. Bail*, 447 N.W.2d 48, 51 (S.D.1989) (citation omitted). And, "[l]iability in tort for breach of that duty may arise as the result of negligence during the performance of the contract, even if there has been no breach of contract." *Id.* (citation omitted).

As the circuit court correctly observed in this case, First Dakota owed a duty of care to Kreisers beyond the contract between the two parties. This case is distinguishable from *Fisher Sand & Gravel Co.* because an independent duty to exercise reasonable care arose from extraneous circumstances not constituting the elements of the contract.[35] Both parties agree that § 1031 exchanges can be incredibly complex. Prior to

---

35. [4] It is also important to note that *Fisher Sand & Gravel Co.* involved a lawsuit against the State of South Dakota. The lawsuit was cognizable under SDCL 31–2–34, which permits a suit "against the South Dakota Department of Transportation [for] any claim, right, or controversy arising out of the work performed, or by virtue of the provisions of any construction contract entered into by the South Dakota Department of Transportation." *Fisher Sand & Gravel Co.*, 1997 S.D. 8, ¶ 9, 558 N.W.2d at 867. We stated that under that statute, "if there is no contract or quasi-contract, there is no lawsuit." *Id.*

the signing of the closing documents, First Dakota advertised that it handled § 1031 exchanges. The advertisement was not limited to forward exchanges. Nevertheless, there is no evidence that Rogers, or anyone else at First Dakota, informed Johnson or anyone else at Kreisers that First Dakota only provided its services in connection with forward exchanges. First Dakota was aware of the different kinds of § 1031 exchanges, but Rogers did not use a checklist or ask any questions of Johnson to gauge his knowledge of § 1031 exchanges so as to ascertain whether Kreisers wanted something other than a forward exchange.

Moreover, because of the complexity of some § 1031 exchanges, it was customary for First Dakota to refer more complex exchanges—like construction exchanges—to other providers; however, in this case First Dakota did not even inquire or verify whether Kreisers was interested in a construction exchange so as to determine whether Kreisers needed a different provider. Additionally, Assam never inquired into the type of exchange that Kreisers desired. Finally, in completing the forms, Reiff, of First Dakota, instructed Larson, of Kreisers, to sign the blank property description form, which she would fill in later. After doing so, she did not show the completed forms to anyone at Kreisers. David Brown, an attorney who owns a company that provides qualified intermediary services in Iowa, testified as an expert witness in this case. He opined that First Dakota breached the standard of care as a qualified intermediary by failing to gather necessary information and failing to make certain it understood what the client was trying to accomplish and how the transaction was structured. This duty of reasonable care existed independent of any contract that was signed between Kreisers and First Dakota.

As a company providing professional services, First Dakota had, at a minimum, an independent legal duty to exercise reasonable care by ascertaining what the client wanted. The subsequent closing contract did not alleviate that duty. Given that independent duty, the circuit court did not err in applying tort law rather than contract law to determine the duty that First Dakota owed to Kreisers.

Economic Loss Doctrine

First Dakota further contends, however, that the economic loss doctrine precludes Kreisers's claim. The economic loss doctrine provides that "purely economic interests are not entitled to protection against mere negligence." *Diamond Surface, Inc. v. State Cement Plant Comm'n*, 1998 S.D. 97, ¶ 22, 583 N.W.2d 155, 160 (citation omitted). The significance of the doctrine is that it "precludes parties under certain circumstances from eschewing the more limited contract remedies and seeking tort remedies." *Ins. Co. of N. Am. v. Cease Elec. Inc.*, 276 Wis.2d 361, 688 N.W.2d 462, 467 (2004). "The prohibition against tort actions to recover solely economic damages for those in contractual privity is designed to prevent parties to a contract from circumventing the allocation of losses set forth in the contract by bringing an action for economic loss in tort." *Tiara Condo. Ass'n, Inc. v. Marsh & McLennan Cos., Inc.*, 110 So.3d 399, 402 (Fla.2013) (citation omitted). The "doctrine draws a legal line between contract and tort liability that forbids tort compensation for 'certain types of foreseeable, negligently caused, financial injury.'" *Terracon Consultants Western, Inc. v. Mandalay Resort Grp.*, 125 Nev. 66, 206 P.3d 81, 87 (2009) (quoting *Barber*

Lines A/S v. M/V Donau Maru, 764 F.2d 50, 52 (1st Cir.1985)). The economic loss doctrine, therefore, sets forth that regardless of whether a tort duty may exist between contracting parties, the actual duty one party owes to another for purely economic loss should be based exclusively on the contract to which they agreed and assigned their various risks. *See Indianapolis-Marion Cnty. Pub. Library v. Charlier Clark & Linard, P.C.,* 929 N.E.2d 722, 729–30 (Ind.2010). Kreisers argues that First Dakota's position stretches the doctrine "too far."

In *City of Lennox v. Mitek Industries, Inc.,* 519 N.W.2d 330, 333 (S.D.1994), this Court adopted the economic loss doctrine. However, in that case our application of the doctrine was limited to commercial transactions under the Uniform Commercial Code. *See id.* We have not yet extended the doctrine to the type of professional services offered in this case. Effectively, First Dakota asks us to extend that doctrine to this case.

In formulating our economic loss rule, we cited Minnesota law, which has declined to extend the economic loss doctrine beyond commercial transactions. *See McCarthy Well Co., Inc. v. St. Peter Creamery, Inc.,* 410 N.W.2d 312, 314–15 (Minn.1987); *see also Mitek Industries, Inc.,* 519 N.W.2d at 333. A number of other jurisdictions have also declined to apply the economic loss rule to purely professional services. *See, e.g., Cargill, Inc. v. Boag Cold Storage Warehouse,* 71 F.3d 545, 550 (6th Cir.1995) (stating that the economic loss doctrine "is associated with 'transactions in goods,' and not transactions in services") (citation omitted); *Cease Elec., Inc.,* 688 N.W.2d at 472 (holding that "the economic loss doctrine is inapplicable to claims for the negligent provision of services"). *But see Terracon Consultants Western, Inc.,* 206 P.3d at 90 (barring a purely economic negligence claim against a design professional under the economic loss doctrine); *2314 Lincoln Park W. Condo. Ass'n v. Mann, Gin, Ebel & Frazier, Ltd.,* 136 Ill.2d 302, 144 Ill.Dec. 227, 555 N.E.2d 346, 353 (1990) (applying the economic loss rule to an alleged claim of architectural malpractice).

Given the nature of the professional services offered by First Dakota to Kreisers, we decline to extend the economic loss doctrine to this case. South Dakota already allows a number of claims, like legal malpractice, to be brought under either breach of contract or negligence. *See Haberer v. Rice,* 511 N.W.2d 279, 286 (S.D.1994) ("A legal malpractice suit may have two causes of action, one which is for breach of contract and another in negligence."). Moreover, the application of the economic loss doctrine to negligence claims like the one in this case has been soundly rejected elsewhere. *See, e.g., Clark v. Rowe,* 428 Mass. 339, 701 N.E.2d 624, 627 (1998) ("The general rule in this country is that the economic loss rule is inapplicable to claims of legal malpractice."); *Collins v. Reynard,* 154 Ill.2d 48, 180 Ill.Dec. 672, 607 N.E.2d 1185, 89 (1992) ("[I]t is singularly inappropriate to attempt to apply the economic loss ... doctrine to attorney malpractice actions."); *see also Congregation of the Passion, Holy Cross Province v. Touche Ross & Co.,* 159 Ill.2d 137, 201 Ill.Dec. 71, 636 N.E.2d 503, 514–15 (1994) (declining to extend the economic loss doctrine to accountant malpractice). The reason for this is that the economic loss rule is usually more appropriate when there is no fiduciary relationship so that the parties can more freely bargain concerning allocation of risk. *See Clark*, 701 N.E.2d at 626 (citation omitted). As Kreisers argues, by extending the economic loss doctrine to this case, we might risk foreclosing future negligence actions for claims like legal malpractice, which quite often only involve claims for purely economic loss. We decline to reach this result, and hold that the economic loss doctrine does not bar Kreisers's claim.

Contract Indemnification

First Dakota next asks us to consider whether the contract indemnification language in the closing documents bars Kreisers's claim. The Indemnification Agreement between Kreisers and First Dakota provides in part that Kreisers agrees to indemnify First Dakota "in connection with the inability of Kreisers's exchange transaction to qualify for tax deferral pursuant to the provisions of Section 1031 of the Internal Revenue Code, for any reason (except for First Dakota's failure to comply with the provisions of the Exchange Agreement or Supplemental Agreement)."

"[T]o relieve a party of the consequences of its own negligence the language of [an indemnification] agreement must be clear and unequivocal." *Bell v. E. River Elec. Power Coop., Inc.*, 535 N.W.2d 750, 753 (S.D.1995) (citations omitted). The circuit court concluded that the contract indemnification was both ambiguous and unhelpful to First Dakota. In concluding that the indemnification provision was unhelpful, the court noted that the Indemnification Agreement provided:

> Kreisers shall, and does hereby agree to indemnify, defend (by counsel reasonably acceptable to First Dakota), protect and hold First Dakota, its general partners, limited partners, officers, employees, attorneys or agents (collectively "Indemnitee") free and harmless from any claim, liability, demand, expense, tax or assessment of any nature or kind, expressed or implied, *whether sounding in tort or in contract that may be asserted against Indemnitee, by any person (other than Kreisers)*....

(Emphasis added). As the circuit court emphasized, the above language appears to exclude Kreisers from the indemnity obligation. Although First Dakota points to a different provision in the agreement to indemnify itself from suit, the two provisions read together at a minimum make the agreement ambiguous.[36] Because our law requires the indemnification language to be "clear and unequivocal," we conclude that the indemnification language does not foreclose Kreisers's negligence claim.

2. Whether the circuit court erred in concluding that Kreisers was not contributorily negligent.

First Dakota argues that Kreisers was negligent in failing to read the closing documents and in failing to have its own attorney and accountant review the closing documents before signing them. Contributory negligence is a question of fact, which

---

36. [5] The circuit court had previously found the indemnification agreement to be ambiguous in denying First Dakota's motion for summary judgment on December 11, 2011.

is reviewed under the clearly erroneous standard. *Wood v. City of Crooks*, 1997 S.D. 20, ¶ 3, 559 N.W.2d 558, 560.

In support of its position that Kreisers was contributorily negligent, First Dakota underscores that both its transmittal letter dated April 13, 2007, and the Agreement of Indemnification advised Kreisers to consult with its own advisers regarding the transaction. However, as the circuit court noted, these documents were the only suggestion presented to Kreisers that they should consult a different representative. Throughout discussions with various individuals at First Dakota leading up to the transmittal of those documents, there is no evidence that any such advisements were made to representatives of Kreisers. Moreover, as the circuit court highlighted, Kreisers already believed that it had an expert in § 1031 exchanges in First Dakota, which never informed Kreisers that its work was limited to forward exchanges. It is important to once again note the complexity of these exchanges. There is no evidence that anyone at Kreisers had any expertise in § 1031 exchanges. Kreisers was putting faith in First Dakota to properly exercise its knowledge and expertise to facilitate the § 1031 exchange. The circuit court's finding that Kreisers was not negligent is not clear error.

First Dakota next argues that Kreisers failed to take reasonable steps to salvage the tax deferral. Both Attorney Assam and Chris Moran of Dakota Homestead Title Insurance testified that, in their opinion, the transaction could have been salvaged as late as July 2007 if the parties had cooperated. However, neither opined that any attempt to salvage the transaction was guaranteed to be successful. Moreover, Moran's testimony was undercut by his own memorandum to Rogers where he stated that any attempt to fix the problem at that late of a date would be a "bad move." The circuit court ultimately relied on the fact that none of First Dakota's expert witnesses were willing to guarantee a fix without substantial risk. The circuit court, therefore, found that it was reasonable for Kreisers to decide not to try to unwind the transaction and re-structure it in an effort to fully qualify under § 1031. Given this reasoning, we find no error with the circuit court's finding on this issue.

3. Whether the circuit court erred in its calculation of damages.

Kreisers asks us to consider whether the circuit court erred in its calculation of damages. "The amount of damages to be awarded is a factual issue...." *Weekley v. Wagner*, 2012 S.D. 10, ¶ 13, 810 N.W.2d 340, 343 (citations omitted). "Damages must be reasonable and must be proved with reasonable certainty." *Id.* (citation omitted). "Reasonable certainty 'requires proof of a rational basis for measuring loss,' without requiring the trier of fact to speculate." *Id.* (quoting *Lord v. Hy-Vee Food Stores*, 2006 S.D. 70, ¶ 31, 720 N.W.2d 443, 454). "This Court reviews the issue of damages under the clearly erroneous standard." *Id.* (citation omitted).

There is no dispute that Kreisers had to pay $172,804 in tax liabilities as a result of the partial failure of the like-kind exchange. Kreisers contends, however, that the circuit court erred in its calculation of certain tax offsets.

In calculating damages, the circuit court considered the testimony of both Zanderson and John Wenande, a certified public accountant and the expert witness for

First Dakota. Wenande testified that the additional taxes paid by Kreisers in 2007 needed to be offset by the additional depreciation available to Kreisers on the increased basis for the newly constructed building as well as the increased basis in the stock of the shareholders of Kreisers. Wenande calculated the net present value of the future tax savings at $49,600. Wenande also determined that a second offset needed to be made for tax savings on the personal tax return of Larson as a result of deducting additional state taxes (from Iowa) he paid in 2007. Wenande calculated that Larson had tax savings of $3,500 in 2008.

While Zanderson agreed with Wenande that there would be some offsets, he differed on the amount. Zanderson believed that Wenande's calculations were speculative. First, Zanderson disagreed with Wenande's assumption of a 33 percent tax rate, testifying that Kreisers's historical tax rate was 23 percent. Additionally, Wenande used a 4.4 percent discount rate, while Zanderson believed a more appropriate rate was 5.08 percent in light of the historical rate of return experienced by Kreisers. Zanderson calculated the offset due to the increased depreciation to be only $3,000. Zanderson also opined that Larson's actual savings were closer to $1,000, instead of the $3,000 savings predicted by Wenande.

There was no dispute that the stepped up basis in the warehouse permits additional depreciation deductions over the useful life of the property. After weighing the opinions of both expert witnesses, the circuit court ultimately found Wenande's opinion regarding certain offsets "to generally be more reliable and on a more sound foundation."

On appeal, Kreisers posits that the "tax benefit rule" illustrates the erroneousness and speculative nature of Wenande's opinion and the circuit court's decision. "The tax benefit rule is a judicially developed principle that is codified in part in the Internal Revenue Code, 26 U.S.C.A. § 111, and prevents plaintiffs from reaping multiple recoveries." *Cody v. Edward D. Jones & Co.*, 502 N.W.2d 558, 561–62 (S.D.1993) (citation omitted). Furthermore, we have stated that "public policy supports disregarding tax benefits in awarding damages." *Id.* at 562. This is because "[t]here is a deterrent value against committing fraud if the fraudulent party realizes he will have to compensate the other party for the full extent of his damages with no offset for any tax benefits the other party may have received." *Id.* (citation omitted).

In response to Kreisers's "tax benefit rule" claim, First Dakota alleges that this issue was not properly raised before the circuit court, and is therefore waived. We have consistently stated that we will not address issues raised for the first time on appeal not raised before the lower court. *Hall v. S.D. Dep't of Transp.*, 2006 S.D. 24, ¶ 12, 712 N.W.2d 22, 26–27 (citation omitted). After a review of the record, it does not appear that Kreisers fully presented this argument before the circuit court. Because the circuit court and First Dakota did not have an opportunity to fully address and consider the application of the tax benefit rule, we decline to reach it here.

The circuit court was therefore left to determine the extent of damages based on the testimony of two competing expert witnesses. We have acknowledged that "[d]amages are speculative, not when the amount is uncertain, but when the fact of damages is uncertain." *Bailey v. Duling*, 2013 S.D. 15, ¶ 35, 827 N.W.2d 351, 363 (citation omitted). And "courts have some leeway in calculating damages...." *Weekley v. Prostrollo*, 2010 S.D. 13, ¶ 24, 778 N.W.2d 823, 830. Ultimately, the fact of damages in this case was not in dispute, and the court found Wenande's opinion to be more reliable on the amount of damages. Accordingly, we conclude that the circuit court did not clearly err in its calculation of damages.

We affirm the circuit court on all issues.[37]

KONENKAMP, ZINTER, SEVERSON, and WILBUR, JUSTICES, concur.

Millard Refrigerated Services, Inc. v. LandAmerica 1031 Exchange Services, Inc.

United States Bankruptcy Court, Eastern District of Virginia
Case 08-03149-KRH

Joint Motion Pursuant to Rule 9019 of the Federal Rules of Bankruptcy Procedure to Approve Stipulation and Settlement Agreement

COMES NOW: (i) Health Care REIT, Inc. ("HCN"); (ii) LandAmerica 1031 Exchange Services, Inc. ("LES"); (iii) the Official Committee of Unsecured Creditors of LandAmerica Financial Group, Inc. (the "LFG Committee"); and (iv) the Official Committee of Unsecured Creditors of LandAmerica 1031 Exchange Services, Inc. (the "LES Committee," and together with HCN, LES, and the LFG Committee, the "Parties") and hereby file this Joint Motion Pursuant to Rule 9019 of the Federal Rules of Bankruptcy Procedure to Approve Stipulation and Settlement Agreement (the "Motion"). In support of the Motion, the Parties respectfully state as follows:

I. JURISDICTION

1. This Court has jurisdiction over this matter pursuant to 28 U.S.C. §§ 157 and 1334. Venue is proper in this district pursuant to 28 U.S.C. §§ 1408 and 1409. This is a core proceeding pursuant to 28 U.S.C. § 157(b). The predicate for the relief sought herein is section 105(a) of title 11 of the United States Bankruptcy Code (the "Bankruptcy Code") and Rule 9019(a) of the Federal Rules of Bankruptcy Procedure (the "Bankruptcy Rules").

II. BACKGROUND

2. On November 26, 2008 (the "Petition Date"), LES and LandAmerica Financial Group, Inc. ("LFG," and collectively with LES, the "Debtors") filed their respective petitions in the Bankruptcy Court for the Eastern District of Virginia.

3. Prior to the Petition Date, HCN contracted with LES whereby LES was to serve as a qualified intermediary for a deferred like-kind property exchange to be consummated under section 1031 of title 26 of the United States Code (the "Internal Revenue Code").

---

37. [6] Because we conclude that First Dakota was negligent, we do not consider whether First Dakota was also guilty of negligent misrepresentation as Kreisers would not be entitled to additional damages on that claim.

4. On December 4, 2008, HCN filed a complaint (the "Complaint") against LES, commencing this adversary proceeding (the "Adversary Proceeding").

5. HCN asserts that funds in the amount of approximately $137 million, which are being held by Centennial Bank as "Escrow Holder" pursuant to two "Exchange Agreements" entered into between HCN and LES, dated June 24, 2008 and October 16, 2008, and two "Qualified Escrow Agreements" entered into between HCN, LES, and Centennial Bank, dated June 24, 2008 and October 16, 2008 (the "Exchange Funds"), are HCN's property and not property of LES's bankruptcy estate.[38]

6. On December 11, 2008, the Court entered an order allowing the LFG Committee to intervene in this adversary proceeding pursuant to Bankruptcy Rule 7024(a).

7. On January 5, 2009, the Court entered an order allowing the LES Committee to intervene in this adversary proceeding pursuant to Bankruptcy Rule 7024(a).

8. On January 16, 2009, the Court entered an order (the "Protocol") in this matter that specifically contemplated settlements. Pursuant to the Protocol, the Adversary Proceeding was designated as the "Lead Case" for escrow plaintiffs. Upon information and belief, there are a limited number of exchangers who executed escrow agreements in connection with the 1031 exchanges.

9. On January 19, 2009, LES filed its Answer and Affirmative Defenses of LandAmerica 1031 Exchange Services, Inc. to the Complaint.

10. On January 23, 2009, the LFG Committee filed its Answer and Affirmative Defenses.

11. On January 27, 2009, the LES Committee filed its Original Answer and Affirmative Defenses of the Official Committee of Unsecured Creditors of LandAmerica 1031 Exchange Services, Inc.

12. Pursuant to the Protocol Order, the Parties have engaged in discovery including the exchange of written discovery and documents, as well as several depositions of LES and HCN witnesses. This discovery has allowed the parties to verify certain key facts, including information regarding the flow of the Exchange Funds.

13. In an effort to resolve the dispute, the Parties have engaged in arm's-length and good-faith negotiations and have reached an agreement (the "Settlement Agreement") which will resolve the Adversary Proceeding and HCN's claims against the Debtors for all purposes in these proceedings. The salient terms of the Settlement Agreement are as follows:

- *Release of Exchange Funds.* Within two (2) days of the Court entering an order granting this Motion, but in no event later than February 25, 2009, LES shall direct and authorize the release of the Exchange Funds, to HCN.

---

38. [1] HCN alleges that approximately $60.73 million of the Exchange Funds are held by Centennial Bank as Escrow Holder in Centennial Bank Account Number 99-700103-7 and approximately $76.75 million of the Exchange Funds are held by Centennial Bank as Escrow Holder in Citibank Account Number 9945292947.

- *The HCN Settlement Payment.* Within 24 hours of the receipt of the Exchange Funds, HCN shall wire $2,000,000 to an account designated by LES.

- *Mutual Release.* HCN shall waive all claims against the Debtors, their estates, the LES Committee, and the LFG Committee related to these proceedings. The Debtors, the LES Committee, and the LFG Committee shall waive all claims against HCN related to these proceedings.

- *Professionals' Fees and Expenses.* The Parties shall each bear their own professionals' fees and expenses.

* * *

III. BASIS FOR RELIEF

A. Legal Standard

14. Bankruptcy Rule 9019 provides that "[o]n motion by the trustee and after notice and a hearing, the court may approve a compromise or settlement." Fed. R. Bankr. P. 9019. Compromises are tools for expediting the administration of the case, reducing administrative costs and are favored in bankruptcy. *See In re Bond*, No. 93-1410, 1994 U.S. App. Lexis 1282, at *9–13 (4th Cir. Jan. 26, 1994) ("To minimize litigation and expedite the administration of a bankruptcy estate, 'compromises are favored in bankruptcy'"); *Fogel v. Zell*, 221 F.3d 955, 960 (7th Cir. 2000); *In re Martin*, 91 F.3d 389, 393 (3rd Cir. 1996). Various courts have endorsed the use of Bankruptcy Rule 9019. *See, e.g., Bartel v. Bar Harbor Airways, Inc.*, 196 B.R. 268, 271 (S.D.N.Y. 1996); *In re Found. for New Era Philanthropy*, No. 95-13729F, 1996 Bankr. Lexis 1892 (Bankr. E.D. Pa. Aug. 21, 1996); *In re Miller*, 148 B.R. 510, 516 (Bankr. N.D. Ill. 1992); *In re Austin*, 186 B.R. 397, 400 (Bankr. E.D. Va. 1995).

15. Before approving a settlement under Bankruptcy Rule 9019, a court must determine that the proposed settlement is fair and equitable, reasonable, and in the best interests of the bankruptcy estates. *See In re Bond*, 1994 U.S. App. Lexis 1282 at *10 ("the bankruptcy court must employ its informed, independent judgment to determine whether the settlement is both fair and equitable"); *In re Three Rivers Woods, Inc.*, 2001 WL 720620 (Bankr. E.D. Va. May 20, 2001) ("a compromise or settlement will most likely gain approval if it is both fair and equitable"); *In re Frye*, 216 B.R. 166 (Bankr. E.D. Va. 1997) ("this court must look at various factors and determine whether the compromise is in the best interest of the estate and whether it is fair and equitable"). To reach this determination, a court must assess the value of the claim that is being settled and balance it against the value to the estate of the approval of the settlement. *See Protective Comm. for Indep. Stockholders of TMT Trailer Ferry, Inc. v. Anderson*, 390 U.S. 414, 424–25 (1968). The Court may consider the options of the trustee and debtor in possession that the settlement is fair and reasonable. *See In re Purofied Down Prods. Corp.*, 150 B.R. 519, 522 (S.D.N.Y. 1993).

B. The Settlement Agreement Is Fair, Equitable, and Reasonable

16. The standard by which a court should evaluate the reasonableness of a proposed compromise and settlement is well established. In addition to considering the proposed terms of the settlement, the court should consider the following factors:

a) the probability of success in litigation;

b) the difficulty in collecting any judgment that may be obtained;

c) the complexity of the litigation involved, and the expense, inconvenience, and delay necessarily attendant to it; and

d) the interest of creditors and stockholders and a proper deference to their reasonable views of the settlement.

See *In re Frye*, 216 B.R. at 174.

(i) The Settlement Agreement Considers the Probability of Success in Litigation

17. First, the Settlement Agreement takes into account the probability of success with respect to the various and complicated state and federal issues surrounding HCN's claims. While the Parties believe that they possess meritorious arguments, they acknowledge that the issues involved in the Adversary Proceeding will be extremely difficult and expensive to litigate and the outcome is difficult to predict. The settlement need not be the best that a party could have achieved, but need only fall "within the reasonable range of litigation possibilities." *In re Telesphere Commc'ns, Inc.*, 179 B.R. 544, 553 (Bankr. N.D. Ill. 1994). As the Settlement Agreement certainly falls within the range of reasonable litigation outcomes, the Settlement Agreement should be approved.

(ii) The Settlement Agreement Considers the Complexity, Time and Expense of Protracted Litigation

18. Second, the complexity, expense, inconvenience, and delay associated with litigation weighs in favor of settlement. Litigating all of the issues resolved by the Settlement Agreement would require the devotion of substantial time and resources, a risk which the Settlement Agreement eliminates. Any litigation would necessarily be protracted, would result in increased administrative costs to the Debtors' estates, would increase HCN's attorneys' fees (which are currently the subject of a pending motion for treatment as administrative expenses, which motion will be withdrawn if this 9019 motion is approved), and would entail considerable future expenses and delay to the detriment of all parties involved. To avoid these costs, the Court should approve the Settlement Agreement. See *U.S. ex rel. Rahman v. Oncology Assocs., P.C.*, 269 B.R. 139 (D. Md. 2001) (approving settlement where creditors supported terms of settlement and were unwilling to risk and bear costs of litigation).

(iii) The Settlement Agreement Considers the Interest of Creditors and Gives Deference to Their Views of the Agreement

19. As both the LFG Committee and the LES Committee are parties to the Settlement Agreement, the views of the creditors are adequately represented and support entering into the Settlement Agreement.

20. For the reasons detailed herein, the Parties request approval of the Settlement Agreement pursuant to Bankruptcy Rule 9019.

IV. WAIVER OF STAY OF ORDER

21. Pursuant to Bankruptcy Rule 6004(h) and any other applicable provisions of the Bankruptcy Rules or Bankruptcy Code, the Parties request that the requirement

that an order granting a motion providing for the sale, use, or lease of property of the estate be stayed for ten days be waived such that an Order granting the Motion will be effective immediately.

* * *

Richmond, Virginia

Dated: February 19, 2009

Revenue Procedure 2010-14

2010-12 I.R.B. 456

SECTION 1. PURPOSE

This revenue procedure provides a safe harbor method of reporting gain or loss for certain taxpayers who initiate deferred like-kind exchanges under § 1031 of the Internal Revenue Code but fail to complete the exchange because a qualified intermediary (QI) defaults on its obligation to acquire and transfer replacement property to the taxpayer.

SECTION 2. BACKGROUND

.01 Under § 1031(a), no gain or loss is recognized on an exchange of property held for productive use in a trade or business or for investment (the "relinquished property") if the property is exchanged solely for property of like kind that is to be held either for productive use in a trade or business or for investment (the "replacement property").

.02 Section 1031 and the regulations under § 1031 allow for deferred exchanges of property. Section 1.1031(k)-1(a) defines a deferred exchange as an exchange in which, pursuant to an agreement (the "exchange agreement"), the taxpayer transfers relinquished property and subsequently receives replacement property. Under § 1031(a)(3), a taxpayer must (A) identify the replacement property within 45 days of the transfer of the relinquished property (the "identification period"), and (B) acquire the replacement property within 180 days of the transfer of the relinquished property, or by the due date of the taxpayer's return (including extensions) for the year of the transfer of the relinquished property, if sooner (the "exchange period").

.03 Section 1.1031(k)-1(g)(4) allows a taxpayer to use a QI to facilitate a like-kind exchange. As required by the written exchange agreement entered into with the taxpayer, the QI acquires the relinquished property from the taxpayer, transfers the relinquished property, acquires the replacement property, and transfers the replacement property to the taxpayer. If a taxpayer transfers relinquished property using a QI, the taxpayer's transfer of the relinquished property to the QI and subsequent receipt of replacement property from the QI is treated as an exchange with the QI.

.04 Under § 1.1031(k)-1(a), if a taxpayer actually or constructively receives money in the full amount of the consideration for the relinquished property. the transaction is a sale and not a deferred like-kind exchange. Section 1.1031(k)-1(f)(2) provides that the determination of whether and the extent to which a taxpayer is in actual or constructive receipt of money or non like-kind property is made under the general rules concerning actual or constructive receipt and without regard to the taxpayer's method of accounting. Generally, actual or constructive receipt of money by an agent of the taxpayer is actual or constructive receipt by the taxpayer. However, § 1.1031(k)-1(g)(4)(i) provides that a QI is not considered the agent of the taxpayer for purposes of determining whether the taxpayer is in actual or constructive receipt of money before the taxpayer receives like-kind replacement property.

.05 The Internal Revenue Service and the Treasury Department are aware of situations in which taxpayers initiated like-kind exchanges by transferring relinquished property to a QI and were unable to complete these exchanges within the exchange period solely due to the failure of the QI to acquire and transfer replacement property to the taxpayer (a "QI default"). In many of these cases, the QI enters bankruptcy or receivership, thus preventing the taxpayer from obtaining immediate access to the proceeds of the sale of the relinquished property. The Service and the Treasury Department generally are of the view that a taxpayer who in good faith sought to complete the exchange using the QI, but who failed to do so because the QI defaulted on the exchange agreement and became subject to a bankruptcy or receivership proceeding, should not be required to recognize gain from the failed exchange until the taxable year in which the taxpayer receives a payment attributable to the relinquished property.

SECTION 3. SCOPE OF REVENUE PROCEDURE

This revenue procedure applies to taxpayers who:

.01 Transferred relinquished property to a QI in accordance with § 1.1031(k)-1(g)(4);

.02 Properly identified replacement property within the identification period (unless the QI default occurs during that period);

.03 Did not complete the like-kind exchange solely because of a QI default involving a QI that becomes subject to a bankruptcy proceeding under the United States Code or a receivership proceeding under federal or state law; and

.04 Did not, without regard to any actual or constructive receipt by the QI, have actual or constructive receipt of the proceeds from the disposition of the relinquished property or any property of the QI prior to the time the QI entered bankruptcy or receivership. For purposes of the preceding sentence, relief of a liability pursuant to the exchange agreement prior to the QI default, either through the assumption or satisfaction of the liability in connection with the transfer of the relinquished property or through the transfer of the relinquished property subject to the liability, is disregarded.

SECTION 4. APPLICATION OF SAFE HARBOR METHOD FOR REPORTING FAILED LIKE-KIND EXCHANGES

.01 *No gain recognized until payment received.* If a QI defaults on its obligation to acquire and transfer replacement property to the taxpayer and becomes subject to a bankruptcy or receivership proceeding, the taxpayer generally may not seek to enforce its rights under the exchange agreement with the QI or otherwise access the sale proceeds from the relinquished property outside of the bankruptcy or receivership proceeding while the proceeding is pending. Consequently, the Service will treat the taxpayer as not having actual or constructive receipt of the proceeds during that period if the taxpayer reports gain in accordance with this revenue procedure. Accordingly, the taxpayer need recognize gain on the disposition of the relinquished property only as required under the safe harbor gross profit ratio method described in section 4.03 of this revenue procedure.

.02 *Gain recognized upon receipt of payment.* A taxpayer within the scope of this revenue procedure may report gain realized on the disposition of the relinquished property as the taxpayer receives payments attributable to the relinquished property using the safe harbor gross profit ratio method described in section 4.03 of this revenue procedure.

.03 *Safe harbor gross profit ratio method.* Under the safe harbor gross profit ratio method, the portion of any payment attributable to the relinquished property that is recognized as gain is determined by multiplying the payment by a fraction, the numerator of which is the taxpayer's gross profit and the denominator of which is the taxpayer's contract price.

.04 *Definitions.* The following definitions apply solely for purposes of applying the safe harbor gross profit ratio method.

(1) *Payment attributable to the relinquished property.* A payment attributable to the relinquished property means a payment of proceeds, damages, or other amounts attributable to the disposition of the relinquished property (other than selling expenses), whether paid by the QI, the bankruptcy or receivership estate of the QI, the QI's insurer or bonding company. or any other person. Except as provided in section 4.05 of this revenue procedure, satisfied indebtedness is not a payment attributable to the relinquished property.

(2) *Gross profit.* Gross profit means the selling price of the relinquished property, minus the taxpayer's adjusted basis in the relinquished property (increased by any selling expenses not paid by the QI using proceeds from the sale of the relinquished property).

(3) *Selling price.* The selling price of the relinquished property is generally the amount realized on the sale of the relinquished property, without reduction for selling expenses. However, if a court order, confirmed bankruptcy plan, or written notice from the trustee or receiver specifies, by the end of the first taxable year in which the taxpayer receives a payment attributable to the relinquished property, an amount to be received by the taxpayer in full satisfaction of the taxpayer's claim, the selling price of the relinquished property is the sum of the payments attributable to the relinquished property (including satisfied indebtedness in excess of basis) received or to be received and the amount of any satisfied indebtedness not in excess of the adjusted basis of the relinquished property.

(4) *Contract price.* The contract price is the selling price of the relinquished property minus the amount of any satisfied indebtedness not in excess of the adjusted basis of the relinquished property.

(5) *Satisfied indebtedness.* Satisfied indebtedness means any mortgage or encumbrance on the relinquished property that was assumed or taken subject

to by the buyer or satisfied in connection with the transfer of the relinquished property.

.05 *Treatment of satisfied indebtedness in excess of basis.* The amount of satisfied indebtedness in excess of the adjusted basis of the relinquished property is treated as a payment attributable to the relinquished property (within the meaning of § 4.04(1) of this revenue procedure) in the year in which the indebtedness is satisfied.

.06 *Treatment of recapture income.* Any required depreciation recapture is taken into account in accordance with §§ 1245 and 1250, except that the recapture income is included in income in the taxable year in which gain is recognized under this § 4 to the extent of the gain recognized in that taxable year.

.07 *Maximum gain to be recognized.* The total gain (including recapture income) recognized under this revenue procedure should not exceed the sum of (1) the payments attributable to the relinquished property (including satisfied indebtedness in excess of basis) and (2) the satisfied indebtedness not in excess of basis, minus the adjusted basis of the relinquished property. Adjustments to the gain determined using the safe harbor gross profit ratio method should be made in the last taxable year in which the taxpayer receives a payment attributable to the relinquished property.

.08 *Loss deduction.* A taxpayer within the scope of this revenue procedure may claim a loss deduction under § 165 for the amount, if any, by which the adjusted basis of the relinquished property exceeds the sum of (1) the payments attributable to the relinquished property (including satisfied indebtedness in excess of basis), plus (2) the amount of any satisfied indebtedness not in excess of basis. A taxpayer who may claim a loss deduction under the preceding sentence may also claim a loss deduction under § 165 for the amount of any gain recognized in accordance with this section 4 in a prior taxable year. The timing of any § 165 loss claimed by the taxpayer is determined under the general rules of § 165 and the regulations thereunder, and the character of any loss is determined under subchapter P of the Code.

.09 *Imputed interest.*

(1) *Sections 483 and 1274.* For purposes of applying the safe harbor gross profit ratio method to a transaction within the scope of this revenue procedure, the selling price, the contract price, and any payment attributable to the relinquished property must be reduced by the amount of any imputed interest allocable to the payment as determined under § 483 or § 1274 and the regulations thereunder, whichever is applicable. For purposes of applying § 483 or § 1274 to a transaction within the scope of this revenue procedure, the taxpayer is treated as selling the relinquished property on the date of the confirmation of the bankruptcy plan or other court order that resolves the taxpayer's claim against the QI (the "safe harbor sale date"). As a result, if the only payment in full satisfaction of the taxpayer's claim is received by the taxpayer on or before the date that is six months after the safe harbor sale date. then no interest is imputed on this payment under either § 483 or § 1274. In addition, the selling price determined under section 4.04(3) of

this revenue procedure (determined without regard to this section 4.09) is used to determine whether § 483 (in general, sales for $250,000 or less) or § 1274 (in general, sales for more than $250,000) applies to a transaction within the scope of this revenue procedure.

(2) § 7872. In the case of a transaction within the scope of this revenue procedure, if exchange funds held by the QI were treated as an exchange facilitator loan under § 1.468B-6(c)(1), and the loan otherwise met the requirements of § 1.7872-5(b)(16), the Service will continue to treat the loan as meeting the requirements of § 1.7872-5(b)(16) until the safe harbor sale date, even if the duration of the loan exceeds six months solely due to the QI default. In addition, if an exchange facilitator loan under § 1.468B-6(c)(1) does not meet the requirements of § 1.7872-5(b)(16) because the loan exceeds $2 million, the Service will not impute additional interest on the loan after the date of the QI default under § 7872. However, interest may be imputed under § 483 or § 1274 pursuant to section 4.09(1) of this revenue procedure.

.10 *Examples.*

Example 1. A, an individual who files federal income tax returns on a calendar year basis, owns investment property (Property I) with a fair market value of $150x and an adjusted basis of $50x. *A* enters into an agreement with *QI*, a qualified intermediary. to facilitate a deferred like-kind exchange. On May 6, Year 1, *A* transfers Property 1 to *QI* and *QI* transfers Property 1 to a third party in exchange for $150x. *A* intends that the $150x held by *QI* be used by *QI* to acquire *A*'s replacement property. On June 1. Year 1, *A* identifies Property 2 as replacement property. On June 15, Year 1, *QI* notifies *A* that it has filed for bankruptcy protection and cannot acquire replacement property. Consequently, *A* fails to acquire Property 2 or any other replacement property within the exchange period. As of December 31, Year 1, *QI*'s bankruptcy proceedings are on-going and *A* has received none of the $150x proceeds from *QI* or any other source. On July 1, Year 2, *QI* exits from bankruptcy and the bankruptcy court approves the trustee's final report, which shows that *A* will be paid $130x in full satisfaction of *QI*'s obligation under the exchange agreement. *A* receives the $130x payment on August 4, Year 2 and docs not receive any other payment attributable to the relinquished property.

A is within the scope of this revenue procedure and thus may report the failed like-kind exchange due to the QI default in accordance with this section 4. *A* is not required to recognize gain in Year 1 because *A* did not receive any payments attributable to the relinquished property in Year 1. *A* recognizes gain in Year 2. *A*'s selling price is $130x (the payments attributable to the relinquished property (the amount specified by the trustee before the end of the first taxable year in which *A* receives a payment attributable to the relinquished property)). *A*'s contract price also is $130x because there is no satisfied or assumed indebtedness. *A*'s gross profit is $80x (the selling price ($130x) minus the adjusted basis ($50x)). *A*'s gross profit ratio is 80/130 (the gross profit over the contract price). *A* must recognize gain in Year 2 of $80x (the payment attributable to the relinquished property ($130x) multiplied by *A*'s gross profit ratio (80/130)). Furthermore, even though the payment attributable to the relinquished property ($130x) is less than the $150x proceeds received by the QI. A is not entitled to a § 165 loss deduction because the payment attributable to the relinquished property exceeds A's adjusted basis in the relinquished property ($50x).

Example 2. B, an individual who files federal income tax returns on a calendar year basis, owns investment property (Property 1) with a fair market value of $160x and an adjusted basis of $90x. Property 1 is encumbered by a mortgage of $60x. B enters into an agreement with QI. a qualified intermediary, to facilitate a deferred like-kind exchange. On May 6, Year 1, B transfers Property 1 to QI and QI transfers Property 1 to a third party in exchange for $160x. At closing, QI uses $60x of the proceeds to satisfy the mortgage on Property 1 and retains the remaining $100x. B intends that the $100x held by QI be used by QI to acquire B's replacement property. On June 1. Year 1, B identifies Property 2 as replacement property. On June 15, Year 1, QI notifies B that it has filed for bankruptcy protection and cannot acquire replacement property. Consequently, B fails to acquire Property 2 or any other replacement property during the exchange period. As of December 31, Year 1, QI's bankruptcy proceedings are on-going and B has received none of the $100x proceeds from QI or any other source. On September 1, Year 2, QI exits from bankruptcy and the bankruptcy plan of reorganization specifies that B will receive $70x in full satisfaction of QI's obligation under the exchange agreement. The terms of the bankruptcy plan of reorganization provide that QI will pay B $35x in October of Year 2 and $35x in February of Year 3. B receives the payments according to the plan and does not receive any other payment attributable to the relinquished property.

B is within the scope of this revenue procedure and thus may report the failed like-kind exchange due to the QI default in accordance with this section 4. Accordingly, B is not required to recognize gain in Year 1 because B did not receive any payments attributable to the relinquished property in Year 1 (the amount of the mortgage satisfied by QI did not exceed B's adjusted basis in Property 1). B recognizes gain in Year 2 and Year 3. B's selling price is $130x (the payments attributable to the relinquished property (the amount specified by the bankruptcy plan before the end of the first taxable year in which B receives a payment attributable to the relinquished property ($70x)) plus the mortgage satisfied by QI (60x)). B's contract price is $70x (the selling price ($130x) minus the satisfied indebtedness not in excess of basis ($60x)). B's gross profit is $40x (the selling price ($130x) minus the adjusted basis ($90x)). B's gross profit ratio is 40/70 (the gross profit over the contract price). In Year 2 and Year 3. B must recognize gain of $20x each year (the payment attributable to the relinquished property ($35x) multiplied by B's gross profit ratio (40/70)). Furthermore, B is not entitled to a § 165 loss deduction because the sum of all payments attributable to the relinquished property ($70x) and the amount of B's satisfied indebtedness not in excess of basis ($60x) exceeds B's adjusted basis in the relinquished property ($90x).

Example 3. The facts are the same as in *Example 2* except B's adjusted basis in Property 1 is $40x. B is within the scope of this revenue procedure and thus may report the failed like-kind exchange due to the QI default in accordance with this section 4. B is considered to have received a payment of $20x in Year 1 because the amount of the mortgage satisfied by QI ($60x) exceeds B's adjusted basis in the relinquished property ($40x). *B* recognizes gain in Year 1. *B*'s selling price is $160x (the amount realized by the QI on the sale of the relinquished property because neither a court order, the bankruptcy plan, nor the trustee specified by the end of Year 1, the first year in which *B* receives a payment attributable to the relinquished property, the amount *B* will receive in full satisfaction of *B*'s claim). *B*'s contract price is $120x (the selling price ($160x) minus the satisfied indebtedness not in excess of basis ($40x)). *B*'s gross profit is $120x (the selling price ($160x) minus the adjusted basis ($40x)). *B*'s gross profit ratio is 120/120 (the gross profit over the contract price). Thus, *B* must recognize gain in Year 1 of $20x (the deemed payment of $20x multiplied by 120/120) and $35x in Year 2 and Year 3 (the payments attributable to the relinquished property received by *B* in those years multiplied by 120/120). Furthermore. *B* is not entitled to a § 165 loss deduction because the sum of the payments attributable to the relinquished property ($90x) and the amount of *B*'s satisfied indebtedness not in excess of basis ($40x) exceeds *B*'s adjusted basis in the relinquished property ($40x).

Example 4. C, an individual who files federal income tax returns on a calendar year basis, owns investment property (Property 1) with a fair market value of $100x and an adjusted basis of $40x. *C* enters into an agreement with *QI*. a qualified intermediary, to facilitate a deferred like-kind exchange. On May 6, Year 1, *C* transfers Property 1 to *QI* and *QI* transfers Property 1 to a third party in exchange for $100x. *C* intends that the $100x held by *QI* be used by *QI* to acquire *C*'s replacement property. On June 1, Year 1, *C* identifies Property 2 as replacement property. On June 15. Year 1, *QI* notifies *C* that it has filed for bankruptcy protection and cannot acquire replacement property. Consequently, *C* fails to acquire Property 2 or any other replacement property within the exchange period. As of December 31, Year 1. *QI*'s. bankruptcy proceedings are on-going and *C* has received none of the $100x proceeds from *QI* or any other source. On September 1, Year 2. *QI* exits from bankruptcy and the bankruptcy plan of reorganization provides that *C* will receive $35x in October of Year 2 in partial satisfaction of *QI*'s obligation under the exchange agreement. The bankruptcy plan also provides that, depending on various facts and circumstances described in the reorganization plan, *C* may receive a payment in February of Year 3. On October 2, Year 2, *QI* pays *C* $35x. On February 3, Year 3, *C* is notified that there will be no Year 3 payment and that the $35x received by *C* in Year 2 represents full satisfaction of *QI*'s obligation under the exchange agreement. *C* receives no other payments attributable to the relinquished property.

C is within the scope of this revenue procedure and thus may report the failed like-kind exchange due to the QI default in accordance with this section 4. Accordingly, *C* is not required to recognize gain in Year 1. *C* recognizes gain in Year 2. *C*'s selling price is $100x (the amount realized by the QI on the sale of the relinquished property because, by stating that *C* may receive a payment in Year 3. the bankruptcy plan did not specify by the end of Year 2. the first year in which *C* receives a payment attributable to the relinquished property, the amount *C* will receive in full satisfaction of *C*'s claim). Because there is no satisfied or assumed indebtedness, *C*'s contract price also is $100x. *C*'s gross profit is $60x (the selling price ($100x) minus the adjusted basis ($40x)). *C*'s gross profit ratio is 60/100 (the gross profit over the contract price). Thus, *C* must recognize gain in Year 2 of $21x (the payment attributable to the relinquished property ($35x) multiplied by 60/100). In Year 3. *C* is entitled to a § 165 loss deduction of $5x, the excess of *C*'s adjusted basis ($40x) over the payments attributable to the relinquished property ($35x). *C* is also entitled to a § 165 loss deduction of $21x in Year 3, the amount of gain that *C* recognized in Year 2.

Example 5. *D*, an individual who uses the cash receipts and disbursements method of accounting and files federal income tax returns on a calendar year basis. owns investment property (Property 1) with a fair market value of $150x and an adjusted basis of $50x. *D* enters into an agreement with *QI*, a qualified intermediary. to facilitate a deferred like-kind exchange. On May 6, Year 1. *D* transfers Property 1 to *QI* and *QI* transfers Property 1 to a third party in exchange for $150x. *D* intends that the $150x held by *QI* be used by *QI* to acquire *D*'s replacement property. On June 1, Year 1, *D* identifies Property 2 as replacement property. On June 15, Year 1, *QI* notifies *D* that it has filed for bankruptcy protection and cannot acquire replacement property. Consequently, *D* fails to acquire Property 2 or any other replacement property within the exchange period. As of December 31, Year 1. *QI*'s bankruptcy proceedings are on-going and *D* has received none of the $150x proceeds from *QI* or any other source. On July 1, Year 2, *QI* exits from bankruptcy and the bankruptcy court approves the trustee's final report, which shows that *D* will be paid, in August of Year 3. $130x in full satisfaction of *QI*'s obligation under the exchange agreement. *D* receives the $130x payment on August 1, Year 3 and does not receive any other payment attributable to the relinquished property. Assume that the selling price of Property 1 is less than $250,000 and that, based on § 483, $5x of the $130x payment is unstated interest.

D is within the scope of this revenue procedure and thus may report the failed like-kind exchange due to the QI default in accordance with this section 4. *D* is not required to recognize gain in Year 1 or Year 2 because *D* did not receive any payments attributable to the relinquished property in those years. Further, § 483 applies to *D*'s Year 3 payment because the payment was due more than 6 months after the safe harbor sale date and *D* received the payment more than 1 year after such date. See § 483(c). Under section 4.09(1) of this revenue procedure, *D*'s selling price is $125x ($130x minus the $5x of unstated interest). *D*'s contract price also is $125x because there is no assumed or satisfied indebtedness. *D*'s gross profit is $75x (the selling price ($125x) minus the adjusted basis ($50x)). *D*'s gross profit ratio is 75/125 (the gross profit over the contract price). *D* must recognize gain in Year 3 of $75x (the payment attributable to the relinquished property ($125x) multiplied by *D*'s gross profit ratio (75/125)). In addition, *D* must include $5x of the $130x payment in income in Year 3 as interest income. See § 1.446-2. Furthermore, even though the payment attributable to the relinquished property ($125x) is less than the $150x proceeds received by the QI. *D* is not entitled to a § 165 loss deduction because the payment attributable to the relinquished property exceeds *D*'s adjusted basis in the relinquished property ($50x).

* * *

Chapter 13

Structuring Reverse Exchanges

I. Commentary

In some situations, property owners are in a position to acquire replacement property before they sell relinquished property. Exchanges arranged in such order are reverse exchanges. Although reverse exchanges may work in theory, no legal authority specifically supports such structures. Instead, several cases provide that the acquisition of replacement property and the subsequent disposition of relinquished property do not qualify for section 1031 nonrecognition, if they are not part of a single transaction.[1] Although section 1031 reporting appears to be an afterthought in those cases, practitioners generally avoid structuring such pure reverse exchanges because no authority directly supports them.

Because the treatment of pure reverse exchanges is uncertain, practitioners developed title-parking reverse exchanges, which the IRS has blessed to a significant extent.[2] The goal of title-parking arrangements is to ensure that the exchanger does not own relinquished property and replacement property at the same time. To avoid the simultaneous ownership of both properties, the exchanger may hire a facilitator to take title to one of the properties. Some situations dictate that the facilitator should take title to the replacement property, in which case the exchange will occur as the last part of the structure. Consequently, such transactions are exchange-last transactions. Other situations dictate that the exchanger should take title to the replacement property immediately, in which case the exchange occurs as the first part of the transaction and the facilitator takes title to the relinquished property. Such transactions are exchange-first transactions.

In Rev. Proc. 2000-37, the IRS provides a safe harbor for doing title-parking reverse exchanges. To come within the safe harbor, the parked property must be held in a qualified exchange accommodation arrangement (QEAA).[3] If the transaction cannot be structured as a QEAA, an exchanger may consider doing a non-safe harbor title-parking exchange. If the transaction is structured outside the safe harbor, courts may respect the formalism of a title-parking arrangement that does not bestow the benefits

---

1. *See, e.g.*, Bezdjian v. Commissioner, 845 F.2d 217 (9th Cir. 1988).
2. *See* Rev. Proc. 2000-37, 2000-2 C.B. 308, as modified by Rev. Proc. 2004-51, 2004-2 C.B. 294 (reproduced in Chapter 15).
3. *See* Rev. Proc. 2000-37, § 4.02.

and burdens of tax ownership on the party holding title.[4] Otherwise, the parties would have to rely upon case law to ensure that the titleholder is the beneficial owner of the property.[5]

Title-parking exchanges are intricate transactions. Attorneys must pay close attention to the transfer and holding of title, consider whether the exchanger will have access to the parked property and how to document such access, determine the flow of money to finance the acquisition of the parked property, and consider how to ensure that the transaction will close at the appropriate time. Title-parking transactions require significant paperwork to account for all aspects of the transactions. A properly-structured title-parking reverse exchange will help the exchanger obtain section 1031 nonrecognition and will protect the parties' legal interests.

II. Primary Legal Authority

Bezdjian v. Commissioner

United States Court of Appeals, Ninth Circuit
845 F.2d 217 (1988)

FACTS

In 1978, the Bezdjians received from Shell Oil Company ("Shell") an offer to sell a gas station (the "Broadway parcel") that the Bezdjians operated under a lease. Shell refused to accept a rental property (the "El Camino property") owned by the Bezdjians in exchange and, instead, insisted on a cash transaction. The Bezdjians consented and bought the Broadway parcel from Shell with the proceeds of a loan that was secured by a deed of trust on their residence and the El Camino property. About three weeks after the Broadway parcel was conveyed to the Bezdjians, they sold the El Camino property to the Leveys, who assumed a mortgage and paid the remainder of the price in cash.

The Bezdjians treated these transactions as a like-kind exchange governed by section 1031 on their 1978 tax return. Upon audit, the Commissioner of Internal Revenue recharacterized the sale of the El Camino property as a taxable transaction and recalculated the Bezdjians' tax liability to reflect their taxable gain. The Commissioner notified the Bezdjians of the resulting tax deficiency and they filed a petition in Tax Court contesting it. The Tax Court found that there was no like-kind exchange and determined that the Bezdjians were liable for the deficiency. The Bezdjians appeal that judgment.

---

4. *See* Estate of Bartell v. Commissioner, 147 T.C. No. 5 (2016).

5. Several cases provide insight into the types of issues attorneys must consider to ensure that the titleholder is the beneficial owner of the property. *See, e.g.,* Oesterreich v. Commissioner, 226 F.2d 798 (9th Cir. 1955); Grodt & McKay Realty, Inc. v. Commissioner, 77 T.C. 1221 (1981), *reproduced supra* Chapter 6; Penn-Dixie Steel Corp. v. Commissioner, 69 T.C. 837 (1978). Property owners may also have other alternatives outside the safe harbor. *See, e.g.,* Priv. Ltr. Rul. 2007-12-013 (Nov. 20, 2006).

ANALYSIS

Section 1031(a) is an exception to the rule requiring recognition of gain or loss upon the sale or exchange of property. *See* I.R.C. § 1001(c) (1978). Section 1031(a) states in pertinent part the following:

> No gain or loss shall be recognized if property held for productive use in trade or business or for investment ... is exchanged solely for property of a like kind to be held either for productive use in trade or business or for investment.

In their brief, the Bezdjians admit that § 1031 requires an exchange. However, they fail to understand that the parties must make an exchange of property or an interest in property for other property of a like kind in order for it to qualify for nonrecognition. Here, the Bezdjians acquired a parcel of real property from Shell and sold another to the Leveys. There is no evidence that either Shell or the Leveys made an exchange with the Bezdjians of anything but cash for real property. The fact that the Bezdjians intended the Broadway parcel to replace the El Camino property in their holdings does not render their transactions an exchange.

The Bezdjians contend that their transactions comprise a "three corner exchange" that qualifies for nonrecognition, as described by the Fifth Circuit in *Biggs v. CIR*, 632 F.2d 1171 (5th Cir.1980). However, *Biggs* is inapposite. In that case, Biggs agreed with Powell to convey real property to Powell in a like-kind exchange. *Id.* at 1178. Biggs arranged a complex series of transactions in which Powell acquired an interest in property that Biggs wanted to own. *Id.* at 1173–74, 1178. Because Powell exchanged this newly acquired interest for Biggs's property, the transaction qualified for nonrecognition under section 1031. *Id.* at 1178. In the final analysis, there was an exchange between the two parties of a property for an interest in property of a like kind. *Id.*

In contrast, no such exchange of property of a like kind occurred between the Bezdjians and either Shell or the Leveys. While the Bezdjians may have wanted to structure such an exchange, there is no evidence that Shell or the Leveys agreed to participate in one. Moreover, the record indicates that the Bezdjians neither conveyed real property to Shell in exchange for the Broadway property nor received real property from the Leveys in exchange for the El Camino property. We conclude that there was no exchange of property of a like kind.

Oesterreich v. Commissioner

United States Court of Appeals, Ninth Circuit
226 F.2d 798 (1955)

FACTS

Petitioner, Walburga Oesterreich, acquired three adjoining lots, 552, 553 and 554, in January, 1926. One of the lots was on the corner of Wilshire Boulevard and Hamilton Drive in Beverly Hills, California.

Wilshire Amusement Corporation was incorporated in 1929 by Albert H. and Albert J. Chotiner, father and son, for the purpose of building a motion picture theatre. They directed a real estate broker, operating in Beverly Hills, to find a suitable location which they could lease and on which they could construct a theatre. The broker learned from Walburga that she would be willing to enter into a lease for the three vacant lots which she owned and he arranged a meeting between the Chotiners and Walburga. After negotiations, Walburga and Wilshire Amusement Corporation entered into an agreement entitled "lease" dated September 11, 1929. The Chotiners decided, in the course of the negotiations, that additional land would be needed for the theatre which they desired to build and for that reason Wilshire Amusement Corporation purchased lot 555 and the northerly 40 feet of lot 556 at a total cost to it of $19,650. Wilshire conveyed that land to Walburga in the fall of 1929.

Walburga is referred to as lessor and Wilshire Amusement Corporation is referred to as lessee throughout the agreement of September 11, 1929. The 'lease' agreement provides for payments called rent to be paid by lessee, Wilshire Amusement Corporation to lessor, the taxpayer. The lessee agreed to pay the lessor total rent of $679,380 payable in monthly installments for a period of 67 years and eight months beginning September 1, 1929 and ending the last day of April, 1997. The rental schedule provided for an annual rental of $7,500 for the first 13 years, $12,000 for the succeeding 18 years and amounts becoming progressively smaller so that the rental for the 68th year was $7,500. The lessee agreed to pay all taxes and similar charges on the property. The lessee agreed to erect a new building on the premises to cost not less than $300,000 and to be completed not later than July 1, 1930. The lessor agreed to join in the execution of notes or debentures and in a deed of trust or mortgage covering the leased premises to secure a loan not to exceed $225,000 to be used in constructing the building. The lessee agreed to take out adequate fire insurance on the building and insurance to protect lessor from claims arising out of the use of the premises. The agreement states that the lessee proposes to sublease a portion of the building for theatre purposes. The lease could be assigned by the lessee upon the terms stated therein and such an assignment would release the lessee of further obligations under the lease. The lessor could declare the lease terminated in case of default continuing longer than a period stated in the lease. The lessee had the right, but was not bound, to tear down any building which might be built on the premises for the purpose of reconstruction in accordance with the terms of the lease should the original building become obsolete or not suited to the purpose of the lessee. Any such replacement was to cost not less than $325,000.

One paragraph of the lease provided that when the lease expired and all conditions met, the

> lessor promises and agrees that she will then, upon the payment to her of the further sum of ten dollars ($10.00) in hand, convey or cause to be conveyed by grant deed to the Lessee free and clear of all encumbrance, all of the real property herein leased, without further or other consideration.

The agreement was recorded in the Official Records of Los Angeles County.

Wilshire Amusement Corporation changed its name to Wilshire-Hamilton Properties, Inc., shortly after September 11, 1929. Wilshire Holding Corporation succeeded to the interest of Hamilton under the agreement of September 11, 1929, in August, 1935.

Wilshire Holding Corporation paid the taxpayer $12,000 in each of the years 1945 and 1946 in accordance with the agreement and entered the amounts so received as rental expense. The taxpayer, on her returns for 1945 and 1946, reported the $12,000 as income from rents. She received a letter from an Internal Revenue Agent in Charge indicating over assessments in her income tax for 1945 and 1946, and enclosing a report in which it was stated that she had reported rental income of $12,000 for the years 1945 and 1946, but investigation showed that the agreement under which these payments were made was "not a lease, but in effect an installment sale of realty under § 44(b) of the Internal Revenue Code (26 U.S.C.A. § 44)," and she overstated her income for each year by $6,206.91 in that connection. She received another letter from the same source dated July 26, 1949, reversing the previous conclusion and stating that the rents were correctly reported as income on her previous tax returns.

The Commissioner determined a deficiency in income tax of $141.16 for 1946 against Walburga Oesterreich and deficiencies against Wilshire Holding Corporation of $1,584 in declared value excess profits tax, $3,097.83 in excess profits tax, for 1945, and $2,798.20 in income tax for 1946.

The Tax Court entered its decision sustaining the Commissioner's determination of deficiency in the taxpayer's income tax for the year 1946.

ANALYSIS

There is only one issue presented by this case. Is petitioner entitled to treat "rental" payments made by "lessee" as long term capital gains or must she treat them as ordinary income? Conversely, is lessee, the Wilshire Holding Corp., entitled to treat these payments as a deductible business expense as defined by Int. Rev. Code § 23(a)(1)(A), 26 U.S.C.A. § 23(a)(1)(A) or merely as non-deductible capital expenditures? The sole issue, therefore, is whether the agreement is a lease or a contract for the sale of land. The courts, in making determinations of this sort, commonly consider the intent of the parties and the legal effect of the instrument as written.

It seems well settled that calling such a transaction a "lease" does not make it such, if in fact it is something else. *Judson Mills*, 11 T.C. 25 (1948); *Robert A. Taft*, 27 B.T.A. 808 (1938). To determine just what it is the courts will look to see what the parties intended it to be. *Benton v. Comm'r*, 197 F.2d 745 (5th Cir. 1952). Both petitioner and Wilshire Holding Corp. have at all times lease. However, the test should not be what the parties call the transaction nor even what they may mistakenly believe to be the name of such transaction. What the parties believe the legal effect of such a transaction to be should be the criterion. If the parties enter into a transaction which they honestly believe to be a lease but which in actuality has all the elements of a contract of sale, it is a contract of sale and not a lease no matter what they call it not how they treat it on their books. We must look, therefore, to the intent of the parties in terms of what they intended to happen.

It is clear that it was intended that title to the premises was to pass to lessee at the end of the 68 year term. The testimony of the parties makes this explicit. Therefore, if the only test in determining whether it was a sale or lease was the passing of title, the parties intended a sale and not lease.

Testimony was offered to the effect that petitioner wanted the bulk of the consideration for the "lease" as soon as possible so that she could enjoy the money during her lifetime. Consequently, the agreement which provided for a tapering off of the rental payments in the later years was tailored to suit her needs and to what the lessees could afford to pay. This was the intent of the parties and this is what went into the agreement. Here we see that what the parties intended and the legal effect of the transaction were one and the same, so we should not consider the intent of the parties apart from the legal effect of the agreement.

The question before us remains whether petitioner is entitled to treat her rental payments as long term capital gains rather than rental income and conversely whether Wilshire Holding Corporation is entitled to deduct the payment as rental expense as defined by § 23(a)(1)(A) which provides as follows:

In computing net income there shall be allowed as deductions:

(a) Expenses

    (1) Trade or Business Expenses

        (A) In General. All the ordinary and necessary expenses paid or incurred during the taxable year in carrying on any trade or business, including ... rentals or other payments required to be made as a condition to the continued use or possession, for purposes of the trade or business, of property to which the taxpayer has not taken or is not taking title or in which he has no equity.

If Wilshire Holding Corporation is either taking title to the property or has acquired an equity, it cannot treat the payments from Wilshire as rental income. It is important to note that these two provisions of § 23(a)(1)(A) are stated in the alternative and the deduction cannot be availed of if Wilshire Holding Corporation has brought itself into either category prohibited by statute. *DuPont v. Deputy*, 22 F. Supp. 589, 599 (D.C. Del. 1938), modified on other grounds, 103 F.2d 257 (3d Cir. 1939), certiorari granted, 308 U.S. 533 (1939), reversed on other grounds, 308 U.S. 488 (1940). In *Helser Machine & Marine Works*, 39 B.T.A. 644, 645, 646 (1939), the court stated,

It is not necessary to hold that by payment of the rental petitioner acquires an "equity", for that word is not easy to define; it is enough that the lease provides a right in the petitioners to take title to the premises for which the rental was paid.

This language was cited with approval in *Judson Mills*, 11 T.C. 25 (1948), at page 33. *See also In re Rainey*, 31 F.2d 197 (D.C. Md. 1927) (non-tax). We find, therefore, that the Tax Court was in error for it ignored this alternative ground of taking title and based its decision on the ground that it believed Wilshire Holding Corporation had not yet acquired an equity in the premises.

There can be no doubt that Wilshire Holding Corporation is acquiring title to the premises. At the expiration of the lease it can acquire the premises now worth $100,000 for the token consideration of $10. Although there have been cases holding that a mere option to buy at the expiration of the time period does turn a lease into a contract of sale, *Benton v. Comm'r*, supra, 197 F.2d 745 (1952); *Indian Creek Coal & Coke Co.*, 23 B.T.A. 950 (1931); *Haverstock*, 13 B.T.A. 837 (1928), it should be noted that in all of these cases, the option price constituted full consideration for the premises or goods acquired. In each of these cases it was always questionable whether or not the options would be exercised. Here there is virtually no question of this, for not only will Wilshire Holding Corporation acquire valuable land for a mere $10 but it will forfeit a $350,000 building now on the premises to the lessor if it does not decide to pay the $10 and take title. The testimony clearly shows that the Wilshire Holding Corporation during all of the original negotiations was very much concerned with what would happen to its building and the land after the lease expired and would not have agreed to the "lease" unless it provided that title would vest in Wilshire.

Another factor leading to the conclusion that the parties at the time of the transaction intended a sale is that the schedule of payments under the so-called lease was not commensurate to the benefit derived by Wilshire from the occupancy and use of the land, for instead of rising toward the end of the lease as the land on Wilshire Boulevard became more valuable the payments decreased.

The alternative criterion under Sec. 23(a)(1)(A) which would prevent Wilshire Holding Corporation from treating the payments as a business expense is whether an equity in the property was acquired. The Tax Court in applying this test held that since the amount due on the remaining portion of the lease greatly exceeded the appraisal value of the property, Wilshire Holding Corporation had not yet acquired an equity. We, however, do not believe that this method of determining whether an equity has been acquired is correct. From 1929 to 1946 Wilshire Holding Corporation paid approximately $160,000 to the lessor. In 1997 it will acquire property appraised at $100,000 in 1946 and worth perhaps ten times as much by 1997. Certainly a part of each payment is going toward the acquisition of this land and to this extent Wilshire Corporation does have an equity. In *Chicago Stoker Corp.*, 14 T.C. 44 (1950), the court said that if the payments made under the "lease" are large enough to exceed the value of the property less depreciation, the lessee is receiving an equity in the property. Although the Stoker case is distinguishable on its facts, the same principle should apply here.

However, even if the Tax Court was correct in holding that Wilshire has not acquired an equity, the alternative ground that they are taking title to the property is sufficient to disqualify the "rental" payments from being treated as a business expense.

Looking at this transaction from a long range view we find that if the opinion of the Tax Court is affirmed, Wilshire Holding Corporation, at the expiration of the "lease", will have acquired a very valuable piece of property for payments written off entirely as business expense while petitioner will have, in effect, sold a valuable piece of property without having been able to treat the proceeds as a long term capital gain.

OPINION

We are of opinion that the Tax Court erred in treating the question of intention of the parties as one of fact collateral to the written instrument. The document was not ambiguous, and evidence as to surrounding circumstances was not required to explain it. The intention of the parties, as expressed in the instrument, was cardinal, as has been said above. The document has here been construed in the light of the applicable statute. No question of fact was involved. One who contracts to purchase real property acquires an equity therein immediately on the signing of the contract to purchase and taking possession. This equity increases with every payment. No comparison of the value of the realty and the amount of rental paid at any given time has any validity.

Estate of Bartell v. Commissioner

United States Tax Court
147 T.C. No. 5 (2016)

OPINION

GALE, JUDGE:

Respondent determined the following deficiencies and penalties with respect to petitioners' Federal income tax:

Petitioners	Year	Deficiency
Estate of George H. Bartell, Jr., etc.	2001	$231,001
George D. and June M. Bartell	2001	167,898
	2002	14,216
David H. and Jean B. Barber	2001	49,604
	2002	19,707
	2003	5,091

These cases have been consolidated for purposes of trial, briefing, and opinion. Unless otherwise indicated, all section references are to the Internal Revenue Code of 1986, as amended and in effect for the years at issue, and all Rule references are to the Tax Court Rules of Practice and Procedure.

The principal issue for decision is whether a property transaction undertaken by the Bartell Drug Co. (Bartell Drug), an S corporation owned by petitioners, qualified for nonrecognition treatment pursuant to section 1031 as a like-kind exchange.

FINDINGS OF FACT

Some of the facts have been stipulated and are so found. The stipulations, with accompanying exhibits, are incorporated herein by this reference. At the time the petitions were filed, all petitioners were residents of Washington State.

Petitioners and Bartell Drug

Bartell Drug owned and operated a chain of retail drugstores during the years at issue and had been doing so in Seattle, Washington, and surrounding areas for more than 100 years. Ownership of the company has remained in the Bartell family since its founding in 1890. During the years at issue, all shares in Bartell Drug were held by petitioners George H. Bartell, Jr.,[6] and his two children George D. Bartell and Jean B. Barber.

The foregoing family members served on the company's board of directors in various capacities and as officers during the period under consideration. Jean B. Barber (sometimes Jean Barber) served as chief financial officer of Bartell Drug, as well as secretary and a director on the board throughout that period.

In conducting its retail business, Bartell Drug owned some of the properties in which its stores operated and leased others. Before the 1980s, most of Bartell Drug's stores were in shopping centers anchored by grocery stores, generally in a strip-mall format with the drugstore space sited between two other merchants. Developers of those centers would typically approach Bartell Drug, offering space in an already-planned complex.

In the ensuing decades, however, two key, and to some degree interrelated, developments affected the business model for retail drugstores. First, grocery stores began including pharmacies within their stores. That innovation both reduced the attractiveness of the grocery-anchored centers for competing drugstores and prompted grocery stores to have developers restrict leasing to such competitive merchants. Second, Walgreen Co. (Walgreens), a national drugstore chain, introduced on a massive scale and to notable success a store format that shifted the paradigm for drug retailing. The emphasis became freestanding corner locations with drive-through pharmacies. Walgreens entered the Seattle area market in the early to mid-1990s, at which point Bartell Drug came under increasing pressure. The national chains Walgreens, Rite Aid Corp., and Safeway, Inc., became increasingly influential and Bartell Drug's chief competitors in the market.

Given the foregoing, Bartell Drug management faced the prospect of the growing obsolescence of its retail locations and sought to formulate a strategy to update its portfolio of owned and leased properties. The changed business climate generally required Bartell Drug to undertake development of new sites itself in order to open freestanding stores. Such a project often necessitated a significantly greater financial commitment, frequently encompassing land acquisition and/or building construction

---

6. [3] George H. Bartell, Jr., died in early 2009 after the filing of the case at docket No. 22709-05. His estate was substituted as a party-petitioner.

costs, than that involved in merely occupying a space built by a third-party developer. Additionally, the properties owned by Bartell Drug at that juncture generally had very low bases, such that outright sale could produce significant taxable gain.

In the early to mid-1990s, Jean Barber was introduced to the concept of section 1031 exchanges through her husband, a real estate broker. Following further investigation and consultation with professional advisers, the Bartell Drug board of directors adopted as a policy and authorized management to pursue a strategy of employing section 1031 exchanges to update the company's real estate portfolio and acquire new store locations. That decision was made in 1998 and was followed by four such exchanges.

In executing the section 1031 exchanges, Bartell Drug worked with Section 1031 Services, Inc., a corporation that provided qualified intermediary services to taxpayers, and a related corporation, Exchange Structures, Inc. Exchange Structures, in turn, set up wholly owned limited liability companies to serve as exchange intermediaries in such transactions. One such limited liability company was EPC Two, LLC (EPC Two), a Washington State entity having Exchange Structures as its sole member. As discussed hereinafter, EPC Two served as the exchange intermediary in the transaction at issue.

Agreement to Purchase the Lynnwood Property

Bartell Drug had operated a small store in Lynnwood, Washington, since the mid-1980s. That store was in a poorly maintained strip mall. By 1999 only a few years remained on the existing lease for the Lynnwood store, and Bartell Drug was interested in considering other properties. The company's real estate manager began looking into potential sites. At the time, it was rumored that Walgreens was also scouting locations in the Lynnwood area, one of which was likewise attractive to Bartell Drug.

That property was a recycling center, owned by Mildred M. Horton,[7] across the street from Bartell Drug's existing Lynnwood store. On April 1, 1999, Bartell Drug's real estate manager had an initial meeting with Mildred Horton and her attorney regarding the property. Further negotiations followed, and as they proceeded Bartell Drug ordered a first commitment for title insurance for the site (hereinafter the Lynnwood property), effective April 21, 1999. The commitment identified Mildred Horton as "Seller" and Bartell Drug as "Buyer/Borrower" and "Proposed Insured". Bartell Drug also contacted an engineering firm about providing a boundary and topographic survey of the Lynnwood property, and the firm responded with a proposal dated April 23, 1999.

The sale negotiations culminated on May 7, 1999, with the execution by Mildred Horton as "Seller" and Bartell Drug as "Buyer" of a Real Estate Purchase and Sale Agreement (sale agreement). The sale agreement recited a total purchase price of

---

7. [4] Mildred M. Horton owned the property both in her individual capacity and as trustee of a testamentary trust established under her deceased husband's will. For simplification, Mildred M. Horton and Mildred M. Horton, Trustee, will be referred to, without distinction, as Mildred Horton.

$1,898,640, payable in cash at closing, and set forth a closing date of August 1, 2000. In addition, the sale agreement specified a series of steps and deadlines to occur in the interim, relating to due diligence, title, survey, inspections, and environmental reports, as well as requirements for periodic earnest money payments totaling $100,000 to be deposited by Bartell Drug in escrow. The sale agreement also contained the following clause:

> 14.5 *Section 1031 Exchange.* Buyer and Seller agree to reasonably cooperate with each other to accomplish any exchange under Section 1031 of the Internal Revenue Code, including permitting assignment of this Agreement to an exchange facilitator; provided that the cooperating party is put to no liability or expense in connection therewith.

After execution of the sale agreement, Bartell Drug began to undertake the steps contemplated therein and related actions aimed at finalizing the acquisition and construction of a drugstore on the Lynnwood property. Bartell Drug ordered a second commitment for title insurance effective May 18, 1999, that modified certain listed exceptions not pertinent here. In July 1999 Mildred Horton and Bartell Drug agreed to extend the period for the company to complete its inspection of the Lynnwood property, so as to allow sufficient time for refining building and site plans. Then, as the extended inspection period drew to a close, Bartell Drug began remission of the stipulated earnest money payments by six checks dated September 1, 1999, through January 31, 2000.

Bartell Drug likewise continued preparations for the construction of a drugstore on the Lynnwood property. On January 5, 2000, Bartell Drug applied to the City of Lynnwood for a building permit for the site. That application listed Bartell Drug as applicant and Mildred Horton as owner of the subject real estate. Bartell Drug also engaged a traffic engineering firm to perform a traffic study and review of site access, and that firm invoiced Bartell Drug for the work on February 15, 2000.

Structuring and Financing the Lynnwood Property Purchase

Meanwhile, Bartell Drug sought to progress on structuring and financing the sale transaction. At some point not clearly disclosed in the record, but before March 2000, Bartell Drug approached Section 1031 Services about the possibility of employing an exchange in connection with the Lynnwood property. At that time, the company anticipated relinquishing an older store in White Center, in King County, Washington, for the exchange. By March of 2000 it had been agreed that EPC Two would take title to the Lynnwood property with a view to effecting a section 1031 exchange. Simultaneously, Bartell Drug had been working with KeyBank National Association (KeyBank) in structuring a multi-component credit package pertaining to both new borrowing facilities and extensions or renewals of existing loans, totaling approximately $15 million. One component of that package was a $4 million facility identified as a transaction loan intended to finance the acquisition of land for and construction of the new store in Lynnwood. The package was approved by KeyBank on February 29, 2000.

KeyBank's commitment letter for the full package, dated March 1, 2000, and sent to Bartell Drug, described the borrower of the $4 million loan as "The Bartell Drug

Company or an entity such as EPC TWO LLC acceptable to the bank with a guaranty provided by The Bartell Drug Company" and the purpose as "to finance the acquisition of land and construction of a new store in Lynnwood, WA. under the benefits of 1031 tax-free exchange." The commitment letter conditioned the financing in the full package upon Bartell Drug's covenant to maintain a tangible net worth of not less than $50 million. KeyBank made an exception to its general loan policy in extending the financing without Bartell Drug having to provide an audited financial statement. Instead, KeyBank was willing to make the loan on the basis of Bartell Drug's financial strength, long operating history, management team, and name recognition. The loan was not secured.

On March 13, 2000, the Bartell Drug board of directors authorized management to proceed in obtaining the facilities, and Jean Barber countersigned the commitment letter on that date. EPC Two, in turn, on March 17, 2000 (in conjunction with the loan documentation detailed *infra*), executed a limited liability company borrowing resolution authorizing the entity to borrow from and to sign promissory notes in favor of KeyBank.

On March 17, 2000, KeyBank as "Lender" and EPC Two by Exchange Structures, its sole member, as "Borrower" executed a Business Loan Agreement in the principal amount of $4 million. The loan was structured as a line of credit and required that a guaranty by Bartell Drug be furnished before the disbursement of any loan proceeds. EPC Two simultaneously executed in favor of KeyBank a promissory note in the principal amount of $4 million and three London Interbank Offered Rate addenda designating the pertinent variable interest rate schedule, as well as a disbursement request and authorization for the funds. The disbursement request recited the specific purpose of the loan as being to "finance construction of new store in Lynnwood". At the same time, Bartell Drug signed a corporate resolution to guarantee and corresponding commercial guaranty of the $4 million note made by EPC Two.

On April 4, 2000, Section 1031 Services sent to Bartell Drug an engagement letter for performance of intermediary services in connection with the section 1031 exchange contemplated for the Lynnwood property. Likewise, on the same date EPC Two sent an engagement letter for performance of "reverse warehousing" services for the exchange. The letters generally discussed fees, transactional agreements and documents, financing, and escrow procedures, with the EPC Two letter advising in particular:

> 2. We take title to the Replacement Property with funds loaned by you and/or a third party lender obtained by you. **Any loan to us from a third party lender must be non recourse to us, although you may personally guarantee the loan.** We provide you with a non recourse note and deed of trust to secure your loan to us. We lease the Replacement Property to you during the warehouse period. You are required under the lease to obtain liability and property insurance, naming us as "additional insured", to pay the property taxes, and to loan us any funds necessary to make mortgage payments.

The basic intermediary fee for a standard two-property exchange was set at $1,500, and 0.5% of the value of the property was specified as the charge for warehousing in a reverse exchange. Under cover of a letter dated April 17, 2000, Bartell Drug returned the countersigned engagement letter. That letter read:

> Enclosed are the executed warehousing and exchange letters. I have talked to Key Bank and they have no problem with issuing a side letter to make the new loan non-recourse to EPC II. However, the bank cannot do this until they receive an executed copy of the Exchange and Cooperation Agreement. I have talked to Dan Pepple, our attorney, and asked him to draft this document. Once we have that document completed, I will contact Key Bank to get the Loan Agreement modified.

As preparations for closing on the Lynnwood property proceeded, a corporate resolution dated July 13, 2000, was executed in which it was represented that the Bartell Drug board of directors in a previous meeting held March 13, 2000, had resolved, inter alia: (1) to enter into a section 1031 exchange transaction with Section 1031 Services to result in the purchase of a retail drugstore in Lynnwood, Washington, and (2) to assign Bartell Drug's rights under the May 7, 1999, sale agreement with Mildred Horton to Section 1031 Services. On July 26, 2000, EPC Two sent to the title insurance company escrow instructions concerning, and various documents to be executed by the parties in connection with, the closing.

During 2000 and 2001, EPC Two was a single purpose entity formed for the exclusive purpose of providing services to Bartell Drug. It was a disregarded entity for Federal income tax purposes at all times relevant to these cases (its sole member being Exchange Services, Inc.), and it had no assets during 2000 and 2001 other than, as more fully discussed hereinafter, a right to acquire the Lynnwood property and then title to the Lynnwood property, subject to various contractual terms governing the property's disposition.

Real Estate Acquisition and Exchange Cooperation Agreement

On July 31, 2000, Bartell Drug and EPC Two entered into a Real Estate Acquisition and Exchange Cooperation Agreement (REAECA) with respect to the Lynnwood transaction. Through the REAECA, Bartell Drug and EPC Two (referred to as SPE in the REAECA) contracted to cooperate in effecting an exchange of current property (i.e., property currently owned by Bartell Drug but to be relinquished) for replacement property. The document set forth the contracting parties' rights and responsibilities in that endeavor. The current property was identified as of that time as the White Center site, and the replacement property as the new Lynnwood property. The REAECA addressed acquisition and ownership of the replacement property, including assignment of the existing purchase agreement, financing, construction of improvements, and leasing; disposition of the current property through cooperation in an exchange via a qualified intermediary (i.e., Section 1031 Services); and transfer of the replacement property to Bartell Drug, including the purchase price attendant thereto.

As regards acquisition of the Lynnwood property, Bartell Drug assigned and EPC Two accepted the rights and obligations under the May 7, 1999, sale agreement with Mildred Horton. The REAECA then specified that EPC Two "shall acquire title to" the replacement property and then "shall cause to be constructed on" the replacement property certain improvements "pursuant to plans and specifications approved by Bartell and undertaken by a general contractor and subcontractors approved by Bartell".

To that end, the REAECA provided that to finance the acquisition of and construction of the improvements to the site, EPC Two would borrow funds from an agreed lender and would have no obligation to become liable for any payments or to advance any funds in excess of those so borrowed or funds supplied by the qualified intermediary from the sale of the current property. Similarly, EPC Two was to have no responsibility: (1) "to investigate, review or otherwise inquire into the nature of any work for which payment is requested, it being expressly agreed that SPE's responsibility is solely to disburse funds on request by Bartell"; or (2) "to review, supervise, inspect or otherwise become involved in the construction" of the improvements.

The REAECA also stipulated that upon substantial completion of the improvements, EPC Two was required to lease the replacement property to Bartell Drug. The lease was to be a triple net lease and was to "provide for rental equal to all debt service payable under any and all" loan agreements with respect to the replacement property.

If Bartell Drug then elected to go forward with an exchange of the current property, that property would be sold to a third party through the qualified intermediary, with the intermediary having been assigned Bartell Drug's rights under such a sale contract and receiving the proceeds thereof. Bartell Drug would next assign to the qualified intermediary its rights and obligations under the REAECA, which included a right to acquire the replacement property. At Bartell Drug's direction, the qualified intermediary would then remit to EPC Two the proceeds from the sale of the current property up to an amount not in excess of the "Purchase Price" of the replacement property. To complete the exchange, the qualified intermediary would direct EPC Two to deed the replacement property to Bartell Drug.

Per the REAECA, the "Purchase Price" for the replacement property was equal to its "Fair Market Value". "Fair Market Value", in turn, was defined:

> "Fair Market Value" of the Replacement Property shall mean the fair market value determined by an appraisal conducted by a nationally recognized real estate appraiser as may be agreed to by Bartell and SPE * * * ; provided, however, that if the Replacement Property is purchased from SPE within twenty-four (24) months after the date on which SPE acquired the Replacement Property, then the "Fair Market Value" shall be deemed to equal its "Acquisition Cost" as hereinafter defined.

The referenced definition of "Acquisition Cost" followed:

> "Acquisition Cost" shall mean the sum of (i) the purchase price paid by SPE to the Seller to acquire the Replacement Property; (ii) all sales, transfer or

similar taxes, and all charges and closing costs paid by SPE in connection with its purchase of the Replacement Property; (iii) all interest and stated fees (including pre-payment fees in connection with mandatory pre-payments) under the Credit Agreements which are not paid as rent pursuant to the Lease, (iv) the cost of construction of all Improvements which are paid by SPE, and (v) any and all unreimbursed costs, liabilities and expenses of any kind incurred by SPE in connection with the acquisition, ownership and operation of the Replacement Property and the completion of the Exchange except for "Excluded Costs" as defined * * *

The REAECA additionally incorporated EPC Two's entitlement to receive from Bartell Drug the .5% fee set forth in the previously described April 4, 2000, letter from EPC Two.

Two indemnity provisions were set forth in the REAECA. One was a general indemnification clause whereby Bartell Drug agreed to indemnify and save EPC Two and/or KeyBank "harmless from all loss, cost, damages, expenses and attorneys' fees suffered or incurred" as a result of any claim, investigation, proceeding, or suit in connection with the ownership or exchange of the replacement property "except to the extent * * * [that party] is liable for such loss as a result of its gross negligence, willful misconduct or breach of its obligations under" the REAECA. The other provision was a specific environmental release and indemnity mandating that Bartell Drug indemnify and hold harmless EPC Two and/or KeyBank for any claims in connection with contamination of the current and replacement properties by any hazardous substance.

Other matters pertaining to security were likewise documented during this period. Contemporaneously with entry into the REAECA, EPC Two on July 31, 2000, executed a deed of trust on the Lynnwood property for the benefit of Bartell Drug. The deed of trust secured Bartell Drug with respect to EPC Two's obligations under the REAECA, which was expressly referenced therein, as well as any liability paid by Bartell Drug under the provisions of its guaranty of payment on the KeyBank loan. Effective August 1, 2000, KeyBank as "Lender" and EPC Two as "Borrower" executed an amendment to the $4 million promissory note. The amendment rendered the note "expressly nonrecourse to Borrower" and stipulated that all payments thereunder were to be made "only from the income and proceeds from the Borrower's interest in the Replacement Property and Improvements to be acquired with the proceeds of the loans(s) evidenced by the Promissory Note".

Closing on the Lynnwood Property

Closing on the Lynnwood property took place on August 1, 2000. The final selling price, incorporating any pertinent amendments to the May 7, 1999, contract, was $1,878,640.[8] Various other charges and expenses were also settled through the escrow

---

8. [5] The $20,000 reduction in the sale price from the amount stated in the May 7, 1999, sale agreement apparently resulted from an addendum to the sale agreement sought by Mildred Horton pertaining to the removal of personal property from the site.

process, and EPC Two received out of the escrow $9,493 in payment of a "Warehousing Lease Fee".[9] On that date, a statutory warranty deed conveying the Lynnwood property from grantor Mildred Horton to grantee EPC Two was recorded. The deed of trust on the property from EPC Two in favor of Bartell Drug was also recorded on August 1, 2000. A final title insurance policy on a fee simple interest in the Lynnwood property, dated August 1, 2000, was issued to EPC Two as the named insured.

Construction of the Lynnwood Store

Work on the new property itself advanced on August 1, 2000, with the commencement of site demolition and the clearing of existing site debris. J.R. Abbott Construction, Inc. (J.R. Abbott), invoiced Bartell Drug for the demolition and clearing on August 31, 2000, and Bartell Drug paid directly the $61,690.23 due in early September of 2000. Bartell Drug was subsequently reimbursed that amount through a construction draw from the KeyBank loan. As the project moved into the phase of store construction, Bartell Drug managed the process. For instance, throughout the following months Bartell Drug was engaged in applying for and obtaining appropriate permits and bonding to enable the work to proceed. In September of 2000, Bartell Drug applied to the City of Lynnwood for a public works permit. On December 20, 2000, the City of Lynnwood issued to Bartell Drug the building permit which had been applied for in January of that year, as noted *supra*.[10]

Performance bonds were required by the City of Lynnwood for the construction of the drugstore. EPC Two executed two commercial surety bond applications dated January 5, 2001, in favor of the City of Lynnwood. Bartell Drug signed those applications as third-party indemnitor. Two performance bonds were issued for the construction listing "EPC TWO, LLC c/o BARTELL DRUG COMPANY" as "Principal" and Travelers Casualty and Security Company of America as "Surety" and were signed on January 8, 2001, only by Bartell Drug and filed with the City of Lynnwood.[11]

Bartell Drug selected J.R. Abbott, the same firm that had performed the demolition, as the contractor for the construction. A contract for the work on the new drugstore dated January 8, 2001, was executed between "EPC Two L.L.C. c/o THE BARTELL DRUG COMPANY" as "Owner" and J.R. Abbott as "Contractor". Both EPC Two and Bartell Drug signed the document via signature blocks labeled "OWNER". All requisite building and similar permits for construction of the drugstore were issued to Bartell Drug.

One key component of the drugstore project was site access. Bartell Drug believed that having two driveway access points was critical, but applicable governmental regulations would have limited the Lynnwood property to one curb cut. Accordingly,

---

9. [6] This $9,493.20 payment equals 0.5% of the original $1,898,640 contract purchase price for the Lynnwood property.

10. [7] All permits issued by the City of Lynnwood in the record list Bartell Drug as "Applicant" and Mildred Horton as "Owner", regardless of the date of application and/or approval.

11. [8] All permits issued by the City of Lynnwood in the record list Bartell Drug as "Applicant" and Mildred Horton as "Owner", regardless of the date of application and/or approval.

Bartell Drug worked closely with the City of Lynnwood to formulate an easement plan involving the drugstore site and the adjacent corner lot. Those negotiations culminated in an Agreement for Joint Access Agreement [sic] dated June 15, 2001, between EPC Two and Bartell Drug as grantors and the City of Lynnwood as grantee. The agreement opened with the following recitals:

> A. *EPC Two LLC holds title to the real property (the "Bartell Parcel")* * * * and The Bartell Drug Company holds the beneficial interest in the Bartell Parcel. Bartell applied to the City for a building permit to develop the Bartell Parcel.
>
> B. As a condition to the issuance of a building permit, the City required Bartell to agree to grant access easements in favor of the adjacent parcel * * *

The agreement then went on to describe the subject easements and was executed by both EPC Two and Bartell Drug.

As construction progressed, periodic payments for the work were typically made in the following manner: (1) J.R. Abbott would send an invoice to Bartell Drug; (2) a Bartell Drug employee would send written authorization to EPC Two for requesting a construction draw from the KeyBank loan in the amount of the invoice; (3) EPC Two would send written authorization to KeyBank for disbursement of funds from the construction loan to be paid by wire transfer to J.R. Abbott; (4) KeyBank would pay J.R. Abbott the amount specified in the EPC Two authorization. During the period from February through July 2001, six such payments were made. Various other expenses, including those incurred after the $4 million loan was depleted, were paid by Bartell Drug directly. A promissory note dated July 6, 2001, was executed by EPC Two in favor of Bartell Drug in the amount of $248,562.33, with respect to at least a portion of the expenses so paid. The note bore no interest for the first 180 days, and thereafter was to bear interest at 7% per annum.

Completion and Leasing of the Lynnwood Store

As the construction phase came to a close, EPC Two as landlord and Bartell Drug as tenant entered a lease agreement for the Lynnwood property and new store effective July 11, 2001. The lease term was for 24 months beginning June 1, 2001. The rent obligation was summarized at the outset of the lease as follows:

> The initial net rent of the Lease shall be $9,493.00, which has been previously paid by Tenant. As of the Commence Date, net monthly rent shall be $2,000.00 per month, with a total net rent under the lease not to exceed $19,413.00. "Net" rent shall mean the amount of rent owing by Tenant after offsets for any interest owed by Landlord to Tenant related to the Premises. * * *

Subsequent provisions set forth further details, e.g.:

> Tenant may offset the rent owing with payments due Tenant under that certain Note payable by Landlord to Tenant of even date herewith. Tenant shall also be responsible for payment of all utilities, taxes and insurance of the Premises, as set forth below. As additional Rent, Tenant shall make all payments due from Landlord on the Loan secured by the Premises to the applicable lender. * * *

The $19,413 amount had been explained by an EPC Two officer in a facsimile accompanying transmission of a draft of the lease with the comment: "The $19,413 'cap' is .5% of the $2,004,066.96 spent on Lynnwood to date plus its acquisition cost of $1,878,640."

Consistent with the REAECA, the lease also incorporated indemnification clauses in favor of EPC Two, one general and one specifically focused on environmental hazards. In the former, tenant agreed to hold landlord harmless against all liabilities arising from acts or omissions of tenant or visitors to the premises. In the latter, tenant undertook to indemnify landlord against all claims related to hazardous materials brought to or used on the premises.

On July 18, 2001, the City of Lynnwood issued a certificate of occupancy for the new Bartell drugstore. In August of 2001, J.R. Abbott sent to Bartell Drug an application and certification for payment for $93,744.05 remaining due on the project. A conditional release and waiver of lien rights for the project, such as any applicable mechanic's or similar lien, contingent upon payment of the $93,744.05, was included with the invoice. Bartell Drug paid the requested amount by check dated August 24, 2001.

Agreement to Sell the Everett Property

Meanwhile, Bartell Drug was also proceeding with steps directed toward the property to be relinquished in the exchange. In August 2000 Bartell Drug had acquired a retail drugstore in Everett, Washington (Everett property), as part of a section 1031 exchange involving the sale of another property. That transaction was accomplished through Section 1031 Services, and a statutory warranty deed from EPC Two to Bartell Drug was recorded on December 27, 2000. In the spring of 2001, Jean Barber requested from KeyBank a six-month extension on the term of the $4 million Lynnwood property loan (otherwise expiring May 15, 2015). KeyBank documentation explaining the request, prepared May 15, 2001, stated:

> [T]he new Lynnwood store under construction, and which is being financed by this loan, is now approximately 80% completed and will not be finished and ready for customers until the month of July. In addition, management needs extra time after completion of the Lynnwood Store to determine the most appropriate repayment source—either from sale/leaseback of the company's White Center Store as originally planned or from the sale of the existing Everett Store, which may or may not be leased back depending on management's negotiations on acquisition of a new Everett Store site. The new maturity date of this loan will afford management more than adequate time to make the best economic and strategic decision for repayment.
>
> Bartell's continues to produce excellent financial results. For the year 2000, * * *

The request was approved, and a modification agreement of the KeyBank loan, dated May 16, 2001, was executed by EPC Two.

On or about September 21, 2001, Bartell Drug entered into a purchase agreement to sell the Everett property to William and Theresa Eng. The transaction was structured as a sale-leaseback, and after a series of amendments negotiated between Bartell Drug and the Engs during September and October, the selling price was stipulated at $4,300,250. Among other provisions, the purchase agreement included a seller exchange clause stating: "Buyer agrees to cooperate should Seller elect to sell the property as part of a like-kind exchange under IRC Section 1031. Seller's contemplated exchange shall not impose upon Buyer any additional liability or financial obligation".

By mid-October of 2001, however, Bartell Drug had received two offers to purchase the Lynnwood property that would have enabled the company to use the site in a sale-leaseback arrangement. Consequently, Bartell Drug management requested from KeyBank an additional extension of the construction loan to negotiate that possibility. KeyBank acceded to the request and a concomitant modification and/or extension agreement dated October 17, 2001, was executed by EPC Two. On November 28, 2001, however, the Bartell Drug board of directors approved the sale of the Everett store, observing that the "proceeds will be used to purchase our store in Lynnwood".

Exchange Agreement

On December 17, 2001, Bartell Drug as "Exchangor" and Section 1031 Services as "Intermediary" executed an exchange agreement for the exchange of relinquished property, identified as the Everett property, for replacement property, identified as the Lynnwood property, in a transaction intended "to qualify for tax-deferred treatment under I.R.C. Section 1031". The exchange agreement provided for the purchase agreement with the Engs and for Bartell Drug's rights under the REAECA to be assigned to Section 1031 Services. Section 1031 Services would then transfer the relinquished property to the Engs, acquire the replacement property from EPC Two, and transfer the replacement property to Bartell Drug. These transfers were to be accomplished through a direct deeding mechanism, i.e., conveyance of title between Bartell Drug and the underlying buyer or seller at Section 1031 Services' direction. The purchase price for the relinquished property would be paid to Section 1031 Services and used by Section 1031 Services to acquire the replacement property from EPC Two. Bartell Drug agreed to indemnify Section 1031 Services from all loss in general and from any claims related to hazardous materials in particular.

By letter dated likewise December 17, 2001, Section 1031 Services sent to Bartell Drug, to the company's attorney, and to the escrow agent for the Lynnwood transaction a substitute exhibit for the REAECA. The exhibit identified the Everett property as the relinquished property for the exchange. Two further letters of the same date were sent by Section 1031 Services to the escrow agent for the approaching closings, transmitting the exchange intermediary's instructions to escrow for the relinquished and replacement property, respectively.

Closing of the Exchange

Finalization of the transfers of the Everett and Lynnwood properties took place between December 26, 2001, and January 3, 2002. On December 26, 2001, Bartell Drug executed an assignment of the purchase agreement for the Everett property, and Section 1031 Services provided notification of that assignment to the Engs. In conjunction therewith, Bartell Drug also executed a special warranty deed conveying the Everett property to entities managed by the Engs. The deed was recorded on December 28, 2001.

On December 27 or 28, 2001, EPC Two executed a statutory warranty deed conveying the Lynnwood property to Bartell Drug, and the deed was recorded on December 31, 2001. On January 3, 2002,[12] Bartell Drug executed an assignment of the REAECA to Section 1031 Services. Section 1031 Services had previously on December 17, 2001, provided notice of the assignment to EPC Two.

Through the respective escrow processes, sale of the Everett property provided a net amount after charges of $4,132,752.09, which was applied toward purchase of the Lynnwood property. From that balance, charges paid out of the escrow included $10,249.81 remitted to Exchange Structures as "Final Rent Payment" and $1,500 remitted to Section 1031 Services as "Exchange Fee". An excess payment of $128,194.05 was due from the buyer, to be furnished by Bartell Drug under the exchange agreement, to complete the transaction.

Tax Reporting and Examination

For 2001 and prior years, Bartell Drug filed with the IRS Forms 1120S, U.S. Income Tax Return for an S Corporation. Included with the 2001 return was a Form 8824, Like-Kind Exchanges, addressing the transfers of the Everett and Lynnwood properties. Bartell Drug reported that the property relinquished in the subject exchange had been acquired on August 1, 2000, and had been transferred to another party on December 28, 2001. The company further reported that like-kind property was actually received on January 2, 2002. The fair market value of the property received was shown as $4,134,592 and the basis of the property given up as $1,329,729, for a deferred gain of $2,804,863.

Schedules K-1, Shareholder's Share of Income, Credits, Deductions, etc., were prepared for each of Bartell Drug's shareholders, i.e., George H. Bartell, Jr., George D. Bartell, and Jean B. Barber, setting forth his or her respective shares of Bartell Drug's items of income and deduction. Petitioners filed Forms 1040, U.S. Individual Income Tax Return, for 2001 and subsequent years at issue reflecting, inter alia, amounts flowing through from Bartell Drug's corporate returns. The gain realized from the sale of the Everett property, having been treated as deferred by Bartell Drug, was not reported by the individual petitioners.

In early 2004, the IRS commenced an examination of Bartell Drug's 2001 corporate return. That audit culminated in a Form 5701, Notice of Proposed Adjustment, dated December 10, 2004, and corresponding Form 886A, Explanation of Items. The single adjustment proposed was the disallowance of tax deferral treatment under section 1031 for the $2,804,863 reported as realized in the like-kind exchange involving the

---

12. [9] Although the pertinent signature is dated "1/3/01", the document refers to the parties' having executed the exchange agreement, which did not occur until December 17, 2001.

Lynnwood and Everett properties. The notices of deficiency underlying the instant cases followed, as the resultant increase in corporate income flowed through to the personal returns of the shareholders.

OPINION

I. Burden of Proof

As a general rule, the Commissioner's determinations are presumed correct, and the taxpayer bears the burden of proving error therein. Rule 142(a); *Welch v. Helvering*, 290 U.S. 111, 115 (1933). However, section 7491(a)(1) may shift the burden to the Commissioner with respect to factual issues affecting liability for tax where the taxpayer introduces credible evidence, but the provision operates only where the taxpayer establishes that he has complied under section 7491(a)(2) with all substantiation requirements, has maintained all required records, and has cooperated with reasonable requests for witnesses, information, documents, meetings, and interviews. *See* H.R. Conf. Rept. No. 105-599, at 239–240 (1998), 1998-3 C.B. 747, 993–994.

Petitioners assert that they have met the record retention, cooperation, and introduction of credible evidence requisites for a shift of the burden of proof. Respondent argues to the contrary. Nonetheless, we find it unnecessary to decide whether the burden should be shifted under section 7491(a). As will be detailed *infra*, the crux of the parties' disagreement as to the outcome of these cases lies not in different views as to what took place but in different positions as to what standard or test should be applied in analyzing whether those events generated taxable income for petitioners. The relevant facts are substantially those gleaned from the documentary record, the bulk of which has been stipulated. Together with a small number of additional documents offered at trial, these materials afford the Court a largely uncontroverted view of what happened. Once the more legal or theoretical question in dispute is answered, the record is not evenly weighted and is sufficient for the Court to render a decision on the merits based upon a preponderance of the evidence, without regard to the burden of proof. Because there is no "evidentiary tie" here, the burden of proof need not be resolved. *See Blodgett v. Commissioner*, 394 F.3d 1030, 1039 (8th Cir. 2005), *aff'g* T.C. Memo. 2003-212.

II. Treatment of the Lynnwood Property Transaction

A. Contentions of the Parties

Petitioners argue that the transaction involving the Lynnwood property is properly treated as a like-kind exchange, thus permitting deferral of income realized upon the disposition of the Everett property. Respondent, conversely, asserts that the transaction in question failed to qualify for section 1031 treatment. Their differences center on whether an exchange for purposes of section 1031 occurred. It has been observed that the "very essence of an exchange is the transfer of property between owners, while the mark of a sale is the receipt of cash for the property". *Carlton v. United States*, 385 F.2d 238, 242 (5th Cir. 1967). A corollary of the requirement of a reciprocal transfer of property between owners is that the taxpayer not have owned the property purportedly received in the exchange before the exchange occurs; if he has, he has engaged in a nonreciprocal exchange with himself. "A taxpayer cannot engage in an exchange with himself; an exchange ordinarily requires a 'reciprocal transfer of property, as distinguished from a transfer of property for money consideration.'" *DeCleene v. Commissioner*, 115 T.C. 457, 469 (2000) (citation omitted).

Respondent maintains that Bartell Drug already owned the Lynnwood property long before the December 2001 disposition of the Everett property, thereby precluding any exchange as of that date. Petitioners contend that Bartell Drug was not then the owner of the Lynnwood property; rather, EPC Two must be treated as the owner. These different results, in turn, are explained by the different tests employed by the parties to answer the ownership question. Petitioners claim that an agency analysis is the appropriate standard and that such an analysis should be employed in a manner consistent with the wide latitude historically permitted in the context of like-kind exchanges. Respondent, on the other hand, advocates application of a benefits and burdens analysis as the traditional test in the myriad of situations raising questions of tax ownership of property.

B. Statutory Principles and Regulatory Developments

Generally, under sections 61(a)(3) and 1001(c), taxpayers must recognize all gain or loss realized upon the sale or exchange of property. Section 1031, however, provides an exception which allows taxpayers to defer recognition of gain or loss on exchanges of like-kind property held for productive use in a trade or business or for investment. The statute sets forth in section 1031(a) the following general rule: "No gain or loss shall be recognized on the exchange of property held for productive use in a trade or business or for investment if such property is exchanged solely for property of like kind which is to be held either for productive use in a trade or business or for investment." This general rule for nonrecognition mandates that qualifying property be exchanged "solely" for other qualifying property. In the event that non-like-kind property, including cash, is received in a transaction otherwise within the purview of the statute, section 1031(b) establishes a regime whereby any gain realized on the exchange is recognized to the extent of the so-called boot, i.e., the nonqualifying property. Any gain not recognized is then deferred through operation of section 1031(d), under which the basis of property acquired in a like-kind exchange equals the basis of the property transferred, less any cash received and loss recognized, plus any gain recognized.

The purpose for the foregoing deferral has been identified in jurisprudence involving section 1031 and its predecessor statutes as resting on the lack of any material change in the taxpayer's economic position. *Commissioner v. P.G. Lake, Inc.*, 356 U.S. 260, 268 (1958); *DeCleene v. Commissioner*, 115 T.C. at 466; *Koch v. Commissioner*, 71 T.C. 54, 63–64 (1978). The new property is substantially a continuation of the taxpayer's investment in the old property, still unliquidated; the taxpayer's funds remain tied up in the same kind of property. *Commissioner v. P.G. Lake, Inc.*, 356 U.S. at 268; *Koch v. Commissioner*, 71 T.C. at 63–64; H.R. Rept. No. 73-704 (1934), 1939-1 C.B. (Part 2) 554, 564.

Given that rationale, courts have frequently interpreted the requirements of section 1031 liberally, exhibiting a lenient attitude toward taxpayers' attempts to come within its terms. *See, e.g., Starker v. United States*, 602 F.2d 1341, 1352–1353 (9th Cir. 1979); *DeCleene v. Commissioner*, 115 T.C. at 467; *Biggs v. Commissioner*, 69 T.C. 905, 913–914 (1978), *aff'd*, 632 F.2d 1171 (5th Cir. 1980). The Commissioner likewise has often taken a similar approach in regulations promulgated and guidance issued under section 1031, even affording various safe harbors for transactions. Secs. 1.1031(a)-1 to 1.1031(k)-1, Income Tax Regs. Such breadth has developed incrementally over time, as will be seen in the discussion *infra*.

The words "like kind" as used in section 1031 are defined to "have reference to the nature or character of the property and not to its grade or quality." Sec. 1.1031(a)-1(b), Income Tax Regs. It is the "kind or class" of the property that must be the same, such that the "fact that any real estate involved is improved or unimproved is not material, for that fact relates only to the grade or quality of the property and not to its kind or class." *Id.*

Historically, there has never been any question that section 1031 as originally enacted covered simultaneous exchanges between two parties. *See, e.g., Starker*, 602 F.2d 1341; *Alderson v. Commissioner*, 317 F.2d 790 (9th Cir. 1963), *rev'g* 38 T.C. 215 (1962); and cases discussed therein. However, following cases finding a broader reach, the statute itself and regulatory directives were likewise widened explicitly to address various deferred exchanges (where the exchange of properties is not simultaneous) and multiparty transactions (where third-party exchange facilitators are used to effect the exchange). For instance, after *Starker*, 602 F.2d 1341, Congress amended section 1031(a) expressly to sanction specified deferred exchanges by adding the following:

(3) Requirement that property be identified and that exchange be completed not more than 180 days after transfer of exchanged property.— For purposes of this subsection, any property received by the taxpayer shall be treated as property which is not like-kind property if—

(A) such property is not identified as property to be received in the exchange on or before the day which is 45 days after the date on which the taxpayer transfers the property relinquished in the exchange, or

(B) such property is received after the earlier of—

(i) the day which is 180 days after the date on which the taxpayer transfers the property relinquished in the exchange, or

(ii) the due date (determined with regard to extension) for the transferor's return of the tax imposed by this chapter for the taxable year in which the transfer of the relinquished property occurs.

Comprehensive regulations were later issued in section 1.1031(k)-1, Income Tax Regs., to facilitate deferred "forward" exchanges (i.e., where the taxpayer receives replacement property after the date of his transfer of relinquished property) within the confines of the statutory time limits. (However, the Secretary expressly declined to provide guidance with respect to deferred "reverse" exchanges (i.e., where the taxpayer receives replacement property before the date of his transfer of relinquished property)). *See* T.D. 8346, 1991-1 C.B. 150, 151. As has been noted by this Court: "These regulations, with their provisions for use of third-party 'qualified intermediaries' as accommodation titleholders, who will not be considered the taxpayer's agent in doing the multiparty deferred exchanges permitted by the regulations, have encouraged the growth of a new industry of third-party exchange facilitators." *DeCleene v. Commissioner*, 115 T.C. at 467.

Nonetheless, even with these regulatory developments, the full reach and range of transactions entitled to protection under section 1031 remained unsettled, as was made clear in the preamble to the regulations:

> Section 1031(a)(3) of the Code and § 1.1031(a)-3 of the proposed regulations apply to deferred exchanges. The proposed regulations define a deferred exchange as an exchange in which, pursuant to an agreement, the taxpayer transfers property held for productive use in a trade or business or for investment (the "relinquished property") and subsequently receives property to be held either for productive use in a trade or business or for investment (the "replacement property"). The proposed regulations do not apply to transactions in which the taxpayer receives the replacement property prior to the date on which the taxpayer transfers the relinquished property (so-called "reverse-*Starker*" transactions.) * * *
>
>   * * *
>
> However, the Service will continue to study the applicability of the general rule of section 1031(a)(1) to these transactions.

T.D. 8346, 1991-1 C.B. at 150–151.

The vacuum in any administrative guidance concerning reverse exchanges was not alleviated until the issuance by the IRS of Rev. Proc. 2000-37, 2000-2 C.B. 308. The revenue procedure addressed specified "parking" arrangements and provided

> a safe harbor under which the Internal Revenue Service will not challenge (a) the qualification of property as either "replacement property" or "relinquished property" * * * for purposes of § 1031 of the Internal Revenue Code and the regulations thereunder or (b) the treatment of the "exchange accommodation titleholder"[13] as the beneficial owner of such property for federal income tax purposes, if the property is held in a "qualified exchange accommodation arrangement" (QEAA) * * *

Id. sec. 1, 2000-2 C.B. at 308.

---

13. Under Rev. Proc. 2000-37, 2000-2 C.B. 308, the "exchange accommodation titleholder" is, generally, a person other than the taxpayer who is subject to Federal income tax and who holds legal title to, or other indicia or ownership of, property intended to be exchanged in a transaction qualifying under sec. 1031. *See* Rev. Proc. 2000-37, sec. 4.02(1), 2000-2 C.B. at 309.

The revenue procedure was effective for qualified exchange accommodation arrangements entered into by an exchange accommodation titleholder on or after September 15, 2000. *Id.* sec. 5, 2000-2 C.B. at 310. Conversely, per the procedure,

> [n]o inference is intended with respect to the federal income tax treatment of arrangements similar to those described in this revenue procedure that were entered into prior to the effective date of this revenue procedure. Further, the Service recognizes that "parking" transactions can be accomplished outside of the safe harbor provided in this revenue procedure. Accordingly, no inference is intended with respect to the federal income tax treatment of "parking" transactions that do not satisfy the terms of the safe harbor provided in this revenue procedure, whether entered into prior to or after the effective date of this revenue procedure.

Id. sec. 3.02, 2000-2 C.B. at 308.

The revenue procedure observed that in the years since the deferred forward exchange regulations were published, taxpayers had attempted to structure a wide variety of reverse "parking" transactions arranged "so that the accommodation party has enough of the benefits and burdens relating to the property" to be treated as the owner. *Id.* sec. 2.05, 2000-2 C.B. at 308. The procedure then imposed time limits paralleling those for deferred exchanges (45 and 180 days) and enumerated specific contractual provisions and/or relationships that would not be considered fatal to treatment of the "exchange accommodation titleholder" as the owner of the replacement or relinquished property for Federal income tax purposes. *Id.* sec. 4, 2000-2 C.B. at 309.

C. Application of Caselaw Principles

Bartell Drug undertook the transaction involving the Lynnwood property before Rev. Proc 2000-37, *supra*, was published on October 2, 2000. *See* Rev. Proc. 2000-37, 2000-40 I.R.B. 308. There is no dispute that Rev. Proc. 2000-37, *supra*, is inapplicable. EPC Two acquired title on August 1, 2000, before the revenue procedure's effective date, and the complete transaction consumed 17 months, well beyond the 180 days that would have been allowed for closing the transaction under it. Hence, each side contends for its respective position on whether a qualifying exchange occurred by drawing on general tax principles and caselaw it considers applicable.

The fundamental question in determining whether section 1031 applies here is whether an exchange occurred. The answer to that inquiry will depend, in this context and as framed by the parties' positions, on whether what happened here should be deemed a self-exchange. A self-exchange, in turn, will be said to have transpired if Bartell Drug would be considered the owner of the Lynnwood property for tax purposes before acquiring title in December of 2001.

Respondent contends that Bartell Drug already owned the Lynnwood property at the time of the disputed exchange because Bartell Drug—not EPC Two—had all the benefits and burdens of ownership of the property; namely, the capacity to benefit from any appreciation in the property's value, the risk of loss from any diminution in its value, and the other burdens of ownership such as taxes and liabilities arising from the property. By contrast, respondent contends, EPC Two did not possess any of the benefits and burdens of ownership of the property; it had no equity interest in the property, it had made no economic outlay to acquire it, it was not at risk with respect to the property because all the financing was nonrecourse as to it, it paid no real estate taxes, and the construction of improvements on the property was financed and directed by Bartell Drug. Moreover, respondent contends, Bartell Drug had possession and control of the property during the entire period EPC Two held title, first by virtue of the REAECA provisions giving it control over the construction of site improvements and then possession through a lease that EPC Two was obligated under the REAECA to extend to it, for rent equal to the debt service on the KeyBank loan plus EPC Two's fee for holding title. Respondent's position is that a benefits and burdens test, which is used in many contexts to determine ownership of property for Federal tax purposes, *see, e.g., Grodt & McKay Realty, Inc. v. Commissioner*, 77 T.C. 1221, 1237–1238 (1981), should be applied in the context of a claim of section 1031 treatment to determine who owns the replacement property, as between a third-party exchange facilitator who takes legal title to it to facilitate an exchange and the taxpayer who ultimately receives it at the time of the exchange.

Petitioners point out, however, that both this Court and the Court of Appeals for the Ninth Circuit, to which an appeal in this case would ordinarily lie, *see* sec. 7482(b), have expressly rejected the proposition that a person who takes title to the replacement property for the purpose of effecting a section 1031 exchange must assume the benefits and burdens of ownership in that property to satisfy the exchange requirement. As the Court of Appeals for the Ninth Circuit pointed out in *Alderson v. Commissioner*, 317 F.2d at 795:

> [O]ne need not assume the benefits and burdens of ownership in property before exchanging it but may properly acquire title *solely for the purpose of exchange* and accept title and transfer it in exchange for other like property, all as a part of the same transaction with no resulting gain which is recognizable under Section 1002 of the Internal Revenue Code of 1954.

We have followed *Alderson* in according section 1031 treatment in a variety of transactions where the taxpayers used a third-party exchange facilitator to take title to the replacement property to effect an exchange of property in form, who was contractually insulated from any beneficial ownership of the replacement property. *See, e.g., Garcia v. Commissioner*, 80 T.C. 491 (1983); *Barker v. Commissioner*, 74 T.C. 555 (1980); *Biggs v. Commissioner*, 69 T.C. 905. When the third-party exchange facilitator has been contractually excluded from beneficial ownership pursuant to the agreement under which he holds title to the replacement property for the taxpayer, that beneficial ownership necessarily resides with the taxpayer once title has been obtained from the seller of the replacement property. And yet the third-party exchange facilitator, rather than the taxpayer, has been treated as the owner of the replacement property at the time of the exchange in the cases cited above. Otherwise, a disqualifying self-exchange could be said to have occurred.

The somewhat formalistic approach of the caselaw on which petitioners rely is perhaps best explained by this Court's observations over 35 years ago in *Barker v. Commissioner*, 74 T.C. at 560–561, 565:

> The touchstone of section 1031 * * * is the requirement that there be an exchange of like-kind business or investment properties, as distinguished from a cash sale of property by the taxpayer and a reinvestment of the proceeds in other property.
>
> The "exchange" requirement poses an analytical problem because it runs headlong into the familiar tax law maxim that the substance of a transaction controls over form. In a sense, the substance of a transaction in which the taxpayer sells property and immediately reinvests the proceeds in like-kind property is not much different from the substance of a transaction in which two parcels are exchanged without cash. * * *
>
> * * *
>
> [T]he conceptual distinction between an exchange qualifying for section 1031 on the one hand and a sale and reinvestment on the other is largely one of form.

Petitioners further point out that settled caselaw has permitted taxpayers to exercise any number of indicia of ownership and control over the replacement property before it is transferred to them, without jeopardizing section 1031 exchange treatment. As we noted in *Biggs v. Commissioner*, 69 T.C. at 913–914:

> [C]ourts have permitted taxpayers great latitude in structuring [section 1031 exchange] transactions. * * * The taxpayer can locate suitable property to be received in exchange and can enter into negotiations for the acquisition of such property. *Coastal Terminals, Inc. v. United States*, 320 F.2d 333, 338 (4th Cir. 1963); *Alderson v. Commissioner*, 317 F.2d at 793; *Coupe v. Commissioner*, 52 T.C. at 397–398. Moreover, the taxpayer can oversee improvements on the land to be acquired (*J.H. Baird Publishing Co. v. Commissioner*, 39 T.C. at 611) and can even advance money toward the purchase price of the property to be acquired by exchange (*124 Front Street, Inc. v. Commissioner*, 65 T.C. 6, 15–18 (1975)). Provided the final result is an exchange of property for other property of a like kind, the transaction will qualify under section 1031.[14]

In *Biggs*, the taxpayer was likewise permitted to advance the funds for the purchase of the replacement property, where title was transferred from the seller to a third-party exchange facilitator and held by it until the exchange was effected. *Id.* at 908–909.

Respondent, however, relies in particular on our more recent decision in *DeCleene*, in which we employed a benefits and burdens analysis in rejecting the taxpayer's claim

---

14. [11] This discussion of the latitude afforded taxpayers in structuring sec. 1031 transactions was later quoted in full with approval by the Court of Appeals for the Ninth Circuit. *Starker v. United States*, 602 F.2d 1341, 1353 n.10 (9th Cir. 1979).

of section 1031 treatment, as support for his contention that a third-party exchange facilitator — here, EPC Two — must hold the benefits and burdens of ownership of the replacement property in order to be treated as its owner at the time of the exchange. In *DeCleene* we concluded, using a benefits and burdens analysis, that the taxpayer had beneficial ownership of the replacement property at the time of the exchange, even though he had arranged for the transfer of legal title to the replacement property to the purchaser of his relinquished property. His purported exchange of the relinquished and replacement properties was therefore no more than an exchange with himself. "A taxpayer cannot engage in an exchange with himself; an exchange ordinarily requires a 'reciprocal transfer of property'". *DeCleene v. Commissioner,* 115 T.C. at 469 (citation omitted).

The taxpayer in *DeCleene* had made an outright purchase of the replacement property (the Lawrence Drive property), which was unimproved land, more than a year before the purported exchange. *Id.* at 459, 468. Then, when approached by a prospective purchaser (WLC) of the property the taxpayer wished to relinquish (the McDonald Street property), the taxpayer was advised he could effect a section 1031 exchange of the McDonald Street property for the Lawrence Street property. *Id.* at 459. In an effort to accomplish an exchange, the taxpayer first transferred the Lawrence Street property to WLC in September — subject to a reacquisition agreement under which WLC agreed to convey the Lawrence Drive property back to the taxpayer by yearend, with a building constructed on it in the interim pursuant to the taxpayer's direction and at his expense.[15] *Id.* at 468–469. WLC purported to purchase the Lawrence Drive property by giving the taxpayer his non-interest-bearing, nonrecourse note for $142,400. *Id.* at 460. The parties agreed that $142,400 was the value of both the Lawrence Drive property in its unimproved state and the McDonald Street property. *Id.* at 463. Once construction of the building on the Lawrence Drive property was complete, but no later than yearend, the parties' agreement called for an exchange of properties whereby the taxpayer would deed the McDonald Street property to WLC and WLC would in turn deed the Lawrence Drive property back to the taxpayer and pay off his $142,400 promissory note (the consideration it gave for the purported purchase of the Lawrence Drive property). *Id.* at 460–461. The exchange of deeds and payment of the note were accomplished three months later as called for under the agreement. *Id.* at 463.

The taxpayer claimed that he had effected a taxable sale of the Lawrence Drive property to WLC, followed by his transfer of the McDonald Street property to WLC in a like-kind exchange for WLC's reconveyance to him of the Lawrence Drive property.[16] The Commissioner determined that the taxpayer had made a taxable sale of the McDonald Street property to WLC.

---

15. [12] The construction loan for the building was nonrecourse to WLC and guaranteed by the taxpayer. *DeCleene v. Commissioner,* 115 T.C. 457, 461 (2000).

16. [13] The taxpayer preferred a taxable sale of his high-basis Lawrence Drive property to a taxable sale of his low-basis McDonald Street property.

In resolving the issue, after noting the historically lenient attitude of courts towards taxpayers in like-kind exchange cases, we put considerable emphasis on the taxpayer's failure to use a third-party exchange facilitator.

> The subject transactions present a case of first impression in this Court. They reflect the effort of * * * [the taxpayer] and his advisors to implement a so-called reverse exchange directly with WLC, *without the participation of a third-party exchange facilitator.* * * *
>
>   * * *
>
> In the case at hand, * * * [the taxpayer] did not just locate and identify the Lawrence Drive property in anticipation of acquiring it as replacement property in exchange for the McDonald Street property that he intended to relinquish. He purchased the Lawrence Drive property *without the participation of an exchange facilitator* a year or more before he was ready to relinquish the McDonald Street property * * *. In the following year, * * * [the taxpayer] transferred title to the Lawrence Drive property, subject to a reacquisition agreement—the exchange agreement—*not to a third-party exchange facilitator,* but to WLC, the party to which he simultaneously obligated himself to relinquish the McDonald Street property. * * *
>
> *In foregoing the use of a third party* and doing all the transfers with WLC, * * * [the taxpayer] and his advisers created an inherently ambiguous situation. * * *

DeCleene v. Commissioner, 115 T.C. at 467–469 (emphasis added).

We analyzed the transaction to determine whether the taxpayer, having acquired the Lawrence Drive property outright and directly held it for more than a year, actually ceased being its owner for tax purposes during the three-month period that WLC held legal title in anticipation of a section 1031 exchange. If not, then the taxpayer had merely engaged in an exchange with himself, rather than the reciprocal exchange of property necessary for section 1031 treatment. *Id.* at 469. We employed a benefits and burdens test to determine the ownership question, concluding that WLC never acquired any of the benefits and burdens of ownership of the Lawrence Drive property, as it acquired no equity interest, made no economic outlay to acquire the property, was not at risk because its obligations in the transaction were all nonrecourse, and was obligated to reconvey the property to the taxpayer. *Id.* at 469–470. As a consequence, "[i]n substance, * * * [the taxpayer] never disposed of the Lawrence Drive property and remained its owner during the 3-month construction period because the transfer of title to WLC never divested * * * [the taxpayer] of beneficial ownership." *Id.* at 471. We therefore concluded that a section 1031 exchange had not occurred.

In contending that *DeCleene* supports his position that EPC Two—a third-party exchange facilitator—had to possess the benefits and burdens of ownership of the Lynnwood property in order for EPC Two to be treated as its owner for tax purposes before the exchange, respondent interprets that case too broadly. Given the *DeCleene* Opinion's explicit and repeated emphasis upon the taxpayer's failure to use a third-party exchange facilitator, it must be said that *DeCleene* did not address the circumstances where a third-party exchange facilitator is used from the outset in a reverse exchange. Moreover, the taxpayer in *DeCleene* had acquired the purported replacement property outright, and held title to it directly without any title-holding intermediary, for more than a year before transferring title to WLC. This feature also distinguishes *DeCleene* from the myriad of cases where taxpayers seeking section 1031 treatment were careful to interpose a title-holding intermediary between themselves and outright ownership of the replacement property. In sum, *DeCleene* does not dictate a result for respondent here.

Our analysis must also take into account the position of the Court of Appeals for the Ninth Circuit, where an appeal in this case would lie absent stipulation to the contrary. *See* sec. 7482(b)(1)(A), (2); *Golsen v. Commissioner*, 54 T.C. 742, 757 (1970), *aff'd*, 445 F.2d 985 (10th Cir. 1971).[17] As previously noted, that Court of Appeals has expressly rejected the contention that the party to the exchange with the taxpayer must possess the benefits and burdens of ownership of the replacement property in order for the exchange to qualify for section 1031 treatment. *Alderson v. Commissioner*, 317 F.2d at 795.

The taxpayers in *Alderson* had executed a contract to sell their Buena Park property to Alloy Die Casting Co. (Alloy) for $172,871.40, pursuant to an escrow agreement under which Alloy had deposited 10% of the purchase price into escrow. The taxpayers then found the Salinas property, and decided that they wished to obtain it to replace the Buena Park property. The taxpayers and Alloy thereupon amended the escrow agreement to provide that Alloy would acquire the Salinas property and exchange it for the Buena Park property "in lieu of the original contemplated cash transaction." *Id.* at 791.

As recounted by the Court of Appeals for the Ninth Circuit, the taxpayers then took a series of steps with respect to the Salinas property—the replacement property—that warrant close scrutiny in view of the arguments respondent has advanced in this case. The taxpayers negotiated the $190,000 sale price of the Salinas property with its owners and then, on August 19, 1957, through written instructions to the Salinas Title Guarantee Co. (Salinas Title) executed on that date,[18] the taxpayers dictated the terms for the disposition of the Salinas property. *Id.* The instructions provided that the taxpayers would make the $19,000 downpayment for the property (which they paid into the Salinas escrow the next day) and that title to the Salinas property would be taken in the name of Salinas Title. *Id.* The instructions further authorized Salinas Title "to deed the Salinas property to Alloy, provided Salinas Title could 'immediately record a deed from Alloy * * * to James Alderson and Clarissa E.

---

17. [14] In *DeCleene* we noted the paucity of applicable sec. 1031 cases in the Court of Appeals for the Seventh Circuit, where the appeal in that case lay. *DeCleene v. Commissioner*, 115 T.C. at 472.

18. [15] These escrow instructions for the disposition of the replacement property were entitled "Buyer's Instructions", the Court of Appeals noted. *Alderson v. Commissioner*, 317 F.2d 790, 791 (9th Cir. 1963), *rev'g* 38 T.C. 215 (1962).

Alderson, his wife [the taxpayers], issuing final title evidence in the last mentioned grantees.'" *Id.*

By deed dated the next day (August 20, 1957), title to the Salinas property was transferred to Salinas Title. *Alderson v. Commissioner*, 317 F.2d at 791. By deed dated August 21, 1957, Salinas Title conveyed the Salinas property to Alloy. *Id.* By deed dated August 26, 1957, the taxpayers conveyed the Buena Park property to Alloy, and by deed dated August 29, 1957, Alloy conveyed the Salinas property to the taxpayers. *Id.* at 791–792. On September 3, 1957, Alloy deposited the $172,871.40 purchase price of the Buena Park property into the Salinas escrow with instructions that it be used to purchase the Salinas property. *Id.* at 792. That amount, together with the $19,000 previously deposited by the taxpayers, slightly exceeded the $190,000 purchase price of the Salinas property, and the excess was refunded to the taxpayers.[19] *Id.* The following day, all of the foregoing deeds were recorded. *Id.*

The taxpayers took the position that they had effected a section 1031 exchange of the Buena Park property for the Salinas property, but the Commissioner disagreed, arguing that they had sold the Buena Park property to Alloy and purchased the Salinas property, in part because Alloy never held a "real" interest in the Salinas property— that is, the replacement property. *Id.* at 795. The Court of Appeals rejected the Commissioner's argument.

> [T]here was no need for Alloy to acquire a "real" interest in the Salinas property by assuming the benefits and burdens of ownership to make the exchange qualify under the statute although * * * [the Commissioner] asserts that failure of Alloy to hold a "real" interest in the Salinas property precluded the transactions involved from being construed as constituting an exchange.

> [O]ne need not assume the benefits and burdens of ownership in property before exchanging it but may properly acquire title *solely for the purpose of exchange* and accept title and transfer it in exchange for other like property, all as a part of the same transaction with no resulting gain which is recognizable under Section 1002 of the Internal Revenue Code of 1954.

Id.

Neither Salinas Title, the third-party exchange facilitator, nor Alloy, the acquirer of the taxpayer's relinquished property, assumed any benefits or burdens of the Salinas property (the replacement property) before the exchange. Salinas Title obtained title to the Salinas property subject to a contractual obligation in the Buyer's Instructions to transfer it to Alloy. Then Alloy obtained title to the property under a contractual obligation that it immediately transfer title to the taxpayers. Consequently, the beneficial ownership of the Salinas property necessarily resided with the taxpayers during the period that Salinas Title and Alloy held bare legal title to the property; it could

---

19. [16] The 10% deposit that Alloy had previously placed into escrow to purchase the Buena Park property was refunded to it. *Alderson v. Commissioner*, 317 F.2d at 792.

be nowhere else. Thus, the taxpayers in *Alderson* held the benefits and burdens of the replacement property before the exchange. Under the theory advanced by respondent in this case, the *Alderson* taxpayers would have engaged in a disqualifying exchange with themselves. The Court of Appeals, however, treated Alloy's nominal ownership of the replacement property as sufficient to establish an exchange for purposes of section 1031.

The transaction in *Alderson* was a forward exchange that spanned approximately three months from the time the taxpayers first executed a contract for the sale of their relinquished property until the deed transfers effecting the exchange of the relinquished and replacement properties were made. Salinas Title held title to the replacement property for only 10 days, and Alloy held it only instantaneously. Yet the same principle that treated a third-party exchange facilitator, holding bare legal title but no beneficial interest in the replacement property, as the owner of that property for purposes of a section 1031 exchange is also evident in *Biggs v. Commissioner*, 632 F.2d 1171, a case where the exchange facilitator held the replacement property much longer.

In *Biggs*, the third-party exchange facilitator held bare legal title but no beneficial interest in the replacement property from the time the replacement property was purchased (with the taxpayer's funds) until title was transferred to the taxpayer—a period of approximately 4 1/2 months. In that case, the taxpayer agreed to sell his Maryland property (the relinquished property) to Powell, but only as part of an exchange for another property. Powell agreed to cooperate in the arrangements for an exchange. The taxpayer identified a replacement property, the Virginia property, executed a sales contract for its purchase in which the purchaser was described as the taxpayer "(acting as agent for syndicate)", and supplied the downpayment. *Id.* at 1173. Powell, however, was "either unable or unwilling" to take title to the Virginia property and so the taxpayer arranged for the title to be transferred to Shore Title Co., Inc. (Shore), a corporation controlled by the taxpayer's attorney. *Id.*

Before the transfer of title, the taxpayer and Shore entered into an agreement concerning the Virginia property that entitled *either* to request that title be conveyed to the taxpayer or his nominee in exchange for the price Shore paid for the property, plus any costs Shore incurred in holding the property, and a commitment by the taxpayer or his nominee to release Shore from, or cause Shore to be released from, any obligations of Shore arising from its acquiring or holding the property. *Id.* On January 9, 1969, the sales contract on the Virginia property was closed and title was transferred to Shore. *Id.* The taxpayer advanced to Shore the remaining cash due the seller, $115,655.14, and Shore assumed liabilities of $142,544.86, both amounts being secured by deeds of trust on the property. *Id.*

Shore then held the Virginia property for the next 4 1/2 months, during which time it entered into a contract to sell the Virginia property to Powell, and Powell thereupon assigned its contract right to purchase the Virginia property to the taxpayer as part of the consideration for an agreement pursuant to which the taxpayer agreed to sell the Maryland property to Powell. *Biggs v. Commissioner*, 632 F.2d at 1174. The various contracts were closed (1) on May 24, 1969, when Shore executed a deed to the Virginia property to the taxpayer and the taxpayer assumed all of Shore's liabilities with respect to the property and released Shore from its obligation to repay the purchase money the taxpayer had previously advanced and (2) on May 26, 1969, when the taxpayer deeded the Maryland property to Powell's assignee. *Id.* at 1175.

The Court of Appeals for the Fifth Circuit and this Court both concluded that a section 1031 exchange had occurred, rejecting two arguments advanced by the Commissioner. The Commissioner argued that no exchange had occurred because Powell never received legal title to the Virginia property (the replacement property), but each Court found Powell's exchange of his right to acquire the Virginia property (rather than title to the property itself) sufficient. *Id.* at 1176–1177; *Biggs v. Commissioner*, 69 T.C. at 914–916. Of greater pertinence here, both Courts also rejected the Commissioner's argument, premised on the fact that the taxpayer had advanced all the funds for the replacement property's purchase, that Shore was the taxpayer's agent. *Biggs v. Commissioner*, 632 F.2d at 1178; *Biggs v. Commissioner*, 69 T.C. at 917. The Court of Appeals recognized that if Shore were treated as the taxpayer's agent "the exchange would have been meaningless" because "in essence, * * * [the taxpayer] would have merely effected an exchange with himself." *Biggs v. Commissioner*, 632 F.2d at 1178. Instead, each Court concluded that Shore took title to the replacement property: "to facilitate an exchange" (Tax Court), *Biggs v. Commissioner*, 69 T.C. at 917, or "to facilitate the exchange" (Court of Appeals), *Biggs v. Commissioner*, 632 F.2d at 1178. The incidents of ownership Shore assumed were thus sufficient for it to be treated as the owner of the replacement property during the period it held title. Otherwise, the taxpayer, who supplied the funds for the replacement property's purchase, would have been the owner and a self-exchange ineligible for section 1031 treatment would have occurred.

Notably for the issue at hand, Shore did not have any beneficial ownership of the replacement property. Shore made no outlay to acquire the replacement property and held title to it subject to contractual provisions that precluded the company from benefiting from any appreciation in the property's value or from being exposed to any risk of loss from a diminution in its value or any liability arising from holding title. The agreement between Shore and the taxpayer, set out in detail in each court's opinion, gave the taxpayer a "call" on the replacement property at any time for consideration equal to the price Shore paid to acquire the property, plus any costs Shore incurred to hold the property, and satisfaction or release of Shore from any obligations it assumed or became bound by as a result of holding title. Shore could likewise "put" the property to the taxpayer for the same consideration. It is thus readily apparent that the taxpayer, not Shore, held the benefits and burdens of ownership of the replacement property during the period Shore held legal title. Nevertheless Shore, a third-party exchange facilitator, was treated as the owner of the replacement property for purposes of satisfying the exchange requirement of section 1031.

Thus, *Alderson* and *Biggs* establish that where a section 1031 exchange is contemplated from the outset and a third-party exchange facilitator, rather than the taxpayer, takes title to the replacement property before the exchange,[20] the exchange facilitator need not assume the benefits and burdens of ownership of the replacement property in order to be treated as its owner for section 1031 purposes before the exchange.

Respondent contends that *Alderson, Biggs,* and the taxpayer-favorable cases we cited in *Biggs* are inapposite because they concerned forward exchanges and a reverse exchange is at issue here. We disagree. First, although *Biggs* is sometimes characterized as involving a forward exchange, the transaction at issue in *Biggs* was actually a reverse exchange as that term has been defined by respondent. In the preamble to the regulations promulgated as section 1.1031(k)-1, Income Tax Regs., governing forward exchanges, the Secretary expressly excluded reverse exchanges from coverage by those regulations, defining reverse exchanges as "transactions in which the taxpayer receives the replacement property prior to the date on which the taxpayer transfers the relinquished property". T.D. 8346, 1991-1 C.B. at 150–151; *see also* Rev. Proc. 2000-37, sec. 2.04, 2000-2 C.B. at 308. In *Biggs,* although the taxpayer and Powell initially executed a "memorandum of intent" covering the sale of the relinquished property on October 25, 1968, they abandoned that agreement after the taxpayer's attorney reviewed it, and instead agreed to have their respective attorneys "work out the terms of a written exchange agreement." *Biggs v. Commissioner,* 632 F.2d at 1173. Thereafter, the sales contract on the replacement property (the Virginia property) was closed (and title transferred to the third-party exchange facilitator) on January 9, 1969, whereas the contract for the sale of the relinquished property (the Maryland property) was not executed until February 27, 1969, and the transfer of the relinquished property did not occur until May 26, 1969. *Id.* at 1174–1175. Consequently, the principles of *Biggs* are applicable to reverse exchanges.

Second, even forward exchange cases, including *Alderson* and those that permit "great latitude" to taxpayers in structuring section 1031 transactions, *Starker,* 602 F.2d at 1353 n.10, analyze the relationship to the replacement property of the taxpayer versus the third-party exchange facilitator, and treat the latter as the owner before the exchange, typically notwithstanding the utterly "transitory", *Barker v. Commissioner,* 74 T.C. at 565, and nominal nature of that ownership. In our view, this analysis of the relationship of the taxpayer to the replacement property, as compared to an exchange facilitator holding bare legal title, is equally applicable in a reverse exchange, as the holding in *Biggs* confirms. *See also DeGroot v. Exchanged Titles (In re Exchanged Titles, Inc.),* 159 B.R. 303 (Bankr. C.D. Cal. 1993) ("[T]he

---

20. [17] Respondent cites in support of his position a number of cases where the taxpayers made outright purchases of the replacement property and then subsequently sought to retrofit the transaction into the form of a sec. 1031 exchange. *See, e.g., Bezdjian v. Commissioner,* 845 F.2d 217 (9th Cir. 1988), *aff'g* T.C. Memo. 1987-140; *Dibsy v. Commissioner,* T.C. Memo. 1995-477; *Lee v. Commissioner,* T.C. Memo. 1986-294. Bartell Drug made no such outright purchase here; it interposed a third-party exchange facilitator between itself and title to the replacement property in contemplation of a sec. 1031 exchange from the outset. These cases are therefore not helpful on the question of whether the third-party exchange facilitator is to be treated as the owner of the replacement property for Federal income tax purposes before the exchange.

transfer of legal title is sufficient to effectuate a reverse I.R.C. § 1031 exchange involving an accommodator[.]").

To be sure, the transaction at issue involved a period before consummation of the exchange during which EPC Two was obligated to, and in fact did, lease the replacement property to Bartell Drug. Bartell Drug leased the replacement property and used it as a drugstore for approximately six months, from the completion of the improvements in early July 2011 until consummation of the exchange at yearend. There was no such leasing of the replacement property to the taxpayer by the exchange facilitator in *Biggs* or *Alderson*. Nevertheless, given that the caselaw has countenanced a taxpayer's pre-exchange control and financing of the construction of improvements on the replacement property while an exchange facilitator held title to it, *see J.H. Baird Publ'g. Co. v. Commissioner*, 39 T.C. 608, 610–611 (1962), we see no reason why the taxpayer's pre-exchange, temporary possession of the replacement property pursuant to a lease from the exchange facilitator should produce a different result.[21]

It is also true that the transaction at issue spanned a greater period than those countenanced in *Alderson* and *Biggs*, which spanned three and 4 1/2 months, respectively. Under the terms of the REAECA, EPC Two as a practical matter could have held title to the Lynnwood property for up to 24 months[22] and in fact EPC Two held title for 17 months. Given the inapplicability of Rev. Proc. 2000-37, *supra*, to the transaction at issue, the caselaw provides no specific limit on the period in which a third-party exchange facilitator may hold title to the replacement property before the titles to the relinquished and replacement properties are transferred in a reverse exchange.[23] We express no opinion with respect to the applicability of section 1031 to a reverse exchange transaction that extends beyond the period at issue in these cases. In view of the finite periods in which the exchange facilitator in these cases could have held, and in fact did hold, title to the replacement property, we are satisfied that the transaction qualifies for section 1031 treatment under existing caselaw principles.

---

21. [18] We note in this regard that the safe harbors extended to reverse exchanges in Rev. Proc. 2000-37, *supra*, cover the exchange accommodation title holder's leasing of the replacement property to the taxpayer, albeit within the time limits imposed therein. *Id.* sec. 4.03(4), 2000-2 C.B. 308, 310.

22. [19] We conclude, given that under the REAECA the purchase price Bartell Drug was obligated to pay for the Lynnwood property went from (i) the acquisition cost of the real property and improvements to (ii) the parcel's fair market value, after EPC Two had held title for 24 months, that the possibility that Bartell Drug would fail to purchase the Lynnwood property before the expiration of that 24 months was too remote to be considered a practical possibility.

23. [20] In scrutinizing the length of the period during which EPC Two held title to the replacement property before its transfer to Bartell Drug, we do not suggest that the transaction at issue failed to comply with the time limits of sec. 1031(a)(3), nor do the parties dispute that point. The 45- and 180-day periods in which the taxpayer must identify the replacement property and receive it, respectively, begin to run on "the date on which the taxpayer transfers the property relinquished in the exchange". Sec. 1031(a)(3)(A) and (B). As the transfer of the Everett property occurred on December 28, 2001, and Bartell Drug received title to the Lynnwood property on December 31, 2001, the taxpayers satisfied those time limits.

For the foregoing reasons, we conclude and hold that Bartell Drug's disposition of the Everett property and acquisition of the Lynnwood property in 2001 qualify for nonrecognition treatment pursuant to section 1031.

To reflect the foregoing,

Decisions will be entered for petitioners.

Penn-Dixie Steel Corp. v. Commissioner

United States Tax Court

69 T.C. 837 (1978)

FACTS

The petitioner, Penn-Dixie Steel Corp. (petitioner), is the successor by merger on May 11, 1973, to Continental Steel Corp. (Continental). It had its principal place of business of Kokomo, Ind., at the time of the filing of the petition herein. The return for the year in question was filed with the Internal Revenue Service Center, Memphis, Tenn., on September 18, 1972. An amendment to that return to submit certain pollution control data was filed on April 3, 1975, with the same Service Center.

Phoenix Manufacturing Co. (Old Phoenix), a division of Union Tank Car Co. (Union), was engaged in the business of producing bars reinforcing concrete and merchant bar products such as flats, rounds, angles, channels, and squares. A continuous supply of steel billets was essential to this business. Continental, which manufactured and sold steel products, including billets, rods, merchant bars, nails, fences, welded fabric, and a variety of industrial wire sizes and finishes, had an excess of semifinished steel in the form of steel billets. Old Phoenix could guarantee a permanent market for that excess steel.

Continental and Union entered an agreement entitled "Joint Venture Agreement" on July 1, 1968, which closed on July 31, 1968. Pursuant to this agreement, a new corporation named Phoenix Manufacturing Co. (Phoenix) was formed. Union transferred to Phoenix assets and liabilities of Old Phoenix having a net value of $17 million in exchange for 50 percent of the stock and an $8.5 million 7-percent debenture due July 31, 1974. Continental made a capital contribution of $8.5 million to Phoenix and received 50 percent of the stock. The treasurer of Phoenix was to invest and reinvest this cash in the highest yielding securities consistent with safety and the maturity date of the Phoenix debenture held by Union. In addition, Continental agreed to enter into a supply contract with Phoenix.

The July 1, 1968, agreement also provided for a put and call. During the period August 1, 1970, to July 31, 1971, Union could put to Continental its Phoenix stock for $8.5 million plus 125 percent of one-half the undistributed profits. Continental could call Union's stock in Phoenix on the same terms during the following year, beginning August 1, 1971, and ending July 31, 1972. The provision regarding undistributed profits was intended to operate as a penalty if profits were not distributed. If neither the put nor call were exercised, both parties would have a right of first refusal to the other party's stock in Phoenix.

Continental would have preferred an outright purchase of Old Phoenix, but Union was unwilling to modify the basic structure of its proposal. Union had considered selling Old Phoenix, but had rejected that option in favor of the joint venture structure in order to (1) avoid capital gains tax by qualifying for tax-free treatment under § 351 and (2) gradually phase in the decline in earnings resulting from the loss of Old Phoenix. Continental accepted Union's terms because Old Phoenix was so well suited to Continental's needs.

The Phoenix board of directors was composed of three representatives of Continental (its president, vice president and treasurer, and secretary) and three representatives of Union (its president and two high-level executives). The secretary of Phoenix was also the secretary of Continental and the treasurer of Phoenix was also the treasurer of Union.

Sometime after July 31, 1968, Penn-Dixie acquired control of Continental. Because Union was concerned that Penn-Dixie was in poor financial condition, its treasurer caused Phoenix as of November 23, 1970, to invest in an $8.5 million 83.4-percent debenture due July 31, 1974, issued by Union.

On February 24, 1971, Continental, Union, and Phoenix executed a supplement to the joint venture agreement of July 1, 1968, and an escrow agreement. Pursuant thereto, Union exercised its put, thereby transferring its 50-percent stock interest in Phoenix to Continental, effective July 31, 1971. Continental purchased the stock by the following series of transactions. The $8.5 million Union 83.4-percent debenture due July 31, 1974, was modified to provide, among other things, for 7-percent interest (83.4 percent prior to February 1, 1971) and a due date of July 31, 1971. Continental executed an interest-free promissory note, in the principal amount of $8.5 million, payable to Phoenix on July 31, 1974, and Phoenix agreed to accept said note in full satisfaction of the modified $8.5 million Union debenture. The net effect of the foregoing transactions was that Phoenix held Continental's $8.5 million note and Continental owned 100 percent of the Phoenix stock. Union continued to hold the $8.5 million Phoenix debenture issued on the original incorporation of Phoenix.

During the taxable year ending January 1, 1972, Continental expended $379,140 for pollution control facilities. Continental purported to make an election to amortize these facilities under § 169, attaching a statement to that effect to its return for such taxable year together with a letter from the Indiana Stream Pollution Control Board dated May 19, 1970, approving the plans and specifications of Continental's pollution control facilities and a letter of June 24, 1971, to the Indiana State Board of Health describing said facilities and their characteristics and reporting on the progress made in putting them into operation. Continental did not attach a statement that the facilities had been certified by the Federal certifying authority or a statement that application had been made to the proper certifying authorities and copies of any such applications. Such applications had not then been made and were not made until early 1973. The United States Environmental Protection Agency application forms were not available until at least 1 year after the final promulgation of the Treasury regulations under section 169 on May 21, 1971.

Certification was received from the Stream Pollution Control Board of the State of Indiana on October 24, 1973, and from the Environmental Protection Agency on November 5, 1973. These documents were brought to the attention of the Internal Revenue Service Appellate Conferee on March 4, 1974, or April 25, 1974. On March 31, 1975, petitioner filed an amended Federal income tax return, supplying copies of the Federal certification and application therefor and the State certification.

ANALYSIS

The first issue is whether the 1968 transaction between Union and Continental constituted a sale to Continental of Union's entire interest in Old Phoenix with payment of one-half the purchase price deferred for 2 or 3 years. The parties agree that if it was a sale, Continental is entitled to an imputed interest deduction of $1,170,450 under section 483. Petitioner, while conceding that Continental's 1968 transaction with Union did not constitute a sale for commercial purposes, contends that it nevertheless constituted a sale for tax purposes in that it shifted the burdens and benefits of full ownership from Union to Continental. *Cf. Merrill v. Comm'r*, 40 T.C. 66, 74 (1963), *affd. per curiam* 336 F.2d 771 (9th Cir. 1964).

It cannot be gainsaid that, in form, the transaction herein did not constitute a sale. Rather, it envisaged the creation of a corporation, intended to satisfy the requirements of section 351, to which assets and liabilities of Old Phoenix and $8.5 million cash from Continental were transferred in exchange for stock and a debenture and in which the equity ownership was given to Continental and Union equally. By the terms of the 1968 agreement, ultimate ownership of the entire equity of Phoenix was to be acquired by Continental if and when Union exercised its put or Continental exercised its call. Thus, in form, Phoenix acquired the assets and liabilities of Old Phoenix from Union in exchange for stock and securities and Continental acquired half of Phoenix's stock in exchange for cash with the opportunity to acquire the other half at a future date.

Petitioner would have us telescope the transaction and consider that Continental acquired all of the assets and liabilities of Old Phoenix from Union in 1968, which it then transferred to Phoenix in exchange for all the stock of Phoenix (Union being given 50 percent of the stock as security for Continental's obligations to it), and paid Union in two installments, the first installment being the transfer to Union of $8.5 million in cash which Union then invested in the Phoenix debenture. Where petitioner finds the second installment is less clear. Presumably, it would have us reconstruct the July 31, 1971, transaction, so as to treat Union as having paid Phoenix $8.5 million in satisfaction of the Union debenture, as modified, to view Phoenix as having lent the $8.5 million to Continental, receiving back the non-interest-bearing note payable on July 31, 1974, and to treat Continental as using this cash to make the second installment payment to Union.[24]

---

24. [2] An alternative reconstruction could view the non-interest-bearing note as having been constructively delivered by Continental to Union and used by Union to satisfy its debenture obligation to Phoenix. Such a reconstruction raises an issue that neither party addressed, namely, the right of Continental to obtain an imputed interest deduction under § 483 in light of the fact that the claimed second installment was paid by delivery of a non-interest-bearing note in favor of Phoenix which was

The parties have locked horns on the issue of whether Union made a completed sale of Old Phoenix to Continental in 1968. In considering this issue, we are mindful of the time-honored principle that the substance and not the form of the transaction is determinative (*see Russo v. Comm'r*, 68 T.C. 135, 143 (1977)) and that we should "look to all the facts and surrounding circumstances to determine the intent of the parties as revealed in their actions and statements, and the economic realities of the transaction." *See Northwest Acceptance Corp., v. Comm'r*, 58 T.C. 836, 845 (1972), *affd. per curiam* 500 F.2d 1222 (9th Cir. 1974). At the same time, we are not unmindful that the transaction herein was structured in an arm's-length transaction between unrelated parties and had obvious tax consequences, beyond the issue involved herein, to Union and a third party (Phonex) who are not before us in this proceeding. *Cf. Freeport Transport, Inc. v. Comm'r*, 63 T.C. 107 (1974). In such a situation, we should proceed with caution and seek strong proof[25] from the party to the transaction who asks us to accede to blandishments that its form be ignored. *See Estate of Rogers v. Comm'r*, 445 F.2d 1020, 1021–1022 (2nd Cir. 1971), *affg. per curiam* T.C. Memo. 1970-192; *Russo v. Comm'r*, supra at 143–144.

Petitioner seeks to have us hold that the benefits and burdens of ownership of Old Phoenix passed to Continental in 1968 and that in reality Phoenix—to which the assets and liabilities of Old Phoenix were transferred—was nothing more than a complacent creature of Continental in carrying out the latter's bidding. The facts simply belie petitioner's contention. The documentation herein is replete with references to the existence of a "joint venture." Union and Continental shared stock ownership of Phoenix. They had equal representation on the Phoenix board of directors. Both in theory and in fact, they shared in Phoenix's earnings until Continental acquired the full stock ownership in 1971. To be sure, Continental seems to have taken the lead in the conduct of Phoenix's operations, but the evidence in this regard falls far short of proving that Phoenix was Continental's amanuensis in the conduct of Phoenix's business.[26]

Petitioner also seeks to fit the instant case to the mold of situations where title remains in the seller as security for the purchase price. *See Clodfelter v. Comm'r*, 48

---

not due until July 31, 1974—3 years after the taxable year before us. Clearly, this fact raises a question as to whether, in any event, "payment" of such imputed interest was made during such taxable year within the meaning of sec. 483 (*see* sec. 483(c)(2); sec. 1.483-1(b)(5), Income Tax Regs.; Williams Co. v. Comm'r, 429 U.S. 569 (1977)) or, if such "payment" was made, whether the imputed interest should be allocated over the period from the date of its delivery to the due date or date it may have actually been paid (*see* Rubnitz v. Comm'r, 67 T.C. 621, 628 and n.8 (1977)). Under the circumstances and in view of our ultimate decision that respondent should in any event prevail, we do not reach this issue and do not express any opinion, directly or indirectly, as to how it should be resolved. We also note that the same problems may be involved in the presumed reconstruction set forth in the body of this opinion in view of the fact that no cash ever actually passed from Continental to Union in respect of the second installment.

25. [3] *See* Peerless Equipment Co. v. Comm'r, T.C. Memo. 1967-181.

26. [4] Grasping at straws, petitioner seeks to persuade us of Continental's overriding control over Phoenix by evidence that usually Union deferred to Continental in the conduct of operations of Phoenix and that Phoenix's accounting system was designed so as to be compatible with that of Continental. We are unimpressed.

T.C. 694, 700 (1967), *affd.* 426 F.2d 1391 (9th Cir. 1970).[27] Thus, petitioner points out that Continental's $8.5 million capital contribution was not part of Phoenix's working capital but, rather, was invested in securities by the treasurer of Phoenix, who was also the treasurer of Union, the implication being that the arrangement was designed to protect the purchase price. But, this is too thin a reed to support petitioner's claim of a mere security arrangement, particularly in light of the fact that Union received, as its own, a share of the net profits and controlled half the seats on the board of directors.

Petitioner seeks to buttress its position by arguing that the possibility that the put or call would not be exercised was so remote that it should be ignored. It argues that the price set at the outset would prove to be advantageous to one party or the other. Thus, if Phoenix was not successful, Union would exercise its put. Similarly, if Phoenix prospered, Continental would exercise its call. We disagree.

Admittedly, every remote contingency and condition need not be satisfied before a sale is deemed to occur. *Herbert J. Investment Corp. v. U.S.*, 360 F. Supp. 825 (E.D. Wis. 1973), *affd. per curiam* 500 F.2d 44 (7th Cir. 1974).[28] But, we are not convinced that there was a sufficient certainty that the put and call would be exercised even if we were to consider such a certainty sufficient to find a sale under all the circumstances herein. Assuming without deciding that a different result might obtain if the put and call were exercisable and expired on the same date (*see* Rev. Rul. 72-543, 1972-2 C.B. 87), the fact of the matter is that a 1-year period would elapse from the date Union's put expired to the date when Continental's call expired. Further, more than 3 years could elapse from the time the joint venture agreement was signed to the date Union's put expired and more than 4 years until Continental's call expired.

We recognize that Continental would have preferred to purchase Old Phoenix outright and would probably not have accepted Union's offer had it not included a call which enabled Continental eventually to acquire 100-percent ownership. Nor do we doubt that, at the time of the 1968 transaction, Continental intended to exercise its call if Union did not exercise its put. But, we are not convinced that such plans would not be subject to reevaluation in light of changing circumstances. We consider it more than a remote possibility that Phoenix might so prosper in the first 3 years that Union would forego the exercise of its put and that the economic outlook for the steel industry could then change sufficiently in the following year to lead Continental to decide not to exercise its call. Alternatively, changes in Continental's own situation might well lead to a change in its position with respect to its call.[29] Finally, it seems

---

27. [5] *See also* White v. Comm'r, T.C. Memo. 1974-69.

28. [6] *See also* Perry v. Comm'r, T.C. Memo. 1976-381. *Cf.* Beaudry v. Comm'r, T.C. Memo. 1972-214, holding that a lease with an option to buy did not constitute a sale, in part, because economic factors did not indicate that the option would necessarily be exercised.

29. [7] A memorandum of the initial stages of negotiations between Continental and Union, dated June 14, 1968, and prepared by the president of Continental, contained the following statement: "At the end of two years, UTC could have right to force us to buy other half. At end of three years, we can compel sale. If neither demand is made, joint venture would continue."

likely that Continental would have resisted Union's attempt to exercise its put if Phoenix's plant had been destroyed in the interim.

In short, the put and call arrangement did not legally, or as a practical matter, impose mutual obligations on Union to sell and on Continental to buy. *See Koch v. Comm'r*, 67 T.C. 71, 82 (1976) (agreement was option, not sale). To be sure, neither party could unilaterally withdraw and prevent a sale, *see Wisconsin Electric Power Co. v. Comm'r*, 18 T.C. 400 (1952), but each party's obligation to act was contingent upon exercise of the put or call, an event which might well fail to occur. *See Hoven v. Comm'r*, 56 T.C. 50 (1971).

The factual situation herein does not even begin to approach the unconditional nature of the obligation involved in *Bradford v. U.S.*, 444 F.2d 1133 (Ct. Cl. 1971), relied upon by petitioner. The same is true, although perhaps to a lesser degree, of *Comtel Corp. v. Comm'r*, 376 F.2d 791 (2d Cir. 1967), *affg.* 45 T.C. 294 (1965), also relied upon by petitioner, in which the Court of Appeals significantly observed that each case "must turn on its own facts" (*see* 376 F.2d at 797). The numerous other cases cited by petitioner are similarly distinguishable.

In sum, while we are left with the definite impression that both parties anticipated that Continental would eventually acquire full ownership of Phoenix, the intent to sell is not synonymous with a sale. *See Hoven v. Comm'r, supra; United States Industrial Alcohol Co. v. Helvering*, 137 F.2d 511, 515–516 (2d Cir. 1943), *revg. in part* 42 B.T.A. 1323 (1940), accepted as to this point in *Woodlawn Park Cemetery Co.*, 16 T.C. 1067, 1079 (1951), and *Wurtsbaugh v. Comm'r*, 8 T.C. 183, 189–190 (1947). The July 1, 1968, transaction simply did not sufficiently commit the parties to constitute a sale.

* * *

Revenue Procedure 2000-37
2000-2 C.B. 308

SECTION 1. PURPOSE

This revenue procedure provides a safe harbor under which the Internal Revenue Service will not challenge (a) the qualification of property as either "replacement property" or "relinquished property" (as defined in § 1.1031(k)-1(a) of the Income Tax Regulations) for purposes of § 1031 of the Internal Revenue Code and the regulations thereunder or (b) the treatment of the "exchange accommodation titleholder" as the beneficial owner of such property for federal income tax purposes, if the property is held in a "qualified exchange accommodation arrangement" (QEAA), as defined in section 4.02 of this revenue procedure.

SECTION 2. BACKGROUND

.01 Section 1031(a)(1) provides that no gain or loss is recognized on the exchange of property held for productive use in a trade or business or for investment if the property is exchanged solely for property of like kind that is to be held either for productive use in a trade or business or for investment.

.02 Section 1031(a)(3) provides that property received by the taxpayer is not treated as like-kind property if it: (a) is not identified as property to be received in the exchange on or before the day that is 45 days after the date on which the taxpayer transfers the relinquished property; or (b) is received after the earlier of the date that is 180 days after the date on which the taxpayer transfers the relinquished property, or the due date (determined with regard to extension) for the transferor's federal income tax return for the year in which the transfer of the relinquished property occurs.

.03 Determining the owner of property for federal income tax purposes requires an analysis of all of the facts and circumstances. As a general rule, the party that bears the economic burdens and benefits of ownership will be considered the owner of property for federal income tax purposes. *See* Rev. Rul. 82-144, 1982-2 C.B. 34.

.04 On April 25, 1991, the Treasury Department and the Service promulgated final regulations under § 1.1031(k)-1 providing rules for deferred like-kind exchanges under § 1031(a)(3). The preamble to the final regulations states that the deferred exchange rules under § 1031(a)(3) do not apply to reverse — *Starker* exchanges (*i.e.*, exchanges where the replacement property is acquired before the relinquished property is transferred) and consequently that the final regulations do not apply to such exchanges. T.D. 8346, 1991-1 C.B. 150, 151; *see Starker v. U.S.*, 602 F.2d 1341 (9th Cir. 1979). However, the preamble indicates that Treasury and the Service will continue to study the applicability of the general rule of § 1031(a)(1) to these transactions. T.D. 8346, 1991-1 C.B. 150, 151.

.05 Since the promulgation of the final regulations under § 1.1031(k)-1, taxpayers have engaged in a wide variety of transactions, including so-called "parking" transactions, to facilitate reverse like-kind exchanges. Parking transactions typically are designed to "park" the desired replacement property with an accommodation party until such time as the taxpayer arranges for the transfer of the relinquished property to the ultimate transferee in a simultaneous or deferred exchange. Once such a transfer is arranged, the taxpayer transfers the relinquished property to the accommodation party in exchange for the replacement property, and the accommodation party then transfers the relinquished property to the ultimate transferee. In other situations, an accommodation party may acquire the desired replacement property on behalf of the taxpayer and immediately exchange such property with the taxpayer for the relinquished property, thereafter holding the relinquished property until the taxpayer arranges for a transfer of such property to the ultimate transferee. In the parking arrangements, taxpayers attempt to arrange the transaction so that the accommodation party has enough of the benefits and burdens relating to the property so that the accommodation party will be treated as the owner for federal income tax purposes.

.06 Treasury and the Service have determined that it is in the best interest of sound tax administration to provide taxpayers with a workable means of qualifying their transactions under § 1031 in situations where the taxpayer has a genuine intent to accomplish a like-kind exchange at the time that it arranges for the acquisition of the replacement property and actually accomplishes the exchange within a short time thereafter. Accordingly, this revenue procedure provides a safe harbor that allows a taxpayer to treat the accommodation party as the owner of the property for federal income tax purposes, thereby enabling the taxpayer to accomplish a qualifying like-kind exchange.

SECTION 3. SCOPE

.01 *Exclusivity.* This revenue procedure provides a safe harbor for the qualification under § 1031 of certain arrangements between taxpayers and exchange accommodation titleholders and provides for the treatment of the exchange accommodation titleholder as the beneficial owner of the property for federal income tax purposes. These provisions apply only in the limited context described in this revenue procedure. The principles set forth in this revenue procedure have no application to any federal income tax determinations other than determinations that involve arrangements qualifying for the safe harbor.

.02 *No inference.* No inference is intended with respect to the federal income tax treatment of arrangements similar to those described in this revenue procedure that were entered into prior to the effective date of this revenue procedure. Further, the Service recognizes that "parking" transactions can be accomplished outside of the safe harbor provided in this revenue procedure. Accordingly, no inference is intended with respect to the federal income tax treatment of "parking" transactions that do not satisfy the terms of the safe harbor provided in this revenue procedure, whether entered into prior to or after the effective date of this revenue procedure.

.03 *Other issues.* Services for the taxpayer in connection with a person's role as the exchange accommodation titleholder in a QEAA shall not be taken into account in determining whether that person or a related person is a disqualified person (as defined in § 1.1031(k)-1(k)). Even though property will not fail to be treated as being held in a QEAA as a result of one or more arrangements described in section 4.03 of this revenue procedure, the Service still may recast an amount paid pursuant to such an arrangement as a fee paid to the exchange accommodation titleholder for acting as an exchange accommodation titleholder to the extent necessary to reflect the true economic substance of the arrangement. Other federal income tax issues implicated, but not addressed, in this revenue procedure include the treatment, for federal income tax purposes, of payments described in § 4.03(7) and whether an exchange accommodation titleholder may be precluded from claiming depreciation deductions (*e.g.*, as a dealer) with respect to the relinquished property or the replacement property.

.04 *Effect of Noncompliance.* If the requirements of this revenue procedure are not satisfied (for example, the property subject to a QEAA is not transferred within the time period provided), then this revenue procedure does not apply. Accordingly, the determination of whether the taxpayer or the exchange accommodation titleholder is the owner of the property for federal income tax purposes, and the proper treatment of any transactions entered into by or between the parties, will be made without regard to the provisions of this revenue procedure.

SECTION 4. QUALIFIED EXCHANGE ACCOMMODATION ARRANGEMENTS

.01 *Generally.* The Service will not challenge the qualification of property as either "replacement property" or "relinquished property" (as defined in § 1.1031(k)-1(a)) for purposes of § 1031 and the regulations thereunder, or the treatment of the exchange accommodation titleholder as the beneficial owner of such property for federal income tax purposes, if the property is held in a QEAA.

.02 *Qualified Exchange Accommodation Arrangements.* For purposes of this revenue procedure, property is held in a QEAA if all of the following requirements are met:

(1) Qualified indicia of ownership of the property is held by a person (the "exchange accommodation titleholder") who is not the taxpayer or a disqualified person and either such person is subject to federal income tax or, if such person is treated as a partnership or S corporation for federal income tax purposes, more than 90 percent of its interests or stock are owned by partners or shareholders who are subject to federal income tax. Such qualified indicia of ownership must be held by the exchange accommodation titleholder at all times from the date of acquisition by the exchange accommodation titleholder until the property is transferred as described in § 4.02(5) of this revenue procedure. For this purpose, "qualified indicia of ownership" means legal title to the property, other indicia of ownership of the property that are treated as beneficial ownership of the property under applicable principles of commercial law (*e.g.*, a contract for deed), or interests in an entity that is disregarded as an entity separate from its owner for federal income tax purposes (*e.g.*, a single member limited liability company) and that holds either legal title to the property or such other indicia of ownership;

(2) At the time the qualified indicia of ownership of the property is transferred to the exchange accommodation titleholder, it is the taxpayer's bona fide intent that the property held by the exchange accommodation titleholder represent either replacement property or relinquished property in an exchange that is intended to qualify for nonrecognition of gain (in whole or in part) or loss under § 1031;

(3) No later than five business days after the transfer of qualified indicia of ownership of the property to the exchange accommodation titleholder, the taxpayer and the exchange accommodation titleholder enter into a written agreement (the "qualified exchange accommodation agreement") that provides that the exchange accommodation titleholder is holding the property for the benefit of the taxpayer in order to facilitate an exchange under § 1031 and this revenue procedure and that the taxpayer and the exchange accommodation titleholder agree to report the acquisition, holding, and disposition of the property as provided in this revenue procedure. The agreement must specify that the exchange accommodation titleholder will be treated as the beneficial owner of the property for all federal income tax purposes. Both parties must report the federal income tax attributes of the property on their federal income tax returns in a manner consistent with this agreement;

(4) No later than 45 days after the transfer of qualified indicia of ownership of the replacement property to the exchange accommodation titleholder, the relinquished property is properly identified. Identification must be made in a manner consistent with the principles described in § 1.1031(k)-1(c). For purposes of this section, the taxpayer may properly identify alternative and multiple properties, as described in § 1.1031(k)-1(c)(4);

(5) No later than 180 days after the transfer of qualified indicia of ownership of the property to the exchange accommodation titleholder, (a) the property is transferred (either directly or indirectly through a qualified intermediary (as defined in § 1.1031(k)-1(g)(4))) to the taxpayer as replacement property; or (b) the property is transferred to a person who is not the taxpayer or a disqualified person as relinquished property; and

(6) The combined time period that the relinquished property and the replacement property are held in a QEAA does not exceed 180 days.

.03 *Permissible Agreements.* Property will not fail to be treated as being held in a QEAA as a result of any one or more of the following legal or contractual arrangements, regardless of whether such arrangements contain terms that typically would result from arm's length bargaining between unrelated parties with respect to such arrangements:

(1) An exchange accommodation titleholder that satisfies the requirements of the qualified intermediary safe harbor set forth in § 1.1031(k)-1(g)(4) may enter into an exchange agreement with the taxpayer to serve as the qualified intermediary in a simultaneous or deferred exchange of the property under § 1031;

(2) The taxpayer or a disqualified person guarantees some or all of the obligations of the exchange accommodation titleholder, including secured or unsecured debt incurred to acquire the property, or indemnifies the exchange accommodation titleholder against costs and expenses;

(3) The taxpayer or a disqualified person loans or advances funds to the exchange accommodation titleholder or guarantees a loan or advance to the exchange accommodation titleholder;

(4) The property is leased by the exchange accommodation titleholder to the taxpayer or a disqualified person;

(5) The taxpayer or a disqualified person manages the property, supervises improvement of the property, acts as a contractor, or otherwise provides services to the exchange accommodation titleholder with respect to the property;

(6) The taxpayer and the exchange accommodation titleholder enter into agreements or arrangements relating to the purchase or sale of the property, including puts and calls at fixed or formula prices, effective for a period not in excess of 185 days from the date the property is acquired by the exchange accommodation titleholder; and

(7) The taxpayer and the exchange accommodation titleholder enter into agreements or arrangements providing that any variation in the value of a relin-

quished property from the estimated value on the date of the exchange accommodation titleholder's receipt of the property be taken into account upon the exchange accommodation titleholder's disposition of the relinquished property through the taxpayer's advance of funds to, or receipt of funds from, the exchange accommodation titleholder.

.04 *Permissible Treatment.* Property will not fail to be treated as being held in a QEAA merely because the accounting, regulatory, or state, local, or foreign tax treatment of the arrangement between the taxpayer and the exchange accommodation titleholder is different from the treatment required by § 4.02(3) of this revenue procedure.

Priv. Ltr. Rul. 2007-12-013

(Nov. 20, 2006)

FACTS

We rely on the facts and conditions set forth in Taxpayer's submissions dated May 22, 2006.

Taxpayer and Related Party are related persons within the meaning of § 1031(f)(3). Taxpayer acquired Relinquished Property on Date 1 and held it as rental property. In Taxpayer's possession, Relinquished Property's fair market value substantially increased.

Related Party wished to acquire Relinquished Property from Taxpayer, and Taxpayer wished to transfer Relinquished Property to Related Party through a like-kind exchange pursuant to § 1031. However, because Related Party did not own like-kind assets that Taxpayer wished to acquire, Taxpayer entered into an agreement with an unrelated third party to acquire Replacement Property. Replacement property is like-kind to Relinquished Property within the meaning of § 1031(a) and § 1.1031(a)-1(b). Replacement Property's fair market value was substantially higher than Relinquished Property's fair market value. The unrelated third party required the closing of the sale of Replacement Property to occur before Taxpayer transferred Relinquished Property to Related Party, and accordingly, Taxpayer structured the transaction as a "reverse" like-kind exchange under the provisions of Rev. Proc. 2000-37, 2002-2 C.B. 308, modified by Rev. Proc. 2004-51, 2004-2 C.B. 294.

On Date 2, Taxpayer and E Corp. entered into a qualified exchange accommodation arrangement described in Rev. Proc. 2000-37. E Corp. is a domestic single-owner limited liability company and wholly owned by D Corp. E Corp. is disregarded as a separate taxpayer pursuant to § 301.7701-3(b)(1)(ii) and has never made nor intends to make an election under § 301.7701-3(c)(1) to be taxed as an association. D Corp. and E Corp. are unrelated to Taxpayer and Related Party. In this reverse like-kind exchange, E Corp. functioned as an exchange accommodation titleholder ("EAT").

In addition, on the same day, Taxpayer loaned to E Corp. $A, which is equal to the purchase price of Replacement Property, and D Corp. granted Taxpayer a security interest in 100-percent of the membership interest in E Corp. as collateral for Taxpayer's loan to E Corp. E Corp. purchased the Replacement Property for $A on Date 3.

On Date 4, Taxpayer entered into an agreement with Related Party to transfer Relinquished Property to Related Party's wholly owned subsidiary, Limited Liability Co. Concurrently, Taxpayer and F Corp., which is an affiliate of D Corp., entered into an agreement to assign Taxpayer's right to receive Relinquished Property sales proceeds, $B, to F Corp. F Corp. is a qualified intermediary ("QI") described in § 1.1031(k)-1(g)(4), and not a "disqualified person" with respect to Taxpayer within the meaning of § 1.1031(k)-1(k). Pursuant to the agreements, Taxpayer transferred Relinquished Property to Limited Liability Co., and Limited Liability Co. paid $B to F Corp.

To complete the exchange, Taxpayer instructed F Corp. to acquire Replacement Property. Accordingly, F Corp. purchased 100-percent of the membership interest in E Corp. from D Corp., subject to E Corp.'s obligation under the loan, for $B. At F Corp.'s direction, D Corp. transferred the E Corp.'s membership interest to Taxpayer and also transferred $B to Taxpayer to pay down the loan. Because E is a disregarded entity for federal tax purposes, a transfer of all the interest in E Corp. is treated as a transfer of the assets of E Corp. As a result, the outstanding balance of the loan was cancelled because Taxpayer in effect became both the debtor and the creditor with respect to such balance.

After the above-transactions, Taxpayer held Replacement Property and Related Party held Relinquished Property. Related Party intends to dispose Relinquished Property within two years of its receipt.

ANALYSIS

Applicable Requirements for Deferral under § 1031.

Section 1031 was initially promulgated to avoid taxing gains that were mere "paper profits," *i.e.*, the taxpayer had realized nothing tangible and to tax them seriously interfered with normal business adjustments. Revenue Act of 1934, § 112.

Section 1031(a)(1) generally provides that no gain or loss shall be recognized on the exchange of property held for productive use in a trade or business or for investment if such property is exchanged solely for property of like-kind which is to be held either for productive use in a trade or business or for investment.

In arranging the like-kind exchange, § 1.1031(k)-1(g)(4) allows taxpayers to use a QI to facilitate a like-kind exchange. A taxpayer's transfer of relinquished property to a QI and subsequent receipt of like-kind replacement property from the QI is treated as an exchange with the QI.

Section 1031(f) was subsequently enacted to accord nonrecognition treatment only to exchanges and conversions where a taxpayer can be viewed as merely continuing his investment. If a related party exchange is followed shortly thereafter by a disposition of the property, the related parties have, in effect, "cashed out" of the investment, and the original exchange would not be accorded nonrecognition treatment. *See* H.R. REP. NO. 101-247, at 1341 (1989), *reprinted in* 1989 U.S.C.C.A.N. 1906, 2811.

Section 1031(f)(1) sets forth special rules for exchanges between related persons. Section 1031(f)(1) provides that if (1) a taxpayer exchanges property with a related person, (2) nonrecognition treatment is offered to the taxpayer in accordance with § 1031 with respect to the exchange, and (3) within two years of the date of the last transfer either the taxpayer or the related person disposes of the property received in the exchange, then there is no nonrecognition of gain or loss in the exchange. In other words, the gain or loss that was deferred under § 1031 must be recognized as of the date of the disposition of the property received in the exchange.

Section 1031(f)(2) provides that certain dispositions will not be taken into account for purposes of § 1031(f)(1). These include any disposition (1) after the earlier of the death of the taxpayer or the death of the related person, (2) in a compulsory or involuntary conversion (within the meaning of § 1033) if the exchange occurred before the threat or imminence of such conversion, or (3) with respect to which it is established to the satisfaction of the Secretary that neither the exchange nor such disposition had as one of its principal purposes the avoidance of Federal income tax.

Section 1031(f)(4) provides that § 1031 shall not apply to any exchange that is part of a transaction, or series of transactions, structured to avoid the purposes of § 1031(f). Thus, if a transaction is set up to avoid the restrictions of § 1031(f), § 1031(f)(4) operates to prevent nonrecognition of the gain or loss in the exchange.

Both the Ways and Means Committee Report and the Senate Finance Committee Print describe the policy concern that led to enactment of § 1031(f)(4):

> Because a like-kind exchange results in the substitution of the basis of the exchanged property for the property received, related parties have engaged in like-kind exchanges of high basis property for low basis property in anticipation of the sale of the low basis property in order to reduce or avoid the recognition of gain on the subsequent sale. Basis shifting also can be used to accelerate a loss on retained property. The committee believes that if a related party exchange is followed shortly thereafter by a disposition of the property, the related parties have, in effect, "cashed out" of the investment, and the original exchange should not be accorded nonrecognition treatment.
>
> ....
>
> Nonrecognition will not be accorded to any exchange which is part of a transaction or series of transactions structured to avoid the purposes of the related party rules. For example, if a taxpayer, pursuant to a prearranged plan, transfers property to an unrelated party who then exchanges the property with a party related to the taxpayer within 2 years of the previous transfer in a transaction otherwise qualifying under section 1031, the related party will not be entitled to nonrecognition treatment under section 1031.

H.R. REP. NO. 101-247, at 1340–41 (1989), *reprinted in* 1989 U.S.C.C.A.N. 1906, 2810–11.

The Parking Transaction under Rev. Proc. 2000-37.

Rev. Proc. 2000-37 sets forth a safe harbor for acquiring replacement property under a qualified exchange accommodation arrangement ("QEAA"), sometimes referred to as a "parking" transaction, to facilitate reverse like-kind exchanges. As provided in this safe harbor, the Service will not challenge either (1) the qualification of property as either replacement or relinquished property (as defined in § 1.1031(k)-1(a)), or (2) the treatment of the EAT as the beneficial owner of such property for Federal income tax purposes, if the property is held in a QEAA as defined in section 4.02 of Rev. Proc. 2000-37.

Taxpayer represents that the exchange satisfies the requirements for deferred exchanges set forth in § 1.1031(k)-1 and the safe harbor for reverse exchanges set forth in Rev. Proc. 2000-37. Accordingly, the only issue in this case is whether nonrecognition treatment under § 1031 would apply to a transaction where (1) Taxpayer purchases like-kind Replacement Property from an unrelated third party via EAT, (2) Taxpayer sells Relinquished Property to Related Party for cash consideration received by a QI, and (3) Related Party disposes Relinquished Property within two years of the acquisition.

Related Party's disposal of Relinquished Property within two years of the acquisition will not trigger taxable gains pursuant to § 1031(f)(1). In the instant case, Taxpayer and Related Party did not engage in a like-kind exchange. Taxpayer transferred Relinquished Property to Related Party through a QI, who also purchased Replacement Property from an unrelated third person for Taxpayer. Taxpayer's transfer of Relinquished Property to the QI and subsequent receipt of like-kind Replacement Property from the QI is treated as an exchange with the QI, who is not related to Taxpayer. Treas. Reg. § 1.1031(k)-1(g)(4).

In addition, § 1031(f)(4) will not apply to prevent nonrecognition of the gain or loss in the exchange. Taxpayer did not transfer Relinquished Property to Related Party as part of a transaction or series of transactions, structured to avoid the purposes of § 1031(f)(1). The related parties in this case did not exchange high basis property for low basis property in anticipation of the sale of the low basis property. Only Taxpayer held property before the reverse like-kind exchange and continued to hold like-kind property after the exchange. Related Party did not hold property before the exchange. Accordingly, Related Party's proposed disposal of Relinquished Property within two years of the acquisition will not result in a "cashing out" of an investment or shifting of basis between Taxpayer and Related Party.

OPINION

Under the given facts and representations, § 1031(f) will not apply to trigger recognition of any gain realized when (1) Taxpayer purchases like-kind Replacement Property from an unrelated third party via EAT, (2) Taxpayer sells Relinquished Property to Related Party for cash consideration received by a QI, and (3) Related Party disposes Relinquished Property within two years of the acquisition.

DISCLAIMERS

Except as provided above, no opinion is expressed as to the Federal tax treatment of the transaction under any other provisions of the Internal Revenue Code and the Income Tax Regulations that may be applicable or under any other general principles of Federal income taxation. Neither is any opinion expressed as to the tax treatment of any conditions existing at the time of, nor effects resulting from, the transaction that are not specifically covered by the above ruling.

This ruling assumes that (1) E Corp. is eligible to serve as EAT within the meaning of Rev. Proc. 2000-37, (2) F Corp. is eligible to serve as QI in this transaction within the meaning of § 1.1031(k)-1(g)(4), (3) Taxpayer and Related Party are related persons within the meaning of § 1031(f)(3), and (4) the transaction satisfies the requirements for deferred exchanges set forth in § 1.1031(k)-1 and the safe harbor for reverse exchanges set forth in Rev. Proc. 2000-37. While this office has not verified any of the material submitted in support of the request for ruling, it is subject to verification on examination. No opinion is expressed as to whether the accommodators used in this transaction are disqualified persons as defined in § 1.1031(k)-1(k), as that would constitute essentially a factual determination.

This ruling is directed only to Taxpayer. Section 6110 (k)(3) provides that it may not be cited as precedent. Pursuant to the Power of Attorney submitted by Taxpayer, a copy of this letter will be sent to Taxpayer's authorized representatives.

Chapter 14

Tax, Legal, and Economic Aspects of Leases

I. Commentary

Leases are fascinating arrangements. They provide the lessor the right to use property and the obligation to pay rent. They provide the lessor the right to receive rent payments and the obligation to allow the lessee to use the property. The lessee may be able to assign its interests under the lease or sublease the property. The lessee may be able to construct improvements on the property. The lessor might sell the property that is subject to the lease. The lease structure may closely resemble a purchase transaction. Entering into a lease, making lease payments, and assigning interests in leases all have tax consequences. The unique nature of leases often makes lease transactions nuanced, and understanding the transaction becomes a fundamental part of analyzing the transaction. Once an attorney determines the nature of a transaction, the tax consequences often become less complicated.

A. General Tax Attributes of Leases

Several general tax attributes of leases will help parties assess whether a lease is more desirable than owning. First, the lessor receives rental payments that are gross income to the lessor.[1] Second, the lessee may deduct rental payments,[2] but must capitalize prepaid rent.[3] What the parties consider to be prepaid rent could be a section 467 rental agreement, and the parties would have to account for the payment under very complicated rules governing such agreements.[4] Third, the lessor, as owner of the property, generally may claim depreciation deductions that are allowed with respect to the leased property.[5] Fourth, a lessee often may claim depreciation deduc-

---

1. *See* I.R.C. §61(a)(5).
2. *See* I.R.C. §162(a)(3).
3. *See* Treas. Reg. §1.263(a)-4(d)(3). *But see* Treas. Reg. §1.263(a)-4(f) (providing a 12-month rule that allows a deduction for prepaid rents that satisfy the requirements of the rule).
4. *See* I.R.C. §467. The specifics of section 467 are beyond the scope of this book, but it could be relevant in many lease transactions that tax lawyers will face in the real estate context. Students should understand generally how section 467 may recast prepaid rent.
5. *See* I.R.C. §167(a).

tions for certain tenant leasehold improvements.[6] Finally, a lessee may recognize gain or loss on the disposition of a lease, the computation of which would be similar to the computation of gain or loss on the disposition of other assets. Some tax aspects of leases deserve specific attention. The following discussion introduces a few concepts of leases.

B. Entering into or Acquiring a Lease

The first question a tax lawyer must consider when examining a lease document is whether the structure is a lease for tax purposes. A document entitled "lease agreement" may not be a lease for tax purposes.[7] The parties to an agreement may seek to obtain the respective benefits of leasing or acquiring property and draft language in the documents that masks the substance of the arrangement. As with other transactions, parties generally must forfeit some economic attributes to obtain tax attributes of leasing or owning property. If a party other than the owner would value the tax attributes of owning the property more than the owner, perhaps the parties will consider a sale-leaseback of the property. The courts have been fairly generous in allowing sale-leaseback structures,[8] but lawyers must still help their clients ensure that the structure reflects their goals.

The right to use property under a lease is intangible property. The lessee may obtain such right by entering into a lease or acquiring the rights from a lessee. The lessee must account for all costs incurred to enter into or acquire a lease.[9] Such costs could include attorney fees, appraiser fees, amounts paid to induce the lessor to enter into the lease, and other costs. If the lessee capitalizes those costs, it must determine whether it can later recover them over the life of the lease or some other period.[10]

C. Accounting for Lease Payments

Typically, the lessor has ordinary income upon receipt of lease payments,[11] and a lessee can deduct rent payments for property used in a trade or business.[12] Prepaid rent can create something of an asymmetrical result, because the law generally requires the lessor to include rent received in gross income upon receipt,[13] but it requires the lessee to capitalize prepaid rent and deduct it over the life the lease.[14] In some instances, different methods of accounting can also create asymmetry if lease payments are de-

---

6. *See* I.R.C. § 168(i)(8).

7. *See* Grodt & McKay Realty, Inc. v. Commissioner, 77 T.C. 1221 (1981), *reproduced supra* Chapter 6.

8. *See, e.g.,* Frank Lyon Company v. United States, 435 U.S. 561 (1978).

9. *See* Treas. Reg. § 1.263(a)-4.

10. *See* Treas. Reg. §§ 1.162-11, 1.167(a)-3.

11. *See* I.R.C. §§ 61(a)(5); 451(a) Treas. Reg. § 1.61-8.

12. *See* I.R.C. § 162(a)(3).

13. *See* Treas. Reg. § 1.61-8(b).

14. *See* Treas. Reg. §§ 1.162-11(a), 1.263(a)-4(d)(3)(i).

ferred. For instance, an accrual method lessee may be able to deduct deferred lease payments ratably over the life of a lease while the cash method lessor defers recognition until receipt of the payments. Congress recognized the potential for such mismatch and the possibility that taxpayers would use the mismatch to create abusive structures, so it enacted section 467 to help eliminate it.[15]

If a lease is a section 467 rental agreement, the lessor and lessee account for the same amount of rent and interest each year as appropriate to account for prepaid or deferred rent and timing of actual payments under the agreement.[16] A leasing structure is a section 467 rental agreement if it provides for deferred or prepaid rents, or the amount of rent will increase or decrease in subsequent years.[17] Taxpayers subject to section 467 must use either (1) constant rental accrual, (2) proportional rental accrual, or (3) rental agreement accrual to determine the amount of section 467 rent for a given tax year.[18] Taxpayers cannot argue for use of constant rental accrual, and proportional rental accrual only applies to disqualified leaseback or long-term agreements that do not provide for adequate interest on fixed rent.[19] Taxpayers may include accrual provisions in an agreement that calls for prepaid or deferred rent. If the lessor and lessee have conflicting interests in the timing of the accruals, the IRS should generally respect their agreed-to accrual provisions. Nonetheless, parties to a lease may fail to include an accrual provision in a rental agreement, which results in unexpected tax consequences to one of the parties. For instance, if a rental agreement provides for

---

15. *See, e.g., General Explanation of the Revenue Provisions of the Deficit Reduction Act of 1984*, p. 285 (Dec. 31, 1984) (identifying the following as an abusive lease transaction: "A sandwich lease transaction—a cash-method partnership (often set up by a syndicator for purposes of the transaction) was simultaneously a lessee under a master lease with the ultimate owner of the property and a lessor under a sublease of the same property. The only practical function of this partnership was to collect rents from the sublessee, the ultimate user of the property, and pass on these rents (minus a fee for its services) to the lessor. The master lease and the sublease were for the same duration and contained substantially identical terms with respect to annual payments of rent: low rents in the early years and much higher rents in the later years. (In one syndicated transaction brought to Congress' attention, the leases provided for annual payments of rent of approximately $4 million in each of the first five years, escalating to approximately $20 million in each of the years 16 through 25.) The sublease provided that the total rent due under the lease accrued ratably over the lease term. The master lease, however, contained no such provision. ¶ The sublessee (an accrual-method taxpayer) would accrue annually a level amount of rent expense reflecting the average rent payable over the term of the lease. The ultimate lessor (also an accrual-method taxpayer) accrued annually only the amount of rental income actually received from the cash method partnership. The partnership in the middle reported exactly offsetting rental income and deductions, except for amounts retained as fees.").

16. *See* I.R.C. § 467(a); Treas. Reg. § 1.467-1(a)(3), (d), (e). For instance, in the early years of a lease, the lessor will be treated as receiving rent payments, even though the lessee does not make payments. The lessee therefore has use of money that otherwise would be paid to the lessor, and section 467 provides that the lessee will have an interest deduction and the lessor will have interest income on a deemed loan, i.e., section 467 loan. *See* Treas. Reg. § 1.467-2, -4(f), *Example 1*. Section 467 does not, however, apply to an arrangement if the aggregate amount of money and property to be received for use of the property does not exceed $250,000.

17. *See* I.R.C. § 467(d)(1); Treas. Reg. § 1.467-1(c).

18. *See* I.R.C. § 467(b)(1), (2), (h); Treas. Reg. § 1.467-1(d).

19. Stough v. Comm'r, 144 T.C. 306 (2015).

prepaid rent, the lessor may have to include the entire amount of prepaid rent in gross income upon receipt, if the agreement does not provide for any other accrual.[20] In such situations, the lessee should be able to claim a deduction under section 467 for the same year that the lessor reports gross income. This type of situation could provide the IRS opportunities to abuse its authority. For example, the IRS might challenge the lessor's treatment of prepaid rent (e.g., require inclusion upon receipt) and, if the tax year for the lessee is closed, prevent the lessee from claiming a deduction for the year of the prepaid rent. Section 467 should prevent that type of abuse in the same manner that it prevents taxpayers from creating abusive structures.

D. Leasehold Improvements

Improvements made to leased property may cause accounting complexity. Every improvement constructed on leased property will raise the question of who qualifies for the depreciation deduction attributable to the improvements.[21] If the lessee constructs the improvements, the parties must consider whether the improvements were rent payments and how the law will treat the transfer of the improvements to the lessor when the lease terminates.[22] If the lessor constructs the improvements, the lessor should treat the improvements like other property the lessor owns.[23]

E. Terminating a Lease

A lessee may wish to discontinue use of property before the end of the lease term. A lessee may be able to get out from under the lease by selling or assigning the right to use the property. Generally, such assignments will require the approval of the lessor. If the lessee assigns the right to use the property, the general rules that apply to property dispositions should apply to the assignment of interests in a lease.[24] If assigning the lease is not an option, perhaps the lessee could sublease the property. The

---

20. *See id.* (citing Treas. Reg. § 1.467-1(c)(2)(ii)(B) as stating that "[if] a rental agreement does not provide a specific allocation of fixed rents..., the amount of fixed rent allocated to a rental period is the amount of fixed rent payable during that rental period").

21. *See* I.R.C. § 168(i)(8) (providing rules governing leasehold improvements); Hopkins Partners v. Comm'r, 97 T.C.M. (CCH) 1560, T.C. Memo 2009-107 (2009) (discussing which party qualifies for the depreciation deduction); Treas. Reg. § 1.162-11(b) (presenting rules (some of which were nullified by section 168(i)(1)) regarding depreciation of leasehold improvements).

22. *See* I.R.C. § 109 (excluding leasehold improvements received upon termination of a lease from the lessor's gross income); I.R.C. § 1019 (governing the basis of leasehold improvements that a lessor receives on termination of a lease); Hopkins Partners v. Comm'r, 97 T.C.M. (CCH) 1560, T.C. Memo 2009-107 (2009) (considering whether improvements were rent substitutes and the tax consequences to the lessee when leasehold improvements transferred to the lessor); Treas. Reg. § 1.109-1 (providing that leasehold improvement that represent rent shall be income to the lessor).

23. *See* I.R.C. § 168(i)(6) (governing the depreciation of improvements).

24. *See* I.R.C. § 1001 *et seq.* (providing rules for computing gain or loss on the disposition of property).

assignment of a lease should relieve the lessee of the obligation to pay rent, subleasing does not relieve the lessee of such obligation.

A lessee may also be able to get out from under a lease by paying the lessor a termination (or cancellation) fee. Assuming the lease is for business purposes, the lessee should be able to deduct a termination fee paid to the lessor.[25] The termination fee is ordinary income to the lessor when received under the theory that it represents payment of future rent, which would be ordinary income to the lessor.[26]

For a variety of reasons, a lessor may be the party who wishes to terminate a lease. If the lessor pays a termination fee, the lessor must capitalize the amount paid.[27] The question becomes whether the lessor must add the termination fee to the basis of the property, recover it over the unexpired term of the terminated lease, or recover it over the life of another lease the lessor might enter into after the termination.[28] The lessee must treat the receipt of a lease-termination payment as a payment received in exchange for selling or assigning the lease.[29]

F. Exchanges of Leasehold Interests

Section 1031 provides that a leasehold of real property with at least 30 years to run can be like kind to other real property.[30] Consequently, a lessee should be able to assign the right to use real property (assuming the right will run for at least another 30 years) in exchange for a fee in other real property. Similarly, the owner of a fee in real property should be able to transfer the fee in exchange for an existing leasehold interest in real

---

25. *See* Cassatt v. Commissioner, 137 F.2d 745 (3d Cir. 1943).

26. *See* Treas. Reg. § 1.61-8(b); Hort v. Commissioner, 313 U.S. 28 (1941). One commentator suggests that section 1234A overturns *Hort. See* Edward J. Roche, Jr., *Lease Cancellation Payments are Capital Gain? Yes! The TRA '97 Change to 1234A Overturned Hort*, 102 J. TAX'N 364 (June 2005) (arguing that under section 1234A, lease termination payments qualify for capital gains if the leased real property is a capital asset). That view is subject to some doubt because section 1234A helps define when a transfer of certain property occurs for tax purposes. S. Rep. No. 105-33, 105th Cong., 1st Sess. 134–35 (1997) ("Extinguishment treated as sale or exchange — The Internal Revenue Code contains provisions that deem certain transactions to be a sale or exchange and, therefore, any resulting gain or loss is to be treated as a capital gain or loss. These rules generally provide for 'sale or exchange' treatment as a way of extending capital gain or loss treatment of those transactions. Under one special provision, gains and losses attributable to the cancellation, lapse, expiration, or other termination of a right or obligation with respect to certain personal property are treated as gains or losses from the sale of a capital asset (sec. 1234A). Personal property subject to this rule is (1) personal property of a type which is actively traded and which is, or would be on acquisition, a capital asset in the hands of the taxpayer (other than stock that is not part of straddle or of a corporation that is not formed or availed of to take positions which offset positions in personal property of its shareholders) and (2) a 'section 1256 contract' which is capital asset in the hands of the taxpayer. Section 1234A does not apply to the retirement of a debt instrument."). When a lessee pays a lessor to terminate a lease, the leased property is not transferred, so section 1234A would not appear to apply to such transactions.

27. *See* Treas. Reg. § 1.263(a)-4(d)(7)(i)(A).

28. *See* Handlery Hotels, Inc. v. United States, 663 F.2d 892 (9th Cir. 1981).

29. *See* I.R.C. § 1241.

30. *See* Treas. Reg. § 1.1031(a)-1(c)(2).

property that has at least 30 years to run.[31] The owner of real property probably cannot use prepaid rent to acquire replacement property as part of a section 1031 exchange.[32] The open question is whether the transferor of a fee in real property can use the proceeds from the sale of that property to enter into a lease. The courts have considered the latter question in the sale-leaseback context.[33] Attorneys must consider whether that authority supports the application of section 1031 to the transfer of a fee in real property to one party in exchange for entering into a lease with another party.

II. Primary Legal Authority

Frank Lyon Company v. United States

United States Supreme Court

435 U.S. 561 (1978)

FACTS

The underlying pertinent facts are undisputed. They are established by stipulations, App. 9, 14, the trial testimony, and the documentary evidence, and are reflected in the District Court's findings.

Lyon is a closely held Arkansas corporation engaged in the distribution of home furnishings, primarily Whirlpool and RCA electrical products. Worthen in 1965 was an Arkansas-chartered bank and a member of the Federal Reserve System. Frank Lyon was Lyon's majority shareholder and board chairman; he also served on Worthen's board. Worthen at that time began to plan the construction of a multistory bank and office building to replace its existing facility in Little Rock. About the same time Worthen's competitor, Union National Bank of Little Rock, also began to plan a new bank and office building. Adjacent sites on Capitol Avenue, separated only by Spring Street, were acquired by the two banks. It became a matter of competition, for both banking business and tenants, and prestige as to which bank would start and complete its building first.

Worthen initially hoped to finance, to build, and to own the proposed facility at a total cost of $9 million for the site, building, and adjoining parking deck. This was to be accomplished by selling $4 million in debentures and using the proceeds in the acquisition of the capital stock of a wholly owned real estate subsidiary. This subsidiary would have formal title and would raise the remaining $5 million by a conventional mortgage loan on the new premises. Worthen's plan, however, had to be abandoned for two significant reasons:

---

31. *See* Rev. Rul. 78-72, 1978-1 C.B. 258.

32. *See* Pembroke v. Helvering, 70 F.2d 850 (D.C. Cir. 1934).

33. *See, e.g.,* Jordan Marsh Co. v. Commissioner, 269 F.2d 453 (2d Cir. 1959); Century Electric Co. v. Commissioner, 192 F.2d 155 (8th Cir. 1951).

1. As a bank chartered under Arkansas law, Worthen legally could not pay more interest on any debentures it might issue than that then specified by Arkansas law. But the proposed obligations would not be marketable at that rate.

2. Applicable statutes or regulations of the Arkansas State Bank Department and the Federal Reserve System required Worthen, as a state bank subject to their supervision, to obtain prior permission for the investment in banking premises of any amount (including that placed in a real estate subsidiary) in excess of the bank's capital stock or of 40% of its capital stock and surplus.[34] See Ark. Stat. Ann. §67-547.1 (Supp.1977); 12 U.S.C. §371d (1976 ed.); 12 CFR §265.2(f)(7) (1977). Worthen, accordingly, was advised by staff employees of the Federal Reserve System that they would not recommend approval of the plan by the System's Board of Governors.

Worthen therefore was forced to seek an alternative solution that would provide it with the use of the building, satisfy the state and federal regulators, and attract the necessary capital. In September 1967 it proposed a sale-and-leaseback arrangement. The State Bank Department and the Federal Reserve System approved this approach, but the Department required that Worthen possess an option to purchase the leased property at the end of the 15th year of the lease at a set price, and the federal regulator required that the building be owned by an independent third party.

Detailed negotiations ensued with investors that had indicated interest, namely, Goldman, Sachs & Company; White, Weld & Co.; Eastman Dillon, Union Securities & Company; and Stephens, Inc. Certain of these firms made specific proposals.

Worthen then obtained a commitment from New York Life Insurance Company to provide $7,140,000 in permanent mortgage financing on the building, conditioned upon its approval of the titleholder. At this point Lyon entered the negotiations and it, too, made a proposal.

Worthen submitted a counterproposal that incorporated the best features, from its point of view, of the several offers. Lyon accepted the counterproposal, suggesting, by way of further inducement, a $21,000 reduction in the annual rent for the first five years of the building lease. Worthen selected Lyon as the investor. After further negotiations, resulting in the elimination of that rent reduction (offset, however, by higher interest Lyon was to pay Worthen on a subsequent unrelated loan), Lyon in November 1967 was approved as an acceptable borrower by First National City Bank for the construction financing, and by New York Life, as the permanent lender. In April 1968 the approvals of the state and federal regulators were received.

In the meantime, on September 15, before Lyon was selected, Worthen itself began construction.

---

34. [1] Worthen, as of June 30, 1967, had capital stock of $4 million and surplus of $5 million. During the period the building was under construction Worthen became a national bank subject to the supervision and control of the Comptroller of the Currency.

In May 1968 Worthen, Lyon, City Bank, and New York Life executed complementary and interlocking agreements under which the building was sold by Worthen to Lyon as it was constructed, and Worthen leased the completed building back from Lyon:

1. Agreements between Worthen and Lyon. Worthen and Lyon executed a ground lease, a sales agreement, and a building lease. Under the ground lease dated May 1, 1968, App. 366, Worthen leased the site to Lyon for 76 years and 7 months through November 30, 2044. The first 19 months were the estimated construction period. The ground rents payable by Lyon to Worthen were $50 for the first 26 years and 7 months and thereafter in quarterly payments:

> 12/1/94 through 11/30/99 (5 years) — $100,000 annually
>
> 12/1/99 through 11/30/04 (5 years) — $150,000 annually
>
> 12/1/04 through 11/30/09 (5 years) — $200,000 annually
>
> 12/1/09 through 11/30/34 (25 years) — $250,000 annually
>
> 12/1/34 through 11/30/44 (10 years) — $10,000 annually.

Under the sales agreement dated May 19, 1968, *id.*, at 508, Worthen agreed to sell the building to Lyon, and Lyon agreed to buy it, piece by piece as it was constructed, for a total price not to exceed $7,640,000, in reimbursements to Worthen for its expenditures for the construction of the building.[35]

Under the building lease dated May 1, 1968, *id.*, at 376, Lyon leased the building back to Worthen for a primary term of 25 years from December 1, 1969, with options in Worthen to extend the lease for eight additional 5-year terms, a total of 65 years. During the period between the expiration of the building lease (at the latest, November 30, 2034, if fully extended) and the end of the ground lease on November 30, 2044, full ownership, use, and control of the building were Lyon's, unless, of course, the building had been repurchased by Worthen. *Id.*, at 369. Worthen was not obligated to pay rent under the building lease until completion of the building. For the first 11 years of the lease, that is, until November 30, 1980, the stated quarterly rent was $145,581.03 ($582,324.12 for the year). For the next 14 years, the quarterly rent was $153,289.32 ($613,157.28 for the year), and for the option periods the rent was $300,000 a year, payable quarterly. *Id.*, at 378–379. The total rent for the building over the 25-year primary term of the lease thus was $14,989,767.24. That rent equaled the principal and interest payments that would amortize the $7,140,000 New York Life mortgage loan over the same period. When the mortgage was paid off at the end

---

35. [2] This arrangement appeared advisable and was made because purchases of materials by Worthen (which then had become a national bank) were not subject to Arkansas sales tax. *See* Ark. Stat. Ann. § 84-1904(*l*) (1960); First Agricultural Nat. Bank v. Tax Comm'n, 392 U.S. 339 (1968). Sales of the building elements to Lyon also were not subject to state sales tax, since they were sales of real estate. *See* Ark. Stat. Ann. § 84-1902(c) (Supp.1977).

of the primary term, the annual building rent, if Worthen extended the lease, came down to the stated $300,000. Lyon's net rentals from the building would be further reduced by the increase in ground rent Worthen would receive from Lyon during the extension.[36]

The building lease was a "net lease," under which Worthen was responsible for all expenses usually associated with the maintenance of an office building, including repairs, taxes, utility charges, and insurance, and was to keep the premises in good condition, excluding, however, reasonable wear and tear.

Finally, under the lease, Worthen had the option to repurchase the building at the following times and prices:

> 11/30/80 (after 11 years) — $6,325,169.85
>
> 11/30/84 (after 15 years) — $5,432,607.32
>
> 11/30/89 (after 20 years) — $4,187,328.04
>
> 11/30/94 (after 25 years) — $2,145,935.00

These repurchase option prices were the sum of the unpaid balance of the New York Life mortgage, Lyon's $500,000 investment, and 6% interest compounded on that investment.

2. Construction financing agreement. By agreement dated May 14, 1968, *id.*, at 462, City Bank agreed to lend Lyon $7,000,000 for the construction of the building. This loan was secured by a mortgage on the building and the parking deck, executed by Worthen as well as by Lyon, and an assignment by Lyon of its interests in the building lease and in the ground lease.

3. Permanent financing agreement. By Note Purchase Agreement dated May 1, 1968, *id.*, at 443, New York Life agreed to purchase Lyon's $7,140,000 6 3/4 % 25-year secured note to be issued upon completion of the building. Under this agreement Lyon warranted that it would lease the building to Worthen for a noncancelable term of at least 25 years under a net lease at a rent at least equal to the mortgage payments on the note. Lyon agreed to make quarterly payments of principal and interest equal to the rentals payable by Worthen during the corresponding primary term of the lease. *Id.*, at 523. The security for the note was a first deed of trust and Lyon's assignment of its interests in the building lease and in the ground lease. *Id.*, at 527, 571. Worthen joined in the deed of trust as the owner of the fee and the parking deck.

---

36. [3] This, of course, is on the assumption that Worthen exercises its option to extend the building lease. If it does not, Lyon remains liable for the substantial rents prescribed by the ground lease. This possibility brings into sharp focus the fact that Lyon, in a very practical sense, is at least the ultimate owner of the building. If Worthen does not extend, the building lease expires and Lyon may do with the building as it chooses. The Government would point out, however, that the net amounts payable by Worthen to Lyon during the building lease's extended terms, if all are claimed, would approximate the amount required to repay Lyon's $500,000 investment at 6% compound interest. Brief for United States 14.

In December 1969 the building was completed and Worthen took possession. At that time Lyon received the permanent loan from New York Life, and it discharged the interim loan from City Bank. The actual cost of constructing the office building and parking complex (excluding the cost of the land) exceeded $10,000,000.

Lyon filed its federal income tax returns on the accrual and calendar year basis. On its 1969 return, Lyon accrued rent from Worthen for December. It asserted as deductions one month's interest to New York Life; one month's depreciation on the building; interest on the construction loan from City Bank; and sums for legal and other expenses incurred in connection with the transaction.

On audit of Lyon's 1969 return, the Commissioner of Internal Revenue determined that Lyon was "not the owner for tax purposes of any portion of the Worthen Building," and ruled that "the income and expenses related to this building are not allowable ... for Federal income tax purposes." App. 304–305, 299. He also added $2,298.15 to Lyon's 1969 income as "accrued interest income." This was the computed 1969 portion of a gain, considered the equivalent of interest income, the realization of which was based on the assumption that Worthen would exercise its option to buy the building after 11 years, on November 30, 1980, at the price stated in the lease, and on the additional determination that Lyon had "loaned" $500,000 to Worthen. In other words, the Commissioner determined that the sale-and-leaseback arrangement was a financing transaction in which Lyon loaned Worthen $500,000 and acted as a conduit for the transmission of principal and interest from Worthen to New York Life.

All this resulted in a total increase of $497,219.18 over Lyon's reported income for 1969, and a deficiency in Lyon's federal income tax for that year in the amount of $236,596.36. The Commissioner assessed that amount, together with interest of $43,790.84, for a total of $280,387.20.[37]

Lyon paid the assessment and filed a timely claim for its refund. The claim was denied, and this suit, to recover the amount so paid, was instituted in the United States District Court for the Eastern District of Arkansas within the time allowed by 26 U.S.C. § 6532(a)(1).

After trial without a jury, the District Court, in a memorandum letter-opinion setting forth findings and conclusions, ruled in Lyon's favor and held that its claimed deductions were allowable. 75-2 USTC ¶ 9545 (1975); 36 AFTR 2d ¶ 75-5059 (1975); App. 296–311. It concluded that the legal intent of the parties had been to create a bona fide sale-and-leaseback in accordance with the form and language of the documents evidencing the transactions. It rejected the argument that Worthen was acquiring an equity in the building through its rental payments. It found that the rents were unchallenged and were reasonable throughout the period of the lease, and that the option prices, negotiated at arm's length between the parties, represented fair estimates of market value on the applicable dates. It rejected any negative inference from the fact that the rentals, combined with the options, were sufficient to amortize

---

37. [4] These figures do not include uncontested adjustments not involved in this litigation.

the New York Life loan and to pay Lyon a 6% return on its equity investment. It found that Worthen would acquire an equity in the building only if it exercised one of its options to purchase, and that it was highly unlikely, as a practical matter, that any purchase option would ever be exercised. It rejected any inference to be drawn from the fact that the lease was a "net lease." It found that Lyon had mixed motivations for entering into the transaction, including the need to diversify as well as the desire to have the benefits of a "tax shelter." App. 296, 299.

The United States Court of Appeals for the Eighth Circuit reversed. 536 F.2d 746 (1976). It held that the Commissioner correctly determined that Lyon was not the true owner of the building and therefore was not entitled to the claimed deductions. It likened ownership for tax purposes to a "bundle of sticks" and undertook its own evaluation of the facts. It concluded, in agreement with the Government's contention, that Lyon "totes an empty bundle" of ownership sticks. *Id.*, at 751. It stressed the following: (a) The lease agreements circumscribed Lyon's right to profit from its investment in the building by giving Worthen the option to purchase for an amount equal to Lyon's $500,000 equity plus 6% compound interest and the assumption of the unpaid balance of the New York Life mortgage.[38] (b) The option prices did not take into account possible appreciation of the value of the building or inflation.[39] (c) Any award realized as a result of destruction or condemnation of the building in excess of the mortgage balance and the $500,000 would be paid to Worthen and not Lyon.[40] (d) The building rental payments during the primary term were exactly equal to the mortgage payments.[41] (e) Worthen retained control over the ultimate disposition of the building through its various options to repurchase and to renew the lease plus its ownership of the site.[42] (f) Worthen enjoyed all benefits and bore all burdens incident

---

38. [5] Lyon here challenges this assertion on the grounds that it had the right and opportunities to sell the building at a greater profit at any time; the return to Lyon was not insubstantial and was attractive to a true investor in real estate; the 6% return was the minimum Lyon would realize if Worthen exercised one of its options, an event the District Court found highly unlikely; and Lyon would own the building and realize a greater return than 6% if Worthen did not exercise an option to purchase.

39. [6] Lyon challenges this observation by pointing out that the District Court found the option prices to be the negotiated estimate of the parties of the fair market value of the building on the option dates and to be reasonable. App. 303, 299.

40. [7] Lyon asserts that this statement is true only with respect to the total destruction or taking of the building on or after December 1, 1980. Lyon asserts that it, not Worthen, would receive the excess above the mortgage balance in the event of total destruction or taking before December 1, 1980, or in the event of partial damage or taking at any time. *Id.*, at 408–410, 411.

41. [8] Lyon concedes the accuracy of this statement, but asserts that it does not justify the conclusion that Lyon served merely as a conduit by which mortgage payments would be transmitted to New York Life. It asserts that Lyon was the sole obligor on the New York Life note and would remain liable in the event of default by Worthen. It also asserts that the fact the rent was sufficient to amortize the loan during the primary term of the lease was a requirement imposed by New York Life, and is a usual requirement in most long-term loans secured by a long-term lease.

42. [9] As to this statement, Lyon asserts that the Court of Appeals ignored Lyon's right to sell the building to another at any time; the District Court's finding that the options to purchase were not likely to be exercised; the uncertainty that Worthen would renew the lease for 40 years; Lyon's

to the operation and ownership of the building so that, in the Court of Appeals' view, the only economic advantages accruing to Lyon, in the event it were considered to be the true owner of the property, were income tax savings of approximately $1.5 million during the first 11 years of the arrangement.[43] *Id.*, at 752–753.[44] The court concluded, *id.*, at 753, that the transaction was "closely akin" to that in *Helvering v. Lazarus & Co.*, 308 U.S. 252 (1939). "In sum, the benefits, risks, and burdens which [Lyon] has incurred with respect to the Worthen building are simply too insubstantial to establish a claim to the status of owner for tax purposes.... The vice of the present lease is that all of [its] features have been employed in the same transaction with the cumulative effect of depriving [Lyon] of any significant ownership interest." 536 F.2d, at 754.

We granted certiorari, 429 U.S. 1089 (1977), because of an indicated conflict with *American Realty Trust v. U.S.*, 498 F.2d 1194 (4th Cir. 1974).

ANALYSIS

This Court, almost 50 years ago, observed that "taxation is not so much concerned with the refinements of title as it is with actual command over the property taxed— the actual benefit for which the tax is paid." *Corliss v. Bowers*, 281 U.S. 376, 378 (1930). In a number of cases, the Court has refused to permit the transfer of formal legal title to shift the incidence of taxation attributable to ownership of property where the transferor continues to retain significant control over the property transferred. *E. g., Comm'r v. Sunnen*, 333 U.S. 591 (1948); *Helvering v. Clifford*, 309 U.S. 331 (1940). In applying this doctrine of substance over form, the Court has looked to the objective economic realities of a transaction rather than to the particular form the parties employed. The Court has never regarded "the simple expedient of drawing up papers," *Comm'r v. Tower*, 327 U.S. 280, 291 (1946), as controlling for tax purposes when the objective economic realities are to the contrary. "In the field of taxation, administrators of the laws and the courts are concerned with substance and realities, and formal written documents are not rigidly binding." *Helvering v. Lazarus & Co.*, 308 U.S., at 255. *See also Comm'r v. P. G. Lake, Inc.*, 356 U.S. 260, 266–267 (1958); *Comm'r v. Court Holding Co.*, 324 U.S. 331, 334 (1945). Nor is the parties' desire to achieve a particular tax result necessarily relevant. *Comm'r v. Duberstein*, 363 U.S. 278, 286 (1960).

---

right to lease to anyone at any price during the last 10 years of the ground lease; and Lyon's continuing ownership of the building after the expiration of the ground lease.

43. [10] In response to this, Lyon asserts that the District Court found that the benefits of occupancy Worthen will enjoy are common in most long-term real estate leases, and that the District Court found that Lyon had motives other than tax savings in entering into the transaction. It also asserts that the net cash after-tax benefit would be $312,220, not $1.5 million.

44. [11] Other factors relied on by the Court of Appeals, 536 F.2d, at 752, were the allocation of the investment credit to Worthen, and a claim that Lyon's ability to sell the building to a third party was "carefully circumscribed" by the lease agreements. The investment credit by statute is freely allocable between the parties, §48(d) of the 1954 Code, 26 U.S.C. §48(d), and the Government has not pressed either of these factors before this Court.

In the light of these general and established principles, the Government takes the position that the Worthen-Lyon transaction in its entirety should be regarded as a sham. The agreement as a whole, it is said, was only an elaborate financing scheme designed to provide economic benefits to Worthen and a guaranteed return to Lyon. The latter was but a conduit used to forward the mortgage payments, made under the guise of rent paid by Worthen to Lyon, on to New York Life as mortgagee. This, the Government claims, is the true substance of the transaction as viewed under the microscope of the tax laws. Although the arrangement was cast in sale-and-leaseback form, in substance it was only a financing transaction, and the terms of the repurchase options and lease renewals so indicate. It is said that Worthen could reacquire the building simply by satisfying the mortgage debt and paying Lyon its $500,000 advance plus interest, regardless of the fair market value of the building at the time; similarly, when the mortgage was paid off, Worthen could extend the lease at drastically reduced bargain rentals that likewise bore no relation to fair rental value but were simply calculated to pay Lyon its $500,000 plus interest over the extended term. Lyon's return on the arrangement in no event could exceed 6% compound interest (although the Government conceded it might well be less, Tr. of Oral Arg. 32). Furthermore, the favorable option and lease renewal terms made it highly unlikely that Worthen would abandon the building after it in effect had "paid off" the mortgage. The Government implies that the arrangement was one of convenience which, if accepted on its face, would enable Worthen to deduct its payments to Lyon as rent and would allow Lyon to claim a deduction for depreciation, based on the cost of construction ultimately borne by Worthen, which Lyon could offset against other income, and to deduct mortgage interest that roughly would offset the inclusion of Worthen's rental payments in Lyon's income. If, however, the Government argues, the arrangement was only a financing transaction under which Worthen was the owner of the building, Worthen's payments would be deductible only to the extent that they represented mortgage interest, and Worthen would be entitled to claim depreciation; Lyon would not be entitled to deductions for either mortgage interest or depreciation and it would not have to include Worthen's "rent" payments in its income because its function with respect to those payments was that of a conduit between Worthen and New York Life.

The Government places great reliance on *Helvering v. Lazarus & Co., supra,* and claims it to be precedent that controls this case. The taxpayer there was a department store. The legal title of its three buildings was in a bank as trustee for land-trust certificate holders. When the transfer to the trustee was made, the trustee at the same time leased the buildings back to the taxpayer for 99 years, with option to renew and purchase. The Commissioner, in stark contrast to his posture in the present case, took the position that the statutory right to depreciation followed legal title. The Board of Tax Appeals, however, concluded that the transaction between the taxpayer and the bank in reality was a mortgage loan and allowed the taxpayer depreciation on the buildings. This Court, as had the Court of Appeals, agreed with that conclusion and affirmed. It regarded the "rent" stipulated in the leaseback as a promise to pay interest on the loan, and a "depreciation fund" required by the lease as an amortization fund designed to pay off the loan in the stated period. Thus, said the Court, the Board justifiably concluded that the transaction, although in written form a transfer of ownership with a leaseback, was actually a loan secured by the property involved.

The *Lazarus* case, we feel, is to be distinguished from the present one and is not controlling here. Its transaction was one involving only two (and not multiple) parties, the taxpayer-department store and the trustee-bank. The Court looked closely at the substance of the agreement between those two parties and rightly concluded that depreciation was deductible by the taxpayer despite the nomenclature of the instrument of conveyance and the leaseback. *See also Sun Oil Co. v. Comm'r*, 562 F.2d 258 (3d Cir. 1977) (a two-party case with the added feature that the second party was a tax-exempt pension trust).

The present case, in contrast, involves three parties, Worthen, Lyon, and the finance agency. The usual simple two-party arrangement was legally unavailable to Worthen. Independent investors were interested in participating in the alternative available to Worthen, and Lyon itself (also independent from Worthen) won the privilege. Despite Frank Lyon's presence on Worthen's board of directors, the transaction, as it ultimately developed, was not a familial one arranged by Worthen, but one compelled by the realities of the restrictions imposed upon the bank. Had Lyon not appeared, another interested investor would have been selected. The ultimate solution would have been essentially the same. Thus, the presence of the third party, in our view, significantly distinguishes this case from *Lazarus* and removes the latter as controlling authority.

It is true, of course, that the transaction took shape according to Worthen's needs. As the Government points out, Worthen throughout the negotiations regarded the respective proposals of the independent investors in terms of its own cost of funds. *E g.*, App. 355. It is also true that both Worthen and the prospective investors compared the various proposals in terms of the return anticipated on the investor's equity. But all this is natural for parties contemplating entering into a transaction of this kind. Worthen needed a building for its banking operations and other purposes and necessarily had to know what its cost would be. The investors were in business to employ their funds in the most remunerative way possible. And, as the Court has said in the past, a transaction must be given its effect in accord with what actually occurred and not in accord with what might have occurred. *Comm'r v. National Alfalfa Dehydrating & Milling Co.*, 417 U.S. 134, 148–149 (1974); *Central Tablet Mfg. Co. v. U.S.*, 417 U.S. 673, 690 (1974).

There is no simple device available to peel away the form of this transaction and to reveal its substance. The effects of the transaction on all the parties were obviously different from those that would have resulted had Worthen been able simply to make a mortgage agreement with New York Life and to receive a $500,000 loan from Lyon. Then *Lazarus* would apply. Here, however, and most significantly, it was Lyon alone, and not Worthen, who was liable on the notes, first to City Bank, and then to New York Life. Despite the facts that Worthen had agreed to pay rent and that this rent equaled the amounts due from Lyon to New York Life, should anything go awry in the later years of the lease, Lyon was primarily liable.[45] No matter how the transaction could have been devised otherwise, it remains a fact that as the agreements were placed in final form, the obligation on the notes fell squarely on Lyon.[46] Lyon, an on-going enterprise, exposed its very business well-being to this real and substantial risk.

The effect of this liability on Lyon is not just the abstract possibility that something will go wrong and that Worthen will not be able to make its payments. Lyon has disclosed this liability on its balance sheet for all the world to see. Its financial position was affected substantially by the presence of this long-term debt, despite the offsetting presence of the building as an asset. To the extent that Lyon has used its capital in this transaction, it is less able to obtain financing for other business needs.

In concluding that there is this distinct element of economic reality in Lyon's assumption of liability, we are mindful that the characterization of a transaction for financial accounting purposes, on the one hand, and for tax purposes, on the other, need not necessarily be the same. *Comm'r v. Lincoln Savings & Loan Assn.*, 403 U.S. 345, 355 (1971); *Old Colony R. Co. v. Comm'r*, 284 U.S. 552, 562 (1932). Accounting methods or descriptions, without more, do not lend substance to that which has no substance. But in this case accepted accounting methods, as understood by the several parties to the respective agreements and as applied to the transaction by others, gave the transaction a meaningful character consonant with the form it was given.[47]

---

45. [12] New York Life required Lyon, not Worthen, to submit financial statements periodically. See Note Purchase Agreement, App. 453–454, 458–459.

46. [13] It may well be that the remedies available to New York Life against Lyon would be far greater than any remedy available to it against Worthen, which, as lessee, is liable to New York Life only through Lyon's assignment of its interest as lessor.

47. [14] We are aware that accounting standards have changed significantly since 1968 and that the propriety of Worthen's and Lyon's methods of disclosing the transaction in question may be a matter for debate under these new standards. Compare Accounting Principles Bd. Opinion No. 5, Reporting of Leases in Financial Statements of Lessee (1964), and Accounting Principles Bd. Opinion No. 7, Accounting for Leases in Financial Statements of Lessors (1966), with Financial Accounting Standards Board, Statement of Financial Accounting Standards No. 13, Accounting for Leases (1976). See also Comptroller of the Currency, Banking Circular No. 95 (Nov. 11, 1977), instructing that national banks revise their financial statements in accord with FASB Standard No. 13. Standard No. 13, however, by its terms, states, ¶ 78, that there are many instances where tax and financial accounting treatments diverge. Further, Standard No. 13 is nonapplicable with respect to a lease executed prior to January 1, 1977 (as was the Lyon-Worthen lease), until January 1, 1981. Obviously, Banking Circular No. 95 was not in effect in 1968 when the Lyon-Worthen lease was executed. Then-existing pronouncements of the Internal Revenue Service gave Lyon very little against which to measure the transaction. The most complete statement on the general question of characterization of leases as sales, Rev. Rul. 55-540, 1955-2 C.B. 39, by its terms dealt only with equipment leases. In that ruling it was stated that the Service will look at the intent of the parties at the time the agreement was executed to determine the proper characterization of the transaction. Generally, an intent to enter into a conditional sales agreement will be found to be present if (a) portions of the rental payments are made specifically applicable to an equity acquired by the lessee, (b) the lessee will acquire a title automatically after certain payments have been made, (c) the rental payments are a disproportionately large amount in relation to the sum necessary to complete the sale, (d) the rental payments are above fair rental value, (e) title can be acquired at a nominal option price, or (f) some portion of the rental payments are identifiable as interest. *See also* Rev. Rul. 60-122, 1960-1 C.B. 56; Rev. Rul. 72-543,

Worthen was not allowed to enter into the type of transaction which the Government now urges to be the true substance of the arrangement. Lyon and Worthen cannot be said to have entered into the transaction intending that the interests involved were allocated in a way other than that associated with a sale-and-leaseback.

Other factors also reveal that the transaction cannot be viewed as anything more than a mortgage agreement between Worthen and New York Life and a loan from Lyon to Worthen. There is no legal obligation between Lyon and Worthen representing the $500,000 "loan" extended under the Government's theory. And the assumed 6% return on this putative loan — required by the audit to be recognized in the taxable year in question — will be realized only when and if Worthen exercises its options.

The Court of Appeals acknowledged that the rents alone, due after the primary term of the lease and after the mortgage has been paid, do not provide the simple 6% return which, the Government urges, Lyon is guaranteed, 536 F.2d, at 752. Thus, if Worthen chooses not to exercise its options, Lyon is gambling that the rental value of the building during the last 10 years of the ground lease, during which the ground rent is minimal, will be sufficient to recoup its investment before it must negotiate again with Worthen regarding the ground lease. There are simply too many contingencies, including variations in the value of real estate, in the cost of money, and in the capital structure of Worthen, to permit the conclusion that the parties intended to enter into the transaction as structured in the audit and according to which the Government now urges they be taxed.

It is not inappropriate to note that the Government is likely to lose little revenue, if any, as a result of the shape given the transaction by the parties. No deduction was created that is not either matched by an item of income or that would not have been available to one of the parties if the transaction had been arranged differently. While it is true that Worthen paid Lyon less to induce it to enter into the transaction because Lyon anticipated the benefit of the depreciation deductions it would have as the owner of the building, those deductions would have been equally available to Worthen had it retained title to the building. The Government so concedes. Tr. of Oral Arg. 22–23. The fact that favorable tax consequences were taken into account by Lyon on en-

---

1972-2 C.B. 87. The Service announced more specific guidelines, indicating under what circumstances it would answer requests for rulings on leverage leasing transactions, in Rev. Proc. 75-21, 1975-1 Cum. Bull. 715. In general "[u]nless other facts and circumstances indicate a contrary intent," the Service will not rule that a lessor in a leveraged lease transaction is to be treated as the owner of the property in question unless (a) the lessor has incurred and maintains a minimal investment equal to 20% of the cost of the property, (b) the lessee has no right to purchase except at fair market value, (c) no part of the cost of the property is furnished by the lessee, (d) the lessee has not lent to the lessor or guaranteed any indebtedness of the lessor, and (e) the lessor must demonstrate that it expects to receive a profit on the transaction other than the benefits received solely from the tax treatment. These guidelines are not intended to be definitive, and it is not clear that they provide much guidance in assessing real estate transactions. *See* Rosenberg & Weinstein, *Sale-leasebacks: An analysis of these transactions after the Lyon decision,* 45 J. Tax. 146, 147 n. 1 (1976).

tering into the transaction is no reason for disallowing those consequences.[48] We cannot ignore the reality that the tax laws affect the shape of nearly every business transaction. *See Comm'r v. Brown*, 380 U.S. 563, 579–580 (1965) (Harlan, J., concurring). Lyon is not a corporation with no purpose other than to hold title to the bank building. It was not created by Worthen or even financed to any degree by Worthen.

The conclusion that the transaction is not a simple sham to be ignored does not, of course, automatically compel the further conclusion that Lyon is entitled to the items claimed as deductions. Nevertheless, on the facts, this readily follows. As has been noted, the obligations on which Lyon paid interest were its obligations alone, and it is entitled to claim deductions therefor under § 163(a) of the 1954 Code, 26 U.S.C. § 163(a).

As is clear from the facts, none of the parties to this sale-and-leaseback was the owner of the building in any simple sense. But it is equally clear that the facts focus upon Lyon as the one whose capital was committed to the building and as the party, therefore, that was entitled to claim depreciation for the consumption of that capital. The Government has based its contention that Worthen should be treated as the owner on the assumption that throughout the term of the lease Worthen was acquiring an equity in the property. In order to establish the presence of that growing equity, however, the Government is forced to speculate that one of the options will be exercised and that, if it is not, this is only because the rentals for the extended term are a bargain. We cannot indulge in such speculation in view of the District Court's clear finding to the contrary.[49] We therefore conclude that it is Lyon's capital that is invested in the building according to the agreement of the parties, and it is Lyon that is entitled to depreciation deductions, under § 167 of the 1954 Code, 26 U.S.C. § 167. *Cf. U.S. v. Chicago B. & Q. R. Co.*, 412 U.S. 401 (1973).

We recognize that the Government's position, and that taken by the Court of Appeals, is not without superficial appeal. One, indeed, may theorize that Frank Lyon's presence on the Worthen board of directors; Lyon's departure from its principal corporate activity into this unusual venture; the parallel between the payments under the building lease and the amounts due from Lyon on the New York Life mortgage; the provisions relating to condemnation or destruction of the property; the nature and presence of the several options available to Worthen; and the tax benefits, such

---

48. [15] Indeed, it is not inevitable that the transaction, as treated by Lyon and Worthen, will not result in more revenues to the Government rather than less. Lyon is gambling that in the first 11 years of the lease it will have income that will be sheltered by the depreciation deductions, and that it will be able to make sufficiently good use of the tax dollars preserved thereby to make up for the income it will recognize and pay taxes on during the last 14 years of the initial term of the lease and against which it will enjoy no sheltering deduction.

49. [16] The general characterization of a transaction for tax purposes is a question of law subject to review. The particular facts from which the characterization is to be made are not so subject. *See* American Realty Trust v. U.S., 498 F.2d 1194, 1198 (4th Cir. 1974).

as the use of double declining balance depreciation, that accrue to Lyon during the initial years of the arrangement, form the basis of an argument that Worthen should be regarded as the owner of the building and as the recipient of nothing more from Lyon than a $500,000 loan.

We however, as did the District Court, find this theorizing incompatible with the substance and economic realities of the transaction: the competitive situation as it existed between Worthen and Union National Bank in 1965 and the years immediately following; Worthen's undercapitalization; Worthen's consequent inability, as a matter of legal restraint, to carry its building plans into effect by a conventional mortgage and other borrowing; the additional barriers imposed by the state and federal regulators; the suggestion, forthcoming from the state regulator, that Worthen possess an option to purchase; the requirement, from the federal regulator, that the building be owned by an independent third party; the presence of several finance organizations seriously interested in participating in the transaction and in the resolution of Worthen's problem; the submission of formal proposals by several of those organizations; the bargaining process and period that ensued; the competitiveness of the bidding; the bona fide character of the negotiations; the three-party aspect of the transaction; Lyon's substantiality[50] and its independence from Worthen; the fact that diversification was Lyon's principal motivation; Lyon's being liable alone on the successive notes to City Bank and New York Life; the reasonableness, as the District Court found, of the rentals and of the option prices; the substantiality of the purchase prices; Lyon's not being engaged generally in the business of financing; the presence of all building depreciation risks on Lyon; the risk borne by Lyon, that Worthen might default or fail, as other banks have failed; the facts that Worthen could "walk away" from the relationship at the end of the 25-year primary term, and probably would do so if the option price were more than the then-current worth of the building to Worthen; the inescapable fact that if the building lease were not extended, Lyon would be the full owner of the building, free to do with it as it chose; Lyon's liability for the substantial ground rent if Worthen decides not to exercise any of its options to extend; the absence of any understanding between Lyon and Worthen that Worthen would exercise any of the purchase options; the nonfamily and nonprivate nature of the entire transaction; and the absence of any differential in tax rates and of special tax circumstances for one of the parties—all convince us that Lyon has far the better of the case.[51]

---

50. [17] Lyon's consolidated balance sheet on December 31, 1968, showed assets of $12,225,612, and total stockholders' equity of $3,818,671. Of the assets, the sum of $2,674,290 represented its then investment in the Worthen building. App. 587–588.

51. [18] Thus, the facts of this case stand in contrast to many others in which the form of the transaction actually created tax advantages that, for one reason or another, could not have been enjoyed had the transaction taken another form. See, e. g., Sun Oil Co. v. Comm'r, 562 F.2d 258 (CA 3 1977) (sale-and-leaseback of land between taxpayer and tax-exempt trust enabled the taxpayer to amortize, through its rental deductions, the cost of acquiring land not otherwise depreciable). Indeed, the arrangements in this case can hardly be labeled as tax-avoidance techniques in light of the other arrangements being promoted at the time. See, e. g., Zeitlin, Tax Planning in Equipment-Leasing

In so concluding, we emphasize that we are not condoning manipulation by a taxpayer through arbitrary labels and dealings that have no economic significance. Such, however, has not happened in this case.

OPINION

In short, we hold that where, as here, there is a genuine multiple-party transaction with economic substance which is compelled or encouraged by business or regulatory realities, is imbued with tax-independent considerations, and is not shaped solely by tax-avoidance features that have meaningless labels attached, the Government should honor the allocation of rights and duties effectuated by the parties. Expressed another way, so long as the lessor retains significant and genuine attributes of the traditional lessor status, the form of the transaction adopted by the parties governs for tax purposes. What those attributes are in any particular case will necessarily depend upon its facts. It suffices to say that, as here, a sale-and-leaseback, in and of itself, does not necessarily operate to deny a taxpayer's claim for deductions.[52]

Hort v. Commissioner

United States Supreme Court
313 U.S. 28 (1941)

We must determine whether the amount petitioner received as consideration for cancellation of a lease of realty in New York City was ordinary gross income as defined in § 22(a) of the Revenue Act of 1932, 47 Stat. 169, 178, 26 U.S.C.A. Int.Rev.Acts, page 487, and whether in any event, petitioner sustained a loss through cancellation of the lease which is recognized in § 23(e) of the same Act, 47 Stat. 169, 180, 26 U.S.C.A. Int.Rev.Acts, page 490.

Petitioner acquired the property, a lot and ten-story office building, by devise from his father in 1928. At the time he became owner, the premises were leased to a firm which had sublet the main floor to the Irving Trust Co. In 1927, five years before the head lease expired, the Irving Trust Co. and petitioner's father executed a contract in which the latter agreed to lease the main floor and basement to the former for a term of fifteen years at an annual rental of $25,000, the term to commence at the expiration of the head lease.

In 1933, the Irving Trust Co. found it unprofitable to maintain a branch in petitioner's building. After some negotiations, petitioner and the Trust Co. agreed to cancel the lease in consideration of a payment to petitioner of $140,000. Petitioner did not include this amount in gross income in his income tax return for 1933. On

---

Shelters, 1969 So. Cal. Tax Inst. 621; Marcus, *Real Estate Purchase-Leasebacks as Secured Loans*, 2 Real Estate L.J. 664 (1974).

52. [19] *See generally* Comm'r v. Danielson, 378 F.2d 771 (3d Cir. 1967), *cert. denied*, 389 U.S. 858 (1967), *on remand*, 50 T.C. 782 (1968); Levinson v. Comm'r, 45 T.C. 380 (1966); World Publishing Co. v. Comm'r, 299 F.2d 614 (8th Cir. 1962); Northwest Acceptance Corp. v. Comm'r, 58 T.C. 836 (1972), *aff'd*, 500 F.2d 1222 (9th Cir. 1974); Cubic Corp. v. U.S., 541 F.2d 829 (9th Cir. 1976).

the contrary, he reported a loss of $21,494.75 on the theory that the amount he received as consideration for the cancellation was $21,494.75 less than the difference between the present value of the unmatured rental payments and the fair rental value of the main floor and basement for the unexpired term of the lease. He did not deduct this figure, however, because he reported other losses in excess of gross income.

The Commissioner included the entire $140,000 in gross income, disallowed the asserted loss, made certain other adjustments not material here, and assessed a deficiency. The Board of Tax Appeals affirmed. 39 B.T.A. 922. The Circuit Court of Appeals affirmed per curiam on the authority of *Warren Service Corp. v. Helvering*, 110 F.2d 723 (2d Cir. 1940). 112 F.2d 167 (2d Cir. 1940). Because of conflict with *Comm'r v. Langwell Real Estate Corp.*, 47 F.2d 841 (7th Cir. 1931) we granted certiorari limited to the question whether, "in computing net gain or loss for income tax purposes, a taxpayer (can) offset the value of the lease canceled against the consideration received by him for the cancellation." 311 U.S. 641 (1940).

Petitioner apparently contends that the amount received for cancellation of the lease was capital rather than ordinary income and that it was therefore subject to §§ 101, 111–113, and 117, 47 Stat. 169, 191, 195–202, 207, 26 U.S.C.A. Int.Rev.Acts, pages 504, 510–514, 524, which govern capital gains and losses. Further, he argues that even if that amount must be reported as ordinary gross income he sustained a loss which § 23(e) authorizes him to deduct. We cannot agree.

The amount received by petitioner for cancellation of the lease must be included in his gross income in its entirety. Section 22(a), copied in the margin,[53] expressly defines gross income to include "gains, profits, and income derived from ... rent, ... or gains or profits and income from any source whatever." Plainly this definition reached the rent paid prior to cancellation just as it would have embraced subsequent payments if the lease had never been canceled. It would have included a prepayment of the discounted value of unmatured rental payments whether received at the inception of the lease or at any time thereafter. Similarly, it would have extended to the proceeds of a suit to recover damages had the Irving Trust Co. breached the lease instead of concluding a settlement. Compare *United States v. Safety Car Heating Co.*, 297 U.S. 88 (1936); *Burnet v. Sanford & Brooks Co.*, 282 U.S. 359 (1931). That the amount petitioner received resulted from negotiations ending in cancellation of the lease rather than from a suit to enforce it cannot alter the fact that basically the payment was merely a substitute for the rent reserved in the lease. So far as the application of $ 22(a) is concerned, it is immaterial that petitioner chose to accept an amount

---

53. [1] Sec. 22(a). "'Gross income' includes gains, profits, and income derived from salaries, wages, or compensation for personal service, of whatever kind and in whatever form paid, or from professions, vocations, trades, businesses, commerce, or sales, or dealings in property, whether real or personal, growing out of the ownership or use of or interest in such property; also from interest, rent, dividends, securities, or the transaction of any business carried on for gain or profit, or gains or profits and income derived from any source whatever."

less than the strict present value of the unmatured rental payments rather than to engage in litigation, possibly uncertain and expensive.

The consideration received for cancellation of the lease was not a return of capital. We assume that the lease was "property," whatever that signifies abstractly. Presumably the bond in *Helvering v. Horst*, 311 U.S. 112 (1940), and the lease in *Helvering v. Bruun*, 309 U.S. 461 (1940), were also 'property', but the interest coupon in Horst and the building in Bruun nevertheless were held to constitute items of gross income. Simply because the lease was "property" the amount received for its cancellation was not a return of capital, quite apart from the fact that "property" and "capital" are not necessarily synonymous in the Revenue Act of 1932 or in common usage. Where, as in this case, the disputed amount was essentially a substitute for rental payments which § 22(a) expressly characterizes as gross income, it must be regarded as ordinary income, and it is immaterial that for some purposes the contract creating the right to such payments may be treated as "property" or "capital."

For the same reasons, that amount was not a return of capital because petitioner acquired the lease as an incident of the realty devised to him by his father. Theoretically, it might have been possible in such a case to value realty and lease separately and to label each a capital asset. Compare *Maass v. Higgins*, 312 U.S. 443 (1941); *Appeal of Farmer*, 1 B.T.A. 711 (1925). But that would not have converted into capital the amount petitioner received from the Trust Co. since § 22(b)(3)[54] of the 1932 Act, 47 Stat. 169, 178, would have required him to include in gross income the rent derived from the property, and that section, like § 22(a), does not distinguish rental payments and a payment which is clearly a substitute for rental payments.

We conclude that petitioner must report as gross income the entire amount received for cancellation of the lease without regard to the claimed disparity between that amount and the difference between the present value of the unmatured rental payments and the fair rental value of the property for the unexpired period of the lease. The cancellation of the lease involved nothing more than relinquishment of the right to future rental payments in return for a present substitute payment and possession of the leased premises. Undoubtedly it diminished the amount of gross income petitioner expected to realize, but to that extent he was relieved of the duty to pay income tax. Nothing in § 23(e)[55] indicates that Congress intended to allow petitioner

---

54. [2] Sec. 22(b). 'The following items shall not be included in gross income and shall be exempt from taxation under this title: ..."(3) The value of property acquired by gift, bequest, devise, or inheritance (but the income from such property shall be included in gross income)." 26 U.S.C.A. Int.Rev.Acts, page 487.

55. [3] Sec. 23(e). "Subject to the limitations provided in subsection (r) of this section, in the case of an individual, losses sustained during the taxable year, and not compensated for by insurance or otherwise (shall be deductible from gross income) — (1) if incurred in trade or business; or (2) if incurred in any transaction entered into for profit, though not connected with the trade or business; or (3) of property not connected with the trade or business, if the loss arises from fires, storms, shipwreck, or other casualty, or from theft. No loss shall be allowed as a deduction under this paragraph

to reduce ordinary income actually received and reported by the amount of income he failed to realize. *See Warren Service Corp. v. Helvering, supra; Josey v. Comm'r,* 104 F.2d 453 (10th Cir. 1939); *Tiscornia v. Comm'r,* 95 F.2d 678 (9th Cir., 1938); *Farrelly-Walsh, Inc., v. Comm'r,* 13 B.T.A. 923 (1928); *Georcke Co. v. Comm'r,* 7 B.T.A. 860 (1927); *Merckens v. Comm'r,* 7 B.T.A. 32 (1927). *Compare, U.S. v. Safety Car Heating Co., supra; Voliva v. Comm'r,* 36 F.2d 212 (7th Cir. 1929); *Appeal of Denholm & McKay Co.,* 2 B.T.A. 444 (1925). We may assume that petitioner was injured insofar as the cancellation of the lease affected the value of the realty. But that would become a deductible loss only when its extent had been fixed by a closed transaction. Regulations No. 77, Art. 171, p. 46; *U.S. v. White Dental Mfg. Co.,* 274 U.S. 398 (1927).

Handlery Hotels, Inc. v. United States
United States Court of Appeals, Ninth Circuit
663 F.2d 892 (1981)

I. BACKGROUND

The plaintiff-appellant, Handlery Hotels, Inc. ("Handlery"), lessor, paid $85,000 to its then lessee, Kreis-Grundy Corporation ("Kreis"), to terminate a lease having an unexpired term of three years remaining. Concurrently, Handlery entered into a new and more favorable lease with Casual Corner of Stonestown, Inc. ("Casual Corner") for a term of twenty years.

Prior to the above transactions Handlery was interested in negotiating with Kreis for an extension of Kreis' existing lease at a higher monthly rental but instead decided to seek a new lease.

Handlery amortized the $85,000 cancellation payment over the three-year unexpired term of the old lease. The Commissioner of Internal Revenue disallowed the three-year amortization period and recomputed the taxes on the basis of a twenty-year amortization period, a period equal to the duration of the new lease. Handlery paid the deficiency and brought this action against the United States for refund.

In the court below, both Handlery and the United States filed motions for summary judgment. The district court denied Handlery's motion and granted the government's motion, holding that the cancellation payment was a cost of obtaining the new lease and therefore should be amortized over the term of the new lease rather than amortized over the unexpired term of the old lease.

The only issue presented in this appeal is whether the lease cancellation payment should be considered a cost of obtaining the new lease and, thus, amortizable over the term of the new lease or a cost of regaining the old leasehold and, thus, amortizable over the remaining unexpired term of the old lease.

---

if at the time of the filing of the return such loss has been claimed as a deduction for estate tax purposes in the estate tax return."

Handlery contends the amortization period should be the unexpired term of the old lease (three years) while the government contends that it should be the term of the new lease (twenty years).

II. DISCUSSION

There are several cases involving lease cancellation payments, but they encompass different fact situations, address a variety of contentions and issues and have conflicting results.

A. General Rule

When the courts were first faced with the question of what should be the tax effect of the lessor's cost in cancelling a lease, the issue was whether it should be considered a business expense and deductible immediately, or a capital expense and therefore amortized.

The first case to address this issue, *Higginbotham-Bailey-Logan Co. v. Comm'r*, 8 B.T.A. 566 (1927), held that cancellation cost was a business expense. Subsequently, *Higginbotham* was overruled by *Miller v. Comm'r*, 10 B.T.A. 383 (1928), which held that the cancellation cost was amortizable over the unexpired term of the old lease.

In *Miller*, the court stated:

> The amount thus expended is a capital expenditure made in order to obtain possession of premises for a period prior to the time the petitioner would have come into possession under the terms of the lease and affords to him no benefits beyond the period for which the payment is made.

10 B.T.A. at 384.

In *Miller*, the taxpayer-lessor contended that the cost was a business expense, and the Commissioner contended it was amortizable over the unexpired term of the old lease. The dissent in Miller suggested that the cost should either be a business expense or amortized over the term of the new lease. Miller has since been recognized as standing for the general rule of amortizing the cancellation cost over the unexpired term of the old lease.

The cases that have followed the general rule of *Miller* are *Borland v. Comm'r*, 27 B.T.A. 538 (1933); *Manhattan Life Insurance Company v. Comm'r*, 28 B.T.A. 129 (1933); *Berger v. Comm'r*, 7 T.C. 1339 (1946); and *Trustee Corporation v. Comm'r*, 42 T.C. 482 (1964); and, by analogy, *Risko v. Comm'r*, 26 T.C. 485 (1956) (cancellation of partnership agreement); *Fry v. Comm'r*, 31 T.C. 522 (1958), aff'd, 283 F.2d 869 (6th Cir. 1960) (remainderman's purchase of life estate); *Rodeway Inns of America v. Comm'r*, 63 T.C. 414 (1974) (cancellation of contract).

In all of the above cases, except *Risko*, *Fry* and *Rodeway*, the lessor cancelled an old lease and entered into a new lease. In *Miller* and *Borland*, the issue as presented by the parties was whether the cancellation cost was a business expense or should be amortized over the unexpired term of the old lease. In *Manhattan*, the Commissioner conceded that, under *Miller*, the cancellation cost was amortizable over the unexpired term of the old lease. In *Berger* and *Trustee*, the issue as presented by the parties was whether the cancellation cost should be amortizable over the term of the new lease or the unexpired term of the old lease.

B. Business Real Estate Trust Exception to the General Rule

An exception to this general rule has arisen where the lessor cancels the old lease and the building on the premises is demolished and a new building erected.

In such a case, the courts have held that the cost of cancellation is actually a cost of acquiring a new asset and should, therefore, be amortized over the life of the new asset. In *Business Real Estate Trust of Boston v. Comm'r*, 25 B.T.A. 191 (1932) and *Houston Chronicle Publishing Company v. U.S.*, 481 F.2d 1240 (5th Cir. 1973), it was held that the cancellation cost was amortizable over the life of the new building. In *Cosmopolitan Corporation v. Comm'r*, 18 T.C.M. 542 (1959), it was held that the cancellation payment was amortizable over the term of the new lease. All of the above cases, except *Houston*, involved a new lease.

In *Latter v. Comm'r*, 20 T.C.M. 336 (1961), the *Business Real Estate Trust* exception was extended to a case where, under the new lease, the lessor was to make extensive improvements (up to the amount of $600,000) to the building. The *Latter* court held the cancellation payment was amortizable over the term of the new lease.

Given the general rule and this exception, *Montgomery Co. v. Comm'r*, 54 T.C. 986 (1970), is irreconcilable. In *Montgomery*, there was no new building erected. The court recognized the general rule but held that the case fell within the *Business Real Estate Trust* exception, presumably applying this exception when a lessor cancels a lease to enter into a more favorable new lease (i.e., extending the exception to the general rule, as was done in the district court in the instant case).

C. Wells Fargo Exception to the General Rule

In *Wells Fargo Bank & Union Trust Co. v. Comm'r*, 163 F.2d 521 (9th Cir. 1947), this court addressed the same issue as it arose in a very peculiar fact situation. The court held, under those facts, that payment for lease cancellation was amortizable over the term of the new lease.

In Wells Fargo the lessor cancelled an existing lease that had four years to go, the lessee having the option to cancel at the end of any year of the term. The lessor's cancellation was for the purpose of entering into a new lease for approximately 81/2 months, having an option to renew.

The total payment for cancellation was $65,000 broken down into a payment schedule spread out over nine months. The monthly rental under the new lease was $10,416.66. If the new lease was renewed, the monthly rental was to remain at $10,416.66 until the end of the first year and thereafter was to be $5,000 per month.

The premium paid by the new lessee during the first year, all rental over $5,000 per month, was intended to cover the cost of cancelling the old lease.

The lessor's income under the new lease reflected a higher income during the first year resulting from the new lessee's payment of the premium. Therefore, amortizing the lessor's cancellation payments over that same year (which covered the term of the new lease) provided for a truer reflection of the lessor's income, rather than amortizing over the unexpired four-year term of the old lease.

D. Analysis

To determine the appropriate amortization period, a determination must be made as to which asset will provide the income generated from the cancellation payment. Basically, the cancellation gives the lessor the ability to relet for the unexpired term. This is because the length of the unexpired term is the major variable in determining the cost of cancellation while the amount for which the lessor can relet is presumably controlled by the fair rental value. If a lessor decides to cancel an old lease, presumably the rental under the old lease is less than fair rental value, and the fair rental value would control the amount for which the lessor could relet today. Therefore, the only time variable that could affect the value of cancelling an old lease would be the length of its unexpired term. This formula supports the general rule that the cost of cancellation is directly related to the unexpired term of the old lease rather than the term of the new lease and therefore should be amortized over said unexpired term.[56]

This general rule may not survive well in a situation where the lessor, instead of reletting, builds a new building on the premises. Under such a situation it is more difficult to isolate the time period over which the cancellation payment generates income because of the great change in the income-producing asset. As such it may be reasonable to hold that when a lessor cancels an existing lease for the purpose of demolishing and rebuilding, the cancellation payment is amortizable over the life of the new asset (the new lease or new building). However, we do not reach this issue as the district court granted the government's summary judgment motion expressly stating that its ruling was not based on any finding of any change in the building on the premises. Based upon the above analysis, it follows that amortization over the unexpired term of the old lease provides a more reasonable reflection of Handlery's income than would amortization over the new lease term.

The instant case is also distinguishable from the *Wells Fargo* case. This court in the *Wells Fargo* case recognized under the facts therein that the monies from which the lessor paid for the cancellation were directly traceable to the premium paid by the new lessee for the term of the new lease. It was further recognized that, under the peculiar facts of that case, amortization of the cost to the lessor over the period of the new lease would provide the true reflection of the lessor's income since with respect to the premium paid by the new lessee, the lessor was merely the intermediary taking the premium from the new lessee and passing it on to the old lessee as a cancellation payment. Therefore said premium should not be considered income to the lessor.

E. Conclusion

Since the amortization term to be applied should provide a true reflection of Handlery's income, we follow the general rule of *Miller, supra,* and hold that the payment

---

56. [1] This analysis assumes that the new lease is as long as or longer than the unexpired term of the old lease.

made by Handlery to cancel the existing lease is amortizable over the unexpired term of the old lease rather than the term of the new lease. The summary judgment granted by the district court is reversed and the case is remanded for further proceedings.

Jordan Marsh Company v. Commissioner

United States Court of Appeals, Second Circuit

269 F.2d 453 (1959)

FACTS

The transactions giving rise to the dispute were conveyances by the petitioner in 1944 of the fee of two parcels of property in the city of Boston where the petitioner, then as now, operated a department store. In return for its conveyances the petitioner received $2,300,000 in cash which, concededly, represented the fair market value of the properties. The conveyances were unconditional, without provision of any option to repurchase. At the same time, the petitioner received back from the vendees leases of the same properties for terms of 30 years and 3 days, with options to renew for another 30 years if the petitioner-lessee should erect new buildings thereon. The vendees were in no way connected with the petitioner. The rentals to be paid under the leases concededly were full and normal rentals so that the leasehold interests which devolved upon the petitioner were of no capital value.

In its return for 1944, the petitioner, claiming the transaction was a sale under § 112(a), Internal Revenue Code of 1939,[57] sought to deduct from income the difference between the adjusted basis of the property and the cash received. The Commissioner disallowed the deduction, taking the position that the transaction represented an exchange of property for other property of like kind. Under § 112(b)(1) such exchanges are not occasions for the recognition of gain or loss; and even the receipt of cash or other property in the exchange of the properties of like kind is not enough to permit the taxpayer to recognize loss. Section 112(e).[58] Thus the Commissioner viewed the transaction, in substance, as an exchange of a fee interest for a long term lease, justifying his position by Treasury Regulation 111, § 29.112(b)(1)-1, which

---

57. [1] § 112. Recognition of gain or loss — (a) General rule. Upon the sale or exchange of property the entire amount of the gain or loss, determined under section 111, shall be recognized, except as hereinafter provided in this section. § 26 U.S.C.A. 112.

58. [2] § 112. Recognition of gain or loss — (b) Exchanges solely in kind — (1) Property held for productive use of investment. No gain or loss shall be recognized if property held for productive use in trade or business or for investment (not including stock in trade or other property held primarily for sale, nor stocks, bonds, notes, choses in action, certificates of trust or beneficial interest, or other securities or evidences of indebtedness or interest) is exchanged solely for property of a like kind to be held either for productive use in trade or business or for investment. (e) Loss from exchanges not solely in kind. If an exchange would be within the provisions of subsection (b)(1) to (5), inclusive, or (10), or within the provisions of subsection (1), of this section if it were not for the fact that the property received in exchange consists not only of property permitted by such paragraph to be received without the recognition of gain or loss, but also of other property or money, then no loss from the exchange shall be recognized.

provides that a leasehold of more than 30 years is the equivalent of a fee interest.[59] Accordingly the Commissioner made the deficiency assessment stated above. The Tax Court upheld the Commissioner's determination. Since the return was filed in New York, the case comes here for review. § 26 U.S.C.A. 7482.

Upon this appeal, we must decide whether the transaction in question here was a sale or an exchange of property for other property of like kind within the meaning of § 112(b) and § 112(e) of the Internal Revenue Code cited above. If we should find that it is an exchange, we would then have to decide whether the Commissioner's regulation, declaring that a leasehold of property of 30 years or more is property "of like kind" to the fee in the same property, is a reasonable gloss to put upon the words of the statute. The judge in the Tax Court felt that *Century Electric Co. v. Comm'r*, 192 F.2d 155 (8th Cir. 1951), certiorari denied 342 U.S. 954 (1951), affirming 15 T.C. 581, was dispositive of both questions. In the view which we take of the first question, we do not have to pass upon the second question. For we hold that the transaction here was a sale and not an exchange.

ANALYSIS

The controversy centers around the purposes of Congress in enacting § 112(b), dealing with non-taxable exchanges. The section represents an exception to the general rule, stated in § 112(e), that upon the sale or exchange of property the entire amount of gain or loss is to be recognized by the taxpayer. The first Congressional attempt to make certain exchanges of this kind non-taxable occurred in § 202(c), Revenue Act of 1921, c. 135, 42 Stat. 227. Under this section, no gain or loss was recognized from an exchange of property unless the property received in exchange had a "readily realizable market value." In 1924, this section was amended to the form in which it is applicable here. Discussing the old section the House Committee observed:

> The provision is so indefinite that it cannot be applied with accuracy or with consistency. It appears best to provide generally that gain or loss is recognized from all exchanges, and then except specifically and in definite terms those cases of exchanges in which it is not desired to tax the gain or allow the loss. This results in definiteness and accuracy and enables a taxpayer to determine

---

59. [3] Reg. 111, § 29.112(b)(1)-1. Property Held for Productive Use in Trade or Business or for Investment.—As used in § 112(b)(1), the words "like kind" have reference to the nature or character of the property and not to its grade or quality. One kind or class of property may not, under such section, be exchanged for property of a different kind or class. The fact that any real estate involved is improved or unimproved is not material, for such fact relates only to the grade or quality of the property and not to its kind or class. Unproductive real estate held by one other than a dealer for future use or future realization of the increment in value is held for investment and not primarily for sale. "No gain or loss is recognized if (1) a taxpayer exchanges property held for productive use in his trade or business, together with cash, for other property of like kind for the same use, such as a truck for a new truck or a passenger automobile for a new passenger automobile to be used for a like purpose, or (2) a taxpayer who is not a dealer in real estate exchanges city real estate for a ranch or farm, or a leasehold of a fee with 30 years or more to run for real estate, or improved real estate, or (3) a taxpayer exchanges investment property and cash for investment property of a like kind."

prior to the consummation of a given transaction the tax liability that will result.

(Committee Reports on Rev. Act of 1924, reprinted in Int.Rev.Cum.Bull.1939-1 (Part 2), p. 250.)

Thus the "readily realizable market value" test disappeared from the statute. A later report, reviewing the section, expressed its purpose as follows:

> The law has provided for 12 years that gain or loss is recognized on exchanges of property having a fair market value, such as stocks, bonds, and negotiable instruments; on exchanges of property held primarily for sale; or on exchanges of one kind of property for another kind of property; but not on other exchanges of property solely for property of like kind. In other words, profit or loss is recognized in the case of exchanges of notes or securities, which are essentially like money; or in the case of stock in trade; or in case the taxpayer exchanges the property comprising his original investment for a different kind of property; but *if the taxpayer's money is still tied up in the same kind of property* as that in which it was originally invested, he is not allowed to compute and deduct his theoretical loss on the exchange, nor is he charged with a tax upon his theoretical profit. The calculation of the profit or loss is deferred until it is realized in cash, marketable securities, or other property not of the same kind having a fair market value.[60]

(House Ways and Means Committee Report, reprinted in Int.Rev.Cum.Bull.1939-1 (Part 2), p. 564.)

These passages lead us to accept as correct the petitioner's position with respect to the purposes of the section. Congress was primarily concerned with the inequity, in the case of an exchange, of forcing a taxpayer to recognize a paper gain which was still tied up in a continuing investment of the same sort. If such gains were not to be recognized, however, upon the ground that they were theoretical, neither should equally theoretical losses. And as to both gains and losses the taxpayer should not have it within his power to avoid the operation of the section by stipulating for the addition of cash, or boot, to the property received in exchange. These considerations, rather than concern for the difficulty of the administrative task of making the valuations necessary to compute gains and losses,[61] were at the root of the Congressional purpose in enacting §§ 112(b)(1) and (e). Indeed, if these sections had been intended to obviate the necessity of making difficult valuations, one would have expected them to provide for nonrecognition of gains and losses in all exchanges, whether the property received in exchanges were "of a like kind" or not of a like kind. And if such had

---

60. [4] Emphasis supplied.

61. [5] In *Century Electric Co. v. Comm'r, supra,* 192 F.2d at page 159, the court thought that in the enactment of 112 § Congress "was concerned with the administrative problem involved in the computation of gain or loss in transactions of the character with which the section deals." But so far as appears from the opinion the attention of the court had not been called to the legislative history of the section set forth earlier in this opinion.

been the legislative objective, § 112(c),[62] providing for the recognition of gain from exchanges not wholly in kind, would never have been enacted.

That such indeed was the legislative objective is supported by *Portland Oil Co. v. Comm'r*, 109 F.2d 479 (1st Cir. 1940). There Judge Magruder, in speaking of a cognate provision contained in § 112(b), said at page 488:

> It is the purpose of § 112(b)(5) to save the taxpayer from an immediate recognition of a gain, or to intermit the claim of a loss, in certain transactions where gain or loss may have accrued in a constitutional sense, but where in a popular and economic sense there has been a mere change in the form of ownership and the taxpayer has not really "cashed in" on the theoretical gain, or closed out a losing venture.

In conformity with this reading of the statute, we think the petitioner here, by its unconditional conveyances to a stranger, had done more than make a change in the form of ownership: it was a change as to the quantum of ownership whereby, in the words just quoted, it had "closed out a losing venture." By the transaction its capital invested in the real estate involved had been completely liquidated for cash to an amount fully equal to the value of the fee. This, we hold, was a sale—not an exchange within the purview of § 112(b).

The Tax Court apparently though it of controlling importance that the transaction in question involved no change in the petitioner's possession of the premises: it felt that the decision in *Century Electric Co. v. Comm'r, supra*, controlled the situation here. We think, however, that that case was distinguishable on the facts. For notwithstanding the lengthy findings made with meticulous care by the Tax Court in that case, 15 T.C. 581, there was no finding that the cash received by the taxpayer was the full equivalent of the value of the fee which the taxpayer had conveyed to the vendee-lessor, and no finding that the lease back called for a rent which was fully equal to the rental value of the premises. Indeed, in its opinion the Court of Appeals pointed to evidence that the fee which the taxpayer had "exchanged" may have had a value substantially in excess of the cash received.[63] And in the *Century Electric* case, the findings showed, at page 585, that the taxpayer-lessee, unlike the taxpayer here, was not required to pay "general state, city and school taxes" because its lessor was an educational institution which under its charter was exempt from such taxes. Thus the

---

62. [6] § 112. (c) Gain from exchanges not solely in kind. (1) If an exchange would be within the provisions of subsection (b)(1), (2), (3), or (5), or within the provisions of subsection (1), of this section if it were not for the fact that the property received in exchange consists not only of property permitted by such paragraph or by subsection (1) to be received without the recognition of gain, but also of other property or money, then the gain, if any, to the recipient shall be recognized, but in an amount not in excess of the sum of such money and the fair market value of such other property.

63. [7] It said, page 157: The assessed value of petitioner's foundry building and land upon which it is located for 1943 was $205,000. There was evidence that in St. Louis real property is assessed at its actual value. There was also evidence introduced by petitioner before the Tax Court that the market value for unconditional sale of the foundry building, land and appurtenances was not in excess of $250,000.

leasehold interest in *Century Electric* on this account may well have had a premium value.[64] In the absence of findings as to the values of the properties allegedly "exchanged," necessarily there could be no finding of a loss. And without proof of a loss, of course, the taxpayer could not prevail. Indeed, in the Tax Court six of the judges expressly based their concurrences on that limited ground. 15 T.C. 596.

In the *Century Electric* opinion it was said, 192 F.2d at page 159:

> Subsections 112(b)(1) and 112(e) indicate the controlling policy and purpose of the section, that is, the nonrecognition of gain or loss in transactions where neither is readily measured in terms of money, where in theory the taxpayer may have realized gain or loss but where in fact his economic situation is the same after as it was before the transaction. *See Fairfield S.S. Corp. v. Comm'r*, 157 F.2d 321, 323 (2d Cir. 1946); *Trenton Cotton Oil Co. v. Comm'r*, 147 F.2d 33, 36 (6th Cir. 1945).

But the *Fairfield* case referred to was one in which the only change in taxpayer's ownership was through the interposition of a corporate title accomplished by transfer to a corporation wholly owned by the taxpayer. And in the Trenton Cotton Oil case, the court expressly relied on *Portland Oil Co. v. Comm'r, supra*, as stating correctly the purpose of § 112(b), but quoted only the first of the two requisites stated in *Portland*. As we have already observed, in that case Judge Magruder said that it was the purpose of § 112(b) "to intermit the claim of a loss" not only where the economic situation of the taxpayer is unchanged but also "*where ... the taxpayer has not ... closed out a losing venture.*"[65] Here plainly the petitioner by the transfer finally closed out a losing venture. And it cannot justly be said that the economic situation of the petitioner was unchanged by a transaction which substituted $2,300,000 in cash for its investment in real estate and left it under a liability to make annual payments of rent for upwards of thirty years. Many bona fide business purposes may be served by such a transaction. Cary, *Corporate Financing through the Sale and Lease-Back of Property: Business, Tax, and Policy Considerations*, 62 Harv. L. Rev. 1.

In ordinary usage, an "exchange" means the giving of one piece of property in return for another[66]—not, as the Commissioner urges here, the return of a lesser interest in a property received from another. It seems unlikely that Congress intended that an "exchange" should have the strained meaning for which the Commissioner contends. For the legislative history[67] states expressly an intent to correct the indefiniteness of prior versions of the Act by excepting from the general rule "specifically and in definite terms those cases of exchanges in which it is not desired to tax the gain or allow the loss."

---

64. [8] Under the leases received back by Jordan Marsh Company, the lessee was required to pay all local taxes.

65. [9] Emphasis supplied.

66. [10] *Trenton Cotton Oil Co. v. Commissioner, supra* (109 F.2d 489).

67. [11] Committee reports on Act of 1924 quoted above in this opinion.

OPINION

But even if under certain circumstances the return of a part of the property conveyed may constitute an exchange for purposes of § 112, we think that in this case, in which cash was received for the full value of the property conveyed, the transaction must be classified as a sale. *Standard Envelope Manufacturing Co. v. Comm'r*, 15 T.C. 41 (1950); *May Department Stores Co. v. Comm'r*, 16 T.C. 547 (1951).

Century Electric Co. v. Commissioner

United States Court of Appeals, Eighth Circuit

192 F.2d 155 (1951)

FACTS

The opinion of the Tax Court and its findings of fact, stated in great detail, are reported in 15 T.C. 581. Petitioner accepts the Tax Court's findings of fact as correct.

Since its organization in 1901 petitioner has been continuously successful in business. In its income tax return for the year 1943 it reported gross sales of $17,004,839.73 and gross profits from sales of $5,944,386.93. On December 31, 1942, petitioner owned land, buildings, and improvements of the total depreciated cost of $1,902,552.16. On December 31, 1943, its actual cash on hand amounted to $203,123.70 During the year 1943 it distributed cash dividends of $226,705.69 and made a contribution to Washington University of $42,500. It also held tax anticipation notes and Series G bonds totaling $2,000,000, readily convertible into cash and sufficient to liquidate its outstanding 1943 tax liability and its two outstanding 90-day bank notes due January 20, 1944.

Petitioner has always operated its business in large part on borrowed capital. In 1943 it had open lines of credit with the Chase National Bank of New York of $300,000, with the Boatmen's National Bank of St. Louis of the same amount, and with the Mercantile-Commerce Bank and Trust Company of $400,000. At the end of 1943 its outstanding loans from the Mercantile bank amounted to $600,000 approved by the authorized officers of the bank. Petitioner has always been able to liquidate its outstanding 90-day bank loans as they become due either by payment or renewal.

The assessed value of petitioner's foundry building and land upon which it is located for 1943 was $205,780. There was evidence that in St. Louis real property is assessed at its actual value. There was also evidence introduced by petitioner before the Tax Court that the market value for unconditional sale of the foundry building, land, and appurtenances was not in excess of $250,000.

As of December 1, 1943, the adjusted cost basis for the foundry building, land, and appurtenances transferred to William Jewell College was $531,710.97. The building was a specially designed foundry situated in a highly desirable industrial location. It is undisputed in the evidence that the foundry property is necessary to the operation of petitioner's profitable business and that petitioner never at any time considered a sale of the foundry property on terms which would deprive petitioner of its use in its business.

Petitioner's explanation of the transaction with the William Jewell College is that in the spring of 1943 a vice-president of the Mercantile bank where petitioner deposited its money and transacted the most of its banking business suggested to petitioner the advisability of selling some of its real estate holdings for the purpose of improving the ratio of its current assets to current liabilities by the receipt of cash on the sale and the possible realization of a loss deductible for tax purposes. Petitioner's operating business was to be protected by an immediate long-term lease of the real property sold.

Petitioner's board of directors rejected this proposition as unsound. But in July 1943, when a vice-president of the Mercantile bank suggested to petitioner's treasurer that it would be a good idea for petitioner to pay off all its bank loans merely to show that it was able to do so, petitioner interpreted this advice as a call of its bank loans. Acting on this interpretation, petitioner borrowed from the First National Bank in St. Louis on the security of tax anticipation notes held by it, funds with which it discharged all its bank loans. Immediately thereafter it re-established its lines of bank credit and began consideration of a sale of the foundry property and contemporaneous lease from the purchaser.

On September 2, 1943, petitioner's board of directors adopted a resolution that the executive committee of the board study the situation "and present, if possible, a plan covering the sale and rental back by Century Electric Company of the foundry property." The decision to enter into the transaction described was communicated to the Mercantile bank, but petitioner never publicly offered or advertised its foundry property for sale. The Tax Court found that petitioner "was concerned with getting a friendly landlord to lease the property back to it, as there was never any intention on the part of petitioner to discontinue its foundry operations." Several offers to purchase the foundry property at prices ranging from $110,000 to $150,000 were received and rejected by petitioner.

At a special meeting of the board of directors of petitioner on December 9, 1943, the president of petitioner reported that the officers of petitioner had entered into negotiations for the sale of the foundry property to William Jewell College for the price of $150,000 with the agreement of said college; "that in addition thereto said Trustees of William Jewell College further have agreed to execute a lease of the property so purchased to Century Electric Company for the same time and on substantially the same terms and conditions which were authorized to be accepted by the special meeting of shareholders of this corporation, held on the 24th day of November, 1943." The stockholders at the November meeting had authorized the sale of the foundry property at not less than $150,000 cash, conditioned upon the purchaser executing its lease of the property sold for a term of not less than 25 and not more than 95 years. The Board by resolution approved the proposed transaction with the William Jewell College, but on condition that "this corporation will acquire from Trustees of William Jewell College, a Missouri Corporation, an Indenture of Lease ... for a term of not less than twenty-five years and for not more than ninety-five years." The resolution set out in detail the terms of the lease from the college to petitioner, approved the form of the deed from the petitioner to the college, authorized the president and secretary of petitioner to execute the lease after its execution by the trustees of the college, and directed "that the president and secretary of this corporation be authorized to deliver said Warranty Deed to said purchaser upon receiving from said purchaser $150,000 in cash, and upon receiving from said purchaser duplicate executed Indenture of Lease on the forms exhibited to this Board." The resolution provided that the deed and lease should be dated December 1, 1943, and effective as of that date.

The deed and the lease were executed and delivered as provided by the resolution of petitioner's board of directors. Neither instrument referred to the other. The deed was in form a general warranty deed, reciting only the consideration of $150,000 in cash. The lease recited among others the respective covenants of the parties as to its term, its termination by either the lessor or lessee, and as to the rents reserved.

As of December 31, 1942, the ratio of petitioner's current assets to its current liabilities was 1.74. The $150,000 in cash received by petitioner on the transaction increased the ratio of current assets to current liabilities from 1.74 to 1.80. The loss deduction which petitioner claims on the transaction and its consequent tax savings would if allowed have increased the ratio approximately twice as much as the receipt of the $150,000.

The questions presented are:

1. Whether the transaction stated was for tax purposes a sale of the foundry property within the meaning of §112 of the Internal Revenue Code, 26 U.S.C.A. §112, on which petitioner realized in 1943 a deductible loss of $381,710.97 determined under section 111 of the code (the adjusted basis of the foundry property of $531,710.97 less $150,000) as petitioner contends; or, as the Tax Court held, an exchange of property held for productive use in a trade or business for property of a like kind to be held for productive use in trade or business in which no gain or loss is recognized under §§ 112(b)(1)[68] and 112(e),[69] and Regulation 111, section 29.112(b)(1)-1.[70]

---

68. [1] Sec. 112. Recognition of Gain or Loss. (b) Exchanges solely in kind. (1) Property held for productive use or investment. No gain or loss shall be recognized if property held for productive use in trade or business or for investment (not including stock in trade or other property held primarily for sale, nor stocks, bonds, notes, choses in action, certificates of trust or beneficial interest, or other securities or evidences of indebtededness or interest) is exchanged solely for property of a like kind to be held either for productive use in trade or business or for investment.

69. [2] (e) Loss from exchanges not solely in kind. If an exchange would be within the provisions of subsection (b)(1) to (5), inclusive, or (10), or within the provisions of subsection (l), of this section if it were not for the fact that the property received in exchange consists not only of property permitted by such paragraph to be received without the recognition of gain or loss, but also of other property or money, then no loss from the exchange shall be recognized.

70. [3] Sec. 29.112(b)(1)-1. Property Held for Productive Use in Trade or Business or for Investment.—As used in section 112(b)(1), the words "like kind" have reference to the nature or character of the property and not to its grade or quality. One kind of class or property may not, under such section, be exchanged for property of a different kind or class. The fact that any real estate involved is improved or unimproved is not material, for such fact relates only to the grade or quality of the property and not to its kind or class.... "No gain or loss is recognized if ... (2) a taxpayer who is not

2. Whether if the claimed loss deduction is denied, its amount is deductible as de-
    preciation over the 95-year term of the lease as the Tax Court held, or over the
    remaining life of the improvements on the foundry as the petitioner contends.

ANALYSIS

On the first question the Tax Court reached the right result. The answer to the
question is not to be found by a resort to the dictionary for the meaning of the words
"sales" and "exchanges" in other contexts, but in the purpose and policy of the revenue
act as expressed in section 112. *Compare Federal Deposit Insurance Corp. v. Tremaine*,
133 F.2d 827, 830 (2d Cir. 1943); *Cabell v. Markham*, 148 F.2d 737, 739 (2d Cir.
1945); *Markham v. Cabell*, 326 U.S. 404, 409 (1945); *Brooklyn National Corp. v.
Comm'r*, 157 F.2d 450, 451 (2d Cir. 1946); *Emery v. Commissioner*, 166 F.2d 27, 30
(2d Cir. 1948). In this section Congress was not defining the words "sales" and "exchanges". It was concerned with the administrative problem involved in the computation of gain or loss in transactions of the character with which the section deals.
Subsections 112(b)(1) and 112(e) indicate the controlling policy and purpose of the
section, that is, the non-recognition of gain or loss in transactions where neither is
readily measured in terms of money, where in theory the taxpayer may have realized
gain or loss but where in fact his economic situation is the same after as it was before
the transaction. See *Fairfield S.S. Corp. v. Comm'r*, 157 F.2d 321, 323 (2d Cir. 1946);
Trenton Cotton Oil Co. v. Comm'r, 147 F.2d 33, 36 (6th Cir. 1945). For tax purposes
the question is whether the transaction falls within the category just defined. If it
does, it is for tax purposes an exchange and not a sale. So much is indicated by
§ 112(b)(1) with regard to the exchange of securities of readily ascertainable market
value measured in terms of money. Gain or loss on exchanges of the excepted securities
is recognized. Under § 112(e) no loss is recognized on an exchange of property held
for productive use in trade or business for like property to be held for the same use,
although other property or money is also received by the taxpayer. Compare this subsection with § 112(c)(1) where in the same circumstances gain is recognized but only
to the extent of the other property or money received in the transaction. The comparison clearly indicates that in the computation of gain or loss on a transfer of property held for productive use in trade or business for property of a like kind to be held
for the same use, the market value of the properties of like kind involved in the
transfer does not enter into the question.

The transaction here involved may not be separated into its component parts for
tax purposes. Tax consequences must depend on what actually was intended and accomplished rather than on the separate steps taken to reach the desired end. The end
of the transaction between the petitioner and the college was that intended by the
petitioner at its beginning, namely, the transfer of the fee in the foundry property
for the 95-year lease on the same property and $150,000.

---

a dealer in real estate exchanges city real estate for a ranch or farm, or a leasehold of a fee with 30
years or more to run for real estate, or improved real estate for unimproved real estate...."

It is undisputed that the foundry property before the transaction was held by petitioner for productive use in petitioner's business. After the transaction the same property was held by the petitioner for the same use in the same business. Both before and after the transaction the property was necessary to the continued operation of petitioner's business. The only change wrought by the transaction was in the estate or interest of petitioner in the foundry property. In Regulations 111, § 29.112(b)(1)-1, the Treasury has interpreted the words "like kind" as used in § 112(b)(1). Under the Treasury interpretation a lease with 30 years or more to run and real estate are properties of "like kind." With the controlling purpose of the applicable section of the revenue code in mind, we cannot say that the words "like kind" are so definite and certain that interpretation is neither required nor permitted. The regulation, in force for many years, has survived successive reenactments of the internal revenue acts and has thus acquired the force of law. *United States v. Dakota-Montana Oil Co.*, 288 U.S. 459, 466 (1933); *Helvering v. R. J. Reynolds Tobacco Co.*, 306 U.S. 110, 116 (1939); and *see Comm'r v. Crichton*, 122 F.2d 181 (5th Cir. 1941).

On the second question the Tax Court held that petitioner was not entitled to depreciation on the improvements on the foundry property over their useful life after December 1, 1943. The answer to this question depends upon whether as a result of the transaction under consideration the petitioner has an identifiable capital investment in the improvements on the land covered by the lease. Petitioner contends that the amount of its claimed loss, $381,710.97, should be apportioned between the land and improvements in proportion to their respective cost bases as of November 30, 1943. This would result in an allocation of $277,076.68 of petitioner's investment in the leasehold to the improvements and $104,634.29 to the land. The difficulty with petitioner's position is that it involves assumptions and inferences which find no support in the record. What the petitioner has done is to exchange the foundry property having an adjusted basis of $531,710.97 on December 1, 1943, for a leasehold and $150,000 in cash. Its capital investment is in the leasehold and not its constituent properties. Accordingly, we agree with the Tax Court that petitioner is entitled to depreciation on the leasehold. The basis for depreciation of the leasehold on December 1, 1943, is, therefore, $381,710.97 under § 113(a)(6) of the revenue code, deductible over the term of the lease.

Cassatt v. Commissioner

United States Court of Appeals, Third Circuit
137 F.2d 745 (1943)

In the early part of January, 1935, Cassatt and Company was obligated on several leases of office space for terms not expiring until 1941. The aggregate prospective rentals for these leases was $1,076,000. A settlement was effected with the various landlords whereby for $346,524.06 the leases were cancelled for the unexpired terms. Of this sum all but $121,575 was paid in January, 1935. The balance was payable before January 15, 1941.

The books of Cassatt and Company were kept and its income tax returns were filed on an accrual basis....

The second question with which we are confronted in this case is whether the Board erred in refusing to permit Cassatt and Company to deduct in computing its 1936 taxable income any portion of the sum of $346,524.06 which it agreed in 1935 to pay to its landlords for the cancellation in that year of its existing leases and any portion of the sum of $73,875.02, which represented the then remaining unamortized part of the cost of certain improvements which it had previously made to the leased premises. It will be recalled that all but $121,575 of the amount payable for the cancellation of the leases was paid in 1935, the remainder being payable during the ensuing six years. It is the taxpayer's contention that the entire cost of cancelling the leases, as well as the unamortized improvement costs should have been amortized over the period of six years during which payments were expected to be received under the contract with Pierce. We think however, that the Board rightly held that the whole amounts here in question were deductible in 1935 and in that year only.

It is clear that the obligation of Cassatt and Company to pay the amount exacted for the cancellation of the leases became fixed and certain in 1935, even though payment of a portion of it was deferred. It was, therefore, deductible in that year (*American National Co. v. U.S.*, 274 U.S. 99 (1927), unless it represented prepayment of an expense which would contribute to the production of income in later years, as for example, a prepayment of rent. *Baton Coal Co. v. Comm'r*, 51 F.2d 469 (3d Cir. 1931). Here, however, the payments were in no sense prepayments of rent for they secured no future tenure from the landlords. On the contrary the consideration for them, the cancellation of the leases, was wholly received by Cassatt and Company in 1935 when possession of the leased premises was given up. The payments were not for the use of property at all and they had no connection with the production of income. They were rather in the nature of damages which had to be paid in order to secure relief from an unprofitable contract. Such payments have been held to be deductible for the year in which they are incurred. *Appeal of Denholm & McKay Co.*, 1925, 2 B.T.A. 444. *Compare Taylor v. Comm'r*, 51 F.2d 915 (3 Cir., 1931), in which this court held that damages received for the cancellation of an installment contract constitute income in the year of cancellation to an accrual basis taxpayer and might not be accrued over the remaining portion of the original term of the contract.

Likewise there is no basis for the taxpayer's contention that the unamortized cost of the improvements to the leased premises should have been further amortized over a period subsequent to the year 1935 when the premises were surrendered. The theory of the amortization of such expenditures is that the improvements which they represent will assist in producing income during the whole term of the lease and that consequently it is fair to charge the expenditures ratably against the income of the whole period of the lease. But when the lease is ended the basis for further amortization of such expenditures is gone and consequently any unamortized portion then remaining must at once be charged off.

The taxpayer, while not seriously controverting the propositions just stated, urges that the Commissioner should have permitted the amortization of the sums here in question over the period of the Pierce contract under the authority given him by Section 43 of the Revenue Act of 1934, 26 U.S.C.A. Int. Rev. Code, §43, in order more clearly to reflect the income of Cassatt and Company. But it appears that the taxpayer did not comply with Article 43-1 of Regulations 86 which implements Section 43 by providing that a taxpayer wishing to take a deduction for a period other than that in which it was paid or accrued shall file his return taking the deduction only for the period when paid or accrued and attach thereto a statement requesting the Commissioner to allocate it to a different period and setting forth the facts upon which he bases his claim for such allocation.[71] This regulation is reasonable and within the Commissioner's authority. *Helvering v. Cannon Valley Milling Co.*, 129 F.2d 642 (8 Cir., 1942). The failure of the taxpayer to comply with it leaves him without standing to invoke the provisions of Section 43. Even if the taxpayer were in a position to seek relief under Section 43, however, we do not think that he has made out a case under that section for he has not shown any necessary connection between the 1935 expense and the 1936 income. But in order to invoke Section 43 it must be made to appear that the expense contributed in some measure to the production of the income from which it is sought to be deducted since otherwise application of the section would permit any loss of one year to be used to offset any gain of a subsequent year. Such a result was clearly not contemplated since it would run counter to the fundamental theory of the revenue acts that income taxation is to be based upon a yearly accounting system. *Burnet v. Sanford & Brooks Co.*, 282 U.S. 359 (1931).

Pembroke v. Helvering

District of Columbia Court of Appeals

70 F.2d 850 (1934)

This case involves income taxes for the year 1925. The decision of the Board of Tax Appeals is reported in 23 B.T.A. 1176.

It appears that Andrew J. Pembroke, the petitioner, was the owner of certain real estate located in the city of Columbus, Ohio, described as 82–90 North Front street, and that the property was held by him for investment. In 1925 Pembroke leased the property to a tenant for a term of 99 years in consideration of an annual rental, payable quarterly in advance, of $8,500 for the first five years and $9,000 thereafter. As part of this transaction Pembroke also received from the lessee a conveyance in fee of certain real estate described as 514–30 West Rich street in the city of Columbus, subject to a $20,000 mortgage. Pembroke received this property as an additional consideration for the execution by him of the 99-year lease.

---

71. [1] This provision has been included in the regulations under all the Revenue Acts since the predecessor of Section 43 first appeared in the Revenue Act of 1924. It must, therefore, be regarded as having the force of law. *Helvering v. R. J. Reynolds Tobacco Co.*, 306 U.S. 110 (1939).

It is contended by petitioner that the transaction was an exchange of property within the purview of section 203 of the Revenue Act of 1926 (44 Stat. 9, 12, 26 USCA 934(b)(1), reading in part as follows:

> "Sec. 203.… (b)(1) No gain or loss shall be recognized if property held for productive use in trade or business or for investment … is exchanged solely for property of a like kind to be held either for productive use in trade or business or for investment.…"

The petitioner claims that in this transaction he exchanged the leased premises with the lessee for the real estate conveyed to him by the lessee, both of which properties were held for investment purposes, and that, according to the provisions of the foregoing statute, no taxable gain resulted to him from it. Accordingly he did not enter the value of the real estate conveyed to him by the lessee as a gain or as income realized in that year.

The Commissioner of Internal Revenue, however, held that the transaction in question was not an exchange of property within the intent of section 203, *supra*, but was simply a lease made by Pembroke to the lessee in consideration of the stipulated rental and of the conveyance of the described real estate to Pembroke by the lessee. In other words, the Commissioner held that the transaction was merely a lease executed by petitioner of the leasehold estate upon consideration of the annual rentals reserved in the lease and the conveyance to him of the described real estate by the lessee. The Commissioner accordingly held that the value of the conveyed real estate should have been returned as income by the petitioner.

The Commissioner found that the net value of the property thus conveyed to petitioner was in the sum of $10,000, and accordingly determined a deficiency in his return for 1925 in the sum of $2,075.68.

An appeal was taken by petitioner to the Board of Tax Appeals upon the claim first above stated, to wit, that the transaction was a mere exchange of parcels of real estate of like kind, and was governed by section 203, supra, and therefore was not subject to income tax assessment, and, furthermore, that the value of the equity in the property transferred, subject as it was to a mortgage of $20,000, did not exceed the sum of $5,000.

The Board after hearing testimony upon the subject, sustained the contention of the Commissioner that the transaction was not covered by section 203, *supra*, and that the value of the property received by petitioner from the lessee was taxable as income. The Board also sustained the valuation of $10,000 which the Commissioner had placed upon the equity in the transferred property. Accordingly, the Board reaffirmed the determination of the Commissioner. This appeal followed.

Upon a review of the record, it seems to us quite manifest that the decision of the Board was correct. The transaction in question plainly was not an exchange of property by the parties, but was a lease by petitioner to the lessee of the designated leasehold estate for which the lessee paid an initial rental by means of the transfer of the property referred to, and stipulated to pay a continuing annual rental throughout the term.

Consequently the value of the equity in the premises conveyed to petitioner at the beginning of the term constituted in effect a payment of rental, and was taxable accordingly. In our opinion, the finding of the Board should not be disturbed. Accordingly the decision appealed from is affirmed.

Stough v. Commissioner

United States Tax Court

144 T.C. 306 (2015)

OPINION

RUWE, JUDGE:

Respondent determined a $300,332 deficiency in petitioners' 2008 Federal income tax and a $58,117.20 accuracy-related penalty under section 6662(a).[72] On one of their 2008 Schedules E, Supplemental Income and Loss, petitioners reported as rents received a $1 million payment from Talecris Plasma Resources, Inc. (Talecris). Petitioners then claimed an offsetting $1 million Schedule E "contribution to construct" deduction (Schedule E deduction). Upon examination respondent disallowed the $1 million Schedule E deduction but increased petitioners' basis in the subject rental property and allowed petitioners $87,868 in additional depreciation.[73] Petitioners no longer contend that they are entitled to the $1 million Schedule E deduction but instead argue that they improperly reported as rents received the $1 million payment.

After concessions by the parties,[74] the issues remaining for decision are: (1) whether the $1 million lump-sum payment made by Talecris during the taxable year 2008 is rental income to petitioners; (2) if the $1 million payment is rental income, whether petitioners may allocate the $1 million payment proportionately over the life of the lease pursuant to section 467; and (3) whether petitioners are liable for an accuracy-related penalty under section 6662(a).

FINDINGS OF FACT

Some of the facts have been stipulated and are so found. The stipulation of facts and the attached exhibits are incorporated herein by this reference.

At the time the petition was filed, Michael H. Stough (petitioner) resided in Wyoming, and Barbara M. Stough resided in Ohio.[75]

---

72. [1] Unless otherwise indicated, all section references are to the Internal Revenue Code in effect for the year in issue, and all Rule references are to the Tax Court Rules of Practice and Procedure.

73. [2] The parties agree that if we sustain respondent's determination as to the $1 million in rental income and disallowance of the $1 million Schedule E deduction, then the $87,868 in additional depreciation is allowable.

74. [3] Petitioners concede: (1) $2,773 in ordinary dividend income; (2) $1,808 in qualified dividend income; (3) $20,699 in interest income; and (4) $34,343 in Schedule E income as set forth in the notice of deficiency. Petitioners further concede a $463 utility expense deduction. Petitioners agree that respondent properly adjusted the total amount of deductions petitioners claimed on Schedule A, Itemized Deductions, for 2008 by increasing the deductions by $14,747.

75. [4] The parties stipulate that petitioners maintained a mailing address in Ohio at the time they filed their petition.

Petitioner is the sole shareholder of an Ohio corporation named Stough Development Corp. (SDC). SDC was incorporated in January 1994 and, for the taxable year at issue, operated as a subchapter S corporation. SDC is a real estate development company primarily in the business of acquiring and developing real estate for use as plasma collection centers.

Talecris, a Delaware corporation and wholly owned subsidiary of Talecris Biotherapeutics Holdings Corp. (Talecris Holdings), also a Delaware corporation,[76] operates plasma collection centers in various locations throughout the continental United States for the purpose of manufacturing and selling plasma protein therapeutics.

On December 15, 2006, SDC and Talecris entered into a development agreement and related guaranty agreement wherein SDC agreed to acquire real property in a location acceptable to Talecris and to construct a plasma collection center pursuant to Talecris' specifications. Attached as an exhibit to the development agreement was a proposed lease to be entered into by SDC and Talecris once the plasma collection center project was complete. The proposed lease required Talecris to lease the plasma collection center from SDC for an initial term of 10 years. Petitioner negotiated the terms of both the development agreement and the proposed lease on behalf of SDC, while James H. Moose acted as the lead negotiator for Talecris.[77]

On September 10, 2007, pursuant to the terms of the development agreement, SDC acquired title via general warranty deed to a parcel of real property in North Carolina (NC property). In order to fund the acquisition of the NC property and to facilitate the subsequent construction of the plasma collection center, SDC took out a commercial loan with PNC Bank. Petitioner was personally liable for the commercial loan. Talecris was not liable on or obligated to make payments under the commercial loan.

On September 24, 2007, SDC transferred to Wintermans, LLC (Wintermans), title to the NC property via general warranty deed. Wintermans is an Ohio limited liability company wholly owned by petitioner and is treated as a disregarded entity for purposes of Federal income tax for the taxable year 2008.

On February 19, 2008, SDC received a certificate of occupancy for the newly constructed plasma collection center. Talecris moved into the plasma collection center sometime in February 2008. Although the proposed lease between Talecris and SDC had not yet been executed when Talecris moved into the plasma collection center, Talecris began paying rent on March 1, 2008.

On June 6, 2008, Wintermans and Talecris executed the proposed lease[78] whereby Talecris agreed to lease the plasma collection center from Wintermans for 10 years.

---

76. [5] On June 1, 2011, Grifols Therapeutics, Inc., a Spanish corporation headquartered in Barcelona, Spain, acquired Talecris Holdings and all of its subsidiaries, including Talecris.

77. [6] Mr. Moose was an executive at Talecris from 2005 to 2010. When Mr. Moose retired from Talecris in 2010 his title was senior vice president.

78. [7] Talecris and SDC executed the December 15, 2006, development agreement with a related guaranty and proposed lease. The final lease of the plasma collection center, executed on June 6, 2008, involved Talecris and Wintermans.

There is no indication and the parties do not argue that the terms of the proposed lease and the final lease differ. The lease required Talecris to pay monthly rent to Wintermans, and the rent would be determined by a mathematical formula based on "project costs" that SDC incurred in acquiring and developing the plasma collection center. Article 1 of the lease defines project costs as "the sum of (a) the Acquisition Costs, (b) the Hard Construction Costs, (c) the Soft Construction Costs, and (d) the Financing Costs." The calculation of monthly rent to be paid by Talecris to Wintermans involves a two-step process: (1) project costs are multiplied by 90% to arrive at "base rent";[79] and (2) base rent is multiplied by 125% and then divided by 12 to arrive at monthly rent.

Section 4.1(a)(v) of the lease allows Talecris, on or before the commencement date, to provide written notice to Wintermans to elect to pay or reimburse Wintermans in a lump sum for any portion of the project costs. Section 4.1(a)(v) of the lease provides:

> (v) Notwithstanding any other provisions of this Lease to the contrary, Tenant may, by written notice given by Tenant to Landlord on or prior to the Commencement Date, elect to pay or reimburse Landlord in a lump sum for any portion of the Project Costs as Tenant may specify in such notice. If Tenant makes such an election, Tenant shall, on or prior to the Commencement Date, make a lump sum payment to Landlord in respect of Project Costs in the amount specified in Tenant's notice of election, and, for purposes of determining the Assumed Term Loan Principal Amount, the Assumed Term Loan Amortization Amount and the Base Rent, the Project Costs and the Maximum Project Costs shall be reduced by the amount of such payment.

Because rent is a function of project costs, a lump-sum payment under section 4.1(a)(v) of the lease would reduce project costs, and consequently, reduce the amount of rent that Talecris owed under the lease. It was within the sole discretion of Talecris to make an election under section 4.1(a)(v) of the lease and to determine the amount of such lump-sum payment.

As of April 1, 2008, there was an outstanding balance of $2,365,400.72 owed by SDC on the commercial loan. On April 17, 2008, Talecris made a $1 million lump-sum payment to Wintermans pursuant to section 4.1(a)(v) of the lease.[80] Petitioners applied the $1 million lump-sum payment to the outstanding balance of the PNC Bank commercial loan.

Talecris issued to Wintermans a Form 1099–MISC, Miscellaneous Income (original Form 1099–MISC), reporting rents of $1,151,493.18 for 2008. This amount represents

---

79. [8] In years 6–10 of the lease, Talecris' base rent increases to 103% of the base rent in effect for the immediately preceding lease year.

80. [9] Although the lease was not executed until June 6, 2008, the parties agree that the $1 million lump-sum payment was made pursuant to section 4.1(a)(v), the terms of which are identical in both the proposed lease and the final lease. It is unclear from the record whether Talecris provided written notice of its election to Wintermans.

$151,493.18 in monthly rent for the plasma collection center along with the $1 million lump-sum payment pursuant to section 4.1(a)(v) of the lease.

Petitioners jointly filed a Form 1040, U.S. Individual Income Tax Return, for 2008. On one of the Schedules E attached to the return petitioners reported rents received of $1,151,493 in connection with the plasma collection center rental. Among the deductions that petitioners claimed on this Schedule E was a $1 million "contribution to construct" expense. Certified public accountant (C.P.A.) Thomas D. Heldman prepared petitioners' Form 1040 for 2008.

On April 16, 2010, respondent began an examination of petitioners' 2008 tax return. In a letter dated November 18, 2010, Michael V. Paul, chief operating officer of SDC, wrote to Staci Baranchak, Talecris' accounts payable manager, requesting, inter alia, that Talecris amend the original Form 1099–MISC issued to Wintermans to treat the $1 million lump-sum payment as a "buy-down reimbursement" of construction cost. At a date not specified in the record, Talecris issued to Wintermans a corrected Form 1099–MISC (corrected Form 1099–MISC), reporting rents of $151,493.18 for 2008.

On January 12, 2011, respondent issued to petitioners a notice of deficiency for 2008, disallowing the claimed $1 million Schedule E deduction but increasing petitioners' basis in the plasma collection center and allowing petitioners $87,868 in additional depreciation.[81] Petitioners timely filed a petition disputing the determinations in the notice of deficiency.

OPINION

As a general rule, the Commissioner's determinations in the notice of deficiency are presumed correct, and the taxpayers bear the burden of proving that the determinations are in error. Rule 142(a); *Welch v. Helvering*, 290 U.S. 111, 115, 54 S.Ct. 8, 78 L.Ed. 212 (1933). Pursuant to section 7491(a)(1), the burden of proof with respect to relevant factual issues may shift to the Commissioner. Specifically, section 7491(a)(1) provides: "If, in any court proceeding, a taxpayer introduces credible evidence with respect to any factual issue relevant to ascertaining the liability of the taxpayer for any tax imposed by subtitle A or B, the Secretary shall have the burden of proof with respect to such issue." Section 7491(a)(2) further provides that the burden of proof shifts to the Commissioner only when the taxpayer has: (1) "complied with the requirements under this title to substantiate any item," and (2) "maintained all records required under this title and has cooperated with reasonable requests by the Secretary for witnesses, information, documents, meetings, and interviews." " 'Credible evidence is the quality of evidence which, after critical analysis, the court would find sufficient upon which to base a decision on the issue if no contrary evidence were submitted.' " *Higbee v. Commissioner*, 116 T.C. 438, 442, 2001 WL 617230 (2001) (quoting H.R. Conf. Rept. No. 105–599, at 240–241 (1998), 1998–3 C.B. 747, 994–

---

81. [10] The basis increase is allocated as follows: (1) $241,999.66 to the land; (2) $626,526.53 to the plasma collection center building; and (3) $131,473.81 to fixtures. This results in additional depreciation for 2008 of $12,737 for the plasma collection center building and $75,131 for the fixtures.

995). Because we decide this case on the preponderance of the evidence, the allocation of the burden of proof does not affect the outcome and need not be decided. *See Knudsen v. Commissioner*, 131 T.C. 185, 189, 2008 WL 4977642 (2008).

1. *Rental Income*

The first issue for decision is whether the $1 million lump-sum payment made by Talecris to Wintermans pursuant to section 4.1(a)(v) of the lease constitutes rental income to petitioners for 2008. Although petitioners initially reported this amount as rental income on one of their Schedules E, they now argue that this reporting was in error and that the $1 million lump-sum payment does not constitute rental income for 2008. Specifically, petitioners argue that the $1 million lump-sum payment was not intended as rent by the parties to the lease but rather was meant to reimburse petitioners for leasehold improvements to the plasma collection center. Respondent argues that "the $1,000,000.00 payment received by the petitioners from * * * [Talecris] is considered additional rental income to the petitioners pursuant to Treasury Regulation § 1 .61–8(c) and was properly reported as such on petitioners' 2008 Form 1040."

Section 61(a) defines gross income to mean all income from whatever source derived, including rental payments received or accrued during the taxable year. Sec. 61(a)(5); sec. 1.61-8(a), Income Tax Regs. Section 1.61-8(c), Income Tax Regs., provides, in pertinent part:

> (c) Expenditures by lessee. — As a general rule, if a lessee pays any of the expenses of his lessor such payments are additional rental income of the lessor. If a lessee places improvements on real estate which constitute, in whole or in part, a substitute for rent, such improvements constitute rental income to the lessor. Whether or not improvements made by a lessee result in rental income to the lessor in a particular case depends upon the intention of the parties, which may be indicated either by the terms of the lease or by the surrounding circumstances. * * *

When a lessee pays an expense or obligation incurred by the lessor in bringing the leased property into existence, there is a direct economic benefit to the lessor to the extent that the lessor is relieved of his or her financial obligations. Under these circumstances there is no ambiguity regarding the financial benefit that the lessor receives. That being the case, there need be no inquiry into the intent of the lessor and lessee unless the lessee's payments were unrelated to the lease. In the instant case there is no question that the $1 million lump-sum payment was made pursuant to the terms of the lease; was optional at the election of the lessee; was to "reimburse" the lessor for "project costs"[82] incurred and paid by the lessor in bringing the property into existence; and reduced the lessee's future rents otherwise due. Given these facts the $1 million lump-sum payment falls within the purview of section 1.61-8(c), Income Tax Regs., as the lessee's payment of the lessor's expenses

---

82. [11] The lease clearly defines "project costs" as the sum of acquisition costs, hard construction costs, soft construction costs, and financing costs. At a minimum, acquisition and financing costs do not constitute a reimbursement for leasehold improvements to the plasma collection center.

and therefore constitutes rent without the need to inquire into the subjective intent of the parties. *See Satterfield v. Commissioner*, T.C. Memo.1975–203, 1975 Tax Ct. Memo LEXIS 170.

Petitioners nevertheless argue that the subjective intent of the parties should control. We disagree because this is not a case of improvements made by a lessee. A lessee's payment for leasehold improvements may or may not result in rental income to the lessor depending on the intent of the parties, which may be indicated by the terms of the lease or by the surrounding circumstances. *Id.; see M.E. Blatt Co. v. United States*, 305 U.S. 267, 59 S.Ct. 186, 83 L.Ed. 167 (1938). There may be situations where an improvement made by a lessee is not intended to compensate a lessor. Indeed, an improvement by a lessee might be worthless or even provide a detriment to the lessor. For example, the useful life of such an "improvement" by the lessee may not extend beyond the term of the lease, in which case it has no value to the lessor and, in fact, may impose a financial detriment if the lessor is responsible for its removal upon termination of the lease. Here the lessee made no leasehold improvements. Rather, the lessee exercised its option to pay $1 million to petitioners in order to reduce the amount of "project costs" for purposes of calculating annual rent.

Even if we were to look into the parties' intentions, the terms of the lease and the surrounding circumstances convince us that the $1 million lump-sum payment was intended as payment for the use of the leased property. First, the operative provision allowing for the lessee's election of a lump-sum payment—section 4.1(a)(v)—is included within article IV of the lease, entitled "RENT". Second, Mr. Moose testified that the purpose of lease section 4.1(a)(v) was to "provide Talecris flexibility in the amount of rental payments that they would be liable for in the future".[83] Third, both parties to the lease treated the $1 million lump-sum payment as rent before respondent's examination of petitioners' 2008 tax return. Talecris reported the $1 million payment as "rent" on the original Form 1099–MISC, and petitioners reported the $1 million payment as rents received on one of their Schedules E. Although the intention of the parties is not determinative in the instant matter, we find that the terms of the lease and the surrounding circumstances indicate that the lessor and the lessee intended the $1 million lump-sum payment to be rent.

2. Section 467

Petitioners argue alternatively that, if we determine the $1 million lump-sum payment to be rental income, they are entitled to report the payment ratably over the 10–year life of the lease pursuant to section 467. In other words, petitioners argue that only a portion of the $1 million lump-sum payment is includible as income for 2008. Respondent argues that petitioners are required to include the entire $1 million payment they received from Talecris in gross income for the year of receipt (i.e., 2008) under section 467. Both parties base their respective arguments on section 467 and

---

83. [12] That Mr. Moose and petitioner testified that they did not consider the lump-sum payment to be "rent" is completely at odds with the terms of the $1 million option and the effect of its exercise.

the regulations thereunder. Neither party cites any caselaw to support those arguments, and the issue is one of first impression in this Court.

Congress enacted section 467 to prevent lessors and lessees from mismatching the reporting of rental income and expenses. H.R. Rept. No. 98–861 (1984), 1984–3 C.B. (Vol.2) 1, 143; Staff of J. Comm. on Taxation, General Explanation of the Revenue Provisions of the Deficit Reduction Act of 1984, at 285–288 (J. Comm. Print 1984). Section 467 provides accrual methods for allocating rents pursuant to a "section 467 rental agreement". In order to qualify as a section 467 rental agreement, an agreement must have: (1) increasing/decreasing rents or deferred/prepaid rents and (2) aggregate rental payments exceeding $250,000. Sec. 467(d)(2); sec. 1.467-1(c)(1), Income Tax Regs. Both parties agree that the lease in this case qualifies as a section 467 rental agreement.[84]

a. *Allocation*

The accrual methods applicable to a section 467 rental agreement are set forth in section 467(b), which provides in part:

SEC. 467(b). Accrual of Rental Payments.—

(1) Allocation follows agreement.—Except as provided in paragraph (2), the determination of the amount of the rent under any section 467 rental agreement which accrues during any taxable year shall be made—

(A) by allocating rents in accordance with the agreement, and

(B) by taking into account any rent to be paid after the close of the period in an amount determined under regulations which shall be based on present value concepts.

Section 467(b)(1)(B) is inapplicable in the instant case, and the parties do not argue otherwise. Therefore, except as provided in section 467(b)(2), the rent determination for any rental period under section 467(b)(1)(A) is made by "allocating rents in accordance with the agreement". Section 467(b)(2) provides for the use of the constant rental accrual method in certain situations. As we explain *infra*, the constant rental accrual method is inapplicable in the situation before us.

Section 467(h) directs the Secretary to "prescribe such regulations as may be appropriate to carry out the purposes of this section". The first case to apply section 467 was *Piccadilly Cafeterias, Inc. v. Unites States,* 36 Fed. Cl. 330 (1996), which was decided before the promulgation of any temporary or final regulations. There the parties' dispute revolved around whether a lease that specified a rent payment schedule could be construed to be an allocation within the meaning of section 467(b)(1)(A). *Id.* at 332–333. In the absence of regulations the Court of Federal Claims held that a rent payment schedule could act as an allocation within the meaning of section

---

84. [13] The lease qualifies as a sec. 467 rental agreement because the rental payments increase in lease years 6–10 and the lease has aggregate rental payments exceeding $250,000.

467(b)(1)(A) and required the taxpayer to report rent in accordance with the rent payment schedule. *Id.* at 335.

Subsequently, on May 18, 1999, the Internal Revenue Service issued final regulations under section 467 that apply to the case before us. T.D. 8820, 1999–1 C.B. 1209. In general these regulations require a lessor and lessee to treat rents consistently and, in certain cases involving tax avoidance, require the parties to account for rent and interest under a prescribed method. Section 1.467-1(c), Income Tax Regs., sets forth rules for allocating rent to a rental period when a section 467 rental agreement contains a specific allocation schedule and also in the absence of such specific allocation schedule. Section 1.467-1(c)(2)(ii), Income Tax Regs., provides:

> (ii) Fixed rent allocated to a rental period. — (A) Specific allocation. — (1) In general. — If a rental agreement provides a specific allocation of fixed rent, as described in paragraph (c)(2)(ii)(A)(2) of this section, the amount of fixed rent allocated to each rental period during the lease term is the amount of fixed rent allocated to that period by the rental agreement.
>
>> (2) Rental agreements specifically allocating fixed rent. — A rental agreement specifically allocates fixed rent if the rental agreement unambiguously specifies, for periods no longer than a year, a fixed amount of rent for which the lessee becomes liable on account of the use of the property during that period, and the total amount of fixed rent specified is equal to the total amount of fixed rent payable under the lease. For example, a rental agreement providing that rent is $100,000 per calendar year, and providing for total payments of fixed rent equal to the total amount specified, specifically allocates rent. *A rental agreement stating only when rent is payable does not specifically allocate rent.*
>
> (B) No specific allocation. — If a rental agreement does not provide a specific allocation of fixed rent (for example, because the total amount of fixed rent specified is not equal to the total amount of fixed rent payable under the lease), *the amount of fixed rent allocated to a rental period is the amount of fixed rent payable during that rental period.* If an amount of fixed rent is payable before the beginning of the lease term, it is allocated to the first rental period in the lease term. If an amount of fixed rent is payable after the end of the lease term, it is allocated to the last rental period in the lease term.

[Emphasis added.]

In applying this regulation to the facts of this case we first find that the lease in question does not "specifically allocate" fixed rent to any rental period within the meaning of section 1.467-1(c)(2)(ii)(A), Income Tax Regs. However, the lease does provide for a fixed amount of rent payable during the rental period (i.e., rent payable pursuant to the terms of the lease). Accordingly, in the absence of a "specific" allocation in the rental agreement, the amount of rent payable in 2008 must be allocated to petitioners' 2008 rental period pursuant to section 1.467-1(c)(2)(ii)(B), Income Tax Regs., which provides that "the amount of fixed rent allocated to a rental period is the amount of fixed rent payable during that rental period." Therefore, petitioners are required to include as gross income the entire $1 million lump-sum payment made pursuant to the terms of the lease for the year of receipt, 2008.

b. *Constant Rental Accrual*

Petitioners argue that they should be permitted to use the constant rental accrual method provided in section 467(b)(2) in order to spread their rental income to other years. However, this method is inapplicable because it was intended to allow the Commissioner to rectify tax avoidance situations, and the regulations provide that this method "may not be used in the absence of a determination by the Commissioner". Sec. 1.467-3(a), Income Tax Regs. No determination was made by respondent concerning tax avoidance. In addition, the constant rental accrual method applies to disqualified leasebacks and long-term agreements. Sec. 1 .467–3(b), Income Tax Regs. The lease sub judice is neither.[85] Finally, any argument that section 467(b)(3)(B), which provides for use of the constant rental accrual method if "such agreement does not provide for the allocation referred to in paragraph (1)(A)", does not apply since we have already held that there was an allocation pursuant to the agreement within the purview of paragraph (1)(A) of section 467(b) and section 1.467-1(c)(2)(ii)(B), Income Tax Regs. Therefore, the constant rental accrual method does not apply to this matter.

c. *Proportional Rental Accrual*

With respect to section 467 rental agreements that do not provide for adequate interest on prepaid or deferred rent, the fixed rent for any rental period is the proportional rental amount. Sec. 1.467-1(d)(2)(ii), Income Tax Regs. Section 1.467-2(a), Income Tax Regs., describes section 467 rental agreements to which the proportional rental method applies:

> (a) Section 467 rental agreements for which proportional rental accrual is required. — Under § 1.467-1(d)(2)(ii), the fixed rent for each rental period is the proportional rental amount, computed under paragraph (c) of this section, if—
>
> > (1) The section 467 rental agreement is not a disqualified leaseback or long-term agreement under § 1.467-3(b); and

---

85. [14] Sec. 1.467-3(b)(2) and (3), Income Tax Regs., provides:

(2) Leaseback. — A section 467 rental agreement is a leaseback if the lessee (or a related person) had any interest (other than a de minimis interest) in the property at any time during the two-year period ending on the agreement date. For this purpose, interests in property include options and agreements to purchase the property (whether or not the lessee or related person was considered the owner of the property for Federal income tax purposes) and, in the case of subleased property, any interest as a sublessor.

(3) Long-term agreement. — (i) In general. — A section 467 rental agreement is a long-term agreement if the lease term exceeds 75 percent of the property's statutory recovery period.

(2) The section 467 rental agreement does not provide adequate interest on fixed rent under paragraph (b) of this section.

As discussed above the lease before us is neither a disqualified leaseback nor a long-term rental agreement, and the parties make no argument to the contrary. Therefore the proportional rental accrual method will apply if the section 467 rental agreement at issue "does *not provide adequate interest* on fixed rent under paragraph (b) of this section." Sec. 1.467-2(a)(2), Income Tax Regs. (emphasis added). Concerning adequate interest on fixed rent, section 1.467-2(b), Income Tax Regs., provides:

> (b) Adequate interest on fixed rent.—(1) In general.—A section 467 rental agreement provides adequate interest on fixed rent if, disregarding any contingent rent—
>
> (i) *The rental agreement has no deferred or prepaid rent as described in § 1.467-1(c)(3);*

[Emphasis added.]

Petitioner argues that the $1 million lump-sum payment is prepaid rent. Section 1.467-1(c)(3)(ii), Income Tax Regs., defines prepaid rent as follows:

> (ii) Prepaid rent.—A rental agreement has prepaid rent under this paragraph (c)(3) if *the cumulative amount of rent payable as of the close of a calendar year exceeds the cumulative amount of rent allocated as of the close of the succeeding calendar year* (determined under paragraph (c)(3)(iii) of this section). [Emphasis added.]

Section 1.467-1(c)(3)(iv), *Example (2)*, Income Tax Regs., provides the following example which is instructive in comparing the " cumulative amount of rent *payable* as of the close of a calendar year" to the "cumulative amount of rent *allocated* as of the close of the succeeding calendar year." (Emphasis added.)

> Example 2.(i) A and B enter into a rental agreement that provides for a 10–year lease of personal property, beginning on January 1, 2000, and ending on December 31, 2009. The rental agreement provides for accruals of rent of $10,000 during each month of the lease term. Under paragraph (c)(3)(iii) of this section, $120,000 is allocated to each calendar year. The rental agreement provides for a $1,200,000 payment on December 31, 2000.
>
> (ii) The rental agreement does not have increasing or decreasing rent as described in paragraph (c)(2)(i) of this section. The rental agreement, however, provides prepaid rent under paragraph (c)(3)(ii) of this section because *the cumulative amount of rent payable as of the close of a calendar year exceeds the cumulative amount of rent allocated as of the close of the succeeding calendar year.* For example, the cumulative amount of rent payable as of the close of 2000 ($1,200,000 is payable on December 31, 2000) exceeds the cumulative amount of rent al-

located as of the close of 2001, the succeeding calendar year ($240,000). Accordingly, the rental agreement is a section 467 agreement.

[Emphasis added.]

The lease entered into between Talecris and Wintermans does not provide for prepaid rent. First, it is necessary to determine "the cumulative amount of rent payable as of the close of * * * [the] calendar year". In 2008 Talecris paid rent to Wintermans totaling $1,151,493.18 ($151,493.18 of monthly rent for the plasma collection center and a $1 million lump-sum payment pursuant to section 4.1(a)(v) of the lease). Therefore, the cumulative amount of rent payable by Talecris as of the close of the 2008 calendar year is $1,151,493.18. Second, it is necessary to ascertain "the cumulative amount of rent allocated as of the close of the succeeding calendar year" (i.e., 2009). As previously held, the lease at issue does not specifically allocate fixed rent to any rental period within the meaning of section 1.467-1(c)(2)(ii)(A), Income Tax Regs. In the absence of a specific allocation, the amount allocated to each year is the amount payable for each rental period. Sec. 1.467-1(c)(2)(ii)(B), Income Tax Regs. Although the record before us does not include the exact amount of rent payable by Talecris for the 2009 calendar year, Talecris did have rent payable during 2009 based on the mathematical formula contained in the lease. It follows logically that the cumulative amount of rent payable as of the close of 2008 ($1,151,493.18) will not exceed the cumulative amount of rent allocated as of the close of 2009 ($1,151,493.18 plus rent payable during 2009). Accordingly, the section 467 rental agreement does not have prepaid rent pursuant to section 1.467-1(c)(3)(ii), Income Tax Regs.

Because the section 467 rental agreement has no prepaid rent, it is deemed to have "adequate interest on fixed rent" under section 1.467-2(b), Income Tax Regs. As discussed above, one requirement for the application of the proportional rental accrual method is that "[t]he section 467 rental agreement does not provide adequate interest on fixed rent". Sec. 1.467-2(a)(2), Income Tax Regs. Pursuant to section 1.467-2(b), Income Tax Regs.,[86] the lease between Talecris and Wintermans does provide for adequate interest on fixed rent. We hold that the proportional rental accrual method does not apply and therefore petitioners must report the $1 million lump-sum payment for 2008.

3. *Section 6662(a) Accuracy–Related Penalty*

Respondent determined that petitioners were liable for a section 6662(a) accuracy-related penalty of $58,117.20 for 2008. Section 6662(a) and (b)(2) imposes a 20% accuracy-related penalty on any portion of an underpayment attributable to a substantial understatement of income tax. Section 7491(c) provides that the Com-

---

86. [15] Sec. 1.467-2(b), Income Tax Regs., provides, in pertinent part:
  (b) Adequate interest on fixed rent. — (1) In general. — A section 467 rental agreement provides adequate interest on fixed rent if, disregarding any contingent rent —
    (i) The rental agreement has no deferred or prepaid rent as described in § 1.467-1(c)(3);
      * * *

missioner bears the burden of production with regard to penalties and must come forward with sufficient evidence indicating that it is appropriate to impose the penalty. *See Higbee v. Commissioner*, 116 T.C. 438, 446, 2001 WL 617230 (2001). However, once the Commissioner meets his burden of production, the burden of proof remains with the taxpayers, including the burden of proving that the penalty is inappropriate because of reasonable cause under section 6664. *See* Rule 142(a); *Higbee v. Commissioner*, 116 T.C. at 446–447.

There is a substantial understatement of income tax for any taxable year if the amount of the understatement for the taxable year exceeds the greater of 10% of the tax required to be shown on the return for the taxable year or $5,000. Sec. 6662(d)(1)(A). Petitioners' understatement of income tax exceeds the greater of 10% of the tax required to be shown on their return or $5,000.[87]

Respondent has met his burden of production in that he has shown that petitioners improperly offset the $1 million lump-sum payment through a Schedule E deduction and that the understatement is substantial. *See Longoria v. Commissioner*, T.C. Memo.2009–162, 2009 Tax Ct. Memo LEXIS 162, at *31.

Petitioners argue that they had reasonable cause because they relied on the advice of their C.P.A., Mr. Heldman.[88] Section 6664(c)(1) provides that the penalty under section 6662(a) shall not apply to any portion of an underpayment if it is shown that there was reasonable cause for the taxpayers' position and that the taxpayers acted in good faith with respect to that portion. *See Higbee v. Commissioner*, 116 T.C. at 448.

"Reasonable cause requires that the taxpayer have exercised ordinary business care and prudence as to the disputed item." *Neonatology Assocs., P.A. v. Commissioner*, 115 T.C. 43, 98, 2000 WL 1048512 (2000), *aff'd*, 299 F.3d 221 (3d Cir.2002). The good-faith reliance on the advice of an independent, competent professional as to the tax treatment of an item may meet this requirement. *Id.* (citing *United States v. Boyle*, 469 U.S. 241, 105 S.Ct. 687, 83 L.Ed.2d 622 (1985)); sec. 1.6664–4(b), Income Tax Regs. Whether a taxpayer relies on the advice and whether such reliance is reasonable hinge on the facts and circumstances of the case and the law that applies to those facts and circumstances. *Neonatology Assocs., P.A. v. Commissioner*, 115 T.C. at 98; sec. 1.6664–4(c)(1), Income Tax Regs. For the reliance to be reasonable, "the taxpayer must prove by a preponderance of the evidence that the taxpayer meets each requirement of the following three-prong test: (1) The adviser was a competent professional who had sufficient expertise to justify reliance, (2) the taxpayer provided necessary and accurate information to the adviser, and (3) the taxpayer actually relied in good faith on the adviser's judgment." *Neonatology Assocs., P.A. v. Commissioner*, 115 T.C. at 99.

We are satisfied that petitioners' 2008 tax return was prepared by a competent professional with sufficient expertise. However, at trial petitioner testified that he

---

87. [16] Petitioners reported a $143,773 tax liability on their 2008 return. The correct liability to be shown was over twice that amount.

88. [17] Petitioners concede that the accuracy-related penalty applies to portions of the underpayment attributable to all adjustments in the notice of deficiency which they previously conceded.

"[b]riefly" reviewed the 2008 tax return before signing it and did not review the Schedule E at issue. Mr. Heldman testified that he did not sit down with petitioners to discuss the prepared tax return before petitioners signed the return. Unconditional reliance on a tax return preparer or C.P.A. does not by itself constitute reasonable reliance in good faith; taxpayers must also exercise "[d]iligence and prudence." *Estate of Stiel v. Commissioner,* T.C. Memo.2009–278, 2009 Tax Ct. Memo LEXIS 273, at *5 (quoting *Marine v. Commissioner,* 92 T.C. 958, 992–993, 1989 WL 47992 (1989), *aff'd without published opinion,* 921 F.2d 280 (9th Cir.1991)). Taxpayers have a duty to read their returns. "Reliance on a preparer with complete information regarding a taxpayer's business activities does not constitute reasonable cause if the taxpayer's cursory review of the return would have revealed errors." *Id.* (citing *Metra Chem Corp. v. Commissioner,* 88 T.C. 654, 662–663, 1987 WL 49292 (1987)). Petitioner was a successful businessman who should have recognized that the $1 million Schedule E deduction for "contribution to construct" was money that, even had it been related to the acquisition and construction of the plasma collection center, would not have been deductible in total in 2008. In fact, the deduction was intended to cancel out the $1 million in rental income that petitioner now claims was improperly reported. Claiming reliance on Mr. Heldman and choosing to not adequately review the contents of a tax return is not reasonable reliance in good faith, and we will not permit petitioners to avoid an accuracy-related penalty for substantially understating their income tax liability. Accordingly, we hold that petitioners are liable for the accuracy-related penalty under section 6662(a).

In reaching our decision, we have considered all arguments made by the parties, and to the extent not mentioned or addressed, they are irrelevant or without merit.

To reflect the foregoing,

Decision will be entered under Rule 155.

Hopkins Partners v. Commissioner

United States Tax Court

97 T.C.M. (CCH) 1560 (2009)

FACTS

Some of the facts and certain exhibits have been stipulated. The stipulations of fact are incorporated in this opinion by reference and are found as facts.

The partnership is an Ohio general partnership formed on September 28, 1995.

The partnership operates the Sheraton Cleveland Airport Hotel (hotel). The hotel is at Cleveland Hopkins International Airport (airport) and is owned by the City of Cleveland, Ohio (city).

The partnership operates the hotel and attendant parking facilities under a leasehold interest assigned to it by its immediate predecessor-in-interest. The leasehold interest was created by a lease from the city to a predecessor-in-interest to the partnership during 1957. Thereafter, various entities which were predecessors-in-interest to the partnership held the leasehold/operator interest through a series of lease concessions and modifications between 1957 and 1990.

The partnership currently has the leasehold right to operate the hotel through November 13, 2048.

The Early Leases

The first lease, the Lease by Way of Concession for a Hotel at Cleveland-Hopkins Airport (1957 lease), was executed on December 12, 1957.

The 1957 lease required the partnership to construct and operate a hotel on the airport premises. The 1957 lease had a total term of 31 years, 4 months.

Under the 1957 lease, title to the hotel passed immediately to the city, and upon termination of the 1957 lease, the hotel premises and all structures and improvements thereon were to remain the property of the city with the exception of furniture, furnishings, fixtures, and equipment that were the personal property of the partnership. After the initial 16-month term, the 1957 lease required the partnership to pay rent of the greater of $4,800 per year or a percentage of gross receipts.

The Supplemental Lease by Way of Concession dated July 30, 1962 (supplemental lease), gave the partnership the use of additional land to be used as parking for customers, and the right to sell food and beverages. The supplemental lease also increased the minimum annual rent to $6,000 per year.

The Second Supplemental Lease dated November 14, 1966 (second supplemental lease), provided additional land for parking; increased the minimum annual rental to $75,000; and extended the term to 35 years from the date of execution. The second supplemental lease also required the partnership to construct an addition to the hotel and to spend $2.8 million on improvements over 5 years.

The Third Supplemental Lease dated March 6, 1969 (third supplemental lease), allowed the partnership to construct hotel additions or improvements on land previously designated for parking.

The Fourth Supplement to Lease by Way of Concession dated January 26, 1984 (fourth supplemental lease), extended the term of the 1957 lease through November 13, 2023, and required the partnership to spend at least $1.25 million on improvements in the initial 5-year period of the fourth supplemental lease and $500,000 on improvements in each subsequent 5-year period. The fourth supplemental lease also provided that all furniture and fixtures would become the property of the city upon termination of the 1957 lease, as amended. The minimum annual rent under the fourth supplemental lease was increased to $150,000 for the initial year of the fourth supplemental lease and was to increase by an additional $9,000 in each subsequent year of the fourth supplemental lease.

The Negotiation of Rent Credits

During the mid-to-late 1980s, the city was enjoying a business and civic rejuvenation following a difficult period. New highway construction facilitated access to the airport. At the same time, the hotel had fallen into disrepair.

The partnership was losing significant amounts of money on the hotel, with projected losses in excess of $500,000 each year through 1997. The partnership was looking for a way to make the hotel profitable. The partnership believed that the rent under the 1969 lease was significantly above the prevailing market rate, and it was seeking rent relief to achieve its objective of making the hotel profitable.

The city was concerned about the condition of the hotel because the hotel was a visitor's first impression of Cleveland. The city wanted the hotel renovated to address the city's concerns and threatened to allow construction of a second hotel on the airport premises if the partnership failed to renovate the hotel. Construction of a second hotel on the airport premises would have put the partnership out of business.

The partnership did not have sufficient cash to make improvements to the hotel, so it attempted to expand its mortgage to cover the cost of improvements. The lender, American Real Estate Group, indicated that it believed the land rent on the hotel was substantially above market and conditioned any additional advance of funds on a substantial reduction in the land rent.

During 1987, the partnership informed the city that the partnership was unable to borrow additional funds to cover the cost of necessary repairs and improvements to the hotel. The partnership proposed a modification of the lease which would have increased the minimum annual rent to $300,000 but would have decreased the percentage rent. The proposed change was expected to result in an overall decrease in rent.

Negotiations regarding the proposed improvements and the change to the rent under the lease ensued between the partnership and the city. The city was in a strong negotiating position because the economic climate in the city at that time was conducive to finding a new operator to construct and operate a new hotel if the city did not obtain the renovations the city wanted.

The partnership submitted to the city a modified proposal in which it again requested that the rent be reduced or, in the alternative, that the cost of improvements be credited against any land rent in excess of $300,000 per year. The city rejected that proposal but later submitted a counterproposal adopting the rent credit approach. The counterproposal allowed the partnership to credit the cost of certain eligible improvements against annual rent in excess of $300,000. The partnership accepted the counterproposal subject to requested changes.

The partnership was concerned with the profitability (or lack thereof) of the hotel and was agreeable to using either a rent reduction or rent credits to achieve its goal of making the hotel profitable. However, the parties believed that the Cleveland City Council, which had to adopt an ordinance approving any lease modification, was unlikely to agree to a rent reduction. Additionally, the parties believed that it was more efficient for the partnership to make improvements than for the city to do so because it avoided the necessity of the City Council's having to approve each step of those improvements. The ultimate decision to structure the leases to include rent credits rather than a rent reduction was motivated by the foregoing concerns, not by tax considerations.

The 1989 Lease Supplement

The Sixth Supplement to Lease by Way of Concession, dated August 11, 1989 (1989 lease supplement), increased the minimum annual rent from $195,000 to $300,000. The percentage rent remained unchanged. However, the 1989 lease supplement entitled the partnership to credits against the percentage rent for certain eligible improvements. Eligible improvements were defined in the 1989 lease supplement and were subject to approval by the city. The partnership was required to spend at least $900,000 every 3 years on eligible improvements. The rent credit in any given year was capped at $400,000, but any eligible improvements made in excess of that limit could be carried forward to future years.

The 1990 Amended Lease

The partnership and the city executed the Amended and Restated Lease by Way of Concession dated December 31, 1990 (1990 amended lease). The 1990 amended lease was effective during the years at issue and remains in effect through trial.

The 1990 amended lease extended the term of the 1957 lease for an additional 35 years. It also permitted the partnership to demolish a portion of the hotel and to convert that area into a parking lot for hotel patrons and public parking patrons.

The 1990 amended lease required the partnership to renovate the hotel tower at a minimum cost of $5 million. The costs related to the renovation were subject to approval by the city and were eligible for rent credits. Additionally, the 1990 amended lease required the partnership to spend $1.5 million on improvements every 3 years. Those expenditures also qualified for rent credits.

The 1990 amended lease increased the maximum amount of rent credit in any given year to $650,000 and allowed any eligible improvements made in excess of that limit to be carried forward to future years.

The Parking Lease

The partnership and the city also entered into a separate Amended and Restated Lease by Way of Concession dated December 31, 1990 (parking lease), allowing the partnership to operate a parking lot on the hotel property. The parking lease was in effect during the years in issue and remained in effect through trial.

The parking lease required the partnership to demolish a portion of the hotel and in its place to construct and operate a parking lot and parking facility.

The parking lease required the partnership to pay annual rent equal to the greater of $100,000 or 10 percent of the gross revenues from parking operations.

The parking lease allowed the partnership a credit against percentage rent for eligible improvements. Any eligible improvements in excess of percentage rent in a given year could be carried forward to be used as a credit against percentage rent in subsequent years.

The 1989 lease supplement, the 1990 amended lease, and the parking lease are sometimes hereinafter referred to collectively as the lease agreements.

The Rent Credit Process

At the start of each year the partnership provided the city with a detailed list of planned eligible improvements. The city had the right to reject planned improvements and occasionally did so. Pursuant to the lease agreements, a failure to comment by the city was deemed an approval.

At the end of each year the partnership submitted to the city a detailed list of expenditures along with documentation of those expenditures. Pursuant to the lease agreements the city had the right to audit the detailed list of expenditures and occasionally rejected items from the list. Eventually, the partnership and the city agreed on what qualified as eligible improvements for that year.

Each year the partnership decided which eligible improvements the partnership would use for rent credit. The partnership documented the eligible improvements the partnership was using to obtain rent credit on a detailed spread sheet provided to the city. In accordance with the lease agreements, title to the eligible improvements vested in the city at the end of the year in which those improvements were credited against rent.

Generally, the partnership elected to receive rent credits for leasehold improvements rather than furniture, fixtures, and equipment (FF & E). The partnership made that election in order to avoid the detailed inventory tracking requirements and the burdensome and unsightly tagging associated with FF & E.

When the partnership made eligible improvements, it accounted for them by recording them on its books as capital assets. Where the partnership received a credit against rent for the full cost of an eligible improvement in the year that the improvement was made, it deducted that cost as a rent expense on its Federal income tax return for that year. When an eligible improvement was not credited against rent in the year it was made, the partnership kept that eligible improvement on the books as a capital asset and depreciated that asset in accordance with §§ 167 and 168. When the partnership received a rent credit for an eligible improvement for which it had claimed a depreciation deduction in a previous year, it treated that as a sale of the eligible improvement for an amount equal to the rent credit and recognized gain, including depreciation recapture, as applicable. The partnership then deducted the cost of the eligible improvement as a rent expense in the year in which it was credited against rent.[89]

The partnership consistently followed the above procedure and that procedure was reviewed by two independent accounting firms.

---

89. [4] Respondent disallowed the partnership's deduction of the cost of eligible improvements as a rent expense in all instances whether the deduction was claimed in the year the improvements were made or in a later year. Respondent's arguments, however, do not distinguish between the two situations, and we note that not all of the arguments are equally applicable to instances where the cost of eligible improvements was deducted in the year they were made (and so were never depreciated) and instances where the partnership depreciated the improvements before using them for rent credit. Since we are not convinced by any of respondent's arguments, we need not consider whether any of the arguments are a basis for disallowing the deduction in one instance but not in the other.

ANALYSIS

Whether the Leasehold Improvements Were a Substitute for Rent

As a general rule, the Commissioner's determinations are presumed correct and the burden of proving an error is on the taxpayer. Rule 142(a); *Welch v. Helvering*, 290 U.S. 111, 115 (1933). In the instant case, the parties agree that petitioner has the burden of proof.

Generally, § 162(a) allows as a current deduction from gross income all the ordinary and necessary expenses incurred in carrying on a trade or business. However, §§ 161 and 261 have the effect of subordinating provisions such as § 162(a) to provisions such as § 263(a)(1), thereby disallowing the current deduction of capital expenditures that otherwise would have been currently deductible trade or business expenses. *Comm'r v. Idaho Power Co.*, 418 U.S. 1, 17 (1974). Unless some other special rule applies (*see, e.g.*, § 263(a)(1)), a taxpayer's deductions for capital expenditures, if allowable at all, generally come by way of amortization or depreciation; i.e., the capital expenditure is deductible over a period of time. Secs. 167, 168, and 169; *INDOPCO, Inc. v. Comm'r*, 503 U.S. 79, 83 (1992).

Capital expenditures are, with limited exceptions, any amounts paid out for new buildings, permanent improvements, and restoration. Sec. 263(a). The parties agree that the eligible improvements in issue are capital expenditures within the meaning of § 263(a).

A taxpayer's entitlement to depreciation deductions for leasehold improvements hinges not on legal title but on a recognized investment in the property. *Gladding Dry Goods Co. v. Comm'r*, 2 B.T.A. 336, 338 (1925); *see also Mayerson v. Comm'r*, 47 T.C. 340, 350 (1966). Consequently, the important question is whether the taxpayer made an investment of capital that the taxpayer is entitled to recover. *Gladding Dry Goods Co. v. Comm'r, supra* at 338 ("The one who made the investment is entitled to its return."). If a lessor makes improvements at the lessor's own expense, the lessor is entitled to depreciation deductions despite the fact that the lessee has the use and enjoyment of the improvements. *Id.* If a lessee makes improvements and the title to the improvements vests immediately in the lessor, the lessor's bare legal title does not preclude the lessee from recovering that lessee's investment through depreciation deductions. *Id.*

Generally, where a lessee makes and invests in improvements on the property leased by the lessee, the lessee is entitled to recover that investment through depreciation deductions rather than through a current business expense deduction. Sec. 1.162-11(b), Income Tax Regs. There is, however, an exception where a lessee places improvements on real estate that constitute a substitute for rent. In that case, § 1.61-8(c), Income Tax Regs., provides that the cost of the improvements made in lieu of rent is rental income to the lessor. Section 1.61-8(c), Income Tax Regs., expressly addresses only the amount to be included in the income of the lessor; it does not address the amounts, if any, that are deductible by the lessee. However, § 1.61-8(c), Income Tax Regs., does make clear that improvements in lieu of rent are rental income to the lessor, and rent is a currently deductible expense for a lessee under § 162(a)(3). Additionally, caselaw provides that, where an improvement is in lieu of rent, the amount invested in the improvement is currently deductible by the lessee as a rent expense. *Your Health Club, Inc. v. Comm'r*, 4 T.C. 385, 390 (1944); *McGrath v. Comm'r*, T.C. Memo.2002-231, *affd. without published opinion* 92 AFTR 2d 6159 (5th Cir.2003). Where improvements are in lieu of rent, the cost of those improvements is actually borne by the lessor through the rent credit, and the lessee has no capital investment to depreciate. *Your Health Club, Inc. v. Comm'r, supra* at 390.

Whether the value of improvements constitutes rent turns upon the intent of the parties to the lease. *M.E. Blatt Co. v. United States*, 305 U.S. 267, 277 (1938); *Cunningham v. Comm'r*, 28 T.C. 670, 680 (1957), *affd.* 258 F.2d 231 (9th Cir.1958); *McGrath v. Comm'r, supra*; see also § 1.61-8(c), Income Tax Regs. The intent of the parties to the lease is derived from the terms of the lease as well as the surrounding circumstances. *Cunningham v. Comm'r, supra* at 680; § 1.61-8(c), Income Tax Regs. Even when the improvements are required by the terms of the lease, they will not be deemed rent unless the intention of the parties to the lease to treat them as rent is plainly disclosed. *M.E. Blatt Co. v. United States, supra* at 277.

We consider in the instant case whether the partnership and the city intended that the eligible improvements be a substitute for rent. Respondent contends that petitioner failed to introduce evidence of the city's intent with respect to the lease agreements, alleging that petitioner relied only on the self-serving testimony of its own agents.[90]

Petitioner did introduce evidence of the intent of the parties to the lease agreements, most notably the lease agreements themselves. Additionally, petitioner introduced the testimony of credible witnesses regarding the lease negotiations and the circumstances surrounding those negotiations. Respondent did not discredit those witnesses at trial, nor did respondent introduce witnesses to rebut the testimony of petitioner's witnesses.

In deciding the intent of the parties to the lease agreements, we first look at the express terms of the documents. Article IV.D of the 1990 amended lease states that the partnership "shall be entitled to receive a credit towards the payment of the annual Percentage Rent, in an amount equal to the cost of eligible improvements ... which have been made and paid for prior to the completion of the lease year". The parking lease, in article IV, paragraph A.5, provides that the partnership "may deduct the cost of eligible improvements made and paid for in a lease year from any Percentage Rent due for that lease year." In *Brown v. Comm'r*, 22 T.C. 147, 148 (1954), *affd.* 220 F.2d 12 (7th Cir. 1955), we held that a similar provision requiring that the cost of improvements "'be credited to the Lessee from the rental due and owing by it under

---

90. [5] Respondent also asserts that petitioner's failure to introduce testimony from the city gives rise to an inference under *Wichita Terminal Elevator Co. v. Comm'r*, 6 T.C. 1158, 1165 (1946), *affd.* 162 F.2d 513 (10th Cir.1947), that the testimony would have been unfavorable. However, *Wichita Terminal* applies to "the failure of a party to introduce evidence *within his possession*". *Id.* (emphasis added). It is inapplicable in this case because petitioner has shown that testimony of the city's agents who negotiated the lease agreements was unavailable.

this lease'" resulted in income to the lessor. The express language of the lease agreements clearly indicates that the parties to those documents intended that the partnership's expenditures for eligible improvements were in lieu of its payment of percentage rent.

When determining whether the parties to the lease intended to treat the cost of improvements as a substitute for rent, consideration must be given to the surrounding circumstances in addition to the express language of the particular lease. *Cunningham v. Comm'r, supra* at 680. One relevant factor is how the parties to the lease treated the expenditure for tax purposes over the course of the lease. *Brown v. Comm'r*, 220 F.2d at 17 (lessee treated the cost of improvements as a rent expense, and the improvements were held to be a rent substitute); *Cunningham v. Comm'r, supra* at 681 (lessee treated the cost of improvements as a capital expense, not a rent expense, and the improvements were held not to be a rent substitute). In the instant case, the partnership consistently treated the eligible improvements, both on its books and in its tax returns, as a deductible rent expense in the year that it obtained a rent credit for the cost of those eligible improvements. That treatment is consistent with the express language of the lease agreements indicating that the eligible improvements were intended by the parties to the lease agreements to be in lieu of rent.

Respondent further argues that "Petitioner's claim that it was the intent of the parties to the lease that the petitioner's capital expenditures were to be made in lieu of rent is further undermined by the fact that the city ... was a tax indifferent party", citing *CMA Consol., Inc. v. Comm'r*, T.C. Memo.2005-16. In *CMA Consolidated*, the presence of a tax indifferent party was a consideration in deciding whether the transaction lacked economic substance, but it is not probative on how the parties intended to structure the transaction.[91] In the instant case, respondent has cited no case standing for the proposition that tax indifference is a consideration in deciding whether the parties to a lease intended capital expenditures to be made in lieu of rent. However, we have considered the tax indifference of the city, and we are persuaded by the record that the city's tax indifference did not play a significant role in the negotiations between the city and the partnership or the city's intent regarding the provisions of the lease agreements.

Accordingly, we conclude that the parties to the lease agreements intended, as evidenced by the express language of the leases and the surrounding circumstances, that the eligible improvements be substitutes for rent. Notwithstanding the intent of the parties to the lease agreements to treat the eligible improvements as substitutes for rent, respondent advances several reasons the eligible improvements should not be treated as deductible rent expenses. We address each of these contentions below.

Whether Rent Credits Must Be Limited in Duration or Amount

Respondent contends that *Your Health Club, Inc. v. Comm'r*, 4 T.C. 385 (1944) and *McGrath v. Comm'r*, T.C. Memo. 2002-231 "can clearly be distinguished in that the rent substitute in both cases was limited to the initial start-up period of the business

---

91. [6] We address the issue of economic substance below in sec. IV.

and the rent substitute made up only a small fraction of the amount claimed as a deduction for rent expense." While respondent correctly points out that in *Your Health Club, Inc.* the rent credit was limited to the initial year of the lease and was just under one-third of the total rent deduction for that year, those limits were imposed by the parties to the lease. In *Your Health Club, Inc.* this Court had no reason to consider a larger credit, and we in no way indicated that a larger credit would have been impermissible. In *McGrath* this Court did limit the amount allowed as a rent substitute. That limitation, however, was based on the intent of the parties to the lease, not on a decision that a larger or longer term rent credit would in all cases be impermissible or incorrect depending on the intent of the parties to other such leases. In *McGrath* we explicitly concluded that neither the lease nor the surrounding circumstances showed that the parties to the lease intended to treat the entire cost of the improvements as a rent substitute. As discussed above, in the instant case, the parties to the lease agreements did intend to treat the eligible improvements as a substitute for rent to the extent of the percentage rent each year. Accordingly, we conclude that respondent's argument that rent credits should be limited in duration and amount is not supported by the cited cases and is inconsistent with the intent of the parties to the lease agreements.

Whether the Transfer of Eligible Improvements Was Illusory

In accordance with article VII.A of the 1990 amended lease and article VII.A of the parking lease, title to eligible improvements vested in the city in the year that those improvements were credited against rent, and the partnership treated each transfer as a deemed sale of the eligible improvement to the city in exchange for the rent credit. Respondent contends that the partnership's transfers of eligible improvements in exchange for rent credits were illusory. In support of that contention, respondent notes that the partnership retained control over and the right to the use of the transferred eligible improvements. Additionally, respondent contends that the partnership could not transfer the eligible improvements to the city because, under the lease agreements, title to those improvements would vest in the city at the end of the lease.

In deciding whether there has been a sale or exchange sufficient to transfer the depreciable interest in an asset from one taxpayer to another, this Court has looked at whether there was a transfer of the benefits and burdens of ownership. *Grodt & McKay Realty, Inc. v. Comm'r*, 77 T.C. 1221, 1237 (1981). *Grodt & McKay Realty, Inc.* lists several factors relevant in determining where the benefits and burdens lie.[92] In the case of leasehold improvements, the balancing factors have been refined by caselaw and the regulations, which provide us with significant guidance in deciding whether

---

92. [7] These factors include: (1) Which party to the transaction has legal title; (2) how the parties to the transaction treated the transaction; (3) whether equity was acquired by the purchaser; (4) whether the purchaser was required to make a present payment; (5) which party to the transaction had the right of possession; (6) which party to the transaction paid property taxes; (7) which party to the transaction bore the risk of loss; and (8) which party to the transaction received the profits generated by the property. *Grodt & McKay Realty, Inc. v. Comm'r*, 77 T.C. 1221, 1237–1238 (1981).

the benefits and burdens (and thus the depreciable interest) lie with the lessor or the lessee.

Depreciation is not predicated upon ownership of property but rather upon an investment in the property. *Mayerson v. Comm'r*, 47 T.C. 340 (1966) (citing *Gladding Dry Goods Co. v. Comm'r*, 2 B.T.A. 336 (1925)). Where leasehold improvements are involved, legal title and the right of possession and enjoyment are not determinative; the important question is whether the lessor or the lessee made the investment in those improvements. *Gladding Dry Goods Co. v. Comm'r, supra* at 338. Generally, where the lessor makes improvements at the lessor's own expense, it is the lessor that has a depreciable interest in the improvements. *Id.* If the lessee makes improvements at the lessee's expense, it is generally the lessee that has a depreciable interest in the improvements. *Id.*; § 1.162-11(b), Income Tax Regs. However, where a lessee makes improvements as a substitute for rent, the lessee has no depreciable interest in those improvements. *Your Health Club, Inc. v. Comm'r, supra* at 390. Such a transaction is not different from one where the lessor paid for the improvements directly and the lessee paid the full rent. *Id.* When the lessor bears the cost of improvements via a rent credit, the lessor has an increased investment in the property, resulting in a higher basis and increased depreciation deductions. *Brown v. Comm'r*, 22 T.C. at 151.

In the instant case, the partnership made the eligible improvements at its own expense. To the extent that it received a rent credit in the year it made the improvements, it appropriately treated the cost of those improvements as a rent expense and deducted that cost currently. *See Your Health Club, Inc. v. Comm'r*, 4 T.C. 385 (1944). To the extent that the partnership did not receive a rent credit in the year that it made the eligible improvements, it had a depreciable interest in those improvements.[93] *See Gladding Dry Goods Co. v. Comm'r, supra* at 338. When the city credited the cost of an eligible improvement made in an earlier year against the partnership's rent, the city assumed the cost of that improvement, and the depreciable interest in that eligible improvement was transferred from the partnership to the city. With the cost of that improvement now borne by the city through the rent credit, the partnership no longer had a capital investment to depreciate. *See Your Health Club v. Comm'r, supra.* Accordingly, we conclude that the benefits and burdens surrounding the eligible improvements shifted from the partnership to the city in the year those improvements were "transferred" and credited against rent.

The partnership properly treated the transfer of its depreciable interest to the city in exchange for a rent credit as a deemed sale. *See United States v. Gen. Shoe Corp.*,

---

93. [8] We note that had the eligible improvements been considered advance rent, the lessor would presumably have had the depreciable interest in those eligible improvements beginning in the year that they were made. However, because the partnership often made eligible improvements in excess of those required under the lease, it was not certain which eligible improvements would eventually be credited against rent. Accordingly, we conclude that the eligible improvements were not advance rent paid in the year they were made.

282 F.2d 9 (6th Cir.1960). The partnership claimed a rent expense deduction equal to the rent credit it received and treated the amount of that rent credit as the amount it realized on the transfer. The partnership recognized gain to the extent that the rent credit exceeded its depreciated basis in the eligible improvement and effectively recaptured any depreciation claimed on the eligible improvement in prior years.

Whether the Rent Credit Arrangement Lacked Economic Substance

Even where a transaction complies with the formal requirements for obtaining a deduction, courts have long looked beyond that formal compliance and analyzed the substance of the transaction. *Knetsch v. U.S.*, 364 U.S. 361 (1960); *Gregory v. Helvering*, 293 U.S. 465 (1935). The taxpayer has the burden of showing that the form of the transaction accurately reflects its substance and that the deduction is permissible. *Comm'r v. CM Holdings, Inc.*, 301 F.3d 96, 102 (3d Cir.2002).

In the instant case, respondent contends that the rent credit provisions in issue lacked economic substance and were not part of a bona fide business transaction. In considering whether a transaction has economic substance, courts look at both the objective economic effect (i.e. whether, absent tax benefits, the taxpayer benefited from the transaction) and the subjective business motivation (i.e. whether the taxpayer was motivated by considerations beyond tax benefits) of the transaction. *Id.*

In the instant case, the hotel was not profitable and was in need of renovation in order to have any hope of becoming profitable. The partnership did not have the funds to renovate the hotel and was unable to borrow funds for the renovations with the lease arrangement structured as it was before 1989. With the introduction of rent credits in the 1989 lease, the annual percentage rent did not change. However, the partnership was able to make improvements to the hotel and credit those improvements against its rent for the year. Clearly, the rent credits provided a financial benefit to the partnership in that the partnership obtained the improvements that it wanted and needed and could reduce its rent on the basis of its cash outlay for the improvements. The negotiation of the lease agreements to include rent credits provided the partnership with a significant benefit independent of any tax considerations.

Petitioner's witnesses testified that the partnership's goal in negotiating rent credits was to find a way to make the improvements to help it make a profit on the hotel. Petitioner's witnesses also credibly testified that tax considerations were not discussed at the time of the negotiations and that it was only later that the partnership considered how the rent credits would be handled for tax purposes.

Petitioner also introduced credible testimony that the parties to the lease agreements chose rent credits over other alternatives for business, not tax, reasons. The mentioned alternatives were for the city to make the improvements at its own expense or to grant the partnership reduced rent and allow (or require) the partnership to make the improvements. Regarding the first alternative, there was concern that the City Council would be unwilling to approve a rent reduction. There was also concern that, if the city made the improvements, it would involve a cumbersome process of obtaining City Council approval repeatedly rather than the single City Council approval needed to modify the lease to include rent credits for improvements made by the partnership. The record shows and we conclude that the partnership's motivation in negotiating rent credits was to turn the hotel into a profitable enterprise and that the parties to the lease agreements had valid business reasons for choosing the rent credit structure over a lease providing for reduced rent.

Respondent makes much of the fact that the city is tax exempt. Where one of the parties is tax exempt, as is the city, there is potential for abuse. However, respondent points to no authority that would support a holding that a transaction involving a tax-exempt party cannot have economic substance. Respondent asserts that a taxable entity similarly situated with the city would not have accepted the lease terms involving rent credits. However, it is clear from the evidence that the city wanted to see the hotel renovated and was not simply going along with the partnership's proposal. For the reasons discussed above, we conclude that a taxable entity in the city's position could have favored the rent credit structure for business reasons, despite that fact that another structure might have produced greater tax savings for it.

We conclude that tax considerations were not a significant motivating factor in the negotiation of the rent credits. On the basis of the record, we conclude that the rent credit arrangements in issue had a subjective business purpose. We also conclude that the rent credit arrangement had objective economic substance.

Whether the Use of Rent Credits Clearly Reflected Income

If a taxpayer's method of accounting does not clearly reflect income, section 446(b) allows the Commissioner to compute taxable income under such method as, in the opinion of the Commissioner, does clearly reflect income. In the instant case, respondent asserts that the partnership's use of rent credits does not clearly reflect income because it "converts depreciable property to rent expense, computed at the historical cost of the asset, thereby inflating its deductions that significantly reduces taxable income". Respondent further alleges that the partnership is "clearly understating income" by taking a current deduction for the cost of long-term eligible improvements.

As respondent notes, a method of accounting clearly reflects income when it results in accurately reporting taxable income under a recognized method of accounting. *RLC Indus. Co. & Subs. v. Comm'r*, 98 T.C. 457, 491 (1992), *affd.* 58 F.3d 413 (9th Cir. 1995). "The Commissioner's determination with respect to clear reflection of income is entitled to more than the usual presumption of correctness, and the taxpayer bears a heavy burden of overcoming a determination that a method of accounting does not clearly reflect income." *Hamilton Indus., Inc. v. Comm'r*, 97 T.C. 120, 128 (1991). The Commissioner has broad discretion but cannot require a taxpayer to change from an accounting method that clearly reflects income merely because the Commissioner considers an alternate method to more clearly reflect income. *RLC Indus. Co. & Subs. v. Comm'r, supra* at 491. If a taxpayer's method of accounting is authorized by the Internal Revenue Code or the underlying regulations and has been applied consistently, the Commissioner cannot arbitrarily require a change or reject the taxpayer's method. *Id.* We review respondent's determination for abuse of discretion. See *Thor Power Tool Co. v. Comm'r*, 439 U.S. 522 (1979).

As discussed above, the method of treating the cost of improvements credited against rent as a deductible rent expense has been accepted by both the courts and the regulations. *See Your Health Club, Inc. v. Comm'r*, 4 T.C. at 390; *McGrath v. Comm'r*, T.C. Memo.2002-231; § 1.61-8(c), Income Tax Regs. In the instant case, respondent correctly points out that by treating the cost of improvements as a rent expense rather than depreciating (or continuing to depreciate) the costs, the partnership does increase its current deductions and reduce its taxable income in the year of the rent credit. However, since the partnership consistently accounted for its eligible improvements using an approved accounting method, respondent is not at liberty to require the partnership to use a different method of accounting, even if respondent believes that another method would more clearly reflect income.[94] *See RLC Indus. Co. & Subs. v. Comm'r, supra* at 491.

Respondent's concern with the use of historical cost is unfounded. It is true that if the eligible improvements were not credited against rent in the year made, the partnership initially depreciated them. However, in the year that the partnership received a rent credit for the eligible improvements, the partnership treated that as a deemed sale of the capital asset for an amount equal to the rent credit it received, which was equal to the historical cost of the eligible improvement. By recognizing gain to the extent that the rent credit exceeded the partnership's depreciated basis in the eligible improvement, the partnership effectively recaptured any depreciation it had previously claimed on that improvement. *See U.S. v. Gen. Shoe Corp.*, 282 F.2d at 12–13. By doing so, the partnership received the same deduction that it would have received if that eligible improvement had been credited against rent in the year it was made. Accordingly, the use of rent credits computed at the historical cost of the improvements did not inappropriately increase the overall deductions; it merely accelerated the time at which the partnership claimed those deductions. While such an acceleration generally would not be permissible for a capital asset, as discussed above, there is an exception that applies in the instant cases that allows the current deduction of capital expenses that are incurred and credited as a substitute for rent. See *Your Health Club, Inc. v. Comm'r, supra* at 390; *McGrath v. Comm'r, supra*; sec. 1.61-8(c), Income Tax Regs.

Accordingly, we conclude that the partnership's method of accounting for eligible improvements made in lieu of rent did clearly reflect income and that respondent abused his discretion in determining that the partnership's method did not clearly reflect income.

---

94. [9] Respondent's proposed accounting method would have the partnership continue to depreciate the eligible improvements even after they are credited against rent. Because the partnership no longer had a depreciable interest in the eligible improvements at that point, respondent's proposed method of accounting is not an authorized method of accounting and would not be a clear reflection of the partnership's income.

Whether the Use of Rent Credits Was an Accounting Method Change

Section 446(e) provides that a taxpayer must secure the consent of the Secretary before changing his method of accounting.

The reason for this rule is that a change in an accounting method will frequently cause a distortion of taxable income in the year of change; therefore, the Commissioner is empowered to prevent such distortion and consequent windfall to the taxpayer by conditioning his consent on the taxpayer's acceptance of adjustments that would eliminate any distortion.... [*Woodward Iron Co. v. United States*, 396 F.2d 552, 554 (5th Cir.1968).]

In the instant case, respondent contends that the partnership's change from depreciating to deducting the cost of an eligible improvement in the year in which the partnership received a rent credit for such improvement is a change in accounting method. We disagree because, as discussed above, when the partnership received a rent credit for the cost of an eligible improvement, the depreciable interest in that eligible improvement was transferred from the partnership to the city. At that point, the partnership, as required by law, *see Your Health Club v. Comm'r, supra* at 390; *Gladding Dry Goods v. Comm'r*, 2 B.T.A. at 338, discontinued depreciating the eligible improvement because it no longer had an investment to depreciate. In the same year, the partnership deducted as a rent expense, as it was entitled to do by law, *see Your Health Club, Inc. v. Comm'r, supra* at 390; *McGrath v. Comm'r, supra*; sec. 1.61-8(c), Income Tax Regs., the value of the interest that it transferred to the city in partial satisfaction of its rent obligation. The partnership appropriately treated that transfer as the deemed sale of the eligible improvement. *See U.S. v. Gen. Shoe Corp., supra* at 12–13. Because the partnership recognized gain on that sale to the extent that its depreciated basis was less than the rent credit, it properly recaptured any depreciation previously claimed and there was no duplication of deductions. The method used by the partnership in treating the matter as a deemed sale was used consistently throughout the term of the lease. Accordingly, we find that the partnership's treatment of eligible improvements did not result in an accounting method change.

Whether Respondent Properly Proposed an Adjustment Under §481(a) for Taxable Year 2000

Where there is a change of accounting method, §481(a) requires adjustments to prevent omissions or duplications and allows the Commissioner to include in the adjustment amounts that are attributable to taxable years for which assessment is barred by the statute of limitations. *Hamilton Indus., Inc. v. Commissioner*, 97 T.C. 120 (1991). As discussed above, because there has been no change of accounting method in the instant case, §481(a) is not applicable.

OPINION

On the basis of the foregoing, we conclude that the partnership and the city intended that eligible improvements be substitutes for rent; the leases in issue had economic substance and were not shams designed merely to reduce taxes; the partnership's treatment of eligible improvements was a clear reflection of income; the change from depreciating to deducting the cost of the eligible improvements in the year of a rent credit was not a change of accounting method; and the partnership appropriately deducted the cost of an eligible improvement as a rent expense in the year in which that eligible improvement was credited against rent.

Revenue Ruling 78-72
1978-1 C.B. 258

Advice has been requested whether a leasehold interest qualifies, under section 1033(f) of the Internal Revenue Code of 1954, as property that is similar or related in service or use to property converted under the circumstances described below.

A, an individual, was the owner of real property located in state X. The property was unimproved and held by A for investment. In February 1976, A conveyed the property to state X in a transaction that constituted an involuntary conversion into money within the meaning of section 1033 of the Code. A immediately reinvested the proceeds received from the involuntary conversion in the acquisition of a leasehold interest in real property improved by an apartment building which then was and still is held for investment. The leasehold interest had an initial term of 25 years and is subject to three 10-year renewal periods optional to A. In addition to the amount invested in the acquisition of the leasehold interest, A's rental obligation for the initial term and any renewal periods is based on a fixed percentage of the monthly gross receipts to A from apartment rentals, net of fees paid to an independent management company engaged by A to administer the operation of the apartment building.

The specific question is whether optional renewal periods should be added to the initial term of the leasehold for the purpose of determining whether the leasehold interest qualifies as 'like kind' property under section 1033(f) of the Code and section 1.1031(a)-1(c) of the Income Tax Regulations.

Section 1033(a)(2) of the Code provides, in effect, that if property is compulsorily converted into money and the taxpayer, during the period specified, purchases other property similar or related in service or use to the property so converted, at the election of the taxpayer the gain shall be recognized only to the extent that the amount realized upon such conversion exceeds the cost of such replacement property.

Section 1033(f) of the Code provides, in part, that if real property held for productive use in trade or business or for investment is compulsorily or involuntarily converted, property of a like kind to be held either for productive use in trade or business or for investment shall be treated as property similar or related in service or use to the property so converted.

Section 1.1033(g)-1(a) of the regulations provides that the principles of section 1.1031(a)-1(b) shall apply in determining whether replacement property is property of a like kind. Section 1.1031(a)-1(b) provides, in part, that the words 'like kind' have reference to the nature or character of the property and not to its grade or qualify. It also provides that the fact that any real estate involved is improved or unimproved is not material, for that fact relates only to the grade or quality of the property and not to its kind or class.

Section 1.1031(a)-1(c) of the regulations indicates, in part, that a leasehold or a fee with 30 or more years to run is like kind with respect to a fee interest in real estate.

In *Century Electric Co. v. Comm'r*, 15 T.C. 581, 591 (1950), *aff'd* 192 F.2d 155 (8th Cir. 1951), *cert. denied*, 342 U.S. 954 (1952), the Tax Court of the United States, indicated that, for like kind exchange purposes, optional renewal periods are included in determining the length of a lease.

In *R & J Furniture Co. v. Comm'r*, 20 T.C. 857, 865 (1953), *acq.*, 1954-1 C.B. 6, which involved a lease with an initial term of 5 years and ten renewal options of 5 years each, the Tax Court of the United States stated that the lease was property of a like kind and the equivalent of a fee interest in real estate under the regulations since the taxpayers had the right to possess, occupy, and use the leased property for a total of 55 years.

In the instant situation, A's lease runs for an initial period of 25 years plus three optional 10-year renewal periods under the same rental terms. Thus, A has the right to possess, occupy, and use the leased property for a total of 55 years.

Accordingly, A's optional renewal periods should be added to the initial term of the lease for the purpose of determining whether the leasehold interest qualifies as "like kind" property under section 1033(f) of the Code and section 1.1031(a)-1(c) of the regulations. On this basis, the leasehold interest acquired by A in 1976 is like kind with respect to the property conveyed to state X. Therefore, for purposes of section 1033(a)(2), the leasehold interest is similar or related in service or use to the converted property.

Chapter 15

Structuring Improvements Exchanges

I. Commentary

An improvements exchange (also referred to as a build-to-suit exchange) is a transaction that entails the exchanger using proceeds from the sale of real property to acquire and improve other real property. Services and materials are not like kind to real property, so they cannot be acquired separately as part of an exchange of real property.[1] Consequently, only the portion of real-property improvements that are complete at the time the exchanger takes possession of the property will be like kind to relinquished real property. Special identification rules apply to property an exchanger identifies that will be produced after the identification.[2] In addition to seeking to use exchange proceeds to construct improvements on property to be acquired, exchangers often look for structures that will allow them to use exchange proceeds to construct improvements on property they already own or control in related entities. The leasehold improvements exchange may provide an opportunity for completing the latter type of transaction.

A. Improvements Exchanges on Property to Be Acquired

Improvements exchanges raise several practical issues. First, if the exchanger wants to have control over the replacement property and the construction of the improvements, the exchanger must either take possession of the property or park title to the property. If the exchanger takes possession, the improvements will not qualify as replacement property. If the exchanger parks title to the property, the titleholder will have control, unless the title parking arrangement can satisfy the Rev. Proc. 2000-37 safe harbor. Second, exchangers are often unable to complete significant improvements on newly acquired property within the 180-day window allowed by the Rev. Proc. 2000-37 safe harbor. Often, before beginning construction, an exchanger must obtain

---

1. *See* Bloomington Coca-Cola Bottling Co. v. Commissioner, 189 F.2d 14 (7th Cir. 1951); Treas. Reg. § 1.1031(k)-1(e)(4).
2. *See* Treas. Reg. § 1.1031(k)-1(e)(3).

permits and approval, which can take several years to obtain. As a result, the Rev. Proc. 2000-37 safe harbor often is not available for improvements exchanges. Third, if the exchanger decides to do a non-safe harbor improvements exchange, the party holding title must have some control over the construction of the improvements. Consequently, the exchanger gives up some control of the property in exchange for more certain tax treatment.

Title-parking improvements exchanges add a layer of complexity that is not inherent in other title-parking arrangements. As with any title-parking transaction, the parties must arrange the financing, acquisition, and control of the parked property. The improvements exchange also requires the exchanger and titleholder to enter into agreements that contemplate the construction that will occur while the titleholder holds the property. Thus, improvements exchanges are fairly complex transactions.[3]

To avoid some of the difficulties inherent in improvements exchanges, an exchanger may acquire property, prepare it to be improved, and then transfer it to a third party to hold during the construction period. Such attempts may not work for a number of reasons. First, the exchanger will often hesitate to transfer sufficient benefits and burdens in the property to the titleholder, so the titleholder will not be the owner of the property for tax purposes.[4] Second, property a taxpayer owns cannot qualify as replacement property. Therefore, if the exchanger transfers property to a third party and reacquires it, the IRS and courts may question whether it is valid replacement property.[5]

Because many of the improvements-exchange structures involve tax risk, exchangers may consider an alternative with lower tax risk. An exchanger will most likely qualify for section 1031 nonrecognition if the seller of the relinquished property constructs improvements before transferring the property.[6] As with other planning strategies, the exchanger must give up control with this strategy to obtain tax certainty. Consequently, the planning strategies available for improvements exchanges are complicated.[7]

B. Leasehold Improvements Exchanges

As a general matter, the most complicated exchange structure is the leasehold improvements exchange. The leasehold improvements exchange allows an exchanger to use exchange proceeds to construct improvements on property owned by a related party. It is a valuable structure because it allows an exchanger and related party to prepare property for improvement before the exchange begins, allowing the exchanger to complete a significant amount of improvements within the 180-day Rev. Proc.

---

3. *See, e.g.,* Estate of Bartell v. Commissioner, 147 T.C. No. 5 (2016) (reproduced in Chapter 13).

4. *See* DeCleene v. Commissioner, 115 T.C. No. 34 (2000).

5. *See id.*; Rev. Proc. 2004-51, 2004-2 C.B. 294.

6. *See* Coastal Terminals, Inc. v. United States, 320 F.2d 333 (4th Cir. 1963); Rev. Rul. 75-291 (1975).

7. *See* Fredericks v. Commissioner, 67 T.C.M. (CCH) 2005 (1994) (allowing a related party to construct improvements that qualified as replacement property, but the exchange occurred prior to the enactment of the rules governing related-party exchanges).

2000-37 title-parking safe harbor.[8] To successfully structure such an exchange, an attorney must consider numerous tax and legal issues. The IRS has privately approved a leasehold improvements exchange,[9] and they have become a common part of section 1031 exchanges. The private letter ruling provides an outline for structuring such transactions.

In structuring a leasehold improvements exchange, a tax attorney must be prepared for both the tax and legal issues such transactions will present. The identification issues that arise with respect to improvements exchanges also arise with respect to leasehold improvement exchanges. Remember, however, that the replacement property will include a long-term leasehold. When drafting the lease of the property from the related party to the exchange accommodation titleholder, recall that the definition of like-kind property provides that leaseholds in real property of more than 30 years can be like kind to real property.[10] Because the construction occurs on property owned by a related party, the tax attorney must consider how to avoid the negative effects of the related-party rules or why they will not taint the transaction. If the transaction is structured within the Rev. Proc. 2000-37 safe harbor, the attorney must ensure that the qualified exchange accommodation agreement, lease, construction contract, and financing all satisfy the safe harbor requirements and protect the exchanger's legal interests.

II. Primary Legal Authority

Bloomington Coca-Cola Bottling Co. v. Commissioner

United States Court of Appeals, Seventh Circuit

189 F.2d 14 (1951)

The question presented by this petition for review is whether the Tax Court correctly upheld the Commissioner's determination that in 1939 the taxpayer sustained a loss upon the sale of real estate which did not come within the scope of § 112(b)(1) of the Internal Revenue Code, 26 U.S.C.A. § 112(b), but was recognizable under § 112(a) thereof for the purpose of computing its excess profits tax credit based on an average base period net income.

The Tax Court held that the transaction was not an exchange protected from tax impact by § 112(b)(1) but was a sale which resulted in a recognizable loss. In this court taxpayer claims "no error with respect to the findings of facts of the Tax Court, but alleges that the Tax Court erred in applying the law to those facts." It makes the point that the payment of $64,500 cash in addition to the transfer of an old bottling

---

8. The IRS prohibits the use of Rev. Proc. 2000-37 safe harbor for leasehold improvement exchanges on property owned by the exchanger. *See* Rev. Proc. 2004-51, 2004-2 C.B. 294. This goes counter to an early suggestion regarding the potential of leasehold improvements exchanges. *See* Bradley T. Borden, *New Safe Harbor Promotes Reverse Exchanges*, 66 Prac. Tax Strat. 68, 77–78 (Feb. 2001).

9. *See* Priv. Ltr. Rul. 2002-51-008 (Sep. 11, 2002).

10. *See* Treas. Reg. § 1.1031(a)-1(c)(2).

plant as consideration for the construction of a new plant did not remove the transaction from the purview of § 112(b)(1) of the Revenue Act of 1938.

FACTS

The material facts are that in 1930 taxpayer, at a cost of $36,000, acquired a bottling plant in Bloomington, Illinois—allocating $30,500 to buildings and $5,500 to land. In 1938, concluding that the plant was inadequate for its needs, taxpayer decided to build a new plant. It decided it had no use for the old plant and wished to dispose of it. With those purposes in mind, it entered into a contract with a contractor to construct a new plant. The new plant was completed in 1939. By the contract the contractor furnished the necessary material and labor, and completed the building in accordance with the plans and specifications prepared by its architect for a total of $72,500. Of this sum the contractor was paid $64,500 in cash and accepted taxpayer's old buildings and the land upon which the old plant was located at a valuation of $8,000, and the old building and land were transferred to the contractor.

Taxpayer, in its 1939 tax return, reported the transaction thusly:

Lot, Cost July 1930	$5500.00
Sold April 30, 1939	1424.55
Loss	4075.45
Limitation	(2000.00)
Building, Cost July 1930	30,500.00
Depreciation on building to April 30, 1939	5,113.21
Net book value April 30, 1939	25,386.79
Sold April 30, 1939	6,575.45
Loss	$18,811.34

Schedule B of taxpayer's 1943 and 1944 excess profits tax return shows the 1939 base period excess profits net income as follows:

1. Normal Tax (or special class) net income	$2,278.25
2. Net capital loss used in computing line 1	2,000.00
***	
4. Net loss from sale or exchange of property other than capital assets deducted in computing line 1 (for taxable years beginning after December 31, 1937)	$18,811.34

The Commissioner in determining the excess profits taxes for the years 1943 and 1944 adjusted the average base period net income for the year 1939 as computed by the taxpayer by deducting the amount of $22,886.79 as a loss not coming within the scope of Sec. 112(b)(1) of the Internal Revenue Code. This resulted in a deficiency of $8,049.19 in 1943 and $8,492.13 in 1944. The taxpayer contested this determination. The Tax Court, finding the facts in detail, sustained the Commissioner.

The Commissioner's determination and its approval by the Tax Court that taxpayer's disposition of the old plant constituted a sale and not an exchange of property for like property must be considered as prima facie correct, and the burden of proving it wrong is upon the taxpayer. We may not reverse the decision unless we can say the decision is clearly erroneous.

ANALYSIS

It is elementary that the language of a revenue act is to be read in the light of the practical matters with which it deals and is to be given its ordinary significance in arriving at the meaning of the statute. *Old Colony R. Co. v. Commissioner*, 284 U.S. 552 (1932).

The applicable statute, 26 U.S.C.A. § 112, provides:

Sec. 112. Recognition of gain or loss —

(b) Exchanges solely in kind — (1) Property held for productive use or investment. No gain or loss shall be recognized if property held for productive use in trade or business or for investment (not including stock in trade or other property held primarily for sale, nor stocks, bonds, notes, choses in action, certificates of trust or beneficial interest, or other securities or evidences of indebtedness or interest) is exchanged solely for property of a like kind to be held either for productive use in trade or business or for investment.

And Treasury Regulations 111, § 29.112(a)-1 states that to constitute an exchange within the meaning of § 112(b)(1) the transaction must be a reciprocal transfer of property as distinguished from a transfer of property for a money consideration only.

A "sale" is a transfer of property for a price in money or its equivalent. "Exchange" means the giving of one thing for another. That is to say, in a sale, the property is transferred in consideration of a definite price expressed in terms of money, while in an exchange, the property is transferred in return for other property without the intervention of money. True, "Border-line cases arise where the money forms a substantial part of the adjustment of values in connection with the disposition of property and the acquisition of similar properties. The presence in a transaction of a small amount of cash, to adjust certain differences in value of the properties exchanged will not necessarily prevent the transaction from being considered an exchange.... Where cash is paid by the taxpayer, it may be considered as representing the purchase price of excess value of 'like property' received." 3 Mertens, Law of Federal Income Taxation, § 20.29, pp. 143, 144.

But this is not a case where the contractor exchanged a completed plant owned by the contractor for property and money, hence the contractor at no time had like property within the meaning of § 112(b)(1) of the Revenue Act. Under these circumstances we would not be warranted in saying that the finding and conclusion of the Tax Court are clearly erroneous. On the contrary, we think the facts adequately support the Tax Court's conclusion that the taxpayer's disposition of its old plant constituted a sale.

Another contention urged is that the loss which was incurred by taxpayer in 1939 on its disposal of its old bottling plant must be disallowed under the provisions of § 711(b)(1)(E), 26 U.S.C.A. § 711(b)(1)(E) on the ground that the property was abandoned. This section provides that deductions for abandonment of property shall not be allowed in the computation of excess profits net income for the base years. And § 29.23(e)-3 of Regulations 111 provides that when, through some change in business conditions, the usefulness in the business of some or all of the capital assets is suddenly terminated so that a taxpayer discards such assets permanently from use in such business, it may claim a loss as prescribed.

In considering the contention that the property had been abandoned it will be enough to say that we agree with the Tax Court: "The old plant was sold for a consideration of $8,000 ... ; it was not abandoned. There are no facts established justifying a finding of abandonment, or that the loss was due to obsolescence. The old plant was an operating plant at the time petitioner (taxpayer) moved to its new building, and its use as a bottling plant could have been continued. The testimony ... was not that the plant was abandoned, but that its sale was determined upon. A claim of loss consequent upon the abandonment of property must be supported by clear and convincing proof of intention to abandon and discard the property (citing case). The record contains nothing to sustain the argument of abandonment, and the facts established are to the contrary. *See Hygrade Food Products Corporation v. Commission*, 144 F.2d 115 (2d Cir. 1944)."

Coastal Terminals, Inc. v. United States

United States Court of Appeals, Fourth Circuit

320 F.2d 333 (1963)

FACTS

A number of years prior to 1957, a group of independent oil jobbers formed the corporation, Coastal Terminals, Inc., for the purpose of having it provide facilities for the storage of oil and other petroleum products. In 1957, and for a number of years prior thereto, Coastal Terminals owned and operated a deepwater oil terminal at North Charleston, S.C., the facility consisting of real estate, tanks, pipe lines and office space. Prior to 1957, Coastal Terminals determined that it was to its advantage, and to the advantage of its oil jobber stockholders, to acquire inland terminal facilities, to be supplied with oil by Plantation Pipe Line. To this end, Coastal obtained options on three sites contiguous to Plantation Pipe Line which would be suitable for the erection of terminal facilities. The first such site, upon which an option was taken in December, 1955, was at Belton, S.C. Later options were taken on sites at Salisbury, N.C., and Doraville, Ga. There was Existing at this time an operating terminal at Wilmington, N.C., which was owned by Coastal Terminals of North Carolina, a separate and distinct corporation of which the taxpayer owned 60% Of the stock and which it hoped to acquire and own outright in the future. Although at that time the taxpayer, Coastal Terminals, had no funds available for the purchase of the sites upon which options had been taken or for the erection of terminal facilities on such sites, as steel was in short supply, the taxpayer obtained commitments from its principal supplier, Chicago Bridge and Iron Company, for the necessary steel, it being understood between Chicago Bridge and Coastal that these commitments might be cancelled if Coastal subsequently found itself unable to finance the purchases. As early as August 1956, Coastal obtained commitments from Chicago Bridge for steel construction at the Belton and Doraville locations.

In the Spring of 1957, Delhi-Taylor Oil Corporation approached Coastal with the view of purchasing Coastal's oil terminal facilities at Charleston. Delhi-Taylor, a Delaware corporation, had its principal offices in Dallas, Texas, and, operating as an independent oil company, was engaged in exploration, production, refining and marketing activities. At the outset, Delhi-Taylor offered to purchase Coastal's terminal facilities at Charleston for $1,000,000.00 cash, and Coastal's asking price was $1,475,000.00. Eventually, Delhi-Taylor offered $1,200,000.00, and Coastal refused to sell for less than $1,400,000.00. At that time it was Coastal's intention to continue in the oil business, but it had no available funds to convert the sites on the Plantation Pipe Line, on which it had taken options, into operating terminals, and Coastal did not consider Delhi-Taylor's offering price of $1,200,000.00 enough to accomplish that end. Since Coastal and Delhi-Taylor could not agree on a sale, the idea of an exchange of properties was suggested and was discussed. These discussions resulted in an agreement that Delhi-Taylor would acquire from Coastal Terminals of North Carolina, its terminal in Wilmington, N.C., the sites at Belton, N.C., Salisbury, N.C., and Doraville, Ga., construct terminals on the sites, and exchange these four terminals for Coastal's deep water terminal in Charleston.

On May 11, 1957, Coastal and Delhi-Taylor entered into a written agreement entitled, "The State of South Carolina, Terminal Purchase and Sale Contract, Charleston, South Carolina". This agreement provided for the sale of taxpayer's Charleston facilities to Delhi-Taylor for a cash consideration of $1,200,000.00, with an escrow deposit of $60,000.00 as earnest money. The agreement further provided:

> ... It is understood that Seller is endeavoring to arrange for an exchange of like properties consisting of terminal facilities at Wilmington, Charlotte and Salisbury, North Carolina and Belton, South Carolina between the parties in lieu of the aforementioned cash consideration or some part thereof, such exchange arrangement to be fully capable of completion on or before July 1st, 1957, but unless Seller shall present, and Purchaser shall at its sole option accept, such arrangement to exchange like property in lieu of payment of the cash consideration aforementioned, prior to the 20th day of June 1957, then this contract shall be closed upon the terms and conditions otherwise elsewhere herein set forth....

IV

Subject to the approval of title by Purchaser's attorneys, and in the event Purchaser's attorneys, and the Surveyor find Seller's title to be good and marketable and free and clear of all liens, encumbrances, restrictions and encroachments, and in the further event that Seller has complied with and performed all other terms and conditions hereof, Purchaser shall close the transaction on or before July 1, 1957..., by paying to the Seller the One Million, Two Hundred Thousand Dollar ($1,200,000.00) purchase price or exchanging property of like kind and value, if such exchange of property can be arranged, less the down payment, or earnest money hereinabove mentioned, at which time Seller will deliver to Purchaser its general warranty deed conveying to purchaser a fee simple title free and clear of all liens, encumbrances, restrictions and encroachments....

This contract was drawn by Delhi-Taylor's counsel, no attorney for Coastal having participated in the preparation of the contract, and Delhi-Taylor was most interested in being assured that it would acquire Coastal's Charleston terminal on July 1, 1957. Notwithstanding the fact that the written agreement apparently gave Delhi-Taylor the option of acquiring Coastal's Charleston terminal, either by purchase for cash or by exchange, the testimony of both Coastal's and Delhi-Taylor's negotiating representatives is clear and positive that a sale for cash could not be agreed upon, and that their definite agreement was for an exchange of properties. Thereafter, Coastal assigned its options to purchase the sites on Plantation Pipe Line to Delhi-Taylor, assigned its commitments for steel from Chicago Bridge and Iron Company to Delhi-Taylor, Delhi-Taylor contracted with Kaminer Construction Company for the construction and installation of pipe connections with the storage tanks, and acquired from Coastal Terminals of North Carolina its existing terminal at Wilmington. The construction of the terminal facilities at the three sites on Plantation Pipe Line proceeded promptly, with Delhi-Taylor checking on the engineering details so that the terminals would be acceptable to Coastal, and by July 1, 1957, the terminals and connections had been substantially completed. On or prior to July 1, 1957, Delhi-Taylor paid for and conveyed the four terminals to Coastal, and Coastal conveyed its deepwater terminal at Charleston to Delhi-Taylor.

The District Judge, sitting as the trier of facts without a jury, found that:

The substance of the transaction was one in which plaintiff owned a deepwater terminal which Delhi-Taylor Oil Corporation wanted to acquire; they were unable to agree upon a sale; that as result of prior corporate investigation and planning, which at the time had no connection with this transaction, plaintiff knew of certain property which it would be willing to accept in exchange for its terminal provided Delihi-Taylor Oil Corporation would acquire and improve the same, and that Delhi-Taylor did acquire and improve the same on its own behalf so that it would be in a position to make an exchange, and that an exchange in fact took place. Plaintiff did not "cash in" and invest the same in another business nor did it receive cash and reinvest the same in like property, but merely exchanged its property with Delhi-Taylor Oil Corporation for like property and continued on as before in its identical business.

Even if it be conceded that upon the testimony different ultimate fact might have been found, we must give due consideration to findings of the District Judge. Rule 52(a) provides that, "Findings of fact shall not be set aside unless clearly erroneous, and due regard shall be given to the opportunity of the trial court to judge of the credibility of the witnesses." Not only are we unable to say that the District Judge's findings of fact were clearly erroneous, but we are of the opinion that upon the evidence his findings were plainly right.

The Government contends that the transaction between Coastal and Delhi-Taylor was a "sale" for gain, the gain from which is recognizable under Section 1002 of the Internal Revenue Code of 1954, which is as follows:

> Except as otherwise provided in this subtitle, on the sale or exchange of property the entire amount of the gain or loss, determined under Section 1001, shall be recognized. 26 U.S.C.A. § 1002.

On the other hand, the taxpayer contends that the transaction was an "exchange" within the meaning of § 1031(a)....

The Government alternately contends that, even if the transaction be deemed an "exchange" within the meaning of § 1031(a), the gain nonetheless is partially taxable under § 1031(b) and (d) to the extent of certain liabilities of the taxpayer assumed by Delhi-Taylor.

* * *

The taxpayer disagrees with this contention and insists that at the time the exchange was agreed upon, it had incurred no obligations to either Chicago Bridge or Kaminer, and that the obligations incident to the undertaking to construct terminals to be exchanged were entirely the obligations of Delhi-Taylor.

ANALYSIS

The purpose of § 1031(a), as shown by its legislative history, is to defer recognition of gain or loss when a direct exchange of property between the taxpayer and another party takes place; a sale for cash does not qualify as a nontaxable exchange even though the cash is immediately reinvested in like property.

We are of the opinion that, upon the evidence, the District Court's findings of fact and conclusions of law were amply sustained by the authorities.

> Whether the transaction constituted a sale or an exchange for income tax purposes depends on the intent of the parties and this intent is to be ascertained from all relevant facts and circumstances, and of necessity the case is largely dependent upon circumstantial evidence.

Sarkes Tazian, Inc. v. U.S., (7th Cir.), 240 F.2d 467, 470.

> ... the transaction must be viewed as a whole, and each step, from the commencement of negotiations to the consummation of the sale, is relevant.

Comm'r v. Court Holding Co., 324 U.S. 331, 334 (1945).

> The transaction here involved may not be separated into its component parts
> for tax purposes. Tax consequences must depend on what actually was in-
> tended and accomplished rather than on the separate steps taken to reach
> the desired end.

Century Electric Co. v. Comm'r, 192 F.2d 155, 159 (8th Cir. 1951).

There was no impropriety or illegality in the undertaking of Delhi-Taylor to exchange property which it did not own at the time of the undertaking. *Howell Tur-
pentine Co. v. Comm'r*, 162 F.2d 319 (5th Cir. 1947), wherein (p. 322) the court quotes
with approval from American Jurisprudence, the following:

> It is not unusual for persons to agree to convey by a certain time notwith-
> standing they have no title to the land at the time of the contract, and the va-
> lidity of such agreements is upheld. In such cases the vendor assumes the risk
> of acquiring the title and making the conveyance, or responding in damages
> for the vendee's loss of his bargain.... Whenever one is so situated with ref-
> erence to the tract of land that he can acquire the title thereto, either by the
> voluntary act of the parties holding the title, or by proceedings at law or in
> equity, he is in position to make a valid agreement for the sale thereof without
> disclosing the nature of this title. 55 Am. Jur., Vendor and Purchaser, § 12.

In accord are *Mercantile Trust Co. & Nelson v. Comm'r*, 32 B.T.A. 82 (1935); *W. D.
Haden Co. v. Comm'r*, 165 F.2d 588 (5th Cir. 1948), and *Alderson v. Comm'r*, 317 F.2d
790 (9th Cir. 1963).

The *Alderson* case, *supra*, so far as we know, is the latest decision on the question
presented in the instant case. The Tax Court (38 T.C. 215) held that the transaction
was a taxable sale and not an exchange within the purview of Section 1031(a) of the
Revenue Code. Counsel for the Government relied heavily on this decision in their
brief in the instant case. However, prior to the argument of this case, the Court of
Appeals for the Ninth Circuit, by its opinion filed May 22, 1963, reversed the decision
of the Tax Court, holding that the transaction was an exchange within the purview
of § 1031(a).

The facts are quite analogous to those of the instant case. The Aldersons (hereinafter
referred to as "taxpayers") entered into an agreement on May 21, 1957 with Alloy
Die Casting Company (hereinafter referred to as "Alloy") to sell their Buena Park
farm property in Orange County, California, to Alloy for $172,871.40, and according
to the terms of the agreement Alloy deposited with Orange County Title Company,
$17,205.00 toward the purchase of the property. From the outset, the taxpayers' desire
was to exchange their Buena Park property for other property of a like kind. They
intended to sell the property for cash only after they were unable to locate a suitable
piece of property to take in exchange. Alloy intended simply to effect a purchase of
the property for cash. Alloy did not learn that petitioners wished to exchange their
property for like property until the latter part of July, 1957. Sometime after the execution of the purchase and sale agreement, taxpayers located certain property in

Monterey County, referred to as the Salinas property, which they desired to obtain in exchange for the Buena Park property. On August 19, 1957, taxpayers and Alloy executed an amendment to their previous agreement providing that the Salinas property would be acquired by Alloy and exchanged for the Buena Park property in lieu of the originally contemplated cash sale transaction. However, the amendment provided that, if this exchange were not effected by September 11, 1957, the original agreement with respect to a purchase for cash would be carried out. On that same day, the daughter and agent of taxpayers delivered to the Salinas Title Guarantee Company, "Buyers' Instructions" reciting that $190,000.00 would be paid for the Salinas property, that $19,000.00 was paid therewith out of taxpayers' money on deposit with the title company, and authorizing the title company to convey the Salinas property to Alloy provided a deed from Alloy to taxpayers could be immediately recorded. The Salinas title company acquired title to the Salinas property for a purchase price of $190,000.00, the funds being provided by the $19,000.00 deposited by taxpayers' daughter, and $172,871.40 being paid to the title company by Alloy, the excess of the amounts deposited being returned to taxpayers. The title company then conveyed the Salinas property to Alloy, who in turn conveyed it by deed to taxpayers, and at the same time the taxpayers conveyed the Buena Park property to Alloy. Taxpayers paid for all documentary stamps on the deeds and all escrow fees.

Upon these facts, the Tax Court held that the transaction was a sale by taxpayers of their Buena Park property to Alloy for cash, and a reinvestment by taxpayers of the purchase price in the Salinas property, Alloy only acting as a conduit through which title to the Salinas property passed.

In reversing the decision of the Tax Court, the Court of Appeals seemed impressed by the fact that, from the outset, it was taxpayers' desire to effect an exchange of property. The Court said:

> Petitioners, on finding the Salinas property, took steps to make it available to Alloy for the exchange by signing buyer's instructions in the escrow of August 19, 1957, opened at Salinas Title, but the fact is, as found by the Tax Court, that petitioners at that time intended to accomplish an exchange of properties and that the Salinas property was "acquired by Alloy" for the sole purpose of such exchange.

> True, the intermediate acts of the parties could have hewn closer to and have more precisely depicted the ultimate desired result, but what actually occurred on September 3 or 4, 1957, was an exchange of deeds between petitioners and Alloy which effected an exchange of the Buena Park property for the Salinas property. It is also noted by the court that the buyer's instructions in the Salinas escrow did not conform to the seller's instructions although the transfer from the original owner of the Salinas property to Salinas Title was, as to the provisions at variance, pursuant to the terms of the buyer's instructions. If Alloy had signed the said "Buyer's Instructions" this litigation

would have been avoided, but even in the circumstances here involved the court concludes that the intended exchange was accomplished.

* * *

In the case at bar, the ultimate objective appears without question to have been the exchange of property of like kind. As the court in the Helvering case (*Gregory v. Helvering*, 293 U.S. 465 (1935)) further observes:

"Putting aside, then, the question of motive in respect of taxation altogether, and fixing the character of the proceeding by what actually occurred, what do we find?" (293 U.S. page 469).

In the instant case we find a plan to exchange the properties within the intent of the statute (§ 1031 I.R.C. of 1954), and the acquiring of the Salinas property by Alloy with the sole purpose of trading same for the Buena Park property which does not make the transaction one within Section 1002, Internal Revenue Code of 1954.

In the instant case, we are of opinion that there was ample evidence to support the conclusion of the District Court that the transaction between Coastal and Delhi-Taylor was an "exchange" within the purview of § 1031(a) and not a "sale" as contemplated by § 1002.

Nor can we agree with the Government's alternate contention that gain to Coastal was recognizable under § 1031(b) and (d) under the theory that Delhi-Taylor's payments to Chicago Bridge and Kaminer for the construction of terminal facilities were payments by Delhi-Taylor of obligations of Coastal. Before any work was done, and in fact, before any binding legal obligations had been incurred by Coastal to either Chicago Bridge or Kaminer, Delhi-Taylor undertook to have these terminals constructed by Chicago Bridge and Kaminer in order to be in position to make the exchange with Coastal. So Delhi-Taylor paid its own legally incurred obligations and not the obligations of Coastal.

DeCleene v. Commissioner

United States Tax Court
115 T.C. No. 34 (2000)

FACTS

Some of the facts have been stipulated and are so found. The stipulations of fact and the accompanying exhibits are incorporated herein by this reference. Petitioners are husband and wife who resided in Green Bay, Wisconsin, at the time they filed their petition.

Since 1969, petitioner Donald DeCleene (petitioner) has owned and operated a trucking/truck repair business. In 1976 and 1977, petitioner purchased improved real property located on McDonald Street, Green Bay (the McDonald Street property). He used the McDonald Street property for his business operations.

In 1993, petitioners owned and worked as employees of DeCleene Truck Repair and Refrigeration, Inc. (Refrigeration). Petitioner served as president. Refrigeration installs and repairs truck refrigeration units and performs general truck repairs. Through December 29, 1993, Refrigeration rented the McDonald Street property from petitioner as its business premises. Petitioner computed his adjusted basis for the McDonald Street property, including the depreciated cost of improvements, as being $59,831 at the time he disposed of that property on December 29, 1993.

In 1992, petitioner was looking for land to which he could move his business.

On September 30, 1992, petitioner purchased 8.47 acres of unimproved real property on Lawrence Drive in De Pere, Wisconsin (the Lawrence Drive property), a suburb of Green Bay. Petitioner described the Lawrence Drive property as a "very good spot" that he "took advantage of". Petitioner promptly sold 2.09 acres of the Lawrence Drive property to an unrelated corporation. Petitioner's adjusted basis of the Lawrence Drive property that he purchased and retained, with allocated fees and other closing costs, was $137,027.

Petitioner partially financed the purchase of the Lawrence Drive property with a $100,000 loan from Bank One, Green Bay, Bank One, Green Bay received petitioner's note and a mortgage on the Lawrence Drive property as security for its loan.

By 1993, petitioner was ready to move his business to a new building to be constructed on the Lawrence Drive property.

After petitioner acquired the Lawrence Drive property, The Western Lime and Cement Co. (WLC) expressed interest in acquiring petitioner's McDonald Street property.

Petitioner discussed WLC's interest in the McDonald Street property with his accountant. The accountant suggested that petitioner could structure a like-kind exchange in which he would quitclaim the Lawrence Drive property to WLC, after which WLC would convey back to petitioner the Lawrence Drive property with a new building built thereon to petitioner's specifications, in exchange for the McDonald Street property.

On September 24, 1993, WLC made an offer-prepared by petitioner's attorney-which petitioner accepted, to purchase the Lawrence Drive property for $142,400; petitioner's acceptance contained an undertaking to "transfer building permit to Buyer on or before September 27, 1993".[11] On September 24, 1993, petitioner quitclaimed

---

11. [2] The copy of the building permit included as Exhibit 39-J in paragraph 67 of the Supplemental Stipulation of Facts replaces paragraph 30 of the Stipulation of Facts, which stated as follows: "Prior to his September 24, 1993 quit claim of title to the Lawrence Drive property to the Western Lime & Cement Co., a permit was obtained in Donald DeCleene's name for construction of a building on the Lawrence Drive property".

Exhibit 39-J is a photocopy that bears a variety of dates: it was originally submitted to and preliminarily approved by the City of DePere Building Inspector on July 29, 1993; it bears the signature of the "Owner/Agent Michael DeCleene V.P. Date 1/12/94"; it was recorded "10/22/93" and bears the notation, "Site Plan approved by Plan Commission on 4-27-93". The name of petitioner as Owner, his mailing address, and telephone number appear on the line of the permit form provided for that information. However, the name, mailing address, and telephone number of WLC have been written in above those of petitioner.

On July 29, 1993, Green Bay Abstract & Title Company, Inc. (the title company), had issued a title commitment with WLC as the proposed insured on the owner's policy in the insured amount

title to the Lawrence Drive property to WLC, and WLC gave petitioner a fully non-recourse noninterest bearing one payment note and mortgage on the Lawrence Drive property in the amount of $142,400. On that same day, petitioner assigned to Bank One, Green Bay, the WLC $142,400 note and mortgage. The WLC $142,400 note was due by its terms "upon the closing of an exchange transaction between" WLC and petitioner, or 6 months from the date of the note, "whichever is earlier".

On September 24, 1993, WLC and petitioner also executed the Exchange Agreement regarding the McDonald Street property and the Lawrence Drive property. The Exchange Agreement was drafted by petitioner's attorney with input from WLC's attorney.

Paragraph 1 of the Exchange Agreement required petitioner to convey by warranty deed the McDonald Street property to WLC, "free and clear of all liens and encumbrances", in exchange for WLC's paying its $142,400 note to petitioner and conveying the Lawrence Drive Property back to petitioner by quitclaim deed.

Paragraph 2 of the Exchange Agreement provided that petitioner would pay all costs relating to the transfers of the McDonald Street and Lawrence Drive properties.

In Paragraph 4 of the Exchange Agreement, petitioner made comprehensive warranties to WLC with respect to the McDonald Street property, but WLC expressly disavowed making any warranties to petitioner with respect to the Lawrence Drive property.

The Exchange Agreement provided that WLC would construct a building on the Lawrence Drive property to petitioner's specifications.

The Exchange Agreement provided that petitioner at the closing of the exchange would pay an amount representing the costs of the building on the Lawrence Drive property, as well as insurance premiums, real estate taxes, interest, and all other "soft" costs WLC might incur incident to the construction of the building.

Petitioner in the Exchange Agreement agreed to indemnify and hold WLC harmless against any damages sustained or incurred in connection with the construction and financing of the Lawrence Drive property.

Petitioner and WLC intended to close on the Exchange Agreement upon completion of construction of the building on the Lawrence Drive property "but not later than December 31, 1993".

Bank One, Green Bay provided financing for the construction of the building on the Lawrence Drive property. On September 24, 1993, Bank One, Green Bay agreed to a construction loan of $380,000, naming WLC as borrower and petitioner as guarantor. This loan was nonrecourse as to WLC. On the same day WLC executed a note and mortgage to Bank One, Green Bay, which provided that WLC had no personal liability on the note secured by the mortgage and that the lender would look solely to the Lawrence Drive property securing the mortgage; petitioner guaranteed the $380,000 construction loan.

---

of $142,400 and Bank One, Green Bay as the proposed insured on the loan policy in the insured amount of $522,400.

Bank One, Green Bay considered petitioner the source of repayment of the September 24, 1993, $380,000 construction loan. In connection with that loan, Bank One, Green Bay never obtained any financial statements from WLC. The check of the creditworthiness of WLC by the Bank One, Green Bay loan officer consisted of calling a branch bank to discuss WLC's business reputation.

The $380,000 note for the September 24, 1993 Bank One, Green Bay construction loan required no interest or principal payments during the time that WLC was expected to be the named borrower on the note; the note did not require payment of interest until March 23, 1994.

On September 24, 1993, the following other events occurred: Petitioner gave Bank One, Green Bay a new mortgage on the McDonald Street property securing a total obligation of $480,000, consisting of both his September 30, 1992, $100,000 note and the WLC nonrecourse note of $380,000 that he had guaranteed; WLC accepted the commitment of Bank One, Green Bay to provide a $380,000 loan for financing construction of the building on the Lawrence Drive property; WLC executed a corporate borrowing resolution authorizing it to borrow from Bank One, Green Bay; WLC executed an application to Bank One, Green Bay for a standby letter of credit in the amount of $380,000 in favor of the title company, which was delegated the task of making progress payments to the contractor under the construction contract; the bank issued its irrevocable standby credit in favor of the title company in that amount.

On September 24, 1993, Landmark Building Systems Ltd. (Landmark) entered into a lump sum construction contract in the amount of $375,688 (subject to certain adjustments) with WLC to construct the building on the Lawrence Drive property. The contract named petitioner, Mike DeCleene (petitioners' son, who works in the family business), and/or a representative of Excel Engineering, as owner's representative. As owner's representative, petitioner and Mike DeCleene had general authority, including the right to approve changes in design or construction, to inspect and approve workmanship and materials, to visit the construction site, and to determine compliance with the contract.

Although the standby letter of credit and the construction contract do not expressly so state, progress payments to the contractor were to be made only with the approval of petitioner or Michael DeCleene as owner's representative. Excel Engineering played a role in the design of the building, but lacked actual authority to sign off as owner's representative.

The construction contract called for substantial completion by December 15, 1993. Between September 24 and December 29, 1993, Landmark worked on the construction of the building on the Lawrence Drive property and substantially completed the building to petitioner's specifications.

On December 28, 1993, 1 day prior to execution and closing of the Assumption, Release and Escrow Agreement described below, Bank One, Green Bay executed a Satisfaction of Mortgage for the mortgage given by WLC to petitioner that petitioner had assigned to the bank in connection with petitioner's quitclaim of the Lawrence Drive property to WLC on September 24, 1993.

On December 29, 1993, Bank One, Green Bay, WLC, and petitioner executed the Assumption, Release and Escrow Agreement, which provided that petitioner assumed and became personally obligated to the bank for all obligations of WLC arising out of the construction note and mortgage, notwithstanding their nonrecourse language; petitioner agreed to be responsible for completion of the construction project; and WLC agreed to pay petitioner $142,400 for the McDonald Street property. Petitioner undertook to use $100,000 of the $142,400 received from WLC "to pay a Note due the Bank in the amount of * * * $100,000" (which had been secured by mortgages on both the Lawrence Drive property and the McDonald Street property) and to escrow the remainder with the bank to pay real estate taxes and any special assessments on the McDonald Street property and to reduce the balance of the construction loan note and mortgage to $360,000, with any surplus of the escrowed funds to be delivered to petitioner. Bank One, Green Bay agreed "to release any liens that it may have on the property located on McDonald Street".

On December 29, 1993, petitioner formally assumed as borrower what had been WLC's nonrecourse $380,000 Bank One, Green Bay note of September 24, 1993; petitioner conveyed the McDonald Street property to WLC by warranty deed. WLC quitclaimed to petitioner its interest in the Lawrence Drive property. WLC directly paid petitioner $142,400 by check to petitioner's order drawn on M & I First National Bank of West Bend, Wisconsin. Petitioner endorsed this check "Pay only to the order of Bank One-Green Bay".

Petitioner and WLC had agreed in the Exchange Agreement that the McDonald Street property, including improvements, and the unimproved Lawrence Drive property each had a value of $142,400. The quitclaim deed of the Lawrence Drive property from petitioner to WLC and the warranty deed of the McDonald Street property from petitioner to WLC each showed that real estate transfer tax of $427.20 had been paid, based on a value of $142,400; the quitclaim deed from WLC to petitioner of the title to the improved Lawrence Drive property showed that real estate transfer tax of $1,140 had been paid, based on a value of $380,000.[12]

Although petitioner had a general desire to complete his acquisition of the improved Lawrence Drive property as soon as possible, he didn't particularly care whether the closing occurred before or after December 31, 1993. WLC wished to have the closing occur before December 31, 1993, because it wanted the Lawrence Drive property removed from its books for insurance valuation purposes before the end of the year.

On their 1993 return, petitioners treated the subject transactions between petitioner and WLC as a sale of the unimproved Lawrence Drive property and a like-

---

12. [3] Although these amounts do not computationally coincide in all respects with the transfer tax figures shown on the buyer's and seller's closing statements, those statements confirm that the transfer taxes on the subject transactions were paid by petitioner.

kind exchange of the McDonald Street property for the improved Lawrence Drive property. Petitioners reported no gain or loss on the disposition of the McDonald Street property. They reported a $5,373 short-term capital gain ($142,400 gross "sales price" less $137,027 basis) on their quitclaim transfer of the Lawrence Drive property to WLC, which is described in Schedule D of their return as a sale of "investment land".

Petitioners' 1993 return includes a Form 8824, Like-Kind Exchanges, which states that petitioners exchanged "land and building" for "land and building". The return discloses no other facts regarding the transactions between petitioner and WLC.

Respondent used petitioner's $59,831 adjusted basis figure for the McDonald Street property in computing the long-term capital gain on the sale of the McDonald Street property determined in the deficiency notice. However, on audit of petitioners' return, an adjusted basis of $61,331 had been established. Respondent's deficiency notice did not back out the gain petitioners had reported on petitioner's quitclaim transfer of the unimproved Lawrence Drive property to WLC, notwithstanding that, under respondent's theory of the case, the Lawrence Drive property has never been disposed of by petitioner.

On April 29, 1998, Bank One, Green Bay, WLC, and petitioner executed an amendment to the Assumption, Release and Escrow Agreement. The amendment recites that the original of that agreement contained a scrivener's error, and recites that WLC would pay petitioner $142,400 "*in satisfaction of the Note and Mortgage*" on the *Lawrence Drive property, that the Lawrence Drive Property "is exchanged per the Exchange Agreement" for the McDonald Street property*, that petitioner will use $100,000 of the $142,400 received from WLC to pay petitioner's $100,000 note to the bank, and that the balance of $42,400 will be escrowed with the bank to pay real estate taxes and any special assessments on the *Lawrence Drive property* (emphases supplied) and to reduce the balance of the construction loan and mortgage to $360,000.

The amendment also sets forth a revision of the provision regarding release of liens by Bank One, Green Bay, reading as follows:

> The Bank agrees to release any liens that it may have on the property located at 625 Lawrence Drive, De Pere, Wisconsin, that are the obligation of the Company [WLC] and against 917 MacDonald [sic] Street, Green Bay, Wisconsin that are the obligation of DeCleene.

The terms of the foregoing transactions among WLC and petitioner and Bank One, Green Bay assured that WLC would pay no amounts thereunder until it received the McDonald Street property, that WLC would have no personal liability with respect to the Lawrence Drive property or financing while the Lawrence Drive property was titled in its name or at any time thereafter, and that all transaction and other costs with respect to the McDonald Street and Lawrence Drive properties would be paid by petitioner.

ANALYSIS

Section 1001(c) provides that the entire gain or loss on the sale or exchange of property shall be recognized. Section 1031(a)(1) provides for nonrecognition of gain or loss on the exchange of certain types of like-kind property, including real property, held for productive use in trade or business or for investment.[13] Section 1031(b) in effect provides that if the property received in an exchange otherwise qualifying for nonrecognition of gain under section 1031(a) includes money or other property ("boot"), then any gain to the recipient shall be recognized, but not in excess of the boot.

Was McDonald Street Sold or Exchanged?

The question posed by respondent's determination is whether the subject transactions were a taxable sale to WLC of the McDonald Street property, as respondent determined, or instead were a taxable sale of the unimproved Lawrence Drive property to WLC, followed 3 months later by petitioner's transfer of the McDonald Street property to WLC in a like-kind exchange for WLC's reconveyance to petitioner of the Lawrence Drive property-now substantially improved-as petitioners reported.

The tax significance of the answer to the question stems from the disparity in the adjusted bases of the McDonald Street and Lawrence Drive properties in petitioner's hands. McDonald Street, which petitioner purchased in 1976–77, had an adjusted basis in his hands substantially lower than his cost of Lawrence Drive, which he purchased in 1992. Petitioner therefore reported as the taxable sale not his permanent relinquishment to WLC of the low-basis McDonald Street property, but rather the first leg of the "repo" transaction that temporarily parked the high-basis Lawrence Drive property with WLC.

Legal and Administrative Background

The primary reason that has been given for deferring recognition of gain under § 1031(a) on exchanges of like-kind property is that the exchange does not materially alter the taxpayer's economic position; the property received in the exchange is considered a continuation of the old property still unliquidated. *See, e.g., Koch v. Comm'r*, 71 T.C. 54, 63–64 (1978). However, § 1031(a) does not go so far in implementing this notion as to be a reinvestment rollover provision, like § 1033 or § 1034. A sale of qualified property for cash requires that gain or loss be recognized under the general rule of § 1001(c); such a sale does not become part of a qualifying exchange under § 1031(a) even though the cash received on the sale is immediately invested in like property. *Compare Coastal Terminals, Inc. v. U.S.*, 320 F.2d 333, 337 (4th Cir. 1963), with *Rogers v. Comm'r*, 44 T.C. 126, 136 (1965), *affd. per curiam* 377 F.2d 534 (9th Cir. 1967).

Petitioners remind us, and we are well aware-as we stated in another § 1031 exchange case in which we held against the taxpayer-that "Notwithstanding the familiar and longstanding rule that exemptions are to be narrowly or strictly construed, … § 1031 has been given a liberal interpretation." *Estate of Bowers v. Comm'r*, 94 T.C.

---

13. [4] Clearly, the Lawrence Drive property, in both its unimproved and improved states, and the McDonald street property were like-kind properties within the meaning of § 1031(a). § 1.1031(a)-1(b)….

582, 590 (1990) (citing *Biggs v. Comm'r*, 69 T.C. 905, 913-914 (1978), *affd.* 632 F.2d 1171 (5th Cir. 1980)). The courts have exhibited a lenient attitude toward taxpayers in like-kind exchange cases, particularly toward deferred exchanges. *See, e.g., Starker v. U.S.*, 602 F.2d 1341 (9th Cir.1979). The Commissioner has also played a facilitating role by issuing regulations that provide safe harbors for deferred exchanges, *see* § 1.1031(k)-1, Income Tax Regs., under the statutory limitations imposed on such exchanges by § 1031(a)(3), as enacted by Deficit Reduction Act of 1984, Pub. L. 98-369, § 77(b), 98 Stat. 596. These regulations, with their provisions for use of third-party "qualified intermediaries" as accommodation titleholders, who will not be considered the taxpayer's agent in doing the multiparty deferred exchanges permitted by the regulations, have encouraged the growth of a new industry of third-party exchange facilitators.

The subject transactions present a case of first impression in this Court. They reflect the effort of petitioner and his advisers to implement a so-called reverse exchange directly with WLC, without the participation of a third-party exchange facilitator. Reverse exchanges have been described as transactions in which the taxpayer locates and identifies the replacement property (and acquires it or causes it to be acquired on his behalf by an exchange facilitator) before he is ready to transfer the property to be relinquished in exchange. The preamble to the deferred exchange regulations, § 1.1031(k)-1, Income Tax Regs., made clear the Commissioner's view that § 1031(a)(3) and the deferred-exchange regulations do not apply to reverse exchanges. See T.D. 8346, 1991-1 C.B. 150, 151.

The Commissioner has recently responded to industry and practitioner requests for guidance[14] by publishing a revenue procedure describing the Commissioner's conditions for qualifying reverse exchanges for nonrecognition of gain under § 1031(a)(1). *See* Rev. Proc.2000-37, 2000-40 I.R.B. 308. Like the deferred exchange regulations that implement § 1031(a)(3), the revenue procedure provides for third-party qualified intermediaries as exchange accommodation titleholders in carrying out the "qualified exchange accommodation arrangements" whose use will qualify reverse exchanges for nonrecognition of gain or loss under § 1031(a)(1). Like the deferred exchange regulations, the revenue procedure provides a safe harbor; it states that "the Service recognizes that 'parking' transactions can be accomplished outside of the safe harbor provided this revenue procedure", but that "no inference is intended with respect to the federal income tax treatment of 'parking' transactions that do not satisfy the terms of the safe harbor". Rev. Proc. 2000-37, 2000-40 I.R.B. 308.

Because the revenue procedure is prospectively effective, it does not apply to the case at hand. See *id.* We therefore have recourse to general principles of tax law to answer the question posed by repondent's determination.

---

14. [5] See, e.g., American Bar Association Section on Taxation, Committee on Sales, Exchanges and Basis, Report on the Application of § 1031 to Reverse Exchanges, 21 J. Real Est. Tax. 44 (1993); Adam Handler, *Pricewaterhouse Coopers Forwards Proposed Guidance on Reverse Exchanges*, 2000 TNT 16-27, Doc.2000-2588 (Jan. 25, 2000); *Safe Harbor Guidance for Reverse Like-kind Exchanges to Come Soon*, IRS Official Promises, Highlights and Documents 1157 (Jan. 25, 2000).

Analysis and Conclusion

In the case at hand, petitioner did not just locate and identify the Lawrence Drive property in anticipation of acquiring it as replacement property in exchange for the McDonald Street property that he intended to relinquish. He purchased the Lawrence Drive property without the participation of an exchange facilitator a year or more before he was ready to relinquish the McDonald Street property and relocate his business to the Lawrence Drive property. In the following year, petitioner transferred title to the Lawrence Drive property, subject to a reacquisition agreement-the Exchange Agreement-not to a third-party exchange facilitator, but to WLC, the party to which he simultaneously obligated himself to relinquish the McDonald Street property.

In forgoing the use of a third party and doing all the transfers with WLC, petitioner and his advisers created an inherently ambiguous situation. The ambiguity is exacerbated by the fact that petitioner and WLC agreed in the Exchange Agreement that the McDonald Street property and the unimproved Lawrence Drive property were of equal value, $142,400. So when WLC paid petitioner $142,400-at the same time that he permanently relinquished the McDonald Street property to WLC-was the payment received by petitioner from WLC the sale price of the McDonald Street property at the December 29 closing, as respondent determined? Or was it the deferred purchase price on petitioner's September 24 quitclaim transfer of title to the unimproved Lawrence Drive property (which petitioner received back on December 29 from WLC with the substantially completed building that had been erected on it in the intervening 3 months), as petitioner reported?

Our approach to answering these questions is to determine for tax purposes whether WLC became the owner of the Lawrence Drive property during the 3-month period it held title to the property while the building was being built on it to petitioner's specifications. If petitioner remained the owner of the Lawrence Drive property during this period, petitioner could not engage in a qualified like-kind exchange of the McDonald Street property for the Lawrence Drive property, and the $142,400 payment received by petitioner would be deemed the sale price of the McDonald Street property. A taxpayer cannot engage in an exchange with himself; an exchange ordinarily requires a "reciprocal transfer of property, as distinguished from a transfer of property for a money consideration". Sec. 1.1002-1(d), Income Tax Regs.

WLC did not acquire any of the benefits and burdens of ownership of the Lawrence Drive property during the 3-month period it held title to that property. WLC acquired no equity interest in the Lawrence Drive property. WLC made no economic outlay to acquire the property. WLC was not at risk to any extent with respect to the Lawrence Drive property because the obligation and security interest it gave back on its purported acquisition of the property were nonrecourse. WLC merely obligated itself to reconvey to petitioner prior to yearend the Lawrence Drive property with a substantially completed building on it that had been built to his specifications and that pursuant to prearrangement he was obligated to take and pay for.

The parties treated WLC's holding of title to the Lawrence Drive property as having no economic significance. The transaction was not even used as a financing device. No interest accrued or was paid on the nonrecourse note and mortgage, which assured that petitioner would get back the Lawrence Drive property after it had been improved. WLC had no exposure to real estate taxes that accrued with respect to the property while WLC held the title; all such taxes were to be paid by petitioner. No account was to be taken under the terms of the reacquisition agreement of any value that had been added to the property by reason of the building constructed in the interim. The construction was financed by petitioner through the bank he was accustomed to dealing with. Petitioner through his guaranty and reacquisition obligation was at all times at risk with respect to the Lawrence Drive property. WLC had no risk or exposure with respect to the additional outlay of funds required to finance construction of the building. WLC had no potential for or exposure to any economic gain or loss on its acquisition and disposition of title to the Lawrence Drive property.

The reality of the subject transactions as we see them is a taxable sale of the McDonald Street property to WLC. Petitioner's purchase in 1992 of the Lawrence Drive property, on which he intended to build a new facility for his business as the replacement for his McDonald Street property, put him in the position of arranging to improve the Lawrence Drive property, as well as to sell the McDonald Street property. Petitioner's prior quitclaim transfer to WLC of title to the unimproved Lawrence Drive property, which petitioners try to persuade us was petitioner's taxable sale, amounted to nothing more than a parking transaction by petitioner with WLC, which contractually bound itself to acquire from petitioner the McDonald Street property that petitioner was going to relinquish permanently, as well as to reconvey to petitioner the Lawrence Drive property as soon as the facility to be built thereon to his specifications was substantially completed.

The reconveyance to petitioner of the Lawrence Drive property was not part of an exchange by petitioner of the McDonald Street property. That reconveyance of the Lawrence Drive property to petitioner merely reunited in his hands the bare legal title to the Lawrence Drive property with the beneficial ownership therein that he had continued to hold all along while the building that he obligated himself to pay for was being built to his specifications.

In support of their claim that petitioner exchanged the McDonald Street property for the improved Lawrence Drive property, petitioners point out that the improved Lawrence Drive property was different from the unimproved Lawrence Drive property that he acquired in 1992 and whose title he transferred to WLC on September 24, 1993. Petitioners state: "Petitioners sold unimproved land (and reported the transaction) and in the exchange got back improved real estate they could continue their business operation in." It's true that unimproved property and improved property are different from each other; they are not "similar or related in service or use" for the purpose of the § 1033 rollover provision. See § 1.1033(a)-2(c)(9), Income Tax Regs. However, the transformation of the Lawrence Drive property while title was parked with WLC does not gainsay our conclusion. In substance, petitioner never disposed of the Lawrence Drive property and remained its owner during the 3-month construction period because the transfer of title to WLC never divested petitioner of beneficial ownership.

Having set forth our analysis and conclusion, we now address the authorities cited by petitioners[15] as favoring their position or as being distinguishable.

Authority in the Court of Appeals for the Seventh Circuit

The only case in the Seventh Circuit-the circuit to which any appeal would lie in the case at hand-that the parties have brought to our attention is *Bloomington Coca-Cola Bottling Co. v. Comm'r*, 189 F.2d 14 (7th Cir. 1951), *affg.* a Memorandum Opinion of this Court dated Aug. 10, 1950. Petitioners try to distinguish the *Bloomington Coca-Cola Bottling Co.* case, but we find it highly instructive.

The taxpayer had originally reported the transaction in issue as a sale at a loss in the year it occurred, 1939, but contended-for 1943 and 1944 excess profits tax purposes-that the transaction had been an exchange under the statutory predecessor of section 1031(a) in which no loss had been recognized. The taxpayer's change in position was attributable to its desire not to reduce its excess profits tax base.

The taxpayer had outgrown its old bottling plant and hired a contractor to erect a new plant, on the taxpayer's land, at an agreed cost of $72,500. Included in the consideration paid by the taxpayer to the contractor was the old bottling plant and the parcel of land on which it was located, at an agreed value of $8,000, plus cash of $64,500. The taxpayer reported on its 1939 income tax return a loss of approximately $23,000 on the sale of the old plant.

As this Court pointed out in its Memorandum Opinion: "Here the contractor was not the owner of the land upon which the new building was constructed, never owned the new building, and never conveyed the new building to the petitioner".

The Tax Court held-and the Court of Appeals affirmed-that the transaction was in effect the purchase of a new facility, and not an exchange of unimproved property for improved property, inasmuch as the taxpayer already owned the land on which the new plant was constructed. The contractor could not be a party to an exchange with the taxpayer because the contractor was never the owner of the property that

---

15. [6] Petitioners contend that their advisers relied on two private letter rulings in structuring the subject transactions: Priv. Ltr. Rul. 78-23-035 (1978), which they characterize as "nearly identical to the facts in our case", and Priv. Ltr. Rul. 91-49-018 (1991), which they cite as "virtually directly on point (even goes farther than our case) on how a transaction can be structured". Petitioners' contentions are unavailing; not only does sec. 6110(j)(3) provide that private letter rulings cannot be cited as precedent, but, unlike the case at hand, the other party to the transaction in both private letter rulings had the risks of ownership during the relevant time period. Similarly, Rev. Rul. 75-291, and Rev. Rul. 77-297, cited in Priv. Ltr. Rul. 78-23-035, don't help petitioners; not only does this Court regard published rulings as having no precedential value, *see* Estate of Lang v. Comm'r, 613 F.2d 770, 776 (9th Cir. 1980), *affg. on this issue* 64 T.C. 404, 406-407 (1975); Intel Corp. & Consol. Subs. v. Comm'r, 102 T.C. 616, 621 (1993); Stark v. Comm'r, 86 T.C. 243, 250-251 (1986), but the facts of both rulings, like Priv. Ltr. Rul. 91-94-018 (1991), are distinguishable from the case at hand in the same dispositive respect.

the taxpayer received in the so-called exchange. The contractor was merely acting as a service provider in the construction of the new plant. The only real property to which the contractor acquired title was the land and old plant that it received as part payment for the construction services it provided.

The subject transactions are similar to those in *Bloomington Coca-Cola Bottling Co. v. Commissioner, supra,* in significant respects. The taxpayer sold its old bottling plant (petitioner sold the McDonald Street property) to the only other party it was dealing with, the contractor (WLC). The taxpayer hired a contractor to build a new facility on land that it owned. In the case at hand, petitioner's conveyance of title to the unimproved Lawrence Drive property and the conveyance of that property back with a substantially completed building on it are to be disregarded; WLC never acquired any of the benefits and burdens of ownership of the Lawrence Drive property. WLC acquired no equity or beneficial interest in the Lawrence Drive property, no risk of loss or opportunity for gain, no exposure to real estate taxes or other carrying charges, no liability even for interest on its nonrecourse secured obligation during the interim period. All we are left with, as in *Bloomington Coca-Cola Bottling Co.,* is that a building was built for petitioner according to his specifications on land that he owned and petitioner was obligated to pay for that building. The taxpayer in *Bloomington Coca-Cola Bottling Co.* and petitioner also sold their old property to the party with whom they dealt in connection with the building of the new facility.[16]

Authorities Relied on by Petitioners

We now turn to the cases petitioners rely on to support their contention that petitioner exchanged the McDonald Street property for the substantially improved Lawrence Drive property: *J.H. Baird Publg. Co. v. Comm'r,* 39 T.C. 608 (1962); *Coupe v. Comm'r,* 52 T.C. 394, 409–410 (1969); *124 Front Street, Inc. v. Comm'r,* 65 T.C. 6 (1975); *Biggs v. Comm'r,* 69 T.C. 905 (1978), *affd.* 632 F.2d 1171 (5th Cir.1980); *Fredericks v. Comm'r,* T.C. Memo.1994-27.

We preface our review of these cases by acknowledging that they all reflect, to some degree, the liberal interpretation in favor of taxpayers that this Court and other courts have applied in cases under § 1031(a)(1). We also observe that none of these cases concerned a reverse exchange and that all of them are highly fact specific and therefore distinguishable from the case at hand. Petitioners have read these cases selectively, emphasizing in each of them what the taxpayer got away with. In so doing, petitioners

---

16. [7] We have found no other like-kind exchange cases in the Seventh Circuit that bear on the issue in the case at hand. However, another Seventh Circuit case worth noting is Patton v. Jonas, 249 F.2d 375 (7th Cir. 1957), which applies the same analysis as the line of Sixth Circuit cases culminating in First Am. Natl. Bank of Nashville v. United States, 467 F.2d 1098 (1972), which hold that "repo" transactions in tax-exempt bonds are to be treated as secured loans so that the purchaser in form is treated as a lender not entitled to exclude the tax-exempt bond interest from its income; this is because the original seller remains the owner of the bonds for tax purposes. *See also* Green v. Comm'r, 367 F.2d 823, 825 (7th Cir. 1966), *affg.* T.C. Memo.1965-272; Commercial Capital Corp. v. Comm'r, T.C. Memo.1968-186. Compare Rev. Rul. 74-27, 1974-1 C.B. 24 (repurchase obligation) with Rev. Rul. 82-144, 1982-2 C.B. 34 (separately purchased and paid-for put).

have lost sight of the cumulative adverse effect on their position of all the facts in the case at hand, which have led to our conclusion that WLC never acquired beneficial ownership of the Lawrence Drive property. It would therefore be a sterile exercise to engage in a detailed recitation of the facts of these cases and a point-by-point refutation of their applicability to the case at hand. A couple of highlights from *J.H. Baird Publg. Co. v. Comm'r, supra,* will suffice.

Petitioners try to make something of the fact that the Court in *J.H. Baird Publg. Co. v. Comm'r,* 39 T.C. at 618, *distinguished Bloomington Coca-Coca Bottling Co. v. Comm'r,* 189 F.2d 14 (7th Cir. 1951), on the ground that "It was clear that the contractor did not own the other property which, it was claimed, was transferred to the taxpayer in the exchange." As already indicated, we have found dispositive in the case at hand that WLC never acquired beneficial ownership of the Lawrence Drive property.[17] WLC merely served as an accommodation party, providing the parking place for legal title to the Lawrence Drive property, while petitioner remained the beneficial owner before and after and throughout the 3-month focal period of the subject transactions.

When petitioner conveyed to WLC title to the Lawrence Drive property, WLC became contractually bound to reconvey it, and petitioner was bound to take it back, prior to yearend (not much more than 3 months). Indeed, under Wisconsin law, both parties were entitled to specific performance of the other party's obligation. See *Anderson v. Onsager,* 155 Wis.2d 504, 455 (Wis. 1990); *Heins v. Thompson & Flieth L. Co.,* 165 Wis. 563 (Wis.1917). It's difficult to imagine commitments more binding than the reciprocal obligations of petitioner and WLC in the case at hand. The conveyance and reconveyance of title to the Lawrence Drive property must be disregarded as having no tax significance because, at the end of the day, petitioner ended up where he started, with title to and beneficial ownership of the Lawrence Drive property.[18]

Computational Questions

Petitioners point out that respondent's deficiency notice, which made an upward adjustment of $82,569 in long-term gain realized and recognized by petitioners on the disposition of the McDonald Street property, which we have found to be the actual sale, failed to back out the short-term gain of $5,373 that petitioners reported on the transfer of title to the unimproved Lawrence Drive property. Petitioners' point is well taken. It should be addressed in the Rule 155 computation.

Similarly, other matters not completely resolved, such as the calculation of additional costs paid by petitioner in connection with the sale of the McDonald Street

---

17. [8] We also observe that *J.H. Baird Publg. Co. v. Comm'r,* 39 T.C. 608, 618 (1962), on which petitioners rely, applied the concept of beneficial ownership in the taxpayer's favor. Petitioners have failed to persuade us that the concept of beneficial ownership is an illegitimate importation into the tax law of qualified like-kind exchanges.

18. [9] In so doing, the subject transactions satisfy the requirements for application of what the Court of Appeals for the Seventh Circuit has characterized as the most restrictive and rigorous version of the step-transaction doctrine: the binding commitment test. *McDonald's Restaurants, Inc. v. Comm'r,* 688 F.2d 520, 525 (7th Cir. 1982), *revg.* 76 T.C. 872 (1981).

property, as well as his adjusted basis in that property, should be addressed in the Rule 155 computation of the gain on the sale.

Penalty Question

The subject transactions were structured by petitioner's accountant and attorneys after petitioner presented them with the accomplished fact of his purchase of the Lawrence Drive property. Petitioners' 1993 income tax return, prepared by petitioner's accountant, reported a taxable short-term gain of $5,373 on the sale of "investment land" and reported a like-kind exchange of "land and building" for "land and building" on Form 8824. The disclosures were bare bones but adequate to trigger the audit that led to the deficiency notice and the case at hand.

Respondent determined that petitioners were liable for an accuracy-related penalty under §6662(a) and (b)(1) or (2). Section 6662(a) imposes a 20-percent accuracy-related penalty on the portion of an underpayment that is due to one or more causes enumerated in §6662(b). Respondent relies on subsections (b)(1) (negligence or intentional disregard of rules or regulations) or (b)(2) (substantial understatement of income tax).

Petitioners argue they are not liable for the penalty. Petitioners point out that a certified public accountant outlined the subject transactions as they were carried out and prepared their return and that the deal was structured and the papers drawn by petitioners' attorneys. Petitioners contend that they reasonably relied on professional advice in the preparation of their return and that they are entitled to relief under the exceptions that apply to a substantial understatement.

Negligence includes a failure to attempt reasonably to comply with the Code. See §6662(c). Disregard includes a careless, reckless, or intentional disregard. *See id.* Negligence is the failure to exercise due care or the failure to act as a reasonable and prudent person. *See Neely v. Comm'r*, 85 T.C. 934, 947 (1985).

No penalty is imposed for negligence or intentional disregard of rules or regulations or a substantial understatement of income if the taxpayer shows that the underpayment is due to reasonable cause and the taxpayer's good faith. See §6664(c); §§1.6662-3(a), 1.6664-4(a), Income tax Regs.

Reasonable cause requires that the taxpayer have exercised ordinary business care and prudence as to the disputed item. *See U.S. v. Boyle*, 469 U.S. 241 (1985); see also *Estate of Young v. Comm'r*, 110 T.C. 297, 317 (1998). The good faith, reasonable reliance on the advice of an independent, competent professional as to the tax treatment of an item may meet this requirement. *See U.S. v. Boyle, supra*; sec. 1.6664-4(b), Income Tax Regs.; *see also Richardson v. Comm'r*, 125 F.3d 551 (7th Cir. 1997), *affg.* T.C. Memo.1995-554; *Ewing v. Comm'r*, 91 T.C. 396, 423 (1988), *affd.* without published opinion 940 F.2d 1534 (9th Cir. 1991).

Whether a taxpayer relies on advice and whether such reliance is reasonable depend on the facts and circumstances of the case and the law that applies to those facts and circumstances. See §1.6664-4(c)(i), Income Tax Regs. A professional may render advice that may be relied upon reasonably when he or she arrives at that advice independently, taking into account, among other things, the taxpayer's purposes for entering into the underlying transaction. *See* § 1.6664-4(c)(i), Income Tax Regs.; *see also Leonhart v. Comm'r*, 414 F.2d 749 (4th Cir. 1969), *affg.* T.C. Memo.1968-98. Reliance is unreasonable when the taxpayer knew, or should have known, that the adviser lacked the requisite expertise to opine on the tax treatment of the disputed item. See § 1.6664-4(c), Income Tax Regs.

In sum, for a taxpayer to rely reasonably upon advice so as possibly to negate a § 6662(a) accuracy-related penalty determined by the Commissioner, the taxpayer must prove that the taxpayer meets each requirement of the following three-prong test: (1) The adviser was a competent professional who had sufficient expertise to justify reliance, (2) the taxpayer provided necessary and accurate information to the adviser, and (3) the taxpayer actually relied in good faith on the adviser's judgment. *See Ellwest Stereo Theatres, Inc. v. Comm'r*, T.C. Memo.1995-610; *see also* Rule 142(a).

OPINION

We conclude on the record before us that petitioners actually relied in good faith on disinterested professional advisers who structured the transactions and prepared their return. Petitioners were justified in their reliance, notwithstanding that we have upheld respondent's determination that the subject transactions did not qualify as a like-kind exchange of the Lawrence Drive property. Accordingly, we hold for petitioners on the penalty issue.

Fredericks v. Commissioner

United States Tax Court
67 T.C.M. (CCH) 2005 (1994)

FACTS

Some of the facts have been stipulated and are so found. The stipulations of fact and attached exhibits are incorporated herein by this reference. Petitioner resided in Santa Ynez, California, when he filed his petition.

On or about January 7, 1980, petitioner and four other individuals acquired interests in Wildridge Apartments, a 305-unit apartment complex, located in Colorado Springs, Colorado. Petitioner held a 90.83-percent interest in Wildridge Apartments and the other four cotenants held a combined minority interest of 9.17 percent. Petitioner acquired his interest in Wildridge Apartments by selling to the four minority owners an undivided 9.17-percent interest in the pending acquisition of Wildridge Apartments for $400,000, by exchanging certain apartment units known as Parkdale and wholly owned by petitioner, and by executing an 18-month "wrap around" note in the amount of $4 million.

In the latter part of 1980, petitioner began attempts to obtain permanent long-term financing for Wildridge Apartments. Petitioner had difficulty obtaining such financing since interest rates continued to rise and lenders "kept backing out." As of September 28, 1981, the interest rate on the 18-month promissory note was 23.5 percent. Under an extension agreement dated September 24, 1982, petitioner was able to extend the original due date (June 7, 1982) on the 18-month promissory note to July 9, 1983, by making a $500,000 payment. On April 12, 1983, the Savings Bank of Puget Sound signed a loan commitment letter for the refinancing of Wildridge Apartments in the amount of $6 million. On May 27, 1983, petitioner signed a promissory note for $6 million, executed a Deed of Trust, Assignment of Rents, and Security Agreement in favor of the Savings Bank of Puget Sound. On June 2, 1983, the loan transaction settled, and, after paying the underlying indebtedness and settlement charges, petitioner received net loan proceeds of $2,020,407.33.

On March 6, 1981, more than 1 year following petitioner's acquisition of Wildridge Apartments, petitioner entered into an "Option Agreement" with the J. and M. Brock Living Trust (Trust) to purchase certain parcels of unimproved real property, consisting of approximately 11 acres located in Buellton, California (Buellton Property).[19] The option period was to end September 6, 1982. Petitioner paid $50,000 for the option. Along with entering into the "Option Agreement", the parties executed (1) "Agreement Re Interpretation of Option Agreement and Purchase Agreement and Escrow Instructions"[20] and (2) "Purchase Agreement and Escrow Instructions."[21]

On August 12, 1982, in consideration of an additional $50,000, the Trust extended the above option to September 6, 1983. The terms of this new option agreement were substantially similar to, and consistent with, the first option and attending agreements. Fred L. Fredericks, Inc. (Company), made the $50,000 payment for the extension of the option. Company later credited petitioner for the $50,000 he paid for the initial option. Petitioner was the sole shareholder of Company. Company conducted business as a licensed building contractor and as a real estate developer.

On February 25, 1982, Fred L. Fredericks Realty, Inc. (FLF Realty), a licensed real estate broker, listed Wildridge Apartments for sale at a price of $9,200,000. Petitioner was the sole shareholder of FLF Realty. In 1983, petitioner retained Paul Hamilton Co., an unrelated company, to sell Wildridge Apartments.

As early as May 4, 1983, petitioner and BHS Realty, Ltd. (BHS Realty), an unrelated limited partnership, had agreed on certain terms of sale of Wildridge Apartments.

---

19. [2] The "Option Agreement" provided that the "option was granted because of the personal involvement" of petitioner, that the option could not be assigned by petitioner, and that "Any such purported assignment shall be void and of no force or effect and shall constitute a default" by petitioner. No such assignment restriction was imposed on the Trust. The Trust gifted a portion of the property, subject to the option, to the Parks and Brock Unitrust.

20. [3] Paragraph 11 of this agreement provides: "This agreement is executed concurrently with the Option Agreement and Purchase Agreement and Escrow Instructions and shall be interpreted therewith as though one document."

21. [4] Paragraph 10 of this agreement provides:

Non-Assignability. Except as provided herein, Buyer may not (a) assign his rights under this Purchase Agreement and Escrow Instructions to any person or entity or (b) designate a nominee or other person or entity to receive title to the Property without the prior written consent of Seller, which consent shall not be unreasonably withheld providing Buyer has a controlling interest in such entity, and such act shall not relieve Buyer from the obligations created herein. Any attempted assignment or designation contrary to the foregoing shall be void and of no force or effect and shall constitute a default by Buyer hereunder.

On or about May 20, 1983, petitioner, on behalf of himself and the minority owners of Wildridge Apartments, and BHS Realty entered into an "Agreement of Purchase and Sale With Closing Instructions" concerning the sale of Wildridge Apartments. The agreed purchase price was $9,180,000. Under §11.11 of the agreement, petitioner disclosed to BHS Realty that prior to the close of escrow, petitioner intended to arrange a like-kind exchange within the meaning of section 1031, whereby petitioner would exchange Wildridge Apartments subject to the terms and provisions of the agreement, for other property owned by Company. In the event this occurred, BHS Realty agreed to purchase Wildridge Apartments from Company. Petitioner signed the agreement and, in his capacity as president of Company, also signed the agreement acknowledging that Company had read and understood all the terms and provisions. Pursuant to section 1.2(a) of the agreement, on or about May 20, 1983, BHS Realty deposited $200,000 in an escrow account with Safeco Title Insurance Co. (Safeco Title).

On June 10, 1983, petitioner entered into an "Agreement of Exchange of Property" with Company, whereby petitioner was to convey Wildridge Apartments to Company. Pursuant to the agreement, Company, as "the owner and developer of certain real property in Buellton, California, consisting of approximately 11 acres",[22] was to (1) construct certain improvements prior to July 1, 1988, including a restaurant, hotel, and movie theater/ice cream parlor complex, and (2) transfer the improved property to petitioner. For its services, Company was to receive the sum of $750,000. Petitioner signed the "Agreement of Exchange of Property" in two capacities, individually and as president of Company. There were no other parties to the agreement.

On June 27, 1983, petitioner conveyed Wildridge Apartments by grant deed to Company. The deed was recorded on July 13, 1983. Company then sold Wildridge Apartments to Wildridge Apartments, Ltd., an unrelated California limited partnership, for $9,180,000. Wildridge Apartments, Ltd., had been created and substituted as purchaser of Wildridge Apartments by the principals of BHS Realty. The conveyance of title to Wildridge Apartments, Ltd., was likewise made by grant deed dated June 27, 1983, and the deed was recorded on July 13, 1983.

On June 30, 1983, pursuant to the escrow instructions, the $200,000 escrow deposit was released to Company from the sales escrow by Safeco Title, the escrow agent. Upon the closing of escrow, Wildridge Apartments, Ltd., (1) executed a "Purchase Money Promissory Note" to Company as holder in the amount of $1,490,000;[23] (2) executed a "Deed of Trust, Assignment of Rents and Security Agreement" dated July 13, 1983, in favor of Company; and (3) paid the balance of the purchase price to

---

22. [5] Company, however, did not own the Buellton Property at the time the agreement was executed.

23. [6] The promissory note was reduced by $10,000 from the original principal of $1,500,000 to $1,490,000. The note bore interest at 12 percent per annum, with the principal and interest due and payable on the first anniversary of July 8, 1983.

Company.[24] On or about July 22, 1983, the minority owners of Wildridge Apartments were paid $245,178 by Company, representing their share of the sale proceeds. On July 14, 1983, Company, through escrow, paid FLF Realty a $125,000 listing commission. On September 19, 1983, Company paid Paul Hamilton Co. a $170,000 sales commission.

On August 26, 1983, Company purchased and acquired the Buellton Property for $1,895,827, consisting of $379,165 in cash and a promissory note for the balance. The Buellton Property was conveyed by grant deeds, consisting of an undivided 20-percent interest from the J. and M. Brock Living Trust and an undivided 80-percent interest from the California Polytechnic State University Foundation for the Parks and Brock Unitrust. The grant deeds were recorded on September 1, 1983.

On December 1, 1984, petitioner and Company entered into an agreement for the lease of the Buellton restaurant parcel. Petitioner leased the restaurant parcel from Company during the months of December 1984 and January 1985. Upon completion of the construction, Company conveyed the restaurant and theater/ice cream parlor parcels to petitioner by grant deed dated December 27, 1984. On September 15, 1986, by grant deed, Company conveyed the hotel to petitioner. Company was credited with its $750,000 contractor's fee for the development of the Buellton Property as follows: $200,000 for the restaurant in February 1985; $100,000 for the theater/ice cream parlor in March 1985; and $450,000 for the hotel in September 1986.

The Buellton Property, with all improvements, had a value based upon cost of $17,484,872, consisting of $2,249,664 for the restaurant, $1,087,506 for the theater/ice cream parlor, and $14,147,702 for the hotel. As provided in the exchange agreement, petitioner expended $271,094 in cash and assumed $8,004,707 in additional debt.

Petitioner filed a joint Federal income tax return for the taxable year 1983 with Paula R. Fredericks, from whom he is now divorced. On his 1983 income tax return, petitioner reported no gain or loss with respect to the Wildridge Apartments. In the notice of deficiency, respondent determined that petitioner failed to report $2,288,390 of capital gain resulting from the sale of Wildridge Apartments.

ANALYSIS

Issue 1. Section 1031(a)

Section 1001(c) requires that the entire amount of the gain or loss on the sale or exchange of property shall be recognized. Section 1031(a), however, provides for the nonrecognition of gain or loss when property held for productive use in a trade or business or for investment is exchanged solely for like-kind property that is to be held for productive use in a trade or business or for investment.[25]

---

24. [7] There is no direct evidence showing how or to whom Wildridge Apartments, Ltd., paid the balance of the purchase price. Respondent does not allege that petitioner received it personally. Therefore, we find Wildridge Apartments, Ltd., paid the balance of the purchase price to Company.

25. [8] Sec. 1031(a) provides:

(a) Nonrecognition of Gain or Loss From Exchanges Solely in Kind.-No gain or loss shall be recognized if property held for productive use in trade or business or for investment

There is no question that Wildridge Apartments and the Buellton Property were of like kind within the meaning of § 1031.[26] The parties disagree, however, on whether petitioner "exchanged" Wildridge Apartments for the Buellton Property. Respondent's determinations are presumed correct, and petitioner has the burden to establish that they are erroneous. Rule 142(a); *Welch v. Helvering*, 290 U.S. 111, 115 (1933).

Essentially, section 1031(a) assumes that new property received in an exchange is substantially a continuation of the old investment. *See Commissioner v. P.G. Lake, Inc.*, 356 U.S. 260, 268 (1958). In an exchange of like-kind property, the taxpayer's economic situation after the exchange is fundamentally the same as it was before the exchange. *Koch v. Comm'r*, 71 T.C. 54, 63 (1978). The Court of Appeals for the Fourth Circuit in *Coastal Terminals, Inc. v. U.S.*, 320 F.2d 333, 337 (4th Cir. 1963), stated:

> The purpose of § 1031(a), as shown by its legislative history, is to defer recognition of gain or loss when a direct exchange of property between the taxpayer and another party takes place; a sale for cash does not qualify as a nontaxable exchange even though the cash is immediately reinvested in like property.

See also Starker v. U.S., 602 F.2d 1341, 1352 (9th Cir. 1979). In *Barker v. Comm'r*, 74 T.C. 555, 561 (1980), this Court noted:

> The "exchange" requirement poses an analytical problem because it runs headlong into the familiar tax law maxim that the substance of a transaction controls over form. In a sense, the substance of a transaction in which the taxpayer sells property and immediately reinvests the proceeds in like-kind property is not much different from the substance of a transaction in which two parcels are exchanged without cash. Yet, if the exchange requirement is to have any significance at all, the perhaps formalistic difference between the two types of transactions must, at least on occasion, engender different results. [Citations omitted.]

Petitioner's intent to exchange Wildridge Apartments is evidenced by the "Agreement of Purchase and Sale With Closing Instructions" entered into between petitioner and BHS Realty.[27] While "matters of taxation must be determined in the light of what was actually done rather than the declared purpose of the participants", *J.H. Baird Pub-*

(not including stock in trade or other property held primarily for sale, nor stocks, bonds, notes, choses in action, certificates of trust or beneficial interest, or other securities or evidences of indebtedness or interest) is exchanged solely for property of a like kind to be held either for productive use in trade or business or for investment.

26. [9] The parties have stipulated that "Wildridge and Buellton were and are real properties. Throughout petitioner's entire period of ownership, these real properties were held by him for productive use in his trade or business or for investment."

27. [10] The Agreement provides:

Section 1031 Exchange. Seller ... intends, prior to the Close of Escrow, to arrange a like-kind exchange, within the meaning of Section 1031 ... whereby Seller shall exchange the Real Property, subject to the terms and provisions of this Agreement, for other property owned by [Company] ... Purchaser agrees ... to purchase the Real Property from the [Company].... In no event shall the Closing Date be extended beyond June 30, 1983 by reason of the exchange.

lishing Co. v. Comm'r, 39 T.C. 608, 615 (1962) (citing *Weiss v. Stearn*, 265 U.S. 242 (1924)), intent is nevertheless relevant to a determination of what transpired. *Barker v. Comm'r, supra* at 564 (citing *Carlton v. U.S.*, 385 F.2d 238 (5th Cir. 1967)); *see also Garcia v. Comm'r*, 80 T.C. 491, 497–498 (1983); *Biggs v. Comm'r*, 69 T.C. 905, 915 (1978), *affd.* 632 F.2d 1171 (5th Cir. 1980).

Courts have afforded great latitude in structuring exchange transactions. *Estate of Bowers v. Comm'r*, 94 T.C. 582, 590 (1990); *Biggs v. Comm'r*, 69 T.C. at 918. While respondent raises many arguments with respect to this transaction, we agree with petitioner that much of this transaction falls within the ambit of cases that have addressed section 1031. *See, e.g., Biggs v. Comm'r, supra* (multiple parties can be involved in the exchange with parties not owning any property at the time of entering into an agreement to exchange);[28] *Starker v. Comm'r, supra* (the transfers need not occur simultaneously);[29] *Barker v. Comm'r, supra* at 562 (a party can hold transitory ownership solely for the purpose of effectuating an exchange); *Mercantile Trust Co. v. Comm'r*, 32 B.T.A. 82, 87 (1935) (alternative sales possibilities are ignored where conditions for an exchange are manifest and an exchange actually occurs); *Alderson v. Comm'r*, 317 F.2d 790 (9th Cir.1963), *revg.* 38 T.C. 215 (1962) (parties can amend a previously executed sales agreement to provide for an exchange); *J.H. Baird Publishing Co. v. Comm'r, supra* (the taxpayer can oversee improvements on the land to be acquired); *Biggs v. Comm'r*, 69 T.C. at 916-917 (the taxpayer can advance money toward the purchase price of the property to be acquired).

Notwithstanding the liberal treatment afforded taxpayers, under certain circumstances, a transaction will be treated as a sale and not as an exchange. For purposes of this case, the transactions will not be treated as an exchange if (1) petitioner received or had control over the sales proceeds from the transaction, *see Coupe v. Comm'r*, 52 T.C. 394, 409 (1969); (2) the transfer of Wildridge Apartments and receipt of the Buellton Property was not part of an integrated plan, *see Biggs v. Comm'r, supra; Greene v. Comm'r*, T.C. Memo. 1991-403; *Anderson v. Comm'r*, T.C. Memo. 1985-205; or (3) Company acted as the taxpayer's agent for purposes of the exchange, *see Coupe v. Comm'r, supra* at 406; *Mercantile Trust Co. v. Comm'r, supra* at 85; *Biggs v. Comm'r*, 632 F.2d at 1178.

A. Receipt or Control Over Wildridge Apartment Sales Proceeds

---

28. [11] In 1989, Congress added § 1031(f) and (g) (exchanges between related parties). Omnibus Reconciliation Act of 1989, Pub. L. 101-239, § 7601(a), 103 Stat. 2370-2371. The transactions in this case occurred before the effective date of this amendment.

29. [12] In 1984, Congress added § 1031(a)(3), which provides that a transfer will not be treated as a like-kind exchange unless the exchange property is (a) identified within 45 days after the transfer of the underlying property, and (b) received by the transferor within the earlier of 180 days after the transfer of the underlying property or the due date for the transferor's tax return on which the exchange would be reported. Deficit Reduction Act of 1984, Pub. L. 98-369, § 77(a), 98 Stat. 596. Sec. 1031(a)(3) applies to transactions after July 18, 1984, or to transactions on or before July 18, 1984, if the exchange property was not received before Jan. 1, 1987. Since petitioner received the Buellton Property before Jan. 1, 1987, § 1031(a)(3) places no time limit on the exchange.

Respondent appears to argue that petitioner was in actual or constructive receipt of the escrow account with Safeco Title.[30] We disagree and hold that there was no actual or constructive receipt of the sales proceeds.[31] Section 1.451-2(a), Income Tax Regs., provides:

> Income although not actually reduced to a taxpayer's possession is constructively received ... [when] it is credited to his account, set apart for him, or otherwise made available.... However, income is not constructively received if the taxpayer's control of its receipt is subject to substantial limitations or restrictions....

On May 20, 1983, petitioner and BHS Realty entered into an "Agreement of Purchase and Sale With Closing Instructions", whereby petitioner agreed to sell Wildridge Apartments to BHS Realty. Section 11.11 provided that petitioner intended to first convey Wildridge Apartments to Company for purposes of arranging a like-kind exchange and that, in the event this occurred, BHS Realty would purchase Wildridge Apartments from Company. Petitioner also signed the agreement in his capacity as president of Company acknowledging that Company had read and understood all the terms and provisions.

Under section 1.2 of the agreement, BHS Realty agreed to pay the purchase price as follows: (1) Upon execution of the agreement, deposit $200,000 in an interest bearing account with Safeco Title, the escrow agent; (2) on or prior to the closing of escrow, assume the obligations of seller under the $6,000,000 note and "First Deed of Trust" held by the Savings Bank of Puget Sound; (3) at the closing of escrow, execute and deliver to seller a "Second Deed of Trust" and promissory note made payable to seller in the amount of $1,500,000 bearing interest at 12 percent per annum, and the principal and interest shall be due and payable on the first anniversary of the closing date; and (4) also on the closing date of escrow, pay the balance of the purchase price in the amount of $1,480,000 together with the $200,000 deposit and interest earned thereon, in cash.

Section 5 of the agreement provides that the closing of escrow shall be on June 30, 1983. Schedule I, paragraph B, of the agreement provides:

> In the event that for any reason other than a default of one of the parties hereto the transactions contemplated hereby are not consummated on or prior to the Closing Date, then the Escrow shall terminate and Escrow Holder shall return the Deposit, together with accrued interest thereon, to Purchaser....

---

30. [13] We assume from the following statement made on brief that respondent raised actual and constructive receipt arguments:

> Had the petitioner and the corporation dealt at arm's length, they would have used separate, inviolable escrow accounts. Instead, they used the same escrow account from which the petitioner received, at his own direction, a premature disbursement of the buyer's $200,000 deposit.

31. [14] While respondent argues that the $200,000 was paid directly to petitioner, we have found, and the parties have stipulated, that the $200,000 was paid to Company. Therefore, petitioner was not in actual receipt of the escrow funds.

Pursuant to the agreement, on May 20, 1983, BHS Realty deposited $200,000 in an escrow account with Safeco Title. On June 10, 1983, petitioner entered into an "Agreement of Exchange of Property" with Company. On June 27, 1983, petitioner, in an individual capacity, and BHS Realty amended the escrow instructions to provide that the escrow holder was directed and authorized to release $200,000 on deposit in escrow, to seller herein subject to the receipt by escrow holder of signed extension of the purchase contract through *JULY 29, 1983*, evidenced by sellers [sic] signature herein....

That same day, petitioner conveyed Wildridge Apartments to Company and Company conveyed Wildridge Apartments to Wildridge Apartments, Ltd. On June 30, 1983, the $200,000 was released to Company from the sales escrow by Safeco Title.

Based on the foregoing, we hold that petitioner was not in constructive receipt of the escrow funds. There were substantial restrictions preventing petitioner's ability to control the escrow funds. Petitioner and BHS Realty agreed that if the terms of the contemplated transactions could not be consummated, the $200,000 deposit plus interest was to be returned to BHS Realty. *See Garcia v. Comm'r*, 80 T.C. at 500; *cf. Klein v. Comm'r*, T.C. Memo. 1993-491.

Also, even though petitioner, in his individual capacity, entered into an amended the escrow instructions on June 27, 1983, petitioner could not have amended the escrow instructions unilaterally; to the contrary, BHS Realty was a necessary party to the amendments. *Cf. Klein v. Comm'r, supra.* Indeed, BHS Realty was a party to the amendments and authorized them. In a letter dated June 27, 1983, BHS Realty authorized Safeco Title to prepare an addendum to the "Agreement of Purchase and Sale With Closing Instructions" providing that the sum of $200,000 was to be released upon a signed extension of the purchase contract.

Furthermore, the $200,000 deposit was not distributed until petitioner had conveyed the title to Wildridge Apartments to Company and Company had in turn conveyed the title to Wildridge Apartments, Ltd. Thus, the $200,000 was distributed to Company only after Company had replaced petitioner as seller under the escrow agreement.[32] *See Garcia v. Comm'r, supra* at 500.

B. Integrated Plan

Respondent argues that petitioner's purported exchange was not an integrated plan and that the "purported exchange consisted of the petitioner's structuring paper transactions around a pre-existing sales contract." Respondent contends that petitioner

---

32. [15] Petitioner acted as a party to the escrow agreement only during the time he held title to Wildridge Apartments, or in other words, while he was the seller of Wildridge Apartments. This is further illustrated by subsequent amendments to the escrow agreement. On July 8, 1983, petitioner, in his capacity as president of Company, and Wildridge Apartments, Ltd., amended the escrow instructions. Thus, by this time, both parties to the original escrow agreement had been replaced by Company as seller and Wildridge Apartments, Ltd., as purchaser. The escrow account was again amended on July 12, 1983, by petitioner, as president of Company, and by Wildridge Apartments, Ltd.

was contractually committed to sell Wildridge Apartments before he attempted the exchange and that the agreement to sell Wildridge Apartments was enforceable independent of any obligation to exchange the Buellton Property. To support this, respondent relies on the "Agreement of Purchase and Sale With Closing Instructions" entered into between petitioner and BHS Realty.

Section 11.11 of the agreement, however, contemplates the type of like-kind exchange that was ultimately carried out.

> 11.11 ... Seller ... intends, prior to the Close of Escrow, to arrange a like-kind exchange, within the meaning of Section 1031 ... whereby Seller shall exchange the Real Property, subject to the terms and provisions of this Agreement, for other property owned by ... [Company] ... Purchaser agrees ... to purchase the Real Property from ... [Company].... In no event shall the Closing Date be extended beyond June 30, 1983 by reason of the exchange.

Furthermore, entering into a sales and escrow agreement before structuring an exchange, would not, in and of itself, invalidate a subsequent exchange. In *Coupe v. Comm'r*, 52 T.C. at 405, we stated:

> It is now well settled that when a taxpayer who is holding property for productive use in a trade or business enters into an agreement to sell the property for cash, but *before there is substantial implementation* of the transaction, arranges to exchange the property for other property of like kind, he receives the nonrecognition benefits of § 1031.... [Emphasis added.]

Respondent also appears to contend that petitioner had substantially implemented the purchase of the Buellton Property prior to structuring an exchange. We disagree. In *Coupe*, this Court applied the "substantial implementation" test to only one side of the transaction-the sale of the taxpayer's property. In *Estate of Bowers v. Comm'r*, 94 T.C. 582 (1990), however, we applied the "substantial implementation" test to the other side of the transaction-the property to be acquired by the taxpayer. In *Estate of Bowers*, we stated that while taxpayers have been given considerable latitude in structuring like-kind exchanges, such latitude is not open-ended. *Id.* at 590.

In *Estate of Bowers*, the taxpayers had entered into an agreement to sell an oil and gas lease to American Quasar Petroleum Co. (Quasar). On May 13, 1982, Quasar endorsed its acceptance of the agreement and made a $400,000 earnest money deposit. The balance of the sales price was to be paid upon delivery of an executed assignment of the lease. The assignment was to be made in 1983. Sometime prior to July 1982, the taxpayers entered into an agreement to purchase a farm from a trust. During 1982, the taxpayer conducted farming operations on the farm. On Schedule F of their 1982 return, the taxpayers reported income, expenses, and depreciation deductions related to their ownership and operation of the farm, resulting in a net farm loss of $130,491.41. *Id.* at 586. In 1983, the taxpayers attempted to restructure the sale of the lease and purchase of the farm as an exchange by (1) having the trust convey the farm to Quasar, and (2) having Quasar assign the farm to the taxpayers in exchange for the taxpayers assigning the oil and gas lease to Quasar.

Due to the taxpayers' 1982 involvement with the farm, we held that taxpayers were "at least in constructive possession of the farm after the ... transactions in July 1982", *id.* at 585, and therefore the transaction was substantially implemented before the taxpayers' "attempt to recast the sale of the lease and the purchase of the farm in the mold of an 'exchange'," *id.* at 591.

The facts before us are distinguishable from those in *Estate of Bowers.* Petitioner, in this case, never acquired legal title to, or constructive possession of, the Buellton Property prior to entering into an agreement to exchange. All that petitioner acquired was an option to purchase the Buellton Property. A similar situation was presented in *Coastal Terminals, Inc. v. U.S.*, 320 F.2d 333 (4th Cir.1963). In *Coastal Terminals*, Delhi-Taylor Oil Corp. (Delhi-Taylor) sought to purchase property owned by the taxpayer. Prior to this, the taxpayer had acquired options to purchase certain real property and had entered into commitments to purchase steel for the construction of terminal facilities. *Id.* at 334. As part of an exchange, the taxpayer assigned the options and commitments to Delhi-Taylor. In the end, Delhi-Taylor conveyed completed terminal facilities to the taxpayer, and the taxpayer conveyed the property desired by Delhi-Taylor. In *Coastal Terminals*, the Court of Appeals for the Fourth Circuit held that the transaction was an exchange. *Id.* at 339.

In our view, the acquisition of an option to purchase real property is not "substantial implementation" of a purchase transaction. Petitioner was under no obligation to exercise the option. Had petitioner desired not to acquire the Buellton Property for purposes of an exchange, petitioner could have simply chosen not to exercise the option. These facts and the facts of *Coastal Terminals* are similar to the situation presented in *Alderson v. Comm'r*, 317 F.2d 790 (9th Cir. 1963), *revg.* 38 T.C. 215 (1962) (entering into a sales contract and later amending the contract to provide for an exchange). The only difference is that the acquisition of an option to purchase involves the other side of the transaction, the purchase of the property desired by the taxpayer.

Respondent points to the fact that the grant deed conveying Wildridge Apartments between petitioner and Company and the conveyance of the grant deed between Company and Wildridge Apartments, Ltd., were executed on the same day and then recorded on the same day. However, the fact that Company held only transitory ownership of Wildridge Apartments is not determinative. In *Barker v. Comm'r*, 74 T.C. 555, 562 (1980), this Court stated:

> it is not a bar to § 1031 treatment that the person who desires the taxpayer's property acquires and holds another piece of property only temporarily before exchanging it with the taxpayer. Similarly, it is not fatal to section 1031 treatment that the person with whom the taxpayer exchanges his property immediately sells the newly acquired property. [Citations and fn. ref. omitted.]

Similarly, in *Alderson v. Comm'r*, 317 F.2d at 795, the Court of Appeals for the Ninth Circuit stated:

> The Mercantile case appears to hold that one need not assume the benefits and burdens of ownership in property before exchanging it but may properly

acquire title *solely for the purpose of exchange* and accept title and transfer it in exchange for other like property ... [Emphasis in original.]

Based on the foregoing, we hold that petitioner structured an integrated four-party exchange: (1) Petitioner was to convey Wildridge Apartments; (2) BHS Realty, and then later Wildridge Apartments, Ltd., was the prospective purchaser of the Wildridge Apartments; (3) J. and M. Brock Living Trust and the Trustee for the Parks and Brock Unitrust were the prospective sellers of the Buellton Property; and (4) Company was the party who received Wildridge Apartments from petitioner, sold it to Wildridge Apartments, Ltd., and then purchased the Buellton Property, made improvements thereon, and transferred it to petitioner.

C. Agent

Respondent contends that Company was a mere conduit or agent for petitioner. In *Coupe v. Comm'r*, 52 T.C. at 406, we agreed that an exchange would be meaningless for purposes of section 1031 if the person with whom the taxpayer made the exchange was acting as the taxpayer's agent. *See also Mercantile Trust Co. v. Comm'r*, 32 B.T.A. 82, 84 (1935).

Company accepted title to Wildridge Apartments, albeit at petitioner's request, in order to facilitate the exchange. Company also accepted title to the Buellton Property for the purpose of facilitating the exchange and for the additional purpose of constructing improvements thereon.[33] *See J.H. Baird Publishing Co. v. Comm'r*, 39 T.C. 608 (1962). This is not a case of petitioner using Company as a "sham" or "straw man". *See Garcia v. Comm'r*, 80 T.C. 491, 500-501 (1983). Company was an active corporation carrying on business as a licensed building contractor and real estate developer. Furthermore, from the proceeds of the sale of Wildridge Apartments, Company purchased the Buellton Property, acquired financing for the purpose of constructing improvements thereon, and transferred title to the property and improvements subject to the Company's obligations for a fee of $750,000. Company was not a mere conduit or agent of petitioner. We have considered respondent's ar-

---

33. [16] The fact that Company was used to facilitate the like-kind exchange does not mean that Company was a mere agent of petitioner. In *Biggs v. Comm'r*, 632 F.2d 1171, 1178 (5th Cir.1980), *affg.* 69 T.C. 905 (1978), the Court of Appeals for the Fifth Circuit stated:

> Finally, we examine the Commissioner's claim that Shore was serving as an agent for Biggs throughout the transactions, and that the accomplishment of the intended exchange was thereby precluded. Admittedly, the exchange would have been meaningless if Shore, acting as Biggs' agent, acquired title to the Virginia property and then executed the deed conveying title to Biggs. For, in essence, Biggs would have merely effected an exchange with himself. However, while the Tax Court refused to find, in contrast to its decision in *Coupe*, that Shore acted as an agent for the purchaser, Powell, it also specifically determined that Shore was not an agent of Biggs. Rather, Shore accepted title to the Virginia property, albeit at Biggs' request, merely in order to facilitate the exchange. We believe that this is an accurate characterization of Shore's role in the transactions. Consequently, we reject the Commissioner's agency notion also.

Undoubtedly, the exchange of the Maryland and Virginia properties could have been more artfully accomplished and with a greater economy of steps. However, we must conclude on the facts before us that the taxpayer ultimately achieved the intended result.... [Citation and fn. ref. omitted.]

guments on this point and find them to be without merit. We, therefore, hold that petitioner is entitled to the nonrecognition treatment of § 1031.

Issue 2. Section 1031(b)

Respondent alternatively argues that if the conveyance of Wildridge Apartments qualifies as a like-kind exchange under § 1031(a), petitioner, nevertheless, failed to recognize gain to the extent of boot received. Section 1031(b) provides:

> If an exchange would be within the provisions of subsection (a) ... if it were not for the fact that the property received in exchange consists not only of property permitted by such provisions to be received without the recognition of gain, but also of other property or money, then the gain, if any, to the recipient shall be recognized, but in an amount not in excess of the sum of such money and the fair market value of such other property.

Respondent contends that by refinancing Wildridge Apartments 1 week after entering into the sales contract with BHS Realty, petitioner received over $2,020,407.33 in "other property or money" representing the amount petitioner "cashed out" of his investment. We disagree.

Section 1031(b) relates to property *received in the exchange* that consists of the exchange property and "other property or money". The only property petitioner received in exchange for his property was the Buellton Property. In addition, petitioner's liabilities were well in excess of the $6 million he owed with respect to the Wildridge Apartments. *See* 1.1031(b)-1(c), Income Tax Regs.; *Garcia v. Comm'r, supra.* Petitioner received the $2,020,407.33 from the Savings Bank of Puget Sound as a result of refinancing Wildridge Apartments. He did not receive it from Company as part of the exchange.

Furthermore, we disagree with respondent's argument that "if the petitioner's sale of the Wildridge apartments and his acquisition of the Buellton property were to be construed as integrated events, his refinancing the Wildridge mortgage should likewise be construed as a part of that plan." Petitioner had reasons for refinancing the mortgage that were unrelated to the exchange. Petitioner's uncontroverted testimony was that he began attempts to secure permanent long-term financing in the same year he purchased Wildridge Apartments (1980). Petitioner also testified that due to rising interest rates he had difficulty obtaining long-term financing. On September 28, 1981, the interest rate on the note was 23.5 percent. In 1982, petitioner made a $500,000 payment on the promissory note and, in consideration of this payment, the note was extended for one more year. On April 12, 1983, the Savings Bank of Puget Sound signed a loan commitment letter for the refinancing of Wildridge Apartments in the amount of $6 million.[34] Furthermore, the settlement of the Savings Bank of Puget Sound loan on June 2, 1983, was timely and significant since the due date of the $3.5

---

34. [17] The Savings Bank of Puget Sound signed the loan commitment letter over 1 month prior to the date in which petitioner entered into the agreement to sell Wildridge Apartments to BHS Realty.

million loan was July 9, 1983. For example, in the event the exchange or sale failed, petitioner nonetheless was in need of refinancing Wildridge Apartments.

OPINION

Accordingly, we hold that petitioner did not receive other property or money other than the Buellton Property in exchange for Wildridge Apartments. Therefore, petitioner is not required to recognize boot pursuant to § 1031(b).[35]

Revenue Ruling 75-291
1975-2 C.B. 332

Advice has been requested whether the transaction described below is an exchange of property in which no gain or loss is recognized pursuant to § 1031(a) of the Internal Revenue Code of 1954.

Y, a corporation, desired to acquire a tract of land and a factory owned by *X*, an unrelated corporation engaged in the business of manufacturing certain products. *Y* entered into a written agreement with *X* for the acquisition of a tract of land and a factory owned by *X*. Pursuant to the agreement, *Y* acquired another tract of land and constructed a factory thereon solely for the purpose of exchanging the tract of land and new factory for *X's* land and existing factory. Under the terms of the agreement, *Y* could terminate the agreement if the costs of purchasing the land and building the factory exceeded a specified amount. *Y* purchased the land, built the factory solely on its own behalf, and consummated the exchange. No personal property was involved in the exchange.

Section 1031(a) of the Code provides that no gain or loss shall be recognized if property held for productive use in trade or business or for investment (not including stock in trade or other property held primarily for sale, nor stocks, bonds, notes, choses in action, certificates of trust or beneficial interest, or other securities or evidences of indebtedness or interest) is exchanged solely for property of a like kind to be held either for productive use in trade or business or for investment.

In the instant case *X* exchanged land and an existing factory for other land and a new factory that *Y* had respectively acquired and built solely for the purpose of making the exchange. With respect to *X*, a taxable exchange is not deemed to arise merely because *Y* acquired the property specifically to complete the exchange, if the transaction otherwise qualifies for nonrecognition of gain under section 1031(a) of the Code. *See Mercantile Trust Company of Baltimore*, 32 B.T.A. 82 (1935), *acq.* XIV-1 C.B. 13 (1935), and *Alderson v. Comm'r*, 317 F.2d 790 (9th Cir. 1963), *rev'g* 38 T.C. 215 (1962), in which the transactions were treated as nontaxable exchanges even though property acquired in exchanges by the taxpayers had been acquired immediately prior thereto by the other parties to the exchanges. In each of those cases, as in

---

35. [18] Based on the foregoing, petitioner is not liable for the addition to tax as determined by respondent.

the instant case, the party acquiring property to be exchanged with the taxpayer did so on his own behalf and not as an agent of the taxpayer.

Accordingly, as to *X*, the exchange of land and factories between *X* and *Y* qualifies for nonrecognition of gain or loss under § 1031(a) of the Code. However, any depreciation recaptured as a result of the exchange of *X*'s property is subject to tax as ordinary income under the provisions of § 1250(d)(4).

On the other hand, *Y* acquired the property transferred to *X* immediately prior to the exchange and did not hold such property for productive use in its trade or business or for investment. Thus, as to *Y*, the exchange does not qualify for nonrecognition of gain or loss under section 1031(a) of the Code.

Revenue Procedure 2004-51

2004-2 C.B. 294

SECTION 1. PURPOSE

This revenue procedure modifies sections 1 and 4 of Rev. Proc. 2000-37, 2000-2 C.B. 308, to provide that Rev. Proc. 2000-37 does not apply if the taxpayer owns the property intended to qualify as replacement property before initiating a qualified exchange accommodation arrangement (QEAA).

SECTION 2. BACKGROUND

.01 Section 1031(a) provides that no gain or loss is recognized on the exchange of property held for productive use in a trade or business or for investment if the property is exchanged solely for property of like kind that is to be held either for productive use in a trade or business or for investment.

.02 Section 1031(a)(3) allows taxpayers to structure deferred like-kind exchanges. Under § 1031(a)(3), property may be treated as like-kind property if it is (A) identified as property to be received in the exchange (replacement property) on or before the day that is 45 days after the date on which the taxpayer transfers the property relinquished in the exchange (relinquished property), and (B) received before the earlier of the date that is 180 days after the date on which the taxpayer transfers the relinquished property, or the due date (determined with regard to extensions) for the transferor's federal income tax return for the taxable year in which the transfer of the relinquished property occurs.

.03 Rev. Proc. 2000-37 addresses "parking" transactions. See sections 2.05 and 2.06 of Rev. Proc. 2000-37. Parking transactions typically are designed to "park" the desired replacement property with an accommodation party until such time as the taxpayer arranges for the transfer of the relinquished property to the ultimate transferee in a simultaneous or deferred exchange. Once such a transfer is arranged, the taxpayer transfers the relinquished property to the accommodation party in exchange for the replacement property, and the accommodation party transfers the relinquished property to the ultimate transferee. In other situations, an accommodation party may acquire the desired replacement property on behalf of the taxpayer and immediately exchange that property with the taxpayer for the relinquished property, thereafter holding the relinquished property until the taxpayer arranges for a transfer of the property to the ultimate transferee. Rev. Proc. 2000-37 provides procedures for qualifying parking transactions as like-kind exchanges in situations in which the taxpayer has a genuine intent to accomplish a like-kind exchange at the time that the taxpayer arranges for the acquisition of the replacement property and actually accomplishes the exchange within a short time thereafter.

.04 Section 4.01 of Rev. Proc. 2000-37 provides that the Internal Revenue Service will not challenge the qualification of property held in a QEAA "as either 'replacement property' or 'relinquished property' (as defined in § 1.1031(k)-1(a)) for purposes of § 1031 and the regulations thereunder, or the treatment of the exchange accommodation titleholder as the beneficial owner of such property…." Thus, taxpayers are not required to establish that the exchange accommodation titleholder bears the economic benefits and burdens of ownership and is the "owner" of the property. The Service and Treasury Department are aware that some taxpayers have interpreted this language to permit a taxpayer to treat as a like-kind exchange a transaction in which the taxpayer transfers property to an exchange accommodation titleholder and receives that same property as replacement property in a purported exchange for other property of the taxpayer.

.05 An exchange of real estate owned by a taxpayer for improvements on land owned by the same taxpayer does not meet the requirements of § 1031. *See DeCleene v. Comm'r*, 115 T.C. 457 (2000); *Bloomington Coca-Cola Bottling Co. v. Comm'r*, 189 F.2d 14 (7th Cir. 1951). Moreover, Rev. Rul. 67-255, 1967-2 C.B. 270, holds that a building constructed on land owned by a taxpayer is not of a like kind to involuntarily converted land of the same taxpayer. Rev. Proc. 2000-37 does not abrogate the statutory requirement of § 1031 that the transaction be an exchange of like-kind properties.

.06 The Service and Treasury Department are continuing to study parking transactions, including transactions in which a person related to the taxpayer transfers a leasehold in land to an accommodation party and the accommodation party makes improvements to the land and transfers the leasehold with the improvements to the taxpayer in exchange for other real estate.

SECTION 3. SCOPE

This revenue procedure applies to taxpayers applying the safe harbor rules set forth in Rev. Proc. 2000-37 in structuring like-kind exchanges.

SECTION 4. APPLICATION

.01 Section 1 of Rev. Proc. 2000-37 is modified to read as follows:

SECTION 1. PURPOSE

This revenue procedure provides a safe harbor under which the Internal Revenue Service will treat an exchange accommodation titleholder as the beneficial owner of property for federal income tax purposes if the property is held in a "qualified exchange accommodation arrangement" (QEAA), as defined in section 4.02 of this revenue procedure.

.02 Section 4.01 of Rev. Proc. 2000-37 is modified to read as follows:

SECTION 4. QUALIFIED EXCHANGE ACCOMMODATION ARRANGE-
MENTS

.01 *In general.* The Service will treat an exchange accommodation titleholder
as the beneficial owner of property for federal income tax purposes if the
property is held in a QEAA. Property held in a QEAA may, therefore, qualify
as either "replacement property" or "relinquished property" (as defined in
§ 1.1031(k)-1(a)) in a tax-deferred like-kind exchange if the exchange otherwise meets the requirements for deferral of gain or loss under § 1031 and
the regulations thereunder.

.03 Section 4.05 is added to Rev. Proc. 2000-37 to read as follows:

.05 *Limitation.* This revenue procedure does not apply to replacement property
held in a QEAA if the property is owned by the taxpayer within the 180-day period
ending on the date of transfer of qualified *indicia* of ownership of the property to an
exchange accommodation titleholder.

SECTION 5. EFFECT ON OTHER DOCUMENTS

Rev. Proc. 2000-37 is modified.

SECTION 6. EFFECTIVE DATE

This revenue procedure is effective for transfers on or after July 20, 2004, of qualified
indicia of ownership to exchange accommodation titleholders (as described in section
4.02(1) of Rev. Proc. 2000-37).

Priv. Ltr. Rul. 2002-51-008

(Sep. 11, 2002)

This responds to your letter, dated January 29, 2002, requesting a ruling on the
proper federal income tax treatment of a proposed like-kind exchange of real property,
as supplemented by letters and submissions dated February 22, March 20, May 16,
June 3, June 14, and August 9, 2002. Taxpayer requests a ruling under § 1031 of the
Internal Revenue Code that no gain or loss will be recognized upon the conveyance of
Relinquished Property (RQ) to Village and the receipt of Replacement Property (RP).

FACTS

Taxpayer is an S corporation, organized under the laws of State A, which operates
Business on a calendar year basis, using the accrual method of accounting. Business
is situated on RQ. Taxpayer owns a fee interest in RQ, with all improvements thereon.

CorpW, an S corporation organized under the laws of State A, currently leases A-
Acres situated on Unimproved Real Property located in City and County under a
Lease and Development Agreement ("Lease"), as amended, with City. Lease's term
is 45 years from the commencement date (which was on or about September 2, 1997),
and one 15-year renewal option.

LLC-W, a State A limited liability company, subleases A-Acres from CorpW and
all rights, title, interest and obligations under Lease, for the entire term of Lease.

LLC-W plans to utilize A-Acres, in part, as the new location for Business that presently exists on RQ. LLC-W is currently developing and constructing the infrastructure required so that Business can be moved to A-Acres.

Taxpayer and CorpW are related parties, each owned half and half by Husband's Trust and Wife's trust, respectively. LLC-W is also related to Taxpayer, owned 45%, 45% and 10%, respectively, by Husband's Trust, Wife's Trust and Minority Member.

Village and Taxpayer entered into an Option Agreement for Sale and Purchase (Sale Agreement) of RQ on December 12, 2001, and December 13, 2001, respectively. Under Sale Agreement, Taxpayers agreed to sell RQ to Village for $B. However, Taxpayer is arranging to have this transaction (the transfer of RQ to Village) structured as a component of a like-kind exchange under § 1031 of the Code. Taxpayer will structure the exchange utilizing the qualified exchange accommodation arrangement (the QEAA) safe harbor provided in Rev. Proc. 2000-37, 2000-40 I.R.B. 308, with an exchange accommodation titleholder (EAT) and its wholly owned subsidiary, Titleholder. Taxpayer will also use the qualified intermediary safe harbor rules of the deferred exchange regulations at § 1.1031(k)-1(g)(4) of the Income Tax Regulations, by entering into an exchange agreement with a qualified intermediary (QI). EAT and QI are both State A limited liability companies, wholly owned by Holding Company, a State B limited Partnership. Initially, the QEAA will be between Taxpayer and EAT. Later, Taxpayer's rights under the QEAA will be assigned to QI to facilitate transfer of RP from EAT to Taxpayer. The additional entity mentioned above, Titleholder, will be established for this exchange transaction, specifically to take title to RP. Titleholder will be a limited liability company, with EAT as its sole member, and disregarded for federal income tax purposes.

The exchange will occur as follows: LLC-W will sublease C-Acres (which is part of A-Acres), at a market rental rate, for a fixed term of 32 years to Titleholder as part of the QEAA. EAT will cause Titleholder to construct RP improvements on C-Acres. Taxpayer will identify RQ within 45 days of Titleholder entering into the sublease as provided in Rev. Proc. 2000-37, in a manner consistent with § 1.1031(k)-1(c).

Under the QEAA, Titleholder will enter into a contract with LLC-W (who will act as Construction Manager and contract on behalf of Titleholder with independent subcontractors) to construct RP improvements based on Taxpayer's plans and specifications. In addition, Titleholder will utilize the Bank Construction Loan (described below) to finance the construction of RP improvements by executing a note payable to Taxpayer, thereby obligating itself to pay Taxpayer for draw requests paid to Construction Manager. The cost to construct RP improvements will approximate $B.

The Bank Construction Loan, in the amount of $E, will be funded by Bank, with Taxpayer as maker and primary obligor. LLC-W and CorpW, together with Husband and Wife, will be guarantors of the Bank Construction Loan.

Subsequent to the commencement of the construction, Taxpayer will assign its rights under Sale Agreement of RQ to QI and give notice of such assignment to all parties to such agreement in writing, all as provided in § 1.1031(k)-1(g)(4)(v) of the regulations. Taxpayer will then transfer RQ to Village, as provided in the exchange agreement with QI. Taxpayer will retain liability on the underlying full recourse mortgage on RQ of approximately $D by agreement with Bank. RQ will then be transferred by QI to Village free and clear. Village will pay the purchase price for RQ to QI and QI will receive and hold in escrow the proceeds from the sale of RQ. RQ constitutes substantially all of Taxpayer's assets. Village will not assume any liabilities of Taxpayer incident to the purchase.

To complete the exchange, Taxpayer will assign its rights to receive RP under the QEAA to QI. Thereupon, QI will direct that EAT transfer RP directly to Taxpayer. EAT will effect this transfer by transferring all of its ownership interest in Titleholder directly to Taxpayer. Through this series of transactions, QI will purchase RP from EAT using all the proceeds from the sale of RQ. EAT (through Titleholder) will use all of the proceeds from the sale of RQ to pay Construction Manager for construction and services and pay the loan from Taxpayer in full. Taxpayer will use the repayment proceeds to fully pay Bank Construction Loan before EAT transfers Titleholder to Taxpayer.

Because Titleholder is a disregarded entity for federal tax purposes, EAT will be deemed to enter into any contract Titleholder enters into and to perform any activity Titleholder performs. Furthermore, a transfer of all the interest in Titleholder will be treated as a transfer of the assets of Titleholder. Therefore, any reference herein to the transfer of RP properly refers to the transfer of all the interests of EAT in Titleholder to Taxpayer.

None of the accommodators to be used to implement the proposed exchange (QI, EAT, Titleholder) are disqualified persons as defined in § 1.1031(k)-1(k). Also, EAT, Titleholder and QI are subject to federal income tax or, if such persons are treated as partnerships or S corporations for federal income tax purposes, more than 90% of its interest or stock are owned by partners or shareholders who are subject to federal income tax. Services to be performed for Taxpayer by EAT, Titleholder and QI, with respect to exchanges of property are intended to facilitate exchanges that qualify for nonrecognition of gain or loss under § 1031.

No later than five business days after the transfer of a qualified indicia of ownership of exchange property (RP) to EAT, Taxpayer and EAT will enter into a written agreement (setting up the QEAA) providing that EAT is holding RP in order to facilitate an exchange under § 1031 and Rev Proc. 2000-37, and that Taxpayer and EAT agree to report the acquisition, holding and disposition of the property as provided in that revenue procedure. The QEAA will specify that EAT will be treated as the beneficial owner of the property for all federal income tax purposes and that Taxpayer and EAT will report the federal income tax attributes of the property on their federal income tax returns in a manner consistent with the terms of the QEAA.

Pursuant to the QEAA, Taxpayer will exchange RQ for RP. RP will be real property that consists of a 32-year sublease of C-Acres and specifically identified buildings and improvements on C-Acres to be utilized as part of the relocated Business. The QEAA will also provide that Titleholder will enter into a fixed term 32-year sublease with LLC-W and pay rent to LLC-W at a market rate of rent for C-Acres of land, which is a portion of A-Acres. All improvements to be constructed on RP will be with the approval of City, County, and Bank where required.

No later than 180 days after the transfer of the qualified indicia of ownership of RP to Titleholder (wholly owned by EAT), Titleholder will be transferred directly to Taxpayer. If the production of the identified RP is not completed by Titleholder on or before the 180-day period has expired, EAT will be required by the agreement to transfer all of its interest in Titleholder prior to the completion to Taxpayer in order to comply with the requirements of Rev. Proc. 2000-37. The agreement between Taxpayer and EAT will expressly limit Taxpayer's rights to receive, pledge, borrow or otherwise obtain the benefits of money or other property held by EAT or Titleholder in a manner consistent with the requirements of § 1.1031(k)-1(g)(4)(ii) and (g)(6). EAT will hold qualified indicia of ownership of RP, as defined in Rev. Proc. 2000-37, (through Titleholder) and such qualified indicia of ownership will be held by EAT at all times from the date of acquisition by EAT until the property is transferred to Taxpayer. At the time the qualified indicia of ownership of the property is transferred to EAT, it is Taxpayer's bona fide intent that the property held by EAT represent RP in an exchange that is intended to qualify for nonrecognition of gain (in whole or part) or loss under § 1031.

In addition to entering into the QEAA, Taxpayer will enter into a written agreement, the exchange agreement, with QI. The exchange agreement will require QI to acquire RQ from Taxpayer and transfer RQ to a purchaser, and to acquire RP and transfer RP to Taxpayer. Pursuant to the exchange agreement, and as provided in § 1.1031(k)-1(g)(4)(iv) and (v), Taxpayer will assign its rights under Sale Agreement (of RQ to Village) to QI, assign its rights under the QEAA to receive RP also to QI, and give proper and timely notice of these assignments to all parties of Sale Agreement and to all parties of the QEAA. Pursuant to these agreements, assignments and notices, RQ will be transferred, through QI, to Village, and Taxpayer will receive, through QI, complete ownership of RP by the transfer of all ownership interest in Titleholder. The exchange agreement between Taxpayer and QI will also require that Taxpayer will have no rights to receive, pledge, borrow, or otherwise obtain the benefits of money or other property (in particular the proceeds resulting from the sale of RQ to Village) held by QI except as provided in § 1.1031(k)-1(g)(6). Furthermore, since Taxpayer will transfer RQ and receive RP simultaneously, the transaction will effectively satisfy the time requirements in § 1031(a)(3). Also, RP will not remain in QEAA for a period exceeding 180 days.

The entire proposed transaction at issue can be summarized in the following steps: (1) Taxpayer will enter into the QEAA with EAT, and will enter into an exchange agreement with QI as described. (2) LLC-W will sublease RP at a fair market rental, for 32 years, to Titleholder, a disregarded entity wholly owned by EAT, as part of a QEAA as defined in Rev. Proc. 2000-37. (3) Taxpayer will lend to Titleholder the funds which it (Taxpayer) will borrow from Husband's Trust, Wife's Trust and Bank to construct improvements necessary on leased property for relocation of Business. (4) Taxpayer will assign its rights under Sale Agreement of RQ to QI and will give required notices of such assignment to all interested parties. (5) Taxpayer will transfer

RQ free and clear through QI to Village, and QI will receive sales proceeds. (6) Taxpayer will assign its position in the QEAA to QI and give required notices of such assignment to all interested parties. (7) QI will use sales proceeds from RQ to pay EAT for all of its interest in Titleholder (which holds all of RP, consisting of leased property and newly constructed improvements to suit Taxpayer's business requirements). (8) EAT will use the proceeds received from QI (the consideration for the transfer of RP (Titleholder)) to pay Construction Manager and to pay the loan from Taxpayer in full (which Taxpayer will, in turn, use to pay the Bank Construction Loan in full). (9) QI will direct EAT to transfer its interest in Titleholder (holding RP) directly to Taxpayer.

RELEVANT LAW

General Requirements for Deferral under § 1031.

Section 1031(a)(1) provides that no gain or loss is recognized on the exchange of property held for productive use in a trade or business or for investment if the property is exchanged solely for property of like kind that is to be held either for productive use in a trade or business or for investment.

In accordance with this provision, for a transaction to have the effect of deferring gain or loss under § 1031, it must (1) constitute an exchange, (2) the property transferred and the property received must be held for productive use in a trade or business or for investment, and (3) the property exchanged must be of a like kind.

Ordinarily, to constitute an exchange, the transaction must be a reciprocal transfer of property as distinguished from a transfer of property for a money consideration only. *See* § 1.1002-1(d) of the regulations. Under the given facts, there will be an exchange in which the taxpayer will receive property for property rather than money for property. The facts also indicate that both the property to be transferred as RQ and the property to be received as RP are properties held or to be held for use in Taxpayer's trade or business.

Section 1.1031(a)-1(b) of the Income Tax Regulations defines like-kind as referring to the nature or character of the property and not to its grade or quality. Section 1.1031(a)-1(c)(2) provides that no gain or loss is recognized if a taxpayer who is not a dealer in real estate exchanges city real estate for a ranch or farm, or exchanges a leasehold of a fee with 30 years or more to run for real estate, or exchanges improved real estate for unimproved real estate.

In the present case, Taxpayer is exchanging a fee interest in improved real estate for a long-term lease of a tract of land for a period of more than 30 years and improvements. Accordingly, such properties are of like kind for § 1031 purposes, provided the requirements of § 1031(a)(3) are satisfied.

Section 1031(a)(3) provides that property received by the taxpayer is not treated as like-kind property if it: (a) is not identified as property to be received in the exchange on or before the day that is 45 days after the date on which the taxpayer transfers the relinquished property; or (b) is received after the earlier of the date that is 180 days after the date on which the taxpayer transfers the relinquished property, or the due date (determined with regard to extension) of the transferor's federal income tax return for the year in which the transfer of the relinquished property occurs.

In addition, under general tax accounting principles, if money or other property is actually or constructively received by a taxpayer or an agent of a taxpayer before receiving like-kind replacement property, the disposition of the relinquished property will be treated as a sale under § 1001 of the Code. Because the transaction at issue in the present case has elements of both a deferred exchange and a reverse (or "parking") transaction, further provisions of the deferred exchange regulations at § 1.1031(k)-1 and Rev. Proc. 2000-37 are applicable for testing whether the transaction qualifies for deferral of gain (or loss) realized under § 1031.

Applicable Deferred Exchange Regulations.

On April 25, 1991, the Service issued final regulations under § 1.1031(k)-1 providing rules for deferred like-kind exchanges under § 1031(a)(3) of the Code. Section 1.1031(k)-1(a) of the regulations provides that a deferred exchange is an exchange in which, pursuant to an agreement, the taxpayer transfers property held for productive use in a trade or business or for investment (the "relinquished property") and subsequently receives property to be held for productive use in a trade or business or for investment (the "replacement property"). In the case of a deferred exchange, if the requirements set forth in § 1031(a)(3) (relating to identification and receipt of replacement property) are not satisfied, the replacement property received by the taxpayer will be treated as property which is not of a like kind to the relinquished property.

Section 1.1031(k)-1(c)(2) of the regulations generally provides that replacement property is identified only if it is designated as replacement property in a written document signed by the taxpayer and hand delivered, mailed, telecopied, or otherwise sent before the end of the identification period to either the person obligated to transfer the replacement property to the taxpayer or any other person involved in the exchange other than the taxpayer or a disqualified person. Examples of persons involved in the exchange include any of the parties to the exchange, an intermediary, an escrow agent, and a title company. An identification of replacement property made in a written agreement for the exchange of properties signed by all parties thereto before the end of the identification period will be treated as satisfying the requirements. Replacement property is identified only if it is unambiguously described. Real property is unambiguously described if it is described by a legal description, street address, or distinguishable name. However, § 1.1031(k)-1(c)(1) provides, in part, that any replacement property that is received by the taxpayer before the end of the identification period will in all events be treated as identified before the end of the identification period.

Section 1.1031(k)-1(d)(1) of the regulations provides, in part, that the identified replacement property is received before the end of the exchange period if the taxpayer receives the replacement property before the end of the exchange period, and the replacement property received is substantially the same property as identified.

Section 1.1031(k)-1(e)(1) of the regulations provides that a transfer of relinquished property in a deferred exchange will not fail to qualify for nonrecognition of gain or loss under § 1031 merely because the replacement property is not in existence or is being produced at the time the property is identified as replacement property. For purposes of § 1.1031(k)-1(e)(1), the terms "produced" and "production" have the same meanings as provided in § 263A(g)(1) and the regulations thereunder.[36]

Section 1.1031(k)-1(e)(2) provides that in the case of replacement property that is to be produced, the replacement property must be identified as provided in § 1.1031(k)-1(c) (relating to identification of replacement property). For example, if the identified replacement property consists of improved real property where the improvements are to be constructed, the description of the replacement property satisfies the requirements of § 1.1031(k)-1(c)(3) (relating to description of replacement property) if a legal description is provided for the underlying land and as much detail is provided regarding construction of the improvements as is practicable at the time the identification is made.

Section 1.1031(k)-1(e)(3)(i) generally provides that for purposes of § 1.1031(k)-1(d)(1)(ii) (relating to receipt of the identified replacement property), in determining whether the replacement property received by the taxpayer is substantially the same property as identified where the identified replacement property is property to be produced, variations due to usual or typical production changes are not taken into account. However, if substantial changes are made in the property to be produced, the replacement property received will not be considered to be substantially the same property as identified. Section 1.1031(k)-1(e)(3)(iii) further provides that if the identified replacement property is real property to be produced and the production of the property is not completed on or before the date the taxpayer receives the property, the property received will be considered to be substantially the same property as identified only if, had production been completed on or before the date the taxpayer receives the replacement property, the property received would have been considered to be substantially the same property as identified. Even so, the property received is considered to be substantially the same property as identified only to the extent the property received constitutes real property under local law.

---

36. [2] Section 263A(g)(1) of the Code states that the term "produce" includes construct, build, install, manufacture, develop or improve. In this regard we note that even before these regulations (§ 1.1031(k)-1(e)) were promulgated, courts permitted taxpayers great latitude in structuring exchange transactions under § 1031 in "build-to-suit" situations. Thus, a taxpayer can locate suitable property to be received in an exchange and can enter into negotiations for the acquisition of such property. *Coastal Terminals, Inc. v. U.S.*, 320 F.2d 333, 338 (4th Cir. 1963); *Alderson v. Comm'r*, 317 F.2d at 790 (9th Cir. 1963); *Coupe v. Comm'r*, 52 T.C. 394 (1969). A party can hold transitory ownership of exchange property solely for the purposes of effecting the exchange. *Barker v. Comm'r*, 74 T.C. 555 (1980). Moreover, the taxpayer can oversee improvements on the land to be acquired, *J.H. Baird Publishing Co. v. Comm'r*, 39 T.C. 608 (1962), and can even advance money toward the purchase of the property to be acquired by exchange. *124 Front Street Inc. v. Comm'r*, 65 T.C. 6 (1975); Biggs v. Comm'r, 632 F.2d 1171 (5th Cir. 1980), *aff'g.* 69 T.C. 905 (1978). The Service has also approved certain exchange transactions in which the replacement property was built to suit the requirements of the exchanging taxpayer. For example, in Rev. Rul. 75-291, 1975-2 C.B. 332, a corporation (X) agreed to exchange its land and factory for land to be purchased by another (Y) and improvements to be constructed thereon. The ruling stated that Y "built the factory solely on its own behalf" and "not as an agent of the taxpayer." X was allowed nonrecognition treatment.

Section 1.1031(k)-1(f)(1) generally provides that a transfer of relinquished property in a deferred exchange is not within the provisions of § 1031(a) if, as part of the consideration, the taxpayer receives money or other property. However, such a transfer, if otherwise qualified, will be within the provisions of either § 1031 (b) or (c). In addition, in the case of a transfer of relinquished property in a deferred exchange, gain or loss may be recognized if the taxpayer actually or constructively receives money or other property before the taxpayer actually receives like-kind replacement property. If the taxpayer actually or constructively receives money or other property in the full amount of the consideration for the relinquished property before the taxpayer actually receives like-kind replacement property, the transaction will constitute a sale and not a deferred exchange, even though the taxpayer may ultimately receive like-kind replacement property.

Section 1.1031(k)-1(f)(2) provides, in part, that except as provided in § 1.1031(k)-1(g) (relating to safe harbors), for purposes of § 1031 of the Code and § 1.1031(k)-1 of the regulations, the determination of whether (or the extent to which) the taxpayer is in actual or constructive receipt of money or other property before the taxpayer actually receives like-kind replacement property is made under the general rules concerning actual and constructive receipt and without regard to the taxpayer's method of accounting. In addition, actual or constructive receipt of money or property by an agent of the taxpayer (determined without regard to § 1.1031(k)-1(k)) is actual or constructive receipt by the taxpayer.

Section 1.1031(k)-1(g)(2) through (g)(5) of the regulations sets forth a variety of safe harbors for use in deferred exchange situations. The use of one of more of these safe harbors in a deferred exchange will shield a taxpayer from actual or constructive receipt of money or other property.

In the present case, Taxpayer will use the qualified intermediary safe harbor as described in § 1.1031(k)-1(g)(4) of the regulations. Section 1.1031(k)-1(g)(4)(i) provides that in the case of a taxpayer's transfer of relinquished property involving a qualified intermediary, the qualified intermediary is not considered the agent of the taxpayer for purposes of § 1031(a). In such a transaction, the taxpayer's transfer of relinquished property and subsequent receipt of like-kind replacement property is treated as an exchange and the determination of whether the taxpayer is in actual or constructive receipt of money or other property before the taxpayer actually receives like-kind replacement property is made as if the qualified intermediary is not the agent of the taxpayer.

Section 1.1031(k)-1(g)(4)(ii) states that the qualified intermediary safe harbor applies only if the agreement between the taxpayer and the qualified intermediary expressly limits the taxpayer's rights to receive, pledge, borrow, or otherwise obtain the benefits of money or other property held by the qualified intermediary as provided in § 1.1031(k)-1(g)(6).

Section 1.1031(k)-1(g)(4)(iii) defines the term "qualified intermediary" as a person, not the taxpayer or a disqualified person (as defined in § 1.1031(k)-1(k)), who enters into a written agreement with the taxpayer (the "exchange agreement") and, as required by the exchange agreement, acquires the relinquished property from the taxpayer, transfers the relinquished property, acquires the replacement property, and transfers the replacement property to the taxpayer.[37]

Section 1.1031(k)-1(g)(4)(iv)(A) provides that, regardless of whether an intermediary acquires and transfers property under general tax principals, solely for purposes of § 1.1031(k)-1(g)(4)(iii)(B), an intermediary is treated as acquiring and transferring property if the intermediary acquires and transfers legal title to that property. Section 1.1031(k)-1(g)(4)(iv)(B) provides that an intermediary is treated as acquiring and transferring the relinquished property if the intermediary (either on its own behalf or as the agent of any party to the transaction) enters into an agreement with a person other than the taxpayer for the transfer of the relinquished property to that person and, pursuant to that agreement, the relinquished property is transferred to that person. Section 1.1031(k)-1(g)(4)(iv)(C) provides that an intermediary is treated as acquiring and transferring replacement property if the intermediary (either on its own behalf or as the agent of any party to the transaction) enters into an agreement with the owner of the replacement property for the transfer of that property and, pursuant to that agreement, the replacement property is transferred to the taxpayer.

Section 1.1031(k)-1(g)(4)(v) provides that solely for purposes of § 1.1031(k)-1(g)(4)(iii) and (iv), an intermediary is treated as entering into an agreement if the rights of a party to the agreement are assigned to the intermediary and all parties to that agreement are notified in writing of the assignment on or before the date of the relevant transfer of property. For example, if a taxpayer enters into an agreement for the transfer of relinquished property and thereafter assigns its rights in that agreement to an intermediary and all parties to that agreement are notified in writing of the assignment on or before the date of the transfer of the relinquished property, the intermediary is treated as entering into that agreement. If the relinquished property is transferred pursuant to that agreement, the intermediary is treated as having acquired and transferred the relinquished property.

The Parking Transaction under Rev. Proc. 2000-37.

On September 15, 2000, the Service issued Rev. Proc. 2000-37, 2000-40 I.R.B. 308, setting forth a safe harbor for acquiring replacement property under a QEAA sometimes referred to as a "parking" transaction. As provided in this safe harbor, the Service will not challenge either (a) the qualification of the property as either replacement or relinquished property (as defined in § 1.1031(k)-1(a) of the regulations) or (b) the treatment of the EAT as the beneficial owner if the property is held in the QEAA as defined in section 4.02 of Rev. Proc. 2000-37. As provided in section 4.02 of the revenue procedure, property is held in the QEAA if all of the following requirements are met:

(1) Qualified indicia of ownership of the property is held by a person (the "exchange accommodation titleholder") who is not the taxpayer or a disqualified person

---

37. [3] Section 1.1031(k)-1(k)(1) of the regulations defines the term "disqualified person" ***.

and either such person is subject to federal income tax or, if such person is treated as a partnership or S corporation for federal income tax purposes, more than 90 percent of its interests or stock are owned by partners or shareholders who are subject to federal income tax. Such qualified indicia of ownership must be held by the exchange accommodation titleholder at all times from the date of acquisition by the exchange accommodation titleholder until the property is transferred as described in section 4.02(5) of Rev. Proc. 2000-37. For this purpose, "qualified indicia of ownership" means legal title to the property, other indicia of beneficial ownership of property under applicable principles of commercial law (e.g., a contract for deed), or interests in an entity that is disregarded as an entity separate from its owner for federal income tax purposes (e.g., a single member limited liability company) and that holds either legal title to the property or such other indicia of ownership;

(2) At the time the qualified indicia of ownership of the property is transferred to the exchange accommodation titleholder, it is the taxpayer's bona fide intent that the property held by the exchange accommodation titleholder represent either replacement property or relinquished property in an exchange that is intended to qualify for nonrecognition of gain (in whole or in part) or loss under § 1031;

(3) No later than five business days after the transfer of qualified indicia of ownership of the property to the exchange accommodation titleholder, the taxpayer and the exchange accommodation titleholder enter into a written agreement (the "qualified exchange accommodation agreement") that provides that the exchange accommodation titleholder is holding the property for the benefit of the taxpayer in order to facilitate an exchange under § 1031 and Rev. Proc. 2000-37 and that the taxpayer and the exchange accommodation titleholder agree to report the acquisition, holding, and disposition of the property as provided in Rev. Proc. 2000-37. The agreement must specify that the exchange accommodation titleholder will be treated as the beneficial owner of the property for all federal income tax purposes. Both parties must report the federal income tax attributes of the property on their federal income tax returns in a manner consistent with this agreement;

(4) No later than 45 days after the transfer of qualified indicia of ownership of the replacement property to the exchange accommodation titleholder, the relinquished property is properly identified. Identification must be made in a manner consistent with the principles described in § 1.1031(k)-1(c). The taxpayer may properly identify alternative and multiple properties, as described in § 1.1031(k)-1(c)(4);

(5) No later than 180 days after the transfer of qualified indicia of ownership of the property to the exchange accommodation titleholder, (a) the property is transferred (either directly or indirectly through a qualified intermediary (as defined in § 1.1031(k)-1(g)(4)) to the taxpayer as replacement property; or (b) the property is transferred to a person who is not the taxpayer or a disqualified person as relinquished property; and

(6) The combined time period that relinquished property and replacement property are held in the QEAA does not exceed 180 days.

Pursuant to section 4.03 of Rev. Proc. 2000-37, property will not fail to be treated as held in the QEAA as a result of any one or more of the following legal or contractual arrangements (listed below, in part, as relevant to the given facts), regardless of whether such arrangements contain terms that typically would result from arm's length bargaining between unrelated parties with respect to such arrangements:

(1) An exchange accommodation titleholder that satisfies the requirements of the qualified intermediary safe harbor set forth in § 1.1031(k)-1(g)(4) may enter into an exchange agreement with the taxpayer to serve as the qualified intermediary in a simultaneous or deferred exchange of the property under § 1031;

(2) The taxpayer or a disqualified person guarantees some or all of the obligations of the exchange accommodation titleholder, including secured or unsecured debt incurred to acquire the property, or indemnifies the exchange accommodation titleholder against costs and expenses;

(3) The taxpayer or a disqualified person loans or advances funds to the exchange accommodation titleholder or guarantees a loan or advance to the exchange accommodation titleholder; and

(4) The taxpayer or a disqualified person manages the property, supervises improvement of the property, acts as a contractor, or otherwise provides services to the exchange accommodation titleholder with respect to the property.[38]

ANALYSIS

The proposed transaction is a parking transaction between related parties (Taxpayer and LLC-W).[39] The qualified exchange accommodation arrangement safe harbor (the QEAA) provided by Rev. Proc. 2000-37 applies to the proposed transaction. Taxpayer will also use the qualified intermediary safe harbor as set forth in the deferred exchange regulations under § 1.1031(k)-1, although the exchange itself is expected to be simultaneous.

In the present case, a qualified indicia of ownership of RP will be held by EAT in compliance with all requirements stated in section 4.02(1) of Rev. Proc. 2000-37. It is and will be Taxpayer's bona fide intent, now and at the time the qualified indicia of ownership of RP is transferred to EAT, that the property held by EAT represent replacement property in an exchange qualifying for nonrecognition of gain (in whole or in part) or loss under § 1031, consistent with section 4.02(2) of Rev. Proc. 2000-37.

---

38. [4] Other types of contractual arrangements, omitted here for want of relevance under these facts, are permissible within the QEAA under section 4.03 of Rev. Proc. 2000-37.

39. [5] [Citing I.R.C. § 1031(f)(1).]

Within five days after the transfer of RP to EAT, Taxpayer will enter into the QEAA with an EAT providing that EAT (through Titleholder) will acquire RP as required by section 4.02(3) of Rev. Proc. 2000-37. Taxpayer represents that EAT will not be a disqualified person as defined by § 1.1031(k)-1(k) of the Code.

In addition, Taxpayer will enter into an exchange agreement with QI to facilitate transfer of RQ to Village in the exchange transaction as permitted by § 1.1031(k)-1(g)(4) of the regulations. Under this provision, a qualified intermediary is not considered the agent of the taxpayer for purposes of § 1031(a). Thus, Taxpayer's transfer of relinquished property through a qualified intermediary and the subsequent receipt or deemed receipt of like-kind replacement property through a qualified intermediary is treated as an exchange.

All timing requirements necessary for property to be held in the QEAA, relating to notice and transfer of qualified indicia of ownership of the property to EAT, will be satisfied. Within 45 days after the transfer of RP to EAT, Taxpayer will identify RQ as required by section 4.02(4) of Rev. Proc. 2000-37. Also, as required by section 4.02(5) of Rev. Proc. 2000-37, no later than 180 days after the transfer of qualified indicia of ownership of RP to EAT, RP will be transferred to Taxpayer. Consistent with section 4.02(6) of Rev. Proc. 2000-37, RQ will not be held by EAT in a QEAA and the total time that EAT will hold RP will not exceed 180 days. Moreover, RP will be received by Taxpayer simultaneously with its transfer of RQ through QI to Village. Therefore, Taxpayer will receive RP before the earlier of: (1) 180 days after the date on which the taxpayer transfers RQ in the exchange, (2) the due date (determined with regard to extension) for Taxpayer's tax return for the taxable year in which the transfer of RQ occurs, or (3) 180 days after the date on which RP is transferred to EAT under the QEAA.

As permitted by section 4.02(1) of Rev. Proc. 2000-37, the qualified indicia of ownership of RP will be held by EAT through Titleholder, another disregarded, single member LLC which it wholly owns. EAT is and will be subject to federal income tax and is not Taxpayer or a disqualified person. LLC-W is subleasing C-acres of the Unimproved Real Property to Titleholder. EAT and Titleholder will construct improvements on such property by one or more contractors hired and supervised by LLC-W. C-Acres (which is subleased from CorpW through LLC-W) together with such improvements, constructed by and for Titleholder, will constitute RP. Once EAT (and Titleholder through LLC-W) completes construction of improvements and the exchange of RP for RQ is completed, Taxpayer will take ownership of Titleholder (the disregarded entity holding title to RP).

Section 1.1031-1(e)(1) of the regulations provides that a transfer of relinquished property in a deferred exchange will not fail to qualify for nonrecognition of gain or loss under § 1031 merely because RP is not in existence or is being produced at the time the property is identified as replacement property. Section 1.1031(k)-1(e)(1) requires a taxpayer to identify RP by providing a legal description of the underlying land that is subject to sublease and as much detail as is practicable regarding the construction of the improvements at the site. In the present case, however, the question of sufficiency of identification of replacement property does not arise because the exchange will be simultaneous, except to the extent the improvements to C-Acres are incomplete when RP is transferred to Taxpayer.

If the production of the identified RP is not completed by EAT on or before the date required to satisfy the requirements of Rev. Proc. 2000-37, EAT will be required by contract to transfer RP to Taxpayer to satisfy those requirements, prior to completion. If this occurs, the identification requirement will be satisfied because Taxpayer will receive RP simultaneously with its transfer of RQ.

Taxpayer will receive no money or other property directly, indirectly or constructively prior to or during the exchange and will receive no economic benefit of money or property other than that derived from the exchange. The only possible exception will be if other property is transferred to Taxpayer incident to the failure of the contractors to timely complete improvements on RP prior to the transfer of Titleholder to Taxpayer. In that event, Taxpayer will have taxable boot in addition to its like-kind replacement property.

OPINION

Accordingly, based on the documents presented, including the exchange agreement with QI, the qualified exchange accommodation agreement with EAT setting up the QEAA, and all other representations made, Taxpayer's transaction will conform with the requirements of the QI and the QEAA safe harbor rules, so that QI and EAT will not be agents of Taxpayer and Taxpayer will not be in actual or constructive receipt of money or other property before receiving RP. Taxpayer will not recognize any gain or loss upon the conveyance of RQ to Village and the receipt of RP. However, if planned improvements are not completed within the exchange period, gain will be recognized to the extent of any boot received in the exchange.

CAVEATS AND EXCEPTIONS

Except as specifically provided above, no opinion is expressed as to the federal tax treatment of the transaction under any other provisions of the Internal Revenue Code and the Income Tax Regulations that may be applicable or under any other general principles of federal income taxation. Neither is any opinion expressed as to the tax treatment of any conditions existing at the time of, nor effects resulting from, the transactions that are not specifically covered by the above ruling. No opinion is expressed as to whether the accommodators used in this transaction are disqualified persons as defined in § 1.1031(k)-1(k), as that would constitute essentially a factual determination. This ruling assumes that QI and EAT are eligible to serve as accommodators.

This ruling is directed only to the taxpayer(s) who requested it. Section 6110(k)(3) of the Code provides that it may not be cited as precedent. Pursuant to a Power of Attorney submitted by Taxpayer, a copy of this letter will be sent to Taxpayer's authorized representatives.

This document may not be used or cited as precedent. Section 6110(j)(3) of the Internal Revenue Code.

Chapter 16

Exchanges and Proximate Business Transactions

I. Commentary

Exchanges often occur in close proximity to business transactions, such as mergers or divisions of a legal entity, liquidation of a partnership or corporation, formation of a new entity, or admission of a new member to an existing entity. Proximate business transactions may affect the holding and use requirements. Recall that an exchanger must hold relinquished property for productive use in a trade or business or for investment.[1] If an exchanger acquires property from a contribution or distribution immediately prior to an exchange, the IRS may argue that the exchanger acquired the property to exchange, not hold for productive use in a trade or business or for investment.[2] An exchanger must also hold replacement property for productive use in a trade or business or for investment.[3] If an exchanger acquires replacement property and immediately contributes it to an entity or distributes it to an owner of an entity, the IRS may argue that the exchanger did not acquire the replacement property with the intent to hold it for productive use in a trade or business or for investment.[4]

Exchangers may rely upon case law to argue that they hold the property with the requisite intent.[5] They must, however, demonstrate that they, and not another party to the proximate business transactions, hold the property. For example, the mere transfer of title from a partnership to a partner does not establish that the partner

---

1. *See* I.R.C. § 1031(a); Regals Realty Co. v. Comm'r, 127 F.2d 931, 933 (2d Cir. 1942) (holding that the intent to sell property disqualifies an intended exchange of such property from section 1031 nonrecognition); Click v. Commissioner, 78 T.C. 225 (1982) (holding that the intent to give replacement property as a gift disqualifies the exchange from section 1031 nonrecognition).

2. *See* Rev. Rul. 77-337, 1977-2 C.B. 305.

3. *See* I.R.C. § 1031(a).

4. *See* Rev. Rul. 75-292, 1975-2 C.B. 333.

5. *See* Magneson v. Comm'r, 753 F.2d 1490 (9th Cir. 1985) (allowing section 1031 nonrecognition even though the exchanger contributed replacement property to a limited partnership in exchange for a general partnership interest immediately following the exchange); Bolker v. Comm'r, 760 F.2d 1039 (9th Cir. 1985) (holding that an exchange following a distribution qualified for section 1031 nonrecognition); Maloney v. Comm'r, 93 T.C. 89 (1989) (allowing section 1031 nonrecognition even though a corporation distributed replacement property immediately following an exchange).

held the property for section 1031 purposes.[6] The parties also must ensure that the same party that transfers relinquished property acquires replacement property.[7]

A common situation is for a tax partnership to have at least one member who would prefer to be cashed out when the tax partnership sells its primary asset. The members of the tax partnership may choose from one of several different structures to effectuate such a goal. For instance, the tax partnership could simply sell the property and allocate the gain among all of the members. If the non-cash-out members would prefer to do a section 1031 exchange with their interests in the proceeds, they would most likely prefer not to recognize gain, so would consider another transaction. The members of the tax partnership may consider specially allocating the gain to the cash-out member, distributing an undivided interest in the property to the cash-out member, taking an installment note and distributing it to the cash-out member, buying the cash-out member's interest in the tax partnership, or borrowing to redeem the cash-out member's interest in the tax partnership. If the tax partnership's property has unrealized section 1250 gain, the cash-out structure may affect which party recognizes that gain,[8] so the members should carefully consider each alternative. If they are unable to structure the cash out fairly, perhaps they have to adjust the cash-out price to account for the gain allocation.

II. Primary Legal Authority

Commissioner v. Court Holding Co.

United States Supreme Court
324 U.S. 331 (1945)

FACTS

The respondent corporation was organized in 1934 solely to buy and hold the apartment building which was the only property ever owned by it. All of its outstanding stock was owned by Minnie Miller and her husband. Between October 1, 1939 and February, 1940, while the corporation still had legal title to the property, negotiations for its sale took place. These negotiations were between the corporation and the lessees of the property, together with a sister and brother-in-law. An oral agreement was reached as to the terms and conditions of sale, and on February 22, 1940, the parties met to reduce the agreement to writing. The purchaser was then

---

6. *See* Comm'r v. Court Holding Co, 324 U.S. 331 (1945) (holding that a corporation was the tax owner of property, even though legal title passed to the shareholders); Chase v. Comm'r, 92 T.C. 874 (1989) (holding that transfer of title did not transfer ownership for section 1031 purposes). *But see* Mason v. Comm'r, 55 T.C.M. (CCH) 1134 (1988) (holding that the partners were the owners of exchange property they held momentarily following the liquidation of a partnership).

7. *See* Tech. Adv. Mem. 98-18-003 (Dec. 24, 1997) (ruling that a transfer by a partnership of property and the receipt by the partners of other property did not qualify for section 1031 nonrecognition).

8. *See* Bradley T. Borden, *Code Sec. 1031 Drop-Swap Cash-Outs and Unrecaptured Section 1250 Gain*, 19 J. Passthrough Ent. 27 (Sep./Oct. 2016).

advised by the corporation's attorney that the sale could not be consummated because it would result in the imposition of a large income tax on the corporation. The next day, the corporation declared a "liquidating dividend", which involved complete liquidation of its assets, and surrender of all outstanding stock. Mrs. Miller and her husband surrendered their stock, and the building was deeded to them. A sale contract was then drawn, naming the Millers individually as vendors, and the lessees' sister as vendee, which embodied substantially the same terms and conditions previously agreed upon. One thousand dollars, which a month and a half earlier had been paid to the corporation by the lessees, was applied in part payment of the purchase price. Three days later, the property was conveyed to the lessees' sister.

The Tax Court concluded from these facts that, despite the declaration of a "liquidating dividend" followed by the transfers of legal title, the corporation had not abandoned the sales negotiations; that these were mere formalities designed "to make the transaction appear to be other than what it was", in order to avoid tax liability. The Circuit Court of Appeals drawing different inferences from the record, held that the corporation had "called off" the sale, and treated the stockholders' sale as unrelated to the prior negotiations.

ANALYSIS

There was evidence to support the findings of the Tax Court, and its findings must therefore be accepted by the courts. *Dobson v. Comm'r*, 320 U.S. 489 (1944); *Comm'r v. Heininger*, 320 U.S. 467 (1943); *Comm'r v. Scottish American Investment Co.*, 323 U.S. 119 (1944), On the basis of these findings, the Tax Court was justified in attributing the gain from the sale to respondent corporation. The incidence of taxation depends upon the substance of a transaction. The tax consequences which arise from gains from a sale of property are not finally to be determined solely by the means employed to transfer legal title. Rather, the transaction must be viewed as a whole, and each step, from the commencement of negotiations to the consummation of the sale, is relevant. A sale by one person cannot be transformed for tax purposes into a sale by another by using the latter as a conduit through which to pass title.[9] To permit the true nature of a transaction to be disguised by mere formalisms, which exist solely to alter tax liabilities, would seriously impair the effective administration of the tax policies of Congress.

It is urged that respondent corporation never executed a written agreement, and that an oral agreement to sell land cannot be enforced in Florida because of the Statute of Frauds, Comp. Gen. Laws of Florida, 1927, vol. 3, Sec. 5779, F.S.A. § 725.01. But the fact that respondent corporation itself never executed a written contract is unimportant, since the Tax Court found from the facts of the entire transaction that the executed sale was in substance the sale of the corporation. The decision of the Circuit Court of Appeals is reversed, and that of the Tax Court affirmed.

---

9. [4] Gregory v. Helvering, 293 U.S. 465 (1935); Minnesota Tea Co. v. Helvering, 302 U.S. 609 (1938); Griffiths v. Helvering, 308 U.S. 355 (1939); Higgins v. Smith, 308 U.S. 473 (1940).

Bolker v. Commissioner

United States Court of Appeals, Ninth Circuit

760 F.2d 1039 (1985)

FACTS

The transaction was consummated as follows. In March 1972, Bolker commenced the liquidation of Crosby. On March 13, 1972, all of the following occurred:

(1) Crosby transferred all its assets and liabilities to Bolker in redemption of all Crosby stock outstanding;

(2) Bolker as president of Crosby executed the Internal Revenue Service liquidation forms;

(3) A deed conveying Montebello from Crosby to Bolker was recorded;

(4) Bolker and Parlex, a corporation formed by Bolker's attorneys to facilitate the exchange, executed a contract to exchange Montebello for properties to be designated by Bolker;

(5) Parlex contracted to convey Montebello to SCS in coordination with the exchange by Bolker and Parlex; and

(6) Bolker, Crosby, Parlex, and SCS entered into a settlement agreement dismissing a breach of contract suit pending by Crosby against SCS in the event that all the other transactions went as planned.[10]

On June 30, 1972, all the transactions closed simultaneously, SCS receiving Montebello and Bolker receiving three parcels of real estate which he had previously designated.

Bolker reported no gain on the transaction, asserting that it qualified for nonrecognition under then-current I.R.C. § 1031(a):

> No gain or loss shall be recognized if property held for productive use in trade or business or for investment (not including stock in trade or other property held primarily for sale, nor stocks, bonds, notes, choses in action, certificates of trust or beneficial interest, or other securities or evidences of indebtedness or interest) is exchanged solely for property of a like kind to be held either for productive use in trade or business or for investment.

The Commissioner sent Bolker statutory notices of deficiency on the ground that the transaction did not qualify under section 1031(a). In the Tax Court, the Commissioner argued two theories: that Crosby, not Bolker, exchanged Montebello with SCS, and in the alternative, that Bolker did not hold Montebello for productive use

---

10. [2] Crosby had filed a breach of contract suit against SCS in 1971 based upon SCS' failure to fulfill a prior contract to purchase Montebello. We do not discuss whether the settlement of this lawsuit as part of the transaction was an exchange of non-like-kind property, because the Commissioner did not raise the argument at trial or on appeal. *See* discussion Part I below.

in trade or business or for investment.[11] The Tax Court rejected both arguments. The Commissioner does not appeal the decision that Bolker individually made the exchange. The Commissioner does not challenge any of the Tax Court's findings of fact; review of the Tax Court's decisions of law is de novo. *California Federal Life Insurance Co. v. Comm'r*, 680 F.2d 85, 87 (9th Cir.1982).

ANALYSIS

I. STOCK FOR PROPERTY

Section 1031(a) specifically excludes from eligibility for nonrecognition an exchange involving stock. The Commissioner argues that Bolker's transactions should properly be viewed as a whole, under the step transaction doctrine, *see Comm'r v. Court Holding Co.*, 324 U.S. 331, 334 (1945) (court may view transaction as a whole even if taxpayer accomplishes result by series of steps), and that so viewed, Bolker exchanged his Crosby stock for property. The Commissioner did not argue this theory in the Tax Court, ... [so w]e therefore decline to address the issue on appeal.

II. THE HOLDING REQUIREMENT

The Commissioner argued unsuccessfully in the Tax Court that because Bolker acquired the property with the intent, and almost immediate contractual obligation, to exchange it, Bolker never held the property for productive use in trade or business or for investment as required by § 1031(a). Essentially, the Commissioner's position is that the holding requirement has two elements: that the taxpayer own the property to make money rather than for personal reasons, and that at some point before the taxpayer decides to exchange the property, he have intended to keep that property as an investment.

Bolker argues that the intent to exchange investment property for other investment property satisfies the holding requirement. Bolker's position also in essence posits two elements to the holding requirement: that the taxpayer own the property to make money, and that the taxpayer not intend to liquidate his investment.

Authority on this issue is scarce. This is not surprising, because in almost all fact situations in which property is acquired for immediate exchange, there is no gain or loss to the acquiring taxpayer on the exchange, as the property has not had time to change in value. Therefore, it is irrelevant to that taxpayer whether § 1031(a) applies. *See, e.g.*, D. Posin, Federal Income Taxation 180 & n. 46 (1983); Rev. Rul. 77-297. The cases generally address the taxpayer's intent regarding the property *acquired* in an exchange, rather than the property *given up*. The rule of those cases, *e.g.*, *Regals Realty Co. v. Comm'r*, 127 F.2d 931, 933-34 (2d Cir. 1942), is that at the time of the exchange the taxpayer must intend to keep the property acquired, and intend to do so with an investment purpose. That rule would be nonsense as applied to the property given up, because at the time of the exchange the taxpayer's intent in every case is to give up the property. No exchange could qualify.

---

11. [3] The Commissioner concedes that the real estate received by Bolker was of like kind to the Montebello property.

The Commissioner cites two revenue rulings to support his position, Rev. Rul. 77-337, and Rev. Rul. 77-297. Revenue rulings, however, are not controlling. *Ricards v. U.S.*, 683 F.2d 1219, 1224 & n. 12 (9th Cir. 1981) (revenue rulings not binding although entitled to consideration as "body of experience and informed judgment"). Moreover, neither ruling is precisely on point here. In Revenue Ruling 77-337, A owned X corporation, which owned a shopping center. Pursuant to a prearranged plan, A liquidated X to acquire the shopping center so that he could immediately exchange it with B for like-kind property. A never held the shopping center, and therefore §1031(a) did not apply. This case differs from 77-337 in two ways. First, the liquidation was planned before any intention to exchange the properties arose, not to facilitate an exchange. Second, Bolker did actually hold Montebello for three months.

In Revenue Ruling 77-297, B wanted to buy A's ranch, but A wanted to exchange rather than sell. A located a desirable ranch owned by C. Pursuant to a prearranged plan, B purchased C's ranch and immediately exchanged it with A for A's ranch. As to A, the exchange qualifies under §1031(a). As to B, it does not, since B never held C's ranch, and acquired it solely to exchange. The same distinctions as in 77-337 apply between this ruling and the facts in *Bolker*. Neither ruling cites case authority for its holdings.

Bolker cites two cases that support his position. In each case, the Tax Court gave §1031(a) nonrecognition to a transaction in which the property given up was acquired with the intention of exchange. However, neither case actually considered the holding issue, which diminishes the persuasiveness of the authority. In *124 Front Street, Inc. v. Comm'r*, 65 T.C. 6 (1975), taxpayer owned an option to purchase real estate. Firemen's Fund Insurance Co. (Firemen's) wanted the property, but taxpayer preferred an exchange to a sale. Firemen's advanced taxpayer the money to exercise its option under a contract providing that taxpayer would exchange the property for property to be acquired by Firemen's. *Id.* at 8-11. Taxpayer exercised its option, and the exchange was consummated five months later when Firemen's had acquired property satisfactory to taxpayer. *Id.* at 12. The issue in the case was whether the transaction was the sale of the option to Firemen's, or an exchange of the property with Firemen's. The court held that it was an exchange, and therefore qualified under §1031(a). *Id.* at 15. The court apparently never considered whether the fact that the optioned property was acquired solely for exchange meant that it was not held for investment under §1031(a). Even without an explicit holding, however, the case does support Bolker's theory that an intent to exchange for like-kind property satisfies the holding requirement.

Rutherford v. Comm'r, 37 T.C.M. (CCH) 1851-77 (1978), is an unusual case with a holding similar to *124 Front Street*. W, a cattle breeder, agreed with R, another breeder, to exchange W's twelve half-blood heifers for twelve three-quarter blood heifers to be bred from the half-blood heifers. W gave R the twelve half-blood heifers. R bred them to a registered bull and gave W the first twelve three-quarter blood heifers produced. *Id.* at 1851-77 to 1851-78. At stake in the case were depreciation deductions. En route to determining R's basis in the half-blood heifers for depreciation purposes, the Tax Court held that the exchange of heifers qualified for nonrecognition under

§ 1031(a). *Id.* at 1851-79. Although the court did not even mention the point, the facts indicate that when by virtue of their birth R "acquired" the three-quarter blood heifers, the property he gave up, he had already contracted to exchange them. Thus, *Rutherford* also supports *Bolker's* position, albeit tacitly.

The Tax Court's holding in this case is based on its recent opinion in *Magneson v. Comm'r*, 81 T.C. 767 (1983) (court reviewed), *aff'd*, 753 F.2d 1490 (9th Cir. 1985). In *Magneson*, taxpayers exchanged property for like-kind property and then by prearrangement contributed the property they acquired to a partnership. Each transaction viewed separately was admittedly tax-free, but in combination raised the issue whether contribution to a partnership satisfies the holding requirement for the acquired property. The *Bolker* Tax Court interpreted *Magneson* as holding that an intent to continue the investment rather than selling it or converting it to personal use satisfied the holding requirement, even if the taxpayer never intended to keep the specific property acquired. In both *Bolker* and *Magneson*, the Tax Court emphasized the admitted nonrecognition treatment accorded each individual step in the transactions, and reasoned that if each step were tax-free, in combination they should also be tax-free, so long as the continuity of investment principle underlying § 1031(a) is respected. *See Bolker*, 81 T.C. at 805-06; *Magneson*, 81 T.C. at 771.

We recently affirmed *Magneson* but our rationale differed from that of the Tax Court. While we recognized the importance of continuity of investment as the basic purpose underlying § 1031(a), *see* H.R. Rep. No. 704, 73d Cong., 2d Sess. 12, *reprinted in* 1939-1 C.B. (pt. 2) 554, 564, we did not hold that that principle justifies the failure to address the specific requirements of § 1031(a). Rather, we based affirmance on our holding that the Magnesons intended to and did continue to hold the acquired property, the contribution to the partnership being a change in the form of ownership rather than the relinquishment of ownership. *Magneson*, at 1495-96. Thus the Magnesons satisfied the specific requirements of § 1031(a). Nothing in *Magneson* relieves Bolker of his burden to satisfy the requirement that he have held the property given up, Montebello, for investment.

Finally, there is nothing in the legislative history which either supports or negates Bolker's or the Commissioner's position. In sum, the Commissioner is supported by two revenue rulings which are neither controlling nor precisely on point. Bolker is supported by two Tax Court decisions which did not explicitly address this issue. In the absence of controlling precedent, the plain language of the statute itself appears our most reliable guide.

The statute requires that the property be "held for productive use in trade or business or for investment." Giving these words their ordinary meaning, *see Greyhound Corp. v. U.S.*, 495 F.2d 863, 869 (9th Cir. 1974) (if Code does not define term, court should give words their ordinary meaning), a taxpayer may satisfy the "holding" requirement by owning the property, and the "for productive use in trade or business or for investment" requirement by lack of intent either to liquidate the investment or to use it for personal pursuits. These are essentially the two requirements courts have placed on the property *acquired* in a § 1031(a) exchange, *see, e.g., Regals Realty*, 127 F.2d at 933-34 (intent to sell disqualifies exchange); *Click v. Comm'r*, 78 T.C. 225, 233–34 (1982) (intent to give as gift disqualifies exchange), so this interpretation would yield the symmetry the use of identical language seems to demand.

The Commissioner's position, in contrast, would require us to read an unexpressed additional requirement into the statute: that the taxpayer have, previous to forming the intent to exchange one piece of property for a second parcel, an intent to keep the first piece of property indefinitely. We decline to do so. *See Starker v. U.S.*, 602 F.2d 1341, 1352–53 (9th Cir. 1979) (refusing to read unexpressed additional requirement of simultaneous exchange into § 1031(a)).[12] Rather, we hold that if a taxpayer owns property which he does not intend to liquidate or to use for personal pursuits, he is "holding" that property "for productive use in trade or business or for investment" within the meaning of § 1031(a). Under this formulation, the intent to exchange property for like-kind property satisfies the holding requirement, because it is *not* an intent to liquidate the investment or to use it for personal pursuits. Bolker acquired the Montebello property with the intent to exchange it for like-kind property, and thus he held Montebello for investment under § 1031(a). The decision of the Tax Court is therefore affirmed.

Magneson v. Commissioner

United States Court of Appeals, Ninth Circuit
753 F.2d 1490 (1985)

FACTS

The Magnesons were the sole owners of an apartment building in San Diego, California (Iowa Street Property). They held the property for productive use in trade or business or for investment within the meaning of § 1031(a). N.E.R. Plaza, Ltd. (NER) was the sole owner of commercial property in San Diego, California, known as the Plaza Property (Plaza Property).

Pursuant to a prearranged transaction consummated on August 11, 1977, the Magnesons transferred their fee interest in the Iowa Street Property to NER in exchange for a ten-percent undivided fee interest in the Plaza Property. Thereafter, on the same day, both the Magnesons and NER transferred their interests in the Plaza Property to U.S. Trust, Ltd. (U.S. Trust), a limited partnership under California law. In exchange

---

12. [5] *Starker*'s specific holding that § 1031(a) does not require simultaneous exchange, 602 F.2d at 1354–55, has been limited by a revision of § 1031(a). Deficit Reduction Act of 1984, Pub. L. No. 98-369, § 77, 98 Stat. 494, 595 (effective July 19, 1984; requiring that property acquired be designated and exchanged within 180 days after taxpayer transfers the property given up). The addition of this requirement, specifically drafted in response to *Starker, see* H.R. Rep. No. 432, 98th Cong., 2d Sess. 1231, *reprinted in* 6B 1984 U.S. Code Cong. & Ad. News 1, 201, does not affect the validity of *Starker*'s refusal to read unexpressed requirements into the then-current version of § 1031(a).

for cash and their ten-percent interest in the Plaza Property, the Magnesons received a general partnership interest in U.S. Trust consisting of a ten-percent equity interest and a nine-percent interest in net profits and losses. U.S. Trust was formed for the purpose of acquiring, holding, and operating the Plaza Property. The Magnesons paid no tax on the gain realized from their exchange of the Iowa Street Property for the Plaza Property, claiming nonrecognition treatment under § 1031(a). They also paid no tax on the gain realized from their contribution of the Plaza Property to U.S. Trust, claiming nonrecognition treatment under § 721.

The parties agree that the contribution of the Plaza Property to U.S. Trust qualifies for nonrecognition of gain under § 721, which provides that "[n]o gain or loss shall be recognized to a partnership or to any of its partners in the case of a contribution of property to the partnership in exchange for an interest in the partnership." The parties also agree that the Iowa Street Property and the Plaza Property are like-kind properties within the meaning of § 1031(a), which in 1977 provided:

> No gain or loss shall be recognized if property held for productive use in trade or business or for investment (not including stock in trade or other property held primarily for sale, nor stocks, bonds, notes, choses in action, certificates of trust or beneficial interest, or other securities or evidences of indebtedness or interest) is exchanged solely for property of a like kind to be held either for productive use in trade or business or for investment.

For purposes of this opinion we will use the phrase "held for investment" when discussing the holding requirement of § 1031(a), because the distinction between productive use and investment is not at issue.

ANALYSIS

I. THE HOLDING REQUIREMENT OF SECTION 1031(a)

The Commissioner argues that the exchange of the Iowa Street Property for the Plaza Property cannot qualify for nonrecognition under § 1031(a) because the Magnesons did not "hold" the Plaza Property for investment. The Magnesons contend that holding the property to contribute to a partnership is "holding" the property for investment. The court found for the Magnesons. The majority concluded that the contribution of the Plaza Property to U.S. Trust was a continuation of the Magnesons' investment unliquidated but in a modified form, and that therefore the Magnesons did hold the Plaza Property for investment. 81 T.C. at 771–72. We review the Tax Court's conclusions of law de novo, noting however that its opinions are entitled to respect because of its special expertise in the field. *California Federal Life Insurance Co. v. Comm'r*, 680 F.2d 85, 87 (9th Cir. 1982).

To qualify for nonrecognition treatment under § 1031(a), the taxpayer must, at the time the exchange is consummated, intend to hold the property acquired for investment. *Regals Realty Co. v. Comm'r*, 127 F.2d 931, 934 (2d Cir. 1942); *see Margolis v. Comm'r*, 337 F.2d 1001, 1003-05 (9th Cir. 1964). Numerous cases have held that the taxpayers' intent at the time of the exchange to liquidate their interest in the property acquired disqualifies the exchange from nonrecognition under § 1031(a). *See, e.g., Regals Realty,* 127 F.2d at 933–34 (intent to sell); *Click v. Comm'r,* 78 T.C. 225, 233–34 (1982) (intent to give as gift); *Lindsley v. Comm'r,* T.C.M. (P-H) 1983-729, at 3047–48 (intent to give to charity); *Land Dynamics v. Comm'r,* T.C.M. (P-H) 1978-259, at 1107–08 (intent to sell). *But see Wagensen v. Comm'r,* 74 T.C. 653, 658–59 (1980) (intent at time of exchange to hold for productive use not negated by desire to give eventually to children). It is stipulated that the Magnesons intended at the time of the exchange to hold the property for contribution to U.S. Trust. Therefore, the Magnesons' exchange can only qualify under § 1031(a) if contributing property to a partnership in return for an interest in the partnership is "holding" the property for investment within the meaning of § 1031(a).

We have found no precedent on point at either the Tax Court or the circuit court level. Revenue Ruling 75-292, 1975-2 C.B. 333, relied on by the Commissioner, addresses a related question: whether a like-kind exchange followed by a transfer for stock under § 351[13] to a controlled corporation qualifies for nonrecognition under § 1031(a). The Service ruled that the property transferred to the corporation was no longer held by the taxpayer, and gain was recognized on the exchange. *Id.* at 334. Revenue rulings, however, are not binding on this court. *Ricards v. U.S.,* 683 F.2d 1219, 1224 & n. 12 (9th Cir.1981) (rulings not dispositive although entitled to consideration as "body of experience and informed judgment"). More significantly, transfer to a corporation in exchange for shares is distinguishable from transfer to a partnership for a general partnership interest in several important ways.

First, a corporation is a distinct entity, apart from its shareholders, whereas a partnership is an association of its partner-investors. Shareholders have no ownership interest in the assets of a corporation; partners own the assets of a partnership. Shareholders have no participation in daily management of corporate assets and very little participation in long-term management; general partners are the managers of the partnership. Thus when the owner of property transfers it to a corporation in exchange for shares, he relinquishes ownership and control of the property. In contrast, he retains both in a transfer to a partnership for a general partnership interest.

Second, a like-kind exchange followed by a § 351 transfer, viewed as a whole, results in the exchange of property for stock. The parenthetical clause of § 1031(a) expressly excludes stock as property eligible for exchange, but there is no such prohibition on exchange of partnership interests. *Long v. Comm'r,* 77 T.C. 1045, 1066–68 (1981) (rejecting Commissioner's argument that partnership interests fit within exclusionary clause as choses in action or evidences of interests). Revenue Ruling 75-292 is therefore inapplicable to this case.

---

13. [2] Section 351 provides, in pertinent part:
   (a) General rule.—No gain or loss shall be recognized if property is transferred to a corporation by one or more persons solely in exchange for stock or securities in such corporation and immediately after the exchange such person or persons are in control (as defined in § 368(c)) of the corporation.

The central purpose of both §§ 721 and 1031(a), as stated by the Treasury Regulations, is to provide for nonrecognition of gain on a transfer of property in which the differences between the property parted with and the property acquired "are more formal than substantial," and "the new property is substantially a continuation of the old investment still unliquidated." Treas. Reg. 1.1002-1(c), T.D. 6500, 25 Fed. Reg. 11910 (1960).[14] The regulations reflect the legislative history of the predecessor of section 1031(a). *See* H.R. Rep. No. 704, 73d Cong., 2d Sess. 12, *reprinted in* 1939-1 C.B. (pt. 2) 554, 564; *Starker v. U.S.*, 602 F.2d 1341, 1352 (9th Cir. 1979) (§ 1031 "designed to avoid the imposition of a tax on those who do not 'cash in' their investments in trade or business property"). Furthermore, as the Tax Court noted, the regulations unequivocally describe section 721 as representing a continuation, not a liquidation, of the old investment. The case law, the regulations, and the legislative history are thus all in agreement that the basic reason for nonrecognition of gain or loss on transfers of property under §§ 1031 and 721 is that the taxpayer's economic situation after the transfer is fundamentally the same as it was before the transfer: his money is still tied up in investment in the same kind of property. *Koch v. Comm'r*, 71 T.C. 54, 63–64 (1978); *see Starker*, 602 F.2d at 1352; *Biggs v. Comm'r*, 69 T.C. 905, 913–14 (1978), *aff'd*, 632 F.2d 1171 (5th Cir. 1980). This principle exactly describes the Magnesons' situation. Before the two transactions, their investment was a fee in-

---

14. [3] The full text of Treas. Reg. 1.1002-1 is as follows:

(a) *General rule.* The general rule with respect to gain or loss realized upon the sale or exchange of property as determined under section 1001 is that the entire amount of such gain or loss is recognized except in cases where specific provisions of subtitle A of the Code provide otherwise.

(b) *Strict construction of exceptions from general rule.* The exceptions from the general rule requiring the recognition of all gains and losses, like other exceptions from a rule of taxation of general and uniform application, are strictly construed and do not extend either beyond the words or the underlying assumptions and purposes of the exception. Nonrecognition is accorded by the Code only if the exchange is one which satisfies both (1) the specific description in the Code of an excepted exchange, and (2) the underlying purpose for which such exchange is excepted from the general rule. The exchange must be germane to, and a necessary incident of, the investment or enterprise in hand. The relationship of the exchange to the venture or enterprise is always material, and the surrounding facts and circumstances must be shown. As elsewhere, the taxpayer claiming the benefit of the exception must show himself within the exception.

(c) *Certain exceptions to general rule.* Exceptions to the general rule are made, for example, by §§ 351(a), 354, 361(a), 371(a)(1), 371(b)(1), 721, 1031, 1035 and 1036. These sections describe certain specific exchanges of property in which at the time of the exchange particular differences exist between the property parted with and the property acquired, but such differences are more formal than substantial. As to these, the Code provides that such differences shall not be deemed controlling, and that gain or loss shall not be recognized at the time of the exchange. The underlying assumption of these exceptions is that the new property is substantially a continuation of the old investment still unliquidated; and, in the case of reorganizations, that the new enterprise, the new corporate structure, and the new property are substantially continuations of the old still unliquidated.

terest in income-producing real estate. They exchanged this property for other income-producing real estate, which they held as tenants in common with NER. The Magnesons and NER then changed the form of their ownership of that real estate from tenancy in common to partnership. They still own the income-producing real estate, and they have taken no cash or non-like-kind property out of the transaction. The Magnesons' transactions therefore fit squarely within the central purpose of § 1031. They exchanged their investment property for like-kind investment property which they continue to hold for investment, albeit in a different form of ownership.

This section of the regulations was subsequently changed due to incorporation of § 1002 into § 1001 as § 1001(c), but was applicable to the taxable year 1977, which is before the court in this case. *See* T.D. 7665, 1980-1 C.B. 319.

The Commissioner, and the dissenting Tax Court judges, argue that the differences between ownership as tenants in common and ownership as a partnership are so substantial that the Magnesons cannot be regarded as having continued to hold the property for investment under § 1031(a) after the partnership contribution. Previous like-kind exchange cases have indeed looked to the nature of the taxpayer's ownership interest as well as to the nature of the property owned to determine if the section 1031(a) requirements are met. *See Estate of Meyer v. Comm'r*, 503 F.2d 556, 557–58 (9th Cir. 1974) (per curiam) (general partnership and limited partnership interests not like-kind property); *Pappas v. Comm'r*, 78 T.C. 1078, 1086–87 (1982) (general partnership for general partnership qualifies as like-kind); *Long*, 77 T.C. at 1064–66 (joint venture for general partnership qualifies as like-kind); *Gulfstream Land & Development Corp. v. Comm'r*, 71 T.C. 587, 595 (1979) (joint venture for joint venture qualifies as like-kind); *cf. M.H.S. Co. v. Comm'r*, 575 F.2d 1177, 1178 (6th Cir. 1978) (§ 1033 condemnation and reinvestment; real property proceeds put into joint venture owning real property; not like-kind because state law converted all joint venture property into personal property of investors so exchange was real for personal and not like-kind); *Koch*, 71 T.C. at 64–65 (unencumbered fee for fee subject to 99-year leasehold interest qualifies as like-kind).

In application of federal tax statutes, state law controls in determining the nature of the legal interest the taxpayer holds in the property sought to be taxed. Federal law does not create or define property rights; it merely attaches tax consequences to the interests created by state law. *Aquilino v. U.S.*, 363 U.S. 509, 512–13 (1960). The dissent and the majority therefore correctly looked to California law to determine and compare the nature of tenancy in common and partnership ownership.

In California, a tenant in common owns an undivided interest in and is entitled to possession and enjoyment of the entire property. *Dimmick v. Dimmick*, 374 P.2d 824, 826 (Cal.2d 1962). Title to his interest is vested in him, he may encumber it or sell it independently of his co-tenants, *Meyer v. Wall*, 270 Cal.App.2d 24, 30 (1969), and the interest is devisable and descendible, *see Wilkerson v. Thomas*, 121 Cal.App.2d 479, 482 (1953). Similarly, a partner is co-owner with his partners, as a tenant in partnership, of specific partnership property. Cal. Corp. Code § 15025(1) (West Supp.1984). A general partner has the right to possess partnership property for the purposes of the partnership, although title is not vested in him. Cal. Corp. Code § 15025(2)(a) (West Supp.1984). However, a partner's interest in specific partnership property is not assignable without concurrent assignment by all other partners, Cal. Corp. Code § 15025(2)(b) (West Supp.1984), nor subject to attachment except for partnership debt, Cal. Corp. Code § 15025(2)(c) (West Supp.1984), nor subject to marital property rights, Cal. Corp. Code § 15025(2)(e) (West Supp.1984). On the death of a partner, his interest in specific partnership property vests in the surviving partners, not in the deceased partner's devisees or heirs. Cal. Corp. Code § 15025(2)(d) (West Supp.1984).

The Tax Court minority concluded from these differences that the transformation of the Magnesons' tenancy in common into a partnership interest "so changed their legal relationship to that property as to disqualify the exchange from § 1031(a) treatment." We disagree. While there are significant distinctions, we do not believe that they are controlling in determining the holding for investment issue. First, we note that the crucial question in a § 1031(a) analysis is continuity of investment in like-kind property. Therefore, the critical attributes in the taxpayer's relationship to the property are those relevant to holding the property for investment. As both tenants in common and as general partners, the Magnesons owned an interest in the Plaza Property. As both tenants in common and as general partners, the Magnesons had the right to possess and control the property. While it is true that § 15025(2)(a) limits their possession and control to partnership purposes, the partnership purpose was to hold for investment. Under these circumstances their control as general partners is of the same nature as their control as tenants in common, in each case holding the property for investment.

The significant differences between the tenancy in common and the partnership interests lie in the voluntary and involuntary alienability of the property. Basically, the tenancy in common interest is freely alienable, but specific partnership property is not. Because the whole premise of § 1031(a) is that the taxpayer's intent is *not to alienate* the property, we believe that alienability distinctions are not dispositive. If at the time of the exchange, as here, the taxpayer intends to contribute the property to a partnership for a general partnership interest, and the partnership's purpose is to hold the property for investment, the holding requirement of § 1031(a) is satisfied despite the limited alienability of specific partnership property.

The Commissioner contends that the Tax Court majority, in focusing exclusively on the continuity of investment principle underlying § 1031(a), ignored the equally important technical requirements of the section itself. Treasury Regulation 1.1002-1(b) provides:

> The exceptions from the general rule requiring the recognition of all gains and losses ... are strictly construed and do not extend either beyond the words or the underlying assumptions and purposes of the exception. Nonrecognition is accorded by the Code only if the exchange is one which satisfies both (1) the specific description in the Code of an excepted exchange, and (2) the underlying purpose for which such exchange is excepted from the general rule.

The Commissioner contends that this double test applies, and that even if this transaction satisfies the "underlying purpose" prong of the test, it still fails to qualify under the "specific description" prong because technically the partnership and not the taxpayers holds the acquired property. This circuit, however, rejected an analogous argument in *Starker*, 602 F.2d at 1352–53, refusing to give such a narrow construction. The Commissioner argued in *Starker* that the language of the regulation quoted above, as applied to § 1031(a), required simultaneous transfer for § 1031(a) nonrecognition. After analyzing the legislative history of § 1031(a) and concluding that it did not support the Commissioner's position, the court stated:

> [T]here is a second sound reason to question the applicability of Treas. Reg. § 1.1002-1: the long line of cases liberally construing section 1031. If the regulation purports to read into section 1031 a complex web of formal and substantive requirements, precedent indicates decisively that the regulation has been rejected.

Starker, 602 F.2d at 1352; *see, e.g., Coastal Terminals, Inc. v. U.S.*, 320 F.2d 333, 336–39 (4th Cir. 1963) (cash option did not preclude section 1031(a) nonrecognition because taxpayer intended to take cash only if no property available); *Alderson v. Comm'r*, 317 F.2d 790, 793 (9th Cir. 1963) (three-corner exchange); *Biggs*, 69 T.C. at 913–14 (four-corner exchange); *124 Front Street, Inc. v. Comm'r*, 65 T.C. 6, 17–18 (1975) (taxpayer can advance money toward purchase price of property to be acquired); *Coupe v. Comm'r*, 52 T.C. 394, 405–09 (1969) (taxpayer can locate and negotiate for the property to be acquired); *J.H. Baird Publishing Co. v. Comm'r*, 39 T.C. 608, 611 (1962) (taxpayer can oversee improvements on the land to be acquired). Applying the *Starker* manner of construing the section, we decline to read into section 1031(a) the requirement that the taxpayer continue to hold the acquired property by the exact form of ownership in which it was acquired. So long as, as in this case, the taxpayers continue to own the property and to hold it for investment, a change in the mechanism of ownership which does not significantly affect the amount of control or the nature of the underlying investment does not preclude nonrecognition under § 1031(a).

II. THE STEP TRANSACTION DOCTRINE

As an alternate position, the Commissioner contends that the step transaction doctrine should be applied in this case and would preclude § 1031(a) nonrecognition. Under this doctrine, the court must view the transaction as a whole even if the taxpayer uses a number of steps to consummate the transaction. *See Comm'r v. Court Holding Co.*, 324 U.S. 331, 334 (1945). A taxpayer may not secure, by a series of contrived steps, different tax treatment than if he had carried out the transaction directly. *Crenshaw v. U.S.*, 450 F.2d 472, 475–78 (5th Cir.1971), *cert. denied*, 408 U.S. 923 (1972). Viewed as a whole, the Commissioner argues that the Magnesons have exchanged their fee interest in the Iowa Street Property for a partnership interest in U.S. Trust, which the Commissioner contends is not like-kind property under this court's decision in *Meyer*, 503 F.2d at 557–58 (general and limited partnership interests not like-kind).

Initially, we note that it may not be appropriate to collapse the steps of this transaction, because it is not readily apparent that the transaction could have been achieved directly. The Magnesons started out with the Iowa Street Property, which was worth one tenth of the Plaza Property. NER owned 100% of the Plaza Property. NER and the Magnesons wanted to end up owning the Plaza Property together in a partnership, and the Magnesons wanted to pay for their share with the Iowa Street Property. The Magnesons could have sold the Iowa Street Property, used the proceeds to buy ten percent of the Plaza Property, and then formed the partnership with NER, but that would have added a step to the transaction, rather than being a more direct route than that taken. Alternatively, NER and the Magnesons could have formed the partnership with the Iowa Street Property and ninety percent of the Plaza Property, and then the partnership could have exchanged the Iowa Street Property for the remaining ten percent of the Plaza Property. Again, this is no more direct than the method by which the Magnesons chose to carry out the transaction. Between two equally direct ways of achieving the same result, the Magnesons were free to choose the method which entailed the most tax advantages to them. *Biggs*, 69 T.C. at 913 (quoted in *Starker*, 602 F.2d at 1353 n. 10).

Even if we apply the step transaction doctrine, and view the transaction as an exchange of the Magnesons' fee interest in the Iowa Street Property for a partnership interest in the Plaza Property, we believe that the transaction qualifies under § 1031(a).[15] The Commissioner argues that this case is controlled by *Meyer*, which held that a general partnership interest and a limited partnership interest were not like-kind although the underlying property in each partnership was like-kind. *Meyer*, 503 F.2d at 558. *Meyer* based its holding on the significant differences between general and limited partnership interests. A general partner has "a broad spectrum of rights and liabilities," *id.* at 557, including, importantly, general liability and rights to management and control. A limited partner's rights are restricted to certain inspection and accounting rights, and the power to dissolve the partnership under certain circumstances. Cal. Corp. Code §§ 15507, 15510, 15515–15517. A limited partner may not actively participate in running the business. He is "primarily an investor, dependent upon the efforts of others to make a profit," and has limited liability. *Meyer*, 503 F.2d at 558. Thus *Meyer* is based on the change in the taxpayer's ability to manage and control the property.

Meyer is not controlling in this case because, as discussed above, the rights of a fee owner and of a general partner to management and control are very similar. Rather than losing any participation in operating the investment property, as did the

---

15. [4] We note that for transactions executed after July 18, 1984, Congress has amended § 1031(a) to exclude the exchange of partnership interests. Deficit Reduction Act of 1984, Pub. L. No. 98-369, § 77, 98 Stat. 494, 595; *see* H.R. Rep. No. 432, 98th Cong., 2d Sess. 1231-34, *reprinted in* 6B 1984 U.S. Code Cong. & Ad. News 1, 201-04 (revision aimed primarily at forbidding tax-free exchange of "burned-out" tax shelter partnership interests).

taxpayer in *Meyer*, the Magnesons as general partners are the managers of their investment, just as they were when they owned the Iowa Street Property in fee simple. Thus, we reject the Commissioner's argument that application of the step transaction doctrine disqualifies this exchange for § 1031(a) nonrecognition.

Finally, we note that a critical basis for our decision is that the partnership in this case had as its underlying assets property of like kind to the Magnesons' original property, and its purpose was to hold that property for investment. Recent Tax Court cases considering the exchange of one partnership interest for another have looked to the underlying assets of the partnerships and required not only that the partnership interests be of like kind, *e.g.*, general for general, or general for joint venture, but that the underlying assets be of like kind. *See Pappas*, 78 T.C. at 1087; *Gulfstream*, 71 T.C. at 594–96. The purpose of this scrutiny is to prevent taxpayers from creating partnerships to hold assets that are not of like kind, and then exchanging the seemingly like-kind partnership interests. In such a case, the partnership form is being used artificially to shield from recognition an exchange that otherwise would not qualify under § 1031(a), *Gulfstream*, 71 T.C. at 595, and the Tax Court properly prescribed scrutiny of the underlying assets to prevent such abuse. In the Magnesons' situation, whether we view the transaction as an exchange followed by a contribution, or as an exchange of real estate for a partnership interest, we will examine the purpose and underlying assets of the partnership acquired to determine if the Magnesons have a continuing investment in like-kind property. The property the Magnesons contributed to the partnership was, of course, of like-kind to their original property. The rest of the partnership property was also like-kind, and the partnership's purpose was to hold real estate investment property, the kind of property that the Magnesons initially owned. Therefore, the Magnesons' ten-percent partnership interest in the underlying assets was entirely in like-kind property to their original investment, and the transaction qualifies under § 1031(a). In contrast, if the Magnesons had made the same initial exchange for like-kind real estate, but had contributed the real estate to a partnership that did not hold it for investment, or that did not have as the predominant part of its assets other like-kind real estate, the exchange would not qualify under § 1031(a). This would be so because once the Magnesons contributed their property, the underlying assets of their investment are the other assets of the partnership, and if those assets are not of like kind to the Magnesons' original real estate investment, the Magnesons have not continued their investment in like-kind property.

OPINION

Our holding in this case is limited to those situations in which the taxpayer exchanges property for like-kind property with the intent of contributing the acquired property to a partnership for a general partnership interest. Further, the taxpayer must show, as the Magnesons have here, that the purpose of the partnership is to hold the property for investment, and that the total assets of the partnership are predominantly of like kind to the taxpayer's original investment.

Regals Realty Co. v. Commissioner

United States Court of Appeals, Second Circuit

127 F.2d 931 (1942)

FACTS

The taxpayer was organized in 1933 by Leonard Marx, a successful real estate speculator, and two associates, to acquire, from a trustee in bankruptcy, the plot and building known as 2-10 East Flagler Street, in Miami, Florida. The price paid was $750, and the purchase was subject to existing leases, and to liens and encumbrances of more than $200,000. Marx succeeded in attracting enough new capital to make alterations and to clear up back interest and taxes, in arranging for a modification of the mortgage, and in concluding favorable leases. By the end of 1934, the property was operating at a profit. Dividends amounting to $5,000 were paid in both 1935 and 1936. In the early part of 1936, representatives of the Burdine Department Store, which was located on an adjoining plot, began negotiations with Marx for the purchase of the taxpayer's property. No definite offer was made, but Marx reported to a stockholders' meeting that he thought he could get $600,000, or about $420,000 above the mortgage. Because the tax upon such a sale would be high, the stockholders decided not to consummate the proposed deal. Marx' testimony on this point was as follows:

> I explained … that if the property was sold we would get $420,000 and under the provisions of the federal tax law we would have to pay that out as our dividends, and we would get that immediately.
>
> Q. Who would get that immediately?
>
> A. The stockholders, and I think out of the $420,000 we would have to pay corporate and individual taxes, and there would be $140,000 left, or something like that; maybe it was $180,000 but it was less than $200,000 anyhow. They said, "Well, there is no sense in the deal for us. What can we buy with $140,000, or, say $150,000 that will give us anything like that income?"

On being informed of this decision, the Burdine people made another proposal. They offered to give the taxpayer $120,000 in cash and a nearby property, located at 26 East Flagler, and worth $300,000, which they had purchased as an addition to their department but which was not suitable for that purpose because of a difference in floor levels. Under this plan, the transfer of 2-10 East Flagler was to be subject to the mortgage. In making this proposal, Burdine's representatives said that the transfer would come within the provisions of § 112(b)(1), so that only the cash received would be taxable. Mr. Marx asked his bookkeeper to look up § 112(b)(1), which "seemed to be just right." He then reported the offer to a stockholders' meeting, saying that 26 East Flagler Street had a higher traffic count than the property at 2-10, that upon the expiration of 1938 of a lease with S. H. Kress, they could probably get a higher rent for the new property, and that "I thought this was a very adequate investment, to replace the investment that we were making, and this was an excellent proposal, this swap, and I felt that they should think it over very carefully before turning it down." He said that, in his opinion, the company would be taxable only on the cash received.

The offer was accepted on July 2, 1936. On August 10, 1936, the Board of Directors met and adopted resolutions to liquidate the company, by distributing the cash received as a liquidating dividend and by selling 26 East Flagler Street. A stockholders' meeting held the same day approved of this action, adding the requirement that the liquidation should be in accordance with § 115(c) of the Revenue Act of 1936, 26 U.S.C.A. Int. Rev. Acts, page 868, which made it possible to treat dividends received on liquidation as return of capital, so that gain thus realized would be taxable at the capital gain rate. In 1937 the taxpayer transferred its property to 26 East Flagler Street Corporation, and distributed the stock of this new corporation to its stockholders.

In arguing that the acquisition of the 26 East Flagler property by the taxpayer was a tax-free exchange under the provisions of § 112(b) quoted above, the taxpayer urges that its sole interest was in making a profitable investment. It points to the refusal to sell 2-10 as evidence of its intention not to convert its property into cash, and says that the exchange rather than a sale was decided upon so that the gain would not have to be recognized. The undisputed desire to avoid a tax on the gain, it says, is strong evidence that it did not intend to sell its property, but intended instead to hold it as an investment.

Against this we have a finding by the Board of Tax Appeals that the taxpayer did not intend to hold the property for investment. For that finding, there is ample support in the record. We have already adverted to the August 10, 1936 resolutions of the directors and stockholders, which spoke of effecting a complete liquidation of the company by selling 26 East Flagler Street. While the minutes were prepared after the meeting and by the taxpayer's counsel rather than by the Secretary, we cannot say that the Board should therefore have decided that they did not reflect accurately the events. Marx said that although the minutes used the word "sell," the intention was only to transfer the property to a new corporation. Yet, on February 10, 1937, according to the minutes of a directors' meeting, Marx "reported that in accordance with the plan of liquidation of the Company, he had been endeavoring to sell the remaining piece of real estate owned by the Company at 26 East Flagler Street, Miami, Florida. He had been unsuccessful in finding a purchaser, and he decided that apparently the time was not propitious for the sale of this property. He, therefore, suggested that, in accordance with the plan of liquidation, this property be sold to the 26 East Flagler Street Corporation, a new company in the process of formulation, in exchange for One Hundred (100) shares of the capital stock of the 26 East Flagler Street Corporation."

The Board had before it other evidence in conflict with taxpayer's assertion that the property was held for investment. Thus, the day following the August 10 meeting, Marx wired a broker, in response to his inquiry about the selling-price of 26 East Flagler, that no price "has been put on building as yet." He repeated this statement in a letter to the same broker two weeks later.

ANALYSIS

We need not go into the evidence in greater detail; enough has been presented to show that there was substantial evidence to sustain the Board's finding as to the

taxpayer's intention, i.e., its finding that the taxpayer did not establish that 2-10 Flagler Street was exchanged for property "to be held ... for investment." We cannot
grant a trial de novo merely because there was evidence on which it might have
based a contrary conclusion; *Helvering v. National Grocery Co.*, 304 U.S. 282, 294
(1938). The Board's finding as to intention is not "a conclusion of law," as in *Midwood
Associates, Inc., v. Comm'r*, 115 F.2d 871, 872 (2d Cir. 1940). Nor is this a case like
Blackmer v. Comm'r, 70 F.2d 255 (2d Cir. 1934), where the only evidence was the
taxpayer's uncontradicted testimony, which was in entire harmony with all the surrounding circumstances.

The taxpayer makes a further argument, namely, that its intention at the time of
the exchange is not relevant on the issue of taxability. To support this argument, it
points to a statement in the Committee Report[16] on the Revenue Act of 1924 (where
the forerunner of §112(b)(1) appeared as Sec. 203(b)(1), 26 U.S.C.A. Int. Rev. Acts,
page 4) that the "intention of the party at the time of the exchange is difficult to determine, is subject to change by him and does not represent a fair basis of determining
tax liability." But that statement must not be wrenched from its context. It explained
the abolition, in the Act of 1924, of the earlier requirement, shown by §202(c)(1)
of the Act of 1921, 42 Stat. 230, that property held for investment must be exchanged
for property to be held for investment, while property held for productive use must
be exchanged for property to be held for productive use. By this requirement, it was
necessary to decide whether the taxpayer's intent was to hold for investment or for
productive use, and it was this examination as to intention which was rejected by
Congress, which said, "If the property received is of a like kind, it is immaterial
whether it is to be held for investment or for productive use." Under the amended
provision, so long as the purpose is one or the other or both, the exchange is tax-
free. But the taxpayer must still acquire the property (a) for investment or productive
use, rather than (b) for inventory, sale, or similar purposes.

OPINION

The intention to hold for a sufficient time to reduce taxes, and no longer, does
not satisfy the statutory test.

Maloney v. Commissioner

United States Tax Court
93 T.C. 89 (1989)

FACTS

When the petitions were filed in the instant cases, petitioners Bonny B. Maloney,
and Robert S. Maloney (hereinafter sometimes referred to as "Maloney"), wife and
husband, resided in New Orleans, Louisiana.

---

16. [2] 68th Cong., 1st sess., Sen. Rept. 398.

Van, a Louisiana corporation, was a calendar year taxpayer. Van was formed in 1966, and its initial business activity, as its name suggests, was the moving and storing of furniture. Sometime in 1977, Van discontinued the active conduct of that business; thereafter, its only activity until its dissolution was the leasing of its assets to related corporations. From the time Van was formed until December 12, 1978, petitioners owned 80 percent of Van's stock and Olga Maloney (hereinafter sometimes referred to as "Olga") owned the remaining 20 percent. Olga was Maloney's stepmother. Maloney's father died in 1978. On December 12, 1978, Maloney acquired the remaining 20 percent of the stock in Van from Olga in exchange for his $125,000 nonnegotiable, noninterest-bearing promissory note. The note was payable in installments over 20 years, beginning January 1, 1984. From then until Van's dissolution, petitioners owned all of Van's stock.

Maloney also had an interest in a number of other corporations, including Maloney Trucking & Storage, Inc., and Gallagher Transfer and Storage (hereinafter sometimes collectively referred to as "the Maloney interests").

One of Van's primary assets was a piece of real estate (hereinafter sometimes referred to as "the I-10 property") located in Jefferson Parish, in or near Metairie, near Cleary Avenue, and extending to the I-10 service road. This is northwest of downtown New Orleans, just outside the New Orleans city limits. Van bought the I-10 property on or about August 15, 1971. At the same time, Van bought land adjoining the I-10 property on the western side. Van's intention at that time was to build a warehouse on this adjoining property and to hold the I-10 property for investment or development. Van built the warehouse on this adjoining property and held the I-10 property for investment.

In mid-1978, Maloney indicated to his attorney, Charles B. Johnson (hereinafter sometimes referred to as "Johnson"), that there was a possible purchaser for the I-10 property. Maloney also mentioned to Johnson that the Maloney interests were considering acquiring a piece of property on Elysian Fields Avenue in New Orleans (that property is hereinafter sometimes referred to as "Elysian Fields"). Elysian Fields is northeast of downtown New Orleans. Johnson advised Maloney that a like-kind exchange would produce more favorable tax results than a taxable sale or exchange. As of August 2, 1978, Maloney intended to consolidate the different businesses with which he was associated. He also intended that operations of the Maloney interests be located on Elysian Fields. Neither Van nor Maloney intended to sell Elysian Fields.

On August 2, 1978, Van entered into an Exchange Agreement (hereinafter sometimes referred to as "the Exchange Agreement") with James Goldsmith and Edward Hernandez (hereinafter sometimes collectively referred to as "Goldsmith and Hernandez"). Under the Exchange Agreement, Van agreed to transfer the I-10 property to Goldsmith and Hernandez. In exchange, Goldsmith and Hernandez were to convey to Van property referred to in the Exchange Agreement as 'the Exchange Property', which was intended to be Elysian Fields. The I-10 property and Elysian Fields are properties of a like kind.

The exchange described in the Exchange Agreement was subject to several conditions. Firstly, Goldsmith and Hernandez did not yet own Elysian Fields, so they were to enter into an agreement to buy Elysian Fields under terms acceptable to Van. Secondly, Goldsmith and Hernandez would have to obtain valid and merchantable title to Elysian Fields, and Van would have to provide valid and merchantable title to the I-10 property. If Goldsmith and Hernandez were unable to acquire valid and merchantable title to Elysian Fields (first condition, above) or were unable to enter into an agreement to purchase Elysian Fields on terms acceptable to Van, then Van would nevertheless be obligated to sell the I-10 property to Goldsmith and Hernandez for cash. Thirdly, the exchange was conditioned on Goldsmith and Hernandez' obtaining a zoning change on the property adjacent to the I-10 property.[17]

On October 15, 1978, Goldsmith and Hernandez entered into an agreement to buy Elysian Fields from Robert Coffin (hereinafter sometimes referred to as "Coffin"). Coffin did not at that time own Elysian Fields; on August 8, 1978, Coffin had entered into an agreement to buy Elysian Fields from Hibernia National Bank in New Orleans (hereinafter sometimes referred to as "Hibernia"). The agreement between Coffin and Hibernia was conditioned on certain zoning changes being made. On October 12, 1978, the Council of the City of New Orleans approved the rezoning upon which the agreement between Coffin and Hibernia was conditioned. The Comprehensive Zoning Ordinance of the City of New Orleans was amended accordingly on April 19, 1979. On November 29, 1978, the Jefferson Parish Council approved the rezoning of the property adjacent to the I-10 property, as contemplated in the Exchange Agreement; the rezoning became effective on December 11, 1978.

In early December, Maloney advised Johnson that there was a possible purchaser for the property adjoining the I-10 property on its western side. Johnson began to consider the possibility of liquidating Van. Shortly thereafter, Johnson and Maloney discussed the possibility of liquidating Van. Maloney reacted favorably. Johnson recommended that Maloney take certain steps before liquidating Van. Firstly, Johnson recommended that Maloney acquire Olga's Van stock. Maloney bought Olga's Van stock on December 12, 1978, as discussed supra. Secondly, Johnson recommended that Maloney contribute additional capital to Van. On December 28, 1978, Maloney borrowed $400,000 and contributed it to Van. The cash so contributed was used in part to provide the $374,112 that Van was to pay to Goldsmith and Hernandez on the exchange.

Maloney made his decision to liquidate Van in mid-December of 1978, within a few days of his discussions with Johnson.

---

17. [3] The Exchange Agreement provided for rezoning of the I-10 property. About 2 months later, the Exchange Agreement was amended to replace that requirement with a requirement for rezoning of certain property immediately to the east of the I-10 property.

On December 28, 1978, the following also occurred: (1) Hibernia transferred Elysian Fields to Coffin; (2) Coffin transferred Elysian Fields to Goldsmith and Hernandez; and (3) Goldsmith and Hernandez transferred Elysian Fields to Van, and in return Van transferred the I-10 property plus $374,112 in cash to Goldsmith and Hernandez.

Van realized gain on the exchange in the amount of $371,144.57.[18]

Soon after Van acquired Elysian Fields, a local funeral home sought to buy Elysian Fields from Van, but Van would not sell the property.

On January 2, 1979, Van's directors (i.e., petitioners and Olga) adopted a plan to liquidate Van under §333, and on January 3, 1979, Van's shareholders (i.e., petitioners) approved that plan. As of January 26, 1979, Van was completely liquidated in full compliance with the requirements of §333, and on that date, all of Van's assets were distributed to petitioners. The fair market values of the assets transferred from Van to petitioners on Van's liquidation were as shown in Table 1.

Table 1

Asset	Amount
Land-Elysian Fields	$900,000.00
Land-Metairie	200,084.00
Building-Metairie	137,416.00
Accounts receivable	91.90
Cash	2,219.97
Total	1,239,811.87

The aggregate value of these assets exceeded Van's income tax liability as determined in the notices of transferee liability issued to petitioners.

On Van's liquidation, petitioners assumed Van's liabilities in the amount of $228,347.15. Petitioners' basis in their Van stock as of the time of Van's liquidation was $529,000.

As previously stated, Van realized gain on the exchange in the amount of $371,144.57. Petitioners realized gain on the liquidation in the amount of $482,464.72, computed as follows:

Property received	$1,239,811.87
Less: liabilities assumed	-228,347.15
Balance	1,011,464.72
Less: basis in stock	-529,000.00
Realized gain	482,464.72

18. [4] The notices of transferee liability show the gain as $371,144.07. The notice of deficiency shows the gain as $371,144. Our finding is in accordance with the parties' stipulation.

After petitioners acquired Elysian Fields, they leased it to Gallagher Transfer and Storage for a term of about 25 or 30 years. Gallagher Transfer and Storage constructed a building on Elysian Fields and uses about 60 percent of the land for its own purposes and subleases about 40 percent to others for parking of cars and trucks. At the end of the lease term, the building constructed by Gallagher Transfer and Storage is to revert to petitioners.

When Van received Elysian Fields in exchange for the I-10 property and cash, it was intended that Van liquidate and distribute Elysian Fields to petitioners and that Elysian Fields be held for investment. It was not intended that Elysian Fields be sold, or used for personal purposes, or transferred by way of gift.

ANALYSIS

Respondent contends that the exchange of the I-10 property for Elysian Fields does not qualify for nonrecognition under § 1031(a) because Van did not hold Elysian Fields for productive use in trade or business or for investment; rather, Van intended to distribute Elysian Fields to its shareholders (petitioners) under § 333.[19] Respondent concedes that, if Van had not been liquidated but everything else (including the later use of Elysian Fields) had taken place as it did, then the exchange would have resulted in nonrecognition of gain under § 1031(a).

Petitioners maintain that an intent to liquidate under § 333 does not necessarily cause a transaction to fail the "holding" requirement of § 1031. They contend that they did not intend to cash out their investment in the property received, and that they therefore qualify for nonrecognition under § 1031.

We agree with petitioners that the exchange qualifies under § 1031.

If (a) Elysian Fields and the I-10 property are of like kind, (b) before the exchange Van held the I-10 property for investment, and (c) after the exchange Van held Elysian

---

19. [5] The parties agree that if we decide that the exchange did not qualify under § 1031, then: (1) Van has additional income for 1978 in the amount of $371,144.57 (see n.4, supra and accompanying text), and a deficiency in Federal corporate income tax in the amount of $115,418.03; (2) petitioners, as transferees of Van's assets (within the meaning of § 6901(a)(1)(A)) are liable for Van's entire deficiency as determined in the notices of transferee liability; (3) Van has additional earnings and profits as of January 26, 1979, in the amount of $371,144.57; and (4) under § 333(e), petitioners' recognized gain on Van's liquidation is increased by the amount of $371,144.57. paraN13665 In order for property to qualify for like-kind exchange treatment, the property must be held either for productive use in trade or business or for investment. However, business property may be exchanged for investment property and vice versa. Sec. 1031(a), § 1.1031(a)-1(a), Income Tax Regs. Accordingly, the distinction between "trade or business" and "investment" is immaterial for our purposes; for convenience, we will use the term "held for investment."

Fields for investment, then under § 1031(a)[20] Van does not recognize any gain on its exchange of the I-10 property for Elysian Fields.[21]

The purpose of § 1031 (and its predecessors) is to defer recognition of gain or loss on transactions in which, although in theory the taxpayer may have realized a gain or loss, the taxpayer's economic situation is in substance the same after, as it was before, the transaction. Stated otherwise, if the taxpayer's money continues to be invested in the same kind of property, gain or loss should not be recognized. H. Rept. 73-704 (to accompany H.R. 7835 the Revenue Act of 1934) p. 13 (1934), 1939-1 C.B. (Part 2) 554, 564. *Biggs v. Comm'r*, 69 T.C. 905, 913 (1978), *affd*. 632 F.2d 1171 (5th Cir. 1980).

Section 333[22] recognizes a taxpayer's continuing investment in the property received (here, real estate), without the interposition of a corporate form. *Bolker v. Comm'r*,

---

20. [6] SEC. 1031. EXCHANGE OF PROPERTY HELD FOR PRODUCTIVE USE OR INVESTMENT.

(a) Nonrecognition of Gain or Loss From Exchanges Solely in Kind. — No gain or loss shall be recognized if property held for productive use in trade or business or for investment (not including stock in trade or other property held primarily for sale, nor stocks, bonds, notes, chooses in action, certificates of trust or beneficial interest, or other securities or evidences of indebtedness or interest) is exchanged solely for property of a like kind to be held either for productive use in trade or business or for investment. [The subsequent amendments of this provision by sec. 77 of the Deficit Reduction Act of 1984 (Pub. L. 98-369, 98 Stat. 494, 595) and by § 1805(d) of the Tax Reform Act of 1986 (Pub. L. 99-514, 100 Stat. 2085, 2810) do not apply to the instant cases. The provision now appears as paragraphs (1) and (2) of § 1031(a).]

21. [7] If cash or other property which does not qualify as like-kind property is included in the exchange, then gain is recognized to the extent of the cash or other property received. Sec. 1031(b); Wagensen v. Commissioner, 74 T.C. 653, 657 (1980). In the instant cases, Van paid cash but did not receive cash, and the parties agree that Elysian Fields and the I-10 property are of like kind.

22. [8] Sec. 333 provides, in pertinent part, as follows:

SEC. 333. ELECTION AS TO RECOGNITION OF GAIN IN CERTAIN LIQUIDATIONS.

(a) General Rule. — In the case of property distributed in complete liquidation of a domestic corporation..., if—

(1) the liquidation is made in pursuance of a plan of liquidation adopted, and

(2) the distribution is in complete cancellation or redemption of all the stock, and the transfer of all the property under the liquidation occurs within some one calendar month, then in the case of each qualified electing shareholder (as define d in subsection (c)) gain on the shares owned by him at the time of the adoption of the plan of liquidation shall be recognized only to the extent provided in subsections (e) and (f)....

(e) Noncorporate Shareholders. — In the case of a qualified electing shareholder other than a corporation—

(1) there shall be recognized, and treated as a dividend, so much of the gain as is not in excess of his ratable share of the earnings and profits of the corporation accumulated after February 28, 1913, such earnings and profits to be determined as of the close of the month in which the transfer in liquidation occurred under subsection (a)(2), but without diminution by reason of distributions made during such month; but by including in the computation thereof all amounts accrued up to the date on which the transfer of all the property under the liquidation is completed; ...

[The subsequent repeal of § 333 by § 631(e)(3) of the Tax Reform Act of 1986, Pub. L. 99-514, 100 Stat. 2085, 2273, does not affect the instant cases.]

81 T.C. 782, 805 (1983), *affd.* 760 F.2d 1039 (9th Cir. 1985). The taxpayer's basis in the property received in a section 333 liquidation is equal to the basis in the stock surrendered, and the gain is not recognized, but is deferred until the investment is cashed out. At that point, the gain is taxed. Id.

In *Magneson v. Comm'r*, 81 T.C. 767 (1983), *affd.* 753 F.2d 1490 (9th Cir. 1985), the taxpayers exchanged property A for like-kind property B, after which the taxpayers contributed property B to a limited partnership. The contribution of property B was nontaxable under section 721. We held that the contribution of property B to the partnership was not a liquidation of the taxpayers' investment, but rather was a continuation of the old investment unliquidated in a modified form. 81 T.C. at 771.

In passing, we note that the term "liquidation" is often used in this context as equivalent to a disposition that "cashes out" the investment. This is the sense that is described as follows in H. Rept. 73-704 (to accompany H.R. 7835, the Revenue Act of 1934) p. 13 (1934), 1939-1 C.B. (Part 2) 554, 564:

> The calculation of the profit or loss is deferred until it is realized in cash, marketable securities, or other property not of the same kind [as the property disposed of] having a fair market value.

This is different from "liquidation" under § 333, where the corporation's shareholders are to receive the exchanged-for property, and not cash. Thus, in *Regals Realty Co. v. Comm'r*, 43 B.T.A. 194 (1940), *affd.* 127 F.2d 931 (2d Cir. 1942), discussed infra, the first holding that section 1031 did not apply was based on the taxpayer's intent to liquidate, in the sense of selling the property for cash, and not based on their intent to liquidate the corporation. In *Bolker v. Comm'r*, 81 T.C. 782 (1983), *affd.* 760 F.2d 1039 (9th Cir. 1985), the corporation was liquidated, but the property was received in kind by the taxpayer; there we held that section 1031 granted nonrecognition.

In *Bolker v. Comm'r, supra*, we dealt with the interplay of §§ 1031 and 333. There, the taxpayer caused his corporation to liquidate under § 333; he then transferred to an unrelated person the property he received in the liquidation, in exchange for property of like kind, and claimed that the exchange was tax-free under § 1031. We concluded, in effect, that the taxpayer is treated as having had the same purpose for holding the property as the taxpayer's corporation had before the § 333 liquidation, as follows (81 T.C. at 805-806):

We believe Magneson entitles petitioner to relief herein. In both Magneson and the instant case, property A was exchanged for property B in a like-kind exchange, both properties being held for business or investment as opposed to personal purposes. In Magneson, the exchange of A for B was immediately followed by a tax-free § 721 transfer; in the instant case, the exchange of A for B was immediately preceded by a tax-free acquisition under § 333. That the tax-free transaction preceded rather than followed the exchange is insufficient to produce opposite results. For, as noted, § 1031's holding for business or investment requirement is reciprocal, equally applicable to properties at both ends of an exchange. Nothing in the policy underlying § 1031 suggests that this minor variation in sequence warrants treating taxpayers dramatically different.

Even aside from Magneson, we believe petitioner is correct. A trade of property A for property B, both of like kind, may be preceded by a tax-free acquisition of property A at the front end, or succeeded by a tax-free transfer of property B at the back end. Considering first the tax-free acquisition of property A through a § 333 liquidation at the front end, it is appropriate to ask why gain is deferred on a liquidation. In short, where a taxpayer surrenders stock in his corporation for real estate owned by the corporation, he continues to have an economic interest in essentially the same investment, although there has been a change in the form of ownership. His basis in the real estate acquired on liquidation is equal to his basis in the stock surrendered, and the gain realized is not recognized but deferred until gain on the continuing investment is realized through a liquidating distribution. At that point, proceeds of the sale are taxed to the extent of the gain.

Section 333 recognizes the taxpayer's continuing investment in the real estate without the interposition of a corporate form. If property A is traded for like-kind property B for business or investment purposes, the taxpayer has not cashed out his venture, and gain or loss should not be recognized. Section 1031 is designed to apply to these circumstances and to defer recognition of gain or loss where the "taxpayer has not really 'cashed in' on the theoretical gain, or closed out a losing venture." *Jordan Marsh Co. v. Comm'r*, 269 F.2d 453, 456 (2d Cir. 1959), *revg. a Memorandum Opinion of this Court*, quoting *Portland Oil Co. v. Comm'r*, 109 F.2d 479, 488 (1st Cir. 1940). Accordingly, we hold that the exchange of the Montebello property qualifies for nonrecognition treatment under § 1031.

The instant cases may be viewed as a variant of Magneson (exchange of like-kind properties followed by a tax-free change in form of ownership) or as a variant of Bolker (interplay of §§ 333 and 1031). In either view, petitioners have satisfied the requirements of § 1031.

Van's purpose was the purpose of petitioners, Van's owners. The acquired property, Elysian Fields, was not liquidated in the sense of being cashed out (as in *Regals Realty Co. v. Comm'r*, 43 B.T.A. 194 (1940), *affd.* 127 F.2d 931 (2d Cir. 1942)); it was not transferred as a gift (as were the residences in *Click v. Comm'r*, 78 T.C. 225 (1982)). Rather, Elysian Fields continued to be held for investment by Van's owners.

The exchange before us reflects both continuity of ownership and of investment intent. Before the exchange, Van owned the I-10 property. After the exchange, Van owned Elysian Fields. Both before and after the exchange, petitioners owned all of Van's stock. After the section 333 liquidation, petitioners owned Elysian Fields directly, without the interposition of the corporate form. Petitioners continued to have an economic interest in essentially the same investment, although there was a change in the form of ownership. *Bolker v. Comm'r*, 81 T.C. at 805. Petitioners at all relevant times intended to continue to use Elysian Fields for investment. Petitioners had Van enter into the exchange because petitioners intended to operate some of their other businesses on Elysian Fields.

If Van had not been liquidated and had used Elysian Fields precisely as its share-holders did, then clearly the exchange would have been nontaxable under § 1031; so respondent concedes. As we understand Magneson and Bolker, the mere addition of another nontaxable transaction (at least, a transaction exempted by § 721 or 333) does not automatically destroy the nontaxable status of the transaction under § 1031.

On the authority of Magneson and Bolker, we conclude that Van's exchange of the I-10 property plus cash, in return for Elysian Fields, is tax-free as to Van under § 1031.

On brief, respondent states that "the evidence in [the instant cases] establishes that Van, an inactive corporation, did not initiate any attempts to acquire the Elysian Fields property, and was not going to use the Elysian Fields property in a trade or business." If we were to accept this view of the situation, and if Van had liquidated before the exchange, then the instant cases would be on all fours with Bolker. It seems, given respondent's view of the facts, that respondent's basic quarrel with what was done in the instant cases is solely as to the order in which the exchange and the liq-uidation took place. We have already stated plainly our position on that point in *Bolker v. Comm'r*, 81 T.C. at 805, set forth supra. Thus, respondent's analysis merely strengthens petitioners' position in the instant cases.

Respondent states as his view that "the intent to liquidate and to distribute property to shareholders is akin to an intent to sell the property or to gift it." We disagree. This has already been decided adversely to respondent. Bolker v. Commissioner, supra.

On brief, respondent directs our attention to the Court of Appeals' opinion in Bolker v. Commissioner, 760 F.2d at 1045, in which that court states that "a taxpayer may satisfy ... the 'for productive use in trade or business or for investment' require-ment by lack of intent either to liquidate the investment or to use it for personal pur-suits." Respondent then states as follows:

> At the time of the exchange, Van intended to liquidate and upon liquidation to distribute all of its property, including the property received in the exchange to its shareholders. Van would then cease to exist. It is incomprehensible that such an intent could be viewed as not being an intent to liquidate its invest-ment. Liquidating its investment is in fact clearly what Van intended to do, and did do.

Respondent appears to have confused two senses of "liquidate." Van did not intend to liquidate Elysian Fields in the sense of receiving for it "cash, marketable securities, or other property not of the same kind having a fair market value." *See* discussion of this point, *supra; see also Zuanich v. Comm'r*, 77 T.C. 428, 443 n.26 (1981), regarding "utraquistic subterfuge." The section 333 liquidation was held not to be a cashing out liquidation in Bolker, and we conclude that it is not a cashing out liquidation in the instant cases.

Respondent cites *Regals Realty Co. v. Comm'r*, 43 B.T.A. at 211, as support for his contention that section 1031 does not allow the property received to be liquidated to the recipient-corporation's shareholder.

In Regals Realty, shortly after the exchange there in issue, the taxpayer decided "to liquidate ... promptly, and in connection therewith TO SELL THE REAL ESTATE WHICH HAD JUST BEEN RECEIVED AND TO DISTRIBUTE THE PROCEEDS OF THAT SALE to complete the liquidation." 43 B.T.A. at 209, emphasis supplied. For one or more reasons, the property was not sold for cash. Instead, in the next year, the property was contributed to a newly-formed corporation in exchange for the newly-formed corporation's stock, and that stock was distributed to the taxpayer's shareholders in the taxpayer's liquidation 43 B.T.A. 204–205. We held that, at the time of the exchange, the taxpayer intended to sell the received property for cash and not to hold the property "for productive use in trade or business or for investment," as the statute requires. Accordingly, we held that the exchange was not tax-free and the taxpayer would have to recognize its gain. 43 B.T.A. at 209–210. *See also Regals Realty Co. v. Comm'r,* 127 F.2d at 933–934.

After so holding, the Board added the following (43 B.T.A. at 210-211):

> Petitioner contends further that the intention should be gauged by what was actually done rather than by the expression of that intent. We are not persuaded that this is correct. But, assuming we were to do so, the result would be the same. For the action actually taken was to dispose of the property to another corporation controlled by the same interests. It may be true that this transaction was in the nature of a tax-free reorganization. Nevertheless it was a transfer from this petitioner and made it impossible for it to "hold" the property as an investment. We think the provisions of 112(b)(1) [the predecessor of sec. 1031] were intended to apply only to the same taxpayer. We are not required to disregard the separate corporate entities of petitioner and its successor at the behest of their creators. *Higgins v. Smith,* 308 U.S. 473 [1940].

This alternative holding was relied on in *Vim Securities Corp. v. Comm'r,* 43 B.T.A. 759, 769 (1941), *affd.* 130 F.2d 106 (2d Cir. 1942), which involved nonrecognition under § 112(f) of the Revenue Act of 1936 (the predecessor of § 1033), and which accordingly is not dispositive of the instant cases. This point is explained in *Magneson v. Comm'r,* 81 T.C. at 772. The alternative holding of Regals Realty was distinguished in *U.S. v. Brager Building & Land Corp.,* 124 F.2d 349, 351 (4th Cir. 1941). The Circuit Court of Appeals for the Second Circuit affirmed the Board in Regals Realty without mention of this alternative holding. Although we have relied on the basic holding of Regals Realty in a number of cases, *e.g., Bolker v. Comm'r,* 81 T.C. at 805; *Magneson v. Comm'r,* 81 T.C. at 781 (1983); *Click v. Comm'r,* 78 T.C. at 231; *Wagensen v. Comm'r,* 74 T.C. at 659, we have not found any case involving §§ 333 and 1031 which has relied on, or even mentioned the alternative holding of Regals Realty.

We need not decide in the instant cases whether we agree with the Regals Realty alternative holding that a section 351 transaction would be incompatible with a section 1031 tax-free exchange. *Compare Magneson v. Comm'r,* 81 T.C. at 773 n.5, with *Magneson v. Comm'r,* 753 F.2d at 1493. We have already held that § 721 and § 333 transactions are not incompatible with § 1031 tax-free exchanges.

OPINION

We conclude that (1) Regals Realty's basic holding is consistent with our holding in the instant cases, and (2) Regals Realty's alternative holding is distinguishable.

Respondent also contends that, from petitioners' perspective, the exchange, in substance, constitutes an exchange of stock for property, which is expressly excluded from the nonrecognition provisions of § 1031(a). The exchange in issue was between Van, on the one hand, and Goldsmith and Hernandez, on the other. Van received only real estate in the exchange. (Van paid $374,112 to Goldsmith and Hernandez, which is boot, and presumably taxable to Goldsmith and Hernandez under § 1031(b); however, Goldsmith and Hernandez are not before us.) Even if petitioners transferred stock to Van in the course of the § 333 liquidation, the like-kind exchange was, from Van's (as well as from petitioners') viewpoint, both in form and in substance, an exchange of real estate.

We hold for petitioners. As a result, (1) Van does not have an income tax deficiency and so petitioners do not have a transferee liability, and (2) Van does not have increased earnings and profits and so petitioners do not have to recognize increased gain on Van's liquidation.

Chase v. Commissioner

United States Tax Court

92 T.C. 874 (1989)

FACTS

Petitioners Delwin G. Chase ("Mr. Chase") and Gail J. Chase ("Mrs. Chase"), resided in Alamo, California, at the time their petition herein was filed. Petitioners filed a joint Federal income tax return for the year at issue.

DISPOSITION OF THE JOHN MUIR APARTMENTS

On January 26, 1978, Mr. Chase formed John Muir Investors ("JMI"), a California limited partnership. JMI was formed for the purpose of purchasing, operating and holding the John Muir Apartments, an apartment building located in San Francisco, California (hereinafter referred to as the Apartments), which were purchased by JMI on March 31, 1978, for $19,041,024. Subsequently, Triton Financial Corporation ("Triton") was added as a general partner of JMI. Triton was a corporation in which petitioner held a substantial interest. Mr. Chase and Triton were general partners who had the exclusive right to manage JMI.

Pursuant to JMI's limited partnership agreement, once limited partners made contributions to JMI, they were prohibited from receiving distributions of property, other than cash, in liquidation of their capital contributions to JMI. A section of the JMI limited partnership agreement entitled 'status of limited partners' provided as follows:

> No limited partner shall have the right to withdraw or reduce his invested capital except as a result of the termination of the partnership or as otherwise provided by law. No limited partner shall have the right to bring an action

for partition against the partnership. No limited partner shall have the right to demand or receive property other than cash in return for his contribution, and no limited partner shall have priority over any other limited partner either as to the return of his invested capital or as to profit, losses or distribution.

After JMI held the Apartments for approximately one year, there developed a high level of speculative interest in San Francisco in purchasing apartment buildings for conversion to condominium units for sale to individuals. This speculative interest caused the value of real estate capable of being converted to condominium units, such as the Apartments, to appreciate. By mid 1979, JMI was attempting to find a buyer for the Apartments.

On January 20, 1980, JMI accepted an offer ("first offer") to purchase the Apartments from an unrelated individual for $28,421,000. Subsequent to JMI's acceptance of the first offer, but prior to the scheduled closing date, petitioners attempted to structure the sale of the Apartments in such a way that they would not have to recognize any taxable gain. To accomplish this, Mr. Chase caused JMI to distribute to himself and his wife a deed to an undivided 46.3527 percent interest in the Apartments in liquidation of petitioners' 46.3527 percent limited partnership interest in JMI. Petitioners attempted to structure the subsequent disposition of the Apartments pursuant to the first offer so that, as to them, such disposition would be treated for Federal tax purposes as a nontaxable nonsimultaneous exchange of real property for other real property.

On February 5, 1980, the first offer expired due to the failure of the buyer to deposit funds into escrow by such date as required by the escrow agreement. However, there was a second offer for the purchase of the Apartments on March 21, 1980, at which time an agent of RWT Enterprises, Inc. ("RWT"), wrote a letter of intent to Triton, one of JMI's two managing general partners, to purchase the Apartments for $26,500,000 ("second offer"). This letter further stated that any broker's commissions would be paid by Triton. This letter did not indicate that RWT believed, or had been informed, that petitioners, individually, had any ownership interest in the Apartments.

In connection with the second offer, on March 26, 1980, an officer of Triton wrote a letter on behalf of JMI, in Triton's role as a managing general partner of JMI, to a brokerage company. This letter stated that JMI agreed to pay a real estate brokerage commission of $250,000 as a result of the sale to RWT and that this commission was the total commission due. Triton did not mention petitioners' undivided ownership interest in the Apartments, or of any duty by petitioners to pay a pro rata portion of such commission.

In preparing to close the sale, an escrow agreement was executed. Under the heading "seller," the escrow agreement was signed, on behalf of JMI, by Mr. Chase. The escrow agreement was not signed by petitioners on behalf of themselves as individual owners of the Apartments.

On June 12, 1980, when Mr. Chase was certain that the sale to RWT was going to close, he recorded the deed from JMI, executed in January 1980, for petitioners' undivided interest in the Apartments.

Petitioners, as with the first offer, attempted to structure the Apartments' disposition so that it would not be taxable to them. To this end, on June 13, 1980, petitioners entered into a Real Property Exchange Trust Agreement ("Exchange Agreement") with RWT and Dudley Ellis ("Mr. Ellis"). Mr. Ellis was a former employee of Mr. Chase who agreed to serve as trustee of a trust (the 'Ellis Trust'), created under the Exchange Agreement. The Exchange Agreement was executed in anticipation of the sale of the Apartments to RWT, and provided that RWT, as purchaser of the Apartments, would transfer to the Ellis Trust petitioners' share of the proceeds. Pursuant to the Exchange Agreement, Mr. Ellis, in his capacity as trustee of the Ellis Trust, agreed to transfer to petitioners "like-kind real property" which Mr. Ellis was to purchase with such proceeds. Specifically, the Exchange Agreement provided that petitioners would locate and negotiate the terms for the purchase of properties to be "exchanged." Petitioners then instructed Marilyn Lamonte, the escrow officer handling the sale, to pay 46.3527 percent of the "net proceeds" from the sale to Mr. Ellis as trustee under the Exchange Agreement.

On July 7, 1980, the John Muir Apartments were sold to Traweek Investment Fund No. 10, Ltd. ("Traweek"), an entity related to, and substituted as buyer by, RWT. The net proceeds of $9,210,876 received from the sale to Traweek were allocated by Lamonte between the Ellis Trust and JMI. The actual payments out of escrow were a check for $3,799,653 to Ellis in his capacity as trustee under the Ellis Trust, and a check for $4,811,223 paid directly to JMI.

Petitioners' instructions to Lamonte, to the effect that Ellis, as trustee, was to be the recipient of 46.3527 percent of "net proceeds" from the sale, were not followed. Rather, the portion of the proceeds distribute to Ellis in trust for petitioners represented an allocation of a distributive share of total net proceeds to petitioners in their capacity as limited partners of JMI in accordance with the terms of the JMI limited partnership agreement and not as a straight allocation of 46.3527 percent of "net proceeds."

From January 1980, until the date of the sale was closed, the expenses of operating the Apartments were paid with funds that were in JMI's operating bank account. Petitioners did not pay, with their own money, any of the expenses from January 1980, when they received a deed to the Apartments through July 7, 1980, the date of sale. Petitioners also did not receive any of the rental income earned during this period, such rent continued to be paid to JMI. Petitioners' relationship with respect to the Apartments, after they were deeded an undivided interest in such, was in all respects unchanged in relation to their relationship to the Apartments as limited partners of JMI.

On June 30, 1981, Ellis, as trustee of the Ellis Trust, assigned to Creston Corporation ("Creston"), as successor trustee of the Ellis Trust, petitioners' share of the proceeds from the sale. Creston was, at the time of such assignment, a corporation wholly owned by Ellis.

By July 23, 1982, Triton, as general partner of entities controlled by petitioner, completed the acquisition of the following three properties which were later acquired from Creston by petitioners: (1) the Snug Harbor Apartments in Dallas, Texas (the

"Snug Harbor property"); (2) a ground lease to commercial real property in Orange County, California (the "Irvine property"); and, (3) certain commercial real estate in Santa Ana, California (the "Woodbridge property").

Creston, as trustee under the Ellis Trust, acquired, and immediately transferred to petitioners, the Snug Harbor property on or about October 27, 1982. Petitioners held the Snug Harbor property for seven months. Creston acquired and then transferred to petitioners, the Irvine property on October 29, 1982. Petitioners, in turn, disposed of the Irvine property on the same date. On October 29, 1982, Creston acquired, and then transferred the Woodbridge property to petitioners, who disposed of the property on the same date. In addition to the above properties, Creston, as trustee under the Ellis Trust, also purchased for petitioners three other properties located in the state of Kentucky.

LIQUIDATION OF THE LOCKWOOD INTEREST

On March 5, 1980, petitioners purchased a 2.92 percent limited partnership interest in JMI from Albert and Hazel Lockwood for $230,000 and a 8.78 percent limited partnership interest from Todd and Karen Sue Lockwood for $690,000 (hereinafter referred to collectively as the "Lockwood interest"). The Lockwood interest was a limited partnership interest in addition to the 46.3527 percent interest previously acquired.

On July 9, 1980, two days after the disposition of the Apartments, petitioners received $929,582 in complete liquidation of their 11.72 percent Lockwood interest. Petitioners reported a short-term capital loss of $783,762 on their 1980 Federal income tax return as a result of this distribution. Petitioners computed their adjusted basis and loss as follows:

Cost of Lockwood interest	$920,000
Distributive share of long-term capital gain reported from the sale of the John Muir Apartments	$850,189
Distributive share of operating loss reported	$(59,845)
Adjusted basis	$1,710,344
Amount realized	$926,582
Less adjusted basis	$1,710,344
Claimed loss	$(783,762)

The $929,582 cash distribution from the liquidation of this 11.72 percent interest liquidated petitioners' entire LIMITED partnership interest in JMI held as of this date. Petitioner, however, continued thereafter to hold an interest in JMI as a GENERAL partner. After this liquidation of the 11.72 percent interest, JMI continued operating as a partnership for the purpose of investing in other real property.

On December 31, 1980, petitioners acquired a 1.31 percent limited partnership interest in JMI from Anthony and Carole Cline.

ANALYSIS

The first issue is whether petitioners met the requirements of § 1031. Section 1031(a) provides that no gain or loss is recognized if property held for productive use in a trade or business or for investment (excluding certain types of property not involved herein) is exchanged solely for property of like-kind. Since the distinction between "trade or business" and "investment" in § 1031(a) is immaterial for our purposes, for convenience, we will use the term "held for investment." Based on a number of theories, respondent contends that petitioners are not entitled to nonrecognition under § 1031(a) or, in the alternative, that petitioners must recognize gain under § 1031(b) to the extent that certain of the property ultimately received by petitioners was not held for investment.

Respondent contends that § 1031(a) is inapplicable because the disposition of the Apartments was, in substance, a sale by JMI, and not an exchange by petitioners of like-kind property. Petitioners contend that we must respect the form in which they structured the disposition of the Apartments, and that such form satisfied the requirements of § 1031(a).

To qualify for nonrecognition, a taxpayer must satisfy each of the specific requirements as well as the underlying purpose of § 1031(a). *Bolker v. Comm'r*, 760 F.2d 1039, 1044 (9th Cir. 1985), *affg.* 81 T.C. 782 (1983). We must determine whether the "exchange" requirement of that section was satisfied. Respondent argues that the substance over form doctrine is applicable to impute the disposition of the Apartments entirely to JMI and concludes that, in substance, petitioners did not "exchange" any part of the Apartments.

The substance over form doctrine applies where the form chosen by the parties is a fiction that fails to reflect the economic realities of the transaction. *Comm'r v. Court Holding Co.*, 324 U.S. 331 (1945); *U.S. v. Cumberland Public Service Co.*, 338 U.S. 451 (1950). In determining substance, we must look beyond the "superficial formalities of a transaction to determine the proper tax treatment." *Blueberry Land Co. v. Comm'r*, 361 F.2d 93, 101 (5th Cir. 1966), *affg.* 42 T.C. 1137 (1964). "Transactions, which did not vary, control, or change the flow of economic benefits, are dismissed from consideration." *Higgins v. Smith*, 308 U.S. 473, 476 (1940). We hold that the substance over form doctrine applies and that, in substance, JMI disposed of the Apartments.

Although the general partners of JMI caused JMI to prepare a deed conveying an undivided 46.3527 percent interest in the Apartments to petitioners, at no time did petitioners act as owners except in their roles as partners of JMI. Petitioners were deeded an undivided interest at the time of the first offer because it appeared that a sale was imminent. When this sale failed to close, however, petitioners' deed remained unrecorded until shortly before the disposition in question. There is no indication that any party to the sale believed that anyone other than JMI held title at the time of RWT's offer to purchase. Further, there is no evidence of negotiations by petitioners on behalf of themselves concerning the terms for the disposition of the Apartments. Also, petitioners never paid any of the operating costs of the Apartments or their share of the brokerage commission. Further, petitioners did not receive, or have credited to them, any of the Apartment's rental income.

Equally important, in apportioning the net sale proceeds, all parties ignored petitioners' purported interest as direct owners. Rather, petitioners received only their distributive share of JMI's net proceeds as limited partners. In addition, the JMI limited partnership agreement provided that no limited partner could demand and receive property other than cash from the partnership. Further, there is no evidence that petitioners were otherwise authorized by the other limited partners to receive a share of the Apartments as a partnership distribution or that the other limited partners were even aware that such a distribution had occurred. We can only conclude that petitioners' failure to respect the form in which they cast this transaction by failing to receive their share of proceeds as direct owners was caused by petitioners' realization that they were not direct owners and could not be so by virtue of the partnership agreement.

Petitioners final argument regarding the substance issue is that JMI's general partners acted as petitioners' agents in negotiating the disposition of the John Muir Apartments to Traweek. This, petitioners argue, explains why they did not appear, individually, as parties in most of the documents to this transaction. We find petitioners' argument, in this regard, both self-serving and unsupported by the record.

Having determined that, in substance, JMI disposed of the Apartments, we must determine whether petitioners are entitled to "exchange" treatment under § 1031(a), which treatment would flow through JMI to all partners in accordance with their distributive share of partnership gain. Sec. 702(a). Petitioners are entitled to nonrecognition of gain under § 1031(a), as a partner of JMI, if JMI has satisfied the requirements of § 1031(a) in disposing of the Apartments.

Section 1031(a) requires that like-kind property be both given up and received in the "exchange." Here, it is clear that JMI transferred investment property but did not receive like-kind property in "exchange." This is because JMI never held the properties that were ultimately received by petitioners as part of the purported "exchange." Accordingly, JMI never "exchanged" like-kind property.

Having concluded that JMI sold the entire interest in the Apartments, and that JMI did not act as petitioner's agent with respect to an undivided interest in such apartment, we hold that petitioners failed to "exchange" like-kind property within the meaning of § 1031(a). Accordingly, petitioners are not entitled to the benefits of that section.[23]

Petitioners argue, alternatively, for the first time on brief, that if § 1031(a) is inapplicable, they now be allowed to elect installment sale treatment under § 453. Petitioners cite *Bayley v. Comm'r*, 35 T.C. 288 (1960), wherein we permitted a taxpayer to elect, in an amended petition, the installment method under § 453, where the issue of nonrecognition under section 1034 was decided adversely to the taxpayer. Peti-

---

23. [2] We do not address respondent's alternative arguments, as those arguments are moot.

tioners' argument fails for two reasons. First, petitioners did not amend their pleadings or raise such issue at trial, but only raised such issue on brief. *See Seligman v. Comm'r*, 84 T.C. 191 (1985) *affd*. 796 F.2d 116 (5th Cir. 1986); *Markwardt v Comm'r* 64 T.C. 989 (1975). Second, since we find that JMI disposed of the Apartments, the election under section 453 can only be made by the partnership. See sec. 703(b); *Rothenberg v. Comm'r*, 48 T.C. 369 (1967). Accordingly, we hold petitioners are not entitled to elect installment sale treatment under section 453.

The final issue is whether petitioners are entitled to claim a short-term capital loss of $783,762 under §731(a)(2) in connection with their receipt of $929,582 in complete liquidation of their Lockwood limited partnership interest on July 9, 1980. This issue is raised because petitioner held a general partnership interest in JMI throughout 1980 and petitioners subsequently reacquired a limited partnership in JMI on December 31, 1980. The general rule contained in §731(a)(2) is that a partner may not recognize a loss from a partnership distribution. Section 731(a)(2) provides an exception to the general rule of nonrecognition, however, if certain requirements are met. First, the distribution must be "in liquidation of a partner's interest in a partnership." Second, no property other than money, unrealized receivables (as defined in §751(c)), or inventory (as defined in section 751(d)(2)) must be received in the liquidating distribution. Third, a loss must be realized. See §731(a)(2).

With respect to the first requirement, both parties refer to section 761(d). That section defines, for purposes of subchapter K, the term "liquidation of a partner's interest" as "the termination of a partner's ENTIRE interest in a partnership by means of a distribution, or a series of distributions, to the partner by the partnership." (Emphasis added.) Respondent argues that under §761(d), in order to terminate one's "entire interest" in a partnership, one must terminate both his general and limited partnership interests. Petitioners argue that §761(d) only requires the termination of either the entirety of one's limited partnership interest or one's general partnership interest. Petitioners further argue that the retention of one's general partnership interest does not prevent, under §731(a)(2), the recognition of a loss upon the termination of one's entire limited partnership interest.

We find, however, that petitioners' argument ignores the plain meaning of the statute which is unambiguous on its face. Section 761(d) provides that the term "liquidation of a partner's interest" means the termination of a partner's entire interest by means of a distribution, or a series of distributions, to the partner by the partnership. When petitioners liquidated their Lockwood interest, Mr. Chase still retained an interest in JMI as a general partner and, therefore, he did not liquidate his "entire interest" in JMI. As to Mrs. Chase, she no longer was a partner in JMI after the distribution in liquidation of the Lockwood interest. Although, as noted by respondent, she became a limited partner in JMI on December 31, 1980, she no longer had any interest in JMI, as of July 9, 1980.

Respondent argues that no loss can be realized because petitioners received non-qualifying property (46.3527 percent interest in the Apartments), as opposed to money, unrealized receivables, or inventory, as part of a series of liquidating distributions, and that petitioners are thus disqualified from realizing a loss. It is unnecessary to reach this argument since we previously held herein that the distribution to petitioners of an interest in the Apartment was, for Federal tax purposes, illusory. Accordingly, we hold that petitioner Gail Chase is entitled to a short term capital loss.

Click v. Commissioner
United States Tax Court
78 T.C. 225 (1982)

FACTS

Petitioner Dollie H. Click resided in Fairfax, Va., at the time of filing her petition herein. Using a single filing status, she filed a Federal income tax return, Form 1040, for the calendar year 1974 with the Internal Revenue Service Center at Memphis, Tenn.

On December 30, 1964, petitioner and her husband purchased approximately 161.250 acres of farmland (hereinafter the farm) in Prince William County, for $110,000. The property was to be held for investment purposes. On September 19, 1967, petitioner and her husband conveyed approximately 4.085 acres of the farm (hereinafter parcel B) to their daughter and son-in-law, Mary and Carlton Highsmith. On June 27, 1967, petitioner and her husband conveyed approximately 2.080 acres of the farm (hereinafter parcel C) to their son and daughter-in-law, John and Sharon Click. Petitioner's remaining parcel consisted of approximately 155.085 acres (hereinafter parcel A).

Petitioner's husband died on September 21, 1972. During the last months of 1972, petitioner received a number of offers to purchase the farm. All of these offers were made by Manassas Realty, on behalf of Williams Properties, Inc., and an undisclosed principal. The undisclosed principal was later identified as the Marriott Corp. (hereinafter Marriott).

On January 9, 1973, petitioner entered into an agreement of lease and purchase option with Williams Properties, Inc., on behalf of its still undisclosed principal, Marriott. Although the agreement provided for the purchase of the entire farm, petitioner's children and their spouses, who owned parcels B and C, neither executed the agreement nor were named as parties to it.

Marriott hoped to acquire the entire farm and certain land adjacent to the farm in order to build a 515-acre amusement park that would contain, inter alia, shops, theaters, and carnival rides. As of June 9, 1973, Marriott had obtained options to purchase an additional 353.46 acres of land surrounding the farm. The farm was the largest single component of the proposed park site, and Marriott considered its acquisition to be a critical and inseparable part of its plans.

In June 1973, Marriott indicated its desire to renegotiate the terms of its January 9, 1973, purchase option because it was not binding on petitioner's children, it contained no subordination provision to allow Marriott to finance improvements, it contained no prepayment provisions, and it was difficult to administer. On June 9, 1973, petitioner and Mr. and Mrs. Highsmith executed with Marriott a 1-year lease and a revised purchase option agreement for parcels A and B. The option agreement gave Marriott until June 9, 1974, to inform the petitioner and Mr. and Mrs. Highsmith of its intention to purchase the property, and until July 9, 1974, to reach settlement on the purchase. In addition, the agreement contained a provision that permitted the sellers, petitioner and her daughter and son-in-law, to opt for partial or full payment through the receipt of "exchange" or "swap" property or properties which the sellers would have the right to designate. Also on June 9, 1973, Mr. and Mrs. John Click entered into a separate agreement with Marriott for the sale of parcel C with settlement to take place on or before July 9, 1974.

During this time, Mr. and Mrs. Highsmith owned and resided in a house on North Ninth Street in Arlington, Va. However, they wanted to move to a new house and so advised petitioner. On petitioner's suggestion, they began looking for a new home to use as "swap" property. Their condition for such property was that it contain a house larger than their house on North Ninth Street. They selected a home, also in Arlington, Va., that was owned by William C. and Bernice Gierisch (hereinafter the Gierisches).

Mr. and Mrs. John Click owned and resided in a house in Fairfax, Va., but they were interested in obtaining a house and more acreage. At petitioner's suggestion, they also began looking for "swap" property. Their condition for such property was that it contain a three-bedroom house with acreage sufficient to maintain a horse. They selected residential property in Clifton, Va., owned by Oscar W. and Margaret Ann Tinney (hereinafter the Tinneys).

The Tinney residence had previously been listed for sale in 1973. Mrs. Sharon Click saw the Tinneys' "for sale" sign and inspected the house several times in 1973. She liked the Tinney residence and wanted to purchase it at that time. However, the Tinneys decided not to sell their house and consequently took it off the market. Subsequently, the Tinneys once again listed their house for sale. Mrs. Click again visited the Tinney residence on several occasions in 1974 prior to the time of Marriott's offer to purchase the house.

On February 22, 1974, Marriott and the Gierisches entered into a purchase agreement for the Gierisch residence. On April 18, 1974, Marriott and the Tinneys entered into a purchase agreement for the Tinney residence. On June 5, 1974, Marriott notified petitioner and Mr. and Mrs. Highsmith of its intent to purchase parcels A and B.

Petitioner did not inspect the Tinney residence until after Marriott had made its offer to purchase and after the house was taken off the market.

On July 9, 1974, the Gierisches and the Tinneys conveyed their houses to Marriott. On the same day, Marriott exercised its option to purchase parcels A and B. Accordingly, petitioner and Mr. and Mrs. Highsmith received from Marriott a promissory note in the amount of $630,925.53, the Gierisch residence valued at $96,152.20, and the Tinney residence valued at $135,816.96 in exchange for parcels A and B. At closing, the three also received the first installment on the promissory note in the amount of $23,647.

Petitioner held all equity rights in the two residences which were received by her in partial satisfaction of the amount due her from the sale of parcel A to Marriott. Petitioner and Mr. and Mrs. Highsmith did not intend that the Highsmiths' legal interests in either the Gierisch residence or the Tinney residence would be in full or partial satisfaction of their conveyance of parcel B to Marriott. Instead, petitioner and the Highsmiths intended that 2.56 percent of the cash paid at closing on July 9, 1974, and a similar percentage of the principal and interest due under the note, would be in satisfaction of their conveyance of parcel B to Marriott.

On July 9, 1974, Mr. and Mrs. Highsmith together received a total of $619 as their pro rata share of Marriott's initial payment ($23,647) on its purchase of parcels A and B.

On or about July 9, 1974, Mr. and Mrs. Highsmith moved into the Gierisch residence, and Mr. and Mrs. John Click moved into the Tinney residence. The Highsmiths sold their North Ninth Street, Arlington, Va., home on or about July 12, 1974. Sometime in August or September 1974, Mr. and Mrs. John Click secured a purchaser for their Fairfax, Va., home. The closing, however, did not occur until December 27, 1974.

During the period from July 9, 1974, through February 8, 1975, Mr. and Mrs. Highsmith took out property damage insurance and paid property taxes on the Gierisch residence. During the same period, Mr. and Mrs. John Click made substantial improvements to the Tinney residence totaling over $5,000. The improvements included a fence for $593.75 to keep their horse enclosed on the property, an automatic garage door opener for $283.36, a well pump and other expenses related to the well for $239.48, a light fixture for $49.69, wall-to-wall carpeting for $1,440, custom draperies for $1,368.02, and wrought iron railings to replace wooden rails for $392. They also paid $781 to prune a tree, $129.71 for gravel for the driveway, and $30 for repair of a canvas awning. Mr. and Mrs. John Click paid for these improvements themselves and did not ask for petitioner's prior approval. At no time did either couple pay rent to petitioner for the respective houses in which they lived.

During this period, petitioner had other investment properties. It was her practice, with the advice and assistance of her attorneys, to take care of arrangements, such as obtaining property insurance, with respect to these properties.

On February 8, 1975, petitioner executed a deed of gift for the Tinney residence to John Click and a deed of gift for the Gierisch residence to Mary Highsmith.

On her 1974 income tax return, petitioner reported that she "exchanged approximately 43 acres of real property acquired in 1961 [sic] and held for investment purposes with a value of $231,968 for two pieces of residential real estate to be held for similar purposes of $231,968.00." She elected to report the remainder of the amount received pursuant to §453.

In his statutory notice, respondent determined that petitioner's exchange of parcel A for the two residential properties and a note and cash does not qualify as a like-kind exchange under section 1031. In the alternative, respondent also determined that the sale and exchange constituted one transaction for purposes of §453.

ANALYSIS

We must determine whether petitioner's exchange of farmland for two residential properties, cash, and a note qualifies for nonrecognition treatment under § 1031. Section 1031(a) provides that no gain or loss shall be recognized if property held for productive use in a trade or business or for investment is exchanged solely for property of a like kind which is also "to be held either for productive use in a trade or business or for investment."[24]

To qualify for treatment under § 1031, three requirements must be satisfied: (1) The transaction must be an exchange; (2) the exchange must involve like-kind properties; and (3) both the properties transferred and the properties received must be held either for productive use in a trade or business or for investment. Sec. 1.1031(a)-1(a) and (c), Income Tax Regs. *Brauer v. Comm'r*, 74 T.C. 1134, 1139–1140 (1980). The parties do not question that the transaction at issue constitutes an exchange. Furthermore, they appear to agree that the farmland and the two residences are like-kind properties because the nature and character of the properties, as distinguished from their grade or quality, are substantially the same. *See generally* § 1.1031(a)-1(b), Income Tax Regs.; *Koch v. Comm'r*, 71 T.C. 54, 65 (1978). The controversy, therefore, centers on whether the two residences received by petitioner Dollie H. Click in the exchange were held for investment.

A taxpayer's intent to hold property for investment must be determined as of the time of the exchange.[25] We must examine the substance of the transaction, rather than the form in which it is cast, when analyzing a purported section 1031 exchange of property. *Wagensen v. Comm'r*, 74 T.C. 653, 660 (1980); *Biggs v. Comm'r*, 69 T.C. 905, 914 (1978). The petitioner bears the burden of proving that she had the requisite investment intent. *Regals Realty Co. v. Comm'r*, 43 B.T.A. 194, 208 (1940), *affd.* 127 F.2d 931 (2d Cir. 1942).

In the instant case, respondent proposes to disallow § 1031 nonrecognition treatment on the theory that petitioner's gifts of the residences were part of a prearranged plan. He alleges that petitioner's intent at the time of the exchange was not to hold the houses for investment, but eventually to gift them to her children. Petitioner counters with the assertion that she had no concrete plan to transfer the acquired property to her children at the time of the exchange. Rather, she stated that she took the property because she wanted "something that would grow in value." As such, she claims that she held the houses as an investment until 7 months after the exchange, at which time she decided to gift them to her children.

---

24. [1] If cash or other property that does not qualify as like-kind property is included in such an exchange, the recipient must recognize gain to the extent of the cash or fair market value of other property received. Sec. 1031(b).

25. [2] *See* Land Dynamics v. Comm'r, T.C. Memo. 1978-259 (holding of property for 22 months after exchange did not establish investment intent); Klarkowski v. Comm'r, T.C. Memo. 1965-328. *See generally* Streer, *Eligibility for Nontaxable Exchange Treatment May Depend on Intent in Holding Property*, 26 Taxation for Accountants 116 (1981).

In *Wagensen v. Comm'r, supra,* we considered a factual setting that appears, at first glance, to be analogous to the case at hand. The taxpayer therein exchanged his ranch for another ranch and cash. Nine months later, he made a gift of the new ranch and some cash to his son and daughter. We held that the taxpayer had no concrete plans at the time of the like-kind exchange to make the later gift. First, the facts showed that he did not initiate discussions with his accountants about a gift until after the exchange. Second, he used the acquired ranch in his ranching business during the period between the exchange and the gift. Accordingly, while we found that the general desire to make a gift prior to the time of the exchange is not inconsistent with an intent to hold the acquired ranch for productive use in business or for investment, we also found that, considering the facts presented, the gift was not part of the exchange transaction. 74 T.C. at 659.

Respondent argues that the *Wagensen* opinion does not control in the instant case because petitioner intended to gift the residences to her children at the time of the exchange, and petitioner never had the requisite investment intent. Furthermore, respondent says that the ranch property exchanged in *Wagensen* was inherently investment or business property, while the houses received herein were personal.[26] Respondent asserts that our holding in *Regals Realty Co. v. Comm'r, supra,* is apposite. In *Regals Realty*, the corporate taxpayer swapped real property used in its trade or business for like-kind real property. Approximately 2 weeks later, the corporation's board of directors decided to liquidate and sell the property. Although it was unsuccessful in finding a purchaser, the corporation eventually transferred property to a new corporation in exchange for the new corporation's stock, and such stock was distributed in liquidation to the taxpayer's shareholders. The Board of Tax Appeals there held that the transaction did not qualify for nonrecognition treatment under the predecessor to section 1031 because "It places an unbearable strain on the credulity to believe that under those circumstances the property acquired was 'to be held' for investment." 43 B.T.A. at 209.

In the instant case, the facts reveal that petitioner suggested to her son and daughter and their spouses as early as mid-1973 that they look for new homes to use as "swap" property. Mr. and Mrs. Highsmith located the Gierisch residence. Mr. and Mrs. John Click located the Tinney residence, which had been the focus of prior inquiry by Mrs. Click in 1973. Such homes suited the personal lifestyles of the two couples and satisfied their desires for larger homes and more land. Only after Marriott made its offer to purchase did petitioner visit the Tinney residence. We cannot believe that petitioner,

---

26. [3] Respondent further argues that the facts in the instant case would not qualify for sec. 1031 treatment based on the substance-over-form analysis put forth in *Wagensen v. Comm'r,* 74 T.C. 653, 660 (1980). There, the Court reasoned that if the form of the transaction had been altered so that the taxpayer gifted an interest in his ranch to his children prior to the exchange, the children's subsequent exchange of the ranch property would have qualified for nonrecognition treatment. Here, however, if petitioner Dollie Click had transferred a portion of her farm property to her children prior to the exchange, and they had exchanged investment farm property for personal residences (in which they planned to live immediately after the exchange), the children would not be entitled to sec. 1031 treatment.

who was an experienced investor, had an investment intent with respect to property that she did not personally select and had never seen prior to its selection.

Further, petitioner, now 72 years old, was working on an estate plan with her attorney in 1973 and 1974 at the same time that the idea for the exchange of properties developed and at the time of the transaction with Marriott. As a woman with a potentially substantial estate, petitioner had been advised with respect to estate and gift tax liabilities that might arise. Based on the evidence presented, we believe that petitioner's estate planning activities are highly indicative of an intent at the time of the exchange to gift the residences to her children.

Finally, petitioner's testimony indicates that she normally took care of her investments and obtained property insurance therefor. Here, the facts indicate that Mr. and Mrs. Highsmith took out property insurance and paid property taxes on the Gierisch residence for the period from July 9, 1974, through February 8, 1975. In addition, during the same period, Mr. and Mrs. John Click paid for a homeowner's insurance policy on the Tinney residence. They also made substantial expenditures for improvements on the Tinney residence. John Click testified that he treated the property as his own, although he knew he was not the owner. He lived in the house rent free during the 7-month period and spent money on the improvements purportedly to protect his mother's investment. A review of the expenditures indicates that many were for improvements that were more in the nature of personal custom features than for general maintenance. In addition, the fact that Mr. Click did not obtain his mother's approval before making the expenditures further belies petitioner's claim that her children lived in the houses as "caretakers" during the period between the exchange and the gift.

Accordingly, we cannot find that petitioner had an investment intent in accepting the homes as "swap" property. Rather, it appears that her primary purpose was to provide larger homes in which her children and grandchildren could reside. From all of the evidence, we believe that petitioner acquired the residences with the intent of making gifts of them to her children and not to hold as investments for eventual sale. While petitioner was certainly a generous and caring parent and grandparent, her concern for the welfare of her family does not qualify the exchange for nonrecognition treatment under § 1031.

Mason v. Commissioner

United States Tax Court

55 T.C.M. (CCH) 1134 (1988)

FACTS

This case was submitted fully stipulated pursuant to Rule 122, Tax Court Rules of Practice and Procedure. Petitioners, Miles H. and Elizabeth D. Mason, are husband and wife who resided at Duluth, Georgia when they filed their petition in this case.

Miles H. Mason ("petitioner") has been a practicing physician since 1948. Beginning in 1957, petitioner entered into numerous business ventures with Larry P. Mc-

Clure, Jr. Petitioner and McClure contributed approximately equal amounts of capital, and McClure managed their investments. Due to a business disagreement, petitioner and McClure entered into a Sales Contract and Agreement (the "Sales Contract") on April 14, 1981, pursuant to which they separated their business interests.

Petitioner and McClure were partners in two partnerships. The assets of one partnership (the "Sky Valley partnership") consisted of property acquired in the area of the Sky Valley resort complex. This partnership used the accrual method of accounting and filed partnership information tax returns for each of the years it was in the business of making investments. The assets of the other partnership consisted of joint venture assets acquired for investment purposes (the "Joint Venture Assets') consisting primarily of parcels of real estate. The parties have stipulated that the Joint Venture Assets were held by petitioner and McClure in a single partnership for Federal income tax purposes. The parties have treated the Joint Venture Assets and the Sky Valley partnership as two independent entities and have presented their arguments on that assumption. As a result, we also assume that the Joint Venture Assets and the Sky Valley partnership are two separate partnerships. As of 1981, petitioner and McClure also owned 100 percent of the stock of two corporations, Sky Valley, Inc. and Resort Campgrounds, Inc.

At the time they agreed to dissolve the partnerships, petitioner and McClure each owned a fifty percent interest in the following entities:

(1) Stock of Sky Valley, Inc.;

(2) Stock of Resort Campgrounds of America, Inc.;

(3) Assets of Sky Valley partnership;

(4) Assets of Joint Ventures.

Pursuant to the Sales Contract, petitioner transferred his stock in Sky Valley, Inc. to McClure in exchange for promissory notes. Petitioner also transferred his stock in Resort Campgrounds of America, Inc. to McClure. Nevertheless, only the treatment of the exchange of Sky Valley partnership assets and of the Joint Venture Assets is before the Court.

The Sales Contract provided for the transfer of the various Sky Valley partnership assets and liabilities and other Joint Venture assets and liabilities resulting in petitioner's and McClure's each receiving a 100 percent interest in a divisible portion of assets and liabilities. Petitioner agreed to convey to McClure "all of his personal and undivided interest in the jointly owned real property lying in the City of Sky Valley and in the immediate vicinity of Sky Valley Resort." McClure agreed immediately upon receipt of petitioners' interest to convey all of the Sky Valley properties to Sky Valley, Inc. Petitioner also transferred his interest in other miscellaneous partnership realty to McClure. McClure agreed to transfer to petitioner his undivided interest in three parcels of real property referred to as the "Bagley Property," the "Jones Property" and the "Jewell Property."[27] Each conveyance was made subject to any outstanding indebt-

---

27. [2] Either McClure or Sky Valley, Inc. also agreed to pay petitioner $50,000 cash. The preamble to the Sales Contract states that as partial consideration for his conveyances to McClure, petitioner

edness on the properties and each partner agreed to assume and pay such indebtedness and hold the other partner harmless from any claim thereunder. The consideration for the exchange of real properties was an exchange and division of jointly owned properties.

Respondent issued his notice of deficiency on May 4, 1987, and petitioners timely filed their petition on July 13, 1987.

ANALYSIS

Section 731(a)(1) provides that no gain will be recognized on a distribution by the partnership to a partner "except to the extent that any money distributed exceeds the adjusted basis of such partner's interest in the partnership immediately before the distribution." Any gain recognized pursuant to §731(a) is treated as a gain from a sale or exchange of the partnership interest by the distributee partner. Section 741 provides "In the case of a sale or exchange of an interest in a partnership, gain or loss shall be recognized to the transferor partner and ... shall be considered as gain or loss from the sale or exchange of a capital asset, except as otherwise provided in §751."

Petitioner argues that the dissolution of the partnerships was accomplished through distributions from the Sky Valley partnership and the Joint Venture Assets and thus falls within §731(a). Because the money that petitioner is deemed to have received pursuant to §752(b) did not exceed his adjusted basis in the partnerships, petitioner argues that no gain or loss should be recognized. Respondent argues that petitioner and McClure intended to exchange partnership interests and, consequently, that §741 governs the transaction.

At issue is whether petitioner and McClure exchanged property owned by them individually following liquidating distributions from the partnerships or exchanged partnership interests which resulted in the termination of the partnerships.

Respondent correctly points out that the regulations under §741 provide that that section may be applicable if one of two partners sells his interest to the other partner despite the partnership's termination pursuant to §708(b). Section 1.741-1(b), Income Tax Regs.;[28] *see Karan v. Comm'r*, 319 F.2d 303, 307 (7th Cir. 1963), *affg.* a Memo-

---

is to receive $50,000 from McClure and Sky Valley, Inc. Later in the contract, however, the $50,000 is listed as a debt solely of Sky Valley, Inc. to petitioner. Because McClure controlled Sky Valley, Inc. after the mutual conveyances, we would view the $50,000 payment in satisfaction of his obligation as coming from him. Respondent, however, did not assert the $50,000 as additional gain to petitioner in his notice of deficiency. We, therefore, assume that the cash came from Sky Valley, Inc., and the exchange between petitioner and Sky Valley, Inc. is not before the Court.

28. [5] Section 1.741-1(b), Income Tax Regs., provides:

(b) §741 shall apply whether the partnership interest is sold to one or more members of the partnership or to one or more persons who are not members of the partnership. Section 741 shall also apply even though the sale of the partnership interest results in a termination of the partnership under §708(b). Thus, the provisions of §741 shall be applicable (1) to the transferor partner in a 2-man partnership when he sells his interest to the other partner, and (2) to all the members of a partnership when they sell their interests to one or more persons outside the partnership.

randum Opinion of this Court; *Kinney v. U.S.*, 228 F. Supp. 656 (W.D. La. 1964), *affd. per curiam* 358 F.2d 738 (5th Cir. 1966). We, nevertheless, do not believe that petitioner and McClure effected a section 741 exchange. We believe that the transaction between petitioner and McClure should properly be characterized for Federal income tax purposes as a pro rata distribution of partnership assets in liquidation pursuant to § 731 followed by a like-kind exchange pursuant to § 1031(a). The Sales Contract's language does not support respondent's view that the parties to it contemplated an exchange of partnership interests.

The Sales Contract pursuant to which petitioner and McClure separated their business interests is replete with terminology indicative of a sale or exchange. The agreement itself is called a SALES Contract. That language does not, however, necessarily suggest a sale or exchange of partnership interests. Indeed, the Sales Contract provides that petitioner and McClure have agreed to "exchange between themselves certain tracts of real property." The Sales Contract refers repeatedly to personal, not partnership, conveyances of property and contemplates exchanges of assets held individually rather than by the partnerships. Although the Sales Contract is silent on whether the exchanges themselves terminated the partnerships or whether the partnerships terminated prior to the partner-level exchanges, we believe that the parties intended to exchange their interests in property and not their interests in the partnerships.[29]

Because the exchanges of property occurred between the individuals in their individual capacities and not as partners, we conclude that the partnerships terminated prior to the partner-level exchanges. Sections 731 and 1031(a), therefore, govern the transaction. The form of the transaction between the individuals comported with the prior dissolution of the partnerships. First, prior to the Sales Contract the individuals in effect received pro rata liquidating distributions from the partnerships pursuant to § 731. Second, the properties held individually were exchanged between the former partners. The Sales Contract, therefore, achieved exchanges of like-kind assets between the former partners. On a § 731 distribution, a partner recognizes gain only to the extent that any money distributed exceeds the partner's basis in his partnership

---

29. [6] Respondent argues that the form of the transaction as evidenced by the Sales Contract was an exchange of partnership interests taxable under § 741, and that petitioners are bound by the form chosen absent "proof which in an action between the parties would be admissible to alter that construction or to show its unenforceability because of mistake, undue influence, fraud, duress, etc." Comm'r v. Danielson, 378 F.2d 771, 775 (3d Cir. 1967), r *evg. and remanding* 44 T.C. 549 (1965), *cert. denied* 389 U.S. 858 (1967). This Court has adopted the "strong proof" rule, pursuant to which a party cannot challenge the form of a transaction that he has chosen absent strong proof that the form did not comport with the intended substance. Lucas v. Comm'r, 58 T.C. 1022, 1032 (1972). The Eleventh Circuit, to which an appeal would lie, however, has adopted the Danielson rule and, if relevant, it would be the applicable rule in this case. *See* Bradley v. U.S., 730, F.2d 718, 720 (11th Cir.), *cert. denied* 469 U.S. 882 (1984); Golsen v. Comm'r, 54 T.C. 742 (1970), *affd.* 445 F.2d 985 (10th Cir. 1971), *cert. denied* 404 U.S. 940 (1971). The Sales Contract does not, however, suggest that the exchanges took place before or upon the termination of the partnerships. The presumptions of the Danielson rule and the strong proof rule are relevant when a party seeks to disavow an agreement that is clear on its face. The Sales Contract nowhere mentions the sale or conveyance of any partnership interest. Neither the Danielson rule nor the strong proof rule is apposite here.

interest. Petitioner received no cash from either partnership. Furthermore, on the termination of the partnership petitioner is deemed to have assumed his pro rata share of partnership liabilities. Petitioner, therefore, did not recognize any gain.

Petitioner would urge us to stop our analysis at that point, but to do so would require us to ignore the exchange of properties that subsequently occurred pursuant to the Sales Contract. Petitioner and McClure exchanged their interests in certain assets, primarily real estate, in a like-kind exchange. Section 1031[30] provides for non-recognition of gain or loss on an exchange of property held for productive use in a trade or business or for investment solely for property of "like kind" which is to be held for productive use in a trade or business or for investment. Thus, petitioner is required to recognize gain only to the extent of any property received that does not qualify as like-kind property. Section 1031(b). Non-qualifying property includes relief from liability so that the excess of liabilities relieved over liabilities assumed in an exchange is gain which must be recognized. Section 1.1031(b)-1(c), Income Tax Regs.; *Long v. Comm'r*, 77 T.C. 1045, 1073 (1981).

OPINION

Pursuant to the Sales Contract, petitioner and McClure exchanged interests in VARIOUS PROPERTIES subject to all outstanding liabilities. McClure assumed liabilities in the amount of $1,696,656 of which $848,328, or 50 percent, represented petitioner's share. Petitioner assumed liabilities in the amount of $1,002,645 of which $501,322.50, or 50 percent, represented McClure's share. In addition, the parties have stipulated that by forgiving McClure's debt to him, petitioner assumed McClure's liability of $100,000. Petitioner also received McClure's share of a note receivable in the amount of $55,675, which was not like-kind property. Petitioner thus assumed McClure's liabilities in the amount of $601,322.50 ($501,322.50 + $100,000) from which McClure's share of the note receivable, $55,675, must be subtracted, leaving a net amount of liabilities assumed of $545,647.50. Petitioner must recognize gain pursuant to § 1031(b) to the extent that his liabilities relieved by McClure in the amount of $848,328 exceeded the liabilities he assumed. Petitioner,

---

30. [7] In 1981, § 1031 provided in relevant part:

SEC. 1031. EXCHANGE OF PROPERTY HELD FOR PRODUCTIVE USE OR FOR INVESTMENT.

(a) NONRECOGNITION OF GAIN OR LOSS FROM EXCHANGES SOLELY IN KIND.—
No gain or loss shall be recognized if property held for productive use in trade or business or for investment (not including stock in trade or other property held primarily for sale, nor stocks, bonds, notes, choses in action, certificates of trust or beneficial interest, or other securities or evidences of indebtedness or interest) is exchanged solely for property of a like kind to be held either for productive use in trade or business or for investment.

(b) GAIN FROM EXCHANGES NOT SOLELY IN KIND.—If an exchange would be within the provisions of subsection (a), of § 1035(a), of § 1036(a), or of § 1037(a), if it were not for the fact that the property received in exchange consists not only of property permitted by such provisions to be received without the recognition of gain, but also of other property or money, then the gain, if any, to the recipient shall be recognized, but in an amount not in excess of the sum of such money and the fair market value of such other property.

therefore, had a long-term capital gain of $302,680.50 on the dissolution of the partnerships.

Decision will be entered for the respondent.

Revenue Ruling 77-337

1977-2 C.B. 305

FACTS

An individual taxpayer, *A*, was the sole owner of the stock of corporation *X*. *X*'s only asset was a shopping center. *A* liquidated *X* pursuant to § 333 of the Code and, as a result, acquired the shopping center. Immediately following the liquidation, in a prearranged plan, *A* transferred the shopping center in exchange for property of a like kind owned by *B*, an unrelated party.

ANALYSIS

Section 333 of the Code provides, in general, that upon the liquidation of a corporation under certain specified conditions, the amount of gain recognized by a qualified electing noncorporate shareholder is computed on each share owned by the shareholder and each share's gain is limited to the greater of the share's ratable share of the corporation's earnings and profits accumulated after February 28, 1913, or the share's ratable share of the sum of the money received by the shareholder plus the fair market value of stock or securities so received that were acquired by the distributing corporation after December 31, 1953. See § 1.333-4(b) of the Income Tax Regulations. In the case of a qualified electing noncorporate shareholder, that part of the recognized gain on a share of stock that is not in excess of the ratable share of accumulated earnings and profits is taxed as a dividend and the remainder of the gain that is recognized is treated as a capital gain. Section 1.333-4(c).

Section 334(c) of the Code provides that the basis of assets (other than money) received in a liquidation to which § 333 applies shall be the same as the shareholder's basis in the stock decreased by money received and increased by gain recognized under § 333 and the amount of unsecured liabilities assumed by the shareholder. See § 1.334-2 of the regulations.

Section 1031(a) of the Code provides, in part, that no gain or loss shall be recognized if property held for productive use in trade or business or for investment (not including stock in trade or other property held primarily for sale) is exchanged solely for property of a like kind to be held either for productive use in trade or business or for investment.

Section 1223(1) of the Code provides, in part, that in determining the period for which the taxpayer has held property received in an exchange, there shall be included the period for which the taxpayer held the property exchanged if the property received has, for the purpose of determining gain or loss from the sale or exchange, the same basis in whole or in part in the taxpayer's hands as the property exchanged.

When property is received by a shareholder in the complete liquidation of a corporation and is thus treated as received in full payment in exchange for stock of the corporation, the period for which the taxpayer holds the property received in the liquidation includes the period for which the taxpayer held the stock of the liquidating corporation. See Rev. Rul. 74-522, 1974-2 C.B. 271.

In Rev. Rul. 75-292, 1975-2 C.B. 333, an individual taxpayer, in a prearranged transaction transferred land and buildings used in the taxpayer's trade or business to an unrelated corporation in exchange for land and an office building owned by the corporation and used in its trade or business. Immediately thereafter, the individual taxpayer transferred the land and office building to the individual's newly created corporation. Rev. Rul. 75-292 holds, in part, that the exchange does not qualify for nonrecognition of gain or loss under § 1031(a) of the Code with respect to the individual taxpayer, because the individual taxpayer did not exchange the land and buildings for property to be held either for productive use in trade or business or for investment. The newly created corporation's eventual productive use of the land and office building in trade of business is not attributable to its sole shareholder.

The proposed transaction between A and B was a prearranged plan whereby X was liquidated to facilitate a further exchange between A and B of their respective properties. The productive use of the shopping center by X prior to the liquidation cannot be attributed to A and, hence, A did not hold an interest in the shopping center for productive use in trade or business or for investment. Compare Rev. Rul. 75-292.

OPINION

Accordingly, A's exchange of the shopping center for B's property does not qualify for nonrecognition of gain or loss under § 1031(a) of the Code.

Any gain or loss resulting from the exchange will be recognized to A to the extent of the difference between A's basis in the shopping center acquired as a result of the liquidation as determined pursuant to § 334(c) of the Code and the regulations thereunder, and the fair market value of B's property at the time of the exchange.

Pursuant to § 1223(1) of the Code and Rev. Rul. 74-522, the holding period of the shopping center acquired by A at the time of liquidation includes the period for which A held the stock in X.

Revenue Ruling 75-292
1975-2 C.B. 333

FACTS

A, an individual, in a prearranged transaction, transferred land and buildings used in A's trade or business to W, an unrelated corporation, in exchange for land and an office building owned by W and used in its trade or business. Immediately thereafter, A transferred the land and office building to Y, a corporation created by A, in exchange for the stock of *Y* in a transaction that qualified under § 351 of the Code. *W* used the land and buildings received from *A* in its trade or business.

ANALYSIS

Section 358(a) of the Code provides, in part, that in the case of an exchange to which § 351, 354, 355, 356, 361, or 371(b) applies, the basis of the property permitted to be received under these sections without the recognition of gain or loss shall be the same as that of the property exchanged with certain specified adjustments.

Section 362(a) of the Code provides, in part, that the basis of property acquired in a transaction to which § 351 applies will be the same as it would be in the hands of the transferor, increased in the amount of gain recognized to the transferor on such transfer.

Section 1031(a) of the Code provides, in part, that no gain or loss shall be recognized if property held for productive use in trade or business or for investment (not including stock in trade or other property held primarily for sale) is exchanged solely for property of a like kind to be held either for productive use in trade or business or for investment.

A did not exchange the land and buildings for property to be held either for productive use in trade or business or for investment. The property he received from *W* was to be transferred to *Y* and was not to be held by *A*.

Accordingly, under the facts of the instant case, the exchange of land and buildings by *A* for land and an office building owned by *W* does not qualify for nonrecognition of gain or loss under § 1031(a) of the Code with respect to *A*. Further, since the land and buildings were assets used in *A*'s trade or business, any gain or loss resulting from the exchange will be subject to the provisions of § 1231 and § 1250, if applicable. The basis to *A* of the land and office building is their fair market value and, pursuant to § 362(a), *Y*'s basis in the land and office building is the same as *A*'s basis therein. *A*'s basis in the *Y* stock is the same as *A*'s basis in the land and office building immediately before the transfer. *See* § 358(a).

OPINION

With respect to *W* the exchange qualifies as an exchange of properties held for productive use in trade or business or for investment under the nonrecognition of gain or loss provisions of § 1031(a) of the Code.

Tech. Adv. Mem. 98-18-003

(Dec. 24, 1997)

FACTS

Taxpayer, a partnership, owned the Relinquished Property and leased it to A, a limited partner of Taxpayer. After leasing the Relinquished Property for approximately 14 years, Taxpayer and A entered into a contract for the sale of the Relinquished Property to A for $w.

Section 9.4(a) of the partnership agreement provided that upon dissolution and liquidation of Taxpayer the managing partner could effect one or more deferred like-kind exchanges under § 1031 through a qualified intermediary. The provision allowed each partner to designate one or more properties which Taxpayer would acquire using the respective partner's share of the net proceeds from the sale of the property. It further stated that none of the individual partners would be considered agents of the partnership for any purpose relating to the deferred like-kind exchange. If the purchase price of a replacement property exceeded that partner's share of the proceeds from the property sale that partner was required to provide the additional funds.

Shortly before the sale was to occur, Taxpayer entered into an exchange agreement with Intermediary, a bank, to act as an intermediary in a deferred exchange of the Relinquished Property. Intermediary assigned its interest in the exchange agreement to A. A purchased the Relinquished Property for $w. After paying closing costs and paying off the debt on the Relinquished Property, Taxpayer received net proceeds of $x. Of this amount, $y was transferred to the Exchange Trust at Intermediary, and $z was distributed to certain partners, including A, in payment for their partnership interests. The Exchange trust subsequently disbursed funds to the closing agents of the other partners to acquire replacement real properties on their behalf which were deeded directly to the individual partners in liquidation of their partnership interests.

ANALYSIS

Section 1031(a)(1) of the Internal Revenue Code provides generally that no gain or loss shall be recognized on the exchange of property held for productive use in a trade or business or for investment, if such property is exchanged solely for property of like kind which is to be held either for productive use in a trade or business or for investment.

Section 1.1002-1(d) of the Income Tax Regulations provides that ordinarily, to constitute an exchange, the transaction must be a reciprocal transfer of property, as distinguished from a transfer of property for a money consideration only.

Taxpayer has not established that the transaction is a exchange with a reciprocal transfer of property. Taxpayer transferred the Relinquished Property, but received no reciprocal transfer of replacement property.

In *Carlton v. U.S.*, 385 F.2d 238 (5th Cir. 1967), taxpayers, who had given an option on their ranch property, negotiated to acquire other ranch property, intending to effect a tax-free exchange. The optionee contracted to buy other property and assigned the contract to taxpayers at the time of sale of taxpayers' ranch. The Fifth Circuit Court of Appeals held that the transaction did not qualify as a tax-free exchange since title to the replacement property never vested in the optionee. Since the optionee never had any property of like kind to exchange, the transfer of the ranch constituted a sale despite the taxpayers' intentions to execute an exchange.

In order for Taxpayer to qualify for nonrecognition treatment under § 1031, the transaction must be in the form of an exchange. Because a sale and a purchase may have the same end result as an exchange, in order for the requirement that the transaction qualify as an exchange to have any meaning, the form of an exchange must be followed. *See Carlton, supra.* In Taxpayer's case, there was no transfer of replacement property to Taxpayer so as to complete an exchange. Instead, Taxpayer received cash, and various real properties were transferred to its partners in payment for the Relinquished Property.

Taxpayer cites Rev. Rul. 90-34, 1990-1 C.B. 154, as authority for its position that the direct deeding of the replacement properties to partners of Taxpayer does not affect the status of the transaction as an exchange by Taxpayer. However, Rev. Rul. 90-34 is distinguishable from Taxpayer's case. The revenue ruling held that X's transfer of property to Y, in exchange for property of a like kind, qualifies as to X for nonrecognition of gain or loss under § 1031 even though legal title to the property received by X is never held by Y. In the revenue ruling Y is the person that receives property and transfers the replacement property to X.

The partners, as recipients of the replacement properties, stand in the same relative position in this transaction as X does in Rev. Rul. 90-34. Taxpayer stands in the same relative position as Y in that revenue ruling. The relevant inquiry here is whether the transaction is an exchange with respect to Taxpayer, not with respect to the partners of Taxpayer.

Further, Rev. Rul. 77-297, 1977-2 C.B. 302, dealt in part with B, an accommodating buyer that acquired replacement property and then transferred the replacement property in exchange for the relinquished property. Rev. Rul. 77-297 held that as to B, the exchange of ranches does not qualify for nonrecognition of gain or loss under § 1031 because B did not hold the replacement property for productive use in a trade or business or for investment. *See also* Rev. Rul. 75-291, 1975-2 C.B. 332, which held that § 1031 does not apply to a taxpayer who acquired property solely for the purposes of exchanging it for like kind property.

OPINION

It is inappropriate to extend Rev. Rul. 90-34 to Taxpayer and its partners. In order for this revenue ruling to apply, the partners would have to be viewed as exchanging their partnership interests in Taxpayer for replacement properties. However, it is Taxpayer that is seeking nonrecognition of gain on the transfer of the Relinquished Property, not nonrecognition of gain on an exchange of the partners' partnership interests in Taxpayer. It is also clear that Taxpayer, and not the partners of Taxpayer, transferred the Relinquished Property. Moreover, even if viewed as an exchange by the partners of Taxpayer, the exchange would fail to qualify for nonrecognition because § 1031(a) does not apply to any exchange of an interest in a partnership. § 1031(a)(2)(D).

Chapter 17

Real Estate Investment Trusts

I. Commentary

Real estate investment trusts (REITs) have become a very popular vehicle for investing in real estate.[1] REITs are subject to a conduit form of taxation. REITs can deduct distributions to shareholders,[2] so they are only taxed on undistributed taxable income and can avoid an entity-level tax by distributing 100% of their taxable income. Conduit taxation thus differs from both passthrough taxation to which tax partnerships are subject and the corporate taxation to which tax corporations are subject. After determining if REIT taxation is appropriate for a real estate venture, the next question is whether the venture can satisfy the REIT classification requirements. Property owners wishing to hold property in a REIT have devised structures such as the UPREIT to enable tax-free contributions to an arrangement that provides the financial benefits of holding stock in a publicly-traded entity.

A. REIT Taxation

To qualify for REIT conduit taxation, an entity must meet the classification requirements discussed below, and it must distribute at least 90% of its taxable income.[3] By distributing all of its income, a REIT can generally avoid entity-level tax by deducting the amount of the distribution from gross income.[4] The distribution requirement distinguishes REITs from other tax entities, such as tax partnerships and tax

---

1. *See* Bradley T. Borden, *Reforming REIT Taxation (or Not)*, 53 Hous. L. Rev. 1 (2015) (hereinafter, *Reforming REIT Taxation*); Bradley T. Borden, *Rethinking the Tax-Revenue Effect of REIT Taxation*, 17 Fla. Tax. Rev. 527 (2015) (hereinafter, *Tax-Revenue Effect*). For additional commentary on the history and policy of REITs, see David F. Levy, Nickolas P. Gianou & Kevin M. Jones, *Modern REITs and the Corporate Tax: Thoughts on the Scope of the Corporate Tax and Rationalizing Our System of Taxing Collective Investment Vehicles*, 94 Taxes: The Tax Magazine 217 (Mar. 2016); Richard M. Nugent, *REIT Spinoffs: Passive REITs, Active Business*, 146 Tax Notes 1513 (Mar. 23, 2015); Richard M. Nugent, *REIT Spinoffs: Passive REITs, Active Businesses*, 146 Tax Notes 1635 (Mar. 30, 2015); Ameek Akosh Ponda, *How Much Gain Would a REIT Defer if a REIT Could Defer Gain?*, 135 Tax Notes 1249 (June 4, 2012).

2. *See* I.R.C. §857(b).

3. *See* I.R.C. §857(a)(1). Distribution of additional REIT stock in lieu of cash can satisfy the distribution requirement. *See* Rev. Rul. 83-117, 1983-2 C.B. 98.

4. *See* I.R.C. §857(b)(2)(B).

corporations, which do not have distribution requirements.[5] Although distributed REIT income is not subject to two levels of tax, the total tax paid on REIT income can be greater than the total tax paid on a tax corporation's income because of the different tax rates that can apply to dividends from the different types of entities and because of the different payout ratios of the two types of entities.

Dividends paid by tax corporations to individuals can qualify for the lowest rates that apply to long-term capital gains.[6] Dividends paid by REITs to individuals do not qualify for favorable treatment, so they are taxed at the highest ordinary rates.[7] If a tax corporation pays out all of its taxable income to individuals, then the total tax on the corporate income will most likely exceed the total tax paid on a REIT's income. Studies suggest that publicly traded tax corporations pay out about 25% of their taxable income, while publicly traded REITs pay out more than 100% of their taxable income.[8] If tax corporations and REITs only paid dividends to individuals at those payout ratios, then the tax paid on REIT taxable income could be greater than the tax paid on a tax corporation's taxable income. Such simple generalizations are typically inadequate to determine the effects of the two types of entities. The analysis of the total tax paid on the respective entities' income requires a more dynamic analysis because tax-exempt and non-U.S. persons also hold stock in each type of entity.[9] Investors should also consider the relative tax effects of investing in a REIT instead of a tax partnership.[10]

Despite the opportunity to avoid the entity-level tax, certain types of income are subject to tax at the entity level of a REIT. First, net income derived from prohibited transactions is taxed at 100%.[11] Prohibited transaction for this purpose means gain from a disposition of property described in section 1221(a)(1) (i.e., dealer property), which is not foreclosure property.[12] Because of the uncertainty about whether property is dealer property, Congress provides safe harbors to exclude gains from the disposition of certain property, including timber, from the definition of prohibited transaction.[13] Second, a REIT must pay tax at the ordinary corporate rate on net income from foreclosure property.[14]

---

5. *See supra* Chapter 4 (discussing the tax treatment of other tax partnerships and tax corporations).

6. *See* I.R.C. § 1(h)(1)(D), (h)(11).

7. *See* I.R.C. § 857(c)(2)(B).

8. *See* Bradley T. Borden, *Counterintuitive Tax Revenue Effect of REIT Spinoffs*, 146 TAX NOTES 381 (Jan. 2015).

9. *See* Borden, *Tax-Revenue Effect, supra*; Ameek Ashok Ponda, *Foreign Pension Plans Investing in Shares of a U.S. REIT*, 74 TAX NOTES 1593 (Mar. 24, 1997). Chapter 19 discusses the possible preferences of non-U.S. tax persons for investing in U.S. real property.

10. *See* Borden, *Tax-Revenue Effect, supra* (comparing the tax revenue effects of investing in REITs and tax partnerships).

11. *See* I.R.C. § 857(b)(6)(A).

12. *See* I.R.C. § 857(b)(6)(B)(iii); Chapter 7, *supra* (discussing the definition of dealer property).

13. *See* I.R.C. § 857(b)(6)(C)–(E).

14. *See* I.R.C. § 856(e) (defining foreclosure property); 857(b)(4)(A) (imposing the tax); Rev. Rul. 77-441, 1977-2 C.B. 240.

B. REIT Classification

If investors decide that a REIT is the ideal form of investment for them, they must ensure that their arrangement will meet the REIT classification requirements. To gain tax treatment as a REIT, an entity must satisfy (1) an organizational test, (2) an asset test, and (3) an income test.[15]

1. Organizational Test

To qualify for REIT taxation, an entity must be a corporation, trust, or association.[16] Because partnerships and limited liability companies can elect to be taxed as corporations,[17] they too can be REITs. The entity must be managed by one or more trustees or directors.[18] The entity must have at least 100 owners, and the interests in the entity must be transferrable.[19] As a general matter, the entity cannot be closely held.[20] The REIT rules adopt a version of the personal holding company ownership requirement for purposes of determining whether an entity is closely held.[21] Under that rule, an entity would be closely held if five or fewer individuals directly or indirectly own more than 50% of the outstanding value of the entity's stock.[22] Typically a qualified retirement trust is treated as an individual for the purposes of determining whether an entity is closely held,[23] but special look-through rules apply to qualified retirement trusts and count the trust beneficiaries as owning the trust's REIT stock.[24] These pension look-through rules allow qualified retirement trusts to be significant owners of REITs. Finally, a REIT cannot come within the definition of financial institution or insurance company,[25] and must otherwise be classified as a corporation for federal tax purposes.[26]

2. Asset Test

To qualify for REIT taxation, at least 75% of the total value of an entity's assets must be represented by real estate assets, cash and cash items, and government securities (but securities cannot represent more than 25% of the value of a REIT's total

---

15. *See* Borden, *Reforming REIT Taxation, supra*.

16. *See* I.R.C. § 856(a).

17. *See* Treas. Reg. § 301.7701-1 to -3.

18. *See* I.R.C. § 856(a)(1).

19. *See* I.R.C. § 856(a)(2), (5). Facilitators will purchase the requisite number of shares comprising a very small, economically insignificant ownership percentage of a REIT to help investors meet the 100-shareholder requirement.

20. *See* I.R.C. § 856(a)(6). A REIT that follows the rules for determining ownership and does not know, and would not have known after exercising reasonable diligence, that it failed to meet ownership requirements shall be treated as satisfying the requirement. *See* I.R.C. § 856(k).

21. *See* I.R.C. § 856(h)(1)(A).

22. *See* I.R.C. § 542(a)(2).

23. *See id.*

24. *See* I.R.C. § 856(h)(3).

25. *See* I.R.C. § 856(a)(4).

26. *See* I.R.C. § 856(a)(3).

assets).[27] REITs focus on holding "real estate assets," so the definition of that term becomes important. Three general types of property come within the definition of real estate asset: (1) real property, (2) shares in other REITs, and (3) debt instruments issued by publicly offered REITs.[28] Real property includes interests in mortgages on real property and interests in real property,[29] which include fee ownership and co-ownership of land or improvements on the land, leaseholds of land or improvements, options to acquire land or improvements, and options to acquire leaseholds of land or improvements.[30] An improvement is a building or other inherently permanent structure.[31] The IRS has published numerous rulings regarding specific types of assets that come within the definition of real property, some of which are not intuitive (which would explain the taxpayer's desire to obtain a ruling).[32]

The IRS has received numerous ruling requests relating to various types of property. In response, the IRS has privately ruled on numerous occasion with respect to those individual requests.[33] The result is a piecemeal response to a broader question of what constitutes real property for REIT purposes. To alleviate the burden of piecemeal ruling and to provide general guidance related to the definition, Treasury decided to address the definition of real property with a more comprehensive definition that is consistent with prior rulings and existing regulations, so it published proposed regulations to that effect.[34] The proposed regulations do three things.[35] First, they define real property as land and improvements to land.[36] Improvements to land include inherently permanent structures (such as buildings) and their structural components.[37] Second, the proposed regulations provide a facts-and-circumstances test for determining whether an item is a distinct asset for purposes of applying the definition of real property.[38] Third, the proposed regulations identify intangible assets that are real property.[39] Under these rules, an intangible asset is real property if it

---

27. *See* I.R.C. §856(c)(4)(A), (B)(i).

28. *See* I.R.C. §856(c)(5)(B).

29. *See id.*

30. *See* I.R.C. §856(c)(5)(C) (excluding mineral, oil, and gas interests from the definition of real property).

31. *See* Treas. Reg. §1.856-3(d).

32. *See, e.g.,* Priv. Ltr. Rul. 2011-43-011 (July 19, 2011) (ruling privately that steel billboard structures are real property).

33. *See* Steven F. Mount, *New Wine in Old Bottles: Has the Definition of "Real Estate Assets" Been Expanded for Real Estate Investment Trusts?,* 54 TAX MGMT. MEMO. 383 (2013).

34. *See* REG-150760-13 (June 2, 2014). *See also* Steve F. Mount, *Definition of "Real Property" for Real Estate Investment Trusts—Prop. Reg. §1.856-10 "Codifies" Current Law,* 55 TAX MGMT. MEMO. 371 (2014); Willard B. Taylor, *Closing the Gap Between Private Rulings and Regulations,* 144 TAX NOTES 597 (2014).

35. *See* Prop. Reg. §1.856-3(a).

36. *See* Prop. Reg. §1.856-3(b).

37. *See* Prop. Reg. §1.856-3(d)(1).

38. *See* Prop. Reg. §1.856-3(e).

39. *See* Prop. Reg. §1.856-3(f).

derives its value from the real property, is inseparable from the real property, and does not produce or contribute to the production of income other than the use or occupancy of space.[40]

The asset test also includes a diversification requirement and other ownership restrictions. Generally, not more than 5% of a REIT's assets (in value) can be represented by the securities of a single issuer.[41] Not more than 20% of the value of a REIT's assets can be represented by the securities of one or more taxable REIT subsidiaries, and not more than 25% of the value of its assets can be represented by nonqualified publicly offered REIT debt instruments.[42] REITs are also prohibited from owning more than 10% of the vote and value of the securities of any single issuer.[43]

3. Income Test

The income test has two subtests that an entity must satisfy to be a REIT. First, at least 95% of an entity's gross income must derive from dividends; interest; rents from real property; gain from the disposition of stock, securities, and real property that is not dealer property; and other types of income from real property.[44] Second, at least 75% of its gross income must derive from rents from real property; interests on obligations secured by real property; gain from the disposition of real property that is not dealer property; dividends and gain from other REIT stock; and other income from real property.[45] Thus, a REIT's income must generally be passive, and a significant portion of it must derive from real property.

Questions regarding the definition of rents from real property often arise, and the definition has changed over the years.[46] The definition of rents from real property has an inclusionary component and an exclusionary component. Under the inclusionary component, rents from real property includes rents from interests in real property; charges for services customarily rendered in connection with the rental of real property;[47] and rent attributable to personal property leased in connection with

---

40. *See* Prop. Reg. § 1.856-3(f)(1). A license or permit can also be intangible real property. *See* Prop. Reg. § 1.856-3(f)(2).

41. *See* I.R.C. § 856(c)(4)(B)(iv)(I).

42. *See* I.R.C. § 856(c)(4)(B)(ii), (iii).

43. *See* I.R.C. § 856(c)(4)(B)(iv)(II), (III).

44. *See* I.R.C. § 856(c)(2).

45. *See* I.R.C. § 856(c)(3).

46. *See, e.g.,* Rev. Rul. 2002-24, 2004-1 C.B. 550 (ruling with respect to services related to providing parking facilities at a REITs rental properties); Paul W. Decker, David H. Kaplan & Ameek Ashok Ponda, *Non-Customary Services Furnished by Taxable REIT Subsidiaries,* 148 Tax Notes 413 (July 27, 2015).

47. "Services furnished to the tenants of a particular building will be considered as customary if, in the geographic market in which the building is located, tenants in buildings which are of similar class (such as luxury apartment buildings) are customarily provided with the service." *See* Treas. Reg. § 1.856-4(b)(1). Examples of such services are furnishing water, heat, light, and air conditioning; cleaning windows, public entrances, exits, and lobbies; performing general maintenance and janitorial and cleaning services; collecting trash; and furnishing elevator services. *See id.*

real property, if such rent does not exceed 15% of the total rent under the lease.[48] Under the exclusionary component, rents from real property generally does not include amounts based upon the income or profits of a tenant; amounts received from a corporation if the entity owns at least 10% of the vote or value of the corporation and any noncorporation if the entity owns at least 10% of the assets or net profits of the noncorporation; and impermissible tenant service income.[49] Leasing property requires providing services related to the property, so managers of REITs must be able to identify and avoid impermissible tenant services.

Impermissible tenant service income is defined broadly but subject to two very important exceptions. Impermissible tenant service income includes any amount a REIT receives directly or indirectly for services it renders to tenants of its property and for managing or operating the property.[50] Under the first exception to this rule, services provided by an independent contractor or the REIT's taxable REIT subsidiary are not treated as provided by the REIT.[51] This exception allows a REIT to hire an independent contractor or taxable REIT subsidiary to provide noncustomary services to tenants and to manage and operate the REIT's property.[52]

The second exception allows a REIT to provide services that do not generate unrelated business taxable income under the tax-exempt rules.[53] This exception allows a REIT to provide services to tenants, so long as the services are not for the convenience of the occupant.[54] Thus, the exception allows the REIT to provide services customarily rendered in connection with the rental of property, such as providing heat and light; cleaning public entrances, exits, and stairways; and collecting trash.[55] The consequences of collecting impermissible tenant services can be draconian,[56] so REIT managers expend great care to ensure that they do not provide such services.

---

48. *See* I.R.C. § 856(d)(1).

49. *See* I.R.C. § 856(d)(2).

50. *See* I.R.C. § 856(d)(7)(A).

51. *See* I.R.C. § 856(d)(7)(C). A partnership of a taxable REIT subsidiary and independent contractor may also provide noncustomary services to REIT tenants. *See* Rev. Rul. 2003-86, 2003-2 C.B. 290.

52. A taxable REIT subsidiary must recognize income for services it provides and pay tax on that income. *See* I.R.C. §§ 11, 856(l)(1). If a REIT receives payments for services that the taxable REIT subsidiary performs and does not pay it to the taxable REIT subsidiary as compensation for those services, a 100% tax applies to the payments, to the extent they come within the definition of redetermined rents. *See* I.R.C. § 857(b)(7). The definition of redetermined rents relies upon section 482 and is subject to several exchanges, or safe harbors. *See* I.R.C. § 857(b)(7)(A)(i)–(vii); Rev. Rul. 2002-38, 2002-2 C.B. 4.

53. *See* I.R.C. § 856(d)(7)(C)(ii).

54. *See* I.R.C. § 512(b)(3); Treas. Reg. § 1.512(b)-1(c)(5). In determining whether services result in something other than rents from real property, courts look at the purpose of the provided services, not the substantiality of the services. *See, e.g.,* Ocean Pines Ass'n, Inc. v. Comm'r, 135 T.C. 276 (2010).

55. *See* Treas. Reg. § 1.512(b)-1(c)(5).

56. *See* I.R.C. § 856(d)(7)(B) (providing that if more than 1% of a REITs receipts are from impermissible tenant services with respect to a property, all of its receipts with respect to such property will be treated as from impermissible tenant services, excluding such receipts from the definition of rents from real property).

Figure 17.1 UPREIT Structure

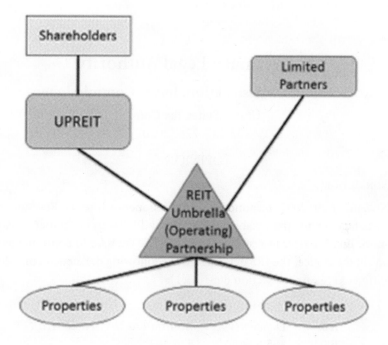

C. UPREITs

Because REITs must be tax corporations, contributions of real estate to a REIT could be a taxable event.[57] This rule discourages property owners from contributing property to publicly traded REITs and would generally prevent them from participating in the benefits to be obtained from owning stock in a publicly traded REIT. The umbrella partnership REIT (UPREIT) structure allows property owners to contribute property to a tax partnership that has a REIT member (see Figure 17.1), so UPREITs have become popular structures.[58] The contribution to the tax partnership can be tax free. Membership interests in the tax partnership are convertible to stock in the REIT, so the members of the tax partnership are able to liquidate their interests in the tax partnership by converting those interests to publicly traded REIT stock and selling the REIT stock. The conversion from interests in a tax partnership to REIT stock is taxable, but the members can stagger their conversions to defer gain recognition, or

---

57. *See* Chapter 4, *supra* (discussing the tax treatment of contributions to tax corporations).

58. *See* Daniel F. Cullen, *UPREITs — Structuring Fractional Interest Tender Offers*, 34 REAL EST. TAX'N 165 (2007); Michael K. Carnevale, James P. de Bree, Mark N. Schneider & Fred T. Witt, Jr., *An Introduction to UPREITs*, 19 TAX MGMT. REAL EST. J. 3 (2003); Brent W. Ambrose & Peter Linneman, *The Maturing of REITs*, 3 WHARTON REAL EST. REV. 37 (1999). In fact, UPREITs became the model for the UP-C, an ownership structure that allows members of any type of tax partnership to gain the economic benefit of being publicly traded without converting to a tax corporation. *See* Gladriel Shobe, *Supercharged IPOs, the Up-C, and Private Tax Benefits in Public Offerings*, 88 U. COLO. L. REV. ___ (2017).

simply retain their interests and participate in the economic performance of the REIT with the other holders of REIT stock.

II. Primary Legal Authority

Ocean Pines Association, Inc. v. Commissioner

United States Tax Court

135 T.C. 276 (2010)

OPINION

MORRISON, JUDGE:

On November 29, 2007, respondent Commissioner of Internal Revenue mailed a notice of deficiency for the taxable years 2003 and 2004 to petitioner Ocean Pines Association, Inc. We refer to respondent as the IRS. We refer to petitioner as the Association. In the notice, the IRS determined the following deficiencies in income tax and additions to tax under section 6651(a)(1):[59]

Year	Deficiency	Addition to Tax Sec. 6651(a)(1)
2003	$65,929	$16,482
2004	94,195	23,549

After concessions, the issues remaining for decision are: (1) whether the Association's operation of a beach club and two nearby parking lots is substantially related to the promotion of community welfare (we hold that the operation is not substantially related, and that therefore the operation is subject to the tax on unrelated-business income), and (2) whether the revenue received by the Association from its members for parking on its two parking lots is exempt from the tax on unrelated-business income as rent from real property within the meaning of section 512(b)(3) (we hold that the revenue is not rent from real property).

BACKGROUND

The parties agreed to submit this case to the Court without trial under Rule 122. We adopt as findings of fact all statements contained in the stipulation of facts. The stipulation of facts and the attached exhibits are incorporated here by this reference. The Association is a homeowners association and nonstock corporation organized and incorporated under the laws of Maryland with its principal office in Maryland. The IRS ruled that it was exempt from federal income tax as an organization described in section 501(c)(4) (civic league or organizations not organized for profit but operated exclusively for the promotion of social welfare).

---

59. [1] Unless otherwise indicated, all section references are to the Internal Revenue Code in effect for the years at issue, and all Rule references are to the Tax Court Rules of Practice and Procedure.

The Association's articles of incorporation state that one of its purposes is "to further and promote the community welfare of property owners in the residential community located in Worcester County, Maryland known as 'Ocean Pines.'" Its membership consists of all of the owners of residential property within the 3,500–acre area known as Ocean Pines. According to the 2000 census, the population of Ocean Pines was 10,496. The Association collects property assessments and other fees from its members and enforces zoning restrictions against its members. It maintains bulkheads, roadways, and parking lots within Ocean Pines. The Association also operates recreational facilities in Ocean Pines that are open to both members and nonmembers, including five swimming pools, a golf course, two marinas, a yacht club, tennis complexes, a soccer field, 10 parks, and five walking trails. The Association provides, through its Recreation and Parks Department, various seminars, sports camps, a children's softball league, swimming lessons, and adult aquatic programs to both members and nonmembers. Some of the recreational facilities and services described above are free. Others are available only for a fee, which is typically higher for nonmembers than members. The Association maintains two volunteer fire stations and a police force. Parking within the Ocean Pines area is free and open to both members and nonmembers.

The Association owns beachfront property approximately eight miles from the Ocean Pines area in Ocean City, an area within Worcester County, Maryland. The Ocean City property consists of two parking lots, containing 300 parking spaces in total, and an oceanfront beach club, known as the Ocean Pines Beach Club. The Association's members who use the parking lots and the beach club commute approximately 15 minutes by car from Ocean Pines to Ocean City. The beach club is open from the beginning of Memorial Day weekend until Labor Day (we refer to this period as the summer months). The beach club is closed during the evenings unless reserved for special events. The beach club allows both Association members and nonmembers to purchase food and beverage services and to use its restrooms for free. However, the swimming pool, gym lockers, and shower facilities are accessible only to Association members. The record does not reveal whether the Association charges a separate fee to its members who use these facilities. In the summer months, the Association limits use of the parking lots to its members who have purchased parking lot permits, and their guests. They may use the parking lots during the day until 4 p.m. Only the Association's members are eligible to purchase permits for the parking lots. The Association's members must pay a weekly or monthly fee depending on the period for which the permit is issued. The Association's employees in Ocean Pines issue the permits. The Association leases the parking lots to third-party businesses during the summer months from approximately 4 p.m. until approximately 3 a.m. The Association also leases the lots during all nonsummer months. It provides no significant services to the third-party businesses. The Association employs a guard daily during the summer months from 8 a.m. until 4 p.m. The guard removes a chain barring entrance to the parking lots at the beginning of each day during the summer months (and replaces it at the end of each summer day) and checks the parking permit decals on the vehicles as they enter the parking lots. If the vehicles do not have permit decals, they are turned away. If any vehicle remains on the parking lot from the periods of use by the third-party businesses, the parking guard places a note on the vehicle demanding that the owner remove the vehicle from the parking lot as soon as possible. The parking guard does not collect fees or park vehicles; the lots offer no valet services. Parking is available upon a first-come, first served basis; i.e., there are no assigned parking spaces. The Association does not maintain common areas in Ocean City, such as beach or bike paths, nor does it levy assessments on the residents or home-owners in Ocean City.

In 2003, the Association received $232,089 in revenue from the two parking lots, $61,024 of which was paid by the third-party businesses. It paid $39,092 in expenses attributable to the operation of the parking lots by the Association (as opposed to the leasing of the parking lots to third-party businesses). It incurred a $20,486 net loss for operation of the beach club in 2003. In 2004, the Association received $266,487 in revenue from the two parking lots, $64,692 of which was paid by third-party businesses. It paid $21,939 in expenses attributable to the operation of the parking lots by the Association. It incurred a $1,741 net loss for operation of the beach club in 2004. The Association timely filed Form 990, Return of Organization Exempt From Income Tax, but did not file the form on which the unrelated business income tax is reported, Form 990–T, Exempt Organization Business Income Tax Return. The Form 990 is not in the record.

The IRS issued a notice of deficiency to the Association on November 29, 2007 (discussed above), determining that the Association owed unrelated business income tax on the net income attributable to the operation of its parking lots. The net income figures used to calculate the deficiency in unrelated business income tax for each tax year at issue included the income from the leasing of the parking lots to third parties and a deduction for the parking lot expenses, but excluded the losses from the operation of the beach club.[60] The IRS determined the late-filing addition to tax in the notice because the Association failed to file a Form 990–T. The Association filed a petition in response to the notice of deficiency. When this case was called from the calendar for the trial session of this Court at Baltimore, Maryland, the parties filed a joint motion for leave to submit the case under Rule 122, which the Court granted, and a stipulation of settled issues. In the stipulation of settled issues, the IRS conceded that

> the revenue received by the Association from the leasing of its Ocean City parking lots to third parties in the evening hours and during the off-season[61] is excepted from § 511 unrelated business taxable income because it satisfies the § 512(b) exception to unrelated business income for the rent from real property.

---

60. [2] As explained below, the IRS now concedes that the losses from the operation of the beach club are deductible against the net income figures used to calculate the deficiency.

61. [3] The revenue referred to in the stipulation of settled issues is the $61,024 paid in 2003 and the $64,692 paid in 2004 by the third-party businesses, unreduced by any expenses allocable to the Association's operation of the parking lots.

The IRS also conceded that the Association was not liable for the late-filing addition to tax under section 6651(a)(1) because it relied on the advice of its accountants in determining that filing a Form 990–T for the years at issue was not necessary. The parties stipulated that the amount of net income from the Association's operation of the parking lots and the beach club potentially subject to the unrelated business income tax is $111,487 in 2003 and $178,115 in 2004. These net income amounts were calculated by excluding the revenue received from the third-party businesses for rental of the parking lots, by including the parking lot fees received from members of the Association, by deducting the losses from the operation of the beach club, and by deducting all of the expenses from the operation of the parking lots.

DISCUSSION

The Association has the burden of proving that the determinations of the deficiencies in the notice are wrong. See Rule 142(a); *Welch v. Helvering,* 290 U.S. 111, 115, 54 S.Ct. 8, 78 L.Ed. 212 (1933). For reasons explained below, we hold that the operation of the parking lots and the beach club is not substantially related to the promotion of community welfare and that the income from operation of the parking lots is not rent from real property within the meaning of section 512(b)(3). Therefore, the income from operation of the parking lots and the beach club is subject to the unrelated business income tax.

I. *Whether the Operation of the Parking Lots and the Beach Club Is Substantially Related to the Promotion of Community Welfare*

Section 501(c)(4) exempts from Federal tax "Civic leagues or organizations not organized for profit but operated exclusively for the promotion of social welfare". Regulations clarify that "An organization is operated exclusively for the promotion of social welfare if it is primarily engaged in promoting in some way the common good and general welfare of the people of the community." Sec. 1.501(c)(4)-1(a)(2), Income Tax Regs. By implication, the regulation defines "exclusively" to mean "primarily". Thus, "an organization will not be denied exemption if it partakes in activities not in furtherance of an exempt purpose so long as such nonconforming activities are insubstantial in comparison to activities which further exempt purpose(s)." *Kentucky Bar Found., Inc. v. Commissioner,* 78 T.C. 921, 923, 1982 WL 11102 (1982). Section 501(c)(4) organizations, like some other types of tax-exempt organizations, must pay income tax on their "unrelated business taxable income". See sec. 511(a)(1). Section 512(a)(1) defines "unrelated business taxable income". It provides:

> Except as otherwise provided in this subsection, the term "unrelated business taxable income" means the gross income derived by any organization from any unrelated trade or business * * * regularly carried on by it, less the deductions allowed by this chapter which are directly connected with the carrying on of such trade or business, both computed with the modifications provided in subsection (b).

Section 513(a) provides that the term "unrelated trade or business" means any trade or business the conduct of which is not "substantially related (aside from the need of such organization for income or funds or the use it makes of the profits derived) to the exercise or performance by such organization of its charitable, educational, or other purpose or function constituting the basis for its exemption under section 501". Accordingly, income is unrelated business taxable income if it is derived from a regularly carried-on trade or business that is not substantially related to the purpose constituting the basis of the organization's exemption under section 501. See sec. 1.513–1(a), (d)(1), Income Tax Regs. For the conduct of a trade or business to be substantially related to the purpose or purposes for which the organization was granted a tax exemption, "performance of the services from which the gross income is derived must contribute importantly to the accomplishment of these purposes." Sec. 1.513–1(d)(2), Income Tax Regs. The parties agree that the parking lot and beach club activity constitute a regularly carried-on trade or business, but disagree as to whether the activity is substantially related to the purpose of promoting community welfare, the purpose constituting the basis of the Association's exemption under section 501(c)(4).

The Association contends that the parking lot and beach club activity "[promote] the community welfare of the property owners" of Ocean Pines, which is one of the purposes of the Association that was set forth in its articles of incorporation. It argues that "the ability to walk on the beach or swim either in the ocean or in the pool at the * * * [beach club] * * * directly promotes the health and wellness (i.e., 'community welfare') of the * * * [Association's] members". The IRS argues, first, that the facilities at the beach club are solely recreational and thus would be nontaxable if operated by a section 501(c)(7) organization (a "club" that is "organized for pleasure, recreation, and other nonprofitable purposes") but are taxable because they are operated by a section 501(c)(4) organization. It argues, second, that the beach club and the parking lots do not promote community welfare because they are not open to the general public. We need not determine whether the IRS's first argument is correct. We agree with the IRS's second argument. We conclude that the operation of the beach club and the parking lots does not promote community welfare because they are not accessible to nonmembers; that is, the general public.

In *Flat Top Lake Association, Inc. v. United States,* 868 F.2d 108, 111–113 (4th Cir.1989), the Court of Appeals for the Fourth Circuit held that a homeowners association that restricts the use of its facilities to its members does not promote the welfare of the community. Although *Flat Top* concerned the question of eligibility for section 501(c)(4) status, as opposed to the question of whether a particular activity of a section 501(c)(4) organization is substantially related to the promotion of community welfare and is therefore exempt from the unrelated business income tax, the two questions are related. As the Tax Court held in *Profl. Ins. Agents of Mich. v. Commissioner,* 78 T.C. 246, 267, 1982 WL 11191 (1982), affd. 726 F.2d 1097 (6th Cir.1984):

> Logically, if * * * activities do not contribute to * * * [an organization's tax-exempt purpose] in the context of determining whether an organization qualifies for exemption, then surely these same activities cannot be said to be related to the organization's exempt purpose in the context of the UBTI provisions.

Applying these principles, a homeowners association generally does not promote community welfare if all of the association's facilities are closed to the general public (i.e., closed to nonmembers of the association). See *Flat Top Lake Association, Inc. v. United States, supra* at 111–113. It follows that if a homeowners association has one facility that is closed to the general public, then that facility is not substantially related to the promotion of community welfare. The income from that facility is subject to the unrelated business income tax unless an exception applies.

The IRS does not contend that the Association's tax-exempt status should be revoked. It concedes that most of the Association's facilities and services are open to the general public. Its contention is that income from the portion of its facilities not open to the general public (i.e., the beach club and the parking lots) is subject to the unrelated business income tax because the operation of these facilities is not substantially related to the promotion of community welfare. We agree. The parking lots and the beach club are not accessible to the general public.[62] Only Association members and their guests may park in the parking lots. Although the beach club allows both Association members and nonmembers to access its food and beverage services and its restrooms, its primary facilities (the swimming pool, gym lockers, and showers) are accessible only to the Association's members. Thus, the operation of the parking lots and the beach club is not substantially related to the purpose of "[promoting] social welfare" within the meaning of section 501(c)(4) because they are not open to the general public. Thus, unless an exception applies, the income attributable to the operation of the parking lots and the beach club is subject to the unrelated business income tax.

II. *Whether Parking Lot Income Is Rent From Real Property Within the Meaning of Section 512(b)(3)*

Section 512(a) provides that unrelated business taxable income is income earned by a tax-exempt organization from an unrelated trade or business it regularly carries on, subject to the modifications in section 512(b). One of these modifications, in section 512(b)(3)(A)(i), is that "rents from real property" are excluded from unrelated business taxable income. The IRS claims that the income from operating the two parking lots is not rent from real property because of statements in legislative reports and because, it says, a regulation explicitly bars income from operation of a parking lot from qualification for the exception. The Association contends that under the regulation, the income from operating the two parking lots is rent from real property. We agree with the IRS.

---

62. [4] The Association argues for these purposes that its membership is so broad that its membership should be considered the general public and therefore its parking lots and beach club (which are open only to its members and their guests) should be considered open to the general public. But the court in *Flat Top* held that a homeowners association that operates for the exclusive benefit of its members "does not serve a 'community' as that term relates to the broader concept of social welfare." *Flat Top Lake Association, Inc. v. United States,* 868 F.2d 108, 111 (4th Cir.1989).

When Congress enacted the unrelated business income tax provisions as part of the Revenue Act of 1950, ch. 994, 64 Stat. 906, the House Ways and Means Committee report stated that the provision of the law excluding rents from real property from unrelated business taxable income was intended to exclude income from passive ownership of assets:

> The tax applied to unrelated business taxable income does not apply to dividends, interest, royalties (including of course, overriding royalties), rents (other than certain rents on property acquired with borrowed funds), and gains from sales of leased property. Your committee believes that such "passive" income should not be taxed where it is used for exempt purposes because investments producing incomes of these types have long been recognized as proper for educational and charitable organizations.

H. Rept. 2319, 81st Cong., 2d Sess. 38 (1950), 1950–2 C.B. 380, 409. It later stated:

> The term "rents from real property" does not include income from the *operation* of a hotel but does include rents derived from a *lease* of the hotel itself. Similarly, income derived from the *operation* of a parking lot is not considered "rents from real property." [Emphasis added.]

Id. at 110, 1950–2 C.B. at 459. The Senate Finance Committee report also included the language above regarding operation of a hotel and a parking lot. S. Rept. 2375, 81st Cong., 2d Sess. 108 (1950), 1950–2 C.B. 483, 560.

The tax on unrelated business income, as enacted in 1950, did not apply to churches and some other tax-exempt organizations. Revenue Act of 1950, sec. 421(b)(1), 64 Stat. 948. In 1969, the Treasury Department recommended extending the unrelated business income tax to all tax-exempt organizations. U.S. Treasury Dept. Tax Reform Studies and Proposals (Part 1) 26–27 (1969). The Joint Committee staff supported the Treasury Department's recommendation, citing its own research on the scope of churches' unrelated business activities. One of the examples of an unrelated business given by the staff was a church's operation of a parking lot. Staff of Joint Comm. on Taxation, Tax-Exempt Organizations 20–21 (J. Comm. Print 1969). The House Ways and Means Committee report on the Tax Reform Act of 1969, Pub.L. 91–172, 83 Stat. 487, incorporated the Joint Committee's examples of proliferating church-operated businesses in describing why it was recommending an expansion of the unrelated business income tax:

> There is inequity in taxing certain exempt organizations on their "unrelated business income" and not taxing others. It has become apparent that organizations now subject to the provision and those not subject to it are equally apt to engage in unrelated business. For example, numerous business activities of churches have come to the attention of the committee. Some churches are involved in *operating* chains of religious bookstores, hotels, factories, companies leasing business property, radio and TV stations, newspapers, *parking lots,* record companies, groceries, bakeries, cleaners, candy sale businesses, restaurants, etc. * * * [Emphasis added.]

The bill in extending the unrelated business income tax to churches provides a period of time* * * for churches to dispose of unrelated business or to spin them off in separate taxable corporations.

H. Rept. 91–413 (Part 1), at 47–48 (1969), 1969–3 C.B. 200, 230–231. Similarly, the report of the Senate Finance Committee stated:

In recent years, many of the exempt organizations not now subject to the unrelated business income tax—such as churches, social clubs, fraternal beneficiary societies, etc.—have begun to engage in substantial commercial activity. For example, numerous business activities of churches have come to the attention of the committee. Some churches are engaged in *operating* publishing houses, hotels, factories, radio and TV stations, *parking lots,* newspapers, bakeries, restaurants, etc. Furthermore, it is difficult to justify taxing a university or hospital which runs a public restaurant or hotel or other business and not tax a country club or lodge engaged in similar activity. [Emphasis added.]

S. Rept. 91–552, at 67 (1969), 1969–3 C.B. 423, 467. The reports suggest that income from operating a parking lot was not exempt from the unrelated business income tax under any provision. The legislative history stated or implied four times that the operation of parking lots yields unrelated business taxable income and not rent from real property.

Section 1.512(b)–1(c)(5), Income Tax Regs., provides that income from the operation of a parking lot is not rent from real property. The regulation provides:

Rendering of services. For purposes of this paragraph, payments for the use or occupancy of rooms and other space where services are also rendered to the occupant, such as for the use or occupancy of rooms or other quarters in hotels, boarding houses, or apartment houses furnishing hotel services, or in tourist camps or tourist homes, motor courts, or motels, or *for the use or occupancy of space in parking lots,* warehouses, or storage garages, does not constitute rent from real property. Generally, services are considered rendered to the occupant if they are primarily for his convenience and are other than those usually or customarily rendered in connection with the rental of rooms or other space for occupancy only. The supplying of maid service, for example, constitutes such service; whereas the furnishing of heat and light, the cleaning of public entrances, exits, stairways, and lobbies, the collection of trash, etc., are not considered as services rendered to the occupant. Payments for the use or occupancy of entire private residences or living quarters in duplex or multiple housing units, of offices in any office building, etc., are generally treated as rent from real property. [Emphasis added.]

The Association, in interpreting the above regulation, argues that income from operating a parking lot is rent from real property unless the services provided by the tax-exempt organization in operating it are "substantial." It states that the services it provides at the lots, i.e. the provision of parking guards to open the lots and to check parking decals, are insubstantial. It compares its level of service to its parking lot customers to the level of service involved in the trash collection mentioned in the regulation. But the test in the regulation for determining whether the services are rendered to the occupant (and therefore disqualify the organization from using the rental exception) is not whether the services provided are substantial, but whether the services are (1) "primarily" for the "convenience" of the occupant and (2) are "other than those usually or customarily rendered in connection with the rental of rooms or other space for occupancy only." And as to the question of whether the services provided by an operator of a parking lot satisfy this test, the regulation also provides guidance. The first sentence of the regulation lists "the use or occupancy of space in parking lots" as an example of "use or occupancy of rooms and other space where services are also rendered to the occupant". The regulation, as we interpret it, determines that the services provided by an operator of a parking lot (at least a typical parking lot) are primarily for the convenience of the customer and are other than those usually or customarily rendered in connection with the rental of rooms or space for occupancy only. Although this conclusion might not apply to a parking lot that is so unusual that it would not be considered a "parking lot" within the ordinary meaning of the term, there is nothing to suggest that the services the Association provides to its parking lot customers are unusual in this context. Thus, the net income the Association earned from operating the parking lots during the summer months does not constitute rent from real property as defined in section 512(b)(3). The net income is subject to the unrelated business income tax.

In reaching our holdings here, we have considered all arguments made, and, to the extent not mentioned above, we conclude they are moot, irrelevant, or without merit.

To reflect the foregoing,

Decision will be entered under Rule 155.

Proposed Regulations on the Definition of Real Estate Investment Trust Real Property

REG-150760-13 (June 2, 2014)

SUMMARY:

This document contains proposed regulations that clarify the definition of real property for purposes of the real estate investment trust provisions of the Internal Revenue Code (Code). These proposed regulations provide guidance to real estate investment trusts and their shareholders. This document also provides notice of a public hearing on these proposed regulations.

* * *

BACKGROUND

This document contains amendments to the Income Tax Regulations (26 CFR part 1) relating to real estate investment trusts (REITs). Section 856 of the Code defines a REIT by setting forth various requirements. One of the requirements for a taxpayer to qualify as a REIT is that at the close of each quarter of the taxable year at least 75 percent of the value of its total assets is represented by real estate assets, cash and cash items (including receivables), and Government securities. See section 856(c)(4). Section 856(c)(5)(B) defines *real estate assets* to include real property and interests in real property. Section 856(c)(5)(C) indicates that *real property* means "land or improvements thereon." Section 1.856-3(d) of the Income Tax Regulations, promulgated in 1962, defines real property for purposes of the regulations under sections 856 through 859 as—

> land or improvements thereon, such as buildings or other inherently permanent structures thereon (including items which are structural components of such buildings or structures). In addition, the term "real property" includes interests in real property. Local law definitions will not be controlling for purposes of determining the meaning of the term "real property" as used in section 856 and the regulations thereunder. The term includes, for example, the wiring in a building, plumbing systems, central heating, or central air-conditioning machinery, pipes or ducts, elevators or escalators installed in the building, or other items which are structural components of a building or other permanent structure. The term does not include assets accessory to the operation of a business, such as machinery, printing press, transportation equipment which is not a structural component of the building, office equipment, refrigerators, individual air-conditioning units, grocery counters, furnishings of a motel, hotel, or office building, etc., even though such items may be termed fixtures under local law.

Section 1.856-3(d).

The IRS issued revenue rulings between 1969 and 1975 addressing whether certain assets qualify as real property for purposes of section 856. Specifically, the published rulings describe assets such as railroad properties,[63] mobile home units permanently installed in a planned community,[64] air rights over real property,[65] interests in mortgage loans secured by total energy systems,[66] and mortgage loans secured by microwave transmission property,[67] and the rulings address whether the assets qualify as either real property or interests in real property under section 856. Since these published rulings were issued, REITs have sought to invest in various types of assets that are not directly addressed by the regulations or the published rulings, and have asked for and received letter rulings from the IRS addressing certain of these assets. Because letter rulings are limited to their particular facts and may not be relied upon by taxpayers other than the taxpayer that received the ruling, see section 6110(k)(3), letter rulings are not a substitute for published guidance. The IRS and the Treasury Department recognize the need to provide additional published guid-

---

63. [2] Rev. Rul. 69–94, 1969–1 CB 189.
64. [3] Rev. Rul. 71–220, 1971–1 CB 210.
65. [4] Rev. Rul. 71–286, 1971–2 CB 263.
66. [5] Rev. Rul. 73–425, 1973–2 CB 222.
67. [6] Rev. Rul. 75–424, 1975–2 CB 269.

ance on the definition of real property under sections 856 through 859. This document proposes regulations that define real property for purposes of sections 856 through 859 by providing a framework to analyze the types of assets in which REITs seek to invest. These proposed regulations provide neither explicit nor implicit guidance regarding whether various types of income are described in section 856(c)(3).[68]

EXPLANATION OF PROVISIONS

Consistent with section 856, the existing regulations, and published guidance interpreting those regulations, these proposed regulations define *real property* to include land, inherently permanent structures, and structural components. In determining whether an item is land, an inherently permanent structure, or a structural component, these proposed regulations first test whether the item is a *distinct asset*, which is the unit of property to which the definitions in these proposed regulations apply.

In addition, these proposed regulations identify certain types of intangible assets that are real property or interests in real property for purposes of sections 856 through 859. These proposed regulations include examples to illustrate the application of the principles of these proposed regulations to determine whether certain distinct assets are real property for purposes of sections 856 through 859.

Distinct asset

These proposed regulations provide that each distinct asset is tested individually to determine whether the distinct asset is real or personal property. Items that are specifically listed in these proposed regulations as types of buildings and other inherently permanent structures are distinct assets. Assets and systems specifically listed in these proposed regulations as types of structural components also are treated as distinct assets. Other distinct assets are identified using the factors provided by these proposed regulations. All listed factors must be considered, and no one factor is determinative.

Land

These proposed regulations define land to include not only a parcel of ground, but the air and water space directly above the parcel. Therefore, water space directly above the seabed is land, even though the water itself flows over the seabed and does not remain in place. Land includes crops and other natural products of land until the crops or other natural products are detached or removed from the land.

Inherently permanent structures

Inherently permanent structures and their structural components are real property for purposes of sections 856 through 859. These proposed regulations clarify that inherently permanent structures are structures, including buildings, that have a passive function. Therefore, if a distinct asset has an active function, such as producing

---

68. [7] One of the requirements for qualifying as a REIT is that a sufficiently large fraction of an entity's gross income be derived from certain specified types of income (which include "rents from real property" and "interest on obligations secured by mortgages on real property or on interests in real property"). Section 856(c)(3).

goods, the distinct asset is not an inherently permanent structure under these proposed regulations. In addition to serving a passive function, a distinct asset must be inherently permanent to be an inherently permanent structure. For this purpose, permanence may be established not only by the method by which the structure is affixed but also by the weight of the structure alone.

These proposed regulations supplement the definition of inherently permanent structure by providing a safe harbor list of distinct assets that are buildings, as well as a list of distinct assets that are other inherently permanent structures. If a distinct asset is on one of these lists, either as a building or as an inherently permanent structure, the distinct asset is real property for purposes of sections 856 through 859, and a facts and circumstances analysis is not necessary. If a distinct asset is not listed as either a building or an inherently permanent structure, these proposed regulations provide facts and circumstances that must be considered in determining whether the distinct asset is either a building or other inherently permanent structure. All listed factors must be considered, and no one factor is determinative.

One distinct asset that these proposed regulations list as an inherently permanent structure is an outdoor advertising display subject to an election to be treated as real property under section 1033(g)(3). Section 1033(g)(3) provides taxpayers with an election to treat certain outdoor advertising displays[69] as real property for purposes of Chapter 1 of the Code.

Structural components

These proposed regulations define a structural component as a distinct asset that is a constituent part of and integrated into an inherently permanent structure, that serves the inherently permanent structure in its passive function, and does not produce or contribute to the production of income other than consideration for the use or occupancy of space. An entire system is analyzed as a single distinct asset and, therefore, as a single structural component, if the components of the system work together to serve the inherently permanent structure with a utility-like function, such as systems that provide a building with electricity, heat, or water.[70] For a structural component to be real property under sections 856 through 859, the taxpayer's interest in the structural component must be held by the taxpayer together with the taxpayer's interest in the inherently permanent structure to which the structural component is functionally related. Additionally, if a distinct asset that is a structural component is customized in connection with the provision of rentable space in an inherently per-

---

69. [8] Section 1.1033(g)–1(b)(3) defines *outdoor advertising display* for purposes of the section 1033 election as "a rigidly assembled sign, display, or device that constitutes, or is used to display, a commercial or other advertisement to the public and is permanently affixed to the ground or permanently attached to a building or other inherently permanent structure."

70. [9] See Rev. Rul. 73–425, 1973–2 CB 222 (holding that a total energy system that provides a building with electricity, steam or hot water, and refrigeration may be a structural component of that building). The IRS and the Treasury Department are considering guidance to address the treatment of any income earned when a system that provides energy to an inherently permanent structure held by the REIT also transfers excess energy to a utility company.

manent structure, the customization of that distinct asset does not cause it to fail to be a structural component.

Under these proposed regulations, an asset or system that is treated as a distinct asset is a structural component, and thus real property for purposes of sections 856 through 859, if the asset or system is included on the safe harbor list of assets that are structural components. If an asset or system that is treated as a distinct asset is not specifically listed as a structural component, these proposed regulations provide a list of facts and circumstances that must be considered in determining whether the distinct asset or system qualifies as a structural component. No one factor is determinative.

These proposed regulations do not retain the phrase "assets accessory to the operation of a business," which the existing regulations use to describe an asset with an active function that is not real property for purposes of the regulations under sections 856 through 859. The IRS and the Treasury Department believe that the phrase "assets accessory to the operation of a business" has created uncertainty because the existing regulations are unclear whether certain assets that are permanent structures or components thereof nevertheless fail to be real property because they are used in the operation of a business. Instead, these proposed regulations adopt an approach that considers whether the distinct asset in question either serves a passive function common to real property or serves the inherently permanent structure to which it is constituent in that structure's passive function. On the other hand, if an asset has an active function, such as a distinct asset that produces, manufactures, or creates a product, then the asset is not real property unless the asset is a structural component that serves a utility-like function with respect to the inherently permanent structure of which it is a constituent part. Similarly, if an asset produces or contributes to the production of income other than consideration for the use or occupancy of space, then that asset is not real property. Thus, items that were assets accessory to the operation of a business under the existing regulations will continue to be excluded from the definition of real property for purposes of sections 856 through 859 either because they are not inherently permanent or because they serve an active function. These distinct assets include, for example, machinery; office, offshore drilling, testing, and other equipment; transportation equipment that is not a structural component of a building; printing presses; refrigerators; individual air-conditioning units; grocery counters; furnishings of a motel, hotel, or office building; antennae; waveguides; transmitting, receiving, and multiplex equipment; prewired modular racks; display racks and shelves; gas pumps; and hydraulic car lifts.

Intangible assets that are real property

These proposed regulations also provide that certain intangible assets are real property for purposes of sections 856 through 859. To be real property, the intangible asset must derive its value from tangible real property and be inseparable from the tangible real property from which the value is derived. Under § 1.856-2(d)(3) the assets of a REIT are its gross assets determined in accordance with generally accepted accounting principles (GAAP). Intangibles established under GAAP when a taxpayer acquires tangible real property may meet the definition of real property intangibles.

A license or permit solely for the use, occupancy, or enjoyment of tangible real property may also be an interest in real property because it is in the nature of an interest in real property (similar to a lease or easement). If an intangible asset produces, or contributes to the production of, income other than consideration for the use or occupancy of space, then the asset is not real property or an interest in real property. Thus, for example, a permit allowing a taxpayer to engage in or operate a particular business is not an interest in real property.

Other definitions of real property

The terms "real property" and "personal property" appear in numerous Code provisions that have diverse contexts and varying legislative purposes. In some cases, certain types of assets are specifically designated as real property or as personal property by statute, while in other cases the statute is silent as to the meaning of those terms. Ordinarily, under basic principles of statutory construction, the use of the same term in multiple Code provisions would imply (absent specific statutory modifications) that Congress intended the same meaning to apply to that term for each of the provisions in which it appears. In the case of the terms "real property" and "personal property," however, both the regulatory process and decades of litigation have led to different definitions of these terms, in part because taxpayers have advocated for broader or narrower definitions in different contexts.

For example, in the depreciation and (prior) investment tax credit contexts, a broad definition of personal property (and a narrow definition of real property) is ordinarily more favorable to taxpayers. A tangible asset may generally be depreciated faster if it is personal property than if it is considered real property, see section 168(c) and (g)(2)(C), and (prior) section 38 property primarily included tangible personal property and excluded a building and its structural components, see § 1.48–1(c) and (d). During decades of controversy, taxpayers sought to broaden the meaning of tangible personal property and to narrow the meanings of building and structural component in efforts to qualify for the investment tax credit or for faster depreciation. That litigation resulted in courts adopting a relatively broad definition of tangible personal property (and correspondingly narrow definition of real property) for depreciation and investment tax credit purposes.

Similarly, in the context of the Foreign Investment in Real Property Tax Act (FIRPTA), codified at section 897 of the Code, a narrower definition of real property is generally more favorable to taxpayers. Enacted in 1980, FIRPTA is intended to subject foreign investors to the same U.S. tax treatment on gains from the disposition of interests in U.S. real property that applies to U.S. investors. Accordingly, foreign investors can more easily avoid U.S. tax to the extent that the definition of real property is narrow for FIRPTA purposes. As in the depreciation and investment tax credit contexts, this situation has led to vigorous debate over the appropriate characterization of certain types of assets (such as intangible assets) that may have characteristics associated with real property but do not fall within the traditional categories of buildings and structural components. See, for example, Advance Notice of Proposed Rulemaking, Infrastructure Improvements Under Section 897, published in the **Federal Register**

(REG–130342–08, 73 FR 64901) on October 31, 2008 (noting that taxpayers may be taking the position that a governmental permit to operate a toll bridge or toll road is not a United States real property interest for purposes of section 897 and stating that the IRS and the Treasury Department are of the view that such a permit may properly be characterized as a United States real property interest in certain circumstances). In the case of FIRPTA, however, Congress modified the definition of real property to include items of personal property that are associated with the use of real property. See section 897(c)(6)(B) (including as real property movable walls, furnishings, and other personal property associated with the use of the real property). Consequently, it is explicitly contemplated in section 897 that an item of property may be treated as a United States real property interest for FIRPTA purposes, notwithstanding that it is characterized as personal property for other purposes of the Code.

In the REIT context, taxpayers ordinarily benefit from a relatively broad definition of real property. Consequently, taxpayers have generally advocated in the REIT context for a more expansive definition of real property than applies in the depreciation and (prior) investment tax credit contexts. In drafting these regulations, the Treasury Department and the IRS have sought to balance the general principle that common terms used in different provisions should have common meanings with the particular policies underlying the REIT provisions. These proposed regulations define real property only for purposes of sections 856 through 859. The IRS and the Treasury Department request comments, however, on the extent to which the various meanings of real property that appear in the Treasury regulations should be reconciled, whether through modifications to these proposed regulations or through modifications to the regulations under other Code provisions.

PROPOSED EFFECTIVE DATE

The IRS and the Treasury Department view these proposed regulations as a clarification of the existing definition of real property and not as a modification that will cause a significant reclassification of property. As such, these proposed regulations are proposed to be effective for calendar quarters beginning after these proposed regulations are published as final regulations in the **Federal Register**. The IRS and the Treasury Department solicit comments regarding the proposed effective date.

SPECIAL ANALYSES

It has been determined that this notice of proposed rulemaking is not a significant regulatory action as defined in Executive Order 12866, as supplemented by Executive Order 13653. Therefore, a regulatory assessment is not required. It also has been determined that section 553(b) of the Administrative Procedure Act (5 U.S.C. chapter 5) does not apply to these regulations, and because the regulations do not impose a collection of information on small entities, the Regulatory Flexibility Act (5 U.S.C. chapter 6) does not apply. Pursuant to section 7805(f) of the Code, this notice of proposed rulemaking has been submitted to the Chief Counsel for Advocacy of the Small Business Administration for comment on its impact on small business.

* * *

§ 1.856-3 Definitions.

* * *

(d) *Real property.* See § 1.856-10 for the definition of *real property.*

* * *

Par. 3. Section 1.856-10 is added to read as follows:

§ 1.856-10 Definition of real property.

(a) *In general.* This section provides definitions for purposes of part II, subchapter M, chapter 1 of the Internal Revenue Code (Code). Paragraph (b) of this section defines real property, which includes land as defined under paragraph (c) of this section, and improvements to land as defined under paragraph (d) of this section. Improvements to land include inherently permanent structures as defined under paragraph (d)(2) of this section, and structural components of inherently permanent structures as defined under paragraph (d)(3) of this section. Paragraph (e) of this section provides rules for determining whether an item is a distinct asset for purposes of applying the definitions in paragraphs (b), (c), and (d) of this section. Paragraph (f) of this section identifies intangible assets that are real property or interests in real property. Paragraph (g) of this section provides examples illustrating the rules of paragraphs (b) through (f) of this section.

(b) *Real property.* The term *real property* means land and improvements to land. Local law definitions are not controlling for purposes of determining the meaning of the term real property.

(c) *Land.* Land includes water and air space superjacent to land and natural products and deposits that are unsevered from the land. Natural products and deposits, such as crops, water, ores, and minerals, cease to be real property when they are severed, extracted, or removed from the land. The storage of severed or extracted natural products or deposits, such as crops, water, ores, and minerals, in or upon real property does not cause the stored property to be recharacterized as real property.

(d) *Improvements to land*—(1) *In general.* The term *improvements to land* means inherently permanent structures and their structural components.

(2) *Inherently permanent structure*—(i) *In general.* The term *inherently permanent structure* means any permanently affixed building or other structure. Affixation may be to land or to another inherently permanent structure and may be by weight alone. If the affixation is reasonably expected to last indefinitely based on all the facts and circumstances, the affixation is considered permanent. A distinct asset that serves an active function, such as an item of machinery or equipment, is not a building or other inherently permanent structure.

(ii) *Building*—(A) *In general.* A building encloses a space within its walls and is covered by a roof.

(B) *Types of buildings.* Buildings include the following permanently affixed distinct assets: houses; apartments; hotels; factory and office buildings; warehouses; barns; enclosed garages; enclosed transportation stations and terminals; and stores.

(iii) *Other inherently permanent structures*—(A) *In general.* Other inherently permanent structures serve a passive function, such as to contain, support, shelter, cover, or protect, and do not serve an active function such as to manufacture, create, produce, convert, or transport.

(B) *Types of other inherently permanent structures.* Other inherently permanent structures include the following permanently affixed distinct assets: microwave transmission, cell, broadcast, and electrical transmission towers; telephone poles; parking facilities; bridges; tunnels; roadbeds; railroad tracks; transmission lines; pipelines; fences; in-ground swimming pools; offshore drilling platforms; storage structures such as silos and oil and gas storage tanks; stationary wharves and docks; and outdoor advertising displays for which an election has been properly made under section 1033(g)(3).

(iv) *Facts and circumstances determination.* If a distinct asset (within the meaning of paragraph (e) of this section) does not serve an active function as described in paragraph (d)(2)(iii)(A) of this section, and is not otherwise listed in paragraph (d)(2)(ii)(B) or (d)(2)(iii)(B) of this section or in guidance published in the Internal Revenue Bulletin (see § 601.601(d)(2)(ii) of this chapter), the determination of whether that asset is an inherently permanent structure is based on all the facts and circumstances. In particular, the following factors must be taken into account:

(A) The manner in which the distinct asset is affixed to real property;

(B) Whether the distinct asset is designed to be removed or to remain in place indefinitely;

(C) The damage that removal of the distinct asset would cause to the item itself or to the real property to which it is affixed;

(D) Any circumstances that suggest the expected period of affixation is not indefinite (for example, a lease that requires or permits removal of the distinct asset upon the expiration of the lease); and

(E) The time and expense required to move the distinct asset.

(3) *Structural components*—(i) *In general.* The term *structural component* means any distinct asset (within the meaning of paragraph (e) of this section) that is a constituent part of and integrated into an inherently permanent structure, serves the inherently permanent structure in its passive function, and, even if capable of producing income other than consideration for the use or occupancy of space, does not produce or contribute to the production of such

income. If interconnected assets work together to serve an inherently permanent structure with a utility-like function (for example, systems that provide a building with electricity, heat, or water), the assets are analyzed together as one distinct asset that may be a structural component. Structural components are real property only if the interest held therein is included with an equivalent interest held by the taxpayer in the inherently permanent structure to which the structural component is functionally related. If a distinct asset is customized in connection with the rental of space in or on an inherently permanent structure to which the asset relates, the customization does not affect whether the distinct asset is a structural component.

(ii) *Types of structural components.* Structural components include the following distinct assets and systems: wiring; plumbing systems; central heating and air-conditioning systems; elevators or escalators; walls; floors; ceilings; permanent coverings of walls, floors, and ceilings; windows; doors; insulation; chimneys; fire suppression systems, such as sprinkler systems and fire alarms; fire escapes; central refrigeration systems; integrated security systems; and humidity control systems.

(iii) *Facts and circumstances determination.* If a distinct asset (within the meaning of paragraph (e) of this section) is not otherwise listed in paragraph (d)(3)(ii) of this section or in guidance published in the Internal Revenue Bulletin (see § 601.601(d)(2)(ii) of this chapter), the determination of whether the asset is a structural component is based on all the facts and circumstances. In particular, the following factors must be taken into account:

(A) The manner, time, and expense of installing and removing the distinct asset;

(B) Whether the distinct asset is designed to be moved;

(C) The damage that removal of the distinct asset would cause to the item itself or to the inherently permanent structure to which it is affixed;

(D) Whether the distinct asset serves a utility-like function with respect to the inherently permanent structure;

(E) Whether the distinct asset serves the inherently permanent structure in its passive function;

(F) Whether the distinct asset produces income from consideration for the use or occupancy of space in or upon the inherently permanent structure;

(G) Whether the distinct asset is installed during construction of the inherently permanent structure;

(H) Whether the distinct asset will remain if the tenant vacates the premises; and

(I) Whether the owner of the real property is also the legal owner of the distinct asset.

(e) *Distinct asset*—(1) *In general.* A distinct asset is analyzed separately from any other assets to which the asset relates to determine if the asset is real property, whether as land, an inherently permanent structure, or a structural component of an inherently permanent structure.

(2) *Facts and circumstances.* The determination of whether a particular separately identifiable item of property is a distinct asset is based on all the facts and circumstances. In particular, the following factors must be taken into account:

(i) Whether the item is customarily sold or acquired as a single unit rather than as a component part of a larger asset;

(ii) Whether the item can be separated from a larger asset, and if so, the cost of separating the item from the larger asset;

(iii) Whether the item is commonly viewed as serving a useful function independent of a larger asset of which it is a part; and

(iv) Whether separating the item from a larger asset of which it is a part impairs the functionality of the larger asset.

(f) *Intangible assets*—(1) *In general.* If an intangible asset, including an intangible asset established under generally accepted accounting principles (GAAP) as a result of an acquisition of real property or an interest in real property, derives its value from real property or an interest in real property, is inseparable from that real property or interest in real property, and does not produce or contribute to the production of income other than consideration for the use or occupancy of space, then the intangible asset is real property or an interest in real property.

(2) *Licenses and permits.* A license, permit, or other similar right solely for the use, enjoyment, or occupation of land or an inherently permanent structure that is in the nature of a leasehold or easement generally is an interest in real property. A license or permit to engage in or operate a business generally is not real property or an interest in real property because it produces or contributes to the production of income other than consideration for the use or occupancy of space.

(g) *Examples.* The following examples demonstrate the rules of this section. *Examples 1* and *2* illustrate the definition of land as provided in paragraph (c) of this section. *Examples 3* through *10* illustrate the definition of improvements to land as provided in paragraph (d) of this section. Finally, *Examples 11* through *13* illustrate whether certain intangible assets are real property or interests in real property as provided in paragraph (f) of this section.

Example 1. Natural products of land. A is a real estate investment trust (REIT). REIT A owns land with perennial fruit-bearing plants. REIT A leases the fruit-bearing plants to a tenant on a long-term triple net lease basis and grants the tenant an easement on the land. The unsevered plants are natural products of the land and are land within the meaning of paragraph (c) of this section. Fruit from the plants is harvested annually. Upon severance from the land, the harvested fruit ceases to qualify as land. Storage of the harvested fruit upon or within real property does not cause the harvested fruit to be real property.

Example 2. Water space superjacent to land. REIT B leases a marina from a governmental entity. The marina is comprised of U-shaped boat slips and end ties. The U-shaped boat slips are spaces on the water that are surrounded by a dock on three sides. The end ties are spaces on the water at the end of a slip or on a long, straight dock. REIT B rents the boat slips and end ties to boat owners. The boat slips and end ties are water space superjacent to land that is land within the meaning of paragraph (c) of this section and, therefore, are real property.

Example 3   Indoor sculpture. (i) REIT C owns an office building and a large sculpture in the atrium of the building. The sculpture measures 30 feet tall by 18 feet wide and weighs five tons. The building was specifically designed to support the sculpture, which is permanently affixed to the building by supports embedded in the building's foundation. The sculpture was constructed within the building. Removal would be costly and time consuming and would destroy the sculpture. The sculpture is reasonably expected to remain in the building indefinitely. The sculpture does not manufacture, create, produce, convert, transport, or serve any similar active function.

    (ii) When analyzed to determine whether it is an inherently permanent structure using the factors provided in paragraph (d)(2)(iv) of this section, the sculpture—

        (A) Is permanently affixed to the building by supports embedded in the building's foundation;

        (B) Is not designed to be removed and is designed to remain in place indefinitely;

        (C) Would be damaged if removed and would damage the building to which it is affixed;

        (D) Will remain affixed to the building after any tenant vacates the premises and will remain affixed to the building indefinitely; and

        (E) Would require significant time and expense to move.

    (iii) The factors described in this paragraph (g) *Example 3* (ii)(A) through (ii)(E) all support the conclusion that the sculpture is an inherently permanent structure within the meaning of paragraph (d)(2) of this section and, therefore, is real property.

Example 4. Bus shelters. (i) REIT D owns 400 bus shelters, each of which consists of four posts, a roof, and panels enclosing two or three sides. REIT D enters into a long-term lease with a local transit authority for use of the bus shelters. Each bus shelter is prefabricated from steel and is bolted to the sidewalk. Bus shelters are disassembled and moved when bus routes change. Moving a bus shelter takes less than a day and does not significantly damage either the bus shelter or the real property to which it was affixed.

(ii) The bus shelters are not enclosed transportation stations or terminals and do not otherwise meet the definition of a building in paragraph (d)(2)(ii) of this section nor are they listed as types of other inherently permanent structures in paragraph (d)(2)(iii)(B) of this section.

(iii) When analyzed to determine whether they are inherently permanent structures using the factors provided in paragraph (d)(2)(iv) of this section, the bus shelters —

(A) Are not permanently affixed to the land or an inherently permanent structure;

(B) Are designed to be removed and are not designed to remain in place indefinitely;

(C) Would not be damaged if removed and would not damage the sidewalks to which they are affixed;

(D) Will not remain affixed after the local transit authority vacates the site and will not remain affixed indefinitely; and

(E) Would not require significant time and expense to move.

(iv) The factors described in this paragraph (g) *Example 4* (iii)(A) through (iii)(E) all support the conclusion that the bus shelters are not inherently permanent structures within the meaning of paragraph (d)(2) of this section. Although the bus shelters serve a passive function of sheltering, the bus shelters are not permanently affixed, which means the bus shelters are not inherently permanent structures within the meaning of paragraph (d)(2) of this section and, therefore, are not real property.

Example 5. Cold storage warehouse. (i) REIT E owns a refrigerated warehouse (Cold Storage Warehouse). REIT E enters into long-term triple net leases with tenants. The tenants use the Cold Storage Warehouse to store perishable products. Certain components and utility systems within the Cold Storage Warehouse have been customized to accommodate the tenants' need for refrigerated storage space. For example, the Cold Storage Warehouse has customized freezer walls and a central refrigeration system. Freezer walls within the Cold Storage Warehouse are specifically designed to maintain the desired temperature within the warehouse. The freezer walls and central refrigeration system are each comprised of a series of interconnected assets that work together to serve a utility-like function within the Cold Storage Warehouse, were installed during construction of the building, and will remain in place when a tenant vacates the premises. The freezer walls and central refrigeration system were each designed to remain permanently in place.

(ii) Walls and central refrigeration systems are listed as structural components in paragraph (d)(3)(ii) of this section and, therefore, are real property. The customization of the freezer walls does not affect their qualification as structural components. Therefore, the freezer walls and central refrigeration system are structural components of REIT E's Cold Storage Warehouse.

Example 6.   Data center. (i) REIT F owns a building that it leases to a tenant under a long-term triple net lease. Certain interior components and utility systems within the building have been customized to accommodate the particular requirements for housing computer servers. For example, to accommodate the computer servers, REIT F's building has been customized to provide a higher level of electrical power, central air-conditioning, telecommunications access, and redundancies built into the systems that provide these utilities than is generally available to tenants of a conventional office building. In addition, the space for computer servers in REIT F's building is constructed on raised flooring, which is necessary to accommodate the electrical, telecommunications, and central heating and air-conditioning infrastructure required for the servers. The following systems of REIT F's building have been customized to permit the building to house the servers: central heating and air-conditioning system, integrated security system, fire suppression system, humidity control system, electrical distribution and redundancy system (Electrical System), and telecommunication infrastructure system (each, a System). Each of these Systems is comprised of a series of interconnected assets that work together to serve a utility-like function within the building. The Systems were installed during construction of the building and will remain in place when the tenant vacates the premises. Each of the Systems was designed to remain permanently in place and was customized by enhancing the capacity of the System in connection with the rental of space within the building.

(ii) The central heating and air-conditioning system, integrated security system, fire suppression system, and humidity control system are listed as structural components in paragraph (d)(3)(ii) of this section and, therefore, are real property. The customization of these Systems does not affect the qualification of these Systems as structural components of REIT F's building within the meaning of paragraph (d)(3) of this section.

(iii) In addition to wiring, which is listed as a structural component in paragraph (d)(3)(ii) of this section and, therefore, is real property, the Electrical System and telecommunication infrastructure system include equipment used to ensure that the tenant is provided with uninterruptable, stable power and telecommunication services. When analyzed to determine whether they are structural components using the factors in paragraph (d)(3)(iii) of this section, the Electrical System and telecommunication infrastructure system—

(A) Are embedded within the walls and floors of the building and would be costly to remove;

(B) Are not designed to be moved, are designed specifically for the particular building of which they are a part, and are intended to remain permanently in place;

(C) Would not be significantly damaged upon removal and, although they would damage the walls and floors in which they are embedded, they would not significantly damage the building if they were removed;

(D) Serve a utility-like function with respect to the building;

(E) Serve the building in its passive functions of containing, sheltering, and protecting computer servers;

(F) Produce income as consideration for the use or occupancy of space within the building;

(G) Were installed during construction of the building;

(H) Will remain in place when the tenant vacates the premises; and

(I) Are owned by REIT F, which also owns the building.

(iv) The factors described in this paragraph (g) *Example 6* (iii)(A), (iii)(B), and (iii)(D) through (iii)(I) all support the conclusion that the Electrical System and telecommunication infrastructure system are structural components of REIT F's building within the meaning of paragraph (d)(3) of this section and, therefore, are real property. The factor described in this paragraph (g) *Example 6* (iii)(C) would support a conclusion that the Electrical System and telecommunication infrastructure system are not structural components. However this factor does not outweigh the factors supporting the conclusion that the Electric System and telecommunication infrastructure system are structural components.

Example 7   Partitions. (i) REIT G owns an office building that it leases to tenants under long-term triple net leases. Partitions are used to delineate space between tenants and within each tenant's space. The office building has two types of interior, non-load-bearing drywall partition systems: a conventional drywall partition system (Conventional Partition System) and a modular drywall partition system (Modular Partition System). Neither the Conventional Partition System nor the Modular Partition System was installed during construction of the office building. Conventional Partition Systems are comprised of fully integrated gypsum board partitions, studs, joint tape, and covering joint compound. Modular Partition Systems are comprised of assembled panels, studs, tracks, and exposed joints. Both the Conventional Partition System and the Modular Partition System reach from the floor to the ceiling.

(ii) Depending on the needs of a new tenant, the Conventional Partition System may remain in place when a tenant vacates the premises. The Conventional Partition System is designed and constructed to remain in areas not subject to reconfiguration or expansion. The Conventional Partition System can be removed only by demolition, and, once removed, neither the Conventional Partition System nor its components can be reused. Removal of the Conventional Partition System causes substantial damage to the Conventional Partition System itself but does not cause substantial damage to the building.

(iii) Modular Partition Systems are typically removed when a tenant vacates the premises. Modular Partition Systems are not designed or constructed to remain permanently in place. Modular Partition Systems are designed and constructed to be movable. Each Modular Partition System can be readily removed, remains in substantially the same condition as before, and can be reused. Removal of a Modular Partition System does not cause any substantial damage to the Modular Partition System itself or to the building. The Modular Partition System may be moved to accommodate the reconfigurations of the interior space within the office building for various tenants that occupy the building.

(iv) The Conventional Partition System is a wall, and walls are listed as structural components in paragraph (d)(3)(ii) of this section. The Conventional Partition System, therefore, is real property.

(v) When analyzed to determine whether it is a structural component using the factors provided in paragraph (d)(3)(iii) of this section, the Modular Partition System—

(A) Is installed and removed quickly and with little expense;

(B) Is not designed specifically for the particular building of which it is a part and is not intended to remain permanently in place;

(C) Is not damaged, and the building is not damaged, upon its removal;

(D) Does not serve a utility-like function with respect to the building;

(E) Serves the building in its passive functions of containing and protecting the tenants' assets;

(F) Produces income only as consideration for the use or occupancy of space within the building;

(G) Was not installed during construction of the building;

(H) Will not remain in place when a tenant vacates the premises; and

(I) Is owned by REIT G.

(vi) The factors described in this paragraph (g) *Example 7* (v)(A) through (v)(D), (v)(G), and (v)(H) all support the conclusion that the Modular Partition System is not a structural component of REIT G's building within the meaning of paragraph (d)(3) of this section and, therefore, is not real property. The factors described in this paragraph (g) *Example 7* (v)(E), (v)(F), and (v)(I) would support a conclusion that the Modular Partition System is a structural component. These factors, however, do not outweigh the factors supporting the conclusion that the Modular Partition System is not a structural component.

Example 8. Solar energy site. (i) REIT H owns a solar energy site, among the components of which are land, photovoltaic modules (PV Modules), mounts, and an exit wire. REIT H enters into a long-term triple net lease with a tenant for the solar energy site. The mounts (that is, the foundations and racks) support the PV Modules. The racks are affixed to the land through foundations made from poured concrete. The mounts will remain in place when the tenant vacates the solar energy site. The PV Modules convert solar photons into electric energy (electricity). The exit wire is buried underground, is connected to equipment that is in turn connected to the PV Modules, and transmits the electricity produced by the PV Modules to an electrical power grid, through which the electricity is distributed for sale to third parties.

(ii) REIT H's PV Modules, mounts, and exit wire are each separately identifiable items. Separation from a mount does not affect the ability of a PV Module to convert photons to electricity. Separation from the equipment to which it is attached does not affect the ability of the exit wire to transmit electricity to the electrical power grid. The types of PV Modules and exit wire that REIT H owns are each customarily sold or acquired as single units. Removal of the PV Modules from the mounts to which they relate does not damage the function of the mounts as support structures and removal is not costly. The PV Modules are commonly viewed as serving the useful function of converting photons to electricity, independent of the mounts. Disconnecting the exit wire from the equipment to which it is attached does not damage the function of that equipment, and the disconnection is not costly. The PV Modules, mounts, and exit wire are each distinct assets within the meaning of paragraph (e) of this section.

(iii) The land is real property as defined in paragraph (c) of this section.

(iv) The mounts are designed and constructed to remain permanently in place, and they have a passive function of supporting the PV Modules. When analyzed to determine whether they are inherently permanent structures using the factors provided in paragraph (d)(2)(iv) of this section, the mounts—

(A) Are permanently affixed to the land through the concrete foundations or molded concrete anchors (which are part of the mounts);

(B) Are not designed to be removed and are designed to remain in place indefinitely;

(C) Would be damaged if removed;

(D) Will remain affixed to the land after the tenant vacates the premises and will remain affixed to the land indefinitely; and

(E) Would require significant time and expense to move.

(v) The factors described in this paragraph (g) *Example 8* (iv)(A) through (iv)(E) all support the conclusion that the mounts are inherently permanent structures within the meaning of paragraph (d)(2) of this section and, therefore, are real property.

(vi) The PV Modules convert solar photons into electricity that is transmitted through an electrical power grid for sale to third parties. The conversion is an active function. The PV Modules are items of machinery or equipment and are not inherently permanent structures within the meaning of paragraph (d)(2) of this section and, therefore, are not real property. The PV Modules do not serve the mounts in their passive function of providing support; instead, the PV Modules produce electricity for sale to third parties, which is income other than consideration for the use or occupancy of space. The PV Modules are not structural components of REIT H's mounts within the meaning of paragraph (d)(3) of this section and, therefore, are not real property.

(vii) The exit wire is buried under the ground and transmits the electricity produced by the PV Modules to the electrical power grid. The exit wire was installed during construction of the solar energy site and is designed to remain permanently in place. The exit wire is inherently permanent and is a transmission line, which is listed as an inherently permanent structure in paragraph (d)(2)(iii)(B) of this section. Therefore, the exit wire is real property.

Example 9. Solar-powered building. (i) REIT I owns a solar energy site similar to that described in *Example 8*, except that REIT I's solar energy site assets (Solar Energy Site Assets) are mounted on land adjacent to an office building owned by REIT I. REIT I leases the office building and the solar energy site to a single tenant. Although the tenant occasionally transfers excess electricity produced by the Solar Energy Site Assets to a utility company, the Solar Energy Site Assets are designed and intended to produce electricity only to serve the office building. The Solar Energy Site Assets were designed and constructed specifically for the office building and are intended to remain permanently in place, but were not installed during construction of the office building. The Solar Energy Site Assets will not be removed if the tenant vacates the premises.

(ii) With the exception of the occasional transfers of excess electricity to a utility company, the Solar Energy Site Assets serve the office building to which they are constituent, and, therefore, the Solar Energy Site Assets are analyzed to determine whether they are a structural component using the factors provided in paragraph (d)(3)(iii) of this section. The Solar Energy Site Assets—

(A) Are expensive and time consuming to install and remove;

(B) Are designed specifically for the particular office building for which they are a part and are intended to remain permanently in place;

(C) Will not cause damage to the office building if removed (but the mounts would be damaged upon removal);

(D) Serve a utility-like function with respect to the office building;

(E) Serve the office building in its passive functions of containing and protecting the tenant's assets;

(F) Produce income from consideration for the use or occupancy of space within the office building;

(G) Were installed after construction of the office building;

(H) Will remain in place when the tenant vacates the premises; and

(I) Are owned by REIT I (which is also the owner of the office building).

(iii) The factors described in this paragraph (g) *Example 9* (ii)(A), (ii)(B), (ii)(C) (in part), (ii)(D) through (ii)(F), (ii)(H), and (ii)(I) all support the conclusion that the Solar Energy Site Assets are a structural component of REIT I's office building within the meaning of paragraph (d)(3) of this section and, therefore, are real property. The factors described in this paragraph (g) *Example 9* (ii)(C) (in part) and (ii)(G) would support a conclusion that the Solar Energy Site Assets are not a structural component, but these factors do not outweigh factors supporting the conclusion that the Solar Energy Site Assets are a structural component.

(iv) The result in this *Example 9* would not change if, instead of the Solar Energy Site Assets, solar shingles were used as the roof of REIT I's office building. Solar shingles are roofing shingles like those commonly used for residential housing, except that they contain built-in PV modules. The solar shingle installation was specifically designed and constructed to serve only the needs of REIT I's office building, and the solar shingles were installed as a structural component to provide solar energy to REIT I's office building (although REIT I's tenant occasionally transfers excess electricity produced by the solar shingles to a utility company). The analysis of the application of the factors provided in paragraph (d)(3)(ii) of this section would be similar to the analysis of the application of the factors to the Solar Energy Site Assets in this paragraph (g) *Example 9* (ii) and (iii).

Example 10. Pipeline transmission system. (i) REIT J owns an oil pipeline transmission system that contains and transports oil from producers and distributors of the oil to other distributors and end users. REIT J enters into a long-term triple net lease with a tenant for the pipeline transmission system. The pipeline transmission system is comprised of underground pipelines, storage tanks, valves, vents, meters, and compressors. Although the pipeline transmission system serves an active function, transporting oil, a distinct asset within the system may nevertheless be an inherently permanent structure that does not itself perform an active function. Each of these distinct assets was installed during construction of the pipeline transmission system and will remain in place when a tenant vacates the pipeline transmission system. Each of these assets was designed to remain permanently in place.

(ii) The pipelines and storage tanks are inherently permanent and are listed as inherently permanent structures in paragraph (d)(2)(iii)(B) of this section. Therefore, the pipelines and storage tanks are real property.

(iii) Valves are placed at regular intervals along the pipelines to control oil flow and isolate sections of the pipelines in case there is need for a shut-down or maintenance of the pipelines. Vents equipped with vent valves are also installed in tanks and at regular intervals along the pipelines to relieve pressure in the tanks and pipelines. When analyzed to determine whether they are structural components using the factors set forth in paragraph (d)(3)(iii) of this section, the valves and vents—

(A) Are time consuming and expensive to install and remove from the tanks or pipelines;

(B) Are designed specifically for the particular tanks or pipelines for which they are a part and are intended to remain permanently in place;

(C) Will sustain damage and will damage the tanks or pipelines if removed;

(D) Do not serve a utility-like function with respect to the tanks or pipelines;

(E) Serve the tanks and pipelines in their passive function of containing tenant's oil;

(F) Produce income only from consideration for the use or occupancy of space within the tanks or pipelines;

(G) Were installed during construction of the tanks or pipelines;

(H) Will remain in place when a tenant vacates the premises; and

(I) Are owned by REIT J.

(iv) The factors described in this paragraph (g) *Example 10* (iii)(A) through (iii)(C) and (iii)(E) through (iii)(I) support the conclusion that the vents and valves are structural components of REIT J's tanks or pipelines within the meaning of paragraph (d)(3) of this section and, therefore, are real property. The factor described in this paragraph (g) *Example 10* (iii)(D) would support a conclusion that the vents and valves are not structural components, but this factor does not outweigh the factors that support the conclusion that the vents and valves are structural components.

(v) Meters are used to measure the oil passing into or out of the pipeline transmission system for purposes of determining the end users' consumption. Over long distances, pressure is lost due to friction in the pipeline transmission system. Compressors are required to add pressure to transport oil through the entirety of the pipeline transmission system. The meters and compressors do not serve the tanks or pipelines in their passive function of containing the tenant's oil, and are used in connection with the production of income from the sale and transportation of oil, rather than as consideration for the use or occupancy of space within the tanks or pipelines. The meters and compressors are not structural components within the meaning of paragraph (d)(3) of this section and, therefore, are not real property.

Example 11. Goodwill. REIT K acquires all of the stock of Corporation A, whose sole asset is an established hotel in a major metropolitan area. The hotel building is strategically located and is an historic structure viewed as a landmark. The hotel is well run by an independent contractor, but the manner in which the hotel is operated does not differ significantly from the manner in which other city hotels are operated. Under GAAP, the amount allocated to Corporation A's hotel is limited to its depreciated replacement cost, and the difference between the amount paid for the stock of Corporation A and the depreciated replacement cost of the hotel is treated as goodwill attributable to the acquired hotel. This goodwill derives its value and is inseparable from Corporation A's hotel. If REIT K's acquisition of Corporation A had been a taxable asset acquisition rather than a stock acquisition, the goodwill would have been included in the tax basis of the hotel for Federal income tax purposes, and would not have been separately amortizable. The goodwill is real property to REIT K when it acquires the stock of Corporation A.

Example 12. Land use permit. REIT L receives a special use permit from the government to place a cell tower on federal government land that abuts a federal highway. Governmental regulations provide that the permit is not a lease of the land, but is a permit to use the land for a cell tower. Under the permit, the government reserves the right to cancel the permit and compensate REIT L if the site is needed for a higher public purpose. REIT L leases space on the tower to various cell service providers. Each cell service provider installs its equipment on a designated space on REIT L's cell tower. The permit does not produce, or contribute to the production of, any income other than REIT L's receipt of payments from the cell service providers in consideration for their being allowed to use space on the tower. The permit is in the nature of a leasehold that allows REIT L to place a cell tower in a specific location on government land. Therefore, the permit is an interest in real property.

Example 13. License to operate a business. REIT M owns a building and receives a license from State to operate a casino in the building. The license applies only to REIT M's building and cannot be transferred to another location. REIT M's building is an inherently permanent structure under paragraph (d)(2)(i) of this section and, therefore, is real property. However, REIT M's license to operate a casino is not a right for the use, enjoyment, or occupation of REIT M's building, but is rather a license to engage in the business of operating a casino in the building. Therefore, the casino license is not real property.

(h) *Effective/applicability date.* The rules of this section apply for calendar quarters beginning after the date of publication of the Treasury decision adopting these rules as final regulations in the Federal Register. John Dalrymple *Deputy Commissioner for Services and Enforcement.*

Revenue Ruling 2004-24

2004-1 C.B. 550

ISSUE

If a real estate investment trust (REIT) provides parking facilities at its rental real properties, under what circumstances do amounts received by the REIT for providing the parking facilities qualify as rents from real property under § 856(d) of the Internal Revenue Code?

FACTS

Situation 1

Corporation R has elected to be a REIT as defined in § 856. R owns commercial real properties such as office buildings, shopping centers, and residential apartment complexes. Each property includes one or more buildings containing space that R rents out for office, retail, or multi-family residential use. Each property also includes parking facilities for the use of the tenants of the buildings and their guests, customers, and subtenants. Each parking facility is located in or adjacent to a building occupied by tenants of R and is appropriate in size for the number of tenants and their guests, customers, and subtenants who are expected to use the facility.

The parking facilities do not have parking attendants. R maintains, repairs, and lights the parking facilities. As needed to manage the REIT itself, R also performs fiduciary functions, such as dealing with taxes and insurance, as permitted by § 1.856-4(b)(5)(ii) of the Income Tax Regulations. No other activities are performed in connection with the parking facilities.

Situation 2

The facts are the same as in *Situation 1* except as follows. At some of R's parking facilities, parking spaces are reserved for use by particular tenants. R assigns and marks the reserved spaces in connection with leasing space in the buildings to the tenants. Any recurring functions unique to the reserved spaces (such as enforcement) are provided by an independent contractor as defined in § 856(d)(3) from whom R does not derive or receive any income within the meaning of §§ 856(d)(7)(C)(i) and 1.856-4(b)(5)(i).

Situation 3

The facts are the same as in *Situations 1* and *2* except as follows.

Although each parking facility is appropriate in size for the expected number of tenants and their guests, customers, and subtenants, some of the parking facilities are available for use not only by those parties, but also by the general public. In addition, the parking facilities have parking attendants. R performs the same activities it performs in *Situations 1* and *2*, but corporation S manages and operates the parking facilities under a management contract with R. S is an independent contractor as defined in § 856(d)(3). Although S typically remits to R parking fees from those using the parking facilities, S receives arm's-length compensation under the terms of its management contract with *R*, and *R* does not derive or receive any income from *S* within the meaning of §§ 856(d)(7)(C)(i) and 1.856-4(b)(5)(i). *S* employs all of the individuals who manage and operate the parking facilities, including the parking attendants. *S* is directly responsible for providing all salary, wages, benefits, administration, and supervision of its employees.

In addition to collecting parking fees from those using the parking facilities, the parking attendants may park cars in order to achieve the maximum capacity of the parking facility or for reasons of safety or security. No separate fee is charged for an attendant to park a car. Occasionally, when necessary, an attendant may provide minor, incidental, emergency service at a parking facility, such as charging a battery or changing a flat tire. No other services are provided at the parking facilities.

LAW

To qualify as a REIT, an entity must derive at least 95 percent of its gross income from sources listed in § 856(c)(2) and at least 75 percent of its gross income from sources listed in § 856(c)(3). "Rents from real property" are among the sources listed in both of those sections. Section 856(d)(1) defines rents from real property to include (subject to the exclusions in § 856(d)(2)) the amounts described in § 856(d)(1)(A), (B), and (C). Section 856(d)(1)(B) refers to "charges for services customarily furnished or rendered in connection with the rental of real property, whether or not such charges are separately stated." Section 856(d)(2)(C) excludes "impermissible tenant service income" from the definition of rents from real property. Thus, to qualify as rents from real property, charges for services must be for services customarily furnished or rendered in connection with the rental of real property and must not be impermissible tenant service income.

Section 1.856-4(b)(1) provides the following guidance on determining whether services are customarily furnished or rendered in connection with the rental of real property:

> ... Services furnished to the tenants of a particular building will be considered as customary if, in the geographic market in which the building is located, tenants in buildings which are of a similar class (such as luxury apartment buildings) are customarily provided with the service.... To qualify as a service customarily furnished, the service must be furnished or rendered to the tenants of the real estate investment trust or, primarily for the convenience or benefit of the tenant, to the guests, customers, or subtenants of the tenant....

Thus, to qualify as a service described in § 856(d)(1)(B), a service furnished at a REIT's property must be customarily provided to tenants of properties of a similar class in that particular geographic market (the geographic market test). Section 1.856-4(b)(1) also mentions the furnishing of parking facilities as an example of a service that is customarily furnished to the tenants of a particular class of buildings in many geographic markets. Reflecting the statutory requirement of "connection with the rental of real property," § 1.856-4(b)(1) also provides that to qualify as a service described in § 856(d)(1)(B), the service must be furnished to the REIT's tenants or their guests, customers, or subtenants.

Section 1.856-4(b)(5)(ii) discusses the fiduciary functions of a REIT's trustees or directors, as follows:

> The trustees or directors of the real estate investment trust are not required to delegate or contract out their fiduciary duty to manage the trust itself, as distinguished from rendering or furnishing services to the tenants of its property or managing or operating the property. Thus, the trustees or directors may do all those things necessary, in their fiduciary capacities, to manage and conduct the affairs of the trust itself. For example, the trustees or directors may establish rental terms, choose tenants, enter into and renew leases, and deal with taxes, interest, and insurance, relating to the trust's property. The trustees or directors may also make capital expenditures with respect to the trust's property (as defined in section 263) and may make decisions as to repairs of the trust's property (of the type which would be deductible under section 162), the cost of which may be borne by the trust.

Thus, § 1.856-4(b)(5)(ii) permits the trustees or directors of a REIT to perform activities needed to manage the REIT itself, as distinguished from rendering services to tenants of the REIT's property or managing or operating the REIT's property.

As noted above, § 856(d)(2)(C) excludes impermissible tenant service income from the definition of rents from real property. Pursuant to § 856(d)(7)(A), impermissible tenant service income means, with respect to any real property, any amount received or accrued directly or indirectly by a REIT for furnishing services to the tenants of the property or managing or operating the property. Section 856(d)(7)(C)(i), however, provides that services rendered or management or operation provided is not treated as furnished by the REIT for this purpose if furnished through an independent contractor (as defined in § 856(d)(3)) from whom the REIT does not derive or receive any income. Thus, amounts received by a REIT for services furnished to its tenants, or for property management or operation, do not constitute impermissible tenant service income if the services or management or operation is furnished through an independent contractor (as defined in § 856(d)(3)) from whom the REIT does not derive or receive any income.

Moreover, pursuant to § 856(d)(7)(C)(ii), an amount is not treated as impermissible tenant service income if the amount would be excluded from unrelated business taxable income under § 512(b)(3) if received by an organization described in § 511(a)(2) (referred to, for purposes of this revenue ruling, as an exempt organization). Thus, services provided directly by a REIT do not give rise to impermissible tenant service income if the charges for those services would be excluded from unrelated business taxable income if received by an exempt organization.

Section 512(b)(3)(A)(i) excludes rents from real property from unrelated business taxable income. Section 1.512(b)-1(c)(5) provides, however, that payments for the use of space where services are also rendered to the occupant are not rents from real property. That section mentions space in parking lots as an example of space where services are also rendered to the occupant. Thus, payments for the use of parking space are not excluded from unrelated business taxable income under § 512(b)(3) if received by an exempt organization.

The conference report underlying the 1986 revision of § 856(d) (the 1986 conference report) provides the following guidance on services performed directly by REITs:

> The conferees wish to make certain clarifications regarding those services that a REIT may provide under the conference agreement without using an independent contractor, which services would not cause the rents derived from the property in connection with which the services were rendered to fail to qualify as rents from real property (within the meaning of section 856(d)). The conferees intend, for example, that a REIT may provide customary services in connection with the operation of parking facilities for the convenience of tenants of an office or apartment building, or shopping center, provided that the parking facilities are made available on an unreserved basis without charge to the tenants and their guests or customers. On the other hand, the conferees intend that income derived from the rental of parking spaces on a reserved basis to tenants, or income derived from the rental of parking spaces to the general public, would not be considered to be rents from real property unless all services are performed by an independent contractor. Nevertheless, the conferees intend that the income from the rental of parking facilities properly would be considered to be rents from real property (and not merely income from services) in such circumstances if services are performed by an independent contractor.

2 H.R. Conf. Rep. No. 841, 99th Cong., 2d Sess. II-220 (1986), 1986-3 (Vol. 4) C.B. 220. Thus, the 1986 conference report indicates that, in some circumstances, REITs may directly perform activities in connection with parking facilities without causing charges for providing the parking facilities to fail to qualify as rents from real property under § 856(d).

The difference between this congressional intent and the treatment of exempt organizations under § 512(b)(3) reflects differences between §§ 856(d) and 512(b)(3), as well as differences between the regulations interpreting those sections. The definition of rents from real property in § 856(d), which applies to REITs, differs significantly in scope and structure from the definition of rents from real property under § 512(b)(3), which applies to exempt organizations. For example, unlike § 512(b)(3), § 856(d)(7)(C)(i) treats services provided by an independent contractor as not provided by the REIT. The definition of rents from real property under § 512(b)(3) does not have a comparable provision.

ANALYSIS

Situation 1

In *Situation 1*, R provides unattended parking facilities at its rental real properties. R maintains, repairs, and lights the unattended parking facilities and performs fiduciary functions permitted by § 1.856-4(b)(5)(ii). These activities are customarily performed at parking facilities located at rental real properties in all geographic markets. No other activities are performed in connection with R's unattended parking facilities. Therefore, the furnishing of R's unattended parking facilities will be treated as meeting the geographic market test of § 1.856-4(b)(1).

R's unattended parking facilities are part of R's rental real properties and are provided for the use of R's tenants and their guests, customers, and subtenants. Each parking facility is located in or adjacent to a building occupied by tenants of R and is appropriate in size for the number of tenants and their guests, customers, and subtenants who are expected to use the facility. Therefore, the furnishing of R's unattended parking facilities meets the requirement of § 1.856-4(b)(1) that services be furnished to the REIT's tenants or their guests, customers, or subtenants. Because it meets both that requirement and the geographic market test, the furnishing of R's unattended parking facilities is a service customarily furnished or rendered in connection with the rental of real property under § 856(d)(1)(B).

The 1986 conference report indicates that the activities performed by R at its unattended parking facilities described in *Situation 1* should not cause charges for providing those parking facilities to fail to qualify as rents from real property under § 856(d). Therefore, although in *Situation 1* payments for the use of parking space are not excluded from unrelated business taxable income under § 512(b)(3) if received by an exempt organization, the furnishing of R's unattended parking facilities will be treated as not giving rise to impermissible tenant service income under § 856(d)(2)(C) and (d)(7). Accordingly, because the furnishing of R's unattended parking facilities qualifies as a service described in § 856(d)(1)(B) and does not give rise to impermissible tenant service income, amounts received by R for furnishing these parking facilities qualify as rents from real property under § 856(d).

Situation 2

In *Situation 2*, the facts are the same as in *Situation 1* except that at some of R's unattended parking facilities, parking is available to tenants on a reserved basis. The furnishing of these parking facilities qualifies as a service described in § 856(d)(1)(B) for the reasons discussed above with respect to *Situation 1*.

The 1986 conference report indicates that income from reserved parking should qualify as rents from real property only if services are performed by an independent contractor. In *Situation 2*, any recurring functions unique to the reserved parking spaces (such as enforcement) are performed by an independent contractor. R assigns and marks the reserved spaces in connection with leasing space to its tenants and provides maintenance, repair, lighting, and fiduciary functions permitted by § 1.856-4(b)(5)(ii). These basic activities performed by R are not services to tenants that the conferees intended to prevent REITs from performing directly at parking facilities. Section 1.856-4(b)(5)(ii) permits the trustees or directors of a REIT to perform activities needed to manage the REIT itself, as distinguished from rendering services to tenants of the REIT's property or managing or operating the property. Therefore, although in *Situation 2* payments for the use of parking space are not excluded from unrelated business taxable income under § 512(b)(3) if received by an exempt organization, the furnishing of *R*'s unattended, reserved parking facilities will be treated as not giving rise to impermissible tenant service income under § 856(d)(2)(C) and (d)(7). Accordingly, because the furnishing of *R*'s unattended, reserved parking facilities qualifies as a service described in § 856(d)(1)(B) and does not give rise to impermissible tenant service income, amounts received by *R* for furnishing these parking facilities qualify as rents from real property under § 856(d).

Situation 3

In *Situation 3*, *R* provides attended parking facilities at its rental real properties. *R* performs the same activities it performs in *Situations 1* and *2*, and *S* manages and operates the attended parking facilities. Attendants at these facilities generally collect parking fees. Attendants may also park cars in order to achieve the maximum capacity of the parking facility or for reasons of safety or security, and no separate fee is charged for an attendant to park a car. Occasionally, when necessary, an attendant may provide minor, incidental, emergency service at a parking facility. These services typically are provided at attended parking facilities at rental real properties in all geographic markets. No other services are provided at *R*'s attended parking facilities. Therefore, the furnishing of *R*'s attended parking facilities will be treated as meeting the geographic market test of § 1.856-4(b)(1).

Some of *R*'s attended parking facilities are available for use not only by *R*'s tenants and their guests, customers, and subtenants, but also by the general public. However, the 1986 conference report indicates that tenant parking facilities also available to the general public should not be precluded from qualifying under § 856(d)(1)(B). *R*'s attended parking facilities are part of *R*'s rental real properties, and each parking facility is located in or adjacent to a building occupied by tenants of *R* and is appropriate in size for the number of tenants and their guests, customers, and subtenants who are expected to use the facility. Because of this proximity to the tenants and appropriate size, the attended parking facilities that also are available to the general public can reasonably be expected to be used predominantly by *R*'s tenants and their guests, customers, and subtenants. For these reasons, the furnishing of *R*'s attended parking facilities will be treated as meeting the requirement of § 1.856-4(b)(1) that services be furnished to the REIT's tenants or their guests, customers, or subtenants. Because it meets both that requirement and the geographic market test, the furnishing of *R*'s attended parking facilities is a service customarily furnished or rendered in connection with the rental of real property under § 856(d)(1)(B).

The 1986 conference report indicates that income from parking that is reserved or available to the general public should qualify as rents from real property only if services are performed by an independent contractor. The only activities that *R* performs in connection with its attended parking facilities are maintenance, repair, lighting, fiduciary functions, and assigning and marking reserved spaces. As noted above, these basic activities are not services to tenants that the conferees intended to prevent REITs from performing directly at parking facilities. All of the other activities involved in furnishing *R*'s attended parking facilities are performed by *S*, an independent contractor as defined in §856(d)(3). Although S typically collects parking fees and remits the fees to R, S receives arm's-length compensation under the terms of its management contract with R, and R does not derive or receive any income from S within the meaning of §§856(d)(7)(C)(i) and 1.856-4(b)(5)(i). S employs all of the individuals who manage and operate the attended parking facilities and is directly responsible for providing all their salary, wages, benefits, administration, and supervision. Therefore, although in *Situation 3* payments for the use of parking space are not excluded from unrelated business taxable income under §512(b)(3) if received by an exempt organization, the furnishing of R's attended parking facilities will be treated as not giving rise to impermissible tenant service income under §856(d)(2)(C) and (d)(7). Accordingly, because the furnishing of R's attended parking facilities qualifies as a service described in §856(d)(1)(B) and does not give rise to impermissible tenant service income, amounts received by R for furnishing these parking facilities qualify as rents from real property under §856(d).

HOLDING

Amounts received by R for furnishing unattended parking facilities, under the circumstances described in *Situations 1* and *2*, and for furnishing attended parking facilities, under the circumstances described in *Situation 3*, qualify as rents from real property under §856(d).

DRAFTING INFORMATION

The principal author of this revenue ruling is Jonathan D. Silver of the Office of Associate Chief Counsel (Financial Institutions and Products). For further information regarding this revenue ruling, contact Mr. Silver at (202) 622-3920 (not a toll-free call).

Revenue Ruling 2003-86

2003-2 C.B. 290

ISSUE

If a joint venture partnership between a taxable REIT subsidiary (TRS) of a real estate investment trust (REIT) and a corporation that qualifies as an independent contractor of the REIT under §856(d)(3)(B) of the Internal Revenue Code provides noncustomary services to tenants of the REIT in the situation described below, will rents paid by the tenants to the REIT fail to qualify as rents from real property under §856(d)?

FACTS

R is a corporation that has elected and qualifies to be treated as a REIT under subchapter M of Chapter 1 of the Code. R owns and operates rental apartment properties in several major metropolitan areas. In 2002, R formed a wholly owned corporation, T, to provide services to tenants of its properties. R and T filed Form 8875 to jointly elect for T to be treated as a TRS of R effective as of the date of T's formation. The services provided to tenants by T are services that are not customarily provided to tenants of rental apartment properties in the metropolitan areas in which R's properties are located.

X is a corporation unrelated, either directly or indirectly, to either R or T. X qualifies as an independent contractor under §856(d)(3)(B). X provides various services to R's tenants and tenants of other rental apartments in the areas where R's properties are located. The services provided by X are noncustomary in the areas where R's properties are located and are primarily for the convenience of tenants.

X and T formed P, which is treated as a partnership for federal income tax purposes, to provide the noncustomary services that formerly were separately provided to R's tenants by either X or T. X and T made equal capital contributions to P. X and T share in all items of P's income, gain, loss, and deduction in proportion to their capital contributions. R's tenants contract directly with P for services. R does not receive any payments related to the services from P, X or tenants. R receives quarterly dividends from T.

LAW AND ANALYSIS

To qualify as a REIT, an entity must derive at least 95 percent of its gross income from sources listed in §856(c)(2) and at least 75 percent of its gross income from sources listed in §856(c)(3). "Rents from real property" are among the sources listed in both of those sections. Section 856(d)(1) defines rents from real property to include rents from interests in real property, charges for services customarily rendered in connection with the rental of real property, and rent attributable to certain leased personal property. However, §856(d)(2)(C) excludes "impermissible tenant service income" from the definition of rents from real property.

Section 856(d)(7)(A) defines "impermissible tenant service income" to include, with respect to any real or personal property, any amount received or accrued directly or indirectly by a REIT for services furnished or rendered by the REIT to tenants of the property. Section 856(d)(7)(B) provides that if impermissible tenant service income from a property for any tax year exceeds 1 percent of all amounts received or accrued directly or indirectly by the REIT during the tax year from the property, the impermissible tenant service income from the property shall include all amounts received or accrued from the property for the tax year. Section 856(d)(7)(C)(i) provides that services furnished or rendered through a TRS or an independent contractor from whom the REIT does not derive or receive any income are not treated as furnished, rendered, or provided by the REIT for purposes of §856(d)(7)(A). Thus, services rendered by a TRS do not give rise to impermissible tenant service income, and services rendered by an independent contractor do not give rise to impermissible tenant service income if the REIT does not receive or derive income from the independent contractor.

R's tenants contract directly with P to perform noncustomary services. Thus, R does not receive directly any payments related to the services from P. Also, R does not directly or indirectly receive income from X, an independent contractor. T is entitled to its share of income from the performance of services in proportion to its interest in *P*, and *R* may indirectly receive this income in the form of dividends from *T*. Under §856(d)(7)(A), amounts received directly or indirectly by a REIT for services furnished or rendered to tenants constitute impermissible tenant service income. However, §856(d)(7)(C)(i) provides an exception for services furnished or rendered through a TRS. *R*'s only interest in *P* is through *T*, which is a TRS. Accordingly, the services provided by *P* are treated as provided by *T* to the extent of *T*'s interest in *P*. Therefore, *R* will not be treated as providing impermissible tenant services to its tenants.

HOLDING

Under the circumstances described above, a joint venture partnership between a TRS of a REIT and a corporation that qualifies as an independent contractor of the REIT under §856(d)(3)(B) may provide noncustomary services to tenants of the REIT without causing the rents paid by the tenants to the REIT to fail to qualify as rents from real property under §856(d).

DRAFTING INFORMATION

The principal author of this revenue ruling is Jonathan D. Silver of the Office of Associate Chief Counsel (Financial Institutions & Products). For further information regarding this revenue ruling, contact Mr. Silver at (202) 622-3920 (not a toll-free call).

Revenue Ruling 2002-38
2002-2 C.B. 4

ISSUE

If a real estate investment trust (REIT) forms a taxable REIT subsidiary (TRS) to provide noncustomary services to tenants of the REIT and no service charges are separately stated from the rents paid by the tenants to the REIT, how is the REIT's income from the services treated under §§856 and 857(b)(7) of the Internal Revenue Code?

FACTS

Situation 1

Corporation *R*, which has elected to be a REIT as defined in §856, owns residential apartment buildings. *R* forms a wholly-owned subsidiary, corporation *T*, to provide housekeeping services to tenants of *R*'s apartment buildings. The services do not qualify as customary services under §1.856-4(b)(1) of the Income Tax Regulations. *R* and *T* jointly elect under §856(l) to treat *T* as a TRS of *R*.

Employees of *T* perform all of the housekeeping services received by *R*'s tenants, including administration and management of the services. *T* pays all costs of providing the services, such as its employees' salaries and the costs of their uniforms, equipment, and supplies. To carry out the housekeeping operations, *T* also rents space in *R*'s apartment buildings in accordance with §856(d)(8)(A). *T* makes no payments to *R* other than its rental payments for that space. The annual value of the housekeeping services provided at each property exceeds one percent of the total annual amount received by *R* from the property.

Charges to the tenants for the house-keeping services are not separately stated from the rents that the tenants pay to *R* for the use of their apartments. *T* does not enter into contracts with the tenants for the performance of the housekeeping services. *R* compensates *T* for providing the services by paying *T* an amount that is 160 percent of *T*'s direct cost of providing the services. *T* reports the full amount of *R*'s payment as gross income on *T*'s federal income tax return.

Situation 2

The facts are the same as in *Situation 1* except that *R* compensates *T* for providing the services by paying *T* an amount that is 125 percent of *T*'s direct cost of providing the services, and that payment is less than the arm's length charge under § 482 for providing the services.

LAW

For taxable years beginning after December 31, 2000, §§ 856 and 857(b)(7) provide special rules for a corporation that is a TRS within the meaning of § 856(l). Those rules, which allow a TRS to provide noncustomary services to tenants of its REIT, govern the relationship between the REIT and the TRS.

To qualify as a REIT, an entity must derive at least 95 percent of its gross income from sources listed in § 856(c)(2) and at least 75 percent of its gross income from sources listed in § 856(c)(3). "Rents from real property" are among the sources listed in both of those sections. Section 856(d)(1) defines rents from real property to include rents from interests in real property, charges for services customarily rendered in connection with the rental of real property, and rent attributable to certain leased personal property. However, § 856(d)(2)(C) excludes "impermissible tenant service income" from the definition of rents from real property. Pursuant to § 856(d)(7)(A), impermissible tenant service income means, with respect to any real property, any amount received by a REIT for services rendered by the REIT to tenants of the property. Section 856(d)(7)(C)(i) provides that services rendered through a TRS are not treated as rendered by its REIT for purposes of § 856(d)(7)(A). Thus, services rendered by a TRS do not give rise to impermissible tenant service income.

Section 857(b)(7)(A) imposes for each taxable year of a REIT a tax equal to 100 percent of "redetermined rents." Section 857(b)(7)(B)(i) provides that redetermined rents mean rents from real property (as defined in § 856(d)) to the extent the amount of the rents would (but for § 857(b)(7)(E)) be reduced on allocation under § 482 to clearly reflect income as a result of services rendered by a TRS to a tenant of its REIT. Section 482 provides that when two or more organizations, trades, or businesses are owned or controlled directly or indirectly by the same interests (controlled organizations), the Secretary may allocate gross income between or among those controlled organizations if the Secretary determines that such allocation is necessary to clearly reflect the income of any of those controlled organizations. Pursuant to § 1.482-

1(b)(1), the standard applied in determining the true taxable income of a controlled organization is that of an organization dealing at arm's length with an uncontrolled organization. Section 1.482-2(b)(3) defines an arm's length charge for services provided between controlled organizations, regardless of whether the services are an integral part of either organization's business activity (the § 482 arm's length charge). Section 857(b) (7)(E) provides that the imposition of tax under § 857(b)(7)(A) is in lieu of allocation under § 482.

Section 857(b)(7)(B)(ii) through (vii) contains exceptions, or safe harbors, from the 100 percent tax on redetermined rents. For example, pursuant to § 857(b)(7)(B) (vi), the definition of redetermined rents does not apply to any service rendered by a TRS to a tenant of its REIT if the gross income of the TRS from the service is at least 150 percent of the TRS's direct cost in rendering the service. Other safe harbors in § 857(b)(7)(B) cover customary services, services giving rise to *de minimis* amounts, services priced comparably to those provided by the TRS to unrelated persons, certain services with separately stated charges, and services excepted by the Secretary.

ANALYSIS

If a REIT forms a TRS to provide non-customary services to the REIT's tenants and no service charges are separately stated from the tenants' rents, a primary question in determining the treatment of the REIT's income from the services is whether they are considered to be rendered by the REIT, or by the TRS, for purposes of § 856(d)(7). If rendered by the TRS and hence described in § 856(d)(7)(C)(i), the services do not give rise to impermissible tenant service income. All relevant facts and circumstances must be considered in determining the provider of the services for this purpose.

In *Situations 1* and *2*, charges to the tenants for the housekeeping services are not separately stated from the rents that the tenants pay to R for the use of their apartments. As a result, the amounts of the rents reflect the availability and use of those services. In other words, R receives greater rental payments than it would have received if the services had not been provided to its tenants. However, the structure of the 100 percent tax on redetermined rents indicates that Congress did not intend the lack of a separately stated service charge, by itself, to cause services to be treated as rendered by a REIT, rather than its TRS. In *Situations 1* and *2*, employees of T perform all of the housekeeping services received by R's tenants, including administration and management of the services. T pays all costs of providing the services, such as its employees' salaries and the costs of their uniforms, equipment, and supplies. T also rents space to carry out the housekeeping operations and makes no payments to R other than its rental payments for that space. For purposes of § 856(d)(7)(C)(i), in those circumstances the services are considered to be rendered by T, rather than R, even though no service charges are separately stated from the tenants' rents. Accordingly, the services do not give rise to impermissible tenant service income and thus do not cause any portion of the rents received by R to fail to qualify as rents from real property under § 856(d).

As rents from real property, those rents are subject to being treated as redetermined rents under §857(b)(7)(B)(i). That section provides that redetermined rents mean rents from real property (as defined in §856(d)) to the extent the amount of the rents would (but for §857(b)(7)(E)) be reduced on allocation under §482 to clearly reflect income as a result of services rendered by a TRS to a tenant of its REIT. Section 482 allows the Secretary to allocate income from a REIT to its TRS to reflect the §482 arm's length charge for the TRS's services. However, the 100 percent tax on redetermined rents is not imposed with respect to services described in a safe harbor of §857(b)(7)(B).

In *Situation 1*, R compensates T for providing the housekeeping services by paying it an amount that is 160 percent of T's direct cost of providing the services, and T reports the full amount of R's payment as gross income on T's federal income tax return. Pursuant to the safe harbor of §857(b)(7)(B)(vi), the definition of redetermined rents does not apply to any service rendered by a TRS to a tenant of its REIT if the TRS's gross income from the service is at least 150 percent of its direct cost in rendering the service. In *Situation 1*, that safe harbor protects R from imposition of the 100 percent tax on redetermined rents. However, if the amount paid by R to T is less than the §482 arm's length charge for providing the services, income is allocable from R to T under §482 to reflect that charge. Section 857(b)(7)(E) does not preclude allocation under §482 of income on which the 100 percent tax is not imposed. Income so allocated from R to T under §482 would be deductible by R under §162 and thus would reduce R's taxable income, but not its gross income. Such allocation under §482 would not cause any portion of the rents received by R to fail to qualify as rents from real property under §856(d).

In *Situation 2*, R compensates T by paying it an amount that is 125 percent of T's direct cost of providing the services, and that payment is less than the §482 arm's length charge. In *Situation 2*, no safe harbor protects R from imposition of the 100 percent tax on redetermined rents. As a result, §857(b)(7)(A) imposes on R a tax equal to the amount that would (but for imposition of that tax) be allocated under §482 from R to T to reflect the §482 arm's length charge for providing the services. In other words, the tax is equal to the amount by which the §482 arm's length charge exceeds the payment from R to T. Pursuant to §857(b)(7)(E), imposition of that tax is in lieu of allocation of the same amount from R to T under §482. Imposition of that tax does not cause any portion of the rents received by R to fail to qualify as rents from real property under §856(d).

HOLDINGS

(1) In *Situation 1*, the housekeeping services are considered to be rendered by T, rather than R, for purposes of §856(d)(7)(C)(i). Accordingly, the services do not give rise to impermissible tenant service income and thus do not cause any portion of the rents received by R to fail to qualify as rents from real property under §856(d). The safe harbor of §857(b)(7)(B)(vi) protects R from imposition of the 100 percent tax on redetermined rents. However, if the amount paid by R to T represents less than the §482 arm's length charge for providing the services, income is allocable from

R to *T* under § 482. Income so allocated from *R* to *T* under § 482 would be deductible by *R* under § 162 and thus would reduce *R*'s taxable income, but not its gross income. Such allocation under § 482 would not cause any portion of the rents received by *R* to fail to qualify as rents from real property under § 856(d).

(2) In *Situation 2*, the housekeeping services are considered to be rendered by *T* for purposes of § 856(d)(7)(C)(i). Accordingly, the services do not give rise to impermissible tenant service income and thus do not cause any portion of the rents received by *R* to fail to qualify as rents from real property under § 856(d). However, no safe harbor protects *R* from imposition of the 100 percent tax on redetermined rents. Section 857(b)(7)(A) imposes on *R* a tax equal to the amount by which the § 482 arm's length charge for providing the services exceeds the payment from *R* to *T*. Imposition of that tax is in lieu of allocation of that amount from *R* to *T* under § 482 and does not cause any portion of the rents received by *R* to fail to qualify as rents from real property under § 856(d).

DRAFTING INFORMATION

The principal author of this revenue ruling is Jonathan D. Silver of the Office of Associate Chief Counsel (Financial Institutions and Products). For further information regarding this revenue ruling, contact Mr. Silver at (202) 622-3920 (not a toll-free call).

Revenue Ruling 83-117

1983-2 C.B. 98

ISSUE

Whether dividend distributions made by a real estate investment trust company (REIT) in cash or shares purchased under a dividend reinvestment plan will qualify for the dividends paid deduction under section 561 of the Internal Revenue Code under the circumstances described below?

FACTS

Situation 1

X, a widely-held REIT under subchapter M of the Internal Revenue Code, established a dividend reinvestment plan. Under the plan, all shareholders may elect to have cash dividends that would otherwise be distributed to them on their common stock reinvested in newly issued common stock of X at a price equal to 95 percent of the stock's fair market value on distribution date. The dividend reinvestment plan is designed as a means for X to raise capital, and the discount of 5 percent that is allowed under the plan approximates the underwriting and other costs that a REIT otherwise would expect to incur in issuing new stock.

Shareholders participate in the plan by completing an authorization card that designates T, a trust company bank, as the participating shareholders' agent to reinvest cash distributions that are first distributed to T, and designates T to hold and vote the shares as each participating shareholder directs. The authorization card must be received by T on or prior to the record date for the next dividend payment. There is no requirement to participate in the plan and shareholders who do not participate receive their cash dividend payments in full. While the plan continues in effect, a participant's dividends will continue to be invested without further notice to T.

Prior to the dividend payment date no cash dividend is available to either X's participating or nonparticipating shareholders. The dividend payment date is the date the participant's option to receive stock becomes effective and a participant receives written notification that T is acting to effectuate the participant's option to receive stock on that date.

Situation 2

The facts are the same as in Situation 1, except that under the dividend reinvestment plan, all shareholders may elect to have cash dividends that would otherwise be distributed to them on their common stock reinvested in newly issued common stock of X at a price less than 95 percent of the stock's fair market value on distribution date.

HELD

Situation 1

X will be entitled to a dividends paid deduction for the amount of any distribution in cash or stock of greater value under section 561 of the Code. The plan treats all shareholders with impartiality by giving all shareholders an equal opportunity to reinvest, and the plan's bargain spread directed at passing to the REIT's participating shareholders underwriting and other costs savings by issuing stock under the plan is relatively small resulting in relatively minor differences in distributions to similarly situated taxpayers.

Situation 2

X will not be entitled to a dividends paid deduction for any part of any distribution in cash or stock of greater value under section 561 of the Code. The plan's bargain spread directed at passing to the REIT's participating shareholders underwriting and other costs savings by issuing stock under the plan is not relatively small, and does not result in relatively minor differences in distributions to similarly situated shareholders.

Revenue Ruling 77-441

1977-2 C.B. 240

Advice has been requested whether, under the circumstances described below, the completion of certain construction will cause the termination of a property's foreclosure status under section 856(e) of the Internal Revenue Code of 1954.

In 1974 a trust, otherwise qualifying as a real estate investment trust within the meaning of section 856 of the Code, made a loan to A for the purpose of financing the construction of an apartment complex on land owned by A. The loan was secured by a first mortgage on the land.

Construction plans submitted by A with the loan application provided for the construction of five detached two-story buildings, a parking lot, swimming pool, clubhouse, and tennis court for the exclusive use of tenants.

In 1975 *A* defaulted in payment of principal and interest on the loan and the trust accepted a deed to the property in full satisfaction of the outstanding indebtedness in lieu of foreclosing the mortgage. The trust subsequently made an election to have the property treated as 'foreclosure property' under section 856(e) of the Code.

At the time of *A's* default each of the five buildings, the parking lot, and swimming pool were 70 percent complete. No construction had begun on the clubhouse or tennis court. The total estimated cost of the clubhouse and tennis court was less than two percent of the total cost of the other components of the apartment project.

After its acquisition of the property, the trust, through an independent contractor, completed construction of the entire project.

The question presented is whether the construction of the clubhouse and tennis court caused the property to lose its status as foreclosure property under section 856(e) of the Code.

Section 856(e)(1) of the Code defines the term 'foreclosure property' as meaning any real property (including interests in real property), and any personal property incident to such real property, acquired by the real estate investment trust as the result of such trust having bid in such property at foreclosure, or having otherwise reduced such property to ownership or possession by agreement or process of law, after there was default, (or default was imminent) on a lease of such property or an indebtedness which such property secured.

Section 856(e)(5) of the Code provides that property shall be treated as foreclosure property for purposes of this part only if the real estate investment trust so elects on or before the due date (including any extensions of time) for filing its return of tax under this chapter for the taxable year in which such trust acquires such property.

Section 856(e)(4)(B) of the Code and section 10.1(b)(2) of the Temporary Income Tax Regulations provide that any foreclosure property shall cease to be such on the first day (occurring on or after the day on which the real estate investment trust acquired the property) on which any construction takes place on such property (other than completion of a building, or completion of any other improvement, where more than 10 percent of the construction of such building or other improvement was completed before default became imminent).

S. Rep. No. 1375, 93rd Cong., 2d Sess. 15 (1974), 1975-1 C.B. 517, 526, states, in part:

> In determining whether 10 percent of construction has been completed, generally the property is to be examined building-by-building. For example, if a REIT acquires on foreclosure a project where two identical apartment buildings are being constructed on one piece of land, if one apartment is 80 percent finished and the other apartment is less than 10 percent finished, the REIT could not complete work on the second building. On the other hand, if an integral part of the first apartment building was a garage not yet begun at the time of foreclosure, the REIT would be able to have the garage constructed

(if the garage and building considered together as one unit were more than 10 percent completed).

In the instant case, the apartment complex is a self-contained project designed with the common recreational facilities (swimming pool, clubhouse and tennis court) as an integral part. The complex with these recreational facilities, when viewed as a single unit, was more than 10 percent complete when default occurred. That is, direct construction costs incurred at time of default on the project were more than 10 percent of the total estimated construction costs. See *S. Rep. No. 1375*, 93rd Cong., 2d Sess. 15 (1974), 1975-1 C.B. 517, 526.

Accordingly, the construction of the clubhouse and tennis court did not cause the property to lose its status as foreclosure property under section 856(e) of the Code.

Priv. Ltr. Rul. 2011-43-011

(July 19, 2011)

Legend:
Taxpayer =
Partnership =
TRS A =

Dear ***:

This is in reply to a letter dated March 14, 2011, requesting rulings on behalf of Taxpayer. The requested rulings concern the qualification of amounts received from the rental of certain properties as "rents from real property" for purposes of § 856(d) of the Internal Revenue Code.

FACTS

Taxpayer is a calendar year taxpayer that uses an accrual method of accounting and that elected to be taxed as a real estate investment trust (REIT) under § 856 of the Code. Taxpayer is the managing general partner of Partnership, owning approximately ***% of the outstanding common units of Partnership. Partnership indirectly owns and operates numerous real properties (the Properties). TRS A is a wholly-owned subsidiary of Partnership that has jointly elected with Taxpayer to be treated as a taxable REIT subsidiary (TRS) of Taxpayer pursuant to § 856(l).

At certain of the Properties, Taxpayer rents space on outdoor steel billboard structures affixed to the Properties (the Steel Billboard Structures). The Steel Billboard Structures range in width from 18 feet to 72 feet and in height from 16 feet to 72 feet. Depending on the Property, the Steel Billboard Structures are mounted either on the roof of the building or on an exterior wall of the building. They may also be freestanding towers.

Issue 1:

A Steel Billboard Structure mounted on the roof of a building is typically braced back to multiple columns installed in the building's structure, i.e., existing structural support columns of the building are exposed and structural steel column extensions are installed above the roof. A horizontal steel frame of wide flange beams is installed connecting the column extensions above the roof plane and supporting the sign.

A Steel Billboard Structure mounted on the wall of a building is constructed by exposing the building's structural columns and spandrel beams. The exterior of the building is removed locally to expose the structural columns and new extensions of structural steel are attached to the existing structure to extend sign connections beyond the exterior face of the building. The exterior of the building is then reconstructed around the new connection.

A tower Steel Billboard Structure is constructed on concrete foundations which are anchored into the earth, often extending 30 feet or more into the earth. A steel mast or columns then extends up from the foundations. If columns are used, it is typical to truss between them with diagonal members from the foundations to the top of the sign, which provides bracing for wind loads on the sign.

Taxpayer represents that the structural components of the Steel Billboard Structures have never been moved and are designed and constructed to remain in place permanently.

Issue 2:

In certain cases, Taxpayer will rent the Steel Billboard Structures directly to end users for fixed amounts under lease agreements (the Rent). Under some leases, the Rent will include payment for certain noncustomary services, such as services relating to the installation of the vinyl signs and maintaining the sign lighting (the Noncustomary Services). In these cases, Taxpayer will enter into a services agreement with TRS A to provide the Noncustomary Services. In addition, Taxpayer may enter into a brokerage agreement with TRS A to provide brokerage services to Taxpayer in connection with the rental of the Steel Billboard Structures to end users.

In other leases, the Rent will not include payment for the Noncustomary Services. Instead, the end users will contract directly with TRS A or unrelated third parties for any services, and will pay arm's length compensation to TRS A or the third parties.

In either case, Taxpayer represents that it will not perform any services in connection with the renting of the Steel Billboard Structures to occupants, other than usual and customary services and activities permitted by landlords with respect to their property or by trustees with respect to Taxpayer. Any noncustomary services will be performed by TRS A. Taxpayer represents that it will compensate TRS A for the Noncustomary Services and any brokerage services on an arm's length basis. Taxpayer further represents that TRS A will use its own employees and bear all of its own costs relating to the Noncustomary Services and the brokerage services, such as its employees' salaries and the costs of their uniforms, equipment, and supplies. TRS A may contract with unrelated third parties to provide some of the Noncustomary Services and/or brokerage services. TRS A will report amounts received from Taxpayer for the Noncustomary Services and brokerage services as gross income on its income tax return.

Issue 3:

Taxpayer will rent certain Steel Billboard Structures that are potential future sites of electric signs to TRS A under lease agreements for rent based on a percentage of gross receipts. Taxpayer represents that the rent paid by TRS A will include only customary services that can be provided by a REIT and will be at a market rate.

TRS A will construct and install on the leased Steel Billboard Structures (1) an aluminum grid for placement of Light Emitting Diode (LED) screens, (2) LED screens, and (3) structures ancillary to such aluminum grid and LED screens (the Electric Signs). TRS A will be the owner of the Electric Signs installed in the Steel Billboard Structures and will be engaged in the electric sign business. TRS A will use its own employees and bear all of its own costs relating to the electric sign business. TRS A may contract with unrelated third parties to provide services relating to the electric sign business.

Taxpayer represents that the Steel Billboard Structure space to be leased to TRS A is unique space at each Property. The remaining space at each Property will be leased to unrelated tenants and will not be comparable in terms of character or use to the Steel Billboard Structure space rented to TRS A. Taxpayer represents that space comparable to the Steel Billboard Structure space does not exist within each Property, but that rent paid by TRS A will be substantially comparable to rent paid by unrelated tenants for similar spaces in the same geographic area.

LAW AND ANALYSIS

Issue 1:

Section 856(c)(2) provides that at least 95 percent of a REIT's gross income must be derived from, among other sources, rents from real property.

Section 856(c)(3) provides that at least 75 percent of a REIT's gross income must be derived from, among other sources, rents from real property.

Section 856(c)(4)(A) provides that at the close of each quarter of its tax year, at least 75 percent of the value of a REIT's total assets must be represented by real estate assets, cash, and cash items (including receivables), and Government securities.

Section 856(c)(5)(B) provides that the term "real estate assets," for purposes of § 856, means real property (including interests in real property and interests in mortgages on real property) and shares (or transferable certificates of beneficial interest) in other REITs that meet the requirements of §§ 856 through 859.

Section 856(c)(5)(C) provides that the term "interests in real property" includes fee ownership and co-ownership of land or improvements thereon, leaseholds of land or improvements thereon, options to acquire land or improvements thereon, and options to acquire leaseholds of land or improvements thereon, but does not include mineral, oil, or gas royalty interests.

Section 1.856-3(b) of the Income Tax Regulations provides, in part, that the term "real estate assets" means real property. Section 1.856-3(d) provides that "real property" includes land or improvements thereon, such as buildings or other inherently permanent structures thereon (including items which are structural components of such buildings or structures). In addition, the term "real property" includes interests in real property. Local law definitions will not be controlling for purposes of determining the meaning of "real property" for purposes of § 856 and the regulations thereunder. Under the regulations, "real property" includes, for example, the wiring in a building, plumbing systems, central heating or central air-conditioning machinery, pipes or ducts, elevators or escalators installed in a building, or other items which are structural components of a building or other permanent structure. The term does not include assets accessory to the operation of a business, such as machinery, printing press, transportation equipment which is not a structural component of the building, office equipment, refrigerators, individual air-conditioning units, grocery counters, furnishings of a motel, hotel, or office building, etc. even though such items may be termed fixtures under local law.

Under section 1.856-3(g), a REIT that is a partner in a partnership is deemed to own its proportionate share of each of the assets of the partnership and to be entitled to the income of the partnership attributable to that share. For purposes of § 856 the interest of a partner in the partnership's assets is determined in accordance with the partner's capital interest in the partnership. The character of the various assets in the hands of the partnership and items of gross income of the partnership retain the same character in the hands of the partners for all purposes of § 856.

Rev. Rul. 71-220, 1971-1 C.B., considers a REIT that develops a mobile home community on land that it had purchased. The community is situated in a planned site that has a country club, marina, parks, churches and schools. When units are delivered they are set on foundations consisting of pre-engineered blocks. The wheels and axles are removed from the units and the units are affixed to the ground by six or more steel straps. Each unit has a carport or screened porch attached to it. In addition, each unit is connected to water, sewer, gas, electric and telephone facilities. Rev. Rul. 71-220 concludes that the mobile homes are "real property" within the meaning of § 856 and section 1.856-3(d).

Rev. Rul. 75-424, 1975-2 C.B. 269, concerns whether various components of a microwave transmission system are real estate assets for purposes of § 856. The system consists of transmitting and receiving towers built upon pilings or foundations, transmitting and receiving antennae affixed to the towers, a building, equipment within the building, and waveguides. The waveguides are transmission lines from the receivers or transmitters to the antennae, and are metal pipes permanently bolted or welded to the tower and never removed or replaced unless blown off by weather. The transmitting, multiplex, and receiving equipment is housed in the building. Prewired modular racks are installed in the building to support the equipment that is installed upon them. The racks are completely wired in the factory and then bolted to the floor and ceiling. They are self-supporting and do not depend upon the exterior walls for support. The equipment provides for transmission of audio or video signals through the waveguides to the antennae. Also installed in the building is a permanent heating and air conditioning system. The transmission site is surrounded by chain link fencing. The revenue ruling holds that the building, the heating and air conditioning system, the transmitting and receiving towers, and the fence are real estate assets. The ruling further holds that the antennae, waveguides, transmitting, receiving, and multiplex equipment, and the prewired modular racks are assets accessory to the operation of a business and therefore not real estate assets.

Rev. Rul. 80-151, 1980-1 C.B. 7, provides two examples that illustrate how the Service will apply the criteria set forth in *Whiteco Industries, Inc. v. Commission,* 65 T.C. 664 (1975) acq., 1980-1 C.B. 1, in determining whether outdoor advertising displays are inherently permanent structures or tangible personal property that qualified for the now-repealed investment tax credit. The criteria, which are in the form of questions, are: (1) is the property capable of being moved, and has it in fact been moved? (2) Is the property designed or constructed to remain permanently in place? (3) Are there circumstances that tend to show the expected or intended length of fixation, that is, are there circumstances that show the property may or will have to be moved? (4) How substantial a job is removal of the property, and how time-consuming is it? (5) How much damage will the property sustain upon its removal? (6) What is the manner of affixation of the property to the land?

The Steel Billboard Structures are substantial structures that are part of the building structures, or separately constructed structures in the case of the tower Steel Billboard Structures, and are designed and constructed to remain permanently in place. The Steel Billboard Structures range in width from 18 feet to 72 feet and in height from 16 feet to 72 feet (typically several stories high). Each of the structures and structural components has never been moved. Because the construction and permanency of the Steel Billboard Structures are substantially comparable to the transmitting and receiving towers in Rev. Rul. 75-424 and the mobile home units in Rev. Rul. 71-220, they are inherently permanent structures. Further, the Steel Billboard Structures are not assets accessory to the operation of a business.

Based on the facts as represented by Taxpayer, we conclude that the Steel Billboard Structures, are "real estate assets" and "interests in real property" for purposes of §§ 856(c)(5)(B) and (C).

Issue 2:

Section 856(d)(1) provides that rents from real property include (subject to exclusions provided in section 856(d)(2)): (A) rents from interests in real property; (B) charges for services customarily furnished or rendered in connection with the rental of real property, whether or not such charges are separately stated; and (C) rent attributable to personal property leased under, or in connection with, a lease of real property, but only if the rent attributable to the personal property for the taxable year does not exceed 15 percent of the total rent for the tax year attributable to both the real and personal property leased under, or in connection with, the lease.

Section 1.856-4(b)(1) provides that, for purposes of §§ 856(c)(2) and (c)(3), the term "rents from real property" includes charges for services customarily furnished or rendered in connection with the rental of real property, whether or not the charges are separately stated. Services rendered to tenants of a particular building will be considered customary if, in the geographic market in which the building is located, tenants in buildings of a similar class are customarily provided with the service. In particular geographic areas where it is customary to furnish electricity or other utilities to tenants in buildings of a particular class, the submetering of those utilities to tenants in the buildings will be considered a customary service. Section 1.856-4(b)(5)(ii) provides that the trustees or directors of a REIT are not required to delegate or contract out their fiduciary duty to manage the trust itself, as distinguished from rendering or furnishing services to the tenants of its property or managing or operating the property. Thus, the trustees or directors may do all those things necessary, in their fiduciary capacities, to manage and conduct the affairs of the trust itself.

Section 856(d)(2)(C) provides that any impermissible tenant service income is excluded from the definition of rents from real property. Section 856(d)(7)(A) defines impermissible tenant service income to mean, with respect to any real or personal property, any amount received or accrued directly or indirectly by the REIT for services furnished or rendered by the REIT to tenants at the property, or for managing or operating the property.

Section 856(d)(7)(B) provides that if the amount of impermissible tenant service income exceeds one percent of all amounts received or accrued during the tax year directly or indirectly by the REIT with respect to the property, the impermissible tenant service income of the REIT will include all of the amounts received or accrued with respect to the property. Section 856(d)(7)(D) provides that the amounts treated as received by a REIT for any impermissible tenant service shall not be less than 150 percent of the direct cost of the REIT in furnishing or rendering the service.

Section 856(d)(7)(C) provides certain exclusions from impermissible tenant service income. Section 856(d)(7)(C) provides that for purposes of section 856(d)(7)(A), services furnished or rendered, or management or operation provided, through an independent contractor from whom the REIT does not derive or receive any income shall not be treated as furnished, rendered, or provided by the REIT, and there shall not be taken into account any amount which would be excluded from unrelated business taxable income under section 512(b)(3) if received by an organization described in section 511(a)(2).

Section 512(b)(3) provides, in part, that there shall be excluded from the computation of unrelated business taxable income all rents from real property and all rents from personal property leased with such real property, if the rents attributable to such personal property are an incidental amount of the total rents received or accrued under the lease, determined at the time the personal property is placed in service.

Section 1.512(b)-1(c)(5) provides that payments for the use or occupancy of rooms and other space where services are also rendered to the occupant, such as for the use or occupancy of rooms or other quarters in hotels, boarding houses, or apartment houses furnishing hotel services, or in tourist camps or tourist homes, motor courts or motels, or for the use or occupancy of space in parking lots, warehouses, or storage garages, do not constitute rent from real property. Generally, services are considered rendered to the occupant if they are primarily for his convenience and are other than those usually or customarily rendered in connection with the rental of rooms or other space for occupancy only. The supplying of maid service, for example, constitutes such service; whereas the furnishing of heat and light, the cleaning of public entrances, exits, stairways and lobbies, and the collection of trash are not considered as services rendered to the occupant.

In Rev. Rul. 2002-38, 2002-2 C.B. 4, a REIT pays its TRS to provide noncustomary services to tenants. The REIT does not separately state charges to tenants for the services. Thus, a portion of the amounts received by the REIT from tenants represents an amount received for services provided by the TRS. TRS employees perform all of the services and TRS pays all of the costs of providing the services. The TRS also rents space from the REIT for carrying out its services to tenants. The revenue ruling concludes that the services provided to the REIT's tenants are considered to be rendered by the TRS, rather than the REIT, for purposes of § 856(c)(7)(i). Accordingly, the services do not give rise to impermissible tenant service income and do not cause any portion of the rents received by the REIT to fail to qualify as rents from real property under § 856(d).

In this case, any noncustomary services provided to tenants at the Steel Billboard Structures will be provided by TRS A, and the fees for the services will be either (a) separately stated from the rents received by Taxpayer and collected and retained by TRS A, or (b) included in the rent received by Taxpayer and Taxpayer will compensate TRS A on an arm's-length basis for providing the services. All costs associated with providing the noncustomary services will be paid by TRS A. Accordingly, income from services provided by TRS A to tenants of Taxpayer at each of the Steel Billboard Structures will be excepted from the definition of impermissible tenant service income, and the amounts received by Taxpayer from tenants of the Steel Billboard Structures will not be treated as other than rents from real property under § 856(d).

Issue 3:

Section 856(d)(2)(B) provides that rents from real property does not include any amount received or accrued directly or indirectly from any person if the REIT owns directly or indirectly: (1) in the case of a corporation, stock possessing 10 percent or more of the total combined voting power of all classes of stock entitled to vote, or 10 percent or more of the total value of shares of all classes of stock of the corporation; or (2) in the case of any person that is not a corporation, an interest of 10 percent or more in the assets or net profits of the person.

Section 856(d)(8) provides that rent received by a REIT from its TRS will not be excluded from rents from real property under § 856(d)(2) if the terms of the limited rental exception of § 856(d)(8)(A) are met. The requirements of § 856(d)(8)(A) are met with respect to any property if at least 90 percent of the leased space of the property is rented to persons other than TRSs of the REIT and other than persons described in § 856(d)(2)(B), but only to the extent that the amounts paid to the REIT as rents from real property (without regard to § 856(d)(2)(B)) from the property are substantially comparable to the rents paid by the other tenants of the REIT's property for comparable space.

In order to meet the limited rental exception of § 856(d)(8)(A), amounts paid to a REIT as rents from real property must be substantially comparable to rents paid by the other tenants of the REIT's property for comparable space. In the instant case, space leased by TRS A is unmarketable for traditional use and is unique at the property. Remaining leases at the property, although all or substantially all leased to unrelated tenants, is not comparable in terms of character or use to the space rented to TRS A. In these circumstances, where no comparable leased space exists within a property, § 856(d)(8)(A) may be satisfied by comparing the rent paid by TRS A to rent paid by unrelated tenants for comparable space in the same geographic area.

Accordingly, we conclude that amounts paid to Taxpayer by TRS A for the rental of the Steel Billboard Structures with respect to which there is no comparable space will not fail to qualify for the limited rental exception of § 856(d)(8)(A) if the rent paid by TRS A is substantially comparable to rents paid by unrelated tenants for comparable space in the same geographic area.

Except as specifically ruled upon above, no opinion is expressed concerning any federal income tax consequences relating to the facts herein under any other provision of the Code. Specifically, we do not rule whether (1) Taxpayer otherwise qualifies as a REIT under part II of subchapter M of Chapter 1 of the Code or (2) whether rents paid to Taxpayer by TRS A satisfy the requirements of § 856(d)(8)(A) concerning comparable rents.

This ruling is directed only to the taxpayer requesting it. Taxpayer should attach a copy of this ruling to each tax return to which it applies. Section 6110(k)(3) of the Code provides that this ruling may not be used or cited as precedent.

In accordance with the Power of Attorney on file with this office, a copy of this letter is being sent to your authorized representatives.

Sincerely,

Jonathan D. Silver
Assistant to the Branch Chief, Branch 2
Office of Associate Chief Counsel (Financial Institutions & Products)

Chapter 18

Loss Limitations

I. Commentary

If a property owner suffers economic loss with respect to a property, generally the property owner's natural desire is to claim a loss deduction to reduce taxable income and tax liability. Tax advisors often look for ways to capture the benefit of tax losses, but they must be aware of rules that might limit the deductibility of losses. Tax law recognizes that some efforts to claim loss deductions may not reflect the economic realities of a property owner's situation. Consequently, tax law has multiple provisions that limit loss deductions. Most real estate advisors will have a general understanding of limits imposed on capital losses and losses from transfers to related parties.[1] Other provisions also limit the deductibility of losses. In particular, the passive activity loss rules and the at-risk rules may limit the amount of loss a property owner, or investor in property, may deduct with respect to property. Consider the general rules of each of those deduction-limiting regimes.

A. Passive-Activity Loss Rules

Parties who invest in real estate ventures often must pay attention to the rules that govern the deductibility of losses from passive activities. Generally, tax law disallows deductions for losses from passive activity incurred by most non-corporate persons.[2] The application of this loss disallowance turns on the definition of passive activity loss. Passive activity loss is the amount by which losses from all passive activities exceed gains from all passive activities.[3] A passive activity is any activity that involves the conduct of a trade or business in which the taxpayer does not materially partic-

---

1. *See* I.R.C. § 1211 (limiting the amount of allowed capital loss to the amount of capital gains plus, in the case of a taxpayer other than a corporation, no more than $3,000); I.R.C. § 267(a) (disallowing a loss on sales or exchanges of property to a related party).

2. *See* I.R.C. § 469(a)(1) (disallowing passive activity credits as well). *See also* I.R.C. § 469(b) (allowing a carryover of disallowed passive losses or credits); I.R.C. § 469(i) (suspending the loss disallowance for certain small rental activities).

3. *See* I.R.C. § 469(d). *See also* I.R.C. § 469(e) (providing rules for determining the amount of income or loss from a passive activity); Carlos v. Comm'r, 123 T.C. 275 (2004) (preventing taxpayers from converting nonpassive income into passive income to ensure passive losses do not offset nonpassive income).

ipate.[4] To avoid the application of the loss disallowance, the ownership of property must constitute a trade or business and the owner must materially participate in trade or business. Fairly detailed rules define material participation.[5] If a property owner wishes to avoid the passive activity loss rules, the property owner must satisfy those rules. To do so, the property owner may be able to combine several trade or business activities or rental activities.[6] Alternatively, property owners may attempt to show that income from others sources is passive, so they can deduct their passive losses against that income.[7]

Rental activity is per se a passive activity,[8] but a real estate professional who materially participates in the rental activity can overcome the passive characterization.[9] A person is a real estate professional if the person performs more than one half of the person's total personal services in real property trades or businesses in which the person materially participates and the person's services in such trades or businesses exceed 750 hours.[10] Generally, the passive loss rules apply to a real estate professional as if each of the professional's interests in real property were a separate activity, but the professional may elect to treat all interests in real property as a single activity.[11] Additionally, the real estate professional must materially participate in the rental activity.[12]

B. At-Risk Rules

Tax law also limits deductions to the amount a property owner has at risk in an activity at the end of the taxable year.[13] The at-risk rules apply to the ownership of real estate.[14] A person is at risk with respect to an activity to the extent of money or the adjusted basis of property contributed to the activity or amounts borrowed with respect to the activity.[15] Generally a person must be personally liable or pledge property as security for an amount to be at risk with respect to borrowed amounts.[16] The one

---

4. *See* I.R.C. §469(c)(1); I.R.C §469(c)(6) (defining trade or business broadly).

5. *See* I.R.C. §469(h)(1); Treas. Reg. §1.469-5T.

6. *See* Treas. Reg. §1.469-4(c).

7. *See, e.g.,* Beecher v. Comm'r, 481 F.3d 717 (9th Cir. 2007).

8. *See* I.R.C. §469(c)(2).

9. *See* I.R.C. §469(c)(7).

10. *See* I.R.C. §469(c)(7)(B). A real property trade or business for this purpose means real property, development, redevelopment, construction, reconstruction, acquisition, conversion, rental, operation, management, leasing, and brokerage trade or business. *See* I.R.C. §469(c)(7)(C); Moss v. Comm'r, 135 T.C. 365 (2010).

11. *See* I.R.C. §469(c)(7)(A) (flush language).

12. *See id.*

13. *See* I.R.C. §465(a)(1).

14. *See* I.R.C. §465(c)(3)(A).

15. *See* I.R.C. §465(b)(1).

16. *See* I.R.C. §465(b)(2). *But see* I.R.C. §465(b)(3)(A) (excluding from the definition of amounts borrowed, amounts borrowed from a person who has an interest in such activity or from a person related to a person who has an interest in such activity); I.R.C. §465(b)(4) (providing that a taxpayer shall not be at risk with respect to amounts protected against loss through nonrecourse financing, guarantees, stop loss agreements, or other similar arrangements); Melvin v. Comm'r, 894 F.2d 1072

exception to this rule is that a real property owner may be at risk with respect to the property owner's share of any qualified nonrecourse financing which is secured by the property.[17] Financing must satisfy four requirements to be qualified nonrecourse financing.[18]

First, the property owner must borrow the financing with respect to the activity of holding real property.[19] Second, the property owner must borrow the financing from a qualified person or the financing must be a loan from or guaranteed by a certain governmental entity.[20] A qualified person is any person in the business of lending money.[21] The person cannot, however, be related to the property owner, be the person from whom the property owner acquired the property, or be a person who receives a fee with respect to the investment in the property.[22] Third, generally no person can be personally liable for the financing.[23] Finally, the financing cannot be convertible debt.[24] Thus, a property owner may be at risk with respect to some nonrecourse financing. If a property owner is a member of an entity taxed as a partner, the property owner's share of the entities qualified nonrecourse financing shall depend upon the allocation of that financing under the section 752 rules.[25]

C. Section 1031 and Nonrecognition of Loss

Section 1031 generally provides that a property owner cannot recognize loss on the transfer of property as part of an exchange that meets the requirements of section 1031, even if the property owner receives boot.[26] If a property owner plans to transfer property with unrealized loss in exchange for like-kind property, the question becomes whether the property owner may structure the transaction to purposely fail some of the requirements of section 1031. The IRS has successfully challenged such efforts,[27] so tax attorneys may have difficulty devising structures that can overcome the section 1031 loss disallowance in the direct exchange context.[28]

(9th Cir. 1990) (holding that partner is protected against losses related to a liability to the extent that he had a right to contribution from his other partners, so the partner could only deduct his pro rata share of the bad partnership loan).

17. *See* I.R.C. § 465(b)(6)(A).

18. *See* I.R.C. § 465(b)(6)(B).

19. *See* I.R.C. § 465(b)(6)(B)(i).

20. *See* I.R.C. § 465(b)(6)(B)(ii).

21. *See* I.R.C. § 465(b)(6)(D)(i) (referencing section 49(a)(1)(D)(iv)).

22. *See* I.R.C. § 49(a)(1)(D)(iv).

23. *See* I.R.C. § 465(b)(6)(B)(iii).

24. *See* I.R.C. § 465(b)(6)(B)(iv).

25. *See* I.R.C. § 465(b)(6)(C).

26. *See* I.R.C. § 1031(a), (c).

27. *See* Redwing Carriers, Inc. v. Tomlinson, 399 F.2d 652 (5th Cir. 1968), *reproduced supra* Chapter 10; Rev. Rul. 61-119, 1961-1 C.B. 395.

28. *But see* Bell Lines, Inc. v. U.S. 480 F.2d 710 (4th Cir. 1973) (holding that a structure was not an exchange where the taxpayer was unaware that the form of the structure did not represent the substance).

II. Primary Legal Authority

Beecher v. Commissioner

United States Court of Appeals, Ninth Circuit
481 F.3d 717 (2007)

COVELLO, DISTRICT JUDGE.

This is an appeal from a decision of the United States Tax Court upholding a tax deficiency determination of the Commissioner of Internal Revenue ("Commissioner").[29] It is brought pursuant to Internal Revenue Code § 7482.[30] The appellants, Gary Beecher and Dolores Beecher ("Beechers") challenge the tax court's ruling that the Beechers cannot apply losses from their various rental properties to offset rental income derived from leases of office space in their home to lessee corporations which they happen to own.

The issues presented are: 1) whether Treasury Regulation § 1.469-2(f)(6), as applied to "C" corporations,[31] is arbitrary, capricious, or contrary to Internal Revenue Code § 469 ("Section 469"); 2) whether Congress's delegation of authority to the Secretary of the Treasury to promulgate regulations pursuant to Section 469 is unconstitutional; and 3) whether the Commissioner must show that a taxpayer was motivated to shelter income as a prerequisite to applying Treasury Regulation § 1.469-2(f)(6).

For the reasons set forth hereinafter, we AFFIRM the decision of the tax court.

I. FACTS

A review of the record reveals the following undisputed material facts.

Gary Beecher and Dolores Beecher are husband and wife. Gary Beecher wholly owns Cal Interiors, Inc., a "C" corporation, that engages in the business of repairing automobile interiors. Dolores Beecher wholly owns S & C Dent Corp., also a "C" corporation, that engages in the business of removing dents from automobiles.

Both Beechers work full time for these corporations, and both corporations' offices are located in the Beechers' home. The corporations pay the Beechers rent for the use of this office space. In addition to renting this portion of their home, the Beechers also own five rental properties.

On their 1997, 1998, and 1999 federal income tax returns, the Beechers reported net income from the leases of the office of $39,307, $23,387, and $22,160, respectively. During these same years, the five other rental properties yielded net losses, such that

---

29. [1] "Within 90 days … after the notice of deficiency … is mailed…, the taxpayer may file a petition with the Tax Court for a redetermination of the deficiency." I.R.C. § 6213(a). "[T]he Tax Court shall have jurisdiction to redetermine the correct amount of the deficiency…." I.R.C. § 6214(a).

30. [2] "The United States Courts of Appeals … shall have exclusive jurisdiction to review the decisions of the Tax Court…." I.R.C. § 7482(a)(1).

31. [3] Under Chapter 1, Subchapter C of the Internal Revenue Code, the income of a "C" corporation is subject to corporate tax, and any distributions that the corporation makes to its shareholders is subject to a second, individual tax. See I.R.C. § 301 et seq.

the combined losses of the five properties exceeded the income derived from the leases of the office. As a result of this combination of income and losses, the Beechers paid no tax on the rental income paid to them by their corporations.

Although rental income is generally characterized as "passive,"[32] the Commissioner determined that the income from the leases of the office was non-passive income, pursuant to the "self-rental" rule of Treasury Regulation § 1.469-2(f)(6).[33] The Commissioner reached this conclusion because the Beechers materially participated in the business activities of the lessee corporations, a fact which the Beechers do not contest. As such, the Commissioner determined that the net income from the leases of the office in their home could not be offset by the losses from the five other rental properties. Because the income from the office leases could not be offset, it was subject to taxation. Therefore, having concluded that the Beechers had incurred a tax liability, the Commissioner issued a notice of deficiency.

The Beechers thereafter filed a petition in the United States Tax Court challenging this determination. The court rendered judgment for the Commissioner, basing its decision on its own precedent, as well as that of the Seventh, First, and Fifth Circuits, citing *Krukowski v. Commissioner*, 279 F.3d 547 (7th Cir.2002), *Sidell v. Commissioner*, 225 F.3d 103 (1st Cir.2000), and *Fransen v. United States*, 191 F.3d 599 (5th Cir.1999).

II. STANDARD OF REVIEW

The Court of Appeals reviews de novo the Tax Court's conclusions of law, including its construction of the tax code. *Biehl v. Comm'r*, 351 F.3d 982, 985 (9th Cir.2003). As a general rule, "the tax decisions of other circuits should be followed unless they are demonstrably erroneous or there appear cogent reasons for rejecting them." *Popov v. Comm'r*, 246 F.3d 1190, 1195 (9th Cir.2001) (internal quotation omitted).

When reviewing regulations, where "there is an express delegation of authority to the agency to elucidate a specific provision of the statute by regulation ... [s]uch legislative regulations are given controlling weight unless they are arbitrary, capricious, or manifestly contrary to the statute." *Chevron U.S.A. Inc. v. Natural Res. Def. Council, Inc.*, 467 U.S. 837, 843–44, 104 S.Ct. 2778, 81 L.Ed.2d 694 (1984); *see Dykstra v. Comm'r*, 260 F.3d 1181, 1182 (9th Cir.2001) (per curiam) (applying the *Chevron* standard in the context of tax regulations).

III. DISCUSSION

Congress enacted Section 469 of the Internal Revenue Code to prevent taxpayers from applying losses from rental properties and other passive business activities to offset and shelter non-passive income, such as wages. *See* S.Rep. No. 99–313, at 716–18 (1986), *reprinted in* 1986 U.S.C.C.A.N. 4075, 4235. Section 469 provides in part:

---

32. [4] "The term 'passive activity' means any activity—(A) which involves the conduct of any trade or business, and (B) in which the taxpayer does not materially participate." I.R.C. § 469(c)(1).

33. [5] "An amount of the taxpayer's gross rental activity income for the taxable year from an item of property equal to the net rental activity income for the year from that item of property is treated as not from a passive activity if the property ... [i]s rented for use in a trade or business activity ... in which the taxpayer materially participates ... for the taxable year...." Treas. Reg. § 1.469-2(f)(6).

"[F]or any taxable year..., neither—(A) the passive activity loss, nor (B) the passive activity credit, for the taxable year shall be allowed." I.R.C. § 469(a)(1). As such, tax-payers are not permitted to take advantage of a net loss from passive activity in a given tax year, but rather must treat such losses as a deduction allocable to passive activity in the next taxable year. I.R.C. §§ 469(a)–(b).

Generally, "[t]he term 'passive activity' means any activity—(A) which involves the conduct of any trade or business, and (B) in which the taxpayer does not materially participate." I.R.C. § 469(c)(1). Moreover, the term "passive activity" also "includes any rental activity...." I.R.C. § 469(c)(2).

When Congress enacted Section 469, it also authorized the Secretary of the Treasury to promulgate regulations concerning passive activity tax shelters, including regulations that recharacterize otherwise passive activities as non-passive. *See* I.R.C. § 469(*l*). Specifically, Section 469 provides that: "The Secretary shall prescribe such regulations as may be necessary or appropriate to carry out provisions of this section, including regulations ... (3) requiring net income or gain from a limited partnership or other passive activity to be treated as not from a passive activity...." I.R.C. § 469(*l*).

Pursuant to this authority, the Secretary issued Treasury Regulation § 1.469-2(f)(6). This regulation provides in relevant part that:

> An amount of the taxpayer's gross rental activity income for the taxable year from an item of property equal to the net rental activity income for the year from that item of property is treated as not from a passive activity if the property ... [i]s rented for use in a trade or business activity ... in which the tax-payer materially participates ... for the taxable year
>
> ....

Treas. Reg. § 1.469-2(f)(6). This regulation is known as the "self-rental" rule. *Krukowski v. Comm'r*, 279 F.3d 547, 551 (7th Cir.2002). "In essence, the regulation provides that when a taxpayer rents property to his own business, the income is not passive activity income." *Fransen v. United States,* 191 F.3d 599, 600 (5th Cir.1999).

A. Validity of the Self-Rental Rule

The Beechers contend that the IRS exceeded its rule making authority by issuing the self-rental rule. They argue that the rule, "as applied to 'C' corporations[is] arbitrary, capricious and contrary to statute and ... thus invalid." Without specifically explaining why this is the case, the Beechers simply incorporate by reference the arguments asserted by tax-payers in the decisions of those courts that previously have addressed this issue. Specifically, they cite *Krukowski v. Commissioner,* 279 F.3d 547 (7th Cir.2002), *Sidell v. Commissioner,* 225 F.3d 103 (1st Cir.2000), and *Fransen v. United States,* 191 F.3d 599 (5th Cir.1999), as well as the lower court decisions in these cases. Notably, the Beechers concede that in each of the cited cases, the Seventh, First, and Fifth Circuits rejected the arguments of the petitioning tax-payers.

The taxpayers in those cases argued, as presumably do the Beechers, that the self-rental rule's recharacterization of certain rental income as non-passive is contrary to the tax code's general classification of rental activity as passive. While the Beechers acknowledge that Section 469 empowers the Secretary to promulgate regulations that recharacterize passive activities as non-passive, they would have this court construe this authority as being very limited. Specifically, they appear to read Section 469 as authorizing the Secretary to recharacterize only two types of activities: 1) limited partnerships; and 2) activities not otherwise classified in Section 469.

Their interpretation, however, has little support in the text of the code. Section 469 directs the Secretary to issue regulations "necessary or appropriate to carry out provisions of this section, including regulations ... requiring net income or gain from a limited partnership or *other passive activity to be treated as not from a passive activity....*" I.R.C. § 469(*l*) (emphasis added). The plain text of Section 469 simply does not bear out the taxpayers' strained interpretation that "other passive activity" refers to passive activity that, unlike rental activity, is not otherwise classified in the code.

To the contrary, the Commissioner asks that we adopt an interpretation that is consistent with the text of the code. Namely, that the provision that provides for "regulations ... requiring net income or gain from a limited partnership or other passive activity to be treated as not from a passive activity," I.R.C. § 469(*l*), refers to regulations that treat income from any passive activity, including a limited partnership, as income from a non-passive activity. Because this case concerns a statute in which "there is an express delegation of authority to the agency to elucidate a specific provision of the statute by regulation," we must afford the Commissioner's interpretation "controlling weight unless ... [it is] arbitrary, capricious, or manifestly contrary to the statute." *Chevron U.S.A. Inc. v. Natural Resources Defense Council, Inc.,* 467 U.S. 837, 843–44, 104 S.Ct. 2778, 81 L.Ed.2d 694 (1984). Applying this standard, we conclude that the Commissioner's construction of Section 469 is valid. As such, the Secretary did not exceed his authority by promulgating the self-rental rule.

Notably, this conclusion is supported by the legislative history of Section 469.[34] The House of Representatives Conference Report reviewing the Secretary's prospective authority under Section 469 states:

> The conferees intend that this authority be exercised to protect the underlying purpose of the passive loss provision, i.e., preventing the sheltering of positive income sources through the use of tax losses derived from passive business activities.... Examples of where the exercise of such authority may ... be appropriate include the following ... (2) related property leases or subleases, with respect to property used in a business activity, that have the effect of reducing active business income and creating passive income....

H.R.Rep. No. 99–841, at 147 (1986), *reprinted in* 1986 U.S.C.C.A.N. 4075, 4235. The example in the report appears to squarely address the present case, and strongly

---

34. [6] As the Beechers' interpretation of Section 469 is without support in the text of the code, arguably there is no need to look further to the legislative history. *See United States v. Daas,* 198 F.3d 1167, 1174 (9th Cir.1999) ("If the statute is ambiguous — and only then — courts may look to its legislative history for evidence of congressional intent.")

suggests that Congress intended the Secretary to issue regulations like the one that the Beechers now contend is contrary to the tax code.

By rejecting the Beechers' argument that the self-rental rule is contrary to Section 469, we join those circuits that already have addressed this question, and uniformly upheld the regulation. *See Krukowski v. Comm'r*, 279 F.3d 547, 552 (7th Cir.2002); *Sidell v. Comm'r*, 225 F.3d 103, 107 (1st Cir.2000); *Fransen v. United States*, 191 F.3d 599, 600–01 (5th Cir.1999). These courts have all held the self-rental rule is a valid regulation in light of the plain text of Section 469, as well as its legislative history. *Krukowski*, 279 F.3d at 552; *Sidell*, 225 F.3d at 107–08; *Fransen*, 191 F.3d at 600–01. Likewise, the First and Fifth Circuits have discounted the notion that the self-rental rule is somehow inapplicable specifically to "C" corporations. *Sidell*, 225 F.3d at 108; *Fransen*, 191 F.3d at 601.[35]

B. Validity of Congress's Grant of Authority to the Secretary

The Beechers next argue that the provisions under which the Secretary promulgated the self-rental rule are unconstitutional. Specifically, they contend that Congress's grant of regulatory authority to the I.R.S. is so "vague" and "uncertain" as to be invalid. We disagree.

Although the Constitution vests exclusively with Congress legislative or decision-making authority, Congress may nevertheless confer "decisionmaking authority upon agencies" so long as it establishes "by legislative [act] an intelligible principle to which the person or body authorized to act is directed to conform." *Whitman v. Am. Trucking Ass'ns*, 531 U.S. 457, 472, 121 S.Ct. 903, 149 L.Ed.2d 1 (2001) (internal quotation omitted, alteration in the original). Here, in Section 469, Congress has directed the Secretary to "prescribe such regulations as may be necessary or appropriate to carry out [the] provisions" of Section 469, including regulations that "specify what constitutes an activity, material participation, or active participation" and regulations "requiring net income or gain from ... other passive activity to be treated as not from a passive activity...." I.R.C. § 469(*l*). Such direction is sufficient to avoid offending the Constitution, and ample when compared to other statutory schemes that courts have held to be lawful. *See, e.g., Am. Power & Light Co. v. SEC*, 329 U.S. 90, 104, 67 S.Ct. 133, 91 L.Ed. 103 (1946) (upholding the statutory delegation of authority to the SEC to modify the structure of holding company systems to ensure that they are not "unduly or unnecessarily complicate[d]" and do not "unfairly or inequitably distribute voting power among security holders"); *New York Cent. Sec. Corp. v. United States*, 287 U.S. 12, 24–25, 53 S.Ct. 45, 77 L.Ed. 138 (1932) (upholding the statutory delegation of authority to the ICC to approve railroad consolidations so long as the mergers are in the "public interest"); *United States v. Dahl*, 314 F.3d 976, 978 (9th

---

35. [7] The Beechers repeatedly note that they were leasing their home office space specifically to "C" corporations. There is no provision in Section 469 or the self-rental rule that would provide for distinct tax treatment for "C" corporations in this context. Why the court should create such a distinction is not self-evident, and the Beechers, for their part, do nothing to explain why such a distinction is warranted here.

Cir.2002) (citing *Whitman v. Am. Trucking Ass'ns*, 531 U.S. 457, 472–76, 121 S.Ct. 903, 149 L.Ed.2d 1 (2001), and upholding the statutory delegation of authority to the U.S. Forest Service to "charge and collect fees for … use of out door recreation sites"). As such, we reject the Beechers' argument that Congress's delegation of authority to issue the self-rental rule under Section 469(*l*) is unconstitutional. In so holding, we join the Seventh Circuit, which has reached a similar conclusion. *See Krukowski v. Comm'r*, 279 F.3d 547, 552 (7th Cir.2002).

C. Validity of the Application of the Self-Rental Rule

Finally, the Beechers contend that even if the self-rental rule is valid, it should not apply to them. Specifically, they argue that the rule is inapplicable because Section 469(*l*) "was enacted specifically to combat 'abusive' tax shelters and does not apply where motivation is for a bona fide business purpose."

The Commissioner concedes that Section 469 was enacted to combat tax shelter abuse, but notes that Congress did not expressly limit its scope "to transactions where a specific tax-avoidance motive was alleged and proved." Further, "[i]t simply would not be feasible for the Commissioner to examine each taxpayer's motive in entering into a related party lease with an active business he controls." As the Tax Court noted below, there is "nothing in the statute or the legislative history" that suggests that the tax-payer must lack a bona fide business purpose in order to fall within the scope of Section 469. The relevant statutory distinction under Section 469 is not between tax-payers who contrive to limit their tax liability and those who do not. *See* I.R.C. § 469(c)(1). Rather, the distinction between passive and non-passive activities is that in the case of passive activities, the "taxpayer does not materially participate" in the business. *Id.* This question hinges on the extent to which the taxpayer is involved in the affairs of both sides of a given transaction, not the taxpayer's motivation for structuring the transaction in a particular manner. *See id.*

Accordingly, the applicability of Treasury Regulation § 1.469-2(f)(6) is not limited to those instances in which a specific tax-avoidance motive is alleged and proved by the Commissioner.

AFFIRMED.

Melvin v. Commissioner

United States Court of Appeals, Ninth Circuit
894 F.2d 1072

Per Curiam:

Marcus Melvin appeals the Tax Court's partial disallowance of a deduction for a bad partnership loan. The Tax Court held that Melvin was "at risk" for, and therefore could deduct under 26 U.S.C. § 465, only for his pro rata share of the loan. The court disallowed the deduction of the remaining portion of the loan, even though Melvin was personally liable for the entire amount, because any portion over the pro rata share was recoverable by right of contribution under California law. We affirm.

FACTS AND PROCEEDINGS

During 1979, Marcus Melvin owned a 71.4286 percent interest in Medici Film Partners ("Medici"), an Oregon general partnership. In 1979, Medici purchased a .872466 percent interest in ACG Motion Picture Investment Fund ("ACG"), a California limited partnership. The ACG partnership agreement provided that all rights and responsibilities of the general and limited partners would be governed by California law. Through his investment in Medici, Marcus owned a .6232 percent share of ACG as a limited partner.

Medici purchased its interest in ACG for $105,000, by making a cash down payment of $35,000 and giving a $70,000 recourse promissory note to ACG for a deferred capital contribution. The note was payable in five equal annual installments of $14,000, plus interest at nine percent per annum, to begin in 1981. Marcus' share of the down payment and recourse note was $25,000 and $50,000 respectively.

In 1979, ACG obtained a $3.5 million recourse loan from the First National Bank of Chicago. The principal was payable in full on December 14, 1981. As collateral, ACG pledged the recourse promissory notes from its 73 limited partners, which reflected their obligations to make deferred capital contributions. The combined face amount of those notes amounted to more than $8 million. Medici's $70,000 promissory note to ACG was among those notes pledged as collateral on the bank loan.

During 1979, ACG incurred a net operating loss of $12,515.318. For the purposes of this appeal, the parties stipulated that ACG had a $3.5 million outstanding recourse obligation at the end of 1979. Marcus and his wife Marilyn filed a joint 1979 tax return which claimed losses of $75,000 for his investment in ACG: $25,000 cash and $50,000 for liability on the note.

The Tax Commissioner first asserted a deficiency in Marcus' income for an unrelated deduction. After the Melvins petitioned for a redetermination of the deficiency, the Commissioner then claimed a deficiency based upon Marcus' ACG investment, arguing that Marcus Melvin was not personally liable for repayment of any portion of ACG's bank loan. Later, the Commissioner conceded that Marcus was liable for his pro rata share of the loan but argued that he was not at risk for anything beyond that. The ACG investment deficiency is the only issue on appeal by the Melvins.

The Tax Court held that Marcus was entitled to deduct his pro rata share of ACG's bank loan, that is, .6232 percent of $3.5 million for a total amount of $46,812, as well as his $25,000 cash contribution to ACG. *Melvin v. Commissioner,* 88 T.C. 63 (1987). It ruled that Marcus was "personally liable" within the meaning of section 465(b)(2) for repayment of the bank loan to the extent of the obligation on Medici's note to ACG because the note was to serve as the ultimate source for repayment if the partnership itself did not have the funds to pay the loan.

The court ruled that Marcus was personally liable for payments on Medici's note in 1979 even though the payments did not have to be made until 1981, two years beyond the taxable year in question. It based its ruling on the fact that Marcus' obligations to pay ACG were definite and fixed and that ACG negotiated the bank loan at arm's length.

Although Marcus was found to be personally liable to the bank on Medici's note, the Tax Court did not allow Marcus to deduct the entire amount of his liability. Relying upon Section 465(b)(4), the Tax Court found Marcus was not at risk for amounts exceeding his pro rata share of his partnership's $3.5 million loan. Section 465(b)(4) excludes deductions for risks that are protected by "loss-limiting arrangements". The court deemed Marcus to be protected against loss by a right of contribution under California law from his other limited partners.

Using a previously "fixed and definite" standard to determine Marcus' personal liability, the Tax Court found that it did not matter whether payment was a result of immediate or prospective protection. The court also found that whether the protection was established by state law or binding agreement between the parties did not matter.

This timely appeal followed.

DISCUSSION

The application of the law to the undisputed facts is reviewed de novo. *Sennett v. Commissioner*, 752 F.2d 428, 430 (9th Cir.1985).

26 U.S.C. §465(a)(1) permits an individual who invests in motion picture films to deduct any loss from his investment, to the extent that he was "at risk" in the activity at the end of the taxable year. A taxpayer is considered to be at risk for the amount of cash contributed and amounts borrowed for the activity. Section 465(b)(1)(A) and (B). With respect to borrowed funds, however, the amounts must have been borrowed for use in the activity and the taxpayer must be personally liable for repayment of such amounts or have pledged property other than property used in this activity as security for such borrowed amount. Sections 465(b)(2)(A) and (B). Furthermore, the taxpayer is not at risk for "amounts protected against loss through nonrecourse financing, guarantees, stop loss agreements, or other similar arrangements." Section 465(b)(4).

Since 26 U.S.C. §465(b)(4) does not specifically define "other similar arrangements", we turn to the legislative history of the section for guidance. Section 465 was added in 1976 to the Internal Revenue Code of 1954 to combat abuse of tax shelters caused by nonrecourse financing, and other "situations in which taxpayers [were] effectively immunized from any realistic possibility of suffering an economic loss even though the underlying transaction was not profitable." *Pritchett v. Commissioner*, 827 F.2d 644, 646 (9th Cir.1987); *Porreca v. Commissioner*, 86 T.C. 821, 838 (1986).

As the Senate Finance Committee explained:

> A taxpayer's capital is not ... "at risk" ... to the extent he is protected against economic loss of all or part of such capital by reason of an agreement or arrangement for compensation or reimbursement to him of any loss which he may suffer. Under this concept, an investor is not "at risk" if he arranges to receive insurance or other compensation for an economic loss after the loss is sustained, or if he is entitled to reimbursement for part or all of any loss by reason of the binding agreement between himself and another person.

S.Rep. No. 938, 94th Cong., 2d Sess. 49 (1976) U.S.Code Cong. & Admin.News pp. 2897, 3439, 3484 ("Senate Report").

The Melvins rely upon the Senate Report to make three arguments as to why a right of contribution from partners under California law is not the type of loss-limiting arrangement contemplated by Section 465(b). First, they argue that the Senate Report left the right of contribution from the list of loss-limiting arrangements and signifies that Congress did not intend the right of contribution to be considered in that category. We are not persuaded because the Senate Report when enumerating examples of those type of arrangements did not contain limiting language and does not constitute an exhaustive list of such arrangements.

Second, the Melvins argue that the Senate Report indicates that Congress intended only to include situations actively arranged by taxpayers rather than the passive assumption through the force of law of the listed types of loss-limiting arrangements: Congress thus intended only to eliminate deductions where an investor has taken steps to limit his risk by arrangement or agreement with another person.

No reason is given why Congress would distinguish between protections "actively" created by an investor from ones "passively" created by state law and we see no basis for making the distinction between those kinds of protections. The legislative history of Section 465 indicates that it was enacted with a broad purpose of preventing any "situation where the taxpayer may deduct a loss in excess of his economic investment." *Id.* at 48 (1976).

Finally, the Melvins argue that Section 465(b)(4) applies only to rights created by contract rather than by tort law. They point out that the Senate Report states: "[a] taxpayer who obtains casualty insurance or insurance protecting himself against tort liability will not be considered not at risk solely because of such insurance protection," *id.* at 50, and thus, they argue, insurance against tort liability was specifically excluded to show that all types of protection under tort law are excluded from Section 465(b)(4). Congress distinguished between rights derived from contract as opposed to tort law, the Melvins argue, because procedures for obtaining reimbursement for torts are too uncertain, cumbersome and protracted to ensure protection against loss. Accordingly, they argue, reimbursement from partners under a right of contribution is uncertain because other partners may not be solvent. They point out further that under California law, a partner must obtain court permission to dissolve a partnership before seeking contribution and such permission is not always obtainable.

We find a dearth of authority for this proposition and conclude that for protection against loss we apply the same principles of logic as used to determine a taxpayer's risk in a transaction.

In *Pritchett*, we held that limited partners were "at risk" under Section 465(b) for a partnership's recourse debt even though the partners were not personally and directly liable to the creditors of the debt.

Instead of focusing on the personal and direct liability aspect we asked who had the ultimate responsibility for the debt and examined the "substance" of the transaction, not its form. *Pritchett,* 827 F.2d at 647. The "economic reality" of the situation is the key factor in determining who is ultimately liable for a debt. *Id.*, quoting *Durkin v. Commissioner*, 87 T.C. 1329, 1379 (1986).

In *Pritchett*, we found the limited partners ultimately responsible for their partnership's debt because they were contractually bound to make additional capital contributions when called upon to do so by general partners to compensate for any deficiency caused by failure to pay off the debt. Even though it was not known whether the general partners would make a cash call upon the limited partners, we held that the limited partners were at risk because the contract made the calls mandatory and "economic" reality ensured that the general partners would enforce their rights. *Id.*

Although *Pritchett* and *Durkin* involved contractual obligations, we find no basis to distinguish those obligations from those derived from tort law. Neither are we persuaded that recovery under tort law is more risky than recovery under contract law. The risk of finding a solvent obligor is present under both theories of law.

Further, the difficulty in dissolving limited partnerships is exaggerated although it is true that no contribution can be asked for until a partnership is dissolved. *Stodd v. Goldberger*, 73 Cal.App.3d 827, 837, 141 Cal.Rptr. 67, 73 (1977).

Under Cal.Corp.Code. Section 15510(1)(c) (West 1977), a limited partner has the same rights as a general partner in dissolving a partnership by decree of the court. Under Sections 15032(1)(e) and (f) of the Cal.Corp.Code, a court is required to decree a dissolution whenever the business of the partnership can only be carried on at a loss or when other circumstances render a dissolution "equitable". If Marcus Melvin were required to pay his obligation under the note to ACG, ACG would have been operating under a loss and a dissolution of ACG would have been required under Section 15032(1)(e).

We conclude that economic reality would dictate enforcement of the Marcus Melvin's statutory right to contribution from his other partners for amounts he would have been required to pay beyond his pro rata share of ACG's loan. As a result, Marcus Melvin would not have been the one who was ultimately liable for those excess amounts because he was protected against those losses within the meaning of 26 U.S.C. § 465(b)(4).

The Melvins finally argue that, even if the Tax Court were correct in holding that a right of contribution is a loss-limiting arrangement, its decision was wrong because no right of contribution existed for limited partners under California law at that time. This issue was not argued below. As a general rule, we will not consider an issue raised for the first time on appeal. *Bolker v. Commissioner*, 760 F.2d 1039, 1042 (9th Cir.1985). Therefore, we decline to address the issue.

The opinion of the Tax Court is AFFIRMED.

Bell Lines, Inc. v. United States

United States Court of Appeals, Fourth Circuit
480 F.2d 710 (1973)

A corporation which trades in old trucks and pays boot in money for new truck' comes under Int. Rev. Code of 1954, § 1031; any gain on the trade-in is not rec nized.[36] There is, however, a capital gain, fully recognizable in the year of the transaction, where a corporation sells old trucks at a profit even though the proceeds are used to purchase new trucks.[37] The two prior sentences are, obviously, simply different characterizations of the same economic event: replacement of property held for productive use in trade or business. But upon such characterizations tax consequences depend.[38] If the transaction is said to be a sale and purchase rather than an exchange, the taxpayer's future basis for depreciation is the actual cost of the new trucks. In this case Bell Lines treated truck replacement in its tax returns as a sale of old trucks and a separate purchase of new ones, and depreciated the new ones at full purchase price. The Commissioner viewed the transaction as a nontaxable exchange of old trucks for new trucks and accordingly adjusted the basis of the new trucks downward, reducing claimed depreciation deductions. In its suit for refund of taxes paid, the taxpayer prevailed in the district court, and the government appeals. We affirm.

Details of the transaction are as follows. The taxpayer, Bell Lines, Inc., as a West Virginia corporation with its principal place of business at Charleston, West Virginia, operated an interstate trucking line during 1959, 1960, and 1961. During this period of time, taxpayer's stock was owned by its officers and directors: John Amos, President; Fred Sclavi, Vice-President and General Manager; Betty Winterholler, Secretary-Treasurer.

In the spring of 1959, taxpayer decided to replace the major portion of its truck tractors. Mack Trucks, Inc., and White Motor Corporation submitted competitive bids, and in the course of bargaining White urged the taxpayer that more could be obtained for the old trucks by selling them to a buyer White had found than by trading them to Mack. Mack immediately offered to buy the old trucks rather than take them as trades. The taxpayer refused Mack's offer and stated that taxpayer was only interested in purchasing new trucks from Mack. Mack, in order to be competitive with White, offered to help taxpayer find a buyer.

Subsequently Mack submitted a proposal for the new tractors with prices quoted without reference to any tradeins. On June 24, 1959, the board of directors of taxpayer

---

36. [1] Int. Rev. Code of 1954, § 1031 provides in relevant part:
   (a) Nonrecognition of gain or loss from exchanges solely in kind.—No gain or loss shall be recognized if property held for productive use in trade or business or for investment (not including stock in trade or other property held primarily for sale, nor stocks, bonds, notes, choses in action, certificates of trust or beneficial interest, or other securities or evidences of indebtedness or interest) is exchanged solely for property of a like kind to be held either for productive use in trade or business or for investment .
   ...
   (d) Basis.—If property was acquired on an exchange described in this section, ... then the basis shall be the same as that of the property exchanged,....
37. [2] Int. Rev. Code of 1954, § 1002 provides: Except as otherwise provided in this subtitle, on the sale or exchange of property the entire amount of the gain or loss, determined under section 1001, shall be recognized.
38. [3] See generally U.S. v. Cumberland Pub. Serv. Co., 338 U.S. 451(1950).

voted to accept the Mack proposal. At the same time the board authorized Sclavi to sell 143 old trucks.[39]

Pursuant to the board's action, taxpayer submitted a purchase order to Mack on June 26, 1959, for 148 tractors, and pursuant to the purchase order taxpayer signed conditional sale agreements—on August 15, 1959, for 40 tractors; on September 15, 1959, for 65 tractors; and on October 15, 1959, for 43 new tractors.

To dispose of taxpayer's used tractors, Sclavi accepted an offer of $650,000 from the Horner Service Corporation, an independent used truck dealership in Vineland, New Jersey. Unknown to the taxpayer, the Horner offer was prompted by an agreement between Mack and Horner. Horner agreed that it would purchase taxpayer's trucks and attempt to resell them, Horner would keep any profit it made, and Mack guaranteed that Horner would not lose money on any truck. Pursuant to this agreement, Mack furnished funds to Horner with which to pay for the taxpayer's used trucks and subsequently took title from Horner of most of the used trucks. Mack on its books treated the transaction as a trade-in.

The taxpayer treated the acquisition of new tractors and the disposition of old tractors as a purchase and sale and reported it as such on its 1959 tax return, paying tax on the capital gain resulting from the disposition of the used tractors. For depreciation of the new trucks, taxpayer used actual cost as the basis for the tax years here in question, 1960 and 1961. The Commissioner determined that the transaction was an "exchange" of tractors for tractors. Under the Commissioner's view, the taxpayer could only use for depreciation purposes a transferred basis, computed under § 1031(d). Since this was less than the basis used by taxpayer, a deficiency was assessed. Taxpayer paid the deficiency and brought this suit for a refund.[40]

The district court found that taxpayer had entered into a contract with Mack for purchase of new trucks and had entered into a separate agreement with Horner for the sale of old trucks. The court further found that none of the officials of taxpayer knew of the arrangements between Mack and Horner. The government argues on appeal that the district court was clearly erroneous in finding: (1) that the transactions between taxpayer and Mack and between taxpayer and Horner were not mutually dependent; and, (2) that taxpayer did not have knowledge of the Mack-Horner arrangement.

---

39. [4] Eventually 144 used trucks were sold. The board's authorization to sell 143 trucks was in apparent response to an offer from a used truck dealer, Udelson, on June 16, 1959, to purchase 143 trucks.

40. [5] The Commissioner had originally assessed a deficiency for the year 1959 based on the useful life (of tractors) used by taxpayer for depreciation in the year of sale. When the Commissioner decided to treat the transaction as an exchange, he was unable to do so for 1959 because the deficiency based on useful life was already before the Tax Court. When the suit for refund of 1960 and 1961 taxes was brought, the district court originally held that the 1959 Tax Court decision estopped the Commissioner from proceeding in 1960 and 1961 to treat the transaction as an exchange. On appeal we held that the issue of sale or exchange had not actually been determined, and accordingly, in light of *Comm'r v. Sunnen*, 333 U.S. 591, 600, (1948), we reversed and remanded. *Bell Lines, Inc. v. U.S.*, No. 71-1823 (4th Cir. 1972).

The officers of taxpayer testified at the trial below. Winterholler stated that she would not have agreed to a trade-in and that taxpayer had never before traded-in tractors. Amos testified that he had no knowledge of the Horner-Mack arrangement and that the purchase by taxpayer of the 148 new trucks was not conditioned on the disposition of the old trucks. Sclavi also testified that the purchase from Mack was not conditioned on sale of the old trucks and that he had no knowledge of the Mack-Horner arrangement. The purchase order agreement of June 26, 1959, and the conditional sales agreements appear to have been fully enforceable against taxpayer regardless of whether it disposed of its used tractors. *See, e.g., Wyckoff v. Painter*, 145 W.Va. 310, 115 S.E.2d 80, 86–87 (1960).

In reviewing the findings of fact of the district judge we are bound by Fed. R. Civ. P. 52(a), which provides in relevant part: "Findings of fact shall not be set aside unless clearly erroneous, and due regard shall be given to the opportunity of the trial court to judge of the credibility of the witnesses." As stated in *U.S. v. National Assoc. of Real Estate Bds.*, 339 U.S. 485, 495 (1950): "It is not enough that we might give the facts another construction, resolve the ambiguities differently, and find a more sinister cast to actions which the District Court apparently deemed innocent."

We think the testimony of taxpayer's officials, if believed, and the evidence of the contracts with Mack are sufficient to support the district court's findings. The district court's findings (1) that taxpayer had a binding agreement with Mack to purchase 148 tractors, (2) that taxpayer had a separate agreement with Horner to buy its used trucks, and (3) that taxpayer was unaware of the side agreement between Mack and Horner are not clearly erroneous.

There remains for us to determine whether on these facts the district court erroneously characterized the transactions as a sale and purchase rather than an exchange. We think not.

In *Coastal Terminals, Inc. v. U.S.*, 320 F.2d 333 (4th Cir. 1963), we held:

> The purpose of Section 1031(a), as shown by its legislative history, is to defer recognition of gain or loss when a direct exchange of property between the taxpayer and another party takes place; *a sale for cash does not qualify as a nontaxable exchange even though the cash is immediately reinvested in like property.* [Emphasis added].

320 F.2d at 337. *See also Leo A. Woodbury*, 49 T.C. 180, 197 (1967), *acquiesced in*, 1969-2 Cum.Bull. XXV; *John M. Rogers*, 44 T.C. 126, 133 (1965).

The court in *Carlton v. U.S.*, 385 F.2d 238 (5th Cir. 1967), stated:

> The very essence of an exchange is the transfer of property between owners, while the mark of a sale is the receipt of cash for the property.... Where, as here, there is an immediate repurchase of other property with the proceeds of the sale, that distinction between a sale and exchange is crucial.

385 F.2d at 242.

It is urged upon us that since Mack supplied funds to Horner to purchase the trucks and later took most of the trucks from Horner, the substance of the transaction is a trade-in or exchange between taxpayer and Mack. The question of sale or exchange often turns upon whether separate steps in a transaction are to be recognized or disregarded.[41] This depends on whether the steps are mutually dependent or merely artificial transactions, as opposed to being steps with legal significance independent of the other steps and supported by legitimate business reasons. 3 Mertens, Law of Federal Income Taxation §§ 20.161, 20.163 (1972).

In the present case we cannot conclude that taxpayer had no legitimate business reasons for selling its old trucks and purchasing new ones. There was evidence it had always purchased without regard to trade-in value of old property, and it is doubtless possible to get a cheaper price where the dealer is not burdened with the necessity of disposing of old property. Moreover, as we have noted, the transactions were not mutually dependent as taxpayer was legally bound to purchase the 148 trucks from Mack whether it had sold the old ones or not. Thus the transaction between taxpayer and Horner may be reasonably viewed as one of substance to be treated separately from the taxpayer-Mack transaction.

That the two transactions were not mutually dependent also distinguishes this case from *Redwing Carriers, Inc. v. Tomlinson*, 399 F.2d 652 (5th Cir. 1968), and Rev. Rul. 61-119, 1961-1 Cum.Bull. 395. In *Redwing Carriers* the taxpayer had used its own wholly owned subsidiary to disguise an exchange as a sale and simultaneous purchase of property. The district court had specifically found that there would have been no purchase of the new equipment had there not been a concurrent and binding agreement for the sale of the old equipment. 399 F.2d at 655. The court thus held the transactions to be within § 1031(a). In Rev. Rul. 61-119 the disposition of old equipment to and acquisition of new equipment from the same dealer where the transactions were reciprocal was held to be an exchange even though accomplished by separately executed contracts.

In distinguishing *Carlton*, the *Redwing Carriers* court stated:

> The most that could be said for the transactional relationship in Carlton was that the sale for cash between the taxpayer and a purchaser had been complementary with the later purchase of like property between the taxpayer and a seller.

399 F.2d at 659.

Cases dealing with whether the replacement of property held for productive use in trade or business results in a sale or exchange have been termed "hopelessly conflict-

---

41. [6] *See Comm'r v. Court Holding Co.*, 324 U.S. 331 (1945); *Gregory v. Helvering*, 293 U.S. 465 (1935); *Alderson v. Comm'r*, 317 F.2d 790, 793–794 (9th Cir. 1963).Where there is a series of steps resulting in a change of property interests, it is vitally important to determine whether each step is to be separately tested against the statutory provisions in determining gain or loss or whether all of the steps resulting in the complete transaction are to be considered in their entirety and effect given to the whole transaction rather than to any of its separate parts. Mertens, *infra* § 20.161, at 731.

ing."[42] However, the result in a case such as this one is controlled by the district court's finding of facts. i.e., whether the replacement transactions were "complementary" or "mutually dependent." The district court's finding below, not clearly erroneous, that the transactions in question were not mutually dependent, precludes our determining that an exchange occurred. Accordingly, the decision of the district court will be

Affirmed.

Moss v. Commissioner

United States Tax Court

135 T.C. 365 (2010)

WELLS, JUDGE:

Respondent determined a deficiency of $8,070 in petitioners' Federal income tax for their 2007 tax year and an accuracy-related penalty pursuant to section 6662(a) of $1,614.[43] We must decide the following issues: (1) Whether the loss of $40,490 claimed on petitioners' Schedule E, Supplemental Income and Loss, should be disallowed because petitioners failed to meet the restrictions on passive activity losses under section 469; and (2) whether petitioners are subject to the accuracy-related penalty pursuant to section 6662(a) for the year in issue.

FINDINGS OF FACT

Some of the facts and certain exhibits have been stipulated. The stipulations of fact are incorporated in this opinion by reference and are found accordingly.

At the time the petition was filed, petitioners lived in Mullica Hill, New Jersey.

Petitioner James Moss (Mr. Moss) works at a nuclear power plant in Hope Creek, New Jersey (Hope Creek plant), operated by Public Service Electric & Gas Co. Mr. Moss is employed as a "nuclear technician—planning". Mr. Moss plans maintenance activities, develops "work packages" that include estimates of job time and equipment to be used, and helps to ensure compliance with Nuclear Regulatory Commission regulations.

During 2007, Mr. Moss was employed full time, 40 hours per week, generally working a shift of 7 a.m. to 3:30 p.m., Monday through Friday, for a total of approximately 1,900 hours. As part of Mr. Moss' duties at the Hope Creek plant, he also had to be available for "call out" time and "standby" time. Call out time occurs where an employee works unscheduled overtime.[44] Standby time occurs where an employee is ordered to await a call for emergency work outside scheduled working hours. During

---

42. [7] Mertens, *supra* § 20.161, at 730–31.

43. [1] Unless otherwise indicated, all Rule references are to the Tax Court Rules of Practice and Procedure, and all section references are to the Internal Revenue Code, as amended, for the year in issue. Amounts are rounded to the nearest dollar.

44. [2] A regular workweek is 5 regularly scheduled basic workdays of 8 hours each. Overtime is all hours worked outside of the regular workweek.

standby time, an employee must be "fit for duty". Mr. Moss' 1,900 hours of work during 2007 included approximately 200 to 300 hours of call out time.

Petitioners own the following rental properties: (1) Four apartments at 301–303 2nd Street, Swedesboro, New Jersey; (2) a single-family home at 1122 Elm Avenue, Wilmington, Delaware; (3) a single-family home at 1009 East 7th Street, Wilmington, Delaware; and (4) a single-family home at 611 East 22nd Street, Wilmington, Delaware (collectively, rental properties).

During his time away from work, Mr. Moss performed activities related to the rental properties. Mr. Moss' activities regarding the rental properties included maintenance, monitoring, eviction of nonpaying tenants, collecting rents, and preparation for new tenants. During 2007, Mr. Moss kept a calendar detailing the dates that he performed the foregoing activities (calendar); however, he failed to include on the calendar the time spent performing such activities. On October 23, 2009, Mr. Moss prepared a summary of the time he spent in connection with the rental properties (summary).

Petitioners timely filed a joint Form 1040, U.S. Individual Income Tax Return, for their 2007 tax year (2007 return). Petitioners' 2007 return was prepared by a certified public accountant (C.P.A.). On Schedule E attached to their 2007 return, petitioners reported a total loss from the rental properties of $40,490. Respondent disallowed $31,318 of the loss, allowing a deductible loss of $9,172.

Petitioners timely filed a petition in this Court seeking a redetermination of their liability for the year in issue.[45]

OPINION

Generally, the Commissioner's determination of a deficiency is presumed correct, and the taxpayer has the burden of proving it incorrect. Rule 142(a); *Welch v. Helvering*, 290 U.S. 111, 115, 54 S.Ct. 8, 78 L.Ed. 212 (1933).[46]

Deductions are a matter of legislative grace, and taxpayers bear the burden of proving that they have met all requirements necessary to be entitled to the claimed deductions. Rule 142(a); *INDOPCO, Inc. v. Commissioner*, 503 U.S. 79, 84, 112 S.Ct. 1039, 117 L.Ed.2d 226 (1992).

Taxpayers are allowed deductions for certain business and investment expenses pursuant to section 162 and 212; however, section 469 generally disallows any passive activity loss for the tax year. A passive activity is any trade or business in which the taxpayer does not materially participate. Sec. 469(c)(1). A passive activity loss is defined as the excess of the aggregate losses from all passive activities for the year over the aggregate income from all passive activities for such year. Sec. 469(d)(1). A rental

---

45. [3] Petitioners also sought a redetermination for their 2006 tax year in their petition to this Court. Because the petition was not timely filed as to that year, we dismissed that portion of the instant case for lack of jurisdiction.

46. [4] Petitioners do not contend that sec. 7491(a) should apply in the instant case to shift the burden of proof to respondent, nor did they establish that it should apply to the instant case.

activity is generally treated as a per se passive activity regardless of whether the taxpayer materially participates.[47] Sec. 469(c)(2).

There are two principal exceptions to the general rule that rental real estate activities are per se passive activities: (1) Section 469(c)(7); and (2) section 469(i). Pursuant to section 469(c)(7), the rental activities of a taxpayer who is a real estate professional are not per se passive activities but are treated as a trade or business subject to the material participation requirements of section 469(c)(1). Sec. 1.469-9(e)(1), Income Tax Regs.

A taxpayer qualifies as a real estate professional and is not engaged in a passive activity under section 469(c)(2) if:

(i) more than one-half of the personal services performed in trades or businesses by the taxpayer during such taxable year are performed in real property trades or businesses in which the taxpayer materially participates, and

(ii) such taxpayer performs more than 750 hours of services during the taxable year in real property trades or businesses in which the taxpayer materially participates [750–hour service performance requirement].

Sec. 469(c)(7)(B). In the case of a joint return, the foregoing requirements for qualification as a real estate professional are satisfied if, and only if, either spouse separately satisfies the requirements. *Id.* Thus, if either spouse qualifies as a real estate professional, the rental activities of the real estate professional are not per se passive under section 469(c)(2).

Section 1.469-5T(f)(4), Temporary Income Tax Regs., 53 Fed.Reg. 5727 (Feb. 25, 1988), sets forth the requirements necessary to establish the taxpayer's hours of participation as follows:

The extent of an individual's participation in an activity may be established by any reasonable means. Contemporaneous daily time reports, logs, or similar documents are not required if the extent of such participation may be established by other reasonable means. Reasonable means for purposes of this paragraph may include but are not limited to the identification of services performed over a period of time and the approximate number of hours spent performing such services during such period, based on appointment books, calendars, or narrative summaries.

We have held that the regulations do not allow a postevent "ballpark guesstimate". *Bailey v. Commissioner,* T.C. Memo.2001–296; *Goshorn v. Commissioner,* T.C. Memo.1993–578.

Respondent does not contend that petitioners have failed to elect to treat all of the rental properties as one activity. See sec. 469(c)(7)(A) (flush language); see also sec. 1.469-9(g), Income Tax Regs. (an election in a prior year is binding for the tax year

---

47. [5] A rental activity is "any activity where payments are principally for the use of tangible property." Sec. 469(j)(8).

it is made and for all future years in which the taxpayer qualifies). Accordingly, we deem that issue conceded.

Petitioners contend Mr. Moss satisfies the section 469 requirements of being a real estate professional. Petitioners provided the calendar and the summary as evidence of Mr. Moss' time related to the rental properties during 2007. The calendar includes a description of the work that he performed on the rental properties and the dates on which that work was performed, but it does not include the amount of time that was spent in the performance of such work. According to the summary, petitioners estimate that during 2007 Mr. Moss spent 112.25 hours traveling to and from the rental properties and 342.75 hours working on the rental properties. Additionally, petitioners contracted with Twin Hills Management to assist Mr. Moss with repairs. Mr. Moss contends that he spent 25.5 hours traveling to and from the rental properties with the Twin Hills employees and 165 hours working alongside them.[48] Mr. Moss contends that he spent 137.75 hours traveling to and from his rental properties and 507.75 hours working on his rental properties, for a total of 645.5 hours.

The total of 645.5 hours is less than the 750–hour service performance requirement of section 469(c)(7)(B)(ii). However, to satisfy the remaining time requirement, petitioners contend that Mr. Moss was "on call" for the rental properties for all of the hours that he was not working at the Hope Creek plant in his regular job. Essentially, petitioners claim that Mr. Moss could have been called to perform work at the rental properties at any time that he was not working at the Hope Creek plant, and, therefore, such on call hours should count toward meeting the 750–hour service performance requirement. We do not agree with petitioners' contention that Mr. Moss' "on call" hours may be used to satisfy the 750–hour service performance requirement. Section 469(c)(7) applies where the taxpayer "*performs* more than 750 hours of services". Sec. 469(c)(7)(B)(ii) (emphasis added); see also sec. 1.469-9(b)(4), Income Tax Regs. ("Personal *services* means any work *performed* by an individual in connection with a trade or business" (emphasis added)). While Mr. Moss was "on call" for the rental properties, he could have been called in to perform services; however, these services were never actually performed by him.[49] Accordingly, we conclude that Mr. Moss' time "on call" for the rental properties does not satisfy any part of the 750–hour service performance requirement.

Additionally, petitioners claim that Mr. Moss' calendar and summary reflect only 75 percent to 85 percent of his time. However, petitioners failed to provide any further information regarding other personal services Mr. Moss may or may not have performed with respect to the rental properties. On the basis of the record, we conclude that petitioners have failed to show that Mr. Moss met the 750–hour service performance requirement of section 469(c)(7)(B)(ii) for the year in issue. Because pe-

---

48. [6] The time related to Mr. Moss' work with Twin Hills is not the result of an estimate but rather was calculated from bills Twin Hills sent during 2007.

49. [7] Apparently, petitioners confuse the 750–hour service performance requirement of sec. 469(c)(7)(B)(ii) with the call out and standby time policies of Mr. Moss' employment at the Hope Creek plant.

titioners have failed to show that Mr. Moss met the 750–hour service performance requirement, we hold that he is not a real estate professional for purposes of section 469(c)(7) and that petitioners' rental real estate activities must therefore be treated as a passive activity under section 469(c)(2). Consequently, it is not necessary to address whether Mr. Moss spent more than 50 percent of his time in the real estate trade or business or whether he materially participated in that business.

The second exception to the general rule that rental real estate activities are per se passive activities is provided in section 469(i)(1), which provides as follows:

> (1) In general. — In the case of any natural person, subsection (a) shall not apply to that portion of the passive activity loss or the deduction equivalent * * * of the passive activity credit for any taxable year which is attributable to all rental real estate activities with respect to which such individual actively participated in such taxable year * * *.

The section 469(i) exception is limited to $25,000. Sec. 469(i)(2). The $25,000 maximum "offset", however, begins to phase out for taxpayers whose adjusted gross income (AGI) exceeds $100,000 and is completely phased out for taxpayers whose adjusted gross income is $150,000 or more. Sec. 469(i)(3)(A). For that purpose, adjusted gross income is derived without regard to "any passive activity loss or any loss allowable by reason of subsection (c)(7)" (modified AGI). Sec. 469(i)(3)(F)(iv). We have said that the active participation standard is met as long as the taxpayer participates in a significant and bona fide sense in making management decisions or arranging for others to provide services such as repairs. See *Madler v. Commissioner,* T.C. Memo.1998–112.

During 2007, Mr. Moss actively participated in the rental properties by personally maintaining them as well as performing other managerial functions. As concluded above, Mr. Moss' rental real estate activities are section 469(c)(2) passive activities, and therefore the losses from the rental property claimed on Schedule E of $40,490 should be added back to petitioners' AGI of $91,166 to determine their modified AGI. See sec. 469(i)(3)(F)(iv). Adding back the Schedule E losses to petitioners' AGI yields a modified AGI of $131,656. Because petitioners' modified AGI exceeds $100,000 by $31,656, the $25,000 allowable loss amount must be reduced by 50 percent for each dollar of modified AGI that exceeds $100,000, or $15,828, to an allowable loss of $9,172. See sec. 469(i)(3)(A). Consequently, on the basis of our holding above and the foregoing calculation, we sustain respondent's determination that petitioners have an allowable loss for their rental real estate activities of $9,172[50] and a disallowed loss of $31,318.[51]

Pursuant to section 6662(a) and (b)(1) and (2), a taxpayer may be liable for a penalty of 20 percent on the portion of an underpayment of tax: (1) Due to negligence

---

50. [8] This is the amount respondent allowed in the notice of deficiency.
51. [9] This is the $40,490 reported as loss on Schedule E minus the $9,172 allowable loss. Any passive activity loss that is disallowed is treated as a deduction allocable to such activity in the next taxable year. Sec. 469(b).

or disregard of rules or regulations or (2) attributable to a substantial understatement of income tax. "Negligence" is defined as any failure to make a reasonable attempt to comply with the provisions of the Internal Revenue Code, and "disregard" means any careless, reckless, or intentional disregard. Sec. 6662(c). "Understatement" means the excess of the amount of the tax required to be shown on the return over the amount of the tax imposed which is shown on the return, reduced by any rebate. Sec. 6662(d)(2)(A). A "substantial understatement" of income tax is defined as an understatement of tax that exceeds the greater of 10 percent of the tax required to be shown on the tax return or $5,000. Sec. 6662(d)(1)(A). The understatement is reduced to the extent that the taxpayer has: (1) Adequately disclosed his or her position and has a reasonable basis for such position, or (2) has substantial authority for the tax treatment of the item. Sec. 6662(d)(2)(B). With regard to the accuracy-related penalty, respondent bears the burden of production pursuant to section 7491(c), and petitioners bear the burden of proof. See *Higbee v. Commissioner*, 116 T.C. 438, 446, 2001 WL 617230 (2001).

The accuracy-related penalty is not imposed with respect to any portion of the underpayment as to which the taxpayer acted with reasonable cause and in good faith. Sec. 6664(c)(1). The decision as to whether the taxpayer acted with reasonable cause and in good faith depends upon all of the pertinent facts and circumstances. Sec. 1.6664-4(b)(1), Income Tax Regs. Relevant factors include the taxpayer's efforts to assess his proper tax liability, including the taxpayer's reasonable and good faith reliance on the advice of a professional such as an accountant. *Id.* Furthermore, an honest misunderstanding of fact or law that is reasonable in the light of the experience, knowledge, and education of the taxpayer may indicate reasonable cause and good faith. Sec. 1.6664-4(b)(1), Income Tax Regs.

On the basis of the record, we conclude that petitioner's understatement will be greater than $5,000. See sec. 6662(b)(2), (d)(1)(A)(ii). Therefore, we hold that respondent has met his burden of production regarding the accuracy-related penalty pursuant to section 6662(a).

As to petitioners' burden, they contend that they qualify for an exception to the accuracy-related penalty. Petitioners contend that the accuracy-related penalty should be waived because they were allegedly mistreated by the Internal Revenue Service (IRS).[52] However, the IRS' treatment of petitioners is not relevant to the reduction of the accuracy-related penalty pursuant to section 6662(d)(2)(B) or section 6664(c). Both exceptions relate to the taxpayer's actions, not the Commissioner's actions. See secs. 6662(d)(2)(B), 6664(c). Accordingly, we conclude that petitioners have failed to prove that they had a reasonable basis or substantial authority for deducting the losses claimed on Schedule E. See sec. 6662(d)(2)(B). Mr. Moss also testified that he relied on his C.P.A. to determine whether he was a real estate professional; however, he also testified that he did not provide his C.P.A. with the number of hours that he

---

52. [10] Petitioners allege that the IRS misaddressed documents, spelled petitioners' name wrong on documents, and would not "give you a straight answer".

spent working on the rental properties. Therefore, we conclude that petitioners have also failed to show that they acted with reasonable cause and in good faith in deducting the losses claimed on Schedule E. See sec. 6664(c)(1). On the basis of the record, we hold that petitioners are liable for the accuracy-related penalty pursuant to section 6662(a) for the year in issue.

The Court has considered all other arguments made by the parties and, to the extent we have not addressed them herein, we consider them moot, irrelevant, or without merit.

On the basis of the foregoing,

Decision will be entered for respondent.

Carlos v. Commissioner

United States Tax Court
123 T.C. 275 (2004)

WELLS, J.

Respondent determined deficiencies in petitioners' Federal income taxes for 1999 and 2000 as follows:[53]

Year	Deficiency
1999	$17,011
2000[n.1]	14,443

n.1 Although respondent initially determined sec. 6662(a) accuracy-related penalties of $3,402.20 for 1999 and $3,276.80 for 2000, respondent concedes that penalties are inapplicable.

The issue to be decided is whether losses from petitioners' rental activity constitute passive activity losses pursuant to section 469.[54]

BACKGROUND

The parties have submitted the instant case fully stipulated, without trial, pursuant to Rule 122. The parties' stipulations of fact are incorporated herein by reference and are found as facts in the instant case.

Petitioners are husband and wife. At the time of filing their petition, petitioners resided in Apple Valley, California.

During the years in issue, petitioners owned two commercial real estate properties in Apple Valley, California. One property was located at 22040 Bear Valley Road (Bear

---

53. [1] Although respondent initially determined corresponding deficiencies of $ 17,011 and $ 16,384 for 1999 and 2000, respectively, the parties have stipulated that the deficiency determined by respondent for 2000 is $ 14,443.

54. [2] All section references are to the Internal Revenue Code, as amended, and all Rule references are to the Tax Court Rules of Practice and Procedure.

Valley Road property), and the other was located at 13685/13663 John Glenn Road (John Glenn Road property). Collectively, the Bear Valley Road property and the John Glenn Road property are referred to as the rental properties. Petitioners also owned all of the stock of two S corporations—Bear Valley Fabricators & Steel Supply, Inc. (steel company), and J & T's Branding Company, Inc. (restaurant).

During 1999 and 2000, petitioners leased the Bear Valley Road property to the steel company and leased the John Glenn Road property to the restaurant.

The steel company agreed to pay rent of $120,000 per year to petitioners for the Bear Valley Road property. The steel company paid the rent, which, after taxes, depreciation, and bank charges, resulted in net rental income to petitioners for the Bear Valley Road property of $102,646 in 1999 and $102,045 for 2000.

The restaurant agreed to pay rent of $60,000 per year to petitioners for the John Glenn Road property. The restaurant failed to pay its designated rent in 1999 and 2000, which, after mortgage interest, taxes, depreciation, and amortization incurred by petitioners, resulted in a net loss to petitioners for the John Glenn Road property of $41,706 in 1999 and $40,169 in 2000.

Petitioners grouped the rental properties together to constitute a single "activity". On Schedules E, Supplemental Income and Loss, of their 1999 and 2000 income tax returns, petitioners netted the income from the Bear Valley Road property and the loss from the John Glenn Road property. For 1999, petitioners subtracted the $41,706 net loss on the John Glenn road property from the $102,646 net income on the Bear Valley Road property, resulting in net rental income of $60,940. Similarly, for 2000, petitioners subtracted the $40,169 net loss on the John Glenn Road property from the $102,045 net income on the Bear Valley Road property, resulting in net rental income of $61,876. Petitioners reported the net rental income as not from a passive activity and reported no passive activity loss.

Respondent disallowed petitioners' net losses on the John Glenn Road property under section 469(a) as passive activity losses.

DISCUSSION

Section 469(a) disallows the passive activity loss of an individual taxpayer.[55] The Internal Revenue Code defines "passive activity" as an activity involving the conduct of a trade or business in which the taxpayer does not materially participate.[56] "Passive

---

55. [3] SEC. 469. PASSIVE ACTIVITY LOSSES AND CREDITS LIMITED.
  (a) Disallowance.—
    (1) In general.—If for any taxable year the taxpayer is described in paragraph (2), nei-
    ther—
      (A) the passive activity loss, nor
      (B) the passive activity credit, for the taxable year shall be allowed.
    (2) Persons described.—The following are described in this paragraph:
      (A) any individual, estate, or trust, * * *.
56. [4] SEC. 469(c). Passive Activity Defined.—For purposes of this section—
  (1) In general.—The term "passive activity" means any activity—
    (A) which involves the conduct of any trade or business, and

activity", however, generally includes any rental activity, regardless of material participation. Sec. 469(c)(2).

Section 469 does not define "activity". See *Schwalbach v. Commissioner*, 111 T.C. 215, 223, 1998 WL 567814 (1998). The Secretary, however, has prescribed regulations pursuant to section 469(1) that specify what constitutes an "activity". Section 1.469-4(c), Income Tax Regs., sets forth rules for grouping tax items together to determine what constitutes a single "activity". That regulation provides: "One or more trade or business activities or rental activities may be treated as a single activity if the activities constitute an appropriate economic unit for the measurement of gain or loss for purposes of section 469." Sec. 1.469-4(c)(1), Income Tax Regs. Whether activities constitute an "appropriate economic unit" depends on the facts and circumstances.[57]

Respondent concedes that petitioners' grouping of the Bear Valley Road property and the John Glenn Road property is an appropriate economic unit. The parties, however, dispute the method for computing passive activity loss within the "activity" grouping.

Section 469(d)(1) defines "passive activity loss" as "the amount (if any) by which — (A) the aggregate losses from all passive activities for the taxable year, exceed (B) the aggregate income from all passive activities for such year." Passive activity loss is computed by first netting items of income and loss within each passive activity and then subtracting aggregate income from all passive activities from aggregate losses. See *id.;* sec. 1.469-2T, Temporary Income Tax Regs., 53 Fed.Reg. 5686 (Feb. 25, 1988).

In carrying out the provisions of section 469, section 469(1)(2) authorizes the Secretary to promulgate regulations "which provide that certain items of gross income will not be taken into account in determining income or loss from any activity (and the treatment of expenses allocable to such income)". While the general rule of section 469(c)(2) characterizes all rental activity as passive, section 1.469-2(f)(6), Income Tax Regs., requires net rental income received by the taxpayer for use of an item of the taxpayer's property in a business in which the taxpayer materially participates to be treated as income *not* from a passive activity (sometimes referred to as the self-rental rule or the recharacterization rule),[58] and provides:

    (B) in which the taxpayer does not materially participate.

  (2) Passive activity includes any rental activity. * * * the term "passive activity" includes any rental activity.

57. [5] Sec. 1.469-4(c)(2), Income Tax Regs., provides:

  (2) Facts and circumstances test. Except as otherwise provided in this section, whether activities constitute an appropriate economic unit and, therefore, may be treated as a single activity depends upon all the relevant facts and circumstances. A taxpayer may use any reasonable method of applying the relevant facts and circumstances in grouping activities * * *.

58. [6] To illustrate the self-rental rule, suppose taxpayer A owns a property and all outstanding stock of B Corp. A materially participates in the operations of B Corp., which generates $100 of income and has $50 of operating expenses in year 1. In year 1, A enters a lease agreement with B Corp. requiring B Corp. to pay $50 of annual rent to A for A's property. B Corp. uses the property in year 1 as its headquarters. If B Corp. were to pay its $50 net income to A in the form of salary, A would have $50 of income not from a passive activity. However, because the $50 of net income is

(f)(6) Property rented to a nonpassive activity. An amount of the taxpayer's gross rental activity income for the taxable year from an item of property equal to the net rental activity income for the year from that item of property is treated as not from a passive activity if the property—

> (I) Is rented for use in a trade or business activity * * * in which the taxpayer materially participates * * *.[59]

Petitioners concede that they "materially participated" in the conduct of both the steel company and the restaurant during 1999 and 2000, and they do not contend that section 1.469-2(f)(6), Income Tax Regs., is either invalid or inapplicable. Petitioners, however, contend that computation of passive activity loss requires the netting of income and loss from *all items* of rental property grouped within the section 469 passive activity and that only after such a computation does section 1.469-2(f)(6), Income Tax Regs., apply to recharacterize passive income as nonpassive. Respondent contends that section 1.469-2(f)(6), Income Tax Regs., requires the removal of self-rental income from the passive activity loss computation and that, after income from the Bear Valley Road property is properly removed from the passive activity loss computation, petitioners are left with no passive income to offset against the passive loss on the John Glenn Road property. We conclude that section 469(d) and the legislative regulations of section 1.469-2(f)(6), Income Tax Regs., support respondent's position.

Section 469(1)(2) explicitly authorizes the promulgation of regulations to remove certain items of gross income from the calculation of income or loss from any activity. Section 1.469-2(f)(6), Income Tax Regs., is a legislative regulation and is entitled to appropriate deference from this Court. See *Chevron U.S.A., Inc. v. Natural Res. Def. Council, Inc.*, 467 U.S. 837, 104 S.Ct. 2778, 81 L.Ed.2d 694 (1984). In *Chevron*, the U.S. Supreme Court stated: "Such legislative regulations are given controlling weight unless they are arbitrary, capricious, or manifestly contrary to the statute." *Id.* at 844. We have previously held that section 1.469-2(f)(6), Income Tax Regs., is not arbitrary, capricious, or manifestly contrary to section 469(1)(2). *Krukowski v. Commissioner*, 114 T.C. 366, 2000 WL 656711 (2000), affd. 279 F.3d 547 (7th Cir.2002); *Shaw v. Commissioner*, T.C. Memo.2002–35; *Sidell v. Commissioner*, T.C. Memo.1999–301, affd. 225 F.3d 103 (1st Cir.2000). The Courts of Appeals for the First, Fifth, and Seventh Circuits have also upheld the validity of section 1.469-2(f)(6), Income Tax Regs. See *Krukowski v. Commissioner*, 279 F.3d 547 (7th Cir.2002); *Sidell v. Commissioner*, 225 F.3d 103 (1st Cir.2000); *Fransen v. United States*, 191 F.3d 599 (5th Cir.1999).

Section 1.469-2(f)(6), Income Tax Regs., explicitly recharacterizes net rental activity income from an "item of property" rather than net income from the entire rental "activity". Both section 469 and the regulations thereunder clearly distinguish between

---

paid to A in the form of rent, it is per se passive income pursuant to sec. 469(c)(2). Sec. 1.469-2(f)(6), Income Tax Regs., recharacterizes the $50 of net rental income as not from a passive activity.

59. [7] As discussed below, sec. 1.469-2(f)(6), Income Tax Regs., is authorized by sec. 469(1)(2).

net income from an "item of property" and net income from the entire "activity",[60] which might include rental income from multiple items of property.[61] Under the authority of section 469(1)(2), the Secretary could have implemented regulations to remove items of gross income equal to net income from the entire activity, but the Secretary instead implemented regulations to recharacterize net income from a specific *item* of self-rental property. The use of the term "item of property" leads us to conclude that respondent's interpretation of the regulation is correct. Accordingly, in the instant case, self-rental income from the Bear Valley Road property is removed from the passive activity loss computation, leaving no passive income to be offset by the passive loss on the John Glenn Road property.

Section 469(d)(1) defines passive activity loss as the excess of losses from *passive activities* over income from *passive activities.* Consequently, recharacterization of "self-rental income" under section 1.469-2(f)(6), Income Tax Regs., as *not from a passive activity* effectively removes the income from the passive activity loss computation. Removal of a single item of income from such computation does not affect the passive characterization of items remaining within the activity. See *Shaw v. Commissioner, supra.* "Under the self-rented property rule, the net rental income from self-rented property is treated as nonpassive income and the net rental losses are treated as passive losses, even though the rental activities are passive activities." *Id.*

Although we have not previously decided whether grouping items of passive income and loss within a single section 469 activity precludes recharacterization under section 1.469-2(f)(6), Income Tax Regs., of income that would otherwise offset the passive loss,[62] we have consistently upheld recharacterization of passive income which would otherwise offset passive loss without considering the effect of the activity grouping. See, e.g., *Krukowski v. Commissioner,* 114 T.C. 355, (2000); *Schwalbach v. Commissioner,* 111 T.C. 215, 219–224, 1998 WL 567814 (1998); *Cal Interiors, Inc. v. Commissioner,* T.C. Memo.2004–99; *Shaw v. Commissioner, supra; Sidell v. Commissioner,* T.C.

60. [8] Sec. 469(1)(2) authorizes the implementation of regulations to remove "certain items of gross income" from the determination of income from an "activity". The designation of an "[item] of gross income" to be removed from such a determination is narrower than and distinct from the term "activity" income (from which the item must be removed). Since sec. 1.469-2(f)(6), Income Tax Regs., designates "net rental activity income for the year from * * * [an] item of property" as the item of gross income to be removed pursuant to sec. 469(1)(2) from the determination of income from the "activity", net rental activity income from an "item" of property is also narrower than and distinct from the broader term "activity" income.

61. [9] The fact that multiple rentals may be grouped together pursuant to sec. 1.469-4(c), Income Tax Regs., to make up a single "activity" further evidences the distinction between net income from an "item" of property and net income from the entire "activity".

62. [10] In *Krukowski v. Commissioner,* 279 F.3d 547, 554 (7th Cir.2002), affg. 114 T.C. 366, 2000 WL 656711 (2000), the taxpayers raised the single activity grouping argument on appeal, but the Court of Appeals did not address the issue because the taxpayers had not elected to treat the rental activities as a single activity on their return. The taxpayers in *Shaw v. Commissioner,* T.C. Memo.2002–35, likewise, belatedly tried to raise the issue of single activity grouping but were not allowed to do so.

Memo.1999–301; *Connor v. Commissioner,* T.C. Memo.1999–185, affd. 218 F.3d 733 (7th Cir. 2000).[63] In each of these cases, we validated application of section 1.469-2(f)(6), Income Tax Regs., to recharacterize specific items of income, leaving remaining items of passive loss with no offset.

In the instant case, we conclude that activity grouping does not preempt the application of section 1.469-2(f)(6), Income Tax Regs. To hold otherwise would undermine the congressional purpose for enacting section 469 and authorizing section 1.469-2(f)(6), Income Tax Regs., to wit: the prevention of sheltering of nonpassive income with passive losses. H. Conf. Rept. 99–841 (Vol.II), at II–147 (1986), 1986–3 C.B. (Vol.4) 1, 147. The conference report accompanying section 469 describes this legislative purpose:

> Regulatory authority of Treasury in defining non-passive income.—The conferees believe that clarification is desirable regarding the regulatory authority provided to the Treasury with regard to the definition of income that is treated as portfolio income or as otherwise not arising from a passive activity. The conferees intend that this authority be exercised to protect the underlying purpose of the passive loss provision, i.e., preventing the sheltering of positive income sources through the use of tax losses derived from passive business activities.

> Examples where the exercise of such authority may (if the Secretary so determines) be appropriate include the following * * * (2) related party leases or subleases, with respect to property used in a business activity, that have the effect of reducing active business income and creating passive income * * *. [*Id.*]

The facts of the instant case appear to fall within the description of activity that Congress intended to prevent.

Petitioners' interpretation of section 1.469-2(f)(6), Income Tax Regs., would effectively allow a taxpayer to subvert Congress's intent. Petitioners' interpretation would allow a taxpayer to convert nonpassive income into passive income against which passive losses could be offset by manipulating the payment of rent from a business controlled by the taxpayer on property rented from the taxpayer to the controlled business.[64] See *Shaw v. Commissioner,* T.C. Memo.2002–35. By converting nonpassive income into passive income in this manner, such a taxpayer would be

---

63. [11] In *Fransen v. United States,* 82 AFTR 2d 6621, 98–2 USTC par. 50,776 (E.D.La.1998), affd. 191 F.3d 599 (5th Cir.1999), the taxpayers similarly challenged application of sec. 1.469-2(f)(6), Income Tax Regs., in an action for refund. The taxpayers argued that sec. 1.469-2(f)(6), Income Tax Regs., is invalid because it contradicts the statutory designation of rental activity income as passive. The court awarded summary judgment to the Commissioner, holding that sec. 1.469-2(f)(6), Income Tax Regs., is consistent with the express congressional purposes of sec. 469 and the authorizing language of sec. 469(1)(3).

64. [12] Because sec. 1.469-2(f)(6), Income Tax Regs., would apply to recharacterize self-rental income under petitioners' interpretation only to the extent such income *exceeds* passive losses within the activity grouping, only the excess would be subject to recharacterization. An amount of passive

able to shelter otherwise nonpassive income with passive losses. Petitioners' interpretation would allow petitioners to shelter nonpassive income from the Bear Valley Road property with passive loss from the John Glenn Road property, contrary to congressional intent.[65]

Accordingly, we hold that net rental income from the Bear Valley Road property constitutes income not from a passive activity. Net rental loss from the John Glenn Road property, however, retains its characterization as loss from passive activity. Consequently, the loss is properly disallowed under section 469(a).[66]

To reflect the foregoing,

Decision with respect to the deficiencies will be entered for respondent; decision with respect to the accuracy-related penalties pursuant to section 6662(a) will be entered for petitioners.

Revenue Ruling 61-119
1961-1 C.B. 395

Advice has been requested whether a transaction of the type described below constitutes a sale of used equipment and the purchase of new equipment or whether it is one integrated transaction constituting an exchange with respect to which section 1031(a) of the Internal Revenue Code of 1954 provides for the nonrecognition of gain or loss.

A taxpayer has equipment used in his trade or business for more than six months for which his adjusted basis is $500. This used equipment has a fair market value of $1,000. Better equipment is now available which the taxpayer desires to acquire. Such equipment has a listed retail price of $10,000 but is regularly sold for $9,000.

Ordinarily, the taxpayer would accomplish the exchange by surrendering the old equipment to the dealer and receiving a trade-in allowance to cover part of the cost of the new equipment. Thus, the dealer would bill the taxpayer for $8,000, representing

---

income *equal* to the amount of passive losses would retain its passive character and, therefore, be sheltered by passive losses within the grouping.

65. [13] The result in this case might appear harsh, since, as respondent's brief recognizes, had the restaurant paid its rent on the John Glenn Road property, petitioners could have properly offset related expenses against that rental income. However, we must base our decision on the facts of the instant case: the restaurant *did not* pay its rent for the John Glenn Road property. Moreover, sec. 469(b) tempers the harshness of disallowing such passive activity losses by allowing them to be carried forward.

66. [14] Petitioners contend that the issue raised by respondent as to whether loss from the John Glenn Road rental should be disallowed as a passive activity loss constitutes a "new matter", distinct from respondent's original contention, set forth in the statutory notice of deficiency, that net income from the Bear Valley Road rental is recharacterized as nonpassive. We need not address this issue, however, because we decide only a legal issue, not a factual one, and the burden of proof therefore does not affect our decision.

the $9,000 sales price of the new equipment minus the $1,000 trade-in allowance for the old equipment. Alternatively, the dealer's invoice might reflect the new equipment at its list price, or $10,000, in which case the trade-in allowance would be shown as $2,000, leaving $8,000 as the balance due from the customer. In either case, the transaction would be treated as a nontaxable exchange, in view of section 1031(a) of the Code, which provides, in part, that no gain or loss shall be recognized if property held for productive use in trade or business is exchanged solely for property of a like kind to be held for the same purpose, and in view of section 1.1031(a)-1(a) of the Income Tax Regulations, which provides, in part, that a transfer of property meeting the requirements of section 1031(a) may be within the provision of section 1031(a) even though the taxpayer transfers in addition property not meeting the requirements of section 1031(a) or money.

In the above situation, therefore, no gain or loss would be recognized even though the taxpayer was allowed $1,000 in the first instance, or $2,000 in the second instance, for the used equipment for which his basis was $500. The taxpayer's unrecognized gain on the trade-in would be applied, in accordance with I.T. 2615, C.B. XI-1, 112 (1932), to reduce his basis of the new equipment for depreciation purposes. Thus, the taxpayer's basis for the new equipment would be $8,500, the purchase price less the unrecognized gain on the used equipment.

The question has been raised whether the foregoing authorities will continue to govern the tax consequences of the transaction if, instead of entering into a direct exchange in the manner outlined above, the parties entered into separate contracts, one covering the sale of the old equipment and the other covering the purchase of the new equipment.

The recognition to be accorded a particular transaction for Federal income tax purposes depends upon the substance of the transaction rather than the form in which it is cast. The Internal Revenue Service and the courts look to what is actually done rather than to the formalities of the transaction or to the declared purpose of the participants in gauging its tax consequences. *See Harry H. Weiss v. Louis Stearn et al.*, 265 U.S. 242 (1924), and *Helvering v. The F. & R. Lazarus & Co.*, 308 U.S. 252 (1939). The courts have held that a sale is to be disregarded where it is a step in a transaction the purpose of which is to make an exchange, and which results in an exchange. *See Century Electric Co. v. Comm'r*, 192 F.2d 155 8th Cir. 1951), *certiorari denied* 342 U.S. 954. *See also* Rev. Rul. 60-43, C.B. 1960-1, 687.

In the instant case the sale of the used equipment and the purchase of the new equipment are reciprocal and mutually dependent transactions. The taxpayer's acquisition of the new equipment from the dealer is contingent upon the dealer taking his used equipment and granting a trade-in allowance equal to or in excess of its fair market value. Moreover, the dealer's acceptance of the old equipment is dependent upon the taxpayer's purchase of the new equipment. Under these circumstances, the transfer of the old equipment to the dealer, irrespective of the form or the technique through which the transfer is accomplished, represents but a step in a single integrated transaction.

Accordingly, it is held that the transfer of the old equipment to the dealer and purchase of the new equipment from him is a nontaxable exchange under section 1031 of the Code, even though the purchaser and the seller execute separate contracts and treat the purchase and sale as unrelated transactions for record keeping purposes.

The fact that the purchase and sale are consummated concurrently, or that the sales price of the new equipment and the trade-in allowance for the old equipment are in excess of the price at which such items are ordinarily sold, may serve as indication that the purchase and sale were not intended as separate or unrelated transactions. However, the absence of either or both of these factors, standing alone, will not be taken to indicate that separate or unrelated transactions were consummated.

Chapter 19

Foreign Investment in U.S. Real Property

I. Commentary

Cross-border transactions and investments have become a part of the everyday practice of a large percentage of real estate tax attorneys. Money from non-U.S. persons continues to flow into various forms of U.S. real estate investments. The tax advisor's role with such investments is helping to ensure that the ownership structure provides the most favorable tax results for all parties, including the foreign investors. This may entail minimizing the foreign investor's income effectively connected to a U.S. trade or business, avoiding the FIRPTA withholding rules, and achieving the most desirable benefits under the appropriate tax treaty. Achieving the foreign investors' objectives may require the use of structures that include so-called "blockers" and "stoppers."

The United States taxes U.S. citizens, resident aliens, and domestic corporations on their worldwide income, with some exceptions.[1] The United states taxes nonresident alien individuals and foreign corporations (i.e., foreign persons) on certain types of U.S.-source income and income effectively connected with a trade or business the person conducts in the United States.[2] The first step in considering the U.S. tax treatment of foreign investment in U.S. real property is identifying who is a foreign person. A nonresident alien individual is any individual who is not a citizen or resident of the United States.[3] A resident alien is an individual who has been lawfully admitted to the United States, has been present in the United States on at least 31 days in the

---

1. *See* I.R.C. §§ 1 (imposing a tax on individual income without restriction), 11 (imposing a tax on corporate income without restriction); Treas. Reg. § 1.1-1(b) (providing that the individual income tax applies to U.S. citizens and resident alien individuals), 1.11-1(a) (providing that the corporate income tax only applies to foreign corporations engaged in a trade or business within the United States to the extent that the income is effectively connected to the conduct of a trade or business in the United States).

2. *See* I.R.C. §§ 871(a) (imposing a tax on certain types of U.S.-source income recognized by nonresident alien individuals), (b) (imposing tax on income recognized by nonresident alien individuals that is effectively connected to a trade or business conducted within the United States), 881(a) (imposing tax on certain types of U.S.-source income recognized by foreign corporations), 882(a) (imposing tax on income recognized by foreign corporations that is effectively connected to a trade or business conducted within the United States).

3. *See* I.R.C. § 7701(b)(1)(B).

current year, and who has been present at least 183 days (determined using a multiplier) during the current and two preceding years, or effectively elects to be a resident alien.[4] A foreign corporation is one that is not domestic.[5] A domestic corporation is one that is created or organized in the United States under U.S. law or the law of any U.S. state.[6] After establishing that a potential investor in U.S. real property is a foreign person, the next step is to determine the general tax rules that will apply to any income the investor recognizes.

One of three general tax systems apply to U.S. income recognized by a foreign person: (1) the tax treatment of U.S.-source income, (2) the tax treatment of income effectively connected to a U.S. trade or business, and (3) the tax treatment of gain from the sale of an interest in U.S. real property. The tax treatment under each system may be subject to treaties. Of course, various ownership structures exist to help foreign investors minimize the tax they pay on income from U.S. property. Income is only subject to one of the systems. Therefore, income that is effectively connected to a U.S. trade or business is subject to that system and is not subject to the system governing U.S.-source income. Income that is not effectively connected to a U.S. trade or business, can be subject to the system governing U.S.-source income.

A. Taxation of U.S.-Source Income Recognized by Foreign Persons

A 30% rate applies to amounts that foreign persons receive from interest, dividends, rents, salaries, wages, premiums, annuities, and other fixed or determinable annual or periodical gains, profits, and income.[7] The tax only applies to the extent such items are not effectively connected to the conduct of a trade or business in the United States.[8] Interest generally is U.S.-sourced if it is on bonds, notes, or other interest-bearing obligations of noncorporate residents or domestic corporations.[9] Dividends generally are sourced in the United States if paid from a domestic corporation,[10] paid by a foreign corporation that is engaged in a U.S. trade or business and at least 25% of its worldwide gross income over a 3-year period is effectively connected with that U.S. trade or business in proportion to that effectively-connected income,[11] and to the extent treated as paid by a domestic corporation.[12] Rents are sourced in the United

---

4. *See* I.R.C. § 7701(b)(1)(A).

5. *See* I.R.C. § 7701(a)(5).

6. *See* I.R.C. § 7701(a)(4).

7. *See* I.R.C. §§ 871(a)(1), 881(a).

8. *See* I.R.C. §§ 871(a)(1) (flush language), 881(a) (flush language).

9. *See* I.R.C. § 861(a)(1). *But see* I.R.C. §§ 861(a)(1)(A) (excluding interest on deposits with a foreign branch of a domestic corporation), (B) (excluding interest paid by a foreign partnership that is not effectively connected to a U.S. trade or business), 884(f)(1) (including interest paid by the branch of a foreign corporation). For definitions of income sourced outside the United States, see I.R.C. § 862(a).

10. *See* I.R.C. § 861(a)(2)(A).

11. *See* I.R.C. § 861(a)(2)(B).

12. *See* I.R.C. § 861(a)(2)(C).

States if they are from property or any interest in property in the United States.[13] Gains, profits, and income from the disposition of U.S. real property is U.S.-sourced income.[14]

Because the 30% tax rate applies to the gross amount of U.S.-sourced items, the tax paid on such items by foreign persons may exceed the ordinary rates that apply to such items when received by U.S. persons. To illustrate, if a property generates $100,000 of rental income and has $65,000 of expenses, a foreign investor would owe $30,000 of tax (30% x $100,000) as tax if the rental income is U.S.-sourced income. A U.S. person, and a foreign person who recognizes the income as effectively connected to a U.S. trade or business, would owe no more than $13,860 (39.6% x ($100,000— $65,000)). Consequently, the tax a foreign person pays on U.S.-source income can be significant. Foreign persons are not, however, required to file tax returns with respect to U.S.-source income.

Treaties between the United States and other countries will often reduce the rates that apply to items of U.S.-source income. For instance, the United States Model Income Tax Convention, the model for U.S. treaties, provides reduced tax rates for dividends and interest recognized by a foreign person.[15]

B. Taxation of Effectively-Connected Income Recognized by Foreign Persons

Foreign persons generally must pay tax at ordinary individual and corporate tax rates, as applicable, on taxable income that is effectively connected with the conduct of a trade or business within the United States[16] and file U.S. tax returns.[17] Because the tax is imposed on taxable income, foreign persons compute their gross income that is effectively connected to a U.S. trade or business,[18] and they are allowed deductions that are effectively connected to the U.S. trade or business.[19] Determining whether this system applies requires first determining whether the foreign person is engaged in a U.S. trade or business and second determining whether the person's income is effectively connected that trade or business.

Foreign persons can elect to treat income from any U.S. real property as income effectively connected to a U.S. trade or business.[20] Furthermore, FIRPTA treats gain or loss from the sale of real property as income effectively connected to a U.S. trade or business.[21] Absent such election, the determination of whether holding property

---

13. *See* I.R.C. §861(a)(4).
14. *See* I.R.C. §861(a)(5).
15. *See* UNITED STATES MODEL INCOME TAX CONVENTION, Articles 10, 11.
16. *See* I.R.C. §§871(b), 882(a).
17. *See* I.R.C. §§874(a), 882(c)(2).
18. *See* I.R.C. §§872, 882(a)(2), (b).
19. *See* I.R.C. §§873(a), 883(c)(1)(A).
20. *See* I.R.C. §§871(d), 882(d).
21. *See* I.R.C. §897(a); *infra* Part I.C.

is a U.S. trade or business requires a factual inquiry under section 864 and its regulations.[22] Because those rules do not include a bright-line definition for owning real property, determining whether foreign ownership of U.S. real property is a U.S. trade or business can be difficult. If a foreign person's activities are limited to collecting rent; paying taxes, insurance, and principal and interest on a mortgage; and doing minor repairs, a court could find that the foreign person's activities are sporadic rather than continuous, irregular rather than regular, and minimal rather than considerable. Based upon such findings, a court could rule that a foreign person performing those limited activities is not engaged in a U.S. trade or business.[23] Performing similar services and acquiring property through a U.S. agent may, however, tip the scales and result in a finding that a foreign person engages in a trade or business in the United States.[24] Because the test for business engagement is fact specific, in some situations, parties may struggle to determine whether a foreign owner of U.S. real property is engaged in a U.S. trade or business.

A foreign person who is a member of a tax partnership shall be treated as engaged in a U.S. trade or business if the tax partnership is engaged in a U.S. trade or business.[25] A foreign person's sale of an interest in a U.S. tax partnership that holds U.S. real property could be treated as income effectively connected to a U.S. trade or business, but the foreign person would bifurcate that gain as appropriate, if the tax partnership holds both U.S. and non-U.S. property.[26]

After determining that a foreign person is engaged in a U.S. trade or business, the next step is to determine whether that person has any income effectively connected to the trade or business.[27] If a foreign person elects to treat ownership of U.S. real property as a U.S. trade or business, all income from that property will be effectively connected to a U.S. trade or business.[28] Otherwise, income is separated into two general categories, and separate rules apply to income that falls within the respective categories.

Category-1 Income includes (1) gain or loss from the sale or exchange of capital assets; (2) fixed or determinable annual or periodic gains, profits, or income; and (3) other U.S.-source items described in 871(a)(1) and 881(a).[29] The regulations refer to Category-1 Income as "fixed or determinable income and capital gains."[30] Items in this category are effectively connected to a U.S. trade or business only if they meet

---

22. *See* Rev. Rul. 88-3, 1988-1 C.B. 268.

23. *See, e.g.*, Herbert v. Comm'r, 30 T.C. 26 (1958), acq. 1958-2 C.B. 6 (ruling with respect to a foreign person who was subject to a tax treaty and owned a single property that had a single tenant).

24. *See, e.g.*, Amodio v. Comm'r, 34 T.C. 894 (1960).

25. *See* I.R.C. §875(1); Treas. Reg. §1.875-1.

26. *See, e.g.*, Rev. Rul. 91-32, 1991-1 C.B. 107.

27. If the person is not engaged in a U.S. trade or business during a taxable year, income allocated to that individual generally will not be effectively connected to a U.S. trade or business. *See* Treas. Reg. §1.864-3.

28. *See* I.R.C. §§871(d)(1), 882(d)(1).

29. *See* I.R.C. §864(c)(2).

30. *See* Treas. Reg. §1.864-4(c).

either an asset-use test or a business-activities test,[31] which show they have a certain nexus to the U.S. trade or business.

Under the asset-use test, income is effectively connected to a U.S. trade or business if it derives from an asset used in, or held for use in, the conduct of that U.S. trade or business.[32] The asset-use test generally applies with respect to passive types of income that do not derive directly from a U.S. trade or business, such as interest income derived from U.S. sources by a foreign person engaged in a U.S. trade or business.[33] Ordinarily, an asset is treated as used in, or held for use in, a trade or business in one of three situations: (1) it is held for the principal purpose of promoting the present conduct of a trade or business in the United States, (2) it is acquired and held in the ordinary course of the trade or business conducted in the United States (such as an account receivable), or (3) it is held in a direct relationship to the trade or business conducted in the United States.[34] An asset is held in direct relation to a trade or business if it is needed in the trade or business.[35]

Under the business-use test, income is effectively connected to a U.S. trade or business if the activities of the trade or business are a material factor in the realization of the income.[36] This test ordinarily applies to passive-type income that arises directly from the active conduct of a U.S. trade or business. The test is of primary significance for the following types of income: (1) dividends or interest derived by a dealer in stock or securities, (2) gain or loss derived from the sale or exchange of capital assets in active conduct of a trade or business by an investment company, (3) royalties derived in the active conduct of a trade or business of licensing patents or similar intangible property, and (4) service fees derived in the active conduct of a trade or business.[37] Property carries a 10-year taint for purposes of determining whether the gain from the disposition of the property was from property used or held for use in a U.S. trade or business.[38]

Category-2 Income consists of all income that does not come within the first category.[39] The regulations refer to Category-2 Income as "income other than fixed or

---

31. *See* Treas. Reg. § 1.864-4(a), (c).

32. *See* I.R.C. § 864(c)(2)(A); Treas. Reg. § 1.864-4(c)(1)(i)(*a*).

33. *See* Treas. Reg. § 1.864-4(c)(2)(i).

34. *See* Treas. Reg. § 1.864-4(c)(2)(ii).

35. *See* Treas. Reg. § 1.864-4(c)(2)(iv)(*a*). Assets held to meet operating expenses of a U.S. trade or business generally are held in direct relation to the trade or business, but assets typically are not held in direct relation to a U.S. trade or business if they are held to (1) provide future diversification, (2) expand the trade or business outside the United States, (3) replace plant in the future, or (4) meet future contingencies. *See id.* An asset is also treated as held in direct relation to a U.S. trade or business if (1) it is acquired with funds generated by that trade or business, (2) the income from the asset is retained or reinvested in the trade or business, and (3) personnel present in the United States and active in the trade or business have significant management or control of the asset. *See* Treas. Reg. § 1.864-4(c)(2)(iv)(*b*).

36. *See* I.R.C. § 864(c)(2)(B); Treas. Reg. § 1.864-4(c)(1)(i)(*b*).

37. *See* Treas. Reg. § 1.864-4(c)(3)(i).

38. *See* I.R.C. § 864(c)(7).

39. *See* I.R.C. § 864(c)(3).

determinable income and capital gains."[40] A "force-of-attraction" rule applies to items in this category, under which, if a foreign person has a U.S. trade or business, all of the foreign person's U.S.-source items, other than the Category-1 Income that is effectively connected under the asset-use test or the business-use test, are treated as effectively connected to the foreign person's U.S. trade or business.[41]

Finally, gain from the sale of interests in U.S. real property is treated as effectively connected to a U.S. trade or business under FIRPTA, as discussed in the next section.

C. FIRPTA

FIRPTA stands for the Foreign Investment in Real Property Tax Act of 1980.[42] Prior to the enactment of FIRPTA, foreign investors only paid tax on capital gains from the sale of real property if the gains were effectively connected to a U.S. trade or business, or, in the case of an individual, if the individual was present in the U.S. for at least 183 days.[43] Foreign investors often preferred that income from the property, such as rent, be effectively connected to a U.S. trade or business, so they could pay tax on the net amount.[44] They could then do some type of planning structure to ensure that the gain on the disposition was not effectively connected and avoid paying tax on that gain.[45] Thus, foreign investors and U.S. investors would be taxed similarly on income from U.S real property, but foreign investors could avoid paying tax on gain from the disposition of U.S. real property. The stated purpose of the act was "to establish equity of the tax treatment in U.S. real property between foreign and domestic investors."[46] Nonetheless, some commentators claim that FIRPTA is a xenophobic attempt to discourage foreign investment in U.S. real property.[47]

The operative provision of FIRPTA treats a foreign person's gain or loss from the disposition of a U.S. real property interest as income effectively connected to a U.S. trade or business.[48] Consequently, the tax imposed on gain recognized by a foreign person from the sale of U.S. real property will be similar to the tax imposed on gain recognized by a U.S. person.[49] For the purposes of this rule, a U.S. real property interest includes an interest in real property located in the United States and an interest in a domestic corporation, unless the taxpayer can establish that the corporation was not a U.S. real property holding corporation during the period the taxpayer held the

---

40. *See* Treas. Reg. § 1.864-4(b).

41. *See* I.R.C. § 864(c)(3); Treas. Reg. § 1.864-4(b).

42. *See* Pub. L. No. 96-499, §§ 1121–25, 94 Stat. 2599, 2682.

43. *See* H.R. Rep. No. 1167, 96th Cong., 2d Sess., 5871, *et seq.*, July 21, 1980.

44. *See id.*

45. *See id.*

46. *See id.*

47. *See, e.g.*, Richard L. Kaplan, *Creeping Xenophobia and the Taxation of Foreign-Owned Real Estate*, 71 Geo. L.J. 1091 (1983); Charles I. Kingson, *The Coherence of International Taxation*, 81 Colum. L. Rev. 1151 (1981).

48. *See* I.R.C. § 897(a)(1).

49. *See* I.R.C. §§ 871(b)(1), 882(a)(1).

interest, or the last five years if shorter.[50] FIRPTA also applies to the disposition of an interest in a tax partnership that holds U.S. real property interests.[51] If the stock of a corporation is publicly traded, the stock is treated as U.S. real property interests with respect to a foreign person only if the foreign person holds more than 5% of the stock.[52] Consequently, gain or loss from the sale of such stock will be treated under FIRPTA as income effectively connected to a U.S. trade or business.

REITs are corporations,[53] so stock in REITs can be treated as U.S. real property interests for purposes of the REIT rules. FIRPTA also applies special look-through rule to distributions from qualified investment entities such as REITs, under which the distributions are treated as gains from the sale of U.S. real property interests to the extent the distributions are attributable to gains recognized by the entity from the disposition of U.S. real property interests.[54] The look-through rule generally only applies if the foreign person owns at least 5% of the corporation's stock,[55] or 10% in the case of a REIT.[56] Additionally, REIT stock will be treated as U.S. real property interests with respect to a foreign person only if that person holds more than 10% of the REIT's outstanding stock.[57] Thus, a foreign person can indirectly own U.S. real property and avoid FIRPTA and avoid being engaged in a U.S. trade or business by limiting its U.S. investments to less than 10% of the outstanding stock of any U.S. REIT. Furthermore, any dividends the foreign person receives from the REIT may be subject to favorable treaty rates.

D. Tax Treaties

The United States has entered into several tax treaties with foreign countries. The purpose of multi-national tax treaties is to eliminate double taxation with respect to taxes on income without creating opportunities for non-taxation or tax avoidance.[58] The provisions of treaties may vary from country to country, and the provisions of various treaties may affect whether and how foreign investors choose to invest in U.S. real property. The United States Model Income Tax Convention provides that the United States can tax income recognized by a foreign person from real property situated in the United States.[59] A foreign person also may elect to be taxed on a net basis of income from real property as if such income were business profits attributable to

---

50. *See* I.R.C. §897(c). A U.S. real property holding corporation is any corporation if the fair market value of its U.S. real property interests are at least 50% of the fair market value of its real property plus the fair market value of any other property the corporation uses or holds for use in a trade or business. *See* I.R.C. §897(c)(2).

51. *See* I.R.C. §897(g).

52. *See* I.R.C. §897(c)(3).

53. *See supra* Chapter 17.

54. *See* I.R.C. §897(h).

55. *See* I.R.C. §897(h)(1).

56. *See* I.R.C. §897(k)(1)(B).

57. *See* I.R.C. §897(k)(1)(A).

58. *See* UNITED STATES MODEL INCOME TAX CONVENTION, Preface.

59. *See id.* at Article 6.

a permanent establishment in the United States.[60] The United States also may tax profits attributable to a foreign person's permanent establishment in the United States.[61] To illustrate how treaties may affect foreign-investor behavior, if dividends from REITs are subject to a lower tax under a treaty,[62] foreign investors who qualify for the treaty rates can pay tax on income from their indirect investment in U.S. real property at the favorable treaty dividend rates.

E. Blockers and Stoppers

Tax planning for foreign investment in U.S. real property often involves the foreign person forming an entity through which to invest in the United States. The entity structure may block or stop certain types of income flowing to the foreign investor, so such entities are often referred to as "blockers" or "stoppers."[63] For instance, tax-exempt organizations generally are not taxed on rents from real property (i.e., rental income is not unrelated business taxable income, or "UBTI"),[64] but they are taxed on debt-financed income.[65] Because most real property is purchased with debt, rents from real property are often debt-financed income for purposes of the UBTI rules. Consequently, tax-exempt organizations (including organizations such as pension funds) would have to pay tax on income that they would receive from typical investments in real property. Tax-exempt organizations may, however, avoid the debt-financed rules by investing in leveraged real property indirectly through a REIT.[66] In such arrangements, the REIT is a blocker for tax-exempt organizations because it blocks debt-financed income from flowing up to them, and foreign tax-exempt organizations may use REITs to invest in U.S. real property. Other foreign investors may also prefer investing through a REIT because REIT dividends might not be income effectively connected to a U.S. trade or business.

Foreign investors may also be able to take advantage of hybrid entities, i.e., entities that are classified one way in one jurisdiction and another way in another jurisdiction. For instance, an LLC is a corporation under Canadian tax law, but it can be a partnership under U.S. tax law.[67] The discussion of complex planning techniques that adopt blocker and stopper entities is beyond the scope of this book, but practitioners who represent foreign investors must become familiar with them.

---

60. *See id.* at Article 6(5).

61. *See id.* at Article 7.

62. *See id.* at Article 10(2), (4).

63. *See* Willard B. Taylor, *"Blockers," "Stoppers," and the Entity Classification Rules*, 64 Tax Law. 1 (2010).

64. *See* I.R.C. § 512(b)(3)(A)(i).

65. *See* I.R.C. §§ 512(b)(4), 514.

66. *See* I.R.C. § 512(b)(1). *But see* I.R.C. § 856(h)(3)(C) (imposing look-through rules on dividends received from pension-held REITs).

67. *See* Bradley T. Borden, *Tax Aspects of Partnerships, LLCs and Alternative Forms of Business Organizations, in* Research Handbook on Partnerships, LLCs and Alternative Forms of Business Organizations (Robert W. Hillman & Mark J. Lowenstein eds.) (Edward Elgar Publishing 2015) (discussing hybrid entities and ways that taxpayers may use them as blockers or stoppers).

II. Primary Legal Authority

Amodio v. Commissioner

Tax Court of the United States

34 T.C. 894 (1960)

TIETJENS, JUDGE:

The respondent determined deficiencies in income tax as follows:

	Docket No. 74297	Docket No. 74211
Calendar year	John Amodio	Inez de Amodio
1951	$20,763.08	
1952	20,555.92	
1953	19,486.81	$4,550.74
1954	14,665.03	365.69

The petitioners are brother and sister. Their proceedings were consolidated as both cases involve the issue whether the petitioners are taxable on the capital gains realized by a trust of which they were the grantors and beneficiaries. This is the sole issue in the case of Inez. Other issues in the case of John are whether he is taxable on a 'net basis' on all dividend, interest, and rental income with respect to all income derived from sources in the United States under the terms of the United States-Swiss tax convention and whether he is taxable on capital gains from sales of capital assets other than those of the trust. By amendment to the petition, John also alleges that through tax payments made on his account by the trustee of the trust and by the Swiss Confederation under the convention and by withholding agents in the United States his taxes for the years involved have been overpaid and asks a determination of such overpayment. Certain facts are stipulated.

FINDINGS OF FACT.

Returns of John Amodio for 1951, 1952, and 1953 and a return for Inez for 1953 were filed with the collector or director of internal revenue at Pittsburgh. Inez filed a return for 1954 with the director for the Upper Manhattan District, New York. John Amodio's return for 1954 was filed with the director of internal revenue at Baltimore, Maryland.

Inez de Amodio was a resident of the United States in 1953 and 1954. John Amodio (also known as John Julio Amodio) is a non-resident alien who resides in Switzerland. These petitioners are daughter and son of Josephine Wainwright de Amodio.

Joseph G. Wainwright, the father of Josephine, arranged for the creation of a trust, herein referred to as the Wainwright trust, on March 14, 1900. The trust corpus was real property in Texas; some in Dallas, some in El Paso. The income from the property was to be paid to Josephine during her lifetime. If upon her death her children had all reached the age of 21 years, all the property was to vest in the surviving heirs. The first trustee was Joseph G. Wainwright, who died in 1902. Other trustees were there-after appointed by the beneficiary. The last trustee was John A. Byerly, appointed in 1934. Josephine died on April 7, 1948, at which time the petitioners, the only children and heirs of Josephine, were both over 21 years of age.

On January 11, 1947, the petitioners entered into an agreement with Byerly concerning their interests in the Wainwright trust. This agreement was referred to as the Amodio trust and provided in general for the administration by Byerly, as trustee, of the property of the Wainwright trust which would come to the petitioners upon the termination of that trust when their mother died. The petitioners were the grantors and equal beneficiaries. The agreement provided that the trustee, as soon as practicable, was to liquidate a sufficient amount of the property to pay each of the petitioners $40,000 in cash. The agreement further provided:

5. Without in any way limiting or restricting the generality of the foregoing provisions, the Trustee shall have powers as follows, with reference to any and each asset at any time constituting a part of the trust estate:

   (e) To consent to the extension, refunding or renewal of any security, obligation, lien, contract or right.

   (f) To improve all or any real property; to erect buildings on all or any real property, in addition to or in substitution for the buildings at any time existing thereon, of such character and cost, and upon such terms of payment, as the Trustee shall deem advisable; to borrow money and create liens upon property and/or rents, for such purpose or for any other purpose; provided, however, that our said Trustee is authorized and empowered to reserve and set aside, at the end of each month, out of the gross current income realized in cash during said period from the property then embraced in this trust, such an amount, not exceeding 5% of said gross current income, as to him shall seem proper. The amount so reserved shall be held and accumulated by him as an improvement fund; and shall be vested by him from time to time, at such intervals and in such manner as shall seem to him to be for the best interests of the trust, in permanent improvements upon the real property embraced in the trust, or in the purchase of additional revenue-yielding property.

   (g) To mortgage real and/or personal property, to such extent, and upon such terms and conditions, and for such purposes, as the Trustee shall deem advisable.

6. We, the settlors, shall be the primary beneficiaries of this trust. We shall be considered the equitable owners of both the income and the corpus of the trust, in equal shares. One-half of the net income of the trust shall be payable to each of us for life. If the first of us to die shall die without leaving lawful issue (heirs of the body) surviving him or her, then, and in that event, all interest in the corpus and income of the trust shall go to and become the exclusive property of the surviving settlor. Upon the death of the survivor of us, this trust shall terminate, and

the interest of the survivor in the trust (whether it be only a one-half interest or the full interest) shall be distributed absolutely free of trust, as specified and directed in his or her will, or if not specifically disposed of in such will, then to the beneficiaries of the residue of his or her estate; or, if such survivor dies intestate, then to such person or persons as would take according to the laws of descent and distribution of the State of Texas, as then existing. Provided, however, that if either of us shall die before the death of the other, leaving lawful issue (heirs of the body) living at the time of his or her death, the share of such deceased settlor in the corpus and income of the trust property shall go to and vest in such lawful issue of such decedent as may be living at the death of such decedent (taking per stirpes and without preference because of any circumstances of sex or order of birth), but such beneficiary or beneficiaries shall not receive any of the trust property corpus (only income from time to time) until the trust is terminated in the manner hereinafter specified. And provided further that this clause 6 shall not affect the right of the survivor to revoke or terminate this trust at any time by his or her sole action under clause 8 hereinafter; but any right of the deceased person to join or be consulted in the termination of the trust, under clause 8 hereinafter, shall not survive to or be enjoyed by the issue of said decedent. During the continuance of the trust, our Trustee hereunder shall continue to act as the Trustee of any of said beneficiaries who may not be sui juris. * * *

8. This trust may be amended in any way or terminated at any time by the joint action of all the beneficiaries of the income from the trust, and such action shall become effective upon the filing in the Deed Records of Dallas County, Texas, of an instrument amending or terminating this trust. * * *

11. The Trustee shall have the power at any time, upon the joint request, in writing, of all beneficiaries of this trust, to make a complete or partial distribution of the corpus of the trust estate to any primary beneficiary or any and each successor beneficiary or any guardian or other legal representative of any beneficiary, of the beneficial interest of such beneficiary in the corpus of the trust estate. Upon the written request of either of us, at any time after the five years from the date the trust property comes into the hands of our Trustee, the Trustee shall pay over to each of us the sum of $5,000 from the corpus of the trust, as soon after such request as the required portion of the trust property can be liquidated. After an additional period of two years from such first $5,000 payment to each of us, upon the written request of either of us, the Trustee shall pay over to each of us an additional sum of $5,000 from the corpus of the trust, as soon after such request as the necessary partial liquidation may be effected. After an additional period of two years from such second $5,000 payment to each of us, upon the written request of either of us, the Trustee shall pay over to each of us an additional sum of $5,000 from the corpus of the trust, as soon after such request as the necessary additional partial liquidation may be effected.

The Amodio trust agreement was accepted by Byerly, as trustee. Shortly thereafter he wrote each of the petitioners as follows:

As a condition of my appointment and acceptance, I have agreed and do now agree that, so long as either of you may live and be capable of acting, no sale or conveyance of trust real property shall be made without the written consent of the Settlor and Settlors (yourselves) then living, first had and obtained; provided, however, that if for any reason, though using due diligence, I should be unable to communicate with or receive written instructions from either or both of you for a period of three months from the date of my inquiry or advice, it is agreed that I shall have full authority and power to make any sale of real property that I, in my sole discretion, may deem for the best interests of the Trust Estate.

Further, I agree not to exercise any of the other powers specifically granted by clauses 5(c), 5(e), 5(f), 5(g), 5(m), 5(o) and/or 5(q) of said trust instrument, or any of them, until after the consent in writing of yourselves or the survivor of you, if one of you shall have died, first had and obtained; provided, however, that if for any reason, using all due diligence, I shall be unable to communicate with or receive written instructions from either or both of you for a period of two months, it is agreed that I shall have full authority and power to exercise any of said powers as I may, in my sole discretion, deem or for the best interests of the Trust Estate; and provided, further, that the failure of either of you to give me specific instructions in writing on the subject of any inquiry or advice concerning the proposed exercise by me of any of the powers enumerated and provided in said clauses 5(c), 5(e), 5(f), 5(g), 5(m), 5(o) and/or 5(q), for a period of two months from the date of my inquiry or advice, shall irrevocably be deemed to be equivalent to written consent by such person to the proposed action by me as Trustee.

Byerly designated Fidelity Trust Company as his agent to manage the Amodio trust. The trust was known as Trust #18372 in Fidelity's records.

The petitioner Inez was born in 1904. She has been married and divorced. She had no children. Petitioner John Amodio was born in 1909, was educated in England, and served in the Royal Volunteer Reserve of the Royal Air Force in World War II. After the war he lived in Switzerland and applied for right of domicile there which was granted him in 1948. He visited the United States late in 1946 with Josephine and Inez. The Amodio trust agreement was drawn up on the occasion of that visit and was signed at Pittsburgh. As a result of some objections by Inez, Byerly wrote the letter quoted above as conditioning his trusteeship. Amodio returned to Europe early in 1947. Josephine died in Switzerland in 1948. Amodio married in 1948 and next visited the United States in 1949, going to Pittsburgh, Dallas, El Paso, and into Mexico. While in Dallas he looked at some real property with a view to purchase. He appointed an agent who contracted on Amodio's behalf to purchase property on Ross Avenue in Dallas. Amodio returned to Europe at the end of 1949. The purchase of the Ross Avenue property was completed by the agent on March 6, 1950. The property contained a 1-story brick building and was acquired at a cost of $48,000, including the assumption of a mortgage in the amount of $18,260.89. At the time of acquisition by Amodio, the entire property was leased for a term of 5 years from June 15, 1949, at a rental of $500 per month.

The collection of the monthly rentals was handled by Moser Company, a Dallas real estate firm. This firm received the checks for the monthly rentals, and, after paying certain expenses and deducting a 5 per cent commission, remitted the balance to Fidelity. Moser Company paid to the City of Dallas in 1951 the amount of a paving assessment against the property and $386 to a roofing company for repairs.

Fidelity received from the Moser Company the monthly remittances constituting the rentals less the deduction of Moser Company's commission and the other disbursements described. From such proceeds, Fidelity made monthly payments of mortgage principal and interest, paid to itself quarterly commission charges, paid premiums on fire insurance and public liability insurance, and paid city and school taxes, State and County taxes, and an assessment of the Dallas Health Department. Pursuant to an option in the lease, the lessee exercised the right to renew the lease for a 5-year period commencing in 1954.

Amodio came to the United States in 1950 for a brief visit and opened an investment account with Brown Brothers Harriman and Co. in New York City. He arranged with Fidelity Trust to have Fidelity prepare and file his United States income tax returns. In September and October 1951 he visited the United States for about 11 days and attended an exhibition of paintings loaned by him to the Dallas Museum. Before arriving he wrote his agent in Dallas expressing a desire to look at other income-producing real property available for purchase. While in Dallas he looked at real property on Greenville Avenue with a view to purchase as an investment and authorized his agent to effect the purchase of this property. From Switzerland he later directed Brown Brothers Harriman and Co. to sell some bonds to provide funds for the purchase of this property, which purchase was effected at the end of 1951. The cost of the Greenville Avenue property was $90,000, including the assumption of a mortgage of $25,500. This property contained a 1-story brick building with 6 rental units. The collection of rentals and the payment of expenses with respect to this property was handled by J.W. Lindsley & Co., a Dallas real estate firm. Certain leases were in force which expired in 1952 or 1953 and which the agent renewed for further terms. The agent secured two new tenants, one for a term commencing in 1952, the other for a term commencing in 1954. The agent collected rentals, deducted commissions of 5 per cent, made mortgage payments of $500 monthly plus interest, and paid insurance premiums and taxes and arranged for repairs in these years.

The rental properties owned by the Amodio trust in the taxable years were parcels of improved real estate in Dallas and El Paso, Texas and Pittsburgh, Pennsylvania. The Texas properties were managed by resident agents who collected rents, made repairs, and acquired tenants.

Amodio did not visit the United States in 1952, 1953, or 1954. While in the United States during 1951 he effected no sales, exchanges, or other dispositions of capital assets.

The rental income and expenses of the Ross Avenue property were:

	1951	1952	1953	1954
Gross rents	$6,000.00	$6,000.00	$6,000.00	$6,000.00
Commissions —Moser	300.00	300.00	300.00	300.00
Commissions —Fidelity	240.00	240.00	240.00	240.00
Assessments	213.15		632.30	
Repairs	386.00		21.80	
Insurance	335.93	6.35	845.76	
Taxes	584.93	584.93	648.70	680.49
Mortgage principal	2,428.11	2,539.68	2,656.33	2,778.34
Mortgage interest	684.69	573.12	456.47	334.46
Available to Amodio	827.18	1,755.91	198.64	1,643.17

The rental income and expenses of the Greenville Avenue property were:

	1952	1953	1954
Rent (agent's commission 5 per cent)	$11,365.00	$10,610.00	$6,890.00
Mortgage payment (plus interest)	6,000.00	6,000.00	6,000.00
Insurance	15.57	883.76	1,216.29
Taxes	1,111.14	1,230.19	1,290.12
Repairs	1,315.19	177.43	105.32
Sent to Amodio	2,162.58	1,836.49	none

In preparing Amodio's United States income tax returns Fidelity computed his net rental income as follows:

	1951	1952	1953	1954
Gross rents	$6,000.00	$17,365.00	$16,610.00	$12,890.00
Depreciation	910.64	3,328.41	3,328.41	3,328.41
Expenses	3,608.05	4,686.56	5,926.21	4,028.22
Repairs		1,315.19	177.43	105.32
Net rents	1,481.31	8,034.84	7,177.95	5,428.05

The returns reported income from the Amodio trust and the Wainwright trust as follows:

	1951	1952	1953	1954
Amodio	$10,560.02	$10,392.06	$10,763.24	11,586.54
Wainwright	1,124.73	1,106.65	679.06	496.38

The returns showed the following additional items of income from dividends and interest and rents from Amodio's agency account, the Amodio trust, the Wainwright trust, and Brown Brothers Harriman and Co. from which tax was withheld at the rate of 15 per cent on dividends and 5 per cent on interest and 30 per cent on rents.

	1951	1952	1953	1954
Agency account:				
Dividends	$1,813.00	$1,949.00	$1,799.00	$2,147.30
Rents		3,197.37	2,936.29	3,272.75
Wainwright:				
Dividends	137.98	173.26	213.52	232.05
Interest	264.33	234.08	175.06	
Rents		1,106.65	679.06	491.39
Amodio trust:				
Dividends	2,006.59	3,974.33	4,337.08	4,732.83
Interest	2,654.05	1,108.69	790.66	412.80
Rents		10,392.06	10,910.15	11,586.54
B.B.H. dividends	23,331.75	24,811.91	20,950.15	21,926.80

Byler filed returns for the Amodio trust for the taxable years 1951 through 1954, which showed the following items:

	1951	1952	1953	1954
Rents	$38,947.13	$40,052.50	$41,701.31	$43,257.00
Depreciation	3,634.71	4,040.79	4,308.03	4,516.41
Repairs				776.00
Other expenses	14,264.23	15,227.60	15,090.79	16,120.20
Net profit	21,048.19	20,784.11	21,526.49	22,620.39
Dividends	4,224.40	8,367.00	9,130.70	9,963.84
Interest	5,532.55	2,334.08	1,653.27	880.09

In 1953 the Amodio trust realized a net long-term capital gain of $33,018.68 and took into account 50 per cent or $16,509.34.

John Amodio was a resident of Switzerland in the years 1951 through 1954. In these years he was engaged in business in the United States through his agents in the ownership and management of income-producing real property. In these years he did not have a permanent establishment in the United States.

The stipulated facts are found as stipulated.

OPINION.

The issue common to both cases is whether the properties constituting the corpus of the Amodio trust should be considered as jointly owned by the petitioners, who were the grantors and equal beneficiaries of that trust. Under the trust instrument the petitioners were each to receive as early as possible $40,000 in cash. Each could withdraw $5,000 in cash from the corpus upon request at 2-year intervals. By joint action they could terminate or amend the trust at any time and revert title to the corpus in themselves in whole or in part. Under the provisions of section 166 of the Internal Revenue Code of 1939[68] the income of any part of a trust is to be included in computing net income of the grantor if the power to revest title in the grantor is held by the grantor alone or in conjunction with any person not having an adverse interest. Under section 676 of the Internal Revenue Code of 1954[69] a grantor is to be treated as owner of any portion of a trust if at any time the power to revest title in him is exercisable by him or a nonadverse party, or both. If the interests of these two petitioners were not adverse to each other, they should be treated under the cited provisions of law as coowners of the property constituting the corpus, the trust should be disregarded as a separate entity and the capital gains and losses of the trust treated as gains and losses of the petitioners.

The petitioners contend that they had interests substantially adverse to each other. The argument is that if one petitioner survives the other, the survivor acquires the entire corpus including the accumulated capital gains, since neither petitioner had children and each was the sole potential heir of the other under the terms of the trust.

The practical effect of the Amodio trust was that the petitioners turned over their interests to the trustee for current management of the properties constituting the

---

68. [1] SEC. 166. REVOCABLE TRUSTS.

Where at any time the power to revest in the grantor title to any part of the corpus of the trust is vested—

(1) in the grantor, either alone or in conjunction with any person not having a substantial adverse interest in the disposition of such part of the corpus or the income therefrom, then the income of such part of the trust shall be included in computing the net income of the grantor.

69. [2] SEC. 676. POWER TO REVOKE.

(a) GENERAL RULE.—The grantor shall be treated as the owner of any portion of a trust, whether or not he is treated as such owner under any other provision of this part, where at any time the power to revest in the grantor title to such portion is exercisable by the grantor or a non-adverse party, or both.

corpus and retained the right jointly to change the terms of the contract or terminate it and take possession of their shares.

In *Welch v. Bradley*, 130 F.2d 109 (C.A. 1, 1942), a mother and daughter were grantors and beneficiaries of a trust of which the mother was trustee. Each could appoint by will the devolution of her share. Together they could terminate the trust and take their respective shares. The daughter was the sole heir of the mother. The court concluded that neither had, as against the other, a substantial interest adverse to the revocation of the trust. The reasoning in the foregoing case is applicable here. The interests of Amodio and his sister were not adverse to each other. The statutes cited clearly apply and the capital gains of the Amodio trust are includible as income of the petitioners as the respondent determined.

This conclusion disposes of the sole issue in the case of Inez. The remaining issues concern the case of John Amodio.

The scheme of taxation of nonresident aliens provided under section 211 of the 1939 Code and section 871 of the 1954 Code distinguished between such aliens engaged in trade or business in the United States and those not so engaged.

The respondent determined that Amodio was taxable as a non-resident alien engaged in trade or business in the United States. The contention is that Amodio was engaged in business in the United States by reason of his ownership and operation of rental real properties, first, the properties owned in his own right and, second, the properties constituting the corpus of the Amodio trust of which he was coowner.

Amodio contends that he was a nonresident alien who resides in Switzerland, that he could not be considered as engaged in trade or business in the United States by reason of the ownership of real property in the United States and that he did not elect, pursuant to provisions of the income tax convention between the United States and the Swiss Confederation (hereinafter referred to as the convention) to be taxed by the United States as so engaged.

Under article IX of the convention,[70] income from real property in the United States, including gains from sales thereof, is to be taxed only in the United States. The pertinent regulation, section 509.111,[71] states that income derived by a nonresident

---

70. [3] T.D. 6149, 1955-2 C.B. 814-836.
 ARTICLE IX
 (1) Income from real property (including gains derived from the sale or exchange of such property but not including interest from mortgages or bonds secured by real property) * * * shall be taxable only in the contracting State in which such property * * * (is) situated.
 (2) A resident * * * of one of the contracting States deriving any such income from such property within the other contracting State may, for any taxable year, elect to be subject to the tax of such other contracting State, on a net basis, as if such resident or corporation or entity were engaged in trade or business within such other contracting State through a permanent establishment therein during such taxable year.
 71. [4] Sec. 509.111 REAL PROPERTY INCOME AND NATURAL RESOURCE ROYALTIES—
(a) GENERAL.—Income of whatever nature derived by a nonresident alien who is a resident of Switzerland, * * * from real property situated in the United States, including gains derived from the

alien residing in Switzerland from real property in the United States is not exempt from United States tax but is taxable under the provisions of the Internal Revenue Code of 1954 generally applicable to nonresident aliens.

According to the convention, article II(1)(F), a "Swiss enterprise" means an industrial or commercial enterprise or undertaking carried on in Switzerland by an individual resident in Switzerland or by a Swiss corporation or other entity. Since Amodio carried on no business activity in Switzerland, he was not engaged in a Swiss enterprise within the meaning of the convention.

The regulations implementing the convention provide in section 509.105(a)(2),[72] that a nonresident alien individual who is a citizen of Switzerland, carrying on an enterprise which is not Swiss, is subject to tax on the income thereof under section 871(c), I.R.C. 1954, if he has engaged in trade or business within the United States at any time during the taxable year.

In *Jan Casimir Lewenhaupt*, 20 T.C. 151 (1953), affd. 221 F.2d 227 (C.A. 9, 1955), we held that a nonresident alien was engaged in business in the United States through his activities connected with the ownership of real property in the United States and the management of such property through a resident agent. We there stated (p. 163):

> The petitioner, prior to and during the taxable year, employed LaMontagne as his resident agent who, under a broad power of attorney which included the power to buy, sell, lease, and mortgage real estate for and in the name of the petitioner, managed the petitioner's real properties and other financial affairs in this country. The petitioner, during all or a part of the taxable year, owned three parcels of improved, commercial real estate. The approximate aggregate fair market value of the three properties was $337,000. In addition, the petitioner purchased a residential property, and through his agent, La-Montagne, acquired an option to purchase a fourth parcel of commercial

---

sale or exchange of such property, (and) rentals from such property * * * is not exempt from United States tax by the convention. Such items of income are subject to taxation under the provisions of the Internal Revenue Code of 1954 generally applicable to the taxation of nonresident alien individuals and foreign corporations. See Article IX of the convention. * * *

(b) NET basis—(1) General.—Notwithstanding the provisions of paragraph (a) of this section, a nonresident alien who is a resident of Switzerland, or a Swiss corporation or other entity, who during the taxable year derives from sources within the United States any income from real property as described in such paragraph may elect for such taxable year to be subject to United States tax on a net basis as though such alien, corporation, or other entity were engaged in trade or business in the United States during such year through a permanent establishment situated therein.

72. [5] Sec. 509.105 Industrial and Commercial Profits—(a) General.—(1) * * *

(2) * * * a nonresident alien individual who is a citizen of Switzerland * * * carrying on an enterprise which is not Swiss, is subject to tax on such income of such enterprise pursuant to section 871(c), * * * Internal Revenue Code of 1954, if such alien * * * has engaged in trade or business in the United States at any time during the taxable year, * * *

property, herein referred to as the El Camino Real property, at a cost of $67,500. The option was exercised and title to the property conveyed to the petitioner in January 1947.

La Montagne's activities, during the taxable year, in the management and operation of petitioner's real properties included the following: executing leases and renting the properties, collecting the rents, keeping books of account, supervising any necessary repairs to the properties, paying taxes and mortgage interest, insuring the properties, executing an option to purchase the El Camino Real property, and executing the sale of the Modesto property. In addition, the agent conducted a regular correspondence with the petitioner's father in England who held a power of attorney from petitioner identical with that given to LaMontagne; he submitted monthly reports to the petitioner's father; and he advised him of prospective and advantageous sales or purchases of property.

The aforementioned activities, carried on in the petitioner's behalf by his agent, are beyond the scope of mere ownership of real property, or the receipt of income from real property. The activities were considerable, continuous, and regular and, in our opinion, constituted engaging in a business within the meaning of section 211(b) of the Code. See *Pinchot v. Commissioner*, 113 F.2d 718.

Amodio contends that the Lewenhaupt case is not applicable in the circumstances of his case. He cites *Evelyn M. L. Neill*, 46 B.T.A. 197 (1942), and *Elizabeth Herbert*, 30 T.C. 26 (1958). In the *Neill* case the taxpayer inherited property which was leased for a long term to a tenant who was required to pay taxes and insurance and to maintain the property and no substantial activity on the part of the taxpayer or her agent was necessary. Under those circumstances it was held that the taxpayer was neither engaged in business in the United States nor maintaining an office or place of business therein.

In *Elizabeth Herbert, supra*, we held that a nonresident alien was not engaged in trade or business in the United States through the ownership of real property in the United States in the circumstances there present. We there stated (p. 53):

In the instant case the real property consisted of one building rented in its entirety to one tenant who has occupied it since 1940, has complete charge of its operation, and is responsible for all repairs except as to outer walls and foundation. This property (the only real property owned by petitioner in the United States) was acquired by petitioner 50 years ago, not as the result of a business transaction entered into for profit (cf. *Fackler v. Commissioner*, 133 F.2d 509) but by gift from petitioner's father when she was a very young girl (see *Grier v. United States*, 120 F.Supp. 395). During the taxable years her only activities, in addition to the receipt of rentals, were the payment of taxes, mortgage principal and interest, and insurance premiums. See *Evelyn M. L. Neill, supra*. The record also shows that petitioner executed a lease of the property in 1940 and a modified renewal thereof in 1946, and made minor repairs to the walls and roof in 1954 and 1955.

We are of the opinion that petitioner's activities with regard to the real property here involved, which might be considered as "beyond the scope of mere ownership of real property, or the receipt of income from real property," were sporadic rather than "continuous," were irregular rather than "regular," and were minimal rather than "considerable." We therefore conclude that petitioner was not engaged in trade or business in the United States' during the taxable years within the meaning of article IX(1) of the United States-United Kingdom tax convention.

In the *Herbert* case the property was acquired by the taxpayer by gift and there were no rental activities in the taxable period, while here Amodio purchased two properties for income-producing purposes, his agents collected rents, paid taxes, insurance, and management fees, arranged leases, and provided for repairs.

Amodio purchased the Ross Avenue property in 1950 for a price of $48,000. He arranged with his agent to look at other real properties for investment and as a result he acquired the Greenville Avenue property at the end of 1951 for a price of $90,000. The gross annual rentals in 1951 were $6,000, in 1952 and 1953 were in excess of $16,000, and were over $12,000 in 1954. The properties were managed by local real estate agents who negotiated or renewed leases, arranged for repairs, collected rents, paid taxes and assessments, and remitted net proceeds to Fidelity after deducting commissions. From the proceeds Fidelity or the local agent paid principal and interest on the mortgages, insurance premiums, and taxes. Fidelity retained its commissions and amounts to be applied on Amodio's income taxes and the remainder was sent to him. The acts of the agents are attributable to Amodio. These activities were beyond the scope of mere ownership of property and the receipt of income. They were considerable, continuous, and regular, as in the Lewenhaupt case. Such activities of a nonresident alien through his agents in the United States constitute engaging in business in the United States. Amodio is taxable as a nonresident alien engaged in trade or business in the United States.

In view of this conclusion it is not necessary to determine whether Amodio is also engaged in business in the United States through his interest in the properties owned by the Amodio trust.

The issue whether Amodio is taxable on capital gains from sales of assets outside the Amodio trust depends upon whether he was engaged in trade or business in the United States. Since he was so engaged in business he is taxable on such gains. Section 211(a) of the 1939 Code and section 871(a) of the 1954 Code, which except such gains of nonresident aliens under certain conditions, are not applicable here.

Amodio further contends that under the convention he was subject to tax on dividend and interest income at rates no greater than 15 per cent and 5 per cent respectively, as provided in articles VI and VII of the convention. The respondent contends (1) that Amodio is not a resident of Switzerland and therefore the convention does not apply, and (2) that if it does apply, Amodio had a 'permanent establishment' in the United States and therefore articles VI and VII are not applicable to him.

The respondent's argument that Amodio is not a resident of Switzerland is stated as follows:

> The United States-Switzerland Tax Convention called for an exchange of certain fiscal information between these countries. The Swiss authorities were informed that United States banks—Brown Brothers and Harriman of New York and Fidelity Trust of Pittsburgh—had withheld 15% and 5% on dividends and interest, respectively, and that the net amounts after withholding were transmitted to Amodio in care of a Swiss bank—Ferrier, Lullin & Cie of Geneva, Switzerland. The American banks withheld 15% and 5% on the theory that Amodio was domiciled in Switzerland and therefore subject to the United States-Switzerland Convention. The Swiss authorities were requested to inquire of Amodio whether he was in fact domiciled in Switzerland, and if not then the Swiss authorities were to withhold an additional 15% and 25% on dividends and interest, respectively, since Amodio would have been erroneously claiming the benefits of the United States-Switzerland Convention. Amodio was informed that if he was actually domiciled in a country other than Switzerland he was to pay additional withholding on income from Swiss authorities was to pay the additional withholdings. It is apparent therefore he made representations to Swiss authorities that he was not seeking the benefits of the United States-Switzerland Convention and was not domiciled in Switzerland.

The respondent refers to a letter to Amodio dated June 18, 1954, by the Swiss Federal Administration, which is translated as follows:

> According to information from American fiscal authorities you have received from the United States through the Fidelity Trust Company in 1951, $22,189.89.
>
> You have claimed the benefits of the Switzerland-United States Convention with respect to the reduced "withholding tax" and therefore we must ask you to let us know your permanent domicile with your exact address.
>
> If you have other than a Swiss domicile we ask you to let us also know. In such a case we will inform the American fiscal authorities that you are not governed by the Switzerland-United States Tax Convention and consequently you are not entitled to the reduction of the 'withholding tax'. This will not be necessary if you will deposit with us for the account of the American fiscal authorities the sum of the reduction of the tax (15% on dividends and 25% on interest). If such should be the case, you must send us at the same time filled out the enclosed Form S-182. The conversion into Swiss Francs is to be made according to the New York market as of the date you pay.

Amodio testified that he has been domiciled in Switzerland since 1948 and intends to remain domiciled there. He testified that he paid the Swiss administration the amounts claimed in the correspondence, and it appears that he did so under the impression he had no choice but to pay. At any rate he is now claiming the benefits of the convention with respect to his income from United States sources. We have no doubt that he was a resident of Switzerland in the taxable years.

Under articles VI and VII of the convention the tax on dividends and interest derived from sources in the United States by a nonresident alien who is a resident of Switzerland shall not exceed 15 per cent and 5 per cent respectively, if such alien has no permanent establishment in the United States.[73]

The respondent argues that Amodio had a permanent establishment in the United States, consisting of the real properties he owned or those of which he was the coowner through the Amodio trust.

The convention and regulations implementing it define "permanent establishment"[74] as meaning an office, factory, worship, or other fixed place of business, and as implying the active conduct of a "business enterprise."

---

73. [6] ARTICLE VI
   (1) The rate of tax imposed by one of the contracting States upon dividends derived from sources within such State by a resident or corporation or other entity of the other contracting State not having a permanent establishment in the former State shall not exceed 15 percent: * * *
ARTICLE VII
   (1) The rate of tax imposed by one of the contracting States on interest on bonds, securities, notes, debentures or on any other form of indebtedness (including mortgages, or bonds secured by real property) derived from sources within such contracting State by a resident or corporation or other entity of the other contracting State not having a permanent establishment in the former State shall not exceed five percent: * * *
74. [7] Sec. 509.104 DEFINITIONS—* * *
   (b) Specific terms.—As used in this Treasury decision—
      (5) Permanent establishment—(i) Fixed place of business.—The term "permanent establishment" means an office, factory, worship, warehouse, branch, or other fixed place of business, but does not include the casual and temporary use of merely storage facilities. It implies the active conduct of a business enterprise. The mere ownership, for example, of timberlands or a warehouse in the United States by a Swiss enterprise does not mean that such enterprise, in the absence of any business activity therein, has a permanent establishment in the United States. Moreover, the maintenance within the United States by a Swiss enterprise of a warehouse for convenience of delivery, and not for purposes of display, does not of itself constitute a permanent establishment in the United States, even though offers of purchase have been obtained by an agent therein of the Swiss enterprise and transmitted by him to the Swiss enterprise for acceptance. The fact that a Swiss enterprise maintains in the United States an office or other fixed place of business used exclusively for the purchase for such enterprise of goods or merchandise shall not of itself constitute such fixed place of business a permanent establishment of such enterprise.
         (iii) Agency.—A Swiss enterprise which has an agency in the United States does not thereby have a permanent establishment in the United States, unless the agent has, and habitually exercises, a general authority to negotiate and conclude contracts on behalf of such enterprise or unless he has a stock of merchandise from which he regularly fills orders on its behalf. If the enterprise has an agent in the United States who has

In *Consolidated Premium Iron Ores Ltd.*, 28 T.C. 127 (1957), we expressed the view (p. 152) that "permanent establishment" implies the existence of an office, staffed and capable of carrying on business from day to day, or a plant or facilities equipped to carry on the ordinary routine of a business activity.

In our opinion the real properties owned by Amodio or of which he was a coowner through the trust cannot be regarded as a 'permanent establishment' within the meaning of the convention. Nor can it be said that his agents managing these properties represent a permanent establishment for this purpose, even though we have concluded that Amodio was doing business through such agents. The convention indicates, in article II(1)(C),[75] that carrying on business dealings through a broker or independent agent acting in the ordinary course of his business as such does not amount to having a permanent establishment. Amodio's agents fall within this description. Accordingly, the tax upon Amodio's dividend and interest income from United States sources is limited to the rates stated in the convention.

Amodio contends further that his liability for income taxes to the United States has been discharged through amounts withheld by agents and additional amounts collected from him by the Swiss Federal Tax Administration and remitted to the United States Treasury on his account. He alleges that his taxes have been overpaid and that he is entitled to refunds and is not liable for deficiencies. The respondent states that there is no evidence that any of the amounts allegedly collected by Swiss fiscal authorities were ever paid over to the United States Treasury, but that an investigation is being made concerning this and credit will be given if such payments have been received.

The liability of Amodio will be subject to recomputation under Rule 50 of this Court as a result of our decisions upon the issues. Any credits available to Amodio may be applied to this liability and if the taxes have been overpaid the amount of

---

power to contract on its behalf, but only at fixed prices and under conditions determined by such principal, it does not thereby necessarily have a permanent establishment in the United States. * * * A Swiss enterprise shall not be deemed to have a permanent establishment in the United States merely because it carries on business dealings in the United States through a commission agent, broker, custodian, or other independent agent, acting in the ordinary course of his business as such.

75. [8] ARTICLE II

(1) As used in this convention:

(c) The term "permanent establishment" means a branch, office, factory, workshop, warehouse or other fixed place of business, but does not include the casual and temporary use of merely storage facilities, nor does it include an agency unless the agent has and habitually exercises a general authority to negotiate and conclude contracts on behalf of an enterprise or has a stock of merchandise from which he regularly fills orders on its behalf. An enterprise of one of the contracting States shall not be deemed to have a permanent establishment in the other State merely because it carries on business dealings in such other State through a commission agent, broker or custodian or other independent agent acting in the ordinary course of his business as such. * * *

the overpayments refundable, subject to the applicable statutes of limitation, can be determined.

Decision will be entered for the respondent in Docket No. 74211. Decision will be entered under Rule 50 in Docket No. 74297.

Herbert v. Commissioner

Tax Court of the United States

30 T.C. 26 (1958)

Kern, Judge:

Respondent has determined deficiencies in petitioner's Federal income taxes for the years 1952 and 1953 in the respective amounts of $5,762.62 and $7,806.09. These deficiencies result from respondent's determination that petitioner (a British subject) '[has] been and [is] engaged in a trade or business through a permanent establishment in the United States and therefore, * * * [does] not qualify for the reductions in the rate of tax provided by the Income Tax Convention between the United States and the United Kingdom.' The 'reductions in the rate of tax' above referred to are those provided by article VI(1) and article IX(1) of the income tax convention which provide that the rate of United States tax on dividends from a United States corporation and or rentals from real property in the United States, received by a subject of the United Kingdom, should be limited to 15 per cent if the recipient is subject to United Kingdom tax on such dividends and rentals and is 'not engaged in trade or business in the United States.' Article II(2) of the convention provides that a resident of the United Kingdom shall not be deemed to be engaged in trade or business in the United States unless he or she 'has a permanent establishment situated therein.'[76]

The petition alleges error in connection with the entire amount of the deficiencies, and also alleges an overpayment of tax in the year 1952 in the amount of $1,207.50.

The parties have filed a stipulation of facts. There has also been filed and made a part of the record herein a deposition of petitioner together with certain exhibits identified therein. The stipulation, the exhibits attached thereto, and the exhibits identified in the deposition are incorporated herein and made a part of our findings of fact by this reference.

Petitioner is an individual who, during the calendar years 1952 and 1953 (and for some years prior thereto and until the present time), was a citizen of the United Kingdom domiciled and resident at Taunton, England. She filed her Federal nonresident alien income tax returns for the years 1952 and 1953 with the director of internal revenue at Baltimore, Maryland, and her departing alien income tax returns for the periods January 1 to December 15, 1952, and January 1 to December 4, 1953, with the Washington office of the Baltimore director of internal revenue.

---

76. [1] The complete text of the convention between the United States and the United Kingdom is set forth in 1947-1 C.B. 209, et seq.

During 1952 and 1953 petitioner owned 119 shares of the stock of the Virginia Hotel Company, there being 681 shares outstanding. Petitioner's sister, Belle Willard Roosevelt, who lives in New York City, also owned 119 shares and their mother owned 341 shares.

The Virginia Hotel Company is a domestic corporation existing under the laws of the State of Virginia. During the calendar years 1952 and 1953 its principal assets were an installment note arising from the sale of the Willard Hotel, Washington, D.C., and two parcels of District of Columbia realty. One parcel is a tract of land at Fourteenth Street and New York Avenue, N.W., improved by the premises known as the Wyatt Building. The other parcel is in the middle of the 1400 block of Pennsylvania Avenue, N.W., improved with a building at 1417-1427 Pennsylvania Avenue and a parking garage.

In each of the years 1952 and 1953 petitioner received dividends on her Virginia Hotel Company stock in the amount of $12,566.40. In these years she also received rents from property located at 613 Fourteenth Street, N.W., Washington, D.C., in the respective amounts of $12,779.84 and $13,641.67. These dividends and rents constituted the only income received by petitioner from United States sources.

Petitioner visited the United States for approximately 2 months in each of the years 1952 and 1953. Prior to 1952 she came to this country every 2 or 3 years, or oftener if there was occasion, for a stay of similar duration. When she made these visits she attended meetings of the stockholders of the Virginia Hotel Company which the corporation usually arranged to coincide with her trips in order that she might 'hear a report of what has been going on.'

During the years 1949 to 1953, inclusive, the offices of the Virginia Hotel Company were located at 1107 Eye Street, N.W., Washington, D.C. On petitioner's return for the years 1949 to 1952, inclusive, in the space provided for her address it is stated 'Address all communications to 1107 Eye Street, N.W., Washington 5, D.C.' On her departing alien income tax return for 1952 she gives as her address 'c/o The Virginia Hotel Co., 1107 Eye Street, N.W., Washington 5, D.C.' On her 1953 returns she gives her address as 1107 Eye Street, N.W., Washington, D.C.

Similarly on a claim for refund relative to the year 1949 petitioner stated 'Address all communications to 1107 Eye Street, Northwest, Washington, D.C.'

The officers or employees of the Virginia Hotel Company keep on file in their offices copies of papers relating to petitioner's interest as a stockholder in that company which they send to petitioner, and also copies of tax returns which are prepared for petitioner without charge by the secretary of that company.

In August 1939 petitioner gave to her sister, Mrs. Roosevelt, an unlimited power of attorney as to any business or property matters which might arise. This power was in full force and effect at all times material hereto. As between petitioner and Mrs. Roosevelt it was understood that the latter would take no action under the power of attorney except as directly authorized by petitioner or in an emergency.

Marjorie Smith was, at all times material hereto, an employee of the Virginia Hotel Company. Marjorie had general instructions from petitioner to prepare her tax returns, and pursuant to that authority did prepare the annual Federal tax returns for the years 1949 to 1952, inclusive. Mrs. Roosevelt signed those returns for petitioner pursuant to the power of attorney without further authorization from petitioner. After they had been signed by Mrs. Roosevelt, Marjorie, by letters on the letterhead of the Virginia Hotel Company, sent the returns to the collector of internal revenue.

In 1907 or 1908 petitioner and her sister, Mrs. Roosevelt, received as a gift from their father a parcel of real estate located at 613 Fourteenth Street, N.W., Washington, D.C. They continued to hold this property throughout the period here involved as tenants in common. During the taxable period and for a number of years before and after, the premises were improved by a 3-story building.

On December 9, 1946, petitioner and Mrs. Roosevelt leased this entire property to Bruce Hunt, Inc., a corporation engaged in the business of selling men's clothing at retail. This lease was a modified extension of an earlier lease agreement between the same parties dated December 17, 1940. The lease extended to June 30, 1957, and provided that the rent was to be in the amount of $1,500 per month plus a percentage of gross sales. The percentage of sales was to be paid annually after the tenant submitted an accounting statement to the lessors.

Among other things, the lease provides that the landlord (petitioner and Mrs. Roosevelt) is to take care of repairs to the foundation and outer walls plus any alterations of a structural nature; that the tenant is to make all other repairs; and that if the tenant refuses to make the repairs chargeable to it, the landlord, his agents or servants has or have the right to enter the premises and make such repairs at the tenant's expense.

The lease also provides that any notice, demand, election, or option by the lessee under the agreement shall be addressed to Mrs. Roosevelt; that in the case of an assignment of the tenant's rights thereunder the landlord must agree in writing thereto; and that the landlord shall pay all real estate taxes and assessments.

At all times material hereto Joseph Wyatt, a cousin of petitioner, was a practicing lawyer in Washington, D.C., and the president of the Virginia Hotel Company. Wyatt advised petitioner in connection with the negotiation of the lease to Bruce Hunt, Inc. Mrs. Roosevelt signed the lease on her sister's behalf, as well as for herself, pursuant to the power of attorney and also pursuant to petitioner's specific instructions after petitioner had approved its terms.

In October 1952 the written lease was modified by an oral amendment increasing the minimum rental and raising the monthly payments from $1,500 to $1,750. Wyatt also negotiated this amendment, represented petitioner relative thereto, and advised her in the premises. The lease was near expiration at the time of hearing herein, and Bruce Hunt, Inc., had not yet exercised its renewal option. Wyatt was conferring with the tenant as to renewal of the lease, acting on behalf of petitioner in that regard and advising her accordingly. Wyatt has never been remunerated in any way for his services to petitioner in connection with this property nor is any remuneration contemplated.

No repairs or renovations to the premises were made by petitioner and Mrs. Roosevelt during the years 1949 to 1953, but in 1954 a portion of the marble store front was replaced at a cost of $585.54. The president of Bruce Hunt, Inc. notified Wyatt that two of the marble facing pieces were damaged. The latter authorized replacement thereof and notified petitioner and Mrs. Roosevelt of the situation. He also requested Commander William Rigdon, an employee of the Virginia Hotel Company, to inspect the store front and to negotiate for the replacement and repairs. Payment was advanced by the Virginia Hotel Company and repayment was promptly made by petitioner and her sister.

In 1955 the rear windows of the premises were removed and bricked up at a cost of $546 and a new roof was put in place at a cost of $880. In these instances the president of the tenant corporation notified Commander Rigdon who in turn notified Wyatt and Paul F. Myers, attorney for the estate of Belle L. Willard, petitioner's mother, who had died on January 28, 1954. At the direction of Wyatt and Myers, Commander Rigdon inspected the premises. Myers then advised petitioner of the need for an estimated cost of the renovations. Mervyn Herbert, petitioner's son, acting on her behalf, authorized that the work be done. Commander Rigdon then made the necessary arrangements. In each case, upon presentation of the bill, payment was advanced by the Virginia Hotel Company, and petitioner and her sister promptly made reimbursement.

During the years in question the monthly rental checks ($1,500 until October 1952 and $1,750 thereafter) from the lessee were drawn to the order of Belle Willard Roosevelt and mailed to her at 1107 Eye Street, Washington, D.C.

Generally such checks were deposited at a Washington bank in an account designated:

> Mrs. Belle Willard Roosevelt, Special,
> 9 Sutton place
> New York 22, New York

The checks were deposited by Marjorie Smith of the Virginia Hotel Company after she endorsed them by typewriter. Checks on this account were made out by Marjorie and forwarded to Mrs. Roosevelt for signature, Marjorie making the entries on the check stubs. The statements for this account were mailed by the bank to Mrs. Roosevelt in New York, and returned by her to Marjorie who then compared them with the entries on the stubs.

After reserving approximately 30 per cent for the payment of such charges as insurance, real estate taxes, interest, and principal on the mortgage, the remainder of the monthly rental payments was disbursed by checks drawn on the account by Mrs. Roosevelt. One check was drawn to the order of Mrs. Roosevelt and two other checks, totaling the amount of the check to Mrs. Roosevelt, were drawn to petitioner's order. Of these two checks to petitioner one was 70 per cent of the total and the other 30 per cent. The large check was sent to England for deposit to petitioner's bank account there, while the smaller check was sent to the National City Bank of New York for deposit to another account of petitioner.

During 1952 and 1953 the tenant paid, in addition to the monthly payments, the further amounts based upon a percentage of sales in accordance with the terms of the lease. This supplemental sum paid in 1952 (based upon 1951 sales) amounted to $7,559.67 and in 1953 (based upon 1952 sales) amounted to $8,000. The $7,559.67 was paid in 6 installments and the $8,000 in 5 installments. These amounts were also paid by checks drawn to the order of Mrs. Roosevelt, mailed to the offices of the Virginia Hotel Company, and deposited to the special account in her name. In this instance no 30 per cent was reserved for the payment of insurance, taxes, and mortgage installments; rather the full amounts were divided between Mrs. Roosevelt and petitioner, one check being drawn to the former and two checks to the latter. Of the two checks to petitioner, as with the monthly rentals, the larger was sent for deposit to her account in London and the other to New York. Her son's secretary keeps a record in England of the checks forward to her as her share of the rental.

On October 5, 1939, petitioner and Mrs. Roosevelt gave the Riggs National Bank, Washington, D. C., a note for $30,000 secured by a deed of trust on the property at 613 Fourteenth Street. The note was payable in semiannual installments of $300 with interest at 4 per cent on the unpaid balance. Wyatt negotiated the loan and deed of trust for petitioner and Mrs. Roosevelt.

During the years 1952 and 1953 petitioner made the following payments relative to the property at 613 Fourteenth Street:

	1952	1953
Second half current year's D.C. real estate taxes	$939.12	$939.12
Note principle (first semiannual installment)	150.00	150.00
Interest on note	228.00	222.00
Plate glass insurance	88.99	83.58
Fire insurance		73.08
Boiler insurance		115.50
First half next year's D.C. real estate taxes	939.12	939.12
Note principal (second semiannual installment)	150.00	150.00
Interest on note	225.00	219.00
Total	2,720.23	2,891.40

The above amounts represent petitioner's one-half of the checks made out by Marjorie Smith on the special account in the name of Mrs. Roosevelt and signed by the latter.

In February 1952 and 1953 the tenant, as required by the lease, mailed or delivered a report of its auditors advising of the amount of sale for the preceding year. Petitioner gave these reports to her son who examined them on her behalf. Copies of business documents and correspondence are kept by petitioner in England either at her home or her son's office.

No independent audit or investigation has been made with respect to the gross sales or percentage rental payments made by the tenant since the making of the current lease by or on behalf of the petitioner of her sister. However in 1946 petitioner and Mrs. Roosevelt employed a certified public accountant who made an investigation of the rental payments due from the tenant for the calendar years 1944 and 1945 under the prior lease which had been extended in a modified form through the taxable years.

During 1952 and 1953 petitioner's mother, Belle Wyatt Willard, owned a substantial amount of real property as well as the majority of the stock of the Virginia Hotel Company. In those years Belle Wyatt Willard was elderly, in fragile health, and unable to manage her own affairs. Under the terms of her mother's will, petitioner had a life interest in one-half of the estate. Sometime prior to 1950 petitioner consulted a New York attorney relative to 'various changes to be made in the Virginia Hotel Company and my mother's properties.'

For the years 1949, 1950, and 1951 petitioner elected to file her Federal income tax returns and be taxed as a nonresident alien engaged in a trade or business in this country.[77]

The arguments of the parties are directed toward two question: management of the Fourteenth Street property was engaged in a trade or business in the United States within the meaning of article IX of the United States-United Kingdom tax convention, and (2) whether petitioner had 'a permanent establishment situated' within the United States during the taxable years within the purview of article II(2) of the tax convention.

The provisions of article IX clearly indicate the recognition by the United States that the ownership and leasing of real property do not constitute per se engaging in trade or business. That article limits the rate of United States tax 'on rentals from real property or from an interest in such property, derived from sources within the United States by a resident of the United Kingdom who is * * * not engaged in trade or business in the United States.' If the ownership and leasing of real property were considered to constitute a trade or business, that provision would be meaningless since on this hypothesis no one could be not engaged in trade or business in the United States who received rentals from real estate located within the United States. That the ownership and leasing of real property, the collection of rentals therefrom, and the performance of certain minimal acts customarily incident to the ownership of real property do not constitute engaging in trade or business is recognized in *Evelyn M. L. Neil*, 46 B.T.A. 197.

However, where the activities of the nonresident alien 'are beyond the scope of mere ownership of real property, or the receipt of income from real property' and are 'considerable, continuous, and regular' it has been held (although not in a case construing the provisions of the United States-United Kingdom tax convention) that such activities of the nonresident alien constitute engaging in a business. See *Jan Casimir Lewenhaupt*, 20 T.C. 151, 163.

In the instant case the real property consisted of one building rented in its entirety to one tenant who has occupied it since 1940, has complete charge of its operation,

---

77. [2] Article IX of the convention contains the following language: 'Provided that any such resident (of the United Kingdom) may elect for any taxable year to be subject to United States tax as if such resident were engaged in trade or business in the United States.'

and is responsible for all repairs except as to outer walls and foundation. This property (the only real property owned by petitioner in the United States) was acquired by petitioner 50 years ago, not as the result of a business transaction entered into for profit (cf. *Fackler v. Commissioner*, 133 F.2d 509) but by gift from petitioner's father when she was a very young girl (see *Grier v. United States*, 120 F.Supp. 395). During the taxable years her only activities, in addition to the receipt of rentals, were the payment of taxes, mortgage principal and interest, and insurance premiums. See *Evelyn M.L. Neil, supra.* The record also shows that petitioner executed a lease of the property in 1940 and a modified renewal thereof in 1946, and made minor repairs to the walls and roof in 1954 and 1955.

We are of the opinion that petitioner's activities with regard to the real property here involved, which might be considered as 'beyond the scope of mere ownership of real property, or the receipt of income from real property,' were sporadic rather than 'continuous,' were irregular rather than 'regular,' and were minimal rather than 'considerable.' We therefore conclude that petitioner was 'not engaged in trade or business in the United States' during the taxable years within the meaning of article IX(1) of the United States-United Kingdom tax convention.

This conclusion relates solely to the interpretation of the pertinent provisions of the tax convention and is not intended to relate in any way to the possibly wider meaning accorded to the word 'business' in some of the provisions of the Internal Revenue Code.

In view of the foregoing it is unnecessary for us to determine whether petitioner during the taxable years had 'a permanent establishment situated' in the United States. The phrase 'permanent establishment' is defined in article II(1)(l) of the tax convention as follows:

The term 'permanent establishment' when used with respect to an enterprise of one of the contracting parties means a branch, management, factory or other fixed place of business, but does not include an agency unless the agent has, and habitually exercises, a general authority to negotiate and conclude contracts on behalf of such enterprise or has a stock of merchandise from which he regularly fills orders on its behalf. An enterprise of one of the contracting parties shall not be deemed to have a permanent establishment in the territory of the other contracting party merely because it carries on business dealings in the territory of such other contracting party through a bona fide commission agent, broker or custodian acting in the ordinary course of his business as such. The fact that an enterprise of one of the contracting party has a subsidiary corporation which is a corporation of the other contracting party or which is engaged in trade or business in the territory of such other contracting party (whether through a permanent establishment or otherwise) shall not of itself constitute that subsidiary corporation a permanent establishment of its parent corporation.

In the light of this definition, it is difficult to conceive what and where petitioner's 'permanent establishment' in the United States might be.

Decision will be entered under Rule 50.

Revenue Ruling 91-32

1991-1 C.B. 107

ISSUE

What are the United States tax consequences of the disposition of a foreign partner's interest in a domestic or foreign partnership that conducts a trade or business through a fixed place of business or has a permanent establishment in the United States?

FACTS

SITUATION 1

FP1, a nonresident alien individual, is a partner in partnership PS1. PS1, which is not a publicly traded partnership within the meaning of section 7704 of the Internal Revenue Code, is engaged in a trade or business through a fixed place of business in the United States. PS1 owns appreciated real and personal property located in Country X. PS1 also owns appreciated personal property located in the United States that is used or held for use in PS1's trade or business within the United States (collectively, the "ECI property"). PS1 does not trade in stocks, securities or commodities. None of the ECI property is a United States real property interest within the meaning of section 897 of the Code. FP1 disposes of his partnership interest in a transaction entered into after March 18, 1986.

SITUATION 2

The facts are the same as those in Situation 1. In addition, FP1 has a distributive share of 25 percent of the income, gain, loss, deduction and credit of PS1. The assets of PS1 consist of the following:

	Basis	Value
Cash	$300,000	$300,000
Real property outside the United States	500,000	1,000,000
Machinery outside the United States	500,000	100,000
Personal property used in its United States trade or business	200,000	500,000
Total	$1,500,000	$1,900,000

FP1 did not contribute property to the partnership in anticipation of deriving a United States tax benefit under these rules from a subsequent sale of his partnership interest. FP1's adjusted basis in his partnership interest is $375,000. FP1 sells its partnership interest for $475,000.

SITUATION 3

FP2, an alien individual resident in Country Y, is a partner in partnership PS2. The United States and Country Y are parties to a treaty whose provisions are identical to those of the Draft United States Model Income Tax Treaty (June 16, 1981) (the Treaty). PS2, which is not a publicly traded partnership within the meaning of section

7704 of the Code, has a permanent establishment in the United States within the meaning of the Treaty. The assets of PS2 consist of immovable and movable property located in Country Y, and movable property located in the United States that are assets of the permanent establishment. FP2 disposes of his partnership interest in a transaction entered into after March 18, 1986.

LAW AND ANALYSIS

SITUATION 1

Section 701 of the Code provides that a partnership is not subject to income tax, but instead its partners are liable for the tax in their separate or individual capacities. Each partner must take into account separately the partner's distributive share of the items of income, gain, loss, deduction or credit of the partnership, as described in section 702 and the regulations thereunder. A partner's distributive share of such items is determined thereunder. A partner's distributive share of such items is determined pursuant to section 704 and the regulations thereunder.

The determination of the source and character of a foreign partner's income from the disposition of a partnership interest depends upon the application of sections 864, 865, 875 and 741 of the Code.

Pursuant to section 875(1) of the Code, a nonresident alien individual or foreign corporation that is a partner in a partnership engaged in a trade or business in the United States is itself considered to be so engaged. Because PS1 is engaged in a trade or business in the United States, FP1 is also so engaged since he is a partner in PS1.

For foreign persons other than a controlled foreign corporation within the meaning of section 957(a) of the Code, section 865 applies to transactions entered into after March 18, 1986. Pub. L. No. 99- 514, section 1211(c)(2), 100 Stat. 2085, 2536. Section 865(e)(2) provides, inter alia, that income from the sale of personal property by a nonresident will be sourced in the United States if the nonresident has a fixed place of business in the United States and if the income is attributable to such fixed place of business. A foreign partner of a partnership that is engaged in a trade or business through a fixed place of business in the United States itself has a fixed place of business in the United States, since the foreign partner is considered to be engaged in such trade or business pursuant to section 875(1). Income from the disposition of a partnership interest by the foreign partner will be attributable to the foreign partner's fixed place of business in the United States. See section 865(e)(3); cf. *Unger v. Commissioner*, T.C. Memo. 1990-15, 58 TCM 1157, 1159. Accordingly, to the extent provided below, income from FP1's disposition of his partnership interest will be sourced in the United States.

Section 864(c)(2) of the Code provides that certain gain or loss from sources within the United States from the sale or exchange of a capital asset is gain that is effectively connected with the conduct of a United States trade or business ("ECI gain"), or is loss that is allocable to ECI gain ("ECI loss"). Factors considered in determining whether the gain or loss is ECI gain or ECI loss within the meaning of section 864(c)(2) include whether the gain or loss is derived from an asset that is used or held for use in the conduct of a trade or business in the United States, or whether the activities of that trade or business were a material factor in the realization of the gain or loss. The rules of section 1.864-4(c)(2) of the regulations apply to determine whether an asset is used or held for use in the conduct of a trade or business within the United States, while the rules of section 1.864-4(c)(3) apply to determine the character of gain or loss realized directly from the active conduct of the trade or business.

Since a foreign partner's gain or loss from the disposition of its interest in a partnership is not gain or loss realized directly from the active conduct of a trade or business within the United States, the character of the foreign partner's gain or loss must be determined pursuant to the rules of section 1.864-4(c)(2) of the regulations. By virtue of its interest in the partnership, the foreign partner is considered to be engaged in a trade or business through the partnership's fixed place of business in the United States. Moreover, the value of the trade or business activity of the partnership affects the value of the foreign partner's interest in the partnership. Consequently, an interest in a partnership that is engaged in a trade or business through a fixed place of business in the United States is an ECI asset of a foreign partner. See section 1.864-4(c)(2) of the regulations.

A partnership, however, may also own property that, if disposed of by the partnership, would produce foreign source income that generally would not be subject to United States tax. Amounts received by a foreign partner from a disposition of its partnership interest may thus be attributable to unrealized gain or loss of the partnership representing the foreign partner's potential distributive share of foreign source items that, if realized by the partnership, generally would not be gain or loss to the foreign partner described in section 864(c).

Subchapter K of the Code is a blend of aggregate and entity treatment for partners and partnerships. Compare section 751 of the Code with section 741. For purposes of applying provisions of the Code not included in subchapter K, a partnership may be treated as an aggregate of its partners or as an entity distinct from its partners, depending on the purpose and scope of such provisions. Rev. Rul. 89- 85, 1989-2 C.B. 218, 219; see *Casel v. Commissioner*, 79 T.C. 424 (1982). The treatment of amounts received by a foreign partner from a disposition of a partnership interest must therefore be considered in connection with the general purpose and scope of section 864(c) and section 865(e). Pursuant to section 865(e)(3) the principles of section 864(c)(5) are applied to determine whether gain or loss from a sale is attributable to an office or fixed place of business for purposes of section 865(e)(1) and (2), so the same analysis applies to both sections 864(c) and 865(e).

Characterizing the entire amount of gain or loss from a foreign partner's disposition of a partnership interest as United States source ECI gain or ECI loss would effectively subject to the tax jurisdiction of the United States items that may not be described in section 864(c) of the Code, a result which Congress did not intend. See S. Rep. No. 1707, 89th Cong., 2d Sess. 17 (1966). Furthermore, treating the gain or loss realized by a foreign partner from the disposition of an interest in a partnership that is engaged in a United States trade or business entirely as United States source ECI gain or ECI loss may be conceptually inconsistent with other sections of the Code. For example, section 897(g) of the Code, which governs the treatment of a foreign partner's disposition of an interest in a partnership that has a United States real property interest, generally treats as ECI gain or ECI loss the amount that is attributable to a United States real property interest of the partnership. This provision evidences the view of Congress that a foreign partner's gain or loss from the disposition of an interest in a partnership that is engaged in a trade or business through a fixed place of business in the United States need not always be treated as ECI gain or ECI loss from United States sources in its entirety.

Accordingly, in applying sections 864(c) and 865(e) of the Code, it is appropriate to treat a foreign partner's disposition of its interest in a partnership that is engaged in a trade or business through a fixed place of business in the United States as a disposition of an aggregate interest in the partnership's underlying property for purposes of determining the source and ECI character of the gain or loss realized by the foreign partner. The determination of the source and the ECI character of gain or loss of a foreign partner from the disposition of a partnership interest will therefore be determined in the manner described below.

A foreign partner's gain or loss from the disposition of an interest in a partnership that is engaged in a trade or business through a fixed place of business in the United States will be ECI (United States source) gain or loss to the extent such gain or loss is attributable to ECI (United States source) property of the partnership. The gain or loss attributable to the ECI property of the partnership is an amount that bears the same ratio to gain or loss realized by the foreign partner from the disposition of its partnership interest as the foreign partner's distributive share of partnership net ECI gain or loss would have borne to the foreign partner's distributive share of partnership net gain or loss if the partnership had itself disposed of all of its assets at fair market value at the time the foreign partner disposes of its partnership interest. In computing the foreign partner's distributive share of net gain or loss of the partnership, net ECI gain or loss and net non-ECI gain or loss are computed separately. Thus, net non-ECI loss will not offset ECI gain, and net ECI loss will not offset net non-ECI gain.

Further, if a foreign partner realizes a loss on the disposition of its partnership interest, and if its distributive share of ECI gain or loss from the deemed disposition of ECI assets by the partnership would be a net ECI gain, then none of the loss realized by the foreign partner on the disposition of the partnership interest shall be ECI loss. If a foreign partner realizes a gain on the disposition of its partnership interest, and if its distributive share of ECI gain or loss from the deemed disposition of ECI assets by the partnership would be a net ECI loss, then none of the gain realized by the foreign partner on the disposition of the partnership interest shall be ECI gain.

In applying these rules, a foreign partner's gain on the disposition of an interest in a partnership that is engaged in a U.S. trade or business will be presumed to be U.S. source ECI gain in its entirety, and a foreign partner's loss on such a disposition will be presumed to be foreign source non-ECI loss in its entirety, unless the partner is able to produce upon request information showing the distributive share of net ECI and net non-ECI gain or loss that such partner would have been allocated if the partnership sold all of its assets. This presumption is a specific application of the general principle that the burden of proof is on the taxpayer.

Note that if a foreign partner contributes property to the partnership in anticipation of a subsequent sale of its partnership interest to derive a United States tax benefit under the approach taken under this ruling, the contribution may be disregarded under general tax principles in determining the tax consequences of the subsequent sale.

For purposes of these rules, the ECI (United States source) property of a partnership does not include United States real property interests held by the partnership. The rules of section 897(g), rather than the rules described in this ruling, govern the treatment of amounts received from the disposition of an interest in a partnership that are attributable to a United States real property interest of the partnership, and are applied before the rules described in this ruling are applied.

SITUATION 2

The character of the $100,000 gain realized by FP1 is determined under section 741 and section 751 of the Code, and is capital gain in this case. FP1's gain from the disposition of his partnership interest that is attributable to the ECI property of PS1 is an amount that bears the same ratio to the gain realized by FP1 from the disposition of his partnership interest as FP1's distributive share of partnership net ECI gain would have borne to his distributive share of partnership net gain if the partnership had disposed of all of its assets at fair market value on the date FP1 disposes of his partnership interest.

Upon a disposition of its ECI asset, the partnership would realize United States source ECI gain of $300,000 (fair market value of PS1's ECI property of $500,000 less basis of $200,000), of which 25 percent, or $75,000, would represent FP1's distributive share. Upon a disposition of all of its non-ECI assets, the partnership would realize a net gain of $100,000 (fair market value of machinery and real property outside the United States of $1,100,000 less basis of $1,000,000), of which FP1's 25 percent distributive share is $25,000.

FP1's gain from the disposition of his partnership interest that is attributable to ECI (United States source) property of the partnership is an amount that bears the same ratio to $100,000 (FP1's gain from the disposition of its partnership interest) as $75,000 (FP1's distributive share of the partnership's ECI (United States source) gain) bears to $100,000 (the sum of FP1's distributive share of the partnership's net ECI gain and net non-ECI gain). Accordingly, the portion of FP1's gain from the disposition of his partnership interest that is attributable to the ECI property of PS1 equals $75,000. Note that if the partnership's assets included United States real property interests, FP1 also would be subject to tax pursuant to section 897(g) on the amount attributable to the United States real property interests of the partnership. In this case, because the appreciated assets other than those used by PS1 in its United States trade or business are located outside the United States, the remaining $25,000 gain realized by FP1 will be foreign source capital gain that is not effectively connected with the conduct of a trade or business in the United States.

SITUATION 3

The Treaty generally exempts from United States tax gain from the disposition of movable property by a resident of the United States treaty partner. See Article 13(3) (Gains) of the Treaty. However, this rule does not apply if such gain is from the alienation of movable property that are assets of a permanent establishment in the United States.

A foreign partner of a partnership that has a permanent establishment in the United States is treated as itself having a permanent establishment. *Donroy, Ltd. v. United States*, 301 F.2d 200 (9th Cir. 1962); see Rev. Rul. 85-60, 1985-1 C.B. 187. More particularly, "the office or permanent establishment of a partnership is the office of each of its partners, whether general or limited." *Unger v. Commissioner*, T. C. Memo. 1990-15, 58 TCM 1157, 1159, citing *Donroy, Ltd. v. United States, supra.* Accordingly, FP2 is considered to have a permanent establishment in the United States because he is a partner in PS2.

The determination whether gain from the alienation of movable property is attributable to a permanent establishment in the United States is generally made by applying principles analogous to those governing whether an item is effectively connected with the conduct of a trade or business in the United States, though the "attributable to" concept of the Treaty is more limited in its scope than the "effectively connected" concept of the Code. See Rev. Rul. 81-78, 1981-1 C.B. 604. The principles applied are substantially similar, however, when the amounts at issue are those that would be described in section 864(c)(2) of the Code if the Treaty were not applied. Accordingly, for the reasons discussed in Situation 1, a disposition of an interest in a partnership that has a permanent establishment in the United States will be treated as resulting in gain that is attributable to the permanent establishment to the extent provided below.

It is appropriate under the Treaty to look to a foreign partner's interest in the assets of the partnership to determine the amount of the foreign partner's gain from the disposition of its partnership interest that is attributable to a United States permanent establishment. Cf. Commentary on Article 1 of the OECD Model Double Taxation Convention on Income and Capital, paragraphs 2-5 (1977). Gain of FP2 from the disposition of its interest in PS2 will thus be subject to United States tax only to the extent such gain is attributable to the unrealized gain of the partnership's assets attributable to the partnership's permanent establishment, and loss will be allocable to FP2's gain from sources within the United States that is attributable to a permanent establishment of FP2. Such gain or loss is to be determined in the manner described in Situation 1.

HOLDINGS

SITUATION 1

Gain or loss of a foreign partner that disposes of its interest in a partnership that is engaged in a trade or business through a fixed place of business in the United States will be United States source ECI gain or will be ECI loss that is allocable to United States source ECI gain, to the extent that the partner's distributive share of unrealized gain or loss of the partnership would be attributable to ECI (United States source) property of the partnership.

SITUATION 2

FP1's gain from the disposition of his partnership interest that is attributable to ECI (United States source) property of the partnership is an amount that bears the same ratio to $100,000 (FP1's gain from the disposition of its partnership interest) as $75,000 (FP1's distributive share of the partnership's ECI (United States source) gain) bears to $100,000 (the sum of FP1's distributive share of the partnership's net ECI gain and net non-ECI gain). Accordingly, the portion of FP1's gain from the disposition of his partnership interest that is attributable to the ECI property of PS1 equals $75,000.

SITUATION 3

Under the Treaty, gain of a foreign partner that disposes of its interest in a partnership that has a United States permanent establishment is gain that is attributable to a permanent establishment and is subject to United States tax under the Treaty, to the extent that the partner's potential distributive share of unrealized gain of the partnership is attributable to the partnership's permanent establishment.

Revenue Ruling 88-3
1988-1 C.B. 268

Rev. Rul. 73-227, 1973-1 C.B. 338, examines the activities of X, the foreign financing subsidiary of a United States parent, and holds that the United States source interest income that X earns is effectively connected with a United States trade or business under section 864(c) of the Internal Revenue Code of 1954.

Section 864(b) of the Code and the regulations promulgated thereunder provide rules for determining whether a foreign taxpayer is engaged in a trade or business within the United States. (These rules may differ in some respects from those used in determining whether a taxpayer is engaged in a trade or business under other sections of the Code.) The determination whether X is engaged in a trade or business within the United States must therefore be made by applying these rules to the facts described in the ruling. Rev. Rul. 73-227, however, does not do so. The ruling simply concludes without discussion of the applicable statute and regulations that X is engaged in a trade or business within the United States. Because the ruling does not discuss and apply the proper legal standard, its conclusion may be unsound.

In addition, the determination whether a taxpayer is engaged in a trade or business within the United States is highly factual. Such a determination is not ordinarily made in an advance ruling. See sections 2.01 and 4.01(2) of Rev. Proc. 87-6, 1987-1 I.R.B. 45.

Accordingly, Rev. Rul. 73-227 is revoked. Determinations under section 864 of the Code must be made by applying the regulations promulgated thereunder to the facts and circumstances of each case.

EFFECT ON OTHER REVENUE RULINGS

Rev. Rul. 73-227 is revoked.

H.R. Rep. No. 1167

96th Cong., 2nd Sess.

July 21, 1980

5. Subtitle E: Foreign Investment in Real Property Tax Act of 1980

PRESENT LAW

General

Under the code, nonresident aliens and foreign corporations engaged in a U.S. trade or business are generally taxed on the U.S. source income of that business in the same manner, and at the same rates, as U.S. persons. (However, their foreign source income not connected with that business is not taken into account in determining the applicable rates of U.S. tax.)

In contrast, the U.S. source income of a nonresident alien or foreign corporation which is not effectively connected with a U.S. business is generally subject to a different tax regime. The code provides that a foreign individual or corporation is ordinarily subject to a 30-percent withholding tax on the gross amount of certain passive income such as rents, dividends, and interest, which is received from U.S. sources and is not effectively connected with a U.S. business. This withholding tax generally satisfied the taxpayer's U.S. income tax liability on the income. Capital gains not effectively connected with a U.S. business are not subject to any U.S. income tax, except in the limited situation of nonresident individuals who were present in the United States 183 days or more during the year, who are taxed at the flat rate of 30 percent on the gains.

Foreign Investment in U.S. Property

Whether a foreign investor in U.S. real property is engaged in a U.S. trade or business depends on all the facts and circumstances. For example, a foreign investor who enters into a single long-term net lease (under which the lessee is responsible for operation of the property and pays the expenses) probably would not be engaged in a U.S. trade or business, whereas a taxpayer who owns and manages a number of commercial buildings would be so engaged.

If a foreign taxpayer is not actually engaged in a U.S. trade or business, he is permitted under the code to elect to be treated as if he were so engaged with respect to all his real property held for the production of income. This election is provided because rental income, unlike other types of passive income, ordinarily has associated with it significant expenses. Therefore, a tax equal to 30 percent of the gross rentals could frequently exceed the entire economic income from the property. If the election is made, the taxpayer may reduce his gross income from the real property by the deductible expenses, such as depreciation, mortgage interest, and real property taxes. The taxpayer is then taxed on the net income at the graduated rates which generally apply to U.S. taxpayers rather than paying 30 percent on his gross rental income. Often, as a result of the election, the investor will pay no tax on the current income because depreciation, mortgage interest, real property taxes and other expenses exceed gross income. (This result would be the same if a U.S. person owned the property.)

However, by making the election, the taxpayer will also subject himself to U.S. tax on any capital gains from the sale or exchange of the property. The election, once made, is binding on the taxpayer in all subsequent years unless consent to revoke it is obtained from the internal revenue service.

Apart from the code election, a number of planning techniques exist whereby a foreign investor may obtain the advantages of being taxed on current income from real property on a net basis. However, unlike the code election, these techniques also offer the opportunity to avoid tax on the capital gain which would result on the sale of the property. Also, unlike the code election, they may be employed on a property-by-property basis. For example, a foreign investor who is actually engaged in a U.S. real estate business will be taxed on current income from the property on a net basis (which might result in no current tax because of the allowable deductions). He may sell the property on the installment basis and receive most or all of the payments in years following the year of the sale. If he is not actually engaged in a U.S. trade or business in later years when the installment payments are received (and has not made the election to be treated as if he were), the gain would not be treated as effectively connected with a trade or business in the later years and would therefore go untaxed.

Secondly, a foreign investor could generally exchange his U.S. real property held for productive use or investment for other property of a like kind, whether within or without the U.S., without recognition of gain. If the property he acquired in the exchange were outside the U.S., the gain he would recognize on the ultimate sale of the property received in the exchange would not be subject to U.S. tax. This would be the case even if the investor were actually engaged in a U.S. trade or business or had made the election to be so treated.

A taxpayer may also obtain the benefits of current taxation on a net basis and exemption from tax on the gain by investing in U.S. real property indirectly through a foreign holding company which either is actually engaged in U.S. business or makes the election. The holding company would be subject to tax on the income it receives from the property, but, as noted earlier, often there would be no taxable income on a current basis. Moreover, the corporation often could reduce or eliminate its taxable income by paying deductible interest to its investors. Ordinarily, dividends and interest paid by a foreign corporation deriving most of its income from U.S. Sources are subject to U.S. withholding taxes. However, these taxes are sometimes waived on a reciprocal basis under tax treaties between the United States and other countries. If the corporation is entitled to such a treaty benefit, income paid currently by the corporation would escape that U.S. tax. (Foreign investors frequently utilize U.S. treaties applicable to the Netherlands Antilles and British Virgin Islands because these treaties contain the necessary waivers or reductions and because these jurisdictions impose low or no taxes on the income.)

The investors in the holding company could avoid U.S. tax on the gain from the sale of the property by either of two methods. First, if the corporation sells the property and follows a plan of liquidation meeting certain requirements, the corporation will not be taxable on the gain under a general rule of the code which exempts liquidating corporation from tax on gains from the sale of property (sec. 337). Moreover, the shareholders and security holders will generally not be taxable when they exchange their stock and securities in liquidation for the proceeds of the sale of the real property because, as foreign investors, they generally are not subject to U.S. capital gains tax. Even though the corporation is engaged in a U.S. trade or business, that business is not imputed to its investors. Since mere ownership or sale of stock is generally not a trade or business, the gains ordinarily would not be effectively connected with a U.S. business and thus would escape U.S. tax.

Second, if the investors instead sell their stock or securities, they would generally not be subject to tax on the gain for the same reasons that they would generally not recognize gain in a liquidation. Assuming that the sales price reflected the appreciated value of the real property, the purchaser of the corporation, even if a U.S. person, could then liquidate it without realizing a gain subject to U.S. tax because his basis in the stock for purposes of determining his gain on the liquidation would be his purchase price for the stock. He would also get a stepped-up basis for the real property equal to his purchase price for the stock.

Finally, some U.S. tax treaties (such as the treaties with the Netherlands Antilles and the British Virgin Islands) provide for a real property election similar to that in the code, but the election may be made on a year-by-year basis. A foreign investor entitled to the benefits of such a treaty and not actually engaged in a U.S. business could use the treaty election to be taxed on a net basis in years prior to the year of sale. In the year of sale, the taxpayer would not make the treaty election and would not be taxed on the gain on the sale of the property because of the absence of a U.S. trade or business.

A number of U.S. tax treaties (not including, however, the protocols with the Netherlands Antilles or the British Virgin Islands) contain reciprocal provisions which prevent the United States from taxing certain types of U.S. source capital gains of foreign investors who are entitled to the treaty benefits. While these provisions reciprocally exempting capital gains generally do not apply with respect to real estate (that is, they do not restrict either country from taxing gains on sales of its real estate derived by residents of the other), they generally would apply with respect to stock in corporations formed or availed of to hold real estate. The code provides that these treaty exemptions are to prevail if they require the exclusion from gross income of gains which the United States would otherwise tax (sec. 894(a); cf. Also sec. 7852(d)).

REASONS FOR CHANGE

The committee believes that it is essential to establish equity of tax treatment in U.S. real property between foreign and domestic investors. The committee does not intend by the provisions of Title IX to impose a penalty on foreign investors or to discourage foreign investors from investing in the United States. However, the committee believes that the United States should not continue to provide an inducement through the tax laws for foreign investment in U.S. real property which affords the foreign investor a number of mechanisms to minimize or eliminate his tax on income from the property while at the same time effectively exempting himself from U.S. tax on the gain realized on disposition of the property.

In order to impose a tax on gains from the sale of U.S. real estate, it is also necessary to impose a similar tax on gain from the disposition of interests in entities which hold substantial U.S. real property. Otherwise, a foreign investor could, as under present law, avoid tax on the gain by holding the real estate through a corporation, partnership, or trust and disposing of his interest in that entity rather than having the entity itself sell the real estate.

EXPLANATION OF PROVISIONS

General (Sec. 962 of Title IX and new Sec. 897 of the Code)

Under the provision, foreign investors are to be taxed on gains on the disposition of U.S. real property. Foreign investors are also to be taxed on gains realized from the sale or exchange of an interest in a real property holding organization (RPHO). In general, an RPHO is a corporation, trust or partnership at least half of the assets of which are U.S. real property interests. An exception is made for portfolio stock investments in publicly-traded corporations. Reporting requirements are established to identify when taxable transactions have occurred. Title IX contains no withholding provisions—neither the purchaser of the property nor any U.S. agent is required to withhold any tax from the seller or to take any other action to ensure that the foreign seller pays the tax due on the sale.

TAX IMPOSED ON SELLER

Amount of Tax

Title IX provides that gain or loss of a nonresident alien individual or a foreign corporation from the disposition of a United States real property interest is taken into account as if the taxpayer were engaged in a trade or business within the United States during the taxable year and as if such gain or loss were effectively connected with that trade or business. Thus, gains are to be subject to tax at the same rates which apply to income received by U.S. persons. In the case of a foreign individual, a loss is to be taken into account under Title IX only to the extent the loss would be taken into account under code section 165(c), which limits deductions for an individual's losses to business losses, losses on transactions entered into for profit, and losses for casualty or theft. Thus, for example, a loss on the sale of the taxpayer's personal residence would not be taken into account. If the foreign investor also has other effectively connected U.S. business activities, gains or losses from those activities during the taxable year are to be combined with gains or losses from U.S. real property interests in determining the investor's U.S. tax liability. However, losses from U.S. real property other than from its disposition could not be taken into account unless the property was actually effectively connected with a U.S. trade or business or the taxpayer had made the election to be so treated.

Although Title IX generally subjects to tax any sale, exchange, or other disposition of a U.S. real property interest, nonrecognition provisions of the code will continue to apply in certain cases. Generally, pending the promulgation of regulations, the nonrecognition provisions are to apply to an exchange of a United States real property interest only where it is exchanged for another such interest the sale of which would be subject to U.S. income taxation. Gain on the sale of an interest is not to be considered subject to U.S. taxation for this purpose if the gain would be exempt under a treaty obligation of the United States and thus exempt from U.S. tax under code section 894(a). However, the treasury department is directed to prescribe regulations which are necessary or appropriate to prevent the avoidance of federal income taxes providing the extent to which nonrecognition provisions shall, and shall not, apply for purposes of the bill. These regulations may, under appropriate circumstances and conditions, provide for nonrecognition even where the taxpayer does not receive in the exchange a U.S. real property interest. Conversely, in appropriate cases, the regulations may provide for the recognition of gain even where such an interest is received. For purposes of these provisions, the term 'nonrecognition provision' means any provision of the code for not recognizing gain or loss.

Direct Interest in U.S. Real Property

The tax is imposed on gains from the disposition of interests in real property (including an interest in a mine, well, or other natural deposit) located in the United States. The term 'interest in real property' includes fee ownership and co-ownership of land or improvements, easements, and options to acquire leaseholds of land or improvements, easements, and options to acquire leaseholds of land or improvements. Such an interest would, for example, include a mineral royalty. Moreover, the term includes partial interests such as life estates, remainders, reversions, and rights of refusal in real property. Movable walls, furnishings, and other similar personal property associated with the use of real property are considered real property for purposes of Title IX.

U.S. Real Property Holding Organizations

Also included in the definition of U.S. real property interests are certain holdings in a U.S. real property holding organization (RPHO). Thus, gain on the disposition of such holdings is subject to the tax. An exception is made to the general rule if the investment is in the form of portfolio stock holdings in a publicly-traded RPHO. Title IX provides that if any class of stock of a corporate RPHO is regularly traded on an established securities market, stock of that class is to be treated as a real property interest only in the case of a person who, at some time during the relevant time periods described below, held more than 5 percent of that class of stock.

An RPHO is a corporation, partnership, or trust, whether domestic or foreign, if at any time during the taxable year, the fair market value of its United States real property interests equals or exceeds value of its United States real property interests equals or exceeds value of its United States real property interests equals or exceeds 50 percent of the sum of (i) the fair market values of its United States real property interests, (ii) its interests in real property located outside the United States, plus (iii) any other of its assets which are used or held for use in a trade or business.

Generally, for purposes of this assets test, if an entity has an interest in another entity, that interest will be treated in its entirety as a U.S. real property interest if the second entity is an RPHO. However, if the second entity is not an RPHO (or, as described above, the interest generally will not be treated as a U.S. real property interest. As an exception to the general rules, if the first entity has a controlling interest in the second entity, special 'look through' rules apply. The bill provides that in such a case, for purposes of the assets test, (i) the value of the controlling interest is not taken into account, (ii) the first entity is treated as holding a pro rata share of the assets of the second entity, and (iii) any assets used or held for use by the second entity in a trade or business shall be treated as so used or held by the first entity. A 'controlling interest' is, in the case of a corporation, 50 percent or more of the total combines voting power of all classes of stock of the corporation, or 50 percent or more of the fair market value of all classes of stock of the corporation; in the case of a partnership, 50 percent or more of the capital or profits interest; or in the case of a trust, 50 percent or more of the beneficial interests in the trust (actuarially determined).

Generally, the holdings subject to the tax are stock in a corporation (other than certain portfolio investments), or an interest (other than solely as a creditor) in a partnership or trust, which, during the shorter of the period (after June 18, 1980) during which the taxpayer held his interest or the 5 years preceding his sale of the interest, is or was an RPHO. However, the interest would not be a U.S. real property interest if the RPHO recognized gain on all its U.S. real property interests prior to sale of the interest in the RPHO. (Also, if the RPHO held an interest in another RPHO, this rule applies even if the interest in the second RPHO was not sold, as long as the second RPHO ceased to be an RPHO by operation of this rule.) Since convertible debt of an RPHO is an interest in an RPHO other than solely as a creditor, such convertible debt is a U.S. real property interest.

For purposes of determining whether the 'look through' rules described above apply, and for purposes of applying the 'portfolio investment' exception described above, constructive ownership rules are provided.

REPORTING REQUIREMENTS

(Sec. 963 of Title IX and new Secs. 6039(c) and 6039(d) of the Code)

Entities which may be RPHOs. — if, at any time during a calendar year, (i) a corporation, partnership, or trust beneficially owns real property interests which constitute more than 40 percent of the fair market value of the assets taken into consideration in determining whether or not it is an RPHO, and (ii) at least one foreign person has an interest (other than solely as a creditor) in the entity, the entity is required to file an information return for the year. The return is to set forth the following information: (i) the name and address of any foreign person who held an interest (other than solely as a creditor) in the entity at any time during the calendar year, (ii) any information regarding the composition of the assets of the entity at such time or times during the calendar year which the treasury may prescribe by regulations, (iii)) any information with respect to transfers during the calendar year of interests in the entity which the treasury department may prescribe by regulations, (iv) whether such entity is an RPHO at any time during the calendar year, and (v) any other information which the treasury may prescribe by regulations. The entity must continue to file these returns for four years after the year in which the reporting requirement otherwise would cease to apply.

If a corporate RPHO would be required to file a return solely because a foreign person owns a class of its stock, and if the stock is regularly traded on an established securities market at all times during the calendar year, no return need be filed unless a foreign person owns more than 5 percent of that class of stock. For purposes of determining whether there is any foreign ownership or, where appropriate, more than 5 percent ownership, constructive ownership rules will apply.

In addition to the information return, the reporting entity is also required to furnish a written statement to every foreign person who held an interest (other than solely as a creditor) in the entity during the calendar year setting forth the name and address of the entity making the return, whether the entity was a United States RPHO at any time during the calendar year and any other information that the treasury may prescribe through regulations. The return is to be furnished to the person having the interest no later than January 31 of the year following the year for which the entity's return was made.

Other returns. — if a foreign person is not subject to the return requirements described above, that person is, except as provided below, required under Title IX to file a return if, at any time during the calendar year, that person beneficially owned a United States real property interest, or during that calendar year or a subsequent calendar year, the person received (or is to receive) an installment payment from an obligation acquired from the disposition of a United States real property interest. The return is to set forth (i) the name and address of the person, (ii) a description of all United States real property interests held by such person at any time during the calendar year and of all installment obligations from United States real property interests, and (iii) such other information as the treasury may prescribe by regulations.

This return requirement does not apply, however, if the person was engaged in a U.S. trade or business during the year, because other return requirements apply under present law in that situation. The requirement also does not apply if the aggregate of the fair market value of the United States real property interests owned by the person at any time during the year, and the face amount of the U.S. real property interest installment obligations, is less than $5,000. The fair market value of United States real property interests is, for this purpose, determined as of the end of the calendar year (or, in the case of any property disposed of during the calendar year, as of the date of the disposition).

The return of a foreign person for a calendar year under this provision is to be filed by April 15 (March 15 in the case of a corporation) of the following calendar year, or at such other time as the treasury may prescribe by regulations.

Failure to Make a Return or Furnish a Statement

A penalty for failure to file a tax return or to furnish a statement required under the rules described above will be imposed in an amount equal to $25 for each day during which such failure continues but not to exceed $25,000. Also, in the case of a failure by a foreign person to file a return required by the rules set forth in 'other returns,' above, the penalty for any calendar year cannot exceed 5 percent of the aggregate of (i) the fair market value of the United States real property interests owned by that person at any time during the year, and (ii) the face amount of the United States real property interest installment obligations.

If it is shown that the failure to file a return or to furnish a notice is due to reasonable cause and not to willful neglect, no penalty will be imposed for that failure.

Miscellaneous amendments (sec. 964 of title ix and secs. 861 and 7605 of the code)

Source of income.—income from the disposition of a United States real property interest will be United States source income.

* * *

United States Model
Income Tax Convention (2016)

CONVENTION BETWEEN THE GOVERNMENT OF THE UNITED STATES OF AMERICA AND THE GOVERNMENT OF _____ FOR THE AVOIDANCE OF DOUBLE TAXATION AND THE PREVENTION OF TAX EVASION WITH RESPECT TO TAXES ON INCOME

The Government of the United States of America and the Government of _____, intending to conclude a Convention for the elimination of double taxation with respect to taxes on income without creating opportunities for non-taxation or reduced taxation through tax evasion or avoidance (including through treaty-shopping arrangements aimed at obtaining reliefs provided in this Convention for the indirect benefit of residents of third states), have agreed as follows:

Article 1

GENERAL SCOPE

1. This Convention shall apply only to persons who are residents of one or both of the Contracting States, except as otherwise provided in this Convention.

2. This Convention shall not restrict in any manner any benefit now or hereafter accorded:

    a) by the laws of either Contracting State; or

    b) by any other agreement to which both Contracting States are parties.

3. a) Notwithstanding the provisions of subparagraph (b) of paragraph 2 of this Article:

        i) for purposes of paragraph 3 of Article XXII (Consultation) of the General Agreement on Trade in Services, the Contracting States agree that any question arising as to the interpretation or application of this Convention and, in particular, whether a taxation measure is within the scope of this Convention, shall be determined exclusively in accordance with the provisions of Article 25 (Mutual Agreement Procedure) of this Convention; and

ii) the provisions of Article XVII (National Treatment) of the General Agreement on Trade in Services shall not apply to a taxation measure unless the competent authorities agree that the measure is not within the scope of Article 24 (Non-Discrimination) of this Convention.

b) For the purposes of this paragraph, a "measure" is a law, regulation, rule, procedure, decision, administrative action or any similar provision or action.

4. Except to the extent provided in paragraph 5 of this Article, this Convention shall not affect the taxation by a Contracting State of its residents (as determined under Article 4 (Resident)) and its citizens. Notwithstanding the other provisions of this Convention, a former citizen or former long-term resident of a Contracting State may be taxed in accordance with the laws of that Contracting State.

5. The provisions of paragraph 4 of this Article shall not affect:

a) the benefits conferred by a Contracting State under paragraph 3 of Article 7 (Business Profits), paragraph 2 of Article 9 (Associated Enterprises), paragraph 7 of Article 13 (Gains), subparagraph (b) of paragraph 1, paragraphs 2, 3 and 6 of Article 17 (Pensions, Social Security, Annuities, Alimony and Child Support), paragraph 3 of Article 18 (Pension Funds), and Articles 23 (Relief From Double Taxation), 24 (Non-Discrimination) and 25 (Mutual Agreement Procedure); and

b) the benefits conferred by a Contracting State under paragraph 1 of Article 18 (Pension Funds), and Articles 19 (Government Service), 20 (Students and Trainees) and 27 (Members of Diplomatic Missions and Consular Posts), upon individuals who are neither citizens of, nor have been admitted for permanent residence in, that Contracting State.

6. For the purposes of this Convention, an item of income, profit or gain derived by or through an entity that is treated as wholly or partly fiscally transparent under the taxation laws of either Contracting State shall be considered to be derived by a resident of a Contracting State, but only to the extent that the item is treated for purposes of the taxation laws of such Contracting State as the income, profit or gain of a resident.

7. Where an item of income, profit or gain arising in one of the Contracting States otherwise would be entitled to the benefits of this Convention in that Contracting State and, under the law of the other Contracting State, a person's tax in respect of such item is determined by reference to the amount thereof that is remitted to or received in that other Contracting State and not by reference to the full amount

thereof, then the relief to be allowed under this Convention in the first-mentioned Contracting State shall apply only to so much of the amount as is taxed in the other Contracting State.

8. Where an enterprise of a Contracting State derives income from the other Contracting State, and the first-mentioned Contracting State treats that income as attributable to a permanent establishment situated outside of that Contracting State, the benefits of this Convention shall not apply to that income if:

   a) the profits that are treated as attributable to the permanent establishment are subject to a combined aggregate effective rate of tax in the first-mentioned Contracting State and the state in which the permanent establishment is situated that is less than the lesser of (i) 15 percent or (ii) 60 percent of the general statutory rate of company tax applicable in the first-mentioned Contracting State; or

   b) the permanent establishment is situated in a third state that does not have a comprehensive convention for the avoidance of double taxation in force with the Contracting State from which the benefits of this Convention are being claimed, unless the first-mentioned Contracting State includes the income treated as attributable to the permanent establishment in its tax base.

However, if a resident of a Contracting State is denied the benefits of this Convention pursuant to this paragraph, the competent authority of the other Contracting State may, nevertheless, grant the benefits of this Convention with respect to a specific item of income if such competent authority determines that such grant of benefits is justified in light of the reasons such resident did not satisfy the requirements of this paragraph (such as the existence of losses). The competent authority of the Contracting State to which the request has been made shall consult with the competent authority of the other Contracting State before either granting or denying a request made under this paragraph by a resident of that other Contracting State.

Article 2

TAXES COVERED

1. This Convention shall apply to taxes on income imposed on behalf of a Contracting State irrespective of the manner in which they are levied.

2. There shall be regarded as taxes on income all taxes imposed on total income, or on elements of income, including taxes on gains from the alienation of property.

3. The existing taxes to which this Convention shall apply are:

   a) in the case of _____:

   b) in the case of the United States: the Federal income taxes imposed by the Internal Revenue Code (which do not include social security and unemployment taxes) and the Federal taxes imposed on the investment income of foreign private foundations.

4. This Convention also shall apply to any identical or substantially similar taxes that are imposed after the date of signature of this Convention in addition to, or in place of, the existing taxes. The competent authorities of the Contracting States shall notify each other of any significant changes that have been made in their taxation laws or other laws that relate to the application of this Convention.

Article 3

GENERAL DEFINITIONS

1. For the purposes of this Convention, unless the context otherwise requires:

   a) the term "person" includes an individual, an estate, a trust, a partnership, a company, and any other body of persons;

   b) the term "company" means any body corporate or any entity that is treated as a body corporate for tax purposes according to the laws of the Contracting State in which it is resident;

   c) the terms "enterprise of a Contracting State" and "enterprise of the other Contracting State" mean, respectively, an enterprise carried on by a resident of a Contracting State, and an enterprise carried on by a resident of the other Contracting State; the terms also include an enterprise carried on by a resident of a Contracting State through an entity that is treated as fiscally transparent in that Contracting State;

   d) the term "enterprise" applies to the carrying on of any business;

   e) the term "business" includes the performance of professional services and of other activities of an independent character;

   f) the term "international traffic" means any transport by a ship or aircraft, except when such transport is solely between places in a Contracting State;

   g) the term "competent authority" means:

      i) in _____: _____; and

      ii) in the United States: the Secretary of the Treasury or his delegate;

   h) the term "_____:" means _____;

   i) the term "United States" means the United States of America, and includes the states thereof and the District of Columbia; such term also includes the territorial sea thereof and the sea bed and subsoil of the submarine areas adjacent to that territorial sea, over which the United States exercises sovereign rights in accordance with international law; the term, however, does not include Puerto Rico, the Virgin Islands, Guam or any other United States possession or territory;

   j) the term "national" of a Contracting State means:

      i) any individual possessing the nationality or citizenship of that Contracting State; and

      ii) any legal person, partnership or association deriving its status as such from the laws in force in that Contracting State;

k) the term "pension fund" means any person established in a Contracting State that is:

> i) generally exempt from income taxation in that Contracting State; and

> ii) operated exclusively or almost exclusively:

>> A) to administer or provide pension or retirement benefits; or

>> B) to earn income for the benefit of one or more persons established in the same Contracting State that are generally exempt from income taxation in that Contracting State and that are operated exclusively or almost exclusively to administer or provide pension or retirement benefits;

l) the term "special tax regime" means any statute, regulation or administrative practice in a Contracting State with respect to a tax described in Article 2 (Taxes Covered) that meets all of the following conditions:

> i) results in one or more of the following:

>> A) a preferential rate of taxation for interest, royalties, guarantee fees or any combination thereof, as compared to income from sales of goods or services;

>> B) a permanent reduction in the tax base with respect to interest, royalties, guarantee fees or any combination thereof, without a comparable reduction for income from sales of goods or services, by allowing:

>>> 1) an exclusion from gross receipts;

>>> 2) a deduction without regard to any corresponding payment or obligation to make a payment;

>>> 3) a deduction for dividends paid or accrued; or

>>> 4) taxation that is inconsistent with the principles of Article 7 (Business Profits) or Article 9 (Associated Enterprises); or

>> C) a preferential rate of taxation or a permanent reduction in the tax base of the type described in part (1), (2), (3) or (4) of subclause (B) of this clause with respect to substantially all of a company's income or substantially all of a company's foreign source income, for companies that do not engage in the active conduct of a trade or business in that Contracting State;

> ii) in the case of any preferential rate of taxation or permanent reduction in the tax base for royalties, does not condition such ben-

efits on the extent of research and development activities that take place in the Contracting State;

iii) is generally expected to result in a rate of taxation[78] that is less than the lesser of either:

A) 15 percent; or

B) 60 percent of the general statutory rate of company tax applicable in the other Contracting State;

iv) does not apply principally to:

A) pension funds;

B) organizations that are established and maintained exclusively for religious, charitable, scientific, artistic, cultural or educational purposes;

C) persons the taxation of which achieves a single level of taxation either in the hands of the person or the person's shareholders (with at most one year of deferral), that hold a diversified portfolio of securities, that are subject to investor-protection regulation in the Contracting State and the interests in which are marketed primarily to retail investors; or

D) persons the taxation of which achieves a single level of taxation either in the hands of the person or the person's shareholders (with at most one year of deferral) and that hold predominantly real estate assets; and

v) after consultation with the first-mentioned Contracting State, has been identified by the other Contracting State through diplomatic channels to the firstmentioned Contracting State as satisfying clauses (i) through (iv) of this subparagraph.

---

78. [1] For inclusion in an instrument reflecting an agreed interpretation: Except as provided below, the rate of taxation shall be determined based on the income tax principles of the Contracting State that has implemented the regime in question. Therefore, in the case of a regime that provides only for a preferential rate of taxation, the generally expected rate of taxation under the regime will equal such preferential rate. In the case of a regime that provides only for a permanent reduction in the tax base, the rate of taxation will equal the statutory rate of company tax generally applicable in the Contracting State to companies subject to the regime in question less the product of such rate and the percentage reduction in the tax base (with the baseline tax base determined under the principles of the Contracting State, but without regard to any permanent reductions in the tax base described in subparagraph (l)(i)(B)) that the regime is generally expected to provide. Therefore, a regime that generally provides for a 20 percent permanent reduction in a company's tax base would have a rate of taxation equal to the applicable statutory rate of company tax reduced by 20 percent of such statutory rate. In the case of a regime that provides for both a preferential rate of taxation and a permanent reduction in the tax base, the rate of taxation would be based on the preferential rate of taxation reduced by the product of such rate and the percentage reduction in the tax base.

No statute, regulation or administrative practice shall be treated as a special tax regime until 30 days after the date when the other Contracting State issues a written public notification identifying the regime as satisfying clauses (i) through (v) of this subparagraph; and

> m) two persons shall be "connected persons" if one owns, directly or indirectly, at least 50 percent of the beneficial interest in the other (or, in the case of a company, at least 50 percent of the aggregate vote and value of the company's shares) or another person owns, directly or indirectly, at least 50 percent of the beneficial interest (or, in the case of a company, at least 50 percent of the aggregate vote and value of the company's shares) in each person. In any case, a person shall be connected to another if, based on all the relevant facts and circumstances, one has control of the other or both are under the control of the same person or persons.

2. As regards the application of this Convention at any time by a Contracting State, any term not defined herein shall, unless the context otherwise requires, or the competent authorities agree to a common meaning pursuant to the provisions of Article 25 (Mutual Agreement Procedure), have the meaning that it has at that time under the law of that Contracting State for the purposes of the taxes to which this Convention applies, any meaning under the applicable tax laws of that Contracting State prevailing over a meaning given to the term under other laws of that Contracting State.

Article 4

RESIDENT

1. For the purposes of this Convention, the term "resident of a Contracting State" means any person who, under the laws of that Contracting State, is liable to tax therein by reason of his domicile, residence, citizenship, place of management, place of incorporation, or any other criterion of a similar nature, and also includes that Contracting State and any political subdivision or local authority thereof. This term does not include any person whose tax is determined in that Contracting State on a fixed-fee, "forfait" or similar basis, or who is liable to tax in respect only of income from sources in that Contracting State or of profits attributable to a permanent establishment in that Contracting State.

2. The term "resident of a Contracting State" includes:

> a) a pension fund established in that Contracting State; and

> b) an organization that is established and maintained in that Contracting State exclusively for religious, charitable, scientific, artistic, cultural, or educational purposes;

notwithstanding that all or part of its income or gains may be exempt from tax under the domestic law of that Contracting State.

3. Where, by reason of the provisions of paragraph 1 of this Article, an individual is a resident of both Contracting States, then his status shall be determined as follows:

a) he shall be deemed to be a resident only of the Contracting State in which he has a permanent home available to him; if he has a permanent home available to him in both Contracting States, he shall be deemed to be a resident only of the Contracting State with which his personal and economic relations are closer (center of vital interests);

b) if the Contracting State in which he has his center of vital interests cannot be determined, or if he does not have a permanent home available to him in either Contracting State, he shall be deemed to be a resident only of the Contracting State in which he has a habitual abode;

c) if he has a habitual abode in both Contracting States or in neither of them, he shall be deemed to be a resident only of the Contracting State of which he is a national;

d) if he is a national of both Contracting States or of neither of them, the competent authorities of the Contracting States shall endeavor to settle the question by mutual agreement.

4. Where by reason of the provisions of paragraph 1 of this Article a company is a resident of both Contracting States, such company shall not be treated as a resident of either Contracting State for purposes of its claiming the benefits provided by this Convention.

5. Where by reason of the provisions of paragraph 1 of this Article a person other than an individual or a company is a resident of both Contracting States, the competent authorities of the Contracting States shall by mutual agreement endeavor to determine the mode of application of this Convention to that person.

Article 5

PERMANENT ESTABLISHMENT

1. For the purposes of this Convention, the term "permanent establishment" means a fixed place of business through which the business of an enterprise is wholly or partly carried on.

2. The term "permanent establishment" includes especially:

a) a place of management;

b) a branch;

c) an office;

d) a factory;

e) a workshop; and

f) a mine, an oil or gas well, a quarry, or any other place of extraction of natural resources.

3. A building site or construction or installation project, or an installation or drilling rig or ship used for the exploration or exploitation of the sea bed and its subsoil and their natural resources, situated in one of the Contracting States constitutes a permanent establishment only if it lasts, or the activities of the rig or ship lasts,

for more than twelve months. For the sole purpose of determining whether the twelve-month period referred to in this paragraph has been exceeded:

> a) where an enterprise of a Contracting State carries on activities in the other Contracting State at a place that constitutes a building site or construction or installation project and these activities are carried on during periods of time that in the aggregate do not last more than twelve months; and

> b) connected activities are carried on at the same building site or construction or installation project during different periods of time, each exceeding thirty days, by one or more enterprises that are connected persons with respect to the first-mentioned enterprise,

these different periods of time shall be added to the periods of time during which the firstmentioned enterprise has carried on activities at that building site or construction or installation project.

4. Notwithstanding the preceding provisions of this Article, the term "permanent establishment" shall be deemed not to include:

> a) the use of facilities solely for the purpose of storage, display or delivery of goods or merchandise belonging to the enterprise;

> b) the maintenance of a stock of goods or merchandise belonging to the enterprise solely for the purpose of storage, display or delivery;

> c) the maintenance of a stock of goods or merchandise belonging to the enterprise solely for the purpose of processing by another enterprise;

> d) the maintenance of a fixed place of business solely for the purpose of purchasing goods or merchandise, or of collecting information, for the enterprise;

> e) the maintenance of a fixed place of business solely for the purpose of carrying on, for the enterprise, any other activity of a preparatory or auxiliary character;

> f) the maintenance of a fixed place of business solely for any combination of the activities mentioned in subparagraphs (a) through (e) of this paragraph, provided that the overall activity of the fixed place of business resulting from this combination is of a preparatory or auxiliary character.

5. Notwithstanding the provisions of paragraphs 1 and 2 of this Article, where a person — other than an agent of an independent status to whom paragraph 6 of this Article applies — is acting on behalf of an enterprise and has and habitually exercises in a Contracting State an authority to conclude contracts that are binding on the enterprise, that enterprise shall be deemed to have a permanent establishment in that Contracting State in respect of any activities that the person undertakes for the enterprise, unless the activities of such person are limited to those mentioned in paragraph 4 that, if exercised through a fixed place of business, would not make this fixed place of business a permanent establishment under the provisions of that paragraph.

6. An enterprise shall not be deemed to have a permanent establishment in a Contracting State merely because it carries on business in that Contracting State through a broker, general commission agent, or any other agent of an independent status, provided that such persons are acting in the ordinary course of their business as independent agents.

7. The fact that a company that is a resident of a Contracting State controls or is controlled by a company that is a resident of the other Contracting State, or that carries on business in that other Contracting State (whether through a permanent establishment or otherwise), shall not be taken into account in determining whether either company has a permanent establishment in that other Contracting State.

Article 6

INCOME FROM REAL PROPERTY (IMMOVABLE PROPERTY)

1. Income derived by a resident of a Contracting State from real property (immovable property), including income from agriculture or forestry, situated in the other Contracting State may be taxed in that other Contracting State.

2. The term "real property" or "immovable property" shall have the meaning which it has under the law of the Contracting State in which the property in question is situated. The term shall in any case include property accessory to real property (immovable property), livestock and equipment used in agriculture and forestry, rights to which the provisions of general law respecting landed property apply, usufruct of real property (immovable property) and rights to variable or fixed payments as consideration for the working of, or the right to work, mineral deposits, sources and other natural resources. Ships and aircraft shall not be regarded as real property (immovable property).

3. The provisions of paragraph 1 of this Article shall apply to income derived from the direct use, letting, or use in any other form of real property (immovable property).

4. The provisions of paragraphs 1 and 3 of this Article shall also apply to the income from real property (immovable property) of an enterprise.

5. A resident of a Contracting State that is liable to tax in the other Contracting State on income from real property (immovable property) situated in the other Contracting State may elect for any taxable year to compute the tax on such income on a net basis as if such income were business profits attributable to a permanent establishment in such other Contracting State. Any such election shall be binding for the taxable year of the election and all subsequent taxable years unless the competent authority of the Contracting State in which the property is situated agrees to terminate the election.

Article 7

BUSINESS PROFITS

1. Profits of an enterprise of a Contracting State shall be taxable only in that Contracting State unless the enterprise carries on business in the other Contracting State through a permanent establishment situated therein. If the enterprise carries

on business as aforesaid, the profits that are attributable to the permanent establishment in accordance with the provisions of paragraph 2 of this Article may be taxed in that other Contracting State.

2. For the purposes of this Article, the profits that are attributable in each Contracting State to the permanent establishment referred to in paragraph 1 of this Article are the profits it might be expected to make, in particular in its dealings with other parts of the enterprise, if it were a separate and independent enterprise engaged in the same or similar activities under the same or similar conditions, taking into account the functions performed, assets used and risks assumed by the enterprise through the permanent establishment and through the other parts of the enterprise.

3. Where, in accordance with paragraph 2 of this Article, a Contracting State adjusts the profits that are attributable to a permanent establishment of an enterprise of one of the Contracting States and taxes accordingly profits of the enterprise that have been charged to tax in the other Contracting State, the other Contracting State shall, to the extent necessary to eliminate double taxation, make an appropriate adjustment if it agrees with the adjustment made by the first-mentioned Contracting State; if the other Contracting State does not so agree, the Contracting States shall eliminate any double taxation resulting therefrom by mutual agreement.

4. Where profits include items of income that are dealt with separately in other Articles of this Convention, then the provisions of those Articles shall not be affected by the provisions of this Article.

5. In applying this Article, paragraph 8 of Article 10 (Dividends), paragraph 5 of Article 11 (Interest), paragraph 5 of Article 12 (Royalties), paragraph 3 of Article 13 (Gains) and paragraph 3 of Article 21 (Other Income), any income, profit or gain attributable to a permanent establishment during its existence is taxable in the Contracting State where such permanent establishment is situated even if the payments are deferred until such permanent establishment has ceased to exist.

* * *

Article 9

ASSOCIATED ENTERPRISES

1. Where:

   a) an enterprise of a Contracting State participates directly or indirectly in the management, control or capital of an enterprise of the other Contracting State; or

   b) the same persons participate directly or indirectly in the management, control, or capital of an enterprise of a Contracting State and an enterprise of the other Contracting State;

and in either case conditions are made or imposed between the two enterprises in their commercial or financial relations that differ from those that would be made between independent enterprises, then any profits that, but for those conditions, would have accrued to one of the enterprises, but by reason of those conditions have not so accrued, may be included in the profits of that enterprise and taxed accordingly.

2. Where a Contracting State includes in the profits of an enterprise of that Contracting State, and taxes accordingly, profits on which an enterprise of the other Contracting State has been charged to tax in that other Contracting State, and the other Contracting State agrees that the profits so included are profits that would have accrued to the enterprise of the first-mentioned Contracting State if the conditions made between the two enterprises had been those that would have been made between independent enterprises, then that other Contracting State shall make an appropriate adjustment to the amount of the tax charged therein on those profits. In determining such adjustment, due regard shall be had to the other provisions of this Convention and the competent authorities of the Contracting States shall if necessary consult each other.

Article 10

DIVIDENDS

1. Dividends paid by a company that is a resident of a Contracting State to a resident of the other Contracting State may be taxed in that other Contracting State.

2. However, such dividends may also be taxed in the Contracting State of which the company paying the dividends is a resident and according to the laws of that Contracting State, but if the beneficial owner of the dividends is a resident of the other Contracting State, except as otherwise provided, the tax so charged shall not exceed:

   a) 5 percent of the gross amount of the dividends if, for the twelve-month period ending on the date on which the entitlement to the dividends is determined:

   i) the beneficial owner has been a company that was a resident of the other Contracting State or of a qualifying third state. The term "qualifying third state" means a state that has in effect a comprehensive convention for the avoidance of double taxation with the Contracting State of the company paying the dividends that would have allowed the beneficial owner to benefit from a rate of tax on dividends that is less than or equal to 5 percent; and

   ii) at least 10 percent of the aggregate vote and value of the shares of the payor of the dividends was owned directly by the beneficial owner or a qualifying predecessor owner. The term "qualifying predecessor owner" means a company from which the beneficial owner acquired the shares of the payor of the dividends, but only if such company was, at the time the shares were acquired, a connected person with respect to the beneficial owner of the dividend, and a resident of a state that has in effect a comprehensive convention for the avoidance of double taxation with the Contracting State of the company paying the dividends that would have allowed such company to benefit from a rate of tax on dividends that is less than or equal to 5 percent. For this purpose, a company that is a resident of a Contracting State shall be considered to own directly the shares owned by an entity that:

> A) is considered fiscally transparent under the laws of that Contracting State; and

> B) is not a resident of the other Contracting State of which the company paying the dividends is a resident;

in proportion to the company's ownership interest in that entity; and

> b) 15 percent of the gross amount of the dividends in all other cases.

This paragraph shall not affect the taxation of the company in respect of the profits out of which the dividends are paid.

3. Notwithstanding the provisions of paragraph 2 of this Article, dividends shall not be taxed in the Contracting State of which the company paying the dividends is a resident if:

> a) the beneficial owner of the dividends is a pension fund that is a resident of the other Contracting State; and

> b) such dividends are not derived from the carrying on of a trade or business by the pension fund or through a person that is a connected person with respect to the pension fund.

4. a) Subparagraph (a) of paragraph 2 of this Article shall not apply in the case of dividends paid by a U.S. Regulated Investment Company (RIC) or a U.S. Real Estate Investment Trust (REIT). In the case of dividends paid by a RIC, subparagraph (b) of paragraph 2 and paragraph 3 of this Article shall apply. In the case of dividends paid by a REIT, subparagraph (b) of paragraph 2 and paragraph 3 of this Article shall apply only if:

> i) the beneficial owner of the dividends is an individual or pension fund, in either case holding an interest of not more than 10 percent in the REIT;

> ii) the dividends are paid with respect to a class of shares that is publicly traded and the beneficial owner of the dividends is a person holding an interest of not more than 5 percent of any class of the REIT's shares; or

> iii) the beneficial owner of the dividends is a person holding an interest of not more than 10 percent in the REIT and the REIT is diversified.

> b) For purposes of this paragraph, a REIT shall be "diversified" if the value of no single interest in real property (immovable property) exceeds 10 percent of its total interests in real property (immovable property). For the purposes of this rule, foreclosure property shall not be considered an interest in real property (immovable property). Where a REIT holds an

interest in a partnership, it shall be treated as owning directly a proportion of the partnership's interests in real property (immovable property) corresponding to its interest in the partnership.

5. In the case of the United States, notwithstanding the provisions of paragraph 2 of this Article, dividends paid by an expatriated entity and beneficially owned by a company resident in _____ that is a connected person with respect to such expatriated entity may be taxed in accordance with the law of the United States for a period of ten years beginning on the date on which the acquisition of the domestic entity is completed. For purposes of applying this paragraph:

   a) no effect shall be given to any amendment to section 7874 of the Internal Revenue Code after the date of signature of this Convention; and

   b) no entity shall be treated as an expatriated entity that:

       i) is a connected person with respect to the domestic entity immediately after the date on which the acquisition of the domestic entity is completed; and

       ii) prior to that date, was never a connected person with respect to the domestic entity.

However, an entity described in the preceding sentence shall become an expatriated entity if, subsequent to the date on which the acquisition of the domestic entity is completed, the entity joins in filing a U.S. consolidated return with either the domestic entity or another entity that was a connected person with respect to the domestic entity immediately prior to the date on which the acquisition of the domestic entity was completed.

6. Notwithstanding the provisions of paragraphs 1 and 2 of this Article, in the case of a company seeking to satisfy the requirements of paragraph 4 of Article 22 (Limitation on Benefits) regarding a dividend, if such company fails to satisfy the criteria of that paragraph solely by reason of:

   a) the requirement in subclause (B) of clause (i) of subparagraph (e) of paragraph 7 of Article 22 (Limitation on Benefits) of this Convention; or

   b) the requirement in clause (ii) of subparagraph (e) of paragraph 7 of Article 22 (Limitation on Benefits) that a person entitled to benefits under paragraph 5 of Article 22 (Limitation on Benefits) would be entitled to a rate of tax with respect to the dividend that is less than or equal to the rate applicable under paragraph 2 of this Article;

such company may be taxed in the Contracting State of which the company paying the dividends is a resident and according to the laws of that Contracting State. In these cases, however, the tax so charged shall not exceed the highest rate among the rates of tax to which persons described in subparagraph (e) of paragraph 7 of Article 22 (Limitation on Benefits) of this Convention (notwithstanding the requirements referred to in subparagraphs (a) and (b) of this paragraph) would have been entitled if such persons had received the dividend directly. For purposes of this paragraph, (i) such persons' indirect ownership of the shares of the company paying the dividends shall be treated as direct ownership, and (ii) a person described in clause (iii) of subparagraph (e) of paragraph 7 of Article 22 (Limitation on Benefits) shall be treated as entitled to the limitation of tax to which such person would be entitled if such person were a resident of the same Contracting State as the company receiving the dividends.

7. For purposes of this Article, the term "dividends" means income from shares or other rights, not being debt-claims, participating in profits, as well as income that is subject to the same taxation treatment as income from shares under the laws of the Contracting State of which the company making the distribution is a resident. The term does not include distributions that are treated as gain under the laws of the Contracting State of which the company making the distribution is a resident. In such case, the provisions of Article 13 (Gains) shall apply.

8. The provisions of paragraphs 1 through 6 of this Article shall not apply if the beneficial owner of the dividends, being a resident of a Contracting State, carries on business in the other Contracting State, of which the company paying the dividends is a resident, through a permanent establishment situated therein, and the holding in respect of which the dividends are paid is effectively connected with such permanent establishment. In such case the provisions of Article 7 (Business Profits) shall apply.

9. A Contracting State may not impose any tax on dividends paid by a resident of the other Contracting State, except insofar as the dividends are paid to a resident of the first-mentioned Contracting State or the dividends are attributable to a permanent establishment situated therein, nor may it impose tax on a corporation's undistributed profits, except as provided in paragraph 10 of this Article, even if the dividends paid or the undistributed profits consist wholly or partly of profits or income arising in that Contracting State.

10.   a) A company that is a resident of one of the Contracting States and that has a permanent establishment in the other Contracting State or that is subject to tax in the other Contracting State on a net basis on its income that may be taxed in the other Contracting State under Article 6 (Income from Real Property (Immovable Property)) or under paragraph 1 of Article 13 (Gains) may be subject in that other Contracting State to a tax in addition to the tax allowable under the other provisions of this Convention.

   b) Such tax, however, may be imposed:

      i) on only the portion of the business profits of the company attributable to the permanent establishment and the portion of the income referred to in subparagraph (a) of this paragraph that is subject to tax under Article 6 (Income from Real Property (Immovable Property)) or under paragraph 1 of Article 13 (Gains) that, in the case of the United States, represents the dividend equivalent amount of such profits or income and, in the case of _____, is an amount that is analogous to the dividend equivalent amount; and

ii) at a rate not in excess of the rate specified in subparagraph (a) of paragraph 2 or paragraph 6 of this Article, but only if for the twelve-month period ending on the date on which the entitlement to the dividend equivalent amount is determined, the company has been a resident of the other Contracting State or of a qualifying third state. The term "qualifying third state" has the same meaning as in clause (i) of subparagraph (a) of paragraph 2 of this Article.

Article 11

INTEREST

1. Interest arising in a Contracting State and beneficially owned by a resident of the other Contracting State shall be taxable only in that other Contracting State.

2. Notwithstanding the provisions of paragraph 1 of this Article:

a) interest arising in _____ that is determined with reference to receipts, sales, income, profits or other cash flow of the debtor or a connected person with respect to the debtor, to any change in the value of any property of the debtor or a connected person with respect to the debtor or to any dividend, partnership distribution or similar payment made by the debtor or a connected person with respect to the debtor may be taxed in _____, and according to the laws of _____, but if the beneficial owner is a resident of the United States, the interest may be taxed at a rate not exceeding 15 percent of the gross amount of the interest;

b) interest arising in the United States that is contingent interest of a type that does not qualify as portfolio interest under the law of the United States may be taxed by the United States, but if the beneficial owner is a resident of _____, the interest may be taxed at a rate not exceeding 15 percent of the gross amount of the interest;

c) interest arising in a Contracting State and beneficially owned by a resident of the other Contracting State that is a connected person with respect to the payor of the interest may be taxed in the first-mentioned Contracting State in accordance with domestic law if such resident benefits from a special tax regime with respect to such interest in its Contracting State of residence;

d) in the case of the United States, interest paid by an expatriated entity and beneficially owned by a company resident in _____ that is a connected person with respect to such expatriated entity may be taxed in accordance with the law of the United States for a period of ten years beginning on the date on which the acquisition of the domestic entity is completed. For purposes of applying this paragraph:

i) no effect shall be given to any amendment to section 7874 of the Internal Revenue Code after the date of signature of this Convention; and

ii) no entity shall be treated as an expatriated entity that:

A) is a connected person with respect to the domestic entity immediately after the date on which the acquisition of the domestic entity is completed; and

B) prior to that date, was never a connected person with respect to the domestic entity.

However, an entity described in the preceding sentence shall become an expatriated entity if, subsequent to the date on which the acquisition of the domestic entity is completed, the entity joins in filing a U.S. consolidated return with either the domestic entity or another entity that was a connected person with respect to the domestic entity immediately prior to the date on which the acquisition of the domestic entity was completed;

e) interest arising in a Contracting State and beneficially owned by a resident of the other Contracting State that is a connected person with respect to the payor of the interest may be taxed in the first-mentioned Contracting State in accordance with domestic law if such resident benefits, at any time during the taxable year in which the interest is paid, from notional deductions with respect to amounts that the Contracting State of which the beneficial owner is resident treats as equity;

f) interest arising in a Contracting State and beneficially owned by a resident of the other Contracting State that is entitled to the benefits of this Article only by reason of paragraph 5 of Article 22 (Limitation on Benefits) may be taxed in the first-mentioned Contracting State, but the tax so charged shall not exceed 10 percent of the gross amount of the interest; and

g) interest that is an excess inclusion with respect to a residual interest in a real estate mortgage investment conduit may be taxed by each Contracting State in accordance with its domestic law.

3. Notwithstanding the provisions of paragraph 1 of this Article, in the case of a company seeking to satisfy the requirements of paragraph 4 of Article 22 (Limitation on Benefits) of this Convention regarding a payment of interest, if such company fails to satisfy the criteria of that paragraph solely by reason of:

a) the requirement in subclause (B) of clause (i) of subparagraph (e) of paragraph 7 of Article 22 (Limitation on Benefits) of this Convention; or

b) the requirement in clause (ii) of subparagraph (e) of paragraph 7 of Article 22 (Limitation on Benefits) that a person entitled to benefits under paragraph 5 of Article 22 (Limitation on Benefits) would be entitled to a rate of tax with respect to the interest that is less than or equal to the rate applicable under paragraph 2 of this Article;

such company may be taxed by the Contracting State in which the interest arises according to the laws of that Contracting State. In these cases, however, the tax so charged shall not exceed the highest rate among the rates of tax to which persons described in subparagraph (e) of paragraph 7 of Article 22 (Limitation on Benefits) of this Convention (notwithstanding the requirements referred to in subparagraphs

(a) and (b) of this paragraph) would have been entitled if such persons had received the interest directly. For purposes of this paragraph, a person described in clause (iii) of subparagraph (e) of paragraph 7 of Article 22 (Limitation on Benefits) shall be treated as entitled to the limitation of tax to which such person would be entitled if such person were a resident of the same Contracting State as the company receiving the interest.

4. The term "interest" as used in this Article means income from debt-claims of every kind, whether or not secured by mortgage, and whether or not carrying a right to participate in the debtor's profits, and in particular, income from government securities and income from bonds or debentures, including premiums or prizes attaching to such securities, bonds or debentures, and all other income that is subjected to the same taxation treatment as income from money lent under the law of the Contracting State in which the income arises. Income dealt with in Article 10 (Dividends) and penalty charges for late payment shall not be regarded as interest for the purposes of this Convention.

5. The provisions of paragraphs 1 through 3 of this Article shall not apply if the beneficial owner of the interest, being a resident of a Contracting State, carries on business in the other Contracting State in which the interest arises through a permanent establishment situated therein, and the debt-claim in respect of which the interest is paid is effectively connected with such permanent establishment. In such case the provisions of Article 7 (Business Profits) shall apply.

6. For purposes of this Article, interest shall be deemed to arise in a Contracting State when the payor is a resident of that Contracting State. Where, however, the person paying the interest, whether a resident of a Contracting State or not, has in a Contracting State a permanent establishment or derives profits that are taxable on a net basis in a Contracting State under paragraph 5 of Article 6 (Income from Real Property (Immovable Property)) or paragraph 1 of Article 13 (Gains), and such interest is borne by such permanent establishment or allocable to such profits, then such interest shall be deemed to arise in the Contracting State in which the permanent establishment is situated or from which such profits are derived.

7. The excess, if any, of the amount of interest allocable to the profits of a company resident in a Contracting State that are:

   a) attributable to a permanent establishment in the other Contracting State (including gains under paragraph 3 of Article 13 (Gains)); or

   b) subject to tax in the other Contracting State under Article 6 (Income from Real Property (Immovable Property)) or paragraph 1 of Article 13 (Gains);

over the interest paid by that permanent establishment, or in the case of profits subject to tax under Article 6 (Income from Real Property (Immovable Property)) or paragraph 1 of Article 13 (Gains), over the interest paid by that company, shall be deemed to arise in that other Contracting State and to be beneficially owned by a resident of the first-mentioned Contracting State. The tax imposed under this Article on such interest shall not exceed the rates provided in paragraphs 1 through 3 of this Article.

8. Where, by reason of a special relationship between the payor and the beneficial owner or between both of them and some other person, the amount of the interest, having regard to the debt-claim for which it is paid, exceeds the amount that would have been agreed upon by the payor and the beneficial owner in the absence of such relationship, the provisions of this Article shall apply only to the last-mentioned amount. In such case the excess part of the payments shall remain taxable according to the laws of each Contracting State, due regard being had to the other provisions of this Convention.

Article 12

ROYALTIES

1. Royalties arising in a Contracting State and beneficially owned by a resident of the other Contracting State shall be taxable only in that other Contracting State.

2. Notwithstanding the provisions of paragraph 1 of this Article:

a) a royalty arising in a Contracting State and beneficially owned by a resident of the other Contracting State that is a connected person with respect to the payor of the royalty may be taxed in the first-mentioned Contracting State in accordance with domestic law if such resident benefits from a special tax regime with respect to the royalty in its Contracting State of residence; and

b) in the case of the United States, royalties paid by an expatriated entity and beneficially owned by a company resident in _____ that is a connected person with respect to such expatriated entity may be taxed in accordance with the law of the United States for a period of ten years beginning on the date on which the acquisition of the domestic entity is completed. For purposes of applying this paragraph:

i) no effect shall be given to any amendment to section 7874 of the Internal Revenue Code after the date of signature of this Convention; and

ii) no entity shall be treated as an expatriated entity that:

A) is a connected person with respect to the domestic entity immediately after the date on which the acquisition of the domestic entity is completed; and

B) prior to that date, was never a connected person with respect to the domestic entity.

However, an entity described in the preceding sentence shall become an expatriated entity if, subsequent to the date on which the acquisition of the domestic entity is completed, the entity joins in filing a U.S. consolidated return with either the domestic entity or another entity that was a connected person with respect to the domestic entity immediately prior to the date on which the acquisition of the domestic entity was completed.

3. Notwithstanding the provisions of paragraph 1 of this Article, in the case of a company seeking to satisfy the requirements of paragraph 4 of Article 22 (Limitation

on Benefits) of this Convention regarding a royalty, if such company fails to satisfy the criteria of that paragraph solely by reason of the requirement in subclause (B) of clause (i) of subparagraph (e) of paragraph 7 of Article 22 (Limitation on Benefits) of this Convention, such company may be taxed in the Contracting State of which the royalty arises and according to the laws of that Contracting State, except that the tax so charged shall not exceed the highest rate among the rates of tax to which persons described in subparagraph (e) of paragraph 7 of Article 22 (Limitation on Benefits) of this Convention (notwithstanding the requirement of subclause (B) of clause (i) of subparagraph (e) of paragraph 7 of Article 22 (Limitation on Benefits)) would have been entitled if such persons had received the royalty directly. For purposes of this paragraph, a person described in clause (iii) of subparagraph (e) of paragraph 7 of Article 22 (Limitation on Benefits) shall be treated as entitled to the limitation of tax to which such person would be entitled if such person were a resident of the same Contracting State as the company receiving the royalties.

4. The term "royalty" as used in this Article means payments of any kind received as consideration for the use of, or the right to use, any copyright of literary, artistic, scientific or other work (including cinematographic films); any patent, trademark, design or model, plan, secret formula or process; or for information concerning industrial, commercial or scientific experience.

5. The provisions of paragraphs 1 through 3 of this Article shall not apply if the beneficial owner of the royalties, being a resident of a Contracting State, carries on business in the other Contracting State in which the royalties arise through a permanent establishment situated therein and the right or property in respect of which the royalties are paid is effectively connected with such permanent establishment. In such case the provisions of Article 7 (Business Profits) shall apply.

6. Royalties shall be deemed to arise in a Contracting State when they are in consideration for the use of, or the right to use, property, information or experience in that Contracting State.

7. Where, by reason of a special relationship between the payor and the beneficial owner or between both of them and some other person, the amount of the royalties, having regard to the use, right, or information for which they are paid, exceeds the amount that would have been agreed upon by the payor and the beneficial owner in the absence of such relationship, the provisions of this Article shall apply only to the last-mentioned amount. In such case the excess part of the payments shall remain taxable according to the laws of each Contracting State, due regard being had to the other provisions of this Convention.

Article 13

GAINS

1. Gains derived by a resident of a Contracting State from the alienation of real property (immovable property) situated in the other Contracting State may be taxed in that other Contracting State.

2. For the purposes of this Article the term "real property (immovable property) situated in the other Contracting State" shall include:

   a) real property (immovable property) referred to in Article 6 (Income from Real Property (Immovable Property));

   b) where that other Contracting State is the United States, a United States real property interest; and

   c) where that other Contracting State is _____,

      i) shares, including rights to acquire shares, other than shares in which there is regular trading on a stock exchange, deriving 50 percent or more of their value directly or indirectly from real property referred to in subparagraph (a) of this paragraph situated in _____; and

      ii) an interest in a partnership or trust to the extent that the assets of the partnership or trust consist of real property situated in _____, or of shares referred to in clause (i) of this subparagraph.

3. Gains from the alienation of movable property forming part of the business property of a permanent establishment that an enterprise of a Contracting State has in the other Contracting State, including such gains from the alienation of such a permanent establishment (alone or with the whole enterprise), may be taxed in that other Contracting State.

4. Gains derived by an enterprise of a Contracting State from the alienation of ships or aircraft operated or used in international traffic or personal property pertaining to the operation or use of such ships or aircraft shall be taxable only in that Contracting State.

5. Gains derived by an enterprise of a Contracting State from the alienation of containers (including trailers, barges and related equipment for the transport of containers) used for the transport of goods or merchandise shall be taxable only in that Contracting State, unless those containers are used for transport solely between places within the other Contracting State.

6. Gains from the alienation of any property other than property referred to in paragraphs 1 through 5 of this Article shall be taxable only in the Contracting State of which the alienator is a resident.

7. Where an individual who, upon ceasing to be a resident (as determined under paragraph 1 of Article 4 (Resident)) of one of the Contracting States, is treated under the taxation law of that Contracting State as having alienated property for its fair market value and is taxed in that Contracting State by reason thereof, the individual may elect to be treated for purposes of taxation in the other Contracting State as if the individual had, immediately before ceasing to be a resident of the first-mentioned Contracting State, alienated and reacquired such property for an amount equal to its fair market value at such time.

Article 14

INCOME FROM EMPLOYMENT

1. Subject to the provisions of Articles 15 (Directors' Fees), 17 (Pensions, Social Security, Annuities, Alimony, and Child Support) and 19 (Government Service), salaries, wages and other similar remuneration derived by a resident of a Contracting State in respect of an employment shall be taxable only in that Contracting State unless the employment is exercised in the other Contracting State. If the employment is so exercised, such remuneration as is derived therefrom may be taxed in that other Contracting State.

2. Notwithstanding the provisions of paragraph 1 of this Article, remuneration derived by a resident of a Contracting State in respect of an employment exercised in the other Contracting State shall be taxable only in the first-mentioned Contracting State if:

   a) the recipient is present in the other Contracting State for a period or periods not exceeding in the aggregate 183 days for all twelve-month periods commencing or ending in the taxable year concerned;

   b) the remuneration is paid by, or on behalf of, an employer who is not a resident of the other Contracting State; and

   c) the remuneration is not borne by a permanent establishment that the employer has in the other Contracting State.

3. Notwithstanding the preceding provisions of this Article, remuneration described in paragraph 1 of this Article that is derived by a resident of a Contracting State in respect of an employment as a member of the regular complement of a ship or aircraft operated in international traffic shall be taxable only in that Contracting State.

Article 15

DIRECTORS' FEES

Directors' fees and other similar payments derived by a resident of a Contracting State for services rendered in the other Contracting State in his capacity as a member of the board of directors of a company that is a resident of the other Contracting State may be taxed in that other Contracting State.

* * *

Article 23

RELIEF FROM DOUBLE TAXATION

1. In the case of _____, double taxation will be relieved as follows:

2. In accordance with the provisions and subject to the limitations of the law of the United States (as it may be amended from time to time without changing the general principle hereof), the United States shall allow to a resident or citizen of the United States as a credit against the United States tax on income applicable to residents and citizens:

a) the income tax paid or accrued to _____ by or on behalf of such resident or citizen; and

b) in the case of a United States company owning at least 10 percent of the voting stock of a company that is a resident of _____ and from which the United States company receives dividends, the income tax paid or accrued to _____ by or on behalf of the payor with respect to the profits out of which the dividends are paid.

For the purposes of this paragraph, the taxes referred to in subparagraph (a) of paragraph 3 and paragraph 4 of Article 2 (Taxes Covered) shall be considered income taxes.

3. For the purposes of applying paragraph 2 of this Article, an item of gross income, as determined under the law of the United States, derived by a resident of the United States that, under this Convention, may be taxed in _____ shall be deemed to be income from sources in _____.

4. Where a United States citizen is a resident of _____:

a) with respect to items of income, profit or gain that under the provisions of this Convention are exempt from United States tax or that are subject to a reduced rate of United States tax when derived by a resident of _____ who is not a United States citizen, _____ shall allow as a credit against _____ tax only the tax paid, if any, that the United States may impose under the provisions of this Convention other than taxes that may be imposed solely by reason of citizenship under paragraph 4 of Article 1 (General Scope);

b) for purposes of applying paragraph 2 to compute United States tax on those items of income, profit or gain referred to in subparagraph (a) of this paragraph, the United States shall allow as a credit against United States tax the income tax paid to _____ after the credit referred to in subparagraph (a) of this paragraph; the credit so allowed shall not reduce the portion of the United States tax that is creditable against the _____ tax in accordance with subparagraph (a) of this paragraph; and

c) for the exclusive purpose of relieving double taxation in the United States under subparagraph (b) of this paragraph, items of income, profit or gain referred to in subparagraph (a) of this paragraph shall be deemed to arise in _____ to the extent necessary to avoid double taxation of such income under subparagraph (b) of this paragraph.

* * *

Article 28

SUBSEQUENT CHANGES IN LAW

1. If at any time after the signing of this Convention, a Contracting State reduces the general statutory rate of company tax that applies with respect to substantially all of the income of resident companies with the result that such rate falls below the

lesser of either (a) 15 percent or (b) 60 percent of the general statutory rate of company tax applicable in the other Contracting State, or the first-mentioned Contracting State provides an exemption from taxation to resident companies for substantially all foreign source income (including interest and royalties), the Contracting States shall consult with a view to amending this Convention to restore an appropriate allocation of taxing rights between the Contracting States. If such consultations do not progress, the other Contracting State may notify the first-mentioned Contracting State through diplomatic channels that it shall cease to apply the provisions of Articles 10 (Dividends), 11 (Interest), 12 (Royalties) and 21 (Other Income). In such case, the provisions of such Articles shall cease to have effect in both Contracting States with respect to payments to resident companies six months after the date that the other Contracting State issues a written public notification stating that it shall cease to apply the provisions of Articles 10 (Dividends), 11 (Interest), 12 (Royalties) and 21 (Other Income).

2. For the purposes of determining the general statutory rate of company tax:

   a) the allowance of generally available deductions based on a percentage of what otherwise would be taxable income, and other similar mechanisms to achieve a reduction in the overall rate of tax, shall be taken into account; and

   b) a tax that applies to a company only upon a distribution by such company, or that applies to shareholders, shall not be taken into account.

* * *

Index

[References are to pages.]